Éirinn & Iran *go Brách*

Éirinn & Iran *go Brách*

Iran in Irish-nationalist historical, literary, cultural, and political imaginations from the late 18th century to 1921

Mansour Bonakdarian

ANTHEM PRESS

Anthem Press
An imprint of Wimbledon Publishing Company
www.anthempress.com

This edition first published in UK and USA 2026
by ANTHEM PRESS
75–76 Blackfriars Road, London SE1 8HA, UK
or PO Box 9779, London SW19 7ZG, UK
and
244 Madison Ave #116, New York, NY 10016, USA

First published in the UK and USA by Anthem Press in 2023

© 2026 Mansour Bonakdarian

The author asserts the moral right to be identified as the author of this work.

All rights reserved. Without limiting the rights under copyright reserved above, no part of this publication may be reproduced, stored or introduced into a retrieval system, or transmitted, in any form or by any means (electronic, mechanical, photocopying, recording or otherwise), without the prior written permission of both the copyright owner and the above publisher of this book.

British Library Cataloguing-in-Publication Data
A catalogue record for this book is available from the British Library.

Library of Congress Cataloging-in-Publication Data: 2025938729
A catalog record for this book has been requested.

ISBN-13: 978-1-83999-667-2 (Pbk)
ISBN-10: 1-83999-667-6 (Pbk)

Cover Concept and Design: Mansour Bonakdarian
Indexing: Mansour Bonakdarian

This title is also available as an eBook.

Published with a generous grant from
The Persian Heritage Foundation (USA)

for
Nasser
(for being there)

ACKNOWLEDGMENTS

I would like to express my gratitude to the Persian Heritage Foundation (USA) for the generous subvention grant that made possible the publication of this book. I am extremely grateful to my brother Nasser Bonakdarian for his continued support over the years, and to my colleagues Dr. Houchang E. Chehabi, Dr. Ian Christopher Fletcher, and Dr. Ali Gheissari for their encouragement of the project. Needless to say, these colleagues bear no responsibility for the information and opinions expressed in this book. My special thanks also to the dedicated staff at Anthem Press for their high standards, tremendous professionalism, and diligence, and to the editorial team at Deanta Publishing Services for their outstandingly meticulous copyediting, as well as the anonymous reviewers of the manuscript for their many helpful comments.

CONTENTS

Introduction		1
Chapter One	"Iran" in Irish Nationalist Antiquarian Imaginations: The Late Eighteenth and Early Nineteenth Century	47
Chapter Two	Thomas Moore's Poetic and Historical Irans: *Intercepted Letters* (1813), *Lalla Rookh* (1817), and *The History of Ireland* (1835)	167
Chapter Three	Irans of Young Ireland Imaginations, 1842–48: From Thomas Osborne Davis' "Thermopylae" to James Clarence Mangan's "Aye-Travailing Gnomes"	211
Chapter Four	Contemporary Affinities: *The Nation* and the Anglo-Iranian War of 1856–57	303
Chapter Five	An Gorta Mór of Others and Nationalist Neglect: *The Nation* and the Iranian Famine of 1870–72	361
Chapter Six	The Ghosts of Iran's Past in Irish Nationalist Imaginations in the Second Half of the Nineteenth Century	381
Chapter Seven	Irish Nationalists and the Iranian Question, 1906–21	467
Chapter Eight	Perspectival Detour: Iranian Familiarity with Ireland and the Irish Question Prior to the Easter Rising	513
Chapter Nine	Nation, History, and Memory: The Irish Free State, Europe-Centered Worlding of Ireland, and James Joyce's *Finnegans Wake* (1939)	563
Conclusion: Historical Apophenia, Affinities, Departures, and Nescience		635
Bibliography of Works Cited		653
Index		697

INTRODUCTION

The title of this book is a play on the Irish expression "Éirinn go Brách," frequently used interchangeably with the more correct "Éire go Brách" (Ireland Forever). Like all other works of history, this project has a history of its own. It originated as a side project long ago while I was revising my University of Iowa dissertation (1991) for publication. The dissertation focused on the opposition in the United Kingdom to London's Iranian policy during 1906–11. That opposition included Irish nationalists of differing political platforms. The revised and amended draft of my dissertation eventually appeared as a book titled *Britain and the Iranian Constitutional Revolution: Foreign Policy, Imperialism, and Dissent* (2006). Along the way, among other tangential projects, I began to explore whether there had been prior episodes of Irish nationalist interest in Iranian encounters with the British Empire. Britain and Russia had been the two leading imperial interlopers in Iranian affairs after the start of the nineteenth century. The earliest episode of contemporary Irish nationalist espousal of Iranian sovereignty I uncovered dates back to the time of the (Second) Anglo-Iranian War of 1856–57, albeit occurring under drastically different circumstances than the Irish nationalist advocacy of Iranian sovereignty after 1906. Moreover, during the course of my research, I came across works of poetry and literature by notable nineteenth-century Irish nationalist authors, such as Thomas Moore and James Clarence Mangan, that variously deployed Iranian settings, among other "oriental" motifs, as a means of commenting on Ireland's history of subjugation by England since the twelfth century, especially since the English Reformation in the sixteenth century. This particular research trajectory subsequently led me to probe not only the ways in which Irish nationalists of varying platforms at different stages since the emergence of nonsectarian Irish nationalism in the late eighteenth century had regarded contemporary Iran in the context of Anglo-Iranian relations, but also the ways in which they may have approached and comprehended Iranian history vis-à-vis the history of Ireland, in terms of manifold formulations of "nation" (including the nation-state), national formations, national identity, and anti-imperialism and territorial sovereignty.

This research led to my unexpected discovery that beginning in the late eighteenth century, around the time a nonsectarian Irish nationalist platform was taking shape, some culturally nationalist Irish antiquarians had designated a nebulous ancient Iran (/Persia) as the alleged ancestral home of Ireland's earliest populations, or as at least as the main source of Ireland's ancient civilization—either introduced directly by Iranian settlers in Ireland or transmitted by other groups arriving in Ireland who had embraced certain Iranian cultural beliefs and practices prior to their arrival. I then came across a range of secondary studies of Irish antiquarianism and various presumed 'oriental' theories of Irish origins, albeit focusing on territories other than "Iran" (in its various historical renderings). These included such pioneering studies as Menahem Mansoor's *Story of Irish Orientalism* (1944) and later works by Clare O'Halloran, Joep (Joseph Theodoor) Leerssen, Colin Kidd, and the detailed seminal study of the subject in Joseph Lennon's 2004 *Irish Orientalism: A Literary and Intellectual History*, all of which also sporadically explore Irish nationalist applications of varying oriental myths of Irish origins, as well as Irish nationalist literary deployments of oriental settings as allegoric means of commenting on Ireland's experience of colonization and resistance and rebellion. While I most certainly have benefitted immensely from these and other studies, as indicated by my voluminous citations of these works throughout the present book, the particular historical scope of my study (temporal and spatial) and my primary objective of engaging with Irish nationalist imaginations through the "Iranian" lens remain distinctive. The present book is an in-depth study of particular *trends* in Irish nationalism from roughly just before the inception of an ideologically nonsectarian Irish nationalist movement in the form of the Society of United Irishmen (1791) until the formation of the Irish Free State (1922) through the particular lens of Irish nationalist imaginations of *other lands* ('Iran' in this case). In the process, the book investigates the presumed historical underpinnings of these multivalent Irish nationalist self-referentialities through the medium of 'Iran' and their implied cultural and political contingencies. In addition, the following chapters chart some of the global circuits through which these Irish nationalist imaginations and representations of Iran in different settings were derived and the channels through which they circulated.

As other studies demonstrate, there were alternative antiquarian theories of Irish origins besides the Iranian (/Persian) model. These other ancient 'oriental' locations were most routinely identified as Scythia or Phoenicia (Carthage), and, to a much lesser degree, as Egypt or Armenia, among other places and cultures. After the late eighteenth century, it was often an amalgam of these cultural-territorial entities that were designated as the source of Irish origins and/or ancient Irish civilization by antiquarians subscribing to competing oriental theories, as in the case of Phoenicians who had embraced Iranian (specifically Persian) cultural practices and beliefs prior to their arrival in Ireland, or a presumably Indo/Iranian, Scythian, Phoenician, Chaldean intermixture. In some cases, these various presumed oriental ancestors of the Irish were identified as continued arrivals of distinct branches of an allegedly identical population group and cultural formation, occasionally with Chaldeans, Persians, and Phoenicians, among other groups, erroneously conflated into common linguistic and cultural units. In connection with competing Irish antiquarian theories of oriental origins, it is important to note at the outset that while Ireland's ancient links to the 'Orient,' among other locations, are now substantiated through genetics, these latest discoveries should not be read back onto the older trends of Irish antiquarianism as somehow verifying and legitimizing those theories of Ireland's oriental origins. The antiquarian models were based on different and highly imaginative, or even possibly at times consciously invented, sets of historical assumptions, deductions, methodologies, and documentation. Moreover, unlike present-day accounts of the extremely gradual migrations across Europe to Ireland, by different paths and in *very* distant times, of peoples whose ancestry had previously settled in what is now the Middle East, Turkey, and/or the Caucasus—there are even disagreements among present-day historians and geneticists on the precise location of those population groups—the antiquarian theories of oriental origins of the Irish maintained historically rapid migrations from the Orient to Ireland. Moreover, these antiquarians insisted on the occurrence of these population dispersions in relatively recent historical times, corresponding to recorded evidence of major ancient empires in various designated oriental locations (with the Orient in this case extending from Central and South Asia to West Asia and North Africa).

The present study is primarily an attempt to engage with Irish nationalism through the prism of Irish nationalist commentaries about other lands and peoples from the time of the inception of nonsectarian nationalist platforms in Ireland after the late eighteenth century until the creation of the Irish Free State in 1922. The only exception to this temporal framework is the section on James Joyce's *Finnegans Wake* (1939), which serves as a means of commenting on the post-1922 shrinking world horizon of nationalist historiography and politics in the Irish Free State. In approaching particular trends in Irish nationalism through the prism of 'Iran,' this study also underscores that Irish nationalism in general during the period (and in many ways even before the emergence of nonsectarian Irish nationalism) always utilized a historiographic paradigm that focused not only on Ireland's domestic past and Anglo-Irish encounters but also simultaneously situated Ireland in the broader world history. This is a process I term "worlding of Ireland." In effect, Irish nationalism was always historiographically cosmopolitan in some configuration, even in the case of incessantly inward-looking and narrowly defined (ethnically and/or religiously) exclusionary expressions of Irish nationalism. Irish nationalists, as nationalists in many other parts of the world, recurrently imagined their own history as being in some form reflected in the histories of peoples and lands elsewhere, no matter how unique they considered their own "national" history. Moreover, they periodically, albeit often highly selectively, expressed past and/or present affinities with other subjugated peoples and lands. These manifold, and often conflicting, cross-referentialities offer alternative heuristic and analytical paths to interrogating the evolution and diverse manifestations of nationalist thought in Ireland during the period covered in this book.

While probing manifold Irish nationalist imaginations and representations of Iran, it is essential to note the present study *is conceived of in the mode of "global history"* and is not solely aimed at readers interested in either Irish studies and/or Iranian studies, but is also aimed at a broader group of readers interested in cross-disciplinary studies of nationalism, imperialism, historiography, and cross-regional formation and circulation of knowledge, among other range of potential audiences. Hence, also some of the very detailed treatment and extensive contextualization of certain subjects in this book for those not already familiar with particular topics or general outlines of specific developments. Needless to say, different readers will find different chapters and details of greater or lesser interest. Before proceeding further, it should also be added that, irrespective of the subject of this book, it is not my intention to somehow historically valorize nationalisms and the category of "the nation." Neither am I in any way suggesting an overarching primacy of 'Iran' as a location appearing in Irish nationalist constructs of ancient Ireland or in Irish nationalist expressions of solidarity with other contemporary struggles against British imperialism, *nor am I implying there was an underlying connection between all the different manifestations of 'Iran' in Irish nationalist imaginations and commentaries over time*, ranging from antiquarian to literary, folklore, and more decidedly "political" (as opposed to narrowly defined "cultural") settings. It is imperative to underscore that periodic *Irish nationalist expressions of contemporary anti-imperialist solidarity and affinity with Iranians were not some kind of a logical corollary of Irish antiquarian claims of Iran-"Erin" ties in ancient times*, even if some Irish nationalists endorsing the territorial sovereignty of contemporary Iran may also have subscribed to antiquarian theories of Iranian origins. The central focus on 'Iran' in this study, with intermittent cross-references and comparisons in regard to other lands and peoples that also featured in Irish nationalist commentaries during the period, provides a historical-analytical vantage point. A number of other territories appeared much more frequently and regularly than Iran in Irish nationalist expressions of cross-territorial anti-imperialist solidarity with contemporary struggles elsewhere—for instance, India, Poland, or Egypt after different stages in the nineteenth century. Nevertheless, the diverse range of Irish nationalist evocations of 'Iran' (both in its broader historical and cultural and the narrower contemporary territorial designations) offers an extended and multifaceted lens for examining various modes of Irish nationalist *self*-framings from the late eighteenth century to 1921 by recourse to world-historical referentialities. Whereas Scythia and Phoenicia, or Armenia on rare occasions, also appeared in Irish antiquarian reconstructions of ancient Ireland, these places had all long ceased to exist as territorial states—although the plight of contemporary Armenian population of the Ottoman Empire occasionally elicited commentary from certain Irish nationalist circles after the late nineteenth century. On the other hand, while the subjugated Polish population of the Russian Empire evoked recurring expressions of solidarity from Irish nationalists of differing platforms after the nineteenth century, Poland did not figure as one of the presumed original homelands of Ireland's ancient population, and contemporary Polish nationalists were not resisting British imperialism. 'Iran' (/ Persia), on the other hand, appeared in a broad range of Irish nationalist commentaries about Ireland itself, from antiquarian claims of origins to literary appropriations and contemporary politics. 'Iran,' too, had periodically ceased to exist as a sovereign state entity, whether under Macedonian/Hellenic rule (331–247 BCE) or from the time of its occupation by Arab-Muslim forces in the seventh century, followed by various Turkic, Mongol, and again Turkic occupations, until it was territorially and politically reconstituted as Iran after the founding of Safavid dynasty in 1501 (albeit on a smaller scale than the ancient Persian empires)—and leaving aside here the Turkic ethnicity of the Safavids. The Safavid Empire was eventually overrun and conquered in 1722 by the Gilzai Pashtun confederacy from present-day Afghan territories. It was not until 1730 that an Iranian military leader succeeded in once again reunifying much of the territory under his control, after which different dynasties continued to rule the country as Iran, with changing territorial frontiers. Hence, in Irish nationalist imaginations after the late eighteenth century, Iran operated as a territorial entity that had existed in ancient times and was still in existence.

In fact, in Irish nationalist poetry by the likes of Thomas Moore or Denis Florence MacCarthy after the second decade of the nineteenth century, the Arab-Muslim occupation of Iran and the imagined Iranian Zoroastrian resistance to foreign occupiers, who were both ethnically and religiously different from ancient Iranians, served as a blatant allegoric analogy for English *Protestant* rule in Ireland after the sixteenth century—following the English Reformation and subsequent creation of the Anglican Church, while the majority of Ireland's population remained Catholic and faced Protestant religious persecution and endured English penal laws in political, social, and economic spheres at different stages. As discussed in great detail later on, this mode of analogy between particular imagined or actual junctures in Iranian and Irish history frequently required varying degrees of historical unfamiliarity or selective amnesia among the intended audiences. For instance, in the case of "The Fire-Worshippers" section of Thomas Moore's 1817 *Lalla Rookh*, the Irish subtext of nonsectarian and cross-ethnic uprisings by the United Irishmen after the late eighteenth century was highly at odds with the ethnoreligious divisions inspiring the hero of Moore's selected Iranian setting. The Iranian Hafed was ultimately an unsuitable match for Moore's eulogization of a multiethnic and nondenominational Irish nationalist platform. This points to the limitations and paradoxes of *worlding* Ireland. As a literary-political substitute for "Erin"[1] (i.e., "Éire"/Ireland), fictionalized Iranian historical settings were meant to represent specific phases in the English colonization of Ireland and various stages of Irish resistance to English rule. Moore's *Lalla Rookh* came to serve as the prototype for the Iran/Erin literary metaphor. This pairing of the two rhyming territorial designations also had a clear poetic advantage. 'Iran' of other historical times too appeared in Irish nationalist literature as historically truncated territorial-cultural allegoric settings for commenting on developments in Ireland following the Anglo-Norman conquests in the twelfth century and, more particularly, English Protestant rule after the sixteenth century. For example, James Clarence Mangan opted for Safavid Iran (1501–1722/36) in a poem titled "To the Ingleezee Khafir, Calling Himself Djuan Bool Djenkinzun" (1846). Simultaneously, as discussed later in the book, in reference to Irish history some Irish nationalist commentators also drew negative associations with 'Iran' of different times, most notably in sympathetic allusions to Spartans resisting the invading Persian army during the Battle of Thermopylae (480 BCE), in which setting Irish nationalists were cross-identified with Spartan forces, and English imperialism was equated with the Persian Empire. Alternatively, in Thomas Moore's 1813 *Intercepted Letters; or, The Twopenny Post-bag* it was contemporary Iranian society that functioned as an allegoric site for indirectly, albeit unambiguously, commenting on continued Protestant persecution of Catholics across the United Kingdom. After the middle of the nineteenth century, developments in contemporary Iran also elicited periodic Irish nationalist condemnation of Britain's continued imperialist aggression in other parts of the world. In the early nineteenth century, England emerged as a leading European imperial power in Iran, in rivalry with Russia—following a brief phase of British rivalry with France in Iranian affairs during the Napoleonic Wars.

In some ways, similar to 'Iran,' Egypt or the Indian subcontinent can also provide long-term and multifaceted historical lenses for probing Irish nationalist self-imaginations by means of references to other territorial, cultural, and political locales in a world-historical setting. Both "India" and Egypt, in their varying modalities, occasionally featured in Irish antiquarian claims of oriental origins of Ireland's Gaelic population, while also appearing (more frequently than Iran) in Irish nationalist expressions of contemporary cross-territorial anti-imperialist solidarities as sites of British domination (India gradually after the late eighteenth century and Egypt after the late nineteenth century). The present study makes no claim of Iran's unparalleled uniqueness as a *longue durée* lens for probing *worlded* Irish nationalist imaginations. In its specifically Iran-themed approach, this book goes beyond explorations of Irish nationalist mythology and literature. While stressing the much greater centrality of Iran in Irish nationalist antiquarianism after the late eighteenth century, and in later nationalist folklore studies of Ireland, than hitherto acknowledged, the present study maps out the extensive scope of largely forgotten or overlooked Irish nationalist appropriations of 'Iran' (past and contemporary). It also underscores the recurring Irish nationalist interest in the Iranian Question after the middle of the nineteenth century (initially in the more "radical" Irish nationalist circles), including the protracted and wide-ranging Irish nationalist advocacy of Iranian sovereignty from 1906 to 1921; again, *without in any way maintaining an underlying link between these different range of interests in, and commentaries on, Iran*. In addition to various historical continuities, transformations, and caesura in Irish nationalist references to, and/or utilizations of, 'Iran'—including changing historiographic, methodological, ideological, and other factors—this study also highlights periodic instances of instrumentalist disregard and conscious neglect of Iran in some Irish nationalist circles, notably in the more so-called radical circles during the large-scale Iranian famine of 1870–72. Occurring only two decades after the Great Famine of 1845–51 in Ireland, the Iranian famine decimated Iran's population on a similar scale as Ireland's population during the Great Famine. By 1851, the theme of "famine" had registered in the collective political memory of 'radical' Irish nationalists as, at best, the epitome of London's neglect of Ireland, if not as an unequivocal indicator of a deliberate English policy of exterminating the Irish. As discussed later, the radical Irish nationalist response to the Iranian famine was in great contrast to the highly sympathetic reaction of the same nationalist circles to contemporary famines in British India. Needless to say, although the present book covers a wide range of assorted Irish nationalist evocations of Iran as well as expressed historical and political affinities and dissociations between the two lands, *it is certainly far from being an exhaustive coverage of Irish-Iranian encounters and exchanges during the period, even in the narrow framework of Irish nationalism.*

As already noted, my examples throughout the book are drawn from the period roughly coinciding with the emergence of nonsectarian Irish nationalism in the late eighteenth century and up to the establishment of the Irish Free State in 1922, with the exception of a section on Joyce's 1939 *Finnegans Wake* that reflects back on Irish antiquarian claims of oriental origins, including the presumably Iranian pedigree, as well as on nineteenth-century Irish nationalist literary uses of the Iran/Erin interchange. Ultimately, the book probes the ways in which Irish nationalist self-referentialities through various mediums of 'Iran' signal different formations and contours of *particular strands* of Irish nationalist imaginations during the period. The opening chapter of the book begins in the late eighteenth century with antiquarian accounts of presumed direct or indirect contacts between ancient Ireland and Iran, and of imagined lasting Iranian cultural and civilizational legacies in Ireland. To put things in perspective, it should be observed that the majority of Irish antiquarians claiming various oriental theories of Irish origins were leading members of the Royal Irish Academy (1785). The central question in this regard is why they should have turned to ancient Iran or to other so-called oriental cultures and/or locations, as the original homeland of the earliest major population settlements in Ireland and as the fountainhead of ancient Ireland's civilization. Chapter One also addresses the formation and circulation of knowledge about ancient Iran in this setting and underscores the remarkable cosmopolitan hermeneutical intertextuality of these antiquarian texts themselves, including not only reliance on 'Iranian' sources available in European translations in various forms but also the incorporation of Persian and Arabic lexicon and script in their publications, foreshadowing, and in some ways transcending, the 1939 polyglot cosmopolitan literary masterpiece of James Joyce, *Finnegans Wake*, which in comparison lacks the use of 'oriental' or other non-Latin script.

Chapter Two examines other modes of Irish nationalist imaginations and representations of Iran at different historical junctures, as a means of commenting on Irish history. Focusing specifically on Thomas Moore—the leading Irish nationalist balladeer, poet, and playwright in the first half of the nineteenth century, as well as an antiquarian—, this chapter examines Moore's allegoric literary deployments of Iranian historical settings as mirroring particular moments in the history of Irish resistance to English domination as well as the ongoing Protestant persecution of Catholics in the United Kingdom. The chapter then proposes that Moore's interest in Iran as an allegorical historical locale was fundamentally related to his antiquarian view of Iranian roots of ancient Ireland's civilization, allegedly transmitted to Ireland by Phoenicians, including the presumably Zoroastrian prototype of Ireland's Round Towers. Chapter Three focuses on disparate historical referentialities to Iran in the poetry of Young Ireland (1842–48), contrasting Thomas Osborne Davis' use of the Hellenic myth of Thermopylae, in which the ancient Persian Empire is cast as an invading imperial aggressor, with the allegoric identification of Iran and Erin in the poetry of James Clarence Mangan. Much of this chapter is devoted to Mangan's works, ranging from his vast body of invented translations of 'oriental' poems, including those ostensibly from the Persian, his selection of an alternative Iranian historical juncture than that of Thomas Moore for condemning the English occupation of Ireland, and the hitherto neglected evidence that shortly before his death in the middle of the nineteenth century Mangan hinted at his own belief in Ireland's ancient ties to Iran.

Chapter Four transitions from Irish antiquarianism and nationalist literature to the first instance of Irish nationalist articulations of anti-"British" solidarity with Iranians, in this case in the instrumentalist form of "the enemy of my enemy is my friend" advocacy of the Iranian *state* during the Anglo-Iranian War of 1856–57 in the pages of the Dublin newspaper *The Nation* (in its post-Young Ireland manifestation). This stance was in contrast to that of the main rival nationalist newspaper, the *Freeman's Journal* (Dublin), which, although voicing concern regarding the legitimacy of initial grounds for British declaration of war against Iran, nevertheless loyally supported the subsequent British war effort and reminded its readers of the presence of Irish military personnel among Britain's imperial forces engaged in the Iranian war. Chapter Five continues to focus on *The Nation*, but this time probing its politically motivated neglect of the Iranian Famine of 1870–72, which proved as deadly as Ireland's most recent Great Famine (1845–51). While relief funds were collected across the United Kingdom for victims of the Iranian famine, with the *Freeman's Journal* among the outlets urging Irish contributions to the eventually meager fund, *The Nation* refrained from expressing sympathy with Iranian victims on grounds that the relief funds collected in the United Kingdom were distributed to the victims through official British channels and, hence, allegedly elevated the stature of the British Empire. As intermittently demonstrated in the following chapters, from early on Irish nationalist expressions of solidarity with other anti-imperialist struggles were highly selective, a phenomenon not that different from expressions of cross-territorial solidarity by most other nationalist groupings in other parts of the world during the period. Chapter Six returns to the theme of presumed ancient connections between Iran and Ireland in the form of persisting oriental theories of Irish origins, even in the aftermath of the notable historiographic shift away from oriental theories by the middle of the nineteenth century. The central focus of this chapter is on Lady Jane Francesca Agnes Wilde's studies of Irish folklore and her assertion of Iranian roots of many of Ireland's continued folk beliefs. This coverage segues to Irish nationalist appeals to varying theories of Aryanism in the latter part of the century. Whereas Aryan theories of linguistic and racial affinities between Ireland and Iran dated back to the late eighteenth century, initially appearing in antiquarian writings of Charles Vallancey, by the late nineteenth-century Aryanism as a racial ingredient of Iran-Erin connections had assumed a (pseudo-)scientific dimension and was itself utilized as a justification for Ireland's independence from England. The remainder of this chapter reflects on Iran-related themes in the Irish Literary Revival of the late nineteenth and early twentieth century, with the Literary Revival engendering its own modes of *worlding* and *deprovincializing* Ireland by means of evoking "repressed cultural memory" and the simultaneous revitalization and/or break with Irish "traditions."

Chapter Seven resumes the topic of contemporary Irish nationalist expressions of political affinities between Ireland and Iran, this time in the aftermath of the Iranian Constitutional Revolution of 1906, in the form of extensive and multilateral Irish nationalist advocacy of Iranian sovereignty in opposition to mounting Anglo-Russian encroachments in Iranian affairs after 1907. This was also the first instance of direct contact between segments of Iranian and Irish nationalists, even if these contacts and the wider Irish espousal of Iranian sovereignty did not yield any publicly enunciated reciprocal Iranian nationalist advocacy of Irish nationalist platforms prior to the Easter Rising of 1916 in Ireland. The chapter also briefly touches on the abortive attempt by militant Irish and Indian nationalists based in the United States to forge an alliance with militant Iranian nationalists under the banner of anti-imperialist Aryanism after 1906. As the allusion to the Pan-Aryan Association suggests, this book is consistently also concerned with interconnected developments in the Irish diaspora (chiefly restricted to Irish communities in the United States in this book, given the extent of my historical expertise). Chapter Eight addresses the absence of Iranian public expressions of support for any Irish nationalist factions prior to 1916—even after the passage of the Irish Home Rule Bill in the British House of Commons in 1912, and despite ample familiarity with the broader Irish Question in many well-informed Iranian nationalist circles after the late nineteenth century. This stand-alone chapter diverges from the central preoccupation of the book with Irish nationalist referentialities to Iran. This chapter explores, on the one hand, the absolute lack of awareness among contemporary Iranians (which remains the case to this day) of the extensive range of Irish nationalist appropriations of 'Iran' during the period covered in this book, as well as the likely reason for the absence of any public expression of support by Iranian nationalists for Irish nationalist platforms prior to 1916—even as Iranian nationalists after the late nineteenth century championed anti-imperialist struggles in India and Egypt, which were also part of the British Empire, alongside numerous other anti-imperialist struggles in other imperial settings. The chapter illustrates that this Iranian neglect was a symptom of an overall Iranian consideration of the Irish Question at the time as a domestic (i.e., provincial) matter within the United Kingdom, and not an imperial state of affairs. This position was largely shared by Iranian nationalist commentators until after the outbreak of the First World War, which created new nationalist fault lines in both Iran and Ireland and engendered a reconsideration of the Irish Question by the more militant Iranian nationalist circles, particularly under the influence of wartime German propaganda. It should be reminded here that, compared to British India or British-occupied Egypt, Ireland was not only geographically and culturally a far more distant location from Iran, but Ireland was simultaneously a British colony and, after 1801, also an integral part of the United Kingdom and, hence, part of the heartland of the British Empire and imperial decision making. Ireland's status in the British Empire was undeniably ambivalent. Ireland not only comprised the oldest substantial English territorial possessions outside mainland Britain, but it was also a European colony of Britain (not forgetting Britain's other European possessions in the Irish Sea, Celtic Sea, North Sea, the English Channel, and the Mediterranean Sea). Among other factors, Ireland was an atypical British imperial dominion in so far as, following its incorporation into the United Kingdom of Great Britain and Ireland in 1801, it was directly represented in the British parliament at Westminster in London. Even Home Rule Irish nationalists enjoyed *organized* partisan representation in the British parliament after 1873, an opportunity not extended to any other British colonial territory.[2] Nor was Ireland among territories with which Iran had long maintained various forms of contact, although at least since the late sixteenth century, there had been increasing indirect commercial contacts between Ireland and Iran within the ambit of the broader Anglo-Iranian relations, as discussed later, and by nineteenth century there were also

Irish and Iranians occasionally traveling to each other's respective territories (Iranian travelers to Ireland being an extreme rarity in comparison). In contrast, Iranians had more extensive familiarity and contacts with some other parts of the British Empire, notably the Indian subcontinent (situated to the southeast of Iran and gradually occupied by Britain after 1757, initially under the direction of the English East India Company) and Egypt (occupied by Britain in 1882). Iranian contacts with both of these territories dated back to ancient times. By the end of the nineteenth century, Britain had also vastly expanded its imperial leverage over coastal regions of the Arabian Sea as well as over Iran's neighboring territories in the Persian Gulf, while periodically attempting to impose London's imperial influence over Afghanistan (bordering Iran to the east).

Chapter Nine looks at the years immediately after the partition of Ireland and the creation of the Irish Free State in 1922, with Northern Ireland remaining part of the United Kingdom and the Free State attaining self-government *within the British Empire*. This chapter addresses two major coinciding *although by no means logically connected*, Europe-centered trends in *worlding* of Ireland in the Free State. One of these was the rapid ascendance of Europe-centered accounts of ancient Ireland—by then the dominant historiographic paradigm that had already assumed increasing cachet since the latter part of the nineteenth century. The other coinciding trend in "Europeanizing" of Ireland examined in this chapter is that of the increasingly Europe-focused foreign policy considerations of the new state. These developments respectively contributed to, on the one hand, the swift disappearance of Iran and other oriental territories and cultures as proposed originary sites of ancient Ireland's population groups and civilization, and, on the other hand, to the diminished preoccupation in the Free State (until at least the 1930s) with non-European matters, with the *notable exception* of India. As explained in the chapter, in addition to the Irish Civil War of 1922–23 and the increasingly (but not comprehensive) inward gaze of competing political factions in the Free State, domestic and regional developments affecting Iran in the aftermath of the First World War also played a part in Iran's disappearance (until 1951) as an object of Irish nationalist expressions of cross-territorial solidarity. This chapter then turns to continued last gasps of oriental theories of Irish origins in some quarters after the creation of the Free State, including Iranian theories, and most notably in Joyce's *Finnegans Wake*.

All of these chapters, with the obvious exception of the chapter on Iranian familiarity with Ireland and the Irish Question, also engage with transformations in Irish historiography and probe the inherent anxieties of various ranges of Irish nationalist modalities (whether as individuals, such as the poet James Clarence Mangan in the 1830s and 1840s, or as collectivities, such as particular Irish nationalist political parties or the Pan-Aryan Association founded in New York in 1906). The Conclusion reflects on various general themes developed in preceding chapters through the prism of the interplay between, and in interstices of, Irish nationalist historical imaginations and memory.

A Partial Thematic Outline and Some Wider Conceptual Contexts

Over the past three-and-a-half decades, there has been a notable increase in comparative studies of Irish nationalism, including in the framework of Ireland's cross-territorial interactions with anti-imperialist struggles in other parts of the globe. On occasion, these studies have also incorporated a range of exchanges between nationalist groups in the Irish diaspora—in such locations, other than Britain itself, as the United States, Canada, India, southern Africa, Australia, or Latin America. Some of these studies have also focused on direct interactions with nationalists from other locations (inside or outside Britain's formal and informal empires) occurring outside their "home" territories, most notably contacts with Indian nationalists in Britain and in North America. There also have been comparative studies of Ireland's partition in 1922 and territorial partitions in other parts of the British Empire, namely India in 1947 and British-administered Palestine in 1948. The present study contributes to these varied ongoing historiographic patterns of worlding the Irish nationalist struggle. It does so by not only concentrating on a region of the world largely overlooked in prior studies of Irish nationalism, but by additionally adopting both a long-term (*longue durée*) view of manifold Irish nationalist commentaries on, and engagements with, other lands and peoples and by expanding its historical horizon beyond *narrowly defined 'political'* expressions of Irish nationalism. Central to the present study is my insistence that Irish nationalists themselves had continuously observed their struggle through varying world-historical prisms and that the worlding of Irish nationalism is not simply a historiographic device of later historians analyzing Irish nationalist trends and outcomes in the past. *None of this, of course, should imply that interconnections between Ireland, India, Egypt, or other parts of the British Empire, or with other regions of the world, such as Iran, were limited to "imperial" or "anti-imperialist" considerations. Similarly, nationalism is not the only lens for examining the broad range of Irish interests in, and references to, Iran and things Iranian during the period covered in this book.*

For Irish antiquarians espousing ancient Ireland's presumed Iranian ethnic makeup and/or cultural heritage, similar to Irish antiquarians endorsing the Phoenician theory of Irish origins, the underlying assertion was that of ancient Ireland's glorious civilization and Golden Age, long before Ireland's gradual colonization by the English after the twelfth century CE (initially by Anglo-Normans). The overwhelming majority of these antiquarians were also adamant that Ireland's oriental ancestors had reached the island by routes bypassing mainland Britain. Such scripting of Ireland's ancient ties to the Orient was unequivocally intended as historical refutation of continued indictments in some English and Anglo-Protestant (as well as Welsh and Scots) circles in Ireland of the enduring savagery of the Irish prior to English domination of Ireland. However, it should be stressed that by the late eighteenth century, there was also a notable presence of Anglo-Protestants in the ranks of Irish nationalist antiquarians subscribing to oriental theories of Irish origins and civilizational Golden Age. Anglo-Protestant participation in varying Irish cultural-nationalist historiographic initiatives predated the formation of nonsectarian and multiethnic Irish nationalist platform of the United Irishmen in 1791.

Examination of Irish nationalist imaginations and representations of 'Iran' during this period additionally provides an as of yet rare case study of how Iranian history (mythologized or otherwise), as well as contemporary developments in Iran, *circulated, were received, perceived, processed, and contextualized* outside Iran itself—including sporadic Irish attempts to grasp contemporary political developments in Iran in light of available information about recent Iranian history. A salient feature of how the Irish imagined, encountered, comprehended, narrated, and/or appropriated Irans of past and present is the specific range of sources and channels through which these engagements were facilitated and processed, some of which are extensively discussed in later chapters. For instance, Irish antiquarians situated ancient Ireland within the ancient Iranian, or more narrowly *Persianate, diasporic sphere*. In other words, ancient Ireland was situated in the category of Persianate, or more broadly Iranian, orbit of historical imagination. This was a perspective unrecognized by, and entirely unknown to, contemporary Iranians—as opposed to the more familiar range of acknowledged Persianate cultures or Iranian peoples existing in such locations as the Indian subcontinent, Central Asia, East Asia, the Caucasus, and some other territories. Irish antiquarian claims of Iranian diasporic and/or indirect cultural presence in ancient Ireland was an imaginative hermeneutics based on a different plausibility scale than such other claimants to a Persianate heritage as the "Shirazis" of Zanzibar, whose assertion of mixed "Persian" descent derived from the widely acknowledged presence of Iranian merchants in the Swahili coast and neighboring islands after the "Middle Ages" (here defined in keeping with present-day mainstream European periodization scheme). There are other examples of population groups self-ascribing themselves onto Persianate or Iranian worlds of different historical eras, whether entirely imaginatively or with some plausible historicity, including the Polish Sarmatianism—as descendants of Irano-Sarmatians who had moved into Eastern European territories in the fourth century BCE, a region over which the Irano-Scythian groups had established their dominance in earlier times—or the Jász population in present-day Hungary—who trace their lineage to the Irano-Alan populations settling in the region after the eight century CE. Irish nationalist antiquarian affirmation of Ireland's ancient ties to Iranian lands was, in effect, an assertion of a diffusionist model of Iranian peoples and/or civilizations now lost to Iranians themselves. In its underlying objective, this Irish antiquarian claim was almost the reverse of 'medieval' (using the mainstream European periodization scheme here) Iranian mythic diffusionist claim, as discussed in Chapter One, or the much later Tamil diffusionist claims, that various ancient population groups around the world had descended from respectively either a primordial Iranian or Tamil people. In the Tamil case, this diffusion followed their departure from their now-lost continental homeland of "Kumarināṭu" (Lemuria), which allegedly had once been located to the south of the Indian subcontinent, stretching westward in the direction of the African continent. Describing maps of this purportedly lost continent of Kumarināṭu, the historian Sumathi Ramaswamy writes:

> The earliest of such maps [...] is entitled "Descendants of Tamilians" (1943) and shows those parts of the globe that we today identify as the Middle East, northeast Africa, the Mediterranean, and southern Europe. Its author, Kandiah Pillai, illustrates the map with an extensive discussion of such "descendants" as Sumerians, Egyptians, Elamites, Babylonians, Cretans, ancient Britons, Phoenicians, Assyrians, Hebrews, Arabs, and Chinese, among others.[3]

Whereas in the Iranian or Tamil models the source of pride rested in being the *ancestors* of other peoples and civilizations, in Irish antiquarian narratives after the seventeenth century it was Irish *descent* from particular groups that constituted the source of civilizational pride.

Irish antiquarian grounding of ancient Ireland in the Persianate, or more broadly Iranian, orbit was also sustained through invoking Ireland's surviving indigenous architectural monuments and other archaeological artifacts and relics as evidence, most pronounced among them the Round Towers. To these ostensible evidentiary records were added specimens of Irish mythology that were presumably derived from Persian/Iranian prototypes, as well as a range of recorded cultural practices in ancient Ireland that seemingly corresponded to Persian/Iranian practices—ranging from "fire-worship" to other rituals evidently conducted by both Iranian magi and Irish druids. As further proof of such ancient ties, some antiquarians cited certain allegedly analogous folk beliefs still surviving in Ireland and Iran. In the case of textual documents on Ireland's ancient ties to Iran, evidence was sifted from such diverse range of works as ancient Hellenic and biblical sources to more recent publications in European languages, including a wide range of Persian and other oriental texts available in English or other European translations (whether in their entirety or in summary form). These Irish antiquarians engaged in (imaginatively) *reading* Irish connections *into* these diverse texts in a practice distinct from conventional hermeneutical *reading of* texts. In epistemological terms, the formation, production, circulation, and reception of knowledge by Irish nationalists concerning Iranian history and/or contemporary conditions in Iran relied on a combination of sources, not all of which were at the time available to, or at least utilized by, Iranians themselves. On the other hand, a range of "historical" sources consulted by Irish antiquarians in producing Iran-centered versions of ancient Ireland also comprised some of the same texts utilized by Iranians in reconstructing their own past (mythic or otherwise). Yet, contemporary Iranians were unfamiliar with Irish claims of ancient Iranian ancestry and/or cultural heritage based on these sources. In effect, Iranians and the Irish were encountering the same historical sources and reading themselves into these texts through distinctively different ontological and hermeneutical lenses.[4] These Iranian sources about ancient Iranian history did not allude to Ireland in any shape or form. However, for a range of Irish antiquarian these sources contained clues (if not absolute proof) of Iranian origins of the Irish and/or of Ireland's ancient civilization. For these antiquarians, ancient Ireland was an *extension* of ancient Iranian history and the sources in question were consulted to that end. As discussed in greater detail in the next chapter, certain historical texts and related documents, including works originally in Persian or in other oriental languages—one of which was produced in the Indian subcontinent in the seventeenth century and titled *Dabestān-e Mazāheb*—were extensively scrutinized by some Irish antiquarians for evidence of Iran-Erin connections in ancient times.

This was a mode of hermeneutical deciphering that rested on, among other techniques, degrees of linguistic conjury (etymological, cognates, grammatical, and semantics) and/or syllogistic abductive inferences. In the act of negotiating new modes of reading and radically reinterpreting existing texts on ancient Iranian history, in order to establish Irish connections otherwise not even implicitly articulated by these texts, these antiquarians inscribed concurrently deductive and inductive narratives of historical progressions and sequences onto existing historical accounts of ancient Iran, in a manner never intended by the authors of those original sources or imagined by contemporary Iranian readers of such sources. In other words, in Irish antiquarian works Ireland's ancient history was grounded in, and simultaneously emerged outside, the pages of these texts. This was a hermeneutical extension of Iranian history beyond what was recorded in the pages of those Iranian texts. Hence, Ireland's presumed ancient ties to Iran, or to other parts of the Orient for that matter, was a *brokered history* that could only have been completed by the Irish following their migration from their Iranian (or other oriental) homeland and could not have been written by those who had remained behind in the Iranian (or other oriental) homeland. As discussed below, the earliest "Irish" accounts of ancient Irish history available to Irish antiquarians in the late eighteenth century were composed around the end of the so-called "late Middle Ages,"[5] along with some still extant oral traditions. Therefore, antiquarians subscribing to the Iranian model had to establish historical correspondence between the existing Irish sources and the available histories of ancient Iran. This was a key historiographic prerequisite in narrating ancient Ireland by means of appending Irish history to the history of ancient Iran (not unlike similar narrations of Ireland's alternative oriental and non-oriental origins). In (re)connecting ancient Ireland to ancient Iran, Irish antiquarians engaged in *future-making* renditions of *existing* historical accounts of ancient Iran. The story of the earliest Iranian population migrations to Ireland, and/or the advent of Ireland's ancient Iranian-influenced civilization, began at the point beyond the threshold where sources on ancient Iranian history fell silent.

In connection with specifically Iranian theories of Irish origins after the late eighteenth century, as opposed to some other oriental theories of Irish origins (such as Scythian or Phoenician), it was also the case that native Irish sources on Irish origins produced since 'medieval' times were also silent on Ireland's ties to Iran. The late eighteenth-century antiquarians asserting an Iranian ethnic and/or cultural pedigree for ancient Ireland were, therefore, engaged in bonding existing historical sources on ancient Iran and Ireland—combining two hitherto disparate histories into a single continuous history and reading into existing Irish sources traces of ancient history of Iran. This was, in effect, also a new hermeneutical engagement with existing Irish histories of ancient Ireland. To this end, Irish antiquarians turned to the latest information available in the West about ancient Iran (including translations from Persian and Arabic) as well as the latest philological theories and language classifications, most notably the Indo-European or "Aryan" theory of linguistic subdivisions. Among many other examples discussed in this book, it was through these various methodological interventions (as resourcefully contorted as their application generally happened to be in the works of Irish antiquarians) and imaginative collation of ancient Iranian and Irish histories that, for instance, the (otherwise legendary) Pishdādiān, and even the more outlandish Mahābādiān, ancestry of ancient Persians became also the ancestors of the (equally fabled) Tuatha de Dananns or of the alleged Milesian progenitors of ancient Ireland's Gaelic population—while also purportedly accounting for such other diffusionist Iranian connections as the design and function of Ireland's Round Towers.

In terms of historiography, this was a *derivative* historical method, with its antiquarian practitioners conceiving their project as reconstructive and resuscitative. Of course, it becomes difficult here to differentiate between, or even gauge, authorial and epistemic "imagination" versus purely premeditated invention and fabrication, leaving aside the robust contemporary contestations among antiquarians belonging to competing camps in oriental or other models of Irish origins over such routine topics as historical evidence, methodology, and other established historiographic interpretive standards. To avoid presuming entirely conscious fictive (re)creations of ancient Ireland by Irish antiquarians (for political or other ends), their works require some degree of contextualization. The idea of "Eastern" roots of the Irish (more precisely the "Gaels," who were regarded as the main ancestral lineage of the earliest large-scale population settlements on the island) reached as far back as the 'Middle Ages.' These earlier accounts were composed by Ireland's monastic scholars. Iran/Persia was a later eighteenth-century addition to the existing inventory of presumed Eastern territorial-cultural locations of Ireland's ancient populations and civilization. The medieval and "early-modern" Irish sources overwhelmingly assigned different formulations of Scythian or Phoenician ancestry to the Irish. Notably, in these earlier accounts "civilization" was first introduced to Ireland with the introduction of Christianity in the fifth century. This implied the early ancestry of the Irish prior to that time had resided in a state of savagery. A major twist to this narrative of Ireland's Eastern origins and much later civilizational development occurred in the seventeenth century. In 1634 Geoffrey Keating, himself a Catholic priest, completed *The History of Ireland (Foras Feasa ar Éirinn*, meaning "the foundation of knowledge concerning Ireland"), which rehabilitated the alleged Scythian ancestry of the Irish contra ancient Greek, as well as medieval Irish Christian and later English, claims of savagery. (It should be added here that in none of the pre-eighteenth century Irish accounts were Scythians classified as belonging to the larger Iranian-speaking population groups that also included the Persians, who at different stages in ancient times had vied with Scythians for regional control and had been defeated by the latter. Although there had been earlier models of Indo-European languages, inclusive of Persian, it was primarily after the late eighteenth century that particular formulations of Indo-European (a.k.a. Aryan) languages gained currency in Western Europe, including in Ireland.)

Keating's and earlier Irish models of Eastern origins were based primarily on biblical (i.e., Mosaic) theory of post-diluvial descendants of Noah populating different adjoining lands somewhere around the Near East, and their descendants in turn subsequently dispersing to all corners of the (known) world in a relatively short span of time, given the prescribed dates for "Creation" itself according to different biblical authorities. With various reconfigurations, this model of population lineages from an ultimately common ancestry, but with different languages, physical characteristics, and civilizational attributes over time—along with all its accompanying anachronistic naming of ethnicities, territories, and cultures—, still carried substantial weight in antiquarian circles across Europe and elsewhere in the late eighteenth century, even if it was not universally accepted. During the eighteenth century, antiquarian accounts of Irish origins generally included manifold versions of the Mosaic model that identified the Irish with different branches of Noah's descendants. But this model was now increasingly, and in some accounts abundantly, supplemented with additional historical models and historiographic methodologies, including recourse to "standard" theories of Indo-European languages, primarily through the medium of the British Sir William Jones (albeit with much earlier roots). As already noted, these new historiographic trends also substantially relied on complementary non-biblical historical accounts of various oriental societies in ancient times. The wide-ranging evidentiary sources of this methodological procedure included works produced by 'orientals' themselves—Eastern or oriental sources in this case meaning sources beyond the existing range of biblical sources, including later commentaries, that had been utilized in Mosaic theories. (This reliance on Eastern histories and the authority of oriental sources for (re)constructing the ancient past of a Western European territory (Ireland) is a grossly overlooked factor in previous studies of Irish antiquarianism.) It is crucial to distinguish this particular reliance on oriental sources as a bedrock of information about the history of a European location (albeit conceived of by many Irish and other antiquarians as an oriental or semi-oriental outpost in Europe) from the growing trend in the West/Europe by the eighteenth century of consulting oriental sources (besides scriptural and other Judeo-Christian religious texts) for compiling histories of oriental peoples and lands themselves, as in the case of such works as Captain John Stevens' 1715 *The History of Persia. Containing, the Lives and Memorable Action of its Kings from the First Erecting of that Monarchy to this Time*, or, a century later, Sir John Malcolm's *The History of Persia from the Most Early Period to the Present Time*. The consultation of extra-biblical oriental sources by Irish antiquarians was a significant pioneering historiographic gesture in reconstructing the ancient past of a Western European territory. As discussed later, this reliance on non-biblical oriental knowledge production, and the accompanying validation of the authoritative attributes of that body of knowledge, occurred at a historical juncture just prior to the appearance of standard historical accounts of oriental societies elsewhere in Western Europe (including Britain) that consigned *some* of the very same oriental sources to the realm of mythology and absurdity, as, for instance, in Sir John Malcolm's 1815 *The History of Persia*.

Well into the twentieth century, the by then few remaining die-hard adherents of oriental theories of Irish origins continued to consult oriental sources for reconstructing the history of ancient Ireland. The best known of these works, published at the cusp of Ireland's division and the partial independence of the Irish Free State, was the 1921 *The Story of the Irish Race* by Seumas MacManus. As discussed in the next chapters, the contrasting and increasingly dominant post-1922 *Europe-centered* historiography of ancient Ireland, which gained official status in the Irish Free State, itself had a much older and complex genesis than what the referent "European history" appears to suggest. This 'Europeanizing' nationalist gesture (leaving aside the earlier "Scandian" theories of Irish origins) had flourished after the middle of the nineteenth century. It asserted the European origin of the Celts, while simultaneously affirming the common Celtic ancestry of all historically documented early settlers throughout the British Isles. This was, above all, initially a product of cross-ethnic nationalist drive for downplaying the seemingly irreducible differences between the ancestry of Ireland's ethnicities that were by then designated as Gaelic, English, Welsh, and Scots. At the time, there were also alternative nationalist claims of a common Celtic ancestry of early population settlements throughout the British Isles, but with the Celts having originated in the Orient. Therefore, at the time of its inception, the Europeanizing Celtic model of ancient Ireland was not an act of deferring to the authority of "Western" knowledge or acknowledging the purported preeminence of the West in world history, even if it ultimately assumed such a political function after 1922, both unintentionally and intentionally.

Apropos of Dipesh Chakrabarty's argument that, in the *postcolonial* era, "Third-World" nationalist historiographies have frequently turned to the history of Europe as an axial "referent,"[6] it is also germane to note that renditions of *ancient* European history well into the nineteenth century, including those of many imperial powers, at times turned to ancient histories of the 'Orient' (real or imagined) for evidentiary material. In the case of Irish models of oriental origins of the Irish, during Ireland's *colonial* phase, it was the history of the Orient that functioned as the key referent for constructing the ancient history of a European territory, both in terms of presumed evidentiary resources and models of historical development and civilizational attributes. This trend notably reached its pinnacle in the late eighteenth and early nineteenth century, at a time when, with a few exceptions, much of what was then designated in Europe as the Orient (e.g., South, Central, and West Asia, as well as North Africa) had not yet come under European imperial domination. At least well into the first half of the nineteenth century, mainstream Western/European historiographic traditions of narrating the origins of Europe's populations relied on what were significantly oriental sources in their inception, keeping in mind also the extensive prevalence of the Mosaic theory of human populations. Hence, the reliance by segments of Irish antiquarians and later historians on other ranges of oriental sources was not entirely unprecedented. What was unique was the non-biblical component of these sources. The main points of contention in the Mosaic theory were those of which branches of Noah's descendants constituted the ancient populations of Ireland and of other parts of Europe, as well as the modes and routes by which they had reached Ireland and other European territories, and when. In fact, Jewish, Christian, and Islamic historiographic traditions are all variously situated in some version of the Old Testament (Hebrew Bible) account of human origins and post-diluvian branching out of the world's populations. In some societies, these versions of human origins and dispersions overtook, incorporated, or coexisted with other existing local accounts of human origins, as in the case of the 'Iranian' territories following the spread of Islam after the seventh century CE. As demonstrated later, in Irish antiquarian accounts of Iranian origins of the Irish, the Mosaic theory was correlated with the earlier available Irish accounts of Irish origins as well as with the newly absorbed knowledge of pre-Islamic Iranian accounts of human creation, along with the new theories of Indo-European languages and population groups. Hence, a distinguishing feature of the specifically Iran-centered strands of oriental theories of Irish origins after the late eighteenth century (including Indo-Iranian, Irano-Scythian, and other such models) was the simultaneous reliance on Persian, Arabic, Sanskrit, and other range of non-biblical oriental sources, alongside biblical and Greco-Roman accounts of ancient history. These forms of Irish antiquarian writing may have been increasingly at odds with the newly emergent European historiographic outlooks by the early nineteenth century (including among some Irish historians), but they certainly were not a unique practice limited to Irish antiquarianism. There were antiquarians in Britain and in other parts of Europe who shared the underlying methodology of such Irish antiquarians as Charles Vallancey, Louisa Catherine Beaufort, Henry O'Brien,

Marcus Keane, and the like—Vallancey himself being an English resident in Ireland, who embraced Irish cultural nationalism. In other words, Irish antiquarians and later historians who adhered to oriental theories of Irish origins were not operating in a historiographic vacuum within Europe, as distinctive as their methodologies and claims may have been.

Joseph Lennon, among others, has noted that "Irish nationalist" orientalism cannot be entirely divorced from the more general patterns of Western orientalism.[7] This verdict also applies to the specifically Iran-centered theories of Irish origins, as well as to broader Irish nationalist commentaries on, and imaginings of, Iran (including contemporary Iran). These Irish nationalist constructs of Iran engaged with, were informed by, and in turn also informed other range of representations of Iran at the time, such as works by other Irish (including unionists), British (including the likes of John Malcolm or Harford Jones Brydges), and the wider European, and by late nineteenth century also American, multivalent and competing "orientalist" perceptions and portrayals of Iran or the Orient at large. Nor should we overlook contributions to these genres of knowledge production by 'orientals' themselves and by other non-European/non-Western sources. During the period covered in this book, there was a growing interest in, and familiarity with, Iranian history and Persian literature among segments of the literate Irish population—including Persian-language literature produced in varying territorial incarnations of 'Iran' in bygone times, as well as occasional contemporary works of Persian literature produced outside Iran, notably in the Indian subcontinent. Persian poetry by far dominated this sphere of literary interest. Historical and mytho-historical works produced by Iranians and by other groups writing in Persian, including in the Indian subcontinent, were also utilized by some Irish and other Western/European antiquarians, poets, and authors to different ends.

In keeping with the Mosaic theory—which retained an authoritative sway in the West well into the middle of the nineteenth century, and even following the publication of Charles Darwin's 1859 *On the Origin of Species*—, many historians and the majority of the population in the British Isles relied on biblical account of human creation and dated the earth's age to roughly 4000 BCE; notwithstanding the much older age of the earth proposed in the eighteenth-century by adherents of the Neptunist theory, the proto-evolutionary theories of the likes of Comte de Buffon (Georges-Louis Leclerc, d. 1788), the growing influence in the nineteenth century of the Plutonist uniformitarian theory of James Hutton (d. 1797), or the first volume of Charles Lyell's *Principles of Geology* (1830), among many other theories in the West that challenged conventional biblical accounts of human origin and the earth's age. Given the dominant "biblical" dating and periodization methods, which also accounted for the presumed regeneration of the human population by descendants of Noah and his wife following their survival of the Great Flood, it is not surprising that practitioners of the Mosaic theory should have deduced a relatively recent time frame for population dispersions around the world following the Flood, including the arrival of the first settlers in Ireland. Famously, in the seventeenth century James Ussher, the Anglican Archbishop of Armagh and Primate of Ireland, had confidently dated the Great Flood to 2349 BCE, while in some other accounts the date for that cataclysmic event was pushed forward to as recently as even 1800 BCE.[8] Therefore, with minor imaginative tinkering and leaps, and not forgetting the particular limitations of historical knowledge at the time—historical knowledge never being devoid of limitations regardless of the latest standard methodologies in the field and its particular setting—, it was not improbably far-fetched for the earlier 'medieval' Irish scholars, or for Geoffrey Keating in the seventeenth century, and even the eighteenth- and early nineteenth-century Irish antiquarians, to assign the arrival of earliest post-diluvian populations in ancient Ireland to a significantly fast-forwarded time frame. This time frame roughly corresponded to historical eras when, alternatively, the Scythian, Phoenician, Egyptian, Persian, Armenian,[9] and other similar range of territorial entities and cultures or 'civilizations' were known to have existed in the Orient. There were also those Irish antiquarians after the eighteenth century who preferred Greek, Scandinavian (Scandian), and other non-oriental models of Irish origins. These rough dating schema of Irish origins became even more nebulous and convoluted when further details were added to underlying narrative structures, such as Scythians passing through Egypt (in the time of Moses) on their way to the Iberian Peninsula and then to Ireland, or when oriental peoples and civilizations with a much less precise documented existence were selected as the ancestors and cultural purveyors of the ancient Irish. The latter was the case, for instance, when antiquarians who subscribed to the broadly Iranian (including Irano-Scythian or Indo-Iranian) or to the more narrowly Persian models of Irish origins sought to also accommodate into the story of Irish origins such (otherwise legendary) Iranian dynasties as the Pishdādiān, or even the earlier Mahābādiān, who were supposed to have existed long before the Persian rulers mentioned in biblical sources and were designated in 'Iranian' sources as the first peoples and dynasties on earth.

The debunking by the likes of the British historian Sir John Malcolm in the nineteenth century of the authenticity of some of the specifically non-biblical accounts of ancient times found in oriental sources, which also happened to be sources consulted by Irish antiquarians, and the mounting emphasis as the nineteenth century progressed on ever more rigorous standards of historical verification and cohesion certainly played a part in the slow demise of Irish theories of oriental origins. Malcolm and others, for example, relegated the Mahābādiān and Pishdādiān to the realm of sheer mythology. Studies of ancient Iran or other 'oriental' territories, such as Malcolm's 1815 *The History of Persia from the Most Early Period to the Present Time*, were significantly facilitated by greater European access to certain regions of the Orient, *in part* due to European imperial expansion and regional rivalries. However, it would be a mistake to presume a direct link between increased European imperialist inroad into the Orient after the late eighteenth century and the gradual demise of Irish antiquarian models of oriental origins by around the mid-nineteenth century—as some sort of conscious or intuitive defensive gesture stemming from Irish national pride and intended to dissociate (colonized) Ireland's past from the past of the Orient that was now being reduced to colonized or semi-colonized status under European imperial hegemony (including British imperialism). For one thing, the question of Irish origins concerned imputed ties between Ireland and the Orient in a distant past, just as those Irish antiquarians who claimed Hellenic roots of ancient Ireland were not deterred by the fact that Greek territories (until 1829) had for centuries been under the imperial control of various Muslim empires. Moreover, European imperialism in the Orient at the time did not apply to Scythia or Phoenicia, which also served as locations of Irish origins in some antiquarian works. In addition, in the case of the Indian subcontinent, and later also Egypt, and Iran, which in the nineteenth century faced varying forms and degrees of intensified European imperialist incursions, as the nineteenth century progressed Irish nationalists actually drew increasing contemporary parallels between their own experience of imperial domination and those of the above-mentioned 'oriental' territories, claiming different forms of nationalist affinities with those territories, rather than seeking to distance themselves from these colonized and semi-colonized regions.

It would be impossible to gauge the precise popularity of oriental or other accounts of Irish origins across the entire spectrum of Irish society and in the Irish diaspora. Yet, it is important to again emphasize that whereas by the second half of the nineteenth century different oriental theories of Irish origins gradually fell out of favor in Irish historical circles, the competing accounts of the origins of the Gaels and other presumed early population groups in Ireland put forth since the 'Middle Ages' were largely within the conceivable historical imaginations and the accepted historiographic conventions of their times, at least until the early decades of the nineteenth century, and notwithstanding contemporary contentions on particular details, sources, and methods of the various accounts. These narratives of Irish origins from the Middle Ages to the nineteenth century should be placed in a broader world-historical context, including different 'creation' (genesis) stories believed by various peoples around the world, or, for example, cartographic conventions in different parts of the world during the time corresponding to the 'Middle Ages' in European periodization scheme (including delineations of terra incognito that were often presumed to abound with monstrosities). For instance, in mainland Britain, next door to Ireland, work such as the twelfth-century *Historia Regum Britanniae* (*The History of the Kings of Britannia*), composed around 1136 by Geoffrey of Monmouth, the Bishop of St. Asaph, was generally accepted as a genuine historical account of England and Wales well into the late sixteenth century. This work maintained the Trojan forces of Brutus founded "Britain" after defeating the indigenous population of giants who inhabited the territory.[10] Similar accounts of ancient Britain were in vogue when Irish antiquarians were debating whether the ancient Irish were descendants of Phoenicians or other so-called Semitic groups, or of Scythians, Persians, Egyptians, or Greeks, among others.[11] The Scottish *Declaration of Arbroath*, addressed in 1320 to Pope John XXII as grounds for Scotland's independence from England, maintained the early Scots were descendants of people originating in "Greater Scythia," even if some present-day historians find this too far-fetched to have been actually believed by the signatories of the Declaration.[12] This was a history of Scottish origins that was later repeated in a different narrative structure by the likes of the Scottish John Pinkerton in his 1787 *A Dissertation on the Origin and Progress of the Scythians or Goths*. Although not as widely acknowledged, there were even accounts of the partially Scythian origins of the Saxon population of England.[13] Alternatively, after the sixteenth century, some English scholars even argued Britons were descendants of the "lost tribes of Israel."[14]

These suppositions were frequently contested by other rival contemporary or later sources, as was the case also with various accounts of Irish origins. Writing in 1586 in his *Britannia: Or a Chorographical Description of Great Britain and Ireland, Together with the Adjacent Islands*, the English antiquarian William Camden disputed the Spanish (i.e., Milesian), or Jewish, Phoenician, or Syrian (i.e., Assyrian) origins of the Irish. He also refuted all assertions of etymological roots of Ireland's name in connection with the aforementioned population groups. Instead, Camden's account of the origins of Ireland's Gaelic population, following a particular Mosaic model of population dispersions around the world, maintained the island's earliest settlers had come over from mainland Britain, more specifically the Scots descendants of Scythians ("Celto-Scytæ") who had already settled in Britain. On the basis of this presumed lineage of the Gaels, Camden confidently divided the population of Ireland into the "barbarous *Irishry*, or more commonly the *wild Irish*" and the law-abiding civilized "*English-Irish*."[15] Among others, a similar castigation of the Irish (i.e., of the Gaelic population) based on their imputed Scythian ancestry was more (in)famously propounded by the English poet and author Edmund Spenser a decade later (see Chapter One), with Spenser holding an administrative post in Ireland for some years. The Irish Geoffrey Keating in the seventeenth century was reacting to such civilizational vilifications of the Gaels and their (alleged) Scythian ancestry in his 1634 *The History of Ireland (Foras Feasa ar Éirinn)*.[16] Beginning with Keating, Irish antiquarianism engaged in a new mode of reframing ancient Ireland within the parameters of known world history, in a manner that specifically claimed a highly civilized pre-Christian (i.e., "pagan") ancient Ireland, while instrumentally challenging the avowed historical and civilizational centrality and hegemony of "England" within the British Isles as propounded by English and other castigators of Ireland's Gaelic population and cultures. As many decidedly Irish nationalist antiquarians after the late eighteenth century also claimed, this revitalized model of Ireland's oriental past claimed that the first great civilization in the British Isles had arrived in Ireland and by a route bypassing mainland Britain. In the case of the Scythian theory of the ancestry of the Gaels, whom Keating and many subsequent Irish antiquarians claimed to have later also settled in Scotland, the meandering route of this migration was, to put it in a very condensed form here, generally from Scythia to Ireland by way of Egypt, and then the Iberian Peninsula along the way. Keating, for his part, also maintained that the passage of the Gaels/Scythians through Egypt coincided with the episode of Moses and his followers crossing the Red Sea. It was further stipulated the descendants of these Scythians eventually reached Ireland three hundred years later, which happened to be "one thousand and eighty years after the deluge."[17]

As already noted, 'Iran' first appeared among the range of oriental locations of Irish origins in the late eighteenth century (either corresponding specifically to ancient Persia or in some accounts appearing as Irano-Scythian, Indo-Iranian, or some other broader 'Iranian' civilizational entity). Alongside the contention of a Persian/Iranian fountainhead of Ireland's glorious ancient civilization in these antiquarian accounts, there also existed Irish nationalist political commentaries that utilized a distinctly divergent representational mode of ancient Persia. This was the persistent portrayal of ancient Persia as a tyrannical and expansionist imperial aggressor state defied by the small Hellenic city-states; most famously in reference to the highly mythologized Spartan last stand against the Persian invaders at the Battle of Thermopylae in 480 BCE. Thermopylae became one of the most hackneyed Irish nationalist historical referentialities—with the unmistakable undertone of Irish resistance against the behemoth of English imperialism, most famously in what would become the unofficial anthem of militant Irish nationalism after the mid-nineteenth century: Thomas Osborne Davis' "A Nation Once Again," composed sometime in the early 1840s. These conflicting Irish nationalist portrayals of ancient Iran/Persia generally coexisted in an uncomplicated manner, particularly given the frequent obscurity in antiquarian models of Iranian origins as to the exact time frame in ancient Iranian and Irish history when Iranian civilization was transmitted to Ireland. Moreover, Charles Vallancey, the leading advocate of the Iranian theory of Irish origins at the turn of the nineteenth century, and a number of other Irish antiquarians set out to discredit some of the extant principal sources of Western/European knowledge about the ancient world that tended to vilify non-Hellenic societies and cultures. The sources in question were Greco-Roman accounts of ancient Persia and other so-called barbarian societies—even as the likes of Vallancey still selectively quoted from Greco-Roman sources when these sources corroborated their conclusions. This historiographic posture was qualitatively different from other modes of Irish nationalist discrediting, or authenticating, of rival sources of information about Iran, as in the case of the coverage of the Anglo-Iranian War of 1856–57 in the Dublin nationalist newspaper *The Nation*. *The Nation* validated official Iranian accounts of the armed conflict in contrast to official British accounts. The much earlier historiographic intercession of Vallancey and others in the oriental antiquarian camps, who in effect were following in the earlier footsteps of Geoffrey Keating's contestation of Hellenic representations of Scythians as barbarians, had broad civilizational implications for Ireland itself.

Similar to Irish antiquarian reliance on extra-biblical oriental sources in reconstructing Ireland's past, the fundamental contestation of ancient Hellenic accounts of Persians as characteristically tyrannical, and/or the persistent privileging of the often generically constructed "Greek" civilization in contrast to Persian culture in subsequent mainstream Western/European accounts of the ancient world (based on Hellenic sources), was yet another significant historiographic intervention in conventional Western/European epistemic practices and knowledge production. This is not to discount an alternative range of earlier and contemporary critiques of Greco-Roman sources in the West/Europe—leaving aside here what is often exaggeratedly termed "Christian" devaluation of so-called pagan knowledge in general. As a random example, in the introductory essay of his 1777 *A Dictionary: Persian, Arabic*, the English John Richardson was principally disinclined to accept the veracity of Hellenic descriptions of ancient Persians.[18] But, the contestation of Greco-Roman debasement of ancient Persian civilization on the part of Irish antiquarians who adhered to Iranian/Persian models of Irish origins was ultimately also an act of challenging Western (in particular English) canonical texts on the presumed civilizational inferiority of ancient Ireland itself. By implication, this historiographic gesture also effectively contested the very notion of what in the post-Enlightenment 'Western' world had become the standard hierarchical historical-civilizational construct of an inherited Greco-Roman based "Western Civilization" (leaving aside here the inherently flawed and fictional premises of any such *longue durée*, singular, and exclusionary civilizational construct). As peripherally hinted at in a 1986 article by Joep Leerssen, along a different trajectory of Orient-Ireland theories of origins,[19] the various theories of oriental origins of the Irish in general positioned Ireland in a liminal geographic-cultural space both *of* and *in-between* the West and the Orient. The purported indigenous Orient-centered cultural heritage of Ireland assigned to the territory an Eastern civilizational identity in a region geographically situated in western Europe (without denying here the contemporaneous existence of non-oriental antiquarian theories of Irish origins). It was precisely this conceptualization of Ireland as being simultaneously of and in-between the West and the Orient that had been seized as a premise by the likes of the English William Camden and Edmund Spenser since the late sixteenth century to castigate the Gaelic Irish and their culture as the most pronounced barbarian counterpart in the British Isles of the purportedly civilized English. Therefore, it is not the least bit surprising that, in the revamped style of Geoffrey Keating, those Irish nationalist antiquarians in the late eighteenth century who subscribed to various versions of Eastern origins of Gaelic civilization should have defended their purported ancient *ursprung* of that civilization. These antiquarians were, in effect, rescripting and reordering existing standard Western/European accounts of the ancient world. Yet, at the same time, the characterization of Ireland as both of and in-between the West and the Orient chafed against Ireland's other, and more contemporary, liminal positioning in world history: that of Ireland as both a British colony and, simultaneously, a major participant in, and in some ways both a beneficiary and a victim of, British imperialism in other parts of the globe, including the Orient. Examples range from the Irish serving as colonial administrators and imperial military personnel to the empire's mixed impact on Irish economy.[20]

As argued in this book, the diverse oriental models of Irish origins gradually fell by the wayside due to two substantial corresponding and subsequently interlinked developments, among a range of other contributing factors discussed in the next chapters. On the one hand, after the early decades of the nineteenth century, there emerged a new "historicist" methodology[21] with more rigorous standards of documentation, verification, and comparative analyses. This historiographic trend eventually traced the earliest definitively corroborated large-scale population settlements in Ireland only as far back as "Celtic" migrations from other parts of Europe, including from mainland Britain, and confirmed the long presence of Celts in continental Europe before their appearance in Ireland, regardless of where the ancestry of the Celts may have originated in very distant times. These recontoured Europe-centered Celticist historiographic models recognized the presence of other earlier population settlements in Ireland. Yet, they maintained the prior appearance of these peoples in other parts of the British Isles before their arrival in Ireland could neither be conclusively refuted nor corroborated, due to lack of available documentation. The Europe-centered Celticist historiographic paradigms dovetailed new trends in Irish architectural history (itself influenced by historicist methods), with George Petrie in the 1830s as the leading Irish pioneer in this regard. The growing endorsement of Petrie's methodology after the

1840s and his verdict that Ireland's Round Towers did not predate the introduction of Christianity to Ireland in the fifth century struck a major blow against a key evidentiary claim in oriental and other theories of Irish origins that maintained the Round Towers were modeled after ancient oriental or other prototypes and introduced by early population settlements in Ireland—even if Petrie's theory did not fundamentally contradict the possibility of oriental descent of Ireland's early population groups and only demolished the archaeological-architectural claim of linkage between these presumed surviving ancient monuments of Ireland and their oriental prototypes. The extent to which these new and continually more rigorous historiographic methods were also influenced in the latter decades of the nineteenth century by Darwinian and other nascent "scientific" theories in comparative anthropology and ethnography is beyond the scope of the present study and is only addressed in passing references later in the book. (*It is in recognition of the expanding influence of more rigorous, albeit imperfect, historicist methodologies after the 1840s that I switch from the use of "antiquarian" to "historian," even if the former more imaginative and deductive methodologies persisted in many studies of ancient Ireland during the remainder of the century, including in works by scholars belonging to the Royal Irish Academy, and notwithstanding the fact that the term antiquarian simply denotes historians of antiquity.*)

The second interrelated major development that pushed the already beleaguered oriental theories of Irish origins to the periphery of Irish historiography was the appearance after the 1840s of a reinvigorated undercurrent of distinctly nonsectarian and multiethnic Irish nationalist platforms, akin to the former platform of the United Irishmen in the late eighteenth century. The catalyst for this revitalized nationalist trend (both republican and Home Rule) was the Young Ireland movement that emerged after decades of O'Connellite nationalist dalliance with the Catholic Church. Irish nationalist antiquarians of previous generations had chiefly come from the miscellaneous ranks of Anglo-Protestant, Anglo-Catholic, Scots-Protestant, Welsh-Protestant, and "Old Irish" of primarily Catholic backgrounds. The principal task of these antiquarians had been the historical recovery of ancient Ireland's cultural/civilizational grandeur and refutation of English allegations of Ireland's persistent barbarity prior to the arrival of Anglo-Normans in the twelfth century. The new generations of Irish historians after the 1840s, some of them also taking their cue from Young Ireland poets such as Thomas Osborne Davis, concentrated instead on undoing the divisiveness of contemporary religious and ethnic distinctions within the "Irish nation," regardless of hostile encounters between different ethnic and denominational groups in the past. This subject also received its fair share of coverage in the poetry of Young Ireland, notably in the works of James Clarence Mangan and Denis Florence MacCarthy. As already noted, the renewed effort to eradicate ethnic (and more obscurely also religious) insularities as authentic markers of belonging to, or exclusion from, the "Irish nation" did not amount to the denial of inter-ethnic and inter-denominational conflicts in Ireland since the twelfth century. In nonsectarian nationalist platforms, national authenticity was exclusively predicated on one's underlying commitment to Irish nationalism, with cultural nationalism as the most basic requirement ("culture" in this setting being an instrumentally crafted, heteroglossic, and highly contested construct). In practice, however, the Old Irish ("Gaels"/"mere Irish") of Catholic persuasion generally enjoyed automatic membership in such constructs of nationhood, unless they publicly expressed opposition to all projects of Irish nationalism (cultural and political). This is also evident in references to the predominantly Catholic ('mere Irish') peasantry as the repository of national folk culture and memory, particularly those in the remaining Gaelic-speaking districts in western counties following the Great Famine of 1845–51. The virtual sacralization of the local population of Aran Islands (as allegedly the most authentic of the Irish) in the Romantic nationalism of the Irish Revival after the late nineteenth century is yet another instance.

In the genre of nonsectarian and cross-ethnic nationalist poetry, there had been transitional figures during the interval between the United Irishmen and Young Ireland. The most pivotal and celebrated of these figures was Thomas Moore in the first half of the nineteenth century. Moore, later also a prominent antiquarian, belonged to the oriental camp in the debate on Irish origins, claiming Phoenician diffusion of Iranian civilization to ancient Ireland. He was deeply steeped in the nondenominational and multiethnic conceptualization of the Irish nation, having been an erstwhile sympathizer of the United Irishmen at the close of the eighteenth century. Moore's most patently Irish nationalist poem (as opposed to his more popular nationalist ballads) was "The Fire-Worshippers" in the 1817 *Lalla Rookh*—a prime example of the liminal literary convention of transfiguring Irish authenticity from "Gaelic-Catholic" to a cross-ethnic and cross-denominational formulation. In this poem, Moore celebrated the love affair of his Persian-Zoroastrian hero with the Arab-Muslim heroine, the latter choosing her lover over her father, who happened to be the Arab-Muslim governor of occupied Iran and the mortal enemy of the poem's hero.

An overlooked upshot of the reinvigorated nonsectarian nationalism after the 1840s (political and/or cultural) is its *receptivity* to the emerging historiographic leverage of Europe-centered Celticist model of Irish origins (without in any way disregarding the coexisting *unionist* contributions to Europe-centered Celticist history of ancient Ireland). This Europe-centered Celticism—as opposed to the more marginal prior Europe-centered accounts of Ireland's ancient population, including the Scandinavian (Scandian) alternative to various oriental theories—focused on the shared distant heritage and ethnic lineage of the ancient populations of Ireland and mainland Britain, not to mention its abandonment of the former overriding emphasis in nationalist antiquarianism on the introduction of civilization to Ireland independently of mainland Britain. The newly emergent Europe-centered Celticist historiographic narrative centered on the distant common ancestry of Old Irish (Gaels/mere Irish) and ancient Britons (regardless of subsequent ethnic admixtures in both cases). The variants of the new model also ditched the former Europe-centered antiquarian supposition of rapid mass migrations to Ireland from the Celtic fringes of continental Europe. Accordingly, the waves of Celtic migrations from mainland Europe across the entire British Isles over a period of many centuries provided the singular most common ancestral denominator of ancient populations of Ireland and Britain, in contrast, for instance, to Picts (who may in fact also have been Celts) and other early population groups on both islands. Needless to say, there was still an inherent ethnicist attribute in this claim of the common Celtic essence of Irish identity, which excluded from "Irishness" certain minority population groups in Ireland, including by the early twentieth century the Jewish migrants from Eastern Europe.

In the early twentieth century, the most frequently cited works in this genre of Europe-centered Celticist historiography of ancient Ireland were those by Eoin MacNeill, Patrick Weston Joyce, Alice Stopford Green, Mary Hayden, and George Aloysius Moonan. The gradual synthesis of the Europe-centered Celticist model of Irish origins and the cross-ethnic Irish nationalist platform received official nationalist endorsement following the establishment of the Irish Free State in 1922, ironically just as Catholicism reaffirmed its hegemonic grip over the criterion of Irish authenticity in the new Irish state—in part thanks to the insistence by Eoin MacNeill and his acolytes on the joint Celtic and (pre-Reformation) Christian identity of Ireland. In a "postcolonial" framing of the disparity between historical writing in the West and in the non-Western world, Chakrabarty has argued:

> That Europe works as a silent referent in historical knowledge becomes obvious in a very ordinary way. There are at least two everyday symptoms of the subalternity of non-Western, third-world histories. Third-World historians feel the need to refer to works in European history; historians of Europe do not feel the need to reciprocate.[22]

Without my addressing in detail here the limitations and oversimplifications concerning historical knowledge production and reception in Chakrabarty's overarching assertion, most notably in the context of *imperial histories* produced in the West/Europe, it can nevertheless be said that Ireland's transition from an overwhelmingly 'Orient'-centered to 'Europe'-centered historical 'referent' (and by no means 'silent' in this case) was already underway during Ireland's colonial existence and assumed greater legitimacy after Ireland's partial postcoloniality in 1922, in the form of the Irish Free State (later Éire and, subsequently, the Republic of Ireland).

Nonetheless, we need to be careful not to essentialize such patterns. As demonstrated in later chapters in the present book, due to distinct developments during the period from 1922 to the 1930s, the dominant Irish nationalist account of Irish "origins" as well as foreign policy considerations and alignments of the Irish Free State became overwhelmingly Europe-centered (the latter designation in the realm of foreign policy also encompassing Britain's so-called white settlement dominions around the world). Yet, Irish nationalists during these years did not entirely abandon their interest in the remainder of the world, most notably in the case of India in regard to ongoing anticolonial struggles in the British Empire. Nor did the officially sanctioned Europe-centered historical narrative of the long gestation and formation of the Irish 'nation' in Ireland's 'postcolonial' era—whether in terms of its partial independence from 1922 to 1949 or as a republic subsequently, and leaving aside here Northern Ireland—terminate Irish nationalist interest in non-European history (past and present); not forgetting also historical referentialities appearing in works of literature and the arts, among other media. Moreover, any random perusal of a wide range of Irish nationalist newspapers in both the Republic of Ireland and Northern Ireland from the late 1960s to the 1980s—ranging from *The United Irishman* (Dublin) to *The Starry Plough* (Belfast), *An Phoblacht* (Belfast), or *Socialist Republic* (Belfast)—will clearly indicate an increasingly "Third Worldist" approach during those years of the crisis in Northern Ireland known as 'The Troubles.'

The fact that many in so-called postcolonial societies may at times turn to particular episode's in 'European'/'Western' history as a model does not denote an absolute aversion to non-European historical referentialities and self-comparison.

A Brief Note on the Broader Historical Setting for the Emergence of Iranian Theories of Irish Origins and Iran-Themed Irish Nationalist Literature

In connection with Irish origins, Iran first acquired antiquarian referential cachet in the late eighteenth century joining the existing list of other oriental and non-oriental designations of Ireland's ancient beginnings. Among other contemporary developments in Ireland that impacted the contours of what can more narrowly be defined as Irish *nationalist* antiquarianism at the time, the appearance of Iranian theories of Irish origins occurred at the historical crossroads of ongoing European Enlightenment search for wide-ranging knowledge from around the globe and the emergence of a broad-based nonsectarian Irish nationalist platform, itself fueled by the secular-oriented, rationalist, and simultaneously universalist precepts within the otherwise heterogenous trends of the Enlightenment (not overlooking the non-European Enlightenment nodes at the time). Orient-centered Irish antiquarianism from the late eighteenth century, notwithstanding the existence of even earlier strands of Irish antiquarianism that had accorded the Gaelic population of Ireland Scythian or Phoenician ancestry, spanned both the European Enlightenment fascination and growing familiarity with the Orient, among other non-European regions of the world, as well as the potent curiosity about non-European/non-Western cultures, histories, and literatures present in the Romantic reaction to the Enlightenment.

What is generically termed the Enlightenment was a broad amalgam of worldviews in different locations around the world and not solely bound to certain regions of Europe,[23] largely (though not entirely) emanating from shared principles of faith in reason and human progress, and variously infused with degrees of universalist and/or particularistic impulses and prioritizations. In some of the leading western European trends of the Enlightenment, a thematic example of the accentuation of *the particular within the universal* is the hierarchical "Euro-centric" (more properly "West"-centric) approaches to non-Western cultures and societies, including the ambiguous redefinition of 'civilization' that now assumed value-laden connotations, as opposed to merely implying urban settlements and modes of life. This was a framing of humanity in a universal world-historical setting that ultimately privileged a particular segment of that humanity and highlighted its purportedly unique and self-contained history as a manifestation of higher cultural, political, societal, scientific, artistic, material, and other achievements in comparison with the rest of humanity, whether or not also ascertaining that other peoples and cultures were intrinsically incapable of similar, let alone higher, levels progress in the long run. The ongoing Irish antiquarian debates on Ireland's ancient civilizational roots were given a new twist in light of, on the one hand, the spread of non-sectarian and cross-ethnic proclivities in Irish nationalism, which were already evident in the decades before the formation of the Society of United Irishmen in 1791 (going back to at least before the 1782 Irish Constitution), and, on the other hand (and more particularly), the prevalent tendency in the broader Enlightenment movement to valorize the ostensibly Greco-Roman heritage of so-called Western Civilization. Although the Enlightenment and Romanticist movements are frequently treated as entirely distinct and mutually antithetical worldviews—with Romanticism generally regarded as a direct reaction to Enlightenment rationality—, in the domain of nationalism the natural law principle of the Enlightenment (which served as the groundwork for faith in rationality and purported 'scientific objectivity') blended without much friction with the Romantic belief in the primacy of feelings and emotions and the preference for so-called traditions (however one chose to define these and without necessarily defending established religions or monarchic system of government). Among other factors in the late eighteenth century, alongside the influence of manifold Enlightenment ideologies, as well as the impact of American and French revolutions, Irish nationalist discourses by the end of the century were simultaneously shaped by the Romantic nationalist outlook of the Prussian Johann Gottfried von Herder (1744–1803). Herder's articulation of the unique characteristics of each nation melded together both the Enlightenment concept of natural law and the Romantic faith in tradition and emotional attachments to one's presumed heritage (language, culture, and so on), as much as Herder otherwise defied the universalist and rationalist principles of the Enlightenment and also recognized historical transformations in language and culture. After all, in his simultaneous rejection of empires and espousal of nations, based on the assertion of unique characteristics of any given people, Herder maintained in the first volume of his two-volume *Ideen zur Philosophie der Geschichte der Menschheit* (1784, 1791), a work that was translated into English in 1800:

> Nature educates families: the most natural state therefore is one nation, with one national character. This it retains for ages, and this is most naturally formed, when it is the object of it's native princes: for a nation is as much a natural plant as a family, only with more branches. Nothing therefore appears so directly opposite to the end of government as the unnatural enlargement of states, the wild mixture of various races and nations under one sceptre. A human sceptre is far too weak and slender for such incongruous parts to be engrafted upon it: glued together indeed they may be into a fragile machine, termed a machine of state, but destitute of internal vivification and sympathy of parts. Kingdoms of this kind, which render the name of fathers of their country scarcely applicable to the best of potentates, appear in history like that type of monarchies in the vision of the prophet, where the lion's head, the dragon's tail, the eagle's wings, and the paws of a bear, combined in one un-patriotic figure of a state. Such machines are pieced together like the trojan horse; guaranteeing one another's immortality, though, destitute of national character, there is no life in them, and nothing but the curse of Fate can condemn to immortality the forced union: for the very politics that framed them are those, that play with men and nations as with inanimate substances. But history sufficiently shows, that these instruments of human pride are formed of clay, and, like all other clay, will dissolve, or crumble to pieces.[24]

The evolving nonsectarian Irish nationalist orientations after the late eighteenth century encompassed both political activities in organized or individual forms (whether or not also inclusive of cultural undertakings) and the more strictly and primarily 'cultural' endeavors (without direct engagement in the narrowly defined 'political' sphere)—without here forgetting other range of nationalist domains, including economic activities, which again could intersect with narrowly defined political and/or cultural spheres. These nationalist endeavors spanned the gamut of republican and non-republican objectives. In both practice and theory, it is of course impossible to always sharply demarcate the narrowly defined political realm (here denoting the ultimate objective of attaining administrative power and/or territorial governance) from the narrowly defined cultural realm (geared toward such projects as establishing or affirming the foundations, parameters, common beliefs and heritage, customs, 'historical memories,' language, and/or other purported range of intersectional and polythetic characteristics and expressions that presumably define 'national' identity). The cultural and political practices and theoretical articulations of nationalism frequently intersected in some form of dialogical manner. Yet, one can still speak of spectrums of political and cultural interconnectedness, including cultural projects by individuals who did not personally aspire for national self-governance, even if their cultural undertakings were applied to that end by others. The most advanced joint expression of political and cultural nationalism in Ireland at the turn of the nineteenth century was articulated by the republican Society of United Irishmen, founded in 1791, with resonance in the Irish diaspora as well. This is not to suggest republicanism as an end goal was necessarily the perfect solution for Ireland's malaise at the time, or that the entire range of United Irishmen's policies and actions were beyond social and/or ethical reproach. Nevertheless, the organization succeeded in building a mass cross-ethnic and nonsectarian following, transcending two of Ireland's most internecine causes of social, political, and cultural schisms—with the origins of this nationalist platform traceable back to political splits and regroupings in Ireland surrounding the 1782 "Grattan's Parliament."

The United Irishmen's cultural range of political propaganda, edification, and indoctrination included a wide array of journalistic activities and collections of poetry.[25] There were, of course, also those aspiring to transcend sectarian and/or ethnic divides in Ireland who opposed the republican agenda of the United Irishmen and republicanism in general or simply avoided any direct public commentary on Ireland's future form of government. In the ranks of these groups were individuals variously immersed in the more narrowly defined 'cultural'-nationalist endeavors. Such cross-ethnic and cross-denominational cultural undertakings predated the formation of the United Irishmen, while crisscrossing with the cultural activities of that organization and would continue after the organization's demise. Overlapping with these cultural activities were particular trends in Irish antiquarianism that, among other things, sought to highlight and celebrate the past cultural and 'civilizational' achievements of Ireland's pre-Norman so-called indigenous population. By the late eighteenth century, these antiquarian projects, dating back to at least the previous century, assumed a clear cultural-nationalist attribute, regardless of the more narrowly defined political-nationalist initiatives of some of the antiquarians in question. A leading figure among these Irish nationalist antiquarians was Charles Vallancey, a Protestant English military officer residing in Ireland. In fact, Vallancey's initial antiquarian accounts of Ireland's ancient grandeur dated to the early 1770s, preceding the emergence of distinctly broad-based nonsectarian and cross-ethnic Irish nationalist political movements. The ideological formation of different strands of cross-ethnic and/or nonsectarian Irish political and/or cultural nationalisms was imbued with different admixtures of universalism and particularism derived from the Enlightenment and trans-Enlightenment worldviews (the latter, for instance, in the case of biblical beliefs in the post-diluvian common ancestry of all humans and the subsequent dispersions of various branches of the human family and emergence of distinct languages and so-called racial traits)—not overlooking the impact of other contemporary political and cultural developments around the world, as in the case of the reverberations in the ranks of the United Irishmen of such events as the American War of Independence (1776–83) or the events of the French Revolution after 1789. These other contemporary political and cultural developments were themselves processed through various lenses of universalism and particularism. A case in point being the occurrence in the poetry of United Irishmen of simultaneous advocacy of Irish nationalism, the French Revolution of 1789 (and more particularly the post-1792 French Republic), the independence of those former American colonies of Britain that comprised the United States of America, alongside a fervent condemnation of the system of enslaving Africans, and "slavery" in general, which continued to be practiced in the independent United States of America.[26] The concurrent intersections and tensions of nationalism and the Enlightenment, not forgetting the trans-rationalist and Romantic dimensions of all forms of nationalism, reverberated in Irish nationalist antiquarianism as well.[27]

It is undeniably impossible to absolutely demarcate the specifically "Irish" essence of Irish antiquarian knowledge production in general (whether that information was produced in Ireland or in the Irish diaspora) from contemporary antiquarian accounts of ancient Ireland produced in mainland Britain and in other parts of the world by *non-Irish* antiquarians, including in continental Europe and North America (not counting here the likes of Vallancey, who resided in Ireland and was involved in the project of Irish cultural reclamation). Nonetheless, there were particular elements that stood out in the more specifically Irish *nationalist* style of antiquarianism during this period, such as the assertion of an indisputable civilizational Golden Age in ancient Ireland independently of contacts with mainland Britain, even if some of these nationalist antiquarians were willing to concede to a common ethnic ancestry of the population of the entire British Isles in ancient times.[28] The Enlightenment's fixation with 'civilization'—a term that now came to be defined in the comparative and, by implication, also hierarchical, idiom of cultural accomplishments and aptitudes, as opposed to its Latin root meaning of "city" or "community" (*civis/civitas*)—and the accompanying emerging concept of 'Western Civilization,' posed an intrinsic challenge to Orient-centered models of Irish nationalist antiquarianism. The Enlightenment concept of Western Civilization not only invented an ostensibly continuous, singular, and exclusively 'Western' civilizational paradigm, but it also insisted on the superiority of Greco-Roman "classical" civilization (again in the singular) over all other cultural expressions and accomplishments around the world in ancient times. Within the Enlightenment tradition itself, including outside Ireland, there were critics of this pattern of hagiographic civilizational contrivance of the West, particularly given the conflation in some circles of the claim of civilizational superiority of the contemporary West with the purportedly higher innate (i.e., "racial") rational capacity of ("white") Western European populations than other groups.[29]

Just as in Ireland, outside Ireland too, there were competing Enlightenment camps in the debates on civilizational attributes of imperialism vs. anti-imperialism.[30] Combined with Ireland's colonized status in Western Europe, along with routine claims of English civilizational superiority by English and other detractors of Ireland's Gaelic past, and the concomitant increasing association of English 'civilization' with the insinuated Greco-Roman heritage central to the motif of Western Civilization, during the eighteenth-century Irish nationalist antiquarians were propelled to engage in a renewed defense of Ireland's ancient past, following in the footsteps of Geoffrey Keating in the previous century, but also resorting to new epistemic formulations, sets of theories, methodologies, and supporting sources and evidence. The revived antiquarian vindication and glorification of the Gaelic past received added momentum and urgency following the tectonic surge in nonsectarian and multiethnic Irish nationalist political initiatives after 1782.[31] In the process, nationalist antiquarians who claimed distinctly 'oriental' roots for the ancient populations and/or cultures of Ireland additionally began to renegotiate and reposition Ireland's place in world history by means of also utilizing alternative non-Western source material for compiling their own accounts of Ireland's past. As well as these interlacing developments, Irish antiquarianism in general was also informed by the Enlightenment interest in the Orient. This Enlightenment interest in the Orient, and in many other regions of the world, was in part augmented due to growing European imperial expansion into the Orient, among other parts of the globe, as the eighteenth century came to a close. This amplified Western imperial presence in the Orient included Britain's expanding direct and indirect imperial leverage in South Asia and the Persian Gulf under the auspices of the privately owned and, after 1773, state-regulated English East India Company (founded in 1600). Continued Western imperial consolidation and new inroads into the Orient, including the short-lived French invasion of Ottoman Egypt in 1798, vastly contributed to the ongoing so-called Oriental Renaissance in the West.[32] Central to this Renaissance was the field of philological studies, some findings of which were selectively applied to Irish antiquarian theories of Ireland's oriental roots. The accelerated scholarly fascination in, and engagement with, the Orient in the West, including the diverse assortment of oriental literatures, was also reflected in the European literary genre of Orient-situated fiction. By the turn of the nineteenth century, this genre carried over into the Romantic literary reaction to the Enlightenment and was reconfigured as the highly popular romantic fad of presumably *oriental-style* literature (whether ultimately disparaging, favorable, or neutral in their representations of the Orient). Irish poets and authors, too, contributed to this literary genre, including works by Irish nationalist authors and poets, in which oriental settings served as means of commenting on Irish history since the early Anglo-Norman conquests of the twelfth century. Thomas Moore's 1817 *Lalla Rookh* straddled both the Enlightenment rationalist and the Romantic antirationalist articulations of Irish nationalism through his deployment of the allegoric vista of the Orient.

On the other hand, James Clarence Mangan's invented translations of ostensibly oriental poems in the 1830s and the 1840s upturned both rationalism and Romanticism as literary modes of probing the category of the 'Irish nation.' While drawing heavily on contemporary Romantic German orientalist literary studies and anthologies, Mangan (d. 1849) in his unprecedented style took to task both the Romantic and Enlightenment pulls in current Irish literature, by simultaneously employing both of these literary types, but in consciously strained arrangements. These tensions at times appeared in the shape of contrasts between the structure, content, form, and tone of prose Introductions to his series of 'translated' poems, or existed as blatant internal contradictions within either the Introductions and/or in the poems themselves. However, following the outbreak of what became the Great Famine of 1845–51, Mangan's poetry assumed an unmistakably emotive Romantic quality of outright nationalist rage and broader human evocation of suffering and trauma—which had been missing from his earlier works or, at best, had been expressed in more layered and sardonic forms. In what was an early instance of a proto-deconstructionist literary strategy, Mangan's oriental pseudo-translations refused to readily own up to whether the Orient in these poems was a disguise for Ireland (given the simultaneous placement of cultural and historical distance and proximity in these 'translations') or if Ireland was itself an Orient to the West of Britain (as the colonized *Other* of England) and, hence, requiring no oriental disguise and already in some ways paralleling the Orient. Mangan's oriental pseudo-translations were ultimately marked by the enigma of whether the Orient and Ireland could even be truly grasped and known by those not belonging to, respectively, the Orient or Ireland in the first place (i.e., by the English, and "England" as a cultural lens, in this case). Language, however, was a major distinguishing feature between the Orient and Ireland in Mangan's works. This was not due to differences between oriental and Irish languages, or of Mangan supposedly having to translate (his invented) oriental poems from their (ostensibly) original languages in order to make them accessible to his general readers in Ireland. Rather, his oriental 'translations' appeared not in Irish language but in English (the language of Ireland's colonizers and the language in which Mangan himself wrote and spoke, similar to most Irish people of his generation who could not speak, let alone read and write, in Irish).[33] As opposed to Moore's *Lalla Rookh*, Mangan's poems in which the Orient served as a camouflage for Irish history of subjugation by, and/or resistance to, England did so in a manner that ultimately also questioned the historical proximity between Ireland and the particular Orient in question. Moreover, Mangan's works in general (prose and poetry), with the exception of the distinctly seething anti-England poems of the last three years of his life, probed the topic of the Irish nation in decidedly unorthodox and unsettling ways, suggesting all identities and nations were highly malleable and all notions of any collective *Self* rested on some element of past inventions and could only be sustained through continual reinventions. At least prior to the widespread ravages of the Great Famine that got underway in Ireland in 1845 and inspired Mangan's most outwardly militant revolutionary nationalist poetry, Mangan's conception of the Irish nation was, in effect, an inherently deferred and belated project emanating from multiple traumas of Ireland's history, but also already laden with the portend of future traumas of identity at the very moment of the Irish nation-state's birth. In his nationalist poetry of the pre-famine era, this inferred intrinsically crisis-ridden future national identity of the Irish was evocative of Mangan's lingering reflection on what constituted 'Irishness' in the past and the present, and what shape Irishness would assume following Ireland's liberation from English domination. In other words, in Mangan's writing, in place of such notions as national heritage, national history, or national memory, the nation was always temporally ruptured; the past yielded no sure guidance for the future, and the aspired future could not accommodate the imagined nation's full baggage of the past. Lastly, and entirely overlooked by other scholars of Mangan, in his Orient/Ireland literary interchanges Mangan exhibited a lingering attachment to oriental theories of Irish origins, more specifically to the Persian (Iranian) model.

Among the many developments in the early nineteenth century that contributed to growing Irish familiarity with Iranian history and literature was the establishment of Anglo-Iranian relations at the start of the century. It was at the close of the eighteenth century that Iran was first drawn into the ambit of British diplomatic and imperial policy making. Along with its proximity to Britain's expanding Indian empire (to the southeast of Iran), Iran bordered the Persian Gulf in the south, where Britain was attempting to bolster its own leverage. Iran also shared a long frontier with the Ottoman Empire to its west, had the expanding Russian Empire to the north, and bordered Afghan territories to the east (with the Afghan lands later also bordering Britain's Indian frontiers in the south and Russia's expanding frontiers in the north). In light of European and extra-European ramifications of the Napoleonic Wars (as a continuation of French Revolutionary Wars of 1792–99), in which Britain was the main challenger to France, British authorities (initially in British India and later in London too) set out to establish diplomatic relations with Iran. The regional impetus for the British diplomatic move included a territorial dispute that had been underway for some time between Iran and Russia (initially over Georgian territory), and Russia's seesawing participation in the French Revolutionary Wars, along with regional challenges faced by the expanding British Empire in the Indian subcontinent (including from Afghan quarters). In late 1799, the governor-general of British India, Lord Mornington (later Marquess Wellesley, and coincidentally a member of the Anglican Irish "Ascendancy"), dispatched John Malcolm as the envoy of British India to the Qajar court in Tehran (the Qajar dynasty ruling Iran from 1796 to 1925). Malcolm was the first "British" representative to the Iranian royal court since the 1562–63 failed mission of Anthony Jenkinson, who served as the representative of England's Queen Elizabeth I to the Safavid royal court of Iran, and was reviled in Mangan's 1846 poem "To the Ingleezee Khafir, Calling Himself Djuan Bool Djenkinzun." Malcolm, who among his other instructions was tasked with enlisting Tehran's assistance to British efforts for curtailing any potential French military threat to British India by way of Iran, Afghan territories, or the Persian Gulf, succeeded in concluding separate political and commercial treaties between the governments of British India and Iran in January 1801.[34] A corollary outcome of this diplomatic engagement and continued future diplomatic contacts between the British Empire and Iran was the further acceleration of interest in, and knowledge production about, Iranian history, society, and cultures in English language throughout the United Kingdom and in British India, particularly in the field of literature (and especially poetry). This had a marked impact on ongoing antiquarian, literary, and, later on, also political, Iran-Ireland associations. As shown in subsequent chapters, this process also drew heavily on knowledge production about Iran in British India by native scholars, whether in English or in other languages, which then circulated in Britain and Ireland (in English translation in the case of works originally appearing in other languages used in the Indian subcontinent, including Persian). John Malcolm and many members of subsequent British diplomatic missions to Iran (much of the latter dispatched directly by the authorities in London after the early nineteenth century) made their own significant contributions to 'European' knowledge of Iranian history, literature, and contemporary society. Besides Malcolm, other members of British diplomatic missions in the early nineteenth century who published wide-ranging works on Iranian history and/or literature included Sir Harford Jones (later Jones Brydges), the British minister to Tehran from 1808 to 1811, and William Ouseley, who accompanied his brother Sir Gore as a member of the latter's ambassadorial staff to Iran (1811–14); the Ouseleys being of Anglo-Irish descent.

It was the year before Malcolm set sail for Iran as the diplomatic envoy of British India that British authorities quelled a large-scale uprising in Ireland led by the republican United Irishmen, who had been anticipating extensive French assistance that did not materialize. The uprising, which got underway in late May 1798 and lasted four-and-a-half months, costing the lives of thousands of combatants and civilians, left a deep and enduring scar on Anglo-Irish relations and marked a major historical trauma in cross-sectarian and cross-ethnic Irish nationalist psyche at large, including many subsequent generations of non-militant and non-republican nationalists—with competing recollections and interpretations of the event in rival Irish nationalist circles to this day. The establishment of Anglo-Iranian relations in 1801, following Malcolm's mission, coincided with London's assumption of direct authority over Irish affairs in the aftermath of the suppression of the 1798 uprising. Under the 1801 Act of Union, the Irish parliament in Dublin (which by then already excluded adult male Catholics, who otherwise met the landed property qualification for parliamentary representation) was formally abolished, and Ireland was placed under London's direct parliamentary control and incorporated into the "United Kingdom of Great Britain and Ireland." In the coming decades, the after-effects of these major political developments in Ireland were also reflected in Irish nationalist literary and political engagements with Iran, as well as in the outlines of Irish nationalist antiquarian debates at large. It was coincidentally after this time frame that the theory of Iranian origins of the Irish reached its zenith, already vigorously vying with other leading oriental and non-oriental theories of Irish origins since the publication of Charles Vallancey's *A Vindication of the Ancient History of Ireland* in 1786. The greater proliferation after 1801 of historical, literary, and other Iran-related information in the United Kingdom and in British India, particularly of ancient Iran (in its broader cultural and territorial definitions, as opposed to only the territory named Iran during the period covered in the present book), along with similar range of information produced in other parts of Europe, as well as the rapidly expanding scholarship after the late eighteenth century on Indo-European branches of languages, further contributed to the evolution of Irish nationalist antiquarian claims of Iranian origins. These developments also variously facilitated the emergence of an Irish nationalist literary genre that allegorically substituted 'Iranian' settings for episodes in Irish history in the form of the Iran/Erin interchange, beginning with Thomas Moore. Meanwhile, in the ongoing antiquarian search for ancient Ireland's civilizational glory in the decades to come, ancient Iran attained preeminence as a most-favored *ursprung* locale. As already noted, theories of Eastern origins of the Irish gradually receded after the 1840s, but they did not entirely vanish. Disparate range of individuals continued to champion oriental theories of Ireland's ancient past. In the late nineteenth century, the leading advocate of Ireland's ancient ties with Iran was the nationalist folklorist, and erstwhile Young Ireland poet and journalist, Lady Jane Francesca Agnes Wilde. Moreover, as discussed in the next chapters, by the middle of the nineteenth century a hierarchically racialized strand of Aryanist discourse (also variously present in earlier Indo-European/Aryan theories of languages and cultures) had become a central component of the Iranian as well as some non-oriental theories of Ireland's Gaelic origins.

From Historical to Contemporary Affinities

As noted earlier, ultimately Irish nationalist antiquarian claims of connections between ancient Ireland and the Orient were intended to sustain the notion of Ireland's Golden Age civilization. Many of these antiquarians and subsequent generations of Irish historians considered this premise a key facet of the cultural project of Irish nationalism. In this regard, Irish nationalists were part of a much broader contemporary global spectrum of nativist and/or nationalist myth-making, or what Eric Hobsbawm and Terence Ranger have called "invention of tradition."[35] As with "modernity" (in its heterogenous manifestations), manifold forms of nationalism too, which are in many ways rooted in modernity, continually (re-)manufacture their own pasts as "tradition." With a precedent in Keating's pre-'Irish nationalist' *The History of Ireland* (1634), in contrast to so-called medieval Irish sources that also traced Ireland's origins to the Orient, the post-eighteenth century Irish nationalist adherents of varying oriental theories of ancient Ireland were engaged in "*self*-orientalizing" gestures aimed at securing Ireland a place of resplendent distinction in ancient world history—contra the equally fabled efforts to historically consign Ireland to a civilizational void before the arrival of Anglo-Normans. The various self-orientalizing maneuvers by these antiquarians and other Irish nationalist commentators in regard to ancient Ireland (without overlooking here the labor of *other* antiquarians, such as Vallancey, who was a recent English resident in Ireland) did not automatically prevent these individuals from making negative commentary about the contemporary Orient. A case in point is Thomas Moore's description (in *Intercepted Letters*, 1813) of contemporary Iran as a site of religious intolerance and persecution by the majority Shi'i Muslim population of the country directed at the minority Sunni Muslim population, even as he later identified ancient Iran as the source of ancient Ireland's civilizational splendor (*The History of Ireland*, volume I, 1835). As Joseph Lennon, too, has pointed out (albeit somewhat tentatively), Irish orientalism, at least in its antiquarian impulse, defies the standard overarching Saidian model of casting Western orientalism as a fundamentally imperialist and malevolent field of knowledge production.[36] In addition to self-orientalizing trends in Irish antiquarian accounts, there existed other modes of Irish nationalist self-orientalizing gestures in their *worlding* of Ireland, including in references to Iran. This was the case with Irish nationalist expressions of solidarity and affinity with certain contemporary anti-imperialist struggles in colonized and semi-colonized regions of the 'Orient'—whether in drawing parallels between Ireland and British-administered India or Egypt, for instance, or in the form of postulating a common racial front in resistance to British imperial aggression under the aegis of the fringe Pan-Aryan Association founded in New York in late 1906, with the primary objective of uniting Irish, Indian, and Iranian nationalists in the struggle against British imperialism. In the middle of the nineteenth century, Irish nationalist interest in Iran extended beyond the ongoing contentious debates on the question of Irish origins or allegoric literary pairings of Iran and Erin. Irish nationalist attention to Iran now began to also focus on contemporary developments in Anglo-Iranian relations, with Irish nationalists of varying political platforms periodically condemning actual or perceived British imperial inroads into Iran (diplomatic, commercial, financial, or military).

Beginning with the Anglo-Iranian War of 1856–57, contemporary Iran was periodically situated in the "Anti-British imperialism" world horizon of Irish nationalism. Prior to the Anglo-Russian Agreement of 1907, Irish condemnations of imperialist encroachment in Iranian affairs at times could be highly selective and skewed, to the point of exempting Russia (i.e., Britain's rival imperial interloper in Iranian affairs since the start of the nineteenth century) from criticism, if not occasionally even insisting Russia was acting as Iran's savior against British mendacity and aggression. Moreover, Irish nationalist expression of solidarity with Iranians during the Anglo-Iranian War of 1856–57 also exposed the deep rifts among competing Irish nationalist worldviews, including in the Irish diaspora that was fast expanding in size following Ireland's Great Famine of 1845–51. The more 'radical' nationalist circles (even if not necessarily militant and/or republican) uniformly condemned the British war effort against Iran, while the more moderate nationalist circles (distinctly committed to parliamentary Home Rule) either expressed support for the British war effort or avoided taking sides in the conflict. The radical nationalist championing of Iran in this conflict, and their simultaneous praise for Russia as Britain's rightful nemesis in Iran, was unmistakably motivated by primarily self-regarding anti-British sentiments and objectives, rather than emanating from some profound concern with Iranian sovereignty by itself. In contrast, the extensive advocacy of Iran's independence after 1907 was undertaken by groups representing a much more comprehensive spectrum of Irish nationalist platforms. The conclusion of the Anglo-Russian Agreement of 1907, during the Iranian Constitutional Revolution (1906–11), set in motion Anglo-Russian cooperation in opposition to Iranian constitutionalist-nationalist camps. The Agreement was ultimately aimed at resolving Russian and British disputes over Tibet, Afghanistan, and Iran and secure the friendship of the two great powers (both of them also allies of France by then) contra German alliance with Austria in Europe. Following the Agreement, St. Petersburg and London began to jointly undermine the nascent Iranian constitutional movement. In this setting, many Irish nationalist circles expressing solidarity with Iranians after 1907 were also championing the rights of the Iranian 'nation,' as opposed to only the sovereign rights of the Iranian state during the Anglo-Iranian War of 1856–57. This is not to say that after 1907 there was a complete absence of chiefly self-interested Irish nationalist objectives in the endorsement of Iranian national and territorial sovereignty. This simultaneous admixture of primarily self-regarding and/or genuinely other-regarding trends in Irish nationalism was evident as far back as the beginnings of Irish nationalist platforms, including in the ranks of the United Irishmen. In contrast to expressed affinities, the present book also addresses episodes of premeditated Irish nationalist neglect of contemporary Iranian developments, on grounds of explicitly stated anti-British political motives. The most salient example of this was the public declaration of disinterest in the plight of Iranian famine victims in 1870–72 by the post-'Young Ireland' Dublin nationalist newspaper *The Nation*.

A Passing Glance at Manifold Paths of Iran/Erin Knowledge Production

As previously noted, Iranians during the period covered in this book, with the possible exception of a few hitherto unknown members of the Iranian émigré community in the Indian subcontinent—not counting the native Parsi population of the subcontinent who traced their origins to Iran—appear to have been entirely unacquainted with Irish nationalist antiquarian and literary referentialities to Iran. There is no documented indication of contemporary Iranian familiarity with Irish claims of Iranian (/Persian) origins (whether such claims were made by nationalist or other Irish antiquarians and later generations of historians and folklorists), or of Irish nationalist literary appropriations of the Iran/Erin analogy, or even of expressions of solidarity with Iran during the Anglo-Iranian War of 1856–57 by a narrow range of Irish nationalists—albeit, after 1907 Iranians acquired degrees of familiarity with post-1907 Irish nationalist expressions of solidarity with Iranian anti-imperialist endeavors. The lack of familiarity with miscellaneous Irish nationalist framings of Iran also applies to Thomas Moore's 1817 narrative poem *Lalla Rookh*, which was the first Irish literary work to deploy Iran as a substitute for Erin (Ireland), with unmistakable Irish nationalist connotations. Even though following the publication of *Lalla Rookh* Moore met two young Iranians studying in England (see Chapter Two), and this poem also attracted the attention of some other Iranians soon after its publication, simply on grounds of the Iranian settings in the first and third sections of the poem, the Iran/Erin correspondence of the poem escaped the attention of Iranian readers.

It was only after the outbreak of the Iranian Constitutional Revolution of 1906-11 that many politically informed Iranians gained awareness of wide-ranging *contemporary* Irish nationalist declarations of anti-imperialist solidarity with Iranians. Even after the Iranian revolution of 1906—most specifically after the conclusion of the 1907 Anglo-Russian Agreement that, among its other arrangements, divided Iran into respective spheres of Russian and British influence—Iranians do not appear to have learned of prior instances of Irish (nationalist or other) appropriations of Iran or of theories of 'Iranian' origins of Irish people and/or Ireland's ancient civilization. Moreover, it was not until the Easter Rising of 1916 in Ireland that certain circles of Iranian nationalists first publicly championed any of the Irish nationalist platforms (notably that of militant Irish republicans in 1916). From 1916 on, Ireland, in its various formulations (including Northern Ireland after the 1922 partition of Ireland), entered the mainstream repository of Iranian anti-imperialist references to worldwide struggles against imperialism past and present, often in highly abstracted historical configurations. A more recent notable instance of wide-ranging Iranian expressions of solidarity with the Irish struggle occurred during the republican paramilitary prisoners' hunger strike in Northern Ireland in 1981.[37] As discussed in detail in Chapter Eight, Iranian unfamiliarity with the broad spectrum of Irish nationalist historical and political references to Iran before 1907 was substantially, but by no means entirely, a symptom of very limited Iranian awareness at the time of Ireland's precise status in the British Empire.

One of the earliest and extremely rare recorded Iranian references to the presumed Iran/Erin connections in ancient times, paralleling Irish antiquarian claims of Iranian origins, appears in the trenchantly satirical book *The Pearl Cannon (Toup-e Morvari)*, written in 1947 by of one of Iran's literary luminaries of the twentieth century, Sadeq Hedayat (1903–51), but not published until 1979. Here, I briefly sketch a number of hypothetical scenarios by which Hedayat may have arrived at this alleged connection, had he in fact been somehow familiar with Irish applications of the Iran/Erin analogy and was not entirely inventing his example. I am engaging in this purely hypothetical investigation as a means of introducing a very cursory random sampling of the wide range of Irish and non-Irish contributions in different parts of the world after the late eighteenth century to the many modes of Iran-Erin historical associations, which are examined in detail in later chapters. As already indicated, Hedayat may very well have simply invented this alleged connection, which he intended as a derisive device in lampooning those he considered quack Iranian etymologists of the Persian language. Still, the nature and content of Hedayat's short statement on Iran-Erin association closely resembles the style and methodology of Irish antiquarians and some later historians, folklorists, and literary figures after the late eighteenth century. In the relevant section of *The Pearl Cannon*, Hedayat included among his deliberately hyperbolic examples of absurd etymological claims the following: "Aran and Iran come from the Magian root 'a'ir' which later appears as Éire and is recorded as Ireland. For this reason it is believed that the Irish have migrated from Iran to their own homeland and have advisedly retained this name."[38] With rare possible exceptions, Hedayat's intended Iranian readers at the time, as well as the majority of subsequent generations of Iranians to this day (and, incidentally, most of the Irish today), would be unaware that Hedayat's choice of a patently fabulous and unreasonable proposition would not have sounded so outlandish to many in the highly literate strata of Irish society from the late eighteenth to early twentieth century (including in the Irish diaspora).

It is again important to note that it is unknown if Hedayat randomly invented his 1947 Iran/Erin etymological taunt, or if he had come across this imputed pseudo-analogy in his readings, conversations, or at a lecture during his many spells of residence outside Iran (in Europe and pre-independence India). He lived in Belgium and France from 1926 to 1930 (later returning to France in 1950, where he committed suicide the following year) and also lived in India from 1936 to 1937. Here, I very briefly offer an entirely speculative range of some of the many possible sources from which Hedayat may have acquired his Iran/Erin etymological quip, in order to introduce a few of the themes covered in the present study and provide a fragmentary vista of the broad spectrum of some intersecting histories and transregional nexuses of knowledge production in the evolution of imputed Iran-Erin connections during the period under discussion. By Hedayat's own time, the small surviving band of Irish adherents of theories of oriental origins of ancient Ireland included the author James Joyce (d. 1941), whom Hedayat rightly regarded as the paragon of modernist literature. Passing random references to Iran (Persia), as well as three parodic mentions of Zarathustra (Zoroaster), a la Friedrich Nietzsche, appeared in Joyce's earlier works: *Dubliners* (1914) and *Ulysses* (1922). But, it was in a particular passage of *Finnegans Wake* (1939) that Joyce fiddled with the Iran/Erin interchange, with other more subtle references to Iran/Erin and more general references to Irans of various historical formations interspersed throughout the book, alongside copious references to other range of oriental locales and subjects, most notably to Phoenician origins of the Irish. With its iconic Joycean style of cosmopolitan text, *Finnegans Wake*, among its many other themes, reflects Joyce's engagement with centuries of Irish literary and historical evocations of varying Orient-Ireland connections in ancient times, including the late eighteenth-century (pseudo-)linguistic antiquarian accounts of the Iranian heritage of ancient Ireland by Charles Vallancey, as well as the 1817 best-selling *Lalla Rookh* by Thomas Moore, and the extensive placement of the Orient in the poetry of James Clarence Mangan, among a range of other such sources.[39] Joyce, who was an adherent of the theory of Eastern origins of the Irish, preferring Vallancey's earlier model of Phoenician progenitors of the Irish to Vallancey's later Iranian model, evidently belonged to the same camp as the likes of Thomas Moore in the nineteenth century, who believed in indirect Iranian cultural transmission to ancient Ireland by means of Phoenician settlers. Allusions to Iran (Persia) or to other regions of the Orient operated as heterotopic, real-yet-unreal, spaces in Joyce's writings, including in *Ulysses*. The nineteenth-century nationalist poet James Clarence Mangan was a major literary influence on Joyce, with Joyce attempting to come to terms with this legacy in two conflicting lectures on Mangan in 1902 and 1907. As in the case of the Orients appearing in the poetry of Mangan in the 1830s and the 1840s, Joyce's oriental mindscapes represented Ireland's 'national' self-hallucination and self-estrangement, as a bifurcated identity that was simultaneously recognizable and yet an unfamiliar phantasmagoria; an Irish self both historically familiar and alien. For instance, the narrator in Joyce's 1904 short story "The Sisters," states while relating a dream, and with the uncertainty of the precise composite location in a dream one often has when awakening from deep sleep, while simultaneously certain of the experience of the place to which the person had been transported while asleep, even if that place has never existed in the narrator's prior wakeful experience or imagination: "I felt that I had been very far away, in some land where the customs were strange—In Persia, I thought."[40] This apparition of Persia in a dream was in fact no other than an Ireland of hyper-wakefulness, an Ireland that was ultimately unfathomable to the waking consciousness; so distant from the narrator's daily experiences that it feels like a foreign place, which the narrator knows to exist but has not in actuality visited.

As already noted, the most pronounced Iran/Erin interchange in Joyce's writing, with the names of both territories appearing coupled together, occurred in his 1939 *Finnegans Wake*. Typical of the underlying structure of the book and its dreams within dreams content, the Iran/Erin association in this case was one of simultaneous correspondence and dissonance, of the recognizable in the unconscious mind but yet forgotten in the waking conscious thought: "the sens of Ere with the duchtars of Iran"—that is, the sons of Ireland with the daughters (*dokhtars*) of Iran.[41] This polyglot book, which was a world-historical rendering of Irish history, abounds with Irish idioms and names that morph into Persian, Arabic, Hindi, Turkish, Hebrew, and other range of 'oriental' terms and names, as well as names and words in other European and non-European languages, alongside a wide range of other non-English vocabulary, often in Joycean style of spelling and transliteration without any explication of their English meanings, and with many of the terms certainly unfamiliar to the average English-language reader, since these were not already common loanwords in English. The book is also replete with references to *One Thousand and One Nights* (a.k.a., *Arabian Nights*), Eastern histories, locations, and personalities, as well as a host of other histories, places, and so on.[42] Certain passages of *Finnegans Wake* are also peppered with allusions to Persian and a wide range of non-English vocabulary, including Persian terms that evoked Vallancey's linguistic claims of Iran-Erin interconnectedness, such as "pedar" (father) and "madar" (mother). Some other examples of references to Iran in *Finnegans Wake*, in a wide array of allusions to the Irish Self (including in scenes of anal sex), are "Come big to Iran. Poo!" or "when the bold bhuoys of Iran wouldn't join up," "Off with your persians!" or "O, O, her fairy setalite! Casting such shadows to Persia's blind!" (the latter a play on window shutters).[43]

Hedayat was fluent in French but had minimal proficiency in English. He was particularly impressed and influenced by the French translation (with a preface by Padraic Colum) of the "Anna Livia Plurabelle" section of *Finnegans Wake*, based on the 1928 English publication of this chapter, of what was then known publicly only as Joyce's "work in progress."[44] But, this section of *Finnegans Wake* does not include passages in which Joyce tinkered with the Iran/Erin word associations, and the first complete French translation of the entire book (by Philippe Lavergne) did not appear until 1982. Therefore, hypothetically, Hedayat may have arrived at his Iran/Erin example after skimming through the original complete English edition of *Finnegans Wake*, which was published in France in 1939—given the censorship laws in the United Kingdom and the book's sexual content. Reportedly, Hedayat had indeed browsed through this English edition.[45] Then again, given Hedayat's rudimentary knowledge of English, and no forgetting the highly abstruse language of Joyce's text, Hedayat may have been apprised of the general content of the English edition of the book by an acquaintance fluent in English, who had read the book in part or in its entirety. Regardless, what is remarkable, whether completely by coincidence, or consciously replicating the form and narrative structure of *Finnegans Wake*, Hedayat's *The Pearl Cannon* happens to be a parodic take on Iranian history, culture, and lore against a backdrop of world history, just as Joyce's work engaged with Ireland's history in a world-historical framework. Yet, it is also hypothetically possible that Hedayat came across the Iran/Erin association by means of an entirely different range of texts than *Finnegans Wake* or some other as of yet unknown "Irish" source. For instance, according to one of Hedayat's acquaintances and biographers, Mostafa F. Farzaneh, Hedayat owned a copy of the American comparative folklorist Alexander Haggerty Krappe's *Mythologie universelle* (1930),[46] in which case Hedayat would certainly have come across references to Iran and Erin. Krappe's book, which included sequential chapters on 'Indian,' Iranian (in the broadest sense), and Celtic mythologies, noted in the chapter on Indian mythology the existence of similarities between certain Iranian (as well as Indian) and Irish myths.[47] Krappe's study was following in the footsteps of much older comparative studies of mythologies and epics that had suggested certain parallels between Irish and Iranian legends. This, in turn, points to yet other possible routes through which Hedayat may have arrived at his Iran/Erin inference, including by means of reading earlier studies on parallels between certain episodes in Irish mythology and the eleventh-century CE Iranian epic *Shāhnāmeh* (*The Book of Kings*)—'Iran' here again denoting broader culturally and geographically historical configurations than present-day Iran, and with *Shāhnāmeh* also widely known and read in the Persianate cultures beyond various territorial incarnations of Iran. *Shāhnāmeh* consisted of Persian epics compiled, supplemented, and composed in verse form by Abul-Qassem Ferdowsi during the late-tenth and early-eleventh centuries. Being based on much earlier versions of many of the epic sequences appearing in it, *Shāhnāmeh* chronicled Iranian history from its (otherwise mythic) origins to the Arab-Muslim conquest in the seventh century CE. In the Introduction to his serialized French translation of *Shāhnāmeh* in mid-nineteenth century, the German-born French orientalist Jules (Julius) Mohl (1800–76) had alluded to the close similarity between the story of Cuchulain and Conla in Ireland's epic of the Ulster Cycle and the story of Rustam and Sohrab in *Shāhnāmeh*. Different volumes of Mohl's translation appeared between 1838 and 1876, with the final published volume just after Mohl's death. Hedayat could very well have read Mohl's work, given Hedayat's keen interest in Iranian mythology, as well as Krappe's references to Mohl.

Alternatively, some of Hedayat's Zoroastrian Parsi interlocuters during his stay in India (1936–37), where he studied Pahlavi script (ancient "Middle Persian") with the prominent Parsi scholar Bahramgor Tahmuras Anklesaria, would certainly have been familiar with the scholarship on similarities between sections of *Shāhnāmeh* and the Ulster Cycle of Ireland. The likes of the prominent Parsi dastur (i.e., Parsi scholar of Zoroastrianism) Jivanji Jamshedji Modi had published material on this subject at the turn of the twentieth century. Bahramgor Tehmuras Anklesaria's father, Tehmuras Dinshaw (also spelled Dinshah/Dinshaji) Anklesaria, had been a close associate of Modi, who in turn cited Anklesaria's research in some of his works. In 1905, Modi published an essay on the resemblance between the Irish and Iranian epics in question. This was based on an 1892 lecture by Modi, titled "The Irish Story of Cucullin and

Conloch and the Persian Story of Rustam and Sohrâb." Referring to earlier European studies on the parallels between these Iranian and Irish epic poems, including Jules Mohl's study, Modi relied on the late eighteenth-century English translation from Irish (Gaelic) of the Cuchulain and Conla saga appearing in Charlotte Brooke's 1789 *Reliques of Irish Poetry*. Brooke, an Irish cultural-nationalist, was incidentally an adherent of the Phoenician theory of Irish origins, while also maintaining Iranian cultural transmission to Ireland in ancient times. Modi in his published lecture repeated the once relatively commonplace nineteenth-century Irish antiquarian misnomer on the origin of Ireland's name:

> The very name of Ireland suggests that the country was originally inhabited by a tribe of the ancient Aryans, the common ancestors of the Irânians of Firdousi [i.e., the compiler of *Shāhnāmeh*] and of other adjoining nations. Again, has not the word Erin, used in the above Irish poem of Cucullin as an ancient name of Ireland, a close resemblance with the name of Irân?[48]

Notes

1. "Erin" is an anglicization of both genitive and dative cases of Éire, the Irish-language name for Ireland (i.e., "Éireann" and "Éirinn"). In Irish nationalist poetry after the late eighteenth century, which was chiefly composed in English language, it was this anglicized designation of Ireland (i.e., 'Erin') that gained currency.
2. On whether Ireland constituted a British "colony," see, among other studies, Declan Kiberd, *Inventing Ireland: The Literature of the Modern Nation*. Cambridge, MA: Harvard University Press, 1995; Terry Eagleton, *Crazy John and the Bishop and Other Essays on Irish Culture*. Cork: Cork University Press, 1998; idem, *Heathcliff and the Great Hunger: Studies in Irish Culture*. New York: Verso, 1995; Clare Carroll and Patricia King, eds., *Ireland and Postcolonial Theory*. Notre Dame, IN: University of Notre Dame Press, 2003; Terrence McDonough, ed., *Was Ireland a Colony? Economics, Politics and Culture in Nineteenth-Century Ireland*. Dublin: Irish Academic Press, 2005; Jennifer M. Regan, "'We Could Be of Service to Other Suffering People': Representations of India in the Irish Nationalist Press, c. 1857–1887," *Victorian Periodicals Review* 41(1), Spring 2006, pp.61–77; Eoin Flannery, *Versions of Ireland: Empire, Modernity and Resistance in Irish Culture*. Cambridge: Scholars Press, 2006; Pauline Collombier-Lakeman, "Ireland and the Empire: The Ambivalence of Irish Constitutional Nationalism," *Radical History Review* 104, 2009, pp.57–76.
3. Sumathi Ramaswamy, *The Lost Land of Lemuria: Fabulous Geographies, Catastrophic Histories*. Berkeley: University of California Press, 2004, p.126.
4. On identity constructs, interpellation, and reading oneself into "authoritative" texts, see Ken Brown and Brennan Breed, "Social Identity and Scriptural Interpretation: An Introduction" in Ken S. Brown, Alison L. Joseph, and Brennan Breed, eds., *Reading Other Peoples' Texts Social Identity and the Reception of Authoritative Traditions*. London: t&tclark (Bloomsbury), 2020, pp.1–32.
5. On the complexities of defining the "medieval" or other such eras in Irish history, see also "Introduction" in Clare Downham, *Medieval Ireland*. Cambridge: Cambridge University Press, 2018, pp.1–3. I am most grateful to one of Anthem's anonymous reviewers for further highlighting the difficulty of applying periodization schemes such as "Middle Ages" (let alone "early" or "late" Middle Ages) to Irish history. In fact, as noted earlier in my Introduction, the same can be said of Iranian and many other histories, given the particular "West"-centric schema and implicit or explicit connotations of "Ancient, Medieval, and Modern" periodization scheme that has evolved since the 'European' Enlightenment in the eighteenth century.
6. Dipesh Chakrabarty, *Provincialising Europe: Postcolonial Thought and Historical Difference*. Princeton: Princeton University Press, 2000, p.28.

7 Joseph Lennon, *Irish Orientalism: A Literary and Intellectual History*. Syracuse: Syracuse University Press, 2004, pp.264–66.
8 Norman Cohn, *Noah's Flood: The Genesis Story in Western Thought*. Reprint. New Haven: Yale University Press, 1999 [1996], pp.95–96 and passim. See also Norman Vance, *Irish Literature: A Social History. Tradition, Identity, and Difference*. Oxford: Blackwell, 1990, p.53.
9 On Armenia and Ireland, see Séamus Mac Mathúna, Maxim Fomin, and Alvard Jivanyan, eds., *Journal of Indo-European Studies*, monograph 61, 2013: "Ireland and Armenia: Studies in Language, History and Narrative," Washington, DC, 2013. In connection with Irish myths of origins in particular, see the editors' Introduction and articles by Séamus Mac Mathúna, Maxim Fomin, Armen Petrosyan, Sergey Ivanov, and John Carey.
10 John Allen Giles, ed., *The British History of Geoffrey of Monmouth*. Translated from the Latin by Aaron Thompson. London: James Bohn, 1842, pp.15, 22–23.
11 See Rosemary Sweet, *Antiquaries: The Discovery of the Past in Eighteenth-Century Britain*. London: Hambledon and London, 2004.
12 Neil Davidson, *Origins of Scottish Nationhood*. London: Pluto Press, 2000, pp.48–51.
13 On claims of the Scythian ancestry of Saxons, see Sharon Turner, *History of the Anglo-Saxons: Comprising the History of England from the Earliest Period to the Norman Conquest*. Volume 1. London, Longman, Hurst, Rees, Orme, and Brown, 1820, pp.114–16.
14 Joseph Jacobs, "Anglo-Israelism" in Isidore Singer, et al., eds., *The Jewish Encyclopedia*. Volume I. New York: Funk and Wagnalls Company, 1901, pp.600–601.
15 William Camden, *Britannia: Or a Chorographical Description of Great Britain and Ireland, Together with the Adjacent Islands*. Volume II. Second edition; Edmund Gibson editor. London: Awnsham Churchill, 1722 [1586], cc.1311-16, 1326-27, 1336, 1415-16, and passim. On Camden's distinct classification of Scottish population of the highlands (as being civilized people similar to the English) and those of the lowlands (barbarous similar to the Irish), see ibid., cc.1158 and passim.
16 See also Christopher Ivic, "'the memorye of their noble ancestors': Collective Memory in Early Modern Ireland" in Oona Frawley, ed., *Memory Ireland. Volume 1: History and Modernity*. Syracuse: Syracuse University Press, 2011, pp.50–51.
17 Geoffrey Keating, *The History of Ireland*. Volume 2. David Comyn translator and editor. London: Irish Texts Society, 1902, pp.13–37 and passim.
18 "A Dissertation on the Languages, Literature, and Manners of Eastern Nations" in John Richardson, *A Dictionary: Persian, Arabic*. Oxford: Clarendon Press, 1777, pp.xi–xiii.
19 Joseph Theodoor Leerssen, "On the Edge of Europe: Ireland in Search of Oriental Roots, 1650-1850," *Comparative Criticism*, vol.8, 1986, pp.91–112.
20 On this theme, see also Joep Leerssen,"Irish Studies and Orientalism: Ireland and the Orient" in C. C. Barfoot and Theo D'haen, eds., *Oriental Prospects: Western Literature and the Lure of the East*. Amsterdam: Rodopi B.V., 1998, pp.167–70.
21 On historicism, as I apply the term in this context, see Jacques Bos, "Nineteenth-Century Historicism and Its Predecessors: Historical Experience, Historical Ontology and Historical Method" in Rens Bod, Rapp Maat, and Thijs Weststeijn, eds., *The Making of the Humanities. Volume II: From Early Modern to Modern Disciplines*. Amsterdam: Amsterdam University Press, 2012, pp.131–47.
22 Dipesh Chakrabarty, *Provincialising Europe*, p.28.
23 Among other works on global Enlightenment*s*, see Sebastian Conrad, "Enlightenment in Global History: A Historiographical Critique," *American Historical Review* 117(4), October 2012, pp.999–1027.
24 John Godfrey Herder (Johann Gottfried von Herder), *Outlines of a Philosophy of the History of Man*. Volume I. Second edition. T. Churchill translator. London: J. Johnson, 1803 [first edition, 1800], pp.448–49.
25 On the broader intersections of Irish culture and nationalist politics at the time, see also Padhraig Higgins, *A Nation of Politicians: Gender, Patriotism, and Political Culture in Late Eighteenth-Century Ireland*. Madison: University of Wisconsin Press, 2010.
26 See, for example, "The Captive Negro," "The Negro's Complaint," "The Dying Negro," "Virtue's Cause," in *Paddy's Resource: Being a Select Collection of Original and Modern Patriotic Songs, Toasts and Sentiments, Compiled for the Use of the People of Ireland*. N.p., 1795, pp.26–28, 36–37, 50–51, 78–79. See also the section on "Toasts and Sentiments" in ibid., pp.93–96.

27 On the Enlightenment in Ireland, see Ian McBride, *Eighteenth-Century Ireland: The Isle of Slaves*. Dublin: Gill & Macmillan, 2007, chapter 2 and passim; idem, "The Edge of Enlightenment: Ireland and Scotland in the Eighteenth Century," *Modern Intellectual History* 10(1), April 2013, pp.135–51.
28 See also Luke Gibbons, "Race Against Time: Racial Discourse and Irish History," *Oxford Literary Review* 13(1–2), 1991, pp.100–103; Colin Kidd, "Gaelic Antiquity and National Identity in Enlightenment Ireland and Scotland," *English Historical Review* 109(434), November 1994, pp.1197–214; Michael Philip Brown and Lesa Ní Mhunghaile, "Futures Past: Enlightenment and Antiquarianism in the Eighteenth Century" in Thomas Bartlett and James Kelly, eds., *The Cambridge History of Ireland: Volume III: 1730-1880*. Cambridge: Cambridge University Press. 2018, pp.380–405.
29 See also Emmanuel Chukwudi Eze, *Race and the Enlightenment: A Reader*. Cambridge, MA: Blackwell, 1997.
30 On this topic, see also Sankar Muthu, *Enlightenment Against Empire*. Princeton: Princeton University Press, 2003, pp.3–6 and passim.
31 For other brief treatments of this topic, see Luke Gibbons, "Towards a postcolonial enlightenment : the United Irishmen, cultural diversity and the public sphere" in Carroll, Clare and Patricia King, eds., *Ireland and Postcolonial Theory*, pp.81–91; Kevin Whelan, "The United Irishmen, the Enlightenment and Popular Culture" in David Dickson, Dáire Keogh, and Kevin Whelan, *The United Irishmen: Republicanism, Radicalism, and Rebellion*. Dublin: Lilliput Press, 1993, pp.269–96.
32 Raymond Schwab, *The Oriental Renaissance: Europe's Rediscovery of India and the East, 1680-1880* (translation of Schwab's 1950 *La Renaissance Orientale* by Gene Patterson-Black and Victor Reinking), New York: Columbia University Press, 1984, pp.16–80 and passim.
33 On the subject of Mangan writing in English see, among other works cited later in this book, David Lloyd, *Nationalism and Minor Literature: James Clarence Mangan and the Emergence of Irish Cultural Nationalism*. Berkeley: University of California Press, 1987, chapter 4 and passim; David Wheatley, "'Fully able / to write in any language—I'm a Babel': James Clarence Mangan and the Task of the Translator" in Sinéad Sturgeon, ed. *Essays on James Clarence Mangan: The Man in the Cloak*. Houndmills, Basingstoke: Palgrave, 2014, pp.33–51.
34 See also Malcolm E. Yapp, *Strategies of British India: Britain, Iran and Afghanistan 1789-1850*. Oxford: Clarendon Press, 1980, p. 19 and passim; Edward Ingram, *In Defence of British India: Great Britain in the Middle East, 1775-1842*. London: Cass, 1984, pp.43–44, 78–87, 91–99, 181, 185–200, 207–11; Denis Wright, *The English Amongst the Persians: Imperial Lives in Nineteenth-Century Iran*. London: I.B. Tauris, 1977, pp.4, 9–24, 32–33, and passim.
35 Eric J. Hobsbawm and Terence O. Ranger, eds. *The Invention of Tradition*. Cambridge: Cambridge University Press, 1983.
36 Edward W. Said, *Orientalism*. New York: Vintage, 1979 [1978]. On Lennon's attempted demarcation of Irish orientalism and Saidian formula of Western orientalism, as well as Lennon's extenuation of the rigidity of Said's stance, see Joseph Lennon, *Irish Orientalism*, pp.121–23 and passim.
37 See Mansour Bonakdarian, "The Easter Rising as a Milestone in Iranian Nationalist Appraisals of the Irish Question," *American Journal of Irish Studies* 14, 2017, pp.51–81; and idem, "Iranian Consecration of Irish Nationalist 'Martyrs': The Islamic Republic of Iran and the 1981 Republican Prisoners' Hunger Strike in Northern Ireland," *Social History* 43(3), August 2018, pp.293–331.
38 The English translation of Hedayat's text is by Iraj Bashiri. See Iraj Bashiri, *The Fiction of Sadeq Hedayat*. Lexington, KY: Mazda Publishers, 1984, p.155. The Persian spelling "اران" could be a reference to Ireland's Aran Islands, or possibly a transliteration of the genitive case of Éire (Ireland) that also appears as "Éireann" (Erin), since Hedayat did not stress the sound of the first vowel in اران. Both Erin and the Aran Islands appear in works by James Joyce, with which Hedayat was familiar. Given the overall structure of *The Pear Cannon*, which offers a survey of European colonialism and informal imperialism around the world, as well as Iran's semi-colonial contemporary status, it is possible that Hedayat's Iran-Ireland example was also intended as an implicit commentary on contemporary Ireland's partial independence from Britain after centuries of colonial rule (with the Irish Free State renamed Éire in 1937,

and later renamed the Republic of Ireland) and Iran's own experience of extensive British imperial leverage at the time.

It is not known if Hedayat had read the letter from the Iranian journalist and sociologist Bahauddin Pazargad that was published in the December 1947 issue of a Tehran journal under the heading "Are all the Irish of Iranian origin?" Sent from New York (dated November 22, 1947), Pazargad related that in the New York State town of Cuba he had met an individual named [David] Gancher, a calculator manufacturer, who was interested in ancient Irish language and claimed to have proven that (1) "all of the Irish are of Iranian descent ... [whose ancestors] had emigrated to Ireland [in ancient times]"; (2) "they had taken with them the name of Iran and Ireland's name in ancient times, too, was 'Iran,' before gradually changing to Éire ..." (3) "they took along the Aryan Pahlavi language that is the root of current Persian language and built the foundation of Irish language on that lexes ...." Bahauddin Pazargad, "Āyā irlandihā hameh irāni-al-asl hasstand?," *Irān va Āmrikā* (Tehran) 26(24), Dey 1326 (December 1947), pp.11–12.

39 See also Lynne A. Bongiovanni, "'Turbaned faces going by': James Joyce and Irish Orientalism," *Ariel: A Review of International English Literature* 38(4), October 2007, pp.25–49. On Joyce and Thomas Moore, see also Emer Nolan, "'The Tommy Moore Touch': Ireland and Modernity in Joyce and Moore," *Dublin James Joyce Journal* 2, 2009, pp.64–77.

40 James Joyce, *Dubliners*. With an Introduction by Laurence Davies. Ware, Hertfordshire: Wordsworth, 2001, p.4. "The Sisters" first appeared in August 1904 in the *Irish Homestead Journal* and was later published in Joyce's collection of short stories *Dubliners* in 1914. See also Ian Almond, "Tales of Buddha, Dreams of Arabia: Joyce and Images of the East," *Orbis. Littererum* 57, 2002, pp.18–30. For an alternative take on theme of the symbolism of the East in this story, see Earl G. Ingersoll, "The Psychic Geography of Joyce's 'Dubliners,'" *New Hibernia Review* 6(4), Winter 2002, pp.98–100.

41 James Joyce, *Finnegans Wake*. Reprint. New York: Viking Press, 1966 [1939], p.358.

42 For a very small random lexical sampling of 'oriental' languages and references appearing in Joyce's book, see the following examples in James Joyce, *Finnegans Wake*: p.4 ("Haroun"), p.5 ("one thousand and one stories"), p.11 ("peri"), p.13 ("Adar"; "Nizam" [i.e., Nisan]; "Tamuz"; ...), p.16 ("mahan"), p.24 ("Guinnghiz Khan"), p.32 ("our king khan?"; "Donyahzade"), p.49 ("Israfel the Summoner"), p.56 ("Muezzin"; "fez"), p.68 ("Houri"; "Aslim-all-Muslim"), pp.138 and 307 ("Darius"), p.177 ("Sheols of houris in chems upon divans"), p.183 ("persianly literature"), p.193 ("Mullah"), p.233 ("jamal, qum, yallah, yawash, yak!"), p.235 ("fateha"; "Osman"; "allah"), p.242 ("Kuran"), p.263 ("Cyrus"), p.292 n.3 ("Bissmullah"), p.302 ("Bhagavat"; "sahib"), p.347 ("Sidarthar"; "Hajiizfijjiz"), p.355 ("Abdul Abulbul Amir"; "emgined Egypsians"), p.356 ("the tarikies"; "aftabournes"; "Oh sard! ah Mah!"), p.357 ("Bissmillafoulties"; "Those sad pour sad forengistanters, dastychappy, dustyrust. Chaichairs."; "hamid and damid"), p.360 ("Bulbul"; "Salam"), p.365 ("Amir"; "villayets"; "kuschkars tarafs"; "bad"; "barran"; "sard"; "Mah"), p.389 ("Fatima Woman history"), p.407 ("aladdin"); p.415 ("this oldeborre's yaar ablong as there's a khul on a khat"), p.417 ("allabath of houris"), p.426 ("ahriman"), p.492 ("Achmed Borumborad, M.A.C.A, Sahib, of 1001 Ombrilla Street, Syringa padham, Alleypulley"; "Djanaral"), p.493 ("Foraignghistan"), p.497 ("durbar"; "shawhs"; "muftis in muslim and sultana reiseines ... jam sahibs"; "salaames"; "Hanzas Khan with two fat Maharashers"), p.532 ("Persians"), p.583 ("Persia's blind"), and numerous appearances of "allah," including as word compounds (e.g., pp.317, 340, 597). Joyce also alluded to such world-historical events as the "Armenian Atrocity" (i.e., the Armenian Genocide in the Ottoman Empire during the First World war). In ibid., p.72.

43 James Joyce, *Finnegans Wake*, pp.144, 358, 491, 532, 583. For decoding these and many other references to Iran/Persia in this work, see the invaluable, albeit far from flawless, guide by Louis O. Mink. *A Finnegans Wake Gazetteer*. Bloomington: Indiana University Press, 1978. On *Finnegans Wake* and Persian terms and Iranian imagery, as well Joyce's influence on Hedayat in general, see also Bernard Benstock, "Persian in *Finnegans Wake*," *Philological Quarterly* 44(1), January 1965, pp.100–109.

44 James Joyce, "Anna Livia Plurabelle" (Samuel Beckett, Alfred Perron, et al., translators), *Nouvelle revue française* 19(212), May 1, 1931, pp.637–46; Philippe Soupault, *Souvenirs de James Joyce*. Parsi: Alger E. Charlot, 1943, pp.59–88.

45 On Hedayat's appreciation of Joyce as a ground-breaking author, as well as his reading of the French translation of "Anna Livia Plurabelle" and skimming through the English edition of *Finnegans Wake*, see Masoud F. Farzaneh, *Āshenā-yi bā Sādeq-eHedāyat. Part I: Āncheh Sādeq-e Hedāyat beh man goft*. Paris (self-published), 1988, pp.57, 275, 277, 330; idem, *Āshenā-yi bā Sādeq-e Hedāyat. Part II: Sādeq-e Hedāyat cheh migoft?* Paris (self-published), 1988, pp.195–98, 201–203. See also Nasser Pakdaman, ed., *Sādeq Hedāyat: Hāshtād-o do nāmeh beh Hassan Chahid Nourāi*. With a Preface by Behzad Noël Chahid-Nourai. Second edition. Paris: Cheshmandaz, 2001, pp.66, 68, 292–93; Michael Beard, *Hedayat's "Blind Owl" as a Western Novel*. Princeton: Princeton University Press, 1999, pp.35–36, 83–84.

46 Masoud F. Farzaneh, *Āshenā-yi bā Sādeq-eHedāyat*, part I, p.127. see also Nasser Pakdaman, ed., *Sadeq Hedayat*, pp.168, 224 n.2.

47 Alexander Haggerty Krappe, *Mythologie universelle*. Paris: Payot, 1930, pp.137–38. Krappe also published an article in 1942 in which he compared ancient Irish and Iranian symbolism and concepts of kingship. However, this was in English and appeared in a highly specialized American journal, which very likely would have been inaccessible to Hedayat. Alexander Krappe, "The Sovereignty of Erin," *American Journal of Philology* 63(4), 1942, pp.444–54.

48 Jivanji Jamshedji Modi, "The Irish Story of Cucullin and Conloch and the Persian Story of Rustam and Sobrâb" in *Asiatic Papers: Papers Read Before the Bombay Branch of the Royal Asiatic Society*. Part I. Bombay: Bombay Education Society, 1905, pp.53–66 (see specially pp.54 and 65). Among other publications by Modi on a similar topic, see also "The Dantes of Iran and Erin," *The Indian Review* (Madras) 23(7), July 1922, pp.451–56 (see especially p.455, c.b.). In this latter work, too, Modi referred to Charlotte Brooke's suggested connection between the Iranian and Irish epic cycles. On Brooke, see also Lesa Ní Mhunghaile, "Anglo-Irish Antiquarianism and the Transformation of Irish Identity, 1750-1800" in David A. Valone, and Jill Marie Bradbury, eds., *Anglo-Irish Identities, 1571-1845*. Lewisburg: Bucknell University Press, 2008, pp.185–86, 192–94.

Chapter One

"IRAN" IN IRISH NATIONALIST ANTIQUARIAN IMAGINATIONS: THE LATE EIGHTEENTH AND EARLY NINETEENTH CENTURY

Irish antiquarians in the late eighteenth century did not invent the idea of Ireland's oriental past. As far back as the 'Middle Ages,' Irish scholars had presumed various oriental origins of the ancient Gaelic population of Ireland. In the Middle Ages, Scythia was the prevalent choice as the originary home of the Gaels, with Phoenicia later becoming the main alternative to this model. The supposition of Eastern origins of some of the earliest population settlements in Ireland can be traced back to sources antedating the initial twelfth-century Anglo-Norman conquests in Ireland. A case in point is the eleventh-century *Lebor Gabála Érenn* (variously translated as *The Book of the Taking of Ireland* or as *The Book of Invasions*), which with some alterations in its different surviving versions largely relied on earlier works by "Irish learned men, the *filid*, whose duty it was to preserve the genealogies and uphold the honour of their kings."[1] Among other (also legendary) oriental ancestors of early populations of Ireland, one recension of *Lebor Gabála Érenn* designated Fénius Farsaid (also appearing as Fenius Farsa)—purportedly a historical Scythian prince—as the ancestor of the Gaels, who reportedly arrived in Ireland following earlier smaller-scale settlements on the island by other population groups and subsequently constituted the major population branch of ancient Ireland.[2] Farsaid's lineage was traced back through his supposed father Baath to Japheth, one of Noah's sons.[3] In the seventeenth century, the oriental pedigree of the ancient Irish continued to be traced to Scythians, notwithstanding the designation of Scythians in ancient Greek and Roman sources as uncivilized and savage, albeit brave.[4] The presumed pedigree of Farsaid and the Scythian designation of the early Gaels, which traced their route from Scythia to Ireland by way of the Iberian Peninsula (more specifically "Spain"), was an early version of what became the "Milesian" model of Gaelic ancestry that continued to be reproduced in different forms well into the twentieth century. The Gaels in this ancestral lineage of the ancient Irish were descendants of Scythian followers of Miledh/Milesius (Míl Espáine) and, hence, designated 'Milesians,' with Miledh/Milesius considered a descendant of Fénius Farsaid.

Whereas the 'medieval' Scythian theory relegated the ancient population of Ireland to a state of general "pagan" savagery prior to the introduction of Christianity to the island after the fifth century, by the seventeenth century some Irish antiquarians were hailing Ireland's ancient pre-Christian oriental past as a civilizational Golden Age. These antiquarians were responding to continued English allegations of Irish barbarity. This latter group of antiquarians provided the ancient Orient-Ireland civilizational template for subsequent generations of what came to be called "Irish nationalist" antiquarians endorsing different models of Ireland's oriental past. Unsurprisingly, these latter-day adherents of the Scythian theory of Irish origins also credited Farsaid with the invention of ancient Irish script, known as Ogham. At the time, writing was regarded as a primary marker of civilizational splendor. In effect, by the seventeenth century concerted effort was underway by some "Gaelic" and "Gaelicized" Irish scholars to defend and civilizationally elevate the presumed Scythian ancestry of the Gaels in reaction to ongoing English vilification of Gaelic Ireland based on ancient Greco-Roman disparagement of Scythians.[5]

The foremost example of this revisionist civilizational vindication and valorization of ancient Ireland was the 1634 *The History of Ireland (Foras Feasa ar Éirinn)* by Geoffrey Keating (Seathrún Céitinn).[6] Written in Irish-Gaelic, and also belonging to the genre of Catholic Counter-Reformation in Ireland,[7] this work systematically challenged the slur of "wild Irish" hurled at the Gaels by a host of English commentators, most famously by William Camden and Edmund Spenser in, respectively, *Britannia: Or a Chorographical Description of Great Britain and Ireland, Together with the Adjacent Islands* (1586) and *A View of the Present State of Ireland* (completed in 1596 and first published in 1633). Keating not only refuted English allegations of contemporary Irish savagery but also disputed the fundamentally negative portrayals of Scythians appearing in ancient Greek and Roman histories, such as the account by Strabo (d. 23 CE).[8] Keating's *The History of Ireland* was, in effect, also a repudiation of accounts found in earlier histories of ancient Ireland compiled by Irish monks, who had portrayed the Scythians as uncultured pagan people in contrast to the future Christianized population of Ireland, irrespective of their presumed Scythian or other descent—with Christianity denoting the only true bedrock of civilization in these accounts. Significantly, Keating was himself of Norman ancestry (known as "Old English" in Ireland's ethnic makeup). To quote Anna Davin, this work by Keating, a "priest and poet of Gaelicized Norman descent, c. 1570–c. 1650," was "[t]he first narrative history of Ireland."[9] In the Introduction to *The History of Ireland*, Keating was categorical about his task:

> [...] as I have undertaken to investigate the groundwork of Irish historical knowledge, I have thought at the outset of deploring some part of her affliction and of her unequal contest; especially the unfairness which continues to be practised on her inhabitants, alike the old foreigners [i.e., descendants of the 'Old English' settlers in Ireland] who are in

possession more than four hundred years from the Norman invasion down, as well as the native Irish who have had possession during almost three thousand years. For there is no historian of all those who have written on Ireland from that epoch that has not continuously sought to cast reproach and blame both on the old foreign settlers and on the native Irish.

Whereof the testimony given by Cambrensis, Spenser, Stanihurst, Hanmer, Camden, Barckly, Moryson, Davies, Campion, and every other new foreigner who has written on Ireland from that time, may bear witness; inasmuch as it is almost according to the fashion of the beetle they act, when writing concerning the Irish. For it is the fashion of the beetle, when it lifts its head in the summertime, to go about fluttering, and not to stoop towards any delicate flower that may be in the field, or any blossom in the garden, though they be all roses or lilies, but it keeps bustling about until it meets with dung of horse or cow, and proceeds to roll itself therein. Thus it is with the set above-named; they have displayed no inclination to treat of the virtues or good qualities of the nobles among the old foreigners and the native Irish who then dwelt in Ireland.[10]

Keating designated the alleged earliest waves of population settlements in Ireland in the following manner: (1) Partholan (Partholón) and his small band of followers (from "Migdonia," possibly Macedonia or Greek territories, according to Keating's nineteenth-century translator John O'Mahony); (2) Descendants of Nemed and their followers (from Scythia), who defeated the indigenous Fomorians ("Fomhoraicc," who in Keating's version, were descendants of African pirates who had long ago settled in northern reaches of Ireland), with the Fomorians later rising up and enslaving some of the Nemedians until the Fomorians were defeated in turn by the next wave of population settlement in Ireland (the Firbolgs); (3) the Firbolgs (related to the Nemedians who had avoided, or escaped from, enslavement by Fomorians and left Ireland, only to return and recapture the land); (4) the Tuatha de Dananns (related to Firbolgs and Nemedians, and hence also Scythians, and coming to Ireland by way of ancient Greek territories, where their various ancestors had first settled); and (5) the Milesians (by way of the Iberian Peninsula), as descendants and followers of Milesius (Miledh/Míl Espáine), who was a descendant of Scythians through Fénius Farsaid and had settled in the Iberian Peninsula, then traveled to Scythia, married a Scythian princess, then served as a military official in pharaonic Egypt and married Scota, a daughter of the Pharaoh Nectanebo II ("Nectonebus"), among his other wives, and returned to the Iberian Peninsula with his followers, who now had also accumulated the knowledge and arts of ancient Egypt. Milesius died in 'Spain,' but his sons and followers proceeded to Ireland.

Keating, singling out the Milesians as the real founders of Ireland's lasting great Gaelic traditions, significantly ruled out the possibility of the Gaels at any point having previously arrived in mainland Britain before reaching Ireland.[11] In keeping with the Judeo-Christian Mosaic account of diverse human populations, Keating identified all of the ancient population groups in Ireland as descendants of Magog's three sons who had eventually found their way to different corners of the world. But, with the exception of the original so-called indigenous Fomorian population of Ireland (presumably descendants of initial African settlers), it was only the Scythian descendants of Magog's son Fénius Farsaid, who had ruled Scythia, that reportedly reached Ireland in waves during the period between "three hundred years after the Deluge [...] and one thousand and eighty years after the deluge."[12] Keating, who also (and we now know mistakenly) identified the Turks as related to Scythians, nonetheless correctly surmised that [Iranian-] Parthians were among groups related to Scythians but (erroneously) labeled [Iranian-] Persians as a distinct branch of people[13]—leaving aside here that, in the Mosaic scheme, all post-diluvian populations ultimately descended from Noah and his wife. Above all, Keating focused on what to him were laudable qualities of Scythians, citing passages from Greek/Hellenic, Roman, and other sources (often in a manner of reading against the grain) in acknowledgment of the "greatness" of Scythians, their "glorious exploits," and, especially, their purported ability to remain "always free from all foreign subjugation," as in the case of their vanquishing the invading Persian emperor Darius I. More importantly, Keating asserted "that other nations received institutions, laws and ordinances from the Scythians, and that they were the first people, who rose to dignity and glory after the Deluge."[14] Despite Keating's attempted rehabilitation of Scythians, and hence the Gaels, English taunts of Gaelic descent from "ancient Scythians, and other barbarous Easterlings" resolutely endured in anti-Gaelic circles as proof of Ireland's civilizational debasement vis-à-vis the English.[15]

From the seventeenth century onward, some Irish antiquarians unambiguously highlighted their commitment to Irish cultural and/or political causes in the "Dedication" section of their publications. For example, the Catholic Rev. James Hely of Trinity College (Dublin) dedicated his 1793 English translation from Latin of the Irish Roderic O'Flaherty's 1685 *Ogygia: seu Rerum Hibernicarum Chronologia* to "The Irish Nation," noting that O'Flaherty (d.1718) had been "deprived of [...] his parental estate, by Cromwell" in retaliation for the earlier Catholic uprising against Protestants in Ireland in 1641, when O'Flaherty had been only a child.[16] (It should also be pointed out that Catholics, such as James Hely, were only admitted to Trinity College, founded by a royal charter in 1592, following the 1778 Catholic Relief Act that removed certain penal laws against Catholics, which had been imposed after the English Reformation in the sixteenth century. The last of the penal laws aimed at Catholics in Great Britain and Ireland—the United Kingdom after 1801—remained in effect well into the nineteenth century.) O'Flaherty had written *Ogygia* following the Stuart Restoration in 1660 and the overthrow of the Cromwellian Puritan Republic. In an unmistakable jointly pro-Catholic and pro-Gaelic rights advocacy, O'Flaherty's own original Dedication was addressed "To His Royal Highness, James, Duke of York and Albany," soon to become the Stuart monarch James II and widely known to have converted to Catholicism. The Stuarts hailed from Scotland and, hence, were considered members of the Celtic sphere related to the Gaelic population of Ireland, some of whom, it was maintained, had also settled in Scottish territories in ancient times. In this Dedication, O'Flaherty beseeched James to promote the publicizing of Ireland's genuine ancient history: "IRELAND, the most ancient nursery of your ancestors, most humbly implores your highness' protection and patronage, in introducing to the knowledge of the world her antiquities." According to O'Flaherty, the Celtic lineage of James could ultimately be traced back to Ireland's Gaelic population who as descendants "from Adam" had reached Ireland as far back as "124 generations, which in a direct line preceded you." O'Flaherty added,

"None, since the creation of the world, has enjoyed the monarchy of Great Britain, before your grandfather, nor obtained the empire of the British isles, (among which we rank Ireland)."[17] Here, O'Flaherty was referring to James VI of Scotland, who in 1603 also assumed the English crown, becoming James I of England and, thereby, reigning as the joint monarch of the Kingdom of Scotland as well as the Kingdom of England (the latter also ruling over the territories of Wales and Ireland).

O'Flaherty and subsequent generations of Irish antiquarians who were committed to defending and celebrating Ireland's ancient past—whether these antiquarians came from the ranks of Catholics or Protestants and whether of so-called Irish, English, Scots, or Welsh descent—were in effect engaged in what they conceived as Speaking Truth to Power. This was reflected in O'Flaherty's Dedication in a later book, completed in 1695 and only privately circulated in manuscript form until its posthumous publication in 1775 by the prominent eighteenth-century nationalist antiquarian Charles O'Conor.[18] Originally titled *Ogygia Vindiciae*, the Dedication of this book (written in the style of "mirror for princes") was addressed to the Catholic Randal McDonnell, the future fourth Earl of Antrim (in northern Ireland) and of Scottish descent. The Dedication commenced with the parable of the ancient Persian king "Darius Hystaspis" who had asked of his gathered counsels *"What was the most powerful in Nature?"* Accordingly, the Persian ruler's preferred answer was given by *"Zorababel*, prince of the Jewish nation under captivity," who stated: *"Truth bears the Power and Sway of all Things."* In keeping with this maxim, O'Flaherty avowedly set out to establish

> THE truth of manifesting the ancient *Irish* to have been the genuine primogenial *Scots*, that occupied *Ireland* a thousand years before our *Saviour*'s birth, and who about five hundred years after his birth, transmitted a colony of *Scots* into the north of *Great Britain*.[19]

In other words, Randal McDonnell was being reminded that although his more recent ancestry may be traced to Scotland, those Scottish ancestors were themselves descendants of originally Irish transplants and that McDonnell was ultimately of Irish-Gaelic descent and, therefore, should be committed to Ireland's welfare.

In the eighteenth century, the historical rehabilitation of Scythians as civilized people was also carried out by some individuals outside Ireland and Britain, and with drastically different agendas. A case in point was the French philosopher and author Voltaire, who in his 1765 *The Philosophy of History* defended the Scythians against their Hellenic and other castigators. However, Voltaire, whose own method for ascertaining the civilized status of Scythians was highly convoluted, happened to belong to the more secular Enlightenment camp that dismissed accounts of the Deluge and the Mosaic theory of human descendants of Noah. Voltaire characterized these accounts as such "disgusting impertinence […] that […] children begin to ridicule them."[20]

In Irish antiquarian debates on oriental origins of the Gaels by the end of the eighteenth century, it was the precise oriental ancestry of Milesian and earlier population settlements in Ireland that constituted the main issue, with most participants in the debate convinced of the civilizational grandeur of ancient Ireland. The different camps were now proposing competing Scythian, Phoenician, Iranian (primarily Persian), and to a much lesser extent "Jewish" (i.e., Hebraic), Armenian, or Egyptian models of the ancestry of the Gaels and/or some of the earlier population settlements in Ireland. Moreover, in some Irish antiquarian accounts after the late eighteenth century, with the greater prevalence of Indo-European theories of languages and, subsequently, also the proliferation of discourses of so-called races, Scythians came to be designated as belonging to the larger family of Iranian peoples (hence the classifications of Scytho-Iranian, Irano-Scythian, or Indo-Scythian, and so on). In these models, Scythians (correctly, in keeping with present-day mainstream hypothesis) were considered as constituting a branch of Iranians distinct from, but ultimately related to, Persians. This was an upshot of philological developments in the field of Indo-European languages at the time. On the other hand, in some other post eighteenth-century versions of Scythian theory of Irish origins, the Scythians were designated as ancestors of Parthians, with the latter in turn identified as being directly related to Persians, thereby rendering the Scythians not only an unambiguously Iranian population group but also as belonging to the same branch of Iranians as the Persians.[21] Earlier, Keating had correctly differentiated between the Persians and the Scythians, although writing in the seventeenth century he would have been unaware of the later identification of both population groups as (linguistic) sub-branches of the broader Iranian peoples (a conclusion drawn from indirect, non-Scythian sources to this day). But, as already stated, by the end of the eighteenth century the Scythians were increasingly identified as a non-Persian-Iranian group, most generally identified as related to Parthians, who ruled the territories of former Persian Empire from 247 BCE to 224 CE, following the collapse of the Macedonian Seleucid Empire that had ruled the region after the death of Alexander the Great, with Alexander's Macedonian-Hellenic forces having overthrown the Persian Achaemenid dynasty in 330 BCE.[22]

In the works of Irish antiquarians and later generations of historians who subscribed to various Iranian models of ancient Ireland, after the late eighteenth century the "Iranian" origins of the Irish, whether in the form of an interchangeably Scytho-Iranian model and/or a strictly Persian model, acquired new (presumed) Indo-European etymological validation. The most prevalent of these etymological proofs was the (mistaken) assumption of the correspondence between near-homophonous names of Iran and Erin (i.e., Ireland), which were regarded as cognates derived from the same root word. Among the many examples discussed throughout this chapter, in an 1858 history of Ireland written by the nationalist Martin A. O'Brennan—with the second volume of the book ambitiously titled *A School History of Ireland, from the Day of Partholan to the Present Time*—the designation "Erin" was traced back to "Iran" or "Irin [...] the primitive name of Persia," a territory which according to O'Brennan (and incorrectly) "at an early epoch included Scythia, [and] was called Iran, *sacred land*," and from which territory the "founders" of Ireland—that is, "Irin, (Holy Land)"—had originated.[23] It would be a grave mistake to regard the likes of O'Brennan at the time as rare eccentrics. A lecture given by O'Brennan at the Mechanics' Institute in Dublin in late 1858 was hailed by the *Cork Examiner* as "decidedly the most deeply-interesting that has been for years delivered in Dublin [...] [attended by] a crowded and respectable audience." The topic of the lecture was "The Bards, the Harp, and Primitive Music of Ireland," with O'Brennan's "praises eloquently bestowed on Charlotte Brookes [sic], who did so much for Irish poetry and songs [...] (and indeed every part of the lecture) was applauded." During the lecture, O'Brennan maintained "Greek and Latin languages were greatly enriched with graceful and vigorous Celtic words. [...] he gave several instances of Greek words as being essentially Iranian or Irish." He then noted "as regards the word Irish there was some mistake," since it should in fact be "Iranian." Accordingly,

> At a very early period, from the mountains west of Hindostan to the Levant was called both Persia and Iran, which signifies "Sacred Land"; and as a colony thence came to this Western Isle, the first settlers gave it the appropriate name "Iran," [...] Iran is made up of two Celtic words—"ir" (sacred), and "an" (land); so called because God created man and held such frequent intercourse with him in Western Asia.

O'Brennan, claiming reliance on Greek sources, added that Scythia had been "a part of Iran," and the Scythians on their way to "Spain," prior to arrival in Ireland, had "imparted some of their own enlightenment to Greece, Egypt, and to Entruria [sic]."[24] O'Brennan was also among the die-hard advocates in the second half of the nineteenth century of the theory of Iranian origin of Ireland's Round Towers, a theory that had enjoyed much wider scholarly consensus from the late eighteenth century to the 1840s (as discussed below).

In these Scythian and Scytho-Iranian models of Irish origins, there were differences of opinion as to whether the Scythian ancestors of the Gaels (the latter-day descendants of Milesians) had come directly from the Scythian homeland or had originated from one of the presumed Scythian satellite territories elsewhere. On the other hand, in the non-Iranian model of Scythian ancestry of the Gaels appearing in Sylvester (Silvester) O'Halloran's influential 1778 *A General History of Ireland*, the Scythians arriving in Ireland were presumed to have originated in "Syria" from whence they migrated to Ireland, and of having shared a common ancestry with Phoenicians.[25] In antiquarian debates on Irish origins at the time, O'Halloran was a leading proponent of the Phoenician (/Carthaginian) model of Milesian migration to Ireland. In his works, the Scythians mentioned in Irish accounts of ancient Ireland as far back as the 'Middle Ages' were rendered Phoenician, with 'Syria' identified as their original homeland. This conferred onto the Scythians the mantle of Phoenician civilization that was more widely celebrated in contemporary European accounts of the ancient world, while also attributing to Scythians the recognizably "imperial" status of the famed sea-faring Phoenicians.[26]

The manifold oriental theories of Irish origins occasionally reverberated in Irish works of literature as well, as in the case of the Phoenician theory of Irish origins appearing in the 1806 *The Wild Irish Girl* by the Anglo-Irish author Lady Morgan (Sydney Owenson)[27] or indirect allusions to Ireland's Round Towers by way of referring to Zoroastrian temples in ancient Iran that appeared in Thomas Moore's 1817 *Lalla Rookh* (which is discussed in the next chapter). The historical identification of ancient Ireland with the Orient by Irish nationalist authors after the late eighteenth century, just as in Keating's work in the previous century, was intended to elevate and privilege Ireland as the earliest civilizational hub in the British Isles. This also bestowed upon the ancestry of Ireland's Gaelic population (and in some accounts the ancestry of even earlier presumed oriental settlers in Ireland prior to the Gaels) the historically foundational role of transmitting civilization to Ireland long before the arrival of the Anglo-Normans in the twelfth century. This claim in no way logically precluded the acknowledgment by these antiquarians that the subsequent embrace of Christianity in Ireland after the fifth century, by way of mainland Roman Britain, constituted yet another principal civilizational ingredient of present-day Ireland, serving as a salient marker of later Irish 'national' character—notwithstanding the competing Christian denominations in Ireland after the sixteenth century. Nonetheless, even in works produced by some antiquarians of ecclesiastical standing, there was now an underlying insinuation in this genre of nationalist antiquarianism of the existence of a civilizational Golden Age in pagan ancient Ireland, including the knowledge of writing and of pre-Christian ethical religious devotion.

Other than definitive theories of Iranian origins, some Irish nationalist antiquarians after the late eighteenth century claimed indirect transmission into Ireland in ancient times of the avowedly sophisticated Iranian civilization by means of population groups exterior to the primordial Iranian homelands, as opposed to direct Iranian migrations to Ireland. In these accounts, the non-Iranian arrivals, prior to reaching Ireland, had come into contact with Iranian civilization and embraced its key attributes. The model of indirect introduction of Iranian civilization to ancient Ireland was most frequently articulated in the form of Phoenician transmission of Iranian cultural practices and beliefs to Ireland. This version had the advantage of rendering the introduction of Iranian traditions to ancient Ireland historically more credible, given the Phoenicians' fame as sea-faring people. These accounts generally also maintained some Iranians had indeed accompanied the Phoenicians on their voyages to Ireland. After all, a majority of oriental models of Irish ancestry insisted on long-distance maritime journeys to Ireland by those ancestors independently of prior arrival in mainland Britain—with the stipulated routes generally including North Africa, across the Mediterranean, and then overland through the Iberian Peninsula, before proceeding to Ireland through the Celtic Sea. The Phoenicians were the most renowned mariners of ancient history, having built a vast maritime empire, including in North Africa (i.e., Carthage). The staunchest adherents of this theory of substantially *Iranianized* (/Persianized) Phoenician settlements in Ireland were John D'Alton (Dalton) and Thomas Moore in the early nineteenth century, with traces of this influence later also surfacing in James Joyce's 1939 literary masterpiece *Finnegans Wake* (as discussed in Chapter Nine). On the other hand, there were equally staunch proponents of direct transfer of Iranian civilization to ancient Ireland by Iranians themselves without other intermediaries. Charles Vallancey in the late eighteenth century was the founding figure of this theory. Vallancey's earliest Iranian model, appearing in 1786, was based on a drastic reworking of Sylvester O'Halloran's Phoenician-Scythian theory. In that work, Vallancey claimed the "original Phoenicians" were in fact no other than Scythians, with Scythians related to Persians and later heavily influenced by the allegedly more sophisticated Persian civilization, such as in the "use of letters" and "fine arts," prior to their arrival in Ireland.[28] In effect,

Vallancey added an Iranian (more precisely, a Persian) foundation to O'Halloran's Scytho-Phoenician theory of Irish origins.

At this point, it should again be noted that the remainder of this chapter deals with the main currents of Irish antiquarianism in the late eighteenth and early nineteenth century within the narrow framework of Irish nationalism. Not all Irish nationalists during this period embraced oriental theories of Irish origins, as intermittently noted in the rest of this chapter. Moreover, there were other antiquarians besides those of nationalist leanings who also subscribed to varying theories of Ireland's oriental origins. Furthermore, not all opponents of Irish nationalism (be they Irish or otherwise) who happened to associate ancient Ireland with the Orient unanimously regarded the ancient Orient as civilizationally retrograde. In addition, as Joseph Lennon too, among others, has noted, different strands of oriental theories of Ireland's heritage, as a substratum of wider debates on Celticism (in its broadest sense) since the seventeenth century, were not solely restricted to self-orientalizing Irish gestures. Nor, were these Celticist debates limited to the British Isles, let alone being solely an Irish nationalist antiquarian pursuit.[29] Others in the West (/Europe) and, it should be added without reservation, in the Indian subcontinent as well, whether or not working within or outside the specifically Celticist debates, were contributing to the theoretical and discursive formations of Irish orientalism.

The Shifting Horizon of Oriental Theories of Irish Origins after the Late Eighteenth Century

From the late eighteenth century, antiquarians of Irish nationalist proclivity (whether in the narrowest cultural and/or the narrowest political sense, and whether sectarian or nonsectarian) either variously reworked, reframed, and re-historicized pre-existing accounts of Irish origins or, alternatively, transformed these earlier accounts by selectively blending some of their components with neoteric models of Irish origins. In the oriental camp, some antiquarians re-*oriented* the formerly designated oriental connections. As noted, for example, Sylvester O'Halloran added a Phoenician twist to former Scythian accounts of Irish origins found in Keating's *The History of Ireland* and in the much earlier *Lebor Gabála Érenn*. The Iranian theories of Irish origins by the likes of Charles Vallancey were yet another form of this re-orienting of Ireland's previously presumed oriental connections. Without in any way accusing these nationalist antiquarians of some type of uniformly conscious fabrication in their re-creations of Ireland's past, or accusing them of greater subjectivity beyond the general patterns of historical subjectivity at the time, it is undeniable that their underlying agenda was to imbue ancient Ireland with the highest civilizational credit and rebuffing the long litany of English taunts of Irish barbarity (in contrast to purported English civility). The internal debate within the broader oriental convention of Irish antiquarianism at this stage, which constituted the prevailing strand of Irish antiquarianism, largely focused on the precise oriental identity and pedigree of the ancient Gaels, and whether the older historical accounts may have confounded the Scythians with some other highly civilized ancient group in the Orient. It was not until the second half of the nineteenth century that sweeping efforts were made by new generations of Irish historians (nationalist and otherwise) to ground Ireland's ancient past in some sort of European footing—notwithstanding the presence after the late eighteenth century of the alternative, but marginal, Scandinavian ('Scandian') model of Irish origins. The Scandian model at the time maintained that the Gaels, of an originally Scythian descent, were part of the Celtic populations who had long settled in Scandinavia, with some of them later arriving in Ireland after first reaching mainland Britain (see below).

In pursuit of further evidence for their particular "place-making" in establishing the identity of the oriental ancestors of the Gaels (to borrow a term used by Sumathi Ramaswamy in a different context),[30] Irish antiquarians turned to the latest available philological, historical, archaeological, and other forms of knowledge production. Rather than merely relying on extant and newly (re-)discovered textual accounts, including works on presumed ancient Irish rituals, these antiquarians sought traces of Ireland's ancestral oriental past in Irish (Gaelic) language itself and in the oldest known surviving edifices in Ireland, as well as in other range of archaeological relics and in popular culture. Language and the architectural design and presumed function of what were supposed to be Ireland's oldest still-extant monuments, the Round Towers, emerged as two of the most emblematic components in attempts to authenticate Ireland's contested oriental pasts. To these "proofs" were anchored other range of potential sources of evidence, whether in the shape of material culture or the available, as well as deduced, information regarding pre-Christian druidic religious practices in Ireland, and so on. The neoteric Iranian theories of Irish origins—centering primarily on the Persian branch of Iranian peoples, who in turn were traced back to what ultimately proved to be purely legendary origins—were chiefly grounded in evidentiary data focusing on language, history, mythology, ancient religious beliefs and practices, surviving folk beliefs and practices, and material culture, including, most markedly, the structural design of the Round Towers. The proliferation of theories of Indo-European languages and growing (albeit often confused) Western familiarity with Zoroastrian religion and ritual practices enhanced the appeal of Iranian (Persian) ancestral links in Irish nationalist antiquarian circles, with competing theories of oriental origins enduring alongside it. By the late eighteenth century, claims of the 'Eastern' ancestry of earliest population groups settling in Ireland—be they the Milesian Gaels or the presumed earlier smaller-scale population settlements—and/or the 'Eastern' origins of Ireland's grand ancient civilization had grown much more heterogeneous. Alongside the more peripheral claims of Egyptian, Armenian, Hebraic, Elamites, and other 'oriental' origins, the newly dominant models were those of Phoenician/Carthaginian or Iranian (ranging from Persians to otherwise entirely legendary groups). But, even these more prevalent models generally appeared in hodgepodge combinations of different and presumably inter-related peoples and cultures (as implausible as many of the suggested interconnections may seem today).

Irish nationalist antiquarian fascination with the prospect of broadly defined 'Iranian' ancestry of the Irish—for example, Persians, Medes, Parthians, and so on, in addition to the increasing identification after the late eighteenth century of Scythians as a branch of Iranian peoples, or often as an admixture of these groups—was extensively facilitated by, and reliant on, the advent of what later came to be known as the theory of "Indo-European" languages. This linguistic category, often inappropriately referred to as the "Jonesian" theory of Indo-European languages after William Jones (1746–94), initially appeared in Jones' works as the "Japhetic" branch of languages. Irish antiquarians in the Iranian camp of Irish origins soon identified Irish (Gaelic) language as closely related to Persian; a number of them claimed Persian as the mother language, while others maintained both languages had sprung from a common root language. Although the theory of Indo-European languages, inclusive of Persian, eventually came to be associated with the British polyglot orientalist William Jones following a lecture he gave in February 1786 at the Asiatic Society of Bengal in Calcutta (founded in 1784), a number of scholars had previously contributed to the development of this theory. Among these were the sixteenth-century Jan van Gorp van der Beke (Jan Goropius Becanus) and the seventeenth-century Marcus Zuerius van Boxhorn, both from the Netherlands, the French Claude Saumaise (Claudius Salmasius), and the Swedish-born German Andreas Jäger. All of these philologists had also designated the extinct Scythian language as the parent of most European tongues. There were also the likes of the Welsh Edward Lhuyd (d.1709) and the French Abraham Hyacinthe Anquetil-Duperron (d. 1805), whose works on the subject predated that of Jones.[31] The term 'Indo-European' itself is believed to have been popularized by the English Thomas Young in 1813, following the classification evidently first coined by Anquetil-Duperron, and later given greater currency by the German Franz Bopp (d. 1867), among others.[32] The theory of a distinct branch of interconnected languages, classified under both labels of Indo-European and "Aryan," gained wider application across Europe and elsewhere following Jones' lectures and publications; soon also fallaciously assuming racial connotations. The theory maintained that most European languages belonged to the same family of languages as Sanskrit and Persian, with all of these languages being related offshoots of an earlier, long-extinct proto-Indo-European (Aryan) language. Based on the dominant biblical Mosaic theory of population dispersions that continued to frame these debates, it was also stipulated at the time that the parent Indo-European language must have originated in the Near East and then spread to Europe. After the late eighteenth century, this parent language was variously referred to as Indo-Iranian, Indo-Scythian, Perso-Scythian, Scytho-Iranian, and so forth. Significantly, Jones, similar to some other linguists before him, identified Celtic languages (a category inclusive of Irish-Gaelic) as a sub-branch of Indo-European languages.[33]

Before the end of the eighteenth century, in Western European and North American circles (and in European communities in other continents) this linguistic connection assumed civilizational, and subsequently racial, connotations, with Indo-Europeans/Aryans designated as civilizationally the most sophisticated of the world's ancient populations, far above other population groups around the world in a hierarchy of cultures and peoples—and with gradations among Indo-Europeans themselves that placed the ostensible contemporary 'Western Civilization' (but excluding the Gaelic Irish) above their distant so-called racial kin in Asia, as well as above the Gaelic Irish in the case of English classifications of Aryan hierarchy. This hierarchical vision of societies and peoples, and the inner-ranking order of Indo-Europeans themselves, became a facet of Celticist debates in Europe and elsewhere. According to the dominant Western model of inner-Aryan gradations, the contemporary so-called racial descendants of Indo-Europeans in Asia were designated as civilizationally inferior to their distant European kin—by having somehow fallen behind, or civilizationally degenerated due to intermixture with other groups, or as a result of other presumed developments, following their initial Golden Age in ancient times. However, there was no clear consensus on the ranking order of the civilizational propensity of different European populations of presumed Aryan descent in terms of their contemporary and historical progress, nor was there unanimity on the standards by which cultural, social, and other presumed modes of civilizational advancement should be gauged. Without overlooking dissenting voices in the West, as in the case of Irish antiquarian proponents of Ireland's oriental Aryan heritage, by the nineteenth century, the mainstream Western Aryanist view in turn spawned yet another internally contested and fringe Aryanist myth aimed at accounting for the professed superiority of European Aryans over their contemporary kin in the Orient. This was a new brand of Aryanism (linguistic, civilizational, and racial) that claimed an originally Nordic ancestral homeland for the Indo-Europeans/Aryans, who had then dispersed to other regions in Europe as well as to parts of Asia. This reversed model of the Aryan circuit claimed a pattern of Aryan diffusion from Scandinavia to the Caucasus and then to southwest Asia and parts of Central Asia—comprising the ancient 'Iranian' territories—as well as to the northern regions of the Indian subcontinent. Accordingly, the comparative historical inferiority of the distant Asian relatives of originally European Aryans was a consequence of their depleted core Aryan civilizational traits (if not also their intrinsic racial capacities) *the further east* they traveled from their original homeland and, hence, their increasing exposure to non-Aryan cultures and peoples with whom they intermingled over time, resulting in their loss of Aryan quintessence. This was in effect a theory of civilizational (and/or racial) degradation due to cultural and racial intermixture. (Presumably, the Western European Aryans, traveling shorter distances away from Scandinavia, had been exposed to comparatively insignificant non-Aryan cultural and racial intermixture, or somehow succeeded to resist those alien influences.) As highly illogical and contradictory as both the mainstream (Asia-centered) and fringe (Scandinavia-centered) Western versions of Aryan racial origins and subsequent development happened to be, one of their common denominators was the fundamental presumption of degeneration through certain forms of cultural integration and/or racial intermixture. There were contemporary commentators who pointed out the absurdity of such claims, some of them also noting the cultural, scientific, and other disparities between western Europe and Asia during the so-called (European) Middle Ages, for instance, which challenged any suggestion of steady historical progress or degeneration.

If approached through the lens of the later Nordic version of Aryan origins, Irish antiquarian claims of oriental 'Aryan' ancestry of the Gaels would have racially rendered the Gaels "lesser" Aryans, since they would have reached Ireland following a period of initially eastward migrations and settlement in Asia. On the other hand, after the late eighteenth century, with the growing ascendance of Aryan theories that traced the origins of the Aryans to Asia, claims of Irish descent from non-Aryan oriental ancestry placed the Gaels beyond the threshold of allegedly most advanced ancient civilizations. Hence, the appeal for Irish antiquarians working within the well-established tradition of oriental origins of the Irish, and who now jointly subscribed to the increasingly popular Aryan theory, to identify an oriental Aryan ancestry for the Gaels within the more prevalent theoretical framing of Asia as the original homeland of the Aryans. Such an oriental formulation of Irish ancestry appeared far less assailable in its claim of Ireland's ancient civilizational glory. Once again, this is not to imply a conscious fabrication of such connections on the part of Irish antiquarians, any more than the general pattern around the globe in regard to other nationalist claims of ancient Golden Age. Seen through the lens of Irish antiquarians endorsing such models, they were merely engaged in revisionist correction of older models in light of the latest discoveries and overlooked details and connections in earlier accounts. These antiquarians maintained the ancestors of the Gaels had reached Ireland during what was still the Golden Age of Aryans in Asia. After the late eighteenth century, even some proponents of the Phoenician theory assigned an Aryan ancestry to (the otherwise Semitic) Phoenicians. Meanwhile, not every Irish nationalist antiquarian bought into the Aryanist discourse, and some continued to outright reject Aryan connections to the Gaelic population of ancient Ireland as well as the increasingly mainstream assertion of Aryan civilizational and/or racial superiority.

The dissemination of the so-called Jonesian theory of Indo-European/Aryan languages generated a new battleground for those wrangling over the superiority of present-day English versus Gaelic cultures and their ancient civilizational foundations. The rival camps deduced elemental links between branches of languages and civilizational and/or racial aptitude and, alternatively, claimed that English or Irish was the more authentic form of Indo-European languages, with some in opposing camps even denying the Indo-European designation of the other language in this debate. In such a setting, some proponents of oriental models of Gaelic ancestry in the ranks of Irish nationalist antiquarians found the Persian, or Scytho-Iranian/Indo-Scythian, and other similar Iranian ('Aryan') models more credible; many among them also insisting the ancient Irish had been the sole custodians of at least the more original and least contaminated Aryan civilization in the British Isles, having reached Ireland without prior stopover in mainland Britain. Accordingly, the English (assuming the legitimacy of their claim of Aryan ancestry) had reached their present-day location from Asia following a protracted overland migration, either losing along the way many of their original civilizational traits due to encounters and interactions with other population groups already in Europe and/or because their

Aryan ancestors had set out for Europe from their original Asian homelands after the gradual decline of the Aryan Golden Age in Asia. This precept rested on the stipulation that the Aryan ancestry of the Gaels had reached Ireland through a very rapid migratory process at the heyday of the Aryan Golden Age in Asia. There were also Irish nationalist antiquarians who accepted the earlier arrival of the Aryans in mainland Britain than in Ireland. But, in this scheme Aryans reaching mainland Britain had left their ancestral homeland prior to the advent of the Aryan Golden Age, in contrast to the later Aryan arrivals in Ireland. In effect, in the framework of contested claims of distinct origins of the English and the Irish—with the origin of the Gaels also featuring in debates concerning the larger Celtic populations of Europe—, English claims of Aryan origins were not necessarily unsettling for the core of Irish antiquarians advocating an oriental Aryan model of Irish origins. The underlying argument remained that Ireland was the first outpost of the Orient's high civilization in the British Isles. This historiographic paradigm of *comparative* world history, dating back to Keating in the seventeenth century, was ultimately aimed at the epistemological resuscitation of the ancient Irish past from the imputed void to which it had been relegated by detractors of ancient Ireland's civilizational standing. As demonstrated in the remainder of the present chapter, this historiographic schema generated its own periodization methods, connecting Ireland's ancient past to certain developments in other parts of the globe, just as 'medieval' Irish monks had done in a different historical setting.

Without initially posing a direct challenge to biblical accounts of population dispersions around the globe, the subsequent development and transmutations of the Jonesian theory of languages gradually parted ways with the Mosaic school. This parting of ways was not necessarily reflected in all accounts of Irish origins at the time. This was a time when pre-Darwinian natural theology still held sway, notwithstanding the Vulcanist and Plutonist rejection of the diluvian account of Noah's Ark; the Vulcanists maintained that the present earth had been formed as a result of primarily cataclysmic volcanic events, while Plutonists favored the model of gradual processes of rock formations over a much longer time period. The main rival geological school of thought to the Vulcanists and Plutonists was the Neptunist model, which maintained rock formations were chiefly due to periods of cataclysmic floods. While some, but certainly not all, Neptunists also believed the age of the earth was much older than claimed in biblical traditions, neither the Neptunists nor the rival Vulcanists or Plutonists categorically rejected all other biblical foundational accounts, as in the case of "Special Creation." Regardless, the majority of those engaged in geology, as well as other commentators in Britain and Ireland, still maintained the earth itself was created in a very recent time, which also placed the presence of humans on earth as god's Special Creation (notwithstanding two entirely different biblical creation stories) in a relatively recent time frame.[34] At the close of the eighteenth century, the Neptunist Richard Kirwan of the Royal Irish Academy, and a leading geologist of his time, vociferously claimed the literal truth of the account of Noah's Flood.[35] Furthermore, in keeping with biblical accounts, most commentators in the United Kingdom (and elsewhere in Europe) still believed all existing humans were the progeny of Noah and his wife, the only humans to have survived the Deluge, with a prior monogenesis Adamite framework still being the dominant view. In this schema, existing human population groups were classified according to their purported patrilineal descent from Noah's sons (i.e., Japheth, Shem, and Ham), with much quibbling over the precise lineage of certain contemporary population groups. Although, under the influence of the 'European' Enlightenment's so-called scientific inquiries, by the late eighteenth century the literal interpretation of the biblical story of the Deluge was coming under greater scrutiny than ever before—as in the case of the proto-evolutionary theory of the French naturalist Comte de Buffon (Georges-Louis Leclerc, 1707–88), as well as in the broader body of Vulcanist and Plutonist writing—, the theory of Japhetic, Shemitic, and Hamitic population distributions survived in Western scientific circles well into the mid-nineteenth century (and continues to hold sway to this day in the more literal camps of Jewish, Christian, Muslim, and other related religious traditions around the world).

Stefan Berger, among others, has reminded us that the teaching of history at European universities until the second half of the eighteenth century had been a subbranch of theology. It was only then that history as a separate discipline began to very gradually take shape.[36] This was a drawn-out process and did not necessarily signal the jettisoning of theological doctrines in teaching, writing, and examining historical narratives. Nor did all historians work within the academe, as in the case of most Irish antiquarians in the late eighteenth and early nineteenth century, including the general membership of the Royal Irish Academy. In the second half of the nineteenth century, by which time history was emerging as a professional academic discipline in its own right, the Irish nationalist genealogist and amateur historian John O'Hart, author of a best-selling history of ancient Ireland titled *Irish Pedigrees; or, the Origin and Stem of the Irish Nation* (1876), retained equal fidelity to both Sylvester O'Halloran's model of conflated Scythian-Phoenician ancestry of the Gaels and to the Mosaic theory of population groups. O'Hart, working outside the academic circles, repeated the old account that Fénius Farsaid (Fenius Farsa) was

> son of Baoth [Baath], son of Magog, son of Japheth, was, according to the [seventeenth-century] Four Masters, the inventor of *Letters*; he was also the grandfather of Gaodhal, a quo the Gaels. This Phœniusa Farsaidh was king of Scythia, and was the ancestor of the Phœnicians: after him the Scythian language was called the "Phœnician."

By the time later editions of *Irish Pedigrees* appeared, O'Hart was also incorporating the ongoing debates on Irish ancestry and on Aryan languages into his revisions of the original text. In the 1892 fifth edition, from which the previous quotation is also taken, O'Hart conformed the Asia-centered Indo-European (/Aryan) theory to the Mosaic model of common descent of all humanity from Noah's sons. Under the section "The Celtic Was the Language of Eden," O'Hart designated what was commonly regarded as the Aryan branch of languages as the original language of all pre- and post-diluvian humanity, adding: "That common primeval language of Man, which some call by the name 'Aryan,' I prefer to call the *Scythian*."[37]

Also of significance in regard to various theories of Iranian origins of the Irish in connection with developments in Indo-European theories of particular branches of languages in the late eighteenth century was the simultaneous and related amplified European intellectual interest in Zoroastrianism, with the earliest systematic European translations of material on Zoroastrian religion appearing at the beginning of that century. The first attempted comprehensive English account of Zoroastrianism, albeit suffering from a range of inaccuracies and substantially reliant on later Muslim sources on Zoroastrian religion, besides its other shortcomings, was *Historia religionis veterum Persarum eorumque magorum* (published in 1700) by the Oxford orientalist Thomas Hyde (1636–1703). The second edition of this work appeared in 1760, titled *Veterum Persarum et Parthorum et Medorum religionis historia*, also known as *De vetere religione Persarum*. However, the most momentous publication on Zoroastrianism in a European language during that century was by far the French translation in 1771 by Abraham Hyacinthe Anquetil-Duperron of Zoroastrian sacred texts and commentaries, known as *Zend Avesta*. Although the authenticity of Anquetil-Duperron's *Zend Avesta* was initially greeted with much skepticism in some British and Irish quarters, notably among leading British orientalists in the Indian subcontinent, it eventually assumed an authoritative status.[38] Both of the translations by Hyde and Anquetil-Duperron, as well as other related works by the latter—even as his translation of *Zend Avesta* still remained suspect in some Irish antiquarian circles—were cited by Irish antiquarians subscribing to various versions of the Iranian model of Irish origins, among a host of other European commentaries on Zoroastrianism appearing in these works.[39] These translations of Zoroastrian material were occurring in the broader context of so-called Oriental Renaissance and the relatively rapid formation of European knowledge about the 'Orient,' initially heavily centered on the Indian subcontinent. Similarly, complete or partial European translations of historical sources produced by 'orientals' themselves now served as routine material consulted by proponents of oriental origins in Irish antiquarian circles. A case in point being the fifteenth-century *Universal History* of Mirkhond, discussed later in this chapter.[40] It is imperative to note that these Irish antiquarians perceived of their projects as also belonging to the wider "Oriental Renaissance," albeit in a uniquely dual position. They not only engaged with the information generated through mainstream currents of this Renaissance as some of their foundational sources but were also appending Ireland's ancient past to that of the Orient's past and, in their own view, vastly contributing to the process of knowledge production about the presumed presence of the Orient in Ireland of ancient times. Based on their generally superficial familiarity with Zoroastrianism and other ancient religions of 'Iranian' and surrounding (and at times intersecting) cultural zones, these antiquarians (erroneously) extrapolated that the primacy of fire in Zoroastrian ritual practices bore a close resemblance to the presumed druidic tradition of fire and sun worship in Ireland, which they then set out to demonstrate through various range of sources and interpretations. This deduced connection was, in turn, expanded from the realm of religious ritual practice to Ireland's most celebrated indigenous surviving monuments predating the arrival of the Anglo-Normans in Ireland: the Round Towers.

Charles Vallancey and the Iranian (Persian) Theory of Irish Origins

The late eighteenth-century pioneers of new oriental models of Ireland's glorious ancient past included the likes of the prominent Catholic eye surgeon Charles O'Conor (1710–91),[41] the renowned Catholic surgeon Sylvester O'Halloran (1728–1807), and Colonel (later General) Charles Vallancey (1725–1812), a Protestant Englishman of French parentage residing in Ireland as a British military surveyor and Ireland's Chief Engineer (of Royal Engineers).[42] All three of these leading Irish antiquarians of the era were committed to the project of Irish cultural nationalism. They were all also initially proponents of some version of the Phoenician thesis of Irish origins. O'Conor and Vallancey, who were founding members of the Royal Irish Academy (1785)—with O'Halloran among early members of the Academy—had also in different ways introduced Persians into their narratives of Ireland's ancient Gaelic past. O'Conor, writing as early as 1753, well before the advent of Jonesian theory of Indo-European languages, had associated Persian and Celtic languages, identifying the Celtic language as the parent language of the language spoken by Scythians and as being related to Persian.[43] In the case of Vallancey's 1786 *A Vindication of the Ancient History of Ireland*, the Persians, as well as Phoenicians, were identified as descendants of Scythians, with the Zoroastrian prophet Zoroaster, "if not a Scythian, at least [having] studied Astronomy in Scythia." Then again, Vallancey designated many other population groups as originally Scythian, ranging from Armenians to Japanese.[44] Casting his net far and wide, in the same work Vallancey concluded the Scythians were the same as the Parthian branch of Iranians and among the earliest of the Celtic populations and that the Persian branch of Iranians and the ancient Irish were ultimately descendants of the (today recognized as non-Iranian) Elamites—who inhabited ancient Elam, which was later ruled by the Persian Empire. Presuming (erroneously) that Elam (also spelled as "Elim" in the same work) was "the ancient name" of Persia. Vallancey also credited Zoroaster with the introduction of "tower" temples, which allegedly became the prototype for Ireland's (presumably ancient) Round Towers.[45]

The allure of Iranian population groups as likely ancestors of the Irish in Vallancey's incrementally developing model of the Persian origins of the Gaels was not solely due to the evolving Indo-European theories of languages, which at the time designated the ancient Iranian lands as either the original homeland of the Indo-Europeans or as among the initial expanding range of the now long-extinct prototype of present-day Aryan languages. In this temporally diffused reconstruction of the ancient ancestry of the Irish, the Persians also had the distinction of being known in history as the main acknowledged imperial rival of Hellenic and Roman states, with extensive surviving Greco-Roman accounts of the Persians. While these accounts generally cast the Persians as *barbarian others* of Hellenic and Roman 'civilizations,' the same sources nonetheless acknowledged the imperial might of the Persians. Vallancey and other advocates of Iranian models of Irish origins dismissed the Hellenic and Roman castigation of

Persian and other Iranian groups, just as Keating in the previous century had rejected the Hellenic and Roman designation of Scythians as barbarians, much in the same manner that Irish nationalists refuted as mere prejudice English claims of civilizational superiority over the Irish. Furthermore, the Persian Achaemenid ruler Cyrus ("the Great") received lofty mention in the Bible as the liberator of the Jews from Babylonian captivity. In addition, by the end of the eighteenth century, there was a notable proliferation of new information about ancient Iranian history, as in the case of *The History of Persia. Containing, the Lives and Memorable Action of its Kings from the First Erecting of that Monarchy to this Time* by John Stevens, published in 1715, that incorporated Iranian and Arab accounts of ancient Iran. The growing contemporary interest in "classical" Persian poetry and increased translations of those poems into European languages also elevated the place of 'Iran' in European literary circles, even if these poems dated from after the seventh century CE, when Iran/Persia ceased to exist as an independent territory for a few centuries (with the poems in question composed by poets from both the territory constituting Persia/Iran as it existed in the eighteenth century as well as from other Persian-speaking regions of the former Persian territory).

Vallancey, with his 1786 *A Vindication of the Ancient History of Ireland*, pioneered the Iranian/Persian theory of ancient Irish origins, gradually fine-tuning his thesis to the point that Persians definitively overshadowed all other groups in his narrative of ancient Ireland by the time of the publication of his 1807 *An Essay on the Primitive Inhabitants of Great Britain and Ireland. Proving from History, Languages, and Mythology, that They were Persians or Indo-Scythæ*. Signs of this steady progression to an indisputably Perso-centric account of ancient Ireland were already present in Vallancey's *A Vindication of the Ancient History of Ireland*. In that work, he designated one of the (presumed) pre-Milesian population settlements in Ireland, that of the (otherwise legendary) Tuatha de Danann, as being incontrovertibly a colony of "the Pishdadians of the Persians" (in actuality, a mythical Persian dynasty). Moreover, in *A Vindication* he characterized the Irano-Scytho-Phoenician ancestry of the Gaels (the latter generally regarded by Irish antiquarians as descendants of Milesians) as already substantially Persianized in culture at the time of their arrival in Ireland.[46] By the time *An Essay on the Primitive Inhabitants of Great Britain and Ireland* appeared, Vallancey had vastly expanded the scope of the Persian ancestry of the Irish, now also inclusive of Milesians who were designated as Persians and Scytho-Iranians/Indo-Scythians.

As previously noted, these antiquarians in the debate on Irish origins turned to the latest developments in the fields of philology, ancient religions, mythology, and what is now called material culture, chiefly in the form of archaeological and extant architectural remains of what were believed to date from the ancient past, along with a continued heavy dose of biblical Mosaic models of post-diluvian population dispersions across the world. As also noted earlier, the antiquarian world-historical recontouring of Ireland's ancient past was occurring within the broader eighteenth-century European debates on Celticism (which in most of its formulations encompassed the Gaels and Gaelic languages, including Irish). That debate, too, was itself now subsumed under the broader debate on Indo-European languages. The various antiquarian re-framings of ancient Ireland were, therefore, a component of a much wider nexus of scholarly investigations, exchange of ideas, and contestations that were also occurring outside Ireland and Britain.[47] By the 1760s, Celtic as a branch of languages was attracting great attention in European philological circles, following a tradition established by the Welsh Edward Lhuyd and the French abbot Paul Pezron earlier in the century, notwithstanding the many extant disagreements on the linguistic origin and dispersion routes of various sub-branches of Celtic language. This debate expectedly segued to the subject of Gaelic and its relation to Celtic.[48] There was also much disagreement among propagators of Ireland's oriental origins as to the precise oriental location (geographic and/or cultural) from which the early population migrations to Ireland had taken place and the precise path they had followed on their journey. Vallancey, for his part, vacillated on the exact primordial geographic derivation of the purported Iranian ancestry of the Irish. This was largely unavoidable, given that he followed the contemporary Iranian practice of tracing the origin of the Persians to the (in actuality mythical) Pishdādiān. Nonetheless, as noted before, there was consensus among these antiquarians that the oriental ancestors of Ireland's Gaelic population had reached the island after a relatively short migratory process and that the ancient Gaels (and, in certain accounts, some of the preceding 'oriental' population migrations to Ireland) had been guardians of a glorious ancient civilization introduced to their new Irish homeland. As also previously noted, in most versions of such narratives another overriding emphasis was that of the Gaels, as harbingers of the earliest recognizable civilization in the British Isles, appearing first in Ireland without any prior contact with mainland Britain. In these accounts, the Iberian Peninsula ('Spain') was the most common choice as the last territory in Europe where the oriental ancestors of the Gaels had briefly settled before reaching Ireland, with some of their kin remaining in the Iberian Peninsula and intermixing with other groups. Once again, this was a rejection of claims that Ireland had been a civilizational void prior to the arrival of Anglo-Normans in the twelfth century, while also challenging 'medieval' Irish Christian narratives of enduring pagan barbarity on the island before the advent of Christianity in the fifth century. Incidentally, in the overwhelming majority of these later accounts of oriental origins, the medieval Norse ("Viking") settlements in Ireland after the ninth century were treated as utterly devoid of civilizational contribution, if not in fact cast as fundamentally destructive.

In addition, in the latter decades of the eighteenth century, Irish nationalist antiquarians were also responding to a key historical-cultural challenge posed by the Scottish Protestant poet James Macpherson's 1760 *Fragments of Ancient Poetry, Collected in the Highlands of Scotland*. In this collection, Macpherson alleged to have discovered an epic set in verse form, which he attributed to a third-century CE Scottish bard named Ossian. The heroic cycle of this poem corresponded to Ireland's foremost epic, the Fenian Cycle, with elements of another major Irish epic, the Ulster Cycle, also appearing in Ossian's version. By the start of the next century, Macpherson's Ossianic Cycle would be proven a forgery beyond doubt.[49] At the time, Macpherson was not alone in the non-English communities of Great Britain and Ireland in attempting to elicit greater ethnic ('national') pride through conscious fabrication of the past. Another famous example from the period is the Welsh Iolo Morganwg (Edward Williams), who in the 1790s invented an old Welsh bardic tradition to a similar end as Macpherson. Macpherson's alleged discovery, soon leading to a fierce debate over the authenticity of the epic, lent further ammunition to those claiming Irish culture was a derivative of what had first appeared on mainland Britain (Scotland in this case). Before Macpherson's work was definitively confirmed to be a forgery, most Irish cultural-nationalists insisted Ossian must simply have recounted an ancient Irish tradition brought over to Scotland in a distant past by Gaelic migrants from Ireland.[50] In this regard, Vallancey and subsequent Irish antiquarians claiming an Iranian (Persian or other) ancestry for the ancient populations of Ireland maintained that elements of the Irish epics in question, particularly a key section of the Ulster Cycle, were originally transmitted to Ireland by Iranian colonists (see below).

Vallancey rejected the Celtic identity of the Gaels, as well as any identification of the Celts with Persians. Notably Vallancey, in contrast to most of his cohorts and his own later works, had initially held that the oriental ancestors of the Gaels first reached Ireland following a brief sojourn in mainland Britain. In his 1786 account, the early Gaels, whom he characterized as "southern Scythians [by which he meant a branch of Persians], seated early on the Persian Gulph and in Touran," and who also comprised "the original Phoenicians," had arrived in England and Wales but were soon forced away by ancient Britons into Scotland and from there to Ireland.[51] This version of the path taken by Iranian ancestors of the Gaelic settlers in Ireland was substantially revised in Vallancey's later writings, with their migratory route now bypassing mainland Britain (i.e., arriving via 'Spain'). Nevertheless, even in his initial rendering of the route, the Iranian migrants had not remained in what later became English territory long enough as to have first transplanted their civilization in England, or elsewhere in Britain for that matter, before reaching Ireland. As one of his primary evidence for Iranian colonization of Ireland in ancient times, Vallancey offered the example of Ireland's surviving Round Towers, the original function of which he characterized as "fire tower[s]." Accordingly, these were irrefutable proof of Persian cultural influence in ancient Ireland (whether through direct Persian migrations or transmitted by other Iranian groups influenced by Persian culture).[52] It was further claimed (inaccurately) that such towers did not exist in England, indicating there had been no prior Iranian long-term settlements in Britain before reaching Ireland. Even though this line of argument could not rule out the possibility of subsequent inauguration of an ostensibly Iranian civilization in mainland Britain, it still rendered Ireland as the first major civilizational hub in the British Isles. As noted, beginning in 1786, and much more emphatically by 1807, Vallancey identified the Gaels as descendants of the larger Iranian population branch, whom he later also dubbed as "Indo-Scythians and the first inhabitants of the British Isles."[53] By 1807, Vallancey was jointly reacting to theories of the Celtic identity of Gaels, which related them to other early population groups in mainland Britain, as well as to the emergent 'Scandian' (i.e., Scandinavian) theory of ancient Irish ancestry put forth by the Protestant Anglo-Irish Reverend Edward Ledwich in his 1790 *The Antiquities of Ireland*. According to Ledwich, the Gaels belonged to the Celtic population, originally of Scythian descent (in its former non-Iranian designation in this case), who by way of migrations through eastern Europe had settled in northern reaches of Europe long before setting out for the British Isles.[54] Ledwich's underlying inference was that of ancient Ireland lacking civilizational splendor, corroborating the ongoing 'wild Irish' vilification of the Gaelic population of Ireland.

Vallancey also turned to philology as yet another tool for incontrovertibly affirming the Iranian heritage of ancient Ireland. In his linguistic-historical conjectures on Persian and other Iranian roots of the early populations of Ireland, he was heavily reliant on William Jones' Indo-European model of languages and related historical commentaries, albeit woven together in a characteristically Vallanceyan style.[55] With hindsight, this reliance on Jones, widely regarded at the time in the British Isles and beyond as the leading authority on Indo-European languages, accounts for some of the confused details in Vallancey's writing, even though Jones did not deal with Ireland; nor did he specifically discuss the Gaels. For instance, one can cite Jones' statement in a published lecture from February 1786 that "*Hindus* [...] had an immemorial affinity with the old *Persians*, *Ethiopians*, and *Egyptians*, the *Ph[o]enicians*, *Greeks*, and *Tuscans*, the *Scythians* or *Goths*, and *Celts*, the *Chinese*, *Japanese*, and *Peruvians*; whence [...] we may fairly conclude that they all proceeded from some *central* country."[56] Whereas Vallancey was by then skeptical of the Celtic connection of the Gaels, Jones nevertheless confirmed, if not in fact being the first to adduce, what became Vallancey's identification of Persians with Phoenicians and a wide array of other (linguistically non-'Aryan') population groups. This example is also important by way of contextualizing what to us today may appear as the bizarrely phantasmagoric imagination of Vallancey and most other Irish antiquarians from the period. William Jones was highly regarded across contemporary Western/European intellectual circles, as well as in some non-European circles (particularly in the Indian subcontinent), as a pioneering figure in philology and was widely quoted as such. While it is undeniable that even by Jones' standards Vallancey's etymological style was highly contortionist, Vallancey was certainly far from being unique in his porous methodology among contemporary antiquarians in Ireland or in much of the rest of the world.

Vallancey emerged as one of the most prolific and renowned theoreticians in what was internally a highly contentious field of tracing Ireland's ancient Gaelic identity to various parts and populations of the Orient. He was, nonetheless, extremely controversial and prone to criticism on grounds of his distinctively extravagant and seemingly inexhaustible etymological acrobatics, even by the contemporary standard of most other antiquarians on different sides of the debate on Irish origins. He frequently made capricious correlations between various languages, accompanied by his inimitable interspersed glossaries, which (as discussed below) appeared in his later works not only in the usual Greek, Latin, and Hebrew scripts common in other antiquarian works concerning Ireland's oriental origins but significantly also in (the Arabic script) Persian and Arabic.[57] As the pioneering proponent of what became an evolving theory of Iranian models of Ireland's great civilizational past, Vallancey's publications were widely consulted by aficionados and detractors alike for many decades to come. While his methodology and conclusions did not meet with the approval of all proponents of competing oriental theories of Irish origins, his stellar presence in the field was also assured by his being a secretary of the antiquities committee of the Royal Dublin Society (1772), a co-founder of Hibernian Antiquarian Society (1779) and a founding member of the Royal Irish Academy (1785).[58] Vallancey's fame was additionally propelled by his becoming the optimal target of *detractors of all oriental theories of Irish origins*, given his more copious output than other proponents of oriental theories and his standing in Irish antiquarian circles. Vallancey was among the growing number of Anglo-Protestant die-hard vindicators of ancient Ireland's civilized heritage. He was, therefore, also a particularly reviled target for Protestant Anglo-Irish and English denigrators of Gaelic and Gaelicized cultures of Ireland, who were still guided in their antiquarian pursuit by highly charged anti-Gaelic and anti-Catholic precepts. The latter agenda also motivated some Presbyterian Scots-Irish detractors of Gaelicized Irish culture, which at the time was heavily influenced by Catholicism in contrast to Scotland's Gaelic tradition. Moreover, Vallancey was representative of a small clique of Britons and Irish Protestants at the time who were sympathetic toward moderate Irish nationalist platforms (primarily cultural, but also at times circumspectly political). He was as vigorous a champion of Irish cultural nationalism and a staunch advocate of reclaiming Irish 'national' pride as the Gaelicized Geoffrey Keating had been in his defense of Ireland's Gaelic population and culture in the seventeenth century, and no less so than Vallancey's contemporary Irish-Catholic antiquarians Sylvester O'Halloran and Charles O'Conor. But, alongside his antiquarian pursuit, Vallancey also fulfilled his official duties as a British military surveyor in his adopted Irish homeland, including during the government's suppression of the republican United Irishmen uprising of 1798; perceiving no contradiction between his military post in the service of British rule in Ireland and his validation of Irish culture and history.[59] This seeming incongruity should not be all that puzzling, given that many Irish antiquarians of so-called Gaelic ethnic background, and predominantly Catholics, also did not subscribe to Irish republican politics during, or in the aftermath of, the failed 1798 uprising. Regardless, some leading Irish nationalists of differing political outlooks in the coming decades, who embraced oriental theories of Irish origins, turned to Vallancey's publications as authoritative antiquarian sources, as did many who shied away from manifestly partisan political platforms.

Beginning in the eighteenth century, what can be termed "patriot" Anglo-Irish Protestant antiquarians, along with a segment of Catholic Gaelic ('mere Irish') as well as Gaelicized 'Old English' nationalist antiquarians, were turning to ancient pre-Norman Ireland as an essential source of Irish cultural-national foundation, with Christianity and other later components subsequently added to that foundational fabric of Irish identity—notwithstanding the frequently virulent and divisive post-Norman *ethnic* and post-English Reformation *religious* divides in Ireland. Charles O'Conor and Sylvester O'Halloran were among the leading eighteenth-century figures of what Anna Davin has labeled "Catholic antiquarianism" in Ireland, which

> had a double political intent, both to rebut the Protestant version of the more recent past, and, "by proving to an English-speaking audience that Ireland had a long and sophisticated culture in literature, music and other arts," to lay claim to political and civil rights, denied previously to Irish Catholics on grounds of their alleged barbarity.[60]

But, alongside this group were also the likes of the Anglican Irish literary antiquarian and renowned compiler and translator of Gaelic poetry, Charlotte Brooke (1740?–93), the celebrated author of the 1789 *Reliques of Irish Poetry*. She was intensely proud of her Irish identity and committed to Irish cultural nationalism, and just as equally determined as the likes of O'Conor to elevate and acclaim Ireland's Gaelic past. Brooke, sharing the stance of her god-father Sylvester O'Halloran, was a proponent of the theory of Phoenician origins of Ireland's ancient glorious civilization, with the sea-faring Phoenicians credited for introducing to Ireland the most sophisticated of ancient cultural traditions and knowledge that *they had acquired from vast regions of the world*. Similarly, she staunchly contested Macpherson's (spurious) claim of the Scottish authorship (Ossian) of what was regarded as Ireland's 'national' epic: the Fenian Cycle. While Brooke as a woman was barred from membership in the Royal Irish Academy and other similar leading scholarly associations in Ireland, she commanded immense scholarly respect from many members of the Academy and beyond. In the Preface to *Reliques of Irish Poetry*, in which she engaged in the standard self-effacing convention followed by many highly talented women of her milieu, who downplayed their own scholarship in comparison with their male counterparts ("lament[ing] […] the limited circle of my knowledge"), Brooke deferred to the historical expertise of "O'CONOR, O'HALLORAN and VALLANCEY,"[61] as divided as these male authorities were by then on details of the oriental origins of the Irish.

As John Patrick Delury has pointed out, "[the post-Norman conquest] History was the nightmare from which the United Irishmen wished to awake," adding that in the eighteenth century,

> Protestants, from Walter Harris to Charles Vallancey, worked with sources from the Gaelic historiographical tradition and spoke of the ancient history of Ireland as if it were their own cultural possession. A handful of Catholic historians, most notably Charles O'Conor, John Curry, and Sylvester O'Halloran, wrote ancient and modern histories of their native land in the English language for a Protestant audience. For the first time, historians from the two traditions worked in personal collaboration on the writing of Ireland's past. They stood in the front trenches in the struggle to bring together the two communities into one nation.[62]

The main fault line in this patriot-nationalist historiographic project of ancient Ireland was the question of the exact origin and civilizational heritage of the ancient Irish. For instance, as noted already, the oriental camp was split between the adherents of competing theories of Phoenician vs. Scythian vs. Iranian, and so on, or other groups vs. a jointly Phoenician and Scytho-Iranian population, among the broad range of proposed nominees. Writing in 1778, O'Halloran identified the Scythians (as presumed descendants of the biblical Magog) as the ancestor of Ireland's Milesians (i.e., Gaels). Also relying on the generally accepted biblical time frames, he dated the start of the Milesian colonization of Ireland (after other earlier smaller groups had already settled there) to the year 2,736 after Creation and located the original Scythian homeland "on the borders of the Mediterranean."[63] His model made no mention of Persia or Persians, or of Medes, Parthians, and other such Iranian groups who had ruled various parts of the territories that later comprised the ancient Persian Empire. On the other hand, O'Conor in his 1753 *Dissertations on the Ancient History of Ireland*, long before the publication of

O'Halloran's work and well before William Jones's popularization of Indo-European theory of languages, had associated the Celtic branch of languages—to which O'Conor correctly assigned Irish-Gaelic—with Persian, among other languages. O'Conor regarded Persian as a later offshoot of "The *Celtic*," which he in turn described as

> the original Language of the Posterity of the Patriarchs, *Gomer* and *Japeth;* and this in After-Ages, branched out into the various Dialects of the Persians, Teutons, *Gauls, Briton* and *Scots.* It was certainly as old and extensive a Language as any on Earth; it was also one of the most copious.[64]

In this account, the Scythians, who were a "Nation bordering on the *Caspian*," had introduced Celtic to Ireland as the main Gaelic population settlement on the island in ancient times.[65] In other words, Persian, along with Gaelic, was derived from the original (presumably Celtic) language of Scythians.

Albeit postulated from highly conjectural premises, O'Conor was in effect, long before Vallancey and the Jonesian Indo-European hypothesis, already suggesting an interconnection between Scythians and Persians, but without identifying them as subgroups of the larger 'Iranian' peoples—and not forgetting also Vallancey's later (erroneous) repudiation of the Celtic classification of Gaelic dialects. In 1775, O'Conor published an English translation from Latin of Roderic O'Flaherty's previously unpublished *Ogygia Vindiciae* (1695), which now appeared as *The Ogygia Vindicated* along with supplementary material, including O'Conor's "A Dissertation on the Origin and Antiquities of the Antient Scots."[66] Appearing prior to Vallancey's gradual shift to the Persian (Iranian) model, in this work O'Conor hailed Vallancey, who was also among the book's subscribers, as a leading authority on ancient Ireland (see below). O'Conor, a co-founder with John Curry of the Catholic Association (a.k.a., the Catholic Committee) in 1756,[67] was defending O'Flaherty's assertion of the existence of Irish literacy prior to the introduction of Christianity to Ireland. This was in reaction to the denial of pre-Christian literacy in Ireland by O'Flaherty's Scottish contemporary Sir George Mackenzie. This dispute had surfaced against the backdrop of seventeenth- and eighteenth-century debates on Gaelic literary traditions of Scotland versus Ireland, occurring within the broader framework of Celticism. O'Conor, while upholding many of the central tenets and the overall scholarship of O'Flaherty, admitted certain unavoidable shortcomings in the latter's work based on information that allegedly should have been available to O'Flaherty at the time. O'Flaherty had claimed a joint Celtic and Scythian origin of the earliest settlers in Ireland arriving "from South and North Britain," with the two population groups constituting "branches from the same stock."[68] O'Conor, both a leading campaigner for Catholic rights and an acclaimed antiquarian on account of his 1753 *Dissertations on the Ancient History of Ireland*, instead asserted that

> Major *Charles Vallancey* [...] [then a member of the Dublin Society; later renamed the Royal Dublin Society] (an English gentleman) has already made very considerable progress in explaining the old language of this island; the rules of its construction, and the Punic [i.e., Phoenician/Carthaginian] original of many of its terms.[69]

However, by 1786, Vallancey was clearly parting ways with this earlier Phoenician model, as evident in his *A Vindication of the Ancient History of Ireland*. The significance of this work in Vallancey's gradual shift to the Persian (Iranian) thesis of Irish origins is repeatedly overlooked in present-day scholarship on Vallancey, with most scholars today remaining fixated on Vallancey's earlier Phoenician model as his paramount theory of Irish origins. A notable exception to this pattern is an essay by Bernd Roling.[70]

A conspicuous feature of Vallancey's publications was his recurring major theoretical turnabouts without abandoning his trademark etymological technique and overall meandering methodology that had previously led him to different conclusions. The point here from our present perspective is not that Vallancey altered his views, but rather that he continued to pursue a widely freewheeling speculative methodology by our standards, not unlike many of his contemporary Irish and other antiquarians. These other antiquarians also drew general abstractions from limited evidence or highly conjectural interconnections. Yet, Vallancey's writings still stand out in this regard, given his almost impulsive disposition to selectively incorporate into his work all range of findings and methodological trends in related fields (old and new) that somehow corroborated his continually evolving antiquarian permutations, without due regard to limits of interpretation. In 1772, Vallancey had sided with the Scytho-Phoenician/Carthaginian theory of Irish origins.[71] In his 1773 *A Grammar of the Iberno-Celtic*, still operating within the Scytho-Phoenician model, he observed: "It is evident then that both the Irish and the Saxons received their letters from the same fountain-head, the Phœnicians." Among others, he cited the work of the seventeenth-century French Samuel Bochart.[72] Vallancey noted that "[Edmund] Spen[s]er, in his View of [the Present State of] Ireland, p.1548, asserts the Irish character [i.e., Irish script] to be Phœnician or Persian, and to be brought by the Milesians from Spain: he denies that the ancient Scythians had the use of letters."[73] Here, Vallancey was rejecting Spenser's view that the Scythian progenitors of Ireland's Gaelic population comprised an uncultured people and that writing had been introduced to Ireland much later by either Phoenicians or Persians, with Spenser designating the latter group as ethnically and culturally distinct from Scythians. Ultimately, in Spenser's estimation even the late appearance of Irish script could not exempt the island's indigenous population from the 'wild Irish' verdict. In the 1786 *A Vindication of the Ancient History of Ireland*, Vallancey substantially altered his previous model and instead settled for an Iranian (in this case Perso-Scythian/Irano-Scythian (Scytho-Iranian)/Indo-Scythian) origin of Gaelic literacy in ancient Ireland; in effect, melding into one people Spenser's otherwise disparate Scythians and Persians. This time around, relying on the work of the contemporary French scientist Jean-Sylvain Bailly, Vallancey wrote:

> The Persians were Scythians, descended from Mount Caucasus, they first settled about the Caspian Sea, then in Armenia, and finally in Persia. The ancient history of the Persians, is the history of these Southern Scythians, the ancestors of the Irish. [...] The learned Mons. Bailly has opened an extensive field of knowledge in the Persian history, proving them to have been originally Scythians.[74]

Dedicated to King George III, Vallancey's 1786 *A Vindication of the Ancient History of Ireland* traced the early population arrivals in Ireland back to the greater Scytho-Persian-Iranian homeland, which in this case was made inclusive of not only the Medes, Parthians, Armenians, Sogdians, and "Indians" (i.e., Indo-Iranians) but also comprised Turanians, Chaldeans, and some other groups. Here, he was clearly following in the footsteps of William Jones' already-quoted erroneous concoction in 1786 of the early Indo-European family of languages, albeit with Vallancey blithely adding his own further extrapolations and adjustments to Jones' mixture. In essence, Vallancey's Indo-European family of languages was a combination of many population groups not necessarily related to one another in terms of language but (anachronistically) having lived at different times in regions that at one point had comprised the vastest expanse of the Scythian Empire, stretching from West Asia and Anatolia into the Caucasus, Central Asia, and the northern reaches of South Asia. Without in any way suggesting that Vallancey was necessarily distorting his evidence in a premeditative mode any more than most other contemporary antiquarians so as to tailor it to his conclusion, this conflation of otherwise linguistically diverse groups as sub-branches of a single language classification nevertheless afforded Vallancey much greater flexibility for drawing on various histories, traditions, and sources in tracing the ancient roots of Ireland's population and civilizational ties, also allowing him some wiggle room in transitioning from a Scytho-Phoenician to a Perso-Scythian model of Irish origins.

In *A Vindication of the Ancient History of Ireland*, Vallancey's version of major waves of early post-diluvian settlements in Ireland followed the same pattern as Keating's narrative, but with a Persian twist now added to the Scythian story (with both groups identified as belonging to the larger Iranian population group). In other words, Vallancey's sequence of major ancient migrations to Ireland from the East followed the established (legendary) model of population arrivals on the island, but with a modified linguistic-ethnic designation of those groups. These were: (1) Partholan and his followers (from Migdon in Scythia, which had been settled by descendants of Magog); (2) Descendants of Nemed and their followers (Nemedians of Scythian origin, by way of the Mediterranean and North Africa, from where a cluster of them moved to Greece and then sailed to Ireland by way of Spain); (3) the Firbolgs ("who were of the possession of the Magi, or Fire-worshippers"—that is, practitioners of pre-Zoroastrian and Zoroastrian religious rituals of ancient Iranian lands); (4) the Tuatha de Dananns (who were identified as Persians, and akin to southern Scythians from "Touran," and hence reportedly the same as "the Pishdad[i]an of the Persians," who brought with them to Ireland the worship of fire and the design of the Round Towers); and (5) the Milesians (descendants of Fénius Farsaid of the "Armenian" branch of Scythians, with Farsaid's name now identified as having allegedly a number of Persian cognates, among them "*Fars* [i.e., Persia] [...] the father of *Parthians* and *Persians*, [...] they descended from the same stock as the ancient Irish"). According to this narrative, Farsaid's Milesian descendants had eventually settled in Spain, then returned to Scythia led by Miledh (a.k.a., Milesius/Míl Espáine), from where they moved to Oman by way of the Persian Gulf, and from there to Egypt, and then back to Spain, before finally settling in Ireland.[75]

This emergent Perso-Scythian (Iranian) connection in Vallancey's account of ancient Ireland was made much more explicit and cardinal by the time of the publication of his 1807 *An Essay on the Primitive Inhabitants of Great Britain and Ireland. Proving from History, Languages, and Mythology, that They were Persians or Indo-Scythæ, Composed of Scythians, Chaldæans, and Indians.* The primary impetus for Vallancey's increasing concentration on the 'Persian' connection was unmistakably the ongoing developments in the field of Indo-European branch of languages, following the rapid proliferation of studies carried out by members of the Asiatic Society of Bengal (Calcutta) in British-controlled territories of the Indian subcontinent.[76] This creative reliance on the latest research in the field of Indo-European languages was also an opportunity for Vallancey to establish himself at the forefront of a new historiographic approach to the study of ancient Ireland. As in his previous publications, his methodology still incorporated the older Mosaic scheme and much of the narrative sequencing of the early population groups of ancient Ireland found in Keating's *The History of Ireland*. These, along with an assortment of other available historical accounts—certain details of which Vallancey intermittently challenged and/or amended when they deviated from his own narrative—were now increasingly combined with Vallancey's revisionist gleaning from recent research on Indo-European languages. And, perhaps most significantly and hitherto overlooked by other scholars, this combination of information was then infused with available translations of sources originally composed in 'oriental' languages (see below), along with a characteristically heavy dose of Vallancey's own incrementally dizzying etymological and historical alchemy.

Vallancey's evolving theory of ancient Ireland's Persian heritage became one of the preeminent and more influential variants of oriental models of Irish origins. A more broadly 'Iranian' theory actually predated Vallancey's writing by nearly two decades and had coexisted for some time alongside Scythian, Phoenician, and other Eastern theories of Irish origins, including some combinations and conflation of these various groups. Vallancey not only made substantial modifications to the former Iranian model but also accorded it a prominence it had previously lacked in debates on Irish origins. For instance, writing in 1764, the leading mid-eighteenth century Welsh linguist Rowland Jones (d. 1774) was among those who had circuitously proposed an Iranian ancestry of the Gaels. According to Jones—who relied on the conventional biblical-inspired rendition of the Japhetic theory of languages and the gradual divergence and distribution of population groups ("nations" in the parlance of the time)—it was the descendants of the three sons of Noah who eventually inhabited the known regions of the biblical world in Asia, Africa, and Europe. Whereas Noah's sons Shem and Ham were designated respectively as ancestors of "Semitic" and "Hamitic" peoples—with Noah himself having already lived a few hundred years by the time his sons were born—it was the descendants of Japheth who eventually inhabited the lands west of the Black Sea, or what would later come to be designated as the heartland of "Europe," with one of Japheth's seven sons, Madai, choosing to stay behind in Asia and settling in a land that came to be named Media after him (i.e., later constituting northern Iranian territories). The remaining sons of Japheth dispersed in different westerly directions in Europe. Based on this account, the descendants of Madai, who were said to have later populated the remainder of what after Rowland Jones' time came to be called the 'Iranian' lands (including

Persia, Bactria, and northern regions of the Indian subcontinent), comprised the non-European Japhetic branch of peoples. (This narrative later provided the basis for the British orientalist and philologist William Jones' Japhetic ("Ya'fet") branch of languages, subsequently called 'Indo-European.') Rowland Jones substantiated his theory by way of referencing such authorities as the first-century CE Jewish-Roman historian Flavius Josephus. Rowland Jones was ultimately also attempting to demonstrate that his own native Welsh language was the original form of many later European languages, maintaining that the Welsh and the early population of Ireland, similar to Britons, were descendants of Japheth's son Gomer, who had settled in Greece and whose descendants had established the "Gentile" branch of nations—Gentiles being equated with 'Europeans.' He rejected the view that the ancient Welsh or the Irish were descendants of Magog or of other sons of Japheth, who had also moved westward via different routes and in different directions. In this scheme, the Irish Gaels, similar to the Welsh, were merely a branch of the Celts. Significantly, and more relevant here, Rowland Jones traced the origins of the Celts to Iranian lands encompassing Persia and Media (as opposed to the Scythian heartland):

> Hence those who placed the first settlements of the Celtes and Cumbri [i.e., the Welsh] in the eastern parts of Asia, behind the Medes and Persians, and in Scythia [i.e., north and east of Media and Persia], as having passed into Europe betwixt the Caspian and Euxine seas [Euxine being the Black Sea] by mount Caucasus, instead of the Thracian Bosphorus, and by the way of Greece, appear to be much mistaken; and though such of them as went by the name of Celto-Scyths might have mixed with the Scythians in their first migrations in Europe, along the Euxine coast towards the Palus Meotis [i.e., Tanais River in Scythia; present-day Don River] and the borders of Scythia, it seems very clear from ancient history, that the founders and first planters of Greece, Italy, ancient Gaul, Britain and Ireland, passed out of Asia into Europe over the Thracian Bosphorus, and thro' Greece.[77]

By 1786, Vallancey had incorporated Scythians into the broader range of Iranian peoples, from whom the ancient Gaelic population of Ireland had presumably descended, while also differentiating the Gaels from the Celts. Furthermore, Vallancey designated Magog as the son of Japheth whose progeny had settled in Ireland.[78] Perhaps even more importantly, in addition to ancient Greek and Latin sources, as well as Christian and Jewish biblical sources and other range of works in Hebrew, Vallancey was the first commentator on Irish origins to cite as evidence a range of non-biblical and non-Hebrew oriental sources available in European translations (in their entirety or in summary form). These works included the Arabic *Rowzat al-Safā fi Sirat al-Anbiyā' wa al-Moluk wa al-Kholafā*, widely known in English as *Universal History* of Mirkhond (Muhammad ibn Khāvandshāh Mirkhvānd, 1433–98), also spelled "Mirkhound" and mistakenly identified by Vallancey as an "Arabian author" on account of the original language in which the text was compiled[79]—Mirkhond was a Persian historian from Central Asia, living in the regions of present-day Uzbekistan and Afghanistan. Vallancey also relied on the Persian epic *Shāhnāmeh*, completed in verse form by

Abul-Qassem Ferdowsi in the eleventh century, as well as such other work as the thirteenth-century Persian *Zardoshtnāmeh* ("The Book of Zoroaster"). Rather than reading actual translations of these works, he referenced them by way of information gleaned from the French Barthélemy d'Herbelot's 1697 *Bibliothèque orientale*. For instance, in the second part of Chapter VIII of *A Vindication of the Ancient History of Ireland* (1786), Vallancey relied on accounts from Persian language 'Iranian' sources (in the broad geo-cultural sense of Iran) to describe the Milesians' decision to return to Spain after having earlier left Spain for their original Scythian homeland, as well as their subsequent migration to Ireland. In this narrative, he remarkably relied on his own rendition of d'Herbelot's summaries of the sources in question for maintaining the (entirely fantastic) claim that the army of the biblical Neo-Babylonian Chaldean king Nebuchadnezzar II had been plundering and laying waste to Spain by the time the Milesians returned there. In this account, which, based on our present-day dating techniques, would also place the Milesian migrations to Ireland in the sixth century BCE, Vallancey identified Nebuchadnezzar as the (otherwise mythical) Iranian epic hero Gudarz. According to Vallancey's historical interjection, Gudarz had earlier driven the Scythians who had settled in Oman (Arabia) out of the region and into Spain.[80] Vallancey then noted the appearance of the Iranian prophet Zoraoster and the collection of his teachings, "*Zend* [sic], or the Bible of the Fire-worshippers [sic]," before introducing a section titled "Irish History *corresponding with the preceding* Persian History."[81] He was adamant that further clues to the earliest particulars of Irano-Scythian migration to Ireland were to be discovered in surviving Persian sources: "We know very little of Asiatic history as yet, particularly of the ancient Persians: the discoveries we may expect from the Asiatic Society [of Bengal, in Calcutta], will undoubtedly one day throw greater lights on the history I am now vindicating."[82] Vallancey acknowledged that on their presumed distant journey to Ireland from the East, the ancestors of the Gaels had also embraced some beliefs and practices of other population groups, such as "Chaldæns and Canaanites," despite having earlier identified Chaldeans as a branch of Irano-Scythian peoples. Yet, the ancestors of the Gaels had retained the core of their original beliefs, rituals, and other knowledge and practices. Among his examples of the heavily Persianized (Irano-Scythian/Indo-Scythian) cultural attributes introduced to Ireland by the original Gaels were literacy, fire-worship, and hence purportedly also Ireland's Round Towers, other monuments, crafts, laws, a wide spectrum of rituals, and history and mythology.[83] He averred: "we find the Persian history, (fabulous or real) to be the history of the ancient Irish[;] can there be more required?"[84]

Leaving aside Vallancey's extravagantly phantasmagoric historiographic method by our contemporary standards, what is extraordinary is his reliance on an entirely new range of oriental "historical" sources, beyond, and in combination with, accounts found in biblical and such other 'Eastern histories,' for reconstructing the history of ancient Ireland, a European territory. This practice of scouring oriental sources, beyond mere biblical and a range of related Hebrew sources, for narrating and verifying Ireland's past was most succinctly framed by Vallancey in the already-quoted phrase 'Irish History *corresponding with the preceding* Persian History' and was soon emulated by a host of other Irish antiquarians—acquiring methodological cachet in establishing Ireland's ancient Iranian heritage, before fizzling out by mid-nineteenth century and giving way to other methodological modes of establishing Iran-Erin connections in ancient times, even if there continued to be some practitioners of Vallancey's method after the mid-nineteenth century, whether or not they acknowledged Vallancey as a precursor. Furthermore, as discussed below, in a comparative world-historical context, it is striking that Iranian mythohistory (in the manifold historical, geographic, and cultural definition of Iran across time), as in the case of (the legendary) Pishdādiān dynasty, was first utilized in the service of *Irish nationalism* after the late eighteenth century, prior to being incorporated into the arsenal of (a distinctly pre-Islamic and Perso-centric formulated) *Iranian nationalism* in the nineteenth century (as opposed to earlier expressions of Iranian and/or Pesianate cultural-historical pride).

As further proof of his conclusions, Vallancey outlandishly imitated William Jones' philological findings. In fact, a great deal of Vallancey's terminology in his writings after 1786 was taken from published texts of Jones' lectures at the Asiatic Society of Bengal and adapted to Vallancey's own historical narrative, with much of Jones' own historical connections and extrapolations no less convoluted and far-fetched than Vallancey's from our standpoint, being riddled with methodological and historical misconceptions—while keeping in mind that Ireland did not feature in Jones' main topics of discussion. Vallancey, however, lacked both Jones' knowledge of languages and his still more meticulous systematic modus operandi. Instead, Vallancey often arbitrarily, and in an entirely unmethodical manner, connected a wide range of oriental languages and Irish-Gaelic by means of homophonous and seemingly cognate-sounding words, and then (and in this regard not unlike William Jones' method) proceeded to establish what we would now call a *genetic* link between the populations speaking those languages. Jones' linguistic model, too, rested on such erroneous genetic framework, following the then dominant Mosaic theory. Still, Jones' approach undeniably exuded a much greater sense of structural organization. Vallancey at times even altered the actual spelling and/or meaning of words, including those in Old Irish. It is unclear if this was due to inadvertent ignorance, pre-meditated stratagem, or merely as a means of simplifying his readers' already daunting task of deciphering the stipulated connections between languages than lose them in detailed explanations of internal changes in languages over time, or a combination of all of the above. He also associated ancient terminology in one language with modern and/or otherwise imported words in another, completely disregarding such factors as word compounds, loan words, altered applications and meanings of words, and so on. This collapsing and conflating of numerous languages and population groups (both spatial and temporal) was not entirely dissimilar to other pre- or post-Jonesian diffusionist theories; with William Jones himself adapting his theory of the diffusion of languages to the existing biblical paradigm of post-diluvian dispersion of population groups. The opening paragraph of the Introduction to Vallancey's 1786 *A Vindication of the Ancient History of Ireland* offers a characteristic example of the contorted methodology throughout his writings, even by mainstream contemporary European antiquarian standards. While claiming Iranian historical sources (in the broad sense of Iran) provided greater clues to Ireland's ancient past, he also notably claimed that 'medieval' Irish manuscripts provided much greater insight than any other source into the early history of Iranian peoples at the time of their dispersions beyond their original homelands (with Armenians also classified as a branch of Persians here). This was avowedly on grounds that the Irish sources in question were works produced and expanded on by Iranians who had continuously ventured westward further and further away from their original homeland and, hence, these works charted the geographic expansion of Iranians that was missing from works produced by those Iranians who did not engage in this westward migration. In effect, the Irish sources related the history and civilizational standing of the Iranian peoples as it was in their homelands in the East at the time the Iranian ancestry of the Irish set out in the direction of Europe, as well as the story of their migration across certain reaches of western Asia, Africa, and Europe, along with the account of their civilizational transplantation in one of the farthest westerly regions of Europe. The Irish sources, in other words, recounted an additional chapter of 'Iran'-centered world history that could not have been written by those who remained behind in the Iranian homelands. To quote Vallancey,

> THE Irish Manuscripts contain a more perfect account of the emigrations of the Armenian-Scythians, or Persians, &c. from the banks of the Caspian and Euxine Sea to Persia; to the Islands of the Mediterranean, to Africa, to Spain, and to the Britannic Isles, than any history hitherto known.
> The detail of these emigrations perfectly correspond with the Punic Annals, translated out of the books of King *Hiemsal*'s library [i.e., the second century BCE Numidian king Hiempsal I] for Sallust; [...] (a) [...] they agree with the most ancient Armenian History, written by *Moses Choronesis* (b), in names and facts, and with the ancient history of the Persians; and, lastly, they correspond with the most authentick Spanish Historians.[85]

Vallancey's conclusions and methodology drew criticism from different contemporary antiquarian circles in Ireland and Great Britain, as well as inside and outside the Royal Irish Academy. These critics included Vallancey's arch-nemesis Edward Ledwich, a proponent of an equally imaginary Scandian (Scandinavian) theory of Irish origin, following a long period of settlement in Scandinavian territories of peoples originally from the East.[86] But, Vallancey at the same time found a great deal of support in various quarters. The prominent Anglo-Irish Protestant 'patriot' politician, Henry Flood, who endorsed historical accounts of pre-Norman Ireland that were sympathetic to Gaelic people and culture recommended in his 1791 last testament (i.e., five years after the publication of Vallancey's *A Vindication of the Ancient History of Ireland*) that Vallancey "should be appointed 'the first professor' of Irish at Trinity College."[87] Within a few years after the publication of Vallancey's *A Vindication*, by which time he was a resolute proponent of the Iranian theory, James Hely of Trinity College had joined the ranks of Vallancey's converts and was steadfastly defending Vallancey against accusations of etymological insouciance. Hely, a scholar of Roderic O'Flaherty's 1685 *Ogygia: seu Rerum Hibernicarum Chronologia*, now deferred to Vallancey as the leading authority on ancient Ireland. In the "Translator's Address" of his 1793 translation from Latin into English of O'Flaherty's *Ogygia*, Hely wrote:

> the constant tradition of our earliest fileas [*sic*] [...] deduce all our first Irish colonies from the oriental Scythians, the most roaming and restless people of the earliest ages. Here [i.e., with Vallancey's recent works] opens a fair and extensive field for useful information—a field, however, untrod by modern antiquarians, save by Col. Vallancey in consequence of the knowledge he acquired of the ancient language of this island, and of his skill in oriental history. He has also discovered a similitude from a number of oriental terms in that language, and from a number of oriental rites in the pagan theology of Ireland. The field thus opened by Col. Vallancey, is made accessible to men fond of adding to the sum of attainable knowledge, and not to gentlemen who employ themselves in endeavouring to detect mistakes in Col. Vallancey's etyrnologies, and, after so glorious an exploit, filling volumes with the superior savageness of our old inhabitants; an assertion, which if a fact, might surely be confined to a single sheet of paper.[88]

It is crucial to note there were other contemporary antiquarians in Great Britain and Ireland who, similar to Vallancey, associated the Scythians with the Persians. For instance, a year after Vallancey's *A Vindication of the Ancient History of Ireland*, the Scottish John Pinkerton in his 1787 *A Dissertation on the Origin and Progress of the Scythians or Goths* identified Scythians as a subsequently nomadic branch of "Persians" who had migrated north of the Araxes (Arras River) following their expulsion from Persian territories.[89] In a hodgepodge contortionist method of his own by our standards, Pinkerton differentiated between the Persians, whose "Farsi" language he associated with "Gothic," and the Medes and Parthians, whose "*Pehlavi*" language he related to "Sarmatic or Slavonic."[90] But, Pinkerton's objective in linking Scythians to Persians was the opposite of Vallancey's. Also capitalizing on recent theories of Indo-European languages, Pinkerton designated the Germanic peoples (Goths) as European descendants of Perso-Scythians and as the historically civilized Europeans, in contrast to the Celts, to which group he assigned the Gaels (contra Vallancey). Pinkerton then described the Celts as

> mere radical savages, not yet advanced even to the state of barbarism; and if any foreigner doubts this, he has only to step into the Celtic part of Wales, Ireland, or Scotland, and look at them, for they are just as they were, incapable of industry or civilization, even after half their blood is Gothic, and remain, as marked by the ancients, fond of lyes, and enemies of truth.[91]

This was a new twist on Camden's and Spenser's disparagement of the Irish as descendants of savage Scythians, with Scythians now divested of both their Gaelic and barbarian baggage, but the Irish, now bereft of a Scythian ancestry, still remaining the 'wild Irish.' Vallancey, nonetheless, later selectively quoted from Pinkerton's book as further corroboration of Vallancey's own conclusions.[92]

Over the coming decades, competing perspectives on Indo-European origins of Ireland's ancient populations and civilization continued to persist in Irish nationalist circles, and while antiquarians and later generations of historians who subscribed to oriental theories of Irish origins increasingly opted for varying formulations of Iranian/ Aryan heritage, others continued to dissent from the Indo-European model in general. For example, writing in 1881 and citing the authority of the prominent early nineteenth-century Irish antiquarian John O'Donovan, and also still relying on the Mosaic model alongside evolving Indo-European theories, the Irish-American Irish nationalist James Joseph Clancy maintained that the Scythian ancestry of Irish Gaels set them apart from the Aryan population groups in Europe:

> the Ancient Irish, the Milesians were of Scythian extraction, being sprung from *Niul*, son of Fenius, the great-grandson of Japhet. *Niul*, a teacher of lang[uag]es, was given in marriage *Scota*, daughter of the king of Egypt, and begot *Gaodhil* (Gael), from whom Milesius was twentieth in descent. *Heber* and *Heremon* were sons of Milesius, and led the colony which settled in Ireland. Strictly speaking, the Irish and French are of Finnish (Scythian) rather than Celtic (i.e., Aryan) origin; but the name "Celt" is universally applied to both peoples to-day.[93]

Nor did all antiquarians embracing the Iranian model of Irish civilization and consulting what they considered as a newly available range of primary oriental sources uncritically take all their cues from Vallancey by simply duplicating his narrative structure and methodology. Louisa Catherine Beaufort and Henry O'Brien, who are discussed later in this chapter, are examples of Irish nationalist antiquarians in the early nineteenth century who were unmistakably influenced by Vallancey in their foundational claims but pursued their own distinctive courses of analyses.

My historiographic interest in this range of Irish antiquarians transcends Joep Leerssen's astute point about the "valuable insights" in terms of "intellectual history" present in the overall Irish antiquarian methodologies and postulations during the period, notwithstanding what Leerssen terms "the fallaciousness of its tenets."[94] As previously stated, a significant component of Vallancey's writing, soon to be replicated in a similar range of works by other contemporary and later generations of Irish antiquarians and historians—most flamboyantly in Henry O'Brien's history of Ireland's Round Towers in the 1830s—was the reliance on a new range of oriental sources for reconstructing the earliest documentable history of the Irish, alongside continued utilization of biblical (inclusive of 'oriental'), classical Greek/Hellenic, Roman, as well as 'medieval' and later Irish texts and other European sources. This assortment of oriental sources rapidly multiplied after the late eighteenth century, given the proliferation of translations into European languages from Persian (including Middle Persian/Pahlavi), Sanskrit, Arabic, and other languages. In his earlier works, Vallancey himself had relied heavily on Judeo-Christian biblical sources and ancient Greek and Roman texts, as in the case of his 1772 *An Essay on the Antiquity of the Irish Language. Being a Collation of the Irish with the Punic Language*. By subsequently supplementing this spectrum of sources with a heavy infusion of the new variety of oriental material, Vallancey laid the groundwork for a distinctly new (albeit chimerical) historiographic method in the study of ancient Ireland.[95] This marked a further epistemological demarcation of Ireland's unique standing in the British Isles. The ability to document ancient Irish history by consulting oriental sources (historical and other), beyond the existing convention of alluding to biblical or other similar early sources, highlighted a clear temporal-cultural overlap between ancient Ireland and the Orient, in ways that were not applicable to the ancient history of England. The new range of oriental sources purportedly confirmed that the presumed ancestors of the Irish at the time of their arrival from the East were not only fully conscious of their oriental roots but were also still directly connected to developments taking place in the Orient (including civilizational facets). Here was allegedly further proof of Ireland's distinctive position in the British Isles as a civilizational fountainhead. In contrast, accordingly, besides a few passing remarks to England in ancient Greek sources, the main written sources consulted in composing the history of ancient England dated from the period after the Roman invasion in 43 CE, with Roman sources claiming to have first brought civilization to the savage tribes of England. At the same time, Vallancey also debunked the legitimacy of existing Western European tradition of dependence on ancient Greek sources as an authoritative reservoir of knowledge about the Persian *Other* of the Hellenic world. Whereas the likes of Keating in the seventeenth century had already challenged ancient Greek accounts of the barbarous character of Scythians, Vallancey was additionally delegitimizing the extant Western convention of exalting the Greek historical tradition as epistemologically and methodologically superior to its contemporaneous oriental accounts of the known world at the time. For instance, as early as 1786 he wrote: "How slender, indeed, were the best pretensions of the Greeks to any real knowledge of the history, language, or manners of ancient Persia!"[96] In 1807, Vallancey went on to characterize the Greek sources in this respect as "grossly ignorant in regard to foreign events" and the product of "a bigoted people, highly prejudiced in their own favour."[97] This was a roundabout attack on ancient Greek and Roman accounts of Ireland, including works by the likes of Strabo and Mela, who described the Irish as living in a state of utter savagery and engaging in such practices as anthropophagy, not dissimilar to accounts of Scythians by the same range of authors.[98] Notably, this condemnation of Greco-Roman ignorance of other peoples and cultures was highly skewed and not extended to unflattering accounts of England in some of the same sources.

Vallancey's condemnation of Greco-Roman sources drastically differed from Keating's reproach in so far as Vallancey's utilization of a new assortment of oriental sources as foundational texts in reconstructing the history of ancient Ireland, and to which he accorded a greater degree of epistemological impartiality and authority in comparison with ancient Greek and Roman sources. The historiographic implications of this turn to oriental sources as primary material for scripting Ireland's remote past are discussed later in this chapter. For now, I will focus on the kinds of new oriental sources that were becoming available to Vallancey and his contemporary and subsequent generations of antiquarian proponents of manifold oriental theories of Irish origins. Vallancey not only selectively and instrumentally incorporated the so-called Jonesian theory of languages into his historiographic method, but he also relied on an assorted range of oriental sources insatiably studied and translated by Jones and other orientalists in the Indian subcontinent (including contributions to this orientalist corpus of knowledge production by "Indian" natives), which launched what came to be called the "Bengal Renaissance."[99] This is not to disregard the contributions to the broader "Oriental Renaissance" by the likes of the French Anquetil-Duperron or by the earlier generations of European orientalists, such as the French Barthélemy d'Herbelot in the seventeenth century,[100] whose *Bibliothèque orientale* was repeatedly quoted by Vallancey, who in turn added his own tangled layers of ethnic, geographic, and linguistic veneers to some of d'Herbelot's existing errors.[101] Among some of the many subjects in *Bibliothèque orientale* that appeared in Vallancey's writings on the Persian origin of the Gaels were d'Herbelot's discussion of Armenians, Scythians, and Parthians, the land of Turan, the fifteenth-century historian Mirkhond, and, most significantly, the (otherwise entirely mythical) ancient Iranian dynasty of Pishdādiān.[102] *Bibliothèque orientale* was largely a summary translation of the Arabic *Kashf al-Zunun 'an Asāmi al-Kutub wa al-Funun* by the seventeenth-century Ottoman historian Mustafa bin Abdullah (a.k.a. Hadji Khalfa "Katip Çelebi").[103] Long after Vallancey, *Bibliothèque orientale* continued to serve as a European/Western historical-cultural primer on what at the time were the predominantly Muslim regions of the Orient in the Near East and North Africa. This was also the case in the Iran-themed Irish nationalist poetry of Thomas Moore and James Clarence Mangan in the first half of the nineteenth century, whose works are discussed in subsequent chapters.

The activities of the Asiatic Society of Bengal led to an unprecedented proliferation of new knowledge about, and translations of, a wide array of oriental sources previously unavailable or largely unknown in the West/Europe, thanks to the synergy of European and native "oriental" scholars engaged in this undertaking. Much of this new body of knowledge, as in the older information available in the West/Europe regarding oriental sources (here excluding some of the Arabic-language sources that may have been available in Muslim-ruled Iberian territories from 711 to 1492 CE), was not devoid of unintended misinterpretations, conscious misrepresentations, mistaken assumptions of epistemic authenticity or hierarchies, and other sets of limitations and deficiencies. Among other attributes of the Oriental Renaissance was also the increased appearance in print of Sanskrit, Arabic, and modern Persian words, phrases, and longer text in their original script in a broad spectrum of Western publications on the Orient (scholarly and otherwise), along with their English pronunciations and/or translations, and etymological or other elucidations. This technological printing innovation, which served as a new style of scholarly claim of linguistic mastery by the authors of the works in question and other related claims of expertise and ultimate command of the subject matter, was emulated in publications by Vallancey and then replicated in publications by a host of other Irish antiquarians—even though Vallancey lacked any degree of fluency in these oriental languages, besides possibly Hebrew, which had previously appeared in printed original script in Irish antiquarian works. For Vallancey and the like, who in practice actually depended on prior translations and explained pronunciations of words and phrases in these oriental scripts by actual experts (whether or not they acknowledged that debt to these experts), this technique was also a *visual* mode of further validating their own authoritative knowledge of the Orient and extolling their distinctive methodology. This was particularly the case in tracing imputed etymological connections between oriental and Irish lexicons—alongside the more common practice of using Irish-Gaelic, Greek,

Hebrew, and other such print types, with the Irish script itself having only originated in the so-called Middle Ages, and not forgetting Hebrew was by then a simultaneously oriental and European/Western language, given its chiefly religious and scholarly use in the Jewish diaspora and varied usage by numerous non-Jewish scholars throughout the West/Europe. In Vallancey's 1786 *A Vindication*, other than the use of Hebrew script, words and phrases in other oriental languages only appeared in their English transliteration. However, in works such as the 1802 *Prospectus of a Dictionary of the Language of the Aire Coti, or Ancient Irish, Compared with the Language of the Cuti, or Ancient Persians, with the Hindoostanee, the Arabic, and Chaldean Languages* and, more extensively, in later works such as the 1804 *Collectanea de Rebus Hibernicis* (Volume 6, Part I) or the 1807 *An Essay on the Primitive Inhabitants of Great Britain and Ireland*, modern Persian and Arabic scripts recurred throughout, serving as an unmistakable visual prop for further corroborating Vallancey's thesis that "the Gael were the Indo-Scythæ of Persia."[104] As widely fanciful as many of Vallancey's etymological claims happened to be, this particular incorporation of oriental script into his writing was a visual-lexicographic technique aimed at lending a greater aura of scholarly erudition and power of persuasion to his work.

This style of multi-script text, peppered with oriental scripts (in addition to Hebrew), was a clear imitation of texts produced by the Asiatic Society of Bengal. Initially developed in the colonial context of British India, this technique was now adopted in the colonial setting of Ireland, but in the service of nationalist historiography. The 1786 *A Vindication* also provided a glossary of "Hindostanic" and Irish terms, but both in English transliteration only (beginning on p. 369). In the 1807 *An Essay on the Primitive Inhabitants*, which also remarkably included Chaldean and "Celestial" alphabets in their purportedly original script (pp. 130–31 and passim), 'Hindostanic' was changed to "Indian or Brahminical," but the lexicon still appeared in English transliteration only (see, for example, pp. 48–49). The continued absence of Devanagari or other "Indian" scripts in *An Essay on the Primitive Inhabitants* (which included the Arabic script in which both Arabic and modern Persian are written, and which was also used in the Indian subcontinent) indicates the technological as well as financial limitations of the printing press in the United Kingdom at the time. The new types of oriental lexicon appearing in Vallancey's and some subsequent Irish antiquarian texts (whether in transliteration or in original scripts), alongside the older use of non-English terminology and Irish-Gaelic, Greek, or Hebrew scripts, rendered these texts even more cosmopolitan. This practice, along with referencing the new range of oriental sources (beyond biblical-related material), in effect expanded the already cosmopolitan base of Irish historiographic tradition, a development that James Joyce took note of in the early twentieth century and incorporated into his own polyglot literary micro-histories of a *worlded* Ireland (as represented by Dublin), most notably in the 1939 *Finnegans Wake*. In this regard, a major difference between *Finnegans Wake* and the works of Irish antiquarians such as Vallancey, besides the actual use of various oriental scripts in the antiquarian texts in question, in place of mere transliterations in Joyce's work, was that whereas Vallancey and the like also provided (actual or invented) English translations of the oriental material appearing in their works, Joyce refrained from translating oriental and other non-English lexicon, including Hiberno-English, appearing in *Finnegans Wake* (see Chapter Nine).

Vallancey's *An Essay on the Primitive Inhabitants* also included a chapter listing alleged specimens of etymological links between Irish-Gaelic and ancient Persian language, appearing in English transliterations and serving as ostensibly indisputable evidence of "the similarity of the Irish language to Zend and to the Pehlvi or old Persian" (Pahlavi was in fact Middle Persian, while 'Zend,' more correctly Avestan, was Old Persian and related to Sanskrit). According to Vallancey, Pahlavi "was the language of the countries, in which the Irish Coti resided."[105] A characteristic example of Vallancey's contorted etymological maneuvers appears in his self-congratulatory discussion of his alleged discovery of the Iranian prototype for the legendary warrior hero of Ireland's Fenian Cycle. There was no inherent risk in this case of offending Irish nationalist sensibilities the way the Scottish poet Macpherson had done with his (contrived) claim of discovering the Scottish original of the Fenian Cycle in the poems of Ossian; Vallancey himself being a vociferous detractor of Macpherson's allegation. In proposing an Iranian prototype for the Irish epic, Vallancey was after all still maintaining an original Irish claim to the Fenian Cycle, albeit tracing its roots to the presumed Iranian homeland of the early ancestors of the Irish before their arrival in Ireland. Instead, the criticisms Vallancey faced in postulating this connection focused on such themes as the extent of the similarity between the Iranian and Irish epics in question and whether one was necessarily a derivative of the other and, if so, in which order. Beginning in his 1786 *Vindication*, Vallancey had identified Fionn mac Cumhaill as the Irish version of the original Iranian hero Esfandiyar (spelled "Asfendyar"), who was killed in battle with another hero, Rustam.[106] Vallancey repeated d'Herbelot's erroneous assigning of Esfandiyar to the (otherwise legendary) first Iranian dynasty, the Pishdādiān, whereas in fact in Iranian epic, as well as in Iranian (mytho-)history at the time, Esfandiyar was a prince of the (otherwise also legendary) Kiāniān dynasty succeeding the Pishdādiān.[107] In his 1807 *An Essay on the Primitive Inhabitants*, Vallancey further elaborated on the subject. Now, by way of continued reliance on d'Herbelot as well as other sources, such as publications by Vallancey's renowned contemporary Anglo-Irish scholar of Iran, Sir William Ouseley, Vallancey referred to works by the Persian historian Abu Jafar Mohammad Tabari (839–923), incorrectly designated "the Livy of Arabian History," and Ferdowsi, "the Persian Homer," among his sources on Iranian mythology. While erroneously conflating the warring territories of Turan and Persia that appeared in Iranian mythology, and in Iranian (mytho-)history at the time, as well as confusing Esfandiyar and Afrasiab, who had appeared in the same entry by d'Herbelot in his *Bibliothèque orientale*, and then also interlacing Pahlavi (Middle Persian) with Arabic language, Vallancey sought to establish etymological correspondence between Persian and Irish languages and a direct link between Irish and Iranian epics. He observed:

> Their great *Fiond*, or *Fionn*, is named frequently *Sogan Fionn*, or Fionn of *Sogan*, a province and city of *Touran*. He is called *Fionn-mac Muhl*, or Umhal Fionn, the son of brass—*umhal* or *muhl* is brass; in Arabic [...] *muhl*. This name has been transformed into *Fionn mac Cumhall* by ignorant poets. He is called *Fiond Rohan* by Campion; and in ancient MSS. In the Seabright collection, *Fiond Ruthan*, pronounced *Ruhan*, (the *t* being aspirated as in the Pehlavi). In Persian history he is named *Rouin Ten*, or body of brass, from [...] *rooi*, brass.

Therefore *Fiond* is evidently the *As-Fend-yar* of Persian history, supposed to be the son of *Kishtasb*, and grandson of *Loharasb*, king of the first dynasty of Persia:—"He was surnamed *Rouin-Ten*, i.e. body of brass, on account of his great strength and courage." (D'Herbelot.) "*Asfendyar* was a *Touranian*."[108]

Vallancey continued this thread of elucidation by further confusing elements of Iranian (mytho-)history based on his reading of entries in d'Herbelot's *Bibliothèque orientale*, including Afrasiab's existing family tree in Iranian (mytho-)historical tradition:

> Now [the Iranian] *Afrasiab*, ninth king of the Pishdadian or first dynasty, was a Turc or Tartar, king of all the country from the Oxus to Gihon to the east and to the north, formerly called *Touran*, and since *Turquestan*. So that *Afrasiab*, whose name, it is allowed, implies father of the *Fars* or *Persians*, is the same as *Fiond mac Umhal*. [...] All fabulous.[109]

It was, indeed, "All fabulous"! In *An Essay on the Primitive Inhabitants*, as he had done previously in *A Vindication*,[110] Vallancey again insisted on the common root of place names Erin and Iran, while repeating his assertion of the overlapping history of the two lands, as reportedly traceable in surviving versions of early Irish accounts written by Irano-Scythian colonists of Ireland: "Most of the transactions of this body, related in their ancient history to have taken place in *Eirin*, (a name of Ireland,) actually took place, when they inhabited *Iran* or Persia."[111] While Vallancey stopped short of equating Erin and Iran as identical names, other Irish antiquarians in the coming decades would make such a claim or, as in the case of the Irish nationalist poet Thomas Moore in his 1817 *Lalla Rookh*, would substitute Iran for Erin as a thinly veiled allegorical camouflage.

Having already identified Armenians as a branch of Iranians *related* to Persians, following William Jones' erroneous ethno-linguistic assumption that coalesced ethnicity with language, the sixth chapter of Vallancey's 1807 *An Essay on the Primitive Inhabitants* was titled "That the Primitive Inhabitants of these Western Isles Came from Persia and Armenia." In this chapter, Vallancey repeated another of Jones' errors by suggesting that the Pahlavi language (in actuality referring to Middle Persian) was related to Chaldean.[112] In the following chapter, Vallancey provided further proof, this time by way of his entirely speculative deduction from Jones' scholarship, that Persians (Irano-Scythians/Scytho-Iranians/Indo-Scythians) had introduced writing to Ireland. Jones, while discussing the cuneiform inscriptions at the ancient ruins of Persepolis in Iran in the 1789 "Discourse Six" during a meeting of the Asiatic Society of Bengal, had stated:

> Many of the *Runick* letters appear to have been formed of similar elements; and it has been observed, that the writing at *Persepolis* bears a strong resemblance to that, which the *Irish* call *Ogham*: the word Agam in *Sanscrit* means *mysterious knowledge*; but I dare not affirm, that the two words had a common origin, and only mean to suggest, that, if the characters in question be really alphabetical, they were probably sacred and sacerdotal, or a mere cypher, perhaps, of which the priests only had the key.[113]

In the 1807 *An Essay on the Primitive Inhabitants*, by which time Vallancey cast himself as the most pioneering contemporary antiquarian and linguistic expert on ancient

Ireland, he listed among the groups of scholars to whom his book was dedicated "The Learned Society of Calcutta" (i.e., the Asiatic Society of Bengal). With great hyperbole, he referred to William Jones (d. 1794) as "my late and departed friend," albeit noting without any perceived irony that Jones "differed from me in a few sentiments, chiefly etymological."[114] Vallancey and Jones had corresponded with one another, and Jones had referred to Vallancey in two of his published lectures at the Asiatic Society: the "Fifth Anniversary Discourse," presented on February 21, 1788, and the "Ninth Anniversary Discourse," presented on February 23, 1792. In the latter lecture, Jones referred to Vallancey in a noncommittal fashion as "Colonel Vallancey, whose learned enquiries into the ancient literature of Ireland are highly interesting."[115] But, in private Jones had described Vallancey's 1786 *A Vindication* to a friend as being 'Very Stupid,' even though not all members of the Asiatic Society of Bengal shared this verdict.[116]

Even more forcefully than in *A Vindication*,[117] Vallancey now made the case that original Zoroastrianism (the major religion of pre-Islamic ancient Iran) was purportedly derived from Chaldean and Brahminical influences and was the prototype of the religion of Indo-Scythian ancestors of the Gaels (i.e., the Milesians), who "did not worship images; they worshipped fire, the sun, moon, planets, &c. but had no images."[118] To this end, he evoked the authority of diverse sources. These included Isaac Newton's *The Chronology of Ancient Kingdoms Amended*—published posthumously in 1728 and referenced by Jones in his 1789 "Sixth Anniversary Discourse," as well as having long been cited in a wide range of previous Irish antiquarian studies, including Charles O'Conor's 1775 translation of O'Flaherty's *The Ogygia Vindicated*.[119] Vallancey's other sources here included William Jones' own writings, the English Thomas Hyde's 1700 *Historia religionis veterum Persarum eorumque magorum* on Zoroastrianism, and works by Vallancey's contemporary Irish antiquarian and erstwhile collaborator William Beauford (Beaufort) before the latter switched to Ledwich's Scandian theory of Irish origin. Vallancey then proffered evidence of the religious connection between Ireland and the ancient Iranian homelands by way of what he classified as the remains of temples of sun worship in Ireland from that time: "After the introduction of Christianity in Ireland these temples were demolished, the intrenchments thrown down, and the ground levelled; the altars only remain."[120] This was yet another assertion of archaeological relics of Iranian settlements in Ireland, alongside the more widely mentioned Round Towers of Ireland that were now traced back to Iranian (by Vallancey) or Phoenician, or *Iranianized*-Phoenician influence by different exponents of oriental theories of Irish origin.

Among the oriental works recently introduced to English readers by members of the Asiatic Society of Bengal and referenced by Vallancey in connection with his theory of the origin of Ireland's Gaelic population and culture was the *Dabestān-e Mazāheb* (*The School of Faiths*), a mid-seventeenth-century Persian text compiled in the Indian subcontinent by a follower of what nowadays is often referred to as the "neo-Zoroastrian" movement led by the Iranian Azar Keyvan. In a lecture at the Asiatic Society on February 19, 1789, William Jones attributed this work to a person by the name of Mohsen Fani ("a native of *Cashmir*"—i.e., Kashmir in the Indian subcontinent), although it is now largely agreed that the author was an Iranian follower of Azar Keyvan by the name of Mir Zulfaqar Ardestani, even if there is no overall consensus on the matter.[121] This Persian text was first press printed in Calcutta in 1809, making it more widely accessible than prior manuscript versions in circulation. The first complete English translation of this text did not appear until 1843, with the title of *Dabistan, or the School of Manners* by David Shea (d. 1836) and Anthony Troyer, both of them members of the Asiatic Society of Bengal. Vallancey only referenced this work once in his 1807 *An Essay on the Primitive Inhabitants* by way of Jones' authority and in connection with Zoroastrianism, without having seen the original text.[122] But, following Vallancey's example, *Dabestān-e Mazāheb* subsequently served as a major primary source for future advocates of the Iranian theory of Irish origins (whether Gaels or earlier settlers). By then, it was a different element of *Dabestān-e Mazāheb* that found its way into Vallanceyan-style works of Irish antiquarianism, namely that of the ancient (entirely legendary) Mahābādiān dynastic era in Iran, preceding the (already legendary) Pishdādiān, and with even more fabulous details. The Mahābādiān dynasty was hailed by Jones as incontrovertibly the "oldest in the world," although Jones could not ascertain "to which of the stocks, *Hindu*, *Arabian*, or *Tartar*, the first Kings of *Iran* belonged, or whether they sprang from a *fourth* race distinct from any of the others."[123]

Vallancey's theory of Persian-Iranian origin of the Gaels, while attracting a growing number of enthusiasts, continued to be debunked by adherents of competing mélange of alternative theories. Moreover, by the start of the nineteenth century, the antiquarian methodology of the likes of Vallancey was lagging far behind the more advanced emergent standards of historical evidence and verification and philological guidelines. For example, in an 1803 review of Vallancey's 1802 *Prospectus of a Dictionary of the Language of the Aire Coti, or Ancient Irish, Compared with the Language of the Cuti, or Ancient Persians*, the anonymous reviewer noted:

> To expose the continual error of his theory, will not cure his inveterate disease. It can only excite hopes of preventing infection, by sh[o]wing that he has reduced that kind of writing to absurdity; and raised a warning monument to all antiquaries and philologians that may succeed him.[124]

Vallancey, nevertheless, continued to enjoy substantial leverage in the field. The debates on Irish origins and the Round Towers were echoed in Irish diasporic communities as well, as in the case of the short-lived 1829 *The Irish Shield and Monthly Milesian* published in New York.[125] By the second half of the nineteenth century, however, all of the various oriental theories of Irish origins (in the sense of rapid migrations to Ireland from the Orient and in relatively recent ancient periods) and former modes of antiquarian methodology were taking a serious battering, even if not completely quashed. In 1852, long after Vallancey's death, William Hamilton Drummond, the Unitarian Irish poet and member of the Royal Irish Academy, commented on Vallancey's etymological and linguistic conjuring and style of exegesis:

> The mode in which the learned Antiquary pursues his argument, is marvelously entertaining. Verily he seems to have taken a lesson on 'comparisons' from that ingenious and renowned dialectician, Captain Fluellen, on whose name the pages of Shakespeare have conferred immortality.[126]

Many other Irish antiquarians of Vallancey's generation were by then subjected to a similar sort of verdict.

Henry O'Brien's Theory of Iranian Origins of the Irish

In its manifold mutations, the hypothesis of the Persian, or more broadly Iranian, origins of Milesians and/or of other early population settlements in Ireland, along with the presumed Iranian roots of Irish language and of Ireland's ancient cultural values and practices, was taken up by other antiquarians and continued well after Vallancey's death in 1812. After Vallancey, the staunchest and also the most controversial and maligned advocate of the Iranian theory of the origin of the Gaels was undoubtedly the young early nineteenth-century Irish antiquarian and steadfast cultural-nationalist Henry O'Brien (1808–35). O'Brien, best known for his *The Round Towers of Ireland* (1834), proposed an alternative Iranian model and was to encounter more robust and disparaging opposition than anything encountered by Vallancey. O'Brien, determined to surpass Vallancey in establishing extensive and incontrovertible proof of Iranian origins of the Gaels and of ancient Irish civilization, wanted it

> emphatically laid down that I do not tread in General Vallancey's footsteps. To his undoubted services, when temperately guarded, I have already paid the tribute of my national gratitude; but, pitying his mistakes, while sick of his contradictions, I have taken the liberty to *chalk out my own road*.[127]

While critical of Vallancey's methodology and analytical premises, O'Brien stressed Vallancey's service to the Irish, whom he unambiguously labeled as "every child of Iran." He wrote:

> though Vallancey, certainly, did not understand the purport of our 'Round Towers,' his view of them, after all, was not far from being correct; and the laborious industry with which he prosecuted his inquiries, and the disinterested warmth with which he ushered them into light, should shield his memory from every ill-natured sneer, and make every child of Iran feel his grateful debtor.[128]

It is unclear if O'Brien in this remark also intended that his contemporary Iranians in Iran itself and its neighboring territories, as well as in other imagined or real Iranian diasporic communities (who also qualified as 'every child of Iran'), should likewise recognize the great service rendered by Vallancey to expanding the world-historical horizon of Iranian history beyond the hitherto reaches of Iranian and Iran-related regional frontiers (including Afghan territories, Central Asia, and parts of the Indian subcontinent)—an Iranian world-historical horizon that purportedly had been shown by Vallancey to also encompass a westerly European territory (Ireland), keeping in mind that contemporary Iranians were completely in the dark about Irish antiquarian debates.

O'Brien's historical methodology was undeniably fantastical in every respect, even by the standards of Vallancey and many of the alternative highly fabulous contemporary spectrums of antiquarian claims of oriental, Scandinavian, or other Mosaic and non-Mosaic theories of Irish origins. With hindsight, O'Brien's brief and tragic appearance on the Irish antiquarian stage was also ill-timed. The publication of his book in 1834, with its bombastic full title of *The Round Towers of Ireland, or the Mysteries of Freemasonry, of Sabaism, and of Budhism, for the First Time Unveiled*, coincided with a sustained uncompromising onslaught from a new, and initially small, circle of Irish historians and other commentators committed to much more rigorous scholarship. The latter mode of scholarly standards was in keeping with intellectual developments elsewhere in the West/Europe and in British India, among other locations, initiating in Ireland an extensive, albeit imperfect, skeptical scrutiny of prior antiquarian accounts. Although these skeptics did not entirely refute oriental or other existing theories of Irish origins, they nonetheless demolished the methodological presuppositions, analytical conclusions, as well as one of the key evidentiary claims of earlier works in the mode of Vallancey, Charles O'Conor, Edward Ledwich, and the like. At the forefront of this onslaught in the 1830s were the Protestant Scots-Irish artist, musicologist, antiquarian, archaeologist, and ordnance surveyor George Petrie (1790–1866) and his close circle of associates affiliated with the influential Tory literary and political journal the *Dublin University Magazine*, founded in January 1833 with the principle objective, as stated in its very first issue, of promoting political conservatism, loyalty to the British crown, and defense of the (Anglican) Church of Ireland. Regardless of its avowed politics, in the coming decades the *Dublin University Magazine* also served as historical, literary, and other outlets for many Irish nationalists of differing ideological outlook, whether cultural and/or political nationalists. Petrie himself belonged to the ranks of Irish Protestants involved in Irish cultural-nationalist endeavors, but without subscribing to any political Irish nationalist platform.

By the time Henry O'Brien's book on the Round Towers appeared, these towers had long assumed a pivotal position in the debate on oriental or other theories of Irish origins, with those in competing oriental camps alleging disparate set of oriental prototypes for the towers and regarding them as indisputable ancient archaeological-architectural evidence of Ireland's ties with different regions of the Orient, as well as further proof of Ireland's civilizational sophistication long before the arrival of the Anglo-Normans on the island. By the time *The Round Towers of Ireland* was published, among the most frequently cited oriental prototypes for the towers were the Zoroastrian or other structures of *seemingly* similar design and *imputed* function in contemporary Iran and surrounding territories, including in Central Asia and the Indian subcontinent. Zoroastrians, moreover, were generally, and wrongly, presumed by these commentators to be fire-worshippers. Petrie challenged all the hitherto purported oriental, Scandinavian, and other such theories of the origins of the Round Towers by adopting a more circumspect historical and broadly contextualized comparative archaeological-architectural methodology. As discussed later, even though Petrie did not directly interrogate or contest the possibility of oriental descent of the Irish in ancient times, he nevertheless delivered a major blow to what had become the central material-culture groundwork and evidential logic of various competing oriental theories. He both trounced claims of ancient origin of the towers and, through complex analyses, refuted their previously suggested functions, even if he ultimately failed to persuade the die-hard proponents of former theories. Henry O'Brien's theory of the Round Towers immediately made him a target of attacks from many quarters, in addition to Petrie and his colleagues. These castigators of O'Brien included the renowned Romantic poet, national balladeer of Ireland, and amateur antiquarian Thomas Moore, who subscribed to an alternative thesis of Iranian origin of the towers, and anonymously and viciously disparaged O'Brien's work in a review essay soon after its publication. In the first volume of Moore's *The History of Ireland* (1835), published a year after O'Brien's book, by which time O'Brien was already deceased, the design of the Round Towers was declared to be of Persian origin, albeit transmitted to Ireland indirectly by way of previously Persianized Phoenicians, who may also have been accompanied by some Persians in their migration to Ireland.[129] The most controversial aspect of O'Brien's model of oriental pedigree of the towers was his insistence that these were not fire, sun, or other such temples, but rather temples dedicated to phallic worship.

In 1833, Henry O'Brien had translated (from the Latin original) the 1831 *Ibernia Phoenicea* (now appearing as *Phœnecian Ireland*) by the Spanish Catholic priest Joaquín Lorenzo Villanueva, which was published in Dublin where Villanueva had settled. O'Brien's translation was dedicated to the Anglican James McEdward O'Brien, the Third Marquess of Thomond. It began:

MY LORD MARQUIS,
  Had I not had the honor of bearing the same name, and of deriving consanguinity and connection from that *ancient* stock, of which your Lordship is, at once, the *deserving* head and the *distinguished* representative, yet—when about to launch into light a work, which purports to unfold the origin of *Ireland*'s early colonization, and seeking for a patron whose *discriminating taste* and *personal acquirements*, would add a charm to the advantages of station and of birth—my eye should instinctively direct itself toward *you*—for, where, in the unbroken catalogue of Iran's proud-born sons, could I find another name so intimately interwoven with her *halcyon* splendors, as that of the *benign patriarch* of the House of Thomond?
  But it is not alone, my Lord, as occupying a princely post, in monarchical succession, among the *Scythian* or later Irish—immortalised by the *glories* of Ceanchora and Clontarf—that *this* homage should be your due; but as the direct descendant of the very *principal* and leader of that *earlier* and *nobler*, and, in every way more *estimable* and *illustrious dynasty*, the Tuatha Danaans, or *true, Iranian, Milesian*, Irish—the incorporation of whom with the Scythians—after the latter, by *conquest*, had wrested from them the soil—gave rise to the compound of *Scoto-Milesians*; which no one has heretofore been able to elucidate.
  These Tuatha Danaans, my Lord, whom your forefather, Brien, conducted into our "sacred island," were the expelled Budhists [*sic*] of Persia—neither Phœnecians nor Celts—whom the intolerance of the Brahmins and the persecution of the Rajas had thrown upon the ocean.[130]

On the frontpiece of this English translation of Villanueva's book, O'Brien was identified as the "Author of the 'prize essay' upon the 'Round Towers' of Ireland." The prize in question was awarded by the Royal Irish Academy and would publicly pit O'Brien against George Petrie. In O'Brien's prefatory section to Villanueva's *Phœnecian Ireland*, titled "To the Public," O'Brien launched into a highly revealing and protracted scathing treatment of Petrie and the Academy.[131] Petrie would later more than amply and pitilessly repay O'Brien's rancor when anonymously reviewing O'Brien's 1834 *The Round Towers*, in the preface to which O'Brien again attacked Petrie (see below). At issue was the highly coveted first prize for an essay on the Round Towers commissioned by the prestigious Royal Irish Academy in 1833, with Petrie's "The Origins and Uses of the Round Towers of Ireland" winning first place along with a monetary award of £50. O'Brien's essay, which became the basis for his 1834 book on the subject, was given the second and unmistakably "consolation" prize of £20. In *Phœnecian Ireland*, O'Brien played his Gaelic ('mere Irish') nationalist card while accusing the Academy of nepotism by awarding the top prize undeservedly to one of its own members (i.e., Petrie):

> *I* had *thought* that the Royal *Irish* Academy were not only a *learned*, but a *just* and a *patriotic* society. *I* had *thought* that having marshalled themselves into an institution, with the *avowed* object of *resuscitating from death* the almost *despaired-of evidences* of our *national history*, they would not alone *foster* every *advance* toward that desirable consummation, but, shower *honors*, and *acclamations*, and *triumphs* upon him, who has not only *infused a vital soul* into those *moribund remains*, but made the history of Ireland, at this moment, the *clearest*, the most *irrefragible*, and withal, the most *interestingly comprehensive chain of demonstrational proofs* in the *whole circle of universal literature*.[132]

Ironically, with the hindsight of the scathing public attack Thomas Moore later anonymously launched against O'Brien in 1834, O'Brien reproduced a song by Moore in one of the footnotes of his Translator's Preface to Villanueva's book, titled "Dear Harp of My Country."[133] O'Brien was writing after the 1829 Catholic Emancipation Act in the United Kingdom and during the time of the campaign led by Daniel O'Connell for the Repeal of the 1801 Act of Union and the restoration of a separate Irish parliament in Dublin.

In his Preface, O'Brien also stated his fundamental differences with Villanueva, including the latter's alleged insufficient familiarity as a *"foreigner"* with the ethnically and denominationally motivated prejudicial falsifications appearing in English accounts of ancient Ireland, both pre- and post-English Reformation.[134] Claiming to be taking "the liberty altogether to erase" what O'Brien perceived as "aberrations" in Villanueva's account, O'Brien also challenged the centrality of Phoenicians' "share [...] in the early splendor" of Ireland. He instead labeled the Phoenicians as

> *only the carriers* of that very ancient and *sacred tribe*, designated emphatically 'Tuatha Dedanan,' that is the 'Dedanite diviners,' who planting themselves in Ireland, after their expulsion from the east, raised the isle—which they *denominated* from their former place of abode—to that pinnacle of literary and religious reputation which made it a *focus* of intellect in the *old pagan world*.[135]

O'Brien dismissed Phoenician and other theories of non-Iranian Irish roots, confidently proposing instead an Iranian origin of Ireland's earliest populations and civilizational glory. Just as Vallancey had done, among his various sources O'Brien too relied on the authority of the seventeenth-century Persian language *Dabestān-e Mazāheb*, by means of William Jones' works and, certainly, also Vallancey's 1807 *An Essay on the Primitive Inhabitants* (in which Vallancey had referred to *Dabestān* on one occasion only)—even if O'Brien, who extensively relied on *Dabestān*, did not acknowledge Vallancey as his initial source of familiarity with the Persian text. He, moreover, accepted Jones' already-mentioned supposition that "the Iranian monarchy must have been the oldest in the world." Significantly, O'Brien, counting himself among descendants of later Milesian arrivals in Ireland ("who were a mixed Scythian colony, [and] implicit followers of Zo[r]oaster"), denied Milesians the highest civilizational attribute among Ireland's ancient settlers; instead describing them as a warrior class of conquerors who initially pillaged the earlier cultural fabric and edifices established by the previous, and more highly civilized, Persian-Iranian settlers, whom he identified as the Tuatha de Danann. It was. accordingly, the Persians/Tuatha de Dananns who had constructed the original Round Towers well before the subsequent *other Iranian* conquerors of the island ('mixed Scythians'/Milesians) eventually adopted some of the same cultural and material practices from the former.¹³⁶ O'Brien, while proposing a theory of Irish descent jointly from the related Persian and Scythian subgroups of Iranian peoples, ruptured the existing linear models of incrementally more advanced civilizational settlements in ancient Ireland up to and including the arrival of Milesians. Instead, he assigned the ultimate civilizational mantle to the pre-Milesian Tuatha de Danann settlers, whose civilizational majesty was later embraced by the militarily superior Milesians after initial territorial conflict and culture clash.

It was in his 1834 *The Round Towers of Ireland, or the Mysteries of Freemasonry, of Sabaism, and of Budhism, for the First Time Unveiled* that O'Brien fully developed his Persian-Iranian theory of Ireland's ancient civilizational grandeur. He dedicated this book

> To the Learned of Europe, to the Heads of its Several Universities, to the Teachers of Religion and the Lovers of History, More Especially to the Alibenistic Order of Freemasons, to the Fellows of the Royal Society, to the Members of the Royal Asiatic Society, to the Fellows of the Society of Antiquaries, to the Editors of the Archæologia Scotica, to the Committees of the Societies for the Propagation of the Gospel and the Diffusion of Useful Knowledge, and to the Court of the Honourable the East India Company.¹³⁷

This self-aggrandizing prop was in keeping with the convention of the time, as in the case of Vallancey's Dedication in 1807 of *An Essay on the Primitive Inhabitants* "To the Professors of Ancient History in the Several Universities of Europe, to all the Societies of Antiquaries, and to the Learned Society of Calcutta [i.e., the Asiatic Society of Bengal]." The single most important institutional network acknowledged in both of these dedications was the Asiatic Society, with which William Jones had been affiliated. In both Vallancey's later works and in O'Brien's *The Round Towers*, the findings of the Asiatic Society played a seminal role in terms of general knowledge production about ancient beliefs and practices in the Indian subcontinent and surrounding regions, as well as contributions to the dynamic theory of Indo-European languages. Most significantly regarding the process of knowledge production occurring in British India in connection with O'Brien's writing was Jones' introduction to European audiences in the late eighteenth century of *Dabestān-e Mazāheb*, which also included an account of the (alleged) extremely ancient text called *Dasātir* (*Edicts*), written in an unknown language. It was supposedly from *Dasātir* that the author of *Dabestān* had acquired his information about the (purported) earliest documented ancient Iranian dynastic era, that of the (otherwise recently invented) dynasty of Mahābāds, which had consisted of 14 extremely long subdynastic epochs, each of which began with a prophet-king and corresponded to cycles of human creation and destruction, followed by the next cycle of regeneration of humanity by the only surviving consecrated couple at the end of each cataclysmic Age, dating back to sextillions of years ago.[138] *Dabestān* also provided a further presumed textual authentication of the previously known (but otherwise entirely mythical) Iranian dynastic era of Pishdādiān, which *Dabestān* claimed to have supplanted that of Mahābādiān (with each of the Pishdādiān dynastic periods also consisting of a number of inner-dynastic cycles). For Vallancey and O'Brien, the Pishdādiān and Mahābādiān *respectively* provided the missing Iran-Ireland historical links (both ethnic and civilizational). Whereas Vallancey, based on accounts available to him at the time, had opted for Pishdādiān ancestry of Persian arrivals in Ireland, O'Brien settled for the recently discovered Mahābādiān ancestry. This choice required pushing the date for the arrival of Persians in Ireland back to a confoundingly distant past, which is precisely what O'Brien did in defiance of biblical tradition. Vallancey's and O'Brien's accounts both followed the premise of William Jones' 1792 lecture "On the Origin and Families of Nations" ("Discourse the Ninth"), in which Jones had insisted "the whole race of man proceeded from *Iràn*."[139] O'Brien was countering Vallancey's supposition in his later works of both the Persian Pishdādiān ancestry of Tuatha de Danann and the subsequent founding of Ireland's most glorious ancient civilization after the arrival of (highly Persianized) Irano-Scythian Milesians.[140] O'Brien pushed back the emergence of Ireland's high civilization to the time of Mahābādiān in the form of Tuatha de Danann arrival on the island and superimposed onto Irish history the narrative plot line of *Dabestān*, in which the Pishdādiān allegedly set out to erase all signs of the prior Mahābādiān dynasty by claiming themselves to be the first real Iranian dynasty and harbingers of a grand civilization, while in actuality merely appropriating many of the much superior civilizational achievements of the Mahābādiān and fusing them with their own less-accomplished civilizational values and practices. O'Brien's model, in effect, also branded the presumed Milesian ancestry of Ireland's majority Gaelic population (including O'Brien himself, as he claimed) as destroyers of the island's foremost Golden Age, thereby making this model even less appealing in mainstream nationalist circles.

The title page of O'Brien's 1834 *The Round Towers* described the book as an expanded version of the "Prize Essay of the Royal Irish Academy." Still smarting from having been denied the first prize by the Academy for his 1833 essay and the Academy's subsequent decision not to publish his essay in its *Transactions of the Royal Irish Academy*, in the Preface to this book O'Brien again engaged in a barbed attack against the Academy, following an introductory commentary on freemasonry's quest for truth in its fight against "bigotry and despotism." He stated:

> it may seem strange that a work, which bears upon its title-page the character of 'Prize Essay,' should not have been published by the Society that have awarded it the prize [...]

I shall take care, now that all vexation has passed over, that no symptoms of asperity shall escape my pen [...] but confine myself strictly to a matter-of-fact detail as to the conduct of the party in the case in question.[141]

The remainder of the Preface, however, made it amply clear O'Brien's fury over the matter had by no means subsided. He proceeded to bitterly reproach the choice of awarding Petrie the first prize, alleging wide-ranging irregularities in the handling of the contest and the final selection of the first prize essay, suggesting that Petrie's essay had been earmarked in advance for the top prize in a patently nepotistic move. O'Brien noted: "I saw at once, that the 'accomplished antiquarian of our city' was Mr. Petrie, the antiquarian artist of the Royal Irish Academy—himself a member of their Council."[142] He lambasted another member of the Academy, in this case an advocate of an alternative oriental theory of Irish origins and the Round Towers, Sir William Betham, for having in private admitted the validity of O'Brien's view on the phallic function of the towers but voting against O'Brien's essay for the top prize.[143] O'Brien informed his readers

it was not only of the gold medal and fifty pounds that I was deprived by this manœuvre, but of the one hundred additional pounds which Lord Cloncurry had offered upon the same subject. Of this the Academy were also the dispensers [...] so that by this stratagem, they assigned to their friend not only their own, but his Lordship's, patronage![144]

As further proof of the Academy's conspiracy against him and favoritism toward Petrie, O'Brien reminded his readers that Petrie's dating of the Round Towers to a period after the introduction of Christianity to Ireland in the fifth century had already appeared in print prior to the contest, in the pages of the *Dublin Penny Journal* (founded in 1832), which O'Brien described as a "periodical" of the Academy[145]—the journal was more accurately owned by John S. Folds and edited by George Petrie and another council member of the Academy, Caesar Otway,[146] on whom O'Brien also heaped invective.

Like most professional and amateur antiquarians in different camps on Irish origins at the time, O'Brien followed the practice of tailoring the evidence to support his conclusions. This was a key factor distinguishing the works of most contemporary antiquarians from Petrie's new analytical approach. Whereas most contemporary antiquarians began from basic suppositions and first principles (whether on grounds of some conviction based on prior accounts and/or new circumstantial evidence) and then rummaged for supporting data, Petrie and his colleagues belonged to the nascent, albeit in many ways still imperfect, historiographic trend that largely moved from the available evidence, that could first be verified as best as possible, to general conclusions. O'Brien's ultimate objective was the same as other adherents of manifold oriental theories of Irish origins: that of confirming the existence of an ancient high civilization in Ireland by way of the Orient, contra the Scandian theory of the likes of Ledwich, William Beauford, and Thomas Campbell, or other theories of Irish origins, and in defiance of allegations of an essentially barbarous identity of the Irish prior to gradual Anglo-Norman conquests beginning during the reign of the English monarch Henry II.[147] In the process, O'Brien located a grand civilization in Ireland further back in time than any other proponent of different oriental theories. Contrary to Vallancey, O'Brien also made a sharper ethnic demarcation between Persian and Scythian sub-branches of Iranian peoples (now with Persians as progenitors of Tuatha de Dananns and Scythians as progenitors of Milesians), albeit maintaining that the Scythians spoke the same Iranian language as the Persians.[148] O'Brien's book was intended to be an all-encompassing encyclopedic assemblage of proofs for designating the earliest known Persians in history, (the in fact entirely mythical) Mahābādiān, as the Tuatha de Danann colony of Ireland, or "the real Hibernians" as he called them.[149] Along the way, he made wide-ranging historical connections between ancient Iranian lands and other territories and cultures, such as identifying the Hellenic deity Apollo as a derivative of Iranian divinities. While not entirely wrong in all of his conjectures, the evidence O'Brien provided was extensively far-fetched at best. His other overriding aim was to establish beyond any shred of doubt the common practice of phallic worship in ancient Iran and Ireland, with the Round Towers as a lasting proof of that practice and having been introduced to Ireland by Persians/Tuatha de Dananns. To this end, O'Brien engaged in a vertiginous and chaotic style that often lacked anything remotely resembling a method, both trespassing our present-day crudest definition of "the limits of interpretation" (to borrow Umberto Eco's phrase) and also outdoing the likes of Ledwich, Vallancey, and Sir William Betham in extravagance of details and range of evidential connections. In his attempted encyclopedic narrative, O'Brien collapsed spatial and temporal boundaries, shredded and re-stitched various histories and cultural beliefs and practices, and adopted the sort of feverish somnambulist etymological acrobatic leaps found in Vallancey's writings.[150] Vallancey, O'Brien, and many other antiquarians simply did not heed William Jones' caveat at the end of the previous century (notwithstanding Jones' own episodic lapses in this regard) "against conjectural etymology in historical researches, and principally against licentiousness of etymologists in transposing and inserting letters, in substituting at pleasure any consonant for another of the same order, and in totally disregarding the vowels."[151]

O'Brien traced the roots of ancient South Asian, Egyptian, and other civilizations back to ancient Iran (identified as the ursprung of all great ancient civilizations). Accordingly, this Iranian civilizational influence, barring the case of Ireland, had spread to other regions during the Pishdādiān dynastic era, after the latter's termination of Mahābādiān dynastic cycle. In this account, Pishdādiān were merely transmitting key elements of Mahābādiān civilization, adopted by Pishdādiān after they vanquished the former, just as Irish descendants of Pishdādiān (i.e., Milesians), who defeated the Tuatha de Danann (the presumed descendants of Mahābādiān) eventually embraced much of the latter's cultural beliefs and values. In effect, descendants of two Iranian groups had reached Ireland in sequence in antiquity and ancient Irish history after the arrival of the Milesians had replicated the pattern of what had already befallen the ancestors of Tuatha de Danann in their original homeland. O'Brien did not elaborate from which other source besides the Mahābādiān, the Pishdādiān dynasty could have derived their own original culture, not to mention their own descent, just as the (invented) *Dasātir* (as covered in *Dabestān*) was also silent on this matter. Instead, O'Brien maintained the Mahābādiān (Tuatha de Danann) had reached Ireland in two waves, the second wave in the form of an Iranian transplant community from India,[152] but without indicating why all these Iranian groups should have undertaken such a long-distance migration to a westerly location in Europe and whether the first wave of arrivals had somehow maintained continued direct or indirect contact with their original homeland by the time the second wave arrived in Ireland. Moreover, contra Vallancey, O'Brien refuted the Zoroastrian (ostensibly 'fire-worship') origin of Ireland's Round Towers, positing instead the thesis of initial phallic worship function of the towers and attributing this practice to the most ancient Persian, and in effect world, civilization of Mahābādiān. His highly ornate and complex method of arriving at this conclusion also included the gendering of the terms Mahābād and Pishdād by way of analogy with Sanskrit terms Lingam and Yoni respectively, with Mahābādiān having celebrated the symbol of male procreativity and Pishdādiān its female form prior to the emergence of Zoroastrianism, after which the existing phallic towers were allegedly turned into astronomical observatories. As further proof of this proposition, O'Brien referenced the fourth-century Puranas from the Indian subcontinent and the *Shāhnāmeh* from 'Iran' (in its broadest cultural configuration), compiled and expanded in verse form in the eleventh century by Abul-Qassem Ferdowsi—with both range of sources believed to contain extremely ancient accounts.[153] While alluding to the biblical Mosaic theory of population groups, O'Brien rendered it and the story of Noah and the Deluge purely "figurative," discussing along the way the cataclysmic-extinctionist theory of the French anti-evolutionary scientist Georges Cuvier (d. 1832) versus contemporary theories of evolution. A combined evolutionary and cataclysmic-extinctionist scheme of the world was required for O'Brien's authentication of the Mahābādiān dynasty by way of *Dasātir* (as recounted in *Dabestān*). Noah now became synonymous with the (otherwise also mythical) ancient Iranian "Kaimours" (Gayōmard/Keyoumars), founder of the (legendary) Pishdādiān dynasty[154]—who previously had been labeled in the Zoroastrian sacred text *Avesta*, and in its exegeses the *Zend* [*Avesta*], as well as in the later compilation of Zoroastrian cosmogony, the *Bundahishn*, as the first, and androgynous, being from whom the first human couple originated,[155] with the couple in actuality being the equivalent of biblical Adam and Eve and not Noah and his wife in the Bible. In effect, in O'Brien's account Noah had long preceded Adam and Eve, rather than the other way around. This reworking of the biblical narrative sequence was essential in accounting for the Mahābādiān predecessors of Pishdādiān.

The Scythians (Milesians/Pishdādiān), whom O'Brien earlier described as Zoroastrians worshippers of fire, were rendered "secular" later in the book, in the sense of their opposition to worship of symbols, and were blamed for outlawing the Persian (Tuatha de Dannan) practice of phallic worship and for initially setting out to demolish the Round Towers, with the surviving towers later converted to astronomical observatories. Based on his distinctive comparative historical approach, and notwithstanding his account of the extremely remote past when the Mahābādiān dynasty existed, O'Brien ironically dated the initial arrival of Mahābādiān (Tuatha de Danann) in Ireland to only c. 1202 BCE (roughly around seven centuries earlier than Vallancey's proposed date for the arrival of Pishdādiān in Ireland). O'Brien then set out to demonstrate a wide range of correspondence between ancient Persian and Irish "institutions" and customs.[156] He further observed:

THUS far have Ireland and Persia kept company together, both equally rejoicing in the common name of *Iran*. But now, when we descend to particulars, this harmony separates. *Ireland* being an island, surrounded on all sides by water—which Persia is not—it was necessary it should obtain a denomination expressive of this accident; or, at all events, when the alteration was so easily formed as by the change of the final *an* into *in*—*an* meaning land, and *in island*—the transition was so natural as at once to recommend its propriety.

Hence it is that though we occasionally meet with *Iran*, as applied to this country, yet do we more frequently find *Irin as* its distinctive term; whereas the latter is never, by any chance, assigned to Persia, the former alone being its universal name. And this is all conformable to the closest logical argumentation, which teaches that every species is contained in its genus, but that no genus is contained in its species; *Irin*, therefore, which is the specific term, may also be called *Iran* the generic, while Iran—except as in *our* instance, where the *extension* of both is identical, could never be called *Irin*: and so it happens that *Ireland* is indifferently called by the names of *Iran* or *Irin*, the latter alone marking its *insular* characteristic; whereas *Persia*, not being so circumstanced, is mentioned only by the general form of *Iran*.[137]

According to O'Brien, Pishdādiān (Scythians/Milesians) even attempted to change the name given to Ireland by Mahābādiān (Persians/Tuatha de Dananns), which was derived from their original homeland 'Iran':

> As to the Iranians the real Hibernians—the true Hyperborean Tuath-de-danaans, or Magic god Almoners—they were hurled from the throne, their sanctified ceremonials trampled in the dust, their sacred harps, which before used to swell to the praises of their Divinity, were now desecrated for the inspiration of the Scythian warriors; and their divine *Boreades*, who ere now composed canticles in adoration of Apollo, were degraded to the secular and half-military occupation of Scythian *bards*.
>
> The name of the island itself, from "Irin," or the "Sacred island," was changed into Scuitte, that is, Scotia or Scythi, or the land of the *Scythians*. Nor was it until the eleventh century of the present era, that, *to remove the ambiguity which arose from the circumstance of there being another country also called by this name* [i.e., Scotland], Ireland assumed its former name, Irin, as its people did Irenses, instead of Scoti.[158]

At the same time, O'Brien even suggested that ancient Iranians themselves were identified in Greek sources as "Irish." Discussing the pre-Hellenic Pelasgi (Pelasgian) population of the Aegean in the remote past, as mentioned in ancient Greek and Roman sources, O'Brien identified the Pelasgi as "another branch of our Tuath-de-danaan." He then claimed these people were also known at the time as "Irish," before further clarifying his view: "This adjective [i.e., 'Irish'] is not here applied to our western *Irin*, *i.e.*, Ireland, but to the eastern Iran, *i.e.*, Persia."[159] In effect, the Tuatha de Dananns arriving in Ireland were already also known as 'Irish' back in their ancestral homeland and in adjoining territories, *alongside* their other ancient designations.

O'Brien's lavish schematic approach to comparative history incorporated an extremely vast range of sources and referentialities from otherwise diverse religions, cultures, time periods, and regions—at times merely expanding or adorning certain ideas about Sabian, Buddhist, Hindu, and other religions found in William Jones' Third, Fourth, and Sixth Discourses, which had also been referenced in some of Vallancey's writing.¹⁶⁰ O'Brien also engaged in excessive etymological reveries, even by the standards of many of his contemporary Irish antiquarians who engaged in their own versions of impulsive philological correlations. These traits alone were sufficient to ensure *The Round Towers* would attract ample critical reception. But, O'Brien went much further, stumping on the toes of all other contemporary Irish antiquarians. He extensively challenged all hitherto existing accounts of ancient Ireland, including the historical stage during which other proponents of oriental theories unanimously maintained a grand civilization had been transplanted to Ireland—that is, during the Milesian colonization of the island. Above all, he not only contested all preceding accounts of the origin of the Round Towers but proposed a new functional model that was highly offensive to conventional moral sensibilities of the Age, and to nationalist antiquarians in particular: that of phallic worship as a component of Ireland's highest civilizational standing in ancient times.¹⁶¹ (Vallancey had previously left open the possibility of manifold range of ritual uses for the towers over time, including phallic worship. But, he had ultimately insisted on their original primary use as temples of ostensibly Zoroastrian "fire-worship.") It was inevitable that many contemporary antiquarian and other commentators, particularly in nationalist circles, should react acrimoniously to O'Brien's theory—which, at least *initially*, also left him without much audible support from the ranks of other established antiquarians and rendered him the most isolated and ostracized claimant of an oriental prototype for the Round Towers. For Petrie and his associates, O'Brien was the ideal strawman for demolishing all current theories of the Round Towers, with Petrie also having a personal score to settle with O'Brien after being subjected to O'Brien's public taunts in connection with the 1833 prize essay of the Royal Irish Academy.¹⁶²

Not surprisingly the reviews of *The Round Towers* were almost unanimously trenchant, to put it mildly. The April 1834 issue of the *Dublin University Magazine*,¹⁶³ with whose editorial staff Petrie was acquainted, included an "anonymous" stinging review. As conventional as it was for reviews to appear anonymously, there could be no mistake about the allegiance of this reviewer. Petrie and his friends repaid O'Brien's personal attacks with unremittingly merciless derision and malice, while also judiciously tearing apart O'Brien's hodgepodge methodology:

> Having dipped a little amongst the stupendous discoveries which it unfolds at every page, we paused for a moment to rub our astonished eyes, and looked round to see if we yet survived in a world of reality. At this moment our glance was arrested by the inscription, in which our author dedicates his great work to all the academies and literary communities in the four quarters of the terraqueous globe, past, present, and to come.¹⁶⁴

Countering O'Brien's accusations of nepotism and procedural irregularities levied against the Royal Irish Academy, the review even denied O'Brien originality in his theory of phallic symbolism of the Round Towers:

> It was known to all who took any interest in the subject what his theory was; and to many how he came by it. The occasion of his writing was, in fact, the accidental discovery of the opinion of another person—the most unprincipled piracy of an essay not his own. It matters not how worthless was the theft; the dupe may be consistently combined with the knave;

he thought the mare's nest of poor Mr. R____n to be a treasure, and stole it accordingly. It is not necessary to dwell on the additional fact, that he was assisted by another, who ransacked libraries for illustrations, while he was himself assiduously engaged in the dignified toil of purloining matter from a rival essay; the means by which his precious compound of piracy, plagiarism, and vicarious labor was amalgamated. Mr. O'Brien has since made it his own, in more than Shakespeare's sense, he stole the "trash," but has added so much of the congenial coinage of his own brain, that its author can scarcely claim it.[165]

Ridiculing the etymological and archaeological methods by which O'Brien had arrived at his particular Persian precedent of the Round Towers, the reviewer added: "His errors are the pitiable result of intellectual disease, acquired by solitary rumination over a single idea, until it has converted itself into a religion in his mind."[166] Yet, *significantly*, the reviewer stopped short of an unconditional denial of any historical connections between Ireland and the Orient, making it clear that he was rebuffing O'Brien's methods and not necessarily dismissing the possibility "that the Irish [language] is identical with the obsolete Persian." The review noted:

Furthermore, we do not deny the existence of those primitive relations of language, of which he would make so much, nor even that they are traceable within certain established limits. Nay more, we freely admit that in cautious hands, and with proper confirmation, they belong to the science of historic research, and throw an ambiguous light on the consanguinity and descent of nations. But it is on the uncertainty of such means we would insist. Such etymologies, correctly used, may be interesting confirmations—they may rivet together or cement authentic materials—but they cannot support the edifice of a theory. The combinations, too, of literal characters may be admitted to be numerically infinite[.] But the capabilities of the organs of speech have narrower limits[;] consequently the same sounds must very variously enter into the composition of every language Mr. O'Brien's reasonings depend on arbitrary assumptions of pronunciation. But the voice of obsolete language cannot be thus resuscitated, even by the sagacious discoverer of the mouthpiece of the oracle of Dodona.[167]

Petrie and his colleagues were striving to set on solid footing the use of archaeological evidence in Irish antiquarianism, in keeping with some of the latest developments in Western European archaeological scholarship, while simultaneously contributing to the development of that mode of scholarship. Their success would be gradual, coming to fruition mostly after the middle of the century. Petrie's emphasis was on verification of the evidence through methodical collection and rigorous interrogation of data and sources, as well as use of intricate comparative analyses, attention to surrounding structures and construction material, hermeneutical examination of historical place names if available, careful assessment of interior and exterior design and potential function of the structures (for instance the interior width of the towers, existence of openings for ventilation, in the event the towers could have functioned as fire temples, and so on), and rejection of purely deductive analogies based on partial similarities in design with other structures.[168]

There was more at stake in continued contestations of Irish origins and Ireland's past civilizational grandeur than only culturally and politically charged Irish nationalist and so-called anti-nationalist disputes (not forgetting many opponents of narrowly defined political Irish nationalism considered themselves English and/or British *nationalists*). Moreover, the nationalist versus anti-nationalist lines in Ireland were often blurred or intersected. Petrie, while firmly opposed to even the more moderate Irish nationalist political platform for the Repeal of the 1801 Act of Union, was staunchly committed to the project of recovering and reclaiming Ireland's historical and cultural heritage and worked to that cultural-nationalist end in close partnership with his circle of friends, some of whom also served as members of his archaeological survey team and were unambiguously Irish nationalist in cultural as well as political spheres. Petrie's most enduring collaboration and friendship in this regard was with John O'Donovan. But, besides the topic of "nationalist" proclivities, for many in the related fields of antiquarianism and archaeology at the time, the methodological clashes and the "origins" battlegrounds were also underlain with weighty concern regarding one's professional and scholarly recognition and reputation (institutional or otherwise), including membership in such organizations as the Royal Irish Academy—which in the 1830s, not unlike many other similar institutions elsewhere in Western Europe, was only haltingly trudging ahead in the direction of the latest so-called scientific methods, with many of the old guard still wielding influence. It is important to keep in mind the gradual progression, as well as the always persisting internal contestations, of the "scientific" method and its standards of verification. After all, not only did the methodology of Petrie & Co. face criticism from some practitioners of the avowedly 'scientific' method later in the century, who otherwise shared Petrie's verdict on the construction and function of the Round Towers, but, as far back as the eighteenth century, most antiquarian advocates of oriental theories of Irish origins had also claimed to abide by the latest contemporary scientific standards in their field. The question is in what ways were those methods construed as being scientific, how they were applied in practice, and their continued susceptibility to *contemporary* mainstream standards of verification and falsifiability, in addition to their analytical and narrative coherence, and the range of supporting evidence and their persuasiveness from the perspective of contemporary scholarly community at large. For some members of the Royal Irish Academy and other range of scholars, their scholarly reputation was also a matter of their livelihood, such as through the sale of publications or securing financial donors for future research and publication projects. As a combination of these factors, and not overlooking personality traits as well, theoretical and methodological disagreements were often fought over bitterly and publicly in print and at lectures. Personal scholarly reputation at times trumped organizational membership, as in the case of Sir William Betham's eventual resignation from the Royal Irish Academy over his fierce objection to growing acceptance in the Academy by 1840 of Petrie's view on the Round Towers; Betham being a resolute advocate of the Phoenician origin of the towers.

Leaving aside the extravagantly fanciful interpretive and etymological underpinning of Henry O'Brien's *The Round Towers*, O'Brien had pinned his main theory of the Iranian (specifically Persian) origin of Ireland's ancient grand civilization on his particular decoding of the original function of the Round Towers, as indicated by the title of his book. The towers were to provide his central and incontrovertible material proof of Persian cultural influence in ancient Ireland. From his critics' point of view, the extensive objections raised to his proposed use of the towers left his formulation of the Iranian theory in shambles, even though Petrie's 'anonymous' review had refrained from entirely dismissing the probability of some unspecified sort of ancient ties between 'Iran'/Persia and Ireland. The subject of the Round Towers was one of Petrie's major archaeological and methodological battlefields in the high-stake antiquarian feud on Ireland's distant past. Petrie, in his 1845 *The Ecclesiastical Architecture of Ireland, Anterior to the Anglo-Norman Invasion*, which was an expanded version of his 1833 prize essay ("The Origins and Uses of the Round Towers of Ireland"), stayed singularly focused on the towers. Unlike Vallancey, Betham, O'Brien, and others, Petrie carefully sidestepped the minefield of Irish origins, approaching the Round Towers chiefly from the standpoint of what we now call "material culture." He engaged in a thorough examination of their comparative architectural design and proximity to other buildings (whether still standing or in ruins) that could be proven to be from roughly similar dates (whether extant in some form or mentioned in surviving local records), as well as similarities or differences in the materials used in the case of remaining edifices, and, more importantly, their potential functional relationship to these other surrounding buildings. He also probed whether there was a pattern in the proximity of the towers to these surrounding structures that recurred in different localities where the towers had once stood or still remained standing. He did not dwell on theories of Irish origins, even as he mentioned the "races" of the ancient "Fir-Bolg," "Tuatha De Danann," and "Milesian" populations of Ireland, albeit identifying Tuatha de Danann as colonists from "Greece."[169]

Petrie, without entirely adhering to empirical logic or even a strict method of so-called scientific verification in certain cases, nonetheless undertook a far more rigorous and corroborative approach than his rivals in the field. If a connection between the towers and other surrounding structures could be established and the other structures, based on available records or their particular design and/or usage, could be roughly dated, then the towers too could be assigned a roughly corresponding date and possibly even a related function. Furthermore, he focused on the most minute as well as the most obvious differences, rather than just apparent similarities, between the Round Towers and other frequently cited examples of seemingly similar structures outside Ireland with which the towers had been compared in previous studies. This enabled Petrie to refute a wide range of presumed connections between the towers and ostensibly similar structures in the Orient and elsewhere. Petrie ultimately demonstrated that the Round Towers were post-Christian edifices and connected to churches in their vicinity (with Christianity having first arrived in Ireland circa the fifth century). His supposition that the towers were primarily used as belfries—not an original idea in itself, but now based on Petrie's methodology and evidentiary approach, rather than mere extrapolation and conjecture—cannot be absolutely proven, given the lack of actual indication of any church bells and the particular design of the towers, unless only handheld bells were rung from the towers, as some of his supporters would later insist. There was also a lack of available so-called medieval written accounts as well as any local folk memory in support of this view. Neither did Petrie explain when and why the practice of building the towers had discontinued, with belfries then attached to the main church edifices.

Nor did he address whether it was possible that churches were for some reason constructed in the vicinity of previously existing towers by using similar material (whether locally available or otherwise), or if they were initially built near such existing towers (made of same or different material), with the older towers later replaced with new resembling structures. Yet, he highlighted the absence of any evidence of burials under or inside the towers in order to dismiss the theory of their sepulchral use, the absence of any sign that the interior of the surviving towers had been continually exposed to flames, as well as the absence of apertures in the structure required for adequate smoke ventilation, in order to refute the theory of fire-worship function of the towers, and so on. Above all, by analyzing the construction material, he established that architecturally the existing towers at the heart of the debate could not have been constructed in earlier times than the fifth century, with the more recent examples dating to around the thirteenth century. A point often overlooked in Petrie's conclusion and its potential appeal to Irish nationalists (particularly Catholics), such as Petrie's close colleague John O'Donovan, was that Petrie's model implied: (1) the towers had originated long before the earliest Norman/English territorial conquests and dated to even before the arrival of the Norse/Vikings in Ireland in the ninth and tenth centuries CE (not forgetting the invading Norse had largely only taken control of coastal regions and not the interior of the island and that they converted to Christianity at a later date than when they launched their initial raids into Ireland). Hence, the towers were of pre-English native design and construction, even if similar edifices in fact existed at a few other locations in Britain and in continental Europe. (2) The earliest towers dated to a period well before the Protestant Reformation in the sixteenth century and, hence, could be considered "Catholic" in terms of any church function associated with them.

By 1834, a year after the publication of Petrie's prize essay, John O'Donovan was convinced of the Christian origin and application of the Round Towers (i.e., serving as belfries).[170] But not all contemporary antiquarians or subsequent historians accepted Petrie's verdict or his evidentiary method, leaving aside the many antiquarians whose existing theories of the towers Petrie had dismissed. Petrie's friend and biographer, William Stokes, noted as late as 1868:

> Theories even more extravagant than those of Vallancey, O'Brien, and Windele have been but recently put forward. The belief that nothing certain is known as to the origin of the towers is still general among the Irish public, whether from ignorance of what has been done, or from the fond belief that the times when the light of Christianity was first taught by a few devoted missionaries to a still uncivilized people, were marked by splendour and by glory.[171]

There were also those in the oriental camp who accepted Petrie's dating of the towers, but continued to insist on principal similarities between the design and imputed function of the towers and a range of ancient oriental structures, mainly the allegedly Zoroastrian "fire temples." This latter group of antiquarians claimed that more ancient and now-extinct original towers had served as the architectural prototypes for subsequent Christian-era Round Towers (a practice supposedly continued even after the

Anglo-Norman invasions), indicating the lasting architectural legacy of oriental influence in Ireland.

In Henry O'Brien's case, his book was selected by Petrie and his associates in the *Dublin University Magazine* for the most frontal and no-holds-barred public vilification, and as their most vulnerable target and, hence, the most fertile opportunity for promoting Petrie's own position, while also settling personal score. Coinciding with this savaging of O'Brien, O'Brien's historical claims were mercilessly targeted in another anonymous review, appearing in the *Edinburgh Review* of April 1834, with an extract of that review reproduced in *The Times* of London in May. In this piece, O'Brien was being attacked by an ardent adherent of a rival theory of oriental origins of ancient Irish civilization, who otherwise did not challenge the idea of an Iranian prototype for the towers, but rather their purported usage and O'Brien's overall approach and key suppositions.[172] This anonymous reviewer was no other than Thomas Moore, who was to shortly publish his own historical version of the Iranian roots of ancient Ireland's civilizational foundation by way of Phoenician intermediaries, and of the Indo-Iranian origin of Ireland's Round Towers (*History of Ireland*, vol. I, 1835). Moore's vilification of O'Brien stemmed from the primary challenge O'Brien posed to Moore's forthcoming work, in so far as O'Brien rejected the major part attributed to Phoenicians as transmitters of Iranian civilization to Ireland—insisting instead on a direct Iran-Ireland link—as well as his dating of the transmission of Iranian (Persian) civilization to Ireland that now long preceded the alleged arrival of Milesians, and O'Brien's insistence on phallic worship during Ireland's civilizational Golden Age. O'Brien had rejected rival claims that so-called Zoroastrian fire temples were the original prototype for the Round Towers, while acceding the towers could later have been adapted to that purpose. In Moore's particular line of assault, O'Brien's riotous historical and etymological imagination proved to be his Achilles' heel.

In effect, O'Brien was immediately subjected to a two-pronged and bitterly derisive attack from distinctly different antiquarian perspectives and on wide-ranging evidential, interpretive, and methodological grounds. In his anonymous 1834 review, Moore disingenuously and selectively alternated between wearing the mantle of an antiquarian expert entirely opposed to oriental theories of Irish origins and the mantle of a more measured and reasonable theory of oriental origins than what O'Brien had proposed, repeatedly rubbishing O'Brien's etymological wonders. Moore branded O'Brien as excelling even Vallancey in the "absurdity" of his theories and methodology. Moore wrote, "So long had Vallancey been accustomed to look at his beloved Ireland through an orientalizing medium, that she grew, at last, to be as completely an Eastern island, in his eye." In reference to Vallancey's transition from Phoenician to ultimately Iranian theories of Irish origins, Moore noted:

> Not content with merely deriving the Irish nation from the ancient Chaldæans, Persians, Scytho-Iberiaus, or whatever other name he chose to give to their progenitors, he seems, at last, to have almost persuaded himself that the offspring has changed but little on the way, and that the Irish continue to be good Chaldæans, Persians, Scytho-Iberians, &c., to this very day.[173]

This assault on Vallancey was not only covertly intended to prepare a more receptive ground for an alternative account of ancient Ireland that Moore was about to publish, but it was overtly a ploy by Moore to garner support for his attack on O'Brien (otherwise, Moore himself belonged to an oriental camp in debates on Irish origins and would allude to continued oriental disposition of the Irish in the 1846 fourth volume of his *The History of Ireland*).[174] Moore then proceeded to wreck O'Brien's assertions:

> That we should have despaired of ever finding another such antiquarian—one so rich in absurdity—will hardly be deemed wonderful. But 'the thing that hath been is that which shall be'; and the cycle of human absurdity, if it does not, like the Periodic year of the Stoics, bring back the same man to say the same foolish thing, brings round others, at least, to say it *for* him. Not only in the work on the 'Round Towers,' now before us, but also in another extraordinary production, entitled 'Nimrod,'[by the English antiquarian Algernon Herbert, published in four volumes between1828 and 1829, and which in fact made a different claim than that of O'Brien's book], as remarkable for its eccentricity as for its omnigenous erudition, there occur speculations respecting Ireland and her past history, which even Vallancey might wish his own; and which show clearly, that to write about that country almost as much unsettles the wits of people as to legislate for it.
>
> [...]
>
> We have now to ascend, even still higher, the cloud-capt regions of Antiquarianism, in order to arrive at Mr[.] O'Brien, who sits supreme in his vocation—'*sedet altus Olympo,*'—overtopping even the old Pelion, Vallancey himself.[175]

After heaping much triumphant scorn on O'Brien's work, Moore concluded this anonymous review with self-flattery and blatant endorsement of his own forthcoming book on ancient Ireland, leaving little room for doubt as to the review's authorship. At this point, Moore suddenly switched from ridiculing oriental theories of Irish origins to insisting not all suggestions of Ireland's ancient civilizational links with the Orient should be dismissed on account of the defects abounding in antiquarianism of the likes of Vallancey and O'Brien. Here, he also favorably referenced the work of the Irish antiquarian John D'Alton (Dalton), a proponent of the (Iranian) Zoroastrian origin of the Round Towers:

> It can hardly be necessary, we trust to say, that to no deficiency whatever of reverence for the high and authentic claims of Ireland to antiquity, nor to any want of deep interest in her history, is the light tone we may seem to have indulged, in the preceding remarks, to be attributed. If some, more ardent than judicious, among her champions, have erred through excess of zeal, and brought ridicule on a good cause by the extravagance of their advocacy, there are some, on the other hand, who have succeeded in shedding over her past times and records that steady light, which alone distinguishes the bounds of truth from those of fiction. By the work of the late venerable librarian of Stowe, the authenticity of the Irish Chronicles is placed beyond dispute; and the Essay of Mr[.] Dalton on the religion, learning, arts, and government of Ireland, abounds with research on these several subjects, alike creditable to his industry and his judgment. Let us hope that the same service which these and other sensible Irishmen have achieved for their country's *ancient* history, will be effected also for the *modern*, by the work which is now expected from Mr[.] Moore.[176]

D'Alton, a member of the Royal Irish Academy, belonged to the antiquarian clique who maintained a Phoenician habitation of ancient Ireland (Phoenicians in his version being conflated with Scythians.) D'Alton also belonged to the Phoenician camp claiming the Phoenicians had previously embraced a syncretic system of beliefs and practices from other groups with whom they had come into contact prior to their arrival in Ireland, including religious and other practices of Iranian peoples (in the broadest sense), most notably Zoroastrian religious performances, which these antiquarians erroneously equated with fire-worship.[177] This model of the diffusion into ancient Ireland of Iranian religious, cultural, aesthetic, architectural, and other so-called civilizational values and practices by way of Phoenicians—who in some of these accounts were accompanied on their journey to Ireland by some Persian 'Iranians'—, as well as the alleged Zoroastrian origin of the Round Towers, was in fact the template Moore adopted in the first volume of his *The History of Ireland* (1835). Following the publication of Moore's *The History of Ireland*, D'Alton in his 1845 book in turn cited Moore as among the authorities substantiating the original function of the Round Towers as fire temples and tracing them to their Zoroastrian prototype.[178] Incidentally, in 1833 D'Alton had been a member of the Royal Irish Academy's council overseeing the selection of "the best Essay on the origin and uses of the round towers" that resulted in the public acrimony between Henry O'Brien and the Academy, following the Academy's award of the best essay prize to Petrie. By his own account, D'Alton was the sole member of the council favoring O'Brien's essay over Petrie's, whose theory of the Christian-era origin of Ireland's Round Towers D'Alton refuted, with D'Alton still insisting in 1845 that O'Brien's original submission should be published in the *Transactions* of the Royal Irish Academy.[179]

Moore later received his own share of condemnation for the remorseless treatment he had meted out to O'Brien in his anonymous review. The satirical journalist Francis Sylvester Mahony (alias "Father Prout") turned his wit and malice against Moore in "The Rogueries of Thomas Moore," appearing in the August 1834 issue of *Fraser's Magazine*.[180] Mahony refuted Moore's claim that O'Brien's theory was an act of plagiarism, disclaiming the purported similarity between O'Brien's model and that of Algernon Herbert in *Nimrod*, which Mahony suggested Moore had not even read.[181] On the other hand, in January of 1842, Moore received a letter signed Connor MacSweeny, accusing Moore of having been a major catalyst in driving O'Brien to complete despair and ultimately early death in 1835, at the age of 27.[182]

O'Brien had anticipated widespread criticism of his 1834 *The Round Towers*. He had already preemptively responded to accusations of "hallucination," "lunacy," and "etymological moonshine" in his book.[183] But, he had not fully appreciated the intensity and bitterness with which his work would be received, not the least on account of his public denunciations of the Royal Irish Academy and Petrie, as well as his rejection of all hitherto models of a grand civilization in ancient Ireland , and his alleged original function of the Round Towers. Besieged by the unrelenting caustic mauling of his book, particularly by Petrie and other members of the Academy, O'Brien threatened legal action against what he construed as the Academy's journal, the *Dublin Penny Journal*, on grounds of defamation of his 'literary character' and his book's alleged consequent loss of sales. The journal had also malevolently rendered the initials for O'Brien's university degree as "Big Ass."¹⁸⁴ In response to O'Brien's legal threat, the editors of the *Dublin Penny Journal* (with Petrie having by then handed over the editorial duties of the journal to Philip Dixon Hardy of the Academy) stood by the journal's rancorous review, only offering a sardonic apology for the personal insult to O'Brien, but by means of further abusing him, including the repeated use of "Big Ass" in this purported apology:

> By a reference to the 98th number of our Journal, the reader will find the review which has excited Mr. O'Brien's bitter ire against us; and here we beg to say, that we do most readily apologize for having translated the A. B. affixed to his name, as *Big Ass*. Our publication had not gone through the press until we wished it expunged, for we felt it was bad taste on our part, and its point could not be seen by the generality of our readers, as it merely referred to Mr. O'Brien having appended the Esquire to his own name, and taken it from Mr. Petrie's, who was certainly at least as well entitled to it. We do, therefore, most unreservedly apologize to the gentleman for having called him a *Big Ass*, and most assuredly shall never be guilty of a like offence in future; but with this exception, we now affirm, on a re-perusal of the work itself, that the review is a fair, impartial, unbiassed judgment—nay more, that it is not as severe or pungent as the work demanded at our hands.¹⁸⁵

Squaring the Round Towers: From Oriental Relics to Oriental Textual Sources of Ireland's Ancient Past

Joep Leerssen, although later substantially revising his earlier unconditional verdict about O'Brien, once maintained:

> The notion of a discrete and unproblematic national epic is perhaps a naïve idealization. The European reading public was overwhelmed, between 1800 and 1840, by a veritable wave of text editions presenting primitive and hitherto forgotten material. [...] There was a blurred, division between genuine material, manipulated material, rank forgery, and even practical jokes; among which circulated also the sincerely well-intentioned but totally erroneous speculations by Freemasons and lunatics.

Leerssen added, "Examples by the Freemason William Betham and the lunatic Henry O'Brien, respectively."¹⁸⁶ Curiously, this sort of judgment is not generally extended to the likes of William Jones and some other members of the Asiatic Society of Bengal, whose often highly fanciful published lectures and research ignited the even more feverish imagination of the likes of Vallancey, O'Brien, and others. Notwithstanding his subsequent considerable reevaluation of O'Brien, Leerssen was by no means the first to brand O'Brien as demented. As noted before, O'Brien had been less than obliquely treated as idiotic by some of his contemporary critics. Following O'Brien's death, William Betham in 1842 outright called O'Brien "insane," while also labeling Betham's long-deceased but still favorite antagonist, Vallancey, "a great dreamer" and "confused." Betham, a contemporary of O'Brien and a leading antiquarian figure of the Royal Irish Academy, was by then not only a veteran proponent of the Phoenician theory of Irish origins but also an advocate of the sepulchral function of the Round Towers—by way of comparing them with allegedly similar Etruscan, Afghan, Indian, Chinese and other structures and establishing a Buddhist precedent for the ancient druidic practices of the Celts in Ireland, according to which argument the Phoenicians had been influenced by Buddhist traditions before reaching Ireland. In 1842, Betham was framing the Phoenician ancestors of the Celts as also the founders of the Etruscan civilization, from whence they had reached Ireland.[187] The field of antiquarianism at the time (and by no means in Ireland alone) will certainly strike many of us today as highly eccentric and fantastically imaginative. Among numerous contemporary examples is the English Godfrey Higgins (1773–1833), a fellow of the Royal Asiatic Society (London) and the author of such works as the well-received and bombastically titled 1827 *The Celtic Druids; or, An Attempt to Shew, That the Druids Were the Priests of Oriental Colonies who Emigrated from India, and Were the Introducers of the First or Cadmean System of Letters, and the Builders of Stonehenge, of Carnac, and of Other Cyclopean Works in Asia and Europe*. Moreover, unless the Royal Irish Academy in 1833 had received no other submissions for its advertised competition of the best essay on the Round Towers than the papers received from Petrie and O'Brien, the fact that O'Brien, rather than some other author, was chosen for the second prize is itself noteworthy, even if this were merely treated as a 'consolation' prize. Nor was the Academy required to award a second prize. In fact, according to D'Alton's description, in his already mentioned 1845 account of the Academy's decision to award the first prize to Petrie, the Academy had received five essay submissions for the competition. It should not be forgotten that many members of the Royal Irish Academy held their own range of what would today strike us as entirely fabulous antiquarian views, with the pattern persisting for years to come, including certain admixtures of biblical and ancient Persian legends. An example of the latter a few years after the publication of O'Brien's *The Round Towers* was a paper by the Reverend Dr. Thomas Hincks of Belfast "On the Years and Cycles of the ancient Egyptians," which was read by the president of the Academy Sir William R. Hamilton on 9th and 23rd of April and May 14, 1838. Hincks' paper treated as historical fact both Noah and the mythical ancient Persian ruler of the Pishdādiān era, Jamshid (/Yima):

> According to the views advocated in this paper, a lunisolar cycle of 600 years was in use prior to the deluge, its epochs being at the autumnal equinox in the years B.C. 3567, 2967, &c. The knowledge of this cycle was preserved by Noah, and diffused through the different nations at the dispersion. It was certainly used in Persia and in Egypt. In the former country, the commencement of the year was fixed at the vernal equinox by Jamshid; the epoch of this change being 7th April, 2007 B.C., when 360 years of the current cycle had elapsed. The Persian years were however reckoned from the first day of the following cycle, that is, from 6th Feb. 1767 [B.C.]; between which and the era of Yezdigerd (16th June, A.D. 632) there elapsed exactly 2400 years of 365 days, that being the form of year introduced by Jamshid.[188]

It is crucial to avoid hasty dismissal of the likes of Henry O'Brien as entirely eccentric and ridiculously insane. The antiquarian views of these individuals, as preposterously delusional as they may appear today, need to be contextualized further. In terms of epistemology, we also should consider that many of these fabulous accounts were no more outlandish than the enduring biblical accounts of Creation, Adam and Eve, the Garden of Eden—with god, snake, and Adam and Eve all communicating in some celestial language—, the Nephilim, Noah, and so on, all of which were still largely processed by many as literal truth. Even long after the publication of Charles Darwin's *The Origin of Species* (1859), many people, including in scientific communities, continued to hold on to literal interpretations of the Bible, including the Deluge and the Mosaic theory of population groups. Among the plethora of other examples of what should appear utterly absurd to us (and in this case also undeniably pernicious and destructive) was the then commonly held views in the United Kingdom and elsewhere on racial hierarchies, the continued belief in many circles of polygenesis theory of human origins (despite simultaneous appeals to the Bible by many who subscribed to such views), and other racial/ethnic fables, as well as beliefs in intrinsic intellectual capacities based on gender and/or social classes, which astoundingly continue to cloud the opinion of many even in scientific communities to the present time. Also still abounding are national, religious, and other myths and teleologies, along with selective interweaving of contradictory and/or unrelated historical material for sustaining certain "traditions" and commemorative projects. All nations and nationalisms and their subsets, dominant or marginalized, resort to pasts that are in some ways fabulously invented and often incongruous. In fact, one of the most common contributing factors to what should strike many of us today as the core fantastical quality of much of antiquarian writing from that era is the predominance of the Mosaic theory of population dispersions. This necessitated making adjustments to presumed dates and locations, identifying corresponding population divisions, assigning historical parallels for biblical tales, rendering the allegoric *historical* and the historical *allegoric*, and/or proposing connections between certain names, terms, and belief systems with particular imaginative periodization schemes, ad nauseam.

As argued in the remainder of this chapter, many of O'Brien's contemporary antiquarians in the United Kingdom held a similarly far-fetched range of views, arrived at by means of no less perplexing methodologies by our standards. Most members of the Royal Irish Academy at the time were not exempt from maintaining such a range of views. Petrie and his small band of close associates were not just taking on the formidable ghost of Vallancey, or the young Henry O'Brien, who had moreover provoked Petrie's fervent personal vendetta and the hostility of the Academy's establishment by his outbursts over the 1833 essay prize of the Academy. Petrie & Co. were, in fact, countering many of the most stalwart and established contemporary figures of the Academy itself. At the same time, while challenging particular historical interpretations of these individuals concerning the age and function of the Round Towers, Petrie and his colleagues readily embraced many of the other (now considered far-fetched) antiquarian suppositions, along with some of the established classification models of Ireland's ancient population settlements: for instance, Firbolgs, Tuatha de Dananns, and Milesians. On the other hand, most other contemporary critics of O'Brien's approach and conclusions were not operating from the same more rigorous analytical standpoint as Petrie and his cohorts. Rather, they engaged in their own alternatively tangled historiographic methods, as in the already noted case of Thomas Moore. The leaps of imagination in continued attempts by antiquarians to authenticate the oriental or some other origins of the Irish deserve more serious consideration, particularly, in light of the primary focus of the present book, given the modes of historical thought and their cultural and/or political underpinnings they reveal. Petrie himself admitted the continued persistence of

Vallanceyan-style opinions and methodologies in the mid-nineteenth century. In 1845, Petrie acknowledged his uphill battle, even as he intensified his iconoclastic efforts:

> It is a difficult and rather unpleasant task to follow a writer so rambling in his reasonings and so obscure in his style, but, *as his followers are still the most numerous class of my readers*, I must get through the labour as well as I can, consoled by the conviction, that little more is necessary to prove the visionary nature of his hypotheses, than to present the arguments on which they rest, in consecutive order. (emphasis added)[189]

Nor, as noted previously, were the debates on Irish origins occurring in a vacuum or in an entirely Ireland-bound context. An example is that of the contemporary debate concerning Dighton Rock in Massachusetts in the United States. In this case, there were parallel debates taking place on the origins of "native" populations of the Americas and claims by the likes of Ezra Stiles after the late eighteenth century of the presence of Scythians and/or Phoenicians in the American continent in ancient times. Some of these theories intersected with debates on Irish origins.[190] Similar debates were raging elsewhere.[191] Additionally, it was not only the likes of Vallancey and Henry O'Brien, following William Jones' example, who sought to variously reconcile the (legendary) Pishdādiān or Mahābādiān Iranian dynastic cycles with the prevailing biblical Mosaic theory. There were prominent contemporary biblical scholars who attempted to do the very same thing. Writing just a few years before O'Brien, the Anglican Rev. William Hales, in charge of Killeshandra rectory in Ireland and formerly a professor of oriental languages at Trinity College, Dublin, had set out to reconcile "*Scriptural and Scientific Principles*" in the fourth volume of the revised edition of his *A New Analysis of Chronology and Geography, History and Prophecy* (1830). Accepting the existence of both Pishdādiān and Mahābādiān, in keeping with *Dabestān-e Mazāheb* by way of William Jones' authority, as well as referencing the discussion of Pishdādiān in Mirkhond's *Universal History*, among a range of other oriental sources, including Ferdowsi's *Shāhnāmeh*, Hales wrote:

> The first *tyrannical* innovation in the pristine *patriarchal* regimen of the first race of mankind began in *Chaldea* and *Babylonia*, as we have seen. And it was afterwards renewed in the second race, by the mighty hunter *Nimrod*, that "arch rebel" in religion and government, who first claimed divine honours, and usurped the domains of his neighbours after the deluge; and whose early celebrity is recorded not only in Scripture, but all over the East and West, in his titles, *Maha Bala*, "the great Master," *Belus*, and *Orion*.
>
> *Artapanus*, in his Jewish history, written about a century before the Christian era, says that *Nimrod* was the only survivor of a race of *giants* who inhabited *Babylonia*, and were destroyed for their impiety by a divine judgment. That he dwelt in a tower at *Babylon*, and was afterwards deified.
>
> *Sir William Jones* also learned from the most intelligent *Mussulmans* [i.e., Muslims] in *India*, that "a powerful monarchy had been established for ages in *Iran* before the accession of *Cayumers*; that it was called the *Mahabadean* dynasty, and that many princes, of whom only seven or eight are named in the *Dabistan*, and among them *Mahbul*, or *Maha Bali*, had raised their empire to the zenith of human glory." *Sixth discourse on the Persians*. Asiat. Research. Vol. II. p. 48, 8vol.[192]

However, contra O'Brien's trans-biblical dating of the Mahābādiān dynastic era, Hales subordinated *Dabestān*'s narrative to biblical stories and presumed time frames. O'Brien discussed Hales' chronology in his book on the Round Towers, challenging it by the standards of "sacred and profane history."[193] Of course, a notable distinction between the fabulous elements of O'Brien's history in contrast to those of biblical accounts—leaving aside that the likes of O'Brien could not compete with god's presumed authorial design and license from the standpoint of the average contemporary Irish Christian reader—was that O'Brien's narrative often lacked even the minimal internal structural coherence present in biblical narratives. This was due to O'Brien's decision to cram into his historical model an astonishingly broad range of information and diverse narratives from various histories and traditions in a synthetic fashion—without overlooking here the fact that passages in different biblical stories themselves assumed their present-day forms over hundreds of years of multiple anonymous authorial and editorial interventions, following their manifold oral and written origins. Furthermore, as already mentioned, O'Brien's attribution of phallic worship to Ireland's most frequently celebrated historical monuments at the time—monuments that had also assumed a hallowed status in nationalist poetry and songs—was anathema in many quarters, in contrast to other suggested "pagan" rituals associated with the towers. Mainstream nationalist sensibilities, whether shaped by broadly Christian (particularly Catholic) and/or other forms of later so-called Victorian values, were aghast at the suggestion that the Round Towers—the much-celebrated relics of Ireland's proclaimed ancient high civilization—had originally functioned as sites of priapic rituals. While Vallancey and some other antiquarians had indicated the towers could later have been used to this end, O'Brien claimed this had been the original and primary purpose of the towers. Petrie's identification of the Round Towers with Christian practices rendered O'Brien's theory even more abhorrent to Petrie's followers and audiences in the moral climate of the milieu, creating a wider psychic chasm between even other proposed non-Christian uses of the towers and that of O'Brien's proposed phallic worship.

In 1855, under the "Antiquarian Notes and Queries" section of the *Ulster Journal of Archaeology* (Belfast), a reader (identified only as "G.H.") strongly objected to an article appearing in an earlier issue of the same journal in which "O'Brien's work [was] mentioned with respect. It is a jumble of ill-connected rubbish." Repeating the then cliché accusation of plagiarism against O'Brien widely shared among supporters of Petrie's view of the towers, and further strengthened by Moore's bogus charge of plagiarism against O'Brien, the reader noted:

> Even the suggestion that the Round Towers were phallic symbols is not new. It originated [*sic*] with Vallancey, and was repeated by the author of a book called 'Nimrod' [...] Upwards of sixty years ago, a writer in the *Anthologia Hibernica* [*sic*] notices what he calls phallic stones in Ireland.[194]

This reader was reacting to an anonymous article that had appeared in the journal earlier in the year. Titled "Notices of the Round Towers of Ulster," that article commenced by quoting the following lines from Moore's "Paradise and the Peri" in *Lalla*

Rookh (with the first word changed from "Whose" to "Those"): "Those Lonely Columns stand sublime, / Flinging their shadows from on high, / Like dials which the wizard, Time, / Had raised to count his ages by!"[195] The article, offering a detailed rebuttal of Petrie's observations on the design of, and material used in, the Round Towers, while still referring to Petrie's research as "admirable," characterized O'Brien's theory "singular, though talented." Also admitting that Vallancey's earlier fire-worship theory of the towers and his etymological method could not be sustained, the author nonetheless defended Vallancey against his later critics such as Petrie, John O'Donovan, and Eugene O'Curry. The author exhorted his readers to remember "that facilities for accurate investigation have been greatly increased since the General [i.e., Vallancey] wrote his papers," adding: "The writer has considered it just to defend General Vallancey from the sweeping charges often made against him. His faults were in some measure those of the period in which he lived."[196] The author then paid tribute to Henry O'Brien:

> It is impossible here to analyse the extraordinary work of O'Brien, which must be read in full to be appreciated. It certainly does not bring conviction to the mind of the accuracy of the opinions advocated; but it must always hold its place amongst Irish archaeological books as one displaying great, it may perhaps be said, misapplied, talent[;] still it is difficult to deny that it is a work which few men could have written; and we cannot avoid the expression of regret that so gifted an individual should have been cut off in early youth, and not have survived until his views were rounded into form by attrition with those of more experienced enquirers.[197]

Relying much more extensively than Vallancey on what little information was by then available in English language about the contents of (the otherwise entirely fictional) *Dasātir* as recounted in *Dabestān*, O'Brien had engaged in a flawed (Peircean-style) abductive method of reasoning, whereby he sought to best explain his theory by means of providing the most suitable range of evidence that fit his claim of ancient Iran-Ireland civilizational connection.[198] Whether or not O'Brien was any more demented than many of his contemporary antiquarians, who believed in a wide array of fables and often engaged in similar vortices of logic, it is undeniable he belonged to the category of more quixotically ambitious antiquarian etymologists of the period, with a philological imagination no less rampant than that of Vallancey. A typical example of O'Brien's self-avowedly groundbreaking exegesis appears following his account of the Mahābādiān precursor (named Mah Ābād) to Pishdādiān's alleged first human ("Kaimours"; Gayōmard/ Keyoumars). Based on the summary account of *Dabestān* appearing in John Malcolm's 1815 *The History of Persia*, and notwithstanding Malcolm's unequivocal designation of both Mahābādiān and Pishdādiān as legendary, O'Brien wrote:

> We only now want a key to unlock the portals of this *Magh-abadean* household; and I flatter myself that *this*, which I am about to tender, will consummate, to an accuracy, that very desirable purpose.
>
> Cain's immediate progeny are they which are included under the above denomination. Their faith and worship are exactly symbolised under its derivative dress. *Magh*, as before explained, is *good*; and *Abad*, an *unit*; that is, when combined, the *Good One*, or *Unit*, the

author of fruitfulness and productiveness—in which light alone, as all-bountiful and all-generous, was he recognised by this family.

This unity of the Godhead was what was *religiously* comprehended under the *Phallic* configuration of the Round Tower erections; and this, furthermore, elucidates that, heretofore enigmatical, declaration of the Budhists themselves, *viz.*, that the pyramids, in which the sacred relics are deposited, *"be their shape what it will, are an imitation of the worldly temple of the Supreme Being."*

But if *Magh-abadean* was the name adopted by them with this spiritual tendency, *Tuath-de-danaan* was that which pictured them a sacerdotal institution. The last member of this compound I have already expounded. It remains that I develope what the two first parts conceal.

Tuath, then, is neither more nor less than a dialectal modification for *Budh*, which, according to the license of languages, transformed itself, otherwise, and indifferently, into *Butt*, Butta, Fiod, Fioth, *Thot*, *Tuath*, *Duath*, *Suath*, Pood, Woad ; and in the two last forms—of which one is Gothic, and the other Tamulic—admitted a final syllable—which was but an insignificant termination—namely, en, making *Pooden* and *Woad-en*; or *Poden* and *Woden*.[199]

There is nonetheless a striking historiographic dimension to O'Brien's outlandish account of Iranian origins of Irish civilization. Similar to Vallancey, O'Brien too extensively relied on the available English translations of oriental sources for reconstructing Ireland's past; notably, in O'Brien's case, on partial English translations of, and commentaries on, the mid-seventeenth century Persian-language text *Dabestān-e Mazāheb*, appearing as "*Dabistan*" in O'Brien's book, and which ostensibly incorporated material from ancient Iranian sources, including the (entirely concocted) *Dasātir*, which was said to have been composed in an unknown language. The first complete translation of *Dasātir* into English by Mulla Firuz Bin Kaus was published in Bombay in 1818. Appearing in two volumes, the first volume consisted of the "original" text in its Persian translation and commentary. The second volume consisted of the English translation. Incidentally, this work was dedicated to Sir John Malcolm. O'Brien does not appear to have been aware of this publication, of which there is no mention in *The Round Towers*. On the other hand, as noted previously, *Dabestān* was not fully translated into English until 1843, long after the publication of O'Brien's *The Round Towers*. That complete translation of *Dabestān* by David Shea and Anthony Troyer was titled *Dabistan, or the School of Manners*. With only partial translations of *Dabestān* available to O'Brien, and the work at the time generally attributed to the Indo-Iranian Mohsen Fani (of Kashmir in the Indian subcontinent), this work was initially popularized in Western European orientalist circles and beyond by Sir William Jones in the late eighteenth century, and was first referenced in connection with Ireland's ancient past by Vallancey, albeit in a very brief application. Jones was introduced to the text in British India in 1787 by the scholar Mir Muhammed Husain (Isfahani) and then in 1789 arranged for its first partial translation into English by another member of the Asiatic Society of Bengal, Francis Gladwin.[200] *Dabestān* provided an inventory of numerous religions in the Indian subcontinent and West Asia, either extant or extinct (actual and invented in hindsight). Some of the information contained in *Dabestān* was allegedly based on an earlier text titled *Dasātir* (*Edicts*, also referred to as *Dasātir-e Āsemāni*; tr. *Heavenly Edicts / Celestial Edicts*), which later turned out to be another fabricated work by so-called neo-Zoroastrian circles.[201] The first part of *Dasātir* was very likely written in Mughal India sometime around the early seventeenth century, long before the gradual English annexation of territories in the subcontinent beginning in 1757 under the authority of the English East India Company. The entire text of *Dasātir*, which purportedly provides an account of ancient Iranian prophets (historical and invented), was most likely contrived by Azar Keyvan, a founder of the neo-Platonic influenced Zoroastrian circle known as "ishrāqiyyun" (Illuminationists). The original text was composed in an invented language, allegedly unrelated to any other known language, and hence considered "heavenly"/"Celestial" or hallowed. A pseudo-translation in the Dari dialect of Persian was rendered in the late eighteenth century. The text covered a concocted pre-Islamic ancient history of 'Iran' (in its broadest historical sense), with that history stretching remarkably far back into time, to long before all hitherto known (and entirely legendary) accounts of the most ancient Iranian past. The text concluded with the Arab-Muslim occupation of Iran in the seventh century CE. It was, hence, only partly based on much earlier Iranian legends that had also appeared in the Iranian heroic epic *Shāhnāmeh*.[202] In its coverage of the history of the earliest Iranian religions, *Dabestān* purportedly relied on the account given in *Dasātir*.

Based on the limited available information in English by the early 1830s concerning the content of *Dabestān*, Henry O'Brien in his *The Round Towers* identified the (otherwise legendary) Tuatha de Danann settlers in Ireland as ancient Persians of the era of the (otherwise legendary) first Iranian prophet Mahābād (Mah Ābād)—who was also identified in *Dasātir* as the very first prophet in the world; in effect corresponding to the biblical Adam, and accordingly being the earliest of the 12 Iranian prophets preceding Zoroaster. In regard to Mahābād, O'Brien primarily reproduced an embellished version of William Jones' sixth and ninth discourses, respectively "on the Persians" (1789) and "On the Origin, and Families of Nations" (1792).[203] O'Brien relied on Jones' then largely undisputed authority for substantiating the authenticity of the two presumably foundational "Iranian" sources to which O'Brien was turning in substantially rewriting the history of ancient Ireland. The authenticity of *Dabestān* and *Dasātir* was affirmed by William Jones, who evidently had not seen a copy of *Dasātir* at the time. The authenticity of these works continued to be largely unchallenged in British, Irish, and other European accounts of Iranian history in the early years of the nineteenth century, even if some of these latter accounts increasingly came to regard the Mahābādiān, and occasionally also the Pishdādiān, dynastic eras as entirely mythical. Highly respected authors of works in this category included the likes of the Scottish Robert Ker Porter (1821) or the prominent Anglo-Irish orientalist expert on Iran, William Ouseley (1819), who also remarked on Sabian religious practices in ancient Iran as mentioned in *Dabestān* and covered in William Jones' commentaries.[204] The Sabian religion or "Sabism" appeared recurrently in O'Brien's *The Round Towers*, as it had also previously occurred in Vallancey's writings, by which both of these authors had in mind the ancient worshippers of celestial bodies (similar to so-called Sabians of Harran), not to be confused with the later followers of Sabean-Mandaean faith. The translator of the first complete English edition of *Dabestān* nearly three decades after Jones' death also attested to the authenticity of the text. This was the Irish David Shea (d. 1836), with Anthony Troyer editing and completing Shea's unfinished translation in the form of the 1843 *Dabistan, or the School of Manners*. In 1832, Shea had also completed a translation of Mirkhond's *Universal History*, which treated the Pishdādiān as genuine Iranian history, notwithstanding the designation of that dynastic era as mythical in some previous English-language publications, such as the Scottish John Malcolm's 1815 *The History of Persia*. It should be added the authenticity of *Dasātir* was also accepted at the time by many Zoroastrian and other contemporary commentators in the Indian subcontinent, Iran, and beyond. It was only after the 1850s that *Dabestān* came to be almost unanimously regarded as a forgery in Western/European orientalist circles, as well as by many leading Parsi scholars of Zoroastrianism;[205] although it continued to be consulted by some authors in the United Kingdom as an authentic source well into the late nineteenth century.[206]

However, all along there also had been categoric skeptics of *Dabestān* and *Dasātir*. In 1819, William Erskine of the Literary Society of Bombay had emphatically refuted the authenticity of both works and challenged Jones' conclusions; notwithstanding Erskine's own errors on such subjects as his presumed absence of ancient Indo-Iranian ethnic affinities or his assumption of Pahlavi (Middle Persian) being completely unrelated to modern Persian. Yet, Erskine acknowledged Jones' continued robust sway in the matter, given Jones' reputation in Western European circles as the inimitable behemoth of oriental studies and the theory of Indo-European languages even long after his death in 1794; an influence that was to continue long after Erskine's critique of Jones. Erskine noted:

> I must entreat you to the confidence with which the works [i.e., *Dabestān* and *Dasātir*] have been brought forward to public notice, the great authority which the name of Sir William Jones carries with it among the generality of readers, the number of speculators who, encouraged by his opinion, and following a slender thread of evidence, have recently written as if they considered the ancient Persians and the ancient Hindus as being beyond all doubt the same race, and the weight assigned to the authority of the history of the Parsi religion, as recorded in the *Dabistán*, especially on the continent of Europe.[207]

Erskine himself had earlier been uncertain of the authenticity of these works. In an 1813 presentation, he twice cited *Dasātir* as a source, without in any way dwelling on its authenticity and only remarking that it was "a work which exists as a riddle in Persian antiquities."[208] It is not known if O'Brien feigned unfamiliarity with Erskine's 1819 refutation of the authenticity of *Dabestān* and *Dasātir* or simply disagreed with Erskine's opinion on the subject. As doubtful as it seems, given that there is no reference in O'Brien's *The Round Towers* to Erskine's particular 1819 published lecture, it is possible O'Brien had somehow not come across this work, despite his extensive reading on the subject. Erskine's detailed 1819 lecture had appeared in the second volume of *Transactions of the Literary Society of Bombay* (1820).[209] O'Brien was no stranger to *Transactions*. In a footnote of *The Round Towers*, he quoted from an earlier work by Erskine, which had appeared in the first volume of *Transactions* (1819), although this particular essay by Erskine did not touch on *Dabestān* or *Dasātir*.[210] O'Brien had extensively rummaged through the available information concerning these presumably Iranian texts as part of his endeavor to provide comprehensive proof of the consanguinity of the ancient Persians and their presumed Irish descendants, as well as of the Iranian origin of the Round Towers.

O'Brien recurrently referred to *Dabestān* in *The Round Towers*. Chapters XV and XIX were particularly devoted to establishing *Dabestān* as incontrovertible proof of his overall historical claims. Just as he had done in his Introduction to the 1833 English translation of Villanueva's *Phœnecian Ireland*, O'Brien reiterated that British accounts of Ireland's ancient past were generally prejudicial. In *The Round Towers*, O'Brien also took to task Greek as well as post-Islamic Arab accounts of ancient Iran, on grounds that those sources had not corroborated the existence of the Mahābādiān dynasty. By contrast, the similar absence of references to Mahābādiān in 'Iranian' sources before the sudden alleged (re)discovery of *Dasātir* and the appearance of *Dabestān* in recent times was explained as being symptomatic of the overriding reliance of post-Muslim-conquest Iranian historians on Arab/Islamic and ancient Greek accounts of ancient Iran—O'Brien also being entirely mistaken about Iranian reliance on Greek sources in this regard. Moreover, according to O'Brien, competing ancient Iranian dynasties had routinely attempted to deny the legitimacy of prior dynasties they had supplanted by obliterating every trace of previous dynasties from historical records (in a dynastic-cultural damnatio memoriae style). In connection with this latter claim, the Pishdādiān dynasty was singled out by O'Brien as the principal culprit in effacing all traces of Mahābādiān from Iranian historical records.[211] To this end, O'Brien even relied on the description given of *Dabestān* in what was the most celebrated and complete history of Iran to appear in any European language up to that date. This was the two-volume 1815 publication by Sir John Malcolm with the full title of *The History of Persia from the Most Early Period to the Present Time: Containing an Account of the Religion, Government, Usages, and Character of the Inhabitants of that Kingdom*. In the first volume of *The History of Persia*, Malcolm discussed the Mahābādiān and Pishdādiān dynastic cycles mentioned in *Dabestān*, as well as references to Pishdādiān in works available prior to the appearance of *Dabestān*, including in the eleventh-century *Shāhnāmeh* of Ferdowsi—a work that later came to constitute the 'national' epic of initially Persians and subsequently most modern-day Iranians of diverse ethnic backgrounds. Malcolm (d. 1833) was widely acknowledged as a leading British, and more broadly "European," authority on Iran following the publication of his 1815 book. He was a long-time employee of the English East India Company, having served in the company's expanding Indian territories first as an ensign and then a military officer (later in life also as a provincial administrator), as well as being appointed the envoy of British India to Iran (1799–1801, 1808, 1810).[212] Notwithstanding O'Brien's citation of Malcolm's book,[213] Malcolm in references to *Dabestān* had characterized the description of Mahābādiān and Pishdādiān dynastic cycles in that work as "fables" and "legends"—most certainly in the case of Mahābādiān and highly likely in the case of Pishdādiān.[214] In regard to Pishdādiān, Malcolm suggested it was possible the outrageously long lives and reigns attributed to each ruler, up to a millennium in one case, leaving aside the fabulous details of their deeds, may in fact have represented the total number of years marking sub-dynastic cycles of direct succession from the line of a given ruler, followed by the transition in the line of succession to another ruler and his line of successors, and so on, as part of larger dynastic cycles, with all of them sharing an identical name, notwithstanding the possibility of even diverse ethnic origins of the rulers of sub-dynastic cycles.[215] But, Malcolm was far less confident than William Jones had been of the actual authenticity of *Dabestān* and *Dasātir*. Malcolm was categoric in his dismissal of the authenticity of *Dasātir*, but uncertain of the authenticity of *Dabestān*, making such qualifying remarks as "if we could rely upon the authenticity of the Dabistan."[216] O'Brien nonetheless insisted on the historicity of both Mahābādiān and Pishdādiān and the authenticity of both *Dabestān* and *Dasātir*. Moreover, O'Brien sought to establish definite ties between the two presumably ancient Iranian dynastic cycles and Ireland's ancient past.

Again, it should be stressed that the verdict of the likes of Malcolm or Erskine on *Dasātir* and *Dabestān* was vehemently challenged by a host of other leading authorities in the field. Writing about the same time as Henry O'Brien, Sir Harford Jones Brydges, another British authority on Iranian history—and a personal rival of Malcolm in both their respective claims of historical knowledge of Iran and in their careers as representatives of the British Empire to the Qajar court in Iran—outright dismissed Malcolm's position on Mahābādiān and Pishdādiān, as well as Malcolm's reservation about the authenticity of *Dabestān*. While there was no reference to Jones Brydges in O'Brien's book, Jones Brydges in his 1833 *The Dynasty of the Kajars*, in a manner not entirely unlike O'Brien's narrative style, averred a conformity between William Jones' description of the Mahābādiān dynasty and biblical accounts of Noah and the Great Flood.[217] In fact, Malcolm himself had even displayed a glimmer of vacillation on the possibility of the historical existence of Mahābādiān, regardless of his stance on the account of that dynasty in *Dabestān*.[218] Two eminent members of the Asiatic Society of Bengal in the 1830s and 1840s, David Shea and Anthony Troyer (the latter invoking comparative philology and engaging in detailed rebuttal of arguments by the likes of Erskine), insisted on the authenticity of both *Dasātir* and *Dabestān*.[219] Interestingly, O'Brien did not mention, and may not have known of, the Dublin-born David Shea's 1832 *History of the Early Kings of Persia, from Kaiomars, the First of the Peshdadian Dynasty, to the Conquest of Iran by Alexander the Great*, which was an English translation of the section on rulers of ancient Iran appearing in the Arabic *Rowzat al-Safā fi Sirat al-Anbiyā' wa al-Moluk wa al-Kholafā* (also known as *Universal History*) by the fifteenth-century Persian historian Mirkhond. Other partial English translations of Mirkhond's *Universal History* were already available since the eighteenth century, including John Stevens' 1715 *The History of Persia*. In fact, O'Brien's familiarity with Mirkhond's work, who is not mentioned in *The Round Towers*, appears to have been limited to information he gleaned from the first volume of John Malcolm's 1815 *The History of Persia*, which amply relied on Mirkhond's work. As already noted, Vallancey referenced Mirkhond once in his 1807 *An Essay on the Primitive Inhabitants of Great Britain and Ireland*, based on information appearing in the French Barthélemy d'Herbelot's 1697 *Bibliothèque orientale*.[220]

Perhaps even more so than referencing ancient Greek, Roman, or biblical and related Hebrew sources, reliance on *Dabestān*, *Dasātir*, and other range of oriental sources by some Irish nationalist antiquarians for reconstructing and reclaiming the history of ancient Ireland, had the advantage of appearing as "neutral" sources in regard to the ethnic and denominational divisions in contemporary Ireland. These sources, since they were themselves silent on the arrival of the early populations in Ireland, could not be accused of favoring one or the other camp in counter-claims of the barbarity or refinement of the ancient Irish, whereas contending antiquarian camps could claim that Greek or Roman sources had already declared the Scythians, the Persians, and so on, as barbarous or, at best, lesser-civilized. The oriental sources in question also offered alternative interpretations of presumed Irish ancestry that were exterior to Ireland's ethnic divisions since the twelfth century. Moreover, in the case of O'Brien's Mahābādiān theory, *Dasātir* (including the coverage of its content appearing in *Dabestān*) supposedly documented the earliest period in world history, long before the rise of Hellenic cultures, offering a unique world-historical lens onto the ancestral ethnic, geographic, cultural, and linguistic setting for one of the earliest population settlements in Ireland. To apply Walter Benjamin's concepts of "after-life" and "reception" of works of art in a completely different setting here, *Dabestān* is an example of works intended for particular audiences that find their way to unexpected audiences and, following their translation (assuming the unintended readers lacked fluency in the original language of those text), are received by audiences who assign to them alternative new meanings, functions, and afterlife, that are radically different from any new range of meanings and/or usage rendered by the presumed "primary" group of audiences. As Vallancey and others had done before him, O'Brien too added his own highly speculative philological deliberations and layering to sources he consulted, whether to accommodate for the Mosaic theory of population groups and/or to explicate other range of connections. Via Jones' account of *Dabestān*, and by simultaneously appealing to the Masonic search for truth and mysterious knowledge, O'Brien was also in effect among the early seekers in the United Kingdom of an Orient-centered theosophical doctrine.

O'Brien, whose work was surreal by our present-day standards, still found it necessary to account for the fantastic details of Mahābādiān and Pishdādiān dynastic cycles and of other similar particulars in different sources he consulted. He treated some such details as mere embellishments, characteristic of all ancient records. Evidently, he also had in mind the Bible (particularly the Hebrew Bible), in which the pre-Deluge personalities lived for many hundreds of years and extremely fantastical events unfolded. According to O'Brien, the competent historian would be able to "glean in the distortion of those maniac *effusions*, the *glimmerings* of that *truth* whence they originally emanated."[221] Among other range of 'Iranian' sources referenced by O'Brien were such works as translations of the Zoroastrian *Zend Avesta*, based on a prior translation by the French orientalist Anquetil-Duperron in the late eighteenth century as well as earlier fragmentary account of Zoroastrian sources by the English Thomas Hyde in 1700. O'Brien's indirect accumulation of historical information from, and about, oriental sources in rewriting Ireland's ancient past also relied on a 1799 essay by Francis Wilford, appearing in the *Asiatic Researches* (the publication of the Asiatic Society of Bengal) and frequently cited by some other Irish antiquarians as well. Wilford's essay covered ancient "Hindu" texts, Egypt, and other territories adjoining the Nile, in an attempt to establish a pattern of cultural-civilizational transmission in very distant ancient times, from the Indian subcontinent to Egypt, and thence to ancient Hellenic territories and beyond, including such practices as phallic worship. Wilford had also claimed that the story of Satyavrata and the flood, appearing in the Indian Puranas, corresponded to the ostensibly later biblical story of Noah. However, what O'Brien avoided mentioning in his *The Round Towers* was that the appended commentary on Wilford's essay by William Jones in the *Asiatic Researches* had discredited Wilford's purported *"evidence"* and his *"conjectural* Etymology."[222] This was an important omission by O'Brien of countervailing information, keeping in mind that O'Brien treated other range of data provided by Jones, the erstwhile president of the Asiatic Society of Bengal, as highly authoritative. O'Brien's omissions of this sort were far from atypical among his contemporary antiquarians. In O'Brien's narrative, the knowledge found in the Puranas and in the great ancient civilizations of the Indian subcontinent were themselves rendered as derivatives of the primal Iranian civilization (more specifically 'Persian' in this case). According to Vahid Fozdar, who examines Wilford's and O'Brien's alternative historical weltanschauungen in a very different setting, the worldviews of these two authors corresponded to the Masonic belief in "humanity's common store of knowledge."[223] Here, we also should not discount the simultaneous influence of Mosaic theory of common origins of humanity.

O'Brien's 1834 book appeared roughly a couple of decades after what can be gauged as the liminal cusp of the very gradual western European transition to more professional and verifiable standards of historical method. One of the important distinctions to note in regard to this transition from the older style of antiquarianism to so-called more scientific historical methodologies and historiographic standards is that of the changing milieu of the composition of texts themselves (i.e., the time of the text) and the temporal narration of the past in those texts (i.e., the time in the text).[224] The milieu of the text's composition was not simply determined by the availability of sources, but also by continually evolving hermeneutical practices and interchange between modes of historical knowledge production and developments in other fields of knowledge, as well as inter-disciplinary theoretical and methodological crossovers. Yet, historiographic transformations are not uniform and do not occur instantaneously. Around the time Henry O'Brien was fine-tuning his Persian theory of ancient Ireland's grand civilization, there were numerous other authors who spawned similar universalist and diffusionist historical accounts. Among these other examples were also some fervent enemies of freemasonry. William Jones' writings on *Dabestān* and *Dasātīr* had provided additional fodder to the already fabulously fertile minds of the likes of the English Evangelical Anglican theologian and biblical historian, George Stanley Faber. In his 1816 highly repetitious three-volume *The Origin of Pagan Idolatry Ascertained from Historical Testimony and Circumstantial Evidence*, Faber—while challenging some of Jones' assertions, such as the designation of Mahābādiān dynasties as the oldest known in human history—made repeated references to Mahābādiān, Pishdādiān, *Zend Avesta*, Zoroaster ("Zeradusht"), and so on. In Faber's account, Zoroaster, reportedly similar to the Buddha, was not a single so-called pagan prophet but, rather, one of many Zoroasters, just as there had been numerous Buddhas. Also discussing the widespread pagan practice of phallic worship, Faber had his own highly inventive categorization and dating scheme for historically locating and cross-identifying individuals, dynasties, and pagan holy texts. For instance, the founder of the Mahābādiān dynasty (spelled "Maha-Bad" in this work) was identified as the "Buddha of Iran," and one of the many Buddhas of the early civilizations:

> The fourteen Menus of the Hindoos are manifestly the same as the fourteen Mahabads or great Buddhas of the ancient Iranians: for the first of them, like the first Menu, is said to have been the author of a sacred book in a heavenly language [i.e., the *Dasātir*].[225]

Unlike Jones, and also unlike Henry O'Brien, Faber classified the Mahābādiān as latecomers in history in keeping with his Mosaic formulation of humanity, and as being post-diluvian descendants of the last of antediluvian survivors: "clearly [...] identified with that Cuthic or Scuthic [i.e., Indo-Scythian] line of kings who were the lords of Asia during fifteen centuries from Nimrod to Thonus Concolerus." In this case, "Maha-Bad, the pretender founder of this dynasty," was "clearly Noah or the Menu Satyavrata of the Hindoos, though blended, like that Menu, with the anterior character of Adam or Menu-Swayambhuva. Nimrod place[d] him at the head of the dynasty, which he himself really founded."[226] Selectively consulting works by Vallancey and the like, in Faber's account the ancient Irish were a mix of "Cuthic," occasional Persians, as well as Indian Pali (accordingly from whom also descended the Pelasgi of the Aegean regions and the population of Palestine, among others), and such other groups whom Faber often cross-identified with one another as descendants of various branches of Noah's sons, who spread across the world at different stages, transplanting their respective, yet intermingled, pagan practices.[227] Given the disparities between Faber's and O'Brien's accounts of Mahābādiān, as well as of ancient Irish and their civilizational practices and origins, O'Brien, who had consulted Faber's works, outright dismissed the accuracy of the latter's scholarship.[228]

The historiographic transformations occurring between the 1810s and 1830s were piecemeal and uneven, rather than marking some radical 'paradigm shift.' In this setting, O'Brien and many others in the context of Irish antiquarianism, or Faber and the like in the broader European antiquarian context, did not constitute a rare minority. As noted, William Jones' faith in the authenticity of both *Dabestān* and *Dasātir* was accepted in much wider and diverse disciplinary circles at the time. As the renowned early twentieth-century British orientalist Edward Granville Browne noted in 1902, Jones, who "was destined to swallow the camel of the *Desátir*—one of the most impudent forgeries ever perpetrated[—]," and who

> however greatly he may have fallen into error in matters connected with the ancient history and languages of Persia, was so eminent in his public career, so catholic in his interests, so able a man of letters, and so elegant a scholar, that his opinion was bound to carry great weight, especially in his own country.[229]

To give just a few more random examples of the range of Jones' continued sway long after his death, one can turn to James Cowles Prichard, the leading British anthropologist and evolutionary theorist in the early nineteenth century. In 1813, Prichard accepted the existence of Pishdādiān, who were mentioned in Mirkhond's *Universal*

History and in Ferdowsi's *Shāhnāmeh*, as well as the existence of Mahābādiān, who were mentioned along with Pishdādiān in *Dabestān* and *Dasātir*.[230] From our point of view, Prichard's accounts of various ancient population groups were no less muddled than those of Vallancey, O'Brien, and many other Irish antiquarians. Among numerous examples, Prichard wrote:

> Both in the European and Oriental histories a long series of wars are recorded to have been carried out between the Persians and the Transoxan nations. The latter are the Turanians or followers of Afrasiab [an otherwise legendary figure appearing as a historical character in *Shāhnāmeh*], who made incursions into Iran [...] The Turanians are the Scythians. According to the oriental history there was a time when the Turanians formed a part of the same nation with the genuine Persians.[231]

He then proceeded to equate the Scythians with the Sarmatic tribes, who "were in all probability allied by kindred to the Medes, Persians and other nations inhabiting that region," before concluding that the Sarmatians "were the ancestors of the Scandinavian nations of modern times."[232] According to Prichard, the Celts, who inhabited ancient Britain and Ireland, engaged in cultural practices identical to the Hindus, including ostensibly "The ancient Irish [...] practice of eating the bodies of their aged relatives."[233] In 1831, three years before the publication of O'Brien's book, Prichard published *The Eastern Origin of the Celtic Nations Proved by a Comparison of Their Dialects with the Sanskrit, Greek, Latin, and Teutonic Languages*, which included similar range of linguistic and historical suppositions.[234] It is important to note here that even prior to Ferdowsi's *Shāhnāmeh* in the eleventh century, the Pishdādiān and their (equally legendary) successor Kiānian dynastic era had been a feature of 'Iranian' historical chronology in the aftermath of the Arab-Muslim conquests of Iranian territories in the seventh century CE, as in the case of the eight-century Mandean religious text *Ginza Rabbā* (*Sidrā Rabbā*), with other similar accounts also appearing in the interval between the composition of Ferdowsi's *Shāhnāmeh* and the appearance of Mirkhond's *Universal History* in the fifteenth century and subsequently.[235]

Attempts by what can be termed "mainstream" authors in the United Kingdom to temporally locate the Mahābādiān and/or Pishdādiān in history, with varying narrative and schematic arrangements, persisted for decades to come. Among these authors was the highly respected Anglican cleric in the United Kingdom, Leveson Venables Vernon-Harcourt. For instance, in his 1838 *The Doctrine of the Deluge, Vindicating the Scriptural Account ...*, Rev. Venables Vernon-Harcourt, former archdeacon of Cleveland (in northeast England) and at the time the chancellor of York, noted in his discussion of the black stone of Ka'ba in Mecca, the most important Muslim site of pilgrimage:

> They say that when Mohammed rebuilt the Caaba [Ka'ba], [the black stone] was placed in the wall out of contempt; but the pilgrims would not give up an adoration which had so long been practiced[,] and to this day it is kissed by all who visit the Caba. Al Shahrestani says that the temple at Mecca was dedicated to Zohal, or Keyvun, who is the same with Saturn; and the author of the Dabistan [*Dabestān*] declares that the black stone was the image of

Keyvun, the Irish Kievin, in Scripture called Chyun, the Remphan, which is interpreted, the God of Time, and consequently the same as Mahadeva and Saturn.²³⁶

Incidentally, Vernon-Harcourt, who added his own interpretation of "Keyvun" (Keyvan) to the narrative of *Dabestān* here, rejected Petrie's theory of Ireland's Round Towers, based on the refutation of that theory put forth by "Miss [Louisa Catherine] Beaufort [, who] has given such good reasons for her opinion"; albeit Vernon-Harcourt also in turn rejected Beaufort's own theory of the Zoroastrian origin of the towers (as presumed temples of fire adoration). Instead, selectively citing the authority of Vallancey and others, and referring to the "Citadel of Tabreez, or Tauris" in Iran as the actual prototype of the Round Towers, he declared the towers to be "Arkite" structures.²³⁷ Other similar random examples from later in the century include Henry Montague Grover, the Anglican rector of Hitcham (Buckinghamshire, England), in his discussion of "The Identity of Cyrus and the Times of Daniel," which appeared in the 1855 volume of the *Journal of Sacred Literature*.²³⁸

Other range of what today will strike us as utterly hodgepodge historical accounts of ancient Ireland, with similar befuddling methodological groundworks as O'Brien's *The Round Towers*, continued to be produced well into the second half of the nineteenth century and even into the early twentieth century, long after this style of historiography had fallen out of favor in leading Irish historical circles. A case in point was the 1867 *The Towers and Temples of Ancient Ireland; Their Origin and History Discussed from a New Point of View* by Marcus Keane, a member of the Royal Irish Academy no less. Keane sought to "reconcile" O'Brien's and Petrie's highly divergent verdicts on the Round Towers, while relying on O'Brien's and Faber's distinct treatment of Mahābādiān and Pishdādiān.²³⁹ By then, as discussed later, the controversy with which Keane's work was greeted was less surprising than in O'Brien's time. But, even Keane found staunch supporters in antiquarian historical ranks.

As noted before, O'Brien's own interpretations were not lacking in admirers during the remainder of his short life following the appearance of his book, with continued enthusiasts well into the early twentieth century. Even though the second edition of *The Round Towers* did not appear until 1898 and his supporters constituted a small minority in antiquarian circles, many others selectively referenced his book as an authoritative source on particular aspects of ancient Irish history and/or the Round Towers. Marcus Keane was one such example. In his 1867 *The Towers and Temples of Ancient Ireland*, Keane relied heavily on O'Brien's work and concurred with O'Brien's description of the original function of the towers, that of phallic worship, in what proved to be Keane's own highly contentious study. Another random example is the 1897 *The God-Idea of the Ancients or Sex in Religion* by Eliza Burt Gamble, the American suffragist and evolutionary theorist (albeit critical of Darwin), who cited O'Brien's Iran-Erin connection as a matter of fact:

> Henry O'Brien, a cultured Irishman, who when in London became, in his own line of investigation, one of the chief contributors to *Fraser's Magazine* while at its best, in response to a call by the Royal Irish Academy for productions relating to the origin and use of

the Round Towers, declared that they were erected by a colony of Tuath-de-danaans, or Lingham worshippers from Persia, who had left their native land because of the victories gained over them by their rivals—the Pish-de-danaans—a sect of Yóni worshippers; in other words, the sect which recognized the female element as the superior agency in reproduction, and who, therefore, worshipped it as divine. In the devastating wars which swept over Persia and the other countries of antiquity prior to the age of the later Zoroaster, the Pish-de[-]danaans were victorious, and, driving from the country the Tuath-de-danaans, or male worshippers, succeeded in re-establishing, and for a time maintaining, the old form of worship. O'Brien claims that the Tuath-de-danaans who were expelled from Persia emigrated to Ireland, and there continued or preserved their favorite form of worship, the Round Towers having been erected by them in conformity to their peculiar religious views. This writer assures us that the old Irish tongue bears unmistakable evidence of the relation existing between these countries. In addition to the similarity of language which is found to exist between ancient Ireland or Iren, and Persia or Iran, the same writer observes that in all their customs, religious observances, and emblems, the resemblance is preserved.[240]

After the late nineteenth century, O'Brien's views also attracted staunch enthusiasts in some theosophical circles.

Notably, both Vallancey and O'Brien, in their distinct theories of Iranian roots of ancient Ireland, rejected the model of 'Celtic' foundation of Ireland's civilization, branding the Celts as later arrivals on the island. At the time of the publication of O'Brien's book, the leading advocate of the Celtic theory of Irish civilization—who also insisted on Ireland's Golden Age independently of mainland Britain—was Sir William Betham, who maintained Phoenicians had introduced civilization to Ireland. A prominent member of the Royal Irish Academy, Betham in his two-volume 1842 *Etruria-Celtica* would further claim Phoenicians had previously established the Etruscan civilization in what later became Italian territories, prior to their reaching Ireland.[241] Earlier, in the same year as O'Brien's *The Round Towers* (1834), Betham's *The Gael and Cymbri* appeared, in which Betham also blamed Vallancey's (Indo-Scythian) Iranian intrusion into the realm of Irish antiquarianism for having initiated a fallacious departure from the Celtic theory of Irish origins.[242] Incidentally, Betham, whose opinion of the Round Towers was also refuted by Petrie in the 1845 *The Ecclesiastical Architecture of Ireland*, emerged as the most outspoken nemesis of Petrie within the Academy. While Vallancey had rejected the Celtic origins of the Gaels, since the late eighteenth century the Persians, or more broadly 'Iranians' (inclusive of Irano-Scythians/Indo-Scythians), had also been designated by some antiquarians and linguists as ancestors of the Celtic migrations across western Europe. For instance, in the first volume of their highly popular and reprinted eight-volume *Pictorial History of England* (1838–41), the literary critic George Lillie Craik (later a professor of English literature at Queen's College in Belfast) and the travel writer and historian Charles Macfarlane were among the many contemporary commentators in the United Kingdom who upheld the Persian origins of the Celtic "race" and of Celtic language. Both authors were Scottish, with Scottish Highlanders considered "Celts." They also categorized the original population of Ireland as Celts and provided examples of prior scholars who had expounded this theory, among them the German-born French antiquarian Simon Pelloutier (d. 1857) in the late eighteenth century. Craik and Macfarlane referenced Henry O'Brien and Vallancey as authorities on the same subject. But, whereas they correctly noted Vallancey's objection to the Celtic theory, they glossed over O'Brien's alternative rejection of the Celtic foundation of Irish civilization:

> Pelloutier, from the numerous and strong resemblances presented by the Druidical and the old Persian religion, concludes the Celts and Persians, as Mr. O'Brien has lately done, to be the same people, and the Celtic tongue to be ancient Persic.[243]

Earlier in the same book, Craik and Macfarlane had noted:

> Colonel Vallancey, who in his latter days adopted the hypothesis that the original Irish people were a colony of Indo-Scythians, and denied that they were either Gauls or Celts, maintained at the same time that the Irish was not a Gallic or Celtic tongue. Mr. O'Brien, who deduces the Irish population from Persia, makes the Irish to have been the ancient language of that country. Finally, Sir William Betham and others, whose system is that Ireland was colonized by the Phœnicians, contend that the ancient Phœnician or Punic language was the same with the modern Irish, and hold themselves to be able to make out that point from the remains of it which we yet possess. [...]
> [...]
> It may also be remarked that there does not appear to be any irreconcilable discordance between the two principal modern theories on the subject of the ancient connexion of Ireland with the East, namely that which attributes the colonization of the country to the Phœnicians, and that which deduces the people, together with their language and their religion, from Persia. It is far from improbable that the Phœnicians were originally a Persian people. The ancient writers generally bear testimony to the fact that the district called Phœnicia, at the extremity of the Mediterranean, was not their original seat. They seem to have found their way thither from some country farther to the east or the south-east.
> [...]
> It is an important part, however, we ought to note, of Mr. O'Brien's theory, that this name [i.e., Erin] is nearly the same word with Iran, the old and still the native name of Persia. Iran, he says, means the Sacred Land and Irin the Sacred Island. In support of this explanation he quotes a statement by Sir John Malcolm, to the effect that he had been told by a learned Persian that Eir or Eer signified in the Pahlavi, or court dialect of Persia, a believer, and that that was the root of the name of the country. The uniform spelling of Erin, or Irin, in the oldest manuscripts, according to Mr. O'Brien is Eirin.[244]

As noted before, by the time O'Brien's *The Round Towers* appeared, there were already undercurrents of a significant, albeit gradual and not abrupt, paradigm shift taking place in Irish, as well as in the broader western European, historiographic methods. The practitioners of the new historiographic methods in Ireland included John O'Donovan, Petrie, and a few others among their colleagues associated with the Ordnance Survey of Ireland, along with a number of individuals unaffiliated with Petrie's circle.[245] In the 1830s, Petrie and, through him, O'Donovan, joined the Ordnance Survey of Ireland, which had been established in 1824.[246] The new historiographic methodology and more rigorous standards of verification pursued by Petrie and his cohorts did not inexorably imply the abandonment of former assumptions of Irish origins, including oriental theories. There were individuals who applied the more refined methodological procedures and still concluded that Ireland's ancient civilizational roots were traceable to the Orient. Louisa Catherine Beaufort (1781–1863) was among the new generation of Irish antiquarians who insisted on the Iranian (Persian) roots of ancient Ireland's civilizational grandeur, while also maintaining Ireland's name ("Erin") was directly derived from 'Iran.' Beaufort had already made her name on the Irish antiquarian stage before the appearance of Henry O'Brien's book and enjoyed great scholarly cachet in antiquarian circles, regardless of differences of opinion on Irish origins. Her presentation at the Royal Irish Academy on October 22, 1827, was published in revised and expanded form in the Academy's *Transactions* the following year as "An Essay upon the State of Architecture and Antiquities, Previous to the Landing of the Anglo-Normans in Ireland," marking the first-ever publication by a woman in the *Transactions*.[247] (Women were not admitted as members of the Academy until 1835, with Maria Edgeworth becoming the first *Irish* female member of the Academy in 1842.) Henry O'Brien, in his 1834 *The Round Towers*, also dismissed Beaufort's ascription of the practice of fire-worship to the towers. O'Brien, instead of at least emulating some of Beaufort's methodological caution (albeit still flawed) in observing certain limitations to historical-archaeological and etymological interpretations, underhandedly begrudged the decision of the Royal Irish Academy to publish Beaufort's essay in 1828, while still refusing to publish O'Brien's 1833 'prize' essay. He insinuated his own essay was, at the very least, on par with Beaufort's recognized scholarship, if not better, while obliquely hinting that Beaufort's gender should have compromised her comparative merit in having her work published in the *Transaction*, while O'Brien still awaited the same opportunity:

> I now address myself to another obstacle which has been advanced by an Irish *lady*, and of the most deserved antiquarian repute, whose classic and elaborate treatise on this identical subject, though somewhat differently moulded, has already won her the applause of that society whose discriminating verdict I now respectfully await.[248]

Although "An Essay upon the State of Architecture and Antiquities" is the only known antiquarian publication by Beaufort, this work indisputably marked a gradual methodological departure in Irish antiquarian claims of oriental origins, as well as signifying a thus far understated transitional juncture in the broader Irish historiographic conventions toward more sober verification standards, narrative coherence, and documentation methods—nearly a decade before Petrie made a more radical intervention in this regard. Beaufort followed a modified synthesis of Jonesian and Vallanceyan style of etymological correspondences (with Vallancey's own works selectively incorporating Jones' ideas) and still pursued a deductive approach in constructing Ireland's ancient past, for which there was no surviving locally documented textual evidence from the period in question. In ascertaining an ancient Iran-Ireland link, Beaufort over-relied, among other features of William Jones' statements, on his passing remark concerning the resemblance between Ireland's ancient Ogham script and the as-of-then yet undeciphered cuneiform inscriptions at Persepolis in Iran.[249] Yet, she adopted a more rigorous method of historical and archaeological verification of her available evidence than most other contemporary Irish antiquarians, even if falling far short of the verification standards that Petrie and his colleagues would soon apply in the field of antiquarian archaeology. Petrie in his 1845 *The Ecclesiastical Architecture of Ireland*, an expanded and updated version of his 1833 prize essay, engaged in a thorough refutation of Scandinavian (Danish in this case), Oriental, and other such theories of the origin of the Round Towers, challenging at length such antiquarian authorities as Charles O'Conor, Vallancey, William Beauford, John Lanigan, John D'Alton, Thomas Moore, and John Windele, besides also demolishing Henry O'Brien's hypothesis. Among leading proponents of the theory that the towers originally had served as edifices of fire-worship ritual, Petrie also disputed Louisa Catherine Beaufort's view of the towers originally functioning as structures for Zoroastrian practice of fire worship (*sic*), introduced to Ireland by Iranian ancestors of the Gaels. But, whereas Petrie had emphatically dismissed the methodological approaches of other antiquarians whose theories he rejected, he made a point of acknowledging the "very elaborate and valuable" quality of Beaufort's overall work, and expressed "respect for the talents and acquirements of that estimable lady."[250] This was not some kid-glove gentlemanly patronizing platitude on grounds of Beaufort's gender. As discussed below, Beaufort was also among the early exponents of an underlying correspondence between particular episodes occurring in 'national' epics of Ireland and Iran (in the broad geographic-cultural and political and historical conceptions of Iran), a view first ventured by Vallancey in a purely speculative manner in the previous century.

As hinted at before, there was nonetheless still a significant shared historiographic dimension to works by Vallancey, Beaufort, and O'Brien, among other examples of Irish antiquarianism at the time, that also intermittently resurfaced later in the century but has been entirely overlooked by present-day scholars working on this milieu of Irish antiquarianism. This is the paradigmatic epistemological practice by these antiquarians of relying on non-European textual sources beyond biblical texts and other similar range of 'oriental' sources—alongside the more general utilization of information available about non-European archaeological relics—for filling in the blank spots in Ireland's ancient past and/or revising existing accounts of that past. Regardless of their faulty methodologies and often fabulous conclusions, this was a consequential historiographic move. This mode of reliance on a new range of oriental sources (in the available partial or complete European translations of those sources) was far different from, for example, the post nineteenth-century Iranian or Indian historians' reliance on Western sources for writing the histories of Iran or the Indian subcontinent, as in the case of Iranian historians consulting John Malcolm's 1815 *The History of Persia*, which itself had relied on both European sources (including ancient Greek and Roman texts) and on Persian and Arabic sources. The approach of the likes of Vallancey, Beaufort, and O'Brien also clearly differed from the more common Western orientalist reliance on oriental sources for reconstructing the histories of the Orient itself, as Malcolm had done. The distinction being made here does not center on the contentious question of hegemonic implications of Western versus oriental historical authority in the heyday of Western imperialism. Rather, the Irish antiquarians in question were writing other (non-European) histories into the history of ancient Ireland and claiming a foundational correlation between that *other* and the Irish *self*. In this regard, their method of incorporating oriental sources differed also from the philological historical models of the likes of William Jones that linked many of the European languages to ancient Persian, Sanskrit, and so on (while also incongruously assuming direct links between the peoples speaking those range of languages, merely on the basis of linguistic affinities). In the process, in a peculiar speculative manner O'Brien, Vallancey, Beaufort, and the like were relying on oriental sources that made no actual mention of Ireland in order to read and incorporate their presumed models of Irish history back into those sources. The manner in which this paradox was addressed, beginning with Vallancey, was to insist on various circumstantial evidences, such as the purportedly identical architectural designs of the Round Towers and certain historical facades in the Orient, as well as other purportedly corresponding material and cultural practices, and overlapping mythologies, and alleged etymological convergences, as in the case of the designations 'Iran' and 'Erin.' For instance, in his later works Vallancey went even further, claiming 'Iran' actually appeared in Ireland's oldest surviving (so-called medieval) historical annals but was misunderstood by most of his contemporary antiquarians as 'Ireland,' when in fact the ancient events chronicled in these Irish sources had taken place in the ancestral Iranian homeland of Ireland's early settlers and not in their new adopted homeland:

> Can it then be wondered at, that the modern Irish are also ignorant of the ancient history of their ancestors? They read many fragments, which, for want of a due knowledge of Oriental geography, they cannot understand. Transactions of their ancestors in Iran they will refer to Eirin, a name of Ireland.[251]

On the other hand, Beaufort argued that one way of proving the Iran-Ireland connection in ancient times consisted of the following method:

> I. By the fables and the facts of Irish history—both of which are most curiously blended with circumstances recorded in that of Persia. Now the earliest history of every nation is the history of the parent country brought with them by the colonists, and transferred to the new country, which in the progress of time gradually becomes the imaginary seat of the various events originally recorded. This is so plainly the case with regard to much of the Irish history, as to excite a strong persuasion that the exact time of the peopling of Ireland might be satisfactorily made out, by ascertaining the period at which the Irish histories cease to be applicable to Persia and Spain, and become appropriate only to Ireland.
>
> Nor could these histories have been invented in support of the claim to Median [i.e., Iranian] descent, because the Irish books and MS. in which they are found, were written long before the annals of Iran had been made known to these countries through modern research.[252]

By incorporating actual or presumed oriental historical sources as supposedly foundational documents of Ireland's ancient past, these antiquarians were narrating European history through both non-European and European records in a manner that dissolved any clear-cut cultural-geographic binary distinctions between the West and the East in ancient times, at least in the case of Ireland—in a manner not even applicable to the somewhat more prolonged geographic diffusionist model of the Mosaic theory, which had also served as the basis for William Jones' account of language distributions across the globe. As hazy as various formulations of Mosaic theory generally happened to be, they followed a more incremental population distribution across the globe from Noah's post-diluvian home base (depending on whether Noah's Ark was believed to have come to rest on top of Mount Ararat in the Caucasus or on a mountain summit elsewhere in western Asia). The historical models of ancient Ireland proposed by Vallancey and most other Orient-centered Irish antiquarians claimed a rapid process of population and cultural transplantation from the Orient to Ireland. To build on Joep Leerssen's phrase "On the Edge of Europe: Ireland in Search of Oriental Roots,"[253] the Ireland of Vallancey, O'Brien, Beaufort, Betham, Moore, et al., was in fact in many ways a continued Eastern presence on one of the most westerly reaches of Europe, not only in terms of distant ancestry but also in a various range of surviving relics, language, legends, and belief systems. To jointly borrow Michel Foucault's concept of "heterotopia,"[254] Mikhail Bakhtin's "dialogic imagination,"[255] and Julia Kristeva's "Intertextuality,"[256] the Irish antiquarians in question were unconsciously or consciously engaged in a project of *dialogical heterotopic intertextuality*. They were selectively pulling threads from the vast canvas of world history in an intertextually dialogical process and producing their own tapestry of alternative heterotopic histories with accompanying historical convergences of time, place, and culture (in dialogue and contestation with other such world-historical tapestries of Irish origins). Simultaneously, to use a Bakhtinian term, many of the Irish antiquarian texts of this genre were "heteroglossic," but not merely because they incorporated a multiplicity of sources from different historical times, regions, and languages, as did many other antiquarian texts in general, or because of the visual assortment of different scripts, including oriental ones, appearing in polyglot texts by the likes of Vallancey. The Irish antiquarian texts in question were also heteroglossic on grounds of their mode of reading and interpreting the range of sources they utilized. These texts eclectically consulted oriental sources that in actuality did not allude to Ireland and Irish history, but were now rendered evidentiary sources revealing information about ancient Ireland. In other words, Irish history, ranging from the ethnicity of early populations of Ireland to the Irish language, Irish cultural beliefs and practices, material culture, and so on, was inserted into the consulted sources that were themselves otherwise silent on such historical connections. This historiographic method of affixing another voice to existing texts (a practice in some ways present as far back as 'medieval' Irish antiquarian manuscripts) engaged in a strategy of fusing histories of separate regions through an instrumentally syncretic process of parallel reading of juxtaposed histories and filling in the lacuna in one history through an abductive intertextual cross-referencing of the other history.

In their intertextual and heteroglossic engagement with former and new range of sources on the subject matter, these antiquarians also produced new modes of "ambivalences" (to borrow from Kristeva again) in the already dynamic narrations of Ireland's ancient past. Kristeva writes: "The term 'ambivalence' implies the insertion of history (society) into a text and of this text into history; for the writer, they are one and the same." She concludes by way of alluding to Bakhtin's work:

Dialogue appears most clearly in the structure of carnivalesque language, where symbolic relationships and analogy take precedence over substance-causality connections. The notion of *ambivalence* pertains to the permutation of the two spaces observed in the novelistic structure: dialogical space and monological space.[257]

Irish nationalist antiquarians were writing the Irish nation and the proclaimed glory of ancient Ireland into world history in dialogic refutation of Ireland's civilizational degeneracy and/or retardation. In this task, by interlinking Ireland's ancient past with other known ancient peoples and territories (whether historical or often mythological as it turns out), they each simultaneously engaged with diverse range of other existing accounts of Irish origins, while ultimately extracting out of this polyphonous dialogue what to them was a singular valid historical narrative in the form of a monologue that precluded other range of interpretations of Ireland's past (and hence also of Ireland's present connections to that past). Each of these monologues was in turn challenged in a dialogic, but not necessarily dialectical, fashion by other antiquarians, producing yet more monologues and consequent dialogues. As discussed in the next chapters, the nineteenth-century Irish nationalist poets Thomas Moore and James Clarence Mangan also deployed distinctive modes of *dialogical heterotopic intertextuality* in their Iran/Erin literary constructs, generating multiple historical and other narrative ambivalences of their own.

Moreover, read against Dipesh Chakrabarty's concept of "provincialising Europe,"[258] albeit applied in a very different historical framework here and evoking a very different range of counter-discourses of "modernity"—that is, in the framework of Irish nationalist counterpoint to English colonization and/or the denigration of pre-Norman Ireland as a civilizational void, characterized by a temporal *lagging-behind England*—, Vallancey, Beaufort, Moore, and much more so, Henry O'Brien, along with a host of other Irish nationalist antiquarians and cultural commentators, treated non-European histories as a constituent civilizational component of ancient European history, while also denying that civilization arrived in Ireland in the heels of English colonization. (This is not to suggest Irish antiquarians were unanimously inattentive to the role of contemporary non-European territories in the development of European territories, whether through imperial or other encounters and exchanges.) These Irish nationalist antiquarians were, in effect, *provincializing England* in civilizational terms at the very moment of the earliest arrival of English (Norman) conquerors in Ireland in the twelfth century, which initiated England's first large-scale territorial possessions outside mainland Britain (as part of what later became Britain's globally expanding empire). Cóilín Parsons, in his study of the Ordnance Survey of Ireland from 1820s to 1840s, with which Petrie, John O'Donovan, and James Clarence Mangan were associated at different stages, develops Edward Said's concept of "contrapuntal" in connection with the survey's stated project. Parsons observes: "As a principle for reading, counterpoint asks us to pay attention to the ways that new narratives emerge from competing themes, and that surprising conjunctions of text and context raise counterintuitive questions."[259] This element of counterpoint also applies to Irish nationalist antiquarianism at large, both in reaction to denigrating accounts of ancient Ireland and competing models of ancient Ireland posited by these antiquarians themselves. It was an outcome of this contrapuntal dialogical exchange that also *new* 'text[s] and context[s]' were introduced into the debate. Moreover, Irish nationalist antiquarians were consciously or unconsciously undermining the broader contemporary hegemonic and universalized narrative of the civilizing propensity of British imperial expansion in different reaches of the globe, including in Ireland—by denying England any civilizational superiority over Ireland before and after the twelfth century. The Orient-centered tradition in Irish antiquarianism since Keating in the seventeenth century—by no means to the complete exclusion of competing genres of Irish antiquarianism or other modes of antiquarianism—produced 'national' histories (initially in the form of the 'nation' defined as a territorial-ethnic-cultural construct and after the late eighteenth century as a multi-ethnic and multi-denominational territorial-cultural construct) that relied extensively on world history and on an increasingly cosmopolitan range of sources for documenting Ireland's oriental roots. These works sought to recover and (re)archive the temporal and spatial traces of the ancestry and cultures of the ancient Irish *before*, and *at the moment of*, as well as *subsequent to* their arrival in Ireland. This included the dissemination of presumed oriental practices and material culture in different regions of the island. Specially after Keating, each of these antiquarian authors also exhibited their own individual signs of "anxiety of influence" (to borrow Harold Bloom's phraseology) and refusal of deference; ultimately cultivating a surfeit of methodological innovations, often in highly contortionist evidentiary manner. In this style of antiquarianism, ancient Ireland was always situated in multiple historical trajectories of 'national' and transnational time and space.

Whither Irans? Contrasting Contemporary Irish and Iranian Nationalist Formulations of Ancient Iran

Significantly, Orient-centered Irish antiquarianism, even while some of its practitioners relied on entirely European sources, provincialized 'Europe' of ancient times—to again borrow Chakrabarty's postcolonial terminology of 'provincialising Europe,' albeit applied in a very different semantic and historical context here. Accordingly, many regions of ancient 'Europe' (here using a much later continental designation) had been an outpost of various oriental civilizations. *Contemporary* Ireland itself in these antiquarian works was simultaneously situated inside Europe (geographically and in terms of many social and political practices and values, among other factors) and outside Europe (in terms of traces of its indigenous culture and traditions). In reference to Indian history and following in the footsteps of Dipesh Chackrabarty's *Provincialising Europe*, but focusing on colonial India instead of Chackrabarty's postcolonial India, Vinay Lal has asserted that within the framework of world history

> British rule appears to have had the effect of erasing the consciousness of India's earlier, more democratic, and certainly more complex engagement with Asia. The most remarkable part of the story, namely the near excision from Indian memory of links to other parts of the globe, and the suspension of other civilizational dialogues, has seldom been told.[260]

Leaving aside here Lal's overarching construct of a territorial and civilizational-cultural entity called "India," among other fundamental exaggerations in his statement, Lal in effect maintains that British imperial domination produced a colonial historical amnesia and erased from memory the Indian subcontinent's prior and complex trans-territorial participation in the Afro-Asian, and one can also add European, commercial, and cultural exchange networks. Moreover, neglecting the subject of historical methodology here and essentializing the modes of education in British India, Lal asserts that the Western-educated Indian elite largely came to view the world through the British lens of world history (if we can assume there was even such a singular British historical lens at the time). Accordingly, this alleged perspective on world history was grounded in Britain's imperial and other range of engagements with the rest of the world, prioritizing those events and regions in world history that were of direct relevance and significance to British history and historical-political consciousness. This type of recurrent reasoning in studies of European imperialism in connection with the Indian subcontinent, the Middle East, or elsewhere, whether by Lal, Chakrabarty, and a host of Saidian and other similarly essentializing commentators, overlooks the frequent instances of local historical (and historiographic) *reactions* to imperialism in the colonized and semi-colonized regions—whether articulated in the form of nationalism or other modalities of identity constructs and resistance—that often operated alongside continued, albeit always dynamic, prior *local* historical and historiographic configurations. These reactive histories generated their own ostensibly *nativist* fictions and accompanying historical and contemporary worldviews that deviated from the presumably hegemonic imperial 'consciousness'—leaving aside here varying modes of counter-imperial consciousness present in so-called imperial metropoles themselves or examples of imperial agents situated in the colonized and semi-colonized regions who sought to "preserve" or "revive" local histories, mythologies, and lore, among many other such examples of alternative worldviews (whether or not such efforts were themselves imbued with other particular forms of *imperial* consciousness, including nostalgia for former "native" empires). Irish nationalist antiquarianism and nationalist historiographies after the late eighteenth century, alongside nationalist literatures, arts, sports, and other modes of "national" self-expression (with the *self* always being multivocal, elastic, and contested), were instances of counter-imperial worldviews (political and/or cultural), among their other potential range of worldviews, given that empire was never the sole defining modality of all experiences and identity formations in colonial and semi-colonial settings. In sharp contrast to the unpersuasive theoretical framings of Lal and Chakrabarty concerning the historical enterprise in India during and after British rule in the subcontinent, and without my homogenizing different local settings, in Ireland there was clearly a wide divide between any identifiable British "imperial" representations of the Irish past and Irish nationalist representations of that past, including the range of sources consulted by Vallancey, Beaufort, O'Brien, and others, notwithstanding other corresponding features of these 'imperial' and anti-imperial historiographies.

As a way of broadly contextualizing and additionally *worlding* Irish antiquarianism in the late eighteenth and early nineteenth century, it can be situated in the framework of persisting legendary accounts of ancient pasts in other parts of Europe and the rest of the world at the time. Moreover, in so far as Iran-centered accounts of ancient Ireland are concerned, it should be pointed out that many contemporary Iranians, as well as many among certain population groups in territories adjoining Iran, also still adhered to legendary traditions of the 'Iranian' past (in the broad geographical, historical, and cultural sense of Iran) *as historical facts*, including the mythical dynasties of Pishdādiān and Kiāniān. Until after the early nineteenth century, Iranians were extensively unaware of the *historical* Achaemenid dynasty that had ruled the region c. 550–330 BCE, or the much earlier Elamites, who had ruled southeastern regions of present Iran. Meanwhile, the Achaemenid Empire was long known to contemporary literate Europeans as a major center of ancient civilizations. This knowledge was primarily acquired through ancient Hellenic sources, even if these sources generally reviled the Persians as less civilized than "Greeks." Well into the late nineteenth century, Iranian historians of ancient Iran relied on a range of *local* and other sources that also included the few 'Iranian' texts consulted by Irish antiquarians who claimed an Iranian heritage for ancient Ireland. Among the sources widely utilized by Iranian historians were Ferdowsi's *Shāhnāmeh* and Mirkhond's *Universal History*, with a number of Iranian historians after the start of the nineteenth century also citing *Dabestān* and *Dasātir*. In addition to these texts and a wide range of other Persian- and Arabic-language sources, Iranian historians after the early decades of the nineteenth century gradually turned to histories of ancient Iran written by contemporary European authors, initially those in Western Europe and in British India.[261] These 'European' histories of ancient Iran, which in actuality transcended any fundamentally *European* configuration of knowledge production, generally incorporated Persian, Arabic, and other regional sources, alongside ancient Greek and Roman sources, while utilizing a wide array of historical methodologies. It was not until at least the second decade of the nineteenth century, in the case of a very small fraction of the more literate, highly informed, and historically minded Iranians exposed to the new genre of Western/European historical accounts of ancient Iran (by the likes of John Malcolm), that a very gradual transformation began to take place in Iranian historical, as opposed to *mytho*-historical, narrations of ancient Iran.[262]

Some of these European sources on ancient Iran were also consulted by Irish antiquarians subscribing to Iranian theories of Irish origins and/or of ancient Ireland's Iranian civilizational foundations through indirect transmission (as in the model of the Phoenician introduction of Iranian culture to Ireland). By relying on these new 'European' historical accounts of ancient Iran, both Iranian and Irish antiquarians at the time engaged in what they construed as the *recovery* (actual in the case of Iran and imaginative in the case of Ireland) of aspects of their "own" histories long absent in previously available historical sources and/or obscured under layers of mythology. The Irish antiquarians in question maintained that segments of ancient Iranian history also comprised the history of the ancient Irish from their *pre-Ireland* existence to their arrival and early settlement in Ireland, whereas for Iranian historians Ireland never featured in either historical or legendary extension of Iranian peoples or cultures to other reaches of the globe.

The fragmentary, as well as legendary, knowledge of ancient Iran on the part of Iranian historians was not entirely due to lack of sources somehow attributable to post seventh-century Arab-Muslim conquest, or to later Mongol and other external or internal incidences of destruction of manuscripts, libraries, or other repositories of information. Rather, it was also symptomatic of inadequate familiarity with a certain range of surviving sources, given the available Hellenic and Roman accounts of ancient Iran, irrespective of their tendentious representations of Persians. Another factor was the inaccurate identification by Iranian historians of the ancient Persian rulers mentioned in Jewish and Christian biblical sources, alongside the continued sway of certain mythological and mytho-historical traditions reinforced through different channels (namely poetry), without discounting the role of contemporary custodians of the predominant religion of Iran (Islam) in selectively devaluing the historical importance of pre-Islamic times, just as the popular embrace of Christianity in Ireland had for centuries devalued the pre-Christian past of the island. For instance, the first known Persian translation of Herodotus' *The Histories* (c.440 BCE) was only completed in 1829 by the Iranian Mirza Mohammad Ebrahim at the East India College in Haileybury (Hertfordshire, England),[263] which is not to say the general contours of Herodotus' work were entirely unknown to Iranians previously, given the wide-ranging Arabic translations, particularly after the ninth century CE, of classical Greek and Roman texts, most notably works on philosophy, politics, geography, sciences, and ethics—during the so-called Islamic Golden Age, which corresponded to the European 'Middle Ages'—with occasional references to works by the likes of Herodotus in some of those translations. Iranians familiar with other languages, too, could have had access to original or translated texts by Herodotus or other Hellenic or Romans authors. The substantial gaps in Iranian familiarity with Iran's ancient past were slowly remedied throughout the nineteenth century, following the introduction of Iranians to such European historical accounts of ancient pre-Islamic Iran as the first volume of John Malcolm's 1815 *The History of Persia*, which only a few Iranians familiar with English language could have read prior to the first complete translation of this volume of Malcolm's history into Persian in 1876 by Ismail Hayrat-Irani in Bombay (British India).[264] Some other Iranians likely had learned about the general contents of the book prior to its translation. The increasing awareness of previously unfamiliar particulars of ancient Iranian history did not inexorably erode the *historical* allure of otherwise legendary and mytho-historical narratives of ancient Iran; both forms of knowledge continued to co-exist in many Iranian scholarly circles as factual past, even if the likes of Malcolm, and later some Iranian historians, dismissed as fables such presumed periods of ancient Iranian history as Pishdādiān or Kiāniān eras. The nineteenth-century transformation in Iranian knowledge of ancient Iran was in many ways the joint outcome of translation projects inside Iran as well as the greater flow of information from, and/or translations of texts from European languages into more familiar regional languages occurring in India, the Ottoman Empire, Egypt, and parts of the Russian Empire; whether conducted by members of Iranian émigré communities—including efforts by the small number of Iranians residing in different parts of western and central Europe later in the century—, or by others fluent in Persian, or by Iranians inside Iran familiar with the languages spoken in surrounding territories. Another major contributing factor to this shift in Iranian familiarity with Iran's ancient past in the nineteenth century was the findings of European archaeologists operating in Iran and in neighboring territories.

In this framework, it is relevant to note that the reading public inside Iran (as opposed to Iranians in the Indian subcontinent) were largely introduced to the Mahābādiān dynastic cycle mentioned in *Dasātir* and *Dabestān* roughly about the same time as, if not even a few decades later than, some European audiences, including Irish antiquarian circles. Long before the invention of Mahābādiān, another legendary ancient Iranian dynasty, the Pishdādiān, was already part of the widely accepted factual history of Iran (in the broadest connotation of Iran). The Pishdādiān recurred in such works as *Shāhnāmeh* or Mirkhond's *Universal History*, among a wide range of other Persian and Arabic sources. The earliest Persian printing of *Dabestān*, which first introduced the Mahābādiān dynastic cycle, appeared in Calcutta in 1809; whereas the first published condensed English coverage of this text had appeared in 1789 (in the form of a published lecture given by William Jones at the Asiatic Society of Bengal in Calcutta). Moreover, given the later emergence of "nationalism" as a discernible *ideology* in Iran than in Ireland, due to particular historical conditions, it was not until the second half of the nineteenth century that the nationalist application of Mahābādiān, and hence the nationalist historical implications of *Dasātir* and *Dabestān*, first surfaced in Iranian nationalist discourses. This was in part due to the active promotion of *Dasātir* and *Dabestān* among key members of Iran's so-called modernist and secular-oriented nationalist coterie by Manekji Limji Hataria, the Zoroastrian Parsi representative from British India overseeing the welfare of the Zoroastrian community in Iran from 1854 to 1890 under the auspices of the Society for the Amelioration of the Condition of Zoroastrians in Persia. The most notable early example of politically instrumentalist absorption of these texts into the manifold discourses of Iranian nationalism through Hataria's influence was the first volume (1868) of *Nāmeh-ye Khosrovān: Dāstan-e Pādeshāhān-e Pārs beh Zabān-e Pārsi ... (Book of Royals)* by Jalal al-Din Mirza, a low-ranking member of Iran's ruling Qajar dynasty.[265] This occurred within a particular pattern of Iranian nationalist historicization of ancient Iran's allegedly pioneering civilizational status as the singular initiator of the Edenic Golden Age *of the World*, intended as a discursive strategy for further instilling national pride among Iranians through various narratives of the halcyon days of Iran (in the broad geo-cultural sense) at its purportedly highest, and unequivocally unique, civilizational standing in the world, followed by subsequent intermittent episodes of "decline," "advancement," and then unmistakable civilizational "loss" in the aftermath of the seventh-century Arab-Muslim conquests. *Nāmeh-ye Khosrovān*, which was intended as a textbook,

> traced Persian dynastic history from the origin of man to contemporary times [...] The author's objective was to offer a brief dynastic history aimed at highlighting the glories of pre-Islamic Iran in contrast to successive Arab and Turkish [and Mongol] invasions that brought about its decline.[266]

Underlining such Iranian nationalist narratives was the insistence on the existing prospect of, and intrinsic national propensity of Iranians for, "renewal" and "progress" of contemporary Iran's status as a member of leading civilized nations of the world.[267]

Nāmeh-ye Khosrovān followed *Dasātir's* and *Dabestān's* chronology of (mythical) ancient Iranian dynastic cycles prior to Alexander the Great's conquest of Iran, beginning with the Mahābādiān and followed by (the equally legendary) Pishdādiān and Kiānian, with no mention of the (historical) Achaemenid dynasty (which in fact had been terminated by Alexander's invasion of the Persian Empire)—even though Jalal al-Din Mirza was admittedly familiar with recent European sources on ancient Iran, from which he also borrowed the stylistic illustrations of Iranian rulers appearing in his book (illustrated by Abdul-Motaleb Isfahani).²⁶⁸ With the proliferation of mounting evidence throughout the nineteenth century of the existence of Achaemenid dynasty, many Iranian historians, and Parsi scholars in India, had earlier attempted to incorporate the Achaemenids into the existing (mytho-)history of ancient Iran (with or without the inclusion of the Mahābādiān, but retaining both the Pishdādiān and Kiānian dynasties).²⁶⁹ Notwithstanding Jalal al-Din Mirza's own presumably Turkic ethnic ancestry (assuming there are such clear-cut ethnic lineages), *Nāmeh-ye Khosrovān* was a vehemently Perso-centric, and in many ways "secular" (albeit with a strongly pro-Zoroastrian tinge), nationalist expression of pride in Iran's ancient past, with a clear reproach of Arab-Muslim invasion of Iran in the seventh century CE as a main marker of Iran's civilizational decline. Jalal al-Din Mirza's example bears some resemblance to the celebration of Ireland's ancient Gaelic past by Irish nationalist antiquarians and subsequent historians, whether of 'Gaelic,' English, Welsh, or Scots ethnic backgrounds. Among the novel aspects of Jalal al-Din Mirza's history were its composition in a presumably purified Persian language, devoid of Arabic and other loan words, and the book's contrast to preceding nineteenth-century (Muslim) Iranian historical surveys of 'Iran' since ancient times, which, while incorporating Pishdādiān and Kiānian dynastic eras, generally provided Qur'anic accounts of Creation and a chronicle of Judeo-Christian-Muslim prophets—frequently, and unsurprisingly, with heavy accent on the life of prophet Muhammad in Arabia. An example of the latter style of history from the period is Rezaqoli Khan Hedayat's 1866 *Ajmal al-Tawārikh*, which in its chronicle of ancient Iranian pre-Islamic dynasties even included the Mahābādiān dynastic cycle, along with Pishdādiān and Kiānian eras, based on *Dasātir* and *Dabestān* and the expressed authority of Azar Keyvan.²⁷⁰

The point here is that following Henry O'Brien's 1834 *The Round Towers*, some Irish antiquarians began to incorporate the (legendary) Mahābādiān of ancient 'Iran' into historical accounts of the origins of the Irish, well before Iranian nationalist and other historians began integrating the Mahābādiān dynastic cycle into their narratives of ancient Iran. In effect, with hindsight, the Iranian nationalist engagement with the Mahābādiān dynasty was a belated historiographic encounter, even if contemporary Iranians do not appear to have had any familiarity whatsoever with Irish antiquarianism. Another important factor in this context is that, whereas Iranians (in the broad sense) were among the intended target audiences of the (forged) neo-Zoroastrian texts *Dasātir* and *Dabestān*, or of the much earlier works such as the epic of *Shāhnāmeh* or Mirkhond's *Universal History*, the Irish antiquarians utilizing these sources for reconstructing Ireland's past were far from even the most remotely imagined audience groups for the authors of those works. In their accounts of ancient Irish history, Vallancey, O'Brien, and other similar range of Irish antiquarians engaged with *Dasātir* and *Dabestān* in a distinct historicizing framework and maneuver than those of Iranian historians—namely, in the context of ancient Ireland and contemporary implications of the presumed Iranian origins of the Irish for the Irish sentiment of national pride (cultural and/or political), in contrast to contemporary Iranian nationalist efforts to revitalize Iranian society, politics, and culture. Jalal al-Din Mirza and similar Iranian historians at the time had no knowledge of prior or ongoing grafting of ancient Irish history onto these (legendary) narratives of ancient Iran. At work here were different constellations of knowledge flow or traveling ideas. Sunil Sharma, albeit discussing a zone of direct and extensive cross-cultural exchanges (that of Iran and Mughal India from the sixteenth to eighteenth centuries), notes an interesting element of disparity in otherwise identical texts circulating in both the Mughal Empire and in Safavid Iran. This observation has broader interpretive application, as in the case of the circulation of *Dabestān*, *Dasātir*, *Shāhnāmeh*, Mirkhond's *Universal History*, and other such works in Iran and in Ireland respectively, while not forgetting also that in the case of *Dabestān* and *Dasātir*, these texts originated outside both Iran and Ireland. The particular texts discussed by Sharma are illustrated manuscripts, narrating the same stories but with different imagery, representing different local visual aesthetics, tastes, and cultural contextualization.[271] In the case of information about *Dabestān*, *Dasātir*, *Shāhnāmeh*, and other such works circulating in Iran and Ireland, and leaving aside the much longer tradition of historical application of *Shāhnāmeh* and Mirkhond's *Universal History* in Iran, as well as the topic of translation of these texts in the case of Ireland, what is of importance here is the respective local frames *of historical arrival* of those texts and their cultural and/or political interpretation and re-installation in keeping with distinct modes of Iranian and Irish nationalist imaginations and objectives. Here were examples of "Traveling Texts" (to borrow from Edward Said[272]) that had accidentally washed ashore in Ireland from 'Iran' and the Indian subcontinent across vast spatial and/or temporal expanse and infused into narratives of ancient Ireland and hailed by a motley group of antiquarians as containing the hitherto missing genealogical record of Irish origins—not forgetting that in the case of *Dasātir* and *Dabestān* at the time, these works were also incorporated more broadly into other ongoing European debates on the origins of languages and races/ethnicities through the initial agency of William Jones. Also of relevance here is Louis Althusser's concept of "interpellation," as developed in connection with "Other Peoples' Texts" by Ken S. Brown and Brennan Breed, in terms of how various groups read themselves into their presumed authoritative texts as if they were the intended addressees of particular passages of those texts.[273] Irish nationalist antiquarians were similarly interpellating the Irish 'nation' into 'Iranian' texts, which these antiquarians now cast as authoritative sources about Ireland's past, in this case also rendering other peoples' texts as their own presumably intended texts.

Then again, all texts and ideas ultimately circulate spatially and temporally beyond their initially intended audiences and are subjected to a range of interpretations independently of the intended expectations of their originators (assuming we can unequivocally identify an original author and context for the creation of the texts in question in the first place[274]). As Hans-Georg Gadamer noted long ago (although he wrongly attributed "objectivity" to history and presumed uniform identity constructs and interpretive acts in every historical Age):

> Every age has to understand a transmitted text in its own way, for the text belongs to the whole tradition whose content interests the age and in which it seeks to understand itself.

> The real meaning of a text, as it speaks to the interpreter, does not depend on the contingencies of the author and his original audience. It certainly is not identical with them, for it is always co-determined also by the historical situation of the interpreter and hence by the totality of the objective course of history.²⁷⁵

There remains the question of the extent to which Irish nationalist antiquarians who incorporated newly available translated oriental sources into their works—with antiquarians in this setting serving primarily as *cultural* and not linguistic translators of those sources—were bound by some acknowledged limits of historical (re-)interpretation. Gadamer, focusing on the role of the *linguistic* translator and acknowledging that "every translation is at the same time an interpretation," added:

> the translator must translate the meaning to be understood into the context in which the other speaker lives. This does not, of course, mean that he is at liberty to falsify the meaning of what the other person says. Rather, the meaning must be preserved, but since it must be understood within a new language world, it must establish its validity within it in a new way.²⁷⁶

The presumed standards of verification versus falsifiability of the original meaning of a text are always open to debate. In the case of historical accounts by Vallancey, Beaufort, O'Brien, and other such antiquarians of differing methodologies, who sought in the (mytho-)history of ancient Orient clues to Ireland's earliest cultures, it is difficult to determine where the boundaries of historical imaginations at the time should be drawn, given the prevalence of similar historical-hermeneutical methodologies by advocates of other theories of Irish origins—unless we somehow ascertain these antiquarians were *all* consciously fabricating and doctoring their proposed historical connections or were *all* simply delusional. At issue here is not the semantic limitations that Vallancey and O'Brien unquestionably trespassed, even by some of the more elastic standards of their own time. Rather, what needs to be addressed is the broader epistemological subject of manifold world-historical imaginations (spatial and temporal) of their milieu, particularly given the continued leverage of the biblical story of Creation and the Mosaic theory of population groups at the time. In the case of *Dasātir* and *Dabestān* specifically, and especially in regard to their nationalist applications in both Iran and Ireland of the nineteenth century, we are dealing with the 'after-life' and 'reception' of those texts in distinct settings, assuming any text (or "work of art" in Walter Benjamin's original formulation) can actually be said to have a particular life span associated with its initial moment of creation and/or availability to the public and its originator's expectations. In the distinct Iranian and Irish nationalist settings for the reception of *Dabestān* and *Dasātir*, there were also different renderings of what Benjamin (in "On the Concept of History") called the "now-time" of received histories. Benjamin wrote (albeit focusing on the ruling classes in his example):

> History is the subject of a construction whose site is not homogenous, empty time, but time filled by the now-time [*Jetztzeit*]. Thus, to Robespierre ancient Rome was a past charged with now-time, a past which he blasted out of the continuum of history. The French Revolution viewed itself as Rome reincarnate.²⁷⁷

Moreover, although Irish antiquarians and Iranian historians in question preceded the emergence of full-fledged historicist traditions in Ireland and Iran respectively, Benjamin's further commentary on now-time is also of great relevance here:

> Historicism contents itself with establishing a causal nexus among various moments in history. But no state of affairs having causal significance is for that very reason historical. It became historical posthumously, as it were, through events that may be separated from it by thousands of years. The historian who proceeds from this consideration ceases to tell the sequence of events like the beads of a rosary. He grasps the constellation into which his own era has entered, along with a very specific earlier one. Thus, he establishes a conception of the present as now-time shot through with splinters of messianic time.[278]

In the now-times of respectively Irish and Iranian historiographies in question, the original intended historical referentiality of *Dasātir* and *Dabestān* (if such an original intent can even be fully ascertained) was appended to the "messianic time" of nationalism.

"Modern" Iranian historiography at the turn of the twentieth century began to slowly break free of this mold of legendary accounts of ancient Iran, as in works produced by Mohammad Hussein Khan Foroughi (Zoka' al-Molk). Foroughi's seminal 1901 comprehensive history of Iran, prepared as a primer for students at the recently founded School of Political Science in Tehran (1899), offered a *corrected* version of ancient Iranian history, based on ancient Greek and Roman accounts and the more recent European histories of Iran. This history commenced with the Achaemenid dynasty and ditched the mythical dynasties. About a few decades earlier, Irish historians, too, were increasingly shedding mythical accounts of Ireland's past. Yet, not only did legendary accounts continue to recur as the actual past in the works of some Irish and Iranian historians for some time to come, but the broader nationalist appeal of the now largely acknowledged *legendary* accounts of the past was never fully cast aside in either Ireland or Iran. Iranian 'secular'-oriented nationalist discourses, whether adhering at this juncture to Foroughi's or Jalal al-Din Mirza's versions of Iran's past, and in contrast to some other modes of Iranian nationalist imaginations, unequivocally located the contemporary center of civilizational advancement in *the West*, with Iran depicted as *an* originator (in the case of Foroughi's history), if not *the* originator (in the case of Jalal al-Din Mirza's history) of advanced civilization in a distant past. Iranian nationalist recourse to ancient mythology was not abandoned outside the more specifically 'modern' historical texts. At the turn of the twentieth century, Ferdowsi's *Shāhnāmeh* gained renewed prominence in Iranian nationalist circles, fervently promoted in the early twentieth century as a *nationalizing* device even by historians who had abandoned Iran's legendary ancient past.[279] For instance, despite promoting a revisionist historiographic approach to ancient Iran, Foroughi was an ardent advocate of the 'national' value of wide propagation of *Shāhnāmeh* with its legendary accounts of the distant 'Iranian' past, beginning with Pishdādiān and Kiāniān dynasties, and with no mention of Achaemenids.[280] A similar sentiment pervaded the Irish Revival movement of the late nineteenth and early twentieth century, as also addressed in subsequent chapters in connection with Iran. This corresponding Irish trend was perhaps most succinctly expressed by the nationalist playwright and poet William Butler Yeats in 1887: "A nation's history is not in what it does, this invader or that other; the elements or destiny decides all that; but what a nation imagines that is its history, there is its heart; than its legends, a nation owns nothing more precious."[281]

Yet, 'national' mythologies, particularly those with episodes of fictional indigenous heroes battling imaginary "foreign" enemies, could also have an alienating effect in multi-ethnic societies with populations identified as presumably autochthonic (the "mere Irish"/Gaels or "Persians," respectively) and other groups now also comprising the nation, who traced their ethnic roots (actual or presumed) to "outside" invaders or other outside groups of times past. One could read the hostilities of the old legends into contemporary ethnic and/or religious, cultural, and other divisions and vice versa, deepening, rather than transcending, presumed or real historical traumas and grudges. Such projections of the past onto the present and vice versa could only further divide the nation and fuel intra-national chauvinisms in place of abetting the nationalist project of forging a common 'national' identity, not the least in resisting imperialism. While there were Iranian nationalists belonging to non-Persian ethnic groups who also played a leading role in perpetuating greater Iranian interest in ancient Persian mythology as a unifying national force, the primary body of Iranian legends utilized in this regard consisted of various episodes in the epic of *Shāhnāmeh*, with a pervasive danger of slippage from the nationally unifying power of this epic to the intra-Iranian sentiments of anti-Arab (and to a lesser extent anti-Turkic) chauvinism. On the other hand, the old legends, if carefully selected or assigned new connotations of a collective Self and the Other, could be crafted to inspire intra-national unity, pride, and resistance to outside forces, albeit with their own accompanying forms of xenophobia and ethnic/'racial' antipathy, as in the case of the Protestant Anglo-Irish Yeats' theatrical productions of cross-ethnic and cross-denominational Irish nationalist plays based on Irish mythology and directed at ongoing English domination of Ireland. Moreover, to avoid the potentially divisive pitfalls of some older legends, nationalists could also invent their very own mythology, as did Lady Isabella Augusta Gregory (née Persse; 1852–1932) and Yeats in *Kathleen ni Houlihan* (1902), again aimed at uniting the Irish across ethnic and confessional lines against continued British hegemony. By the end of the nineteenth century, Iranian nationalist literati also began to produce their own jointly invented and borrowed mythology, which, rather than looking back at Iran's presumed Golden Age prior to its ostensible decline following the Arab-Muslim invasions of the seventh century CE, turned its gaze to Iran's present predicaments. A case in point was the 1895 *Sālārnāmeh* by Mirza Aqa Khan Kermani, which heavily borrowed from *Shāhnāmeh* but continued that epic narrative up to and including the Iran of Kermani's own time (with an unequivocally "Aryanized" tinge).

However, there was a key distinction between the overwhelming Iranian nationalist literary recourse to existing legends, particularly those appearing in *Shāhnāmeh*, on the one hand, and Irish nationalist appeals to both invented mythology and the older traditions of Ulster or Fenian mythic cycles, on the other hand. This contrast between Irish and Iranian nationalist turn to mythology was astutely noted by Edward Granville Browne, the Cambridge Orientalist and leading British advocate of the Iranian Constitutional Revolution of 1906–11, who was also a supporter of Irish Home

Rule. In his 1914 *The Press and Poetry of Modern Persia*, Browne praised Irish nationalist poetry and literature since the Young Ireland movement in the mid-nineteenth century, and especially Yeats' play *Kathleen ni Houlihan*—which, it should again be added, was written with the substantial assistance of Lady Gregory and first performed in 1902, albeit much of the credit for the work unduly went to Yeats. In the latter play, Ireland was presented as an old woman, Kathleen (also spelled Cathleen), calling on her children to defend and protect her against aggressors. Browne, also highly acclaiming the Irish nationalist Alice Milligan's long poem *Hero Lays* (1908), noted:

> In Persia [...] ([in] early eleventh century of the Christian era) the great Firdawsi displays in the "Epic of the Kings" or *Shâh-Nâma* [...] spirit of pride in his nation and race and that love of heroic deeds and high achievements which the Arabs call *Hamâsa*. Such poetry in ancient times is, however, so far as my studies go, always of the triumphant, victorious, and imperialistic type; while of the more subtle and moving patriotic verse of the conquered and helpless nation (that verse wherein Ireland stands supreme), which can only strive to maintain its spiritual life under the more or less galling yoke of the foreign invader, and must sustain its sense of nationhood by memories of a glorious past and hopes of a happier future, there is hardly a trace in Persian or Arabic until this present century.[282]

The variants of Iranian nationalist historiography that celebrated pre-Islamic ancient Iran were laden with a similar sense of loss and nostalgia as in Irish nationalist historicizations of a glorious ancient Ireland (regardless of their particular claims of origins). But, in this regard, too, there was a subtle difference between Irish antiquarians of the late eighteenth and early nineteenth century and Iranian historians of the latter part of the nineteenth century. Whereas Irish antiquarians looked back to Ireland's professedly bygone civilizational splendor primarily as a means of countering English and other allegations of Irish barbarity prior to the arrival of Normans in Ireland (if not also claims of continued Gaelic-Irish barbarity to the present time), Iranian nationalist historians of 'secular' orientations (but not necessarily all groups of nationalists) pointed to their country's past ancient civilizational magnificence, not in response to any allegations of Iran's ancient barbarity (as Hellenic or Roman sources had previously alleged), but primarily as an act of bemoaning their own professedly subsequent civilizational deficit and malaise—generally blamed on Arab and Mongol invasions—and as a potential stimulant for a future-oriented revival of Iran's civilizational glory. To this end, many Iranian 'secular' nationalists sought to absorb and emulate certain cultural, political, and other such attributes of contemporary Western European societies, in addition to Western technology—which also appealed to some Iranian nationalists with strong religious convictions—in order to prevent Iran's further decline and likely colonization by European powers (namely England and Russia). In contrast, as discussed in greater detail in the next chapters, the post-United Irishmen nonsectarian Irish nationalist cultural discourses regarded contemporary Ireland as a largely neglected imperial outpost of England in the British Isles: once a 'nation,' now reduced to a 'province.' If anything, the Irish Revival after the late nineteenth century manifested a strong tendency to "de-Anglicize" Ireland by ridding Ireland of English cultural practices and, instead, reviving indigenous culture, including language and sports. As similar or different as

Irish and Iranian nationalist historiographies and cultural practices happened to be in these settings, they were not entirely dissimilar to the existing range of nationalist historiographies and cultural practices elsewhere around the world, particularly those in other colonized and semi-colonized territories. A common feature of all anti-imperialist *nationalist* histories is their claim of uniqueness, their own foundation myths, their celebration of a certain stage in their past as a Golden Age, lamentation of 'national' decline at some subsequent stage, and their regenerative appeal for a collective revival,[283] all of which include varying forms of 'invention of tradition.' In contrast to Iran, in the case of Ireland, it was in fact the nation's foundation story that was highly contested in nationalist circles, until at least the early part of the twentieth century.

The important question, with distinct answers based on different settings, is why do nations as "imagined communities" (to borrow Benedict Anderson's phrase[284]) turn to, resurrect, and/or invent certain traditions at particular historical junctures—whether these nations are initially conceived of in top-down, bottom-up, or some other fashion. Highly instructive in thinking through the competing theories of specifically 'Iranian' roots of ancient Ireland is Sumathi Ramaswamy's 2004 *The Lost Land of Lemuria: Fabulous Geographies, Catastrophic Histories*. Ramaswamy's book examines the history of an allegedly lost land where the Tamil people originated, in the manner of purported "lost continents" such as Atlantis. "Lemuria," believed to have been a vast continent south of the Indian subcontinent and stretching east in the direction of Australia and west toward the eastern coast of Africa, first appeared in print in 1864 in an essay on zoology in a British publication, without any reference to the Tamil people. Among the early claimants of Lemuria as a lost homeland was the late nineteenth-century Theosophical Society founded by Madame Blavatsky, which designated Lemuria the homeland of the Third Root-Race of beings in the evolutionary process of the modern Fourth Root-Race of human beings (the Fourth Root-Race, in turn, evolving into future and higher Root-Races).[285] Although the various articulations of Lemuria ("Kumarikkaṇṭam" in the Tamil language) concern a lost place of origins, as opposed to Irish antiquarian claims of an originary homeland of the Gaels in 'Iran' or other parts of the Orient, or Scandinavia—that is, territorial entities that could still be geographically mapped in some form—, there is nonetheless a striking correspondence between the Tamil belief in Lemuria and Irish assertions of a long forgotten, yet retrievable, Iranian origin of the Irish. Tamil accounts of Lemuria as their ancestral land after the turn of the twentieth century were a reaction to both colonial and Indian "Aryanist" downgrading of Tamil culture. There was a similar logic to Irish versions of Iranian or other so-called oriental *history-making* since the late eighteenth century. In both cases, the particular claims of ancestral homelands occurred in the framework of entry onto the modern stage of nationalist politics. On the one hand, there was the Tamil ethno-nationalism in reaction to Aryanist "Indian" ethno-nationalism. On the other hand, there was a burgeoning cross-ethnic, and later also cross-denominational, Irish cultural nationalism that was responding to colonial and other vilifications of the presumably indigenous Irish culture.[286] (This Irish endeavor had somewhat ambivalent roots in earlier works such as Keating's 1634 *The History of Ireland* (*Foras Feasa ar Éirinn*) and Roderic O'Flaherty's 1685 *Ogygia*. While Keating's vindications of the cultural-ethnic identity of Gaelic and

Gaelicized Irish paralleled the later antiquarian cultural-'nationalist' undertaking, O'Flaherty was also defending the Catholic faith.) In the mode of Michel Foucault's concept of 'insurrection of subjugated knowledges,' Ramaswamy writes of the Tamil myth of Lemuria:

> I propose that this preoccupation with the lost—and with the vanished, the disappeared, the hidden and the forgotten—is an inevitable, even irresistible, condition of modernity, but that its poetics and politics vary across life-worlds, ideologies, disciplines. I suggest that high modernity has not been merely preoccupied with progress and advance, but also with loss and disappearance. Correspondingly, loss is good to think in regard to what it means to be modern.
>
> And so, this is as well a book about disenchantment. Or more correctly, it is about the refusal to give up (entirely) on enchantment in a late-modern world where disenchantment is offered as the desirable norm to which we should all aspire as true moderns. As the rationalizations and intellectualizations of our physical and human sciences disavow truths that once mattered and discard wonders that had once captivated, the world is leached of magic, mystery, and marvel. How is a lost place made in the wake of such disenchantment? This, too, is one of my concerns.
>
> [...]
>
> I consider Lemuria as a *place-world* that is the product of varied *labors of loss* underwritten by place-making imaginations that I characterize as *fabulous* and *catastrophic*. The history that I document is necessarily *off-modern*, *eccentric*, and *oppositional*, as it foregrounds matters that have been marginal in their own time in their own place, or have been deemed unworthy of the professional scholar's attention.[287]

In the case of Irish antiquarianism, the disparate oriental theories of Irish origins were certainly not "marginal in their own time in their own place," given the predominance and prominence of the practitioners of these theories in the ranks of the Royal Irish Academy and outside the Academy until at least the 1840s. Nor were these theories considered "*off-modern*" by their practitioners, many of whom wrapped themselves in the purportedly scientific garb of the (European) Enlightenment thought, not to mention the 'modern' foundations of nationalism. Modernity is not ready-made, it grows out of what came before and is always tinged in its present state with some elements of the past or so-called 'tradition,' which itself is always in the process of transmuting. Modernity, then or now, has never initiated a complete caesura with what continually precedes it and is generally labeled 'tradition.' As the process of modernity evolves, it always constantly extends into the future and produces its own past flow of so-called traditions as well.[288] Neither has modernity been geo-culturally instantaneous nor foundationally singular in its composition, theoretical manifestations, and practices.[289] As far as Ireland's relation with England and colonial modernities are concerned, Ireland was both a recipient of and a contributor to Britain's imperial modernities (intellectually, administratively, militarily, infrastructurally—including shipbuilding—, commercially, financially, culturally, and in many other ways), while also functioning within the broader parameters of global modernities that were not solely circumscribed by its ties to the British Empire. In fact, Irish nationalist antiquarianism was an instance of the manifold and evolving Irish anticolonial modernities, no matter how intersecting and often interdependent nationalist and imperial modernities happened to be. To paraphrase Ramaswamy's final sentence in the above quotation and apply it to the Irish context under consideration, it can be said that by the early twentieth century, the *older* mode of Irish antiquarianism was discarded as "*off-modern, eccentric,* and *oppositional,* [...] [and] deemed unworthy of the professional scholar's attention."

Irish nationalist antiquarians of the late eighteenth and early nineteenth centuries, too, were concerned with the lost and the forgotten: that of resurrecting ancient Ireland's civilizational sophistication and enchantment. They, too, were engaged in what ultimately proved to be 'labors of loss,' a term originally used by Georges Bataille and here applied in its different usage by Ramaswamy: "labors of loss are those disciplinary practices, interpretive acts, and narrative moves which declare something as lost, only to 'find' them through modernity's knowledge protocols, the very act of discovery and naming constituting the originary loss."[290] One major difference between Lemuria and Irish antiquarian accounts of ancient Ireland is that while Lemuria is consigned to a time "before any *surviving* recorded history,"[291] Irish antiquarians claimed various range of existing recorded evidence for much, if not all, of the ancient past they claimed to be recovering. Central to Irish nationalist historiography, to borrow Dilip Menon's phrase from another colonial context,[292] was the notion of Ireland's long glorious history in contrast to the "abbreviated time" of colonialism since the gradual Norman conquests after the twelfth century. (In these nationalist narratives, the Norse settlements and the (pseudo-)historical accounts of ancient colonizations of parts or all of Ireland by Tuatha de Dananns or by Milesians, for instance, were exempted from the category of colonialism as applied to England.) If the abbreviated time of colonialism was a "political" time in Irish nationalist historiography, then the pre-colonial era (i.e., pre-Norman conquests), and particularly the proclaimed ancient Golden Age of Ireland, was rendered doubly political—both on grounds of Ireland's ancient superiority to England and in contrast to the colonial time of England's subjugation of Ireland. The ancient past in these antiquarian accounts was always elastically extended into colonial time (up to the present), and colonial time was overshadowed by the longevity of, and pride in, that past. The advent of Irish nationalist modernity (as obscure as such beginnings are) was inexorably followed by more 'modern' modes of historical interrogation of the past; not the least due to the persistence of heated antiquarian clashes over the unsettled question of Irish origins and Ireland's antiquity, rendering that foundational past contested and ambivalent. After the 1840s, the former styles of Irish antiquarianism, which were still manifested in works by Thomas Moore, William Betham, and many others, were increasingly challenged (although not entirely obliterated) by another expression of modernity—what Max Weber later termed in a different context the "disenchantment" (*Entzauberung*) effect.[293] By the 1840s, more rigorous historical methods of verification, source selection, comparative historical analyses, among other features, were strangulating the extensively speculative antiquarian modes of analyses, with even the designation "antiquarian" gradually sounding outmoded and eventually dropped in favor of "historian" by many scholars of ancient history. By the latter part of the nineteenth century, this new style of historiography, albeit with its own flaws and disenchantments, and constantly evolving, was in clear ascendance, as former methodologies receded from the scene, but did not entirely vanish. Nonetheless, despite incremental methodological refinements, the question of Irish origins itself remained largely unsettled until the end of the century.

The notion of a lost ancestral homeland akin to Atlantis or Lemuria was by no means absent from Irish accounts of origins, most famously in the case of Roderic O'Flaherty's 1685 *Ogygia*, which was defended by some subsequent antiquarians.[294] However, the likes of Vallancey, Beaufort, O'Brien, Betham, and Moore were not so much engaged in *actual* "place-making," in the sense of seeking to establish the existence of an ancestral homeland now cartographically absent from the world's landmass, as is the case with Lemuria, but rather a place-making in the sense of retracing the story of Ireland's ancient origins to the Orient and providing an *ontic mapping* of the departure from the Orient and arrival in Ireland of the ancestry of the Irish, in what was ultimately a project of ancestral *culture-making* or civilizational grounding. Theirs was not a recuperative account of a vanished ancestral homeland, but that of retrieving and reclaiming Ireland's ties to specific lands and ancient cultures in the Orient. In the Iran-Erin setting, Irish antiquarians were (imaginatively) re-branching ancient Iranian history (in competing narrative forms and plots, including in Thomas Moore's version of indirect Iranian civilizational diffusion to Ireland by way of Phoenicians), in a manner entirely unbeknownst to contemporary Iranians themselves. These reconstructed new chapters in *the world history of Iran* remained 'nationally' confined to contemporary Ireland and the Irish diaspora (with Ireland's very origins also constituting a form of diaspora). In contrast to Lemuria's 'labors of loss,' the Irish antiquarian search for oriental roots was a resuscitative undertaking of allegedly documented history and surviving traces and relics, and hence an act of recall and remembrance through existing textual archives, artifacts, and beliefs and practices. This was a labor of recovery and genealogy counteracting the ruinous effects of not merely *natural time* but also *political time* as in the alleged depletion of the nation's memory of its distant past wrought by English colonialism. (In this context, the introduction of Christianity to Ireland in the fifth century was pragmatically left out of the narrative of historical erasures and induced amnesia of Ireland's more distant past.) Seen in this light, the efforts of the likes of Vallancey, Beaufort, Henry O'Brien, and others also involved their assemblage of alternative archives of forgotten or overlooked historical documents of Ireland's ancient past—by means of inserting pages from the (actual or mythic) ancient histories of 'Iranians' or other 'oriental' peoples in place of the missing pages in Ireland's existing history. In the broader resuscitative projects of oriental origins of the Irish in general, the Round Towers served as the foremost marker of what Pierre Nora has termed "sites of memory."[295] These towers now served as sites of 'national' pride and as presumed historical reservoirs for both reactivating national memory and defying castigating accounts of Ireland's pre-Norman civilization, while simultaneously also functioning as national "sites of mourning" (to borrow Jay Winter's concept from a different context[296])—as reminders of the vanished Golden Age. Gradually (but not entirely) new modes of methodology deployed in mainstream Irish nationalist historiographic debates bulldozed over the oriental theories of Irish origins. George Petrie's discrediting of oriental theories of the origin of the Round Towers called into question more than ever before the remainder of ascribed oriental ties of ancient Ireland by diverse groups of Irish antiquarians. In the meantime, other forms of presumed textual and oral evidence of connections between ancient Ireland and Iran found their way into the debate on Irish origins. Following the highly contentious debates in the latter decades of the eighteenth century surrounding Macpherson's claim of the Scottish origin of the Ossianic Cycle, by the middle of the nineteenth century Irish nationalists increasingly turned to Ireland's heroic epics as a means of propagating a national-cultural "revival" and a collective sense of pride in Gaelic traditions (with the old legends often remolded into new forms). This move, which was accelerated after the emergence of the Young Ireland circle in the 1840s, reached its pinnacle at the turn of the twentieth century. As a component of this renewed nationalist emphasis on Irish heroic cycles, beginning in the late eighteenth century a debate got underway as to whether Ireland's heroic cycles, and mythologies in general, also contained traces of the origins of the Irish. As discussed in the next chapters, it was in this setting that Vallancey suggested the main frame of the Fenian Cycle was derived from an ancient Iranian epic, while Louisa Catherine Beaufort later alleged that one of Ireland's central heroic tales appearing in the Ulster Cycle, that of Cuchulain (Chuchulain / Cú Chulainn) and his son Conla (Conlaoch), must have originated in Iranian lands.

The Persistence of Oriental Theories of Irish Origins and the Emergent Aryanist Constructs of the Gaels

It is important to keep in mind the highly dynamic nature and continually changing parameters of debates on Irish origins over time. Not only were there wide-ranging gradations to competing claims of oriental origins of the Irish, including in the specifically Iranian and even more narrowly Persian models, but there were also disparate range of participants, with the debates frequently segueing from one particular context to another and assuming new tenor in keeping with other developments over time, alongside commentaries by individuals outside Irish antiquarian circles. An example of this from the second half of the nineteenth century (1862 in this case) is the comparative civilizational verdict of the English (and Catholic) Lord Acton, the Naples-born John Emerich Edward Dalberg-Acton, a prominent historian, an editor of the Catholic periodical *The Rambler* (later renamed the *Home and Foreign Review*, 1862–64), and a holder of an Irish seat (for Carlow) in the British parliament from 1859 to 1865.[297] Acton, without disclaiming the self-orientalizing gesture of Irish antiquarians in question by merely avoiding the subject, and acquiescing to Irish cultural superiority in the twelfth century over the Anglo-Norman invaders of Ireland, posited a very mixed civilizational characterization of ancient Orient itself (in this case also inclusive of East Asia). Given the period when he was writing (see below), Acton was operating within the standard currents of blinkered classification of different so-called ethnicities as either inherently capable of civilizational achievement, as in the case of ancient "Persia" in his model, or incapable of such achievement *on their own*, bizarrely as in the case of "Chinese" and "Hindoos." He averred an originally derivative, and *ever since* inert, Irish racial and accompanying civilizational trait (i.e., as ethno-civilizationally Celtic). Regarding the Celtic civilization itself as a derivative, rather than an original and/or evolving, civilization, Acton contrasted the Celts with, among others, the ancient Persians—the latter identified as belonging to one of the major civilizational fountainheads in history and, hence, as originators of civilizations. Acton was defending Catholicism, and Irish Catholics in particular, against accusations of spiritual depravity by another English historian, Goldwin Smith. In a widely quoted statement, Acton wrote in an article in the March 1862 issue of *The Rambler*:

> Mr[.] Goldwin Smith mistakes the character of the invasion of Ireland because he has not understood the relative position of the civilisation of the two countries at the time when it occurred. That of the Celts was in many respects more refined than that of the Normans. The Celts are not among the progressive, initiative races, but among those which supply the materials rather than the impulse of history, and are either stationary or retrogressive. The Persians, the Greeks, the Romans, and the Teutons are the only makers of history, the only authors of advancement. Other races possessing a highly developed language, a copious literature, a speculative religion, enjoying luxury and art, attain to a certain pitch of cultivation which they are unable either to communicate or to increase. They are a negative element in the world; sometimes the barrier, sometimes the instrument, sometimes the material of those races to whom it is given to originate and to advance. Their existence is either passive, or reactionary and destructive [...]. The Chinese are a people of this kind. They have long remained stationary, and succeeded in excluding the influences of general history So the Hindoos; being Pantheists, they have no history of their own, but supply objects for commerce and for conquest. So the Huns [...].
>
> To this class of nations also belong the Celts of Gaul. The Roman and the German conquerors have not altered their character as it was drawn two thousand years ago. They have a history, but it is not theirs; their nature remains unchanged, their history is the history of the invaders. The revolution was the revival of the conquered race, and their reaction against the creations of their masters. But it has been cunning only to destroy [...].
>
> The Celts of these islands, in like manner, waited for a foreign influence to set in action the rich treasure which in their own hands could be of no avail. Their language was more flexible, their poetry and music more copious, than those of the Anglo-Normans. Their laws, if we may judge from those of Wales, display a society in some respects highly cultivated. But, like the rest of that group of nations to which they belong, there was not in them the incentive to action and progress which is given by the consciousness of a part in human destiny, by the inspiration of a high idea, or even by the natural development of institutions. Their life and literature were aimless and wasteful.[298]

Acton's refutation of Goldwin Smith's judgment on Gaelic culture points to the continued persistence of virulent 'British' strains of the 'wild Irish' fable that no longer necessarily resorted to orientalizing of ancient Ireland (as in the case of earlier tracing of Irish ancestry to Scythians *while* labeling the latter savages). In this context, Acton was also engaged in demarcating what Partha Chatterjee would later define in a different context as "spiritual" versus "material" civilizational domains.[299] Debates on race and civilization were themselves continually evolving and assuming different connotations and applications. By the end of the nineteenth century, with the so-called "whitening" of the Irish-Gaelic "race" in mainstream British racial classifications, a new variation of the 'wild Irish' parable was taking shape in British imperial discourses, targeting not so much the Gaelic and Gaelicized Irish and/or Irish Catholics, but specifically Irish nationalists of *all backgrounds*, as being irrationally hostile to civilizational progress, with England ostensibly as the purveyor of that progress in Ireland. By then, chafing against this assertion of English civilizing mission was also the memory of the Irish Great Famine of 1845–51, which many opponents of Irish nationalism blamed on the Irish themselves. A much later example of British imperialist vilifications of Irish nationalists as fundamentally hostile to societal advancement was the exchange that took place during a special foreign affairs debate in the British House of Commons on July 10, 1912. The joint Anglo-Russian imperial intrusion in Iranian affairs was a foremost topic in this debate. By then, following the 1906 Iranian Constitutional Revolution and the 1907 Anglo-Russian Agreement (as discussed in Chapter Seven), a broad multi-party opposition had formed in the United Kingdom to counter London's and St. Petersburg's meddling in Iranian affairs contra the Iranian constitutionalist-nationalist camps. The opposition to London's Iranian policy included members of the "Home Rule" Irish Parliamentary Party. The 1912 parliamentary debate on Iran focused on the joint British and Russian promotion of a trans-Iranian railway scheme to be constructed by an international consortium without consultation with Iranian authorities. This was occurring in the immediate aftermath of the Anglo-Russian suppression of the Iranian Constitutional Revolution in late December of 1911. Most Iranian nationalists and their supporters in the United Kingdom feared the proposed railway was a preliminary step in the direction of Iran's formal partition between Britain and Russia. A participant in the 1912 British parliamentary debate was the prominent Irish Parliamentary Party member of parliament (MP) John Dillon, a leading critic of London's Iranian policy among his many other extra-Irish anti-imperialist endeavors.[300] In a contemptuous statement singling out Dillon in the Iranian debate, the Conservative (Unionist) MP Mark Sykes noted:

> The hon. Member cannot possibly forget anyone who brings order and prosperity to a distracted country. I can perfectly well understand it, because order and prosperity in countries like Ireland and Egypt are opposed to the kind of politics in which [Irish] Nationalists take a part.[301]

By the time Acton's article appeared in the 1862 issue of *The Rambler*, debates on Irish origins had become highly racialized, with contending camps primarily arguing whether the Gaels (categorized as Celts or otherwise) and other early population groups settling in ancient Ireland belonged to the Aryan branch of so-called races, with the Aryan race placed at the apex of the racial hierarchy in mainstream Western/European racial discourses and variously assigned its own contested internal ranking order. The controversy over Irish origins was not fully resolved in the nineteenth century. As the leverage of older antiquarian theories began to recede in scholarly circles, the Aryan thread in those theories (oriental or otherwise) gained greater momentum in the second half of the century, also initiating a new range of explicitly Aryan-centered theories and counter-theories of Ireland's oriental roots, in a similar highly politicized nationalist form as before. There now emerged extensively racialized and contentious Aryanist platforms that, despite their highfalutin claims of scientific objectivity, remained anchored in many of the late eighteenth-century Aryanist suppositions and continued the former pattern of mangling the various branches of human languages under the unsubstantiated guise of racial affinities and differences among population groups. Among numerous examples of this range of theories, which continued to insist on Persian, Irano-Scythian, and/or Phoenician and other similar oriental origins of the Gaels in the framework of the more highly accentuated Aryanist discourses in the second half of the century, was the 1868 *An Illustrated History of Ireland* by Margaret Anna Cusack, a nun, prolific author, and moderate Irish nationalist, who was an Anglican convert to Catholicism before reverting back to Anglicanism. In this book, and in her subsequent widely researched and highly analytical works by the standards of the day, she also relied on a broad range of earlier antiquarian sources, alongside Petrie's publications.[302] Also citing biblical authority, Cusack assigned a Scythian-Phoenician "Aryan" origin to the first Celtic settlers in Ireland, who in her account arrived after the earlier "Assyrian" settlers in Ireland led by Partholan, who in turn had arrived on the island following other earlier population settlements.[303] More than two-and-a-half centuries after Keating's *The History of Ireland*, some Irish historians continued to confidently resound the theory of Scythian colonization of Ireland in ancient times in one form or another. However, by the time Cusack's book appeared, the horizon of Mosaic theories of population groups in debates on Irish origins was rapidly shrinking, although not entirely vanishing.

The Irish nationalist genealogist John O'Hart, in the first volume of his 1892 edition of the by-then highly popular *Irish Pedigrees; or, the Origin and Stem of the Irish Nation*, which also claimed a Scythian ancestry for Ireland's ancient Gaelic population, similarly incorporated into his particular model the now-prevalent Aryanist discourse. O'Hart utilized the post eighteenth-century European association of Scythians with ancient Parthians (linguistically an Iranian group). *Irish Pedigrees* had originally appeared in 1876 but was significantly revised by 1892. Citing the 1768 *Dictionary* of Dr. John O'Brien, the Bishop of Cloyne, O'Hart noted: "In his Dictionary Dr. O'Brien states that the word 'Scythian' is derived from the Celtic word *sciot*, which, in the Irish language signifies a dart or arrow; and this derivation seems probable, as the Scythian nations, particularly the Parthians, were all famous archers."[304] O'Hart then identified the Celts as the most ubiquitous and enduring ancestry of the ancient Irish and as belonging to the "Caucasian" race (another designation for Aryans), into which category O'Hart casually lumped together different population groups that had historically inhabited western and southern Asia[305]—notwithstanding over a century of post-Jonesian philological re-classifications, including by the likes of the prominent Oxford linguist Friedrich Max Müller in the second half of the nineteenth century. O'Hart, who incidentally embraced the biblical belief in monogenesis and, at least in theory, advocated racial equality ("God has made of one blood all nations of men and the most positive identity exists among them all"), almost randomly tossed into the same racial cauldron as the Celts multitudes of distinct linguistic and cultural groups. Entirely misunderstanding the Persian suffix "-stan" (implying land/territory) with "tan," and stirring in a mélange of Mosaic and Jonesian and post-Jonesian ethnic-racial categorization of Caucasians, while also resorting to a Vallanceyan style hyper-etymological method, which in this case simultaneously moved along different trajectories of time and space, O'Hart noted:

The Celts were the first inhabitants of Europe after the Deluge.

The Celts were of the Caucasian race—a race which included (with the exception of the Lapps and Finns) the ancient and modern Europeans and Western Asiatics, such as the Assyrians, Babylonians, Medes, Persians, Scythians, Parthians, Arabs, Jews, Syrians, Turks, Afghans, and Hindoos. To these must also be added the European colonists who have settled in America, Australia, and other parts of the world. [...]

In his Irish Dictionary [1768], Dr. [John] O'Brien derives from the Celtic many names of countries terminating in *tan*: as Britan or Britain; Aquitain, in Gaul; Lusitan or Lusitania, the ancient name of Portugal; Mauritan or Mauritania, the land of the Moors; Arabistan, the land of the Arabs; Turkistan, the land of the Turks; Kurdistan, the land of the Kurds; Farsistan, Luristan, etc., in Persia; Caffristan and Afghanistan, the lands of the Caffres and the Afghans; Hindostan, the land of the Hindoos; etc.

A great affinity between the Celtic and the Sanscrit languages has also been shown by many etymologists; and the word "Sanscrit," itself, has been derived from the Celtic word *Seanscrobhiha* [sanskrivta], which signifies "old writings," and has the same signification in the Irish language. As the Sanscrit is one of the most ancient of languages, we can therefore form an idea of the great antiquity of the Celtic.[306]

This work, retaining the Fénius Farsaid (ostensibly Japhetic) line of Gaelic descent, reiterated the Scoti (Scuti, that is Scythian) etymological affinities of Gaelic language (notwithstanding the historical absence thus far of evidence for a Scythian script and vocabulary, with the exception of a few hazy comments by Herodotus), categorized the Gaels as a Celtic population group and conflated Parthians (whose empire from 247 BCE to 224 CE included Iranian territories at large) as a branch of Scythians (rather than both population groups belonging to the larger Iranian linguistic group).[307] Notably, however, O'Hart denied a significant cultural legacy attributable to the allegedly Parthian-Scythian settlers in ancient Ireland. Instead (and this time correctly differentiating Persians and Parthians as two branches of Iranian groups), he highlighted the continued cultural relevance in Ireland of a population group arriving after the initial Parthian settlers, that of the *Persianized* Scythians, who evidently had either arrived directly from Persian territories after having settled there for some time or after a period of resettlement in Greek territories. While interjecting his own version of Aryan/Caucasian racial theory into this model, in his reconstruction of the lineage of the ancient Irish O'Hart relied heavily on much earlier works, including new editions of the seventeenth-century *Annals of the Four Masters*. Most significantly, among the surviving relics of O'Hart's alleged Persian cultural heritage in ancient Ireland were, once again, the Round Towers:

4. *The Firbolgs or Firvolgians*, who were also Scythians, divided Ireland amongst the five sons of their leader Dela Mac Loich [...]. The Firvolgians ruled over Connaught down to the third century [...] and the sovereignty of Connaught was then transferred to the Milesians [...]. The Firbolg race never after acquired any authority in Ireland, being reduced to the ranks of farmers and peasants; but they were until very numerous, and to this day a great many of the peasantry, particularly in Connaught, are considered to be of Firbolg origin.

5. *The Tuatha de Danans*, also of the Scythian family, invaded Ireland thirty-six years after the plantation by the Firbolgs. According to some annalists, they came originally from Persia, and to others, from Greece; and were located chiefly at Tara in Meath, at Croaghan

in Connaught, and at Aileach in Donegal, The Danans being highly skilled in the arts. the Round Towers of Ireland are supposed to have been built by them. [...].[308]

In the second volume of the 1892 edition of *Irish Pedigrees*, while discussing the many possible derivations of Ireland's name, O'Hart was much more categorical about his own identification of the Tuatha de Danann as a Persian colony:

> Vallancey supposed "Erin" to be the same as "Iran," the ancient name of Persia; and [Henry] O'Brien, in his book on the "Round Towers," maintains the same opinion: namely, that "Erin" or "Irin" is the same as "Iran" or Persia, and says that, in the Persian language, it signifies *the sacred land*, and that it got this name from the colony of Tua-De-Danans who came to Ireland from Iran or Persia; and it may be observed that the old Irish historians state that Ireland got the name "Eire" from one of the Danan queens.[309]

By 1892, when the fifth edition of John O'Hart's *Irish Pedigrees* was published, in which O'Hart now insisted on the Aryan roots of the Gaelic population of Ireland, in addition to the Aryan origins of the Round Towers and the alleged derivation of Ireland's name (i.e., Erin), a wide range of other ostensibly surviving traces of ancient civilizational affinities between Iran and Ireland were being postulated in some Irish nationalist circles. As discussed in subsequent chapters of the present book, in the latter decades of the nineteenth century the search for the origins of the Irish and of ancient Irish cultures was further reinvigorated by increased attention to folklore and other past and current cultural traditions, with varying presumed oriental connections also proposed in this context. Among the leading publications in the field of Irish folklore studies in the latter part of the nineteenth century were works by Lady Jane Francesca Agnes Wilde, the principal proponent of the theory of ancient Iranian roots of some of Ireland's foremost surviving folk beliefs and practices (see Chapter Six). These latter claims also found resonance in other spheres of Irish cultural nationalism, which included individuals affiliated with theosophical circles in the Irish Literary Revival.

These later expressions of ancient affinities between Ireland and Iran also utilized Aryanist discourses of race and civilization. In the latter quarter of the nineteenth century, many English theoreticians of racial hierarchy were already incorporating the Gaelic "mere Irish" into the Aryan category of racial divisions and classifying them as lesser 'white' peoples within the British imperial configuration, with "Aryan" and "whiteness" in this equation treated as being synonymous.[310] A similar development was taking place in the United States, where the Irish—specifically the Catholic Irish-Americans of presumed Gaelic background—had been regarded as less than white in the dominant white racialist theories.[311] As a confluence of these varied Aryanist propensities in the early years of the twentieth century and continuing into the First World War, as discussed in more detail in Chapter Seven, particular oriental theories of Irish origins (either explicitly or in consciously ambiguous forms) were instrumentalized with a specifically "pan-Aryan" inflection by some radical Irish nationalists, with the aim of building cross-territorial anti-British solidarity, namely between the Irish, Indians, and Iranians. For instance, in the opening years of the twentieth century, militant Irish nationalist circle in the United States, who adhered to Aryanist ideologies, formulated a (anti-"British Empire") pan-Aryan platform. This was carried out in collaboration with segments of militant Indian nationalists in the United States and, abortively, was also aimed at attracting the "racial" solidarity of Iranian nationalists in a united anti-British front. By then, however, a particular model of Irish origins, claiming a *European*-Celtic origin of the Gaels, in common with other early population settlements in the remainder of the British Isles, had assumed general scholarly consensus in Ireland and in the ranks of Irish nationalist historians. Nevertheless, Dr. Edmund Crosby Quiggin, the prominent Celtic scholar at Caius College, University of Cambridge, noted the continued persistence of competing legendary accounts of Ireland's earliest inhabitants at the time. In his entry under the "Early History" of Ireland in the eleventh edition of the *Encyclopædia Britannica* (1910), Quiggin wrote with some overstatement:

> Although innumerable histories of Ireland have appeared in print since the publication of Roderick O'Flaherty's *Ogygia* (London, 1677), the authors have in almost every case been content to reproduce the legendary accounts without bringing any serious criticism to bear on the sources. This is partly to be explained by the fact that the serious study of Irish philology only dates from 1853 and much of the most important material has not yet appeared in print. In the middle of the 19th century [John] O'Donovan and [Eugene] O'Curry collected a vast amount of undigested information about the early history of the island, but as yet J[ohn] B. Bury in his monograph on St Patrick [1905] is the only trained historian who has ever adequately dealt with any of the problems connected with ancient Ireland. Hence it is evident that our knowledge of the subject must remain extremely unsatisfactory until the chief sources have been properly sifted by competent scholars. A beginning has been made by Sir John Rhys in his "Studies in Early Irish History" (*Proceedings of the British Academy*, vol.i), and by John [Eoin] MacNeill in a suggestive series of papers contributed to the *New Ireland Review* (March 1906-Feb 1907). Much might reasonably be expected from the sciences of archaeology and anthropology. But although Ireland is as rich as, or even richer in monuments of the past, than most countries in Europe, comparatively little has been done owing in large measure to the lack of systematic investigation.[312]

The continued allure of oriental theories surfaced in other range of commentaries on Irish identity in the early decades of the twentieth century, including in James Joyce's cosmopolitan and politically *supra-nationalist* works of literature (see Chapter Nine).

In the meantime, as addressed in subsequent chapters, during the nineteenth century Iran elicited other forms of 'historical' referentiality in Irish nationalist circles. These ranged from disparate allusions to Iranian history in Irish nationalist poetry, as a means of framing Ireland's history under English rule, to the coverage of the [Second] Anglo-Iranian War of 1856–57 in the pages of the Dublin nationalist paper *The Nation* in its post-Young Ireland phase.

Notes

1 Myles Dillon, "Lebor Gabála Érenn," *Journal of the Royal Society of Antiquaries of Ireland* 86(1), 1956, p.62.
2 See, among other works, Joseph Lennon, *Irish Orientalism*, p.30.

3 Geoffrey Keating, *The History of Ireland, from the Earliest Period to the English Invasion*. John O'Mahony translator. New York: P.M. Haverty, 1857, p.147; John Carey, "The Ancestry of Fénius Farsaid," *Celtica* 21, 1990, pp.104–12. Citing, among other works, a 1913 study by the German Celtic scholar Kuno Meyer, John Carey notes: "The association of the Gaels with Scythia seems to be an old one [...]. Various scholars have plausibly suggested that the link goes back to etymological speculations equating the names *Scotti* [Scotia/Scoti; the Roman designations for Ireland] and *Scythae*." Ibid., pp.107–108.

4 See also Helmut Humbach and Klaus Faiss, *Herodotus's Scythians and Ptolemy's Central Asia: Semasiological and Onomasiological Studies*. Weisbaden: Ludwig Reihert, 2012; Siän Jones and Paul Graves-Brown, "Introduction: Archaeology and Cultural Identity in Europe," and Colin Renfrew, "Prehistory and the Identity of Europe, or, Don't Let's be Beastly to the Hungarians," and Andrew P. Fitzpatrick, "'Celtic' Iron Age Europe: The Theoretical Basis" in Paul Graves-Brown, Siän Jones, and Clive Gamble, eds., *Cultural Identity and Archaeology: The Construction of European Communities*. New York: Routledge, 1996, pp.10, 132, 244.

5 See, among other works, Colin Kidd, "Gaelic Antiquity and National Identity," pp.1199–204.

6 On Keating and his milieu, see Bernadette Cunningham, *The World of Geoffrey Keating: History, Myth and Religion in Seventeenth-Century Ireland*. Dublin: Four Courts Press, 2000.

7 Nicholas Canny, "The Formation of the Irish Mind: Religion, Politics and Gaelic Irish Literature 1580-1750," *Past & Present* 95(1), May 1982, pp.100–103.

8 Geoffrey Keating, *The History of Ireland* (1902 edition), vol.I, pp.3, 5, 9, and passim; William Camden, Britannia, vol.II; Edmund Spenser, *A View of the State of Ireland as it Was in the Reign of Queen Elizabeth*. Reprint. Dublin: L. Flin and Ann Watts, 1763, pp.46, 60, 64, 97, and passim; For a few other examples of denigrating English accounts of so-called indigenous Gaelic population of Ireland based on the latter group's presumed Scythian ancestry, see David Dickson, "No Scythians Here: Women and Marriage in Seventeenth Century Ireland" in Margaret MacCurtain and Mary O'Dowd, eds., *Women in Early Modern Ireland*. Edinburgh: Edinburgh University Press, 1991, pp.223–35; John Patrick Montaño, *The Roots of English Colonialism in Ireland*. Cambridge: Cambridge University Press, 2011, pp.26, 34, 105, and passim. On the 'wild Irish,' see also Edward D. Snyder, "The Wild Irish: A Study of Some English Satires against the Irish, Scots, and Welsh," *Modern Philology* 17(12), April 1920, pp. 687–725; Lesa Ní Mhunghaile, "Anglo-Irish Antiquarianism," pp.183–84. On Keating's repudiation of 'wild Irish' allegations, see also Bernadette Cunningham, *The World of Geoffrey Keating*, pp.114–16 and passim.

9 Anna Davin, "Introduction" (Irish History Feature), *History Workshop*, no. 31, Spring 1991, p.96. See also Bernadette Cunningham, "'Foras Feasa ar Éirinn' and the Historical Origins of Irish Catholic Identity," *New Hibernia Review* 5(4), Winter 2001, pp.144–47.

10 Geoffrey Keating, *The History of Ireland* (1902 edition), vol.I, pp.3, 5. See also idem, *The History of Ireland* (1857 edition), pp. xvii–xxi. On Stanihurst, Campion, Spenser, Davies, and Keating's quoted characterization of these individuals' portrayal of the Irish, see also Christopher Ivic, "the memorye of their noble ancestors," in Oona Frawley, ed., *Memory Ireland*, vol.I, pp.50–51 and passim.

11 Geoffrey Keating, *The History of Ireland* (1857 edition), pp.114–28, 135, 175–80, 183–85, 189–91.

12 Ibid., pp.xli, 147–68.

13 Ibid., pp.149–51.

14 Ibid., pp.xvii–Lxxii, 150.

15 Norah Carlin, "Extreme or mainstream?: the English Independents and the Cromwellian reconquest of Ireland, 1640-1651" in Brendan Bradshaw, Andrew Hadfield, and Willy Male, eds., *Representing Ireland: Literature and the Origins of Conflict 1534-1660*. Cambridge: Cambridge University Press, 1993, p. 221. See also Reinhard Lupton, "Mapping mutability: or, Spenser's Irish Plot" in ibid., p.95.

16 Roderic O'Flaherty, *Ogygia, or a Chronological Account of Irish Events*. Volume I. James Hely translator and editor. Dublin: W. McKenzie, 1793, pp.v, xi.

17 Ibid., pp.xiii–xiv, xvi. See also Roderic O'Flaherty, *The Ogygia Vindicated, Against the Objections of Sir George MacKenzie*. With "A Dissertation on the Origin and Antiquities of the Ancient Scots, and Notes, critical and explanatory, on Mr. O'Flaherty Text" by Charles O'Conor, translator and editor. Dublin: G. Faulkner, 1775, pp.l–li.

18 On O'Flaherty, see also Joseph Lenon, *Irish Orientalism*, pp.75–80.
19 Roderic O'Flaherty, *The Ogygia Vindicated*, pp.xlix–li.
20 Voltaire, *The Philosophy of History*. Reprint. No translator. Glasgow: Robert Urie, 1766 [1765], pp.64–67. Voltaire, who dedicated the book to Catherine the Great of Russia, pointed out the Russian Empire at the time also encompassed the ancient Scythian homeland, before asserting a presumed historical and ethnic correspondence between Scythians and contemporary Russians (namely the so-called enlightened Russian rulers since the time of Peter the Great) as further proof of the unjustifiable historical maligning of ancient Scythians as savages.
21 John O'Mahony's commentary in Geoffrey Keating, *The History of Ireland* (1857 edition), p.148, n.5.
22 On medieval European accounts of Parthians as 'exiles from the Scythians,' and their identification in English accounts with the Irish and the Welsh, see Robert Bartlett, "Ancient Iran in the imagination of medieval West" in Ali Ansari, ed.., *Perceptions of Iran: History, Myths and Nationalism from Medieval Persia to the Islamic Republic*. London: I.B, Tauris, 2014, pp.43–44.
23 Martin A. O'Brennan, *O'Brennan's Antiquities*. Volume I. Second Edition. Dublin: n.p., 1858, pp.179, 358, 375, passim; idem, *A School History of Ireland, from the Day of Partholan to the Present Time*. Volume II. Dublin: n.p., 1858, pp.1, passim.
24 *Cork Examiner*, December 22, 1858, p.4 c.c.
25 Sylvester O'Halloran, *A General History of Ireland, from the Earliest Accounts to the Close of the Twelfth Century ....* Volume I. London: A. Hamilton, 1778, pp.vii–viii, 39–40.
26 Claire Lyons, "Sylvester O'Halloran's General History: Irish Historiography and the Late Eighteenth-Century British Empire." PhD dissertation, National University of Ireland, Galway, 2011, pp.203–208, 218, 233–36.
27 On *The Wild Irish Girl*, see also Clare O'Halloran, "Harping on the Past: Translating Antiquarian Learning into Popular Culture in Early Nineteenth-Century Ireland" in Melissa Calaresu, Filippo de Vivo, and Joan-Pau Rubies, eds., *Exploring Cultural History: Essays in Honour of Peter Burke*. Farnham, UK: Ashgate, 2010, pp.327–43; Luke Gibbons, "Romantic Ireland: 1750–1845" in James Chandler, ed., *The Cambridge History of English Romantic Literature*. Cambridge: Cambridge University Press, 2009, pp.182–83 and passim.
28 See, for example, Charles Vallancey, *A Vindication of the Ancient History of Ireland*. Dublin: Luke White, 1786, pp.336–38 and passim.
29 Joseph Lennon, *Irish Orientalism*, pp.62–71. Among other works, see also Joep Leerssen, *Remembrance and Imagination: Patterns in the Historical and Literary Representation of Ireland in the Nineteenth Century*. Notre Dame, IN: University of Notre Dame Press, 1997, pp.11–12; Mary Helen Thuente, *The Harp Re-Strung: The United Irishmen and the Rise of Irish Literary Nationalism*. Syracuse: Syracuse University Press, 1994, pp.26–34; Stiofán Ó Cadhla, *Civilizing Ireland: Ordnance Survey 1824-1842, Ethnography, Cartography, Translation*. Dublin: Irish Academic Press, 2007, pp.56–57.
30 On 'place-making,' see Sumathi Ramaswamy, *The Lost Land of Lemuria*.
31 On Jones, also known as the "Persian Jones," see Raymond Schwab, *The Oriental Renaissance*, pp.33–64 and passim; Garland Hampton Cannon, "Sir William Jones's Persian Linguistics," *Journal of the American Oriental Society* 78(4), October–December 1958, pp.262–73; Javed Majeed, *Ungoverned Imaginings: James Mill's* The History of British India *and Orientalism*. Oxford: Clarendon Press, 1992, pp.11–46; Joseph Theodoor Leerssen, "On the Edge of Europe," p.93; Joseph Lennon, *Irish Orientalism*, p.83; Lyle Campbell, "Why Sir William Jones Got it All Wrong, or Jones' Role in How to Establish Language Families," *Anuario del Seminario de Filologia Vasca Julio de Urquijo / International Journal of Basque Linguistics and Philology*, 40, 2006, pp.246, 256–57, and passim; Lyle Campbell and William J. Poser, *Language Classification: History and Method*. Cambridge: Cambridge University Press, 2008, pp.33–34; Mark Aronoff and Janie Rees-Miller, eds., *The Handbook of Linguistics*. Second edition. Wiley Blackwell, 2007, pp.101–103; Michael J. Franklin, *'Orientalist Jones': Sir William Jones, Poet, Lawyer, and Linguist, 1746-1794*. Oxford: Oxford University Press, 2011 (see particularly pp.274, 333–45, 354). On the "Indo-Scythian hypothesis and the rise of comparative philology" and the early designation of 'Indo-Scythian' by the French humanist Claude Saumaise (Claudius Salmasius) in 1643, see Vivien Law, "Language and its students: the

history of linguistics" in Neville Edgar Collinge, ed., *Encyclopedia of Language*. London: Routledge, 1990, p.441.
32 Raymond Schwab, *The Oriental Renaissance*, chapter 7.
33 See William Jones' Third Anniversary Discourse (1786) in William Jones, *The Works of Sir William Jones*. Volume I. Anna Maria Jones editor. London: G.G. and J. Robinson, Pater-Noster-Row, and R.H. Evans, 1799, p.26.
34 See, among other works, John Wilson Foster, "Encountering Traditions" in John Wilson Foster, ed., *Nature in Ireland: A Scientific and Cultural History*. Montreal: McGill-Queen's University Press, 1997, pp.23–30, 63–66; Christopher Moriarty, "The Early Naturalists" in ibid., 71–72; Patrick N. Wyse Jackson, "Fluctuations in Fortune: Three Hundred Years of Irish Geology" in ibid., 93–94; J.H. Andrews, "Paper Landscape: Mapping Ireland's Physical Geography" in ibid., 206–207; Martyn Anglesea, "The Art of Nature Illustration" in ibid., 499–501; Jonathan Jeffrey Wright and Diarmid A. Finnegan, "Rocks, skulls and materialism: geology and phrenology in late-Georgian Belfast," *Notes and Records: The Royal Society Journal of the History of Science* 72(1), 2017, pp.28–35; Peter Woodman, *Ireland's First Settlers: Time and the Mesolithic*. Oxford: Oxbow, 2015, pp 45–48; Thomas R. Trautmann, *Aryans and British India*. Berkeley: University of California Press, 1997, chapter 2; Brian Young, "'The Lust of Empire and Religious Hate': Christianity, history, and India, 1790-1820" in Stefan Collini, Richard Whatmore, and Brian Young, eds., *History, Religion, and Culture: British Intellectual History 1750-1950*. Cambridge: Cambridge University press, 2000, pp.98–102; and John Burrow, "Images of time: from Carlylean Vulcanism to sedimentary gradualism" in ibid., chapter 9.
35 Richard Kirwan, *Geological Essays*. London: D. Bremner, 1799, pp.54–86.
36 On the evolution of history as a separate discipline during the (European) Enlightenment as well as the subsequent development of "national traditions" in early nineteenth-century Europe, see Stefan Berger and Christoph Conrad, *Past as History: National Identity and Historical Consciousness in Modern Europe*. Houndmills, Basingstoke: Palgrave, 2015, chapters 2 and 3.
37 John O'Hart, *Irish Pedigrees; or, the Origin and Stem of the Irish Nation*. Volume I. Fifth edition. Dublin: James Duffy and Co., 1892 [1876], pp.27–28 (see also p.9).
38 Raymond Schwab, *The Oriental Renaissance*, pp.716–17, 30–31, and passim.
39 See, for example, Charles Vallancey, *A Vindication*, pp.196, 198–205, and passim; idem, *An Essay on the Primitive Inhabitants of Great Britain and Ireland. Proving from History, Languages, and Mythology, that They were Persians or Indo Scythæ, Composed of Scythians, Chaldæans, and Indians*. Dublin: Graisberry and Campbell, 1807, pp.6, 23, 35, 40, 81, 174, and passim.
40 See, for example, Charles Vallancey, *An Essay on the Primitive Inhabitants*, p.19.
41 Luke Gibbons and Kieran O'Conor, eds., *Charles O'Conor of Ballinagare*. Dublin: Four Courts Press, 2012. See, in particular, John Wrynn, "Charles O'Conor as a 'philosophical historian'" and Clare O'Halloran, "'A revolution in our moral and civil affairs': Charles O'Conor and the creation of a community of scholars in late eighteenth-century Ireland" in ibid., pp.72–78 and pp.79–96 respectively.
42 See also Lesa Ní Mhunghaile, "Anglo-Irish Antiquarianism," pp.184–88. On Vallancey in general, see, among other works, Walter D. Love, "Edmund Burke and an Irish Historiographical Controversy," *History and Theory* 2(2), 1962, pp.180–98; idem, "The Hibernian Antiquarian Society: A Forgotten Predecessor to the Royal Irish Academy," *Studies: An Irish Quarterly Review* 51(203), Autumn 1962, pp.419–31; Joseph Theodoor Leerssen, "On the Edge of Europe," pp.91–112; idem., "Irish Studies and Orientalism," in C. C. Barfoot and Theo D'haen, eds., *Oriental Prospects*, pp.161–73; Clare O'Halloran, *Golden Ages and Barbarous Nations: Antiquarian Debate and Cultural Politics in Ireland, c.1750-1800*. Cork: Cork University Press, 2004, pp.41–70; Colin Kidd, "Gaelic Antiquity and National Identity," pp.1197–214; John Patrick Delury, "Ex Conflictu Et Collisione: The Failure of Irish Historiography, 1745 to 1790," *Eighteenth-Century Ireland / Iris an dá chultúr* 15, 2000, pp.9–37; Brita Irslinger, "Geographies of Identity: Celtic Philology and the Search for Origins in Ireland and Germany" in Joachim Grage and Thomas Mohnike, eds., *Geographies of Knowledge and Imagination in 19th Century Philological Research on Northern Europe*. Newcastle upon Tyne: Cambridge Scholars, 2017, pp.174–92; Joseph Lennon, "Antiquarianism and Abduction: Charles Vallancey as Harbinger of Indo-European Linguistics," *European Legacy* 10(1), February 2005, pp.5–20; idem, *Irish Orientalism*, pp.81–101 and passim; Thomas R.

43 Trautmann, *Aryans and British India*, pp. 93–97; Ian McBride, *Eighteenth-Century Ireland*, pp.401–404; Tony Ballantyne, *Orientalism and Race: Aryanism in the British Empire*. Houndmills, Basingstoke: Palgrave, 2002, p.36; Norman Vance, *Irish Literature*, pp.68–69, 81–84, and passim.
43 Charles O'Conor, *Dissertations on the Ancient History of Ireland*. New edition. Dublin: G. Faulkner, 1756 [1753], pp.25–26, 29, passim.
44 Charles Vallancey, *A Vindication*, pp.xi, xlviii, 49 (appearing in place of xlix).
45 Ibid., pp.340–50.
46 Ibid., pp.xlviii, 168, 170, 181, 339, 438–39, passim.
47 On 'Celticism' and 'orientalism,' see also Joep Leerssen, "Celticism" in Terence Brown, ed., *Celticism*. Amsterdam: Editions Rodopi B.V., 1996, pp.1–20. Clare O'Halloran, *Golden Ages and Barbarous Nations*, pp.41–70; Colin Kidd, "Gaelic Antiquity and National Identity," pp.1197–214; Joseph Lennon, *Irish Orientalism*, pp.62–71, 80–88, and passim; idem, "Irish Orientalism: An Overview" in Carroll, Clare and Patricia King, eds., *Ireland and Postcolonial Theory*, pp.129–57; Thomas R. Trautmann, *Aryans and British India*, p.94; Daniel R. Davis "Introduction" in Paul Pezron, *Celtic Linguistics, 1700-1850. Volume I: The Antiquities of Nations*. Edited with a new Introduction by Daniel R. Davis. London: Routledge, 2000, pp.xx–xxiii.
48 See Daniel R. Davis "Introduction" in Paul Pezron, *Celtic Linguistics*, vol.I, pp.xiv–cvi, xxii–xxiii; Colin Kidd, *British Identities Before Nationalism: Ethnicity and Nationhood in the Atlantic World, 1600-1800*. Reprint. Cambridge: Cambridge University Press, 2004 [1999], pp.66–70, 196–97.
49 Among other works, see Clare O'Halloran, *Golden Ages and Barbarous Nations*, chapter 2; idem, "Irish Re-Creations of the Gaelic Past: The Challenge of Macpherson's Ossian," *Past and Present*, no.124, August 1989, p.82 and passim; Kevin Hart, *Samuel Johnson and the Culture of Property*. Reprint. Cambridge: Cambridge University Press, 2004 [1999], pp.136–55; David Sandner, *Critical Discourses of the Fantastic, 1712-1831*. Farnham, Surrey: Ashgate, 2011, pp.55–57; Mary Helen Thuente, *The Harp Re-Strung*, pp.31–33 and passim; Lesa Ní Mhunghaile, "Anglo-Irish Antiquarianism," p.188.
50 See, for example, Roderic O'Flaherty, *The Ogygia Vindicated*, Preface, pp.xiii–xx. See also Howard Gaskill, ed., *The Reception of Ossian in Europe*. London: Thoemmes Continuum, 2004.
51 Charles Vallancey, *A Vindication*, pp.438–39. See also pp.335–39, 400–401.
52 Ibid., pp.438–39. See also p.339.
53 Charles Vallancey, *An Essay on the Primitive Inhabitants*, p.164, 335–37, 438–39.
54 Edward Ledwich, *The Antiquities of Ireland*. Second Edition. Dublin: John Jones, 1804 [1790], pp.21–24, passim. See also Joseph Lennon, *Irish Orientalism*, pp.133–34; Lesa Ní Mhunghaile, "Anglo-Irish Antiquarianism," pp.186–87.
55 For different takes on Vallancey and Indo-European theory of languages, see Joseph Lennon, *Irish Orientalism*, pp., pp.89–111; Thomas R. Trautmann, *Aryans and British India*, pp. 93–98, 127. Whereas Lennon presumes Vallancey's continued commitment to his former Phoenician theory of Irish origins, Trauttman assumes Vallancey was an adherent of the Celtic origin of the Gaels.
56 William Jones' Third Anniversary Discourse (1786) in Jones, *The Works of Sir William Jones*, vol.I, p.34.
57 See, for example, Charles Vallancey, *An Essay on the Primitive Inhabitants*, pp.154–57, 173–85, passim.
58 Among many other works, see Walter D. Love, "The Hibernian Antiquarian Society," pp.419–20, passim; John Patrick Delury, "Ex Conflictu Et Collisione," pp.29–35; Joseph Lennon, "Antiquarianism and Abduction," pp.5–20; Joseph Theodoor Leerssen, "On the Edge of Europe," p.99.
59 See also John Harwood Andrews, "Charles Vallancey and the Map of Ireland," *Geographical Journal* 132(1), March 1966, pp.48–61. For an alternative, and overtly Saidian-style, "colonialist" conflation of Vallancey's military survey work in Ireland and his antiquarian objectives, see William O'Reilly, "Orientalist Reflections: Asia and the Pacific in the Making of Late Eighteenth-Century Ireland," *New Zealand Journal of Asian Studies* 6(2), December 2004, pp.127–47.

60 Anna Davin, "Introduction," p.98. See also Colin Kidd, *British Identities Before Nationalism*, chapter 6 ("The weave of Irish identities, 1600–1790").
61 Charlotte Brooke, *Reliques of Irish Poetry: Consisting of Heroic Poems, Odes, Elegies, and Songs, Translated into English Verse; with Notes Explanatory and Historical, and the Originals in Irish Character, to which is Subjoined an Irish Tale*. Reprint, with "A Memoir of Her Life and Writings" by Aaron Crossly Seymour. Dublin: J. Christie, 1816 [1789], Preface, p.cxxix.
62 John Patrick Delury, "Ex Conflictu Et Collisione," pp. 9–10 (see also pp.25–26). On this subject, see also Sean J. Connolly, *Divided Kingdom: Ireland 1630-1800*. Oxford: Oxford University Press, 2008, pp.426–31.
63 Sylvester O'Halloran, *A General History of Ireland*, vol.I, pp.vii–viii of "Preliminary Discourse," and 45–53.
64 Charles O'Conor, *Dissertations*, p.29.
65 Ibid., pp.10, 25–26, 34, 94, 163.
66 Roderic O'Flaherty, *The Ogygia Vindicated*.
67 Anna Davin, "Introduction," pp.98–100.
68 Roderic O'Flaherty, *The Ogygia Vindicated*, pp. xxvii, xxv. See also Colin Kidd, *British Identities Before Nationalism*, pp. 65, 156–58; Joseph Theodoor Leerssen, *Mere Irish & Fíorghael: Studies in the idea of Irish nationality, its literary expression and development*. Amsterdam: John Benjamins, 1986, pp.321–24 and passim.
69 Roderic O'Flaherty, *The Ogygia Vindicated*, pp.ii, xxv, xxvii–xxviii.
70 Bernd Roling, "Phoenician Ireland: Charles Vallancey (1725–1812) and the Oriental Roots of Celtic Culture" in Karl A.E. Enenkel and Konrad Adriaan Ottenheym, eds., *The Quest for an Appropriate Past in Literature, Art and Architecture*. Leiden: Brill, 2018, pp.755, 760, 766.
71 Charles Vallancey, *An Essay on the Antiquity of the Irish Language. Being a Collation of the Irish with the Punic language. With a Preface proving* Ireland to be the Thule *of the Ancients. Addressed to the Literati of Europe*. Dublin: S. Powell, 1772.
72 Charles Vallancey, *A Grammar of the Iberno-Celtic, or Irish Language*. Dublin: G. Faulkner, T. Ewing, and R. Moncrieffe, 1773, p.12.
73 Ibid., p.14.
74 Charles Vallancey, *A Vindication*, pp.xlvi–xlvii. See also Clare O'Halloran, "An Irish Orientalist in London: Charles Vallancey (1726-1812)" in Joep Leerssen, A. H. van der Weel, and Bart Westerweel, eds., *Forging in the Smithy: National Identity and Representation in Anglo-Irish Literary History*. Amsterdam: Editions Rodopi B.V., 1995, pp.161–74.
75 Charles Vallancey, *A Vindication*, pp.27–28, 40–41, 130–33, 159, 167–70, 252–53, 256, 257–60, 269–73, 279, 291–300.
76 On the Asiatic Society, see also David Kopf, *British Orientalism and the Bengal Renaissance*. Berkeley: University of California Press, 1969; Raymond Schwab, *The Oriental Renaissance*, chapter 3 and passim; Clare O'Halloran, "An Irish Orientalist in London," pp.164–68; Joseph Lennon, *Irish Orientalism*, pp.97–102.
77 Rowland Jones, *The Origin of Language and Nations, Hieroglyfically, Etymologically, and Topografically Defined and Fixed, After the Method of an English, Celtic, Greek and Latin English Lexicon*. London: J. Hughs, 1764, Preface (unnumbered page 25). On Rowland Jones' linguistic intervention, contribution, and contextualization, see also Daniel R. Davis, "Introduction" in Paul Pezron, *Celtic Linguistics*, vol.I, pp.xv–xviii.
78 Charles Vallancey, *A Vindication*, p.49 and passim. For William Betham's later objection to Vallancey's position and Betham's alternative claim of "Phoenician" Celtic heritage of Ireland, see William Betham, *The Gael and Cymbri: An Inquiry into the Origin and History of the Irish Scoti, Britons, and Gauls, and of the Caledonians, Picts, Welsh, Cornish and Bretons*. Dublin: William Curry, Jun, and Co., 1834, pp.15–16, 44–45, and passim.
79 Charles Vallancey, *An Essay on the Primitive Inhabitants*, p.19.
80 Charles Vallancey, *A Vindication*, pp.299–303.
81 Ibid., pp.318–19, 323, 435, and passim.
82 Ibid., p.323.
83 Ibid., pp.338–41, 349, 355–57, 398–99, 403, 438–39, 454, 463, 468, 477, 479, and passim. See also Charles Vallancey, *An Essay on the Primitive Inhabitants*, pp.152–53, 164, and passim.
84 Charles Vallancey, *A Vindication*, p.339.

85 Ibid., p.i. On the same theme, see also Vallancey's later writings, as in the case of *Prospectus of a Dictionary of the Language of the Aire Coti, or Ancient Irish, Compared with the Language of the Cuti, or Ancient Persians, with the Hindoostanee, the Arabic, and Chaldean Languages*. Dublin: Graisberry and Campbell, 1802, pp.xxxix–xlii, and passim.
86 On Vallancey and Ledwich, see also Joseph Lennon, *Irish Orientalism*, pp.9, 109–10, 133–34.
87 James Kelly, "The Last Will and Testament of Henry Flood: Context and Text," *Studia Hibernica*, no.31, 2000/2001, p.45. See also pp.46, 48.
88 Roderic O'Flaherty, *Ogygia, or a Chronological Account of Irish Events*, vol.I, p.viii. Vallancey was among the subscribers of this book.
89 John Pinkerton, *A Dissertation on the Origin and Progress of the Scythians or Goths*. London: John Nichols, 1787, pp.18, 24–31, 34–35, passim.
90 Ibid., pp. 18, 38.
91 Ibid., p.69.
92 Charles Vallancey, *An Essay on the Primitive Inhabitants*, pp.141–42, 165–70.
93 James Joseph Clancy, *The Land League Manual. With Portraits and Sketches of Parnell and Davitt*. New York: Thomas Kelly, 1881, p.118 n.*.
94 Joseph Theodoor Leerssen, "On the Edge of Europe," p.91.
95 For some other self-proclaimed novel aspects of Vallancey's approach, see Clare O'Halloran, "An Irish Orientalist in London," pp.170–73.
96 Charles Vallancey, *A Vindication*, p.v.
97 Charles Vallancey, *An Essay on the Primitive Inhabitants*, p.xiii.
98 J.F. Killeen, "Ireland in the Greek and Roman Writers," *Proceedings of the Royal Irish Academy. Section C: Archaeology, Celtic Studies, History, Linguistics, Literature* 76, 1976, pp. 207–15.
99 See David Kopf, *British Orientalism and the Bengal Renaissance*.
100 See Raymond Schwab, *The Oriental Renaissance*.
101 Barthélemy d'Herbelot de Molainville, *La Bibliothèque orientale, ou Dictionnaire universel contenant generalement tout ce qui regarde la connossance des peuples de l'Orient*. Paris: Compagnie des Libraires, 1697.
102 See, for example, ibid., pp.65–66, 128, 317, 383, 702–703, 895.
103 See Nicholas Dew, *Orientalism in Louis XIV's France*. Oxford: Oxford University Press, 2009, chapters 1 and 4 in particular.
104 Charles Vallancey, *An Essay on the Primitive Inhabitants*, p.vii.
105 Ibid., p.173. The (Sassanian-era) Middle Persian script was first deciphered by the French Silvester de Sacy in 1793 and the cuneiform (Achaemenid-era) Old Persian was decoded in stages by a wide range of European scholars until its full decipherment by the English Henry Creswicke Rawlinson in 1846–47.
106 Charles Vallancey, *A Vindication*, pp.355–57.
107 See Barthélemy d'Herbelot de Molainville, *La Bibliothèque orientale*, p.138. For d'Herbelot's entry on Pishdādiān and their designation as the first dynasty, see ibid., pp.702–703.
108 Charles Vallancey, *An Essay on the Primitive Inhabitants*, pp.41–42, 46.
109 Ibid., p.43.
110 Charles Vallancey, *A Vindication*, pp.49, 176.
111 Charles Vallancey, *An Essay on the Primitive Inhabitants*, p.161. See also p.xii.
112 Ibid., pp.139–41, 173–74. Jones had stated in his "Sixth Anniversary Discourse," delivered at the Asiatic Society of Bengal in 1789 that "*Assyrian* was the parent of *Chaldaick* and *Pahlavi*." William Jones, *The Works of Sir William Jones*, vol.I, p.92.
113 William Jones, *The Works of Sir William Jones*, vol.I, p.86. See also Charles Vallancey, *An Essay on the Primitive Inhabitants*, pp.151–53; Charles Vallancey, *A Vindication*, pp.58–60, and passim.
114 Charles Vallancey, *An Essay on the Primitive Inhabitants*, pp.14, 15 n*.
115 William Jones, *The Works of Sir William Jones*, vol.I, pp.53, 268.
116 See Clare O'Halloran, "An Irish Orientalist in London," pp.168–69.
117 Charles Vallancey, *A Vindication*, p.399.
118 Charles Vallancey, *An Essay on the Primitive Inhabitants*, p.39.
119 See, for example, Roderic O'Flaherty, *The Ogygia Vindicated*, pp.xxviii–xxix.
120 Charles Vallancey, *An Essay on the Primitive Inhabitants*, pp.39–41. On Beauford and Vallancey, see also Walter D. Love, "The Hibernian Antiquarian Society."

121 William Jones, "Sixth Anniversary Discourse" in William Jones, *The Works of Sir William Jones*, vol.I, pp.78, 81, 87, 91. This source is also mentioned in other works by Jones. On the disputed authorship of *Dabestān-e Mazāheb*, see Fath-Allah Mojtaba'i, "Dabestān-e maḏāheb," *Encyclopaedia Iranica* (http://www.iranicaonline.org/articles/dabestan-e-madaheb).
122 Charles Vallancey, *An Essay on the Primitive Inhabitants*, p.174.
123 William Jones, "Sixth Anniversary Discourse" in William Jones, *The Works of Sir William Jones*, vol.I, p.78.
124 *Edinburgh Review* 2(3), April 1803, p.118. During his long antiquarian career, Vallancey also ultimately failed to convince the highly influential Anglo-Irish conservative politician and author, Edmund Burke, of the validity of either of Vallancey's earlier Phoenician or later Iranian theories. Burke believed it was more plausible that Ireland was first settled by people migrating from mainland Britain, than from Spain or elsewhere. Walter D. Love, "Edmund Burke," pp.183–98; Frederick Peter Lock, *Edmund Burke, Volume II: 1784-1797*. Oxford: Clarendon Press, 2006, pp.109–13; John C. Weston, Jr., "Edmund Burke's Irish History: A Hypothesis," *PMLA* 77(4), September 1962, pp.400–402.
125 See, for example, "History of Ireland. Chapter IX." in *The Irish Shield and Monthly Milesian* (New York) 1(8), August 1829, pp.273–82; "History of Ireland. Chapter IX." in ibid. 1(9), September 1829, pp.313–15; and "Ancient Sepulture of the Irish" in ibid. 1(12), December 1829, pp.448–49.
126 William Hamilton Drummond, *Ancient Irish Minstrelsy*. Dublin: Hodges and Smith, 1852, p.82 n.*.
127 Henry O'Brien, *The Round Towers of Ireland, or the Mysteries of Freemasonry, of Sabaism, and of Budhism, for the First Time Unveiled*. London: Whittaker and Co., 1834, p.19.
128 Henry O'Brien, *The Round Towers* (1834 edition), p.13.
129 I discuss Moore's Iran-related poetry and historical writing in great detail in the next chapter. Here, among other works, see also Joseph Theodoor Leerssen, "On the Edge of Europe," p.108; and Joseph Lennon, *Irish Orientalism*, pp.112–13.
130 Joachimo Laurentio Villanueva (Joaquín Lorenzo Villanueva), *Phœnecian Ireland*. Henry O'Brien translator and editor. London: Longman & Co., 1833, pp.v–vi.
131 Ibid. pp.xii–xxxii.
132 Ibid., p.xxii.
133 Ibid., pp.viii–ix.
134 Ibid., pp.xxiv–xxxii.
135 Ibid., pp.xix–xx.
136 Ibid., pp.xx–xxiii.
137 Henry O'Brien, *The Round Towers* (1834 edition).
138 William Jones, "Sixth Anniversary Discourse," delivered on February 19, 1789, in William Jones, *The Works of Sir William Jones*, vol.I, pp.78, 87–89. On Mahābādiān, see also John Malcolm, *The History of Persia from the Most Early Period to the Present Time: containing an Account of the Religion, Government, Usages, and Character of the Inhabitants, of that Kingdom*. Volume I. London: John Murray, 1815, pp.7–12; William Erskine, "On the Authenticity of the *Desatir*, with Remarks on the Account of the Mahabadi Religion Contained in the Dabistan" (read on May 25, 1819) in *Transactions of the Literary Society of Bombay*. Volume II. London: Longman, Hurst, Rees, Orme, and Browne; and John Murray, 1820, pp.342–76; idem, "On the Sacred Books and Religion of the Parsis" (read on April 27, 1819) in ibid., pp.303, 313; James Baillie Fraser, *An Historical and Descriptive Account of Persia: From the Earliest Ages to the Present Time. With a Detailed View of its Resources, Government, Population, Natural History, and Character of its Inhabitants, Particularly of its Wandering Tribes; Including a Description of Afghanistan and Beloochistan*. Edinburgh: Oliver and Boyd, 1834, pp.101–102, 144–46; Edward Granville Browne, *A Literary History of Persia. Volume I: From the Earliest Times until Firdawsi*. Reprint. London: T. Fisher Unwin, 1908 [1902], pp.53–57; Fath-Allah Mojtaba'i, "Dabestān-e maḏāheb"; idem, "Dasātīr," *Encyclopaedia Iranica* (http://www.iranicaonline.org/articles/dasatir); Mohamad Tavakoli-Targhi, *Refashioning Iran: Orientalism, Occidentalism, and Historiography*. Houndmills, Basingstoke: Palgrave, 2001, pp.86–94.
139 William Jones, "Discourse the Ninth," delivered on February 23, 1792, in William Jones, *The Works of Sir William Jones*, vol.I, p.137.
140 See, for example, Charles Vallancey, *A Vindication*, pp.167–78, 207, 253–54.

141 Henry O'Brien, *The Round Towers* (1834 edition), p.x.
142 Ibid., p.xvi.
143 Ibid., pp.xxv–xxvi.
144 Ibid., pp.xvii–xviii.
145 Ibid., p.xviii. For the detailed crux of O'Brien's accusations against the Royal Irish Academy concerning the Academy's selection of Petrie's essay as the winner, see also the "Introduction" by W.H.C. in Henry O'Brien, *The Round Towers of Ireland, or the History of Tuath-de-Dananas*. Reprint of O'Brien's 1834 *The Round Towers of Ireland, or the Mysteries of Freemasonry* …. With an "Introduction" by W.H.C. Calcutta: Thacker, Spink, and Co., 1898, pp.xii–xxvii.
146 See Laurel Brake and Marysa Demoor, general eds., *Dictionary of Nineteenth-Century Journalism in Great Britain and Ireland*. Ghent: Academia Press, 2009, pp.182–83.
147 Henry O'Brien, *The Round Towers* (1834 edition), pp.13, 48, 59–60, 273–74, 321, 331–33, 406, 471–72. See also Walter D. Love, "Edmund Burke," pp.182–83, 184–98; idem, "The Hibernian Antiquarian Society," pp.423, 428, and passim.
148 Henry O'Brien, *The Round Towers* (1834 edition), pp.297, 383, 386, 393–94, 399, 426–30.
149 Ibid., p.429.
150 See also Seán O'Reilly, "Birth of a Nation's Symbol: The Revival of Ireland's Round Towers," *Irish Arts Review Yearbook* 15, 1999, pp.27–30; Joscelyn Godwin, *The Theosophical Enlightenment*. Albany: State University of New York Press, 1994, pp.19–22.
151 William Jones, "Discourse the Ninth," delivered on February 23, 1792, in William Jones, *The Works of Sir William Jones*, vol.I, p.139. See also p.138.
152 Henry O'Brien, *The Round Towers* (1834 edition), chapter XX and pp.285 and passim, 441–43.
153 Ibid., pp.257–63, 282–83 and passim.
154 Ibid., chapter XX, especially pp.272–73, 276–78.
155 According to this Iranian tradition, the first human couple (Mashya and Mashyana) were born of Keyoumars' semen and gave birth to seven sets of twins, the first set being devoured and the next six twins going on to populate different regions of the world. In *Shāhnāmeh*, however, Keyoumars was the first ruler on earth by the grace of god, who ruled over all humans and animals, and was also the disseminator of civilization. See also Ehsan Yarshater, "Iranian National History" in Ehsan Yarshater, ed. *The Cambridge History of Iran. Volume 3(1): The Seleucid, Parthian and Sasanian Periods*. Reprint. Cambridge: Cambridge University Press, 2003 [1983], pp.416–35.
156 Henry O'Brien, *The Round Towers* (1834 edition), pp.435–43 and passim.
157 Ibid.), p..429. See also p.127.
158 Ibid., p..429. See also pp. 430–31, 252, 520, and passim.
159 Ibid., pp.85–86. See also pp. 120–29, 184–85, and passim.
160 See William Jones, *The Works of Sir William Jones*, vol.I.
161 For example, Sir William Betham later called the suggested practice of phallic worship "the obsceneties of Siva." William Betham, *Etruria-Celtica: Etruscan Literature and Antiquities Investigated*. Volume II. Dublin: Philip Dixon Hardy and Sons, 1842, p.204. See also pp.191–92. Many decades later, in an article on "The Round Towers" by a Reverend P. Power in the *Journal of the Ivernian Society* (Cork), O'Brien's theory of the Round Towers was still referred to as "certain obscene worship" (vol. 6, no. 22, January–March 1914, p.85).
162 See also Joep Leerssen, *Remembrance and Imagination*, pp.108–20.
163 "Round Towers of Ireland," *Dublin University Magazine* 3(16), April 1834, pp.375–86. See also Seán O'Reilly, "Birth of a Nation's Symbol," pp.27–30.
164 "Round Towers of Ireland," *Dublin University Magazine* 3(16), April 1834, p.375.
165 Ibid., p. 378.
166 Ibid., p.382.
167 Ibid., pp.382–83.
168 On this topic, see also Cóilín Parsons, *The Ordnance Survey and Modern Irish Literature*. Oxford: Oxford University Press, 2016, pp.14–16 and passim; Marian Bleeke, "George Petrie, the Ordnance Survey, and Nineteenth-Century Constructions of the Irish Past" in Janet T. Marquardt and Alyce A. Jordan eds., *Medieval Art and Architecture after the Middle Ages*. Newcastle upon Tyne: Cambridge Scholars, 2009, pp.129–48; Paul Walsh, "George Petrie:

His Life and Work" in Próinséas Ní Chatháin, Siobhán Fitzpatrick, and Howard Clarke, eds., *Pathfinders to the Past: The Antiquarian Road to Irish Historical Writing, 1640–1960*. Dublin: Four Courts Press, 2012, pp.44–71. See also John Healy, *Irish Essays: Literary and Historical*. Dublin: Catholic Truth Society of Ireland, 1908, pp.64–72; Charlotte Salter-Townshend, "Round Towers and the Birth of Irish Archaeology: George Petrie and Changing Perceptions of Irish Archaeology in the 19th Century," *Archaeology Online*, September 2013. On archaeology and nationalisms in general, see also among other works Bruce G. Trigger, "Alternative Archaeologies: Nationalist, Colonialist, Imperialist," *Man*, new series, 19(3), September 1984, pp.355–70; Yael Zerubavel, *Recovered Roots: Collective Memory and the Making of Israeli National Tradition*. Chicago: University of Chicago Press, 1995, chapters 4 and 5, and passim; Nadia Abu El-Haj "Reflections on Archaeology and Israeli Settler-Nationhood," *Radical History Review* 86, Spring 2003, pp.149–63.

169 See, for example, George Petrie, *The Ecclesiastical Architecture of Ireland, Anterior to the Anglo-Norman Invasion; Comprising an Essay on the Origin and Uses of the Round Towers of Ireland, which Obtained the Gold Medal and Prize of the Royal Irish Academy*. Second edition. Dublin: Hodges and Smith, 1845, pp.103, 127, 129.

170 Patricia Boyne and John O'Donovan, "Letters from the County Down: John O'Donovan's First Field Work for the Ordnance Survey," *Studies: An Irish Quarterly Review* 73(290), Summer 1984, p.113.

171 William Stokes, *The Life and Labours in Art and Archæology, of George Petrie, LL.D., M.R.I.A.* London: Longmans, Green, & Co., 1868, pp.156–57.

172 [Thomas Moore], "[Review of Henry O'Brien's] *The Round Towers of Ireland; or the Mysteries of Freemasonry, of Sabaism, and of Budhism, for the First Time Unveiled*," *Edinburgh Review* 59(119), April 1834, pp.143–54. On *The Times* article (May 3, 1834, p.7), see also the entry for May 5, 1834 in Thomas Moore, *Memoirs, Journal, and Correspondence of Thomas Moore*. Volume 7. Edited by Lord John Russell. London: Longman, Brown, Green, and Longmans, 1856, p.31.

173 [Thomas Moore], "[Review of Henry O'Brien's] The Round Towers of Ireland," pp.144–45.

174 See, for instance Thomas Moore, *The History of Ireland*. Volume IV. London: Longman, Rees, Orme, Brown, Green, & Longman, 1846, pp.202–203.

175 [Thomas Moore], "[Review of Henry O'Brien's] The Round Towers of Ireland," pp.145–46.

176 Ibid., pp.153–54.

177 On D'Alton's writings on the subject, see for instance John D'Alton, "Essay on the Ancient History, Religion, Learning, Arts, and Government of Ireland" ("Introduction" and "Period First. From the Birth of Christ to the Arrival of St. Patrick, A.D. 431"), *Transactions of the Royal Irish Academy* (Dublin), vol.16, part II, 1831, pp.3–170 under the "Antiquities" section. See specially pp.82–89, 141–44.

178 See, for example, D'Alton's remarks on "the exact similitude" between the Round Towers and purportedly ancient Zoroastrian towers surviving in Iran and India in John D'Alton, *The History of Ireland: From the Earliest Period to the Year 1245*. Volume II. Dublin: privately published, 1845, pp.30–32. On the ostensible Zoroastrian origin of the Round Towers, see also ibid., pp.43–44, where, in support of his model, D'Alton cited a diverse range of other sources, including the study of Zoroastrianism in *Historia religionis veterum Persarum eorumque magorum* (1700) by Thomas Hyde.

179 See ibid., pp.32–34.

180 See Fergus Dunne, "The Politics of Translation in Francis Sylvester Mahony's 'The Rogueries of Thomas Moore,'" *European Romantic Review* 23(4), August 2012, pp.456, 463–67; Joep Leerssen, *Remembrance and Imagination*, pp.121–26. On Francis Sylvester Mahony ("Father Prout") see Terry Eagleton, "Prout and Plagiarism" in Tadhg Foley and Seán Ryder, eds., *Ideology and Ireland in the Nineteenth Century*. Dublin: Four Courts Press, 1998, pp.13–22.

181 *Fraser's Magazine* 10(56), August 1834, pp.195–96, 201.

182 Wilfred S. Dowden, ed. *The Journal of Thomas Moore. Volume 5: 1836-1842*. Newark: University of Delaware Press, 1988, p.2227.

183 Henry O'Brien, *The Round Towers* (1834 edition), p.129.

184 *Dublin Penny Journal* 2(98), May 17, 1834, p.361 n.*.

185 Ibid. 3(156), June 27, 1835, pp.410–11.

186 Joep Leerssen, "Ossian and the Rise of Literary Historicism" in Howard Gaskill, ed., *The Reception of Ossian in Eu*rope, pp.116–17. Leerssen's diagnosis of O'Brien in this case is contrary to Leerssen's earlier assertion that such works should not be judged according to present-day historical standards, but should rather be approached on the basis of their discursive stance in the broader debate on the barbarian or civilized nature of the Irish in ancient times. See, for example, Joseph Theodoor Leerssen, "On the Edge of Europe," p.91. Leerssen later again significantly modified his harsh assessment of O'Brien. See Guy Beiner with Joep Leerssen, "Why Irish History Starved: A Virtual Historiography," *Field Day Review* 3, 2007, p.81. For an earlier commentary on this mode of seesawing disparity in Leerssen's earlier works in general, see also Niall Ó Ciosáin, "Review: Round Towers and Square Holes: Exoticism in Irish Culture," *Irish Historical Studies* 31(122), November 1998, pp. 262–64.
187 William Betham, *Etruria-Celtica*, pp.31, 179–205, and passim.
188 *Proceedings of the Royal Irish Academy* 1(11), 1838, pp.160–62, and ibid. 1(12), 1838, pp.169–71. The quoted text appears on pp.169–70.
189 George Petrie, *The Ecclesiastical Architecture of Ireland*, p.21.
190 See, among other works, Douglas Hunter, *The Place of Stone: Dighton Rock and the Erasure of America's Indigenous Past*. Chapel Hill: University of North Carolina Press, 2017, pp.70–81, 86–88.
191 For a brief discussion of nineteenth-century claims in Brazil and Canada of Phoenician presence in those territories in ancient times, see Eleftheria Pappa "Tropicalismo in Classics. Contemporary Brazilian Approaches to the Value of Classical Antiquity in Higher Education: Between Colonial Legacy and Post-Colonial Thinking," *Journal for Critical Education Policy Studies* 18(2), 2020, pp.377–78.
192 William Hales, *A New Analysis of Chronology and Geography, History and Prophecy: in which Their Elements are Attempted to be Explained, Harmonized, and Vindicated, upon Scriptural and Scientific Principles; tending to Remove the Imperfection and Discordance of Preceding Systems, and to Obviate the Cavils of Sceptics, Jews, and Infidels. Volume IV: Profane Chronology.* Second edition. London: G.J.G. and F. Rivington, 1830, p.18. See also ibid., pp.xxxi, 22 n.*, 30–32 n.*, and passim.
193 Henry O'Brien, *The Round Towers* (1834 edition), pp.432–35.
194 *Ulster Journal of Archaeology* (Belfast) 3(1), 1855, p.250.
195 "Notices of the Round Towers of Ulster," *Ulster Journal of Archaeology* 3(1), 1855, p.14. See Thomas Moore, *Lalla Rookh: An Oriental Romance*. New edition with a new preface. New York: C.S. Francis & Co., 1849 [1817]. p.134.
196 "Notices of the Round Towers of Ulster," *Ulster Journal of Archaeology* 3(1), 1855, pp.19, 21–22.
197 Ibid., p.23.
198 On abductive reasoning in this sense, see also Joseph Lennon, *Irish Orientalism*, pp.101–102 and 114; idem, "Antiquarianism and Abduction," pp.5–20; Allan Megill, *Historical Knowledge, Historical Error: A Contemporary Guide to Practice*. With contributions by Steven Shepard and Phillip Honenberger. Chicago: University of Chicago Press, 2007, pp.129–32.
199 Henry O'Brien, *The Round Towers* (1834 edition), pp.247–48. On John Malcolm's verdict on the entirely mythical nature of Mahābādiān and Pishdādiān, see John Malcolm, *The History of Persia*, vol.I (1815 edition), pp.7–30. Living in British India, Malcolm was a follower of the newly emergent more sober approach to historiography in the United Kingdom and Western Europe.
200 David Shea and Anthony Troyer, eds. and trans., *Dabistan, or the School of Manners*. Volume I. Paris: Oriental Translation Fund of Great Britain and Ireland, 1843, pp.iii–viii. See also Edward Granville Browne, *A Literary History of Persia*, vol.I, pp.53–56; Mohamad Tavakoli-Targhi, *Refashioning Iran*, pp.28–29, 88, 93–94, 171 n.64; and Fath-Allah Mojtaba'i, "Dabestān-e maḍāheb."
201 Fath-Allah Mojtaba'i, "Dasātīr"; Aditya Behl, "Pages from the Book of Religions: Encountering Difference in Mughal India" in Sheldon Pollock, ed., *Forms of Knowledge in Early Modern Asia: Explorations in the Intellectual History of India and Tibet, 1500–1800*. Durham: Duke University Press, 2011, pp.210–39.
202 Fath-Allah Mojtaba'i, "Dabestān-e maḍāheb"; idem "Dasātīr"; Carl W. Ernst, "The *Dabistan* and Orientalist Views of Sufism" in Jamal Malik and Saeed Zarrabi-Zadeh, eds., *Sufism East and West: Mystical Islam and Cross-Cultural Exchange in the Modern World*. Leiden: Brill, 2019,

pp.33–52; Henry Corbin, "Āzar Kayvān," *Encyclopaedia Iranica* (http://www.iranicaonline.org/articles/azar-kayvan-priest).
203 See "Sixth Anniversary Discourse: on the Persians" and "Discourse the Ninth: On the Origin, and Families of Nations" in William Jones, *The Works of Sir William Jones*, vol.I, pp.73–94 and 129–42.
204 William Ouseley, *Travels in Various Countries of the East; More Particularly Persia*. Volume I. London: Rodwell and Martin, 1819, pp.110–11, 126, 142, 299, 410–15, 429, 448, and passim; Robert Ker Porter, *Travels in Georgia, Persia, Armenia, Ancient Babylonia, etc., During the Years 1817, 1818, 1819, and 1820*. Volume I. London: Longman, Hurst, Rees, Orme, and Brown, 1821, pp.xiii–xiv, 567. *Dabestān* and the Pishdādiān had also appeared in William Ouseley's *Epitome of the Ancient History of Persia. Extracted and Translated from the Jehan Ara, a Persian Manuscript*. London: Cadell and Davis, 1799, pp.xxii, 70–71. The Persian text mentioned in the latter publication by Ouseley was *Tarikh-e Jahan-Ara*, a late-sixteenth century historical work by Qazi Ahmad al-Qaffari.
205 See, for example, "*Brief Notices of Persian, and of the Language called Zend*. By John Homer, Esq., M.R.A.S., formerly President of the Society. Communicated by the Rev. Dr. [John] Wilson, Honorary President" (presented on January 20, 1853), *Journal of the Bombay Branch of the Royal Asiatic Society* 5(18), July 1853, pp.95, 102–103; Jivanji Jamshedji Modi, "A Glimpse into the Work of the Bombay Branch, 'Royal Asiatic Society, during the last 100 years (November 1804 to 1904) from a Parsee point of view," *Journal of the Asiatic Society of Bombay* 21(59), 1905, pp.183–87.
206 See, for instance, pp.9–12 in the anonymously published article (by the English author Keningale Cook): "An Aryan Ancestor," *Dublin University Magazine*, new series, 2(7), July 1878, pp.1–13; and p.178 in Keningale Cook, "An Aryan Ancestor," *Dublin University Magazine*, new series, 2(8), August 1878, pp.177–91.
207 William Erskine, "On the Authenticity of the *Desatir*," p.394. See also pp.342–48, 373. As a side note, it should be added here that critiques of William Jones on this subject by Erskine or by John Malcolm were on a different scale than what can be termed Euro-centric dismissal by the likes of James Mill of Jones' broader commentary on ancient civilizations of the East. Mill, the English Utilitarian philosopher and disparager of what by then had come to be generically designated "Hinduism" by European/Western commentators, wrote in the first volume of his famous *The History of British India* (1817–26):

> It was unfortunate that a man so pure and warm in the pursuit of truth, and so devoted to oriental learning, as Sir William Jones, took up, with that ardour which belonged to him, the theory of a high state of civilization in the principal countries of Asia. [...]
> Beside the illusions with which the fancy magnifies the importance of a favourite pursuit, Sir William was actuated by the virtuous design of exalting the Hindus in the eyes of their European masters; and thence ameliorating the temper of the government; while his mind had scope for error in the vague and indeterminate notions which it still retained of the signs of social improvement. The term civilization was by him, as by most men, attached to no fixed and definite assemblage of ideas. With the exception of some of the lowest states of society in which human beings have been found, it was applied to nations in all the stages of social advancement.

James Mill, *The History of British India*. Volume I. London: Baldwin, Cradock, and Joy, 1817, p.431
208 William Erskine, "Observations on Two Sepulchural Urns Found at Bushire, in Persia" (read on July 6, 1813) in *Transactions of the Literary Society of Bombay* (Volume I). London: Longman, Hurst, Rees, Orme, and Browne; and John Murray, 1819, pp.195, 197.
209 William Erskine, "On the Authenticity of the *Desatir*," pp. 342–76.
210 Henry O'Brien, *The Round Towers* (1834 edition), p.353 n.*; William Erskine, "Account of the Cave-Temple of Elephanta" (read on November 2, 1813) in *Transactions of the Literary Society of Bombay* (Volume I). London: Longman, Hurst, Rees, Orme, and Browne; and John Murray, 1819, p.210.
211 Henry O'Brien, *The Round Towers* (1834 edition), pp.252–53. See also ibid., pp.249, 253–56, 311. See also the reaction to O'Brien's claims in the review of his book in *Dublin University Magazine* 3(16), April 1834, pp.383–84.

212 Mansour Bonakdarian and Manoutchehr Eskandari-Qajar, "Malcolm, Major-General Sir John (1769-1833)," *Encyclopaedia Iranica* online, October 2021 (https://referenceworks.brillonline.com/entries/encyclopaedia-iranica-online/malcolm-sir-john-COM_362631)
213 Henry O'Brien, *The Round Towers* (1834 edition), pp.245–47.
214 John Malcolm, *The History of Persia*, vol.I (1815 edition), pp.6–31, 181–90, 199, 204, 205, 247, 248–49.
215 Ibid., p.11.
216 Ibid., chapters 2, 3, and 7, 11; idem, *The History of Persia from the Most Early Period to the Present Time: containing an Account of the Religion, Government, Usages, and Character of the Inhabitants of that Kingdom*. Volume I. Second revised edition. London: John Murray, 1829, Appendix.
217 "Preliminary Matter" in Harford Jones Brydges, *The Dynasty of the Kajars. Translated from the Original Persian Manuscript Presented by His Majesty Faty Aly Shah* [...]. London: John Bohn, 1833, pp.xvi–xxii, and passim. Incidentally, in another work, Jones Brydges mockingly noted "striking similarities between the Persians and the Irish" in terms of temperaments and behavior. Harford Jones Brydges, *An Account of the Transactions of His Majesty's Mission to the Court of Persia in the Years 1807-11, to Which is Appended, a Brief History of the Wahauby*. Volume I. London: James Bohn, 1834, pp.123, 133-34.
218 John Malcolm, *The History of Persia*, vol.I (1815 edition), pp.10 n.†, 11. See also, Harford Jones Brydges, *The Dynasty of the Kajars*, "Preliminary Matter," p.xxi.
219 David Shea, *History of the Early Kings of Persia, from Kaiomars, the First of the Peshdadian Dynasty, to the Conquest of Iran by Alexander the Great*. London: Oriental Translation Fund of Great Britain & Ireland, 1832 (English translation from the Arabic original of the section on rulers of ancient Iran appearing in the fifteenth-century *Rowzat al-Safā fi Sirat al-Anbiyā' wa al-Moluk wa al-Kholafā*, also known as *Universal History*, by Muhammad ibn Khāvandshāh Mirkhvānd), pp.iii–iv, 439–40; and Anthony Troyer's "Preliminary Discourse" in David Shea and Anthony Troyer, eds. and trans., *Dabistan, or the School of Manners*, vol.I., pp.xx xi–lxv. As previously noted, this translation of *Dabestān* was initiated by Shea and completed by Troyer following Shea's death in 1836.
220 Charles Vallancey, *An Essay on the Primitive Inhabitants*, p.19.
221 Henry O'Brien, *The Round Towers* (1834 edition), pp.133–34.
222 Francis Wilford, "On Egypt and Other Countries adjacent to the Ca'li' River, or Nile of Ethiopia, from the Ancient Books of the Hindus" (including a commentary by William Jones, the president of the Asiatic Society of Bengal) in *Asiatic Researrches; or Transactions of the Society Instituted in Bengal*. Volume 3. London: J. Sewell and Co., 1799, pp.295–468. See also Henry O'Brien, *The Round Towers* (1834 edition), pp.92–93, 114, 161, 220, 243–44, 248, 259–61, 275, 326–27, 345–46, 350, 449, 451.
223 Vahid Fozdar, "'That Grand Primeval and Fundamental Religion': The Transformation of Freemasonry into a British Imperial Cult," *Journal of World History* 22(3), 2011, pp.505–506, 511, 513, 518.
224 The binary conception of text and time here is somewhat different from that theorized by Günther Müller and further developed by Paul Ricoeur as "time of narrating" and "narrated time." See Paul Ricoeur, *Time and Narrative*. Volume 2. Kathleen McLaughlin and David Pellauer translators. Chicago: University of Chicago Press, 1985 (originally published in French in 1984), pp.77–81. On transformations in antiquarian and historical methodologies in England at the time, see also Philippa Levine, *The Amateur and the Professional: Antiquarians, Historians and Archaeologists in Victorian England, 1838–1886*. Cambridge: Cambridge University Press, 1986, pp.3–6 and passim.
225 George Stanley Faber, *The Origin of Pagan Idolatry Ascertained from Historical Testimony and Circumstantial Evidence*. Volume I. London: F.C. and J. Rivington, 1816, pp.122–23.
226 Ibid., vol.III, pp.441–43.
227 Ibid., pp.447, 48 n.4, 490–94, 510, 586, 596–98, 599–600, and passim.
228 Henry O'Brien, *The Round Towers* (1834 edition), pp. 224, 226.
229 Edward Granville Browne, *A Literary History of Persia*, vol.I, pp.53, 56–57.
230 James Cowles Prichard *Researches into the Physical History of Man*. London: John and Arthur Arch, 1813, pp.455–69.
231 Ibid., pp.476–77.
232 Ibid., pp.479–80.

233 Ibid., pp.528–34.
234 See also Tony Ballantyne, *Orientalism and Race*, pp.38–40.
235 See, for example, Louis Herbert Grey, "The Kings of Early Irān According to the Sidrā Rabbā," *Zeitschrift für Assyriologie und verwandte Gebiete* 19, 1905-1906, pp.272–87; or the fourteenth-century Hamdollah Mostufi Qazvini's *Tārikh-e Gozideh*. Abdul-Hussein Nava'i, editor. Tehran: Amir Kabir, 1339 (1960/1961). According to Mostufi Qazvini's *Tārikh-e Gozideh*, which continued to influence Iranian historical writing well into the nineteenth century (with some later dilutions of the distinction Qazvini made between Persians and Turks), Persians were classified as descendants of Shem's lineage through Shem's son Elam, with Arabs and Jews being descendants of Shem's son Arpachshad. All "Africans" were descendants of Ham's sons, while all Europeans, including Greeks, were descendants of Noah's son Japheth, as were Mongols, Turks, the Chinese, the Rus, Bulgars, Khazars, and other groups (through different sons of Japheth). *Tārikh-e Gozideh*, pp.24–26.
236 Leveson Venables Vernon-Harcourt, *The Doctrine of the Deluge, Vindicating the Scriptural Account from the Doubts which Have Recently Been Cast Upon it by Geological Speculations*. Volume II. London: Longman, Orme, Brown, Green, and Longmans, 1838, pp.217–18. See also p.364.
237 Ibid., pp.397–404. Here Vernon-Harcourt made the serendipitously correct etymological equation between the English and Persian cognate terms: the English "Ark" (from the Latin "arca," meaning "chest") and the Persian "arg"/"ark" (meaning citadel, and possibly related to the Latin "arx," itself a cognate of arca). He was, however, extremely wrong about the age of the *arg* citadel wall in Tabriz, the original foundation of which only dates to the fourteenth century CE.
238 Henry Montague Grover, "The Identity of Cyrus and the Times of Daniel," *Journal of Sacred Literature*, new series 7(14), January 1855, pp.364–31. The journal was edited by the prominent evangelical biblical scholar John Kitto until his death in November 1854 and by the Reverend Henry Burgess subsequently. Kitto, incidentally, had earlier served as a member of a Christian mission to Iran and the Ottoman territories.
239 Marcus Keane, *The Towers and Temples of Ancient Ireland; Their Origin and History Discussed from a New Point of View*. Dublin: Hodges, Smith and Co., 1867, pp.6, 231, 235–36 n.*, 317, 321–22, 327, and passim.
240 Eliza Burt Gamble, *The God-Idea of the Ancients or Sex in Religion*. New York and London: G.P. Putnam's Sons, 1897, pp.303–304.
241 For a very different reading of Betham in this regard, see Joseph Lennon, *Irish Orientalism*, p.112.
242 William Betham, *The Gael and Cymbri*, p.11 (see also pp.xi, 12–16, 25, and chapter II).
243 George Lillie Craik and Charles Macfarlane, *The Pictorial History of England: Being a History of the People, as Well as a History of the Kingdom*. Volume I. London: Charles Knight and Co., 1838, p.70. Subsequent editions of the book vary in content and thematic organization. The section on religion in the 1841 edition began with the English Reformation and entirely omitted earlier religious beliefs and practices, whereas the passage in reference to Pelloutier and O'Brien appeared on p.65 of the 1846 New York edition, which followed the thematic arrangement of the 1838 edition.
244 Ibid., pp.15–17.
245 See also Elizabeth Tilley, "The Royal Irish Academy and Antiquarianism" in James H. Murphy, ed., *The Oxford History of the Irish Book. Volume IV: The Irish Book in English, 1800-1891*. Oxford: Oxford University Press, 2011, pp.470–76.
246 On the Ordnance Survey, see also Cóilín Parsons, *The Ordnance Survey*; Patrick J. Duffy, "Ordnance Survey Maps and Official Reports" in James H. Murphy, ed., *The Oxford History of the Irish Book*, vol.IV, pp.553–52; Joep Leerssen, *Remembrance and Imagination*, pp.100–108.
247 Louisa Catherine Beaufort, "An Essay upon the State of Architecture and Antiquities, Previous to the Landing of the Anglo-Normans in Ireland," *Transactions of the Royal Irish Academy*, 15, 1828, pp. 101–241.
248 Henry O'Brien, *The Round Towers* (1834 edition), pp.87–88 (and pp.83–87). See also Tony Ballantyne, *Orientalism and Race*, pp.37–38.
249 See William Jones, "Sixth Anniversary Discourse," delivered on February 19, 1789, in William Jones, *The Works of Sir William Jones*, vol.I, p.86.

250 George Petrie, *The Ecclesiastical Architecture of Ireland*, pp.35–36. Among advocates of fire-worship theory, Petrie subjected Windele to a particularly severe criticism, slighting him for relying among other so-called authorities on certain details of O'Brien's 1834 *The Round Towers*. While O'Brien rejected the use of the towers for fire worship, he had noted the towers, other than phallic worship, later occasionally also served "sepulchural purposes," which was among the secondary functions of the towers accepted by Windele. Ibid. pp.11–97. On Petrie's rejection of existing alternative theories of the origin of the towers see also William Stokes, *The Life and Labours*, pp.141–43, 146–50, 415–16, and passim.
251 Charles Vallancey, *An Essay on the Primitive Inhabitants*, p.xii. See also p.161.
252 Louisa Catherine Beaufort, "An Essay upon the State of Architecture and Antiquities," pp.102–103.
253 Joseph Theodoor Leerssen, "On the Edge of Europe," pp.91–112.
254 Foucault coined this concept in 1967. See Michel Foucault, "Of Other Spaces: Utopias and Heterotopias" in Neil Leach, ed., *Rethinking Architecture: A Reader in Cultural Theory*. New York: Routledge, 1997, pp.330–36.
255 Bakhtin first coined the term in the mid-1930s. See Mikhail M. Bakhtin, "Discourse in the Novel" in Mikhail M. Bakhtin, *The Dialogic Imagination: Four Essays by M.M. Bakhtin*. Michael Holquist editor, and Caryl Emerson and Michael Holquist translators. Austin: University of Texas Press, 1981, pp.269–371.
256 Kristeva first used the concept in 1966 in connection with Mikhail Bakhtin's concept of "dialogism." See Julia Kristeva, "Word, Dialogue and Novel" in Julia Kristeva, *The Kristeva Reader*. Toril Moi editor. New York: Columbia University Press, 1986, p.39.
257 Julia Kristeva, "Word, Dialogue and Novel," pp.39, 43.
258 Dipesh Chakrabarty, *Provincialising Europe*.
259 Cóilín Parsons, *The Ordnance Survey*, p.36.
260 Vinay Lal, "Provincializing the West: World History from the Perspective of Indian History" in Benedikt Stuchtey and Eckhardt Fuchs, eds., *Writing World History, 1800-2000*. Oxford: Oxford University Press, 2003, p.282 (in the section of Lal's essay that is titled "Europe as the Lodestar of History: The Diminishing Horizons of 'World History' in Colonial India").
261 See also Ehsan Yarshater, "Iranian National History" in Ehsan Yarshater, ed. *The Cambridge History of Iran*, vol.3(1), pp.359–480; idem "Iran iii. Traditional History," *Encyclopaedia Iranica* (http://www.iranicaonline.org/articles/iran-iii-traditional-history).
262 See also Ehsan Yarshater, "Iran iii. Traditional History," *Encyclopaedia Iranica* (http://www.iranicaonline.org/articles/iran-iii-traditional-history).
263 *Gentleman's Magazine* (London), new series, vol.22, June 1829, p.542. on Mirza Mohammad Ebrahim, see Michael H. Fisher, "Persian Professor in Britain: Mirza Muhammad Ibrahim at the East India Company's College, 1826-44," *Comparative Studies of South Asia, Africa and the Middle East* 21(1&2), 2001, pp.24–32: idem, *Counterflows to Colonialism: Indian Travellers and Settlers in Britain 1600-1857*. New Delhi: Permanent Black, 2004, pp.133–34.
264 Ismail Hayrat-Irani, *Ketāb-e Tārikh-e Irān Ta'lif-e Navāb-e Mostetāb Ser Jān Malkom Sāheb Bahādor*. Volume I. Bombay: n.p., 1876. The second volume was published in Bombay in 1884 (1302 A.H.). Both volumes were subsequently reprinted in India and Iran.
265 Jalal Pour-Fath-Ali Shah Qajar (Jalal al-Din Mirza), *Nāmeh-ye Khosrovān: Dāstan-e Pādeshāhān-e Pārs beh Zabān-e Pārsi keh Soudmand-e Mardān, beh-vizheh Koodakān asst: az Āqāz-e Ābādiān tā Anjām-e Sāssāniān*. Volume I. Tehran: n.p., 1285 A.H.(1868), pp.11–20 in particular; Mohamad Tavakoli-Targhi, "Contested Memories: Narrative Structures and Allegorical Meanings of Iran's Pre-Islamic History," *Iranian Studies* 29(1&2), Spring 1996, pp.149–75; Abbas Amanat, "Pur-e ḵāqān wa andiša-ye bāzyābi-e tāriḵ-e melli-e Irān," *Iran Nameh*, 17, Winter 1999, pp.5–54; idem, "The Kayanid crown and Qajar reclaiming of royal authority," *Iranian Studies* 34(1–4), 2001, pp.17–30; Abbas Amanat and Farzin Vejdani, "Jalāl-al-Din Mirzā," *Encyclopaedia Iranica* (iranicaonline.org/articles/Jalal-al-Din Mirza); Firoze M. Kotwal, Jamsheed K. Choksy, Christopher J. Brunner, and Mahnaz Moazami, "Hataria, Manekji Limji," *Encyclopaedia Iranica* (iranicaonline.org/articles/hataria-manekji-limji); Afshin Marashi, *Nationalizing Iran: Culture, Power, & the State, 1870-1940*. Seattle: University of Washington Press, 2008, pp.56–65.

266 Abbas Amanat, "Historiography viii. Qajar Period," *Encyclopaedia Iranica* (http://www.iranicaonline.org/articles/historiography-viii).
267 On the subject of Iran's standing among the most civilized nations of the world at the time, see also, Charles Kurzman, "Weaving Iran into the Tree of Nations," *International Journal of Middle East Studies* 37(2), May 2005, pp.137–66; Mansour Bonakdarian, "Negotiating Universal Values and Cultural and National Parameters: Iran and Turkey at the First Universal Races Congress (London, 1911)," *Radical History Review*, 92, Spring 2005, pp.118–32, as well as the critique of West-centric definitions and constructs of 'modernity' in Iranian national historiography discussed in Mohamad Tavakoli-Targhi, "Early Persianate Modernity" in Sheldon Pollock, ed., *Forms of Knowledge in Early Modern Asia*, pp.257–90.
268 Jalal Pour-Fath-Ali Shah Qajar (Jalal al-Din Mirza), *Nāmeh-ye Khosrovān*, vol.I, p.10.
269 See, for example, Palanji Barjorji Desai, "The Ostracism of the Achæmenids from the Pahlavi Works and the Shâh Nameh" in Jivanji Jamshedji Modi, ed., *The K. R. Cama Memorial Volume: Essays on Iranian Subjects Written by Various Scholars in Honour of Mr. Kharshedji Rustamji Cama on the Occasion of His Seventieth Birthday*. Bombay: Fort Printing Press, 1900, pp.29–39.
270 Rezaqoli Khan Hedayat, *Ajmal al-Tawārikh*. Tabriz: Aqa Reza and Karbala'i Mohammad Hussein publishers, 1283 A.H. (1866), pp.2–6, 10–17.
271 Sunil Sharma, "Woven Worlds and Painted Pictures: The Persian Book in India." Lecture presented at the Library of Congress, June 11, 2014 (https://www.loc.gov/today/cyberlc/feature_wdesc.php?rec=6468); and Sunil Sharma, *Mughal Arcadia: Persian Literature in an Indian Court*. Cambridge, MA: Harvard University Press, 2017, pp.13–15.
272 Edward W. Said, "Traveling Theory" in Edward W. Said, *The World, the Text, and the Critic*. Cambridge, MA: Harvard University Press, 1983, pp.226–47.
273 Ken Brown and Brennan Breed, "Social Identity and Scriptural Interpretation," pp.15–16, 31–32.
274 Brennan W. Breed, "Anchor or Spandrel: The Concept of the Original Context" in Brennan W. Breed, *Nomadic Text: A Theory of Biblical Reception History*. Bloomington: Indiana University Press, 2014, pp.75–92.
275 Hans-Georg Gadamer, *Truth and Method*. Joel Weinsheimer and Donald G. Mar translators. Second revised edition. London: Continuum, 2004, p.296.
276 Ibid. p.386.
277 Walter Benjamin, *Selected Writings. Volume 4: 1938-1940*. Howard Eiland and Michael W. Jennings editors, and Edmund Jephcott, et al., translators. Cambridge, MA: Harvard University Press, 2003, p.395.
278 Ibid., p.397.
279 See also Ali M. Ansari, *The Politics of Nationalism in Modern Iran*. Cambridge: Cambridge University Press, 2012, pp.55–60. See also pp.23–24.
280 Mohammad Hussein Khan (Zoka' al-Molk) Foroughi, *Doureh-ye Ebtedā'i az Tārikh-e Ālam. Volume I: Tārikh-e Irān*. 1318 A.H. (1901), pp.7–9, 13–50. See also Abbas Amanat, "Historiography viii. Qajar Period"; Farzin Vejdani, *Making History in Iran: Education, Nationalism, and Print Culture*. Stanford: Stanford University Press, 2015, pp.40–43.
281 Quoted in William Butler Yeats, *The Collected Works of W.B. Yeats. Vol. XII: John Sherman and Dhoya*. Richard J. Finneran editor. New York: Macmillan, 1991, pp.xi–xii.
282 Edward Granville Browne, *The Press and Poetry of Modern Persia. Partly Based on the Manuscript Work of Mirzâ Muhammad Ali Khân "Tarbiyat" of Tabriz*. Cambridge: University Press, 1914, p.xxxiii, n.1, xxxiii, xxxvii.
283 Anthony D. Smith, *National Identity*. Reno: University of Nevada Press, 1991, chapter 3 (see especially pp.50, 65–67).
284 Benedict Anderson, *Imagined Communities: Reflections on the Origin and Spread of Nationalism*. London: Verso, 1983.
285 Sumathi Ramaswamy, *The Lost Land of Lemuria*, pp.21–25, 55–71, 172–74, and chapter 4
286 See also Anna Davin, "Introduction," pp.98–100.
287 Sumathi Ramaswamy, *The Lost Land of Lemuria*, pp.1, 4.
288 On this subject, see also the clarification of modernity and off-modern in ibid., pp.9–10.

289 Among numerous other works, see also Stuart Hall, "Introduction" in Stuart Hall and Bram Gieben, eds., *Formations of Modernity*. Cambridge: Open University, 1992, pp.1–16; Arjun Appadurai, *Modernity at Large: Cultural Dimensions of Globalization*. Minneapolis: University of Minnesota Press, 1996.
290 Sumathi Ramaswamy, *The Lost Land of Lemuria*, p.7.
291 Ibid., p.5.
292 Dilip Menon, "Writing History in Colonial Times: The Space and Time of Religious Polemic in Late 19th and Early 20th Century Southern India." Presented at the Center for South Asian Studies, University of Michigan, November 16, 2015 (https://www.youtube.com/watch?v=vMzMoG96YlQ).
293 See Max Weber's 1919 "Science as a Vocation" in Max Weber, *From Max Weber: Essays in Sociology*. Hans H. Gerth and C. Wright Mills, eds. and trans. With a new Preface by Bryan S, Turner. New London: Routledge, 2009, pp.139, 159.
294 On this subject, see also Vallancey, *A Vindication*, chapter I, p.3.
295 Pierre Nora, ed. *Realms of Memory: Rethinking the French Past. Volume I: Conflicts and Divisions*. New York: Columbia University Press, 1996 (originally published in French in 1984).
296 Jay Winter, *Sites of Memory, Sites of Mourning: The Great War in European Cultural History*. Cambridge: Cambridge University Press, 1995.
297 See also Roland Hill, "Lord Acton and the Catholic Reviews," *Blackfriars* 36(429), December 1955, pp.469–82.
298 "Mr. Goldwin Smith's Irish History," reproduced in John Emerich Edward Dalberg-Acton, *The History of Freedom, and Other Essays*. John Neville Figgis and Reginald Vere Laurence editors. London: MacMillan and Co., 1907, pp.240–42.
299 Partha Chatterjee, *The Nation and Its Fragments: Colonial and Postcolonial Histories*. Princeton: Princeton University Press, 1993, chapter 6 and passim.
300 Dillon, a Catholic and, at the time, second only in stature in the Irish Parliamentary Party to the party leader John Redmond, was also the father of future historian of Ireland Myles Dillon. John Dillon himself was the son of John Blake Dillon, a founding member of Young Ireland and a co-founder, with Charles Gavan Duffy and Thomas Osborne Davis, of *The Nation* in 1842 and, later in life, a parliamentary advocate of Irish self-government within the British Empire.
301 [Great Britain] *Parliamentary Debates* (Commons), 5th series, vol.40 (1912), c.1977. Also notable in the statement by Sykes, particularly given his unionist politics and opposition to Irish Home Rule, was his paradoxical designation of Ireland as a "country" and its identification with Egypt, a British protectorate. A wide range of Iranian constitutionalist press, published inside and outside Iran, regularly reproduced translated summaries or entire texts of British parliamentary proceedings concerning Iranian developments (generally based on the regular reports of parliamentary debates appearing in *The Times* of London). Among other examples, a summary of the parliamentary exchange between Dillon and Sykes appeared in *Habl al-Matin* of Calcutta (August 19, 1912, no.10, p.5). Sykes would later also serve as the British negotiator of the 1916 Sykes-Picot Agreement that divided up the Arab provinces of the Ottoman Empire between Britain and France, which came to be ruled as "mandates" following the end of the First World War.
302 On Cusack, see Patrick Maume, "Margaret Cusack and Catholic-Nationalist History" in James H. Murphy, ed., *The Oxford History of the Irish Book. Volume IV: The Irish Book in English, 1800-1891*. Oxford: Oxford University Press, 2011, pp.484–96.
303 Margaret Anna Cusack, *An Illustrated History of Ireland: From the Earliest Period*. London: Longmans. Green, and Co., 1868, pp.31–42 (note also pp.1–11); idem, *The Student's Manual of Irish History*. London: Longmans. Green, and Co., 1870, pp.3–20.
304 John O'Hart, *Irish Pedigrees*, vol.I (1892 edition), p.14.
305 Ibid., pp.12, 14.
306 Ibid., p.12.
307 Ibid., pp.14, 44–47.
308 Ibid., p.46.
309 John O'Hart, *Irish Pedigrees; or, the Origin and Stem of the Irish Nation*. Volume II. Fifth edition. Dublin: James Duffy and Co., 1892 [1876], p.63.
310 On this topic, to which I return later, see Michael de Nie, *The Eternal Paddy: Irish Identity and the British Press, 1798–1882*. Madison: University of Wisconsin Press, 2004; Robert J.C.

Young, *Colonial Desire: Hybridity in Theory, Culture and Race*. New York: Routledge, 1995, pp.68–89; Catherine Hall, "The Nation Within and Without" in Catherine Hall, Keith McClelland, and Jane Rendall, eds., *Defining the Victorian Nation: Class, Race, Gender and the Reform Act of 1867*. Cambridge: Cambridge University Press, 2000, pp.204–20; Amy E. Martin, "'Becoming a Race Apart': Representing Irish Racial Difference and the British Working Class in Victorian Critiques of Capitalism" in Terrence McDonough, ed., *Was Ireland a Colony?*, pp.186–211.

311 Noel Ignatiev, *How the Irish Became White*. New York: Routledge, 1995; David R. Roediger, *The Wages of Whiteness: Race and the Making of the American Working Class*. New York: Verso, 1999.

312 Edmund Crosby Quiggin, "Ireland: Early History," *The Encyclopædia Britannica*. 11th edition, 1910, vol.14 (Hugh Chisholm editor). New York: The Encyclopædia Britannica Company, p.756.

TWO
THOMAS MOORE'S POETIC AND HISTORICAL IRANS: *INTERCEPTED LETTERS* (1813), *LALLA ROOKH* (1817), AND *THE HISTORY OF IRELAND* (1835)

By the time Henry O'Brien's *The Round Towers* appeared in 1834, Thomas Moore (1779–1852), who participated in the public pillorying of O'Brien, was awaiting the publication of the first volume of his *The History of Ireland*, which offered an alternative oriental account of Irish origins. Appearing in 1835, this first volume of what became a four-volume history of Ireland from the earliest times until the middle of the seventeenth century covered the period up to the Norse invasions (beginning in the late eighth century). As already noted in the previous chapter, Moore's book too was destined to be assailed by George Petrie for its particular theory of the Round Towers. At the time of the publication of *The History of Ireland*, Moore was already a distinguished Romantic poet and dramatist, the pre-eminent Irish nationalist balladeer, an indefatigable champion of Catholic rights in the United Kingdom, and a supporter of the campaign to repeal the 1801 Act of Union. The Dublin-born Moore, who spent most of his life in England, continued to be regarded as "The National Bard of Ireland" in most Irish nationalist quarters even after the emergence of the Young Ireland literary circle in 1842 with its new divergent patterns of nationalist poetic sensibility. The Young Ireland poet Michael Joseph Barry dedicated his 1845 edited volume of nationalist poetry to Moore, with the collection containing some of Moore's own works.[1] The poet and a founding member of Young Ireland, Thomas Osborne Davis (d. 1845), who was originally to have edited the aforementioned collection of nationalist poems, hailed Moore "as our greatest poet." Davis, who was otherwise critical of Moore's grandiloquent style, wrote of Moore in the Young Ireland mouthpiece *The Nation* (Dublin):

He is immeasurably our greatest poet, and the greatest lyrist, except Burns and Beranger that ever lived; but he has not given songs to the middle and poor classes of Irish. The Irish-speaking people have songs by the thousand, but they (especially the political ones) are too despairing; the poor who are limited (and, therefore, in some sort barbarized) to English alone, have only the coarsest ballads, wherein an occasional thought of frolic, or wrath, or misery, is utterly unable to redeem the mass of threadbare jests, ribaldry, mock sentiment from the heathen mythology, low thoughts, and barbarous misuse of the metres and rhymes of the language. The middle classes are forced to put up with snatches from those above and below them, and have less music than either.[2]

In the nineteenth century, alongside journalism and prose fiction, poetry (including ballads and songs) was by far the most favored mediums of Irish nationalist expression; ballads in particular, given their added accessibility to, and appeal among, both the highly literate and the less literate members of society—with Ireland enjoying a relatively high degree of literacy (i.e., in English language) after the 1830s.[3]

Born into a middling Catholic family, by his adult life Moore increasingly veered in the direction of deism, with a broadminded commitment to Catholic and Protestant inter-denominational tolerance and coexistence.[4] Marrying the Anglican Elizabeth "Bessy" Dyke and raising their children as Anglicans, Moore's social network consisted of many prominent Anglicans, including political figures such as the Whig Lord John Russell (also a future Liberal prime minister, 1865–66) and Lord Moira (a.k.a. Marquess of Hastings, the governor-general of British India from 1813 to 1823). Moore, regardless of his personal religious orientation, remained firmly committed to defending the rights of Catholics in the United Kingdom. He was an erstwhile sympathizer of the republican United Irishmen, who staged an unsuccessful uprising in 1798 and had been an acquaintance of the leader of the failed 1803 United Irishmen rebellion, Robert Emmet, who was executed following the suppression of that rising. Moore and Emmet had known each other during their university days in Dublin (Trinity College), from which Moore graduated in 1799.[5] Following the failed 1798 large-scale United Irishmen uprising, the Irish parliament in Dublin, which had excluded Catholics, was closed down, and in 1801 Ireland was incorporated into the United Kingdom of Great Britain and Ireland under the Act of Union—with Ireland now represented at the Westminster parliament in London. By the opening years of the nineteenth century, Moore had abandoned radical politics and was committed to the moderate and non-violent platform of the Repeal movement (a.k.a. "Home Rule," meaning campaigning for the repeal of the Act of Union and the restoration of a separate Irish parliament *within* the British Empire, albeit with equal political representation for Catholics and Protestants). Notwithstanding his occasional glorification of past republican nationalist heroes in his highly popular *Irish Melodies* and in "The Fire-Worshippers" section of his 1817 narrative poem *Lalla Rookh*, Moore now focused on the peaceful promotion of both inter-denominational harmony and political equality among Protestants and Catholics (i.e., Catholic Emancipation) and Irish Home Rule.[6]

In three of Moore's poems, Iranian settings served as surrogate historical backdrops for either Irish resistance to English domination or the ongoing plight of Catholics in the

United Kingdom. The earliest of these was an epistolary poem on the theme of contemporary persecution of Catholics in the United Kingdom in the form of "Letter VI: From Abdallah, in London, to Mohassan, in Ispahan," appearing in Moore's 1813 *Intercepted Letters; or, The Twopenny Post-bag. To Which are Added, Trifles Reprinted*. In this poem, Moore followed the continued convention in Britain and Ireland of utilizing the "Persian Letters" mode of allegorically commenting on one's own society through the gaze of a culturally *Other* observer, which had attained great popularity since the publication of Montesquieu's 1721 *Lettres persanes*. Montesquieu's work was first translated into English in 1722 by John Ozell as *The Persian Letters*, with the earliest example of a highly successful adaptation of the genre in Britain and Ireland being the English Whig politician George Lyttelton's 1735 *Letters from a Persian in England to His Friend at Ispahan*, initially published anonymously.[7] Other such examples included the anonymous 1736 *Remarks of a Persian Traveller on the Principal Courts of Europe with a Dissertation upon that of England, the Nation in General, and the Prime Minister. Written Originally in the Persian Language, and now Translated into English and French* (published in London by John Hughs). An early instance of using the 'Persian Letters' literary device for commenting on Irish society was "A Letter from a *Persian* in *Ireland* to His Friend in *Sheraz*," appearing in the short-lived Dublin weekly paper *The Meddler* (1743–44).[8] The paper, published by Peter Wilson, vaguely stated its principal objective in the Enlightenment parlance of promoting "the common good" and "virtue."[9] *The Meddler*'s "A Letter from a *Persian* in *Ireland*," a lackluster attempt at emulating the style of *Lettres persanes*, was written by an imaginary Iranian traveler in Ireland, named Aram, and was addressed to his friend Helim back in Iran. The letter criticized the indolent habits of the wealthy Irish, characterized the Irish in general as being hypocritical champions of truth while regularly lying, criticized men of the upper classes for publicly and excessively indulging in the use of snuff, while lambasting the women of the same classes for wearing "artificial Hair, which the better Sort purchase from the Meaner, and have it molded into the strangest and most unnatural Forms, you can imagine." The letter also criticized the practice among upper-class men of wearing wigs. It ended with a double-entendre, rebuking the purportedly prevalent infidelity among married men of the upper classes in Ireland by way of equating it with the Muslim practice of polygamy. Aram informed his friend:

> But my *Helim*, tho' these People have many strange and barbarous Customs, they have nevertheless several that are praise-worthy. It is not indeed permitted by the Laws of this Country for a Man to have more than one Wife; yet those of the first Rank, soon after they are married, take a second, whom they keep in Private; which gives me great Reason to hope, that they may in time become Mussulmans, and obey the precepts of our Prophet by encreasing [*sic*] their Wives to the number of four, that number which Nature, and Reason, as well as his Wisdom, have prescribed.[10]

Over a century-and-a-half later, Iranian writers, with their own variations of travelogue- and correspondent-style critiques of Iranian society, would also adopt the *Lettres persanes* format by reversing the nationality as well as the travel location of the principal correspondents in this genre. Among other examples was the "English Letters" genre that first appeared in 1909–10 in serialized form ("Letter from a Briton to a Friend") in the social-democratic constitutionalist and nationalist Tehran newspaper *Irān-e Nou*.[11]

Moore's 1813 *Intercepted Letters*, published under the pseudonym "Thomas Brown, the younger," was a collection of simulated letters written in verse form and criticizing various aspects of social and political status quo in the United Kingdom. Reprinted 14 times in the first year of publication alone, *Intercepted Letters* consisted of alleged letters first discovered in a lost mailbag by a member of the Society for the Suppression of Vice—established in 1802 by politically conservative and evangelical Anglican groups with the objective of suppressing immorality and socially and politically subversive beliefs, particularly in published form. Reportedly, the letters were eventually sold by the "Suppressors" to a friend of "Thomas Brown," from whom the author had acquired them.[12] This work appeared during what became the closing stages of the Napoleonic Wars (1799–1815), with Britain having been at war since 1793 (first with revolutionary France and then with the Napoleonic Empire), with a brief interlude during 1802–03 (Peace of Amiens). This was a time when extensive restrictions were imposed on political and social dissent. Moreover, while before the end of the eighteenth century some of the remaining penal laws imposed on Catholics since the sixteenth century had been revoked, namely under the 1778 Catholic Relief Act, other penal laws and the more general Protestant discriminatory attitudes toward, and treatment of, Catholics continued. Whereas the Catholics were a majority in Ireland (albeit with the Anglican Ascendancy in control of Irish affairs), Catholics formed a minority in the predominantly Protestant Britain and in the United Kingdom as a whole, with the Church of England (Anglican Church) as the official church in England, as well as in Wales (where it operated under the designation of the Church of Wales) and in Ireland (where it was named the Church of Ireland). "Letter VI" of *Intercepted Letters*, "From Abdallah in London to Mohassan in Ispahan," served as a device for indirectly commenting on the condition of Catholics in the United Kingdom during Moore's own time. The fictional editor of *Intercepted Letters* informed the readers in a footnote:

> I have made many inquiries about this Persian gentleman [i.e., Abdallah], but cannot satisfactorily ascertain who he is. From his notions of Religious Liberty, however, I conclude that he is an importation of Ministers; and he is arrived just in time to assist the P[rince] and Mr. L[eckie] in their new Oriental Plan of Reform—See the second of these Letters—How Abdallah's epistle to Ispahan found its way into the Twopenny Post-Bag is more than I can pretend to account for.[13]

As to why Abdallah would have composed letters to his friend Mohassan back in Iran in English language, one would have to ask Moore. Moore made it clear in the remainder of this section of the letter that Abdallah was a Shi'i Muslim, emphasizing the enmity between the majority *ithna' ashari* (Twelver) Shi'i and the minority Sunni Muslim populations of Iran. This was intended to parallel the Protestant oppression of minority Catholics in the United Kingdom; hence also the references in the above quotation to Prince Regent (later George IV) and the Tory historian and proponent of British imperial and naval expansion, Gould Francis Leckie, whom Moore knew and who opposed

Catholic Emancipation. Despite the abrogation of most penal laws against Catholics in the United Kingdom by 1813, Catholics continued to face political and other disabilities. Among other prohibitions, they were barred from holding parliamentary seats (leaving aside here the required landed property qualification for holding a parliamentary seat, and by adult males only). They were also excluded from high state and military offices, which required an oath of allegiance to both the monarch and the Church of England (known as the Oath of Supremacy) and were still disqualified, along with all other non-Anglicans, from attending English universities (which at the time consisted of Oxford and Cambridge only). Moreover, Catholics were subject to paying tithes to the Anglican establishment (until 1871). The compulsory payment of the tithe by Catholics to the established Anglican Church in Ireland (i.e., the Church of Ireland) constituted a leading grievance of the Catholic establishment and the majority of Ireland's population, who happened to be Catholics. These disabilities and levies eventually provided the momentum for the extensive campaign following the end of the Napoleonic Wars led by Daniel O'Connell (1775–1847) and the subsequent founding of the Catholic Association in 1823 that culminated in the Catholic Relief Act of 1829, which allowed (adult male) Catholics who met the required property qualification to stand in parliamentary elections. Moore was a supporter of this campaign but personally disdained O'Connell, whom Moore considered a demagogue groveling to the Catholic establishment for financial and publicity support.[14]

In the 1813 letter "From Abdallah in London to Mohassan in Ispahan," which was among Moore's various literary endorsements of the rights of Catholics *during* the Napoleonic Wars, the Iranian author and, by implication, the contemporary dominant Shi'i religious establishment in Iran were cast as intolerant; the latter allegorically serving as a stand-in for the Church of England. In another footnote to Abdallah's letter, Moore quoted from the Italian Giovanni Mariti, whose work he would also cite in the 1817 *Lalla Rookh*. Making use of Mariti's comment on the fable that "The Shiites [i.e., Shi'i] wear green slippers, which the Sunnites consider as a great abomination," Moore's Abdallah expressed:

Yet, spite of tenets so flagitious,
(Which must, at bottom, be seditious;
As no man living would refuse
Green slippers, but from treasonous views;
Nor wash his toes, but with intent
To overturn the Government!)
Such is our mild and tolerant way,
We only curse them twice a day,
(According to a Form that's set)
And, far from torturing, only let
All orthodox believers beat 'em,
And twitch their beards, where'er they meet 'em.
[...]
The same mild views of Toleration
Inspire, I find, this button'd nation
Whose Papists (full as giv'n to rogue,
And only Sunnites with a brogue)

Fare just as well, with all their fuss,
As rascal Sunnites do with us.[15]

Despite Moore's analogy in this poem between the persecution of Sunni Muslims in contemporary Iran and of Catholic Christians in the United Kingdom, Islam in general (as also evident in Moore's *Lalla Rookh* discussed below) or the *contemporary* Iranian state, society, and cultures ordinarily were not cast in a sympathetic light in Irish nationalist works of literature *prior* to the emergence of the Young Ireland movement in the 1840s. After that point, different Irish nationalist poets provided both antipathetic and sympathetic versions of Iran's past and present, and of Islam as both a religion of conquest and a religious-cultural marker of resistance to European imperialism. The general pre-1840's literary pattern of allegoric references to Iran following the gradual consolidation of Islam as the dominant religion of that territory, initially in the form of Sunni Islam after the Arab-Muslim invasion in the seventh century, was not inconsistent with the cultural elevation of pre-Islamic Iran in Irish antiquarian claims of Iranian origins of Irish civilization—leaving aside the many elisions and conflations of historical time and space appearing in those antiquarian works. Yet, as discussed in detail later on, it is imperative to note Moore's later allegoric condemnation of Arab-Muslim invasion of Iran was not a wholesale castigation of Islam. This can be attested by the Muslim faith of the fictional narrator of the tales appearing in *Lalla Rookh* and his wife-to-be—i.e., Feramorz (/Aliris) and Lalla Rookh—or the Arab-Muslim lover (i.e., Hinda) of the hero of "The Fire Worshippers" segment of the narrative poem, or the Iranian hero of "The Veiled Prophet of Khorassan" segment of the poem, named Azim. What Moore condemned in this long narrative poem was religious intolerance in all shapes as well as attempted eradication of indigenous cultural and religious practices by foreign occupiers. As discussed in the next chapter, whereas after the 1840s the Young Ireland poet Denis Florence MacCarthy was to follow Moore's example of celebrating Iran's native Zoroastrian resistance to Arab-Muslim rule in the seventh century, as Moore did in his "The Fire-Worshippers" section of the 1817 *Lalla Rookh* (discussed below), the Young Ireland poet James Clarence Mangan would part ways with this temporal allegoric focus on Iranian history. In contradistinction to Moore's characterization of a homogenized Islam in various sections of *Lalla Rookh* in general, and of Shi'i Islam in particular in the case of *Intercepted Letters*, Mangan (d. 1849) cast (Shi'i) Islam of sixteenth-century Safavid-ruled Iran as the essence of Iranian cultural-nativist resistance to alleged English imperialism at the time. There were also Young Irelanders who condemned the pre-Islamic ancient Persian empire of the Achaemenid era as a virulent imperialist force, notably in the most influential Young Ireland poem by a founding member of the movement Thomas Osborne Davis: "A Nation Once Again." Davis drew an analogy between the ancient 'Greek' resistance to imperialist aggression by the Persian Empire and Irish resistance to English imperialism. As already noted, and discussed in some depth later in this chapter, there was also an antiquarian dimension to Moore's interest in ancient pre-Islamic Iran, which would appear in the first volume of his *The History of Ireland* (1835).

Moore's best-known Iran-centered poems occurred in his most enduring and commercially successful work, the 1817 narrative poem *Lalla Rookh: An Oriental Romance*. In two sections of the four-part *Lalla Rookh*, Moore turned to Iran in much greater allegoric detail and thematic centrality than he had in "Letter VI" of *Intercepted Letters*. In Iran-centered sections of *Lalla Rookh*, instead of focusing on *intra*-Islamic sectarian religious persecution, Moore concentrated on the motif of alien military, political, religious, and cultural aggression and oppression, by symbolically casting Iran in the aftermath of Arab-Muslim occupation in the seventh century as Ireland under English rule, since the sixteenth century more specifically. Moreover, while Moore had by then abandoned militant nationalism, *Lalla Rookh* marked his most extensive foray thus far into the subject of radical nationalist politics, a topic he also subsequently, albeit now critically, explored in his satirical *Fudge Family* epistolary poems (1818, 1823) and *Memoirs of Captain Rock* (1824).

Moore's 1817 *Lalla Rookh*

Moore had already commenced work on the widely researched *Lalla Rookh* by around September 1811, well before the publication of *Intercepted Letters* in 1813.[16] Although completed in 1816, *Lalla Rookh* was published in 1817, after the publisher (Messrs. Longman) decided to postpone publication in light of the general economic crisis in the immediate aftermath of the termination of the Napoleonic Wars in 1815. This was meant to secure higher sales and revenue for the publisher, given the large sum already paid to Moore by Messrs. Longman, and simultaneously avoid undermining the literary credibility of Moore's work in consequence of lower sales than anticipated. When published, the book was a spectacular literary success in terms of its immediate public reception and sales, despite many reviewers complaining of its excessively ornate imagery, loquacious details, and heavily adorned style. Even many of these same reviewers still found much to praise about the work.[17] Going through numerous editions, including in the United States, and translated into a number of European languages in the coming years, *Lalla Rookh* remained Moore's most financially successful achievement ever.[18] This work belonged to the broader genre of imaginary and supposedly oriental-style works produced by some poets in the ranks of the Romantic literary circle, such as poems by one of Moore's most famous literary friends, Lord Byron.[19] Interspersed with prose segments, *Lalla Rookh* comprised of four separate poems: "The Veiled Prophet of Khorassan," "Paradise and the Peri," "The Fire-Worshippers," and "The Light of the Haram." With the latter section being primarily an idealized romance, the remaining three sections also conveyed blatant political allegories. While "Paradise and the Peri" centered around the theme of Hindu resistance to early Muslim rule in the Indian subcontinent,[20] the first and third sections of the book, "The Veiled Prophet of Khorassan" and "The Fire-Worshippers," were situated in fictionalized "Iranian" historical settings as a vehicle for commenting on two distinct episodes in the history of uprisings in Ireland against English rule. Both poems were set in Arab-Muslim occupied former Iranian territories. Significantly, in place of the more common English designation of 'Persia' at the time, Moore used 'Iran,' the indigenous name of the territory, which had also appeared frequently in Irish antiquarian texts as far back as Vallancey's works and had gained greater currency than before following the dissemination of Sir William Jones' philological works. Given the homophonous designations of Iran and Erin (i.e., Ireland), references to 'Iran' in *Lalla Rookh* served as thinly veiled allegoric substitutes for commenting on historical developments in Ireland. Moreover, as discussed later in this chapter, Moore was a believer in the Iranian origin of Ireland's ancient civilization (by means of Phoenician transmission) and the common etymological root of the names of both territories.

Both of the Iranian settings deployed in *Lalla Rookh* centered on the subject of resistance and rebellion by the occupied native population in reaction to alien military, political, and religious domination; reminiscent of Ireland's experience of English domination as well as the simmering religious tensions between the majority Catholic and the minority, but dominant, Protestant communities of Ireland since the sixteenth century—even if, paradoxically, "The Fire-Worshippers" was intended to champion the inter-denominational and cross-ethnic platform of the United Irishmen uprisings against English rule in 1798 and 1803. Lalla Rookh of the title, meaning "Tulip Cheek" in Persian,[21] is the name of a fictional daughter of the otherwise historical Mughal emperor Aurangzeb (r. 1658–1707); the Mughal Empire (founded in 1526) controlling much of the Indian subcontinent prior to the gradual English colonization of the subcontinent by the English East India Company after 1757. In the story, princess Lalla Rookh is engaged to Aliris, the young king of Bukhara in Central Asia. She and her retinue journey from Delhi to Kashmir, where she is to meet for the very first time and marry Aliris. Along the way, a poet named Feramorz joins the royal convoy and entertains the princess and her entourage with various tales that constitute the four sections of *Lalla Rookh*, with prose description of the journey and various reactions to Feramorz's tales comprising the remainder of the book. Lalla Rookh's puritanical chamberlain, fittingly named Fadladeen ("virtue of faith" in Arabic) and representing sectarian religious intolerance that Moore opposed, disapproves of Feramorz's tales but is unable to induce the princess to banish the poet. During the journey, Lalla Rookh finds herself falling in love with Feramorz and is anguished by her feelings for the poet while already betrothed to the king of Bukhara, whom she is about to meet and marry. To her immense relief and joy, she discovers at the end of the book that Feramorz is no other than Aliris in disguise. It has been suggested that Moore's choice of name for the poet Feramorz includes the sound of Moore's own name, and it is generally acknowledged that the fictional poet "echoes" Moore's own sentiments.[22] It is also possible that the combined Aliris/Feramorz name choices were suggestive of al-"Iris" (i.e., "Irish") and Moore. Whether Moore was aware when selecting Feramorz's name, the pre-Islamic Persian name "Faramarz" incidentally signifies one who forgives his enemies, a temperament evocative of Moore's own statement of *Lalla Rookh*'s intended underlying message of tolerance.[23]

In his choice of the Iran/Erin analogy in "The Veiled Prophet of Khorassan" and "The Fire-Worshippers," as a metaphoric device for commenting on particular episodes in Irish history under English occupation, Moore imaginatively utilized different periods in the history of Arab-Muslim occupied former Iranian territories, and hence also distinct Iranian cultural and religious terrains.[24] Feramorz's tales commence with "The Veiled Prophet of Khorassan," in which the historical eighth-century 'Iranian' Hashim ibn Hakim "al-Muqanna" (i.e., "the veiled one") was transformed into Moore's villain "Mokanna," the false prophet. The historical al-Muqanna, who was also a chemist and had reportedly disfigured his face in an explosion during an experiment (hence his wearing a veil), had staged a four-year long religious-nativist uprising against the Baghdad-based Arab (and Sunni-Muslim) Abbasid caliphate, with the rebellion centered in Transoxania (where Bukhara, in present-day Uzbekistan, is situated). The rebellion got underway in 776 CE under the banner of al-Muqanna's heterodox messianic faith that fused elements of Islam with so-called indigenous religious attributes, the latter also including neoteric doctrines. With the defeat of the rebellion, al-Muqanna poisoned himself, after killing his wife as well as his favorite slave. He had requested that his followers incinerate his corpse. But, they failed to completely cremate his body.[25] Moore's detailed historical research for *Lalla Rookh* surpassed that of the rest of his contemporary Romantic authors in the United Kingdom who were similarly engaged in the 'oriental-style' literary genre, including the works of his friend Byron. Moore's information concerning the historical al-Muqanna was largely acquired from the French Barthélemy d'Herbelot's 1697 *Bibliothèque orientale*, which relied on earlier Muslim sources.[26] The anti-hero Mokanna of Moore's poem is a contemptuous and malevolent self-serving manipulator, who dupes his followers with the joint promise of earthy emancipation and salvation in the afterlife, while furtively pursuing his own self-aggrandizing objective of seizing territorial power. Unbeknownst to his followers, Mokanna suffers from facial deformity, which he hides behind a silver veil, claiming instead that no mortal could survive the experience of glancing at his supernaturally "dazzling" countenance.[27] It is very likely that Moore opted for the English rendering of al-Muqanna's name as 'Mokanna,' not only as a means of disencumbering an otherwise hard-to-pronounce name for his average reader but also to give the name an Irish sound, echoing such clan names as McKenna, without necessarily prompting the reader to presume any direct correspondence between the latter and Mokanna's name. Other similar Irish literary specimens of this style of near-homophonous oriental-Irish naming included, later in the century, James Clarence Mangan's fictional warrior bard, 'Al Makeenah,' evocative of both Moore's Mokanna and the McKenna clan name.[28]

Lalla Rookh: "The Veiled Prophet of Khorassan"

"The Veiled Prophet" revolves around three central characters, all of whom are identified as Iranians living in the former Iranian territories now under Arab-Muslim occupation. These are the veiled prophet Mokanna, Azim (a patriotic youth), and Zelica (Azim's long-lost lover and now Mokanna's principal harem maiden). Mokanna, who has founded a messianic faith, has staged an uprising against the Arab-Muslim Abbasid Caliph "Mahadi" under the banner of eternal salvation and freeing Iranian territories from the yoke of foreign tyrants. Azim had previously served in the Caliph's army and participated in the invasion of Empress Irene's Byzantine Empire ("Greece"). Captured in battle, after serving some years in captivity, Azim returns to his homeland now with a resolute determination to liberate 'Iran' from Abbasid domination. (Incidentally, the historical al-Muqanna had earlier joined the Abbasid forces and had also spent time in detention.) Moore attributed Azim's so-called nationalist transformation to Azim's exposure (during his captivity) to the "Greek" predilection for liberty—a highly exaggerated, and in this case also utterly anachronistic gesture, of both uniform equation of ancient Hellenic cultures with democracy and conflation of ancient 'Greece' with the Byzantine Empire. This was symptomatic of the wider Hellenophilia in the United Kingdom at the time, particularly in some Romantic circles. Returning to his homeland, Azim learns of Mokanna's rebellion against the Caliph and resolves to join Mokanna's forces:

> O, who could, even in bondage, tread the plains
> Of glorious Greece, nor feel his spirit rise
> Kindling within him? who, with heart and eyes,
> Could walk where Liberty had been, nor see
> The shining foot-prints of her Deity,
> [...]
> And now, returning to his own dear land,
> Full of those dreams of good that, vainly grand,
> Haunt the young heart—proud views of human-kind,
> Of men to Gods exalted and refined—
> False views, like that horizon's fair deceit,
> Where earth and heaven but seem, alas, to meet!—
> Soon as he heard an Arm Divine was raised
> To right the nations, and beheld, emblazed
> On the white flag MOKANNA's host unfurled,
> Those words of sunshine, "Freedom to the World."
> At once his faith, his sword, his soul obeyed
> The inspiring summons; every chosen blade
> That fought beneath that banner's sacred text
> Seemed doubly edged, for this world and the next;
> And ne'er did Faith with her smooth bandage bind
> Eyes more devoutly willing to be blind,
> In virtue's cause;—never was soul inspired
> With livelier trust in what it most desired,
> Than his, the' enthusiast there, who kneeling pale
> With pious awe, before that Silver Veil,
> Believes the form, to which he bends his knee,
> Some pure, redeeming angel, sent to free
> This fettered world from every bond and stain,
> And bring its primal glories back again![29]

Eventually, Azim and his former lover Zelica are reunited in Mokanna's palace after Azim arrives there to join Mokanna's army. The young lovers had been separated after Azim set out to fight in the Caliph's occupation force in Byzantine territories. Neither lover had ceased to yearn for the other, but Zelica, assuming Azim was killed in battle, ended up as part of the false prophet Mokanna's entourage, becoming his favorite harem girl, "sworn bride," and "priestess."[30] Witnessing the splendor and opulence of Mokanna's palace, Azim grows suspicious of the sincerity of the veiled prophet's stated platform of religious salvation and Iran's liberation. Zelica then warns Azim of the veiled prophet's narcissistic and malevolent agenda, after Mokanna discloses his true self to Zelica.[31] Failing to convince Zelica to escape with him, Azim now joins the Caliph's army instead of Mokanna's forces, with the sole objective of destroying Mokanna, and without any underlying allegiance to the Caliph, whom Azim considers a foreign occupier of his homeland. Killing Mokanna would both release Zelica from the oath of loyalty she had taken to the false prophet and, at the same time, terminate a misguided rebellion that was exploiting the genuine and valid 'nationalist' and religious aspirations of the Iranian people. Once the main battle between the forces of Mokanna and the Caliph gets underway, Mokanna's army initially gains the upper hand, but Azim manages to rally the Caliph's scattered forces and turns the tide against the insurgents. With his army defeated, Mokanna poisons all of his remaining followers inside his palace and reveals his face and motives to his dying followers, before plunging himself into a bath of acid. Zelica is now the only person still alive in the palace. Already despairing of having been duped by the false prophet and ashamed of herself in Azim's estimation, Zelica wishes to speed up her own death than wait for Mokanna's poison to take effect. She dons Mokanna's discarded silver veil and leaves the palace in the hope of being mistaken for the veiled prophet and killed by the Caliph's forces, unaware that Azim has joined the rival army. Azim, seeing the veiled figure approaching, rushes forth with a spear, seeking the distinction of killing the false prophet. Zelica hurls herself toward the spear and is mortally wounded. Azim realizes he has inadvertently fatally wounded his lover. The lovers embrace, and the dying Zelica urges Azim to live (i.e., to abandon warfare) and to pray for and love Zelica till they are reunited in the afterlife.[32]

As I have already argued in another publication,[33] the closest Irish match for Moore's Mokanna and the latter's revolt as portrayed in *Lalla Rookh* is the 1641 uprising led by Sir Phelim O'Neill (1604–53), Moore's most despised Irish-Catholic historical personality. Sir Phelim led the Catholic uprising of 1641 that later culminated in the 1642–52 Confederate War between Catholic forces, with some backing from a number of European Catholic states, and English and other Protestant forces, with the Confederate War overlapping and intersecting with the English Civil War of 1642–49.[34] Whereas Moore defended the objectives and conduct of the Confederate War, even as he censured the outside meddling of the Papal nuncio in the affair, he vehemently condemned the 1641 prelude to that event, which had been marked by intense savagery and indiscriminate slaughter of Protestants by Sir Phelim's Catholic forces. For Moore, Sir Phelim's uprising, akin to the fictional Mokanna's rebellion, was ultimately a self-serving act, with both Sir Phelim and Mokanna surreptitiously conspiring to attain political-military supremacy by manipulating the otherwise legitimate "nativist-nationalist" and religious grievances of people who flocked to join their insurrection. Sir Phelim, who was removed from his leadership position by his relative Owen Roe O'Neill with the advent of the Confederate War, was deprecated by Moore for his incitement of indiscriminate and virulent Catholic hatred toward Protestants. Although Moore had alluded to Sir Phelim in an earlier work, Moore's direct public expression of contempt for Sir Phelim's purported self-aggrandizing manipulation of Catholic suffering and his participation in sectarian atrocities appeared following the publication of *Lalla Rookh*, first in concise form in the 1824 *Memoirs of Captain Rock* and then in ample detail in the 1846 fourth volume of *The History of Ireland*. In the latter work, Moore chiefly relied on available partisan accounts of the 1641 uprising that vigorously deprecated Sir Phelim O'Neill: the first volume of Thomas Carte's 1736 *An History of the Life of James Duke of Ormonde, from His Birth in 1610, to His Death in 1688*; the third volume of Thomas Leland's 1773 *History of Ireland from the Invasion of Henry II*; as well as such works as Sir John Temple's 1646 *The Irish Rebellion; Or, An History of the Irish Papists to Extirpate the Protestants in the Kingdom of Ireland*.[35] In the fourth volume of *The History of Ireland*, Moore noted the enduring and distinctly sectarian collective memories of Sir Phelim's atrocities:

> To the protestant the story, or legend, of the Irish massacre is from his childhood familiar; being, too often, the only remarkable event in our history with which he deigns to become acquainted; while, to the catholic, it brings a feeling of retrospective shame.[36]

In "The Veiled Prophet," Moore had creatively reworked the historical al-Muqanna's heterodox messianic religion. It was now transformed into Mokanna's debased form of a denominational faith that had key attributes in common with the Muslim faith of the Arab occupiers, and with Mokanna's followers also beseeching the same god as the Arabs ("Allah" in Arabic and rendered as "Alla" in Moore's poem), even as Moore simultaneously identified indigenous Iranians rushing to join Mokanna's forces as "Worshippers of Fire" (i.e., presumably Zoroastrians). This implied association between Mokanna's newly established faith and the religion of the Arabs closely corresponded to what Moore later described as Sir Phelim's perversion of Catholicism, with both Catholicism and Protestantism being denominations of the same Christian faith.[37]

Read metaphorically, Azim in "The Veiled Prophet" represents Moore's alter ego, with Moore creating an indigenous Iranian (i.e., Irish) character who seeks to eradicate the self-serving fanatical and false prophecy of Mokanna (i.e., hubristic self-serving Irish-Catholic bigots posing as defenders of violated Catholic rights). Mokanna masquerades as the liberator of indigenous Iranian people oppressed by religiously and ethnically foreign occupiers. As in *Intercepted Letters* and his other works, Moore was again underscoring his abhorrence of inter-denominational prejudice and intolerance. He opposed retaliatory and indiscriminate religious and ethnic chauvinism, no matter how valid the grievances of a group might be. In a prose segment of "The Veiled Prophet," which describes the poet Feramorz joining princess Lalla Rookh's entourage, Moore wrote:

> Without a moment's delay, young FERAMORZ was introduced, and FADLADEEN [Lalla Rookh's chamberlain], who could never make up his mind as to the merits of a poet, till he knew the religious sect to which he belonged, was about to ask him whether he was a Shia or a Sooni [i.e., Shi'i or Sunni], when LALLA ROOKH impatiently clapped her hands for silence.[38]

In the poem, Azim sought to eternally eradicate Mokanna and the deceptive prophecy with which he manipulated the rightful aspirations of the oppressed. In the process, Azim unintentionally, but inevitably, destroys Zelica, his ultimate and eternal love, and hence also metaphorically symbolizing his homeland (i.e., Iran/Erin)—in a heterosexually feminized classification of Ireland in this case. It is Zelica's beauty (i.e., the allure of Ireland) that Mokanna uses as his paramount bait for ensnaring brave male recruits willing to fight and die for their homeland and indigenous traditions. But, the Zelica that Azim slays is an Ireland that had been duped by Mokanna in her state of loss of reason: "'twas grief, 'twas madness did it all!"[39] Unwittingly turned into an instrument of Mokanna's ambition, she now wished to vanish as a physical object of desire following the recovery of her reason and plagued by shame, so that Azim can truly love her again as an ideal.[40] Zelica, the venerated Ireland of persecuted people, who have been manipulated by a false prophet and enticed to commit religious bloodbath, destroys herself—unable to return to her ostensibly unsullied "primal" state. With this act, Ireland terminates any hope of regaining her independence in this life cycle. But, she acquires Azim's eternal love and serves as his source of national inspiration and devotion. Zelica's final appeal to Azim is to cease self-destructive violence and to continue living in the world *as is*, in anticipation of eventual reunion with his love: "'But live, my AZIM;—O! to call thee mine / ' [...]—dream divine! / 'Live, if thou ever lov'dst me, if to meet / 'Thy ZELICA hereafter would be sweet, / 'O, live to pray for her—[...]."[41] After Zelica's death, Azim abandons warfare and dedicates himself to the memory of Zelica until his natural death, when he will be buried next to Zelica's tomb and reunited with her, signifying Azim's reception and eternal embrace by the soil of his homeland. Paralleling Moore's own feeling toward his native land, "The Veiled Prophet" ends with Azim's enduring love of Ireland, but without being able to restore her to her so-called authentic and independent essence in this life. Yet, Azim is assured at the time of his death that Zelica (Ireland) "was blessed":

> Time fleeted—years on years had passed away,
> [...]
> An aged man, who had grown aged there
> By that lone grave, morning and night in payer,
> For the last time knelt down—and, though the shade
> Of death hung darkening over him, there played
> A gleam of rapture in his eye and cheek,
> That brightened even Death—like the last streak
> [...]
> His soul had seen a Vision, while he slept;
> She, for whose spirit he had prayed and wept
> So many years, had come to him, all dressed
> In angel smiles, and told him she was blessed!
> For this the old man breathed his thanks, and died—
> And there, upon the banks of that loved tide,
> He and his ZELICA slept side by side.[42]

Lalla Rookh: "The Fire-Worshippers"

The third section of *Lalla Rookh*, "The Fire-Worshippers," is the tale of an abortive Iranian-Zoroastrian uprising against Arab-Muslim occupation of Iran in the seventh century, with the Zoroastrian religion selected by Moore as the core marker of native Iranian identity. In "The Veiled Prophet" too, Moore intermittently, and inconsistently, had identified indigenous Iranians as simultaneously Muslim and "Worshippers of Fire," a frequent European misunderstanding at the time regarding Zoroastrian beliefs and practices. As already noted, in keeping with some other contemporary Irish antiquarians, Moore believed Zoroastrian fire temples were the prototype of Ireland's Round Towers, a subject he later elaborated on in the first volume of *The History of Ireland* in 1835 (see below). Moore played on this conjecture throughout "The Fire-Worshippers,"[43] also alluding to Zoroastrian fire temples (i.e., the Round Towers of Ireland) as "their lost country's ancient fanes."[44] This imputed correspondence between ancient Iran and Ireland, along with the patent Iran/Erin allegoric interchange throughout the poem, augmented the proximity of the subject matter explored in the poem through the lens of a particular moment in Iranian history as a parallel for Irish history—notwithstanding some major dissimilarities glossed over by Moore. Thanks to "The Fire-Worshippers," *Lalla Rookh* rapidly acquired cachet as one of the most recognized Irish nationalist literary specimens, alongside Moore's highly popular editions of *Irish Melodies*. By the end of the century, however, the book would recede into near-oblivion, only to attain revived interest again in the past few decades, in some scholarly circles to be more precise. In a letter to his publisher Thomas Longman on November 23, 1837, Moore himself predicted that in the long run his "'Melodies,' will beat the mare, Lalla, hollow."[45] "The Fire-Worshippers" presents a highly essentialized fictional adaptation of inter-religious animosity between Iran's Zoroastrian natives ("Ghebers," as Moore called them, following the conventional idiom in the United Kingdom at the time) and their religiously and ethnically alien conquerors. This poem has conventionally been acknowledged since *Lalla Rookh*'s initial publication as denoting Irish resistance to English rule during the period marking the United Irishmen uprisings of 1798 and/or 1803, regardless of ongoing debates over Moore's intended Irish historical model for the poem's hero—leaving aside here the disparity between the cross-confessional and cross-ethnic feature of the United Irishmen and the poem's concentration on inter-religious and inter-ethnic conflict between Iranian Zoroastrians and Arab Muslims, among other historical incongruities. The ostensibly deep-seated inter-religious and inter-ethnic conflict in "The Fire-Worshippers" is tempered only by the love affair between Hafed, the Zoroastrian hero, and Hinda, the daughter of the tyrannical Arab-Muslim governor of Iran, "Al Hassan."[46] Hinda and Hafed represented previously antagonistic religious and ethnic/national identities, as well as younger-generation descendants of so-called natives and occupiers, capable of transcending the mutual seething bigotry and xenophobia, as well as the indiscriminate conquered- and conqueror-complexes of their forebears. This love affair, also mirroring Moore's own marriage to an Anglo-Protestant woman, was the principal allusion in the poem to the cross-ethnic and cross-sectarian nature of the republican United Irishmen movement ('mere Irish,' 'Old English,' English, Welsh, and Scots of variously Catholic, Anglican, Presbyterian, and other Christian denominational backgrounds, as well as deists and atheists).

In a patently circuitous reference to Robert Emmet—who was executed following the failed uprising he led in 1803 and had been a friend of Moore during their university days—and the many who had lost their lives before Emmet for the cause of a generically defined cross-denominational Irish struggle for independence since the late eighteenth century, Moore offered the following eulogy for the doomed Iranian hero of "The Fire-Worshippers":

> 'Tis come—his hour of martyrdom
> In Iran's sacred cause is come;
> And, though his life hath passed away
> Like lightning on a stormy day,
> Yet shall his death-hour leave a track
> Of glory, permanent and bright,
> [...]
> And hither bards and heroes oft
> Shall come in secret pilgrimage,
> And bring their warrior sons, and tell
> The wondering boys where Hafed fell; And swear them on those lone remains
> Of their lost country's ancient fanes,
> Never—while breath of life shall live
> Within them—never to forgive
> The' accursed race, whose ruthless chain
> Hath left on Iran's neck a stain
> Blood, blood alone can cleanse again![47]

Moore's lines echoed Emmet's own expressed hope during his speech from the dock following his arrest in 1803: "I wish that my memory and name may animate those who survive me, while I look down with complacency on the destruction of that perfidious government."[48] A number of commentators since 1817 have suggested that Hafed and his Arab-Muslim lover Hinda represent Robert Emmet and his lover Sarah Curran, both of them Anglicans (with Curran's father being a staunch supporter of the Anglican Ascendancy and British rule in Ireland). Alternative Irish nationalist martyrs have also been proposed as Moore's model for Hafed. For example, toward the end of the nineteenth century, Lady Jane Francesca Agnes Wilde ("Speranza" of the Young Ireland days) sided with those who maintained Hafed was patterned after one of the leaders of the 1798 United Irishmen uprising, Lord Edward FitzGerald (also a member of the Anglican Ascendancy, and already married in his case).[49] In fact, Moore equally memorialized both Emmet and Fitzgerald in his various popular melodies and, later, also composed a biography of Fitzgerald (1831). It is perhaps more accurate to regard "The Fire-Worshippers" as a mélange representation of the general spirit of both United Irishmen uprisings of 1798 and 1803, with Emmet as the prototype for Moore's Iranian hero, albeit with traces of Fitzgerald and others, and with the lovers in the poem simultaneously marking Moore's own cross-denominational marriage to Bessy.

The Irish nationalist allegoric application of Iran/Erin analogy was most clearly articulated in "The Fire-Worshippers" in the phrase "FOR GOD and IRAN," a highly recognizable resonance of the Irish nationalist idiom "for God and Ireland"; leaving little room for doubt in the minds of general readers of *Lalla Rookh* in the United Kingdom of Moore's intended simile.[50] In the Preface to the 1841 sixth volume of his *The Poetical Works*, Moore publicly commented for the first time on his intended Irish historical analogy in "The Fire-Worshippers":

> But, at last, fortunately, as it proved, the thought occurred to me of founding a story on the fierce struggle so long maintained between the Ghebers [i.e., Zoroastrians], or ancient Fire-worshippers [sic] of Persia, and their haughty Moslem masters. From that moment, a new and deep interest in my whole task took possession of me. The cause of tolerance was again my inspiring theme; and the spirit that had spoken in the melodies of Ireland soon found itself at home in the East.[51]

However, he avoided any direct public commentary on the intended historical connotation of "The Veiled Prophet of Khorassan," given the avowedly shameful episode in Irish-Catholic history and in Ireland's bloody communal past the latter poem evoked.[52] "The Fire-Worshippers" established a literary precedent for manifold subsequent Iran/Erin pairings in Irish nationalist poetry and prose, as well as for utilization of other episodes in Iranian history as referential devices for commenting on certain periods in Irish history. For instance, this latter mode of coupling Iran and Ireland later appeared in different arrangements in the poetry of James Clarence Mangan during his Young Ireland years in the 1840s (see the next chapter), or in a distinct prose form and stripped of any precise historical referentiality, in James Joyce's 1939 *Finnegans Wake* (see Chapter Nine).[53] Meanwhile, other Irish nationalist poets and writers after Moore replicated his analogy between Iranian-Zoroastrian resistance to Arab-Muslim invasion of Iran in the seventh century, on the one hand, and various episodes of Irish resistance to English domination after the twelfth century, on the other hand, as well as the persecution of the largely Catholic population of Ireland ('mere Irish' and 'Old English') by Protestant settlers and so-called indigenous converts to the Anglican faith after the mid-sixteenth century. A case in point is the poem titled "The Clan of Mac Caura" published in 1850 by Denis Florence MacCarthy, an erstwhile contributor to the Young Ireland mouthpiece *The Nation*. The poem, from which I quote later in this chapter, appeared in the closing stages of the "Great Famine" in Ireland and in the aftermath of the failed 1848 Young Ireland uprising. MacCarthy followed the conventional English designation of Zoroastrians at the time as "Guebre" ("Ghebers" in Moore's work, among other variant spellings).[54]

Overlooked in Moore's "The Fire-Worshippers," and in subsequent commentaries on the poem, is the fact that the Iranian Sassanian state, which was overrun by Arab-Muslim forces in the seventh century, had itself been an aggressive imperial state, albeit in decline at the time of the Muslim invasion, and with periodic state policy of persecuting non-Zoroastrian religious groups. The choice of Arab-Muslim occupied Iran in "The Fire-Worshippers" was, therefore, ultimately an historically unsuitable proxy for Ireland of post sixteenth century, or even the Ireland of the twelfth century. Moreover, in "The Fire-Worshippers" Moore drew an analogy between the early phase of Iran's conquest by a foreign power and Ireland of late eighteenth and/or early nineteenth century (i.e., long after the earliest stage of gradual Anglo-Norman conquests in Ireland initiated in the twelfth century). The implied historical correspondence, as tortuous as it was in its allusion to the United Irishmen uprisings, would not have worked in reference to Ireland of the twelfth century. Leaving aside here that Ireland at the time of the early Anglo-Norman conquests was not administratively a single unified territory, the Irish and the English in the twelfth century also shared the same religious denomination (i.e., Roman Catholic Christianity).

In "The Veiled Prophet" and "The Fire-Worshippers" Moore was presenting two distinct, albeit related, propensities in Irish history of resistance to English domination since the sixteenth century. The poems mirrored alternative dimensions of Ireland's history of resistance to English rule with contrasting 'nationalist' subtexts. Whereas "The Veiled Prophet" was Moore's warning against the dangers of Catholic *sectarian* uprisings against English rule, "The Fire-Worshippers" reflected Moore's endorsement of cross-denominational and cross-ethnic Irish nationalism, even if by the time Moore began work on *Lalla Rookh* he had long abandoned militant and republican nationalist politics and was advocating a peaceful campaign for Irish Home Rule within the British Empire (hence also Zelica's final words to Azim in "The Veiled Prophet").

Lalla Rookh and Expanded Contemporary Contacts between Iran and the United Kingdom

In composing *Lalla Rookh*, Moore carried out extensive research on various aspects of the history of 'Iran' (in the broadest geographic, historical, and cultural sense) and the remainder of Near Eastern territories, as well as on the Indian subcontinent and Central Asia, as indicated by the sources cited throughout the book. In addition to the fad of orient-themed literature in the United Kingdom in the early nineteenth century, the publication of *Lalla Rookh* also coincided with the surge in translations of literature and poetry by oriental authors themselves, including a number of adept translations into English from the Persian. This occurred alongside the rapid proliferation of historical and other studies of oriental lands and cultures. The wide-ranging examples include James Mill's controversial multi-volume *The History of British India* (1817–26) or John Malcolm's already-mentioned accomplished two-volume *The History of Persia* (1815). Malcolm couched his primary objectives in writing a general history of Persia ('Iran') from ancient times to the present in the following terms:

> WHILST the Annals of almost every Nation that can boast of any political importance have been illustrated by eminent British Writers, Persia seems hitherto to have been generally neglected. It must, therefore, be allowed to be highly desirable that this blank in our Literature should be filled up, and that the English reader should be made acquainted with the history and condition of a people, who have in most ages acted a conspicuous part on the theatre of the world; and who have of late acquired peculiar claims to our attention, from the nature of their relations to British India, and from the renewal of their intercourse with the States of Europe.[55]

For many decades to come, Malcolm's work served as a primary source of reference in the United Kingdom and beyond for commenting on Iranian history, including in related observations by Irish nationalists. Malcolm's book was consulted by Moore in composing *Lalla Rookh*. In the Preface to the 1841 sixth volume of *The Poetical Works of Thomas Moore* (also appearing in the 1842 American edition of *Lalla Rookh* and in subsequent editions of that work), Moore claimed that Malcolm (d. 1833), allegedly an undisputed authority on Iranian history, had once publicly praised Moore's historically accurate portrayal of Iran of the seventh and eight centuries CE.[56] Boasting of his own erudite historical recreations of Iranian territories of the period, in his self-flattery Moore also mentioned the prominent Anglo-Irish orientalist Sir William Ouseley (d. 1842) as having attested to Moore's extensive knowledge of Iranian history, although pointing out "an exception to the general accuracy for which he gives me credit." Reportedly, Ouseley had noted that Moore's sole error in otherwise presumably accurate depiction of Iran during the seventh and eight centuries had been Moore's assumption that Zoroastrians cremated their dead.[57]

It is imperative not to forget the wider spectrum of oriental-style Romantic literary genre in the United Kingdom around the time Moore's 1817 *Lalla Rookh* was published, as well as the broader Iran-related literary milieu in the United Kingdom and works on Iranian literature and oriental-style literature produced in other parts of Europe. English-language publications on 'Iranian' literature (classical Persian in this case and from Iranian lands in their former broadest cultural-territorial designation and beyond)[58] also included works published in British India. Among notable contemporary examples of these English publications in general were such works as James Atkinson's *Soohrab; a Poem, Freely Translated from the Original Persian of Firdousee, Being a Portion of the Shahnamu of that Celebrated Poet*, published in Calcutta in 1814, at which time Atkinson was an employee of the English East India Company. This was a translation of a segment of the epic cycle of *Shāhnāmeh* (*The Book of Kings*), compiled and supplemented in verse form by the poet Abul-Qassem Ferdowsi in the early eleventh century, based on much earlier versions. *Shāhnāmeh* chronicled "Iranian" history from its (otherwise mythic) origins up to the Arab-Muslim conquest in the seventh century CE. (By the end of the nineteenth century *Shāhnāmeh* would be hailed anachronistically by Iranians and some Persian-speaking populations in other territories as their seminal "national epic.") As noted, Moore had commenced work on *Lalla Rookh* in late 1811. There is no mention of Atkinson's work in the original edition of Moore's book or in his prefaces to later editions. But Moore was certainly familiar with general features of the Iranian epic from other translations and/or summary accounts, particularly of the most renowned hero of the epic, Rustam. In addition to general references in *Lalla Rookh* to d'Herbelot's 1697 *Bibliothèque orientale* and Malcolm's 1815 *History of Persia*, which contained information on Ferdowsi's *Shāhnāmeh*, Moore specifically cited Joseph Champion's *The Poems of Ferdosi* (originally published in Calcutta in 1785 and reprinted in London in 1788) and William Ouseley's 1795 *Persian Miscellanies*, as well as some other general reference to *Shāhnāmeh*.[59] He very likely also had learned about other segments of *Shāhnāmeh* from the three-volume *Oriental Collections* (1797–1800) edited by Ouseley.

The 1814 publication of a partial translation of *Shāhnāmeh* by Atkinson—and even more so his later abridged translation of the entire work, appearing as *The Shâh Nâmeh of the Persian Poet Firdausí* in 1832, long after the publication of *Lalla Rookh*[60]—would draw further attention to similarities between a particular episode in the Iranian epic in question and a main segment in Ireland's Ulster Cycle. A direct connection between *Shāhnāmeh* and another of Ireland's major epics, the Fenian Cycle, had been suggested previously by Charles Vallancey in his 1783/1784 "A Vindication of the Ancient History of Ireland," then appearing as a long treatise in *Collectanea de Rebus Hibernicis*, the publication of the Dublin-based Hibernian Antiquarian Society, a precursor to the Royal Irish Academy (1785). This work by Vallancey appeared in book form in 1786 (i.e., *A Vindication*). Vallancey's hypothesis, however, was based on his characteristically confounding etymological and historical correlations. While also referring to Rustam (spelled as both "Rostam" and "Rustam"), Vallancey concentrated on the similarity between another major character in *Shāhnāmeh*, named Esfandiyar, and the legendary Irish warrior hero Fionn mac Cumhaill.[61] It was, however, the close correspondence between the Iranian story of Rustam and his son Sohrab in *Shāhnāmeh*, on the one hand, and the Irish story of Cuchulain and his son Conla in the Ulster Cycle, on the other hand, that became the focus of much scholarly and literary commentary after the early nineteenth century. Among the early Irish proponents of an underlying connection between the two epics was Joseph Cooper Walker (d. 1810), a member of the Royal Irish Academy. Quoting comparative passages from William Ouseley's *Persian Miscellanies* (on *Shāhnāmeh*) and Charlotte Brooke's *Reliques of Irish Poetry* (on the Ulster Cycle), Walker in the posthumously published 1818 expanded edition of his *Historical Memoirs of the Irish Bards* asserted: "The similitude, between the pathetic Irish tale of Conloch, and the story of Rustam, as related by the Persian poet, Ferdusi, in his heroic poem, entitled Shah Nameh, is almost too strong to admit of its being supposed accidental."[62] The extraordinary similarity between these particular segments of the two epics appears to have escaped Moore's attention. But, the partial 1814 translation of *Shāhnāmeh* by Atkinson and his 1832 abridged translation of the entire work (*The Shâh Nâmeh of the Persian Poet Firdausí*) helped draw further attention to the similarities between the Iranian and Irish myths in question. For the Irish antiquarian Louisa Catherine Beaufort, writing in 1828, even before Atkinson's *The Shâh Nâmeh*, this connection demonstrated beyond doubt the Iranian origin of the Irish story of Cuchulain and Conla, hence serving as additional proof of Iranian roots of Irish civilization.[63]

In addition to literature and history, the manifold imaginations of the Orient circulating in the United Kingdom during these years were also shaped by the rapidly expanding diplomatic, commercial, missionary, and imperial encounters, as well as increased travel between the territories in general. This included people from the Orient visiting the United Kingdom (the overwhelming majority of them being men). Among other examples, these oriental visitors ranged from occasional travelers to diplomats, as well as lascars and ayahs from the Indian subcontinent, or small number of permanent immigrants. In the early nineteenth century, compared to some of Iran's neighboring territories, such as Russia, the Ottoman Empire, or the Indian subcontinent, very few Europeans (including Britons and Irish) traveled to or resided in Iran. These included members of diplomatic corps, their families and/or domestic staff, their other military and non-military entourage, alongside some commercial agents, military advisers engaged by the Iranian government, rare travelers, or members of Christian missionary organizations. In comparison, an even smaller number of Iranians visited the United

Kingdom during the early part of the nineteenth century. The few Iranian travelers at the time primarily consisted of members of diplomatic missions, along with a few (male) students sponsored by Iranian authorities after the second decade of the century.

On May 12, 1819, Moore met two Iranian students studying at Oxford, as part of a group of six students dispatched to England in 1815 by the Iranian crown prince Abbas Mirza. Both students reportedly expressed their admiration for *Lalla Rookh*. One of the students, whose name Moore recorded in his memoirs and met again on May 20 and June 6, was Mirza Jafar (one of two Iranian students by that name), to whom Moore referred following their second meeting as "my friend Giafer."[64] Following their third meeting in London (for breakfast), Moore identified this Mirza Jafar as "Meerza Jiafer Jabeeb," who was about to take his exams at the University of Oxford later in the month, hence clarifying that this particular Jafar was studying medicine—Moore evidently either personally misspelt as 'Jabeeb' the Arabic-Persian pronunciation of "tabib"/"tabeeb," meaning doctor, or this was a misprint in his posthumously published journal.[65]

Another Iranian in the United Kingdom at the time, who arrived in London in 1819, was the Iranian envoy Mirza Abul Hassan Khan "Ilchi" Shirazi. This was Abul Hassan Khan's second visit to England, by which time he already enjoyed much public and literary fame and notoriety in the United Kingdom, further piquing British public curiosity about Iran. Moore's *Lalla Rookh* was published between Abul Hassan Khan's two visits, 1809–10 and 1819–20. Abul Hassan Khan's second trip to England generated even more public and press fanfare than his first visit, not the least on account of his female companion during this trip, who was swiftly dubbed by the British press as the "Fair Circassian." He also became a subject of some contemporary European and American satirical works, with the latter category of works largely relying on press information reaching the United States from the United Kingdom. The most famous example of these lampoons was by James Justinian Morier, also an erstwhile British diplomatic staff in Iran. These were the highly popular *The Adventures of Hajji Baba of Ispahan* (1824) and its somewhat lesser acclaimed sequel *The Adventures of Hajji Baba, of Ispahan, in England* (1828). In these works, Morier ridiculed Iranians and Iranian cultural mores in general, with greater space devoted to parodying Abul Hassan Khan in *The Adventures of Hajji Baba, of Ispahan, in England* in the form of the absurd character "Mirza Firouz" (see my discussion of Mirza Abul Hassan Khan Shirazi in Chapter Eight). This latter sequel followed the 'Persian Letters' style with which Moore had experimented in his 1813 *Intercepted Letters*. It is not known if Moore's Iranian traveler 'Abdallah' in "Letter VI" of the 1813 *Intercepted Letters* was in any way inspired by Abul Hassan Khan's first visit to England, where Moore lived at the time. Whereas Moore mentioned in his memoirs having watched "the procession of the Persian ambassador to Carlton House [the residence of Prince Regent in London]" on May 20, 1819 (during Abul Hassan Khan's second visit to England), there is no mention of Abul Hassan Khan's prior visit in Moore's memoirs.[66] Incidentally, in *Lalla Rookh*, among his wide range of sources, Moore had relied on James Justinian Morier's 1812 *A Journey Through Persia, Armenia, and Asia Minor, to Constantinople, in the Years 1808 and 1809* (appearing in Moore's citations as "Morier's Travels").[67] During his second journey to the United Kingdom, Abul

Hassan Khan also visited Dublin in November 1819, where he immediately became a public sensation—Irish newspaper reports of his celebrity status in London, including the elaborate public and official receptions he attended, long preceding his actual visit to Ireland. Following this visit, Abul Hassan Khan even featured in works of Irish fiction (see Chapter Eight).

As indicated by the two Iranian students Moore met in London, a number of Iranians soon after *Lalla Rookh*'s publication had learned about the Iranian settings of two sections of this narrative poem and the overall plotline of the book. However, it is not known if Moore discussed the underlying Iran/Erin allegorical motif of those particular sections of the poem with these students. If Moore explained this allegoric device to either or both of the Iranian students, it does not appear that information was subsequently widely shared with other Iranians, given that later generations of Iranians seem to have taken the references to Iran at face value, rather than recognizing them as allegoric depictions of Irish history. It is unknown if Mirza Abul Hassan Khan also obtained a copy of *Lalla Rookh*. Moore's belief, based on hearsay, that *Lalla Rookh* had been translated into Persian and was circulating in Iran was clearly a mistake. As of yet, there is no evidence of even partial translations of the work in public circulation inside Iran during Moore's own lifetime, although, given its Iranian settings the poem could likely have been at least partially translated in summary prose form for private circulation within the royal court and possibly in some other circles not long after its publication. In addition to the aforementioned Iranian students, a few other Iranians conversant in English appear to have also obtained copies of the book—which is not to suggest other affluent Iranians may not have done so also, simply for owning a copy in their personal library collections, even if unable to read the book themselves. The Scottish traveler James Baillie Fraser wrote in his 1826 *Travels and Adventures in Persian Provinces* that an engineer by the name of Mohammad Reza Mirza in the service of Fraser's Iranian host in the city of Rasht (i.e., the governor of the city) had loaned Fraser his copy of Moore's *Lalla Rookh*. Mohammad Reza Mirza happened to be another one of the students previously dispatched to England by the Qajar crown prince Abbas Mirza. Fraser added that Mohammad Reza Mirza had brought the book from England, and the numerous penciled notes in the margins of its pages indicated Mohammad Reza Mirza's close reading of the poem.[68] Increasing number of Iranians conversant in a range of European languages were to read Moore's book in the coming decades, either in the original English or in available translations in other European languages, including French, given the book's rapid fame in Iranian circles interested in European literature, particularly those with references to Iran. However, no Persian translation of *Lalla Rookh* appeared in Iran or in neighboring Persian-speaking territories (including Persian-speaking communities in India and the Ottoman Empire, both with robust Persian publishing markets, India in particular). By the twentieth century, many literate Iranians had some general familiarity with the overall narrative gist of *Lalla Rookh*, albeit evidently still unaware of its allegorization of Irish history, and there were occasional references to and discussions of the book in print, as in the case of a very concise summary of its prose sections highlighting Fadladeen's intolerance that appeared in a major Tehran newspaper in 1917.[69] Contemporary information conveyed to Moore by third parties regarding the public reception of *Lalla Rookh* in Iran were outright exaggerations or fabrications. Based on an account by a "Mr. Stretch," who claimed to have obtained the information from "the nephew of the Persia ambassador" in France, Moore even believed the "Bendemeer's Stream" song appearing in "The Veiled Prophet," with the river also mentioned in "The Fire-Worshippers," was sung in Persian by Iranians who presumed it was an originally Persian song. For Moore, this was yet another sign of his accurate portrayal of Iranian settings in *Lalla Rookh*.[70] Aside from the hyperbole, Moore unfortunately also got some historical details of "Bendemeer" wrong. The term refers to the Band-e Amir dam over the Kor River in what is now the Fars province in Iran, which is believed to have been constructed in the *tenth century*—hence after the time frames of both Iran-centered sections of *Lalla Rookh*.

Thomas Moore and the Lingering Specter of Oriental Origins of Ireland's Round Towers

Lalla Rookh's remarkable success in terms of sales and reprints was also of great emotional consolation for Moore, who for years had dreaded being outpaced by his friend and literary competitor Lord Byron—that is, in both literary productivity and in the deployment of oriental settings.[71] Moore had feared by the time he completed *Lalla Rookh* the so-called oriental-style Romantic poetry, or what John D. Yohannan later aptly called "pseudo-Oriental" poetry,[72] would already have become passé due to Byron's copious production of poems in that genre.[73] Whereas it has often been suggested that Moore was apprehensive that Byron's use of oriental settings would deprive Moore of an "original" oriental location for *Lalla Rookh*, Moore had actually decided from the start to situate his oriental narrative poem in territories uncharted by Byron, who stayed focused on the lands then under Ottoman control, including Greek territories. But, the choice of Iranian and Indian settings in *Lalla Rookh* was not merely an attempt by Moore to avoid treading in the same familiar terrain appearing in the poems by Byron and other Romantic poets working in the same genre. Significantly, Moore's choice of locations for his narrative poem was a direct consequence of his belief in the 'Iranian,' or more broadly Indo-Iranian, roots of Ireland's ancient civilization.

Byron was aware of Moore's anxiety in regard to Byron's saturation of the oriental-style genre of Romantic poetry in general. Byron was also familiar with the general outlines of oriental theories of Irish origins. Dedicating in print his 1814 *The Corsair* to Moore as a means of consoling his friend, Byron noted:

> It is said [...] that you are engaged in the composition of a poem whose scene will be laid in the East; none can do those scenes so much justice. The wrongs of your own country, the magnificent and fiery spirit of her sons, the beauty and feeling of her daughters, may there be found [...]. Your imagination will create a warmer sun, and less clouded sky; but wildness, tenderness, and originality are part of *your national claim of oriental descent*, to which you have already thus far proved your title more clearly than the most zealous of your country's antiquarians.[74] (Emphasis added.)

During an 1879 speech in Liverpool in celebration of the centenary of Moore's birth, Alexander Martin Sullivan, the Irish nationalist MP, lawyer, journalist, and editor and proprietor of the Dublin newspaper *The Nation* at the time, stated:

> In 1817 Lalla Rookh—probably his most considerable poetical work—appeared. Even in this 'Oriental Romance' Moore contrived, under a very slight disguise, to present Ireland and her struggles for liberty to the sympathies of the reader, the 'Iran' of the 'Fire Worshipper' being 'Erin'; the theory that the Irish round towers were of Persian origin being in Moore's time strongly pressed by some historiologists.[75]

Sullivan did not mention that Moore himself was one such 'historiologist.' Although Joseph Lennon correctly notes that Moore's "most significant Orientalist work, *Lalla Rookh* (1817), does not mention Ireland's Oriental origin legends,"[76] Moore nevertheless provided intermittent hints of his belief in the presumed ancient historical connection between Iran and Erin by referring to "towers" throughout *Lalla Rookh*. For Moore, the Round Towers were emblematic of ancient Ireland's magnificent civilization and its ties to the Orient. The towers had also featured in his seminal nationalist poem "Let Erin Remember the Days of Old" (*Irish Melodies*, 1808). In "The Fire-Worshippers" section of *Lalla Rookh*, there were interspersed references to 'towers' of Zoroastrians (whom Moore, too, erroneously labeled as Worshippers of Fire). Moore belonged to the antiquarian camp that considered the ancient Zoroastrian temples of Iranian lands as the prototype of Ireland's Round Towers, hence one of his key motives in writing the scathing review of Henry O'Brien's book in 1834, given O'Brien's designation of the Round Towers as structures of phallic worship ritual.[77] Moreover, unlike Vallancey, Beaufort, O'Brien, and other similar adherents of Iranian origins of ancient Irish civilization, Moore believed that Iranian cultural practices had been introduced to Ireland by means of *already-Iranianized* Phoenicians who frequented the island.

For Moore, similar to many other Irish nationalist antiquarians at the time, the Round Towers served as both ancient 'national' monuments of Ireland and proof of fire-worship in pre-Christian Ireland. In the 1835 first volume of what became his four-volume *The History of Ireland* (1835–46), Moore set out to explicitly confirm the ancient Iranian origin of the towers.[78] In other words, in the interval between the publication of *Lalla Rookh* and *The History of Ireland* in 1835, Moore had retained his conviction in Ireland's oriental roots, even more strongly than before it appears. Moore's emphasis on sound scholarship in his commentaries on Vallancey or O'Brien was, in effect, an act of self-promotion and an assertion of antiquarian originality. He dismissed the etymological acrobatics of his predecessors in favor of his own style (of ultimately conjectural methodology). *The History of Ireland*, which he had pre-advertised in his anonymously penned astringent review of O'Brien's book the previous year, opened with a long description of early inhabitants of Ireland and their religious and cultural practices, addressing along the way some of the ongoing controversy surrounding the origins of the Irish.

Moreover, contra Charles Vallancey, O'Brien, Beaufort, and the like, Moore denied Iranians had directly populated Ireland in ancient times, although allowing for the possibility that a few Iranians may have accompanied the Phoenicians to the island.

Nevertheless, he was emphatic that ancient Iranian belief systems, cultural practices, and devotional rituals and architectural styles had permeated Ireland and formed the bedrock of ancient Ireland's high civilization. Alternative theories of Phoenician origins of the Irish that attributed Ireland's ancient civilizational features directly to Phoenicians, as espoused by Vallancey himself before he switched to the Iranian model, remained in circulation well into the second half of the nineteenth century as one of the prevalent theories of Irish origins—with William Betham (d. 1853) being its leading proponent during Moore's lifetime. A key premise for the continued allure of these alternative theories of Phoenician origins in antiquarian circles in the 1830s, or for Moore's theory of Phoenicians as mere transmitters of otherwise Iranian civilization, was the Phoenicians' confirmed historical reputation as sea-faring people and their recorded founding of colonies as far west as the north-western coast of the African continent (i.e., Carthage), as also attested by ancient Hellenic and Roman sources. The view that Phoenicians had reached Ireland via Carthage, as opposed to directly navigating from their original homeland in West Asia (e.g., Tyre, Sidon, etc.), also eliminated the likelihood of their prior arrival and/or settlement in nearby mainland Britain before reaching Ireland. In these "Carthaginian" accounts of Phoenician migrations to Ireland, the Iberian Peninsula ('Spain') was generally singled out as the principal preceding Phoenician colony before they reached Ireland. This narrative accorded Ireland the distinction of being the earliest center of high civilization in the British Isles. Accordingly, further evidence that Phoenician had not also sailed to England from the Spanish coast was the *alleged* absence of identical Round Towers anywhere in mainland Britain, with the exception of Scotland, which these theories claimed to have been erected by later settlers from Ireland. As previously noted, the underlying claim made by the majority of Irish nationalist antiquarians subscribing to varying theories of oriental origins (including the manifold Iranian models) was that ancient Irish civilization had not been a derivative "Britain-first" cultural formation. Given the sea-fearing renown of the Phoenicians, the variants of the Phoenician theory required far less imaginative license, in comparison with claims that Persians or other Iranian groups had accomplished the same pattern of colonizing Ireland on their own, particularly by means of by-passing mainland Britain and arriving in Ireland via the Iberian Peninsula (which would have required more advanced long-distance sea-faring technology, as opposed to overland migration across the European continent followed by navigation to Britain and then to Ireland).

The first volume of Moore's *The History of Ireland*, which covered the period from ancient times to the rapid spread of Christianity in Ireland by the seventh century, opened with a long description of the early inhabitants of Ireland and their religious and cultural practices, addressing along the way the controversy surrounding the origins of the Irish. Moore was outright dismissive of the Milesian myth. Moreover, he ascertained that the first settlers in Ireland, as well as in "Gaul, Britain, and Spain," were Celtic peoples who had spread westward from their original territories in West Asia across the European continent to constitute "the first inhabitants of the western parts of Europe." He then immediately clarified it would be "rash" to therefore presume that the subsequent population arrivals in Ireland and "Britain" in ancient times should also have been identical. Brushing aside Vallancey's "false zeal and fantastic speculation" (not forgetting also the rejection of Celtic origins of the Irish in Vallancey's later works), Moore stopped short of questioning the supposition of oriental origins of later, and avowedly, highly civilized settlers in ancient Ireland after the earlier arrival of the Celts. In Moore's version, the most notable post-Celtic population settlement in early Ireland was that of the Phoenicians, who comprised the next major population group on the island. He also noted the Phoenicians reaching 'Spain' prior to their settlement in Ireland had already "bec[o]me intermixed with the original race, or Celts" then living in Spain. Moore specified that the Phoenicians had arrived in Ireland from the "Gallician coasts of Spain" around 1000 BCE.[79] This was a reworking of the existing disparate Phoenician theories of Irish origins. Above all, in Moore's account the Phoenicians were *the* harbingers of Ireland's glorious ancient civilization by having previously absorbed the highest civilizational values and practices of the Age from Iranians, long before the appearance of even the Hellenic civilization. Moore interchangeably used both 'Iran' and 'Persia' in his account. His theory, therefore, differentiated between the ethnic make-up, on the one hand, and the cultural heritage, on the other hand, of ancient Ireland's civilizational foundation. The civilizational properties the Phoenicians introduced to Ireland had previously belonged to another ethnic group: the Iranians. In his claim of Ireland's pre-Norman civilizational preeminence, Moore developed his own style of versatile conjuring and selective plucking from a wide range of sources. He wrote, for instance,

> By Plutarch it is stated, that an envoy despatched by the emperor Claudius to explore the British Isles, found, on an island, in the neighbourhood of Britain, an order of Magi accounted holy by the people[;] and, in another work of the same writer, some fabulous wonders are related of an island lying to the west of Britain, the inhabitants of which were a holy race; while, at the same time, a connection between them and Carthage is indistinctly intimated.[80]

As further proof of Phoenician migration from the Iberian Peninsula to Ireland, with the emphasis here being on 'Spain' as the transit route, Moore noted:

> So irresistible, indeed, is the force of tradition, in favour of a Spanish colonization, that every new propounder of an hypothesis on the subject is forced to admit this event as part of his scheme. Thus, [George] Buchanan [in the eighteenth century], in supposing colonies to have passed from Gaul to Ireland, contrives to carry them first to the west of Spain; and the learned Welsh antiquary, [Edward] Lhuyd [d.1709], who traces the origin of the Irish to two distinct sources, admits one of those primitive sources to have been Spanish. In the same manner, a late writer, who, on account of the remarkable similarity which exists between his country's Round Towers and the Pillar-temples of Mazanderan [i.e., Mazandaran province on the south Caspian littoral in Iran], deduces the origin of the Irish nation from the banks of the Caspian, yields so far to the current of ancient tradition, as, in conducting his colony from Iran to the West, to give it Spain for a resting-place. Even [Thomas] Innes [d.1744], one of the most acute of those writers who have combated the Milesian pretensions of the Irish, yet bows to the universal voice of tradition in that country, which, as he says, peremptorily declares in favour of a colonisation from Spain.[81]

Moore's mention of the Persian magi in the guise of Phoenician holy men, similar to his subsequent references to Iranian cultural traits, was intended to demonstrate the presumed absorption by Phoenicians of Iranian values prior to their reaching Spain and then Ireland. This Iranian-Phoenician connection was essential for Moore's hypothesis of the fire-worship function of the Round Towers, modeled after the purported practice of ancient Iranians (i.e., the Zoroastrian religion). According to Moore, the early Celtic population of Ireland, while initially engaging in "primitive system of idolatry," gradually intermixed with Phoenicians (themselves having earlier intermixed with other Celts in Spain) and subsequently absorbed "a number of rites and usages belonging to much later and less simple modes of worship" introduced by Phoenician settlers, with these now-Irish Phoenicians continuing their commercial contact with Iranian lands, among other locations, during the early period of their colonization of Ireland. The more contact these Phoenicians maintained with Iranian lands ('Persia' specifically), the more Iranianized they continued to become over time after their initial settlement in Ireland. Identifying these different Celtic, early Iranianized-Phoenician, and the later predominantly Iranian stages of cultural development in Ireland, Moore wrote:

> There may be traced, indeed, in the religious remains of the Irish, the marks of three distinct stages of superstition; namely, that first rude ritual which their Celtic progenitors brought with them from the East; next, the introduction of images somewhat approaching the human shape; and, thirdly, those monuments of a more refined system of fire-worship which still embellish this country. While some of their rites and names of deities are traceable directly to the Phœnecians, there are other religious customs which seem to have been derived, through the means of this people, from Persia. It was on the whole the description of religion likely to spring up in a country into which a variety of modes of devotion and doctrine had been imported; and it is well known that the Phœnecians, with that utter indifference to diversity of worship which forms one of the most striking differences between the Pagan and the Christian religionist, set no limit to the varieties of creed and ritual, with which, in their career over the globe, they furnished their colonies. Being in constant communication with Persia, for the sake of the Eastern trade, it was even a part of the commercial policy of this people to encourage an intercourse, on religious subjects, between their Eastern and Western customers, of which they themselves should be made the channel, and so convert it to their own advantage in the way of trade.
>
> The mixed nature, indeed, of the creed of the ancient Irish seems to be intimated in their mode of designating their own priesthood, to whom they applied as well the Persian as the Celtic denomination; calling them indifferently either Magi, or Druids. Thus, those Magi described, in the Lives of St Patrick, as warning the king against the consequences of the new faith, are, in the ancient Hymn of [Saint] Fiech, on the same subject, denominated Druids.[82]

Presumably the fact that the Phoenicians based in Ireland did not, in turn, transmit their so-called indigenous or extant Celtic Irish cultural practices to Iran in these continued exchanges "between their Eastern and Western customers" was itself a sign of the higher civilizational sophistication of Iranians (Persians in this case) over the Celts, who had also settled in mainland Britain. According to Moore, among the customs imported into Ireland by Phoenicians was the Iranian practice of historical documentation:

In a like manner, according to the historian Ctesias, [...] it was enjoined to the Persians, by an express law, that they should write down the annals of their country in the royal archives. In Ireland this practice of chronicling events continued to be observed to a late period; and not only at the courts of the different Kings, but even in the family of every inferior chieftain, a Seanachie, or historian, formed always a regular part of the domestic establishment. To this recording spirit, kept alive, as it was, in Christian times, by a succession of monastic chroniclers, we owe all those various volumes of Psalters and Annals with which the ancient literature of Ireland abounds.

To reinforce his own case here, Moore, while also referring to works by William Jones, William Ouseley, and other such range of philological and/or historical experts, even found it necessary to cite Vallancey among his sources, albeit circumspectly. This was in connection with Moore's attribution of the origin of the Round Towers to similar towers used for the alleged purpose of 'Fire-worship' in ancient Iran and by Parsee Zoroastrians settlers in parts of the Indian subcontinent at later periods.[83] In fact, as already noted, Moore was convinced of this ostensibly shared common religious identity of ancient Iran and Ireland while writing *Lalla Rookh* two decades earlier. In the first volume of *The History of Ireland*, as a means of underscoring the unadulterated Phoenician transfer of Iranian religious beliefs and rituals to Ireland, Moore even suggested the possibility of some Iranian magi having reached Ireland onboard the Phoenician vessels. This Iranian influence was further elucidated in the following manner, lapsing on one occasion into the same sort of etymological waffle that Moore accused Vallancey and O'Brien of concocting:

On the strength of the remarkable resemblance alleged to exist between the pillar-temples near Bhaugulpore [in the Indian subcontinent] and the Round Towers of Ireland, a late ingenious historian does not hesitate to derive the origin of the Irish people from that region; and that an infusion, at least, of population from that quarter might, at some remote period, have taken place, appears by no means an extravagant supposition. The opinion, that Iran and the western parts of Asia were originally the centre from whence population diffused itself to all the regions of the world, seems to be confirmed by the traditional histories of most nations, as well as by the results both of philological and antiquarian enquiries. To the tribes dispersed after the Trojan war, it has been the pride equally both of Celtic and of Teutonic nations to trace back their origin. The Saxon Chronicle derives the earliest inhabitants of Britain from Armenia; and the great legislator of the Scandinavians, Odin, is said to have come, with his followers, from the neighbourhood of the Euxine Sea [i.e., the Black Sea]. By those [e.g., Philipp Clüver (d.1622), Johann Georg Keysler (d.1743), and Simon Pelloutier (d.1857)] who hold that the Celts and Persians were originally the same people, the features of affinity so strongly observable between the Pagan Irish and the Persians will be accounted for without any difficulty. But, independently of this hypothesis, the early and long-continued intercourse which Ireland appears to have maintained, through the Phœnecians, with the East, would sufficiently explain the varieties of worship imported to her shores, and which became either incorporated with her original creed, or formed new and distinct rallying points of belief. In this manner the adoration of shaped idols was introduced; displacing, in many parts—as we have seen, in the instance of the idol Crom-Cruach—that earliest form of superstition which confined its worship to rude erect stones. To the same later ritual belonged also those images of which some fragments have been found in Ireland, described as of black wood, covered and plated with thin gold, and the chased work on them in lines radiated from a centre, as is usual in the images of the sun. There was also another of these later objects of adoration, called Kerman Kelstach, the favourite idol of the Ultonians [i.e., residents of Ulster], which had for its pedestal, as some say, the golden stone of Clogher [known as "Cermand Cestach"], and in which, to judge by the description of it, there were about the same rudiments of shape as in the first Grecian Hermæ. Through the same channel which introduced these and similar innovations, it is by no means improbable that, at a still later period, the pillar-temples of the Eastern fire-worship might have become known; and that even from the shores of the Caspian a colony of Guebres [i.e., Zoroastrians] might have found their way to Ireland, and there left, as enigmas to posterity, those remarkable monuments to which only the corresponding remains of their own original country can now afford any clue.[84]

Moore's choice of 'Kerman Kelstach' as one of many conventional spellings of the name of the alleged gold-covered stone idol 'Cermand Cestach,' reportedly destroyed in the sixteenth century, was no mere coincidence. It evoked the name of the ancient and extant Iranian city of Kerman (in present-day southeastern Iran) and a major center of Zoroastrianism, which was also mentioned a number of times in *Lalla Rookh*.[85] The city had been a stronghold of Zoroastrian defiance of the gradual spread of Islam in Iran after the seventh-century Arab-Muslim conquests and continued to be one of the remaining major centers of Iran's rapidly declining Zoroastrian community, only second in that respect compared to the city of Yazd to its north (with Yazd also mentioned in *Lalla Rookh*; appearing as "Yezd").

Given the highly contentious and often politically charged field of Irish antiquarianism, the first volume of Moore's *The History of Ireland* was greeted with controversy as well. The book was received with much acerbity and scorn in some circles, including in the anonymous review appearing in the June 1835 issue of the *Dublin University Magazine*, which echoed the tone of Moore's own anonymous review of Henry O'Brien's book the previous year. This time around, however, there was an unmistakably malignant sectarian (Anglican) tenor to the review, with the reviewer attacking Moore's alleged Catholic bias.[86] As Joep Leerssen, too, has noted, Moore's *The History of Ireland* was the "first major, ambitious national history [of Ireland] in the nineteenth century."[87] It was one of a series of histories of constituent parts of the United Kingdom commissioned as part of the Cabinet Cyclopaedia edition published by Longman, Rees, Orme, Brown, and Green, alongside such works as *The History of Scotland* by Walter Scott and *The History of England* by James Mackintosh. By the mid-1830s, the influence of nationalism had become a conspicuously entrenched feature of debates on territorial (i.e., 'national') histories. The reviewer of Moore's book in the *Dublin University Magazine* squarely blamed Moore's covert religious-nationalist project for what the reviewer described as a "partisan" and concocted narrative. For the reviewer, this volume of Moore's history was nothing short of a distorted polemical fabrication of the past. Exposing the reviewer's own partiality, the review noted:

> As a historian, we have no confidence in Mr. Moore. Even had he not warned us against his prejudices, which we consider rather sectarian than national, and his fierce and sullen

hatred of those who dissent from him, we should have found in the manner in which he has treated his subject sufficient reason to distrust him. He gives up the innocent Milesian fictions, and in return for the sacrifice he reiterates the mischievous fable of a papal supremacy. We do not know that the records of fraud contain any instance of imposture so palpable and so defenceless as this; so destitute of all support; so discountenanced by positive evidence, and so obstinately and unartificially defended.[88]

At the time, the *Dublin University Magazine* was accused by many Catholic Irish nationalists of being a mouthpiece of Anglo-Irish interests. Whether or not this was the case, the reviewer of Moore's book concentrated for much of the remainder of the review on sectarian religious divides in Ireland, refuting Moore's assertion of the Catholic ("Romish") identity of the church in Ireland prior to Anglo-Norman conquests. Instead, the reviewer maintained the early church in Ireland had adhered to principles very much resembling the post sixteenth-century Anglican Church of England.[89] Primarily concerned with debunking what the reviewer termed Moore's "Popish" proclivity ("He is evidently enslaved to the Romish superstition"), the review notably did not challenge the oriental origins of the Irish. In fact, it maintained that in place of the fiction of the spread of Christianity to Ireland by emissaries of the Roman Church, "We are persuaded that the Gospel was preached first, or most successfully by missionaries of Asiatic, not Roman derivation, and that the people, because of their origin and their habits, were prepared to receive more cordially the eastern teachers."[90] To presume 'Asiatic' proselytizers had introduced Christianity to Ireland implied direct or indirect contacts between Asia and the island in much more recent times (i.e., the Christian era) and via 'Britain' as the route of transmission. The supposition of 'Asiatic' proselytizers introducing Christianity to Ireland had been firmly propounded much earlier by Edward Ledwich (and some scholars today maintain *Egyptian* Coptic Christianity influenced early monastic forms of Christianity in Ireland). While Moore did not deny the presence of "Greek and Asiatic missionaries" in Ireland, he was steadfast that the main tenor of early Christianity in Ireland had been Roman.[91] Curiously, there is no mention of any reviews of the first volume of *The History of Ireland* in Moore's published memoirs, edited by his friend Lord John Russell after Moore's death. Moore only mentioned an unnamed "Irishman" writing to him to express disappointment at Moore's jettisoning of the Milesian theory of Gaelic origins.[92]

In defiance of Petrie's position in his 1833 Royal Irish Academy prize essay and subsequently, and brushing off the review in the *Dublin University Magazine* of the first volume of *The History of Ireland*, in the second volume of his *The History of Ireland* (1837) Moore again rejected, with unmistakable national pride, the Christian origins and use of the Round Towers.[93] Following the publication of the fourth volume of *The History of Ireland* in 1846, a year after the publication of Petrie's *The Ecclesiastical Architecture of Ireland*, Moore was made a member of the Royal Irish Academy. The dispute over the Round Towers, and particularly that of their Christian versus pre-Christian origin, dragged on for a few more decades, even as Petrie's verdict gained more and more leverage following the publication of *The Ecclesiastical Architecture of Ireland*, in which Petrie also targeted Moore's theory of the Round Towers.[94] There were no clear dividing lines in this multifaceted and multivalent debate. Similarly, it took a long time to dissuade many members of the public inured to Eastern theories of the towers of such beliefs. For instance, among a broad array of contending opinions later in the century, in 1879 a reader of the monthly magazine *Catholic Progress*, published in London and Dublin by the Young Men's Catholic Association, avowed the veracity of the "eastern origin" of the Round Towers and their initial use "as temples by the fire-worshippers [...], which coincides with the practice observed by the Guebri or Parsi of Persia." The article cited Vallancey, John D'Alton (Dalton), and John Lanigan as authorities on the subject "in opposition to the idea advanced by Mr. Petrie and his followers that the Round Towers were Christian belfries."[95] Even though Moore had clearly distanced himself from much of Vallancey's and other similar inferences and methods, Vallancey's influence was still noticeable in some antiquarian circles during the middle of the nineteenth century and later. The Irish journalist Samuel Carter Hall and his Irish wife, the novelist Anna Maria (née Fielding), in their discussion of the Round Towers in the third volume of their highly popular 1843 history of Ireland (*Ireland: Its Scenery, Character, &c.*), declared Vallancey the progenitor of the tradition that equated the Round Towers with so-called fire-worship or sun-worship towers of the East. Clearly under Vallancey's methodological and linguistic influence, the Halls situated Moore squarely within that same tradition. While categorically shifting the cultural and religious influences in ancient Ireland further East to the Indian subcontinent, with Iran now chiefly a subsidiary developmental cultural stage in the transmission of those influences to Ireland, the Halls wrote:

> The tower and low square temple were equally common to the Persians, with whom, as well as, indeed, with most of the other early pagan nations, fire or the sun formed a main object of adoration. In India the presiding genius of fire is still named Agni, a name curiously corresponding with that of the Irish tower, *Tur-aghan* or *Aidhne*, being pronounced nearly as *Agni*. And the columnar temples belonging to the ancient worship of that element still subsist there. The similarity of name and design led Vallancey to recognise the almost identity of the western and oriental towers; and he it was who first announced the real origin and purpose of the former, so long involved in darkness. He has been followed by some of the ablest writers on Irish antiquities that have hitherto appeared; by [William] Webb, [Isaac] Weld, [Charles] O'Conor, [John] Lanigan, [John] Dalton [D'Alton], [Henry] O'Brien, [William] Beauford, [Thomas] Moore, and [William] Betham, who agree in their adscription as sun temples; whilst O'Brien and Betham only hesitate in supposing that all were fire temples. Their sepulchral purpose was only guessed at by O'Brien. Sir William Betham is cognizant of it by the discoveries recently made.
>
> Independently of language, the similarity of structure above alluded to would have supposed an identity of design, and offered ground for a reasonable presumption of analogous purpose. We know that the Indian towers were *Mithratic*, that is, consecrated to solar worship; and therefore, and for the other reasons mentioned, derived from language and similarity, we are coerced to consider those of Ireland as similar.
>
> We cannot here be expected to open up the question of early Irish colonisation, but those acquainted with Irish and Asiatic antiquities, are well aware of the many analogies in language, religion, letters, architecture and usages, between Ireland and the cradle of

mankind. The Cabiric religion has left vestiges in Ireland, by which a connexion between that country, through Chaldea and Persia, with India, can be satisfactorily traced.[96]

Similarly, the ongoing and even less settled debate in the United Kingdom on the origins of ancient populations of Ireland continued well into the twentieth century, frequently with certain nationalist overtones among Irish historians. To demonstrate this continuum, for instance the 1838 entry on "Gael, Gaelic" in the *Penny Cyclopædia of the Society for the Diffusion of Useful Knowledge* (London) discussed the etymological, ethnographic, and linguistic complications of affirming the origins of the Gaels, the Gaelic language, and of the even earlier pre-Gaelic 'Irish' identities. This entry, which mentioned the first volume of Moore's *The History of Ireland*, could only establish with certainty the cacophonous and inconclusive nature of current debates:

> Whence came the Irish, supposing them to be Gael—from India? or Persia? or Phœnicia? or Spain? or France? or England? or Scotland? Were the Scots or Milesians of Ireland a Gallic or Germanic people? What is the origin of the present Highlanders of Scotland? Are they the progeny of a comparatively recent Irish colonization, as has of late been generally agreed, and as their own traditions have always asserted? or are they the descendants of the antient Caledonians, assumed on that supposition to be Gauls, and to have been the original population of the whole island, who were, probably a short time before the commencement of the Christian æra, driven from South to North Britain before a new immigration from the continent? All or most of these may be considered as questions still doubtful and disputed.[97]

In a somewhat similar vein, the 1870 *Chambers's Encyclopædia* (Edinburgh), under the entry for "History" of Ireland, reiterated the continued ambiguities surrounding Irish origins:

> *History*—According to ancient native legends, I. [i.e., Ireland] was in remote times peopled by tribes styled Firbolgs and Danauns, eventually subdued by Milesians or Gaels, who acquired supremacy in the island. The primitive inhabitants of I. are now believed to have been of the same Indo-European race with the original population of Britain. Although I., styled *Iernis*, is mentioned in a Greek poem five centuries before Christ, and by the names of *Hibernia* and *Juverna* [by] various foreign pagan writers, little is known with certainty of her inhabitants before the 4th c. after Christ, when, under the appellation of Scoti, or inhabitants of *Scotia*, they became formidable by their descents upon the Roman province of Britain. These expeditions were continued and extended to the coasts of Gaul till the time of Laogaire MacNeill, monarch of Ireland (430 A.D.).[98]

Nonetheless, by the middle of the nineteenth century, Petrie and his close colleagues John O'Donovan (1809–61) and Eugene O'Curry (1796–1862), who were equally contemptuous of Vallancey and the like, had unmistakably delivered a serious blow to former styles of antiquarianism.[99] The account of the gradual triumph of Petrie & Co.'s new historical and archaeological methods over former styles of antiquarianism was most famously celebrated by Rev. Patrick MacSweeney in his 1913 *A Group of Nation*

Builders: O'Donovan-O'Curry-Petrie. MacSweeney, of St. Patrick's College, Maynooth, hailed the innovative triumvirate as "national heroes," who had undertaken "patriotic research" so as to bind Ireland's future to its past "by the strong links of knowledge and love," in a move that MacSweeney characterized as the "battle for intellectual freedom."[100] Accusing Moore of "propagating a legend," MacSweeney wrote of the Royal Irish Academy in the early nineteenth century in general:

> Unfortunately its exposition was undertaken [...] by men who, foreigners by birth and faddists by nature, were but little competent to understand [Ireland]. The school of Vallancey and of Betham produced one useful result—it awakened the undying opposition of Petrie, O'Donovan, and O'Curry, and thus gave birth to their immortal work, which in O'Donovan's words consisted of 'distinguishing History from Fable.'[101]

MacSweeney deployed the particular late nineteenth-century positivist 'scientific' parlance, before proceeding to the subject of earlier debates concerning the Round Towers prior to the 1840s and hailing the triumph of Petrie & Co. over what MacSweeney described as the unfounded concoctions of O'Brien, Betham, Windele, Vallancey, and others. MacSweeney also anachronistically further padded Petrie's qualification as an archaeologist in reference to the Round Towers debates of the 1830s and 1840s, by noting Petrie's *later* range of expertise in the field:

> Petrie's friends, the Scandinavian antiquaries, [Christian Jürgensen] Thomsen and [Jens Jacob Asmussen] Worsaae were the founders of scientific archaeology. To them is due the classification of the protohistoric period into Stone, Bronze, and Iron Ages; and Ireland, thanks to Petrie, was from the beginning to benefit by a knowledge of this fundamental classification. Petrie was, therefore, a pioneer. Since his time archaeological investigation, owing to the fruitful use of the comparative method, has developed enormously.[102]

Although, following Petrie's intervention in the Round Towers controversy, along with other range of contributions by John O'Donovan, Eugene O'Curry, and others, the status of former antiquarian methods gradually declined, those former methods did not entirely disappear, and there were many later generations of archaeologists, folklorist, and historians who still worked in the shadow of some of the older antiquarian beliefs and procedures. The concerted mid-nineteenth-century assault on former methodologies of Vallancey and his counterparts inside and outside the Royal Irish Academy (which differed in essence and tenor from former critiques of such methodologies by rival camps in Irish antiquarianism) was not tantamount to the wholesale rejection of all oriental theories and methodological hypotheses, some of which had roots in much earlier seventeenth-century endeavors by the likes of Geoffrey Keating and Roderic O'Flaherty, if not also in 'medieval' Irish annals. A case in point is the serialized column titled "Half Hours with Irish History" appearing after late 1857 in the *Irish Literary Gazette* (published simultaneously in Dublin, Cork, Belfast, and Galway), beginning in the November 7, 1857, issue of the paper (vol.1, no.15). In its second installment of this special column, the *Irish Literary Gazette* reiterated the position first propounded by Moore in his 1835 first volume of *The History of Ireland*: that the Phoenicians had introduced to Ireland religious practices derived from Iran (Persia).[103] In the fourth installment of the special column, the gazette asserted that the practice of the "first fire-worshippers of Ireland" most certainly originated in India and Persia, territories where England was now imposing its imperial might in different degrees.[104] This column, incidentally, appeared in the aftermath of the Anglo-Iranian War of 1856–57, which had ended eight months earlier, on March 4, 1857 (see Chapter Four).

Petrie's close colleague, the Catholic cultural-nationalist Eugene O'Curry, who later also served as the chair of archaeology and history at the Catholic University of Ireland (Dublin; founded in 1851), was dismissive of "the gross fabrications of Vallancey."[105] But, O'Curry did not contest the 'medieval' annalists' ascription of what O'Curry now in a revisionist manner termed a "comparatively civilized" Scythian ancestry of so-called Nemedian and Milesian populations of ancient Ireland, among other range of similar assertions by O'Curry.[106] He was also of the opinion that:

> It must occur to every one [sic] who has read of Zoroaster, of the Magi of Persia, and of the sorceries of Egypt mentioned in the seventh chapter of Exodus, that Druids and Druidism did not originate in Britain any more than in Gaul or Erinn. It is indeed probable that [...] the European Druidical system was but the offspring of the Eastern augury, somewhat less complete, perhaps, when transplanted to a new soil than in its ancient home.[107]

MacSweeney himself, in his 1913 *A Group of Nation Builders*, was not outright rejecting the supposition of Ireland's ancient connections with the Orient. There was a notable twist to MacSweeney's account. By then, the latest so-called scientific methods and discoveries were coincidentally pointing toward similar conclusions as that of Vallancey and other adherents of oriental theories of Irish origins, *albeit* by reliance on a much sounder methodology, rather than relying on the etymological contortionism, wild leaps of conjecture, and speculative deduction characteristic of Vallancey and many other late eighteenth- and early nineteenth-century Irish antiquarians. Furthermore, the new discoveries by the early twentieth century recounted very gradual and protracted human migration processes than the extremely rapid patterns of population (re)settlements from the Orient in Ireland that appeared in works by Vallancey, O'Brien, Betham, D'Alton, Moore, and the like. MacSweeney wrote:

> The filiation between East and West, which is being brought about by modern scientific Archaeology, may appear to have a kind of resemblance to the guess-work of the school of Vallancey, but it is in reality a distinct and independent result attained by a method which is the very negation of his method.[108]

It is essential to reiterate here that Petrie himself, as his friend and biographer William Stokes too pointed out in 1868, was convinced of a range of ancient connections between the Orient and Ireland, even as he demolished the reveries of oriental origins of the Round Towers, among other theories of the pre-Christian antiquity of the towers, including the Scandinavian (Scandian) model. Writing under the influence of the evolving Aryan racial theory in the second half of the nineteenth century, Stokes belonged to the camp that identified the ancient Celtic population of Ireland as a branch of the Indo-European "Aryan family" that had indisputably originated in the East. Praising Petrie's expertise in other branches of historical knowledge of Ireland, in addition to archaeology, Stokes also noted Petrie's expertise in musicology and his election in 1851 as the president of the newly founded Society for the Preservation and Publication of the Melodies of Ireland. Stokes pointed out:

> Thus firmly convinced of the historical interest of this ancient Irish music, Petrie points out specimens, where they occur, of airs connected with fairy legends, and bearing a strong affinity to Eastern melodies. The lullaby tunes, especially, have a close resemblance to those of Hindostan and Persia. He points to three classes of music, said to have been brought into the country by the Tuatha de Danann, a mythic, or heroic race, supposed to have invaded Ireland many centuries before Christ. The origin of many airs bearing a Gothic or Scandinavian character, he traces to the long occupation of the Island by the Danes and Northmen [i.e., after the ninth century CE], and the blending of the Teutonic with the Celtic races, in ages now remote. Those airs, which are peculiarly Irish in expression, Petrie analyzes with a power possessed by none but himself.[109]

Stokes then added that the first volume of Irish airs collected by Petrie for the society included a lullaby, which Petrie classified as belonging to the category of "music said to have been introduced into Ireland by that heroic or mythological race called the Tuatha de Danann." Commenting on this lullaby, Petrie had written:

> Further, with reference to this air, I would observe that its strong affinity to the lullaby tunes of Hindostan and Persia will scarcely fail to strike the investigators of national melody; and connected as it thus is with a fairy legend, this affinity must be regarded with interest by those who trace such superstitions to an Eastern origin.[110]

Petrie had earlier accepted the existence of both Firbolgs and Tuatha de Dananns, albeit at the time siding with the supposition of their 'Greek' origins.[111]

Between 1848 and 1851, the six-volume *Annals of the Kingdom of Ireland by the Four Masters*, edited and translated into English by John O'Donovan, was published. This new edition of the *Annals of the Four Masters* was based on the seventeenth-century work of a Franciscan monk supervising the project, Michael O'Clery, and his colleagues Conary O'Clery, Cucogry [or *Peregrine*] O'Clery, and Ferfeasa O'Mulconry, who together from 1632 to 1636 completed in Irish language a compilation of earlier, chiefly 'medieval,' annals of Ireland's past, along with a number of subsequent works to which were added their own historical contribution up to the year 1616.[112] O'Donovan's edited translation of the *Annals* was based on a surviving manuscript purchased for the Royal Irish Academy in 1831 by George Petrie. *Annals of the Kingdom of Ireland*, which had become the seminal Irish language historical documentary source covering the Ireland of so-called medieval to early modern periods, was compiled and composed by individuals who firmly believed in otherwise legendary accounts of ancient Ireland. Michael O'Clery in his dedication of *Annals* to his patron Fergal (Ferall) O'Gara, a chieftain in Sligo county, had written:

> 'I perceived the anxiety you suffer from the cloud which at present hangs over our ancient Milesian race; a state of things which has occasioned the ignorance of many, relative to the lives of the holy men, who, in former times have been the ornaments of our island; the general ignorance also of our civil history, and of the monarchs, provincial kings, tigherns (lords), and toisachs (chieftains), who flourished in this country through a succession of ages, with equal want of knowledge in the synchronism necessary for throwing light on the transactions of each. [...] In truth every benefit derivable from our labours is due to your protection and bounty; nor should it excite jealousy or envy that you stand foremost in this as in other services you have rendered your country; for by your birth you are a descendant of the race of Heber, which gave Ireland thirty monarchs, and sixty-one of which race have died in the odour of sanctity.'[113]

The fact that what were taken to be the best available native-language historical accounts of 'medieval' and 'early modern' Ireland, including the eleventh century *Lebor Gabála Érenn* (*The Book of Invasions*), or similarly Geoffrey Keating's 1634 *Foras Feasa ar Éirinn* (which also relied on *Lebor Gabála Érenn*)—all of which were collated and/or written by individuals whose own grasp of earlier eras in Irish history were steeped in mythology—raises certain fundamental methodological and historiographic questions regarding the *historicity* of these authors' chronicles of *their own respective eras* as well.

In 1914, Francis Joseph Brigger of the Royal Irish Academy noted what he considered as the unequivocal triumph of Petrie's theory of the Round Towers in scholarly circles: "It is now admitted by all Irish authorities of any repute, and that beyond dispute, that the Round Towers, the glory of Ireland, were built by Irish people as Christian monuments," with their origin predating the "Dane, Norman, [and] English" invasions of the island.[114] Brigger's essay was appearing in *The Glories of Ireland*, published in 1914 and edited by Joseph Dunn and Patrick Joseph Lennox of the Catholic University of America in Washington, DC. This collection of essays on Ireland's history (in keeping with the latest historical methodologies) also included essay contributions from non-professional historians such as the radical Irish nationalists Roger Casement and Alice Milligan. Interestingly, Casement in his opening chapter of the collection on "The Romance of Irish History" did not venture into pre-Christian history of Ireland. A number of other essays in the collection referred to Tuatha de Dananns, Milesians, and Aryans, but without specifying the ethnic origins of Tuatha de Dananns or Milesians.[115] On these occasions, as well as in Casement's decision to start his historical reflections on Ireland's past after the introduction of Christianity, there is an unmistakable indication of conscious avoidance of the still unsettled question and active minefield of Irish origins, including both the facticity of certain ancient population groups mentioned in 'medieval' annals, and treated as historical by later antiquarians (such as Tuatha de Dananns or Milesians), and the precise origins of those population groups.

Notes

1 Michael Joseph Barry, ed., *The Songs of Ireland*. Second edition. Dublin: James Duffy & Sons, 1846. The collection, which in its new 1846 Preface was identified by Barry as "a National Collection," (pp.19, 20) consisted primarily of nationalist songs that in the original 1845 Preface had been characterized as "songs [...] of a political tendency" (p.16). See also the *Cork Examiner*, March 5, 1852, p.4, cc.d–f. For other examples of contemporary celebration of Moore, see also *Cork Examiner*, March 5, 1852, p.4 cc.d–f; ibid., December 29, 1852, p.4 cc.d–f. The *Cork Examiner* was an O'Connellite paper, with Moore having been personally averse to Daniel O'Connell (d. 1847), despite their shared stance on the repeal of the Act of the Union.

2 Barry, ed., *The Songs of Ireland*, pp.35–36. Robert Burns (1759–96) was considered Scotland's "national" poet, while the French Pierre-Jean de Béranger (1780–1857) was regarded by many of his contemporaries as the greatest lyricist.

3 See also the Introduction by James Kelly and Susan Hegarty and the chapters by James Kelly, Nicholas Wolf, and Ciaran O'Neill in James Kelly and Susan Hegarty, eds., *Schools and schooling, 1650–2000: New perspectives on the history of education*. Dublin: Four Courts Press, 2017; Nicholas Wolf, *An Irish-Speaking Island: State, Religion, Community, and the Linguistic Landscape in Ireland, 1770–1870*. Madison, WI: University of Wisconsin, 2014, chapter 4 ("Education and Established Church").

4 See [Thomas Moore], *Corruption and Intolerance: Two Poems. With Notes. Addressed to an Englishman by an Irishman*. London: J. Carpenter, 1808, pp.42, and 51 n.*; Thomas Moore, *Memoirs, Journal, and Correspondence of Thomas Moore*. Volume 8. Edited by Lord John Russell. London: Longman, Brown, Green, and Longmans, 1856, pp.197, 198; [Thomas Moore,] *Travels of an Irish Gentleman in Search of Religion. With Notes and Illustrations, by the Editor of "Captain Rock's Memoirs." In Two Volumes*. London: Longman, Rees, Orme, Brown, Green, & Longman, 1833; Moore's comment on "Jesuitism" in Thomas Moore, *Memoirs, Journal, and Correspondence of Thomas Moore*. Volume 2. Edited by Lord John Russell. London: Longman, Brown, Green, and Longmans, 1853, p.73; Stephen Gwynn, *Thomas Moore*. London: MacMillan and Co., 1905, pp.61–62, 70; Ronan Kelly, *Bard of Erin: The Life of Thomas Moore*. Dublin: Penguin, 2008, p.501 and passim; Javed Majeed, *Ungoverned Imaginings*, pp.90–92; Norman Vance, *Irish Literature*, p.116; Jeffrey Vail, "Thomas Moore in Ireland and America: The Growth of a Poet's Mind," *Romanticism* 10(1), 2004, p.59.

5 Mary Helen Thuente, *The Harp Re-Strung*, pp.171–76; Ronan Kelly, "Another Side of Thomas Moore," *History of Ireland* 11(3), Autumn 2003, pp.39–43.

6 See also Mary Helen Thuente, *The Harp Re-Strung*, pp.171–92; Emer Nolan, "Introduction" in Thomas Moore, *Memoirs of Captain Rock, The Celebrated Irish Chieftain, with Some Account of His Ancestors. Written by Himself*. Edited and with an Introduction by Emer Nolan, and with annotations by Seamus Deane. Dublin: Field Day, 2008, p.xiv; Ronan Kelly, "Another Side of Thomas Moore," pp.39–43; Shelley E. Meagher, "Nineteenth-century Ireland and the Orient: Tom Moore's Lalla Rookh" in Ruth Connolly and Ann Coughlan, eds., *New Voices in Irish Criticism 5*. Dublin: Four Courts Press, 2005, pp.145–53; Jeffrey Vail, "Thomas Moore in Ireland and America," pp.41–42, 43, 58, and passim; Jane Moore, "Nineteenth-century Irish Anacreontics: the literary relationship of James Clarence Mangan and Thomas Moore," *Irish Studies Review* 21(4), 2013, p.393; William O'Neill, "Joyce's Esthetic and Some Earlier Irish Writers," *Études irlandaises* 21(1), 1996, p.35.

7 For a random example of Lyttelton's book being advertised in late eighteenth-century Irish nationalist newspapers (with the name spelled "Littleton"), see *Northern Star* (Belfast), May 25, 1793, p.1 c.c. On Lyttelton's book, see also Pauline Kra, "Montesquieu's Lettres persanes and George Lyttelton's Letters from a Persian in England," *Studies on Voltaire and the Eighteenth Century*, 304 (1992), pp.871–74.

8 *The Meddler* (Dublin) 1(11), March 15, 1743–44, pp.2–4. The dating of the paper follows both the Julian calendar that remained in use in Britain and Ireland until 1752 as well as the Gregorian calendar, which replaced the Julian calendar following the 1751 Act of Parliament. In the Julian calendar, the new year began on 25 March (Lady Day). Therefore, this issue of the paper would have been March 15, 1744, in the Gregorian calendar, with the new year beginning on January 1. Each issue of the paper consisted of four pages, with the

first issue dated January 5, 1743–44 (i.e., January 5, 1744, in the Gregorian calendar) and the last issue (vol.1, no.25) dated June 21, 1744.
9 Ibid., 1(1), January 5, 1743–44, pp.1–3.
10 Ibid., 1(11), March 15, 1743–44, p.4.
11 The nineteen-part serialized installments appeared in *Irān-e Nou* from Shaval 9, 1327 (October 24, 1909), pp.2–3 to 20 Jamādi al-Awal 1328 (May 29, 1910), pp.2–3. The Western calendar date appearing in the latter issue of the paper is incorrect and should be May 30.
12 Thomas Brown [Thomas Moore], *Intercepted Letters; or, The Twopenny Post-bag. To Which are Added, Trifles Reprinted*. Third edition. London: J. Carr, 1813, pp.ix–x.
13 Thomas Brown [Thomas Moore], *Intercepted Letters*, p.26. See also Thomas Moore, *The Poetical Works of Thomas Moore. As Corrected by Himself in 1848*. Volume I. New York: Robert Martin, 1851, p.339 n.22.
14 Moore to Lady Donegal, April 10, 1815, in Thomas Moore, *Memoirs, Journal, and Correspondence of Thomas Moore*, vol.2, pp.73–74; Stephen Gwynn, *Thomas Moore*, 68–69; Emmer Nolan, "Introduction" in Thomas Moore, *Memoirs of Captain Rock* (Emer Nolan, ed., 2008), p.xiv.
15 Thomas Brown [Thomas Moore], *Intercepted Letters*, pp.29–30. It is somewhat ironic that Moore retained "Green slippers" as an emblem of the bigoted Shi'i majority population of Iran in this poem, given that green also symbolized Ireland.
16 Moore, *Lalla Rookh*, p.7; Lord John Russell's editorial note in Thomas Moore, *Memoirs, Journal, and Correspondence of Thomas Moore*, vol.2. pp.111–12. It appears Moore was working on the poem by September 1811. See Moore's letter of September 11, 1811 to Miss Godfrey in Thomas Moore, *Memoirs, Journal, and Correspondence of Thomas Moore*, vol.8, pp.92–93; letter of September 20, 1811 from Samuel Rogers to Moore in ibid., pp.94–95. In an 1812 letter to Lady Donegal, Moore clearly identified the oriental poem on which he was working at the time as "Lalla Rookh." Ibid., p.113. The letter does not bear a date, but, Lady Donegal's reply to the letter is dated August 28, 1812. Ibid., pp.117–19. See also ibid., pp.194, 205; Howard Mumford Jones, *The Harp That Once-: A Chronicle of the Life of Thomas Moore*. New York: Henry Holt and Company, 1937, p.152. Ronan Kelly perceptively notes that "Letter VI" of *Intercepted Letters* was "presumably, [...] an early return on all his Eastern reading for Lalla Rookh." Ronan Kelly, *Bard of Erin*, p.235.
17 For a sampling of reviews, see *Edinburgh Review* 29(57), November 1817, pp.1–35; *Edinburgh Monthly Magazine* 1(3), June 1817, pp.279–85; *Literary Gazette* 19, May 31, 1817, pp.292–95; *British Review and London Critical Journal* 10(19), August 1817, pp.30–54; *Critical Review* 5(6), fifth series, June 1817, pp.560–81; *Eclectic Review* 8, new series, October 1817, pp.340–53. For the opinion of Moore's close friends on this subject, see also "Byron to Mr. Murray," September 15, 1817, in Thomas Moore, ed., *Letters and Journals of Lord Byron: With Notices of His Life*. Volume II. Reprint. New York: Harper, 1831 [1830], p.102; Lord John Russell, "Preface" in Thomas Moore, *Memoirs, Journal, and Correspondence of Thomas Moore*. Volume 1. Edited by Lord John Russell. London: Longman, Brown, Green, and Longmans, 1853, pp.xvi, xxv; Stephen Gwynn, *Thomas Moore*, pp.83–85, 86–87. See also Allan Gregory, "Thomas Moore's Orientalism" in Peter Cochran, ed., *Byron and Orientalism*. Newcastle: Cambridge Scholar's Press, 2006, pp.173–82.
18 Moore was offered £3,000 for the work by Messrs. Longman, reportedly before even sharing a single line of the poem with the publisher. See Moore's letter of May 22, 1815 to Samuel Rogers in Moore, *Memoirs, Journal, and Correspondence*, vol.8, p.194. On the brisk sale of the first edition of the book, see ibid., pp.229, 277. Among other works, see also William Keach, "'Trade and Poesy' in Moore's Lalla Rookh: an oriental romance," *La Questione Romantica*, nos.18–19, Autumn 2005, pp.91–98. According to Róisin Healy, *Lalla Rookh* enjoyed great popularity in Poland. Róisin Healy, *Poland in the Irish Nationalist Imagination, 1772-1922: Anti-Colonialism within Europe*. New York: Palgrave Macmillan, 2017, pp.85–88.
19 On Moore's particular mode of oriental-style literature, see also Andrew Rudd, "'Oriental' and 'Orientalist' Poetry: The Debate in Literary Criticism in the Romantic Period," *Romanticism*, 13(1), 2007, 53–62. On narrative uses of Iran and of the Persian literary influences in English-language Romantic literature, as well as the Orient at large in English literature since Elizabethan times, see Hasan Javadi, *Persian Literary Influence on English Literature*. New edition. Costa Mesa, CA: Mazda, 2005; and the collection of essays in C.C. Barfoot

and Theo D'haen, eds., *Oriental Prospects*, particularly Barfoot's "English Romantic Poets and the 'Free-Floating Orient'" in ibid., pp.65–96.

20 Given that "Paradise and the Peri" was a story of Hindu resistance to Muslim rule, being narrated by the Muslim Feromarz/Aliris (poet/husband-to-be) to the fictional daughter of the actual eighteenth-century Mughal Muslim ruler of much of the Indian subcontinent (Emperor Aurangzeb), the continued general scholarly neglect of the subversive undertone of this section of the book in the overall plot of Moore's text is perplexing. On the general theme of resistance to imperialism in this section of Moore's poems, see also Julia M. Wright, *Ireland, India and Nationalism in Nineteenth-Century Literature*. Cambridge: Cambridge University Press, 2007, 98; Padma Rangarajan, "*Lalla Rookh* and the Afterlife of Allegory," *English Language Notes* 54(1), Spring/Summer 2016, 80; Andrew Rudd, "'Oriental' and 'Orientalist' Poetry," pp.53–62.

21 See also Thomas Moore, *Lalla Rookh*, p.19 n.2.

22 Jeffrey Vail maintains "the name 'Feramorz' contains Moore's own surname." Jeffrey W. Vail, "'The Standard of Revolt': Revolution and National Independence in Moore's Lalla Rookh," *Romanticism on the Net* 40, November 2005, n.p. See also Stuart Curran, *Poetic Form and British Romanticism*. New York: Oxford University Press, 1986, p.144; Marilyn Butler, "Orientalism" in David B. Pirie, ed., *The Penguin History of Literature. Volume 5: The Romantic Period*. London: Penguin, 1994, p.426; Shelley Meagher, "Politics and Persian Mythology in Irish Poetry," *La Trobe Journal* (Melbourne), no.91, June 2013, p.78.

23 On tolerance, see also Thomas. Moore, *The Poetical Works of Thomas Moore, Collected by Himself.* Volume VI. London: Longman, Orme, Brown, Green, & Longmans, 1841, p.xvi; idem, *Lalla Rookh*, p.12.

24 See also Shelley Meagher, "Politics and Persian Mythology," pp.76–85.

25 Oleg G. Bolshakov, "Central Asia Under the Early ᶜAbbasids" in Muhammad S. Asimov and Clifford E. Bosworth, eds., *History of Civilizations of Central Asia. Volume IV. The Age of Achievement: A.D. 750 to the End of the Fifteenth Century. Part One: The Historical, Social and Economic Setting*. Paris: UNESCO Publishing, 1998, pp.41–44; Patricia Crone, "MOQANNA" (2011, 2012) *Encyclopaedia Iranica* (https://iranicaonline.org/articles/moqanna). See also Edward Granville Browne, *A Literary History of Persia*, vol.I, pp.318–23 (Browne mentioned Moore's "Veiled Prophet" on p.318); Elton Daniel, *The Political and Social History of Khurasan Under Abbasid Rule, 747-820*. Minneapolis: Bibliotheca Islamica, 1979, pp.137–47; Alan White, "An Appalling or Banal Reality," *Variaciones Borges* 15 (2003), pp.47–91.

26 *Lalla Rookh*, p.26 n.1. See also Moore's account of d'Herbelot's description of al-Muqanna's "doctrine" in ibid., p.33 n.1. Given Moore's interest in Napoleon Bonaparte, it is unknown if Moore was aware of Napoleon's short story on al-Muqanna. See Andrew Martin, "The Mask of the Prophet: Napoleon, Borges, Verne," *Comparative Literature* 40(4), Autumn 1988, pp.318–34.

27 Thomas Moore, *Lalla Rookh*, p.27.

28 On Al-Makeenah, see Mangan, "The Time of the Barmecides," *Dublin University Magazine* 13(76), April 1839, pp.483–501. As Melissa Fegan too has noted, "Mangan's self-association with the impostor Al Mokanna, the Veiled Prophet of Khorassan of Moore's *Lalla Rookh*, is alluded to by the editors of the *Collected Works* [with Jacques Chuto as general editor]." Melissa Fegan, "'Every Irishman is an Arab': James Clarence Mangan's Eastern 'Translations'," *Translation and Literature*, 22 (2013), p.198.

29 Thomas Moore, *Lalla Rookh*, pp.30–31. Mokanna's white flag was in fact a reference to the color of the historical al-Muqanna's standard. See ibid., pp.28 n.1, 85 n.4, 87, 89; Oleg G. Bolshakov, "Central Asia Under the Early ᶜAbbasids" in Muhammad S. Asimov and Clifford E. Bosworth, eds., *History of Civilizations of Central Asia*, vol. IV, pp.38, 41–43; Farhad Daftary, "Secterian and National Movements in Iran, Khurasan and Transoxania During Umayyad and Early ᶜAbbasid Times" in ibid., pp.56. Leaving aside that Moore made no distinction between ancient Athenian "democracy" and the eight-century Byzantine Empire, where Azim was held captive during the war, in these lines there is an unmistakable "clash of civilizations"-style demonization of the Muslim caliphate in contrast to a homogenized Greek civilization.

30 Thomas Moore, *Lalla Rookh*, pp.35–51, 53.

31 Ibid., pp.51, 54–55, 62–64.

32 Ibid., pp.73–80, 89–90, 95–96, 101, 105, 106–107, 109–110.

33 Mansour Bonakdarian, "Locating Ireland in Iran of Thomas Moore's 'The Veiled Prophet': Allegory, History, and Unsettled Interpretive Trajectories," *European Romantic Review* 30(5–6), November 2019: 519–40.
34 On the Confederate War, see also Micheál Ó Siochrú, *Confederate Ireland, 1642-1649: A Constitutional and Political Analysis*. Dublin: Four Courts Press, 1999; Pádraig Lenihan, *Confederate Catholics at War, 1641-1649*. Cork: Cork University Press, 2000; Eamon Darcy, *The Irish Rebellion of 1641 and the Wars of the Three Kingdoms*. Woodbridge: Royal Historical Society, 2013.
35 See, for example, Thomas Moore, *The History of Ireland*, vol.IV, p.231. See also Moore, *Memoirs of Captain Rock* (Emer Nolan, ed., 2008), pp.xxiii, xvi; Thomas Moore, *Memoirs, Journal, and Correspondence of Thomas Moore*. Volume 4. Edited by Lord John Russell. London: Longman, Brown, Green, and Longmans, 1853, pp.142, 165.
36 Thomas Moore, *The History of Ireland*, vol. IV, p.230.
37 Thomas Moore, *Lalla Rookh*, pp.3–32, 87–88.
38 Ibid., p.57.
39 Ibid., p.77. See also p.98.
40 "Shuddering she went—a soul-felt pang of fear, / A presage that her own dark doom was near, / Roused every feeling, and brought Reason back / Once more, to writhe her last upon the rack." Ibid., p.104.
41 Ibid., pp.110–11.
42 Ibid., p.111.
43 See, for example, ibid., pp.146–47, 151, 175, 176, 177, 179, 185, 191.
44 Ibid., p.214.
45 Thomas Moore, *Memoirs, Journal, and Correspondence*, vol.8, p.277. See also Stephen Gwynn, *Thomas Moore*, p.90. Emer Nolan, "Preface" in Thomas Moore, *Memoirs of Captain Rock* (Emer Nolan, ed., 2008), p.xxviii; Emer Nolan, *Catholic Emancipations: Irish Fiction from the Thomas Moore to James Joyce*. Syracuse: Syracuse University Press, 2007, pp.1–10.
46 "Oh her—a maid of ARABY—/A Moslem maid—the child of him,/Whose bloody banner's dire success/Hath left their altars cold and dim,/And their fair land a wilderness!" *Lalla Rookh*, pp.202–203. Ironically, Hafed is the Arabic pronunciation of the Arabic male name that appears as "Hafez" ("Hafiz") in its Persian pronunciation. In its Islamic usage, it also signifies one who has memorized the Qur'an. It is possible, though uncertain, Moore chose the name given its connotation of one who remembers/recalls. Moore was familiar with the fourteenth-century Persian poet Hafez (Hafiz), and the name choice reflects Moore's fondness of that poet, who is mentioned on a few occasions in *Lalla Rookh*. Moore most likely came across the the Arabic pronunciation of Hafez's name in d'Herbelot's *La Bibliothèque orientale* (p.416), in which d'Herbelot noted in an entry "Hafedh ou Hafez, [...] Poëte Persien, [...]" with Moore deciding that the Arabic pronunciation "Hafed" (with the final sound letter dropped here) had a more rhythmic ring to it in English language than Hafez, and was also less likely to constantly remind his better-informed readers of the poet Hafez, which could distract them. In fact, Moore selected Arabic names for both of his "Iranian" heroes in this book (Azim in "The Veiled Prophet," and Hafed). Whereas Azim's name is contextually sound, given the time period in which that poem was set (i.e., almost a century after the Arab-Muslim occupation of Iran), Hafed's name is incongruous, given that his insurgency was occurring not long after Iran's occupation in the seventh century. It is also not clear if Moore deliberately chose names beginning with the letter "H" for the main characters of "The Fire-Worshippers," including Hinda and Al-Hassan.
47 Ibid., pp.213–14.
48 Timothy Daniel Sullivan, Alexander Martin Sullivan, and Denis Baylor Sullivan, eds., *Speeches from the Dock; or, Protests of Irish Patriotism*. New York: P.J. Kennedy, Excelsior Catholic Publishing House, 1904, p.45.
49 Lady (Jane Francesca) Wilde, *Notes on Men, Women, and Books*. London: Ward and Dawney, 1891, p.226.
50 Thomas Moore, *Lalla Rookh*, p.193. See also, among other works, Ronan Kelly, *Bard of Erin*, pp.289–91.
51 Thomas. Moore, *The Poetical Works of Thomas Moore, Collected by Himself*, vol.VI, p.xvi. This commentary was reproduced in subsequent editions of Lalla Rookh, as in the case of the

1842 American edition. See Thomas Moore, *Lalla Rookh*, p.12. The "melodies of Ireland" here is a reference to Moore's various volumes of *Irish Melodies*.
52 See Mansour Bonakdarian, "Locating Ireland in Iran of Thomas Moore's 'The Veiled Prophet'."
53 In Joyce's *Finnegans Wake*, other than his unique style of cosmopolitan text, in addition to Moore's and Mangan's influence there was also a clear allusion to Charles Vallancey's late eighteenth century pseudo-etymological claims of ancient historical links between Ireland and 'Iran' (in the broadest sense of the latter). On Joyce and Moore, see Emer Nolan, "'The Tommy Moore Touch'," 64–77. See also Bernard Benstock, "Persian in *Finnegans Wake*," 100–109.
54 Denis Florence MacCarthy, *Ballads, Poems, Lyrics, Original and Translated*. Dublin: James McGlashan, 1850, p.155.
55 See the preface in John Malcolm, *The History of Persia*, vol.I (1815 edition), p.vii.
56 Thomas. Moore, *The Poetical Works of Thomas Moore, Collected by Himself*, vol.VI, p.xix; Thomas Moore, *Lalla Rookh*, p.13. The Scottish Sir John Malcolm was an officer (and later an administrator) in British India, who had been dispatched as the representative of the governor-general of British India to Iran in 1800, 1808, and 1810—during the Russo-Iranian War that coincided and intersected with the British war effort against France during the Napoleonic Wars. See Mansour Bonakdarian and Manoutchehr Eskandari-Qajar, "Malcolm, Major-General Sir John (1769-1833)." In June 1819 Moore had visited Sir John Malcolm's wife Isabella Charlotte (née Campbell) in England, while Malcolm himself was still living in India. Moore noted in his memoirs: "She played for me the Persian air [...] and some others, rather pretty." Thomas Moore, *Memoirs, Journal, and Correspondence of Thomas Moore*, vol.2, p.318.
57 Thomas. Moore, *The Poetical Works of Thomas Moore, Collected by Himself*, vol.VI, pp.xix–xx; Thomas Moore, *Lalla Rookh*, pp.13–14.
58 Iran as a unified territory under a single so-called indigenous independent administration (however one defines indigenous in such contexts) did not exist from the seventh to the sixteenth century. Even after the sixteenth century, with the territory then known as Iran having vastly shrunk in size, people living in a number of other adjoining territories could claim historical entitlement to the past cultures and customs of ancient 'Iran' (as much as any contemporary group can ever claim the past), with post sixteenth-century Iran simply being the largest of these territories.
59 Thomas Moore, *Lalla Rookh*, pp.13, 23–24, 114, 237, 242, 156 n.1, 177, and passim.
60 See also the anonymous and lengthy scathing review of Atkinson's *The Shâh Nâmeh of the Persian Poet Firdâusí*, which reproached Atkinson's omission of certain key sections of the Iranian epic and his failure to deliver an appropriately elegant poetic translation in the *British Critic* 13(26), 1833, pp.361–92.
61 Charles Vallancey, *A Vindication*, pp.357- 62 (see also pp.79, 259, passim). See also, Vallancey, *An Essay on the Primitive Inhabitants*, pp.41–43, passim.
62 Joseph Cooper Walker, *Historical Memoirs of the Irish Bards*. Volume I. Second edition. Dublin: J. Christie, 1818, pp.365–68.
63 Louisa Catherine Beaufort, "An Essay upon the State of Architecture and Antiquities," p.108. It is not known if Beaufort had discussed the similarity between the Iranian and Irish epics during her October 22, 1827 presentation at the Royal Irish Academy, which she later expanded for publication in 1828.
64 Thomas Moore, *Memoirs, Journal, and Correspondence of Thomas Moore*, vol.2, pp.308. 313, 323. Of their meeting on June 6, Moore wrote that Mirza Jafar "Showed me some curious Persian MSS." On these Iranian students in general, see also Nile Green, *The Love of Strangers: What Six Muslim Students Learned in Jane Austen's London*. Princeton: Princeton University Press, 2016. Green, who refers to Mirza Jafar's joy of reading *Lalla Rookh*, does not mention this student meeting Moore. See ibid., pp.278–79.
65 Thomas Moore, *Memoirs, Journal, and Correspondence of Thomas Moore*, vol.2, p.323.
66 Ibid., p.311.
67 See *Thomas Moore, Lalla Rookh*, pp.28 n.5, 97 n.3, and 168 n3. Morier's *A Second Journey through Persia, Armenia, and Asia Minor, to Constantinople, between the Years 1810 and 1816* was not published until 1818. Incidentally, Moore first met Morier in London on May 23, 1819 during a

dinner with a group that included another British diplomat Stratford Canning. Moore and Morier met again in Paris in 1821, where Moore and his family were living at the time after Moore fled England until a substantial financial litigation against him could be resolved. See Thomas Moore, *Memoirs, Journal, and Correspondence of Thomas Moore*, vol.2, p.313; as well as entries for July 3 and July 5, 1821, in Thomas Moore, *Memoirs, Journal, and Correspondence of Thomas Moore*. Volume 3. Edited by Lord John Russell. London: Longman, Brown, Green, and Longmans, 1853, pp.247, 249.

68 James Baillie Fraser *Travels and Adventures in Persian Provinces on the Southern Banks of the Caspian Sea*. London: Longman, Rees, Orme, Brown, and Green, 1826, pp.128–29, 139. See also *Lalla Rookh*, p.14; Thomas. Moore, *The Poetical Works of Thomas Moore, Collected by Himself*, vol.VI, pp.xx–xxi.

69 *Assr-e Jadid* (Tehran), 7 Rabi' al-Awal 1335 (January 2, 1917), p.8.

70 Thomas Moore, *Memoirs, Journal, and Correspondence of Thomas Moore*, vol.3, p.167; idem, *The Poetical Works of Thomas Moore, Collected by Himself*, vol.VI, pp.xx–xxi; Thomas Moore, *Lalla Rookh*, pp.14, 67 n.3.; John D. Yohannan, "The Persian Poetry Fad in England, 1770-1825," *Comparative Literature* 4(2), Spring 1952, pp.155–56. Moore was living in France at the time.

71 For Moore's anxiety in this regard, see also his 1813 letter to Mr. Power in Thomas Moore, *Memoirs, Journal, and Correspondence of Thomas Moore*, vol.1, pp.349–50.

72 John D. Yohannan, *Persian Poetry in England and America*. Delmar, New York: Caravan Books, 1977, p.35. On uses of the Orient in English-language Romantic poetry, see also Wallace Cable Brown, "Thomas Moore and English Interest in the East," *Studies in Philology* 34(4), October 1937, pp.576–88; Hasan Javadi, *Persian Literary Influence on English Literature*, pp.84–94; George M. Wickens, "*Lalla Rookh* and the Romantic Tradition of Islamic Literature in English," *Yearbook of Comparative and General Literature*, no.20 (1971), pp.61–66; Allan Gregory, "Thomas Moore's Orientalism," pp.174–75, 182.

73 See also Shelley Meagher, "Politics and Persian Mythology," p.76.

74 George Gordon Byron (Lord Byron,) *The Corsair, A Tale*. Reprint. Boston: West & Blake, 1814, pp.3–4. This narrative poem would become Byron's best-selling work. It should be noted that Byron's character of "Don Juan," in the 1819–24 poem by the same name, bears much resemblance to Moore's Mokanna.

75 Alexander Martin Sullivan, *Speeches and Addresses in Parliament, on the Platform, and at the Bar, 1859 to 1881*. Second edition. Dublin: T.D. Sullivan, 1882, p.162.

76 Joseph Lennon, *Irish Orientalism*, p.155.

77 See also Fergus Dunne, "The Politics of Translation," pp.463–65.

78 Thomas Moore, *The History of Ireland*. Volume I. London: Longman, Rees, Orme, Brown, Green, & Longman, 1835, 17, 19, 22–40. See also Shelley Meagher, "Politics and Persian Mythology," pp.77, 80; Jerry C.M. Nolan, "In Search of an Ireland in the Orient: Tom Moore's *Lalla Rookh*." *New Hibernia Review* 12(3), Autumn 2008, pp.72, 76, 90. The fourth and final volume of Moore's *The History of Ireland*, published in 1846, ended with the death of Owen O'Neill in 1646 during the Confederate War.

79 Thomas Moore, *The History of Ireland*, vol. I, pp.1–18.

80 Ibid., p.14.

81 Ibid., pp.17–18. See also pp.10–13. As his source by "a late writer" on the resemblance between the Round Towers and the "Pillar-temples of Mazanderan," Moore cited a generically unidentified "Popular History of Ireland, by Mr. Whitty, part I," a source to which he referred again on another occasion on p.249 n.*. It is, however, unclear who this particular 'late' Mr. Whitty was (not to be confused with the journalist and author Michael James Whitty, 1795–1873), or if such an author actually existed. Moore may in fact have been plagiarizing information that had previously appeared in Henry O'Brien's and/or L.C. Beaufort's and Vallancey's works. In fact, O'Brien had ambiguously cited "Whitty," without any indication of the work in question and in connection with other related subjects in his 1833 translation of Joaquín Lorenzo Villanueva's book (*Phœnecian Ireland*): in the Translator's Preface (pp.ix n.†, xi) and in O'Brien's translator's note at the bottom of p.285. O'Brien, could very well have invented this source or merely meant 'whitty" as in "clever and insightful" in praise of his own ideas—in which case, Moore's reference to 'late' author could in fact be no other than O'Brien, with Moore realizing O'Brien's facetiousness. The similarity between the Round Towers and edifices of presumed 'fire-worship' in Mazandaran had

been mentioned in Henry O'Brien's 1834 *The Round Towers* (p.513), without any reference to 'Whitty' in that work. The similarity between the structures in Mazandaran and the Round Towers was earlier noted in Louisa Catherine Beaufort's 1828 "An Essay upon the State of Architecture and Antiquities" (p.200) by way of citing the work of the eighteenth-century English reformer and traveler Jonas Hanway, who had visited Iran and had remarked on what he assumed to be ancient Iranian fire-temple towers in the "Mazanderan" province as well as in the neighboring Russian Caucasus (i.e., Baku) in the first volume of his two volume 1753 *An Historical Account of the British Trade Over the Caspian Sea; With a Journal of Travels from London Through Russia into Persia* ..., to which were appended two additional volumes on Iranian history. Hanway was cited by Beaufort in her essay again in other Iran-related connections. Vallancey had earlier cited Hanway in reference to Vallancey's view of the similarity between the Round Towers and structures found in contemporary Iran and surrounding areas, but Vallancey did not mention the Mazandaran province, referring instead to such structures around Baku. See "III. A Second Essay on the Round Towers of Ireland" in Charles Vallancey, *Collectanea de Rebus Hibernicis*, vol 6, part I, p.137. O'Brien, in his 1834 *The Round Towers* (p.72 n.*) challenged what by then had become almost a convention of citing Hanway as proof that the presumed ancient Iranian structures, which Hanway identified as fire-worship edifices, bore a close resemblance to Ireland's Round Towers: "It is most unaccountable how Hanway, after seeing this evidence of an *actual* fire-temple, should, notwithstanding, commit the egregious blunder of calling the Round Towers—which differed from it as much as a *maypole* does from a rabbit-hole—fire-temples also. Yet has he been most religiously followed by Vallancey, [William] Beauford, Dalton. &c., who could not open their eyes to the mistake."

82 Thomas Moore, *The History of Ireland*, vol. I, pp.19–20. See also pp.21–34, and passim.
83 Ibid., pp.26–34.
84 Ibid., pp.31–33.
85 Thomas Moore, *Lalla Rookh*, pp.147n.1, 172, 174, 175n.1, 206, and 218.
86 *Dublin University Magazine* 5(30), June 1835, p.628 c.a.
87 However, grossly underestimating Moore's belief in the oriental origins of ancient Ireland and the historicity of the Tuatha de Dananns, Milesians, and so on, Leerssen goes on to claim: "Moore finds it difficult, however, to dismiss completely the source material, tenable or not, from the legendary and pseudo-historical native tradition. The rehearsal of early mythical conquests was too ingrained, and there was no alternative information available. As a result, Moore, and indeed most nineteenth century historians after him, opts for a Hegelian *Aufhebung*: he enshrines the discredited legends in his text by taking critical account of their legendary nature ...." Joep Leerssen, "Setting the Scene for National History" in Stefan Berger and Chris Lorenz, eds., *Nationalizing the Past: Historians as Nation Builders in Modern Europe*. Houndmills, Basingstoke: Palgrave Macmillan, 2010, pp.80–81. Furthermore, the obvious ingredient missing in Leerssen's comparison between Irish and Belgian Nationalist historiographies in regard to their respective configurations of their 'national' pasts, as well as between Irish historiography in this regard, on the one hand, and German or French historiographies, on the other hand, is Ireland's colonial status, at least as comprehended by Irish nationalists. What Leerssen overlooks is the primary focus in Irish nationalist antiquarianism of the eighteenth and early nineteenth centuries on establishing Ireland's ancient civilizational distinction from, and superiority over, ancient England.
88 *Dublin University Magazine* 5(30), June 1835, p.616. On this topic, see also Ronan Kelly, "Thomas Moore and Irish Historiography" in in Karen Vandevelde, ed., *New Voices in Irish Criticism 3*. Dublin: Four Courts Press, 2002, pp.70–75.
89 *Dublin University Magazine* 5(30), June 1835, pp.627–29.
90 Ibid., p.627 c.b.
91 Thomas Moore, *The History of Ireland*, vol.I, pp.297–302, and passim.
92 Entry for June 10, 1835 in Thomas Moore, *Memoirs, Journal, and Correspondence of Thomas Moore*, vol.7 pp.93–95. See also February 25, 1836 in ibid., p.144; February 29, 1836 in ibid., p.148; August 3, 1836 in ibid., p.164.
93 Thomas Moore, *The History of Ireland*, vol.II, pp.59–61.
94 George Petrie, *The Ecclesiastical Architecture of Ireland*, pp.67–70 and passim.

95 "The Round Towers of Erin" (signed "E."), *Catholic Progress*, 8(93), September 1879, pp.278-79.
96 Samuel Carter Hall and Anna Maria Hall, *Ireland: Its Scenery, Character, &c*. Vol. III. London: Jeremiah How, 1843, p.200.
97 *Penny Cyclopædia of the Society for the Diffusion of Useful Knowledge*. Vol. XI. London: Charles Knight and Co., 1838, p.32.
98 *Chambers's Encyclopædia: A Dictionary of Universal Knowledge for the People*. Vol.V. Edinburgh: W. & R. Chambers, 1870, p.426.
99 See, among other works, Stiofán Ó Cadhla, *Civilizing Ireland*, pp.174-77 and passim; Paul Walsh, "George Petrie: His Life and Work" in Próinséas Ní Chatháin, Siobhán Fitzpatrick, and Howard Clarke, eds., *Pathfinders to the Past*, pp.44-71.
100 See the "Foreword" in Patrick MacSweeney, *A Group of Nation Builders: O'Donovan-O'Curry-Petrie*. Dublin: Catholic Truth Society of Ireland, 1913.
101 Ibid., pp.9-10, 22. See also pp.18-19, 25, 38.
102 Ibid., pp.86, 88-90, 106, 107-20.
103 *Irish Literary Gazette* (Dublin, Cork, Belfast and Galway), November 21, 1857, p.264.
104 Ibid., December 5, 1857, p.296.
105 Eugene O'Curry, *On the Manners and Customs of the Ancient Irish: A Series of Lectures*. Volume II. Edited with an Introduction by William Kirby Sullivan. Dublin: W.B. Kelly, 1873, p.179. See also William Kirby Sullivan, "Introduction" in Eugene O'Curry, *On the Manners and Customs of the Ancient Irish: A Series of Lectures*. Volume I. Edited with an Introduction by William Kirby Sullivan. Dublin: W.B. Kelly, 1873, p.dxxxvi. The first volume of O'Curry's book is, in fact, entirely Sullivan's long "Introduction" to O'Curry's lectures. Sullivan (d.1890), was the president of Queen's College, Cork, and a member of the Royal Irish Academy.
106 Eugene O'Curry, *On the Manners and Customs of the Ancient Irish*, vol.II, pp.94, 110, 184, 188, 233.
107 Ibid., p.206.
108 Patrick MacSweeney, *A Group of Nation Builders*, pp.113-14.
109 William Stokes, *The Life and Labours*, pp.324-25, 331-33.
110 Ibid., p.336. See also George Petrie, *The Petrie Collection of the Ancient Music of Ireland. Arranged for the Piano-Forte*. Volume I. Dublin: M.H. Gill, 1855, p.73.
111 George Petrie, *The Ecclesiastical Architecture of Ireland*, pp.78, 127, 174-75, 192-93, 196-97, and passim. See also Patrick MacSweeney, *A Group of Nation Builders*, 1913, pp.122-23, 129.
112 John O'Donovan, *Annals of the Kingdom of Ireland by the Four Masters, from the Earliest Period to the Year 1616*. Volume I. Dublin: Hodges and Smith, 1848, p.xix. See also Dermot McGuinne, "John O'Donovan's Edition of *The Annals of the Kingdom of Ireland by the Four Masters*" in James H. Murphy, ed., *The Oxford History of the Irish Book*, vol.IV, pp.477-83.
113 John O'Donovan, *Annals of the Kingdom of Ireland by the Four Masters*, vol.I, 1848, p.x. On the *Annals*, see also Bernadette Cunningham, *The Annals of the Four Masters: Irish History, Kingship and Society in the Early Seventeenth Century*. Dublin: Four Courts Press, 2009.
114 Francis Joseph Brigger, "The Ruins of Ireland" in Joseph Dunn and Patrick Joseph Lennox, eds., *The Glories of Ireland*. Washington, D.C.: Phoenix, 1914, pp.89, 91, 94.
115 Ibid., pp.56, 64, 71, 110, 210, 262, 71, 291. By the time this collection appeared in late 1914, the First World War had erupted, with Casement, then in Germany to procure German assistance for militant Irish nationalist activities against British rule in Ireland, and his militant nationalist colleagues in Ireland (i.e., members of the Irish Republican Brotherhood) and in the diaspora (in the United States in particular, as affiliates of Clan na Gael) focused on unifying the Irish in opposition to Britain in the global war that was raging.

Chapter Three

IRANS OF YOUNG IRELAND IMAGINATIONS, 1842–48: FROM THOMAS OSBORNE DAVIS' "THERMOPYLAE" TO JAMES CLARENCE MANGAN'S "AYE-TRAVAILING GNOMES"

Commenting on the early phase of the Royal Irish Academy, the prominent twentieth-century Irish nationalist author and playwright William Butler Yeats wrote in 1937:

> A generation before *The Nation* newspaper was founded [in 1842,] the Royal Irish Academy had begun the study of ancient Irish literature. [...] The Academy persuaded the English Government to finance an ordnance survey on a large scale; scholars, including the great scholar [John] O'Donovan, were sent from village to village recording names and their legends. [...] the Royal Irish Academy and its public with equal enthusiasm welcomed Pagan and Christian; thought the Round Towers a commemoration of Persian fire-worship. [...][1]

Yeats did not mention that by 1842 Petrie's position on the Round Towers (first articulated in 1833) was steadily gaining ground in the Royal Irish Academy, even if Petrie's most comprehensive study on the topic *The Ecclesiastical Architecture of Ireland* did not appear in print until 1845. From 1833 to 1846, Petrie was in charge of the Ordnance Survey, mentioned by Yeats, with which O'Donovan and Eugene O'Curry too were affiliated. Nor did Yeats elaborate that many scholars and other commentators continued to latch on to varying oriental theories of ancient Ireland, regardless of their perspectives on the origin of the Round Towers. As already noted, in some circles the former competing oriental theories of the likes of Vallancey, Sylvester O'Halloran, Louisa Catherine Beaufort, Betham, Lanigan, D'Alton (Dalton), Henry O'Brien, Windele, Thomas Moore, and others continued to hold sway, even if often in revised forms. These views were frequently echoed in the "national" and provincial press in Ireland. Examples of the latter include the *Cork Examiner*, founded in 1841 as an O'Connellite pro-Catholic rights and pro-Repeal movement newspaper.[2] Certainly outside the Academy, no abrupt paradigm shift was detectable regarding the old antiquarian views of the Round Towers. Nor did the appearance of the Young Ireland nationalist movement and its newspaper *The Nation* in 1842, which was committed to cross-ethnic and cross-confessional Irish nationalism, mark any seismic departure from older oriental theories of Irish origins in general. The Young Ireland coterie, with their own dynamic brand of Romantic nationalism, remained divided on the supposed oriental heritage of ancient Ireland, as well as on the subject of the Round Towers.

Young Ireland had its origins in a small literary circle of Irish nationalists based in Dublin, who came together in 1839–40 to advocate Daniel O'Connell's campaign for the Repeal of the Union (i.e., for Irish Home Rule within the British Empire, with a separate parliament in Ireland, inclusive of Catholic members). In 1842 this group became affiliated with the newly founded nationalist paper *The Nation* under the editorial direction of Charles Gavan Duffy and Thomas Osborne Davis. The paper was intended to serve as the mouthpiece of the Repeal movement and propagate nonsectarian Irish nationalism, even though O'Connell had forged close ties with the Catholic establishment in Ireland. Within a year, *The Nation* emerged as one of the two largest circulation nationalist newspapers in Ireland.[3] The much older and now staunchly O'Connellite *Freeman's Journal* (founded in Dublin in 1763) was the largest circulation nationalist paper in Ireland, as well as being one of the major Irish newspapers in general. In the coming years, Duffy and Davis, along with John Blake Dillon, William Smith O'Brien, and John Mitchel emerged as leading figures of the group that came to be known as Young Ireland. With the exception of Duffy and Dillon, all other founding figures of the movement were Protestants. The group eventually broke with O'Connell in 1843, after the latter called off a "Monster Meeting" in Clontarf (north of Dublin), organized by O'Connell's Repeal Association (formed in 1840). O'Connell's decision was in response to a warning from the authorities that they would resort to force to prevent the meeting. O'Connell, who was committed to non-violent social and political transformation, despite using pugnacious rhetoric, wished to avoid bloodshed. He was, nonetheless, arrested on charge of sedition even after calling off the meeting. Young Ireland, in parting ways with O'Connellites, embraced a more radical platform, rejecting O'Connell's position that the Repeal movement should proceed gradually and peacefully, without any recourse to physical force. Within a short time, Young Ireland gravitated toward a categorically "secular"-oriented republican nationalism, albeit with a decidedly non-violent and chiefly literary leaning at the time. The movement was immediately shunned by the Catholic establishment in Ireland, which was both a major sponsor of O'Connell's campaign and disapproved of both republicanism and 'secular'-oriented nondenominational nationalist platforms. The publication of a poem in *The Nation* on April 1, 1843, signaled the movement's clear break with O'Connell's Repeal campaign and tactics. Appearing anonymously, the poem, titled "The Memory of the Dead," was written by the Presbyterian Irish nationalist John Kells Ingram.[4] This would be Ingram's only work to appear in *The Nation*, nor was he an actual member of Young Ireland himself. Commencing with an unmistakable reference to the failed

United Irishmen uprising of 1798, the poem proceeded to celebrate the memory of that event as the "guiding light/ [...] / Though sad as theirs your fate":

The Memory of the Dead

Who fears to speak of 'Ninety-Eight'?
Who blushes at the name?
When cowards mock the patriot's fate
Who hangs his head for shame?
He's all a knave or half a slave
Who slights his country thus;
But a *true* man, like you, man,
Will fill your glass with us.

[...]

They rose in dark and evil days
To right their native land;
They kindled then a living blaze
That nothing shall withstand.
Alas! that might can vanquish right—
They fell and pass'd away;
But true men, like you, men,
Are plenty here today.

Then here's their memory! May it be
For us a guiding light,
To cheer our strife for liberty
And teach us to unite.
Though good and ill be Ireland's still,
Though sad as theirs your fate,
Yet true men be you, men,
Like those of Ninety-Eight.[5]

Thomas Osborne Davis and "Iran" of "Marathon" and "Thermopylae"

Among leading Irish nationalist figures in the 1840s who rejected the Zoroastrian (allegedly "fire-worship") or other Eastern precedents for, and resemblances to, the Round Towers was Thomas Osborne Davis (d. 1845), a cofounder of *The Nation* and its affiliated Young Ireland circle. Confessing his own earlier fanciful acceptance of "oriental" and "pagan" origins of the Round Towers, Davis now ridiculed such suppositions and instead echoed Petrie's refutation of the opinions of Vallancey and others concerning the towers.[6] Having now turned away from Vallanceyan-style methodology and much of that mode of antiquarianism, Davis nonetheless defended these antiquarians for having inspired pride in Ireland's ancient past:

They excited the noblest passions—veneration, love of glory, beauty, and virtue. They awoke men's fancy by their gorgeous pictures of the past, and imagination strove to surpass them by its creations. They believed what they wrote, and thus their wildest stories sank into men's minds. To the exertions of [Joseph Cooper] Walker, O'Halloran, Vallancey, and a few other Irish academicians in the last century, we owe almost all the Irish knowledge possessed by our upper classes till very lately. It was small, but it was enough to give a dreamy renown to ancient Ireland; and if it did nothing else it smoothed the reception of [Edward] Bunting's music, and identified Moore's poetry with his native country.

While, therefore, we at once concede that Vallancey was a bad scholar, O'Halloran a credulous historian, and Walker a shallow antiquarian, we claim for them gratitude and attachment, and protest, once for all, against the indiscriminate abuse of them now going in our educated circles.[7]

Yet, Davis' acknowledgment of the failings of Vallancey, O'Halloran, Walker, and their cohorts did not amount to a comprehensive rejection of Ireland's ancient ties to the Orient. While he looked back to ancient Athenian-style republicanism (albeit without enslaved peoples) as a template for the future virtuous Irish republic,[8] Davis nevertheless turned to the 'Orient' in search of Ireland's ancient roots. Relying on descriptions in the Scottish Samuel Laing's 1836 *Journal of a Residence in Norway*, Davis added a new twist to the existing Asian/Milesian renditions of Irish origins. He opted for Scythian origins of the Irish, that of Indo-Scythians (or what Davis called "Sanscritic") to be precise, and then culturally and ethnically blended in the much later Norse invaders of territories in the British Isles (from the late eighth to mid-ninth centuries CE) with the presumed early ancestors of the Gaels. Remarking on the mistaken belief of Vallancey and others that Milesians had arrived from the Orient—which was a gross oversimplification of Vallancey's more general oriental theory of Irish origins—Davis stated his own conviction in the oriental origins of Ireland's pre-Milesian populations:

One of the commonest errors, attributing immense antiquity, oriental origin, and everything noble in Ireland to the Milesians, originated with these men; or, rather, was transferred from the adulatory songs of clan-bards to grave stories. Now, it is quite certain that several races flourished here before the Milesians, and that everything oriental, and much that was famous in Ireland, belonged to some of these elder races, and not to the Scoti or Milesians.[9]

In another setting, Davis conceded that Milesians, too, were indeed of oriental descent after all, of Indo-Scythian (or Indo-Iranian) roots, to be exact:

It seems highly probable that the Milesians themselves—that Scotic (or Scythian) race who gave our isle the name of Scotia Major—reached our shore, having sailed from the Baltic. They were old Sea Kings.

[…]

There are strong reasons for believing that these people came from the east, through Muscovy, and preferring the fish-filled bays and game-filled hills of Norway and Sweden to the flat plains of Germany, settled far north. Such is the tradition of the country and the expressed opinion of all their writers. The analogy of their language to the Sanscrit, their polygamy and their use of horse-flesh, all tend to prove that they were once an equestrian tribe in Upper Asia.[10]

For Davis, the ancient Indo-Scythian arrivals in Ireland, who shared a common heritage with the later Norse invaders of the British Isles, constituted only one of the original Irish stock. There were other preceding and subsequent *substantial* arrivals of population groups in Ireland in ancient times according to Davis, such as Phoenicians, whom he also seems to have identified with Indo-Scythians. To this end, and appearing under the heading "Ethnology of the Irish Race," Davis was relying on the new so-called science of craniological ethnography spearheaded by Dr. (later Sir) William Robert Wills Wilde in his studies of Irish origins in the 1840s.[11] Moreover, while endorsing Petrie's stance on the Round Towers and rejecting Vallancey's claim of the towers having initially served as fire temples, Davis conceded that Vallancey's more general theory of fire-worship in ancient Ireland and its strong resemblance to the "custom exist[ing] among the Parsees or Guebres of Persia" (i.e., Zoroastrians) was a "plausible" analogy.[12] Given Davis' own Protestant Welsh-Irish parentage, it is not surprising he should have been attracted to Laing's particular rendering of Scythian migrations westward, which also allowed for a wide dispersion of this group throughout the British Isles in later periods in the form of Norse (Danes/Vikings) invasions. This formulation of a common ancestral origin of Ireland's ancient Milesian and 'medieval' Norse populations, on the one hand, and the shared ancestry of these Irish people with descendants of the Norse in mainland Britain, on the other hand, was a significant intervention in debates on Irish origins. It raised the possibility that some of the English, Welsh, and Scots settlers in Ireland following the Anglo-Norman conquests after the twelfth century, and more notably after the sixteenth century, already shared at least *some* common ancestry with the majority of descendants of Ireland's older pre-twelfth century population.

This formula reduced the ethnic divide between the Gaelic ('mere Irish') population of Ireland and at least some of the descendants of later arrivals in Ireland from mainland Britain. In effect, the 'Irish' in general, regardless of how far back they could trace their ancestry's presence on the island, for the most part shared some degree of common ethnic pedigree and, therefore, as a 'nation,' shared at least some element of an ethnically identical lineage—allowing also in this scenario for generations of ethnic intermixing following the Norse settlements on mainland Britain. It was hence imperative to imagine the future Irish nation in-the-making not on grounds of ethnic identities but in terms of common ideals and a common desire to govern the *national self* independently of London's control. Prior to Davis, there had been a number of antiquarians who had posited different theories of shared, if not uniformly common, ancestry of the Gaelic population of Ireland and some population groups on mainland Britain. But, all of these earlier theories, most pronouncedly in the form of Celtic theory of Irish origins, had made an either/or choice regarding the oriental or Scandinavian (Scandian) or other European ancestral origins of the Celts. Davis, on the other hand, was proposing a blurred oriental descent for both the Milesian Gaels and the Norse (i.e., Scandinavians), without directly venturing into the Celtic debate, and also leaving room for the hypothesis of Ireland being the location of the earliest population settlements in the British Isles (by those who were common ancestors of the Gaels and the Norse); hence also Ireland's unique civilizational standing in the British Isles in ancient times.[13] Such a vague stance left room for stipulating the arrival of descendants of the same peoples in mainland Britain at a later date, their intermixing with other population groups in mainland Britain over time, and the relocation of descendants of some of this latter population to Ireland in various stages following the Anglo-Norman conquests. Leaving aside the leaps and bounds of this theory, Davis' conflation of oriental and Scandinavian theories of Irish origins, as well as his assertion of a later Scandinavian ancestry for many English, Scots, and Welsh, was a radical departure from existing debates on Irish origins. Largely overlooked by historians working on theories of Irish origins today, this was an early specimen of what by the end of the century became the increasingly prevalent theory of *some kind of a shared ancestral lineage* between Irish population of Gaelic ancestry and other post-Gaelic major population arrivals on the island, particularly after the Norman invasion. The conventional version of this model by the end of the century would be that of some degree of shared *Celtic* ancestry of the Gaels and many of the subsequent major population settlements in Ireland, regardless of the debate on whether the Celts had themselves first hailed from the Orient (in a relatively short time frame) or from some part of the European continent (after a long period of settlement there). These theories constituted a new historical-political initiative for diffusing ethnic divisions among the contemporary population of Ireland in pursuit of the project of forging a 'nation.' It is unclear whether Davis' model served as a palimpsest for some of the future versions of a shared Celtic ancestry and/or heritage of the majority of Irish, whose ancestry could be traced to pre-Norman and post-Norman population arrivals on the island. Yet, Davis' model also accommodated his thesis of Ireland's protracted *cultural* cross-fertilizations, given the earlier Phoenician and/or Scythian arrivals on the island, or the much later partly Norse arrivals from mainland Britain, and, thereby, by implication, also downplaying religious and other communal divisions as central cultural markers of contemporary Irish identity. Davis' historical narrative dovetailed the nonsectarian nationalist platform propounded by the expanding Young Ireland circle. Rejecting inter-communal hostilities, Young Ireland rebranded the Irish 'nation' as those wishing to identify with Ireland as the national homeland to which they belonged and toward whose self-government and collective welfare they endeavored—a goal that transcended all other presumed differences as members of the Irish *national* community (even though Davis devoted little attention to class or gender dimensions of the nation).[14] The Young Ireland project of nation-building was not dissimilar to that of the United Irishmen half a century earlier and in some ways presaged the French philosopher Ernest Renan's 1882 "What is a Nation?," which characterized the nation as "a daily plebiscite."[15] As David Dwan has pointed out in connection with Young Ireland's emphasis on "civic virtue," the movement was preoccupied with manifold (European) Enlightenment conceptions of "the common good."[16]

Davis' ultimate emphasis in his narrative of Irish ethnicity was not to dwell on the ethnic makeup of the Irish but to break away from the persisting and divisive fixation on the question of origins. For him, the nation was grounded not so much in its past, but rather in its present orientation and futurity. In his poetry, too, Davis offered a narrative of the continual miscellany of major population arrivals in Ireland since the earliest times, who now with equal merit comprised the population of the land. This was perhaps best underscored in the poem "Celts and Saxons" (see below). The decisive point was who among the Irish was willing to belong to an independent nation and what they were willing to do toward that collective goal. In effect, for Davis and most of his Young Ireland colleagues it was *nationalism that begot the nation* by consciously and communally molding the present in order to create the future national 'common good,' in opposition to English exploitation and maladministration of Ireland. In other respects, this nationalist project too, like all other nationalist projects, invented its conception of the nation and that nation's "national history." While Davis avoided any clear-cut racialization of the Irish, some Young Irelanders later embraced racially deterministic discourses—the most infamous example being John Mitchel after his emigration to antebellum slave-owning United States. But, in the days of pre-1848 Young Ireland uprising the focus of the movement and its literary undertakings were aimed at inspiring the Irish to consciously "imagine" their community anew as a collective nation (to borrow Benedict Anderson's general expression of 'imagined communities' here). Davis wrote in his undated poem "Celts and Saxons" (composed in the early 1840s):

I.
We hate the Saxon and the Dane,
    We hate the Norman men—
We cursed their greed for blood and gain,
    We curse them now again.
Yet start not, Irish born man,
    If you're to Ireland true,
We heed not blood, nor creed, nor clan—
    We have no curse for you.

II.
We have no curse for you or your's,
    But Friendship's ready grasp,
And Faith to stand by you and your's,
    Unto our latest gasp—
To stand by you against all foes,
    Howe'er, or whence they come,
With traitor arts, or bribes, or blows,
    From England, France, or Rome.

III.
What matter that at different shrines
    We pray unto one God—
What matter that at different times
    Our fathers won this sod—
In fortune and in name we're bound
    By stronger links than steel;
And neither can be safe nor sound
    But in the other's weal.

IV.
As Nubian rocks, and Ethiop sand
   Long drifting down the Nile,
Built up old Egypt's fertile land
   For many a hundred mile;
So Pagan clans to Ireland came,
   And clans of Christendom,
Yet joined their wisdom and their fame
   To build a nation from.

V.
Here came the brown Phœnician,
   The man of trade and toil—
Here came the proud Milesian,
   A hungering for spoil;
And the Firbolg and the Cymry.
   And the hard, enduring Dane,
And the iron Lords of Normandy,
   With the Saxons in their train.[17]

It was only in such a context that Davis could imaginatively and historically connect himself and all other Irish as members of a nation, regardless of their actual or presumed ancestry or the time frame when their ancestors happened to first arrive in Ireland. Hence, his use of the plural "we" and "our":

> THERE was once civilization in Ireland. We never were very eminent to be sure for manufactures in metal, our houses were simple, our very palaces rude, our furniture scanty, our saffron shirts not often changed, and our foreign trade small. Yet was Ireland civilized. [...] For there was a time when learning was endowed by the rich and honoured by the poor, and taught all over our country. Not only did thousands of natives frequent our schools and colleges, but men of every rank came here from the Continent to study under the professors and system of Ireland [...] Ireland was equally remarkable for piety.[18]

The present-centered and future-oriented nationalist project of Young Ireland required alternative creative reconceptualizations and reconfigurations of the past, *if* the past was to be considered in this formulation at all. This is not to suggest the past was to be a forgotten affair for Davis and his associates. Nationalists had to be selective in their recourse to the past, avoiding an obsession with memories of past ethnic and confessional divisions that threatened to internally splinter the nation in-the-making by amplifying its past internecine traumas, while simultaneously recollecting the injustices inflicted on Ireland by English *government*. The objective was to construct an Irish past grounded in a new ontological historicity: a nonsectarian collective within the imagined parameters of a nation aspiring to invent itself. In such an undertaking the present was not entirely subordinate to the past. In fact, the present determined the past (not unlike other presentist narrations of the past devised by a broad range of nationalist projects elsewhere). The only past that truly mattered consisted of selective episodes that inspired and enabled national formation, struggle for independence, and common national welfare. At issue here was not so much the cultural baggage that each new wave of population arrivals in Ireland had brought with them. Instead, the past was to remind the Irish of particular chapters in their history that could continually inspire them to aspire toward and build their own nation-state. The goal was to contrive a unifying national 'culture' *now*, including the promotion of learning the Irish language as a distinctive marker of national identity and the proper medium of both conveying the new *national* culture and connecting the *nationalized* Irish with Ireland's nationally-sustaining past, regardless of their presumed ethnic descent.[19] The past was to be a "life-affirming" past (to borrow from Friedrich Nietzsche's 1873 *On the Use and Abuse of History for Life*), a past that promoted national unity. This mode of nationalist remembrance required a re-coding of one's *acquired* historical memory, if not also of one's *personal* memory. Different members of Young Ireland undertook to realize this challenge in distinct ways. Hence, also, ample celebratory references by Young Ireland poets to the 1798 uprising and lesser focus on pre-United Irishmen chapters in Ireland's long history of uprisings after the twelfth century. For nonsectarian nationalists, Ireland's pre-1798 history was a slippery slope and a dangerous minefield. For instance, Davis' poem "Oh! For a Steed" exposed some of the pitfalls of celebrating Ireland's pre-1798 episodes of so-called national heroism. In contrast to his poem "Celts and Saxons," which exhorted the contemporary Irish to transcend transmitted historical memories of past invasions that had led to Ireland's current ethnic admixture, as in the case of the Norse (Danes), the poem "Oh! For a Steed" celebrated Irish resistance to outside invaders, as in the case of "when Brian [Boru] smote down the Dane."

Significantly, inspirational historical chapters for nurturing the nation were not to be limited to Ireland's own past. The Irish could also draw inspiration from the (mytho-) history of other nations. Young Ireland poets, most notably James Clarence Mangan, routinely incorporated borrowed histories of other 'nations' into their poems as a source of inspiration for the Irish (see below). Yet, this cosmopolitan world-historical mode of Irish nationalist engagement with the past—as opposed to the world-historical configuration of ancient Ireland in antiquarian works—did not entirely eliminate the potential pitfalls of Ireland's own divisive sectarian history. One could always allegorically read the inner divisions and conflicts of other 'nations' onto Irish history in a range of ways.

Nowhere in Davis' listings of various historical admixtures of the Irish nation did ancient Iran make a direct appearance; although such an admixture may have been implied by the previously mentioned example of his designating a distant Indo-Scythian ancestry for some of the early population settlements in Ireland, and might also be gleaned from his somewhat generic reference to Ireland having been "In the Pagan times [...] a sanctuary of Magian or Druid creed," hence a reference to traces of Zoroastrian and/or pre-Zoroastrian ancient Iranian religious practices in Ireland (i.e., through the medium of the magi).[20] Davis' most emotive reference to ancient Iran, however, appeared in his best-known borrowed chapter from the (mytho-)history of another so-called nation, intended as an inspiration for the Irish. This was an 'Iran' of the Achaemenid Persian Empire (c.550–330 BCE) cast in negative light as an oppressive, enslaving, and territorially expansionist and civilizationally destructive imperialist state, whose victims were the subject of Davis' acclamation and commemoration. This Iran (Persia), without Davis mentioning the actual name of the territorial state, appeared in Davis' highly celebrated and most popular Irish nationalist poem to date: "A Nation Once Again." Composed sometime in the early 1840s, in this poem the "Greeks" (as an ahistorically homogenized single nation as well as excessively characterized as freedom loving and egalitarian), in resisting the invasion of the much more powerful Persian and allied forces, served as Davis' intended historical equivalent for the Irish nation's quest for sovereignty. This particular temporal-spatial typecasting of Iran was Davis' way of reproducing and recontextualizing an already existing and highly mythologized tradition in parts of Europe/the West that demonized the ancient Persian Empire as the cultural Other of a comparatively more civilized (and highly essentialized) ancient 'Greece.' This stereotyping trend was further galvanized following the cultivation of the fable of "Western Civilization" during the course of the multivocal eighteenth-century Enlightenment movement in Europe. For Davis, as already noted, ancient 'Greece' (namely Athens) also represented a model of republicanism to be emulated by the Irish nation for its avowed spirit of virtuous citizenry and civic duty. The first stanza of Davis' "A Nation Once Again" began:

> When boyhood's fire was in my blood
> I read of ancient freemen
> For Greece and Rome who bravely stood
> Three hundred men and three men
> And then I prayed I might yet see
> Our fetters rent in twain
> And Ireland long a province be
> A nation once again[21]

The "Three hundred men" in this poem was a reference to the semi-mythical account of the resistance at the Thermopylae Pass in 480 BCE by reportedly only 300 Spartan survivors of the original pan-Greek army fighting a Persian invasion force of allegedly over 100,000 men (and in some accounts many times that number). Accordingly, while all but one of the Spartan fighters perished in the battle, they nonetheless managed to slow down the Persian invaders on land, while a joint naval force of allied Greek states destroyed the superior flotilla of the Persians and their allies and turned the tide of the war against the invading forces—in actual history a few Greek territories had joined the Persian side in the war. Davis' recourse to this recurrent myth in European accounts of the battle at Thermopylae Pass did not necessarily amount to any generic castigation of Iranians (Persians in this case) as the *Other* of the West. This can be gauged from his reference to the "three men" in the same line of the poem after his mentioning "Three hundred men." The "three men" was a reference to the last stand of Roman defenders of the Sublicius Bridge against the forces of the Etruscan ruler of the "Italian" city of Clusium in 508 BCE. Davis' underlying concern was to champion the cause of the underdogs defending their native lands against militarily superior aggressors.[22]

At least among the more literate public in the United Kingdom, there was extensive familiarity with the legend of the Battle of Thermopylae, which also appeared in school texts and in the Greek language curricula of public schools and universities.[23] Additionally, there was a long tradition of European (including Irish) references to Thermopylae as a model act of resistance against all apparent odds when confronting a more superior hostile force and defending liberty against tyranny. The most notable among recent English-language literary works during Davis' lifetime that paired the ancient Persian Empire as a tyrannical state and a culturally retrograde force in opposition to a homogenized so-called 'Greek' civilization was a section in the third canto of Lord Byron's incomplete narrative poem *Don Juan* (published in installments between 1818 and the year of Byron's death, 1824). In this case, the focus was on the Battle of Marathon fought between the Achaemenid Persian Empire and Athens in 490 BCE. The Hellenophile Byron, also an avid defender of the Greek War of Independence from Ottoman control (1821–29) which he joined shortly before his death from illness, wrote:

The mountains look on Marathon—
   And Marathon looks on the sea;
And musing there an hour alone,
   I dream'd that Greece might still be free;
For, standing on the Persians' grave,
I could not deem myself a slave.[24]

Ironically, and inconsistent with the above portrayal of the ancient Persians, the sixteenth and final canto of Byron's poem opened with the following (equally mythologized) proverb that many in radical Irish nationalist circles would repeat in the coming decades as their own revolutionary credo:

THE antique Persians taught three useful things,
   To draw the bow, to ride, and speak the truth.
This was the mode of Cyrus, best of kings—
   A mode adopted since by modern youth.
Bows have they, generally with two strings;
   Horses they ride without remorse or ruth;
At speaking truth perhaps they are less clever,
But draw the long-bow better now than ever.[25]

Both of these Byronic depictions of ancient Persians, as either a tyrannical barbaric state or as noble people, recurred to different ends in Irish nationalist allegorizations of Ireland's history. Among other range of Irish nationalists, besides Davis, who also resorted to the myth of Thermopylae were the likes of the poet Edward Walsh in his 1845 "Ode to the Liberator" (in honor of Daniel O'Connell),[26] or Patrick Tynan, the controversial member of the militant Irish National Invincibles, formed in 1881 as a breakaway faction of the Irish Republican Brotherhood (1858). From his safe refuge in New York City in the aftermath of the 1882 murders carried out by the Invincibles in Phoenix Park, Dublin, Tynan wrote:

The Nationalists are the men who believe that the only possible solution of the struggle with the British usurper is the absolute and complete independence of Ireland. They do not ignore the lessons of history, by believing there is any stepping-stone, or mid-position, between subjection and liberty. As followers of Theobald Wolfe Tone and Robert Emmet, as descendants of the men of 1798, they hope to place their country among the nations of the earth. They were nationalists who surrounded Miltiades at Marathon, when he gained his glorious victory over the hordes of Darius, the Persian monarch. They were nationalists, those heroic three hundred Spartans, who under the immortal Leonidas held Thermopylae for Hellas, when the hosts of Xerxes crossed the ridge of Anopaia, and died to preserve the imperishable glory of freedom for Greece. He was a nationalist, the Spartan Denekos, who hearing from a Trachian, just before the battle, that when the Persians shot their arrows the sun was darkened, answered back merrily: "Our friend from Trachios brings good news; we Spartans love to fight in the shade." They were nationalists, upon whose tomb was inscribed:

> Tell the Spartans, at their bidding,
> Stranger, here in death we lie.[27]

Among numerous other later examples, the historian, proponent of the Irish language, and republican nationalist, Eoin MacNeill (1867–1945) characterized Thermopylae as signifying the spirit of nationalism as a distinctive collective identity:

Herein lies the justification of nationality, of intense, distinctive and highly developed nationality. In it resides the elemental power of transformation. To it belongs the philosopher's stone. If the Greek people had possessed but a feeble individuality as a people, if they had resembled Cretans and Phoenicians and Persians, if they had not felt instinctively that they had something precious in themselves, something that was worth Thermopylae, then it would never have been written in a later age that:

> Greece and her foundations are
> Built beneath the tide of war,
> Throned on the crystalline sea
> Of thought and its eternity.

In every intense and distinctive development of a nation, there dwells the actuality or the potentiality of some great gift to the common good of mankind; and I rejoice, I am sure we all rejoice, to see, in these days of clashing and crashing empires, that the clear idea of nationality, as if by the wonderful recreative power that is in nature, is rising in the esteem of good men all over the world, above and beyond the specious and seductive appeal of what has been called "the wider patriotism."[28]

It should go without saying, as discussed later, that the appeal to the myth of Thermopylae on the part of Irish nationalists in no way hindered their simultaneous championing of Iran's own contemporary anti-imperialist struggles. MacNeill, "rejoic[ing]" the anti-imperialist "idea of nationality" spreading "all over the world," would not have excluded contemporary Iran from his envisioned list. In a manner analogous to Thomas Davis' utilization of Thermopylae, MacNeill's castigation of the ancient Persian Empire did not indicate a permanent historical demonization of Iran and a static essentialization of Iranians across time. There were a range of other generic and scattered Irish nationalist references to the authoritarian character of the Achaemenid Persian Empire. A case in point is the reference to "satraps" (provincial governors in the Achaemenid Empire) appearing in an 1886 article titled "*At Last!*" by the Fenian John Boyle O'Reilly in reference to the "magistrates" prosecuting Fenian prisoners.[29]

The references to Thermopylae in Irish nationalist commentaries were frequent and prosaic enough to have elicited a sarcastic remark in 1914 from the renowned Irish composer and conductor, and also a fervent unionist opponent of Irish nationalism, Charles Villiers Stanford. In reference to the 1848 failed Young Ireland uprising, also known as the "Fenian uprising," Stanford reversed the Irish nationalist identification from that of the Spartans to the Persians at Thermopylae: "It lasted a few minutes only, and a wag compared the Fenians to the Persians, pointing out that the Persians fled from Greece, but the Fenians fled from Tallaght (the village name is pronounced Talla)."[30] Needless to say, history and mythology, such as the Battle of Thermopylae, could be interpreted and politically utilized in different ways by Irish nationalists themselves, as demonstrated in a 1911 article by Standish James O'Grady, the Anglican Irish author, literary critic, historian, and conservative cultural-nationalist, who opposed both religious sectarianism and Irish political nationalism, republicanism in particular. O'Grady, characterizing Thermopylae as "the greatest event in all history," sought to highlight the contribution made to the Spartan last stand against the advancing Persian forces by the internally persecuted and semi-colonized population of Sparta, who were omitted from most contemporary accounts of the event. This was a circuitous appeal by O'Grady for acknowledging and reciprocating the manifold contributions made by Irish Catholics to the survival and welfare of the United Kingdom and the British Empire (including, it should not be forgotten, Irish recruits in the British imperial military). Conceding the presence of a larger Spartan force at Thermopylae than generally acknowledged, O'Grady in turn comparatively compensated for this adjustment by further inflating the size of the Persian and allied forces. He then noted that the Spartan army included many Helots (individuals of serf-like status, mostly descendants of people captured long ago from other Hellenic territories), along with Thespians and Thebans—suggesting that the size of the Spartan force cited in most versions of the battle ('300') only evidently accounted for the "free" Spartans in charge of an army of a largely subjugated soldiers, as well as allied forces of Sparta from Thespiae and Thebes. O'Grady estimated the size of the Persian-led forces as 300,000 and the total number of 'Greeks' they encountered as around 60,000, including 35,000 Helots; underscoring that at Thermopylae "there perished not only the 300 Spartans, but also 3,000 Spartan Helots! Xerxes [the Persian emperor] counted the slain, and found them 4,000. There were 300 Spartans, 750 Thespians, a few Thebans: the rest, 3,000, were Helots." O'Grady concluded his article with a profoundly loaded statement: "History would seem to be a kind of liar."[31] This was jointly aimed at Irish political nationalists—whose loyalty to the British Empire O'Grady sought to enlist and whom he wished to convince would fare much worse if not governed by London—as well as at unionists at large—particularly those in the ranks of Anglo-Irish Ascendency, whom O'Grady considered either dismissive of, or oblivious to, the many genuine grievances of Irish Catholics, despite the latter's continued contributions to the British Empire. In its epistemological grounding,

O'Grady's version of Thermopylae and his intended tempered cultural nationalism was at odds with what Eugene O'Brien has uniformly characterized as a common "aetiology of nationalism" that is grounded in the "use of the suffix 'centric,'" which "is an index of the essentialism that is at the heart of nationalism."[32]

Returning to Thomas Davis, he again identified ancient Achaemenid Iran with tyranny, brutality, and imperialist oppression in another undated poem from the early 1840s, titled "A Second Plea for the Bog-Trotters" (bog-trotter meaning 'mere Irish'):

I.
The *Mail* says, that Hanover's King
Twenty Thousand men will bring,
And make the "base bog-trotters" sing
   A *pillileu*;
And that O'Connell high shall swing,
   And others too.

II.
There is a tale of Athens told,
Worth at least its weight in gold
To fellows of King Ernest's mould
   (The royal rover),
Who think men may be bought and sold,
   Or ridden over.

III.
Darius (an imperial wretch,
A Persian Ernest, or Jack Ketch,)
Bid his knaves from Athens fetch
   "Earth and water,"
Or else the heralds' necks he'd stretch,
   And Athens slaughter.

IV.
The Athenians threw them in a well,
And left them there to help themsel',
And when his armies came, pell-mell,
   They tore his banners,
And sent his slaves in shoals to hell,
   To mend their manners.

V.
Let those who bring and those who send
Hanoverians, comprehend
Persian-like may be their end,
   And the "bog trotter"
May drown their knaves, their banners rend,
   Their armies slaughter.[33]

In this poem, the references to Persia, the Persian emperor Darius I, and Athens (along with some other Hellenic city-states, it should be added) were in connection with the Battle of Marathon in 490 BCE. Yet, it is crucial to reiterate that Davis' celebration of different episodes of ancient 'Greek' resistance to Iranian (Persian) invaders was devoid of any supposition of a historically stagnant and civilizationally virulent Iranian trait. For Davis, imperialism, Western or non-Western, was a civilizationally deleterious force and, above all, an act of oppression that should be resisted, even though he did not venture to tackle examples of Athenian or Spartan imperialism. In his contemporary world, it was largely a number of European/Western powers that were imposing their imperial might across the globe, including in Europe itself. Davis excoriated these contemporary instances of imperial aggression in such poems as "Oh! For a Steed" or "A Ballad of Freedom." In these poems no distinction was made between the rights of those resisting British, Russian, French, or other imperialist powers, be it by the Irish, Poles, Algerians, Afghans, Circassians, and so on. In addition, he condemned other instances of oppression, such as the plight of the indigenous population of the United States, among many other groups around the world whose rights were violated and whose lives were destroyed. If anything, Davis advocated an ethical and empathetic cross-solidarity between the oppressed 'nations.' His poem "Oh! For a Steed," which mentioned the ancient Battle of Marathon, also decried *contemporary* American, Austrian, British, and Russian imperialism. In "The Sack of Baltimore," recounting the raid on the Irish town by that name in 1631 and taking of captives into slavery by the "Algerine" (i.e., the Barbary Coast Muslim pirates), it was the "Algerians" who were condemned. On the other hand, in "A Ballad of Freedom" Davis championed the right of contemporary Algerians to resist French imperialism: "Hurrah for Abdel-Kader!" (i.e., the leader of the Algerian struggle from 1832 to 1847 against French occupation). Ultimately, as expressed in the closing line of this poem, Davis was advocating "Hurrah for Human Freedom!"[34]—as complicated as that desire was in the framework of nationalism, with often complex intersecting matrices of competing identity and national and/or nativist constructs in subjugated regions.

A subject overlooked by Davis and his colleagues when dissociating contemporary ethnic make-up of the Irish nation (Gaelic, Norse, English, Scots, Welsh, and other) since the time of both Norse (Danes/Vikings) and much earlier Anglo-Norman invasions of Ireland—for claiming a multi-ethnic united Irish front against England's continued domination of Ireland—was the ontological effect of time and location (the latter defined here as cultural-historical and sociopolitical spaces) shaping the personal experiences and received memories of individuals, which determined what to these individuals constituted "colonialism" from a nationalist perspective. In other words, exactly how relevant is the past to the present time and future time of nationalist projects, and which particular phases and aspects of the past are relevant in that context? At issue here is whether temporal and spatial distance from the initial phases of colonization and its more experientially and visibly deleterious and discriminatory encounters rendered the after-effects of colonialism less malignant and more tolerable in nationalist historiography, if not also even an object of glorification in some instances (as I note below)—not forgetting, of course, the long process of large-scale land confiscations and other forms of dispossession in Ireland by the English state or by English, Welsh, and Scots settlers, as well as post sixteenth-century religious tensions in Ireland and the consequent penal laws and their continued, social, economic, and political legacies even after their revocation. In effect, to which time-scale in imperial encounters do nationalisms belong and respond to? To put it differently, using Walter Benjamin's previously discussed concepts of 'now-time' and 'messianic time,' are nationalisms in colonial and semi-colonial settings entirely products of colonialism/imperialism, or do nationalisms also in turn imagine and construct what they brand and historicize as colonialism/imperialism? Which pasts do the "now-times" of different nationalist projects select for framing their own existence? As Benjamin noted: 'History is the subject of a construction whose site is not homogenous, empty time, but time filled by the now-time [*Jetztzeit*].' It is the now-time of nationalism that reads itself into the past and constructs the past with the promise of a future renewal, or what Benjamin described as 'conception of the present as now-time shot through with splinters of messianic time.' This concept is even more relevant regarding antiquarian claims of Ireland's glorious ancient civilization (whether allegedly transferred from the Orient or from some other stipulated location). Regardless of the presumed original homeland of various major ancient population settlements in Ireland following the prior appearance of the earliest humans on the island, all subsequent population groups had ultimately arrived in Ireland as colonizers. This was readily acknowledged in contemporary antiquarian as well as 'medieval' Irish accounts, regardless of whether these post-"primitive" population settlements, identified in various sources as harbingers of civilization, happened to be Scythian and/or Phoenician, Armenian, Persian, Europe-centered Celts, and followers of Milesius (Miledh/Míl Espáine) or some other group. Even if some antiquarians dismissed as entirely legendary the accounts of certain presumed earliest population groups on the island (the magical Fomorians and subsequent arrival of Partholan (Partholón) and his followers, or the Nemedians), at the very least according to all antiquarian theories of Irish origins the Firbolgs were living on the island prior to the introduction of 'civilization' by later population arrivals. These later population arrivals, the Tuatha de Dananns and/or the Milesians, were in effect colonizing occupiers (the very badge of vilification attached to English rule in Ireland), who according to different accounts either eradicated or subjugated the pre-existing groups (also applicable to accounts of Milesian arrivals following the earlier Tuatha de Danann settlements in Ireland). Yet, it was to these latter groups that different antiquarians respectively assigned credit for the introduction of civilization to the island and/or identified as the ancestry of Ireland's Gaelic population. The earliest ancestors of the Irish in these accounts, whether the Nemedians, Fomorians, Tuatha de Danann, or Milesians, had themselves arrived as waves of colonizers, building in sequence a composite civilization, of which some distinguishable features had *putatively* survived well into the time of Norse and later Anglo-Norman conquests (whether in terms of architecture or folk beliefs and practices).

(Mytho-)histories of Irish origins centered on a time that not only long preceded Norse and Norman invasions but even stretched back as far as when 'Ireland' itself was *pre-Irish*, in the blurred time-scape of the arrival of the earliest ancestors of the Irish who had started out elsewhere. The selective nationalist remembrance of Ireland's ancient past was determined by the now-time of nationalist rejection of English rule, just as Young Ireland's now-time of multiethnic collective Irish resistance to continued English rule determined which aspects of the past in Anglo-Irish encounters should be deemed worthy of nationalist remembrance or forgetting. Here, a distinction needs to be made again between the otherwise overlapping concepts of 'cultural' and 'political' nationalism, with cultural modes of nationalism not always necessarily committed to attaining self-government in the near future. Young Ireland espoused a vision of a future "virtuous" Irish community that allegedly could not exist under English domination, whereas many cultural nationalists who shunned political nationalism believed in the possibility of reviving—in actuality *(re-)inventing*—indigenous Irish culture under continued English rule, as did Standish James O'Grady in the next century.

There was, of course, a major difference between Ireland's ancient episodes of colonization in antiquarian accounts and its post-Norman occupation. Ireland had become the one and only *home* territory of the ancient Tuatha de Dananns or Milesians following their settlement on the island, rather than being administered as part of an imperial realm that was centered in another territory as in the case of English rule over the island. It was only in the aftermath of Anglo-Norman invasions that Ireland (initially parts, and later all, of the island) had come to be governed as a satellite realm of an outside territorial power. Davis did not clearly articulate the distinction between these two modes of colonization. Yet, it was precisely somewhere in-between these distinct patterns of colonization that the likes of Davis imagined their own identity as Irish, and more importantly as Irish nationalists. These were descendants of English, Welsh, and Scots settlers in Ireland, dating as far back as the twelfth century, for whom Ireland and not England, Britain, or the United Kingdom constituted their chosen 'national' homeland; a homeland that should not simultaneously exist as an imperial outpost and dominion of another territory (i.e., as a 'province' in Davis' parlance)—in marked contrast to the vision of Ireland shared by many other descendants of former English, Scots, and Welsh settlers in Ireland, who preferred to maintain political ties with London and opted for a multi-centered cultural identity, with its own cosmopolitan fabric. The fundamental disparity between ancient and post-Norman colonization of Ireland (with the intermediate Norse episodes of more localized colonization developing along both patterns) was enunciated in the late nineteenth century by the Irish-American James Joseph Clancy. A Parnellite Home-Rule and "Land League" nationalist, Clancy was attacking the 1881 three-volume *The English in Ireland in the Eighteenth Century* by the English historian James Anthony Froude. Clancy, subscribing to one of the older antiquarian mélanges of oriental origins of the Irish (in this case Scythian, Phoenician, and Egyptian) and insisting on the pre-Christian oriental prototype of the Round Towers (the earliest of which he dated to "three thousand years ago"), claimed pre-Norman patterns of Ireland's colonization had always resulted in a distinctly Irish identity of the colonizers:

> Four distinct waves of colonization are recorded to have reached pre-Christian Erin, the latest of them being the Milesian, which element gradually subjugated, overshadowed, and absorbed the earlier occupants The product was a simple, upright, patriarchal people—courageous, clannish, ardent, imaginative, with merits and defects peculiarly their own.[35]

Clancy further observed:

> The modern Irish, Froude tells us, are at once a "most mixed and most homogeneous race. They are descendants of N[e]medians, Milesians, Norse, Vikings, Dutch, German, British and Saxon slaves, Norman adventurers, and refugees of all countries." Quite true; and herein we find an impregnable argument, for the modern Irishman (always excepting the garrison), no matter how many currents mingle in his veins, loathes and abominates British misrule.[36]

As already noted, in Irish nationalist allegories of resistance and heroism there were multiple and often contradictory representations of 'Iran' of identical historical time periods. This included ethical narrations of the same ancient Iran that sharply contrasted with the barbarous, cowardly, and tyrannical Persian Empire of the Thermopylae myth or the Battle of Marathon. Later in the century, for instance, there were militant Irish nationalists who claimed to draw ethical inspiration from ancient Iran of the Achaemenid era (based on information from certain ancient Hellenic sources), just as Byron had done in the previously mentioned example from his poem *Don Juan*. This was irrespective of these Irish nationalists' perspective on Irish origins or their occasionally simultaneous allegoric allusions to the battles of Thermopylae and Marathon. These purported ethical qualities were themselves mythical in proportion, as in the case of the ascribed sublime ancient Persian practice of truthfulness, honor, and valor—which contrasted sharply with the frequent extravagantly reductionist British *and* Irish descriptions of the low moral standing of Persians in ancient times by way of merely repeating the otherwise culturally and militarily hostile and highly selective ancient Hellenic accounts of the Persians.[37] Among those militant Irish nationalists later in the century who held a favorable ethical impression of ancient Persians and claimed their own observance of those same ethical principles (leaving aside here the potentially gendered attributes of those principles) was a leader of the Irish Republican Brotherhood (IRB), John O'Leary (d.1907), who had been drawn to the Young Ireland movement in his late teens and engaged in direct nationalist activities following the suppression of the failed Young Ireland uprising of 1848. The older O'Leary's nationalist ethics, according to William Butler Yeats, dictated "A man was not to lie, or even to give up his dignity, on any patriotic plea." Yeats added: "and I have heard him say, 'I have but one religion, the old Persian: to bend the bow and tell the truth.'"[38] Implied here were O'Leary's twin commitments to nationalist militancy and Speaking Truth to Power. The editors of a more recent collection of Yeats' works, Richard J. Finneran and George Bornstein, contend: "The remark that 'I have but one religion, the old Persian [...]' was not original with O'Leary but rather one that he quoted from the narrator of Charles Kinsley's [1881] novel *Westward Ho!*"[39] O'Leary's Persian maxim had actually originally appeared in *The Histories* of Herodotus (c.440 BCE), notwithstanding the Greek author's overall condescending attitude toward Persians, and this maxim was repeated by Xenophon (d. 354 BCE). Among other sources in the nineteenth century, the alleged Persian motto was recirculated in some European/Western literate circles by way of its appearance in the opening part of Lord Byron's Canto XVI of the unfinished *Don*

Juan, A Poem (in progress 1823), first published in 1824.[40] In fact, O'Leary's appeal to the ostensibly ancient Persian custom of "drawing the bow" and "speaking the truth" was not a novel Irish nationalist innovation and had precedent in earlier Irish republican circles, long before Lord Byron further popularized it. In 1795, for example, the Dublin-based freemason republican paper *Sentimental and Masonic Magazine*, edited by John Jones, and seeking to impart virtuous republican moral qualities on its readership, had written under the heading "On Good Faith":

> He who lyes offends against heaven, and offends himself: a lye has something so odious, that is a shock to the character of a gentleman, whatever can be said to mitigate it. The very nations which the Greeks treated as barbarians, had an abhorrence of lyes and frauds. Herodotus says, "The Persians have an infinite contempt for those who falsify their word; and they train their children from five to twenty-five years old, in nothing but to draw the bow, to ride on horseback, *and to speak truth.*"[41]

This account of the prized ancient Persian mores, in contradistinction to the more commonplace negative ancient Hellenic representations of Iranians, was reinforced in some European/Western circles following the edited English translations by Friedrich Max Müller of *Zend Avesta* later in the nineteenth century, as well as the appearance of the expression in such works as Friedrich Nietzsche's *Thus Spoke Zarathustra* (1883–85), in which it was actually debased as an ethical error, given its appeal to morality.

Clearly fond of this imputed ancient Persian "religious" edict, at the end of the century O'Leary attributed the same characteristics, now suffused with the Christian ethics of charity, to John O'Mahony (d. 1877), a former Young Irelander, scholar, and one of the founders of the Fenian movement (1858)—the American affiliate organization of the IRB and the core organization of the Irish republican movement in the United States until IRB's break with the Fenian movement in 1871 and IRB's subsequent collaboration with a new break-away branch of former Fenians in the United States, called the Clan na Gael (i.e., Family of the Gaels). Praising O'Mahony, O'Leary wrote: "He had, in short, the old Pagan Persian virtues of truthfulness and courage to a high degree, with the Christian value of charity superadded."[42] For O'Leary, this imagined Iranian quality had become the standard gauge of people's character. Commenting on James Stephens (d. 1901)—a leader of the Young Ireland uprising of 1848 and a founder of the IRB (1858), who in 1863 had appointed O'Leary a co-editor of the IRB-controlled *Irish People* (Dublin, 1863–65), which was managed by Stephens—, O'Leary wrote:

> He was, for instance, a stern stickler for absolute truth in theory, but one suspected, and even sometimes knew, that his practice and his theory, like those of many better and worse men, were too often at variance. To what extent that other Pagan and Persian virtue with which I have so largely credited John O'Mahony was present in or absent from Stephens' composition, I find it rather hard to decide even now.[43]

By the late nineteenth century, O'Leary's 'old Persian' motto became a staple of avowed ethical quality in some militant Irish nationalist circles. Underscoring another cosmopolitan feature of Irish nationalism, it is safe to say that instead of appealing to the purported ancient Persian maxim as the appropriate Irish republican model of virtue, Irish nationalists could just as easily have extracted a comparable model from Irish history and/or Irish mythology. As a side note, in his 1896 book O'Leary also made an unpersuasive, albeit clearly cautionary, comparison between Queen Victoria's visit to Dublin in 1849, the year after the failed Young Ireland uprising and during the Great Famine (and also in the aftermath of revolutions that had swept across continental Europe), and the Iranian monarch Nasser al-Din Shah's visit to Paris in 1873. The shah, who also visited Britain during his 1873 trip (and again in 1889), attracted large crowds and much press fanfare during his European tour and became the subject of the famous Bracey Vane English music-hall song "Have You Seen the Shah?" as well as the burlesque operetta "Kissi-Kissi, or the Pa, the Ma, and the Padishah" by Francis Cawley Burnand. The shah, who was knighted by Queen Victoria in 1873 (the Order of the Garter), was assassinated in May 1896 by an Iranian political dissident, the same year in which O'Leary's book appeared. Writing in a sardonic tone ahead of Queen Victoria's upcoming Diamond Jubilee celebrations (1897), O'Leary's comparison of the shah in 1873 with the Queen in 1849 was intended to underscore the alleged collective Irish aloofness, if not antipathy, toward British monarchy. Greatly understating the public excitement generated by the shah's exotic appeal in Paris in 1873, O'Leary claimed the British Queen (who in 1877 had also assumed the title "Empress of India") had been in 1847 just as alien an object of curiosity for the Irish population she ruled as the shah had been to the French:

> I had the felicity, for the first and last time, of seeing her Britannic Majesty on her first visit to this country, in the year 1849, and I can certify that on that occasion she was received with considerable curiosity, and, as far as one could judge, a total absence of all other feelings. She passed down the broadest street in Dublin, or perhaps in Europe, amid a gaping crowd, but, as far as I could at all see or hear, without a single cheer or other sign of sympathetic interest. And her Majesty did not like her position, if one were to judge by her looks, and no wonder either. I saw a very similar scene some twenty years after in Paris, at the reception of the Shah of Persia, who was gazed upon by vast crowds, which made not the slightest pretence of regarding him in any other light than that of a mere curiosity, the big diamond in his hat attracting quite as much attention as its wearer, and no doubt, a great deal more regard. But the Shah, unlike the other potentate, was apparently sublimely indifferent as to how he was regarded by any such mere profanum vulgus. I am perhaps diverging somewhat from Fenianism, but scarcely so far as I seem. Royal visits and lying descriptions of them, and sentimental gush over their possible and impossible effects, may help Britishers and West Britishers to throw dust in each other's eyes, but they most certainly do not make, or tend to make, the "mere Irish," or the Irish "fall down and almost worship," but rather stand up, and scoff or scowl, as their special temperaments or moods at the time being may urge them.[44]

The Man in the Cloak and Oriental Pseudo-Translations

By the 1840s, other periods in Iranian history, besides the disparate references to ancient Iran—whether as the fountainhead of Ireland's earliest grand civilization or as an imperial menace to 'Greece'—were being utilized by Irish nationalists as a means of commenting on Ireland's history. These alternative Irans of other eras had first appeared in Moore's 1813 *Intercepted Letters* as a general critique of Protestant persecution of Catholics in the United Kingdom and, much more importantly, in his 1817 *Lalla Rookh* in the form of seventh- and eight-century occupied former Iranian territories that served as settings for commenting on Ireland under English domination. Contemporary Iran, as in *Intercepted Letters*, also continued to resurface in Irish nationalist commentaries, fictional or otherwise, most notably following the outbreak of the Anglo-Iranian War of 1856–57 (see Chapter Four). In much of these other temporal configurations, Iran served as an empathetic device for condemning British imperialism in Ireland. In the Young Ireland circle, it was the poet James Clarence Mangan (1803–49) who spearheaded this trend in the pages of *The Nation*. The remainder of this chapter focuses on the uses and representations of 'Iran' as a territorial and/or cultural entity in the poetry of Mangan, as well as Mangan's other imagined Iranian motifs in his invented "translations" of oriental poems. By focusing here on this very narrow selection of Mangan's otherwise incredibly wide-ranging and multi-layered literary works, I am merely continuing my central theme of probing the ways in which Irish nationalist appropriations of 'Iran' reflect on Irish nationalist modes of historicizing and imagining Ireland. Hence, it is not my intention to reduce Mangan's entire oeuvre and range of interests to either just nationalism or the particular interpretations I will be drawing based on my primary thematic focus. My analyses also extend to Mangan's tormented engagement with oriental theories of Irish origins, as well as his conflicted self-positioning as a nationalist. Interrogating Mangan's references to Iran provide further indication of his ambivalence toward nationalism and its simultaneous recourse to both historical recovery and amnesia. David Lloyd, shrewdly noting "The cultural field [...] becomes a primary site of struggle both before and after independence in Ireland," states:

> Mangan's writings have always been recognized as relating uneasily to Irish nationalism, particularly given its demand for a literature devoted to the production of an authentic Irish identity. He has generally been considered as a failed exemplar of nationalist writing, and his failure or minor status is most often attributed to is historical position: his writing is minor by virtue of the minority status or "underdevelopment" of Irish literature at that time. My contention is, rather, that the "failure" of Mangan's work should be seen in terms of its recalcitrance to the demands of nationalists as of imperialist aesthetics for the production of a major writing in conformity with a canon whose function is to produce identity. Mangan's is minor writing, but a minor writing in the positive sense of one whose very "inauthenticity" registers the radical non-identity of the colonized subject.[45]

Commentators on James Clarence Mangan are unanimous on his commitment to Irish 'cultural nationalism,' even if they are divided on the extent of his commitment to political nationalism, and militant nationalism in particular.[46] Although Mangan's Iran-inflected works represent a very slender sampling of his vast output of poetry and prose, two of these poems nonetheless decidedly ground him in the sphere of *political* nationalism after 1846, with a categorical turn to republican militancy during the last three years of his life, even if we are to assume that his association with Young Ireland and the movement's mouthpiece *The Nation* after 1842 did not somehow already mark his turn to political nationalism. Mangan's meteoric, but brief and turbulent, fame in the mid-nineteenth century as a leading Young Ireland poet heralded a new direction in English-language poetry in general, and in Irish nationalist poetry more specifically, prefiguring James Joyce's modernist and polyglot cosmopolitan style more than half a century later. Joyce (d. 1941) was conscious of his debt to Mangan, even as he criticized Mangan in a lecture given in 1902 and in a 1907 essay that Joyce did not get an opportunity to present, with the latter being a revised draft of the 1902 lecture and assuming a less critical tone toward Mangan.[47] Yet, Mangan failed to captivate the more mainstream and conventional Irish nationalist literary sensibilities that still preferred the Romantic mood and tone of Thomas Moore's stylistically anodyne melodies and poetry, with Moore outliving Mangan and continuing to be considered the paragon of Irish nationalist poetry for decades to come. William Butler Yeats (1865–1939), assuming the mantle of Ireland's leading nationalist poet at the turn of the century, and no fan of Moore's style, was himself in 1895 still conventional enough in poetic taste and conformist in his penchant for mainstream standards of aesthetic beauty, to write:

> [Mangan] with happiness and cultivation might have displaced Moore. But as it was, whenever he had no fine ancient song to inspire him, he fell into rhetoric which was only lifted out of commonplace by an arid intensity. In his 'Irish National Hymn,' 'Soul and Country,' and the like, we look into a mind full of parched sands where the sweet dews have never fallen. A miserable man may think well and express himself with great vehemence, but he cannot make beautiful things, for Aphrodite never rises from any but a tide of joy. Mangan knew nothing of the happiness of the outer man, and it was only when prolonging the tragic exultation of some dead bard, that he knew the unearthly happiness which clouds the outer man with sorrow, and is the fountain of impassioned art.[48]

This was, in fact, a major shift in Yeats' tone toward Mangan. Only a few years before, in 1892, Yeats had written in his self-celebratory poem "To Ireland in the Coming Times": "Nor may I less be counted one / With Davis, Mangan, Ferguson."[49] Interestingly, like Moore and Mangan before him, Yeats too would turn to Persian poetry and, more broadly, to other range of oriental literature in general for inspiration, as discussed later. But, these three poets channeled their oriental inspirations in distinctly different ways. In Mangan's case, the favored poetic medium of engaging with oriental literature was that of creative self-plagiarizing.

Mangan has aptly been described as Ireland's first modernist poet[50]—more fittingly, it should be said a pioneering modernist poet in general—while also branded as a "postmodern puzzlemaker" by Seamus Heaney (following Heaney's change of mind, in the same article no less, regarding Mangan's literary style).[51] James Joyce was the next Irish author after Mangan to profoundly unsettle *English*-language literary canonicity—without our ignoring Oscar Wilde's *mastery* of the English canon, which was also unsettling to that canon, given that Wilde was Irish. In 1902, Joyce remarked: "Mangan, it must be remembered, wrote with no native literary tradition to guide him."[52] In 1907, Joyce added: "Although he wrote such admirable English, he refused to work for English magazines or journals; although he was the spiritual focus of his age, he refused to prostitute himself to the rabble or become a mouthpiece for politicians."[53] Mangan was engaged in his unique and continually experimental style of poetry well before the emergence of Young Ireland. But, it was his contributions to *The Nation* (Dublin), beginning with the very first issue of the paper on October 15, 1842, that marked his transition to writing poetry with overtly nationalist quality and secured him a degree of recognition as a nationalist poet.[54] A regular contributor to *The Nation*, Mangan dissociated himself from the paper in 1847, opting for a more militant form of republican nationalism nearly two years into what came to be known as the Great Famine—previously the "Great Famine" in Irish history referred to the famine of 1740–41. For years before he joined *The Nation*, Mangan had been composing *invented* translations of poems purportedly from oriental languages, including Persian (works of classical poetry in Persian by 'Iranians' and non-'Iranians'), Arabic (from different Arab-speaking territories and different time periods), and more frequently Turkish (both Ottoman and non-Ottoman), alongside the occasional "Hindostanee," Chinese, and other range of contrived translations from non-European and European languages. The latter also included invented translations from German, a language in which Mangan was actually fluent and from which language he also made genuine, albeit revised, translations. In his short autobiographic self-obituary, published posthumously in 1850, Mangan termed this style of creative self-plagiarism "the antithesis of plagiarism," characteristically, even attributing this phrase to "a friend of mine" in yet another act of self-plagiarizing. Another of his preferred appellations for his concocted translations was "anti-plagiaristic productions."[55] Had he given himself credit for authoring the original poems he otherwise claimed to be translations from poems originally composed in oriental languages, he would merely belong to the 'oriental-style' literary tradition in English language, which dated back to the eighteenth century and included works by the likes of Moore.

In the late nineteenth century, the Irish author Oscar Wilde famously protested, Caliban-like: "French by sympathy, I am Irish by race, and the English have condemned me to speak the language of Shakespeare."[56] But Mangan went beyond protesting his dependence on English as a medium of everyday and literary expression. In his pseudo-translations, Mangan not only claimed a polyglot mantle (not forgetting his actual fluency in German and various degrees of familiarity with a few other European languages), but he also posed as *translator* of works into English language, rather than *creator* of works in English (without my denying the authorial creativity and originality of translators). Most of his readers, who would have been unaware the poems he passed off as works of others were in fact his own creations, would at best regard him as an accomplished multilingual translator, even allowing for translators' creative input in the process of translation (including word choices, cultural expressions, and so on). Mangan's continually innovative and multi-layered self-plagiarizing style, which carefully crafted and subverted many of the existing literary canonicities, was imbued with an inherent contradiction between his simultaneous quest for public renown and adoration, on the one hand, and for self-effacement and concealment, on the other hand. As one of Mangan's biographers Sinéad Sturgeon puts it, "'The Man in the Cloak' [...] one of the Irish writer's favourite *nome de Plume*s," is indicative of Mangan's "lifelong obsession with the veiling of identity and—since to conceal one's identity is also to complicate and intensify it—the conviction that the self is at once hidden, unstable, and multifarious."[57]

In his simultaneous self-effacement and self-projection, Mangan was playfully precise as to how he wished others to perceive and describe him. In a pseudonymous 1841 essay titled "My Bugle, and how I Blow it. By THE MAN IN THE CLOAK,"[58] he elucidated why this particular author should be called "The Man in the Cloak":

> Thirdly—That I am the Man *in* the Cloak. In other words, I am by no manner of means the Man *of* the Cloak, or the Man *under* the Cloak. The Germans call me *Der Mensch mit dem Mantel*, the Man with the Cloak. This is a deplorable error in the nomenclature of that otherwise intelligent people; and I am speechless with astonishment that they should have fallen into it. Why? Because my cloak is not part and parcel of myself. The cloak is outside, and the man is inside, as Goldsmith said of the World and the Prisoner; but each is a distinct entity; of that I am satisfied; on that point I, as the Persians would say, tighten the girdle of assurance round the waist of my understanding, though, perhaps, there is no waste of my understanding whatever.[59]

Writing in the language of English conquerors, Mangan's unique style and real or invented polyglot productions unmoored him as much as possible from any extant tradition of English writing,[60] in contrast to other contemporary and past Irish nationalist authors working in the medium of English language, such as Moore. Irish authors writing in English language, and notably Irish nationalist authors, even while acknowledged as being Irish, were nonetheless contributing to and enriching *English* literature.[61] After the appearance of Young Ireland, much breadth and ink than ever before were to be expended by Irish nationalists on the comparative merits of writing in Irish (Gaelic) or in English. Even many of those in this debate who considered Irish as the only legitimate national language of Ireland conceded that given the small size of Ireland's Irish-speaking population and the even smaller size of Irish-reading population,[62] for the time being English was the only language in which they could reach the majority of the Irish. The likes of Mangan also had to contend with the reality that they themselves lacked any degree of fluency in Irish language. Mangan's purported translations into English, by the mere essence of the works being labeled as "translations," was a creative way of writing in English but separating the works in question from the canon of English literature (in its broadest sense) through their alleged non-English origins—especially in the framework of English literature in the United Kingdom, as opposed to works in English produced by authors in North America, Australia, New Zealand, southern Africa, India, and elsewhere. Fergus Dunne points out that "Paul de Man has [...] argued that 'translation canonizes its own version more than the original was canonical.'"[63] Even allowing for de Man's overgeneralization and assuming that Mangan's invented translations at least generated some ambiguity regarding the language to which they authentically belonged (i.e., the original or the translated language), these invented translations would still have been regarded as doubly removed from the genus of English literature. The very category of "translation" always denotes a difference from other works in the same language. Moreover, without the readers' ability to read the alleged original work in the original language, translations always remain suspect in terms of the boundary between the translators' innovation and the authenticity of what is expressed in translation in the name of the original work. Meanwhile, other than Mangan's usual practice of attributing the poems in question to entirely concocted as well as historical and semi-historical oriental and other poets, there were still other techniques by which he underscored the linguistic and cultural *otherness* of the poems for English-language readers. These methods ranged from his inclusion of pseudo-*transliterations* at the beginning of some of the poems, in the purported languages from which he claimed to be translating, to abundant insertion of footnotes elucidating terms, names, places, concepts, and practices, which marked a sharp distance between the supposed cultural source and setting of the poems and his English readers, including in his 'translations' from the Irish.

As already discussed in previous chapters, around the time of the emergence of distinctly nonsectarian and cross-ethnic Irish nationalist platforms in the late eighteenth century (cultural and/or political), allusions to 'Iran' in connection with Ireland's ancient past appeared in a range of Irish antiquarian texts with markedly Irish nationalist overtones. The specifically Irish nationalist *literary* placements of Iran, primarily as a textual device for allegorically commenting on historical or contemporary conditions in Ireland, was initiated by Thomas Moore in the second decade of the nineteenth century. Alongside the more usual European interest in Persian poetry (works produced by 'Iranian' or other Persianate poets), various Iranian and other 'oriental' motifs had long appeared in so-called *European* literature dating back to the ancient Hellenic Age, including in *collage translation* forms. The most popular and enduring of such works in the first half of the nineteenth century were different translations of *One Thousand and One Nights* (a.k.a. *Arabian Nights*), following Antoine Galland's first translation of the work in a European language (French in his case) in the early eighteenth century. These trends were further driven by the Romantic literary tradition, as in the case of the fourth (final) section of Moore's *Lalla Rookh*, titled "The Light of the Haram." As many of his other contemporary authors who variously worked with and through elements of oriental literatures, Mangan too elaborately engaged with oriental literatures in his early poetry, including the utilization of "his familiarity with the *Arabian Nights' Entertainments* and the Oriental fictions of his contemporaries to create the appropriate atmosphere" in his poems and prose centered in the Orient.[64] In addition, after the opening years of the nineteenth century, there was a profusion of English language travel, historical, and journalistic accounts of so-called oriental societies, including Iran, alongside translations of oriental literature ("classical" poetry in particular). A similar pattern was manifest in a number of other Western European languages in which some Irish readers were well-versed. Moreover, contemporary and historical descriptions of Iranian society, politics, cultures, and Persian literature (Iranian or non-Iranian), along with lengthy reviews of books related to Iran or Persian literature in general, could be perused in the pages of the press, ranging from *The Times* of London to the London periodical the *Annual Register*, founded in 1759 (which early on was edited by the Irish-born conservative-Whig political commentator and future politician Edmund Burke), or the *Edinburgh Review* (founded in 1802), *Blackwood's Edinburgh Magazine* (founded in 1817), among other British journals, as well as in miscellaneous Irish press ranging from the newspaper *Freeman's Journal* (Dublin, 1763) to periodicals such as the *Dublin University Magazine* (founded in 1833), or the *Dublin Penny Journal* (1832–36), along with a range of Irish provincial press. There was also the widespread practice of periodicals reproducing articles originally appearing in other periodicals or providing partial or entire serialized reproductions of books. As a random example, in March 1834 the *Dublin Penny Journal* published an anonymously authored article titled "Historical and Descriptive Account of Persia" based on a report originally appearing in the *Edinburgh Cabinet Library*, which itself had very likely acquired the information from another journal or newspaper.[65]

Both literary and historical references to 'Iran' appeared in Mangan's poetry, including in works other than his oriental pseudo-translations or essays on oriental literatures.[66] This is also reflective of the lingering influence on Mangan's writings of the antiquarian hypotheses of the likes of Vallancey, on the one hand, and the Iran/Erin literary device pioneered by Moore, on the other hand; albeit, now formulated in the unique and characteristically discordant "Manganesque" form.[67] In his Iran-themed writing, Mangan worked *with*, *through*, and *against* both of these influences.[68] In a somewhat similar balancing act of concurrent proximation and distancing, James Joyce later grappled with Mangan's literary influence.[69] Mangan utilized the Iran/Erin metaphor for different effects than in Moore's *Lalla Rookh*. The two poets, who were raised as Catholics and were coincidentally sons of grocers (with both of them later financially assisting their families),[70] had widely divergent religious and nationalist temperaments, as well as social standing, education, lifestyles, and social networks. They were both advocates of Catholic rights, but while they both also rejected Catholic religious chauvinism and periodically struggled with the denominational faith of their upbringing, Mangan's relationship with Catholicism was much more troubled than Moore's. On occasion, this bordered on outright condemnation of the faith. Whereas Moore after his younger days remained a temperate cultural-nationalist and politically a moderate proponent of the Repeal of the Union, Mangan in the last years of his life increasingly veered toward both cultural *and* political nationalist *militancy*, even while going through bouts of skeptical frustration with nationalism along the way. Overall, from the time of his association with the Young Ireland circle in 1842, Mangan expressed his nationalist sentiment in an unmistakably acrimonious and acerbic tone in contrast to Moore's restrained and romantically adorned mournful lamentations (the latter with the recurring refrain of "'Tis gone and Forever" in reference to a fully independent Ireland).[71]

It is undeniable that Mangan was consciously tapping into the enduring 'oriental-style' Romantic literary vogue of the previous decades in the United Kingdom.[72] He cited works by Byron[73] and was extensively familiar with Moore's poetry, among other major Romantic figures producing works in ostensibly oriental settings and/or styles. In an exchange with a friend, Mangan offered a backhanded compliment to Moore's *Lalla Rookh* by way of playing on the similarity between Moore's name and "Moorish," referring to the poet as 'Tom Moorish.'[74] Many of Mangan's early pseudo-translations of oriental poems exploited the Romantic genre, while also playfully undermining it. These Romanticist traces were consciously abandoned in his post-1846 nationalist poems. In his most famous Iran-located allegoric, and unequivocally bitter, political nationalist poem, "To the Ingleezee Khafir, Calling Himself Djuan Bool Djenkinzun" (1846), Mangan was clearly rejecting Moore's ornate flowing style and pathos, which had been reproduced in Mangan's early 'oriental' poetry, albeit with Mangan's inimitable playful touch. Another distinction between Moore's and Mangan's oriental poems, including Mangan's earlier works, was the latter's choice of time frames in oriental histories when drawing analogies with Irish history, be these Ottoman, Iranian, or other settings. In what could only have been a calculated decision to distance himself from Moore's legacy, Mangan steered clear of the subject of Arab-Muslim conquest of Iran in the seventh century CE and of Iranian-Zoroastrian resistance that had become associated with Moore's allegoric pairing of Iran/Erin. Other than the fact that Mangan's earlier pseudo-translations of Persian poems concentrated on 'classical' Persian poetry of the post-Islamic era (from 'Iran' and other territories), Mangan's "To the Ingleezee Khafir" relied on the Islam-inspired—"Twelver"(*ithna' ashari*) Shi'i Islam in this case—cultural underpinning of purported Iranian defiance of an outside power (England). Moreover, this poem's denunciation of English imperialism was far more transparent than even in Moore's "The Fire-Worshippers" section of *Lalla Rookh*.

Well before the founding of Young Ireland and its publication *The Nation* (1842), Mangan's oriental poems had been appearing in various Irish journals, including the *Dublin University Magazine*. This highly acclaimed journal had been founded as a Protestant-unionist mouthpiece in 1833, but it catered to a wide array of literary and non-literary works in general (including a range of what can be classified as 'cultural' Irish nationalist expressions, including George Petrie's works), so long as these were not overtly anti-Protestant or outright opposed to the 1801 Act of Union. References to Moore's *Lalla Rookh* appeared in the first three of Mangan's "Literæ Orientales" series in the *Dublin University Magazine*.[75] Installments of "Literæ Orientales" appeared in this journal once in 1837, twice in 1838, and once during each of the years 1840, 1844, and 1846. Published anonymously, their authorship should have been well-known to most readers soon after the first installments. Mangan's concocted translations from oriental languages were not restricted to this series and appeared in other settings as well. In his "Literæ Orientales," Mangan cited as his sources the likes of the seventeenth-century Barthélemy d'Herbelot, the philologist Sir William Jones (critically on a number of occasions), as well as the likes of the contemporary Anglo-Irish expert on Iran and Persian literature, Sir William Ouseley, all of whose works had been consulted by Moore in *Lalla Rookh*.[76] Mangan, however, extensively consulted other range of sources for his invented Persian poems as well. Nor were his pseudo-translations limited to so-called Persian poems; they comprised mostly of purported Turkish and Arabic works.

There was undeniably a notable difference between Moore's and Mangan's textual familiarity with the Orient and oriental literatures. David Lloyd writes in a somewhat slight characterization of the footnotes appearing in Mangan's publications that indicate the extent of his research on Orient-related subjects:

> The plethora of notes in Moore's work gives an indication of how the sensuous exoticism of the verse is supported by the exoticism of the intellect, with the intention [...] of allowing the reader to feel carried more effectively into an authentic Orient. Turning, on the other hand to Mangan's [...], one perceives how many of his references merely 'unveil' pieces of common knowledge disguised in the text by the 'Oriental' nomenclature.

Lloyd adds,

> The difference between Moore's notes and Mangan's lies in their opposed functions. Moore provide a set of sources that substantiate the authenticity of the Oriental scenario. [...] In Mangan's case, the notes perform quite the opposite role, actually undermining one's sense of mastery of a certain field; while accumulating a vast capital of ostensibly authenticating sources, they turn the reader's investment of labor into a depletion of his resources. Both the poems and the articles absorb their readers in a quest for origins which, since those origins are perpetually falsified, becomes unendingly protracted. At times, Mangan's play reaches the point of deliberate s*elf*-parody.[77]

This interpretation, however, is only valid if the reader is aware that Mangan's poems were invented translations. In fact, many contemporaries and later generations of readers took at face value that the poems Mangan attributed to fictional oriental poets, or speciously to actual oriental poets, were genuine translations, notwithstanding Mangan's own later public acknowledgment of his self-plagiarizing technique. These readers included Lady Jane Francesca Agnes Wilde (d. 1896; née Elgee), an erstwhile Young Ireland contributor of nationalist poems to *The Nation* from 1846 to 1848, and later in the century a leading folklorist and a highly regarded cultural personality by many key figures of the Irish Literary Revival. Lady Wilde (who is discussed in Chapter Six of the present book) was a fervent admirer of Mangan's poetry and one of the latter-day and most vociferous proponents in the late nineteenth century of the Iranian theory of Irish origins.[78] In 1893, expressing her disappointment with the many shortcomings of a book of selected poems recently published by the Irish Commissioners for Education, titled *Selections for Irish Children*, she highlighted Mangan's absence in the volume, noting:

> Then we have numerous specimens from a poet of Blackwood, called "Delta"; but of the learned original mind of [James] Clarence Mangan, there is no trace whatever. Poor Mangan; who spent a weary, sad life illustrating all literatures from Ireland to Irân! and who lives consecrated in the martyrology of genius, though allowed no place in the Pantheon of Marlborough Street.[79]

Many of the early "oriental" poems by Mangan focused on Ottoman or Arab historical-cultural settings, rather than on Iranian motifs and locales. Or, if these poems alluded to Iran and Iranians (in the broadest sense of the term), they did so in a jumbled and *deliberately* careless manner that conflated Persians with Arabs, in a manner which Vallancey occasionally had done in his earlier writings (e.g., the 1786 *A Vindication of the Ancient History of Ireland*). This also accounts for Mangan's 1840 deliberate misstatement that Vallancey had suggested "every Irishman is an Arab" (see below). This conflation was a conscious move on Mangan's part for maintaining a desired internal narrative coherence and thematic simplicity in some of his poems, while at the same time provocatively signaling an underlying incongruity and, therefore, the very inauthenticity of his invented poems. He was, in effect, cajoling his more adept readers to see through his slippages and subterfuge, prodding them to doubt the authenticity of his so-called translations. Otherwise, not only did he engage in a detailed and meticulous compilation of historical data about his subject matter, but he also stressed in his "Literæ Orientales" the difference between Persian and Arabic literature and their respective cultural-historical underpinnings according to his interpretation. In fact, as I argue later, the periodic blurring of histories (cultural time and space) was a trademark of Mangan in connection with his unsettled engagement with history in general (most centrally the history of Ireland) as well as with nationalism (national identity in particular).

Mangan's occasional pattern of conflated oriental histories is evident, for example, in the first of the poems listed in a passage by one of Mangan's early biographers, David James O'Donoghue. Writing in the late nineteenth century, O'Donoghue was substantiating with some embellishment the literary finesse of Mangan's oriental poems:

> A few of the poems like "The Time of the Barmecides," "The Karamanian Exile," and "The Wail and Warning of the Three Khalendeers," have already won their way to the admiration of thousands of Irishmen. With the single exception of Edward Fitzgerald, in his "Quatrains of Omar Khayyam," no writer has come near to Mangan's richness of imagery; while the variety of rhyme and metre, and fulness of melody in these "Literæ Orientales," which ran through various numbers of the [Dublin] *University Magazine*, are his own.[80]

Of the above-mentioned poems, "The Karamanian Exile" was centered around the city of Karaman in the eponymous Anatolian principality, once ruled by the Turkic Karamanid princes and captured by the Ottomans in 1468 CE. "The Wail and Warning of the Three Khalendeers" (i.e., "qalandars"; itinerant dervishes)—with the three kalandars (/qalandars) appearing in *One Thousand and One Nights* (a.k.a., *The Arabian Nights*)—was also situated in the Ottoman Empire. On the other hand, "The Time of the Barmecides" was based on the eighth-century CE Barmakid family hailing from the formerly Iranian territories of the Arab-Muslim Abbasid Empire (r. 750–1258). Mangan's 'Barmecides' were designated as Arabs, instead of being ethnically Persian. The historical Barmakids, evidently also previously Buddhists prior to their conversion to Islam, with their ancestral roots in Balkh (present-day Afghanistan),[81] served as advisers and high officials of Abbasid rulers from roughly 750 CE and assisted with the consolidation of Abbasid control over their newly conquered territories, before falling out of favor with the caliph Harun al-Rashid in 803 CE. The Barmakids would have been known to some of Mangan's readers, who were familiar with the popular *One Thousand and One Nights*, in which they were identified as *Persians*, with one of the stories describing their fall from caliphal favor. The Barmakids had also appeared in other contemporary English-language poems, as in the case of the English poet Felicia Heman's 1828 "The Mourner for the Barmecides," albeit without any precise ethnic identification.[82] Mangan, however, chose to identify them in a footnote to his poem as "the most illustrious of the Arabian nobility."[83] Also noteworthy is Mangan's anachronistic reference in this same poem to the "Karamanian sword," which alluded to Karaman (formerly known as Laranda) in Anatolia, (re)named after the Karamanid Turkish dynasty that ruled the region from the mid-thirteenth century until the late fifteenth century, and hence the impossibility of a sword in the ninth century being designated "Karamanian."

"The Time of the Barmecides" first appeared in combined prose and verse form as part of Mangan's satirical "A Polyglott Anthology" in the *Dublin University Magazine* in April 1839, with its authorship attributed to "THE OUT-AND-OUTER" (possibly a play on the word "author"), and was slightly revised the following year. "A Polyglott Anthology" included a wide range of purported translated poems, including from the Irish—some of the latter being actual or partly actual translations, very likely based on existing English-language translations, given Mangan's lack of any degree of fluency in Irish language at the time. The text of this anthology consisted of a dialogue between two German speakers (without being identified as Prussian, Austrian, etc.), with the English translation of the names assigned to them portending Joyce's style in *Finnegans Wake* (1939). One of these individuals was "The Herr Hoppandgoön Von Baugtrauter, a celebrated traveler" (a hopping-goon of[/from] bogtrotter?)—in which case, given the pejorative designation of the 'mere Irish' as "bogtrotters," this moniker calls into question this person's identification as a German, unless this character represents Mangan himself, who was fluent in German, but ironically never even left Ireland other than in his imagination and literary forays. The other interlocutor was "The Herr Poppandgoöff Von Tutschemupp, a distinguished critic" (a humping-goof of[/from] tush-'em-up?). The target of Mangan's caricature in the latter name was unmistakably his leading source of information on oriental literatures, the Austrian Joseph Freiherr von Hammer-Purgstall (1774–1856).[84] The Barmakids ("Barmekiden" in German) were discussed in various works by Hammer-Purgstall, including in his translation of *One Thousand and One Nights* and in the second volume of his *Rosenöl, erstes Fläschchen oder, Sagen und Kunden des Morgenlandes aus arabischen, persischen und türkischen Quellen gesammelt*, published in 1813 in Stuttgart. A key exchange in the dialogue between the two German-speaking characters in Mangan's "A Polyglott Anthology" occurs toward the middle of the story, with Von Tutschemupp remarking "The nationality of Ireland appears to be fast vanishing," to which Von Baugtrauter replies "It has vanished." Recounting episodes from his travels, Von Baugtrauter mentions that in Delhi (i.e., in British India) he had once come across a Fakir dressed in rags, who had quoted a line by the eighteenth-century English poet Alexander Pope. Von Tutschemupp responds: "I should like to hear a German beggar quoting the *Gulistan* of SAADI"—the latter referring to the famous thirteenth-century CE Persian poet Sa'di, well-known in European/Western literary circles familiar with Persian poetry at the time. Von Baugtrauter, who recites many a poem with different historical and geographical provenances, recites "The Time of the Barmecides" in the early segment of his tales, which are themselves overlain with cross-historical referentialities. In "The Time of the Barmecides," the poem's longing for youth, strength, and the bygone days of valor and armed resistance to outside occupiers can be read as evocative of Irish nationalist nostalgia and Mangan bemoaning the loss of national defiance, heroism, and the *will* to resist. For instance: "Then youth was mine, and a fierce wild will, / And an iron arm in war," or "At hand my tried Karamanian sword / Lay always bright and bare; / For those were days when the angry blow / Supplanted the word that chides." It is significant that this poem was presented in the first person, so that the speaker in the poem was, in effect, also bemoaning his own eventual inability or, more properly, loss of ability, to resist foreign aggressors; a recognition of the fact that he could no longer 'Supplan[t] the word that chides' with any effective 'angry blow.' The poem closed with the refrain "And I mourn for the times gone long ago, / For the Times of the Barmecides!"[85] This early pseudo-oriental poem by Mangan is also evocative of Thomas Moores' already noted despairing refrain of "'Tis gone and Forever." In the 1840 revised edition of "The Time of the Barmecides" appearing in "Literæ Orientales. No. IV," Mangan added the following refrain to the end of the stanza with "At hand my tried Karamanian sword": "When hearts could glow—long, long ago, / In the Time of the Barmecides."[86] In contrast to Mangan's later "To the Ingleezee Khafir" (1846), the 1839 and 1840 "The Time of the Barmecides" functioned as an even more remote allegoric substitution of the Orient for Ireland than in Moore's *Lalla Rookh*, in which at least the Iran/Erin analogy was much more clearly evident through the homophonous sound of the two territorial designations; not forgetting that the various sections of Moore's narrative poem were far longer than Mangan's poems and offered greater room for metaphoric interchanges between the Orient (including the Indian subcontinent) and Ireland.

In the 1839 "A Polyglott Anthology," Von Baugtrauter also informs Von Tutschemupp that he had copied the "The Time of the Barmecides" from the scrapbook of a teenage wife of a local king in Transoxania, with this "ancient Arabic song" attributed to "AL MAKEENAH, a warrior who had survived the glory of the Barmecidian nobles fifty-eight years." Von Baugtrauter later mentions that for this transgression, the jealous king had killed his wife, having her sewn inside a sack and thrown into a river, while having Von Baugtrauter "*caged* [...] for six months."[87] For adept contemporary readers, Mangan's fictitious Arab warrior bard, 'Al Makeenah,' could of course be transliterated as an homonymic Irish clan name, such as McKenna, and was a clear ironic reference to the name of Moore's anti-hero in "The Veiled Prophet of Khorasan" section of *Lalla Rookh*: the false prophet "Mokanna"—not forgetting that Moore's historical model for Mokanna was Hashim ibn Hakim "al-Muqanna,"[88] who had led a four-year-long abortive uprising against the Arab-Muslim Abbasid caliphate starting in Transoxania in 776 CE and that Lalla Rookh was betrothed to the young king Aliris of Bukhara in Transoxania. In actuality, of course, 'Al Makeenah' was no other than Mangan, the masked poet of Dublin; 'the man in the cloak.' References to Moore's veiled prophet Mokanna recur in a number of Mangan's pseudo-oriental poems, including in some of his explicatory footnotes to these poems. There were other instances of this style of parody of names in Mangan's works, as in the case of his invented "Arabian biographer" named "Ibn Khallahan," sounding very similar to "Callaghan"/"Callahan" or possibly even the Irish poet Jeremiah John Callanan (1795–1829), while playing on the name of the renowned North African ("Tunisian") Muslim historian Ibn Khaldun.[89]

The April 1840 installment of "Literæ Orientales" ("No. IV") in the *Dublin University Magazine*, which also included the revised version of "The Time of the Barmecides," consisted of a sampling of Mangan's "Arabian, Persian, and Turkish Poetry." In his expository essay on the different styles of oriental poetry in question, Mangan identified Persian poetry as marked by airiness, grace, a spirit of triumphant joyousness, alternating with gloom and apprehension, though never verging on despair, gaiety, sadness, mingled gaiety and sadness, wit, melody of versification, bacchanalian mirthfulness; and in the more elaborate poems metaphysical subtlety, luxuriance of descriptive power, and prodigality rather than energy of language.

Following this description, which was in fact a description of Mangan's own pseudo-translated Persian poems at that stage, he included the poem "The Days of Nourooz'iz" (i.e., "The Days of Norouz," the pre-Islamic Iranian new year, the start of which corresponds to the vernal equinox on March 20–21). He claimed the poem was his translation of a "Kasseedeh [i.e., *qassideh* style] from the Deewaun [*divan*] of Aboul-Kazim [...]: it is strictly speaking, a *song*, and was meant for the *Kimantzee* [the bowed string instrument *kamancheh*], or lute. The festival-time of Nourouziz [here spelled differently than in the title of the poem] which it celebrates occurs in Spring." Another avowedly Persian "song" in the same series, titled "Night is Nearing," was attributed to "Baba Khodjee," with the remaining poems being mostly "Turkish" and "Arabian."[90] Mangan's pseudo-translations from Turkish poetry were by far the most prevalent of his oriental 'translations' in the "Literæ Orientales" series. In 1837, in the very first installment of his "Literæ Orientales," Mangan acquiescently quoted his contemporary Austrian orientalist Joseph Freiherr von Hammer-Purgstall's verdict that "Persian poetry is the sun, Turkish the sunflower; the last naturally turns towards the first, and is indebted to it for its hues and growth."[91] Mangan reiterated this opinion in the 1844 fifth installment of "Literæ Orientales": 'Persian poetry has always been the sun to which the sunflower of Ottoman poetry has turned.'[92] Yet, pre-Ottoman and Ottoman Turkish 'translated' poetry took up the largest space in what became Mangan's six-part "Literæ Orientales" series, followed in volume by 'translations' from the Arabic. The prevalence of the pseudo-translations of Turkish poems (including actual poems previously translated into German that Mangan otherwise claimed to be translating from their original) was to some degree a reflection of Mangan's primary reliance on German language publications by Hammer-Purgstall. Hammer-Purgstall's more recent works focused rather heavily on Turkish literature, as opposed to his pre-1830s publications.[93] It was largely from Hammer-Purgstall's works that Mangan also adapted his own historical descriptions of various genres of oriental poetry and his biographical accounts of the lives and milieus of real and invented oriental poets. Furthermore, Hammer-Purgstall's translations of oriental poems into German served as a palimpsest for Mangan's own invented English translations. In effect, the Austrian orientalist's translations of actual poems became a reservoir for Mangan's self-plagiarism. In keeping with his subversive wit, Mangan on occasion even challenged the quality of Hammer-Purgstall's translations from Turkish, providing instead his own concocted translations as more accurate and authentic. Another possible reason for the preponderance of Turkish 'translations' in the six installments of "Literæ Orientales," or the many pseudo-translations from Arabic in these series, may have been Mangan's attempt to carve out a niche for himself as a translator of 'oriental' poetry in English language, at a time when translations from Persian were rapidly proliferating in the United Kingdom, as in the case of James Atkinson's already mentioned 1814 *Soohrab; a Poem, Freely Translated from the Original Persian*, his 1832 *The Shâh Nâmeh of the Persian Poet Firdausí*, and his translation of Nezami-Ganjavi's *Lailā and Majnūn: A Poem* (1836), or the sampling of verses from Persian poems by Ferdowsi ("Firdousee"), Sa'di ("Sa'dee"), Nezami [Ganjavi], Hafiz, Rumi ("Moolah of Room") and others appearing in both volumes of John Malcolm's 1827 *Sketches of Persia, from the Journals of a Traveller in the East*, among numerous examples.

Joseph Lennon has noted that in the "Literæ Orientales" series "Mangan domesticated the Orient as if it were his own native land," but his engagement with the Orient was a far cry from colonial modes of orientalism.[94] However, with Mangan posing as a translator of oriental poems, the very insinuation that he somehow 'domesticated the Orient' requires a more layered and intrinsically deconstructive reading. While Mangan composed a compendium of oriental 'translations' in "Literæ Orientales" series, he was emphatic on the distinctive qualities and the different styles, moods, sounds, and evocations of the Turkish (Pre-Ottoman and Ottoman), Persian, and Arabic poetry. Influenced also by Johann Gottfried Herder's (d. 1803) concept of national peculiarities of each 'nation,'[95] Mangan was quick to add that so-called oriental poetry in actuality consisted of distinct "national characteristics of the diverse poetries of the East"; thereby challenging the very generic rubric of the terms 'Orient' and 'oriental':

> We have for conciseness' sake included all these poetries under the general term Oriental, but it should be understood that although there are many common traits and resemblance among them, there are also a sufficient number of distinguishing qualities to confer upon each a character of its own. The Arabian, Persian and Turkish poetries do not constitute one literature. It is questioned even whether they be the offspring of the same parent literature. Augustus Schlegel it is true supposes the Turkish to be sprung from the Persian; but he rejects the assumption that there is any bond between the Persian and Arabic; and Von Hammer[-Purgstall] attempts to establish an individuality for each of the three, though he too admits that Turkish poetry derives no inconsiderable share of its beauty and excellence from its judicious imitation of first-rate Persian Models.[96]

As noted, most of Mangan's purported translations of oriental poems were entirely or largely his own creations, with their authorship and provenance attributed to others, including to some actual poets. On occasion Mangan also speciously claimed to have indirectly translated these poems from existing translations in other European languages, doubling the effect of his self-plagiarism. Most of his purported indirect translations were from supposed prior German translations of oriental poems; German being one of the languages in which Mangan was genuinely proficient by the 1830s. In these cases, Mangan frequently noted: "Original not found!"[97] Whereas, in fact, the asserted prior translations in other European languages were nowhere to be found either, since these too never existed. There was a degree of similarity here between Mangan's format and the 'Persian Letters' genre, including Moore's "Letter VI" in his 1813 *Intercepted Letters*, in which invented letters in ostensibly European translations of the originals were attributed to Iranian or other so-called oriental or alternative groups of cultural *Others*. But there was also a major difference. Whereas in the 'Persian Letters' format, readers were fully aware of the fictitious nature of the interlocuters in question, Mangan's poetic contrivance was not as self-evident to average readers.

Mangan's translations of Persian poems in the "Literæ Orientales" series in the *Dublin University Magazine* that were attributed to 'Iranian' poets (in the broad territorial and cultural constructs of Iran) included the following: (1) "Saying," attributed to the actual fourteenth-century Kamal al-Din Khujandi ("Kemalledin Khogendi") in the "Literæ Orientales, No. I" (September 1837, p. 286); (2) "My Eyes," attributed to the sixteenth-century "Abulfazl. A Persian Born. OB. 1562" (the name was possibly based on Abul-Fayz Faizi ibn Mubarak, the South Asian-born Mughal chief minister and Persian-language poet in the court of Emperor Akbar and, therefore, not actually an Iranian); and (3) "Treacherous Black Guards" attributed to "Ali Baba. A Persian. OB. 1595" (the invented name was most likely a reference to the character Ali Baba and the Forty Thieves in *One Thousand and One Nights*, with the story first included in the collected tales in Galland's translation), appearing in "Literæ Orientales, No. II" (March 1838, pp. 301, 302); as well as two undated "Persian" poems: (1) "The Days of Nourooz'iz" attributed to "Aboul- Kazim," along with (2) the unattributed "Night is Nearing," both of which appeared in "Literæ Orientales. No. IV" (April 1840, pp. 380, 387—no dates were provided for any of the Turkish, Arab, and Persian poets or their poems in this installment). The invented poet Aboul-Kazim of "The Days of Nourooz'iz," with the name also appearing in the poem itself as "Kazim" was in fact a play on Mangan's own name, with the initial and final letters of the name ("K" and "m") producing the initial sounds of Mangan's first and last names: "Clarence Mangan" (Clarence being Mangan's adopted and preferred name[98]). Hence Mangan's jibe at not being duly appreciated and financially rewarded for his efforts in the following quatrain of the poem: "Kazim! each pearlet thy poesy strews is / Cheap at a diadem's value, or whose is? / Bankrupt of taste is the dunce who refuses / Verses like thine when their theme is Nourooz'iz!"[99]

A number of Persian poems attributed to Ottoman and other Turkish poets also appeared in various installments of this series. Moreover, the likes of actual classical ('Iranian') Persian poets "Nizami" (Nezami-Ganjavi; born and died in Ganja, present-day Republic of Azerbaijan), "Saadi" (Sa'di), "Hafiz" (Hafez), Nur al-Din Abd al-Rahman Jami (from present-day Afghanistan), along with a few others, appear in Mangan's explanatory historical prose texts. In the fifth installment of "Literæ Orientales" (1844), he also listed the historical thirteenth- to fourteenth-century mystical 'Iranian' poets "Djelal-ed-Deen Rûmeh" (Moulana Jalal al-Din Mohammad Rumi; 1207–73 CE, born in Balkh, present-day Afghanistan, and died in Seljuq-controlled Konya in Anatolia, during the time of Ilkhanid Mongol rule over the region). Additionally in the same installment, he listed "Alla-ed-Defflet" (the historical Ala al-Dawla Semnani; 1261–1336 CE) and "Sheikh Saadr-ed-Deen" (the historical Sufi philosopher Shaykh Sadr al-Din Qunavi; 1207–74 CE, who lived in Seljuq-controlled Konya in Anatolia) as among the luminaries of Persian poetry of that Age.[100] Other Persian translations by Mangan appeared in different settings, as in the case of the 1847 poem "Jealousy," published in the *Dublin University Magazine* and written in the form of a dialogue between an older possessive and mistrustful husband (Ali Shah) and his young wife (Aminah), whom he suspects of amour.[101] This otherwise anemic entertaining poem, particularly keeping in mind that it was published in the midst of the Great Famine, was clearly yet another desperate attempt by the then acutely penurious Mangan to eke a living. The poem was attributed to the invented poet "Selim-il-Anagh," the last part of whose name, denoting the place of his birth or residence, closely resembles the Irish Annagh/Anagh, in both County Cavan and County Westmeath—that is, in Kilkenny West—, and formerly comprising the Barony of Anagh in County Tyrone, Ulster. This was very likely Mangan's Persianized rendering of the name of the eighteenth-century Jacobite Irish poet Eoghan Rua O Suilleabhain (Owen Roe O'Sullivan), who had lived in Annagh (with some similarity also in the sounds of Selim and Sullivan). A poem titled "Lullaby" (sung by a father to his son), which Mangan in his translations from Irish attributed to O'Sullivan, bears certain inverse parallels to "Jealousy."[102]

Further signaling to his more adept readers the inauthenticity of his (invented) translated poems, which were otherwise his own authentic creations, Mangan often also appended to these 'translated' poems invented English transliterations of ostensibly original oriental phrases or sentences. These supposedly Turkish, Arabic, or Persian words appeared in descriptive footnotes or as introductory prose quotations at the beginning of his poems. At times, he attained this effect by stringing up relatively close transliterations of certain words which he evidently found in dictionaries or in other range of publications offering English or other European-language pronunciations of original words, including Hammer-Purgstall's works. Most often, however, these transliterations were mere invented gibberish. This was a parody of Hammer-Purgstall's practice of sporadically including German transliteration of a line from a poem he had translated at the start of that particular poem.[103] Mangan, while pushing the bounds of incredulity by incorporating this yet another dubious textual layer to his mock translations, ironically convinced some commentators of even later generations that he may possibly have acquired at least a degree of proficiency in some oriental languages, despite Mangan's own admission to the contrary in his posthumously published autobiography in 1850 (see below). For instance, in addition to the already mentioned Lady Wilde, these included the prominent scholar of Mangan Rudolf Patrick Holzapfel. Writing in 1967, Holzapfel noted: "We can also be reasonably sure that he learned to work with and transliterate—perhaps even translate—Arabic. He might have done this first through the German, however."[104]

Mangan, by calling into question the authenticity of his translation projects through various clues of their inauthenticity, was in fact calling into question the very concept of authenticity itself, as it pertained to him not only as a translator of oriental poems but, more significantly, as an Irish individual. He was underscoring his own intrinsic cultural-national bifurcated and simultaneously melded identity, as well as the identities of most of his Irish readers, who were bereft of what should have been a mother tongue (Irish) and were only capable of daily communication in what was considered an adopted language (English). This sensibility is perhaps best captured in the final (and untitled) poem appearing in Mangan's April 1840 fourth installment of "Literæ Orientales." In contrast to the 'translated' poems appearing in this article, this last poem represented the views of the 'anonymous' author of "Literæ Orientales." It opened with the lines: "Where art thou, Soul of Per-Version? / Where be thy fantasies jinglish? / Why lies intact so much Prussian and Persian, / And whither has fled the phrase, 'Done into English?'"[105]

Mangan's interjection of not only made-up and real Turkish, Arabic, Persian, as well as Chippewa ("Chippewawian"), German, Italian, and other languages in his 'translated' poems was a reminder of the ultimate foreignness of these other languages (some more foreign than others) from the perspective of his English readers, requiring their translation into English before they could be rendered intelligible; the same way Irish texts had to be first translated into English before they could be understood by most Irish, including Mangan. Mangan even claimed a number of translations from Irish, in which language he is attested to have lacked more than an intermediate fluency even later in life. In these 'translations,' Irish stood out as the most alien of Mangan's translated languages. Whereas select lines from all other real or fabricated foreign poems (ranging from Persian to German) appeared at the beginning of some of Mangan's translations in the form of transliterations written in the more familiar Latin script, Irish phrases in his translations from Irish were written in the Irish insular Gaelic (Latin) script of the poem's time. For the English *and Irish* reader with no knowledge of Irish language, this more insular visual presence in the text rendered his translations from Irish doubly alien, denying the untrained reader even the pretense of being able to pronounce the foreign words. Mangan made Irish the most-difficult-to-decipher of all of these translated languages for his readers who could read English but not Irish, in what unequivocally was meant to establish the simultaneous cultural-historical proximity and distance between most Irish and the English (with "Irish" here being inclusive of also descendants of English settlers in Ireland). At the same time, Mangan was underlining the inability of any English translation of an Irish poem, including his own 'translations,' to capture the essence of the Irish original. For the average reader in the United Kingdom, and especially in Ireland, Mangan in effect made Irish (as a linguistic medium of cultural expression) appear more exotic and esoteric than any oriental or other language.

Hafiz, but Almost *All His*: Mangan's "Literæ Orientales"

The fourteenth-century Persian poet 'Hafiz' (Khajeh Shams al-Din Mohammad Hafez) was of particular interest to Mangan, although it is not known if he first encountered Hafiz's poetry in Hammer-Purgstall's 1812 *Der Diwan von Mohammed Schemsed-din Hafis* or in a different source, with Hammer-Purgstall's translation being "the first complete translation of Hafiz's *Divān* in any Western Language."[106] In the first installment of "Literæ Orientales" (1837), Mangan stated grandiosely, "It is acknowledged that no poet has as yet made his appearance in Arabia, China, Tartary, India, or the Ottoman Empire, who has succeeded in transferring the laurel from the brows of SHEMSEDDIN MOHAMMED HAFIZ to his own."[107] Although poems attributed to Hafiz did not actually feature in any of Mangan's installments of "Literæ Orientales" over the years, Mangan credited this Persian poet for a number of poems published in other settings. Examples include Mangan's comical 1848 "An Ode of Hafiz" during the Great Famine, in which the Persian poet allegedly faults the prophet of Islam for erring ("When you cursed the swine and the wine") and then concludes: "But I almost think, to save my bacon, / I'd 'go the whole hog,' and give up the wine!"[108] This was also Mangan's vicarious admission, given his utterly dire destitute circumstances during the famine, that the impecunious Mangan, notorious for his love of liquor, now had to settle for any trifle of food over all other pleasures. As well as being considered highly eccentric, because of his attire and mannerisms, Mangan was well-known by his acquaintances for his dependence on alcohol, and by certain accounts also addiction to opiates at some stage in his life.[109] This poem was a clear case of Mangan assigning his own creation to Hafiz, but the distinction between the authentic and inauthentic attributions to Hafiz in Mangan's works was not always so evident. As Ellen Shannon-Mangan notes, Mangan's recourse to masking, inventing, other-attributing, or pseudonymous and anonymous authorship, make "formidable the task [...] of determining if a poem 'could be,' 'may well be,' or 'can't possibly be' by Mangan," as in the case of the "four-quatrain verse" appearing in the *Weekly Dublin Satirist* of April 4, 1835, titled "'An Oriental Poem' and signed 'Hafiz.'"[110] In fact, the poem in question, with Hafiz's trademark references to "Solomon and Sheba," is not an actual translation from any of Hafiz's known *Rubā'iyāt* (four-quatrain verses). In a now widely repeated quotation, according to Mangan's erstwhile Young Ireland and subsequent revolutionary republican friend, John Mitchel, "Somebody asked [Mangan] why he gave credit to Hafiz for such exquisite gems of his own poetry; because, he said Hafiz paid better than Mangan—and any critic could see that they were only *half his*."[111] However, despite Mangan's periodic allusions to Hafiz, Louise Imogen Guiney correctly noted in late nineteenth century:

> His custom was to leave Hafiz alone, with Saadi and Omar [Khayyam], these being persons somewhat familiar to the general [readers]. The poets he courts are more preciously private to himself [...] Some of their names stand out memorably bright, and only just beneath those of the splendid phantom Mirza Schaffy, and the Haji-Abdu el-Yazdi, who had some reality so long as Sir Richard Burton lived.[112]

Mangan also at times recreated 'oriental poems' as patchworks of existing lines or images taken from different actual poems existing in European translations, collating them into newly fashioned collage poems. Cóilín Parsons notes that Mangan engaged in a similar style in a few of his translations from Irish, as in the case of combining segments of poems by the eighteenth-century Aogán Ó Rathaille.[113] On another occasion, when translating a German poem by Friedrich Schiller, Mangan "imported" into the translation "a palpable echo of two famous lines of [Percy Bysshe] Shelley," while in another poem he combined resonances of lines taken from the poetry of Schiller and Byron.[114] Whereas in Mangan's patchwork poem of Ó Rathaille all the lines were taken from Ó Rathaille's own poems, in his oriental collage poems none of the oriental poets from whose works Mangan borrowed some elements (lexically and/or metaphorically, or in terms of mood and tone) could claim the entirety of the new collage poem as ultimately their own creation. These poems operated at multiple layers of authorial estrangement, displacement, and dislocation. Nor were these poems in terms of language and cultural production completely 'oriental' or 'Western.' They were simultaneously always *both* and *neither*; and textually intersecting and yet incongruent. Moreover, these poems were imbued with what Roland Barthes in 1967, and in an entirely different setting, termed "the Death of the Author." At the same time, the poems also corresponded to Jacques

Derrida's concepts of "trace" or "residue" of the past in the present (first discussed in his *Speech and Phenomena* and *Of Grammatology*, both published in French in 1967), denoting the indebtedness of all creativity to prior creations, whether or not acknowledged. Mangan's frequent recourse to writing anonymously or pseudonymously was also an implicit admission of traces of works by others in his writing and the impossibility of his absolute authorial claim.

Translators aim to excavate and map in a new idiomatic, rhythmic, and expressive form, among other qualities, the work undergoing translation. For Mangan, however, any translation of a poem by Hafiz, for example, yielded merely another version of a single original poem. Each translator's quest for originality and authenticity in the task of translation produced yet another divergent reproduction of the original (as was also the case with Mangan's translation of Schiller's poem mentioned below). Pushed to the extreme, this multiplying effect of the quest for translational originality would at some point clash with, and unmoor itself from, the original, abandoning the quest for authenticity in order to attain originality and producing an *entirely* new poem—which may well retain some similarities to the original poem, whether in terms of traces of imagery, mood, concepts, objects, and so on. The latter effect was precisely what Mangan set out to achieve in his so-called translations of oriental poems. No other translation of any actually existing oriental poems, which Mangan also 'translated' by merely revising them, could ever rival Mangan's translations and hence challenge his originality, if those other existing actual translations sought to remain as true to the original text as possible (i.e., quest for authenticity). Nor could any other translator ever attempt to originally translate what were otherwise Mangan's entirely invented poems, since their purported oriental originals never existed—as Mangan himself claimed on occasion: 'original not found.' As Harry Harootunian points out in his discussion of Walter Benjamin (who was writing nearly three-quarters of a century after Mangan), for Benjamin

> translation [was] an "afterlife" of the original moment, as an activity that "issued" not from the life of the original as such but later on, to constitute a difference separate from the original but still owing its existence to it. Under the terms of this operation, "the life of the original attains" in translation to its "ever-renewed latest and most abundant flowering."[115]

Seen in this light, Mangan's invented translations as ostensible afterlives of non-existing or only partially existing originals were also an invention of history, in so far as the past or the present to which the original supposedly belonged did not itself exist outside Mangan's invention. "Original not found" was an echo of Mangan's conviction of "history not found." To put it differently, history, in the sense of the past as it happened and leaving aside even the competing perspectives and agendas of those in the past who recorded the events as they occurred, was cognitively irrecoverable in the present, since at best only traces of it remained.

For Mangan, all historical narrations were ultimately acts of interpretation and translation from present-oriented perspectives and understanding of either fragmentary remains of the past or were instrumentalist narrations of entirely imagined and invented pasts serving present-day objectives. Hence, claims of authenticity were always present- and future-oriented invented impositions onto the past. All origins, as well as claims of originality (including original translations), were present-anchored and future-oriented performance, the intended performative effects of which would only vanish with time, since those in the future too would interpret and translate their past from their respective present-oriented cognitive-ontological instrumentalist stance, forming their own origins from selective fragments of their chosen pasts, or wholly re-imagining their pasts (consciously or unconsciously). History was at best a mere repetition of the ever-changing present's claim to a past and the alleged continuity of that past into the present, just as 'translation' presupposes an 'original' and insists on some form of attachment and correspondence between the two versions. Here was Mangan's insurmountable friction with history: he sought to transcend and reject the past, and yet felt trapped in that past, if for no other reason than his attempt to surmount it, whether in terms of literary tradition, assumptions of Irish authenticity, or Ireland's colonial status. Wrestling with the past was to writhe about in a quagmire. The simultaneous urge for ultimate reconciliation with history in some form, whether as an escape from the imagined embrace of the past or the recognition of irreconcilability of the present, the past, and the future, is also reflected in Mangan's literary style. As Seamus Deane has noted,

> The only completion available to Mangan is the non-completion of the fragment, the impossibility of finding a vantage-point from which his life can be viewed as something which forms a whole—which is a 'history.' […] He plays with the notion of establishing a narrative and then disestablishes it, […] Mangan keeps switching the text's intentionality.[116]

It can be added that Mangan's repeated revisions of many of his works, even after their initial publication—hence the existence of different published versions of some of his works—were not only attempts to amend the past (in this case his own recorded past), but were also suggestive of his fixation with marking a break between the present and the past, while recognizing the impossibility of such a break even through re-creation and disguise, if not through a process of occlusion and erasure. Specifically in his re-writing of his previously published poems, there was a marked process of regeneration of a work in multiple new forms, of new translations and, hence, new interpretations of the supposed originals, of the past always fragmenting and multiplying in altered present re-creations, and constituting new works that were whole in their own originality, while never fully free of their earlier lingering specter (at least in the shape of past translations by the same author, when the original poems did not actually exist), and always potentially prone to future re-working and re-creation, and therefore perpetually incomplete.

In the "Literæ Orientales" series, Mangan also facetiously devalued his own oriental 'translation' project by initially expressing doubt about the overall quality of oriental poetry in Turkish, Arabic, and Persian and their appeal to European audiences. In this context, Mangan playfully placed himself both inside and outside the category of 'European,' or, more appropriately, situated himself as an Irish individual both inside and outside the category of his English-language readers. His suggested reason for this aporia was the alleged underlying tendency of oriental poetry toward "mysticism." By using the plural "we" when deriding those readers who expressed categoric disparaging verdicts on Eastern literatures in general—such as claiming their ostensible *uniform* lack of rational thought and/or logically coherent narrative structure, in contrast to the presumed hallmarks of Western literature—Mangan was also targeting the frequent English charge of the Irish proclivity toward superstition and dogma (particularly by the 'mere Irish' Catholics). The East in this context was synonymous with Ireland. In the 1838 second installment of "Literæ Orientales," Mangan wrote:

> Our next article will probably terminate our review of Ottoman Poetry. It will depend upon circumstances whether we shall afterwards enter upon Persian and Arabic. At present we have no great inclination to either. To acknowledge the truth, at the close of our paper, *we dislike Eastern poetry*. Its great pervading character is mysticism—and mysticism and stupidity are synonymous terms in our vocabulary. No luxurious of imagination can atone for the absence of perspicuity. A poet above all men should endeavor to make words the images of things. He should not disdain to graduate in the school of the logician.[117]

Two years later, in his fourth installment of "Literæ Orientales," he underscored the limitations of *cultural* translation and made a plea for the difficult, but indispensable, necessity of a profoundly sympathetic encounter with the literary products of *Other* cultures, the Orient (i.e., Ireland) in this case. This seemingly near-impossible task of empathetic immersion in the cultural weltanschauungen of Others required an epistemological reconfiguration. Mangan was also attacking Western engagements with the Orient (i.e., Ireland) that were historically *static* in their judgment, given the fact that the Others in question here belonged to not only different spatial, but also to different temporal, frames of the *past* (since Mangan claimed to be translating *classical* Turkish, Arabic, and Persian works of poetry). Applied to Ireland, this was a critique of the inability of those English commentators prone to making uniform and statically disparaging assessments of Irish literature to transcend their bigotry and appreciate Irish poetry and aesthetic sensibilities. By extension, Mangan's pseudo-translations of oriental and other poems, too, were in fact works of 'Irish' poetry, given that they were produced by an Irish poet (Mangan), albeit in English language. These were simultaneously far removed in content and form from earlier and contemporary works of other Irish poets, whether writing in Irish or in English. Mangan was simultaneously taking to task the ability of English observers as competent translators of Irish culture, as well as of contemporary Irish as purveyors of Ireland's past.

Mangan's exegesis in the 1840 fourth installment of "Literæ Orientales" on the necessity of empathetic cultural immersion for appreciating the Other, as impossible as it is to ever attain absolute cultural conversion (again assuming there is such a thing as cultural authenticity in the first place), deserves to be quoted in detail. The anonymous author of "Literæ Orientales," vouching for his own ability to produce premium idiomatic and expressive English translations from oriental languages, admitted that mere translation will always fail to capture the underlying cultural nuances of the original work in question. Here, Mangan concentrated on ontological and epistemological dimensions of cultural encounters between the West and the East (and hence also cultural encounters between England and Ireland, leaving aside that the geographic orientation of England-Ireland was the reverse of West-East). Also making a pun regarding the distinctly different meanings of otherwise identical sounding terms (Ottoman and ottoman, the latter denoting footstool, and with the former inclusive of the latter, but not the other way around) and inserting a French phrase while insisting on reading works of oriental literature in their original languages, Mangan wrote:

> Our conclusion is a matured one: we state, and we challenge the entire world of linguists and littérateurs to refute the statement, that Oriental Poetry is not fairly readable in an English translation—that there is practicability of idiomatically translating it with effect into any of our languages. We do not question the qualifications of the translator for his office; he may be a man—though the contingency seems remote and phantomy—to rival [John] Anster: all that we mean to aver is that Oriental Poetry appareled in a western dress becomes essentially unrecognisable, forfeits its identity, ceases to be an intelligible object of apprehension to the understanding. It must be read in the oriental, and *ce qui est plus et pire*, it must be studied in it; for the bare reading will not answer. The student is not to flatter himself into the belief that because he has rattled through a Persian grammar and skimmed [John] Richardson's Dissertation the business is accomplished and he has nothing more to do but take his MS. in hand and loll on his ottoman. A severe initiation awaits him. He must for a season renounce his country, divest himself of his educational prejudices, forego his individuality, and become, like Alfred Tennyson, "a Mussulman true and sworn." Over the wide gulf by which we of Europe are severed from the Eastern nations in religious worship, modes of thought and habits of feeling, and in the governments, customs and social systems that spring out of these and react upon them sans intermission, no bridge is thrown—the enthusiast must plunge into its depths and scale the opposite steep, [...] he must first disencumber himself of all the old rags of his Europeanism and scatter them to the winds [...][118]

Leaving aside the scoff at Tennyson and the compliment paid to Mangan's friend Anster in this passage, by substituting England for "Europe" and Ireland for "Eastern," Mangan's statement could well apply to English encounters with his own country and culture: "Over the wide gulf by which we of Europe are severed from the Eastern nations in religious worship, modes of thought and habits of feeling." In this framework, contrary to the suggestion by other scholars of Mangan that to "renounce his country" was merely indicative of Mangan's ambivalence toward Irish nationalism, he was in effect urging the *English* to momentarily shed *their* national prejudice toward the Irish as well. It was, after all, the English who were in need of refinement: "for a season renounce[ing] his country, divest[ing] himself of his educational prejudices, forego[ing] his individuality." Mangan opposed all forms of self-centric nationalist chauvinism, English or Irish. He added that the translator must go "beyond the extreme outer porch or Ethnic Forecourt" (the latter also a pun on the Four Courts building in Dublin that served as the center of British legislation in Ireland):

> must be satisfied to accept sounds for symbols, influences for ideas, and dreams for tangibilities. He must in fine begin his poetical education afresh [...] and after a series of years, (industry, commentators and opium in the meantime assisting), he may perhaps be able to boast that he has measured the height, length, breadth and circumference of the Great Temple in which the imagination of Bakki [the Ottoman poet Mahmud Abdülbāki] and the soul of Hafiz are enshrined, and beyond the extreme outer porch or Ethnic Forecourt

of which none save those who have served a like probationary apprenticeship to the Genius of Orientalism have ever been permitted to advance.[119]

But, almost immediately, Mangan stressed the fundamental vast divide between European and Eastern temperaments, which by the end of this thematic thread was slyly transformed into the divide between the mainstream of English Protestants and Irish Catholics, with "Englishman" replacing the West and a slippage occurring between the "Mooslem" (Muslim) who "has more *faith*" and "catholic philosopher." Playing on English stereotypes of the Irish, as being prone to superstition, emotional irrationality, unrestrained fatalism, and so on, as well as the recurrent contradictory portrayals of the Irish as simultaneously scheming, shrewd, insensitive, and the like, Mangan concluded:

> Eastern Poetry is at best what the old schoolmen would have called an *ens rationis*—a lawless, unfixable, ghostlike thing, irreducible to rule, unamenable to criticism, [...] It is occasionally graphic enough—can on most occasions be admired for euphony—and may at intervals exhibit sublimity—but the great irradiating light of Imagination is not there [...]. Indeed, if we were to succinctly describe the difference between this poetry and our own we should say that the latter depends chiefly upon *Expression*, but the former chiefly upon *Impression*. [...] what we mean to assert is that whereas in the West strict attention to the modes and accidents of Expression is indispensable to the production of Impression, in the East it seems almost wholly superfluous. How the Mohammedan poet treats his theme is a matter of slight consequence. The only thing likely to puzzle his readers would be mystification; and that he cannot employ, because he knows nothing about it: in his darkest opacities his good faith and single-mindedness are still transparent: he may be sometimes silly; he is always serious [...] Among us, with whom coherence and consistency of thought and diction are fast growing into a positive nuisance, this incongruous combination would be at once ascribed to mental imbecility [...] The truth is that the Mooslem has more *faith*, humanly speaking than the Englishman. It is an easier task to satisfy him. [...] He takes the higher ground. He knows that the Abstract and the Possible hold unconditional charters from the hand of Deity, [...] He is a philosopher—not a pur-blind analyst of some incontrovertible axiom—not a groping investigator into noon-day facts—but a genuine, generous, downright, unsophisticated, catholic philosopher.[120]

It is in this light, and not forgetting the irony of Ireland being located to the west of Britain and frequently identified by the English as culturally more akin to the East than to the West (in a cultural-political mapping of West and East), that Mangan's concluding comments in this installment of "Literæ Orientales" should be read. Moreover, despite Mangan's ultimate rejection of Charles Vallancey's methodology, as discussed again below in connection with Mangan's 1848 "Irish National Hymn," Mangan was enthralled with the Iran/Erin (Orient/Ireland) correlation. In his ever-looping similes, he ended the fourth installment of his "Literæ Orientales" by conflating Persians and Arabs as ethnic groups, contrary to his own earlier statement on the subject, and then of Arabs with the Irish by way of a witty reference to Vallancey. Notable also in the previous passages quoted above is the clear distinction Mangan made between the English and the Irish (as opposed to "we"), while simultaneously equating the "English and Irish" in so far as their common lack of familiarity with "foreign literature, Eastern and Western" (meaning here also the average English-speaking Irish reader's lack of familiarity with Irish literature itself, also applicable to Mangan himself):

> Before encasing our pen we cannot avoid adverting with regret to the apathy of our contemporaries, English and Irish, on the subject of foreign literature, Eastern and Western. Is it not shameful that we should have been left to fight our Oriental battle single-handed? According to Vallancey every Irishman is an Arab. Yet, what Irishman has come forward to second our exertions? The whole of the reviewing press has nobly sustained us—indeed has lauded us altogether beyond our deserts; and we thankfully acknowledge the obligation. But what we want and demand is active cooperation.[121]

Here was a crucial essence of Mangan's invented oriental translations: the average highbrow English reader was, in fact, more likely to be familiar with classical Persian poetry than with Irish poetry and literature, having greater acquaintance with the literature of *the East over there*, than *the East over here* (albeit cartographically situated to the west of Britain). Mangan's self-plagiarized oriental poems, while characterized by veiling and masquerading, were at the same time an act of discarding the pretense of the possibility of perfect cultural translation, a rejection of the efficacy of any Western attempt at literary mapping and surveying of the Orient that could yield some authentic grasp of oriental literatures, as many of Mangan's contemporaries claimed. In a similar vein, in his translations from Irish, he underscored the inability of English language to reliably decipher poetry originally produced in Irish language, with language and culture determining one's engagement with the world in Mangan's view; hence also his own inability to come to terms with Irishness, given his inadequate grasp of the Irish language. At a different level, this formula also implied the inability of Mangan and his Irish contemporaries to fully grasp Ireland's *past*—even if they had been fluent in Irish language, they were not grounded in the Irish culture of the past (again assuming the possibility of cultural authenticity in the first place), and the Irish language they spoke now was continually shedding its previous cultural nuances and accumulating new ones.

Mangan had already lampooned Vallancey in his 1839 "A Polyglott Anthology," published under one of Mangan's pennames: "THE OUT-AND-OUTER." In that piece, Mangan's invented German scholar. "The Herr Hoppandgoön Von Baugtrauter" (which, as noted before, may in fact represent Mangan), also translated into German poems attributed to an Irish-American named Felix O'Gallagher ("F. O'G."; i.e., fog), originally composed in both Irish and English. Here Mangan was supposedly translating into English the German translations not only of originally Irish compositions but also of originally English compositions in his characteristic translational looping. In Baugtrauter's German translation of O'Gallagher's Irish poem, Mangan wrote: "And, as from every adverse facts VALLANCEY / Proved us mere Irish to be Orientals, / Nature makes Grinning Schools turn men out Sentimentals."[122] David Wheatley, focusing like most other commentators on Vallancey's earlier writings only, notes:

> Among the most fanciful strands of contemporary antiquarianism was Charles Vallancey's belief in the Phoenician origin of the Irish language. Mangan's reference to Vallancey in an

1839 epigraph suggests that his [i.e., Mangan's] translations were not without ethnological ambitions of their own, 'Prov(ing) us mere Irish to be Orientals.'

Wheatley adds,

> Mangan's interest in exotic foreign literatures is by no means unique for the period ([Maria] Edgeworth includes a fragment of Estonian poetry in *Castle Rackrent* [published in 1800]), but his forays into translation were more than fantastical caprices. While Charles Gavan Duffy and John Mitchel decried his wilder translations as "apocrypha" and "perversions," they are central to Mangan's work and his whole conception of authorship.[123]

It needs to be clarified here that Wheatley's reference to the objection made to Mangan's translations by the prominent Young Ireland leader Charles Gavan Duffy is only directed at certain topics in Mangan's so-called translated poems and not to Mangan's insinuated theory of oriental origins of the Irish. Duffy, in a footnote to his "The Laurence's Address" appearing in Timothy Daniel Sullivan's 1879 edited first volume of *Penny Readings for the Irish People*, cited Henry O'Brien as one of his sources when identifying the name of ancient Ireland as "Iran or Irin."[124] Other than Mangan's fascination with Vallancey's theory of oriental origins of the Irish, there is yet another overlooked aspect to Mangan's engagement with Vallancey. Whereas Vallancey relied on European translations of Persian sources, which he could not read in the original language (and some of which were entirely mythical or were later proven to be forgeries), in order to document Ireland's missing ancient past, Mangan in his pseudo-translations from oriental languages, in which he too lacked any familiarity (including Persian), produced phony English documentation of non-existing oriental literature.

Mangan's "An Extraordinary Adventure in the Shades" is a stunning literary prose piece that beyond question is one of the earliest modernist literary specimens, on par with such other rare contemporary modernist masterpieces as works by the German Karl Georg Büchner (from Hesse), as distinct as their styles happened to be. Published in the Dublin *Comet* in 1833, years before the appearance of his "Literæ Orientales," Mangan played around with a combination of his own name and his oriental preoccupation with a generically termed "Araby" (a la Vallancey). The piece was written from the perspective of a narrator, who in a drunken stupor and hallucinatory state in a Dublin pub, called the Shades Tavern, assumes he is gazing upon Mangan. The narrator refers to the other person as "no other than a revivification of Maugraby, the celebrated Oriental necromancer."[125] The name—in addition to "Maghrib," denoting "west" in Arabic language (hence Ireland as the projected "Orient" in the West) as well as the Arabic geographical designation for the region of North Africa extending from present-day Libya to the farthest north-westerly reach of the continent—may have also been intended as a contraction simultaneously evocative of "Mangan"+"grabby," given Mangan's pecuniary circumstances and financial reliance on friends, as well as 'Mangan'+'Araby' (hence also "Irish Mangan" through a presumed Vallanceyan lens). The narrator draws a parallel between Ireland of *the future* and the Near East of *ancient times*. As a result of Maugraby's expanding large nose, which the drunken narrator hallucinates to be taking over the pub and then the rest of the city, the narrator imagines that in *future* Ireland Dublin would be clustered with non-European *ruins of the past*: "Dublin would, in its melancholy destiny, be assimilated by the historian of a future age, with Persepolis, Palmyra, and Nineveh!"[126] "An Extraordinary Adventure in the Shades" was published five years before Mangan joined the first topographical survey of Ireland overseen by Petrie (as part of the Ordnance Department's general survey). Mangan's vision of the future ruined Dublin in this 1833 piece was chiefly consistent with what Cóilín Parsons has correctly characterized as the theme of ruins in Mangan's 'translations' from the Irish after he joined the topographical division of the Ordnance Department in 1838, such as Mangan's re-working of Eugene O'Curry's translation of the poetry of Mac Liag's (d. 1015).[127] According to Parsons,

> Mangan trades in evanescence—there is a constant threat that the visible will become invisible, or that the extant material remains of the history of Ireland will be pushed off the map entirely. Remains becomes traces and walls become shadows as Mangan builds up his own archive of disappearances, walking a fine line between the tyranny of fact and the heterodox possibilities of the imagination. Translations and forgeries afford the perfect medium in which to elide the distinctions between the visible world and its invisible alternatives, and ruin poems in particular conjure up a landscape filled with inescapable reminders of alternative paths to the present, each of which has been suspended rather than terminated.[128]

In "An Extraordinary Adventure in the Shades," however, it was not a fear of Ireland's absolute *disappearance* from the map, but rather the anxiety of the present-day capital of colonial Ireland appearing on future maps as a site of historical ruin belonging to a distant past, classed together with the monumental ruins of some of the paramount, but tumbled, long ago civilizations. Ironically, all the ancient ruins listed by Mangan had been centers of 'oriental' *empires*, unlike Dublin of Mangan's day, when Ireland was an imperial outpost. This Dublin, no less existing as a ruin in a presumably future independent Ireland, required a novel imaginative cartography that was both spatially and temporally curved, so that it could accommodate past and future ruins of cities in a new geographic realignment of West and East, with *Ireland's future* approaching the *past of somewhere else* in the East. Unlike Vallancey's model of Ireland's ancient ties with the Orient, Mangan's inebriated narrator was hallucinating *Ireland's future reunion with its oriental lineage* and not an Orient at its civilizational height, but a bygone Orient now laid to waste with other cultures and civilizations having long supplanted the former cultures in the region, and with only traces remaining of that past prior to its ruin. This marked the improbability of Ireland ever coming to terms with its own history. But, much to the relief of Mangan's drunken narrator, the narrator later realizes the person he had been contemplating was not Maugraby after all. Mangan's nose, therefore, fortunately did not botch Ireland's national future, nor entirely sabotage Ireland's encounter with history.

In connection with Mangan's oriental pseudo-translations and prose commentaries, David Lloyd has shown that "irony," "parody," and "refraction" permeate these works.[129] In "An Extraordinary Adventure in the Shades," too, it is a perpetual mode of historical refraction that Mangan channels into his pairing of Ireland and the Orient. Mangan's rejection of unconditional creative originality was a simultaneous act of embracing and refusing 'the modern' (notwithstanding his own unmistakably 'modernist' oeuvre), of the always compromised rootedness of the present in the past, the inheritances and debts accumulated from others, and the ultimately always borrowed, selectively incorporated, and reinvented quality of not just literary creativity, but also of *identities* and *histories*. At the same time, the past itself was an imagination and creation of the present. The 'modern' invented its own contrapuntal "tradition," as much it was shaped by the past and hence unable to break free from 'tradition.' Nationalism was to Mangan a bricolage of selected fragments of a refractive history (including histories of Others), with nationalist history imparting its own range of inheritance that, in turn, imposed onto the present the debts of the past, which were to continue into the future, albeit in constantly reconstructed and reframed modes. For Mangan, the interconnected subjects of origins, authenticity, and translation (including taking fragments from histories of *Others* and rendering them as being analogous to episodes in *Irish* history in his own works), as well as the interchange between languages, traces, authorial entitlement, and the 'modern,' were intrinsically applicable to Ireland's highly contentious and unsettled national history.[130]

In 1838 Mangan secured employment at the Ordnance Department (of Ireland's Ordnance Survey) through George Petrie and John O'Donovan, whom he had known since the early 1830s. Mangan had previously eked a living as a scrivener (an act of copying originals). Petrie most certainly also arranged for the publication of Mangan's "Literæ Orientales" series (starting in 1837) in the *Dublin University Magazine*, the editors of which he knew. Petrie, who was in charge of the topographical division of the Ordnance Department, established in 1833, had recruited O'Donovan to assist him with the very first government topographical Ordnance Survey of Ireland, and from 1838 until the closure of the topographical division in December 1841 Mangan was tasked with transcribing documents for the department under Petrie's supervision.[131] There were a number of interesting parallels between Mangan's oriental translations, his engagement with nationalism and Irish history, and the Ordnance Survey's fieldwork and archival project. Cóilín Parsons notes that, in assigning placenames on the topographical map, the survey failed to fully establish the former Irish placenames in their pre-Anglicized pronunciation forms, and in many cases the former Irish names could not be established with any certainty. The survey instead settled for its own particular renaming of locales, what Parsons calls O'Donovan's "fourth language":

> But the Survey did not translate placenames into a recognizable language. The target language is neither modern Irish nor English, nor even Hiberno-English, but an idiom peculiar to the maps. This fourth language, which Thomas Davis—himself a proponent [sic] of the place of the English language in the development of the Irish nation—labels barbarous, was not one that anyone spoke.[132]

Mangan's gibberish English transliterations of lines purportedly taken from oriental languages resembled such a fourth language. In Mangan's case, however, this was a conscious decision. Not only could he not understand the oriental languages from which he was 'translating,' but even if he had managed to gain fluency in those languages, he could never be certain that in his translations he was reproducing in English the authentic recovered temporal and spatial cultural nuances of those poems, assuming those works even existed in the first place. Mangan's sense of the ultimate futility of constant surveying, documenting, and archiving of Ireland by the topographical division of the Ordnance Department was also evident in his approach to 'translation' of oriental and other poetry. In a similar vein, Mangan did not believe there was a singular narrative of Ireland's past that could be recovered and authenticated—just as in his reference to some of the poems he claimed to be translating from other existing translations he added: 'Original not found.' Even the most thorough systematic and fastidious effort at recovery, as in the case of O'Donovan's topographic endeavor, yielded placenames that would have been unrecognizable to the inhabitants of those places in the past. For Mangan, the historical-cultural *here* and *now* and its language could bear some traces of the *there* and *then* (to borrow Jacques Chuto's expression, which is quoted later in the present chapter), but it could never fully reproduce that of which only traces remained. In a nationalist context, these traces of the past both burdened and destabilized the forward-oriented nationalist project here and now. There was the nostalgic recognition of the continually disappearing Irish past due to the passage of time in general, as well as due to post-Norman cultural displacements as part of broader imperial and trans-imperial temporal transformations. There was additionally the unsettling nationalist realization, even if suppressed, of the impossibility of authentically comprehending the past through its traces alone, particularly traces that also bore residues of English cultural impositions. In this regard, as Parson has perceptively noted, there is also a major contrast between Mangan's 'translated' poetry in general (including from the Irish) and the Ordnance Survey's archaeological undertaking:

> If it is the aim of the Survey to provide a thick description of human geography and unearth the archeology of Ireland, Mangan's poems tend in the opposite direction: Tara is dematerialized, Timoleague is in ruins, and Kincora is lost. The opposite is the case if we look at the landscape itself, which is richly populated with the remains of the past, reminders of what [David] Lloyd evocatively calls the multiple "temporalities of modernity" that characterize postcolonial landscape and culture. For Mangan, however, the modernizing process of the Survey ensures that "[a]ll that is solid melts into air." [...] This dissolution of the material remains of the past in Mangan's ruin poetry might indeed be read as a key moment when "man is compelled to face with sober senses, his real conditions of life, and his relation with his kind." Mangan is no historical materialist, but what he does take cognizance of is that his "relation with his kind" is being fundamentally altered by the archiving process of the Survey. The transfer of knowledge of the history and landscape of the island from oral to written sources, from ancient manuscript to government document, is a Derridean process of "consignation in an external place," of confining knowledge and rendering it outside the space of life and politics. Archiving is also, as Ann Laura Stoler points out, an "epistemological experiment," a cross section of "contested knowledge," fraught with the problems of classification and recognition that produce more uncertainties, and greater claims for the necessity of information. As the Survey seeks, almost maniacally, to fill out its knowledge of all of Ireland's history and archeology, as its shelves swell with unpublished and unpublishable reams of information, Mangan slowly and carefully strips it all away, projecting futility and loss where his colleagues see productivity and recovery.[133]

As far as 'nation' was concerned, Mangan was in some ways resonating aspects of what also became Thomas Davis' formulation of the nation, which focused on the present and the future, rather than the past, while also presaging James Joyce's verdict in the next century that an independent Ireland would have to be either a reconstruction of *existing* cultures and an amalgam of divergent histories or an entirely reinvented historical-cultural entity. Ironically, however, Joyce stated in his 1902 and 1907 essays on Mangan (with some rephrasing in 1907): "With Mangan a narrow and hysterical nationality receives a last justification" and "history of his country encloses him so straitly."[134] But, in fact, for Mangan there was no possibility of a return to a pre-colonial Irish identity or a recovery of pre-English domination 'Irish' culture, even if such a past could ever be fully and authentically resuscitated. The years during which Mangan worked at the Ordnance Department convinced him of this. Many Irish villages surviving from long ago, and other similar locales, had been renamed in English, or had long ago assumed Anglicized pronunciations of their original names, with local populations unable to recall the former Irish names or the previous pronunciations of the now-Anglicized Irish names. The very terrain of Mangan's country was *accented* at best, or entirely *translated*, with no assuredly authentic trace of the original remaining. Similarly, Irish language and Irish identities, too, were accented and translated. Only *translations* of the past existed, without any proof of wholly corresponding originals. Cóilín Parsons writes:

> Mangan's discomfort with the politics of recovery with which he himself was complicit led him to construct a canon of poetry that explored the negative shadows of the Survey's positivist drive. The result, in many of Mangan's translations from Irish, is that the material becomes dematerialized, and the real becomes spectral—his ruin poems in particular offer not praise of enduring monuments, but fantasies of destruction. This dematerialization in Mangan's work expresses one the central features of every attempt to archive and preserve—it is the contradiction at the heart of the idea of the creation of an archive that Jacques Derrida identified.[135]

Judging by his poems and prose, Mangan appears to have regarded history as always fractured and dismembered, resisting total recall. Ireland's ancient history, riddled with major lacuna—including most notably any collectively shared or coherent account of Ireland's ancient past—, and even its more recent history, with competing nationalist and "anti-nationalist" recalls of traumas and pride, were instances of the impossibility of any singular and total historical recollection of Ireland's past. Even more fundamentally, nationalist histories required conscious episodic acts of amnesia and recollective alterations and rearrangements of the past for generating even the least degree of cohesive narrative continuum of the 'national,' leaving aside the many coexisting and competing nationalist historical narratives in the first place. It was in part to overcome the historical surfeit of competing and inherently contentious nationalist narratives of Ireland's past that Mangan so often turned to particular moments in non-Irish history, offering his readers not always a historical mirror, but, at times, also a kaleidoscopic historical cornucopia from which they were expected to deduce Mangan's intended fragmentary references to particular stages in Ireland's history, without interrogating the *before* and *after* of those truncated episodes in Irish and Other histories. Perhaps the best example of Mangan's reliance on the history of other lands and peoples as a mode of commenting on conditions in Ireland is his 1846 poem "Siberia," composed during the Great Famine (see below). Mangan's extensive allusions to conditions in Ireland by way of commenting on events and/or settings in other parts of the world, past and present, produced an additional cosmopolitan layering of Mangan's works, in a way Thomas Moore had never intended. This cosmopolitanism, also evident in Mangan's invented translations from oriental and other languages, positioned Mangan as both Irish and cosmopolitan, even though he never traveled outside Ireland and refrained from submitting his works for publication in periodicals published outside Ireland.

Mangan's view of the impossibility of total or even partially coherent historical recovery and archiving of the *past* was accompanied by a pronounced anxiety about the inevitability of *future* displacement and disillusionment. He even inserted these anxieties into some of the poems that were his bona fide translations, as in the case of his 1834 licentious translation of the German "Der Pilgrim" ("The Pilgrim") by the eighteenth-century Württembergian poet Friedrich Schiller. In Mangan's translation, signed "Clarence," the youthful narrator of this poem fails miserably in his endeavor to "ever speed to the glorious East" in search of its much vaunted "eternity's life-giving chalice." He is, instead, carried away by the highly symbolic "green waves" of a river (green symbolizing Ireland) to a place of deracination, desolation, and inescapable permanent gloom. The poem ended with the following stanzas:

> In the end I came to a rushing river,
>   Whose green waves rolled to the shores of the East;
> And, strong in the faith of a fervent believer,
>   I cast myself far on his heaving breast.
>
> But woe is me! the billows but bore me
>   To the barren and wreck-strewn region I tread:
> Dark skies are o'er me, wild wastes are before me,
>   And my goal is lost, and my soul is dead.
>
> For man is vanity! Danger and pain
>   Encompass his paths from year to year;
> Earth woos the proud heights of heaven in vain,
>   And the *There* of existence but mocks the *Here*.[136]

Schiller's original final line had simply read "Und das dort ist niemals hier" ("And *the there* is never *here*").

John Bull Scorned: Mangan's Iranian "Khizzilbash"

Mangan's "Literæ Orientales" largely consisted of simulated translations from Turkish, attributed to the likes of the historical sixteenth-century Ottoman poets Mahmud Abdülbāki ("Baki") or Lamii Çelebi. Some of the so-called Turkish, Arabic, and Persian poems in the "Literæ Orientales" series were implicitly evocative of Ireland's encounter with English colonialism. But, when it came to explicit condemnation of English colonialism through oriental allegory, Mangan settled for Thomas Moore's Iran/Erin interchange in the latter's distinctly political Irish nationalist poems allegorically set in "Iranian" historical contexts. This was the case with Mangan's 1846 "To the Ingleezee Khafir, Calling Himself Djuan Bool Djenkinzun," which first appeared in *The Nation* (Dublin), independently of the "Literæ Orientales" series or "A Polyglott Anthology," and is today frequently consulted by scholars of Mangan in its incomplete form. The line "IRAN's nation and race" in this poem referenced both Moore's allegoric device (re "nation") and Vallancey's historical link (re "race"). In a later poem, "Irish National Hymn," published in May 1848 in the radical nationalist Dublin newspaper *The United Irishman*, Mangan strictly resorted to Vallancey's Iran/Erin connection in ancient times. "Irish National Hymn," also appearing individually and independently of Mangan's earlier oriental series of poems, was an unequivocally revolutionary call to arms. Both of these poems by Mangan decidedly celebrated resistance to English colonialism, with "To the Ingleezee Khafir" vicariously offering an example of an allegedly past Iranian resistance to English imperialism, and "Irish National Hymn" urging the Irish to prepare for and join an impending uprising. These poems were composed during what came to be known as Ireland's Great Famine of 1845–51, also known as "an Gorta Mór" (the Great Hunger), during which Mangan died (June 1849) destitute and suffering from cholera and acute malnutrition. The two Iran-themed poems reflect Mangan's sharp turn to militant political nationalism at a desperate juncture in Irish history, during which time he also embraced John Mitchel's physical-force nationalist stance in 1847, marking a clear break with the earlier prevalent moral force tendency in the Young Ireland camp.[137] Both poems, therefore, challenge the supposition of Mangan's continued aversion to *political* nationalism and/or his consistently pessimistic attitude toward Irish nationalism in general (cultural and or political),[138] which is not to say he fully overcame his troubled relationship with nationalism and nationality as a yardstick of individual identity. In 1848, Mangan started writing for Mitchel's newly founded and unambiguously titled *The United Irishman* (launched in February of that year and adopting the mantle of the organization that had launched the 1798 uprising in Ireland). The paper was suppressed by the authorities just ahead of the dismal uprising on July 29, 1848, by the militant wing of Young Ireland affiliated with Mitchel—Mitchel was arrested ahead of the uprising. "To the Ingleezee Khafir" and "Irish National Hymn" are also indicative of Mangan's changed attitude toward history and historical documentation (including histories of other lands) as potentially inspiring and life-affirming, as well as signaling his more optimistic faith in the future-oriented potential of Irish nationalism (in its republican revolutionary manifestation), even if this faith stemmed from his utter desperation.

Yet, in light of the famine ravaging Ireland, his mood of nationalist optimism alternated with intense bouts of pessimism and a sense of futility, as evident from his poem "Siberia" (*The Nation*, April 18, 1846). In "Siberia," the Russian empire's frozen wasteland of political exile[139] became the familiar existential experience of the average Irish person suffering from the famine, including the then utterly indigent Mangan. The experience of hunger during the famine (and the cold in the frostier and wet times of the year) was agonizingly amplified in this poem by echoing the misery of life in Siberia. Accordingly, the Irish were condemned to the most abject form of life in *exile* while living in their own *homeland*, once again reflecting Mangan's equivalences of the *there* and *here*. There could be no confusion as to the intended parallel for the Czar (Tsar) in this poem and of Mangan's call to action: "Therefore, in those wastes / None curse the Czar. / Each man's tongue is cloven by / The North Blast, who heweth nigh / With sharp scymitar." Without rebellion, the Irish, in their own land no less, merely exited on the precarious threshold of agonizing death similar to exiles in Siberia: "When man lives, and doth not live, / Doth not live—nor die."[140] As Ciara Hogan, too, has noted, a similar mood of Ireland's misery pervades Mangan's 1847 "Song of the Albanian."[141] Mangan's now unmistakably future-oriented nationalist poems, at times with a prophesizing tone, also included "The Warning Voice" (*The Nation*, February 21, 1846—with the year erroneously appearing in the paper as 1847), "Soul and Country" (*The Irishman*, April 28, 1849), and the already mentioned 1848 "Irish National Hymn."[142] Desperate to earn some meager income, Mangan continued with his entertaining 'oriental' and other poems during these years, such as the 1848 "Ode of Hafiz," and, at least on one occasion during these years, in the poem titled "An Invitation" (1846), he even made the survivalist recommendation that the suffering Irish emigrate to the Americas, instead of urging them to revolt against British rule.[143]

The 1846 "To the Ingleezee Khafir" was among Mangan's earliest and outright furious militant poems. Compared to Moore's Iran-centered sections of *Lalla Rookh* (1817), in which Iran allegorically served as a stand-in for Ireland, with the Arab-Muslim Umayyad and Abbasid Empires representing English imperialism, Mangan's poem reduced the metaphoric historical distance and any potential allegoric ambiguity by means of setting up an encounter between an Iranian warrior and a direct representative of the English monarchy. In this respect, Mangan's poem was closer to Thomas Osborne Davis' "A Ballad of Freedom," in which Davis referred to contemporary Afghan resistance to British imperialism,[144] or to "Afghanistan" by the Young Irelander Denis Florence MacCarthy (written in 1842 in the aftermath of the Anglo-Afghan War of 1839–42 and published in 1850).[145] MacCarthy also noted the savage British devastation of the Afghan city of Ghazni, which he reminded his readers had once been fêted by the tenth- to eleventh-century Persian poet Abul-Qassem Ferdowsi.[146] MacCarthy, it should be reminded, was also among Irish nationalist poets who replicated Thomas Moore's similitude between ancient Iranian-Zoroastrian temples and Ireland's Round Towers.[147] A major difference between Mangan's and Moore's, or MacCarthy's, Iran/Erin interchange was that Mangan was revising Moore's formula by inventing an instance of *successful* Iranian deterrence of an alleged foreign imperialist incursion (the English state in the sixteenth century in this case), other than Mangan's clear designation of a historical Englishman as the imperialist intruder. Mangan's Iranian character in "To the Ingleezee Khafir" (the presumed nationalist *Other* of the English imperialist) was not a mirror image of the Irish *Self*. The poem, set in sixteenth-century Iran, invited Mangan's readers to *contrast* Ireland's ongoing experience of English subjugation with a past episode of successful Iranian defiance of presumed English imperial aggression. Mangan undercut any easy parity and cross-identification between the Irish and Iranians in this poem. Unlike Moore, Davis, MacCarthy, and others, Mangan set up a narrative device of concurrent Irish nationalist proximity to and distancing from the Iranian subject of the poem. This reflected Mangan's recognition of the complications involved in using the history of Anglo-Iranian encounters as a surrogate for the history of Anglo-Irish encounters, not the least given the different outcomes of those encounters in the past. In particular, Mangan destabilized the possibility of any facile Irish Catholic identification with the sixteenth-century Iranian *Other*, who was presumably resisting the Protestant English state. By the end of the poem, the Iranian scorning the representative of the English crown confused the pope as the religious guide of English Protestants. This was a trademark refractive Manganesque literary device. John Mitchel, who devoted no space to the discussion of Mangan's oriental poems in his edited volume of Mangan's poetry and only provided a very thin sampling of those poems in the section titled "Apochrypha," ironically included "To the Ingleezee Khafir" in this same section of the book, which otherwise consisted of two Ottoman, one Arabic, and one Spanish pseudo-translations by Mangan.[148] As with some other works by Mangan, there are slightly different versions of this poem, given Mangan's habitual revisions of his works in different publications. Significantly, however, beginning with Mitchel's edited volume, the third and final section of "To the Ingleezee Khafir" was expunged from many subsequent posthumously published versions of this poem, or only partially reproduced.[149] In Mitchel's case, this censorship was doubtless due to Mangan's reference to "Pope Urban" in that final section of the poem. Mitchel may have misunderstood the lines, by being inattentive to the punctuation and erroneously assuming the Iranian character in the poem was slandering the pope as well, or he may have found objectionable the correlation between the pope and a "Mufti" (denoting an Islamic legal expert, with the title nowadays chiefly used among Sunni sects of Islam)—with the Unitarian Protestant Mitchel always careful not to tread on Catholic sensibilities. Or, it is also possible Mitchel (over-sensitively) wished to remove from the poem any direct reference to Ireland's distinct Christian sects, given his commitment to nonsectarian nationalism. Ironically, Mitchel's complete omission of this section also expunged from the poem Mangan's recourse to the Iran/Erin simile: "IRAN's nation and race" (see below).

"To the Ingleezee Khafir, Calling Himself Djuan Bool Djenkinzun" was first published anonymously under the section "Poet's Corner" in Young Ireland's weekly *The Nation* on April 18, 1846, during the first year of the devastating famine. The poem was allegedly sent to the paper by "A learned friend."[150] It was identified as being a "translation of 'a particularly genuine Persian poem.'" The poem was an unmistakable attack on British 'colonial' rule in Ireland by way of targeting English imperialism in general, in this case allegedly in the form of a foiled English act of aggression in sixteenth-century Iran. This 'translated' poem, which included descriptive footnotes, was attributed to an Iranian by the name of "Meer Djafrit" (i.e., Mir Jafar, and also evocative of the Arabic word "afreet"/demon) and addressed to the English 'Djaun Bool Djenkinzun' (i.e., "John Bull" Jenkinson). Given Meer Djafrit's self-identification as a "Khizzilbash" (the Turkic Qizilbash tribal forces serving in the Iranian Safavid Empire's military at the time), Meer Djafrit would have been ethnically an Iranian-Turk and a Shi'i Muslim (similar to Iran's Safavid rulers from 1501 to 1722). The poem immediately proceeded with Meer Djafrit's castigation of the Christian English *Other*:

TO THE INGLEEZEE KHAFIR, CALLING HIMSELF DJAUN BOOL DJENKINZUN.

I

Thus writeth Meer Djafrit—
   I hate thee, Djaun Bool,
Worse than Márid or Afrit,
   Or corpse-eating Ghool.
I hate thee like Sin,
   For thy mop-head of hair,
Thy snub nose and bald chin,
   And thy turkeycock air.
Thou vile Ferindjee!
   That thou thus shouldst disturb an
Old Moslim like me,
   With my Khizzilbash turban!
Old fogy like me,
   With my Khizzilbash turban!

II

I spit on thy clothing,
   That garb for baboons!
I eye with deep loathing
   Thy tight pantaloons!
I curse the cravat
   That encircles thy throat,
And thy cooking-pot hat,
   And thy swallow-tail'd coat!
Go, hide thy thick sconce
   In some hovel suburban;
Or else don at once
   The red Moosleman turban.
Thou dog, don at once
The grand Khizzilbash turban!

III

Thou vagabond varlet!
   Thou swiller of sack!
If our heads be all scarlet
   Thy heart is all black!
Go on to revile
   IRAN's nation and race,
In thy fish-faggish style!
   He who knows with what face
Thou can'st curse and traduce
   Thine own Mufti, Pope Urban,

May scorn thine abuse!
   Of the Khizzilbash turban—
Scorn all thine abuse
   Of the Khizzilbash turban![151]

Mangan's phrase "IRAN's nation and race" evoked Moore's Iran/Erin 'national' allegoric interchange, albeit in a satirically caustic and more ambiguous Manganesque style, while also obliquely resonating Vallancey's ethnic association ('race') between Iran and Erin in ancient times. It is telling that Mangan used both 'nation' and 'race' in this phrase, denoting a distinct racial-ethnic origin of the 'mere Irish' with which he was identifying the core of the Irish nation, notwithstanding Mangan's commitment to cross-denominational and cross-ethnic Irish nationalism. In the event his intended comparison between the sixteenth-century Iranian Qizilbash and Irish nationalist antipathy toward England should elude his readers, Mangan provided certain clues in the footnotes to the poem. "(1) The Oriental poets up to the 17th century, as to the Irish up to the 10th, almost always introduced their own names into their poems." In keeping with his trademark invented translations, in footnote 6 Mangan gave the Persian equivalent of "Thou dog" as "*Ei Gaour!*" In actuality, this English transliteration of the Persian term denoted an "infidel" from the point of view of Iranian Muslims. This was one of the many variations of the English spelling of the term that had originated from *gabr* (possibly from the Arabic original *kafir* and initially applied by Muslims in reference to Zoroastrians, before gaining wider usage). Mangan then provided the Irish equivalent for the supposed Persian term as "*A Gadar*," which means a hunting dog.[152] In other words, he sought to establish a feigned etymological correspondence between Irish and Persian lexicons here, by restocking the Persian word with an invented meaning. As elaborated later in the present chapter, this seemingly snide allusion to Vallanceyan-style lexical maneuverings was not an absolute rejection by Mangan of all things Vallanceyan. In footnote 8, by clarifying that "Iran, as our readers may be aware, is the ancient name of Persia" and implicitly inferring the homophonous similarity of Iran to 'Erin,' Mangan alleged in reference to Iran: "The Turks and Arabs, however, commonly call it *Djemistan*, or the Land of *Djem*, the oldest Persian monarch on record" (i.e., the mythical Iranian king Jamshid/Jam, reputed to have once ruled the world before losing his cosmic effulgence after telling a lie—with Mangan himself no less fibbing in this poem). This was Mangan's playful display of his anonymous made-up translator's historical erudition and authority. The translator also noted that some of the lines uttered by the Qizilbash in the Persian original are "remarkably pointed," offering in footnote 7 his own made-up gibberish transliteration from "Persian" (with traces of actual Turkish).[153]

Ellen Shannon-Mangan classifies "To the Ingleezee Khafir" as one of "Mangan's final two hate poems," alongside "Siberia."[154] Other samples of Mangan's poetics of hate from the same year include his extensively reworked "translation from German" of the 1841 poem by the Prussian Georg Herwegh, titled "The Song of Hatred" ("Das Lied vom Hasse"). This latter poem, with its universal call for armed revolts against tyranny and shedding of blood to break "the chains of the world" ("Be your sharp swords early and late Red!"), and its appeal to generic concepts of "Freedom" and "Justice" for all, was selected as a representative example of Mangan's political poetry in the obituary for Mangan written by the editor of the *Democratic Review* (London), George Julian Harney (a republican socialist and former Chartist). The other poem by Mangan that Harney included in this obituary was "For Soul and Country," which according to Harney "was written by poor Mangan but a short time before his decease" (published in the Dublin paper *The Irishman*). This was an unmistakably revolutionary poem in the spirit of the most Jacobin poems in the United Irishmen's editions of *Paddy's Resource* (1795–98), even as Mangan lamented he himself may not survive to see what was certain to be the inevitable and imminent independence of Ireland, unless god had died: "My countrymen my words are weak, / My health is gone, my soul is dark / My heart is chill—."[155] As Joyce remarked later, "Mangan can tell of the beauty of hate."[156]

In "To the Ingleezee Khafir," the Qizilbash—his geographic, temporal, and cultural distance notwithstanding—was cast as sharing with Irish nationalists an antipathy toward English imperialism. But, the Qizilbash's blanket castigation of the English and of English cultural practices, such as some men shaving off their beard or wearing top hats and tailcoats, also simultaneously marked his cultural distance from the Irish, many of whom shared those same English cultural practices. The reference to the pope was a further mechanism of dissociation aimed at Irish Catholic readers of the poem. These dissonant final lines abruptly and unexpectedly disconnected any hitherto empathetic Irish Catholic reader from the Iranian Qizilbash, inducing perplexity at the insinuated association between John Bull and the papacy. This latter correlation in the poem carried a *double entendre*. Not only was the religious authority of the pope equated with that of a 'Mufti,' but the pope was also associated with both the Anglican faith of Jenkinson and with the English imperial state: "John Bull"—the latter appellation in Mangan's time also commonly used as a moniker for the English East India Company ("John Bull Company").

As depicted by Mangan in this poem, Safavid Iran was repelling the intrusive force of the very same outside interloper that had colonized Ireland, even if, as discussed below, the historical "Djaun Bool Djenkinzun" (Jenkinson) was in reality only an individual commercial agent of an English company, who was also leading a small diplomatic mission that was actually bearing a message of goodwill from the English monarch to the ruler of the powerful Safavid Empire. The poem is indicative of Mangan's wide reading and meticulous research for his subject matter. What other scholars of Mangan have thus far overlooked regarding "To the Ingleezee Khafir" (not to mention some strange speculations concerning Jenkinson's identity) is the historical setting of this poem. In fact, the same can be said of many existing historical analyses of Mangan's other oriental poems. While Mangan invented his poems, he did not always invent (at least not entirely) the historical settings for them. As already noted, "The Karamanian Exile" or "The Time of the Barmecides," for example, were based on actual historical events. Here was another shared ground between Mangan and Moore. They both engaged in detailed historical research of their subject matters, as counterintuitive as this seems in Mangan's case, given his ambivalent attitude toward both history and literary authenticity. Ironically, in the case of "To the Ingleezee Khafir" any advanced level of historical familiarity with Mangan's subject matter on the part of his readers would unravel Mangan's intended effect of the confrontation between his Iranian and English characters. "Djaun Bool Djenkinzun" was a conscious, historically informed reference to Anthony Jenkinson (d. 1611), an early English traveler to Iran in 1562–63, and in this poem metonymically standing for England (i.e., "John Bull"—an anachronistic designation here, since the character of John Bull was only invented in the early eighteenth century). In 1846 John Bull was also appearing in British narratives and visual depictions of the Irish famine as the ostensibly caring Britain concerned with and aiding the Irish, who had condemned themselves to famine and were in need of the moral, financial, and rational guidance of the English—as in the case of cartoons appearing in *Punch* (London).[157] Mangan even took care to spell Jenkinson's name in a manner evocative of Persian pronunciation of the name (and/or Turkish pronunciation, given the Turkic ethnicity of the Iranian interlocuter in the poem). This unfamiliar pronunciation to English ears was yet another means of establishing not only the foreignness of the Iranian Qizilbash ('Meer Djafrit') for Irish readers but also, and more significantly, through an elliptical effect, the foreignness of the English Jenkinson in Iran (i.e., the foreignness of the English in Ireland; with English here standing for England and not the Irish of English ethnic descent). During his travel to Iran, Jenkinson represented the Muscovy Company, an English private joint-stock chartered company established in 1555 with a monopoly for trading in "Russian" territories. He was also on a diplomatic mission from Queen Elizabeth I (r. 1558–1603) to the Safavid court in Iran, with his diplomatic deputation being rebuffed by the Iranian ruler Shah Tahmasp I. Jenkinson's travel narrative initially appeared in a multi-volume collection of English travel accounts published by Richard Hakluyt between 1598 and 1600 (*The Principal Navigations, Voyages, Traffiques, and Discoveries of the English Nation*).[158] Among other English-language sources by the time Mangan composed this poem, a brief account of Jenkinson's diplomatic mission, a reproduction of his letter of introduction to the Iranian court from Queen Elizabeth (taken from Hakluyt's book), and a description of the Iranian ruler's snubbing of the English embassy had appeared in the first volume of Sir John Malcolm's influential 1815 *The History of Persia* (reprinted in 1829), which also referred to the Qizilbash (spelled "Kûzel-bash" and "Kuzzil-bâsh" in the 1815 and 1829 editions respectively). Malcolm also recounted that the shah had reportedly inquired of Jenkinson whether he was a "Gaur" (i.e., an infidel) or a Muslim, with Gaur being another variation of Mangan's '*Gaour!*' (appearing as "Gower" in Jenkinson's original account). Malcolm added that Jenkinson was treated by the shah as an "unclean" "infidel" and then noted the shah's "bigoted attachment to his religion."[159] The discussion of the 'Kuzzil-bâsh' in Malcolm's book (translated as 'red heads') occurs in the pages just preceding the account of Jenkinson's admittance to, and speedy dismissal from, the Iranian royal court.

Mangan's allusion to the pope in the poem was to Pope Urban VIII (Maffeo Barbarini). Mangan explained in footnote 9 of the poem: "From this line it is clear that these verses cannot be older than the earlier part of the 17th century, as Pope Urban VIII (the last of the name) deceased in 1644."[160] Given that Urban VIII did not assume the office of papacy until 1623, more than half a century after Jenkinson's travel to Iran, the Qizilbash in Mangan's poem should not have known of the future pope. The appearance of Pope Urban VIII in this poem is further evidence of Mangan's characteristic style of generating ambivalence about the authenticity (in this case also the historicity) of his poems by introducing deliberate narrative and/or historical, conceptual, and other disruptions and disjuncture, as a means of undermining uncomplicated engagement with history, or of subverting the readers' expectation of straightforward narrative coherence in the text. Incidentally, Pope Urban VIII was first mentioned in connection with Jenkinson's travel only in a footnote by the editors of the 1886 reprint of Jenkinson's account (long after Mangan's death), with the pope's name spelled "Maphaeus Barberino." In this edition of Jenkinson's voyage, the pope was solely mentioned in connection with one of his uncles (Raphael), who had conducted business in Russia about the time Jenkinson was carrying out his duties for the Moscovy Company in Russia, prior to crossing over into Iran.[161] This reference to the pope would, therefore, not have been available to Mangan; although Mangan may somehow have realized the connection between the pope and Raphael Barberino, who was mentioned by Jenkinson in his original travel account. There is also no mention of the pope in Malcolm's history; nor, for that matter, is there any mention of Qizilbash in Jenkinson's account of his travel through Iran. But, Pope Urban VIII's name had resonance in the history of Anglo-Irish and Protestant-Catholic relations in Ireland. It was in the last years of the pope's life that a Catholic uprising broke out in Ireland (beginning in 1641), with the pope subsequently extending his religious endorsement to the Catholic forces in what became the Confederate War of 1642–52.

Other than Malcolm's *The History of Persia*, references to the Qizilbash had appeared in other English language and European sources by the time Mangan's poem appeared, For instance, in 1828 the Scottish traveler and author James Baillie Fraser[162] had published his three-volume *The Kuzzilbash: A Tale of Khorasan*. This was a fictional work, purportedly a translation of an authentic Persian manuscript by a Qizilbash, named "Ismael Khan," who supposedly had served in the military force of Nader Shah, the founder of the Afsharid dynasty in Iran (r. 1736–47) after the collapse of the Safavid dynasty and an "Afghan" interregnum. Oddly, Fraser gave the birth year of Ismael Khan as 1740 (i.e., seven years before the assassination of Nader Shah), possibly a deliberate move by Fraser to alert his readers of the inauthenticity of his purported translation—in a move similar to Mangan's later invented "original" works and pseudo-translations, including "To the Ingleezee Khafir". Fraser, in clarifying the meaning of *Kuzzilbash* in his "Introduction" referred to Malcolm's *The History of Persia*.[163] It is indeed likely Mangan was familiar with Fraser's work, given the similarity between a passage from this book and an 1839 poem by Mangan that was set in a different historical time and location (although this could have been purely coincidental, or they both may have relied on another source). The opening stanza of Mangan's 1839 "The Time of the Barmecides" reads:

> My eyes are dimmed, my hair is grey, / I am bowed by the weight of years; / I would I were stretched in my bed of clay, / With my long-lost youth's compeers! / For back to the Past, though the thought brings woe, / My memory ever glides— / To a long, long time, long time ago, / To the time of the Barmecides.[164]

The opening lines of the very first chapter of Fraser's 1828 story read:

> In the name of the most merciful God, &c. &c. [...] My beard is now white with the snow of age, my eyes are dim, and my arms have lost the vigour of youth: but the wisdom bought by many perils, may avail to warn the unwary from the snares of destruction, and teach them how to pluck the rose of safety from among the rude thorns of danger.
>
> The counsels of a wise and valued friend induced me to accustom myself, from an early age, to commit to writing an account of such remarkable occurrences as fell under my observation from time to time [...] became the means of fixing passing events upon the tablet of my memory, and enabled me to amuse the friends of my latter years, with the tales of days long since gone by.[165]

Qizilbash characters had appeared in other poems by Mangan prior to "To the Ingleezee Khafir," as in the case of the 1845 "Bagdad is Taken," attributed to an Ottoman poet "Moostafa Kaikidjee" (Qizilbash spelled as "Kizzilbash" on that occasion). This poem centered around the Ottoman capture of Baghdad from Safavid Iran in 1638 during the reign of the Safavid ruler Shah Safi. Another Qizilbash made an appearance in Mangan's 1847 'translation' from the Persian of the poem "Jealousy," attributed to 'Selim-il-Anagh' (on this occasion spelled "Kuzzilbash," identical to Fraser's spelling).[166]

It would have been readily apparent to Mangan's readers that the "Ingleezee Khafir" of the title (i.e., the English 'kafir'/infidel) and the "vile Ferindjee" (the despised "farangi," i.e., European/Western Christian foreigner—the Persian pronunciation of the Arabic term derived from "Franks") were allusions to the post sixteenth-century Anglican Ascendency in Ireland; notwithstanding Qizilbash's confusion regarding the pope, and the fact that the Qizilbash was not directly targeting Jenkinson's faith ('Thine own Mufti, Pope Urban, / May scorn thine abuse!'). Moreover, any of Mangan's readers with some familiarity with the historical setting of the poem (Jenkinson's mission to the Safavid court in the sixteenth century) would have known that Jenkinson represented the English monarch Queen Elizabeth I on his visit to Iran, with Elizabeth's long reign (1558–1603) encompassing such events as the failed anti-English (Geraldine) Desmond Rebellions in Ireland and the concomitant anti-Catholic establishment of Protestant plantations in Ireland (including the Plantation of Munster), the extensive religious persecution of Catholics throughout the queen's dominion, and the failed Nine Years' War (a.k.a. Tyrone's Rebellion) led by Hugh O'Neill and other Irish clan leaders, which resulted in further expansion of English hegemony in Ireland. It is even possible that the repeated phrase "Khizzilbash turban," which Mangan explained in a footnote as denoting the red (scarlet) turban worn by Qizilbash forces, was an allusion to the standard of O'Neill (Earl of Tyrone) which consisted of the Red Hand.

Mangan's Appropriation of Truncated Histories and Recollective Disenchantments

As noted before, Islam (regardless of its internal divisions) generally had not been depicted in a sympathetic light in Irish nationalist literature prior to Mangan, even though Moore in "Letter VI" of his 1813 *Intercepted Letters* expressed a parity between the persecution of Catholics in the United Kingdom and the minority Sunni population of contemporary Iran. Otherwise, Moore in different sections of his 1817 literary magnum opus *Lalla Rookh* presented a generic Islam in either unsympathetic or antipathetic light, in contradistinction to Zoroastrianism in the case of 'Iran' or to Hinduism in the case of the Indian subcontinent—even if any overall castigation of Islam in this work was blurred by interspersed prose sections in which Moore's alter-ego, the poet Feramorz (/Aliris), was also identified as a Muslim (albeit proud of the Zoroastrian heritage of his homeland), as well as by periodic condemnation of inter-denominational tensions and intolerance among Muslims (notably in reference to Lalla Rookh's chamberlain Fadladeen, portrayed as a Sunni bigot). Similarly, in "The Clan of Mac Caura," published two years after the failed Young Ireland uprising of 1848 by Denis Florence MacCarthy (a former Young Irelander), the ongoing Irish resistance to English rule was allegorized as the failed resistance of Iran's Zoroastrians ("Guebre") against Arab-Muslim invaders, notwithstanding both MacCarthy's and Moore's commitment to non-sectarian varieties of Irish nationalism. MacCarthy wrote:

> Proud should thy heart beat, descendant of Heber,
> Lofty thy head as the shrines of the Guebre,
> Like them are the halls of thy forefathers shattered,
> Like theirs is the wealth of thy palaces scattered.
> Their fire is extinguished—thy banner long furled—
> But how proud were ye both in the dawn of the world!
> And should both fade away, oh! What heart would not sorrow
> O'er the towers of the Guebre—the name of Mac Caura![167]

MacCarthy, similar to Moore and some other Irish nationalists, was also convinced of direct or indirect ties between Ireland and Iran in ancient times ("But how proud were ye both in the dawn of the world!"), adding that the "Shrines of the Guebre" in the poem (also appearing as 'towers of the Guebre') represented "The Round Towers" of Ireland, and noting: "The Mac Carthys trace their origin to Heber Fionn, the eldest son of Milesius, King of Spain, through Oilioll Olium, King of Munster, in the third century."[168]

Mangan, although explicitly casting the predominantly 'Twelver' (*ithna' ashari*) Shi'i religion of sixteenth-century Safavid Iran as the principle cultural marker of his Qizilbash character, who was purportedly defying English imperialism ("Old Moslim like me, / With my Khizzilbash turban!"), nevertheless upended any blasé sympathy between Irish Catholics and the Muslim Qizilbash by way of throwing Pope Urban VIII into the mix, while also casting the Qizilbash as a religious bigot. To borrow Clifford James Geertz's concept of "thick description," and leaving aside the anachronistic allusion to Pope Urban in Mangan's poem, the final section of the poem exposes the core religious bigotry of the Qizilbash by taking a closer and deeper look at his cultural sensibility, not unlike the anti-Protestant bigotry of many Catholics who had rebelled in Ireland in 1641 (in the leadup to what became the later Confederate War of 1642–52), among numerous other examples of such bigotry in Irish history—leaving aside here the disparity of power relations between a Qizilbash, who was serving the mighty Safavid Empire, and Irish Catholics subjected to England's imperial yoke and Protestant persecution. Looked at through the lens of multi-layered inter-cultural *translation*, Mangan's "To the Ingleezee Khafir" is riven with textually destabilizing and historically and culturally ambivalent referentialities.

In Moore's "The Fire-Worshippers" and MacCarthy's "The Clan of Mac Caura," Iran of seventh century served as a surrogate setting for the seemingly repetitive historical episodes of doomed, albeit venerated, Irish armed resistance to English imperialism. Unlike Moore's or MacCarthy's accounts of the ultimately abortive Iranian-Zoroastrian resistance to foreign aggressors, Mangan's Qizilbash in "To the Ingleezee Khafir" had scorned and repelled the ostensible foreign threat. Mangan's Iranian historical setting was also dissimilar to that of Moore's *Lalla Rookh* by utilizing an actual historical episode of *English encounter* with Iran (albeit blown out of proportion metonymically and in terms of Mangan's insinuated English intent). Moreover, Mangan's Iranian castigator of English imperialism was a Muslim, rather than a Zoroastrian (in Moore's "The Fire-Worshippers") or a follower of al-Muqanna's heterodox religion (in Moore's "The Veiled Prophet"). Mangan's Qizilbash was, no less, a Shi'i Muslim, similar to the majority of Mangan's and Moore's contemporary Iranians, with Moore having equated contemporary Shi'i persecution of Iran's minority Sunni Muslim population with Anglican persecution of Catholics in the United Kingdom. On the other hand, earlier in an 1845 pseudo-translation by Mangan from the German titled "The Last Words of Al-Hassan" and attributed to "a Heyden" (the German term "Heiden" meaning "heathen"), Mangan had cast the Shi'i as victims of the puritanical Sunni sect in Arabia ("Wahabee") and of the Sunni Ottoman state ("Osmânlee"), while allegorically representing the Anglican persecution of Catholics. "The Last Words of Al-Hassan" jointly drew on Mangan's contemporary German poet and playwright Heinrich Heine's 1822 Romantic poem and famous 1821 play (published in 1823), both titled "Almansor." In Heine's play, the lead character of the tragedy, Almansor, and his servant Hassan bemoan the Christian devastation and desecration of Muslim holy places and the burning of Muslim books (including the Qur'an) in the aftermath of the Christian conquest of the last Muslim stronghold in Iberia in 1492 (i.e., the fall of Granada). The 'Last Words,' in Mangan's title, alludes to Hassan's now famous statement (albeit not his last) in Heine's play: "Das war ein Vorspiel nur, dort wo man Bücher verbrennt, verbrennt man auch am Ende Menschen" ("It was only a prelude, where books are burned, in the end people too will be burned").[169] In Mangan's 1845 poem, the insinuated Christian bigotry of Heine's play was transformed into an inner-religious sectarian bigotry among Muslims, with a clear allusion to sectarian tensions among Protestants and Catholics in Ireland. In this poem, in which prophet Muhammad's cousin and son-in-law Ali signifies Shi'i Muslims, the "Venerable Stone" of Ka'ba in Mecca is very likely a reference to the ceremonial coronation Stone of Destiny (Lia Fáil) on the Hill of Tara that was once the seat of Ireland's High Kings:

I have seen the standard of Ali stained
   With the blood of the Brave and Free
And the Kaaba's profaned
   By the truculent Wahabee.
[...]

My bride in the harem of the Osmânlee,
   Myself in the Lampless Land!
      'Llah Hu!
My bride in the harem of the Osmânlee,
   Myself in the Dark Dark Land!

We weep for the Noble who perish young,
   Like flowers before their bloom—
[...]
By the dread firmàn of Heaven's Deewàn—
All are born for the Dark Dark land![170]

Here were again some of the complications and contradictions of using *other people's histories* as a means of commenting on Ireland's history, given the tenuousness of historical equivalences. The Shi'i or the Sunni (not unlike Moore's and MacCarthy's Zoroastrians), depending on location and time frame, could not indefinitely function as a stand-in for the Catholic experience in post-sixteenth century Ireland or in nineteenth-century United Kingdom. Such allegoric maneuvers could only be sustained by taking selective slices from those other histories and also selectively applying them to one's own history (leaving aside here whether anyone can actually claim the distant past as one's *own* history).

The narrative structure of "To the Ingleezee Khafir" impeded any direct cross-identification by Irish nationalists (and Catholics among them in particular) with Mangan's Iranian Qizilbash. Moreover, the Qizilbash's imputed effective deterrence of English imperialism could not be transferred to any moment in Ireland's extant history of resistance to English rule. Mangan's poem served as a roundabout Irish nationalist gratification at the humiliation of Ireland's haughty English rulers by an Iranian in the sixteenth century. The Irish nationalist allegory in this case could only function as a temporary and vicarious revanchist salve and a comic relief for Mangan's contemporary Irish nationalists, while at best encouraging Irish nationalist confrontation with English imperialism. Such an allegoric take on Mangan's poem also required total ignorance of, or conscious suspension of knowledge about, Iranian history in the sixteenth century and subsequent history of Anglo-Iranian relations (particularly since the start of the nineteenth century). Iran's sixteenth-century Safavid state (founded in 1501) was an expansionist imperial power, unlike Ireland of pre-Norman conquests (leaving aside that "Ireland" was not a unified territory at the time). The Qizilbash tribal forces had aided the Safavid seizure of power and territorial expansion. The Qizilbash also represented the brutality with which the ethnically Turkic Safavid dynasty had carried out the initial wave of its compulsory mass conversion to Twelver (*ithna' ashari*) Shi'i Islam of Iran's population, who at the time had been predominantly Sunni (regardless of whether they were ethnically Persian). Within a few generations, the overwhelming majority of Iranians had embraced Shi'i Islam, whether through compulsion or due to other as of yet unclear voluntary motives. In other words, rather than corresponding to the Irish experience under English imperial rule, Mangan's Qizilbash and the Safavid state he represented were analogous to the English state in the sixteenth century and its attempts following the English Reformation to eradicate Catholicism throughout the British Isles, and in Ireland in particular (albeit failing to match the success rate of the Safavid conversion policy, with the majority of the Irish remaining Catholic). Mangan's poem clearly did not take into account the domestic Iranian symbolism of the religiously repressive and intolerant Qizilbash protagonist confronting the English "Khafir." The same Qizilbash, who had shored up the powerful Safavid state, capable of unifying 'Iran' and resisting much of the subsequent outside incursions into the country (though not all), was an instrument of Twelver Shi'i intolerance toward Iran's Sunni and other non-Twelver Shi'i Muslim, Zoroastrian, Jewish, various Christian, and other religious communities. The Qizilbash forces, as the main military arm of the Safavid state, were on par with the army of the Anglicizing English state after the [Protestant] English Reformation of 1534 under Henry VIII, a policy pursued with more vehemence in Ireland under Elizabeth I and reaching its pinnacle during the puritanical Cromwellian Commonwealth Republic in the mid-seventeenth century. An in-depth historical investigation of Mangan's selected moment in Iranian history (again to use Geertz's concept of 'thick description') would unravel any intended Irish nationalist narrative trajectory in the poem, while also undermining the very notion of historically stable categories of nation and nationhood, or of enduring national and cultural identities and core characteristics of a presumed nation.

The Islam appearing as the alien religious marker of expansionist imperialism in the first three verse sections of Moore's *Lalla Rookh* had become, in the setting of Mangan's Iran of the sixteenth century, an essential fabric of mainstream Iranian identity, first in the form of Sunni Islam (in former 'Iranian' territories ruled by various Arab, Turkic, and other groups prior to the Safavid seizure of power) and subsequently in the form of Twelver Shi'i Islam, following the Safavid consolidation of power and (re-)unification of much of former Iranian lands. Not many generations after the initial Arab-Muslim occupation of Iran in the seventh century, most Iranians had already converted to Islam. In addition, Iran had ceased to exist as an independent territorial state from the seventh century until the Safavid dynasty in the sixteenth century, with its population by the sixteenth century being ethnically even more diverse than in the past, following periods of Arab, Turkic, Mongol, and again Turkic rule and other invasions or coerced and peaceful population resettlements—the latter also variously including Armenians and Georgians from the Caucasus or mercantile communities from the Indian subcontinent. It was, in other words, the Safavids (an ethnically non-Persian group) who "revived" Iran as a unified territorial state after many centuries of so-called "foreign" domination. The Safavid state itself was an expansionist imperial power in the sixteenth century, while the Iran of Mangan's own time in the nineteenth century was a much smaller territory than the ancient Persian Empire of Moore's and MacCarthy's poems or the Safavid Empire of Mangan's poem—with many other population groups in the territories adjoining Iran in the nineteenth century having as valid a claim to pre- and post-seventh-century 'Iranian' historical and cultural heritage, including ancient legends and Persian poetry. After the seventh-century Arab-Muslim domination, the majority of the population of formerly Iranian territories had gradually embraced not only a new religion but also a new (Arabic) script, and Persian language had become saturated with Arabic loan-words and sounds, as well as a range of vocabulary borrowed from other languages. All of these factors further underscore the historical malleability and syncretic underpinnings of all presumed cultural and national identities. Then again, as Paul Ricoeur has noted, "everything that compounds the fragility of identity also proves to be an opportunity for the manipulation of memory, mainly through ideology."[171]

Moreover, relations between England and the Safavid state had not been fundamentally antithetical over time. While Anthony Jenkinson's official mission to the Safavid court proved abortive, the Safavid state was later highly receptive to private English overtures, as in the case of commercial undertakings by the English East India Company (EIC; founded in 1600), which was granted special trading privileges in Iran in 1616—at the time posing no apparent military-political threat to Iran's sovereignty. The Safavid state even relied on the EIC's naval assistance (along with that of the Dutch East India Company) to drive out the Portuguese from the Persian Gulf. Safavid royal decrees (*farmans*) for trading privileges were granted to the EIC in 1616, 1622, and 1623 by Shah Abbas I (r. 1587–1629) as he prepared to attack and expel the Portuguese forces from Hormuz Island in the Persian Gulf with EIC's military aid. The Iranian state and the EIC subsequently shared the Portuguese spoils and arranged for joint collection of customs on the island, and the EIC also received preferential status in Iran's silk trade.[172] These were not the only examples of the Shi'i Safavid state's tolerance of Mangan's English 'Ferindjee' infidels. Besides private English commercial undertakings in Iran by the EIC and the presence of other European merchants across the country, and military cooperation with the EIC, the Safavid court of Shah Abbas I engaged a small band of private English military adventurers led by the Sherley (also spelled Shirley) brothers, Robert and Anthony. The brothers also served the Safavid state in diplomatic capacity.

As already noted, Mangan's "To the Ingleezee Khafir" ultimately relied on an inherently ruptured cross-historical affinity between sixteenth-century Iran and Ireland *since the sixteenth century* through the poem's reference to the pope during the Qizilbash's scorning of the English. Similarly, the poem's underlying defiant tone could only sustain its comic effect if the forward passage of historical time could be suspended. Had Mangan in his distinct use of Iran/Erin allegory taken a broader slice of Iranian history, extending to the time when he was composing his poem in 1846, his readers would have encountered an Iran that was increasingly succumbing to competing Russian and British imperial leverage. Britain had waged a successful military offensive against Iran in 1838 (with Irish soldiers, no less, in the ranks of the invading British imperial force), and Russia had annexed vast territories after 1804. Moreover, both European powers enjoyed special economic privileges in the country and diplomatically intervened in Iranian affairs, including in the process of royal succession.

Any sentiment of lasting elation at the Qizilbash's bravado in Mangan's poem against the English intruder required a truncated and frozen recollection of history. Such fragmented and warped utilizations of historical time are in fact a symptom of all national histories and are also often essential for representing "enduring" *nationalist* traumas of the past. All acts of recollection require degrees of simultaneous forgetting and, at least temporary, dissociation from other memories. As already noted, Mangan's employment in the Ordnance Department had reinforced his continually dissecting approach to history. The marvel of the Qizilbash's cultural self-confidence in Mangan's poem and the Qizilbash's complacent sneering victory, in purportedly thwarting the extension of English hegemony over Iran, only held its power of enchantment without the infusion of other range of synchronic or diachronic historical retrospection (whether of the Safavid state's religious intolerance and expansionist nature, or of Iran's subsequent capitulation to English and Russian imperial influence, etc.). Furthermore, as gratifying as the idea of an Iranian Qizilbash reviling an alleged agent of English imperialism in the past may have been for Mangan's nationalist readers, the poem was yet another reminder of continued English domination of Ireland and the repeatedly failed attempts by the Irish to rid themselves of the English imperial yoke. In Mangan's post-1846 militant nationalist poetry of 'hate,' there was a limit to creative plagiarism, self-plagiarism, and subversion of authenticity. If Mangan were to directly allude to English imperial aggression in Ireland without recourse to metaphoric casting of England (as Moore or MacCarthy, too, had done by substituting Arab-Muslim Empires for England), Mangan would have had to completely invent some episode of (long-term) successful Irish repulsion of English colonization; offering an entirely fictional historical account that would have been immediately recognized as inauthentic by his Irish and British readers, while also slighting Irish nationalist historical memory. Hence the appeal and advantage of turning to *fragments* from *histories of other 'nations'* for trouncing English imperial aggression.

To use Pierre Nora's concept of "Tyranny of Memory," albeit applied in a different manner and context here, Ireland's unmediated history of encounters with England exercised a 'Tyranny of Memory' over competing Irish nationalist projects. While past uprisings and campaigns, particularly nonsectarian episodes since the emergence of the United Irishmen in 1791, were commemorated as acts of resistance and heroism by Irish nationalists, these were also simultaneously reminders of repeated failure and as of yet deferred victory. The land was, after all, still occupied, even if under the always fluid spatial-political and social configurations of colonialism and its nationalist rivals. The allure of this recollective enterprise for nationalist projects was the forging of a direct correlation between "traces" of the past and "obligation" of the present, to borrow Paul Ricoeur's concepts in regard to memory. Ricoeur notes that the "work of memory, work of mourning" entails

> the twofold aspect of duty, as imposing itself on desire from outside and exerting a constraint experienced subjectively as obligation. [...] Extracting the exemplary value from traumatic memories, it is justice that turns memory into a project; and it is this same project of justice that gives the form of the future of the imperative to the duty of memory.

Hence, it can be said the labor of memory in the Irish nationalist setting was underlain with the desired interchange in the present between what Ricoeur terms 'trace,' "heritage," "debt," and 'obligation.'[173] To add a spatial dimension to Ricoeur's formulation as well, it can be said nationalists were also committed to replacing the geography of colonialism with that of nationalism, as different strands of nationalism envisioned a self-governing or a completely independent Irish nation. Just as in Moore's fictional *Lalla Rookh* future generations of Iranian nationalists would visit the rock upon which Hafed had lay dying (as a nationalist 'site of memory,' to borrow Pierre Nora's concept), in order to keep alive the desire for the liberation of their homeland from Arab-Muslim conquerors, so were Irish locations (and artifacts and objects) instrumentally imbued with the power of nationalist recollection and were hoped to continually proliferate the desire for 'national' liberation. As Moore put it in an already quoted section of "The Fire-Worshippers" following Hafed's death: 'And hither bards and heroes oft / Shall come in secret pilgrimage, / And bring their warrior sons, and tell / The wondering boys where Hafed fell; / And swear them on those lone remains / Of their lost country's ancient fanes.' But, as Aleida Assmann has noted in the context of colonial and postcolonial spaces:

> It is often the very same site that yields contrasting and irreconcilable narratives, depending on the point of view of the historical agents and non-agents. [...] This contestation can take different shapes. There is the polarity between the hegemonic and imperial narrative versus a subversive or liberating counter-narrative; there are usable and unusable, self-reinforcing and awkward narratives; and there is even the asymmetry of ardent remembrance practised on one side and total amnesia on the other. We will have to distinguish not only between the colonial power and the colonized, but also between political, that is, imperial or national memory on the one hand, and social and individual memories on the other. While political memories define, support, and enforce a collective identity, social memories generally do not; social memories are embodied—they exist as a network between individuals, they are much more varied, and lack an effectively homogenized symbolic shape and profile. Social memory affords room for internal variations whereas political memory gains its clear profile in a context of struggle and contestation.
>
> To distinguish between different shapes of memory, then, we have to pay attention to symbolic strategies. The creation of effective and affective symbols is of paramount importance for binding individuals together and compelling them to commit themselves to common goals. Without such symbols and commitments, there is little chance of constructing long-term memories and collective identities. In the creation of symbols, memory often draws more heavily on imagination than on historiography. From the point of view of memory, the question is not so much what exactly happened in the past, but how the event can become representative of an enduring experience. In a similar way, the *lieux de mémoire* [sites of memory] project the past into the present. They are constructions of past events which are made accessible in the present. The *lieux de mémoire*, then, are not so much about how history actually took place, but how history is rooted in the hearts, minds, and imaginations of subsequent generations.[174]

Irish nationalist literary and other forms of commemoration of failed struggles of the past not only pointed to the heroism of previous generations of nationalists, their willingness to sacrifice themselves for the next generations, and the continued desire on the part of the Irish to free themselves from England's domination, but were also intended to cultivate in Irish minds the idea of an inherited 'national' debt and of an obligation to fulfill the ultimate mission of those who sacrificed in the past for the sake of both present and future generations. Militant Irish nationalist alignments of the interconnected past-present-future concept of debt-leading-to-obligation generally occluded the periodic successes of moderate nationalists and/or non-violent pro-Catholic rights campaigns by the likes of Daniel O'Connell. Discussing Martin Heidegger's *Being and Time* (1927), Ricoeur further clarified:

> the idea of debt is not a simple corollary to the idea of trace; the trace has to be followed back; it is a pure referral of the past to the past; it signifies, it does not obligate. In as much as it obligates, the debt does not exhaust itself in the idea of burden either: it relates the being affected by the past to the potentiality-of-being turned toward the future. In [Reinhart] Koselleck's vocabulary, it relates the space of experience to the horizon of expectation.[175]

If Ireland's history lacked examples of effective victories over the English aggressor, one could rummage the history of others in search of such an example to at least dispel the myth of England's invincibility.[176] Mangan's fictional Qizilbash of "To the Ingleezee Khafir," by way of turning to *world history*, was intended to serve as further confirmation that England had been defeated elsewhere (*there and then*) and hence could also be eventually defeated in the as of yet unwritten future chapter of Ireland's national history (*here and then*).[177]

Mangan's National Hymn: Ireland's Self-Liberation and Iran's Aye-Travailing Gnomes

The foremost specimen of historical fragmentation in Mangan's works was his own country, the ancient past of which even lacked a unanimous general account among nationalists committed to corroborating Ireland's Golden Age. This was not a mere symptom of selective inclusion and exclusion of highly contested past events as part of a carefully crafted nationalist strategy of partial and instrumentalist recall of the past. Mangan's view of insurmountable challenges in recovering Ireland's distant past with any degree of certitude was reinforced during his years of employment at the Ordnance Department. Ireland's ancient past was a blank book in the pages of which generations of monks and later antiquarians and historians had hurriedly inscribed, crossed out and redacted, edited, and re-inscribed discordant, and at times ultimately confounding and indecipherable, renditions and interpretations of that past. Existing accounts of Ireland's ancient past were admittedly at best disjointed, contested, and largely unverifiable patchworks from the perspective of the latest standards of historical and archaeological methodology endorsed by the likes of Petrie and John O'Donovan. Ireland was a nation-in-the-making that admittedly lacked its own commonly held foundational creation story. Many present-day commentators have ascertained that Mangan was at best dismissive of, if not cynical toward, wide-ranging oriental theories of Irish origins spawned by the likes of Vallancey. Mangan's friend and colleague at the Ordnance

Survey, John O'Donovan, related a similar opinion of Mangan in an 1834 letter to another colleague. O'Donovan reported that when he had expressed his concern to Mangan that the survey's findings "will be condemned in the North by all those who are tinged with the notions of Vallancey and [William] Beauford," Mangan's advice was "to refute them, 'first break into immoderate horselaugh, and then suddenly altering from gay to grave, from lively to severe, with one immortal and terrific frown desire them to go to the Devil for drivelling twaddlers.'"[178] But, Mangan's engagement with oriental theories of Irish origins was far more complex, tortuous, and variegated. He was certainly scathing of the meandering and contorted techniques of Vallancey and the like. Yet, Mangan obstinately refused to endorse Petrie's and O'Donovan's verdict of the Christian-era origin of the Round Towers. Mangan stated as much in an entry on George Petrie in his 1849 series "Sketches of Modern Irish Writers," even if in a jocular tone:

> I am dissident [...] from Dr. Petrie's theory of the origin and uses of the Irish Pillar Towers. That they are of Cha[l]dean construction, and were intended by their architects to promote the objects of astrological science, are points upon which I have satisfied myself.[179]

Even if we treat Mangan's accreditation of the Chaldean origin of the Round Towers as a form of irony, he was nevertheless sincere about his divergence from Petrie's theory. The astrological, or more properly astronomical, function of the Round Towers at some stage in their use, which Mangan, similar to many earlier antiquarians or the likes of Canon Ulick Joseph Bourke later in the century (in his 1875 *The Aryan Origins of the Gaelic Race and Language*) called 'Pillar Towers,' had been widely proposed by a diverse group of former antiquarians from Charles O'Conor to Vallancey, John Lanigan, Henry O'Brien, and Thomas Moore, as the singular, or coexisting, or modified later range of functions assigned to the towers. Here Mangan was alluding to the influence of Vallancey's *initial* version of oriental roots of ancient Irish civilization, prior to Vallancey's turn to the predominantly Iranian model of Irish origins. Vallancey had even still maintained in his 1786 *A Vindication of the Ancient History of Ireland* that "The original religion of the Irish, (who were Scythians and Persians) was *Sabism*, which beg[a]n in *Chaldea* and spread into Scythia, Media, and Persia," with two distinct Sabian modes of worship allegedly brought to Ireland by the Tuatha de Danann and Milesians respectively: one "with" and the other "without" images. Vallancey had used the distinct terms "tower" and "pillar stone" to designate the different functions of the towers as fire temples and of the pillar stones as structures for charting "the revolution of the planets."[180] Incidentally, Henry O'Brien had used the terms "Pillar Towers," "Round Pillars," and "Round Towers" interchangeably in his 1834 *The Round Towers*, although Mangan made no mention of O'Brien.[181] David Lloyd may have been too hasty when concluding:

> collapsed towers which recur so frequently in Mangan's writings in turn figure the collapse of the myth of origins that had been associated with the celebrated round towers of Ireland. Petrie's *Ecclesiastical Architecture of Ireland*, by proving that the origin of the towers was monastic rather than prehistoric, exploded what both Thomas Davis and an anonymous writer

in the *Dublin University Magazine* regarded as the middle-class faith that the towers revealed the origins in "indefinite antiquity" of Irish civilization. A more entire fatality of Petrie's findings was the antiquarian Henry O'Brien's *The Round Towers of Ireland* [...]. O'Brien's argument [...] reads like an elaborate parody of the fundamental forms of nationalist thinking, while his etymological methods seem like a burlesque of the "science of origins." What O'Brien's Vallanceyan philological researches "unveil" is not only the Oriental origins of the Gaelic language but, furthermore, the origins of the round towers in the phallic worship of Edenic man, which indicates the real meaning of the Tree of Knowledge and the cause of the Fall.[182]

On the other hand, Ellen Shannon-Mangan has characterized Mangan's rejection of Petrie's verdict on the Round Towers, as a tongue-in-cheek stance. She writes, "Mangan seems never to have felt as close to Petrie as he clearly did to O'Donovan," adding:

his apparent contrariness in disagreeing with Petrie and siding with his opponents on the Oriental origin of the round towers of Ireland was the whole joke. While the intent of these passages may be misunderstood now, Petrie would have seen them as making fun of their old enemy and antiquarian rival, Sir Thomas [*sic*; should be "William"] Betham, and his method of unraveling the mystery of the round towers and other ancient marvels.[183]

O'Donovan's previously mentioned 1834 letter merely reflects Mangan's periodic playful jostling with Vallancey's excessive and meandering philological, methodological, and other cogitations. But, Mangan did not entirely reject Vallancey's historical inferences, nor the validity of oriental origins of the Irish.

While parodying Vallancey in some of his works, and anxious not to subject himself to the ridicule of his Petrieite cohorts at the Ordnance Survey, Mangan still tenaciously flirted with Vallancey's various theories of Irish origins as late as 1848. In that year it was Vallancey's later model of the predominantly Iranian origin of Ireland's Golden Age that surfaced in Mangan's "Irish National Hymn" (discussed below). Mangan's 1848 allusion to the Iranian origin of Irish civilization should not be conflated with his invented translations of oriental poetry, or with his interest in oriental literatures in general. Yet, as previously noted, the appearance of the line "IRAN's nation and race" in Mangan's 1846 "To the Ingleezee Khafir" already marked his ongoing conflicted engagement with Vallancey's later theory of Irish origins. In addition, Vallanceyan-style etymological equivalences were notably present in Mangan's post-1846 decidedly Irish nationalist poems and in a much less flippant and non-sardonic manner than before. Mangan injected oriental terminology and/or imagery into a few of his famine-era 'translations' from the Irish, as in the 1846 "A Vision of Connaught in the Thirteenth Century," which first appeared in *The Nation* and under Mangan's own name. In a footnote to this poem, he explained the line that reads 'O, my Lord and Khan' in the following manner: "Identical with the Irish Ceann, Head, or Chief; but I the rather gave him the Oriental title, as really fancying myself in one of the regions of Araby the Blest."[184] Here, Mangan was again deliberately melding Turkish, Persian, and Arabic under the rubric of 'Araby,' as he had done in his previously mentioned 1840 reference in "Literæ Orientales. No. IV" to Vallancey's theory of Irish origins: 'every Irishman is an Arab.' In another footnote to a much earlier 'translation' from the Turkish ("Panegyric of Sultan Suleiman"), Mangan had elaborated: "*Khan* (chief, head—precisely our Hiherno-Celtic Ceann), is Tartarian" (i.e., Turkic).[185] The term 'khan' was in fact originally Mongol-Turkic and was also used in Turkish and Persian to denote a tribal chief.

Mangan's engagement with the Orient consisted of two distinct modes of strategic self-orientations. One was his literary utilization of the genre of Romantic oriental-style literature in English; which in Mangan's case also entailed his attempted avoidance and, when not possible, his concealment of reliance on existing oriental-style "English" literature, in addition to German and other sources, notwithstanding his occasional references to English authors. This is most evident in his "Literæ Orientales" series, as well as in "Anthologia Germanica" series and "A Polyglott Anthology." Long before William Butler Yeats in 1893 called for an "Irish literature separate and independent from British culture,"[186] Mangan had already attempted such a maneuver by turning to Irish, Oriental, German, and a wide range of other literary cultures, even if inventing many of his translations.[187] He had circumvented as much as possible direct engagement with, and grounding in, 'British culture' and literature. As Richard Haslam has pointed out, a similar style of winding detours and evasion is evident in Mangan's posthumously published (and unfinished) autobiography in connection with his adaptation from the Protestant Anglo-Irish Charles Robert Maturin's 1820 novel *Melmoth the Wanderer*. On that occasion, Mangan used Maturin's work indirectly by way of plagiarizing Honoré de Balzac's French adaptation of Maturin's work (in Balzac's *Melmoth Réconcilié*, 1835).[188] This instance of *actual* plagiarism was Mangan's roundabout way of identifying with Maturin social isolation. In the 1849 series titled "Sketches of Modern Irish Writers," Mangan equated Maturin's solitary existence with that of the thirteenth-century Persian poet Sa'di ("the 'Lonely Man of Shiraz'"); the imputed solitude ascribed to Sa'di in fact being a reference to Mangan's own existence. Mangan, despite his many acquaintances and occasional close friendships, was generally a solitary figure, feeling intense alienation from his surroundings. As he put it,

> An inhabitant of one of the stars, dropped on our planet, could hardly feel more bewildered than Maturin habitually felt in his consociation with beings around him. He had no friend—companion—brother, he, and the 'Lonely Man of Shiraz' might have shaken hands, and then—parted. He—in his own dark way—understood many people; but nobody understood him in *any way*.[189]

Closely identifying with different modalities of mood and temperament he associated with the Anglo-Irish Maturin, or with Sa'di, Hafiz (Hafez), and other range of actual oriental poets of bygone days, Mangan nevertheless created a literary distance between himself and those poets and writers through the literary mechanism of indirect plagiarizing, or self-plagiarizing, so as to retain his own originality and avoid being completely absorbed by the persona of his imagined authorial doppelgängers across geographic, cultural, and temporal realms.

Mangan's other strategic literary self-orientation toward the East was indicative of his tortuous engagement with Vallancey's theories of Irish origins. In this regard, in addition to the line 'IRAN's nation and race' in the 1846 "To the Ingleezee Khafir," there are other clues demonstrating that, at least after 1846, if not much earlier, Mangan had embraced Vallancey's Iranian hypothesis of the origin of Irish civilization. This is amply clear in a letter Mangan wrote, evidently in 1846, to James McGlashan, the Dublin publisher and former editor of the *Dublin University Magazine*. By then in an ever more desperate pecuniary circumstance during the famine, Mangan insisted in the letter that he had forsaken liquor. He additionally pretended in this letter to have now mastered Persian and then invoked Vallancey's theory in support of the importance of teaching Persian to the Irish:

> The [Trinity] College has lately received a large accession of Oriental works. Although you may not entirely credit it, it is a fact that I have made great progress in the Persian language, and I am ready to teach it to such of my countrymen as are willing to do credit to the Vallancey-an notion of their Oriental descent. If you would care to introduce Hindoo poetry to your readers, I could supply you with it.[190]

Here was another instance of what Ricoeur described as the interchange between trace, heritage, debt, and obligation. Leaving aside the wide chasm between modern Persian and ancient Persian (not that such a language was even spoken during the mythical Iranian Pishdādiān dynasty that Vallancey had identified as the civilizational bedrock of ancient Irish culture), Mangan was obviously trying to desperately eke a living by suturing the present to the past. In regard to another aspect of Mangan's engagement with the past, Joseph Lennon, also turning to Ricoeur's concept of 'trace' and Walter Benjamin's distinction between "now" and "the present," has noted perceptively: "At some of his most visionary moments, Mangan overtly aligns antiquity and futurity."[191] An overlooked striking example of this futurity of the past appeared as a narrative device in Mangan's 1848 poem titled "Irish National Hymn," in which Mangan alluded to Iran—again specifically using the term 'Iran,' as he had done in "To the Ingleezee Khafir," instead of the more common English designation of 'Persia' at the time. This time, however, the Iran/Erin connection drastically diverged from Moore's prior allegoric historical parity between the two territories. In this 1848 poem, Mangan was affirming Ireland's ancient ties to Iran as proposed by Vallancey, L.C. Beaufort, Henry O'Brien, and others.

"Irish National Hymn," appearing in John Mitchel's militant nationalist *The United Irishman* (Dublin) on May 13, 1848, opened with lines exulting Ireland's otherwise ambivalent ancient past: "O! Ireland! Ancient Ireland! / Ancient! yet for ever [*sic*] young! / Thou our mother, home and sireland— / Thou at length has found a tongue— / Proudly thou, at length, / Resistest in triumphant strength ...." The fourth and fifth stanzas of the poem played on Ireland's ancient ties to Iran by inventing an Iranian legend ("Eastern story") and then relating that legend to Mangan's prophecy of Ireland's forthcoming revolution:

IV.
Deep, saith the Eastern story,
   Burns in Iran's mines a gem,

For its dazzling hues and glory
　　Worth a Sultan's diadem.
　　　But from human eyes
　　　　Hidden there it ever lies!
The aye-travailing Gnomes alone,
　　Who toil to form the mountain's treasure,
　　May gaze and gloat with pleasure without measure
Upon the lustrous beauty of that wander stone.

V.
So is it with a nation
　　Which would win for its rich dower
That bright pearl, Self-Liberation—
　　It must labour hour by hour.
　　　Strangers, who travail
　　　　To lay bare the gem, shall fail:
　　Within itself must grow, must glow—
　　Within the depths of its own bosom
Must flower in living might, must broadly blossom,
The hopes that shall be born ere Freedom's Tree can blow.

The poem appeared at a time when Ireland had sunk deeper into the Great Famine, and in the midst of revolutions breaking out in continental Europe following the February 1848 revolution in France, and nearly two months prior to the failed Young Ireland (/ Fenian) uprising in Ireland led by Mitchel's revolutionary associates (including William Smith O'Brien and Thomas Francis Meagher), while Mitchel himself was in prison. The poem concluded with the following prophetic lines that underscore Mangan's unequivocally militant nationalist gravitation at the time: "The Time, the Hour, the Power are near— / Be sure thou soon shalt form the vanguard / of that illustrious band whom Heaven and Man guard:— / And these words come from *one whom some have called a Seer*" (emphasis in the original).[192]

While Mangan got the time and the hour right, it was not so with 'the Power.' As it transpired, those joining the 'vanguard' in the 1848 uprising in Ireland turned out to be a small ill-fated 'band,' whom 'Heaven and Man' failed to 'guard' against the English state. This uprising, too, came to form yet another instance of militant Irish nationalist commemorative marker of trace and heritage for beckoning future generations of the Irish to fulfill their debt and obligation to past generations.

Ellen Shannon-Mangan notes that Mangan contributed three poems to the short-lived *United Irishman*; adding:

> The third and last was by title the most ambitious of all Mangan's nationalist poems, for he wrote it to be the "Irish National Hymn." It was also the last of his stirring original poems of Irish nationalism, the slightly later "Tribune's Hymn for Pentecost" being more prayer to "the always-faithful God" than a challenge to Ireland.[193]

David Lloyd, however, questioning Mangan's ability as a "seer" and characterizing the fourth stanza of the poem as "the oriental fable which intrudes into the 'Irish National Hymn,'" interprets the poem as being ultimately ironic. He writes: "If, as the poem suggests, the Young Irelanders are to be seen as the 'aye-travailing gnomes,' labouring 'hour by hour' for 'That bright pearl, self-liberation,' a possible reading is that they remain so gazing and gloating at this alchemical stone, which they themselves may even have 'formed,' but may never actually grasp."[194] Reading against Lloyd's interpretation, one can in fact *contrast* 'The aye-travailing Gnomes' protecting the Iranian 'gem' with 'Strangers, who travail / To lay bare the gem' of Ireland's 'Self-Liberation.' In Mangan's estimation, the prospect of failure ("fail") was directed at the efforts of 'Strangers' (i.e., the English state and other opponents of Irish nationalism) for exposing and preventing Irish revolutionary activities, rather than auguring yet another (albeit ultimately doomed) Irish nationalist uprising, under the heading of 'Irish National Hymn' no less. Moreover, Iran's 'aye-travailing Gnomes' should be equated with 'the vanguard / of that illustrious band whom Heaven and Man guard,' given the correspondence between the gem and Self-liberation. Leaving aside possible interpretations of the various symbolisms in this poem, it is significant that Mangan inserted an entire stanza based on an invented Iranian legend into what he identified as Ireland's 'National Hymn.' Without any presumed connection between Iran and Ireland, this would have been a major intrusion of a foreign element into the interiority of a simultaneously nationalist and *nationalizing* poem, and of an exterior component bucking the substance of a domestic tale. Had there been no intended connection between Iran and Erin in Mangan's poem, he could simply have chosen or invented an Irish parable instead. However, conjuring Vallancey's Iran-Erin historical tie, Mangan devised an Iranian legend to illustrate his portended revolutionary Irish nationalist project of Ireland's imminent independence (hence also the doubleness of the invented Iranian fable, which related to both Ireland's presumed distant past and its impending future). The contextual effect of the Iranian fable in this poem was indisputably more than mere stylistic oriental aura and a cosmetic lyrical device. After all, this was his most decisive outwardly revolutionary Irish nationalist poem. Given the subject and tone of the poem, this was clearly no setting for Mangan's tongue-in-cheek parrying with the convoluted methodology of Vallancey. As in the case of his Iran/Erin analogy in "To the Ingleezee Khafir" ('IRAN's nation and race'), Mangan in "Irish National Hymn" was drawn to the antiquarian union of Iran and Ireland, this time in a somber tone that was reflective of the revolutionary underpinning of the poem and also symptomatic of the ongoing mass suffering in Ireland from the famine, including Mangan's own utterly miserable existence. It seems, with an awakened urge for a nationalist revolution, Mangan's nativist faith in Ireland's oriental roots was also stirred. This was in sharp contrast to Mangan's seesawing ambivalence toward both nationalist violence and antiquarian theories of Irish origins exactly a year prior to the publication of the "Irish National Hymn." For instance, preceding the second installment of his "Anthologia Hibernica" (No. II) in the *Dublin University Magazine* of May 1847, there was an anonymous poem by Mangan addressed to himself ("To Clarence Mangan"):

Various and curious are thy strains, O, Clarence Mangan!
  Rhyming and chiming in a very odd way:
[...]
For the Bards are the pulse of the big heart of Erin,
  Throbbing wildly, now quick, now slow;
[...]
Thou, too, art a Bard—and thy Spirit's River
  Is fed by each streamlet from her Founts of Song;
[...]
Go wander in thy strength thro' the scenes of Erin's history;
  Pour thy glad waters round many an abbey's walls;
Let the fields of old triumphs be green again with verdure,
  And awake the echoes of the princes' halls.
I sometimes doubt if I have Irish blood in me,
  So often in these mazes do I lose my clue,
Mixing Danes with Milesians, and the clear-faced Saxon
  With the hairy-dirty children of Boru.
I have small faith in *Punic* etymologies:
  I sometimes fancy Petrie and St. Patrick are the same:
I doubt that Betham knows all the tongues of Babel,
  Or that William Smith O'Brien is a Hebrew name.
I do not care a button for Young Ireland, or Old Ireland;
  But, as between the two, I rather like old Dan,
And I wish the Nation would let the agitation
  Die a humbug as it first began![195]

Mangan Shifting the Sands of *Here and Now* and *There and Then*

The majority of Mangan's 'translated' oriental poems were not necessarily or transparently political in content—even if many of them ultimately dealt with underlying politics of historical, cultural, and linguistic identity formations.[196] Mangan continuously grappled with, and worked through, the question of identity in complex forms. After all, he was labeled an Irish*man*, was born into the Catholic faith, was a poet, and a resident of the United Kingdom, and, hence, also "British"—the latter designation itself an unequivocal expression of imperialist semantic violence that rendered Ireland and *Irishness* invisible under the collective rubrics of "Britain" and "Britons" (which signified England, Wales, and Scotland), not to mention such territorial designations as "the British Isles" that encompassed Ireland. Mangan, drawn to Irish nationalism, was also a European, a human, and an impoverished educated male member of the lower-middle class.[197] He was both socially ostracized and self-marginalized. Moreover, within the United Kingdom Mangan was provincial (while belonging to a major European and imperial world power) and, therefore, also a *provincial* author in the United Kingdom, writing in English. At the same time, in the setting of Ireland itself, he was a metropolitan author (a Dubliner), a nationalist poet who personally did not venture beyond the borders of Ireland[198] and abstained from publishing his works in English periodicals published outside Ireland,[199] yet produced an exceptionally cosmopolitan oeuvre of actual and invented translations with a globally accented literary imagination, spanning more varied territorial, cultural, linguistic, and historical terrains than any of his literary contemporaries in the United Kingdom writing in English (including other Young Ireland poets who covered a wide range of territories in their expression of anti-imperialist solidarity, such as Thomas Davis). Mangan was an author working in the imperially transnational medium of English language, a colonized subject far more fluent and expressive in English language than in his own so-called national mother tongue (a Caliban, to conjure Shakespeare's character from *The Tempest*). Yet, as an "anti-British" Irish nationalist (culturally early on, and both culturally and politically toward the end of his life), he also belonged to a population from whose ranks were recruited a substantial proportion of the imperial military might of the expansionist British Empire. Hence, leaving geographic and cultural distances aside, as a colonized subject he shared certain identity features with the so-called indigenous subjects of the British Empire in India and elsewhere; even as Ireland occupied a unique place in the British Empire, as both constituting the earliest major English territorial conquests outside mainland Britain and being incorporated under the 1801 Act of Union into a parliamentary merger with Britain, among its other distinctive features as a British colony. At the same time, Mangan continually struggled with what it meant to be Irish *now* and what Irishness might have represented at different stages in the past, prior to and after the twelfth-century English conquests in Ireland, as well as the shape Irishness would assume in a future independent Ireland. Jacques Chuto has noted:

> Exiled in time and space, longing for an ideal *There* and *Then* [...] Instead of assuming, for reasons that seem to be mainly sentimental, that Ireland was always first and foremost among the poet's preoccupations, it would be more to the point to say that Mangan, willy-nilly, was mainly preoccupied with himself.[200]

For Mangan, the foundations of his Irish identity remained slippery and nebulous, with coexisting and mutual pulls of historical authenticity and inauthenticity, with simultaneous originality and invention also marking his 'translations' from oriental, Irish, and other languages.

In addition to contemporary indeterminate and polymorphous accounts of Irish antiquity, even if Mangan ultimately settled for an oriental theory of Irish origins, many of Ireland's more recent historical structures as well as folk memories were fast dissolving into thin air, along with the shrinking size of Ireland's Irish-speaking population (a process that was dramatically intensified following the Great Famine). Mangan's tenure at the Ordnance Survey reinforced such a perspective of Ireland's fast-disappearing past. Ireland's *national* future also remained uncertain. Here was yet another trauma of inherited national history, exacerbating the colonial tyranny of the present and upending any banal sense of Irish rootedness in *here and now* and future *there and then*. Mangan's deracinated existence (leaving aside that no person is ever singularly or fully rooted in any given identity construct) was both a symptom of so-called history and personal choice. He both refused and was denied the comfort of cultural and social entrenchment, struggling also with the added anguish of his works failing to garner the fame and reputation to which he rightly felt entitled, while at the same time passing off many of his own creations as works of others. As James Joyce, indisputably a literary semi-offspring of Mangan, noted in his two essays on Mangan in 1902 and 1907 (with the latter revised draft distinctly more sympathetic), and with some echoes of Mangan's own commentary on Maturin: "Mangan has been a stranger in his country, a rare and unsympathetic figure in the streets, where he is seen as going forward alone like one who does penance for some ancient sin."[201] Not only were nation and nationalism incapable of taming this aspect of Mangan's sense of (self-)estrangement, but they in fact aggravated this sentiment. In the first installment of his "Literæ Orientales" (1837), Mangan wrote:

> The mind, to be sure, properly to speak, is without a home on the earth. Ancestral glories, genealogical charts, and the like imprescriptible indescribables are favorite subjects with the composite being Man, who also goes now and then the length of dying in idea for his fatherland—but for Mind—it is restless, rebellious—a vagrant whose barren tracts are by no means confined to the space between Dan and Beersheba. It lives rather out of the world. As a stranger said at the sermon, when asked why he did not weep with the rest of the congregation, it "belongs to another parish." It is apt, when in quest of its origin, to remount quite as far as the Welshman who across the middle of his pedigree wrote, *About this time the earth was created*. It is a Cain that may build cities, but can abide in none of them. It repudiates every country on the map; it must do so; it should; it would not be Mind if it did otherwise.[202]

In 1849, just weeks before his death, Mangan composed what remained an incomplete short autobiography, appearing in August 17, 1850, issue of recently founded and short-lived (post-Fenian rising) newspaper the *Irishman* (Dublin). The piece was to appear as part of his biographical series titled "Sketches of Modern Irish Writers" in the same paper, which espoused radical nationalist and working-class agendas. This autobiography, in effect serving as Mangan's self-obituary, was written in the third person by someone "intimately acquainted with Mr. Mangan." In this piece, Mangan wrote of his compulsion ("I *must*") to compose translations from familiar and unfamiliar languages and to experiment with form:

> Mangan understands eight languages, and has translated from many besides that he does not understand. He has been also overmuch addicted to a practice akin to this, that of fathering upon other writers the offspring of his own brain. [...] I cannot commend it. A man may have a right to offer his property to others, but nothing can justify him in forcing it upon them. I once asked Mangan why he did not prefix his own name to his anti-plagiaristic productions, and his reply was characteristic of the man: "That would be no go; nohow you fixed it: I *must* write in a variety of styles; and it wouldn't do for me to don the turban, and open my poem with a *Bismillah*; when I write a poem to the Arab Mohir-Ibn-Mohir—Ibn Khalakan is the man from whom it should come; and to him I give it." "And do you really sympathise with your subject?" I demanded. "Yes, always, always," was his answer: "When I write as a Persian, I feel as a Persian, and am transported back to the

days of Diemsheed [Jamshid] and the Genii; when I write as a Spaniard, I forget, for the moment, everything but the Cid, the Moors, and the Alhambra; when I translate from the Irish, my heart has no pulses except for the wrongs and sorrows of my own stricken land."[203]

Mangan's recourse to 'orientalism' made a dialogic mockery of any potential present-day insinuation that by claiming the Orient as *one's own* Mangan and other non-"orientals" like him were presumably engaged in an ultimately imperialist encounter with the Orient, or of any equally preposterous suggestion that Mangan's equation of the Orient with the fabulous, such the 'Genii' in the above quotation, implied a reductionist and essentialist approach to the Orient as being somehow superstitious, irrational, and so on. Moreover, there was something significant in the above-quoted passage from Mangan's autobiography. He was claiming to be actually *writing* as a Persian or a Spaniard when he invented his Persian or Spanish poems, but only capable of *translating* from the Irish. Translation entails working with an existing text in a different language, as creative as the translator might be in producing a distinctly new work—all translations being in some ways different from that which is translated (in rhythm, word choices, mood, cultural reception, etc.). Many translators also rely on existing translations of the original work where possible (including those rendered into other languages in which the translator has some proficiency), either as a means of comparison for the sake of precision and/or originality or as a way of working through more intricate translational idiomatic and form choices. Mangan never attained an adequate degree of proficiency in Irish language necessary for a comprehensive translation on his own. This was a language (his ostensible 'national' mother tongue no less) that required, for example, a different mode of translation than his translations from German, in which Mangan was fluent. His English translations from the original Irish were largely reworkings of what had already been rendered into English by his friends and others proficient in Irish. These were not direct linguistic translations; instead, they involved a process of revising and modifying existing English texts to produce yet another *English* text with different effects, at times by means of inserting idioms or lines from other poems for the sake of originality, enhancement, or contextual effect. He was, in effect, translating from the English (the language of Ireland's colonizers) into English (the language understood by most Irish) in works that were aimed at Irish readers and not intended to appear in periodicals published in England.

Moreover, just as Mangan continually revised some of his previously published poems and prose writing, he also approached all texts as always potentially accessible to conversion and never finalized, or as theoretically "heteroglossic" texts (to borrow Mikhail Bakhtin's much later concept). This was not entirely different from the common convention of periodicals publishing abridged versions of works by different authors without their prior permission for that particular form of abridgment, or of edited selections of Mangan's own works appearing after his death, as in the case of John Mitchel's editorial deletion of the final section of "To the Ingleezee Khafir" or Mitchel's classification of this poem under the section he titled "Apochrypha," among other range of stylistic and contextual editorial decisions—or, for that matter, of my own selective and largely fragmentary and narrowly contextualized reading of Mangan's vast body of works in the present book. Authorial ownership of texts, with or without copyright, is always susceptible to revisions (by the author or by others), reinterpretation, recontextualization, other alterations, misquotation, as well as fraudulent plagiaristic pilfering. As with history and memory, texts too become 'traces' that can disappear and may reappear at some point, or remain in circulation to be re-encountered, (re-)received, rejected, translated, and applied and utilized in contested forms and distinct contexts by diverse audiences (temporal, spatial, cultural, political, gendered, social, etc.). For Mangan and many of his readers, the Irish language being translated into English was a major part of what constituted their cultural grounding, if not also a component of their 'national' *ursprung*. But, it could only be rendered sensible for them in another language (specifically English), regardless of the degree to which what was made accessible in English was true to the original text. For Mangan, engagement with history was also always an act of translation, re-classification, interconnections, re-connections, deletions and redactions, and additions, with always changing goals and/or tactical stipulations for the historical re-narrations and their re-staging aimed at different audiences. These parallel approaches to textuality and historicity, both of which directly pertained to the question of identity (authorial, national/ethnic, political, religious/secular, gendered, and other), were brought together by Mangan in his Irish, oriental, and other pseudo-translations.

Leaving aside Mangan's social class, religious background, and other range of so-called 'identity' determinants (whether *acquired* and selectively retained or discarded, or *chosen*), so far as both his inadequate fluency in Irish language and his being ethnically labeled Irish were concerned his 'national' voice could only be expressed in the only language in which he had been fluent since childhood (i.e., English), and a language which in this case came with a historical baggage of colonial encounters (as opposed to mere learning of another language, including English, in some alternative setting). Just as the Anglo-Irish, as the hyphenated caption also suggests, had embraced varying degrees of what were presumed to be 'Irish' cultural values and practices, the 'mere Irish' had become Anglicized in a different range of cultural practices and mores, not least of all in terms of the daily language of communication in case of the majority of the Irish. In fact, the 'mere Irish' (a.k.a. 'Gaelic'-Irish)—as presumed descendants of the indigenous pre-Norman conquest population of the island, and overlooking here the Norse and other prior and subsequent intermixing of populations—now also comprised a hyphenated identity in their own land as a legacy of the arrival of English, Welsh, and Scots settlers whose prior ethnic-territorial identities were now combined in compound forms with "-Irish," thereby requiring a similar category of hyphenated identification for descendants of the earlier indigenous population. It was also in what was frequently labeled by the 'Gaelic' population of Ireland as the "language of the English colonizer" that various Irish nationalist platforms were generally communicated to most of the Irish. Mangan's own 'national' identity, as all national identities in fact are, was an identity in limbo, historically and *by choice*.[204] After all, the hyphenated Gaelic-Irish in Mangan's time primarily denoted the presumed location of one's ancestral homeland, rather than being automatically also a marker of the 'national' mother tongue one spoke (which many 'mere Irish' could no longer speak) or of cultural practices (given the vast spectrum of cultural syntheses and fluidity among different Irish communities).

Here was also another irony of the title of Mangan's "A Polyglott Anthology." Through invented oriental translations, Mangan could reinvent himself as an author masquerading as a scholar of oriental languages (and as a native German-speaking scholar at that), and/or project himself and Ireland onto other histories, while projecting those histories back onto Ireland's history and onto his own personal experiences as a poet. He could reanimate and transform Ireland's *here and now* and *there and then* (Ireland of the past in this case) by a range of *there* and *then* (past and present) taken from other histories. But, the gap between *here* and *there* and *now* and *then* could never be entirely overcome or glossed over; nor did Mangan aim at such glossing over. As Schiller had remarked in his already quoted poem "The Pilgrim": 'And *the there* is never *here*.' Terry Eagleton writes in a somewhat severe assessment of Mangan:

> Mangan's literary career was also a parodic commentary on a scholarly reverence for fact, which had not, after all, proved of unequivocal value to the Irish. In a society where the scrupulous collecting of social data had played its part in political control as well as in social enlightenment, the scholar's passion for fact could not be seen as entirely ideologically innocent. In any case, the facts in question were often enough rebarbative, distilling a human wretchedness belied by the impassive spirit in which they were studied. Just as the political revolutionary wants to change the facts, so Mangan felt free to reinvent them. While scholars bend their energies to what is the case, radicals turn them to what might be [...]
>
> If Mangan was an author, he was also an anti-author, who published only one book and stole much of the rest of his material. [...] If one of his registers is the overpitched rhetoric of nationalism, the other is a vein of extravagant aimlessness to which, seen as a social condition, nationalism was one political response. It is hard for him to be serious and witty together, so that the seriousness lapses too often into portentousness and the wit degenerates into facetious trifling. His humour is really a kind of frenetic desperation, in which it is not hard to detect a certain colonial futility and self-involvement. [...] Mangan and Petrie may well have occupied the same office, but their sensibilities, like their politics, were worlds apart.[205]

Alternative *time-spaces* appearing in Mangan's works of poetry and prose were frequently imbued with purposeful comparisons and contrasts to his contemporary Ireland. In the 1833 "An Extraordinary Adventure in the Shades," it was the vision of a future ruined Dublin being consigned to the list of great ruins of the ancient Near East. His 1846 "Siberia" was set in an *elsewhere-here* and in a *timeless-present* means of framing the famine ravaging Ireland at the time. In his much noted 1846 Ireland-centered "A Vision of Connaught in the Thirteenth Century," the alternative time-scape at first functioned as a therapeutic nationalist arrangement—the account of Cahal of the Red Hand, the celebrated king of Connaught (Connacht) who waged repeated defensive wars against English encroachment—before turning into a gloomy nightmare of subsequent English-occupied Connaught and the famine ravaging Ireland in Mangan's own time ("A SKELETON"). The narrator of the poem then awakens of all places in the German Grand Duchy of Hesse-Darmstadt of Mangan's own time ("Of the castled Maine [i.e., Mainz-Kastel, also the site of a major battle during the Napoleonic Wars], / One Autumn eve, in the Teuton's land").[206] As mentioned before, the poem also makes a

Vallanceyan-style allusion to Ireland's ancient oriental ties by using the idiom of 'Khan,' further adding to the confusion of the time-space in the poem (including in a cultural-linguistic sense):

> [...]
> Anon stood nigh
> By my side a man
> Of princely aspect and port sublime.
> Him queried I,
> "O, my Lord and Khan,
> What clime is this, and what golden time?"
> [...]
> 'Twas then the time,
> We were in the days,
> Of Cáhal Mór of the Wine-red Hand
> [...]
> I again walked forth;
> But lo! the sky
> Showed fleckt with blood, and an alien sun
> Glared from the north,
> And there stood on high,
> Amid his shorn beams, A SKELETON!
> It was by the stream
> Of the castled Maine,
> One Autumn eve, in the Teuton's land,
> That I dreamed this dream
> Of the time and reign
> Of Cáhal Mór of the Wine-red Hand![207]

The *there and then* time-spaces could never temper the plight of *here and now*, particularly after the failed 1848 Young Ireland/Fenian uprising in the midst of the Great Famine. The failure of the 1848 uprising, a revolt which Mangan had portended in his "Irish National Hymn," was yet another disappointing frustration of Ireland's repeatedly deferred transition to the status of an independent nation-state. James Joyce, himself a believer in oriental origins of the Irish (vacillating between Vallancey's earlier Phoenician and later Iranian/Persian theories, among other similar versions),[208] wrote of Mangan with great exaggeration in the first decade of the twentieth century (1902 and 1907): "All his poetry remembers wrong and suffering and the aspirations of one who has suffered and who is moved to great cries and gestures when that sorrowful hour rushes upon the heart."[209] Exaggeratedly characterizing Mangan as "a romantic, a would-be herald, a prototype for a would-be nation," Joyce added in 1907, in an inordinately caustic judgment:

> The history of his country encloses him so straitly that even in his moments of high passion he can but barely breach its walls. He, too, cries out, in his life and in his mournful verses, against the injustices of despoilers, but never laments a deeper loss than the loss

of plaids and ornaments. He inherits the latest and worst part of a tradition upon which no divine hand has drawn out the line of demarcation, a tradition which dissolves and divides against itself as it moves down the cycles. And because this tradition has become an obsession for him, he has accepted it with all its griefs and failures and regrets which he would bequeath just as it is: the poet who hurls his anger against tyrants would establish upon the future an intimate and far more cruel tyranny.[210]

Joyce also stated, albeit in a much more fundamentally extreme binary denominational tone than Mangan would have used:

Mangan will be accepted by the Irish as their national poet the day the conflict between Ireland and the foreign Powers, the Anglo-Saxon and the Roman Catholic; reaches a settlement that will give rise to a new civilization, either indigenous or purely foreign.[211]

Joyce did not elaborate on what constituted Ireland's present-day indigenous civilization or how an absolute foreign purity could be attained by survivors of the aforementioned 'conflict.' Mangan's previously discussed unfinished autobiography (i.e., self-obituary), composed weeks before his death, concluded with the line: "If it be not too late, possibly Mangan may yet be rescued and restored to society; but when a fly is rapidly sinking in a glass of water, and not a soul in the house besides himself, it is difficult for him to forbear conjecturing that he must go to the bottom."[212] These lines, practically capturing Mangan's last gasps for life and his self-identification as a largely neglected Irish nationalist and literary figure, were his admission of having spent his adult life as a social outcast and forsaken renegade. The sinking fly also signified the bitter breakdown of Mangan's earlier desperate hope, prior to the 1848 uprising, that this time around the nationalist uprising in Ireland might succeed.

Following his death in 1849 during the famine, Mangan fast vanished from Irish literary memory, notwithstanding the posthumous publication of some of his previously unpublished works. He did, however, enjoy sporadic spells of recollection and tribute as a major Irish poet. Mangan's prose writing remained largely neglected in these recollective endeavors until the publications of David James O'Donoghue's *The Life and Writings of James Clarence Mangan* (Edinburgh, 1897) and *The Prose Writings of James Clarence Mangan* (Dublin, 1904). In 1859, John Mitchel spearheaded the intermittent efforts to recognize Mangan as one of Ireland's greatest poets, editing *Poems by James Clarence Mangan* (New York). Mitchel was then a former leading Young Ireland figure and now a militant republican nationalist (Fenian) living in the United States, and had been a close associate of Mangan in the period leading up to the failed Young Ireland uprising in 1848. Toward the end of the century, Mangan gained even greater, albeit short-lived, public prominence as a major Irish poet following the appearance of his collected works edited by as diverse a range of authors, such as the United States-based Fenian John Boyle O'Reilly (*Poetry and Song of Ireland*, New York, 1887), the London-born Irish journalist, author, and biographer David James O'Donoghue, as already noted, and the American poet, cultural critic, and prominent scholar of seventeenth-century English poetry Louise Imogen Guiney (*James Clarence Mangan: His Selected Poems, with a*

Study, Norwood, Massachusetts, 1897).[213] Although Mangan again fast faded from public literary memory in his native country, he received due recognition, even if not always entirely flattering, as an eminent poet from some of Ireland's leading literary figures after the latter decades of the nineteenth century, among them Lady Wilde, W.B. Yeats, and James Joyce. It was, hence, with great exaggeration that Stephen Lucius Gwynn[214] noted in his 1906 book *The Fair Hills of Ireland*:

> Every educated man and woman of the Irish race at home and abroad knows the name and the tragic story of Clarence Mangan; yet how few remember the hedge school poet of the eighteenth century, not less interesting and by far more typical a figure, whose line, with Mangan's translation of them, I have set at the head of these pages.[215]

Gwynn, who in the previous year had published a biography of Thomas Moore,[216] was here referring to the late eighteenth- and early nineteenth-century Donnchadh Rua Mac Con Mara (Red Donough McNamara). Even in scholarly literary circles, Mangan again largely sank into oblivion until James Kilroy's 1969 edited volume of *The Autobiography of James Clarence Mangan*, despite the fact that as early as 1950 the *Official Guide: Dublin*, issued by the Tourist Board of the Republic of Ireland, stated: "James Clarence Mangan, who is regarded as the greatest of the Anglo-Irish poets, was born in Dublin in 1803. Here he lived his unhappy life and wrote the songs which made his name immortal."[217]

Notes

1 William Butler Yeats, *Essays and Introductions*. Reprint. New York: Collier Books, 1986 [1968], pp.511–12.
2 See, for example, "Researches Amongst the Round Towers," *Cork Examiner*, September 29, 1841, p.1, c.c; "Editorial," ibid., November 5, 1841, p.1, c.c; "Round Towers," ibid., November 26, 1841, p.3, c.d; "The Round Towers of Ireland," ibid., February 7, 1845, p.4, cc.b-c. The *Cork Examiner*, incidentally, also covered the 1841 formal resolution to the Anglo-Iranian conflict over Herat (1839) and periodically commented on Catholic missionary activities in Iran.
3 It is estimated that by 1843 the paper had "a readership possibly as high as 250,000." Michael Foley, "Colonialism and Journalism in Ireland," *Journalism Studies* 5(3), 2004, p.377. On Irish nationalist journalism, see also Marie-Louise Legg, *Newspapers and Nationalism: the Irish Provincial Press, 1850-1892*. Dublin: Four Courts Press, 1999; and Ann Andrews, *Newspapers and Newsmakers: The Dublin Nationalist Press in the Mid-Nineteenth Century*. Liverpool: Liverpool University Press, 2014.
4 See also Sean Ryder, "Young Ireland and the 1798 Rebellion" in Laurence M. Geary, ed., *Rebellion and Remembrance in Modern Ireland*. Dublin: Four Courts Press, 2001, pp.135–47.
5 John Kells Ingram, *Sonnets and Other Poems*. London: Adam and Charles Black, 1900, pp.6–7, 104–106. A few words and some of the punctuation in this version of the poem differ from the original version.
6 Thomas Osborne Davis, *Literary and Historical Essays*. Edited by Charles Gavan Duffy. Dublin: James Duffy, 1846, pp.62–79; Thomas Osborne Davis, "Historical Monuments of Ireland" in Thomas Osborne Davis, *Prose Writings of Thomas Davis*. Edited and with an Introduction by Thomas William Rolleston. London: Walter Scott, 1889, pp.80–82. See also George Petrie, *The Ecclesiastical Architecture of Ireland*, pp.11–33.
7 Thomas Osborne Davis, "Irish Antiquities" in Thomas Osborne Davis, *Prose Writings of Thomas Davis*, p.88.

8 On Davis' interest in a vaguely defined republican "Greece" see also David Dwan, *The Great Community: Culture and Nationalism in Ireland*. Dublin: Field day, 2008, pp.51 and passim.
9 Thomas Osborne Davis, "Irish Antiquities" in Thomas Osborne Davis, *Prose Writings of Thomas Davis*, p.88.
10 Thomas Osborne Davis, *Literary and Historical Essays*, pp.54–55. See also ibid., pp.29, 33, 36–38, 45, 54–57, 67–74, and passim. On Davis and historiography, see also Helen Mulvey, *Thomas Davis and Ireland: A Biographical Study*. Washington, DC: Catholic University of America, 2003, chapter 6.
11 See Davis' "Ethnology of the Irish Race" in Thomas Osborne Davis, *Literary and Historical Essays*, pp.80–88.
12 Ibid., p.68.
13 Ibid., pp.39–47.
14 See also David Dwan, *The Great Community*, pp.59–67 and passim.
15 Ernest Renan, *What Is a Nation? and Other Political Writings*. M.F.N. Giglioli translator. New York: Columbia University Press, 2018, chapter 9.
16 On the nationalist platform of Young Ireland and 'the common good,' see David Dwan, *The Great Community*, pp.53, 64, and passim.
17 Thomas Osborne Davis, *The Poems of Thomas Davis*. Thomas Wallis editor. Dublin: James Duffy, 1857, p.28.
18 Thomas Osborne Davis, *Literary and Historical Essays*, p.39.
19 Davis, "Our National Language" and "O'Donovan's Irish Grammar" in ibid., pp.173–82, 183–86. See also Jean-Christophe Penet, "Thomas Davis, 'The Nation' and the Irish Language," *Studies: An Irish Quarterly Review* 96(384), Winter 2007, pp.433–43.
20 Thomas Osborne Davis, *Literary and Historical Essays*, p.39.
21 Thomas Osborne Davis, *The Poems of Thomas Davis*. Edited and with an Introduction by John Mitchel. New York: D. & J. Sadlier & Co., 1866, pp.93–94.
22 For a highly contrasting interpretation of this poem by Davis, see Toby H. Loeffler, "'Erin go bragh': 'Banal Nationalism' and the Joycean Performance of Irish Nationhood," *Journal of Narrative Theory* 39(1), Winter 2009, p.30.
23 See also Charles Gavan Duffy, *Thomas Davis: The Memoirs of an Irish Patriot, 1840-1846*. London: Kegan Paul, Trench, Trubner, & Co., 1890, pp.8–9.
24 George Gordon Byron, *Don Juan*. New edition. Boston: Phillips, Sampson, and Co., 1858, p.137.
25 Ibid., p.487; idem, *The Complete Works of Lord Byron*. Volume III. J.W. Lake editor. Paris: Baudry, 1825, p.247.
26 "Ode to the Liberator" appearing under the section "The People's Festival," *Cork Examiner*, June 13, 1845, p.3, c.b. Walsh also "wrote a great deal for *The Nation* between 1843 and 1848," although he evidently "disliked Thomas Davis." David James O'Donoghue, *The Poets of Ireland: A Biographical and Bibliographical Dictionary of Irish Writers of English Verse*. Dublin: Hodges Figgis, & Co., 1912, pp.469–70.
27 Patrick J.P. Tynan, *The Irish National Invincibles and Their Times*. London: Chatham and Co., 1894, pp.6–7. Prior to the 1894 edition, Tynan's book had been privately circulated for six years. It is interesting that the book was published in London as well as in the United States (see the "Publisher's Note to the English Edition," p.v). Tynan was the disputed "Number One" in connection with the 1882 Phoenix Park murders.
28 Eoin MacNeill, *Phases of Irish History*. Dublin: M.H. Gill & Son, 1920, pp.226–27.
29 *Parry's Literary Journal* (Salt Lake City, US) 2(11), August 1886, p.324. This article had originally appeared in the *North American Review* (Boston).
30 Charles Villiers Stanford, *Pages from an Unwritten Diary*. London: Edward Arnold, 1914, pp.93–94.
31 Standish James O'Grady, "An Event of World History," *Irish Review* 1(4), June 1911, pp.161–64; "An Event of World History" in Standish James O'Grady, *Selected Essays and Passages*. With an Introduction by Ernest A. Boyd. Dublin: Talbot Press, 1918, pp.291–95. On O'Grady, see also Lawrence J. McCaffrey, "Components of Irish Nationalism," in Thomas E. Hachey and Lawrence J. McCaffrey, eds., *Perspectives on Irish Nationalism*. Lexington: University Press of Kentucky, 1989, p.13; Jerry C.M. Nolan, "Standish James O'Grady's Cultural Nationalism," *Irish Studies Review* 7(3), 1999, pp.347–57; Patrick Maume, "Standish

James O'Grady: Between Imperial Romance and Irish Revival," *Éire-Ireland* 39(1&2), Spring/Summer 2004, pp.11–35.
32 Eugene O'Brien, "The Epistemology of Nationalism," *Irish Studies Review* 5(17) Winter 1996/1997, p.15.
33 Thomas Osborne Davis, *The Poems of Thomas Davis* (1866 edition), pp.201–202. Darius I ("the Great"; r. 522–486 BCE) was the Persian emperor who ruled over the vastest expanse of the Achaemenid Empire. Prince Ernest Augustus, the fifth son of George III, and ruler of Hanover from 1837 to 1851, was a renowned anti-Catholic who had opposed the 1829 Catholic Emancipation Act and encouraged the use of force to quell Catholic disturbances in Ireland. Jack Ketch was the notorious legendary seventeenth-century executioner.
34 Thomas Osborne Davis, *The Poems of Thomas Davis* (1857 edition), pp.11–13, 16–19, 115–18. On Davis, nationalism, internationalism, and cosmopolitanism, see also Terry Eagleton, *Heathcliff and the Great Hunger*, pp.91, 259–60.
35 James Joseph Clancy, *The Land League Manual*, p.118. See also pp.115–18, 120–21, 128.
36 Ibid., p.308.
37 There were also somewhat routine British and Irish depictions of the deficient contemporary Iranian "national character," as repeated among other sources in the highly acclaimed two-volume *The History of Persia* (1815) by the Scottish John Malcolm. Many commentators in the United Kingdom and elsewhere followed Malcolm's example of characterizing Iranians as consistently lacking strong moral rectitude throughout history. According to Malcolm this was due to the population of the territory having been invariably subjected to tyrannical rule.
38 William Butler Yeats, *The Collected Works of William Butler Yeats*. Volume 8. Stratford-on-Avon: Shakespeare Head Press, 1908, p.94; William Butler Yeats, *Essays and Introductions*, p.247.
39 William Butler Yeats, *The Collected Works of W.B. Yeats. Volume IV: Early Essays*. Richard J. Finneran and George Bornstein eds. New York: Scribner, 2007, pp.429–30 n.5.
40 George Gordon Byron, *Don Juan*, p.487; idem, *The Complete Works of Lord Byron*, vol.III, 1825, p.247.
41 *Sentimental and Masonic Magazine* (Dublin), vol.6, January 1795, p.3. On Jones and freemasonry in late eighteenth-century Ireland, see also Seán Murphy, "Irish Jacobitism and Freemasonry," *Eighteenth-Century Ireland/ Iris an dá chultúr*, 9, 1994, pp.75–82.
42 John O'Leary, *Recollections of Fenians and Fenianism*. Volume I. London: Downey & Co., 1896, p.103.
43 Ibid., p.117.
44 Ibid., vol.II, p.61.
45 David Lloyd, *Nationalism and Minor Literature*, p.xi.
46 On Mangan, see also John Mitchel, "James Clarence Mangan: His Life, Poetry, and Death" in James Clarence Mangan, *Poems by James Clarence Mangan. With Biographical Introduction by John Mitchel*. New York: P.M. Harvey, 1859, pp.15–16; David James O'Donoghue, *The Life and Writings of James Clarence Mangan*. Edinburgh: Patrick Geddes and Colleagues, 1897, pp.19, 86, 89–90, 111, 207; the anonymous review of two books on Mangan's poetry, appearing in the American edition of *Literature* (New York), no.12, January 8, 1898, pp.10–11; James Kilroy, *James Clarence Mangan*. Cranbury, New Jersey: Associated University Press, 1970, pp.28–29, 33–34; and David Lloyd, "James Clarence Mangan's Oriental Translations and the Question of Origins," *Comparative Literature* 38(1), Winter 1986, p.23; idem, "Great Gaps in Irish Song: James Clarence Mangan and the Ideology of the Nationalist Ballad," *Irish University Review* 14(2), Autumn 1984, pp.179–90; Ciara Hogan, "'Lost Hero of the Past': Ruin, Wound, and the Failure of Idealism in the Poetry of James Clarence Mangan," *Études irlandaises* 35(1), 2010, pp.131–46; idem, "Cultural Nationalism and the 'Cashless Bard': Class and Nation in the Poetry of James Clarence Mangan" in Olivier Coquelin, Patrick Galliou, and Thierry Robin, eds., *Political Ideology in Ireland: From the Enlightenment to the Present*. Newcastle: Cambridge Scholars Press, 2009; Hasan Javadi, *Persian Literary Influence on English Literature*, pp.xii, 69, 71; John D. Yohannan, "The Persian Poetry Fad in England," p.159.
47 For the text of Joyce's lectures, see Kevin Barry, ed. *James Joyce: Occasional, Critical, and Political Writing*. With an Introduction by K. Barry, and translations from Italian by Conor

Deane. Oxford: Oxford University Press, 2000, pp.53–60, 127–36. See also William O'Neill, "Joyce's Esthetic," pp.33–41.

48 William Butler Yeats, ed., *A Book of Irish Verse: Selected from Modern Writers*. Revised edition. London: Methuen and Co., 1900 [1895], p.xxii.

49 See Sinéad Sturgeon, "Introduction. James Clarence Mangan: The Man in the Cloak" in Sinéad Sturgeon, ed., *Essays on James Clarence Mangan*, p.7. On Yeats and Mangan, see also Mary Helen Thuente, *W.B. Yeats and Irish Folklore*. Dublin: Gill and Macmillan, 1980, pp.18, 30, 37, 159, and passim.

50 Enda Duffy, "Critical Receptions of Literary Modernism" in Joe Cleary, ed., *The Cambridge Companion to Irish Modernism*. Cambridge: Cambridge University Press, 2014, pp.196, 197,199. See also David Lloyd, *Nationalism and Minor Literature*, pp.xi–xii, 23–26, 199–201, 210–14.

51 Seamus Heaney, "Singing High: James Clarence Mangan," *Poetry Ireland Review* 77 (2003), p.14. On page 11 of this article, Heaney had ironically written: "while much in Mangan's sensibility is modern, much in his writing still belongs in a previous era."

52 Kevin Barry, ed. *James Joyce*, p.56. See also the 1907 version of this line in ibid., p.133.

53 Ibid., p.134.

54 See also David Wheatley, "Introduction" in James Clarence Mangan, *Poems*. David Wheatley editor. Oldcastle, Ireland: Gallery Press, 2003, p.13.

55 Appearing in the *Irishman* (Dublin) of August 17, 1850, this piece is reproduced in Jacques Chuto, Peter Van de Kamp, Augustine Martin, and Ellen Shannon-Mangan, eds., *The Collected Works of James Clarence Mangan. Prose: 1840-1882*. Dublin: Irish Academic Press, 2002, pp.223, 224; and in Sean Ryder, ed., *James Clarence Mangan: Selected Writings*. Dublin: University College Dublin Press, 2004, pp.7, 413. See also David Wheatley, "Fully able / to write in any language—I'm a Babel" in Sinéad Sturgeon, ed. *Essays on James Clarence Mangan*, pp.37–38. Mangan's mode of creative plagiarism differed from the style of the late twentieth-century American post-feminist author Kathy Acker, given that Acker's works appeared under her own name as her creations and she was admittedly plagiarizing the works of others, such as Dickens. One similarity between the two, however, is that Acker too invented Persian sentences in her *Blood and Guts in High School* (1984) by patching together words evidently looked up in the dictionary, as did Mangan when incorporating phrases in putative Oriental languages into his writing.

56 Richard Ellmann, *Oscar Wilde*. New York: Alfred A. Knopf, 1988, p.352 n.*.

57 Sinéad Sturgeon, "Introduction. James Clarence Mangan: The Man in the Cloak" in Sturgeon, ed. *Essays on James Clarence Mangan*, p.1. On Mangan's preoccupation with veiling and masking in his poems too, see David Wheatley, "Fully able / to write in any language—I'm a Babel" in ibid., pp.41–43; David Wheatley, "Introduction" in James Clarence Mangan, *Poems* (David Wheatley ed.), p.11. See also, in particular, David Lloyd, *Nationalism and Minor Literature*, pp.195–214; Matthew Campbell, "Lyrical Unions: Mangan, O'Hussey and Ferguson," *Irish Studies Review* 8(3), December 2000, p.325.

58 Charles Patrick Meehan, ed., *Essays in Prose and Verse by James Clarence Mangan*. Dublin: James Duffy & Sons, 1884, pp.43–57. See also David James O'Donoghue, ed., *The Prose Writings of James Clarence Mangan*. Dublin: O'Donoghue & Co., 1904, pp.279–90. O'Donoghue noted that the piece was "Originally written for the *Belfast Vindicator* (hence the reference towards the close to a 'Vindicator of Talent'), in which it appeared on March 27, 1841. It was subsequently reprinted in *The Nation*, November, 1844." See ibid., "Notes," unnumbered page 331.

59 Charles Patrick Meehan, ed., *Essays in Prose and Verse*, p.52; David James O'Donoghue, ed., *The Prose Writings of James Clarence Mangan*, p.286.

60 David Wheatley makes the point that Mangan was indebted to English literary tradition, as in the case of Coleridge. Wheatley, "Introduction" in James Clarence Mangan, *Poems* (David Wheatley ed.), p.14.

61 For different assessments of this theme, see David Lloyd, *Nationalism and Minor Literature*, chapter 4; Matthew Campbell, "Lyrical Unions," pp.328–329; David Wheatley, "Fully able / to write in any language—I'm a Babel" in Sinéad Sturgeon, ed. *Essays on James Clarence Mangan*, pp.35–38.

62 For the range of concerns that Irish language was in crisis, see also Nicholas Wolf, *An Irish-Speaking Island*, p.8. Joep Leerssen, "Language Revivalism before the Twilight" in Joep Leerssen, A. H. van der Weel, and Bart Westerweel, eds., *Forging in the Smithy*, pp.135–39.
63 See Fergus Dunne, "The Politics of Translation," p.470.
64 Melissa Fegan, "Every Irishman is an Arab," p.200. See also p.195.
65 *Dublin Penny Journal* 2(99), March 22, 1834, pp.298–300.
66 On this topic, see also David Lloyd, *Nationalism and Minor Literature*, pp.110–14, 122–25, 129–32.
67 The term "Manganesque" appears to have been first coined by David James O'Donoghue in his 1897 *The Life and Writings of James Clarence Mangan* (p.xxii) and was also used the same year in Louise Imogen Guiney, *James Clarence Mangan: His Selected Poems, with a Study. With a Dedication to Sir Charles Gavan Duffy*. Norwood, MA: Norwood Press, 1897, p.106. Guiney and O'Donoghue were familiar with, and referred to, each other's research on Mangan in their respective publications (see p.234 in O'Donoghue's book and p.34 in Guiney's book). For more recent use of the term see, for example, Ellen Shannon-Mangan, *James Clarence Mangan: A Biography*. Dublin: Irish Academic Press, 1996, pp.45, 133, and passim. Shannon-Mangan's book is the most exhaustive biography of Mangan to-date.
68 On the broader scope of Mangan's engagement with Moore's works, see Jane Moore, "Nineteenth-century Irish Anacreontics," pp.387–405.
69 On Joyce and Mangan, see Heyward Ehrlich, "'Araby' in Context: The 'Splendid Bazaar,' Irish Orientalism and James Clarence Mangan," *James Joyce Quarterly* 35 (2–3), Winter-Spring 1998, pp.309–31. Note also Ehrlich's discussion of Joyce's working through Moore's versus Mangan's legacies in ibid., pp.320–26; notwithstanding Ehrlich's erroneous conflation of Arabic, Persian, and Turkish, as in the case of his identification of "Khan" as an Arabic lexicon on p.324.
70 David James O'Donoghue, *The Life and Writings of James Clarence Mangan*, p.3; David Wheatley, "Introduction" in James Clarence Mangan, *Poems* (David Wheatley ed.), p.11.
71 In addition to the recurrence of this phrase and sentiment in Moore's various editions of *Irish Melodies*, see for example Moore's poem appearing in his October 31, 1814, letter addressed to the publisher of his *Irish Melodies*, William Power, in *Memoirs, Journal, and Correspondence of Thomas Moore*, vol.2, p.46. The opening lines of this verse would be echoed in "The Fire-Worshippers" in *Lalla Rookh* in the form of Hinda's lamentation in the immediate aftermath of Hafed's death, capturing Moore's own sentiment concerning the ineffectiveness of pursuing any future revolutionary and republican solution to Ireland's status in the British Empire: "High burst in air the funeral flames, / And IRAN's hopes and hers are o'er!" Thomas Moore, *Lalla Rookh*, p.231. On this theme, see also Emer Nolan, "Preface" in Thomas Moore, *Memoirs of Captain Rock* (Emer Nolan, ed., 2008), p.xiv; Matthew Campbell, "Lyrical Unions," p.336 in particular; Luke Gibbons, "Romantic Ireland: 1750–1845" in James Chandler, ed., *The Cambridge History of English Romantic Literature*, pp.195–97.
72 On this point, see also Seamus Deane, *Strange Country: Modernity and Nationhood in Irish Writing since 1790*. Oxford: Clarendon Press, 1997, pp.135–37.
73 See also Patricia Coughlan, "'Fold over Fold, Inveterately Convolv'd': Some Aspects of Mangan's Intertextuality" in Birgit Bamsbäck and Martin Croghan, eds., *Anglo-Irish and Irish. Literature: Aspects of Language and Culture* Volume 2. Uppsala: S. Academiae Ubsaliensis, 1988, pp.191–200.
74 Heyward Ehrlich, "'Araby' in Context," p.325; Melissa Fegan, "Every Irishman is an Arab," p.200.
75 See the reference to Moore's "AL MOKANNA, the Veiled Impostor of Khorasan" and a line from *Lalla Rookh* appearing in "Literæ Orientales, No. I," *Dublin University Magazine* 10(57), September 1837, pp.290, 292; references to "The Paradise and the Peri" in "Literæ Orientales, No. II," *Dublin University Magazine* 11(63), March 1838, pp.297 n.++, 311 n.*; references to Mokanna of *Lalla Rookh* again in "Literæ Orientales, No. III," *Dublin University Magazine* 12(69), September 1838, p.336 n.S. On Mangan's "Literæ Orientales" in general, see also Ellen Shannon-Mangan, *James Clarence Mangan*, pp.173–74, 186–91, 218–19, 265–66; Jacques Chuto, Peter Van de Kamp, Augustine Martin, and Ellen Shannon-Mangan,

eds. *The Collected Works of James Clarence Mangan*, pp.1–7, 107–11, 154–57; Sean Ryder, ed., *James Clarence Mangan*, pp.54–60, 62–67, 70–76, 82–88, 140–52, 204–15.

76 See, for example, "Literæ Orientales, No. I," *Dublin University Magazine*, vol.10, no.57, September 1837, p.280; Louise Imogen Guiney, *James Clarence Mangan*, pp.91–92; David James O'Donoghue, *The Life and Writings of James Clarence Mangan*, p.89 (O'Donoghue confuses William Ouseley with his brother Sir Gore); David Lloyd, *Nationalism and Minor Literature*, pp.122–24; Melissa Fegan, "Every Irishman is an Arab," pp.203, 205.

77 David Lloyd, *Nationalism and Minor Literature*, pp.118–19.

78 See, for example, her two-volume 1887 *Ancient Legends, Mystic Charms, and Superstitions of Ireland*.

79 Lady Wilde, *Social Studies*. London: Ward & Downey, 1893, p.293. As I discuss later, various theories of the Eastern origins of the Irish continued to circulate in different forms well into the twentieth century, some of them echoing Vallancey's theories and methodology, but without referring to his works, and combining Vallanceyan-style antiquarianism with selective adaptations of more recent anthropological, archaeological, historical, and other findings.

80 David James O'Donoghue, *The Life and Writings of James Clarence Mangan*, p.90.

81 Richard W. Bulliet, "Naw Bahār and the Survival of Iranian Buddhism," *Iran* 14, 1976, pp.140–45.

82 For a comparison between Heman's and Mangan's poems, see Matthew Campbell, *Irish Poetry Under the Union, 1801-1924*. New York: Cambridge University Press, 2014, pp.119–20. On James Joyce's later reference to Mangan's 'Barmecides,' in Joyce's 1922 *Ulysses*, see also R. Brandon Kershner, "'Ulysses' and the Orient," *James Joyce Quarterly* 35(2 & 3), pp.289–91.

83 *Dublin University Magazine* 13(76), April 1839, p.485.

84 For Mangan's reliance on Hammer-Purgstall's works, see also Jacques Chuto as quoted in David Lloyd, "James Clarence Mangan's Oriental Translations," p.26.

85 *Dublin University Magazine* 13(76), April 1839, pp.483–501.

86 "Literæ Orientales. No. IV. Arabian, Persian and Turkish Poetry," *Dublin University Magazine* 15(88), April 1840, p.390.

87 *Dublin University Magazine* 13(76), April 1839, p.484.

88 See also Melissa Fegan, "Every Irishman is an Arab," p.198.

89 'Ibn Khallahan' appeared in Mangan's explanatory note for the final poem in "Literæ Orientales. No. IV. Arabian, Persian and Turkish Poetry," *Dublin University Magazine* 15(88), April 1840, p.394. See also Sean Ryder, ed. *James Clarence Mangan*, p.88.

90 "Literæ Orientales. No. IV. Arabian, Persian and Turkish Poetry," *Dublin University Magazine* 15(88), April 1840, pp.377–394.

91 "Literæ Orientales, No. I," ibid. 10(57), September 1837, p.282 n.* (see also p.281). For Hammer-Purgstall's comment, see Joseph Freiherr von Hammer-Purgstall, *Geschichte der Osmanischen Dichtkunst bis auf unsere Zeit*. Volume 1. Pesth: Conrad Adolph Hartleben, 1836, p.51.

92 "Literæ Orientales, No. V," *Dublin University Magazine* 23(137), May 1844, p.535. See also Sean Ryder, ed. *James Clarence Mangan*, p.140; Jacques Chuto, Peter Van de Kamp, Augustine Martin, and Ellen Shannon-Mangan, eds. *The Collected Works of James Clarence Mangan. Prose: 1840-1882*, p.107. During the time frame covered by Mangan in this installment of "Literæ Orientales" Anatolia had lapsed from (Turkic) Seljuk control to Mongol control.

93 For examples of Hammer-Purgstll's earlier works on Persian literature, see *Encyklopädische Uebersicht der Wissenschaften des Orients, aus sieben arabischen, persischen und türkischen Werken übersetzt. Den Freunden und Kennern der orientalischen*. (1804); *Schirin. Ein persisches romantisches Gedicht nach morgenländischen Quellen* (1809); *Morgenlaendisches kleeblatt, bestehend aus parsischen hymnen, arabischen elegien, türkischen eklogen* (1819); *Juwelenschnüre Abul-Maani's (des vaters der bedeutungen), das ist bruchstücke eines unbekannten persischen dichters* (1822). Hammer-Purgstall continued to produce works on Persian poetry and literature, as in the case of his 1838 *Mahmud Schebisteri's Rosenflor des Geheimnisses. Persisch und Deutsch herausgegeben*. On Hammer-Purgstall and Persian poetry, see also "Literæ Orientales, No. I," *Dublin University Magazine* 10(57), September 1837, p.280; and "Literæ Orientales, No. II," ibid. 11(63), March 1838, pp.291–312. In the latter work, Mangan savaged Hammer-Purgstall, whom he later also mocked as the character of "Herr Poppandgoöff Von Tutschemupp, a distinguished critic" in his "A Polyglott Anthology," ibid. 13(76), April 1839, pp.483–501 (published under one of Mangan's many pseudonyms, "THE OUT-AND-OUTER").

94 Joseph Lennon, "'Antiquity and Futurity' in the Writings of James Clarence Mangan" in Sinéad Sturgeon, ed. *Essays on James Clarence Mangan*, p.67.
95 The second volume of Mangan's *Anthologia Germanica* included three 'translations' of poems attributed to Herder, with the first poem "The Fair and Faithless One of Grailov" being an account of the Ottoman invasion of Eastern Europe. See James Clarence Mangan, *Anthologia Germanica. German Anthology: A Series of Translations from the Most Popular of the German Poets*. Volume II. Dublin: William Curry, Jun. and Company, 1845, pp.41–56. For Herder's influence on the Young Ireland movement, see also Eva Stöter, "'Grimmige Zeiten': The Influence of Lessing, Herder and the Grimm Brothers on the nationalism of the young Irelanders" in Tadhg Foley and Seán Ryder, eds., *Ideology and Ireland in the Nineteenth Century*, pp.173–80.
96 "Literæ Orientales. No. IV. Arabian, Persian and Turkish Poetry," *Dublin University Magazine* 15(88), April 1840, p.379. See also Jacques Chuto, Peter Van de Kamp, Augustine Martin, and Ellen Shannon-Mangan, eds. *The Collected Works of James Clarence Mangan. Prose: 1840-1882*, p.5.
97 See David Wheatley, "Fully able / to write in any language—I'm a Babel" in Sinéad Sturgeon, ed. *Essays on James Clarence Mangan*, pp.40–41.
98 On Mangan's choice of the name 'Clarence,' see also Sinéad Sturgeon, "'False, fleeting, perjured Clarence': Pseudonymity and Criminality in the Writings of James Clarence Mangan," *Canadian Journal of Irish Studies* 36(2), Fall 2010, pp.76–99.
99 "Literæ Orientales. No. IV. Arabian, Persian and Turkish Poetry," *Dublin University Magazine* 15(88), April 1840, p.381.
100 "Literæ Orientales, No. V," ibid. 23(137), May 1844, p.535. Mangan again mentioned Rumi (this time spelled "Rumee") in reference to the mystic poet's lack of religious prejudice in what became the final installment of "Literæ Orientales" ("No. VI"), ibid. 27(157), January 1846, p.47.
101 Ibid. 30(180), December 1847, pp.668–69. See Jacques Chuto, Rudolf Patrick Holzapfel, and Ellen Shannon-Mangan, eds. *The Collected Works of James Clarence Mangan. Poems: 1845-1847*. Dublin: Irish Academic Press, 1997, pp.419–20.
102 For the poem attributed to O'Sullivan see Louise Imogen Guiney, *James Clarence Mangan*, 1897, pp.152–55. Another translation of a poem by O'Sullivan ("Shane Bwee; or the Captivity of the Gaels") appeared in James Clarence Mangan, *Poems by James Clarence Mangan*, pp.344–46.
103 See, for example, Joseph Hammer[-Purgstall], *Der Diwan von Mohammed Schemsed-din Hafis*. Volume I. Stuttgart: J.G. Gottaschen, 1812. On the more general subject of these transliterations, see also Jacques Chuto, "Militant Nationalist Verse from 1798 to 1848," *Études irlandaises* 4(1), 1979, p.250.
104 Rudolf Patrick Holzapfel, "Mangan's poetry in the 'Dublin University Magazine': a bibliography," *Hermathena*, no.105 (Autumn 1967), p.45.
105 Literæ Orientales. No. IV. Arabian, Persian and Turkish Poetry," *Dublin University Magazine* 15(88), April 1840, p.394. See also Sean Ryder, ed. *James Clarence Mangan*, p.88.
106 J.T.P. de Bruijn, "Hammer-Purgstall, Joseph Freiherr von," *Encyclopaedia Iranica* (http://www.iranicaonline.org/articles/hammer-purgstall). See also David Lloyd, *Nationalism and Minor Literature*, pp.126–27.
107 "Literæ Orientales, No. I," *Dublin University Magazine*, 10(57), September 1837, pp.281–82.
108 Ibid. 32(191), November 1848, p.539. See also Sean Ryder, ed. *James Clarence Mangan*, p.293.
109 In his autobiographic self-obituary, he denied being an "opium-eater," noting: "He never swallowed a grain of opium in his life, and only on one occasion took—and then as a medicine—laudanum." See Jacques Chuto, Peter Van de Kamp, Augustine Martin, and Ellen Shannon-Mangan, eds. *The Collected Works of James Clarence Mangan. Prose: 1840-1882*, p.223; Sean Ryder, ed. *James Clarence Mangan*, p.413.
110 Shannon-Mangan, *James Clarence Mangan*, p.152.
111 John Mitchel, "James Clarence Mangan: His Life, Poetry, and Death" in James Clarence Mangan, *Poems by James Clarence Mangan*, p.20. It appears Mangan made this statement to his friend, the academic John Anster. See Sean Ryder, ed. *James Clarence Mangan*, p.411. See also David James O'Donoghue, *The Life and Writings of James Clarence Mangan*, pp.19, 86, 89–90, 111, 207; the anonymous review of two books on Mangan's poetry appearing in the

American edition of *Literature* (New York), no.12, January 8, 1898, pp.10–11; J. Yohannan, "The Persian Poetry Fad in England," p.159; James Kilroy, *James Clarence Mangan*, pp.28–29, 33–34; David Lloyd, "James Clarence Mangan's Oriental Translations," p.23; Hasan Javadi, *Persian Literary Influence on English Literature*, p.69.

112 Louise Imogen Guiney, *James Clarence Mangan*, pp.94–95.
113 Cóilín Parsons, *The Ordnance Survey*, pp.108–109.
114 Louise Imogen Guiney, *James Clarence Mangan*, pp.36–37, 38.
115 Harry D. Harootunian, "The Benjamin Effect: Modernism, Repetition, and the Path to Different Cultural Imaginaries" in Michael P. Steinberg, ed. *Walter Benjamin and the Demands of History*. Ithaca: Cornell University Press, 1996, p.71. For a slightly different take on Benjamin, De Man, and translation, see Anne MacCarthy, *James Clarence Mangan, Edward Walsh and Nineteenth-Century Irish Literature in English*. New York: Edwin Mellen, 2000, pp.84, 110–11. On the afterlife of Mangan's works, see also "Crossing Over: On James Clarence Mangan's 'Spirits Everywhere'" in David Lloyd, *Counterpoetics of Modernity: On Irish Poetry and Modernism*. Edinburgh: Edinburgh University Press, 2022, pp.49–64.
116 Seamus Deane, *Strange Country*, p.128.
117 "Literæ Orientales, No. II," *Dublin University Magazine* 11(63), March 1838, p.312.
118 "Literæ Orientales. No. IV. Arabian, Persian and Turkish Poetry," ibid/ 15(88), April 1840, p.377. See also David Lloyd, "James Clarence Mangan's Oriental Translations," p.25; Jacques Chuto, Peter Van de Kamp, Augustine Martin, and Ellen Shannon-Mangan, eds. *The Collected Works of James Clarence Mangan. Prose: 1840-1882*, pp.1–2.
119 "Literæ Orientales. No. IV. Arabian, Persian and Turkish Poetry," *Dublin University Magazine* 15(88), April 1840, pp.377–78. See also Jacques Chuto, Peter Van de Kamp, Augustine Martin, and Ellen Shannon-Mangan, eds. *The Collected Works of James Clarence Mangan. Prose: 1840-1882*, p.2.
120 "Literæ Orientales. No. IV. Arabian, Persian and Turkish Poetry," *Dublin University Magazine* 15(88), April 1840, pp.378–79. See also Jacques Chuto, Peter Van de Kamp, Augustine Martin, and Ellen Shannon-Mangan, eds. *The Collected Works of James Clarence Mangan. Prose: 1840-1882*, pp.2–3.
121 "Literæ Orientales. No. IV. Arabian, Persian and Turkish Poetry," *Dublin University Magazine* 15(88), April 1840, pp.393–94. See also See also Jacques Chuto, Peter Van de Kamp, Augustine Martin, and Ellen Shannon-Mangan, eds. *The Collected Works of James Clarence Mangan. Prose: 1840-1882*, p.7; Melissa Fegan, "Every Irishman is an Arab" p.207.
122 "A Polyglott Anthology," *Dublin University Magazine* 13(76), April 1839, pp.490–91.
123 In connection with Mangan's 'ethnological ambitions,' Wheatley also notes, "and perhaps it was in the same spirit that Joyce made 'Mangan's sister' the love-object of his narrator who travels to the Araby bazaar in *Dubliners*." "Introduction" in James Clarence Mangan, *Poems* (David Wheatley ed.), pp.12–13. See also Melissa Fegan, "Every Irishman is an Arab" pp.195–214.
124 Charles Gavan Duffy, "The Laurence's Address: To the Irish Princes at Peace with the Invader" in Timothy Daniel Sullivan, *Penny Reading for the Irish People*. Volume I. Dublin: T.D. Sullivan, 1879, pp.245, 248.
125 Charles Patrick Meehan, ed., *Essays in Prose and Verse*, p.79.
126 Ibid., p.84.
127 Eugene O'Curry, *On the Manners and Customs of the Ancient Irish*, vol.II, p.118.
128 Cóilín Parsons, "Anarchive: James Clarence Mangan among the Ruins," in Parsons, *The Ordnance Survey*, p.108. On fragmentation and the theme of ruins in Mangan's poetry, see also Luke Gibbons, "Race Against Time," pp.108–109.
129 David Lloyd, "James Clarence Mangan's Oriental Translations," pp.20–35.
130 For different views on this subject, see also David Lloyd, "Translator as Refractor: Towards a Re-Reading of James Clarence Mangan as Translator," *Dispositio* 7(19–21), 1982, pp.158–60; idem, "James Clarence Mangan's Oriental Translations," pp.20–35; Joseph Lennon, "'Antiquity and Futurity' in the Writings of James Clarence Mangan" in Sinéad Sturgeon, ed. *Essays on James Clarence Mangan*, pp.73–75.
131 Cóilín Parsons, *The Ordnance Survey*, pp.87–88.
132 Ibid., p.56. See also p.51.
133 Ibid., pp.111–12.

134 Kevin Barry, ed. *James Joyce*, pp.59, 60, 135, 136.
135 Cóilín Parsons, "Anarchive: James Clarence Mangan Among the Ruins," in Parsons, *The Ordnance Survey*, p.83.
136 *Dublin University Magazine* 3(168), June 1834, p.694.
137 See also John Mitchel's biography of Mangan in James Clarence Mangan, *Poems by James Clarence Mangan*, pp.15–16.
138 For the debate on Mangan's nationalism, see also Jacques Chuto, "James Clarence Mangan: In Exile at Home," *Études irlandaises* 1(1), 1976, pp.35–50; Jacques Chuto "Militant Nationalist Verse from 1798 to 1848," *Études irlandaises* 4(1), 1979, pp.262–64; Ciara Hogan, "Lost Hero of the Past," pp.140–41; Matthew Campbell, "Lyrical Unions," p.333; Sinéad Sturgeon, "Introduction" in Sinéad Sturgeon, ed., *Essays on James Clarence Mangan*, pp.4–5.
139 Róisín Healy has suggested that in this poem Mangan may also have had in mind the Polish nationalists deported to Siberia. Róisín Healy, *Poland in the Irish Nationalist Imagination*, p.134.
140 James Clarence Mangan, *Poems by James Clarence Mangan*, pp.432–33.
141 Ciara Hogan, "Lost Hero of the Past," p.140.
142 See also James Clarence Mangan, *Poems by James Clarence Mangan*, pp.430–31, 437–41, 446–48.
143 See also James Clarence Mangan, *Poems by James Clarence Mangan*, pp.436–37.
144 See also the discussion of Thomas Osborne Davis' "A Ballad of Freedom" in Jacques Chuto, "Militant Nationalist Verse," p.247.
145 See also Julia M. Wright, *Ireland, India and Nationalism*, pp.174–81.
146 Ibid., pp.178–79.
147 See, for example, "The Clan of Mac Caura" (1850) in Denis Florence MacCarthy, *Ballads, Poems, Lyrics*, p.155.
148 James Clarence Mangan, *Poems by James Clarence Mangan*, pp.418–49. Mitchel's selected poems were overwhelmingly from Mangan's *Anthologia Germanica*, appearing as "German Anthology" in this edited volume.
149 See, for example, ibid., pp.428–29; John Boyle O'Reilly, ed., *Poetry and Song of Ireland*. New York: Gay Brothers & Co., 1887, pp.410–11; David James O'Donoghue, *The Life and Writings of James Clarence Mangan*, p.161.
150 *The Nation*, April 18, 1846, p.427, c.b.
151 Ibid., April 18, 1846, p.427, c.b. See also Jacques Chuto, Rudolf Patrick Holzapfel, and Ellen Shannon-Mangan, eds., *The Collected Works of James Clarence Mangan. Poems: 1845-1847*, pp.159–60; Sean Ryder, ed. *James Clarence Mangan*, pp.214–15.
152 In the 1845 pseudo-translation of an ostensibly German poem, attributed to the invented poet "Heyden" and titled "The Last Words of Al-Hassan," appearing in "Anthologia Germanica—No.XIX," Mangan had also given the equivalent of "Giaour" as "Literally *dog*, (the Irish *Gadhar*), and figuratively *infidel*." "Anthologia Germanica—No.XIX—Miscellaneous Poems," *Dublin University Magazine* 25(145), January 1845, p.99 n.*. The poem is reproduced in Sean Ryder, ed. *James Clarence Mangan*, pp.160–61. The term in reference to Zoroastrians had appeared in a sympathetic light in the form of "Ghebers" in Moore's *Lalla Rookh* and, following Moore's example, as "Guebre" in Denis Florence MacCarthy's 1850 "The Clan of Mac Caura," among other range of Irish nationalist poetry. On "The Last Words of Al-Hassan," see the remainder of the present chapter.
153 For a very different interpretation of these footnotes, see Melissa Fegan, "Every Irishman is an Arab" p.211.
154 She notes "the inimitable 'Siberia' [...] has always been recognized as one of his finest poems, while the former ['To the Ingleezee Khafir'], although much less has been said about it, is an outstanding example of the poet's sarcastic wit at play, a masterpiece of its kind." Ellen Shannon-Mangan, *James Clarence Mangan*, p.316.
155 *Democratic Review of British and Foreign Politics, History, & Literature* (London), vol.1, August 1849, pp.117–20.
156 Kevin Barry, ed. *James Joyce*, p.59.
157 See also Melissa Fegan, *Literature and the Irish Famine, 1845-1919*. New York: Oxford University Press, 2002, p.50.
158 In 1886 this work appeared as part of the multi-volume collection published by the Hakluyt Society. For the text of the letter from Queen Elizabeth to Shah Tahmasb (dated April 25,

1561), see Anthony Jenkinson and other Englishmen, *Early Voyages and Travels to Russia and Persia*. Volume I. E. Delmar Morgan and C.H. Coote editors. London: Hakluyt Society, 1886, pp.112–14.
159 John Malcolm, *The History of Persia*, vol.I (1815 edition), pp.511–13 and passim.
160 *The Nation*, April 18, 1846, p.427, c.b.
161 See the reprint of Hakluyt's book appearing as: Anthony Jenkinson and other Englishmen, *Early Voyages and Travels to Russia and Persia*. Volume II. E. Delmar Morgan and C.H. Coote editors. London: Hakluyt Society, 1886, p.183. For the account of Jenkinson's voyage to Iran, see ibid., pp.112–56.
162 See also Denis Wright, "Fraser, James Baillie," Encyclopaedia Iranica (iranicaonline.org/articles/fraser-).
163 James Baillie Fraser, *The Kuzzilbash: A Tale of Khorasan*. Volume I. London: Henry Colburn, 1828, p.9.
164 "A Polyglott Anthology," *Dublin University Magazine* 13(76), April 1839, p.485.
165 James Baillie Fraser, *The Kuzzilbash: A Tale of Khorasan*. Volume I. London: Henry Colburn, 1828, pp.11–12.
166 For this poem, see Jacques Chuto, Rudolf Patrick Holzapfel, and Ellen Shannon-Mangan, eds. *The Collected Works of James Clarence Mangan. Poems: 1845-1847*, pp.419–20.
167 Denis Florence MacCarthy, *Ballads, Poems, Lyrics*, p.155.
168 Ibid., p.379.
169 Heinrich Heine, *Tragödien, nebst einem lyrischen Intermezzo*. Berlin: Ferdinand Dümmler, 1823, p.148.
170 "Anthologia Germanica—No.XIX—Miscellaneous Poems," *Dublin University Magazine* 25(145), January 1845, pp.98–99. The poem is also reproduced in Jacques Chuto, Rudolf Patrick Holzapfel, and Ellen Shannon-Mangan, eds., *The Collected Works of James Clarence Mangan. Poems: 1845-1847*, pp.3–4; and in Sean Ryder, ed. *James Clarence Mangan*, pp.160–61.
171 Paul Ricoeur, *Memory, History, Forgetting*. Kathleen Blamey and David Pellauer translators. Second edition. Chicago: University of Chicago Press, 2006 [2004] (originally published in French as *La mémoire, l'histoire, l'oubli* in 2000), p.448.
172 John Malcolm, *The History of Persia*, vol.I (1815 edition), pp.531–37, 544–52, 559; Percy Sykes, *A History of Persia*. Volume II. London: MacMillan and Co., 1915, pp.259–62, 273–83, 363–37; John Piggot, *Persia: Ancient and Modern*. London: Henry S. King & Co., 1874, pp.205–207; William Noel Sainsbury, ed., *Calendar of State Papers. Colonial Series. Volume 6: East Indies, China and Persia, 1625-1629*. London: Her Majesty's Stationary Office, 1884, passim; Laurence Lockhart, "European Contacts with Persia, 1350-1736" in Peter Jackson and Laurence Lockhart, eds., *The Cambridge History of Iran. Volume 6: The Timurid and Safavid Periods*. Reprint. Cambridge: Cambridge University Press, 2006[1986], pp.393–96; Ronald Ferrier, "Trade from Mid-14th Century to the End of the Safavid Period" in ibid., pp.444–53; Colin Paul Mitchell, "Shāh 'Abbās, the English East India Company and the Cannoneers of Fārs," *Itinerario* 24(2), 2000, pp.104–25; Peter Good, "The East India Company's *Farmān*, 1622-1747," *Iranian Studies* 52(1–2), 2019, pp.181–97.
173 Paul Ricoeur, *Memory, History, Forgetting*, pp.88–89.
174 Aleida Assmann, "How History Takes Place" in Indra Sengupta, ed., *Memory, History, and Colonialism: Engaging with Pierre Nora in Colonial and Postcolonial Contexts*. London: German Historical Institute, 2009, pp.161–62.
175 Paul Ricoeur, *Memory, History, Forgetting*, p.381.
176 On a related subject, see also Ricoeur's discussion of Maurice Halbwachs' working through the historical memory of the "nation," "universal history," and 'the universal memory of human species' in ibid., p.397.
177 On the concept of 'there and then' in Mangan's poetry, see also Jacques Chuto, "James Clarence Mangan," p.44; Patricia Coughlan's reference to Mangan's works in which the "setting [...] is an elsewhere, whether of time or space," in Patricia Coughlan, "'Fold over Fold" in Birgit Bamsbäck and Martin Croghan, eds., *Anglo-Irish and Irish Literature*, p.196.
178 Quoted in Cóilín Parsons's *The Ordnance Survey*, p.83.
179 Reproduced in Sean Ryder, ed. *James Clarence Mangan*, p.408. See also Joseph Lennon, "'Antiquity and Futurity' in the Writings of James Clarence Mangan" in Sinéad Sturgeon, ed. *Essays on James Clarence Mangan*, pp.58–59.

180 See, for example, Charles Vallancey, *A Vindication*, pp.398, 399, 403, 409, 463, 467, 468–73, 547–58.
181 Henry O'Brien, *The Round Towers* (1834 edition), pp.17–19, 34, 165, and passim.
182 David Lloyd, *Nationalism and Minor Literature*, p.193.
183 Ellen Shannon-Mangan, *James Clarence Mangan*, p.120.
184 *The Nation*, July 11, 1846, p.619, c.a (appearing under "Poet's Corner"). On this poem, see also Sean Ryder, ed. *James Clarence Mangan*, p.228; Patricia Coughlan, "'Fold over Fold" in Birgit Bamsbäck and Martin Croghan, eds., *Anglo-Irish and Irish Literature*, p.196.
185 "Literæ Orientales, No. II," *Dublin University Magazine* 11(63), March 1838, p.308 n.*
186 Ralph Pordzik "A Postcolonial View of Ireland and the Irish Conflict in Anglo-Irish Utopian Literature since the Nineteenth Century," *Irish Studies Review* 9(3), 2001, p.332.
187 See also Matthew Campbell, "Lyrical Unions," pp.327,330, 336.
188 Richard Haslam, "Broad Farce and Thrilling Tragedy': Mangan's Fiction and Irish Gothic," *Éire-Ireland* 41(3&4), Fall/Winter 2006, p.229 and passim. See also Patricia Coughlan, "'Fold over Fold" in Birgit Bamsbäck and Martin Croghan, eds., *Anglo-Irish and Irish Literature*, pp.192, 195.
189 Reproduced in Sean Ryder, ed. *James Clarence Mangan*, p.404.
190 Reproduced in Jacques Chuto, Peter Van de Kamp, Augustine Martin, and Ellen Shannon-Mangan, eds. *The Collected Works of James Clarence Mangan. Prose: 1840-1882*, p.279.
191 Joseph Lennon, "'Antiquity and Futurity' in the Writings of James Clarence Mangan" in Sinéad Sturgeon, ed. *Essays on James Clarence Mangan*, pp.69–72. On this topic, see also Luke Gibbons, "Romantic Ireland: 1750–1845" in James Chandler, ed., *The Cambridge History of English Romantic Literature*, pp.199–201.
192 *The United Irishman* (Dublin), May 13, 1848, p.211, c.a. Among other posthumous collections of Mangan's works, this poem also appeared in John Mitchel's 1859 edited volume of Mangan's poems: James Clarence Mangan, *Poems by James Clarence Mangan*, pp.446–48. In this collection, the poem was included in the section titled "Miscellaneous," with Mitchel describing the poem as possessing "rich metaphor and allegory, and [...] in the form of noble lines" (ibid., p.16). The poem also appeared as the opening selection classed under "Original Poems. II. Pro Patria" in Louise Imogen Guiney, *James Clarence Mangan*, pp.295–97.
193 Shannon-Mangan, *James Clarence Mangan*, pp.377–78. Here, Shannon-Mangan only reproduces the opening and closing sections of the poem.
194 David Lloyd, "Great Gaps in Irish Song," pp.186–87.
195 "To Clarence Mangan," *Dublin University Magazine* 29(173), May 1847, p.623. The title "Anthologia Hibernica" was most likely a conscious pun by Mangan on the name of a periodical by the same title published by Richard Edward Mercier in late-eighteenth century Dublin. Of that periodical, Máire Kennedy writes that it "was devoted to science, history, and literature" as part of Ireland's Enlightenment movement. Máire Kennedy, "Reading the Enlightenment in Eighteenth-Century Ireland," *Eighteenth-Century Studies* 45(3), Spring 2012, pp.367, 369–71.
196 See also David Wheatley, "Fully able / to write in any language—I'm a Babel" in Sinéad Sturgeon, ed. *Essays on James Clarence Mangan*, pp.33–51.
197 On the significance of his class identity, see also Ciara Hogan, "Cultural Nationalism and the 'Cashless Bard,'" pp.82–102.
198 David Lloyd, "James Clarence Mangan's Oriental Translations," p.20.
199 John Mitchel wrote:

> For this Mangan was not only an Irishman—not only an Irish papist—not only an Irish papist rebel;—but throughout his whole literary life of twenty years, he never deigned to attorn to English criticism, never published a line in any English periodical, or through any English bookseller, never seemed to be aware that there was a British public to please. He was a rebel politically, and a rebel intellectually and spiritually—a rebel with his whole heart and soul against the whole British spirit of the age. The consequence was sure, and not unexpected. Hardly anybody in England knew the name of such a person; and the only critique of his volumes called "German Anthology" which I have ever met with, is a very short and contemptuous notice in the *Foreign Quarterly*, for October, 1845, wherein the austere critic declares Mr. Mangan's method of rendering the German to

be, 'not gilding refined gold, but plating it with copper; not painting the lily white, but plastering it with red ochre.'
John Mitchel, "James Clarence Mangan: His Life, Poetry, and Death" in James Clarence Mangan, *Poems by James Clarence Mangan*, p.8.

200 Jacques Chuto, "James Clarence Mangan," p.44.
201 Kevin Barry, ed. *James Joyce*, pp.54–55, 131.
202 "Literæ Orientales. No. I," *Dublin University Magazine* 10(57), September 1837, p.274.
203 Reproduced in Jacques Chuto, Peter Van de Kamp, Augustine Martin, and Ellen Shannon-Mangan, eds. *The Collected Works of James Clarence Mangan. Prose: 1840-1882*, p.224; and Sean Ryder, ed. *James Clarence Mangan*, pp.413–14.
204 On this topic, see also "Introduction" in James Clarence Mangan, *Poems* (David Wheatley ed.), pp.14–15. Wheatley writes: "Equally modern in Mangan is his scepticism about the unitary self capable of receiving [...] a [final] revelation, preferring as he did the elective ventriloquism of translation—whether or not the original ever existed."
205 Terry Eagleton, *Scholars and Rebels in Nineteenth-Century Ireland*. Oxford: Blackwell Publishers, 1999, pp.131–32.
206 On this poem, see also Matthew Campbell, *Irish Poetry Under the Union*, pp.121–22; Cóilín Parsons's *The Ordnance Survey*, pp.99–101; Jacques Chuto, "James Clarence Mangan," pp.43–44.
207 Reproduced in James Clarence Mangan, *Poems by James Clarence*, pp.433–35.
208 While as Lynne A. Bongiovanni correctly points out that in text of a 1907 intended lecture Joyce claimed Irish language had derived from Phoenician (Bongiovanni, "Turbaned faces going by" p.25), in his 1939 *Finnegans Wake* Joyce toyed with the Iran/Erin simile. See Chapter Nine in the present book. See also Joseph Theodoor Leerssen, "On the Edge of Europe," pp.108–109.
209 Kevin Barry, ed. *James Joyce*, pp.58, 135. Joyce also noted in 1907, "I know of no other piece of English literature where the spirit of revenge has attained such heights of melody." Ibid., p.134.
210 Ibid., pp.135–36. This was a slightly revised version of what Joyce had written in 1902. See ibid., p.59.
211 Joyce, "James Clarence Mangan (1907)" in ibid., p.130.
212 Reproduced in Jacques Chuto, Peter Van de Kamp, Augustine Martin, and Ellen Shannon-Mangan, eds. *The Collected Works of James Clarence Mangan. Prose: 1840-1882*, pp.222–25; Sean Ryder, ed. *James Clarence Mangan*, pp.411–15; and idem, "Male Autobiography and Irish Cultural Nationalism: John Mitchel and James Clarence Mangan," *Irish Review*, no.13, Winter 1992/1993, pp.72–73, 76–77.
213 For additional detail on these publications, see also Jaques Chuto, "James Clarence Mangan" in James H. Murphy, ed., *The Oxford History of the Irish Book*, vol.IV, pp.432–41.
214 Gwynn was a leading Irish Parliamentary Party "Home Rule" nationalist MP, author, and literary critic. He emerged as a leading Irish nationalist champion, alongside John Dillon, of the Iranian constitutional movement of 1906-11 contra London's and St. Petersburg's official forward policy in Iran (see Chapter Seven in the present book).
215 Stephen Gwynn, *The Fair Hills of Ireland*. Dublin: Maunsel and Co., 1906, p.8. See also p.1. This book was simultaneously published by Macmillan & Co. in London and New York.
216 Stephen Gwynn, *Thomas Moore*. London: MacMillan and Co., 1905.
217 *Official Guide: Dublin*. Dublin: Bord Fáilte Éireann, 1950, p.54

Chapter Four

CONTEMPORARY AFFINITIES: *THE NATION* AND THE ANGLO-IRANIAN WAR OF 1856–57

With the exception of allegoric social, cultural, and political referentialities to contemporary Iran in the 'Persian Letters' genre of Irish literature, including in Moore's 1813 *Intercepted Letters,* prior to 1856 it was Irans of past historical and/or imaginary settings that featured in Irish nationalist commentaries in connection with Ireland itself (namely in antiquarian and literary works). In 1856 contemporary Iranian developments became a subject of Irish nationalist political observation and commentary in the framework of the Irish Question, more specifically in so-called radical nationalist circles. This marked the start of what became periodic Irish nationalist expressions of solidarity with variously configured "Iranian" acts of resistance to outside aggression, initially in the form of defending the Iranian state, which was itself engaged in an act of territorial aggression, and subsequently in the form of expressed camaraderie with varying Iranian popular expressions of anti-imperialist nationalism (as well as with Iranian anti-autocratic endeavors). In 1856 Britain and Iran went to war for the second time; the first occasion having been the brief Anglo-Iranian War of 1838 that resulted in a British military victory and subsequent commercial and other privileges in Iran under the eventual peace treaty of 1841. The 1856 Anglo-Iranian conflict occurred just as the ravages of the devastating Irish famine of 1845–51 had subsided. It also coincided with the closing stages of the Crimean War (1854–56), in which Britain and France had joined the Ottoman state in curbing Russia's territorial aggression against the Ottoman Empire and foiling St. Petersburg's control of the Black Sea.[1] During the latest Anglo-Iranian War, British troops dispatched to Iranian territory from neighboring British India also included, alongside the native Indian sepoys, Irish soldiers and officers (Protestants and Catholic), as had been the case in the 1838 armed conflict between Iran and the British Empire. In Ireland and in the Irish diaspora (notably in the United States) the more "radical" Irish nationalists seized the Anglo-Iranian War as an opportunity to condemn what they characterized as Britain's continued imperialist aggression around the world, by also circuitously redirecting attention to continued English occupation and alleged maladministration of Ireland.

The Anglo-Iranian War of 1856–57 (or the "Second Anglo-Persian War" as it came to be known) was waged by Britain as a means of reversing Iran's military operations for capturing Herat and its adjoining "Afghan" territories. These territories were last directly controlled by an Iranian state in the eighteenth century and were since governed by competing Durrani/Abdali Pashtun (Pathan) clan factions with different degrees of allegiance to, or defiance of, the Iranian state. Herat was also coveted by the rival Ghilzai Pashtun confederacy that controlled 'Afghan' territories to the east and south, stretching southward to the frontiers of British India. Attempts to capture Herat in the previous decades by rulers of Iran's Qajar dynasty (1796–1925) had met with failure, with one such campaign in 1837–38 leading to the "First Anglo-Persian War." British administrators were concerned with the destabilizing regional effect of Iranian-controlled Herat to the northwest of existing Afghan territories, which British policy makers regarded as a major buffer zone between British India to the south and the Russian Empire to the north. British military intervention in 1838 forced Iran to halt its offensive against Herat, but without unequivocally renouncing Tehran's claim to that territory and its environs under a delayed peace treaty concluded between Iran and Britain in 1841.[2] In late 1851 the Iranian monarch Nasser al-Din Shah (r.1848–96) found a renewed opportunity for seizing Herat, exploiting a request by the new ruler of Herat (Sayyid Mohammad Khan) for military assistance against the invading forces of 'Afghan' rulers of Kandahar and Kabul. Iranian troops captured Herat, eliciting in response a British military warning to Tehran. To avoid another war with Britain, on this occasion Tehran withdrew its troops from Herat. Following a coup in Herat in 1855, the new Iranian-backed ruler of Herat, Mohammad Yusuf of the Sadozai clan (related to the Durrani/Abdali tribe), turned to Iranian authorities for assistance against his local and regional rivals, as well as for impeding the territorial ambition of the Afghan strongman Dost Mohammad Khan, the Barakzai ruler of Kabul who was fast consolidating his hold over the remainder of 'Afghan' territories. In the same year, Dost Mohammad Khan, a former adversary of Britain's expansionist policy in the region, had resumed diplomatic relations with British India. He had previously been captured by British invading forces in 1840 during the First Anglo-Afghan War and held in India for nearly two years. In 1855, Dost Mohammad Khan and British authorities in India concluded a treaty of friendship, primarily directed against Russian ambitions in the region, while also intended to bolster Dost Mohammad Khan's ability to curtail Iran's influence in Herat. In 1856, Dost Mohammad Khan set out to capture Herat, having already extended his control over other Afghan territories in the previous year, including Kandahar. It was the Iranian military intervention in Herat at the behest of Mohammad Yusuf for defending his newly gained territory, and with Russian encouragement of the Iranian monarch, that sparked off the Second Anglo-Iranian War, with Britain attempting to prevent Tehran's seeming ambition of eventually establishing direct control over Herat.

The military conflict between Iran and Britain got underway with the declaration of war on November 1, 1856, by the governor-general of British India (Lord Charles

John Canning). This was followed by the dispatch of naval forces from British India to the Persian Gulf and the landing of British forces in southern Iran later in the month, occupying first the Iranian island of Kharg and then the major southern port city of Bushire by December, with further British reinforcements and expeditionary forces continuing to arrive in early 1857 and expanding their inland zone of occupation. In the meantime, Dost Mohammad Khan took up arms against Iranian forces and their local allies in Herat. The war between Britain and Iran ended after the signing of the Treaty of Paris on March 4, 1857, with Tehran pledging to respect Afghan sovereignty over Herat, although the armed hostilities between Britain and Iran continued until April 5, due to delay in communications—in the absence of a telegraph line between London and Calcutta before 1870, as well as the absence of means of rapid communication between Calcutta and British imperial forces in southern Iran and the Persian Gulf.

Anglo-Iranian diplomatic relations had already ruptured prior to the British declaration of war over Herat. In 1855, the British legation in Tehran had been embroiled in drawn-out caustic exchanges with Iranian authorities. The cause of the dispute was the employment by the legation since 1854 of a dismissed Iranian official, Mirza Hashem Khan, and his subsequent appointment as an employee of the British mission in Shiraz in central Iran, despite vehement objections from Iranian authorities. Before long, the quarrel came to center around Tehran's contention of improper relations between Mirza Hashem's wife and the new British representative in Tehran, Charles Murray, as well as with Murray's predecessor, the British chargé d'affaires William Taylour Thomson. Further complicating matters, Mirza Hashem's wife happened to be a sister-in-law of the Iranian monarch.[3] Murray, unable to resolve the situation to London's satisfaction following a protracted and barbed series of accusations and counter-accusations between him and Iranian authorities, pulled down the legation flag on November 20, 1855, and shortly thereafter left Iran in keeping with his earlier ultimatum. Murray's departure took place almost exactly a year before Britain declared war against Iran over Herat. With the British declaration of war in late 1856, the Mrs. Hashem episode was resurrected by the British press critical of London's justification for the latest war. *The Times* of London—in an uncharacteristic deviation from its usual stance of defending London's official foreign policy—along with a host of regional papers, such as the *Leeds Mercury*, regarded the prior debacle surrounding the so-called Mrs. Hashem affair as the actual premise for London's military action against Tehran.[4] In the British press, the war came to be variously dubbed as "the great Mrs. Hashem question,"[5] "a silly quarrel about a Persian woman,"[6] or "Mrs. Hashim's case,"[7] among other such appellations. These captions implied that Britain's expressed concern over Herat was a pretext for finally settling score with Iranian authorities over the presumed diplomatic offence caused to Murray and the subsequent rupture of diplomatic relations between the two countries—with some commentators in Britain convinced of the veracity of Murray's amorous relationship with Mrs. Hashem. Most other critics of the British Whig prime minister Lord Palmerston's Iranian war effort, including many members of the British parliament, maintained Murray had no business in the first place of getting mixed up in a quarrel with Iranian authorities over Mirza Hashem and/or the latter's wife.

At the time of the outbreak of military hostilities between Iran and Britain in late November of 1856, Lord Palmerston (Henry John Temple) did not even enjoy the full backing of his own cabinet, nor could he count on the broad support of the Conservative opposition,[8] in what the former Peelite Whig chancellor of the exchequer, William Gladstone, termed the "Persian Squabble."[9] The initial rupture in Anglo-Iranian diplomatic relations by Murray had happened to coincide with, and further escalated, the already fierce foreign policy debates in Britain (inside and outside the parliament) in condemnation of Palmerston's overall conduct of foreign affairs. This included the ongoing vehement Radical onslaught in Palmerston's own party against his handling of the Crimean War (1854–56), with the Anglo-Iranian War occurring just as the Crimean War was coming to an end. The closing stages of the Anglo-Iranian War, in turn, coincided with the early phase of what became the Second Anglo-Chinese War of 1856–60 (a.k.a. the "Second Opium War"). The diplomatic and subsequent military conflict between London and Tehran also overlapped with the rapidly worsening diplomatic row between London and Washington from 1854 to 1856 concerning their respective expressed "interests" in Central America, which was further exacerbated by the botched British scheme to recruit mercenaries in the United States for the war effort in Crimea in violation of the US neutrality laws, among other sources of the diplomatic rift between London and Washington at the time.[10] As outlandish as it sounds, Palmerston was even briefly convinced Tehran and Washington may join forces against Britain.[11]

The British parliamentary opposition to Palmerston's Iranian policy, which included members of Palmerston's own party, condemned the Iranian war on grounds of its unconstitutionality, with no parliamentary consultation prior to the declaration of war. Additionally, the opposition maintained the war would prove detrimental to British imperial interests by politically alienating Iran and expediting Russia's increased leverage in Iran and, consequently, leading to expanded Russian influence in the region as a whole. The opposition moreover condemned the financial burden of waging yet another war just as Britain was concluding an exorbitant war in Crimea. It was, in fact, to circumvent the process of parliamentary authorization for military action against Tehran that Palmerston had disingenuously arranged for the authorities in British India to initiate the official declaration of war, even though ultimately such a declaration would have required London's prior endorsement, since it concerned British India's external affairs. Palmerston's parliamentary critics also censured Charles Murray's altercation with the Iranian government prior to the termination of diplomatic relations between the two countries, with Murray and his predecessor, the chargé d'affaires Thomson, accused of unwarranted meddling in matters pertaining to an Iranian woman (Mrs. Hashem), who also happened to be related to the shah. Murray and Thomson were blamed for having allegedly violated both Iranian customs and Islamic law.[12] These critics further insisted the initial break in relations between London and Tehran had aggravated the eventual outcome of the conflict over Herat. Significantly, the main front of the British opposition to Palmerston's Iranian policy came from the Radical wing of the prime minister's own Whig (later Liberal) Party and was spearheaded by the Radical MP Austen Henry Layard, who had engaged in condemnation of London's relations with Tehran as early as March 1856 (almost nine months before war finally broke out between the two countries). The Radical campaign, also enjoying the support of William Gladstone,[13] marked the first instance of a fervent Radical challenge to their own party's policy toward Iran, foreshadowing the Radical campaign against Sir Edward Grey's Iranian policy in the next century (see Chapter Seven).

The Anglo-Iranian War developed into a constitutional debate in the House of Commons. Following Iran's defeat in the conflict and the peace negotiations in March 1857, on July 8, 1857, the prominent Radical MP, John Arthur Roebuck (born in India and a supporter of Irish Home Rule),[14] alleged that the entire conduct of the war by the British government had been an unconstitutional undertaking: "A war had been declared, an expedition had been undertaken, a peace had been made" without consulting the Parliament.[15] Roebuck, backed by a number of Radicals and Gladstone (with Layard having lost his Parliamentary seat by then), also accused Palmerston's of pressuring Iran into closer ties with Russia. The Anglo-Iranian War came to a close shortly before the opening stages of the Indian uprising (a.k.a., "Sepoy Mutiny") which erupted in May 1857—with the Indian uprising, incidentally, constituting the earliest examples of prolonged radical Irish nationalist championing of the Indian "nation."[16] Palmerston's (British) Radical parliamentary critics, now joined by a number of Conservative MPs, also held the Iranian war variously responsible for the outbreak of disturbances in India. Contrary to the government's denials, Roebuck and other critics maintained that the absence from India of Indian imperial forces who had been dispatched to southern Iran (i.e., "British," including Irish, and native Indian soldiers) had provided the rebellious sepoys an opportunity to mutiny: "denuding India of the forces of England [which had endangered] the very existence of our Indian Empire."[17] This expressed concern with India's security on the part of the Radical opposition was in objection to the deployment of British-Indian forces outside Indian frontiers (i.e., for aggressive rather than defensive military operations). Moreover, this stance also targeted the British Foreign Office's stated logic of waging war against Iran—that is, to maintain India's security. In the end, Roebuck's parliamentary resolution for censuring the government failed to be carried (with an overwhelming vote of 352 to 38 in favor of Palmerston).[18] Although parliamentary and extra-parliamentary debates concerning the military expenditure of the war against Iran continued for some time, after the defeat of Roebuck's parliamentary motion the (British) Radical focus shifted to the situation in India and other overseas developments, chiefly the ongoing British intervention in China.[19]

The Irish Press Coverage of the Anglo-Iranian War

Based on parliamentary and press reports, London's instigation of the Anglo-Iranian War was unpopular across a broad spectrum of British public opinion. Yet, with the exception of the Radical press and Radical MPs, much of the British press, including *The Times*, while critical of London's initial premise for the war, covered the conduct of the war itself either with increasingly patriotic tenor in support of 'British' forces or, at the very least, maintained a neutral stance in their reporting of the war. Neutrality and patriotism were the general pattern in the Irish press coverage of the war too, with the notable exception of *The Nation* among the Dublin-based Irish nationalist press with relatively wide circulation. *The Nation* emerged not only as a vehement critic of London's war effort against Iran but also as an enthusiastic proponent of what it characterized as the Iranian state's justifiable military campaign against British imperial aggression. *The Nation*'s highly critical coverage of the British war effort differed drastically from the onslaught against Palmerston's government by British Radical outlets, in so far as *The Nation* also made use of the war as a means of commenting on Ireland's colonial status and the avowed continued British misrule in Ireland.

Just as Britain's military operations against Iran got underway, the December 1856 issue of the conservative unionist Irish periodical *Dublin University Magazine* carried a long article on the evolution of Anglo-Iranian relations and the Herat Question. The article was highly critical of Murray's conduct: "Hardly had the Hon. Mr. Murray arrived at his new post, before he found himself involved in a miserable zenana [i.e., harem] intrigue, the only object of which was to divert his attention from more serious public affairs." Nonetheless, the article maintained Iran was incontrovertibly the guilty party in the latest Herat dispute between London and Tehran:

> The ostensible motive for the siege [of Herat by Iranian forces] is similar to that put forward by Russia for interfering in the internal administration of Turkey. A considerable number of the inhabitants of Herat, being descendants from a colony established by Nadir Shah [the eighteenth-century Iranian ruler], profess the Sheeah [i.e., Shi'ism] [...] and have consequently been subjected to some persecution by the prevailing Soonnites [i.e., Sunnis]. The Shah, therefore, comes forward as the protector of his co-religionists and demands the possession of Herat as [...] "a material guarantee" for their toleration and freedom from insult throughout Afghanistan. On the same grounds a French or Austrian army might lay claim to Dublin or Cork, for the purpose of defending the Roman Catholics of Ireland from Protestant tyranny. But there remains for England the same necessity as of aforetime, for the preservation of Herat. [...]
>
> The same necessity existing, the same means are being adopted for rescuing this advanced post of our Indian empire from the grasp of Russianized Persia. Probably as we write these lines, 5,000 British troops are encamped on Karrak [Iran's Kharg Island in the Persian Gulf] and the adjacent islands, while a steam flotilla commands the waters of the Persian Gulf.[20]

The more staunchly conservative unionist *Belfast News-Letter* was even more critical of the manner in which London had declared war on Iran, but it too placed the ultimate blame for the conflict on Tehran. After the outbreak of the war the *News-Letter* followed the same pattern of patriotic reporting as its ideological press cohorts across the United Kingdom, such as *The Times* of London and the *Irish Times* (Dublin). The "O'Connellite"-style Home-Rule Irish nationalist press (Daniel O'Connell having died in 1847), as in the case of the wide-circulation Dublin newspaper the *Freeman's Journal*, relied on the same British and international news sources as the mainstream press across the United Kingdom and avoided any tendentiously Irish nationalist editorialized coverage of the event. The *Freeman's Journal*, with larger circulation than *The Nation*, was chiefly supportive of British military operations during the war, even if it did not categorically legitimize the manner in which the war was conducted. Nationalist politics notwithstanding, the paper's position was not all that surprising, given the presence of Irish personnel in the ranks of Britain's imperial Indian military force engaged in the war. As a generally temperate Home Rule Irish nationalist mouthpiece, always careful not to alienate the moderate nationalist community at large or the Catholic establishment, the paper was in fact pursuing an "Irish" patriotic platform that on such occasions could not easily be disentangled from London's platform of imperial-patriotism. Moreover, the *Freeman's Journal* was to some extent also pragmatically obligated to adopt a cautious tone in its coverage of the Iranian war, given that it served as the mouthpiece of the Irish Home Rule faction in the British parliament, which relied on Palmerston's Whig Party to push through Irish reforms—even if such consideration did not stop the paper from attacking Palmerston's unmistakably mendacious rationalization of the Second Chinese War.

The coverage of the Iranian war by the *Freeman's Journal* was in sharp contrast to the coverage of the war in the pages of *The Nation*, which provided more frequent, and much more detailed, reporting of the armed conflict and resorted to overtly anti-'British' commentaries and outright condemnation of "English" imperialism, with clear echoes of the Irish Question. To this end, *The Nation* found it necessary to evade the subject of Irish military personnel engaged in the British military campaign against Iran. An example of the vastly different style and tone in the coverage of the war by these two Dublin-based Irish nationalist papers was the way in which they reported the British capture of the Iranian port city of Bushire. Whereas the *Freeman's Journal* provided a straightforward account of the British operation,[21] *The Nation* provided a highly editorialized and censorious commentary (as discussed below). On rare occasions when the *Freeman's Journal* editorialized its reportage of the war, it resounded London's official line. For instance, in its December 15, 1856, issue early in the conflict, the paper reported that "some of the Bombay journals" (with Bombay being the center of India's Zoroastrian Parsi population who considered Iran as their ancestral home) had characterized the outbreak of military hostilities against Iran by "Sahib Company"—that is, the English East India Company, which at the time maintained, and paid for, Britain's 'Indian' military forces under the supervision of the governor-general in Calcutta—"as an act of piracy." The editorial quickly added that it was understood, "With our imperfect information," that "Persia is manifestly the aggressor, and whether instigated or not by Russia to seize Herat, and whether the possession of the 'Gate' [i.e., Herat's potential as a presumed Russian gateway toward India] by either power would lead to a descent on the Indus, it is clear the Shah has violated treaties [e.g., the 1853 treaty between Iran and Britain]."[22] The *Freeman's Journal* was not entirely averse to making passing objections to London's handling of the military conflict. In late December 1856, for example, the paper commented on Palmerston's aggressive foreign policy around the globe, albeit without in any way absolving Tehran of ultimate responsibility for the outbreak of the Anglo-Iranian War. What was notable in this article, however, was the paper's careful identification of "England" as the power engaged in different conflicts around the world that were endangering the personnel of the "British army," which included Irish members. It further reminded its readers that the invading British force routed by the Afghans in 1839–42 had also been dispatched by 'England':

> And so we are drifting into another Chinese war? England appears to have her hands full already. There is Russian question, and the Swiss question, and the Persian question, and now we have the Chinese question, together with a "small affair" on the Kohat frontier of India, from which five thousand men were reported to have marched on Cabul [Kabul]. This expeditionary corps, we suppose, is intended to watch the approach of the Persians towards Affghanistan, should they be so unwise as to enter the memorable defiles in which a British army was annihilated. So England, under Lord Palmerston, has a variety of irons in the fire. No sooner is one taken out than another is thrust in. A war with Persia was quite sufficient for the [English East India] Company. The Shah has not yielded to the pressure on his commerce in the only maritime outlet of his empire [i.e., the Persian Gulf]. The Persians have a very small foreign trade, and whatever they have is carried on inland, so that the occupation of the Gulph is not attended with the same injurious consequences as if their commerce had been greater. While the expedition was on its way, for which the [English East India] Company borrowed several lace [i.e., lakh] of rupees and are likely to borrow many more, the startling news had arrived that hostilities had broken out with China.²³

The *Freeman's Journal* occasionally reported criticisms of the legitimacy of London's "Persian War" voiced by other quarters, thereby indirectly criticizing certain aspects of Palmerston's conduct of the war. On January 14, 1857, for instance, it reported on a public meeting at the Droitwich Town Hall (Worcestershire, England) presided by the Lord Mayor. During this meeting, the local Tory MP, Sir John Pakington, also a former secretary of state for war and the colonies, condemned the government's continued imposition of the war tax after the termination of the Crimean War. Pakington then expressed his "grave doubts as to the policy which had led to the war with Persia, and as to the justice of our attacks upon the Chinese," adding: "The war with Persia was the subject on which they had least information."²⁴ The paper reported a similar January 22 meeting called for by the Lord Mayor of Dublin.²⁵ It, moreover, published a report of the January 19 public meeting at the Music Hall in Birmingham in condemnation of Iranian and Chinese wars, attended by some of the city's influential political, civic, and religious personalities.²⁶ On February 26, 1857, following weeks of reporting on the Anglo-Iranian conflict and the recent round of mediations between Britain and Iran, initiated by France and other states, the *Freeman's Journal* reported the conclusion of "Peace with Persia," seizing the occasion to again criticize Palmerston's original declaration of war against Iran without parliamentary consultation. However, the paper refrained from even remotely absolving Iran of responsibility for the outbreak of the conflict. It merely relayed Tehran's desperate efforts to end the war. Interestingly, this report also contained an unmistakably roundabout gibe aimed at the sort of coverage of the conflict appearing in *The Nation*, which was the *Freeman's Journal*'s main rival Irish nationalist outlet. In its reporting of the war, *The Nation*, pursuing a more 'radical' Home Rule stance at the time in comparison with the *Freeman's Journal*, had repeatedly repackaged dubious rumors (disseminated by a correspondent of *The Times* of London) with the objective of highlighting Britain's desperate quandary in the Iranian war. The *Freeman's Journal* ridiculed this brand of reportage as gullible drivel (*"gobe mouche"*):

> The war with Persia is brought to an end, and glorious visions of promotion in the Indian army are rudely dissipated. Lord Palmerston was not unwilling to terminate the difficulty, in which his unconstitutional conduct involved him, by accepting the friendly offices of the Emperor Napoleon—Russia strained energetically in the direction of peace—and poor Persia made every effort to release herself from the grips of a new and formidable foe, who had resolved to deal with her southern [region] in the same fashion as Russia did with her northern provinces. Persia was really alarmed at the aspect of affairs in Bushire, notwithstanding the great aggregate meeting at Teheran, where holy war was announced, and so many thousand Shutes [Shi'i] swore by the bones of Zoroaster [*sic*] to exterminate the invaders! The British set sedulously to work to lay the foundation of a permanent occupation. [...] The Emperor of France having just concluded a commercial treaty with Persia, and being otherwise in high favour at the Court of Teheran, stepped in between the belligerents, and had sufficient influence to induce Lord Palmerston not to prove over exigent in his demands. The arrangement would have been sooner effected had it not been for the garrulity of the *Times* correspondent, who conjured up an imaginary treaty, just concluded between Russia and Persia, in which the latter ceded to the former a large slice of territory on the frontier with Turkey, which would enable Russia to command the high road to Erzeroum and place the Asiatic provinces of the Sultan at her future disposal. Every person conversant with Russian policy knew that such a treaty was fiction. [...] None but the veriest *gobe mouche* believed in such a treaty as the *Times* correspondent fished up somewhere—just such a parchment as Mr. Disraeli once saw in the archives of the French Foreign-Office! [...] The fact of completing the negotiation with the Persian Ambassador [i.e., Farrokh Khan] is the most conclusive answer to the fiction of the *Times*.²⁷

Significantly, none of the reporting on the Iranian war in the *Freeman's Journal*, including its occasional accounts of Conservative or Radical parliamentary and extra-parliamentary condemnations of Palmerston's handling of affairs, in any way reflected back on the Irish Question. This was in sharp contrast to the coverage of the war in the pages of *The Nation*, with the paper's persistent attacks on the British side in the conflict marked by distinctively 'Irish nationalist' vigor and venom. *The Nation* responded to the outbreak of the Anglo-Iranian War with a clearly anti-British posture, and its frequently lengthy editorialized accounts of the conflict often implicitly redirected the attention of its readers to English domination of Ireland. It decidedly portrayed the Iranian government (and ambiguously the Iranian people) as unjustly victimized by British imperialism.

The Nation and the Blending of Constitutional Politics and Revolutionary Rhetoric

Before proceeding with *The Nation*'s coverage of the Iranian war and the inferred affinity between Irish nationalists and Britain's Iranian enemy in 1856–57, it is important to first situate the paper's reporting of that war in the context of the paper's long-standing pattern of similar coverage dating back to its very founding in 1842. Following the abortive uprising by the militant faction of Young Ireland in 1848, many leading radical nationalists were rounded up by the authorities or went into hiding and exile. *The Nation* was closed down by the authorities and its editor Charles Gavan Duffy was detained, with Duffy having endorsed the uprising with great hesitancy. *The Nation* was revived the following year after Duffy's release from prison. Duffy rapidly gravitated away from radical nationalism, turning his attention to electoral politics and land reform. He even secured a seat in the House of Commons from 1852 to 1855. In 1855, before moving to Australia, Duffy transferred the majority ownership of *The Nation* to the O'Connellite nationalist (i.e., parliamentary Home Rule) Alexander Martin Sullivan (1830–84), also an occasional contributor to *The Nation* since 1853.[28] At the time of the Anglo-Iranian War, the paper (published as a weekly) was overseen by Sullivan. Duffy's co-partner in the paper, John Cashel Hoey stayed on as the editor-in-chief until his resignation in 1857, when he too sold his share of the paper to Sullivan.[29] Incidentally, at the time Sullivan belonged to the camp of Eastern origins of ancient Ireland's presumably Milesian settlers, as descendants Scythians in his view.[30]

The Nation's unmistakably anti-British tenor in reporting the Iranian war, along with its coverage of the earlier Crimean War, the ongoing diplomatic wrangling between London and Washington, and the later Chinese War and the Indian uprising, and other such developments around 1856–57, remained characteristic of the paper's future coverage of London's conflicts in other parts of the world as well. This was in part indicative of the paper's oscillation between physical force and moral force polarities of Irish Home Rule nationalism, even as A. M. Sullivan himself publicly steered toward constitutional politics (i.e., parliamentary Home Rule campaign). The paper retained the confrontational tone of the Young Ireland days of Davis & Co.—with remnants of former leading Young Irelanders still in the United Kingdom having themselves for the most part mellowed into pursuing parliamentary politics by 1855, instead of joining the nascent post-1848 revolutionary republican movements.[31] Even as *The Nation* served as a pro-constitutional Home Rule ("Repeal") mouthpiece under Sullivan's ownership, it continued its former strident and pugnacious criticism of ongoing British imperial aggression around the globe, with Sullivan himself during his subsequent parliamentary career joining the pro-Indian reform lobby (the Constitutional Society of India) and vehemently condemning such acts of British imperial violence as that against the Zulus in southern Africa in 1879–80.[32] The overtly anti-'British' tone of *The Nation* under Sullivan's ownership, in comparison with the *Freeman's Journal*, was also a symptom of the competition between the two papers for securing a wider nationalist readership. On the one hand, this was a matter of difference in style of expression in the ranks of moderate constitutional Irish nationalists, just as Daniel O'Connell had recurrently used belligerent rhetoric in his otherwise non-violent campaign for Home Rule. Whereas *The Nation* tended to accentuate the growing Irish disloyalty to British rule in the hope of attaining Home Rule, the *Freeman's Journal* stressed the loyalty, as well as military and other contributions, of the Irish to the preservation of Britain's *existing empire* as a propensity deserving of British reciprocation by means of granting Ireland self-government; even as the *Freeman's Journal* continually criticized the nature of British administration of Ireland. On the other hand, the difference in tone between the two papers also reflected the generally blurred boundaries of radical versus moderate nationalist dispositions and ultimate objectives.[33] Moreover, the different degrees of sensitivity on the part of these papers to the opinion of the Catholic establishment should be taken into account as well, with the latter shunning radical politics. The *Freeman's Journal* was determinedly more cautious in appeasing the Catholic Church. Otherwise, the *Freeman's Journal* too occasionally resorted to intensely indignant and castigating tone toward British authorities, not only in some Irish matters (such as the 1879–82 Land War in Ireland), but also in regard to some extra-Irish developments (as in the case of the British occupation of Egypt in 1882)—without discounting here the dynamism of Irish nationalist platforms and tactics over time, or of domestic Irish developments during the periods the *Freeman's Journal* adopted a highly critical tone toward British foreign and extra-Irish imperial policies. In addition, *The Nation*'s commentaries on the Anglo-Iranian War and other similar developments in 1856–57 were also a manifestation of the eclectic scope of Irish nationalist pronouncements of cross-national or cross-territorial sympathies and solidarities. At the time, *The Nation* was willing to cast its instrumentalist embrace much wider geographically than the *Freeman's Journal*.

To gauge the militant rhetoric of *The Nation* during the Anglo-Iranian War, the paper's reports should be compared not only with its main rival nationalist mouthpiece in Ireland, the *Freeman's Journal*, but also with the outright-revolutionary republican Irish nationalist press in the diaspora, with the United States as the main center of revolutionary Irish nationalist activities after the failed 1848 uprising in Ireland. By the time the Iranian war rolled around, with the conflict also bearing on Anglo-Russian rivalry in the region, militant Irish nationalism in general had undergone significant metamorphoses. The uprising staged in Ireland in 1848 by the breakaway radical wing of the Young Ireland was a dismal failure, occurring under famine conditions and with inadequate preparations and lack of even rudimentary level of popular organization, along with other political and tactical miscalculations—which is not to suggest the majority of Irish population resentful of British rule would otherwise have joined the uprising, especially considering the hostility of the Irish Catholic establishment to republicanism and armed struggle, with Catholics constituting the overwhelming majority of Ireland's population. Unlike the successful French Revolution of 1848, or the failed revolutions of that year elsewhere in continental Europe, the Irish uprising fizzled out before it had even gotten underway. With the Young Ireland movement, including its non-violent faction, rapidly melting away in the climate of post-1848 suppression, imprisonment, transportation, voluntary exile, and/or disillusionment, the center of physical force revolutionary Irish republicanism shifted to the United States, where some former leaders of the 1848 uprising also settled. The diasporic Irish nationalist communities in the United States enjoyed much greater propaganda freedom in their advocacy of unfettered revolutionary violence in Ireland, than did their diasporic cohorts in places such as mainland Britain, Australia, Canada, or southern Africa, which were located within the British Empire. The Irish famine of 1845–51 resulted in rapid increase in the size of Irish diasporic communities throughout the United States, while also considerably fueling antipathy toward British rule in these expanding diasporic communities. Militant Irish nationalists in the United States conducted a vigorous and extensive recruitment campaign among the newly arriving Irish, even though until at least

1918 their efforts failed to win over the hearts and minds of the majority of Irish population disposed toward nationalist politics (whether in the United States or in Ireland itself), who preferred non-violent means—with the Catholic hierarchy in the (otherwise republican) United States also opposed to violent revolutionary tactics and rhetoric.

By the mid-1850s, some surviving organizers and participants of the 1848 rising, who had either managed to evade arrest or had been released from confinement, or had succeeded to flee from locations to which they had been transported following their conviction, were busy forging a new brand of Irish nationalist militancy with networks in both the Irish diaspora and Ireland. There were also the likes of John Blake Dillon, a founding member of Young Ireland, who had half-heartedly joined the 1848 rising but had now abandoned radicalism. Dillon returned to Ireland from the United States in 1855, following a pardon, and embraced parliamentary Home Rule politics, similar to Duffy. In 1858, some leaders of various post-1848 militant Irish nationalist tendencies joined forces, forming the Irish Republican Brotherhood (IRB), headquartered in Ireland and with branches in the Irish diaspora. IRB's counterpart in the United States was called the Fenian Brotherhood, with New York as the main center of its activities and its branches soon spreading across the United States and to other Irish diasporic locations. Both of the main organizations were frequently referred to interchangeably by the public as "Fenians." The core of these interconnected militant organizations had already been in the making by the time the Anglo-Iranian War broke out in 1856. The US branch of the organization had its roots in the Emmet Monument Association, founded in New York in 1855 by John O'Mahony, Michael Doheny, and Michael Corcoran, which, among other initial campaigns, had sought to build up American public support for Russia during the Crimean War of 1854–56, while attempting in vain to obtain Russian military support for an insurgency in Ireland.[34] Among many other examples of such militant Irish nationalist activities in the United States prior to the formation of the Fenian Brotherhood, in 1856 the authorities in Cincinnati, Ohio, foiled a plan by William George Halpin and his associates to send a small band of Irish-American armed volunteers to Ireland to help stage an uprising.[35]

Washington's diplomatic quarrel with London over British attempts to recruit volunteers in the United States to fight in the Crimea, in violation of US neutrality laws, was also exploited by US-based militant Irish nationalists, who conspired to legally entrap the agents involved in the British recruitment scheme. The crisis eventually resulted in the expulsion of four British diplomatic staff from the United States.[36] Another point of contention between London and Washington at the time was the military operations carried out by a band of mercenaries in the Mosquito Coast (Nicaragua and Honduras) and the neighboring territories, lasting from 1855 to 1857. The mercenaries were led by the veteran American filibuster William Walker, who even briefly succeeded in establishing himself as the president of Nicaragua, following which he also authorized the re-introduction of slavery in the country. From London's point of view, Walker's raids, and the extent of official US support he enjoyed at the time, were a transparent challenge to British interests in the region, where Britain had colonial possessions and imperial influence, particularly in Belize to the north of Honduras. Meanwhile, in keeping with the famous Irish nationalist pronouncement, attributed to Daniel O'Connell and frequently taken out of its historical context, that "England's difficulty is Ireland's opportunity," militant Irish nationalists regarded any considerable threat to British imperial interests—hence Britain's military preoccupation in other parts of the globe—as advantageous to Irish nationalists and a possible opportunity for an uprising in Ireland. It was in keeping with this objective that some militant Irish nationalist circles publicly supported Walker's armed intervention in the Mosquito Coast, notwithstanding Walker's mercenary-imperialist freebooting and his outright violation of other countries' territorial sovereignty; nor forgetting his pro-slavery stance, which did not sit well with all of his Irish nationalist advocates. The latter quandary accounts for the frequent omission of references to Walker's pro-slavery policy in radical Irish nationalist reports that celebrated his campaigns. Which is not to suggest all militant Irish nationalists were personally averse to slavery, as evident from the political career of the likes of John Mitchel. Mitchel, a former radical Young Irelander and a leader of the 1848 rising, who had been detained by British authorities prior to that uprising, arrived in the United States in 1853 following his escape from the British penal settlement in Van Diemen's Land (Tasmania). In the United States, Mitchel became an outspoken defender of the institution of what was called "African slavery" in the southern states.

Radical Irish nationalist mouthpieces in the United States, such as the *Irish News* and the *Irish-American*, both published in New York, eagerly championed Walker's military campaign. Among these, the *Irish News*, a weekly newspaper founded in 1856 by Thomas Francis Meagher, a former contributor to *The Nation* (Dublin) in its Young Ireland days and a leader of the 1848 uprising, provided some of the most sympathetic coverage of Walker's recent exploits in Nicaragua. Meagher, who had also managed to make his way to the United States after escaping from Van Diemen's Land, where he was serving transportation for life, was ostensibly opposed to the institution of slavery in theory, but nonetheless tolerated the system in the American south for the time being, arguing enslavement needed to be eradicated gradually. Soon after the Democratic candidate James Buchanan won the US presidential election in November 1856, Meagher wishfully hoped to be appointed the US ambassador to Nicaragua (among his choice of a number of Latin American territories). Presumably, Meagher considered this a fair reward for having stringently endorsed in the pages of the *Irish News* Buchanan's presidential campaign that included the latter's anti-abolitionist stance.[37] The Irish diaspora constituted a considerable electoral base in some US cities. Mitchel and Meagher are reminders of the limits of Irish nationalist expressions of solidarity with the sovereign rights of other nations (Nicaragua in this case) and/or of other oppressed peoples (the enslaved population in the United States and in Walker's briefly controlled Nicaragua). Such constricted Irish nationalist vista on the rights of others went as far back as the likes of Theobald Wolfe Tone, a leader of the 1798 United Irishmen uprising, and continued well into the twentieth century.[38] As with nationalists from other territories, many Irish nationalists too were highly selective and self-serving in their prioritization of the rights of other peoples. While the inter-Irish collective vision of the United Irishmen had resonated some of the precepts of more universalist trends in the "European" Enlightenment thought, this did not automatically translate into the adherence of all

Irish nationalists (republican or otherwise) to such universal principles of rights, even overlooking gender and labor rights.

Similar in tone to leading militant Irish nationalist newspapers in the United States, *The Nation* (Dublin) too lauded as heroic Walker's rag-tag band of mercenaries in the 'Nicaraguan' conflict, which included Irish-Americans. Covering one of Walker's raids in Costa Rica under the heading of "Young Ireland in Nicaragua," the paper reproduced a report from the New York *Sun* of a communique transmitted by a purportedly "young soldier of freedom" serving in Walker's army:

> During one period of the battle, a body of Walker's troops took possession of a church, from which a large force of the enemy vainly attempted to dislodge them. It is utterly untrue that any damage was done to the building, or any images or paintings destroyed. The party who occupied it were nearly all Irish Catholics, and under the command of General Walker's brother—who since died—a member of the Catholic religion. [...] The great bulk of Walker's army were composed of Irishmen, who, on hearing of English interference on behalf of Costa Rica, were anxious to cross weapons with the old enemy on the streets of Rivas, and ready to 'give 'em Jessie.'[39]

Ever sensitive to the opinion of the Catholic establishment and its political sway in Ireland, this was also an opportunity for *The Nation* to add an Irish-Catholic and anti-"English imperialism" twist to Walker's opportunistic exploits. The *Freeman's Journal*, by contrast, had been providing disinterested accounts of Walker's adventurist military feats, without lapsing into elation about the affair or deliberating on the presence of Irish soldiers of fortune in Walker's army. For its part, the moderate nationalist *Cork Examiner* in an article condemning London's latest wars in Iran and China, riled against Walker and the support he enjoyed in Washington, which it regarded as no less imperialistic than British wars of aggression.[40]

As a detour here, albeit related to the subject of *The Nation*'s emphasis on the presence of Irish Catholics in the ranks of Walker's army, the generally unacknowledged and privileged position accorded to Irish Catholics in Irish nationalist politics needs to be stressed. Irish nationalist opposition to British rule in Ireland itself since the late eighteenth century, including post-1848 trends in Irish republicanism, had continued to be overwhelmingly inclusive in their formulations of the "Irish nation," in both (Christian) cross-denominational and cross-ethnic definitions. In addition to certain generally excluded minority communities in Ireland in these formulations of the Irish nation, such as the very small Jewish population (primarily descendants of Jewish émigrés from Eastern European territories after the late nineteenth century), there were some other limitations to the inclusiveness of Irish nationalist platforms, leaving aside the topics of gender and "race" here. For instance, in 1857, around the time of the Anglo-Iranian War, the militant republican nationalist and scholar John O'Mahony in the United States completed a new annotated English translation of Geoffrey Keating's 1634 *Foras Feasa ar Éirinn*, appearing as *The History of Ireland*. The original text had been produced in the context of Catholic Counter-Reformation,[41] and was first translated into English in 1723 by Dermod O'Connor. O'Mahony, finding O'Connor's translation "so unlike what Dr. Keating actually wrote,"[42] provided a decidedly nationalist preface along with a nationalist historical interpretation of the original work. O'Mahony, in a similar manner as Thomas Osborne Davis earlier, insisted he was only hostile toward those who tyrannized "the oppressed natives of Ireland," regardless of their religious and ethnic background, and was emphatic that "In Ireland [...] the foreign element has [...] long since merged into the Gael—so have some of the descendants of the more recent conquerors."[43] However, not all individuals residing in Ireland were to be automatically accorded membership in the envisioned republican model of the future independent nation. As David Dwan has shown, the Young Ireland republican vision of an independent Irish nation, for instance, demanded an underlying commitment to the welfare of that nation (the "common good" as defined by Young Ireland) as the precondition for "citizenship."[44] Dwan has rejected Joep Leerssen's claim that Young Ireland nationalism was undergirded by an ethnic foundation.[45] However, it seems they are both partially correct. While Young Ireland and most other republican and non-republican nationalist movements in Ireland after the late eighteenth century avoided an ethnic delineation of the Irish nation—insofar as those of Gaelic, Scandinavian, English, Welsh, and Scots ancestry, for the most part—those designated as having Gaelic ancestry ('mere Irish') were certainly regarded in the Young Ireland and some other nationalist circles as being historically the more authentic members of the Irish nation. To put it differently, in Irish nationalist debates on the ethnic inclusivity of the Irish nation, it was never the status of those of presumed Gaelic ancestry that was subject to deliberation. They were regarded as simply belonging to the land. This is not to say that those of Gaelic ethnicity opposed to nationalist principles, or to Young Ireland's vision of a "community" in pursuit of a 'common good,' were to be automatically tolerated without some form of coercion in the future independent Irish republic as conceived by republican nationalists. (In the case of Home-Rule nationalist vision of a self-governing Ireland within the British Empire, the topic of national belonging and coercion of unionists and other non-'nationalists' assumed a much more nebulous dimension.) Moreover, on the cultural front of nationalism, for many nationalists it was Gaelic language and Gaelic "traditions" (ranging from supposed folk beliefs to literature and sports) that were to be resuscitated as the 'national' language and culture, leaving aside here the fiction of cultural purity and authenticity.

The Nation's coverage of the Nicaraguan conflict, similar to that of the 'radical' Irish republican press in the United States, was indicative of the extent to which some nationalist circles were willing to disregard imperialist implications of Walker's raids or of Washington's Latin American policies, so long as those occurrences challenged and clashed with Britain's imperial interests. As in the case of developments in the Mosquito Coast, or Russia's war effort in the Crimea, or the Second Anglo-Chinese War, among other examples from the period, *The Nation*'s coverage of the Anglo-Iranian War of 1856–57 was unmistakably molded by the paper's stance toward England as Ireland's long-standing oppressor, with no due regard for the intricacies of the Herat Question as seen from different perspectives, notably from the point of view of those in Herat itself. While it is indisputable that British involvement in the Herat conflict was motivated by primarily imperial interests, the fate of Herat itself in the conflict between Britain and Iran (and Russia by extension) cannot be swept aside. In effect, Herat was caught between competing forward policies of Britain, Iran, the Afghan strongman

Dost Mohammad Khan, as well as Russian imperial strategy, with Britain backing Dost Mohammad Khan and Russia prodding Tehran. Without entirely denying some degree of possible genuine of sympathy on the part of *The Nation* with the Iranian side in the Anglo-Iranian War, the paper's coverage of the war unquestionably served as yet another opportunity to denounce (by proxy) direct British rule in Ireland. In this case, too, there were parallels between *The Nation*'s coverage of the Iranian war and reports of that conflict appearing in some of the militant republican Irish nationalist outlets in the United States. The latter included *The Citizen* (1854–57), founded in New York by John Mitchel and John McClenahan, among others, and edited by McClenahan at the time of the Anglo-Iranian War, following Mitchel's departure from New York to Tennessee in 1855.[46] In its first report of military preparations in British India for waging war against Iran and assisting Dost Mohammad Khan to capture Herat, *The Citizen* described the real motive behind the pending war as the underlying desire of "British robbers" "to steal another slice of Indian territory,"[47] without specifying which particular Indian territory the paper had in mind or how exactly the present Herat Question related to further British territorial expansion in India. The bottom line was to use the Anglo-Iranian conflict as yet another opportunity for denouncing British imperial aggression and continued intervention around the globe.

Similar to reports in *The Citizen*, *The Nation*'s coverage of British conflicts around the world and of other related international affairs were opportunities for situating the Irish nationalist struggle in a broader world setting of British imperialism—no matter how selective and ironic this approach was at times in the framework of *general* resistance to imperialism. But, the Iranian and Chinese wars, each in its own distinct setting and with differing stated rationales for British involvement in the conflicts, were far different from the circumstances in the Crimea or Walker's mercenary operations. *The Nation*'s reporting of Iranian and Chinese wars was in the form of the paper's expressed solidarity with acts of anti-imperialist resistance against *direct British aggression* in different parts of the world, and also assumed a much more pronounced tenor in the paper's coverage of the Indian uprising of 1857. These were all examples of *worlding* the Irish nationalist struggle against English rule *through contemporary events*, as opposed to *historical* references such as Thomas Moore's analogy between English rule in Ireland and the Arab-Muslim occupation of Iran in the seventh century or of Mangan's purported sixteenth-century Iranian resistance to English imperial aggression in his poem "To the Ingleezee Khafir." The pattern of identifying the Irish struggle with contemporary episodes of resistance against imperial aggression elsewhere in the world, as tortuous as the parallels often were, had been a marked feature of *The Nation* in its early Young Ireland days (1842–48), as in the case of some of the already mentioned poems by Thomas Osborne Davis or the paper's reporting of world events. Whether or not a conscious effort, this was another mode of *deprovincializing* Ireland, a theme to which I return in some detail later. Suffice it to mention here that the worlding of the Irish struggle defied attempts to relegate the Irish Question to the realm of an internal "provincial" (i.e., sub-national) political dispute within the United Kingdom. This worlding process connected the Irish struggle to, and situated it within, the broader sphere of anti-imperialist (more specifically anti-'British') assertions of national sovereignty around the world (colonial or otherwise). The very first news item appearing under "The Overland Mail" section in the inaugural issue of *The Nation* on October 15, 1842, with Duffy as its chief editor, consisted of a report titled "India, Affghanistan [sic], and China," which provided examples of the worldwide virulence of British imperialism and violations of sovereign rights of other 'nations.' The examples in this instance ranged from Britain's ongoing colonial rule in India to its recent war in China (also known as the [First] "Opium War," 1839–42), and its military aggression in "Afghanistan" (1839–42), with the latter resulting in a trouncing defeat of the invading British forces.[48] The same issue of the paper included additional reports on the disastrous outcome of British military intervention in Afghanistan. With a more than a subtle nod to the legitimacy of armed resistance against imperialism, the paper peddled the large-scale fatalities of British forces in a tone sharply contrasting with reports of the Afghan war in the mainstream British press, which were obsessed with the carnage as an allegedly gratuitous slaughter of units of Britain's 'Indian' army by the purportedly savage Afghans. *The Nation* reported: "Nor shall we believe, till we have better authority than the fancies of the truculent Briton, that the laws of nature will be suspended to the vengeance or the evasion of an army which invaded with no pretext save a lie, and no design save aggrandizement, the territories of an independent and unoffending people."[49]

In the radical Irish nationalist press, as in the pages of *The Nation* of Young Ireland days and after, there was a notable feature to this process of worlding the Irish struggle. When denouncing British acts of aggression in other parts of the world, there was frequently a glossing over, and at times unconvincing omission, of the sizeable participation of Irish officers and soldiers in Britain's imperial military machine. The above 1842 report of the Afghan war in *The Nation* of Young Ireland days not only entirely exempted Irish personnel of participation in British military operations in Afghanistan but also implausibly insinuated an expansive Irish sentiment of fellow-feeling with victims of British imperialism elsewhere. It insisted: "Irish soldiers had refused to fight the Affghans [sic]."[50] Around that time, the Young Ireland leader Thomas Osborne Davis composed his already noted poem "A Ballad of Freedom," in which he also celebrated the Afghan victory over British forces. Meanwhile, the authorities in the United Kingdom and the public alike (including in Ireland, where some of Britain's 'Indian' military personnel engaged in the Afghan war hailed from) were still in a state of collective shock over the near complete decimation of the 4,500-strong British force and its accompanying 12,000 camp aides and family members during their retreat from Kabul in early winter of 1842. In 1843, the personal account of one of the few British survivors of the event, Lady Florentia Sale (née Wynch), the wife of the officer Robert Sale, became an immediate bestseller upon its publication: *A Journal of the Disasters in Affghanistan, 1841–2*.

Leaving aside the incredulous nature of *The Nation*'s denial in 1842 of Irish presence in the British military force engaged in Afghanistan—particularly since 'British' commanding officers on that occasion included the likes of the famed Anglo-Irish Sir John Keane[51]—the paper's account also evaded the fact that the 'Irish soldiers' in question already belonged to a 'British' occupation force: that of the British imperial army in

India, which also consisted of native Indian sepoys and sowars (native infantry and cavalry serving under European officers); not forgetting the extensive Irish participation in the English East India Company's gradual colonization of the Indian subcontinent after 1757 in the first place. *The Nation*, in its 1842 reporting of the Afghan war, must also have counted on its readers' unfamiliarity with, or amnesia, regarding the pivotal role played in the Great Game between Britain and Russia in Afghan territories and other parts of Central Asia by the likes of the two fabled and widely reported Irish cousins, Arthur Conolly (born in London) and William Hay Macnaghten (born in Calcutta), both of them agents of the English East India Company (with Macnaghten killed in Kabul in 1841 and Conolly killed in Bukhara in June 1842).[52] This style of distorted reporting and selective omissions, resurfacing again and again in subsequent radical Irish nationalist commentaries on Britain's imperial military engagements, including during the Anglo-Iranian War of 1856–57, had another implication that clearly escaped the attention of the editors of *The Nation* and of other Irish nationalist press expressing similar views. By attempting to exonerate the Irish 'nation,' this style of journalism implicitly cast a negative light on Indian and other colonial "natives" serving in British imperial forces. This pattern of privileging the Irish nation consequently debased other colonized peoples in the British Empire in comparison (as being more willing than the Irish to serve as lackeys of British imperial expansion), and inadvertently counteracted Irish nationalist expressions of anticolonial affinities with Indians and other colonized subjects of the empire. The majority of routed British forces in Afghanistan in 1839–42 were Indian sepoys and sowars. Similarly, in the Iranian war of 1856–57 Indian soldiers comprised more than half of the 5,670 British fighting personnel, as well as most of the accompanying support staff.[53] This particular manner of reporting the conflicts involving imperial forces from British India, which in fact included a sizeable Irish presence, in effect implied Indians were both far more willing to carry out England's imperialist bidding than their Irish counterparts and that they ultimately were incapable of the same degree of anticolonial sympathy with other victims of British imperialism than their Irish counterparts. This inferred contrast between Irish soldiers and the reminder of British imperial forces was to presumably underscore the substantial degree of historical and cultural anti-imperialist proclivity among the Irish 'nation.' Whereas by the early twentieth century there were indeed rare examples of overt anti-imperialist politicization among some Irish soldiers, as in the case of the 1920 Connaught Rangers Mutiny in Punjab, India, in opposition to the martial law declared in Ireland during the Irish War of Independence,[54] these were atypical occurrences and certainly did not mark a uniform sentiment among the Irish military personnel in Britain's imperial military force across the globe. As it happened, within a short time after the conclusion of the Anglo-Iranian War in 1857, it was a large body of Indian sepoys and sowars across British India who staged an unprecedented, and the most extensive ever, rebellion staged by imperial forces against British rule in the entire history of the British Empire (including the successful rebellion in the American colonies from 1776 to 1783 that was led by former military personnel in the British colonial army, among them leading officers such as George Washington). The Indian rebellion of 1857 was eventually crushed with the assistance of loyal native forces, including the Nepalese Gurkhas, as well as English, Irish, Scots, Welsh, and other European recruits.

The Nation's Coverage of the Anglo-Iranian War of 1856–57

In its reporting of the Iranian war, *The Nation* initially reproduced the same official British accounts of the affair appearing in most other papers in the United Kingdom, albeit with its own added commentaries. In its account of the origins of the war, *The Nation* essentially reiterated the same narrative of developments leading up to the disruption of diplomatic relations between Tehran and London as that voiced by Palmerston's Radical critics and the mainstream press. This was followed by allegation of the unconstitutionality of Palmerston's declaration of war; again echoing Palmerston's Radical critics in parliament. But, unlike British Radicals and other critics of Palmerston in the United Kingdom, *The Nation*'s accounts of the Iranian military campaign for capturing Herat, and of the subsequent Iranian armed confrontation with British forces in the Persian Gulf and southern Iran, assumed an unmistakably pro-Tehran and anti-"British Empire" tone. In this respect, the paper's weekly sustained reporting of the Anglo-Iranian crisis was unambiguously and outspokenly a denunciation of British imperial aggression in general, ultimately intended to guide the readers' attention back to England's continued aggression against the Irish 'nation.' Gradually, the paper provided increasingly extensive reportage of the official Iranian version of developments. These Iranian accounts also periodically appeared in some other British and Irish papers, corresponding to, and further corroborating, the stance of Palmerston's (British) Radical critics inside and outside the British parliament. Becoming a more regular feature of *The Nation*'s coverage of the conflict, these Iranian accounts were often accompanied by the paper's own Irish nationalist perspective on British imperialism. This method of lambasting Britain's handling of affairs also often included hyped up, or entirely concocted, scenarios of grave military challenges facing British forces in the conflict and/or of consequential damage to Britain's regional standing and long-term interests.

The Nation's reporting on Iran at this time was restricted entirely to the coverage of the war and other related matters. This reporting was significant on a number of grounds, particularly because the Iranian crisis offered the very first occasion of a protracted sympathetic Irish nationalist media focus and commentary on developments in *contemporary* Iran. As noted before, it was no longer the Iran of some mythological or historical past that was capturing Irish nationalist imaginations, even if *The Nation*'s representations of contemporaneous Iran at times assumed fantastic, quasi-mythic proportions. The suggested cross-territorial affinity between Ireland and Iran appearing in *The Nation*'s coverage of the war was also markedly different from the civilizational, ethnic, and other historical affinities claimed in Iran-centered Irish antiquarian works. The focus was now on the shared "anti-English"/"anti-British" political stance of Irish nationalists and the Iranian state. *The Nation*'s subtextual representation of both contemporary Iran and Ireland as victims of British imperialism was a novel form of expressed affinity between Ireland and Iran, which was to resurface in a much more pronounced manner and across a much wider spectrum of Irish nationalist platforms during the

Iranian Constitutional Revolution of 1906–11 (as discussed in Chapter 7), albeit with the Iranian 'nation' as the object of expressed Irish nationalist solidarities on the latter occasion. During the war of 1856–57, *The Nation*'s avowed anti-British solidarity with Iran was couched in terms of defending the territorial sovereignty of the Iranian *state*. This was in part due of the absence of any full-fledged nationalist *movement* in Iran in the mid-nineteenth century and the absolutist character of the Iranian state (even if Tehran lacked full centralized state control over many Iranian provinces). However, *The Nation*'s articulated affinity between the two lands—notwithstanding their different historical frames—bore a striking similarity to Mangan's poem "To the Ingleezee Khafir," in which, as previously discussed, the enemy of sixteenth-century Iran was unambiguously cast as British imperialism ('*John Bull*' Jenkinson). Just as in Mangan's poem, *The Nation* too evoked the specter of Anglo-Irish encounters by focusing on a world historical context of British imperial aggression in general. Ultimately, *The Nation*'s commentaries on British aggression against Iran were meant to function as a mnemonic device, reminding the paper's readers once again of England's colonization of Ireland and amplifying anti-England sentiments. More significantly, similar to Mangan's poem, and in this regard also similar to Moore's "The Fire-Worshippers" in *Lalla Rookh*, *The Nation* too underlined the religious-cultural divide between Iran and the foreign imperial aggressor it was confronting. On this occasion, similar to Mangan's poem (rather than Moore's poem), it was again (Shi'i) Islam that was cast as the core essence of Iranian cultural identity. But, whereas Mangan had been conscious of how the Shi'i Iranian hero of his poem could simultaneously evoke Irish nationalist sympathy while also undermining that very sympathy due to his cultural-religious alienness, *The Nation* does not appear to have pondered this same quandary in its religious characterizations of the Iranian state.

The maxim of 'England's difficulty is Ireland's opportunity' did not necessarily denote an immediate prospect of Ireland attaining Home Rule or full independence; this could be a drawn-out process. England's loss of imperial reputation was a sufficiently welcome consequence in the short-run. A discernible concern of *The Nation* was the final outcome of the conflicts in both southern Iran and Herat. A military defeat for Britain in southern Iran, and/or a victory for Iran in the Herat theatre of war against British-backed Afghan forces, would signal a major blow to British imperial and military prestige. The same concern was evident in the paper's reporting of the Second Anglo-Chinese War that broke out shortly before the end of the Iranian war, by which time the authorities in British India (which also supplied the invading forces of the Chinese war) appeared militarily and financially overstretched. Contrary to the stance of Palmerston's Radical critics in Britain, in its early expectant reporting of the Iranian war *The Nation* was ecstatic about the possible decline of British hegemony in India, given the paper's overblown anticipation of a Russian counter-offensive in Iran and in Afghanistan (not forgetting the recent Russian defeat in the Crimean War). It was hoped a direct Russian participation in the conflict would also elicit internal challenges to British rule in India. As things transpired, the paper's expectation of an irreversible damage to Britain's imperial prestige eventually proved overblown in the case of both Iranian and Chinese wars, if not also in the aftermath of the momentous challenge to British imperial rule in India in 1857–58.

Similar to the reporting of the First Afghan War by the paper during its former Young Ireland days, throughout its coverage of the Iranian conflict too *The Nation* sought to deflect attention away from the Irish presence in the British imperial military force dispatched to Iranian territories. This was an exceptionally rare and extreme case of radical Irish nationalist denial of Irish participation in the Iranian war. Even the likes of the diasporic militant Irish nationalist press, such as *The Citizen* (New York), readily acknowledged the presence of Irish personnel in the British occupation force in southern Iran.[55] In Ireland itself, the moderate Home Rule nationalist papers, such the *Freeman's Journal* and the *Cork Examiner*, also periodically alluded to the large presence of Irish military personnel in Britain's 'Indian' force. The *Cork Examiner*, in fact, highlighted this Irish participation under the heading "The Irish in the Persian War." It wrote: "Our readers must have remarked that in the attack on Bushire, which ended in its capture, Irishmen played a most distinguished part, and certainly bore the heaviest share of the casualties; for nearly all the officers killed on that occasion were Irish, and the list of the men shewed, as usual, that Irishmen had even more than their fair proportion of hard knocks." The *Cork Examiner*, despite its condemnation of the origins of the Iranian war, nevertheless noted "the gallant conduct of a young Irish nobleman, Lord Dunkellin, who by his courage and coolness in a moment of extreme danger, well maintained the chivalrous character of his native West [i.e., western Ireland]."[56] In addition to "Irish patriotism" and concern with the welfare of Irish military personnel now that the war was underway, irrespective of whether Britain was justified in initiating the armed conflict, the point being underscored by the *Cork Examiner* was that of Ireland deserving Home Rule within the empire on grounds of its continued substantial contributions to, and sacrifices for, preserving the empire.

In its coverage of the war, *The Nation* also attempted to occlude the presence in the ranks of Palmerston's critics of Irish supporters of British rule in Ireland. In addition to British Radicals and the likes of Gladstone inside and outside the British parliament, there were other political figures critical of Palmerston's handling of Iranian affairs. These included the Irish MP for Enniskillen, and a prominent barrister, James Whiteside. Whiteside, a Conservative Protestant-unionist, was nonetheless renowned for having defended the likes of leading Irish nationalists Daniel O'Connell and William Smith O'Brien.[57] In its reports of the Anglo-Iranian conflict *The Nation* steered away from any in-depth discussion of Palmerston's parliamentary critics. Even on those occasions when the paper's regular columns on parliamentary proceedings indicated the Iranian war was debated in both houses of parliament, the paper only addressed the topic in passing and in very general terms, without specifying the nature and tenor of the opposition to Palmerston's policy.[58] This omissive style of reporting was evidently intended to deny Irish opponents of Irish nationalism any degree of moral rectitude in questioning Britain's alleged imperial aggression in other parts of the world, as well as denying them political prominence in the pages of the paper. Whiteside's exclusion from *The Nation*'s reporting of the parliamentary opposition to the war is all the more noteworthy considering the paper's naming of Palmerston's other parliamentary critics, some of whom happened to be stalwart opponents of Irish Home Rule, but were not Irish themselves. The paper adopted a similar style in its later reporting of parliamentary debates on the Chinese war, naming the likes of the British Conservative opponent of Irish Home Rule, Lord Edward Stanley (Earl of Derby), while avoiding the names of Irish members of parliament opposed to Irish Home Rule who were equally critical of that war.[59]

There was also a similarity between *The Nation*'s commentaries on the subject of Anglo-Russian imperial rivalry during its coverage of the Iranian war and the routine vindication of Russian imperialism appearing in the more militant and republican diasporic Irish nationalist press in the United States—in light of the recent Crimean War and more than half a century of Anglo-Russian rivalry in western and central Asia, including in Iran. *The Nation* was chiefly unconcerned with, and on occasion eagerly reveled in, the prospect of expanded Russian imperial hegemony in the region at the expense of British imperialism. This rendered *The Nation* an opponent of British imperialism, but not of imperialism in general, in contrast to the paper's earlier Young Ireland years. During the paper's coverage of the Anglo-Iranian conflict, what was disregarded in the overtly optimistic scenario of Russia's expanded regional leverage was the danger posed by Russian imperial hegemony to the territorial sovereignty of Iran, the Afghan states, and possibly even a future independent India, should Britain be forced to withdraw from India at some point. Here lay the underlying limitation of *The Nation*'s expressed solidarity with Iran, which is further proof of the paper's ultimately self-serving (i.e., Irish nationalist) stake in the Anglo-Iranian War. Similar to many militant diasporic Irish nationalist mouthpieces, as was evident not only during the Crimean War but also in their advocacy of Walker's wars of aggression in the Mosquito Coast and neighboring territories, *The Nation* too stopped short of categorically castigating all forms of imperialism and refrained from espousing a comprehensive platform of respect for territorial and/or national sovereignty of all peoples. This ultimately self-centric worldview was certainly not unique to some Irish nationalist circles. As discussed later, during the Iranian Constitutional Revolution of 1906–11 Iranian constitutionalist-nationalists who were familiar with outlines of the Irish Question tactically refrained from commenting on Irish developments, while on the other hand openly expressing sympathy with many other nationalist struggles around the world; even as Irish nationalists of varying ideological orientations were publicly advocating the Iranian revolution. Irish nationalist articulations of cross-territorial solidarity were certainly not uniformly and fundamentally self-interested. Prominent Irish nationalist figures of wide-ranging outlooks, such as Daniel O'Connell in the early nineteenth century, Thomas Osborne Davis in the mid-nineteenth century, John Dillon in the late nineteenth and early twentieth century, or Frederick Michael Ryan in the early twentieth century, among many others, unquestionably rose above the parochialism of Irish-centric nationalist worldviews. As far as *The Nation*'s stance during the Crimean War was concerned, the constitutional-nationalist Timothy Daniel Sullivan, Alexander Martin Sullivan's brother and a future editor of the paper, later commented in his autobiography:

> THE outbreak of the war with Russia, in March, 1854, caused a great quickening of the hopes of Irish Nationalists and gave cheer to their hearts. England was now at war with

a first-class European power, and who could tell what developments might take place ere the close of the conflict? The situation, however, from their point of view, was grievously complicated by the fact that, under the guidance of Napoleon the Third, France became an ally of England, and thus the triumph of Russia would involve the humiliation of an old friend. They knew, moreover, that Russia was the chief actor in the partition of Poland, a crime as cruel as England's conquest and oppression of Ireland; but even so, they gave their sympathies and best wishes to the power at war with the misrulers of their own country.[60]

This combined anti-British and pro-Russian stance of *The Nation* during the Crimean War carried over to its reporting of the Iranian war.[61]

Long before the outbreak of the Anglo-Iranian War, *The Nation* had already been reporting intermittently on the siege of Herat by Iranian troops. On January 12, 1856—in light of both the Iranian capture of Herat and its environs as well as a recent Russian military success on the Crimean War front—the paper was euphoric enough to write prematurely under the heading "The 'Gate of India'": "England has sustained an irretrievable disaster in the capture of Herat by Persia—and politicians already speculate upon the end of which this is the beginning." After describing the strategic significance of Herat and mentioning Iranian attempts (allegedly "supported by Russia") to capture the territory since 1832, only to be forced by Britain "to beat a retreat" on previous occasions, the article connected the latest Iranian offensive in Herat to the Crimean War. The report suggested that not only was the Iranian incursion instigated by Russia, but that it had also been planned to coincide with the recent Russian capture of the strategically significant Ottoman city of Kars in the Crimean conflict (in November 1855), thereby considerably augmenting Russia's leverage in the region at Britain's expense purportedly.[62] Prior to this report, the paper had commented on such other regional developments as the Santal ("Santhal") uprising in northeast India against British administration of the region, among other intended targets of the rebellion (June 1855–January 1856). The fall of Herat to Iranian forces was presented as a welcome sign of the crumbling of British influence in Asia vis-à-vis Russia. In celebrating what it projected as potential unraveling of British rule in India, *The Nation* was adopting a blasé attitude toward the alleged mounting Russo-Iranian grip over Afghan territories. This was a far cry from the paper's Young Ireland phase, when it staunchly championed Afghan sovereignty during the Anglo-Afghan War of 1839–42 (with the paper having been founded in October 1842). This was not a matter of historical amnesia. The common denominator in 1839–42 and 1856–57 remained the paper's attack against British imperial aggression (with Britain having been the culprit in the earlier Afghan war). Although the paper, now under A. M. Sullivan's control, was much more Irish-centric in selectively prioritizing and dismissing the sovereign rights of other peoples/territories, the newly found admiration for Russia in certain Irish nationalist circles during the 1850s was also in sharp contrast to the conventional Young Ireland platform. Young Ireland's Thomas Osborne Davis, in his 'A Ballad of Freedom' for instance, had denounced British imperialism in general, including the recent British aggression in Afghanistan in 1839–42, and celebrated the Afghan resistance led by Dost Mohammad Khan ("Hurrah for Dost Mohammed!"), while simultaneously condemning other cases of European imperialism around the globe, including Russian aggression in Poland and in Circassia. Russia's treatment of Polish and Circassian populations certainly had not markedly improved by the time the Crimean and Anglo-Iranian wars got under way. Moreover, Davis had characterized the Russian state as being internally a malignant force as well: "The Russian, lord of million serfs, and nobles serflier still."[63] *The Nation* under Sullivan's ownership was simply oblivious to such details in 1856–57.

Even if during the Anglo-Iranian War *The Nation* could rationalize its stance on the Herat Question—on grounds of the now drastically transformed political realignments in Afghan territories compared to 1839–42, including the alliance between British India and Dost Mohammad Khan—it would still be hard pressed to deny continued Russian autocracy at home and imperial aggression abroad. As far as developments in Afghan territories were concerned, the Afghan hero of 1839, Dost Mohammad Khan (who had been captured and exiled by the British in that year and later allowed to return and resume power), was now challenging Iranian influence in Herat and surrounding territories, having forged to that end a military pact with his erstwhile arch-enemy (British India). But, this fact by itself could not mitigate Iran's aggressive forward policy in Herat. *The Nation* even wishfully anticipated that Dost Mohammad Khan's diplomatic and military pact with Britain would not withstand the pressure of Russian maneuvering. It wrote in January 1856:

> Herat, that superb city, which the Oriental poets love to designate "the Pearl of the Universe," has indeed fallen before the chivalry of Persia—and so another bulwark of British dominion in India has vanished for ever. It is amusing to observe with what nonchalance English journalists affect to treat this terrible disaster, and their reliance upon the speedy co-operation of **DOST MOHAMMED** and the other Candahar [Kandahar/Qandahar] chiefs—as if the wily old Ameer [i.e., Dost Mohammad Khan] and his colleague [sic] will not be delighted to have an opportunity of breaking with the English enemy from whom they suffered so much! It is believed that the **DOST** can readily place himself at the head of an army seventy thousand strong, and he has already set about organizing his fortress. What a convenient ally for the Czar! Curiously enough, we are reminded, that the every path now mapped out by Muscovite genius is strewn with the traditions of former illustrious conquests. For 2,000 years invading armies have traversed this region, and found it the vulnerable point through which they could penetrate the heart of India. "Alexander the Great took Herat—then the *Aria* of the ancients—and thence crossed Cabool [Kabul] to the Indus," observes a contemporary. "In 1398 Tamerlane came by the same route with his hordes, and made himself master of Cabool. In 1520 the celebrated Baber [Babur] founded at Delhi the empire of the Moguls [Mughals], and the undisputed sovereignty of that city. By the same course came the Sultan of Gheisned [i.e., the Ghaznavid ruler Mahmud in the eleventh century], who planted the religion of Islam in India [sic]. By the same route a little more than a century since [i.e., 1738-39], Nadir Shah [the Iranian ruler] penetrated victoriously to the foot of the Himalayas. There is, indeed, an eastern proverb, we are told, which says that no one can be king of Hindostan [India] without first becoming the lord of Cabool—a saying which, like every other proverb, is the result of wisdom and experience."
>
> Here are historic omens of victory bright enough to sustain the grim warriors of the North—and so England trembles for her hold upon the fair Land of the Sun [i.e., British India]. With

her native army [sepoys and sowars] requiring another army to preserve its allegiance—with the santhal tribes in actual revolution, and discontent spreading like a prairie-fire among the other Native States—is it impossible to predict the doom of "our" empire in India?[64]

The Nation, in one of its earlier (February 1856) reports on the cessation of diplomatic relations between London and Tehran—in the form of a "statement [...] said to be a correct version of the dispute between Persia and Great Britain"—had echoed the official British account of Murray's altercation with Iranian authorities that led to diplomatic rupture between the two countries. Recapping the account of Mirza Hashem's employment in British diplomatic service in Iran, and dismissing the allegations made by Iranian authorities against Murray, the report, which was directly quoted in *The Nation* without identifying its original source, concluded: 'Mr[.] Murray had no alternative left but to insist upon the liberation of the Mirza's wife, and the immediate retraction of the vile calumny which [the Iranian chief minister] had spread, or to strike his flag. As Persia refused the former, British honor compelled him to adopt the latter.'[65] But, following news of British preparations for military action against Iran later that year, the paper completely reversed its stance on the Mirza Hashem and Mrs. Hashem affair. Just as its reporting of developments respecting Herat put a positive spin on the Iranian siege and capture of that city, the paper now also echoed Tehran's version of the roots of the Anglo-Iranian conflict. *The Nation* cited Iranian, Russian, and other pro-Iranian accounts of diplomatic tensions between Tehran and London leading up to the war. These sources included the French-language Russian paper *Journal de St. Petersburg* and translations of reports from the Persian-language Iranian state-controlled weekly *Rouznāmeh-ye Vaqāye'-e Ettefāqiyeh* (tr. "Current Events Newsletter"), which was generally identified in English-language sources as the *"Teheran Gazette."* Translated texts of these Persian-language reports, as well as of other Iranian sources on the Anglo-Iranian conflict, mostly appeared in *The Nation* by way of quoting from already available English translations in a wide range of British press as well as in larger-circulation Irish newspapers. These existing English translations were themselves often indirect translations of Persian sources that were previously translated from Persian into other European languages, before being translated a second time into English. These other European periodicals included the *Ost Deutsche Post* (Vienna) or the *L'Indépendance Belge* (Brussels), both of which *The Nation* on occasion also cited as its direct sources.[66] Irish newspapers generally acquired their reports of foreign affairs from the same press sources as British newspapers, if not actually reproducing material from the major newspapers published in England, such as *The Times* of London. In its coverage of the situation in Herat and of the Anglo-Iranian War, *The Nation* also relied on the English-language press in India, as did some other Irish papers, but to a different effect. As early as March 1856 (i.e., well before the formal British declaration of war against Iran in November of that year), *The Nation* was already reporting on British military preparations in India and in the Persian Gulf, based on information appearing in the *Bombay Times*, the *Delhi Gazette*, and other Indian sources.[67] *The Nation* did not always identify its sources of information, as in the case of its brief account of the (falsely) rumored secret treaty between Iran and the United States, which is not to suggest it made up the report.[68]

In its coverage of the official Iranian account of the quarrel between Tehran and Murray, on October 25, 1856, *The Nation* reproduced a report "originally published in the Persian language, [which] appeared a short time since in *Le Nord*. It may be regarded as an official expos[é] of the origin of the rupture between the Schah [*sic*] of Persia and the British Government."[69] This was followed by *The Nation*'s editorial assessment of the account provided by *Le Nord*, a paper published in Brussels and known as a mouthpiece of the Russian government. According to *Le Nord*, Murray had been the real culprit in the eventual debacle from the start, by first insisting on retaining Mirza Hashem as a British consular staff in the city of Shiraz, where Britain at the time did not even enjoy a consular status in the first place, and then for having had the audacity to interfere on behalf of Mirza Hashem's wife after Iranian authorities placed her in the custody of one of her relatives. The report read, "What a great impropriety on the part of a foreign minister, to speak officially, in the East, of a Mussulman [Muslim] woman, and, above all, of the near relative of the sovereign! The Mussluman people are so susceptible on the question of women, that the least imprudence on the part of a European is sufficient to create the most fanatic and dangerous irritation."[70] This line of commentary aired by a press organ of the Russian government was all the more provocative given the Griboyedov Incident of 1829, which *Le Nord* carefully and conveniently evaded, given its implications in Russo-Iranian relations, while unmistakably hinting at that incident for those in international diplomatic and other expert circles familiar with the event. Palmerston's critics in Britain recurrently referred to Griboyedov's case as a historical precedent that should have taught Murray where to draw the line when meddling in Iranian affairs. Following the cessation of the Russo-Iranian War of 1826–28—the second major war fought between the two countries in the early nineteenth century, which resulted in further vast territorial losses by Iran to Russia and granted Russia various commercial and diplomatic privilege in Iran—a Russian mission arrived in Tehran to collect the first installment of the considerable war indemnity to which Iran had agreed in the peace talks. The Russian mission was led by the diplomat and author Alexander Sergeyevich Griboyedov. Once in the Iranian capital, Griboyedov was informed that a handful of Christian women (Armenian and/or Georgian) from the Caucasian territories now under Russian control were forcibly converted to (Shi'i) Islam and held in Iranian harems against their will. Intoxicated with a sense of victor complex, Griboyeddov decided to "rescue" the women without prior consultation with Iranian authorities. Breaking into the alleged harems in Tehran, the staff of the Russian mission took away for questioning at the Russian mission's complex two women suspected of having been forcefully converted and kept in the harems. This incited a furious mob attack against the Russian mission led by incensed Shi'i clerics, who viewed the Russian action as an insult to their faith as well as a violation of the sanctity of the harem, and an affront to Iranian sovereignty; not to mention their seething rage at the hubris of a foreign Christian power that already had extensively humiliated Iran in the battlefield for the second time in recent memory. After the besieged Russian guards at the Russian mission grounds opened fire on the angry crowd, the mob attacked the Russian headquarters and massacred Griboyedov and nearly the entire staff of the mission, whose bodies were then mutilated.[71]

The above-mentioned editorial commentary in *The Nation*, based on the reproduced article from *Le Nord*, went on to claim that instead of admitting Murray's responsibility for adversarial relations between London and Tehran, Britain was disingenuously exploiting Iranian military operations in Herat as a pretext for military confrontation with Iran. The article spuriously maintained Herat was "within the dominion of Persia," giving the Iranian state "indisputable" "right to occupy it [...] as plain as England's right to occupy Plymouth or Liverpool." The report also erroneously or falsely maintained that until recently British maps of the region unequivocally situated Herat within Iranian frontiers, only for the territory to be suddenly included in the latest maps within the domain of the Kabul-based Afghan state of Dost Mohammad Khan. *The Nation* continued, "Geography to the winds! The Society of Useful Knowledge to the devil! Herat shall be in whatever degrees of longitude I, England, think proper; and in order that there may no longer be any obscurity on this important point, I declare Herat the property of DOST MAHOMED, and will protect him in the possession of it! [...] the world's map shall be as the British Government shall regulate it."[72] The reproduced article from *Le Nord* concluded by calling on the Congress of Paris, which had met earlier in 1856 to draft the peace accord for terminating the Crimean War, to obstruct the impending British military action against Iran: "Stunned by the contemplation of England's stupendous audacity, we are unable to dwell on England's frightful rapacity and over arching [sic] despotism. But in the sacred name of truth and justice we ask how long is the civilized world going to endure this monstrous tyranny? Shall Persia fall? And shall the arm that was stretched forth on the fraudulent pretence of protecting the Sultan [i.e., British military cooperation with the Ottoman Empire during the Crimean War], be permitted perfidiously to crush the Schah [sic]?"[73]

Both *The Nation*'s muddled cartographic assertion of Herat's disputed sovereignty and London's post-1856 rationalization of Dost Mohammad Khan's jurisdiction over the territory were equally dismissive and negligent of Herat's hitherto autonomous status and local sovereignty for decades. *The Nation* did not specify to which earlier British maps in support of Iranian sovereignty over Herat its reproduced article was alluding. It was certainly the fact that much earlier British maps had categorically located Herat and its environs within Iranian frontiers, as in the case of the map by Aaron Arrowsmith appearing in Sir John Malcolm's 1815 *The History of Persia*. However, more recent British maps, as in the case of an 1834 map (published in 1842) of "Central Asia; comprising Bokhara, Cabool, Persia, The River Indus, & Countries Eastward of It" by John Arrowsmith (Aaron Arrowsmith's nephew, who had taken over his uncle's firm), situated Herat outside Iranian frontiers, as part of various separately governed territories comprising "Afghanistan."[74] This later map was produced four years before Tehran's previous attempted siege of Herat, which led to the Anglo-Iranian War of 1838. But, in the follow-up 1841 peace treaty with Britain, Iran refused to formally renounce its claim to Herat. The 1841 treaty was concluded in the midst of the first Anglo-Afghan War of 1839–42, when Dost Mohammad Khan was considered a threat to British interests in the region, and well before the 1855 friendship pact between the latter and the authorities in British India.[75] Under the 1841 peace treaty with Britain, Iran also granted Britain "most-favored nation" status in trade with that country, placing the British Empire on the same footing as Russia, which had obtained a similar standing in trade with Iran in 1828, following the Second Russo-Iranian War. Notwithstanding the Herat boundaries in John Arrowsmith's map, London did not in principal contest Tehran's ultimate claim to Herat in the 1841 treaty. That treaty did not revoke the terms of an earlier 1814 Anglo-Iranian Treaty concerning relations between Tehran and Herat. In 1814, Britain had undertaken to mediate disputes between Tehran and Herat *only* if called upon to do so by *both parties* in the dispute, but otherwise lacked the discretionary authority to interfere in affairs between Tehran and Herat. In late 1851, the beleaguered governor of Herat (Sayyid Mohammad Khan) requested Iran's military intervention against hostile overtures from the rulers of Kandahar and Kabul, placing himself under Tehran's protection. With Iranian military preparations underway, Britain diplomatically intervened to halt the impending Iranian armed involvement in Herat. At the time, Justin Sheil was the British representative in Tehran (of whom more will be said later in this chapter). Britain then pressured Tehran in a new Anglo-Iranian Treaty of January 25, 1853, to renounce, under vague terms, any future military interference in Herat, *unless* Herat was attacked by a "foreign" power and presumably requested Iranian assistance. Even then Iranian troops were not to enter the city itself and Tehran was to abstain from meddling in Herat's internal affairs. This 1853 treaty further stipulated, "The Persian Government engage to abandon the pretension and demand [...] or any other mark whatever of Herat being subject to Persia." But, the treaty significantly concluded with yet another ambiguous clause: "The above [...] engagements are in force so long as no interference of any sort shall occur on the part of the British Government; but, if otherwise, they will be invalid."[76] The indeterminate reference to British 'interference' in the latter clause could be broadly interpreted as any direct or indirect British involvement in determining Herat's territorial future, as in the case of British support for Dost Mohammad Khan's capture of the city and its environs in 1856, or British military intervention in Iran itself in 1856–57, even if Tehran had taken the first step in the latest crisis by attempting to militarily protect the governor of Herat who was reliant on Iranian support.

All of the above cartographic and diplomatic ambiguities and prior developments point to the complexity of the Herat Question by 1855. Nor should we discount the wishes of the people and/or different governors of Herat regarding the future governance and sovereignty of the territory—as in the case of, for example, the internal political upheavals in the city and the considerable resistance offered to Iranian forces by the population of Herat in 1856. The Herat Question spanned a multifaceted range of intersecting local and regional geopolitical ambitions and counterclaims, with regional contestants including Iran, the rulers of Kandahar and Kabul before 1856 (with the territories united into a single Afghan state by the time of the outbreak of the Anglo-Iranian War), as well as Russia, and British authorities in India (and, by implication, the British Empire in general). In the process, whereas *The Nation* insinuated (direct) British rule was unpopular among the Irish, and hence illegitimate, in its reporting of the Anglo-Iranian War the paper ironically obscured the wishes of the people of Herat (*There*) concerning the fate of their territory, so that the paper could draw a preferred parallel between Iran (*There*) and Ireland (*Here*) in opposition to London. The gist of the October 25, 1856, editorial in *The Nation* was that of unjustified British aggression around the globe, with the subtext of delegitimizing (direct) British rule in Ireland, while also circuitously questioning London's authority to *map* Ireland as a territory within the United Kingdom. *The Nation*'s representational style of an overarching and essentialized British imperial aggression around the globe relied on drawing selective parallels and connections between *here* and *there* and *now* and *then* in a manner that was distinct from, but not entirely dissimilar to, the worlding maneuvers of Irish nationalist antiquarians who had extrapolated Ireland's ancient Golden Age by means of associating ancient Ireland with various (historical or fabled) civilizations in distant lands (oriental or other), or Moore's and Mangan's respective poetic constellations of Iran/Erin.

The Iranian war of 1856–57 fit *The Nation*'s existing pattern, under A. M. Sullivan's ownership, of fervent denunciations of British imperial arrogance and aggression around the globe, examples of which prior to the Iranian war included a September 1856 article titled "THE BULLY ENGLAND." It cited the British occupation and administration of the Indian subcontinent, Ceylon, Borneo (in the case of the latter by "Sir JAMES BROOKE—now Rajah BROOKE"), New Zealand, Central America, and Ireland itself, as well as such recent incidents as the Crimean War and the alleged British plan of "now [...] domineering over Europe." This article commenced with an explicit disparagement of the English state, which the paper accused of repeated 'Crimes against humanity': "The hypocrite of the nations has too long been permitted to be the bull too. Crimes against humanity—crimes against the public law—crimes heinous, black, and perfidious, and such as cannot be laid to the charge of any other nation, Christian or Pagan, ancient or modern, she has been allowed, even within this nineteenth century, unchecked and unreproved, audaciously to perpetuate."[77] This article is furthermore important in connection with another aspect of *The Nation*'s periodic reporting of Iranian military advances on Herat in the coming months, with the population of Herat ravaged by famine after the city was placed under siege by Iranian troops and their regional allies. 'THE BULLY ENGLAND' article had underlined Ireland's Great Famine of 1845–51 as the epitome of England's destructive policies in general and its widespread crimes in Ireland: "In Ireland—but why speak of her?—we have seen two millions and a half of people swept like weeds from off the face of the land. The world opened her heart and her hand; gave Ireland her pity and her alms; but lifted no arm to shield or to revenge."[78] The theme of famine and hunger in Irish nationalist discourse was already a sacrosanct historical memory and a permanent political stigma attached to England, with the famine treated as quintessential indicator of Ireland's collective suffering under English administration—without forgetting the earlier Great Famine of 1740–41, now known as "Year of Slaughter." Yet, in its reporting of the Iranian assault on Herat in 1856, during which the mass starvation of the besieged population was deliberately exploited by the Iranian army as a military tactic for forcing the city into submission, *The Nation* avoided passing judgment on the Iranian strategy, nor did it voice any discernible sympathy with the suffering population of the besieged city; this occurring only five years after the end of the Great Famine in Ireland. The Iranian army had initially been invited to the city in December 1855 by the new Tehran-backed governor of Herat, Mohammad Yusuf, who had seized power in a coup. Mohammad Yusuf had sought Tehran's assistance against domestic and regional rivals. In spring of

1856, Iranian forces, which had taken control of Herat's environs, encountered unanticipated resistance from the population of the city and were forced to retreat. In the meantime, Mohammad Yusuf dissociated himself from Iranian forces positioned outside the city gates. Further complicating the Iranian plan, in June Mohammad Yusuf was ousted by Issa Khan, who turned to the Afghan strongman Dost Mohammad Khan for assistance.[79] Repeatedly failing to force their way into the city, Iranian forces placed Herat under siege and set out to starve its inhabitants into submission. The city finally fell to the Iranian army and its regional allies on October 26, following weeks of famine.[80] Quoting from other sources, *The Nation* nonchalantly reported: "the fall of Herat by famine. The Governor and his family have been put to death."[81] Even if in absolute numeric terms the human toll and duration of the artificial famine devastating Herat's population were nothing remotely close to the scale of the Great Famine in Ireland or of other major famines, the paper's lack of ethical judgment on the matter, while cheering Iran's military action, was still a politically callous act.

In November 1856 Britain finally declared war on Iran, after many weeks of preparations by the authorities in British India. Lieutenant-General Sir James Outram returned to India from England to take charge of the British invasion force, which for the time being was under the command of Major-General Foster Stalker.[82] With the British occupation of the Iranian island of Kharg in the Persian Gulf looming large on the horizon, *The Nation* eagerly hoped for a Great Power intervention in the conflict in opposition to Britain. Other than Russia, the paper also yearned for French assistance to Iran, notwithstanding France's recent joint military action with Britain against Russia in the Crimean War. On November 29, 1856, the "Foreign Intelligence" section of the paper carried a translated report from the French newspaper *La Presse* that the island of Kharg in actuality belonged to France "in virtue of a treaty concluded in 1769 between [Claude] Pyrault, our consul at [Basra in Ottoman Iraq]," and the Iranian state during the reign of Karim Khan, the founder of Iran's short-lived Zand dynasty (r.1751–94).[83] Karim Khan had in fact encouraged a French occupation of Kharg (i.e., by the French East India Company, just before its dissolution), but had not acceded to the permanent French ownership of the island—as a means of rebuffing attempts by the English East India Company to capture the island, after the Dutch East India Company and then the local Arab ruler of Kharg were expelled from the island by the Zand state. However, in the end France chose not to occupy Kharg and the matter came to pass. The article reproduced in *The Nation* nevertheless continued: "This treaty is doubtless but little known; but that consideration does not diminish its importance, since no ulterior convention has abolished or modified it." Regardless of the French origin of this information, this was a peculiarly wishful and simultaneously astounding attempt by *The Nation* to drum up support for Iranian sovereignty, by professing an island claimed by Iran, and facing impending British occupation at the time, in actuality belonged to France and not to Iran. Even the remotest prospect that France might emerge as an enemy of Britain in the Iranian conflict, whether in alliance with Russia or independently, was quickly dashed. Within three weeks, *The Nation* reported that "France has endeavoured to persuade Persia to yield to England."[84] In fact, unbeknownst to the public, at the time the French government was considering whether it should join Britain in China in what later came to be known as the Second Opium War (1856–60), which had commenced in October, or to continue pursuing diplomatic exchanges with Peking for obtaining an official Chinese apology and reparations for the recent execution of a French Christian missionary in China. In December 1857 France joined Britain in the Chinese war.

A more probable scenario was *The Nation*'s anticipation of Russian assistance to Tehran, St. Petersburg being London's main European imperial rival in the region and having encouraged the Iranian military advance on Herat, as well as having recently suffered a defeat in the hands of Britain and its allies in the Crimea. The paper enthusiastically reported various rumors, followed by almost immediate denials, of Russian military buildup for countering any British incursion into Iranian territory.[85] In the case of Russia, too, it was soon obvious St. Petersburg had no intention of committing itself to a military pact with Tehran in direct confrontation with Britain, even if Russia continued to encourage Tehran's forward policy in Herat, in the hope of some deferred Russian exploitation of the situation. Quoting from the German *Hamburgische Börsenhalle*, on December 27 *The Nation* admitted "The statement made by several foreign journals of a convention having been concluded between Persia and Russia, by which the latter is bound to assist the former, is completely unfounded."[86] Still, the paper continued to rummage for any sign of possible Russian intervention, diplomatic and/or military. On January 17, 1857, *The Nation* relayed reports from various French newspapers of continued Iranian victories against Dost Mohammad Khan's forces around Herat and of last-minute diplomatic endeavors by Tehran to halt the imminent military confrontation with Britain—that is, the mission of Farrokh Khan (Amin al-Molk) as the Iranian envoy to France in search of a peaceful settlement of the conflict. The paper also reported the false rumor of the arrival of British troops in Kabul to assist Dost Mohammad Khan, along with news of British naval proceedings in the Persian Gulf and their "inciting the Governors of the provinces to separate from the Shah." *The Nation* then provided an account of the alleged Iranian request for Russian military assistance, while repeating the incorrect report of recent dispatch of Russian forces to northern Iran by way of the Caspian Sea "to counterbalance the probable results of the English expedition to the Persian Gulf."[87] On this occasion, *The Nation*'s enthusiasm for a Russian military showdown with Britain made the paper even neglectful of the fact that the rumored Russian military arrivals in northern Iran would in actuality constitute a retaliatory Russian *occupation* of Iranian territory in response to the British occupation of southern Iran; hence, potentially further undermining Iranian sovereignty in the long run, rather than directly aiding Iran in its war against Britain.

Following the British invasion of Iranian territories in December 1856, *The Nation* stepped up its efforts to legitimize Iran's military advance on Herat, as a means of branding London's war against Iran an unwarranted act of aggression. In early January 1857, relying on a translation in another paper of a report originally appearing in the official Iranian mouthpiece *Rouznāmeh-ye Vaqāye'-e Ettefāqiyeh* ("*Teheran Gazette*") on November 5, 1856, *The Nation* asserted Tehran's ostensibly neutral and placatory stance on Herat's future, evidently unconcerned that the '*Teheran Gazette*' was distorting the details and sequence of the Herat conflict. *The Nation* reported:

[...] the siege of Herat was undertaken to prevent the Governor, Esa Khan [Issa Khan], from surrendering the town to the Emir Dost Mohammed Khan. This proceeding, the Gazette adds, was perfectly consistent with the treaty of Herat concluded between Great Britain and Persia [i.e., the treaty of 1853]. Notwithstanding all that has passed, the Persian Government has not lost sight of the preservation of its friendship with Great Britain, and is ready to withdraw its troops from Herat on condition that the British Government shall take measures at Candahar [Kandahar], Affghanistan [sic], and Herat itself to secure that each of those countries shall remain forever under the rule of its own government.[88]

Leaving aside Tehran's unrealistic request that Dost Mohammad Khan also relinquish his control over Kandahar—which would break up and vastly shrink Dost Mohammad Khan's recently incorporated Afghan territory and significantly diminish his overall regional leverage—the report in *The Nation* was intended as a reminder that Iran was acting in accordance with its 1853 joint undertaking with Britain, while Britain was in breach of that treaty. Even under the most liberal interpretation of the 1853 Anglo-Iranian Treaty over Herat, which recognized Tehran's option of military intervention if Herat was threatened by an outside force, Tehran was still clearly in violation of other terms of the 1853 treaty. If in 1856–57 it could be argued Iranian forces, which actually had already marched on Herat before Issa Khan seized power as the governor of the city with Dost Mohammad Khan's patronage, had done so to prevent an anticipated foreign intervention in the city, the treaty had nonetheless also stipulated that, even when repelling a foreign military advance on Herat, Iranian forces should refrain from entering the city itself. *The Nation*'s report insisted Iran had all along displayed paramount flexibility and willingness to settle the matter diplomatically and withdraw its army from Herat's environs. In this re-scripting of events and treaties, the onus in the Anglo-Iranian conflict rested entirely on London's shoulders.

The fighting between British and Iranian forces got underway following the British capture of Kharg Island on December 3, 1856. Attempting to characterize the war as a one-sided imperialist act of coercion, *The Nation* immediately noted the superiority of Britain's military strength in the conflict, evocative of the paper's regular characterization of London as 'The Bully England.' Expectedly, the paper exempted Iran from a similar frame of analysis in regard to Tehran's military operations in Herat and surrounding areas. Then again, *The Nation* portrayed those Iranian military operations as being both defensive and legitimate. To highlight England's barbarity, the paper also noted the savagery of British military actions in other settings, notwithstanding London's bogus pretention of justice and civilization. These other cases included the ongoing British military pacification efforts in the Peshawar Valley on the frontier of India and Afghanistan—a territory that Britain had occupied just a few years earlier and would remain a hotbed of anti-British rebellions for almost a century until the British withdrawal from India in 1947, after which the territory became part of the newly created country of Pakistan.[89] More significantly, however, *The Nation* noted the interaction between imperialism and control of information, in a particular configuration of power/knowledge to be more precise; in this case that of British military actions around the globe and control of journalistic reports reaching the public across the British Empire and beyond. Under the caption "FALL OF BUSHIRE," following the British capture of Bushire in the southern Iranian mainland on December 10, 1856, *The Nation* alluded to the drawn-out siege of Sevastopol during the Crimean War. This siege, lasting from October 1854 to September 1855, cost the lives of nearly 200,000 combatants and civilians from both sides of the conflict, mostly from wounds, hunger, the weather, and disease, before the joint armies of Britain, France, Ottoman Empire, and their other allies, finally captured the city. *The Nation* then commented on the disparate manner in which British military engagements in the Crimea and the war effort now underway in Iran were presented to the British public. Alluding to the candid reporting of the Crimean War by the Irish-born correspondent of *The Times* of London, William Howard Russell, which had played a major role in forcing the prime minister Lord Aberdeen out of office in January 1855, *The Nation* wrote:

> That was an ugly business before Sebastopol [*sic*]. Snow and mud and the Russians to contend with, and the French as witnesses; it was a horrid business. The Great Britons lost amazingly by it; they got beaten, and every one [*sic*] knew it, there was the sting of the affair, but before Bushire its all right—a less powerful foe, and no one to tell the truth to Europe, for sometime at all events. This indeed is a pleasing state of things. Only for the French and those abominable reporters we would have heard splendid stories of the British successes in the Crimea, the soldiers would have been knocking down Russian forts as if they were made of paper, and the affairs at Balaklava and the Redan would only have been a couple of larks played off by a few pleasant fellows, who returned laughing with all their might after having frightened the Russians out of their lives. Well, we have now received accounts of the taking of Bushire, and we may suppose it must have been a very smart affair when the Great Briton is forced to tell the sort of story we quote to-day:—"on approaching Bushire (says the *Bombay Times*) the place was shelled by the war steamer Assaye. The bulk of the Persian force fled, but a force of 800 men seemed determined to fight it out. They sallied out, and at one time had obtained possession of a gun. The vanguard, which had marched too much ahead, were compelled to make a rapid countermarch. The English troops seemed anxious to make a dash, and unfortunately charged with the bayonet, sacrificing valuable lives that might have been spared had the shelling been continued. Colonel [James] Stopford of the 64th fell bleeding. He was shot through the heart, and was pierced by many wounds. Lieutenants [Mathews Corsellis] Utterson and [William Blackburn] Warren of the 20th were killed by his side."
>
> We wish William Russell had been there to give us a sketch of that capture of a gun and that "unfortunate" charge with the bayonet. As he was not present we must only accept the hints and guess the meaning of the Bombay organ. "A flag of truce," we are told, "was taken to the town by Captain [Felix] Jones with a summons to surrender. The Governor was allowed till noon the following day to give his answer; but the flag of truce was fired on, and the envoy could not approach his mission. An apology was, however, almost immediately sent by the Governor." But the valiant Britishers had made their preparations for attack and they would not be disappointed. On the morning of the 10th of December the fleet commenced to dismantle the earthworks and throw shells into the place; the Persians sent off a flag of truce, asking for twenty-four hours' delay; the request would not be listened to by the British heroes. From this narrative it is plain that the firing of the Persians on the English flag of truce was either an accident or a mistake. The Governor apologised for it the moment he became aware of the occurrence, but the British admiral wanted no peaceable

submission; the envoy and his flag were a sham, his summons to surrender was intended only as a piece of acting, Bushire was to be destroyed, and 3,000 men were to be sacrificed that British officers might have decorations and an increase of pay, and England might recover in India the name of terror she lost in the Baltic, at Kars, and the Redan. [...]"[90]

In the same issue (January 31, 1857), the paper printed another article under the heading "THE PERSIAN WAR."[91] This article began with a very brief composite and exaggeratedly dazzling survey of Iranian history, geography, population, and economy, and then went on to suggest, in an even more exaggerated manner, that the ultimate British objective in the war might be the conquest of Iran: "The spoil then is no insignificant temptation to extend the area of Anglo[-]Saxon civilization." On the other hand, the same article downplayed the significance of recent British victories against Iran, despite the superior "force of the English armaments dispatched." It noted that the Kharg Island was "a mere pilot station" and Bushire "for the last ten years, had sunk from the commercial status it held" and was "doubtless, badly defended." This ignored the fact that Bushire, regardless of its infrastructural and other neglect by Iranian authorities, was Iran's major commercial port in the Persian Gulf and, until the recent cessation of relations between London and Tehran, had served as the seat of the British Residency in the Persian Gulf since 1775 under the jurisdiction of authorities in British India (with the Residency originally established in 1763, but withdrawn in 1768, before its resumption in 1775). *The Nation*, moreover, surmised that should the British occupation of Bushire last, "a few months will be sufficient to decimate them [i.e., the British occupation forces]: for so pestilential are the vapours of the Gulf, and so intolerable the heat of the climate, that Europeans have never been able to resist their combined influence." The article again suggested forthcoming Russian military assistance to Iran and restated the charge of British military aid to Dost Mohammad Kahn in Afghanistan—by this time, with the Peshawar Treaty of January 27, 1857, a military pact had indeed been concluded between British India and Dost Mohammad Khan in opposition to Iranian operations around Herat. The paper then once more highlighted the general brutality of British imperial rule, noting that in the preceding years Britain's Indian army had "carried desolation and massacre through villages" in the Peshawar Valley and, despite even opposition from some senior military commanders in India, Britain was bent on pursuing in the valley "the last act of policy (which would seem incredible were not the early annals of Ireland in existence)." Accordingly, this policy "was to establish a series of forts and garrisons 'to prevent the barbarians [allegedly the population of the valley as seen through British eyes] from cultivating their fields, and so to starve their families.'"[92] Keeping in mind the paper's earlier insouciant reporting of the Iranian tactic of starving Herat's population during the siege of that city, the policy of deliberate mass starvation was evidently inhumane when carried out by Britain, but less so when committed by Britain's enemies. The reference to British dispossession of fields in the Peshawar Valley was evocative of English/Protestant plantations in Ireland after the sixteenth century. Furthermore, insisting, "The current war is but the commencement of a new struggle between Russia and England in the East," with the implication that Russia was currently fighting a war against Britain by proxy (i.e., Iran), the paper prognosticated that even if the war should conclude very soon as rumored, another armed conflict between Britain and Iran would resume before long: "The interests at stake are too vast to admit of this, and in the event of its continuance, all the chances of success are on the Russian side."[93] According to these articles, in one form or another the future spelled doom for regional ambitions of the malignant British Empire.

In its subsequent reporting of the Anglo-Iranian War, *The Nation* was adamant on Tehran's refusal "to submit to the orders from Downing Street," even while mentioning the visit of the Iranian representative Farrokh Khan to Paris in the hope of French mediation for terminating the war, the success of which the paper cavalierly doubted. *The Nation* also continued to routinely situate British military operations against Iran in the broader global context of aggression by "Bully of the Nations,"[94] while intermittently still pondering the prospect for the resumption of former antagonism between Britain and France over the Iranian Question (i.e., at the start of the nineteenth century during the Napoleonic Wars). The paper once more erroneously informed its readers that the Kharg Island, now seized by British forces, belonged to France by a treaty: "It is said that two treaties—one of which dates so far back as 1708, under Louis XIV, and the other in 1808—exist, by which the Island of Karak, now occupied by the British, has been ceded conditionally [by Iran] to France. Thus the complication becomes greater; and it is certain that French diplomacy at Teheran refrained altogether from offering support to the pretensions of England."[95]

Sir Justin Sheil and Lady Mary Leonora Woulfe Sheil

Although other newspapers in the United Kingdom also periodically reproduced extract translations of articles appearing in the *Rouznāmeh-ye Vaqāye'-e Ettefāqiyeh* ("*Teheran Gazette*"), *The Nation*'s lengthy reproductions of the official Iranian perspective on the crisis, particularly without critical editorial commentary as was generally the case in other papers, was highly exceptional. This situated *The Nation* among the very few public outlets in the United Kingdom that echoed and endorsed the official Iranian line. In late February 1857, yet another detailed version of Tehran's account of developments appeared in *The Nation*, based on the translation of an article from *Rouznāmeh-ye Vaqāye'-e Ettefāqiyeh*, which *The Nation* had procured from an unnamed Calcutta paper. This article covered such topics as Tehran's decision to send a military force to Herat, the breakdown of diplomatic relations between Tehran and London, Tehran's attempts to avoid a war with Britain, the course of the current war, and Iranian efforts underway to diplomatically bring the war to a close. The article expectedly blamed the conflict on London's "bad faith and of the infraction of treaties." It condemned the British support for Dost Mohammad Khan's expansionist policy in Kandahar and his encroachment by proxy on Herat (i.e., by backing the new governor of the city). The article also mentioned Sir Justin Sheil, the former British representative in Iran (1844–54), who was succeeded by Murray following a temporary spell by the British chargé d'affaires William Taylour Thomson. This was the first direct reference in *The Nation* to Justin Sheil in connection with the Iranian crisis. Sheil, who had held other consular positions in Tehran from 1836 until assuming the post of the British envoy extraordinary and minister plenipotentiary, was identified in the reproduced article as a major culprit in the course of events leading to the current war. The official Iranian statement, again conflating the terms of various Anglo-Iranian treaties and insisting on Britain's ultimate recognition of Iranian sovereignty over Herat in 1814 and the British pledge not to interfere in affairs between Iran and Herat unless called upon by both parties to mediate their differences, added:

> The first infractions of these treaties by British agents took place in the reign of the late King Mohammad Shah, at the Siege of Herat [i.e., 1837-1838]. The English Government sent vessels of war into the Persian Gulf, which act compelled the King to raise the siege. His Majesty, not wishing to break off friendly intercourse with England, renounced at that time the capture of Herat. At a later period, Mr[.] Sheil assumed a cold and threatening manner, but the Court of Teheran, always appreciating the friendship of England, contracted, relative to Herat, a new arrangement [i.e., treaty of 1853], based upon the internal relations of the country, such as they existed in the days of Kamran [Shah Durrani] and of Yar Mohammed Khan. It was said then that the English should not interfere in any case, or in any manner, in the affairs of Herat, and that they should not have any relations with the chiefs of the said town. It is to be observed that that treaty must be null and void according to all international law, which stipulates that a treaty between two powers shall be ratified, and the ratifications exchanged—these conditions were not fulfilled.
>
> Moreover, Mr[.] Sheil himself annulled that arrangement, and his successors have imitated his example; this is proved by official documents that have been communicated to us. It was by acts that Mr[.] Sheil infringed the arrangement agreed upon; he sent one of his confidants Sultan Khan, to Herat, and he commenced relations that he had no business to enter into, for it had been expressly stipulated that a copy of the arrangement agreed upon should be sent to the government of Herat. To the observations made then by the Teheran Cabinet to Mr[.] Sheil that his conduct was contrary to stipulations, he replied officially that he did not regard himself bound not to hold communication with Herat, and that he should communicate with that town whenever and as often as he pleased without informing the Persian Government. In fact, these communications were entertained without interruption. After Mr[.] Sheil, the Charge d'Affaires, Mr. Thompson [Thomson] even took advantage of the departure of Molla Akram, the Secretary of the Governor of Herat, to entertain him outside the town and to give him money and a letter from Seid [Sayyid] Mohammad Khan.[96]

This official Iranian statement, substantially differing in its details from the official British version of events,[97] then provided further inventory of British duplicity leading up to the war.

It is noteworthy that Justin Sheil's name had not previously appeared in *The Nation* in connection with the diplomatic breakdown between Tehran and London, notwithstanding repeated references to Sheil by both Iranian authorities and many British critics of Palmerston's Iranian policy over the preceding months. These accounts held Sheil responsible for initial deterioration of relations between Tehran and London that led to the final cessation of relations in 1855 during Murray's tenure at the British legation. We can only speculate, with great caution, as to whether *The Nation*'s lack of prior references to Sheil in its coverage of the Iranian crisis was a conscious editorial decision by

A. M. Sullivan and his staff. If this was a deliberate move, then the most likely reason would be Sheil's family connections. Justin Sheil hailed from a prominent Irish Catholic family and had married into yet another distinguished family in Ireland, with members of both families having played leading roles in the campaign of Daniel O'Connell's Catholic Association earlier in the century. Justin Sheil's brother Richard Lalor Sheil (d. 1851) was a co-founder of the Catholic Association (1823), while Stephen Woulfe, the father of Justin Sheil's wife Lady Mary Leonora Woulfe Sheil, had been a leading Irish MP and supporter of O'Connell's Catholic Emancipation campaign, despite eventually breaking with O'Connell over other matters.[98] On the other hand, another possible explanation could be the already mentioned effort by the paper, until at least this stage, to deny any substantial Irish involvement in British imperial aggression around the globe. Yet, neither of these hypotheses account for why the paper had now overcome its hesitance and decided to finally mention Sheil's involvement in the developments.

As a brief side note in connection with Sheil, it is worth mentioning not only did the parliamentary and extra-parliamentary critics of Palmerston's Iranian policy in the United Kingdom recurrently allude to Sheil's part in the erosion of relations between the two countries, but one of these critics in particular, the Radical MP Austen Henry Layard, took advantage of the recently published book on Iran by Sheil's wife as yet another opportunity for condemning the British invasion of Iran. Layard wrote an anonymous 40-page joint review of two new publications on Iran, appearing in the *Quarterly Review* of April 1857, just as the Iranian conflict had concluded. The reviewed books were the 1856 translation by William Jesse of the French-language travelogue of Joseph Pierre Ferrier, titled *Caravan Journeys and Wanderings in Persia, Afghanistan, Turkistan, and Beloochistan*—edited by Henry Danby Seymour, one of Layard's Radical allies in the Iranian debate—[99] and Lady Sheil's 1856 *Glimpses of Life and Manners in Persia*.[100] To those who had closely followed the Iranian debate in the United Kingdom, there could be little doubt as to the actual authorship of the joint review. Segments of Layard's review were almost verbatim duplication of an earlier parliamentary speech by him. Besides the general readership, review articles such as this were intended as additional source of information for individuals on different sides of political debates in Britain. For instance, the prominent Peelite-Whig British politician, William Gladstone, who sided with Layard and other critics of Palmerston over the entire handling of "the Persian Squabble," evidently had read book reviews to further familiarize himself with the Iranian Question.[101] Among its other features, Lady Sheil's book had the distinction of being the earliest first-hand account of Iran by a European/Western woman, and an Irish woman no less who happened to be married to someone involved in the diplomatic disputation with Tehran prior to the recent war. She provided an account of her life in Iran from October 1849 to April 1853, her impressions of the people, their customs, religions, as well as the country's terrain, diverse climate, styles of architecture, among many other features, and a narrative her journey through other lands on her way to and from Iran. The book had appeared in print following the cessation of diplomatic relations between Tehran and London and rising tensions between the two countries over Herat just prior to the outbreak of the Anglo-Iranian War. Lady Sheil was clearly conscious of the greater marketability of her book in the United Kingdom at this juncture:

"There seemed at one moment a prospect that Persia would hold, as friend or foe, a prominent position before the English public. This anticipation led first to the production of these pages. Even now the altered aspect of political affairs may not perchance have deprived them of all interest." She also opened the first chapter of the book with the observation that, "At this moment, when public attention is so much directed to the East, I have thought my recollections of the scenes I have visited may not be without interest to a few readers."[102] Following her own narrative, the book included appended notes "written by my husband," since in her words, "There are in Persia subjects not accessible to female inquiry."[103] In actuality, this was not solely due to conditions in Iran, but was also to a large extent in keeping with so-called respectable middle-class and gendered mores of her own Victorian society at the time, which largely considered political and certain other matters of "public" nature off limits to women.

While Lady Sheil did not directly address the Mrs. Hashem affair, she promptly underscored her first-hand familiarity with the lives of Iranian women as the most distinctive quality of her book: "One advantage I enjoyed over many preceding travellers in Persia. I have been able to see the anderoons or harams of the Shah and some of the principal personages of his Court; and to judge, to a certain extent, with my own eyes, of the condition of women in that portion of the East."[104] Yet, the publication of Lady Sheil's book afforded further opportunity for the British opposition to Palmerston's Iranian policy to allude to the Mrs. Hashem affair. In addition to the uniqueness of the book's authorship and its content, press commentaries on the book in the United Kingdom solidly anchored it within the general corpus of travel and historical accounts of Iran that informed British conceptions of Iranian women; in this case a work covering the daily lives of Iranian women (of affluent classes) written from the more intimate perspective of another woman, who also happened to be from the United Kingdom and adhered to more conventional British middle-class mores.[105] For Palmerston's critics, including the press, Lady Sheil's book indirectly shed greater light on the Mrs. Hashem affair. This was apparent in Layard's anonymous review of the book, in which Layard attacked the course of British diplomacy with which Lady Sheil's husband had been directly connected. Layard's prime target, however, was Murray. He dexterously extracted from Lady Sheil's book just the sort of information necessary to pillory Murray for his alleged recklessness and flippancy when meddling in the private family affair of an Iranian man (Mirza Hashem), with inexorable diplomatic consequences. After devoting some space to Lady Sheil's discussion of Iranian (Shi'i Muslim) marriage customs and the purportedly prevalent infidelity and fickle affections among both married men and women of higher Iranian social strata in towns and cities,[106] Layard corroborated Lady Sheil's view that "Mohammedan women [...] enjoy more liberty than among us"—that is, greater opportunity to engage in adultery, which was generally attributed by such Western commentators to gender segregation and practice of women veiling in public in Muslim societies at large.[107] Layard then steered the discussion to the case of Mrs. Hashem. He underscored the extreme sensitivity and jealousy of "Oriental" men "on the subject of their women when a European is in any way concerned," and reminded the readers of likely dangers involved when European men meddled in the affairs of Oriental women. His choice example, as in his previous statements on the subject in other settings, was the 1829 Griboyedov affair, which had attracted much press attention in Britain and was also mentioned in Lady Sheil's book.[108] Not averse to civilizationally hierarchical and essentialist remarks about 'orientals,' Layard was insinuating that either something genuinely illicit had occurred between Murray and Mrs. Hashem, or that Murray had been foolish enough to give credence to such an impression by his heedless and arrogant conduct, which had expectedly roused suspicion and offended local sensibilities in Iran, ultimately resulting in a diplomatic fracas and war:

> Notwithstanding the latitude given to their wives—a latitude favourable to intrigue—the Persians, like all Orientals, are extremely sensitive on the subject of their women when a European is in any way concerned. Lady Sheil describes the massacre of the whole Russian mission, under M. Grubraëdoff [Griboyedov], with the exception of one attaché, some thirty years ago. The circumstances which gave rise to this outbreak of popular fury arose upon the demand of the Russian Minister that several Georgian women, who were in the harem of the Shah and of his principle noblemen, should be delivered up to him, on the plea of their being Russian subjects. In a significant note to a passage in M. Ferrier's work (p.153), Sir John Login confirms from his own knowledge a statement we have often heard repeated upon almost equally good authority, that our disasters in Afghanistan were not altogether unconnected with the jealousy felt by the wild chiefs of that country in the intercourse of our officers with their women. It is well known that the differences between ourselves and Persia, which have unfortunately ended in a war, commenced with a lady, of whom we shall have to say a word hereafter. It is not perhaps inconsistent with our experience of human nature, and especially of that division of it of which we are treating, to presume that this very jealousy felt by the men of any communication whatever between their women and Europeans, is the cause of the great curiosity shown by the former to see and converse with the forbidden race. Lady Sheil has described how the ladies of Teheran flocked to the English doctor, a privileged person in all parts of the East, under the pretense of consulting him upon imaginary ills, but really with a view to indulge an appetite, often felt in Persia, as elsewhere, for gossip and scandal. Eastern women, indeed, are always eager to avail themselves of any excuse to see a "Frank." 'You wish to see the women,' said an indigenous British vice-consul to an English traveller; "well, keep a monkey or a peacock, and you will always have the yard of your house full of them." The suggestion was adopted, and with the fullest success—no husband venturing to do more than remonstrate against the gratification of so reasonable curiosity as that of seeing a strange animal.[109]

The Nation and Jihād against Britain

Soon after the British invasion of Bushire in December 1856, Tehran had pursued peace talks with London through French arbitration, after Tehran's initial offer of direct negotiations with London through their respective ambassadors in Istanbul was rebuffed by Palmerston. In the end, on March 4, 1857, the government of the shah accepted the key British terms for an armistice, albeit resisting additional British demands intended to further humiliate the Iranian state and elevate London's diplomatic standing in Iran above all other foreign powers. Due to delay in communications—in the absence of direct telegraph lines between London and British India at the time, as well as between

British India and southern Iran—British military operations in Iran continued for nearly another month, with forces under the command of General Henry Havelock advancing on Mohammareh (Khorramshahr) on the southern Iranian-Ottoman frontier and capturing the town on March 27, followed by the capture of Ahvaz on April 1. Among other terms of the Treaty of Paris (March 4), signed by the Iranian representative Farrokh Khan and the British ambassador to France, Lord Cowley (Henry Wellesley), which was formally ratified by both sides on May 2 in Baghdad (Ottoman Empire), Britain was to withdraw from Iranian soil and Iran was to evacuate Herat and its outlaying region and recognize the independence of the territory. (Herat was eventually incorporated into Dost Mohammad Khan's unified Afghan realm in 1863.) Moreover, all future disputes between Iran and Herat (hence, after 1863 also bearing on relations between Iran and Afghanistan) were to be mediated by Britain. Britain was further permitted to establish consular offices in all Iranian locations where Russia maintained consulates, in addition to other parts of the country, and Charles Murray was to be received ceremoniously by Iranian authorities and resume his post as the British representative.[110] In short, the outcome of the brief war between Iran and Britain was a substantial victory for London and, in the short run, signaled Russia's diminished regional leverage. The British ambassador to the Ottoman Empire conducting the initial peace talks with the Iranian envoy was the Anglo-Irish Stratford Canning (Viscount Stratford de Redcliffe), whose cousin happened to be the governor-general of India at the time (Charles John Canning), with the Irish Henry Blosse Lynch leading the subsequent negotiations resulting in the Paris peace accord on March 4, 1857. (Lynch, then residing in Paris, had previously served with distinction in military and diplomatic posts in British India and the Persian Gulf. Incidentally, Thomas Kerr Lynch, one of Henry's brothers, and a co-founder along with another brother, Stephen, of the Euphrates and Tigris Steam Navigation Company (1861), was later appointed the Iranian Consul-General in London in December 1867.[111])

In its coverage of the peace negotiation, *The Nation* again avoided any details of the talks that could draw much attention to the Irish personnel serving in Britain's imperial operations. On February 28, 1857, it reported the particulars of the French mediation underway between the two countries that shortly culminated in a peace treaty, without mentioning the British negotiators, whose names appeared in other press reports.[112] It was to be expected that in the absence of a telegraph line between the United Kingdom and Iran, or a direct line between the United Kingdom and India, many of the reports of the Iranian war appearing in the Irish and the British press should be somewhat dated. On April 4, 1857, *The Nation*, without identifying the original source of the news item, published summary details of General James Outram's "8th of February" [actually 7th of February] assault on Khushab in southern Iran and the casualty figures for the British imperial force.[113] On the other hand, *The Nation* also deliberately delayed reporting certain events on occasions when the paper desperately hoped for a different turn of events than indicated by the information available to the press in the United Kingdom. To the end, the paper anticipated some form of adverse outcome for London in the Iranian conflict. Even though by February 1857 the faintest likelihood of Russia, let alone France, being militarily drawn into the conflict in opposition to Britain had fast dissipated, the paper continued to wish otherwise. Taken off guard by the speedy and unexpected resolution of the Anglo-Iranian War, *The Nation* adopted the hopeful tone that the conflict may not be entirely over yet, and Britain might still suffer humiliation. On March 7, 1857, following one of its reports on the concurrent Chinese War, the paper correctly stated that the Paris peace accord between London and Tehran still lacked "definitive" ratification by both governments. It then fancifully asserted that Russia was pressing ahead with its "preparations [...] on the Caspian to assist her neighbor" and, therefore, "the difficulty is not likely to be settled in so facile a manner." The paper again also bizarrely expressed hope that France, which had mediated the peace settlement, may somehow resort to hostilities against Britain over the Kharg Island. *The Nation* intimated that the peace treaty had "strangely" omitted Kharg from the list of occupied Iranian territories to be evacuated by British forces and "England appeared determined to hold possession" of the island. It added: "It is possible that the old Treaty, by which it was rendered to France, has been disinterred, and that Louis has asserted his prior claim to check the rapacity of the Briton, and increase his prestige in the East. Indeed, the Island is a point of too much importance to France to be delivered up, without a remonstrance, at least, against the piratical tendency of his Ally [i.e., Britain]."[114] Similar expectation that the Iranian conflict may be far from over, and that Russia may yet intervene militarily in support of Iran, was echoed in militant diasporic Irish nationalist outlets, as in the case of the New York papers the *Irish-American* and *The Citizen*.[115]

More significantly, the same issue of *The Nation* that hoped France may possibly wreck the prospect of a peace settlement between Britain and Iran, also carried the translation of a January 1857 Iranian royal decree ("firman") addressed to the Iranian people for public mobilization in the form of a *jihād* (holy war) for resisting the British invasion.[116] The decree called on all Iranian Muslims to resist British aggression following the occupation of Bushire in December 1856. Ironically, it was after the conclusion of the peace treaty that *The Nation* could publish the text of the Iranian royal decree, given the usual delays in communication between Iran and Western Europe and the fact that *The Nation* would have had to obtain the English or some other European translation of the Iranian royal decree from another source. With the original Persian text having appeared in *Rouznāmeh-ye Vaqāye'-e Ettefāqiyeh* ("*Teheran Gazette*"), the article in *The Nation* included a somewhat embellished translation of the royal decree (obtained from a secondary source)—although not specified by *The Nation*, the date of the report in the Iranian newspaper was January 14, 1857. The translation of the text of Nasser al-Din Shah's decree, which had been read in the name of the monarch at the main mosque in Tehran (Masjed-e Shah) and addressed to all Iranian Muslims in general, and those of Shi'i persuasion in particular, denounced Britain as the aggressor and violator of existing treaties between the two countries and condemned London for its unwillingness at the time to consider Iranian offers for peaceful resolution of the crisis. Other than its in-depth coverage of the war, *The Nation* appears to have published this now outdated text—the English translation of which certainly could not have been available in the press much sooner—chiefly as a reminder to its readers that, regardless of the final outcome of the conflict, Iranians as a 'nation' were courageously united in defense of their country's sovereignty against British aggression; leaving aside here the exclusion of Iranian non-Muslims from the intended audience of the shah's decree (which was calling for a Muslim holy war). This was a rare opportunity for the paper to portray the war not as a mere conflict between two governments, but as the righteous struggle of people whose "national" rights were violated by an imperialist power. (*The Nation* had refrained from applying a similar interpretation to the population of Herat resisting the Iranian capture of their city.) The report of the Iranian royal decree in *The Nation* offered a synecdochic rhetorical shift between, on the one hand, the sovereign rights of the Iranian people and, on the other hand, the Iranian state, with the shah as the surrogate representatives of the Iranian nation here:

'After acts so injurious, and threats uttered against our government in contempt of all justice, taking into consideration the hostility of the British government, we wish to preserve intact our honour and our religion. We place all our hopes in God, and we will resist by every means (emedje istadeim) [in the original Persian text: *"dar in rāh tā hameh-jā istādeh-am"* / in this path I stand ready in every respect].

'You all, inhabitants and fellow-believers, who for so many years have given me so many proofs of your devotion and your courage, I call on you! You will place your foot firmly in the road of honour, and you will assist me to defend with valour and energy our honour and dignity, which may have been [!] my rule of conduct as they have been that of my ancestors.'

The reading of the firman was received with immense applause. The Sadrazam [i.e., *sadr-e a'zam* / chief minister] was commissioned to transmit to his Majesty the expression of the devotion of the entire population.[117]

From the point of view of *The Nation*, the most evident attraction of the reproduced translation of the Iranian royal decree in condemnation of British aggression was doubtless the joint emphasis in the decree on territorial sovereignty, faith/god, and national honor. While *The Nation* was committed to nonsectarian cross-communal Irish nationalism, joint references to god and nation (the latter in various formulations of popular and territorial sovereignty) were paradigmatic of most currents of Irish nationalism during the period—with unionist communities in Ireland having their own distinct renditions of "for god and nation." Notwithstanding the general disparagement of Islam by both Catholic and Protestant establishments at the time, the Iranian royal decree echoed the principal ingredients of mainstream constitutional or revolutionary Irish nationalist platforms, give or take additional objectives and different tactics championed by different groups. As previously noted, in "The Fire-Worshippers" section of Thomas Moore's 1817 *Lalla Rookh*, the fictional Iranian hero Hafed had raised the battle cry of "FOR GOD and IRAN" as the transparent echo of "For God and Ireland." The most popular of the radical Irish nationalist anthems at the time of *The Nation*'s coverage of the Iranian war was "A Nation Once Again," composed in the early 1840s by Thomas Osborne Davis. That poem coupled a nondenominational godly virtue with Ireland's right to exist as a nation: "For freedom comes from God's right hand / And needs a godly train // And righteous men must make our land / A Nation once again."[118] In contrast to Moore's sectarian setting (i.e., Zoroastrian/Catholic v. Muslim/Protestant foreign occupation), Davis's poem evoked god as a nonsectarian component (albeit largely interpreted as a "Christian" god) of Young Ireland's nationalist ethos of what David Dwan in a different setting has called Young Ireland's vision of a common "virtue."[119] This Young Ireland tradition of nonsectarian evocation of god dated back to the founding of the Society of United Irishmen in the late eighteenth century. On the other hand, Mangan's 1846 fictional Qizilbash in "To the Ingleezee Khafir" was an Iranian (Shi'i) Muslim proudly spouting his loathing of the "vile Ferindjee" Khafir (i.e., the European/Christian infidel). The god of the Iranian monarch's 1857 decree in fact operated at a different level from these Irish parallels, since the shah was exhorting Iranian Muslims against not only the "English" Christian invaders, but ultimately also against the remainder of the British occupation force in southern Iran, which included cross-denominational Christians from other parts of Britain as well as Ireland, along with Hindu, Sikh, and Muslim sepoys and sowars. While the shah did not directly attack the religious beliefs of the invaders, it would have been clear to his Iranian audience that he regarded the *English state* as the actual aggressor and was identifying that non-Muslim entity as the infidel against whom Iranian Muslims should wage a holy war on their own territory in southern Iran and the Persian Gulf.

Cross-Territorial Affinities and the Worlding of the Irish Question

In 1857 Iran formally consented to renounce its territorial claim to Herat, although it again militarily intervened in the territory following a border dispute that erupted between Herat and Afghanistan in 1862 (over the Farah province). On that occasion, Tehran unsuccessfully attempted to prevent Herat's capture by Dost Mohammad Khan's Afghan forces, with the Iranian army even pushing deep into Afghan territory before Dost Mohammad Khan, with British assistance again, managed to repel the Iranian forces and annex Herat shortly prior to his death in 1863. In the coming decades, St. Petersburg continued to pursue its own expansionist objectives in the region. It waged yet another war against the Ottoman Empire (1877–78), while also closing in on Iran's northeastern frontier and also annexing territories bordering Afghanistan to the north. Moreover, by the end of the century St. Petersburg steadily acquired greater influence in the Iranian court. Britain, in the meantime, waged yet another costly war in Afghanistan (1878–80). This time, however, it at least succeeded in gaining leverage over Afghanistan's foreign affairs under the Gandamak Treaty of 1879.[120]

More immediately for Britain, just as the British military operations on the Iranian mainland were winding down in 1857 following the Paris peace treaty, a large-scale and rapidly spreading armed uprising against British rule broke out in India in May 1857, involving large numbers of British sepoy and sowar forces. Outram, Havelock, and their forces were recalled from southern Iran to India to aid in the suppression of what became an exceedingly lethal and mutually gruesome conflict before the rebel forces were finally crushed the following year. Now, it was the Indian uprising (better known in the United Kingdom as the "Sepoy Mutiny"), alongside other ongoing British conflicts, as in China, that afforded *The Nation* further opportunities for denouncing British imperial aggression, misrule, and savagery. Of course, for the paper India as a colony of Britain offered closer parallels to the Irish Question. In the coming decades there continued to be periodic reports in *The Nation* and in other range of Irish nationalist press of Iran-related news in connection with British policy and/or other modes of leverage in the region—including the coverage of popular oppositions in Iran to the Reuter and subsequent tobacco concessions granted by Nasser al-Din Shah to British subjects in 1872 and 1890 respectively. These Irish sources also covered such developments as the Iranian famine of 1870–72, or the European visits of Nasser al-Din Shah (1873, 1878, 1889) and that of his successor Mozaffar al-Din Shah (1902), and some other occasional Iran-related news. In addition, there was continued Iran-related coverage of literary, antiquarian, and other topics of cultural and historical interest. The next occasion that Iran became the subject of sustained contemporary political reporting and sympathetic commentary in the pages of Irish nationalist press, and in a much more extensive and vociferous manner than in 1856–57, was during the Iranian Constitutional Revolution of 1906–11 (see Chapter Seven).

In contrast to *The Nation*'s pro-Russian stance during the Crimean War, the paper's coverage of such events as the Iranian or Chinese wars, and much more notably that of the Indian uprising, was indicative of varying modes of selective expressions of affinity between segments of Irish nationalists and wide-ranging formulations of "anti-imperialist" resistance elsewhere around the world. It was states and/or peoples resisting *British* military action that were deemed worthy of the paper's solidarity in the 1850s, and not the Ottoman state facing Russian territorial aggression in the Crimea (particularly since Britain militarily aided the Ottoman state) or the people of Herat facing Iranian military siege of their city in 1856–57. Certainly not all Irish nationalists followed the same pattern as *The Nation* (and most contemporary militant Irish nationalist papers published in the United States). Regardless of whether in different settings Irish nationalist expressions of fellow-feeling with states or peoples elsewhere were empathetic in principle or purely tactical overtures,[121] these cross-identifications with the struggles of other peoples and the drawing of historical and/or contemporary parallels between those other struggles and the Irish Question (in the form of campaigns for either Home Rule or full independence) were ultimately modes of worlding the Irish Question. Different forms of imperialism as well as anti-imperialist nationalisms generated their own distinctive and contrasting versions of world history and accompanying modes of defining and locating contemporary world events in the framework of respectively empire-centered or anti-imperialist world histories. The competing empire-centered world histories in this process, as in the case of mainstream British, French, Russian, American, or Ottoman, among other examples, often clashed with one another in their self-placement in the world. The same can be said of anticolonial/anti-imperialist world-historical narratives within particular imperial or cross-imperial settings—as, for instance, on occasions when competing ethnic/racial, religious, territorial, and other such claims, either internally, cross-regionally, or in opposition to some other groups, produced a range of dichotomous alternative world-historical self-framings and narratives. There was also an amalgam of other ideological influences on anti-imperialist historical narrations, as in the case of, for example, the influence of Karl Marx and Friedrich Engels after the mid-nineteenth century in certain contexts. Marx and Engels, incidentally, wrote on the Irish Question, India, the Second Chinese War, as well as on the Anglo-Iranian War. Marx wrote a number of articles on the latter topic for the *New York Tribune* (appearing on February 14, May 22, and June 24, 1857), and Engels contributed a related article to the same paper (appearing in the February 19, 1857, issue).[122]

Irish nationalist references to Iran, ranging from mytho-historical connections to literary adaptations of Iranian settings for Irish motifs and journalistic coverage of contemporary developments, which variously asserted particular forms and degrees of interconnections and/or equivalence between Ireland and Iran, were components of manifold strategies of Irish self-emplotment in a world-historical context. Even if often ultimately self-directed and self-regarding, a significant feature of this pattern of *worlding the nation* was its underlying cosmopolitan and trans-national configuration. This cosmopolitan grounding of the nation went beyond the mere acknowledgment of conceptual and aspirational universality of nationalist and other forms of resistance to colonialism/imperialism around the world. The *avowedly* empathetic modes of worlding the nation, alongside simultaneous assertions of the historical particularity of that nation (in terms of its distinctively unique core features and experiences), was a delicate balancing act of claiming national *particularity* while *universalizing* of the nation's past heritage and/ or present colonial condition and continued struggle for autonomy or independence, requiring repeated narrative adjustments, elisions, and re-scripting. A case in point in connection with the Anglo-Iranian War of 1856–57 was *The Nation*'s characterization of the Dost Mohammad Khan, who in the pages of *The Nation* since the paper's founding in 1842 (initially as the Young Ireland outlet) was transformed from a hero (as the ruler of Kabul resisting British occupation during the First Anglo-Afghan War) to a villain (as the Afghan leader backed by Britain, who in 1856–57 challenged the Iranian territorial claim over Herat). The 'Hurrah for Dost Mohammed!' in the Young-Irelander Thomas Osborne Davis' "A Ballad of Freedom" was transformed into "the wily old Ameer" of *The Nation* under A. M. Sullivan's ownership during the Iranian war. In other words, expressed cross-territorial affinities and various forms of inscribing the Irish struggle in world-historical contexts were always temporally as well as spatially contingent and malleable; just as Mangan or Moore too had selectively deployed fragments of the histories of other peoples and territories as a means of commenting on developments in Ireland. In this scripting of Ireland in a world-historical context, the imputed heroes of the *there* and *then* could become the villains of *there* and *now*. This was not necessarily on the basis of ultimate aspirations of the individuals in question (given, for instance, the constancy of Dost Mohammad Khan's ambition to consolidate his hold over Afghan territories), but on grounds of their changed function in, and suitability for, Irish nationalist condemnations of British imperialism—just as after the Anglo-Russian Agreement of August 1907 Russia was once again (as in the pre-Crimean War years) cast as a malignant imperialist power and a domestically tyrannical state in those 'radical' Irish nationalist circles that in the interim had championed Russian imperial rivalry with Britain. What had changed about Dost Mohammad Khan between 1842 and 1856 was not his territorial expansionist objectives, but his mode of interaction with British India in pursuit of his ambition. After all, Dost Mohammad Khan was not an Irish nationalist serving the 'nationalist' interests of Irish people. This style of seesawing Irish nationalist identification with, and dissociation from, the same individuals or states was distinct from the extensive range of divergent Irish nationalist cross-references to 'Iran' across a very broad historical, cultural, and political timeline, ranging from a very remote ancient Iran as the originary home of the Irish in some antiquarian accounts to ancient imperial Iran of Thermopylae in Davis' "A Nation Once Again," the Arab-Muslim "colonized" Iran of seventh and eight centuries in Thomas Moore' *Lalla Rookh*, or alternatively Moore's Iran of the early nineteenth century in *Intercepted Letters*, or the defiantly independent and powerful sixteenth-century (Shi'i Muslim) Safavid state of James Clarence Mangan, or the (Shi'i Muslim) Qajar state of *The Nation* in 1856–57 that was purportedly victimized by Britain (*The Nation* ignoring the potential Russian threat to Iranian sovereignty during the same time frame).

Yet, overlooked or consciously glossed over in Irish nationalist political allusions to 'Iran,' with the exception of antiquarian models of Iranian origins in this case, or in Irish nationalist references to Dost Mohammad Khan, and the many other such politically motivated circuitous world-historical self-referentialities by means of alluding to others, was the historically inconstant polythetic identity of peoples and the changing political fabric of any nation, state, or territory across time, including Ireland. Also overlooked or consciously ignored in this connection was Ireland's own past and present record of abetting the preservation and expansion of British Empire, even as Irish nationalists resisted English domination and denounced British aggression elsewhere. In effect, one's 'national' self-perception can be diametrically at odds with the historical perceptions that other 'nations' form of the particular nation in question. I return to this topic in Chapter 8, when probing contemporary Iranian perceptions of Ireland. In fact, in ongoing historical debates concerning the rival Pro-Treaty and Anti-Treaty Irish nationalist camps following the establishment of the Irish Free State in 1922—which primarily tend to focus on Ireland's partition, as well as on the Free State's self-governing status within the British Empire, and the hostilities between the two Irish nationalist camps that erupted into the Irish Civil War of 1922–23—what is generally neglected is the fundamental disagreement between the antagonistic nationalist camps in 1922 over Ireland's continued acceptance of the onus of, and contribution to, the maintenance of Britain's vast Empire and the potential for future participation by the Free State in London's imperial inroads into other parts of the globe and/or in British suppression of nationalist or other range of anti-imperialist movements in the existing empire. Given that during the Second Anglo-Iranian War of 1856–57, *The Nation* was committed to attaining Home Rule for Ireland (i.e., self-government within the British Empire), it is unclear how accomplishing that objective would have entirely released Ireland from the burden of contributing to the maintenance of the British Empire and any future British imperial aggression around the world. Even if, following the attainment of Home Rule, nationalists were to demand that Irish military recruits only be stationed in Ireland for defensive imperial purposes, Ireland would still be making an array of other contributions to preserving, if not also expanding the British Empire, contra nationalist and/or nativist objectives in other parts of the existing empire and beyond. In the case of republican nationalists, on the other hand, who wished to sever all imperial ties with Britain, what was continually evaded since the emergence of the United Irishmen, was the fact that the Irish nationalist struggle was not only directed at London and the politically unionist Irish camps, but also at some level it was a struggle directed against a large cross-section of other Irish who were currently serving as personnel in, or were in some other form beneficiaries of, Britain's imperial machinery, not all of whom necessarily sympathized with unionist politics.

From alternative Irish nationalist perspectives there was yet another appealing feature of worlding Ireland's history of relations with England by way of drawing parallels with events and developments in other lands throughout history. As already hinted at, this was yet another mode of deprovincializing Ireland, which had come under full control of the English crown in 1541, during the reign of the Tudor monarch Henry VIII and following the failed 1534–35 uprising in Ireland led by Thomas Fitzgerald, the 10th Earl of Kildare. Since then, with the establishment of the Kingdom of Ireland, under direct rule of the English crown, all of Ireland had been governed from London, notwithstanding the legislative power of the parliament in Dublin. This marked the beginning of Ireland's status as a "province" of the English crown, which was further accentuated following the annulment of the Irish parliament in Dublin and the creation of the United Kingdom of Great Britain and Ireland in 1801—leaving aside that by then Catholics had already been barred from the Irish parliament for nearly a century (the Irish House of Commons in 1692, and House of Lords in 1716), and would remain barred from the post-1801 parliament of the United Kingdom until the Catholic Emancipation Act of 1829. Hence, Thomas Osborne Davis' already-mentioned famous expression of Ireland's *future* status after independence as a 'nation,' rather than a 'province': 'And Ireland long a province be / A nation once again.' By worlding the Irish experience of colonization, Irish nationalists were positioning Ireland on par with India and other British colonies that otherwise could not be considered as a province within the United Kingdom (even if designated as imperial dominions), or were claiming 'national' equivalence with independent and semi-independent nations such as Iran ('nation' here implying a territorial state and/or people). By drawing selective parallels between Ireland's experience and those of other real or alleged victims of British imperialism, Ireland too was definitively cast as a victim of English imperial aggression and as illegitimate sphere of English sovereignty, and hence already *not* a province. This is a topic to which I return in greater detail in later chapters. As previously noted, these anti-imperialist modes of worlding the Irish nation by drawing parallels with other territories and populations hinged on simultaneous expressions of proximity and distance as well as historical recollection and amnesia, given the frequently dissonant representations of those other territories and peoples over an extended time frame. In this worlding of the Irish nationalist struggle, there were also differing styles of selectively and rhetorically deflecting the historical peculiarities of each 'nation,' such as the absence of Ireland's prior historical existence as a single unified independent realm at the time of its imperial subjugation by England, in contradistinction to the case of Iran of the seventh century, sixteenth century, or nineteenth century, for instance—even if Iran had ceased to exist as a unified and/or independent territory for some extended periods of time in the interval, without forgetting also that many Afghans, Central Asians, and others also have as valid a historical claim to 'Iran' of earlier times as do those living in the territory now called Iran (while also recognizing here that all such claims to the past are no more than primarily invented 'national' self-projections onto the past or other modes of "identity" fictions). The most pervasive deflective rhetorical tactics of Irish nationalists were those of claiming *natural* and/or *cognitive* justifications (the latter in the sense of national "awakening") for Ireland's warranted self-government within the empire or full independence from Britain. The socialist Irish nationalist James Connolly, a leading participant in the Easter Rising of 1916 during the First World War, was to write a few week before the uprising that the Irish nation was a natural entity transcending its political history, and that Ireland, by the mere grace of its geographic situation, was always already a distinct nation (a divinely ordained one, no less). Contrasting Ireland's purported natural existence as a nation with that of Belgium, the sovereignty of which Britain had safeguarded since 1839 and the invasion of which by German forces in 1914 served as London's public pretext for entering what became the First World War, Connolly wrote:

> And yet Belgium as a nation is, so to speak, but a creation of yesterday—an artificial product of the schemes of statesmen. Whereas, the frontiers of Ireland, the ineffaceable marks of the separate existence of Ireland, are as old as Europe itself, the handiwork of the Almighty, not of politicians. And as the marks of Ireland's separate nationality were not made by politicians so they cannot be unmade by them.
>
> As the separate individual is to the family, so the separate nation is to humanity. The perfect family is that which best draws out the inner power of the individual, the most perfect world is that in which the separate existence of nations is held most sacred. There can be no perfect Europe in which Ireland is denied even the least of its national rights [...].[123]

Taking a different rhetorical approach, in 1917 the republican Irish nationalist Robert Wilson Lynd combined the notion of Ireland as a (presumably) pre-existing unified geographic entity with the concept of national 'awakening'; the latter by itself seen as adequate logical grounds for deserving national independence. Lynd wrote in *If the Germans Conquered England, and Other Essays*, a war-time anti-British and pro-German propaganda piece that also endorsed Irish nationalist solidarity with Iranian nationalists, among other range of anti-imperialist nationalist struggles:

> You may always take it that a Nationalist who shows signs of Chauvinism is an Imperialist in the making. By his Chauvinism he has already betrayed the central principle of Nationalism, which is to respect the personality of every other nation as one wishes the personality of one's own nation to be respected. Therefore, when one speaks of Nationalism as a political theory and not a catchword of party politics, one is thinking of Nationalism like Mazzini's—the Nationalism which urges countries like Finland, Persia, India, Poland, Egypt, Georgia, and Ireland to strive not for mastery over other nations, but for an equal place in an international brotherhood of peoples.[124]

He added:

> One may meet the Imperialist half-way, however, and admit to some extent the "geographical expression" argument. Grant, for instance, that Italy was once a "geographical expression." The question that immediately arises is: "Does the Imperialist hold it would have been better for Italy to have remained so and never to have awakened into nationhood?"

If he thinks that it is better to remain a geographical expression than a free nation, why does he (supposing, for instance, he is an Englishman) recoil from the thought of subjection of England to some foreign Power? And, if it is better to be a nation than a geographical expression, then surely he is bound to aid Poland, India, Persia, Egypt, Ireland, and all other trammelled peoples as far as in him lies, in their struggle for a place among the free nations.[125]

Moreover, the process of *worlding the nation* in this context required other modes of selective remembrance and forgetting of certain aspects of, and particular episodes in, Irish history itself.[126] For instance, Irish nationalist claims of a shared experience of victimization under British colonization with Indians or Egyptians (the latter after 1882) overlooked such major historical and contemporary differences as Ireland's direct parliamentary representation in the United Kingdom since 1801, including direct Irish nationalist representation at Westminster after 1829. Indians and Egyptians did not enjoy that privilege, nor could they rise to the highest commands of the British imperial military or administration, as could the Irish (including Catholics after 1829). Similarly, compared to the Indian subcontinent or Egypt, where Irish military personnel had participated in the occupation of those territories (initially in the service of the English East India Company in the case of the Indian subcontinent) and in the subsequent preservation and/or expansion of British hegemony in those territories, as well as in the suppression of nationalist challenges to British rule, Indian or Egyptian military personnel were not deployed in suppressing nationalist or other disturbances in Ireland. These were important factors in *The Nation*'s glossing over, and even denial, of Irish participation in the British military invasion of southern Iran in 1856–57.

Despite their comparative and cosmopolitan frames of affiliative referentiality and analyses, anti-imperialist *nationalist* self-emplotments in world-historical settings were often primarily self-regarding (in the case of the Irish as well as those from other territories). Yet, there were notable exceptions to this rule as well. Among the Irish, as noted before, examples of individuals from widely differing nationalist platforms who embraced unequivocal internationalist and transnational perspectives included the likes of John Dillon (1851–1927) and Frederick Michael Ryan (1876–1913), whose trans-Irish commitments are discussed in later chapters. It is important here to differentiate these individuals in terms of their expression of anti-imperialist affinities—notwithstanding the wide gulf between Ryan's socially progressive views and Dillon's aversion to feminist and working-class politics, in addition to their different narrowly defined 'nationalist' outlooks, among other contrasts—from the likes of the members of Irish Transvaal Brigade (a.k.a., Irish Commandos/MacBride's Brigade), who joined the Boer armed resistance against British occupation in southern Africa during the Boer War of 1899–1902. For the Brigade, Ireland's independence from Britain remained the ulterior motive; seeking primarily to encumber the British Empire when and where possible, while also gaining experience in paramilitary guerrilla warfare and building international support networks for a future armed struggle in Ireland—not forgetting the complexities of the Boer War and the Boer practice of enslaving Black Africans, which Dillon too overlooked his pro-Boer stance at the time.

The wide-ranging patterns of Irish nationalist self-identification and fellow feeling with other peoples around the world who were also resisting imperialism or struggling against other forms of oppression can be traced back to the late eighteenth century. This was a markedly different proclivity than the earlier anti-English sentiments and/or the anti-Protestant cross-identification in some Irish Catholic circles with Catholic states and populations in other parts of Europe—not forgetting also the earlier evidently widespread Irish Catholic receptivity to the idea of being ruled by a British monarch so long as the monarch was a Catholic, as in the case of those Irish Catholics rallying to support the ousted Stuart monarch James II at the end of the seventeenth century. Among other developments, after the late eighteenth-century Irish nationalist expressions of solidarity with the rights of other perceived victimized nations and/or groups of people was to a large extent a manifestation of combined influences of universalist and so-called secular trends (at least in the sense of being nondenominational) in the European Enlightenment thought, notwithstanding the simultaneous pull of religion in the personal lives of many of these individuals. This development impacted and crisscrossed with domestic political realignments in Ireland vis-à-vis London, including the 1782 "Grattan's Parliament" and the founding of the cross-denominational and cross-ethnic Society of United Irishmen (1791). Among related influences in other parts of the British Empire and elsewhere around the world were the reverberations of such occurrences as the American War of Independence and the French Revolution, themselves variously products of different trends in the Enlightenment thought.[127] As previously noted, the expansive range of cross-territorial sympathies and solidarities, sometimes primarily tactical and at other times reflecting deeply held convictions, were in some cases marked by both tacit or explicit inner tensions, if not outright contradictions. For instance, in the same pamphlet the United Irishmen could express solidarity with the former American colonies that had rebelled against English rule, while simultaneously condemning the enslavement of peoples of "African" descent and slavery in general, with the former American colonies of England having preserved the institution of slavery.[128] On a different level, these wide-ranging world-historical self-positioning gestures by Irish nationalists offered an additional mode of connecting Ireland to other parts of the world, besides Ireland's place in the global economy, consumption patterns and fashion, the sciences, literary styles, the arts, imperial service, and manifold intellectual circuits, as well as travel, emigration and immigration, overseas missionary activities, and so on. Moreover, by at least the latter decades of the nineteenth century, varying Irish nationalist platforms were in turn eliciting anti-imperialist nationalist expressions of solidarity from groups in other parts of the world, as in the case of Indian or Egyptian nationalists, in what constituted yet another mode of worlding the 'Irish nation' (i.e., being *worlded* by others in this setting). However, as discussed later, it was not until after the outbreak of the 1916 Easter Rising in Ireland that Iranian nationalists first began to publicly express solidarity with Irish nationalists (the militant republican camps specifically).

It was also in the framework of Irish nationalist world-historical perspectives of cross-territorial anti-imperialist solidarities that what has been termed 'Irish orientalism' assumed a new mode of self-orientalizing attribute by the start of the twentieth century, at least in militant republican circles in the United States, connecting Ireland not to the ancient Orient of a distant past, as earlier generations of antiquarians had done, but to the contemporary Orient as an anti-imperialist gesture grounded in an avowed *racial affinity*. As discussed in Chapter 7, this occurred in the form of "pan-Aryanism" directed against British imperial hegemony, albeit failing to garner support among Iranians nationalists. The next chapter deals with an instance of ultimately self-centric Irish nationalist engagement with developments occurring in Iran nearly a decade-and-a-half after the terminations of the Second Anglo-Iranian War. The focus of that chapter, too, is A. M. Sullivan's nationalist newspaper *The Nation* (Dublin). On this occasion, however, Iran, instead of being an object of the paper's expressed sympathy, became an object of its deliberate, politically calculated and publicly admitted, neglect.

Notes

1 On Irish nationalist responses to the Crimean War, see also David Murphy, *Ireland and the Crimean War*. Dublin: Four Courts Press, 2002; Paul Huddie, *The Crimean War and Irish Society*. Liverpool: Liverpool University Press, 2015.
2 On the Herat war, among other works, see also Mansour Bonakdarian, "Construing the Enemy: Diplomacy, Culture, Gender, and National Sovereignty in British Debates on the Anglo-Iranian War of 1856-57" (forthcoming); idem, *Britain and the Iranian Constitutional Revolution*, pp.7–9; Abbas Amanat, "Herat vi. The Herat Question" (2003, 2012), *Encyclopaedia Iranica* (http://www.iranicaonline.org/articles/herat-vi); Jean Calmard, "Anglo-Persian War (1856-57)" (1985, 2011), *Encyclopaedia Iranica* (http://www.iranicaonline.org/articles/anglo-persian-war-1856-57); Vanessa Martin, "Social Networks and Border Conflicts: The First Herat War 1839-1841" in Roxane Famanfarmaian, ed., *War and Peace in Qajar Persia: Implications Past and Present*. New York: Routledge, 2008, pp.110–21: Firoozeh Kashani-Sabet, *Frontier Fictions: Shaping the Iranian Nation, 1804-1946*. Princeton: Princeton University Press, 1999, pp.30–33; Evgeny Sergeev, *The Great Game, 1856-1907: Russo-British Relations in Central and East Asia*. Baltimore: Johns Hopkins University Press, 2013, pp.52–55, 71–77. On the First Anglo-Iranian War in 1838, see also; "Past and Present State of Afghanistan—Chap IV," *Dublin Monthly Magazine*, vol.1, part 2, August 1842, pp.96–109 (p.103 in particular).
3 Charles Murray to Earl of Clarendon, November 28, 1855, no.15, F.O.539/6, f.17 (United Kingdom, The National Archive, London). See also the Persian originals and Persian translations of exchanges between Iranian and British representatives in the Mirza Hashem Khan and Mrs. Hashem affair in Mahmoud Gharavi, *Majerā-ye Dowlat-e Ingilis va Mirzā Hāshem Khān*. Tehran: Nashr-e Tarikh-e Iran, 1363 (1984); Barbara English, *John Company's Last War*. London: Collins, 1971; Robert Grant Watson, *A History of Persia from the Beginning of the Nineteenth Century to the Year 1858*. London: Smith, Elder and Co., 1866, pp.420–23; Denis Wright, *The Persians Amongst the English*. London: I.B. Tauris, 1986, p.111.
4 See, for example, *The Times*, January 21, 1857, p.11, c.d.
5 Ibid., January 21, 1857, p.11, c.d.
6 *The Quarterly Review* 101(202), 1857, p. 533. This reference appeared in an anonymous review (in ibid., pp.501–41) of Lady Mary Leonora Woulfe Sheil's 1856 *Glimpses of Life and Manners in Persia*.
7 See *Fraser's Magazine* 56(332), August 1857, p. 136.
8 "This Irano-British war of 1856-7 did not have full cabinet support in England, and was not viewed enthusiastically in India where many believed in the principles of 'masterly inactivity', Mindful of what had happened in Afghanistan. [...] *The Times*, in a leading article entitled 'Where Herat is, we neither know or care', mirrored the views of many people in England who were unfamiliar with the issues involved and saw no reason for war with Iran." Rose Greaves, "Iranian Relations with Great Britain and British India, 1798–1921," in Peter Avery, Gavin Hambly, Charles Melville, eds., *The Cambridge History of Iran. Volume 7: From Nadir Shah to the Islamic Republic*. Cambridge: Cambridge University Press, 1991, pp.394–95. Although some of the Tory press, such as the *Blackwood's Edinburgh Magazine* blamed the war

on joint machinations of the Iranian state and Russia and defended the British military action against Iran (*Blackwood's Edinburgh Magazine* 81(496), February 1857, pp.137–52), the prominent Russophobe Tory-Radical MP, David Urquhart, accused Palmerston of a rash policy that would "bind Persia and cast her at the feet of Russia." *Diplomatic Review* 4(23), January 14, 1857, p.183.

9 William Ewart Gladstone, *The Gladstone Diaries. Volume V: 1855-1860*. Henry Colin Gray Matthew editor. Oxford: Clarendon Press, 1978, p.115.

10 James Blennerhasset Conacher, "British Policy in the Anglo-American Enlistment Crisis of 1855-1856," *Proceedings of the American Philosophical Society* 136(4), December 1992, pp.533–76.

11 After receiving "false reports concerning the pourparlers of the Persian-American treaty," in the winter of 1856 Palmerston informed his foreign secretary, Lord Clarendon: "The 'Yankees,' he heard, were to send ship to protect the Persians. What was this but '"impudent intermeddling' in affairs with which America had no concern?" Herbert C.F. Bell, *Lord Palmerston*. Volume II. Reprint. Hamden, CT: Archon, 1966 [1936], p.142.

12 The Radical MP Austen Henry Layard was among the critics who made frequent references to this topic. Layard also referred to the massacre of the Russian mission by a fanatical Iranian mob in Tehran in 1828 as an important historical precedent that Murray should have taken into account in his presumably insolent affront to Iranian religious and cultural sensitivities. Although the Iranian government never alluded to the 1828 incident in its dealings with Murray, this was precisely the kind of historical parallel the Iranian chargé d'affaires in Constantinople had in mind when suggesting that Murray should be grateful for the absence of a major disturbance in the aftermath of his supposed 'intrigue.' See [Great Britain] *Parliamentary Debates* (Commons), 3rd series, vol.140, 1856, cc. 1713–24. On Layard and Palmerston, see also Jasper Ridley, *Lord Palmerston*. New York: E.P. Dutton, 1970, pp.440–41.

13 In the early 1850s Gladstone was breaking out of his former Tory Peelite political orientation and joining force "with the Radicals Molesworth and Roebuck on colonial affairs." Henry Colin Gray Matthew, *Gladstone 1809-1874*. Oxford: Clarendon Press, 1986, p.81.

14 Roebuck, along with Gladstone, had played a central role in parliamentary attacks on government's conduct of the Crimean War and in objection to the diplomatic dispute with the United States. Known as "'Tear'em' Roebuck," he had gained further clout as a Radical when his motion for a vote of "no confidence" in Lord Aberdeen's government during the Crimean War was carried by a majority of 157 votes in the Commons; forcing Aberdeen's resignation. See Olive Anderson, *A Liberal State at War: English Politics and Economics During the Crimean War*. New York: St. Martin's Press, 1967, p.43.

15 [Great Britain] *Parliamentary Debates* (Commons), 3rd Series, vol.146, 1857, cc.1132–33. Roebuck added that "never in the whole history of the House of Commons was a more important subject submitted to its consideration." Ibid., c.1577. See also ibid., cc. 1609, 1638–39.

16 See, for example, Jennifer M. Regan, "'We Could Be of Service to Other Suffering People'," pp.61–77; Matthew Kelly, "Irish Nationalist Opinion and the British Empire in the 1850s and 1860s," *Past and Present* 204(1), August 2009, pp.130–31, 135, 137–38, 141, 143–50. For earlier and subsequent Irish nationalist commentaries on British India, see also Niamh Lynch, "Defining Irish Nationalist Anti-imperialism: Thomas Davis and John Mitchel," *Éire-Ireland* 42(1 & 2), Spring/Summer 2007, pp.82–107; Pauline Collombier-Lakeman, "Ireland and the Empire," pp.57–76.

17 [Great Britain] *Parliamentary Debates* (Commons), 3rd Series, vol.146, 1857, c.1578.

18 Other than Roebuck and the Radical Acton Smee Ayrton, who proposed and seconded the resolution, 16 Radicals, 14 Conservatives, 7 Liberal Conservatives (Peelites), and 1 pro-Palmerston Whig supported the resolution. See [Great Britain] *Parliamentary Debates* (Commons), 3rd Series, vol.146, 1857, c.1655. Some MPs who supported Palmerston in the vote, such as the Conservative Spencer Horatio Walpole, shared the Radical view that Palmerston had violated parliamentary procedures, but held that "At the same time, I am by no means insensible of the great danger, in the present state of affairs [i.e., the rebellion in India], of making divisions in this House." Ibid., cc.1616–17.

19 It should be noted that the leading Radical, Richard Cobden, regarded the Anglo-Iranian War of 1856–57 as an example of interventionist foreign policy that diverted attention from

domestic problems. He remarked in 1857: "Our privileged oligarchs can do as they like, as Palmerston, their real tool, has for a couple of months distracted public attention from matters by holding the Persian war in terrorem over us." John Atkinson Hobson, *Richard Cobden: The International Man*. New York: Henry Holt and Company, 1911, p.200.
20 "Our Political Relations with Persia," *Dublin University Magazine* 48(288), December 1856, pp.645–46.
21 "Capture of Bushire," *Freeman's Journal*, January 30, 1857, p.2.
22 Ibid., December 15, 1856, p.2. See also ibid., December 17, 1856, p.2.
23 Ibid., December 31, 1856, p.2.
24 Ibid., January 16, 1857, p.4.
25 Ibid., January 21, 1857, p.2; ibid., January 23, 1857, p.2.
26 Ibid., January 21, 1857, p.3.
27 Ibid., February 26, 1857, p.2.
28 Alexander Martin Sullivan, *New Ireland: Political Sketches and Personal Reminiscences*. Volume I. Fifth edition. London: Sampson Law, Marston, Searle, & Rivington, 1878, pp.371–72; Justin McCarthy, Charles Welsh, Maurice Francis Egan, Douglas Hyde, Lady Gregory, and James Jeffrey Roche, eds., *Irish Literature*. Volume 9. Philadelphia: J.D. Morris & Company, 1904, p.3323. "Alexander Martin Sullivan" in Thomas Power O'Connor, ed., *The Cabinet of Irish Literature: Selections from the Works of the Chief Poets, Orators, and Prose Writers of Ireland*. Volume IV. London: Blackie and Son, 1880, pp.228–33. The journalist Thomas Power O'Connor was then a Parnellite Home Rule Irish nationalist MP.
29 Alexander Martin Sullivan, *New Ireland*, vol.I, p.371; "John Cashel Hoey" in T.P. O'Connor, ed., *The Cabinet of Irish Literature*, vol.IV, pp.251–53; "Sketch of the Life of Alexander M. Sullivan" by "T.P.G." in Alexander Martin Sullivan, *The Story of Ireland: A Narrative of Irish History from the Earliest Ages to the Insurrection of 1867 [...] Continued to the Present Time by James Luby, of New York*. New edition. New York: P.J. Kennedy, 1898, pp.v–ix. This was a posthumous American edition of A. M. Sullivan's 1885 publication.
30 Alexander Martin Sullivan, *The Story of Ireland*, pp.11–20.
31 On parliamentary, as well as even imperial, careers of some of these leading former Young Irelanders, see Alexander Martin Sullivan, *New Ireland*, vol.I, pp.152–54. Sullivan subsequently claimed, with abundant embellishment, that a faction of the early Young Ireland movement had been unmistakably out-and-out "O'Connellite Repealers" and had remained so all the way through the 1848 uprising, as opposed to the republican revolutionary fervor brewing within the movement. See Sullivan's "Forty-Eight," which had originally appeared in the first volume of Sullivan's 1878 *New Ireland*, (pp.116–30) and was reproduced under the entry for "Alexander Martin Sullivan" in T.P. O'Connor, ed., *The Cabinet of Irish Literature*, vol.IV, p.230. See also Matthew Kelly, "Irish Nationalist Opinion and the British Empire," pp.136, 150–51.
32 Pauline Collombier-Lakeman, "Ireland and the Empire," p.66; Paul Townend, "Between Two Worlds: Irish Nationalists and Imperial Crisis, 1878–1880," *Past and Present* 194(1), February 2007, pp.163–64; idem, *The Road to Home Rule: Anti-Imperialism and the Irish National Movement*. Madison: University of Wisconsin Press, 2016, chapter 2.
33 See Oliver MacDonagh, "Ambiguity in Nationalism: The Case of Ireland" in Ciaran Brady, ed., *Interpreting Irish History: The Debate on Historical Revisionism, 1938-1994*. Blackrock, Ireland: Irish Academic Press, 1994, pp.105–21.
34 On the anticipated, but unrealized, Russian assistance to the Emmet Monument Association and the association's pro-Russian stance at the time, see David Murphy, *Ireland and the Crimean War*, pp.1–11.
35 Halpin, who rose to the rank of a Lieutenant-Colonel in the Union Army during the American Civil War of 1861–65, later became a member of the Fenian military council (at the rank of a general) and was arrested by British authorities in 1867 for his role in the failed Fenian/Irish Republican Brotherhood uprising in Ireland in that year and sentenced to 15 years in prison on charge of treason-felony. He obtained early release in 1871 on grounds of his US citizenship. See Kirk C. Jenkins, *The Battle Rages Higher: The Union's Fifteenth Kentucky Infantry*. Lexington: University of Kentucky Press, 2003, passim; Brian Jenkins, *Fenians and Anglo-American Relations during Reconstruction*. Ithaca: Cornell University Press, 1969; Desmond Ryan, *The Fenian Chief: A Biography of James Stephens*. Dublin: Gill and Son, 1967. See also

John Y. Simon, ed., *The Papers of Ulysses S. Grant. Volume 20: November 1, 1869–October 31, 1870*. Carbondale, IL: Southern Illinois University Press, 1967, pp.115–18. For the text of Halpin's and other defendants' trial in 1856, see William G. Halpin and other defendants, *In the District court of the United States for the southern district of Ohio. United States vs. W. G. Halpin, David Reidy, Edward Kenifeck, Samuel Lumsden, et al. Charged with conspiracy, for exciting insurrection in Ireland, and aiding it by an armed force from the United States. Preliminary examination before the Hon. H. H. Leavitt, sitting as commissioner*. Cincinnati: Moore, Wilstach, Keys & Overend, 1856.

36 Laurence Fenton, "Charles Rowcroft, Irish-Americans, and the 'Recruitment Affair', 1855–1856," *Historical Journal* 53(4), December 2010, pp.963–82.

37 Paul R. Wylie, *The Irish General: Thomas Francis Meagher*. Norman: University of Oklahoma Press, 2007, pp.98–104. Incidentally, prior to his presidential nomination Buchanan had served as the American ambassador in London.

38 See, for example, Terry Eagleton, *Crazy John and the Bishop*, pp.288–90; Bill Rolston, "Bringing it all Back Home: Irish Emigration and Racism," *Race & Class* 45(2), 2003, pp.39–53; Mary Buckley, "John Mitchel, Ulster and Irish Nationality (1842-1848)," *Studies: An Irish Quarterly Review* 65(257), Spring 1976, pp.36, 39, 42, 43; Paul R. Wylie, *The Irish General*, pp.98–104; Cormac Ó Gráda, *Jewish Ireland in the Age of Joyce: A Socioeconomic History*. Princeton: Princeton University, 2006.

39 *The Nation*, August 2, 1856, p.775, cc.c-d.

40 *Cork Examiner*, February 4, 1857, p.3.

41 See also Nicholas Canny, "The Formation of the Irish Mind," pp.100–103.

42 Geoffrey Keating, *The History of Ireland* (1857 edition), p.5.

43 Ibid., pp.10–12.

44 David Dwan, *The Great Community*, chapter 2.

45 Ibid., p.15; idem, "Romantic Nationalism: History and Illusion in Ireland," *Modern Intellectual History* 14 (3), 2017, pp.717–45; Joep Leerssen, *Remembrance and Imagination*, pp.22–24.

46 Bryan P. McGovern, *John Mitchel: Irish Nationalist, Southern Secessionist*. Knoxville: University of Tennessee Press, 2009, pp.98–107.

47 *The Citizen* (New York), November 8, 1856, p.707. For the paper's continued coverage of different stages of the Anglo-Iranian War, see, for example, ibid., November 22, 1856, p.739; ibid., December 6, 1856, p.776; ibid., February 21, 1857, p.115; ibid., March 7, 1857, p.147; ibid., March 14, 1857, p.163; ibid., March 21, 1857, p.179.

48 *The Nation*, October 15, 1842, p.6, c.a. See also Joseph Lennon, *Irish Orientalism*, pp.216–18.

49 *The Nation*, October 15, 1842, p.9, c.a. On the coverage of the Anglo-Afghan War in Britain, see also Antoinette Burton, "On the First Anglo-Afghan War, 1839-42: Spectacle of Disaster" (http://www.branchcollective.org/?ps_articles=antoinette-burton-on-the-first-anglo-afghan-war-1839-42-spectacle-of-disaster).

50 *The Nation*, October 15, 1842, p.9, c.c.

51 The Dublin O'Connellite nationalist outlet, the *Freeman's Journal* had not only periodically reported on Keane's career and his capture of Afghan cities, but also on Keane's role in the massacres of Afghan prisoners by British forces. See, for instance, *Freeman's Journal*, December 10, 1839, p.3; January 2, 1840, p.2; June 8, 1842, p.2.

52 See, for example, "Colonel Stoddart and Captain Conolly," *Cork Examiner*, April 15, 1844, p.3, c.g; "Colonel Stoddart and Capt. Conolly," ibid., April 17, 1844, p.4, c.d.

53 Micheal Codfelter, *Warfare and Armed Conflicts: A Statistical Encyclopedia of Casualty and Other Figures, 1492-2015*. Jefferson, NC: McFarland, 2017, pp.220, 222.

54 See, for example, "'The Remains Ireland's Loneliest Martyr': The Commemoration of the Connaught Rangers Mutiny" in Michael Silvestri, *Ireland and India: Nationalism, Empire and Memory*. Houndmills, Basingstoke: Palgrave Macmillan, 2009, pp.139–74.

55 See, for example, *The Citizen* (New York), February 28, 1857, p.131.

56 *Cork Examiner*, February 6, 1857, p.2. See also ibid., February 2, 1857, p.4. Notwithstanding the paper's opposition to the Iranian war, it occasionally reproduced reports from other sources that branded Iran as the aggressor without any editorial commentary, as in the case of a report from the London *Observer* (itself based on other reports). See *Cork Examiner*, January 23, 1857, p.3.

57 Patrick Maume, "Unionists and Patriots: James Whiteside, the Irish Bar and the Dilemmas of the Protestant Nation in Victorian Ireland" in Allan Blackstock and Frank O'Gorman,

eds., *Loyalism and the Formation of the British World, 1775-1914*. Woodbridge, UK: Boydell Press, 2014, pp.145–61.
58 See, for example, *The Nation*, February 21, 1857, p.408, c.a; or the paper's reporting of the "Queen's speech" read at the opening of the new session of the houses of parliament in ibid., February 7, 1857, p.376, c.a.
59 Ibid., February 28, 1857, p.424, c.a.
60 Timothy Daniel Sullivan, *Recollections of Troubled Times in Irish Politics*. Dublin: Sealy, Bryers & Walker, 1905, p.20. On the paper's coverage of the Crimean War, see also ibid., pp. 21–23.
61 Writing on Irish nationalist reactions to imperial affairs following the outbreak of the 1857 uprising in India, Matthew Kelly makes the erroneous observation that *The Nation* and other "advanced Irish nationalist opinion" throughout the 1850s had been continually pro-French and primarily anti-Russian, even if delighting in Russian challenges to British imperial might. This ignores the coverage of the Crimean War and the Iranian war by *The Nation*. Matthew Kelly, "Irish Nationalist Opinion and the British Empire," pp.131, 139–40.
62 *The Nation*, January 12, 1856, pp.309, cc.b-c.
63 Thomas Osborne Davis, *The Poems of Thomas Davis* (1857 edition), pp.16–19. On Irish nationalists and Poland, see also Róisin Healy, *Poland in the Irish Nationalist Imagination*.
64 *The Nation*, January 19, 1856, p.328, c.b.
65 Ibid., February 9, 1856, p.372, c.a.
66 See, for example, ibid., January 12, 1856, pp.309, cc.b-c; March 1, 1856, p.421, c.c.
67 See, for example, ibid., March 8, 1856, p.445, c.a; October 18, 1856, p.115, c.c; November 8, 1856, p.173, c.d, November 15, 1856, p.179, cc.c-d and p.192, cc.b-c.
68 Ibid., May 17, 1856, p.598, c.d.
69 Ibid., October 25, 1856, p.137, cc.a-c.
70 Ibid., p.137, c.a.
71 On the Griboyedev incident, see also Laurence Kelly, *Diplomacy and Murder in Tehran: Alexander Griboyedov and Imperial Russia's Mission to the Shah of Persia*. Reprint. London: I.B. Tauris, 2006 [2002]. The Griboyedov affair was a widely-known event in European and American circles in the nineteenth century. For instance, in his account of travel through Iran in 1870, the soon to be famous explorer and brutal exploiter of the African continent, Henry Morton Stanley, made a special note of the event, with some of his own embellishments. Henry Morton Stanley, *My Early Travels and Adventures in America and Asia*. Volume 2. Second edition. London: Sampson Low, Marston and Company, 1895, pp.313–16.
72 *The Nation*, October 25, 1856, p. 137, c.b.
73 Ibid., p.137, c.c.
74 John Arrowsmith, "Central Asia; comprising Bokhara, Cabool, Persia, The River Indus, & Countries Eastward of it [...] By his obliged Servant, J. Arrowsmith. June 1834. (Map) 29. London, Pubd. 15 Feby. 1842, by J. Arrowsmith, 10 Soho Square" in the Digital Public Library America map collection: (https://dp.la/search?q=john+arrowsmith+persia).
75 See, for example, the 1843 map by the Scottish Alexander Keith Johnston. (http://www.cais-soas.com/CAIS/Images2/persian_gulf/Persia_A_K_Johnston_National_Atlas_1843WM.png)
and the 1852 map by the Liverpool firm of (Scottish) George Philip and Son (http://www.cais-soas.com/CAIS/Images2/persian_gulf/British_map_of_Persia__Kabul_by_Philip_George_and_Son_1852WM.png).
76 Reproduced in Clements Robert Markham, *A General Sketch of the History of Persia*. London: Longmans, Green, and Co., 1874, pp.537–38.
77 *The Nation*, September 20, 1856, p.57, cc.b-c.
78 Ibid., p.57, c.b.
79 See also ibid., November 22, 1856, p.195, cc.c-d.
80 See also Clements Robert Markham, *A General Sketch of the History of Persia*, p.504.
81 *The Nation*, November 15, 1856, p.192, cc.b-c. The same news item was repeated in ibid., November 22, 1856, p.208, c.b. See also an earlier report on the siege of Herat in ibid., November 8, 1856, p.164, c.a.
82 See also ibid., November 29, 1856, p.224 c.d. For the text of the November 1, 1856, proclamation of war by the British governor-general in India, see ibid., December 20, 1856, p.259 c.c.

83 Ibid., November 29, 1856, p.211 c.a.
84 Ibid., December 20, 1856, p.269 c.d.
85 See, for example, ibid., December 20, 1856, pp.259 cc.b-c., 269 c.d.
86 Ibid., December 27, 1856, p.288 c.d.
87 Ibid., January 17, 1857, p.323 cc.c-d.
88 Ibid., January 3, 1857, p.292 c.a. See also *Rouznāmeh-ye Vaqāye'-e Ettefāqiyeh*, 26 Rabi' al-Thāni 1273 (December 24, 1856), pp.1–6.
89 On Britain and the Peshawar Valley, see also Richard Gott, *Britain's Empire: Resistance, Repression and Revolt*. London: Verso, 2011, pp.412–16.
90 *The Nation*, January 31, 1857, p.360 cc.a-b.
91 Ibid., p.361 cc.a-b.
92 Ibid., p.361 cc.a-b.
93 Ibid., p.361 cc.a-b. For additional reports of the rumored Russo-Iranian understanding, see also ibid., February 21, 1857, p.405 c.a. For reports of the concern in the French press regarding developments in the Persian Gulf, see ibid., February 7, 1857, p.371 cc.b-c.
94 Ibid., February 7, 1857, p.377 cc.-c-d.
95 Ibid., p.377 cc.-c-d. See also ibid., February 14, 1857, p.395 c.d.
96 Ibid., February 21, 1857, pp.404 cc.c-d-405 c.a.
97 For the published text of official British correspondence with Iranian authorities in connection with Sheil and Herat, as well as the subsequent Mirza Hashem and Mrs. Hashem affairs, the termination of diplomatic relations between the two countries, the latest Herat war, the Anglo-Iranian War, and the eventual peace accord, see [Great Britain] *Correspondence Respecting Relations with Persia*. London: Harrison and Sons, 1857.
98 "Sheil, Richard Lalor" in Charles Knight, ed. *Biography, or Third Division of "The English Encyclopedia."* Volume 5. London: Bradbury, Evans, & Co., 1867, pp.468–69. This entry was compiled from the two-volume 1855 *Memoirs of the Right Honourable Richard Lalor Sheil* by W. Torrens McCullough. One of the sons of Justin and Lady Sheil, Edward Sheil, would emerge as a leading Irish Home Rule MP later in the century. See also Brendan McNamara, "An Irishwoman in Tehran, 1849-1853: Identity, Religion, and Empire" in Houchang E. Chehabi and Grace Neville, eds., *Erin and Iran: Cultural Encounters Between the Irish and the Iranians*. Boston: Ilex, 2015, pp.173–75. Incidentally, in 1843 a British resident in Iran, Edward Burgess, noted that Justin Sheil doubted he would be appointed British representative in Iran (i.e., as minister plenipotentiary), partly on account of Richard Lalor Sheil's Irish nationalist politics. Burgess informed his brother Charles in a letter: "Col[.] Sheil is now acting as Chargé d'Affaires and has been since Sir John McNeill's departure, but he does not expect to be confirmed, because his brother is on the wrong side in politics and moreover the said Colonel [...] wants to get home." Benjamin Schwartz ed., *Letters from Persia. Written by Charles Burgess and Edward Burgess, 1828-1855*. New York, New York Public Library, 1942, p.53. See also ibid., p.69.
99 Joseph Pierre Ferrier, *Caravan Journeys and Wanderings in Persia, Afghanistan, Turkistan, and Beloochistan; with Historical Notices of the Countries Lying between Russia and India*. William Jesse translator and Henry Danby Seymour editor. London: John Murray, 1856. Seymour had traveled to Iran in 1847. See also Benjamin Schwartz ed., *Letters from Persia*, p.94.
100 Lady Mary Leonora Woulfe Sheil, *Glimpses of Life and Manners in Persia*. London: John Murray, 1856.
101 William Ewart Gladstone, *The Gladstone Diaries*, vol.V, pp.115, 189, 217, 288.
102 Lady Sheil, *Glimpses of Life and Manners in Persia*, p.1.
103 See the "Preface" in ibid.
104 Ibid., p.1.
105 For a more detailed and complex discussion of Lady Sheil's book in the framework of gender, nation, cross-cultural perceptions and representations, see my forthcoming "Mediating Gender Roles & 'Private' and 'Public' Spaces and Spheres in 'Other' Lands: Victorian Narratives of British and Native Women in Iran."
106 "In the towns, and especially in the capital, Isfahan and Shiraz, the morals of both men and women are of the very worst description. Lady Sheil hints at this state of things in Teheran, and states that there was scarcely a lady whom she could with propriety visit. This general corruption is to be attributed to the dissolute habits of men, and want of respect for the

marriage tie, and the facility of divorce." *Quarterly Review* 101(202), April 1857, p.507. For Lady Sheil's discussion of different types of marriage contracts in Iran, including temporary marriages, as well as polygamy, and the lives of women of upper classes, see her *Glimpses of Life and Manners in Persia*, pp.141–46, passim.

107 The somewhat contradictory assertion that women of upper ranks in Iranian cities were both domestic slaves and, yet, simultaneously enjoyed far too great a degree of freedom (as potential so-called adulteresses) was a recurrent motif in many other publications on Iran by European/Western (including British and Irish) authors at the time. These authors maintained that the combination of the austerity of arranged marriages, polygamy, and the harem system, afforded women greater opportunity and freedom for adultery. Many of these same writers saw the veil as a means of concealing women's identity in public, thereby making it possible for them to avoid detection in their affairs. It should be noted Lady Sheil was somewhat more nuanced in her assessment of the overall restricted lives of Iranian women, stating that women of higher social rank and royal lineage *could* exercise some degree of authority over their husbands.

108 Lady Sheil, *Glimpses of Life and Manners in Persia*, pp.183–85.

109 *Quarterly Review* 101(202), April 1857, pp.508–509.

110 [Great Britain] *Correspondence Respecting Relations with Persia*. London: Harrison and Sons, 1857, pp.237–39.

111 *London Gazette* (Official Public Record), December 13, 1867, p.6820.

112 *The Nation*, February 28, 1857, p.421 c.a; March 14, 1857, p.452 c.c.

113 Ibid., April 4, 1857, p.507 c.d.

114 Ibid., March 7, 1857, p.441 c.d.

115 See, for example, *Irish-American*, March 14, 1857, p.1 c.h; ibid., March 21, 1857, p.2 c.e; and the identical reports appearing in *The Citizen*, March 14, 1857, p.163 c.a; ibid., March 21, 1857, p.179 c.b.

116 On the declaration of *jihād* during the war, see also Firoozeh Kashani-Sabet, *Frontier Fictions*, pp.59–61.

117 *The Nation*, March 7, 1857, p.436 c.d. This English translation of the Iranian royal decree differed in some details from the Persian original. In the Persian text, while calling on Iranians to unite in repelling "English" aggression in the name of "the valiant nation and state of Iran and Islam" ("mellat va dowlat-e ghayour-e irān va eslām"), the Iranian people were addressed by the monarch as his "valiant servants and subjects" ("noukarān va ro'ayā-e ghayour-e mā"). See *Rouznāmeh-ye Vaqāye'-e Ettefāqiyeh*, 18 Jamadi al-Awal 1273 (January 14, 1857), pp.1–2.

118 Thomas Osborne Davis, *The Poems of Thomas Davis* (1866 edition), pp.93–94. In 1867, 'For God and Ireland' resonated in the nationalist hymn "God Save Ireland" composed by A. M. Sullivan's brother Timothy Daniel Sullivan, also a future proprietor and editor of *The Nation*.

119 David Dwan, *The Great Community*, chapter 2.

120 James Alfred Norris, "Anglo-Afghan Wars ii. Second Anglo-Afghan War (1878-80)," *Encyclopaedia Iranica* (http://www.iranicaonline.org/articles/anglo-afghan-wars#pt2). See also Evgeny Sergeev, *The Great Game, 1856-1907*, chapter 2.

121 For other examples later in the century of the inner ambiguities of Irish nationalist expressions of solidarity with other groups in opposition to British imperial aggression, see Paul Townend, "Between Two Worlds," pp.149–52, 154–56; idem, *The Road to Home Rule*, pp.81–82, 106–108, and passim.

122 See also Kevin B. Anderson, *Marx at the Margins: On Nationalism, Ethnicity, and Non-Western Societies*. Chicago: University of Chicago Press, 2010, pp.2–3, 15, 205–208, and passim.

123 *Workers' Republic* (Dublin), February 12, 1916, reproduced in James Connolly, *Labour and Easter Week: A Selection from the Writings of James Connolly*. Desmond Ryan editor, with an Introduction by William O'Brien. Dublin: Sign of the Three Candles, 1949, pp.145–46.

124 Robert Lynd, *If the Germans Conquered England, and Other Essays*. Dublin: Maunsel and Company, 1917, p.147.

125 Ibid., pp.150–51.

126 Among the many examples, see also the essays in Ian McBride, ed., *History and Memory in Modern Ireland*. Cambridge: Cambridge University Press, 2001.

127 On some of the major transformations in Ireland's political milieu during the late eighteenth century, see also Padhraig Higgins, *A Nation of Politicians*. The possible impact of such other contemporary events as what eventually became the Haitian Revolution in the formerly French-controlled Saint-Domingue from 1791 to 1804, or developments in the Spanish Americas and elsewhere around the world, remain to be explored.

128 On praise for the United States of America, see "Virtue's Cause," among other poems in *Paddy's Resource* (1795), pp.78–79. For declarations of sympathy with enslaved Africans, see "The Captive Negro," "The Dying Negro," and "The Negro's Complaint" in ibid., pp.26–28, 36–37, 50–51.

Chapter Five

AN GORTA MÓR OF OTHERS AND NATIONALIST NEGLECT: *THE NATION* AND THE IRANIAN FAMINE OF 1870–72

Without question, the most traumatic event in nineteenth-century Ireland that affected practically the entire population in some way was the Great Famine of 1845–51. The Irish famine, also known among its many designations as "an Gorta Mór" in Irish (i.e., the Great Hunger), is generally estimated to have resulted in more than a million deaths and directly contributed to the emigration of nearly twice as many people—often under horrific conditions in their long voyage to distant lands—with large-scale emigration from Ireland continuing for decades to come. By the close of the nineteenth century, Ireland's population of four-and-a-half million was just over one-half of the island's population at the start of the century.[1] The Great Famine, having directly touched the lives of nearly the entire population of the island in some form—as victims, observers, and/or those working to ameliorate the mass suffering of the population, and so on—became ingrained in the transmitted "historical" memory of subsequent generations of the Irish, constituting one of the most enduring components of so-called collective memory of the Irish at large, both in Ireland and in Irish diasporic communities. For the majority of those leaving Ireland during the famine and in the years immediately following the catastrophe, the famine was the most direct cause of their geographic and accompanying forms of dislocation, whether or not these emigrants found greater economic and/or social opportunities in their new diasporic settings, including in mainland Britain. Whereas in mainland Britain, the Irish transplants continued to be identified as "Irish," or as ethnic sub-categories of the Irish population (such as "Anglo-Irish"), the diasporic Irish population elsewhere often assumed, or were accorded, new hyphenated identity labels (such as "Irish-Americans"). For the remaining ordinary Irish, whether or not internally displaced by the famine, the very soil and localities of Ireland were saturated with the melancholy memory of suffering and death. For decades, following the sharply dwindling population of villages and towns through death and the large-scale exodus of survivors during the famine, parts of the island, particularly in the hardest-hit western provinces, remained largely depopulated virtual ghostlands.[2] With or without visible signposts, much of the land was pervaded with corpses of famine victims in rapidly expanded cemeteries and the remembrance of immense suffering and loss. The extensive depopulation of those provinces worst affected in terms of fatalities and/or emigration (including internal migration to larger towns and urban centers) also resulted in a substantial decline in the size of the island's Irish-speaking population.[3]

As a pivotal event in Irish "remembrance" (including among pre- and post-famine Irish diasporic communities as well as Irish nationalists and unionists alike), that large-scale devastation became deeply embedded in wide-ranging nationalist historical narratives of Ireland's victimization, with differing patterns and degrees of memory retrieval, suppression, and invention. The famine was all the more powerful a symbol of "national" suffering for the entire spectrum of Irish nationalists—in this case, commonly in a formulation of the "nation" that occluded the unionists—given that the victims of the catastrophe had been ordinary people, irrespective of politics and religion, including children, who perished in astounding numbers across the island. The famine was cast by nationalists as a cataclysmic mass-scale martyrdom of innocent civilians, directly attributed to British misrule of Ireland. The dead and the suffering survivors were alternatively portrayed as either casualties of London's negligence and incompetence or as deliberate sacrificial victims of the English Minotaur. Following an initial phase of bewilderment, the famine gradually surfaced in some specifically "radical" (militant or otherwise) Irish nationalist commentaries as the epitome of London's allegedly genocidal policies in Ireland. This narrative style was not entirely dissimilar to James Clarence Mangan's comparison in his 1846 poem "Siberia" of the famine that was ravaging Ireland and the agony of existence in the frigid Siberian wasteland, where opponents of the tsarist autocracy and Russian criminals were exiled. Radical nationalist allegation of a calculated British policy of starving the Irish en masse was categoric about London's intent to wipe out as many Irish as possible (Catholics in particular) and depopulate the land. The Great Famine, repeatedly recalled, reconstructed, and reframed to this day, was fused in the "collective" memory of republican Irish nationalists with the anguished recollection of the failed Young Ireland rising of 1848 in the midst of the famine and at a time of widespread revolutions across many parts of Europe. Particularly in light of the dismal Young Ireland rising of 1848, the assertion of an official British plot to exterminate the Irish by means of exploiting the famine was considered by radical Irish nationalists as an invaluable recruitment strategy (albeit without noticeable immediate success).

Following the Great Famine, episodes of large-scale famine elsewhere in the British empire evoked empathetic responses from the Irish at large, with Irish nationalists expressing varying degrees of historical affinity with those other sufferers, as joint victims of British neglect or conscious malice. The theme of famine, not only in Ireland in times past, but also in other British dominions, increasingly assumed a central narrative magnitude in radical Irish nationalist claims of London's political and ethical ineligibility to govern its colonized peoples. The most frequent Irish nationalist cross-references to famines in other parts of the empire in this regard were the recurring large-scale famines in British India.⁴ In fact, by the end of the nineteenth century joint references to famines in Ireland and India by Irish and Indian nationalists constituted a common paradigm of assailing British mismanagement and/or callous neglect of colonized lives, with sketches and photographs of starving Irish and/or Indians periodically appearing in the nationalist press in both territories. In these famine narratives, the overriding target was British imperial rule. Better known nineteenth-century examples of Irish nationalist cross-identification with victims of famines in India occurred during the Orissa Famine of 1865–67 and the Great Indian Famine of 1876–78—the Orissa Famine also overlapped with the foiled June 1866 Irish republican (Fenian) raid into the British dominion of Canada from across the border in the United States and the follow-up abortive March 1867 uprising in Ireland by the Irish Republican Brotherhood (a.k.a., "the Fenian Rising"). During the famines in other British colonies, as well as a number of famines elsewhere, Irish nationalist outlets, such as *The Nation* or the *Freeman's Journal*, not only expressed great sorrow and fellow-feeling with the victims, but also urged Irish contributions toward relief funds for those victims. In the case of other British colonies, in addition to being an expression of cross-nationalist camaraderie among alleged victims of London's imperial disregard, these gestures were also in some way an indication of the broader Irish acknowledgment and ethical reciprocation of the extensive international relief aid sent to Ireland during the Great Famine of 1845–51. Incidentally, those relief efforts had also included donations from the Iranian state. For instance, in his 1851 book Thomas D'Arcy McGee noted: "The Czar, the Sultan, and the Pope, sent their roubles and their Pauls. The Pasha of Egypt, the Shah of Persia, the Emperor of China, the Rajahs of India, conspired to do for Ireland, what her so-styled rulers refused to do—to keep her young and old people living in the land."⁵ McGee was a former O'Connellite nationalist turned revolutionary Young Irelander in 1848, and had emigrated to the United States after the failed Young Ireland uprising of 1848, later settling in Canada where he also became the proprietor of the short-lived Irish nationalist newspaper the *New Era* (Montreal, May 1857 to May 1858) as well as becoming a Canadian politician. By emphasizing the contributions of various foreign heads of states or princes to the Irish famine relief fund, McGee was condemning what most Irish at the time believed to have been Queen Victoria's callous attitude toward the famine victims of her own Irish realm and her purportedly paltry personal financial contribution to the relief fund.

Occurring almost two decades after the Great Famine in Ireland, and three years after the Orissa Famine of 1865–67 that elicited widespread Irish sympathy (including in the Irish diaspora), was the Iranian famine of 1870–72. This famine broke out in the summer of 1870 (initially in southern provinces) and rapidly escalated after the spring of 1871. The Iranian famine proved as deadly as the Irish and Orissa famines in terms of the total number of lives lost (estimated at c.1,500,000), also representing a similar proportion of deaths out of the total population comparable to that of Ireland in 1845–51, if not actually a higher ratio of fatalities than in Ireland—an estimated 20–25 percent of Iran's total population of c.7,000,000 perished,⁶ even though some contemporary reports in the United Kingdom put the total population of Iran prior to the famine as low as 4,000,000.⁷ Moreover, compared to the Irish famine, the casualties of the Iranian famine occurred in a much shorter time span. The Iranian famine evoked worldwide sympathy and prompted extensive international relief efforts, including in the United Kingdom, where following the rapid intensification of the famine by the spring of 1871 it attracted regular national and local press coverage, with the London newspaper the *Morning Post* taking the lead.[8] In the Irish nationalist press, however, the Iranian famine failed to induce as much sympathy. In the case of the Dublin nationalist newspaper *The Nation*, the Iranian famine even met with an acknowledged outright dismissive posture. In the spring of 1871, similar to the remainder of major newspapers throughout the United Kingdom, the leading foreign news item regularly appearing in the main moderate Home-Rule Irish nationalist paper the *Freeman's Journal* (Dublin) and its more radical rival Home-Rule mouthpiece *The Nation* concerned the closing stages of the Franco-Prussian War (July 1870–May 1871), including reports of the regional and global geo-political significance and outcomes of that war. The latter developments included German unification, the affairs of the Third French Republic (founded following the Prussian capture of Napoleon III in the Battle of Sedan in September 1870), and the short-lived Paris Commune of March–May 1871, which was brutally crushed by the Third Republic—both of the above Irish nationalist newspapers denounced the revolutionary Commune as "Communistic."[9] Preoccupation with such other international events, however, cannot account for the trifling attention devoted to the Iranian famine by *The Nation* in particular, whether in the spring of 1871 or during the remainder of that famine.

The foremost organized Iranian famine relief effort in the United Kingdom was that directed by the City of London's Mansion House under the auspices of "Persian Famine Relief Fund." Supervised by the Lord Mayor of the City (Sir John Gibbons in 1871 and Sir Sydney Hedley Waterlow in 1872–73), the City of London's Mansion House fund also served as the repository for similar contributions collected across the kingdom by other municipalities.[10] There were also individual aid efforts undertaken by the likes of Sir Moses Haim Montefiore (d.1885), who made substantial contributions to the Mansion House campaign while also independently encouraging and coordinating private charitable donations by members of Europe's Jewish communities for the expressed purpose of assisting Jewish victims of the Iranian famine, including funds raised in parts of the Russian Empire.[11] Other range of small- and large-scale donations received by the Mansion House relief fund included a considerable sum from an anonymous donor, as well as money raised by the Order of Freemasons (the United Grand Lodge of England) or by the Fishmongers' Company in the City of London, while money was also raised through such occasional charity events as a football match after the end of the famine between the Lloyd's and the Stock Exchange teams at Kennington Oval in January 1873.[12] Donations also arrived from other parts of the United Kingdom, including Ireland, as in the case of £25 from Alexander Findlater of the renowned philanthropic Dublin Presbyterian mercantile family.[13] The Mansion House Persian Famine Relief Fund also received contributions from other parts of the British Empire as far away as New Zealand and Australia.[14] Individuals in India provided aid to Iranian victims either through the City of London' Mansion House (by means of banks) or by sending funds directly to Iran through various channels.[15] The Mansion House Persian Famine Relief

Fund also received contributions from other parts of Europe, as in the case of "1,000 Prussian Thalers ['£146 6s. 10d.']" from the German Emperor Wilhelm I.[16] At times, fundraising for Iranian famine victims in the United Kingdom and in other parts of the British Empire and beyond also relied on exhorting sympathy for one's co-religionists in Iran, as in the case of emphasizing the plight of Jewish, Zoroastrian, or Christian victims—notwithstanding denominational differences between the overwhelming majority of Christian sects in the United Kingdom and in Iran, where Christians consisted primarily of Armenian, Chaldean Assyrian, and Nestorian Assyrian sects, who had more immediate co-religionists in neighboring territories, including in British India, than they did in the United Kingdom. In such more narrowly targeted appeals on behalf of the famine victims, the particular groups in question were frequently mentioned in contradistinction to Iran's predominantly Muslim population (Twelver Shi'i as well as other sects), who generically (hence erroneously) were categorized as ethnically "Persians"; implying that non-Muslim populations of Iran were somehow not strictly Iranian, given the common application in the United Kingdom at the time of the terms 'Persia' and 'Persian' as denoting 'Iran' and 'Iranian.'[17] The pleas for international help on behalf of particular religious minority groups inside Iran during the Iranian famine ranged from the already-mentioned international Jewish campaign for aiding the Jewish victims of the famine to an appeal by the small Armenian enclave in Singapore for a donation from the King of Siam (Thailand) to relieve the suffering of Armenian victims of the famine.[18]

The appeals in the United Kingdom for funds on behalf of Christian victims of the Iranian famine were also indicative of denominational competition between certain fundraising groups, reflecting also existing sectarian rivalries regarding Christian missionary endeavors in distant lands. Different denominations appealed to their own members in raising funds for Iranian famine victims. In this case, Catholic organizations had an edge in the Iranian setting, given that there existed in Iran small communities of indigenous Catholics, whereas there were no Anglican, Presbyterian, Methodist, or other such *native* Protestant communities; even if different Christian denominational missionary organizations from the United Kingdom ultimately sought to reach as vast a population group in places such as Iran in the hope of winning converts—a project that ultimately met with repeated failure for all Christian missionary groups active in Iran. An example is an advertisement for "A Persian Mission" appearing in the *Freeman's Journal* a year after the worst phase of the Iranian famine had subsided. The advert was aimed at raising funds in Ireland for the mission in Iran as well as for those still suffering the effects of the famine. It identified the intended target group in Iran as the small Catholic community (comprised chiefly of members of the Chaldean Assyrian and the much smaller Catholic Armenian Rite churches).[19]

In the end, the funds collected by the City of London Mansion House and other organizations in the United Kingdom for Iranian famine victims paled in comparison with money raised through the same channels for victims of the earlier Orissa Famine in British India or for victims of two other recent disasters *outside* the British Empire (see below). While the Iranian ambassador in London, Mohsen Khan ("Mo'in al-Molk," later "Amin al-Molk") attended a number of Mansion House fund-raising events after having initially denied a major famine was ravaging his country,[20] it was the Iranian consul-general in London who was tasked with the regular liaising of relief efforts.[21] The Iranian consul-general happened to be the Irish Thomas Kerr Lynch, who along with Edwyn Sandys Dawes served as an honorary joint secretary of the Persian Famine Relief Fund committee headquartered at the Mansion House.[22] With rare exceptions, all contributions toward the Iranian famine relief collected and received in the United Kingdom were transmitted to Iran via British Foreign Office channels and in care of the British minister in Tehran, Charles Alison. To better coordinate the international aid effort, the Iranian government had set up a relief commission consisting of diplomatic representatives of Britain (Alison), Russia, the Ottoman Empire, and France. The British vice-consul in Tehran after July 1871, Henry Hardy Ongley, was deputized by Alison to oversee the day-to-day conduct of British aid efforts. Funds arriving from the United Kingdom were then transferred largely to the Anglo-Irish Anglican Rev. Robert Bruce of the Church Missionary Society active in central Iran, with other Anglican missionaries and even the staff of the British-owned Indo-European Telegraph Department in various parts of Iran taking part in regional distribution of funds. Rev. Bruce and his wife Emily had reached Iran in 1870 on their way back to India from the United Kingdom, but had decided to stay in Iran and assist the famine victims.[23] Bruce continually appealed "to the Christian charity of persons in England and Ireland" and received donations from Ireland by means of the London Mansion House, which were largely raised through Anglican institutions. Mostly by means of the *Church Missionary Intelligencer*, but also in the pages of some newspapers, Bruce kept Anglican and other readers in the United Kingdom apprised of the crisis in Iran and of the relief activities he and his wife oversaw.[24]

Ireland, Politics, and the Coverage of the Iranian Famine of 1870–72

Among the many developments in Ireland itself, the Iranian famine coincided with another round of widespread potato disease in Ireland during 1871. Although this latest blight did not result in a famine as had the potato blight in 1845–51, it nevertheless generated occasional press references to that devastating famine.[25] On the other hand, the latter phase of the Iranian famine overlapped with large-scale sectarian and political violence in Belfast. These clashes were triggered in August 1872 by Protestant-unionist (i.e., the Orange organizations) attacks on separate parades organized by supporters of detained Fenians as well as by Home Rule nationalists, with the parades taking place following the Repeal of the Party Processions Act the previous year. The Act removed the 1850 ban on distinctly denominational and partisan parades across Ireland, with the Orange parades having already resumed a few years earlier despite the ban. Moreover, the Ancient Order of Hibernians, a secret and sectarian Catholic Irish nationalist organization, was also now publicizing its presence in Ireland and retaliating against Protestant-unionist attacks.[26] These riots were occurring in the aftermath of the abortive 'Fenian Rising' in Ireland in 1867, waged by the Irish Republican Brotherhood, as well as the latest episodes of failed Fenian raids into Canada from the United States (in 1870 and 1871), and the deadly clashes between Irish Orange organizations and

Catholics in New York in 1870–71, which further galvanized extremist political tensions in Ireland. The wider sectarian and political tensions across Ireland during the period were further aggravated by recent conflicts over the rights of agricultural tenants and the broader land question in Ireland, including extensive violence by remnants of the sectarian Catholic Ribbonists. The land crisis resulted in a series of land reforms introduced by the Liberal prime minister William Gladstone (i.e., the 1870 Irish Land Act).

As in the rest of the United Kingdom, the Irish press reported on the Iranian famine with varying frequency and at different length. These news outlets ranged from the conservative and pro-Protestant unionist *Irish Times* (Dublin) to the more blatantly sectarian Anglican and unionist *Belfast News-Letter*, or the conservative pro-landlord *Dublin Evening Mail*, the Dublin-based moderate Home Rule nationalist paper the *Freeman's Journal*, the more radical Dublin-based Home Rule mouthpiece *The Nation*, and a host of provincial papers such as the unionist *Cork Constitution* or the Home Rule nationalist *Cork Examiner*. In comparison with reports of the Anglo-Iranian War of 1856–57, regular news of the Iranian famine reached Ireland much faster. This was due to the completion of a telegraph line in 1868 by the Indo-European Telegraph Department, connecting London with British India and passing through Iran. In their reporting of the Iranian famine, it is no surprise that sectarian Protestant papers in Ireland, such as the *Belfast News-Letter*, highlighted relief efforts carried out in Iran by Protestant groups, most notably by Anglican missions, as well as by a number of official British representatives in Iran, including the Persian Gulf Resident in Bushire, Colonel Lewis Pelly.[27] On the other hand, the Home-Rule and nonsectarian nationalist press, such as the *Freeman's Journal*, were by no means entirely averse to mentioning the role of British diplomatic staff in relieving the suffering of famine victims in Iran or of the Mansion House campaign in London, even if these nationalist papers avoided overemphasizing the specifically Protestant aid distribution efforts underway in Iran when mentioning Rev. Robert Bruce and others.[28]

In reports of the Iranian famine appearing in the nationalist press in Ireland there was no mention of Ireland's Great Famine of 1845–51 or of the earlier devastating famine of 1740–41 ("Year of Slaughter"), or of any other Irish historical example. It is tempting to attribute this factor to the hallowed status of the Great Famine in nationalist memory and lore—presuming it was felt the Great Famine would somehow be historically devalued and rendered less exceptional in nationalist memory through its equation with other similar catastrophic events elsewhere in the world. There are plenty of examples throughout history of nations or other narrowly defined population groups guarding the putative distinctiveness and exceptionalism of their own "victimhood" as a badge of extraordinary suffering deserving special historical recognition and respect, whether or not also utilizing that claim as a cover or outright flagrant license for victimizing other groups with expected impunity. An alternative line of explaining the absence of allusions to Ireland's Great Famine in Irish nationalist coverage of the Iranian famine is that of the lingering collective trauma of the Great Famine and the likely desire not to be readily reminded of such a 'national' calamity, which was otherwise deeply etched into personal and/or 'collective' (or "social") memories of the population—'collective' as well as 'social' memory here also denoting the absorption of knowledge of past events transmitted through various channels independently of personal experience. This latter explanation is all the more enticing, given the fact that the remainder of the Irish press, too, avoided drawing any parallels between the Irish and Iranian famines. Yet, in actuality, neither of the above hypothetical scenarios accounts for the Irish nationalist disinclination to draw some form of analogy between the Iranian famine and the Great Famine in Ireland. One way of gauging the reaction of the Irish press to the Iranian famine, and particularly the reaction of Irish nationalist newspapers of varying ideological proclivities, is to contextualize these range of responses in comparison with the coverage in the same newspapers of other large-scale famines, disasters, or crises across the world roughly around the same period.

Vincent Comerford notes the prevailing Irish mood of silence on personal experiences of the Great Famine and of the hushed collective recollections of the event during the first decade after the more immediate horrors of that famine subsided. He writes, the "first monograph history of the Great Famine" was Canon John O'Rourke's 1875 *The History of the Great Irish Famine of 1847*,[29] although there were occasional brief commentaries on the Great Famine in earlier works published in Ireland or in the Irish diaspora, as in the case of Thomas D'Arcy McGee's 1851 *A History of the Irish Settlers in North America*, published in Boston. In the chapter titled "The Black Forty-Seven" in the first volume of his 1877 *New Ireland*, Alexander Martin Sullivan, the proprietor of *The Nation*, was to note the dearth of monograph-length accounts of the Great Famine: "In truth, until the appearance a few years since of the Rev. Mr. O'Rourke's excellent volume, the 'History of the Irish Famine,' the only competent record of the events of that time was the 'Report of the Society of Friends' [i.e., Quaker] Irish Relief Committee."[30] But, this did not denote absolute silence on the topic, particularly by Irish nationalists (and not forgetting also the allusions in the pages of *The Nation* to Ireland's Great Famine in connection with British policy in parts of India around the time of the Anglo-Iranian War of 1856–57, as discussed in the previous chapter). For instance, as Comerford too points out, John Mitchel had already accused London of a deliberate policy of eradicating the Irish during the Great Famine. In an article written in the United States in 1858 for the *Southern Citizen* (Knoxville, Tennessee), Mitchel branded London's policy during the famine as "extermination." This article was later reproduced as a brief chapter in Mitchel's 1861 *The Last Conquest of Ireland (Perhaps)*, which was published in Scotland and in which Mitchel, in his newly found white supremacist creed, appealed to the indignation of "White men."[31] In fact, in 1848, in the midst of the Great Famine, Mitchel's short-lived *The United Irishman*, as well as another short-lived militant nationalist Dublin paper the *Irish Tribune*, had both accused British authorities of taking advantage of the famine to wipe out what the authorities allegedly regarded as Ireland's excess population.[32] While, in contrast to Mitchel and other militant Irish republican nationalists, most so-called moderate Home Rule Irish nationalists blamed London of incompetence and blundering policies in coping with the Great Famine, rather than harboring a genocidal scheme, A. M. Sullivan, who pursued parliamentary Home Rule politics while resorting to militant rhetoric, shared Mitchel's verdict of London's intentional policy of decimating Ireland's population. Well before the Iranian famine, while commenting in 1867 on the Orissa Famine in India, *The Nation* had drawn various comparisons between that famine and the Great Famine in Ireland, pondering the hidden British agenda for allowing purportedly preventable large-scale famines to occur in

India. The paper also stated unequivocally that in Ireland during the famine of 1845–51 London's "object was transparent enough—it was the speediest, cheapest, and *safest* way of ridding the country of its population to make room for sheep and black cattle."[33]

The Iranian famine occurred in the interval between the two already-mentioned major famines in British India: the Orissa Famine of 1865–67 and the Indian "Great Famine" of 1876–78.[34] In Irish nationalist coverage of both Indian famines there were recurrent references to Ireland's own past experiences of famine. Whether in quoting other sources, or in their own editorial commentaries, cross-references to Ireland's Great Famine in connection with the famines in India appeared in the *Freeman's Journal* and *The Nation*. This was also the case in their coverage of even earlier Indian famines, such as the 1861 famine in the northwestern provinces.[35] As in the Iranian famine, nearly a million-and-a-half people perished during the Orissa Famine. A key difference between the two distant famines from Irish nationalist point of view was that Orissa was located in the British Empire, with British authorities in India and London ultimately held accountable for the handling of the famine and for their lack of preemptive preparations, given the frequent recurrence of famines in India. In this setting, allusions to Ireland's Great Famine and calls for Irish contributions to Indian relief funds were more than mere expressions of empathetic cross-identification with England's other suffering colonial subjects. The Orissa Famine and other large-scale Indian famines were occasions for circuitously reminding Irish readers of Ireland's own similar suffering under British administration; just as during the Anglo-Iranian War of 1856–57 *The Nation*'s reporting of that war was intended to indirectly draw attention to the history of English imperial aggression in Ireland. Direct and inferred allusions to Ireland's Great Famine in the coverage of Orissa and other Indian famines appearing in the Irish nationalist press were ultimately an expression of Irish nationalists' eternal recollection of the Great Famine and London's culpability in one form or another. As *The Nation* put it, "Ireland still remembers."[36] As mentioned before, the theme of famine became a key medium of cross-identification between Ireland and India under English domination in an extensive range of Irish nationalist condemnations of British imperial rule.[37] Another case of a large-scale famine that attracted attention in Ireland in the 1870s and spurred Irish contributions toward the relief funds was the Chinese Famine of 1876–79.[38] Similar to the Iranian famine, this famine, too, occurred outside Britain's formal imperial territories.

Compared to Indian famines, the coverage of the Iranian famine in the same range of Irish nationalist press, from *The Nation* to the *Freeman's Journal*, as well as in provincial and diasporic nationalist newspapers, was exceedingly infrequent and cursory at best. In the case of *The Nation*, which trailed far behind the *Freeman's Journal* in this regard, this markedly scant attention to the famine in Iran was all the more striking given the paper's initial acknowledgment of the gravity of the event and its extensive decimation of Iran's population, which in the words of a report from the *Times of India* (Bombay) reproduced in the paper was "severe beyond comprehension."[39] *The Nation*'s subsequent decided silence on the Iranian famine was an unmistakably conscious act, owing to the fact that the funds raised throughout the United Kingdom for Iranian famine victims and channeled through the Mansion House in the City of London were forwarded to Iran via the British Foreign Office and then distributed in Iran by the British minister in Tehran,

Alison, through various networks, but primarily by Rev. Bruce and other Anglican missions across Iran. The broad involvement of British authorities in the Iranian famine relief, which otherwise was mentioned *casually* in the periodic coverage of the crisis appearing in the *Freeman's Journal*, was the principal reason *The Nation* avoided devoting attention to the Iranian famine or expressing any degree of actual sympathy with its victims. It needs to be pointed out that relief funds collected in the United Kingdom for past and subsequent Indian famines too were transmitted to India through the Mansion House in the City of London, with the funds distributed in India via the office of the British Viceroy (Sir Charles John Canning in 1861, Sir John Laird Mair Lawrence in 1865–67, and Lord Lytton (Robert Bulwer-Lytton) in 1876–78). Whereas in the case of India it was to be expected that British authorities would in some form be involved in relief efforts, Iran was situated outside the British Empire and, from *The Nation*'s point of view, any official British involvement in aid efforts in that country cast a humanitarian aura on British authorities, without simultaneously enabling the paper to blame British authorities for the outbreak of that famine. In contrast to reports of Indian famines, or of the Anglo-Iranian War of 1856–57 for that matter, *The Nation*'s coverage of the Iranian famine could not render England a culprit in the crisis. To the contrary, it would have amounted to an acknowledgment of British munificence in responding to human suffering. *The Nation* was very forthright in highlighting this particular angle as the basis for its politically motivated decision to ignore the Iranian famine and the related famine relief efforts steered by the Mansion House. The paper explicitly underscored its stance on the matter by condemning the ostensibly disguised British motive for assisting Iranian victims; suggesting the British aid effort was calculated to ultimately benefit Britain geo-politically. In making this assertion, *The Nation* also casually conflated the British government and the British people: "Famine is raging in Persia. [...] In London, a movement for giving the sufferers assistance has been set on foot, but, as might have been expected, the motive of it appears to have been not quite praiseworthy. The Shah can benefit British dominion in India considerably, and hence, most probably, the desire of the British public—and, it is rumored, of the British Government also—to relieve the starving inhabitants of Persia."[40] In this terse and unsympathetic declaration of the paper's position regarding the Iranian famine relief efforts underway in the United Kingdom, *The Nation* was no doubt also responding to such earlier statements appearing in the British press by the likes of Henry Creswicke Rawlinson, a military officer and prominent orientalist with prior service in British India and an erstwhile British military instructor attached to the Iranian army earlier in the century. In 1871, Rawlinson had helped launch the London Mansion House famine relief fund for the Iranian victims and appealed to as broad a spectrum of public sentiment in the United Kingdom. In the process, Rawlinson had stated, with much exaggeration regarding past Anglo-Iranian relations: "[H]e was sure that the present appeal would not be disregarded, particularly when it was recollected that Persia was a very old ally of this country, and that, having regard to her position between our Indian possessions and the Russian empire, she was likely to occupy a very prominent position in our future political history."[41]

The Nation, in its insinuation of a uniformly hidden imperialist agenda behind the charitable activities of the "British public" now assisting Iranian victims, rather than proposing the possibility of such a motive on the part of only some individuals involved, practically noted its reluctance to devote much space to the Iranian famine. The few other reports of the famine appearing in the paper in the coming months tended to be passing accounts, lacking any emotional tone and even casually repeating the commonplace British press opinion that the Iranian government and the overwhelming majority of the country's population "indeed, seem to submit to their multiplied ills with Mahommedan fatality."[42] This characterization of Iran's majority Muslim population and of the Iranian monarch (Nasser ad-Din Shah, who had also reigned during the Anglo-Iranian War of 1856–57) was in sharp contrast to the paper's pronouncements during the Anglo-Iranian War (see Chapter Four). Keeping in mind also *The Nation*'s apathetic attitude toward the famine in Herat during the Iranian siege of the city in 1856, at which time *The Nation* was championing Iran's war effort against Britain, the paper's treatment of the much larger scale and deadlier famine in Iran in 1870–72 was yet another indication of the ever-present potential among many nationalists (in Ireland and elsewhere) to lapse into selective and hierarchical ethos of humanity. Among other reasons for *The Nation*'s disinclination to devote attention to the Iranian famine, let alone join the widespread press efforts in the United Kingdom to solicit funds for victims of the disaster, appears to have been the steady coverage of the famine by the Irish unionist press, such as the *Belfast News-Letter*, that highlighted the fund-raising efforts headquartered in the City of London for assisting the famine victims and the role of British diplomatic staff in distributing the aid in Iran.

Another means of gauging *The Nation*'s response to the Iranian calamity, and substantiating its unmistakably deliberate policy of neglecting that famine, is to examine the paper's neglect of some other contemporary international disaster relief efforts, such as that for victims of the August 1871 hurricane in the West Indies (with many of the islands also situated within the British Empire), which killed hundreds of people and destroyed thousands of homes, in contrast to the paper's simultaneous enthusiastic endorsement of relief efforts for the Great Chicago Fire of October 10, 1871, in the United States, which killed around 300 people and left homeless well over a hundred thousand people (nearly a third of the city's population). In its first report of the Chicago fire, *The Nation* expressed hope that "Ireland, we are sure, will cheerfully contribute her mite [*sic*] to make light the burden, should it be necessary."[43] This was followed in the next weekly issue of the paper by a very detailed (even if the paper characterized it as "abridged") account taken from the *Freeman's Journal* of a meeting at the Dublin mayoral Mansion House for setting up a relief fund for the Chicago victims, along with the names of some of the existing donors, and a report of a similar relief fund established in Cork. In this reproduced news report, the Liberal (and Catholic) MP for Tipperary, Denis Caulfield Heron, was quoted as reminding others gathered at the Mansion House in Dublin:

> Of the 30,000 [*sic*] citizens of Chicago, one-third of whom were now sufferers, at least 100,000 were of the Irish race (hear, hear). Charity knew neither country nor creed, and they were also united to the people of Chicago by the ties of sympathy and of gratitude. When was there distress in Ireland that America did not send forth a helping hand where was the Irish emigrant that ever forgot the old country at home? (Hear, hear). Dublin that

day was to do for Chicago in its unhappiness what America, including Chicago, had done for Ireland in the hour of her distress (applause).[44]

The Irish-American population of Chicago, and of the United States in general, and their continued ties to Ireland was clearly among the leading incentives of *The Nation* in rushing to support the Chicago relief efforts—not to mention the importance also of the sizeable portion of Irish-American population committed to, and in various ways assisting, different Irish nationalist platforms. For *The Nation* "Charity" clearly seemed *to know* both "country" and "creed." A multi-page report of the Chicago fire and the suffering unleashed by it appeared in *The Nation* the following week,[45] followed by further reports of Irish contributions to the Chicago relief fund and the paper's resolute encouragement of further donations,[46] notwithstanding the fact that the primary fund-raising effort in Ireland for this disaster was spearheaded by the Mansion House in Dublin and handled under the auspices of general funds collected and transmitted by the Mansion House in the City of London.[47]

On the other hand, in contrast to the Chicago fire and somewhat similar to the Iranian famine, the West Indies hurricane, which attracted some donations from Ireland, failed to elicit as much attention or sympathy in the pages of *The Nation* as it did in many other Irish papers. This was more than a mere reflection of the overall relative dearth of public contributions toward Iranian and West Indian relief efforts throughout the United Kingdom (in comparison with funds raised for the Chicago fire or for a few other contemporary disasters around the world). In November 1871, the *Belfast News-letter* noted the general pattern of neglect throughout the United Kingdom of the Iranian famine and of the hurricane in West Indies, comparing the public reaction to these events with the public's eagerness to assist those in need in France in the aftermath of the Franco-Prussian War of 1870–71 and the more recent victims of the Chicago fire:

> The metropolitan subscription for the relief of the Chicago Fund continues to increase at the rate of upwards of £1,000 per day, and the aggregate of the United Kingdom will, no doubt, "foot up," as the Yankees say, to about a-quarter of a million. This sum, added to the £680,000 raised for the sick and wounded French, will represent something like a million contributed by the British public to those two objects alone within little more than a twelvemonth. This extraordinary sympathy is the more remarkable when it is remembered that two other urgent appeals made to the generosity of the public have been almost disregarded. The harrowing details of the shocking famine in Persia have produced but a few hundred pounds, while the cry of our fellow-subjects for relief consequent on the hurricane in the West Indies has elicited but four thousand pounds. No one, of course, grudges what Chicago has got, but it must be conceded that the wealthy among us have, for some reason or other, failed to appreciate the equally pressing needs of others for whom earlier appeals were made.[48]

By March 1872, the total contributions received by the London Mansion House for the Iranian relief fund from across the United Kingdom and from abroad amounted to only c. £14,000.[49] What the *Belfast News-Letter* failed to mention was that the Irish nationalist press, *The Nation* in particular, had also "failed to appreciate the equally pressing needs" of those suffering in Iran and in the Caribbean. Further research is needed to ascertain the cause of *The Nation*'s inadequate response to the hurricane in the West Indies, which unlike famines in Ireland and India could not be pinned on either avowedly deliberate genocidal policy or continued callous neglect on the part of British authorities. It remains unclear whether the paper's neglect of the destruction caused by the hurricane was due to the fact that the hurricane had also affected the Caribbean colonies of other states besides England (and hence the paper could not single out England as a culprit in some form), or if the paper's lack of interest was in some way related to the fact that the majority of the victims in the British West Indies consisted of former enslaved peoples of African descent and their descendants, or whether there was some other explanation.

When the Persian Famine Relief Fund headquartered in London was being established on October 26, 1871, Henry Creswicke Rawlinson had hoped the fund would evoke the same generosity of spirit and donations in the United Kingdom as the Istanbul fire of 1870, the Orissa Famine of 1865–67, and the current French and Chicago relief efforts.[50] What is unmistakable is not only the far lesser space devoted to the Iranian famine in Irish nationalist newspapers, but the premeditated neglect of the event by *The Nation* and its detached attitude to the suffering of the victims. A weekly publication at the time, in its June 10, 1871, issue, the paper relayed verbatim a report on the famine from the previous month's issue of the *Times of India*. This report also alleged, without specifying the location of the incident in Iran, that the starving Muslims ("Mussulmans") had "killed and eaten" a victim and that "fathers and mothers are said to be devouring their own children."[51] This reported incident of anthropophagy by the *Times of India* appears to have been one of the earliest of such reports to reach the United Kingdom, with similar accounts multiplying in the coming months. Noteworthy in this regard is also the blasé repetition by not just *The Nation*, but also by a broad range of other Irish press, of the purportedly unique Muslim proclivity among Iranian famine victims for cannibalism, leaving aside whether most accounts of anthropophagy during the Iranian famine were accurate or apocryphal. The *Belfast News-Letter* reproduced the exact same report from the *Times of India* on the same day as *The Nation*, with the same emphasis on specifically Muslims engaging in the practice of consuming human flesh, including the devouring of their own children.[52] The very same report was carried a few days earlier in the pages of the British press,[53] and was also repeated in the *Freeman's Journal* two days after the appearance of the identical report in *The Nation* and the *Belfast News-Letter*. The *Freeman's Journal*, now mentioning a particular location, noted: "At Yezd some fifty children have been killed and eaten by the starving Mahomedan [Muslim] population."[54] Documented cases of anthropophagy have occurred during major famines throughout history and across the world, including consumption of one's own relatives under extremely desperate physically and psychologically traumatic conditions.[55] What is curious about the Irish press reports (in general) of cannibalism during the Iranian famine and the recurrent stated identification of the practice with the majority Muslim population of Iran is the blotting-out of episodes of cannibalism during Ireland's own Great Famine of just over two decades earlier, including reported consumption of children by parents. Other than contemporary evidence of cannibalism during the Great Famine in Ireland,[56] no lesser a militant nationalist figure than John Mitchel had commented in 1860 on the occurrence of anthropophagy during that famine: "[I]nsane mothers began to eat their young children, who died of famine before them."⁵⁷ Incidentally, the press in Britain and in some other parts of the world occasionally drew parallels between Irish and Iranian famines, including incidences of anthropophagy. For example, under the section "A Letter to the Young," *Old Jonathan: The District and Parish Helper*, a pan-Protestant periodical published in London, noted:

> A very painful famine has prevailed for a long time in Persia, by which the people have been reduced to most distressing want and privation, resorting, in consequence, to means for maintaining life that are dreadful to think of—mothers eating their own children, and such like. Can anything be more agonizing to think of? If you, my dear young friends, had witnessed the dreadful effects of famine as I did, in the years '46 and '47 in Ireland, you would be the better able to judge of the awful state of things resulting therefrom. Oh, that God may, in great mercy, continue to preserve our own dear England from such hapless circumstances!⁵⁸

The particular style of reporting cases of cannibalism during the Iranian famine in the Irish press, and in the Irish nationalist press in particular, was not symptomatic of what one might construe as post-traumatic denial or deflection (conscious or otherwise) of one's own presumed 'national' mortification by means of accentuating the same elements of degradation and horror in nationally (and in this case also culturally and religiously) *Other* groups. *The Nation*'s allusion to cannibalism during the Iranian famine and the paper's categorically insouciant tone in response to that disaster was again in sharp contrast to the paper's coverage of the Orissa Famine of 1865–67. In reporting on the Indian famine, *The Nation* not only recurrently drew fundamental analogies between that famine and Ireland's Great Famine of 1845–51, but it even characterized the Indian famine as much grislier than Ireland's suffering: "We alone in Ireland are the only other people in the world who have passed through such a terrible ordeal [...]. But even we have had nothing to endure that bears comparison to this horrible tragedy—this fearful carnival of death."⁵⁹ On another occasion, the paper wrote of the Orissa Famine: "[S]o appalling in its consequences, so terrible in its details, that the agony of Ireland and the sufferings by former famines in India pale into utter insignificance in comparison."⁶⁰ In the framework of this expressed Irish cross-identification with Indian victims of British imperialism, *The Nation* cited incidences of cannibalism as an indicator of the depths of suffering to which Indian famine victims had been driven, with British authorities ultimately to blame for the horror.⁶¹ In the case of the Iranian famine, Britain could not be held accountable for the occurrence of cannibalism or for the outbreak of the famine itself, and hence for any other imputed genocidal policy. To the contrary, all available reports indicated the important part played by British official channels in soliciting and distributing international aid to Iranian victims.

The detached reporting of the Iranian famine by the Irish nationalist press remained paradigmatic of Irish nationalist press reports of other subsequent contemporary developments in Iran until the outbreak of the Iranian Constitutional Revolution of 1906–11, with the exception of occasional, albeit cursory, sympathetic commentaries in support of the Iranian 'nation' during the Iranian Tobacco Protest of 1891–92 (a popular nationwide upheaval in Iran directed at a comprehensive tobacco concession granted by the Iranian government to a British subject). Within months after the Iranian famine subsided in early 1873, the Iranian monarch Nasser al-Din Shah embarked on his first exorbitant European tour, during which he visited England. This visit occurred in the aftermath of an astounding concession the shah had granted to the British Baron Julius de Reuter during the famine in 1872. The wide-ranging Reuter concession was intended to develop Iran's infrastructure, while counter-balancing the growing Russian influence in Iran, as well as financially bolstering the Iranian state in the short run and financing the exorbitant expenditures of the royal court, including the shah's upcoming European tour. In exchange for £40,000 and 60 percent of the revenues of the country's customs, the control of which was now transferred to Reuter, the latter was granted an exclusive monopoly for the collection of all customs, construction of railways, tramways, major roads, telegraph lines, irrigation works and canals, and extraction of all minerals (except gold, silver, and precious stones) for the next seventy years, as well as a monopoly to launch an Iranian national bank and establish all industrial factories in the country.[62] Stirring great astonishment around the world, the concession, which did not enjoy London's official backing, was met with widespread opposition across Iran, as well as objections from Russia, and was eventually cancelled by Iranian authorities in 1873 to avert a potential revolution. The Reuter concession and the shah's European visit attracted ample, albeit politically detached, coverage in the Irish press. *The Nation*'s recollection of the recent Iranian famine of 1870–72 was so indifferent and fleeting that in one of the paper's reports of the shah's stay in England in 1873, which the paper used as an opportunity to comment at length on conditions in Ireland, it completely disregarded the devastation wreaked by the Iranian famine. It wrote:

> Persia, much as it has suffered, has not lost a third of its population as Ireland has within thirty years, yet in Persia there is no boasting about the "constitution," and nothing at all said about the blessings of liberal legislation. The Persians, too, at the worst, have no foreign masters—"their tyrants are their countrymen;" yet the Shah never ventures to describe them as "spoilt children," or the victims of over-indulgence. He will find that we manage things far better here. With less real liberty than the Persians, we are still paraded as reveling in the full blaze of freedom. With more destitution amongst us than they, we are represented as thriving and comfortable. The Shah needs no one to teach him how to grind the faces of the poor; but if he wants to learn how that operation can be conducted under the mask of liberal professions and in the name of progress and good government, how the cant of constitutionalism can cover the extinction of liberty, he had better come to Ireland for the lesson.
>
> But to Ireland, we make bold to say, he will not come; and, indeed, we are not particularly concerned about it. To keep him in the blaze of English gala-making suits his entertainers better, and we are quite willing they should monopolise the Shah. We should like, however—not to be entirely behindhand in the race of courtesy—to make a small contribution to the presentations which his Majesty will receive during his stay amongst our neighbours. The gift would not be a very expensive one, but it might serve to temper some of the views of English love of freedom which are pressed upon him with such self-sufficiency by his hosts. A copy of Daniel Reddin's affidavit from the Crown Office, a copy

of the Irish Census Returns, and of the Irish Coercion Acts, from Thom's, would form a very neat presentation, and would prove, we have no doubt, far more useful to the Shah than all the diamond snuff-boxes and illuminated addresses which he will carry back to Ispahan from the shores of Albion.[63]

Notes

1 Cormac Ó Gráda, *Black '47 and Beyond: The Great Irish Famine in History, Economy, and Memory*. Princeton: Princeton University Press, 2000; Christine Kinealy, *The Great Irish Famine: Impact, Ideology and Rebellion*. Houndmills, Basingstoke: Palgrave, 2001; Stuart McLean, *The Event and Its Terrors: Ireland, Famine, Modernity*. Stanford: Stanford University Press, 2004; John Crawley, William J. Smyth, and Mike Murphy, eds., *The Atlas of the Great Irish Famine*. Cork: Cork University Press, 2012; Luke Gibbons, *Limits of the Visible: Representing the Great Hunger*. Cork: Cork University Press, 2015; Melissa Fegan, *Literature and the Irish Famine*.

2 See also the Irish Famine Project (https://www.irishfamineproject.com/data.html); as well as Terry Eagleton, *Heathcliff and the Great Hunger*, chapter 1.

3 At the same time, due to large-scale population migrations from the countryside to large towns and cities during the famine, there was a proportionate increase in the size of the urban Irish-speaking population of Ireland in the immediate years after 1845. See Nicholas Wolf, *An Irish-Speaking Island*, p.4.

4 On the "intensified" Irish nationalist "sense of equivalence" with the population of British India due to the shared experience of "Famine," see Matthew Kelly, "Irish Nationalist Opinion and the British Empire," pp. pp.137–38.

5 Thomas D'Arcy McGee, *A History of the Irish Settlers in North America: From the Earliest Period to the Census of 1850*. Boston: American Celt, 1851, p.137. See also Christine Kinealy, *Charity and the Great Hunger in Ireland: The Kindness of Strangers*. London: Bloomsbury. 2013, pp.10, and passim.

6 Shoko Okazaki, "The Great Persian Famine of 1870-71," *Bulletin of the School of Oriental and African Studies, University of London* 49(1), 1986, pp.183–92 (see especially pp.184–85); John Gurney and Mansour Sefat-gol, *Qom dar Qahti-e Bozorg-e 1288 Qamari*. Qom: Ketabkhaneh-ye Bozorg-e Hazrat-e Ayatollah-e Ozma Mar'ashi-Najafi, 2008, pp.17–30, 180–86, and passim; Charles P. Melville, "The Persian Famine of 1870-1872: Prices and Politics," *Disasters* 12(4), 1988, pp.309–25.

7 See, for example, *Morning Post* (London), October 26, 1871, p.6.

8 For the paper's regular announcement of the "Famine in Persia General Fund in Aid of the Sufferers," see for example ibid., December 13, 1871, p.1; December 18, 1871, p.1; January 16, 1872, p.1; January 27, 1872, p.1; February 9, 1872, p.1; March 2, 1872, p.1; April 6, 1872, p.1; May 25, 1872, p.1.

9 For a random sampling of the coverage of the final stages of the Franco-Prussian War and the subsequent defeat of the Paris Commune by the Third Republic see, for example, *Freeman's Journal*, August 25, 1871, p.3; ibid., October 26, 1871, p.3; *The Nation*, December 2, 1871, p.1227; ibid., June 17, 1871, p.591. See also Michael McCarthy, "The Franco-Irish Ambulance Brigade 1870-71," *Old Limerick Journal* (Limerick), vol. 25, Summer 1989, pp.132–38.

10 On the launch of the Mansion House 'Persian Famine Relief Fund,' see also *Freeman's Journal*, October 26, 1871, p.3.

11 Other prominent members of the British Jewry who responded to the famine relief effort were Albert Abdullah David Sassoon and Messrs. Rothschild & Sons. See, for example, *The Penny Illustrated Paper and Illustrated Times* (London), July 12, 1873, p.23; *Spectator* (London), October 28, 1871, pp.1292–93; *Morning Post* (London), October 30, 1871, p.4. See also Louis Loewe, ed., *Diaries of Sir Moses and Lady Montefiore: Comprising Their Life and Work as Recorded in Their Diaries from 1812 to 1883*. Volumes I and II. Chicago: Belford-Clarke Co., 1890, passim; Daniel Tsadik, *Between Foreigners and Shi'is: Nineteenth-Century Iran and its Jewish Minority*. Stanford: Stanford University Press, 2007, pp.82–88; Abigail Green, "Sir Moses Montefiore and the Making of the 'Jewish International'," *Journal of Modern Jewish Studies* 7(3), November 2008, p.294; "Source 38 The Great Famine of 1871–2 in Iran and the Beginning of Organized

Activity Abroad on Behalf of Iranian Jews. From the Report of the Persian Famine Relief Fund, Published by the Board of Deputies of British Jews, London 1873, pp. 8–16" in David Yerosushalmi, *The Jews of Iran in the Nineteenth Century: Aspects of History, Community, and Culture*. Leiden: Brill, 2009, pp.321–45.

12 See, for example, *Morning Post* (London), September 18, 1871, p.1; December 23, 1871, p.6; January 24, 1873, p.6.

13 Alex Findlater, *Findlaters: The Story of a Dublin Merchant Family, 1774-2001*. Dublin: A. & A. Farmer, 2001, p.41.

14 See, for example, *New Zealand Herald* (Auckland), June 6, 1872, p.2; *The Argus* (Melbourne), May 23, 1872, p.5.; ibid., May 24, 1872, p.4; *The Standard* (London,), September 5, 1872, p.6; *Morning Post* (London), September 5, 1872, p.3. See also Christina Twomey and Andrew J. May, "Australian Responses to the Indian Famine, 1876-78: Sympathy, Photography and the British Empire," *Australian Historical Studies* 43(2), 2012, p.248.

15 Substantial Indian donations came from the likes of the Aga Khan, the Rao of Kutch, and the Maharaja Holkar, and included more extensive famine relief efforts by the likes of the Zoroastrian Parsi Mehrban brothers of Bombay. On relief assistance from India, see *Morning Post* (London), December 8, 1871, p.3; ibid., December 9, 1871; *Pall Mall Gazette* (London), December 9, 1871, p.7; *Dublin Evening Post*, August 1, 1871, p.3.

16 *Morning Post* (London), May 2, 1872, p.3.

17 See, for example, Rev. Robert Bruce's appeal on behalf of the victims in the Armenian Christian village of "Feridan" near Isfahan in the *Belfast News-Letter*, January 8, 1872, p.3; or the report of the activities in Australia of "the Jewish residents of St. Kilda [...] for the purpose of devising means to alleviate the distress of the Jews in Persia" in *The Argus* (Melbourne), May 6, 1872, p.4.

18 See the anonymous letter-to-the-editor by an Armenian resident of Singapore, detailing the appeal from Rev. Petros of the Armenian Church to King Chulalongkorn of Siam, in *The Straits Times* (a.k.a. *Daily Times*, Singapore), January 6, 1872, p.1. See also ibid., January 4, 1872, p.1. The tiny, but influential, Armenian community in Singapore was primarily of Iranian-Armenian ancestry, among them the reputed founder in 1845, and original proprietor, of *The Strait Times*, Catchick Moses. See Nadia Wright, "The Armenians of Singapore: An Historical Perspective," *Armenian Weekly* (https://armenianweekly.com/2015/01/06/armenians-of-simgapore).

19 *Freeman's Journal*, 6 October 6, 1873, p.1.

20 See also the *Irish Times*, December 27, 1871, p.2 c.b; ibid., September 18, 1872, p.2 c.a; *Belfast News-Letter*, December 28, 1871, p.3; *Freeman's Journal*, October 27, 1871, p.4; *Morning Post* (London), October 26, 1871, p.6, ibid., January 19, 1872, p.1; ibid., March 18, 1872, p.7. Mohsen Khan had publicly denied the outbreak of famine in Iran in a long letter-to-the-editor (dated July 29, 1871) in *The Times* (London), July 31, 1871, p.5 c.e. The press throughout the United Kingdom extensively rebuked Mohsen Khan for his initial denial. See, for example, the *Freeman's Journal* (Dublin), October 27, 1871, p.4.

21 See, for example, *Morning Post* (London), November 23, 1871, p.5; December 23, 1871, p. 6.

22 See, for example, *Morning Post* (London), November 23, 1871, p.5; December 13, 1871, p.1; December 18, 1871, p.1; January 16, 1872, p.1; January 27, 1872, p.1. Dawes was a shipping magnate and the owner of ships christened the Shiraz and the Ispahan in the service of the British India Steam Navigation Company's operations in the Persian Gulf. The original honorary secretary of the committee, who continued to be addressed by that title in the committee's public appeals and reports, was Major John Underwood Bateman-Champain of the Indian Army.

23 See, for example, *Irish Times* (Dublin), December 27, 1871, p.2; *Morning Post* (London), March 28, 1872, p.1; ibid., November 23, 1871, p.5. On Rev. Bruce, see also Edward John Lake, *The Church Missionary Society atlas*. Sixth edition. London: Church Missionary House, 1879, p.56; *Church Missionary Gleaner* (London) 17(199), July 1890, pp.109–10; Heidi A. Walcher, *In the Shadow of the King: Zill al-Sultān and Isfahān Under the Qājārs*. London: I.B. Tauris, 2008, pp.206, passim; Robin E. Waterfield, *Christians in Persia: Assyrians, Armenians, Roman Catholics and Protestants*. Reprint. New York: Routledge, 2011 [1973], pp.148–49, passim. Among numerous other contemporary sources that mentioned Rev. Bruce's aid efforts in Isfahan and the surrounding region in central Iran, see also Rev. John Haskell Shedd, "Communications

from the Missions. Famine in Persia," *The Foreign Missionary* (New York) 30(3), August 1871, pp.72–76 (Shedd was an American Presbyterian missionary); Sir Frederic Goldsmid, "Notes on Recent Persian Travel," *Journal of the Royal Geographical Society* (London), vol.44, 1874, pp. pp.192–203; "The Persian Famine—Ispahán, 1871-72" in Rev. Arthur Lewis, *George Maxwell Gordon, M.A., F.R.G.S.: The Pilgrim Missionary of the Punjab. A History of His Life and Work, 1839-1880*. Second edition. London: Seeley & Co., 1889, chapter 6; William Brittlebank, *Persia During the Famine: A Narrative of a Tour in the East and of the Journey Out and Home*. London: Basil, Montagu, Pickering, 1873. As part of his journey from England to India and back, Brittlebank traveled through Iran in 1872, starting out in southern cities of Bandar Abbas and Bushire and then heading north via Shiraz, first to Isfahan in central Iran, among other towns and cities, before reaching Tehran and then continuing north to Rasht and Enzeli, before crossing the Caspian into the Russian Empire on his return trip to England.

24 See, for example, *Church Missionary Intelligencer: A Monthly Journal of Missionary Information* (London), new series, vol.VIII, 1872, pp.46–48, 314–20. See also Robert Bruce, "Persia, in its Relation to the Kingdom of God. Part IV: The Church Missionary Society's Persia Mission," *Church Missionary Intelligencer and Record* (London), new series, vol.VII, February 1882, pp.102–14; *Morning Post* (London), November 23, 1871, p.5.
25 See, for example, the *Belfast News-Letter*, August 26, 1871, p.3. This report appeared on the same page of the paper as a report of "The Famine in Persia."
26 Mark Radford, *The Policing of Belfast, 1870-1914*. London: Bloomsbury, 2015, pp.74–78.
27 See, for example, the *Belfast News-Letter*, November 23, 1871, p.3.
28 See, for example, *Freeman's Journal*, August 25, 1871, p.3; October 26, 1871, p.3.
29 Vincent Comerford, "Grievance, Scourge or Shame? The Complexity of Attitudes to Ireland's Great Famine" in Christian Noack, Lindsay Janssen, and Vincent Comerford, eds., *Holodomor and Gorta Mór: Histories, Memories and Representations of Famine in Ukraine and Ireland*. Reprint. London: Anthem Press, 2014 [2012], pp.51–73 (for the quoted text see p.52).
30 Alexander Martin Sullivan, *New Ireland*, vol.I, pp.140–41.
31 John Mitchel, *The Last Conquest of Ireland (Perhaps)*. Author's edition. Glasgow: R. & T. Washbourne, 1882 [1861], pp.117, 120, and passim. On Mitchel, see also Melissa Fegan, *Literature and the Irish Famine*, pp.17–21 and passim.
32 Ann Andrews, *Newspapers and Newsmakers*, p.124.
33 *The Nation*, February 23, 1867, p.426.
34 On donations collected in Ireland for the Indian famine of 1876–78, see also William Digby, *Famine Campaign in Southern India (Madras and Bombay Presidencies and Province of Mysore), 1876-1878*. Volume II. London: Longmans, Green, and Co., 1878, pp. 43 n.1, 44, 47, 94, 101, 112, 463.
35 See, for example, *Freeman's Journal*, April 6, 1861, p.4; ibid., October 15, 1866, p.3; ibid., March 2, 1874, p.3; *The Nation*, February 23, 1867, pp.426–27; ibid., July 6, 1867, pp.729–30; ibid., August 24, 1867, p.14; ibid., September 15, 1877, p.1. See also Jennifer M. Regan, "We Could Be of Service to Other Suffering People," p.67.
36 *The Nation*, July 6, 1867, p.729.
37 See, in addition, Peter Gray, "Famine and Land in Ireland and India, 1845-1880: James Caird and the Political Economy of Hunger," *Historical Journal* 49(1), 2006, pp.193–215; Jill Bender, "The Imperial Politics of Famine: The 1873-74 Bengal Famine and Irish Parliamentary Nationalism," *Éire-Ireland* 42(1 & 2), Spring/Summer 2007, pp.132–56; Jane Ohlmeyer, "Ireland, India and the British empire," *Studies in People's History* 2(2), 2015, pp.181–84; Barry Crosbie, *Irish Imperial Networks: Migration, Social Communication and Exchange in Nineteenth-Century India*. Cambridge: Cambridge University Press, 2012, pp.185–93 and passim; Howard Brasted, "Indian Nationalist Development and the Influence of Irish Home Rule, 1870-1886," *Modern Asian Studies* 14(1), 1980, p.61; Melissa Fegan, *Literature and the Irish Famine*, p.30. On India and Ireland, see also Joseph Lennon, *Irish Orientalism*, pp.193–203; Scott B. Cook, *Imperial Affinities: Nineteenth Century Analogies and Exchanges Between India and Ireland*. New Delhi: Sage, 1993, particularly pp.78–79 in connection with famine.
38 For random examples of solicitation of, and contributions to, the Chinese Famine relief fund in Ireland, see *Freeman's Journal*, June 18, 1878, p.4 c.f; ibid., July 2, 1878, p.1 c.f; ibid., August 30, 1878, p.5 c.f; ibid., October 5, 1878, p.6 c.g; *The Nation*, August 24, 1878, p.1, c.d.
39 *The Nation*, June 10, 1871, p.561, c.c.

40 Ibid., November 11, 1871, p.1138 c.b.
41 *Morning Post* (London), October 26, 1871, p.6.
42 See, for example, *The Nation*, December 23, 1871, p.1307, c.a
43 Ibid., October 14, 1871, p.1029.
44 Ibid., October 21, 1871, p.1065.
45 Ibid., October 28, 1871, pp.1084–86.
46 See also, for example, the letters-to-the-editor in ibid., December 16, 1871, p.1281.
47 See, for example, *Daily News* (London), November 4, 1871, p.5 c.c.
48 *Belfast News-Letter*, November 1, 1871, p.3 cd.
49 *Morning Post* (London), March 18, 1872, p.7.
50 *Spectator* (London), October 28, 1871, pp.1291, 1292–93; *The Sun and Central Press* (London), October 25, 1871, p.6.
51 *The Nation* (Dublin), June 10, 1871, p.561 c.c.
52 *Belfast News-Letter*, June 10, 1871, p.3 c.f. See also ibid., July 28, 1871, pp. 3 c.a; August 26, 1871, p.3 c.f.
53 See, for example, *Morning Post* (London), June 7, 1871, p.3.
54 *Freeman's Journal* (Dublin), June 12, 1871, p.6.
55 Among the many studies, see also Najwa al-Qattan, "When Mothers Ate Their Children: Wartime Memory and the Language of Food in Syria and Lebanon," *International Journal of Middle East Studies* 46(4), November 2014, pp.719–36. One of the many eyewitness accounts of the Iranian famine was by Charles James Wills, a medical officer attached to the (British) Indo-European Telegraph Department in Iran from 1866 to 1881. In his overarchingly sensationalist account of his stay in Iran, Wills too noted cases of cannibalism during the Iranian famine. Charles James Wills, *In the Land of the Lion and Sun or Modern Persia*. London: William Clowes and Sons, 1883, p.254. For Wills' account of the aid provided by the Persian Famine Relief Fund in London, see ibid., pp.252–55.
56 See also Cormac Ó Gráda, *Eating People is Wrong, and Other Essays on Famine, Its Past, and Its Future*. Princeton: Princeton University Press, 2015, pp.31–37 and passim.
57 John Mitchel, *The Last Conquest of Ireland*, p.121.
58 *Old Jonathan: The District and Parish Helper* (London), vol.4, June 1872, p.46.
59 *The Nation*, February 23, 1867, p.426.
60 Ibid., July 6, 1867, p.729.
61 See, for example, ibid., February 23, 1867, p.426; August 17, 1867, p.820.
62 See, among other works, Charles Issawi, *The Economic History of Iran 1800-1914*. Chicago: University of Chicago Press, 1971, p.177.
63 *The Nation* (Dublin), June 21, 1873, p.392. Daniel Reddin was a "Fenian" involved in the rescue of Irish Republican Brotherhood prisoners in Manchester in 1867. He was captured and subjected to brutal treatment by the prison medical officer who disbelieved Reddin's claim of suffering paralysis in his legs while in detention.

Chapter Six

THE GHOSTS OF IRAN'S PAST IN IRISH NATIONALIST IMAGINATIONS IN THE SECOND HALF OF THE NINETEENTH CENTURY

Debates on Ireland's (in fact mythical) oriental origins and other similar accounts of ancient Ireland continued well into the early part of the twentieth century, even if by the middle of the nineteenth century a gradual consensus was taking shape on more rigorous historiographic standards, including more stringent methods of comparative and evidential verification. These improved historiographic standards also benefitted from advancements in philological and archaeological research criteria taking place around the same time, as flawed as some of these developments happened to be by our standards (without implying here that present-day standards are somehow perfect). The frequently intersecting fields of archaeology, philology, and history continued to serve as battlegrounds in ongoing debates on Ireland's ancient past in the second half of the nineteenth century, by which time the question of ancient Irish identities and Irish mythology also extended into emergent and inter-related fields of ethnography, anthropology, and folklore studies, which at the time were methodologically far less scrupulous compared to archaeology or even history. The ravages of the Great Famine of 1845–51 provided added impetus for studies in Irish folklore and other so-called traditions that seemed to be fast disappearing.

By the mid-nineteenth century, Petrie's (d.1866) assertion of the Christian origin of the Round Towers was rapidly gaining consensus in scholarly circles and among leading commentators. Petrie's verdict was even validated in such works as the 1864 *Handbook for Travellers in Ireland*, appearing as part of the prominent London publisher John Murray's series of handbooks of countries around the world and of different constituent parts of the United Kingdom. The *Handbook*, going through subsequent editions, noted with some confusion that, among other hypotheses, the Round Towers were believed by some to have been of Danish origin, while

Their Phoenician, Persian, or Indo-Scythian origin was advocated warmly by General Vallancey, who considered them to have been fire temples,— places from which to proclaim the Druidic festivals, gnomons, or astronomical observatories, Phallic emblems, or Buddhist temples. These opinions, embracing what is called the Pagan doctrine of the Round Towers, were afterwards followed by O'Brien, Lanigan, Miss Beaufort, and Mr. [John] Windele." The *Handbook* then went on to assure its readers: "The opinions which Dr. Petrie has so ably argued out, and which are now generally received, are that the round towers were designed for the double purpose of belfries and castles [*sic*].[1]

Yet, Petrie's position continued to have its resolute detractors in the coming decades, some of them highly regarded individuals in scholarly circles. In the second half of the nineteenth century, the Round Towers as presumed architectural signposts of Ireland's ancient ties with the Orient also continued to fascinate a wide range of Irish nationalist commentators (cultural and/or political), including the likes of Marcus Keane of the Royal Irish Academy, canon Ulick Joseph Bourke, also a member of the Academy, the prominent folklorist Lady Jane Francesca Agnes Wilde, and the journalist and revolutionary republican nationalist Edmond O'Donovan. More relevantly here, the broader theory of 'Iranian' origins of the Irish and of the Round Towers also continued to have ardent advocates.

In his 1867 *The Towers and Temples of Ancient Ireland; Their Origin and History Discussed from a New Point of View*, Marcus Keane argued the so-called Nemedians who had arrived in Ireland prior to the Tuatha de Dananns, as well as the latter, along with the much earlier Fomorians, belonged to the same population group and were of an Cuthite-Iranian origin:

> The name by which the Colony is designated—Nemedians—I am disposed to think is derived from "NEMEADH," holy or consecrated, rather than from "Nemed," the proper name of their Chief or King. This interpretation agrees with what would appear to be the pretensions of the first apostates, for Persia was called "Iran," interpreted to mean in the [Pahlavi] language, "Sacred land, or land of believers;" and the ancient name of Ireland was "Irin"—"the Sacred Island."[2]

Leaving aside Keane's elucidation of the term 'Iran,' which in actuality means "of the Aryans" (subsequently "land of the Aryans"), and ignoring the fact that the designation 'Iran' would not have historically existed yet at the time the (otherwise mythical) Fomorians and Nemedians (or the Tuatha de Dananns for that matter) had supposedly reached Ireland, Keane's main objective was to demonstrate the resemblance between the Round Towers, as well as other presumed ancient structures in Ireland, and those found in West Asia and in the Indian subcontinent, which he regarded as prototypes of the Irish constructions. According to Keane, the oriental influence in this regard had even spread to the Americas at some later time, with Inca structures found in Peru reportedly substantiating this claim. Keane's sources included the likes of Vallancey, Henry O'Brien, the late eighteenth-century English antiquarian Jacob Bryant,[3] and the early nineteenth-century English biblical scholar George Stanley Faber. Keane provided an assortment of allegedly existing proofs of Ireland's ancient connections with the Orient, ranging from fire-worship to accounts of (the otherwise entirely legendary) 'Iranian' dynasties of Mahābādiān and Pishdādiān. According to Keane, the substantial pre-Celtic population arrivals in Ireland—in this model namely the Nemedians and Tuatha de Dananns—were Cuthian (Cuthite) "descendants of Ham" that purportedly included Iranians, Scythians, Babylonians, Canaanites, and a few other ancient groups. Although the term 'Milesian' does not occur in Keane's book, he was in effect claiming it was the pre-Milesian population groups hailing from the Orient who had introduced high civilization to Ireland. This also implied that subsequent major population arrivals in ancient Ireland (whether or not designated as Milesians) were Celtic peoples. This non-Celtic model of Ireland's ancient grand civilization paralleled Vallancey's and O'Brien's distinct theories, albeit with its own peculiar fusion of different population groups into a singular Cuthite-Iranian category. Like many earlier antiquarians, Keane also claimed Erin and Iran were derived from the same root and that the ancient Irish language, prior to its intermixture with the Celtic language, was a variation of Cuthite dialects that supposedly included Sanskrit. Keane also endorsed O'Brien's identification of the Round Towers as ancient structures of Phallic worship.[4] Henry O'Brien's supposition of the phallic ritual function of the Round Towers and of putatively similar ancient towers in 'Iranian' lands continued to be repeated in such works as the anonymously authored and privately published 1889 pamphlet titled *Phallic Objects, Monuments and Remains: Illustrations of the Rise and Development of the Phallic Idea (Sex Worship) and Its Embodiment in the Works of Nature and Art*, which adamantly refuted Petrie's theory. The author of this work was the English occultist, freemason, and cleric Hargrave Jennings.

The reason Keane focused on the Nemedians in his above-quoted text was to prove that a pre-Celtic population had introduced Cuthite cultural practices and a distinctly pagan religious architectural style and, more particularly, "buildings of stone and mortar" to Ireland. This was to validate the pre-Christian origin of Ireland's Round Towers in light of what he considered as the "fact" that the Celtic population of Ireland prior to the arrival of the Normans in the twelfth century had only constructed wooden structures and could not have built the stone edifices of the towers according to available information.[5] This argument did not explain why the Celts could not have learned masonry skills from the Tuatha de Danann, who had supposedly arrived after the Nemedians and were later supplanted by the Celts. According to Keane, the Tuatha de Dananns were skilled builders of stone structures. Nor did his narrative address why the descendants of the Tuatha de Dananns should have ceased to build stone structures of any kind after the arrival of the Celts, unless we were to assume the Celts had exterminated all human and cultural traces of their predecessors on the island, with the exception of the Round Towers and other such structures. Keane was among a dying breed of entirely old-school Irish antiquarians. Although writing in the second half of the nineteenth century, Keane's methodology and theoretical framework belonged to earlier generations, devoid of sufficient dialogue with the latest linguistic, historiographic, ethnographic, and other theories; albeit referring to Friedrich Max Müller on one occasion. This style was in sharp contrast to works produced in the latter part of the century by the likes of canon Ulick Joseph Bourke or Lady Wilde that insisted on the Iranian roots of ancient Ireland while engaging with the latest theories and methodologies, whether utilizing or challenging them.

The ongoing debate over the etymological derivation of Ireland's name ('Erin') continued to be permeated by assumptions of 'oriental origins' in a range of other works on

Irish history in the second half of the century, among them John O'Hart's previously mentioned popular 1876 *Irish Pedigrees; or, the Origin and Stem of the Irish Nation*, which went through numerous editions:

> THE name "Eiré" became the chief appellation of Ireland. From "Eire" have been derived the names *Eri*, *Eiriu*, *Eirin*, and lastly *Erin*: hence, the inhabitants of Ireland have been denominated, in Irish, *Eirionach* and *Eirionaigh*, Latinized "Erigena," "Erigenᴊ," and "Erinenses." As shown by O'Conor, Keating, and O'Flaherty, "Eria," which is only another form of "Eire," or "Erin," was also an ancient name applied to Egypt, and likewise to the island of Crete in Greece, now called Candia. The origin of the names "Eirin" and "Ierne" has been variously explained by antiquaries. Rochart [sic; Samuel Bochart] and Villaneuva considered that Ierne was derived from the Ph[o]enician words "Iberin" or "Iberne," which signified the most remote bounds or habitations, as Ireland was then the most remote part of the known world; and Rochart [sic] was of opinion, that, as the Greeks did not visit Ireland in those early ages, they got the name "Ierne" from the Ph[o]enicians—the only people who had intercourse with Ireland in those remote times, and are therefore considered to have given Ireland the name "Ierne," which appears to be derived from the Irish "Eire" or "Eirin." According to Dr. O'Conor, Camden, and others, the name "Eirin" signifies the Western Isle: derived from the Irish "Iar," *the west*, and "in," *an island*, as being the most western isle of Europe. Vallancey supposed "Erin" to be the same as "Iran," the ancient name of Persia; and O'Brien, in his book on the "Round Towers," maintains the same opinion: namely, that "Erin" or "Irin" is the same as "Iran" or Persia, and says that, in the Persian language, it signifies the *sacred land*, and that it got this name from the colony of Tua-De-Danans who came to Ireland from Iran or Persia; and it may be observed that the old Irish historians state that Ireland got the name "Eire" from one of the Danan queens. Charles O'Conor, in his "Dissertations," considers that "Eire" or "Eri" was derived from *Erithnea*, the name of the country of the Erithneans, who were Ph[o]enicians, and a colony of whom came to Ireland. Others derive "Ierne" from the Greek "Ieros," sacred, and "nesos," *an island*, thus signifying the sacred isle, the same as the Insula Sacra of the Roman writers. According to old Irish annalists, Egypt was anciently called "Eria," which is only another form of the word "Eire" or "Erin."[6]

Edmond O'Donovan and the Continued Allure of Oriental Theories of Irish Origins in the Late Nineteenth Century

In connection with Iran-centered assumptions of Ireland's oriental roots, Keane, Henry O'Brien, L.C. Beaufort, Vallancey, or the likes of Lady Wilde later in the century, relied entirely on textual accounts of Iran. Unlike them, Edmond O'Donovan, who made only passing comments on the potential oriental origins of the Irish, made his assertion based on personal observations while traveling through Iran. Edmond (also spelled "Edmund") O'Donovan (1844–83) happened to be the best-known Irish nationalist traveler to Iran in the nineteenth century, with an extensively documented account of his visit to that country in his published travel narrative. He was a journalist and war correspondent for the *Daily News* (London) and would be killed in the Sudan while covering the anti-British and anti-Egyptian "Mahdist" uprising there in 1883. The son of the preeminent Irish antiquarian John O'Donovan (d.1861), Edmond O'Donovan was a member of the Irish Republican Brotherhood (IRB), having been detained by

British authorities prior to traveling to Iran. He arrived in Iran in late 1880, following an adventuresome journey through Central Asian provinces of the Russian Empire, where, according to O'Donovan, he was held captive for a few months by the Turkmen tribes of Merv on suspicion of espionage. He traveled through northern Iran, including Tehran, until early 1881.[7] O'Donovan's account of his travels through Russian territories, Iran, and then the Ottoman Empire was published as the two-volume *The Merv Oasis* (1882). With abundant boastful passages describing his adventures and courage, the book provided detailed descriptions of the topography, towns, local produce, peoples, and cultural practices in the territories he passed through, as well as of historical sites, local and frontier politics, and such particulars as the raids into Iranian territory by Turkmen tribes (spelled "Turcoman" in the book) situated on the Russian side of the Russo-Iranian frontier (as distinct from Iran's own Turkmen population), for the purpose of capturing women for ransom, as forced wives, or for enslavement. These descriptions were primarily disparaging of *contemporary* 'oriental' peoples, cultures, and dominant religious practices, including O'Donovan's observations of the Shi'i Muslim *taziyeh* passion plays.[8] Later in the century O'Donovan was repeatedly cited by no less an emerging authority on Iran as the British George Nathaniel Curzon (a Conservative imperialist MP and later a Viceroy of British India). In the first volume of his 1892 two-volume *Persia and the Persian Question,* Curzon referred to O'Donovan as an earlier traveler to Iran from the United Kingdom who had provided valuable observations and "whose literary accomplishments equal those of any other writer on Persia."[9]

As noted before, O'Donovan's father, John, had belonged to George Petrie's coterie in the controversy during the 1830s–50s surrounding the origins of Ireland's Round Towers. Edmond O'Donovan, while earlier sharing his father's and Petrie's designation of Ireland's Round Towers as indisputably Christian ecclesiastical edifices, was nonetheless taken by the allure of oriental theories of Irish origins as he journeyed through Iran, including his speculation that the Round Towers might, after all, be modeled after oriental prototypes. This is evident from his conflicting published commentaries on a number of structures he observed in Iran that seemingly resembled the Round Towers, as well as his other occasional statements in *The Merv Oasis*. In one case, while relating the scenery near Damghan ("Damkhan") in northeastern Iran, and relying on the church/mosque functional analogy, he alluded to Petrie's position that, whether or not churches in the vicinity of Ireland's Round Towers had survived, the Round Towers had once been part of larger ecclesiastical complexes. O'Donovan observed "two lofty *minars*, or minarets, as they are more commonly styled in the West. One of them was close by my road, so that I had an opportunity of examining it with a little attention as I passed." Coming across other such minarets during his travels, O'Donovan added:

> [...] I mention this fact chiefly because my servant told me that in the more southerly provinces, as Yezd there were exactly similar buildings of a date long antecedent to the rise of Mahomedanism [i.e., Islam]. What truth may be in his statement I had no means of ascertaining, but the Damkhan minar is unquestionably Mahomedan. During the archaeological discussions on the Irish 'Round Towers,' which excited such attention some forty years ago, much stress was laid on the reported existence of 'fire towers' in Persia similar to the Irish buildings. General Vallancey, in the last century, first called attention to the matter, and

argued that the Irish towers were erected by sun worshippers with the same purpose as the Persian towers had been by the Guebres [i.e., Zoroastrian] before the advent of Mahomed. The Persian tower which I saw was most certainly a Mahomedan minar, [t]hough the mosque attached, being built of sun-dried bricks, might easily be destroyed, and thus leave the tower standing alone, perhaps to puzzle future generations of archaeologists.[10]

While on the one hand supporting Petrie's position on the Christian ecclesiastical origin of the Round Towers, O'Donovan was clearly astonished by what he considered as remarkable resemblance between some of the Iranian minarets and the Round Towers, exhibiting sporadic reservation about Petrie's theory. Toward the end of the first volume of *The Merv Oasis*, O'Donovan described the holiest Shi'i center of pilgrimage in Iran, the shrine of Imam Reza in the northeastern city of Mashhad, which immensely fascinated him. He mentioned a few of the mosques in the compound, in addition to the main Gowharshad mosque (constructed in 1418), noting among them "one evidently very ancient mosque, whose name I have not been able to make out, which, as it stands, is a good specimen of Persian mismanagement and neglect." He then commented on a minaret standing some distance away from all the existing mosques, the underlying implication of which was his *reservation* about the presumed connection between mosques and the minarets and, hence, also between church structures and the Round Towers in Ireland as claimed by Petrie:

> Close alongside this mosque is a minar [i.e., minaret] of very rich appearance, built entirely of enamelled bricks, some placed obliquely with the others so as to form ornamental designs. This tower is completely detached from the main building, is perfectly plain in outline, and tapers slightly towards the summit. It is from seventy to eighty feet in height, and, in its form and isolation from the mosque itself, forcibly reminded me of the Irish round towers. In fact, take away the colour, it was similar to the old tower of Kildare.[11]

Even though the tower in Kildare stands in proximity to a church, in this architectural comparison O'Donovan was suggesting the possibility of minarets having existed as autonomous structures prior to later construction of mosques next to many of them and/or the incorporation of the earlier architectural design of minarets into the designs of mosque complexes at some later point. However, he glossed over the topic of whether the minaret in question might have been constructed in pre-Islamic times (i.e., pre-seventh century) or may, at least, have been architecturally modeled after earlier pre-Islamic Iranian edifices. Nor did he address whether historically it was in Iranian or other now-Muslim territories that mosques with minarets had first appeared. Given O'Donovan's comparison between the minaret in Mashhad and the Round Tower of Kildare, any imputed ancient cultural-aesthetic connection between Ireland and the Orient would have had to occur in much earlier times than the advent of Islam in the seventh century, or of even the introduction of Christianity in Ireland in the fifth century. He was clearly unaware that the earliest structure at the shrine of Imam Reza in Mashhad only dates to the ninth century CE, with subsequent reconstructions and additions made under Ghaznavid, Seljuk, Ilkhanid, Timurid and later dynasties.

On other occasions in the book, O'Donovan displayed even greater susceptibility to the lure of oriental theories of Ireland's ancient past. Among the similarities he deduced between Iran and Ireland was that of a game he observed being played in Iran: "I have seen the elder boys playing at 'hockey,' or 'hurling,' as it is called in Ireland, just in the same way that it is played at home."[12] Although O'Donovan did not specify to which Iranian game he was alluding, traditional "indigenous" Irish sports were at the time regarded in Irish nationalist circles (cultural and/or political) in both Ireland and in the Irish diaspora as a key cultural ingredient of Irish national identity. The Gaelic Athletic Association was founded in Ireland in 1884, a year after O'Donovan's death, to actively and systematically promote these Irish sports and to standardize their rules. Earlier in the book, O'Donovan had already remarked on what in his view were other inexplicable similarities between the Orient and Ireland, fleetingly dabbling in pseudo-philological conjectures and comparative racial taxonomy. Describing the Yomut Turkmen tribe (even though Turkmens are a population group that even then was considered non-Persian and non-Aryan in the European racial nomenclature), and confounding Turkish, Arabic, and Persian words, O'Donovan wrote in his own Vallanceyan style:

> There is nothing known to Western Europeans to which I could compare a Turcoman village, save, perhaps, those collections of beehives one sees along the Spanish shore of the Bidassoa. A *kibitka* is exactly like an enormous beehive, and one is exactly like another. They are in reed and felt what the 'beehive houses' in stone are in the remnants of ancient Celtic architecture. *A propos* of Turcomans and Celts, there seems a curious resemblance between the name of the individual from which that of the village is taken, and a similar patronymic at home [i.e., Ireland]. Hassan-Kouli (Ghouli) means 'the servant of Hassan,' just as Easterns style themselves 'servant of God,' 'of Mohammed,' or 'of Ali,' that is, according to some authorities. Some say the 'Ghouli' means a lake. In Scotland we have the word gillie—a servant; and in Ireland the name 'Giola Patrick,' i.e., 'the servant of St. Patrick.' I do not know what philologists will say to this. My attention was drawn to it by the wonderful resemblance of the inhabitants to those of the west of Ireland. The physiognomy is the same, and the military attitude and humoristic tendencies of both races are strikingly similar. The independent clan organisation and the elective system of choosing the chief form other points of resemblance, and the nomadic shepherd life is similar to that of the early inhabitants of the Celtic districts of the British Isles.[13]

Unaware that "Ghouli" ("gouli" in actuality) was the truncated Turkish form of the Arabic "gholām" (servant), and further confusing that term with the Turkish word "gol" for pool or pond, O'Donovan was here comparing a Turkish (i.e., not Indo-European) abbreviated form of an Arabic (i.e., Semitic) term that in its original form sounded nothing like "gillie" or 'Giola.' In the second volume of the book, O'Donovan remarked:

> Near the Nadir Tepé [in Iran] is an ancient tomb held in high veneration. At different points within view of this tomb are cairns of stones, each passer-by adding one as a salute to it, saying salaam, as the expression is. A similar tribute is paid to an ancient lignum vitæ tree not far off, and in its case the peasants also attach a fragment of their dresses to the sacred tree. In the Kurd districts of Anatolia I have noticed a similar custom, which forcibly

reminded me of the practice of the Irish peasants of the south and west in the vicinity of holy wells.[14]

These passing observations in O'Donovan's book were yet further reminder of the persisting allure of oriental theories of Irish origins in the late nineteenth century and beyond.

Digression: Other Irish Travelers in Iran in the Nineteenth Century

The Irish nationalist journalist Edmond O'Donovn was among the growing number of Irish travelers to Iran during the century, some of whom left behind published records of their sojourn to that country. The very first recorded traveler from Ireland to have reached 'Iranian' territory appears to have been "Brother James of Ireland" who accompanied the Bohemian Franciscan monk Odoric of Venetia in the early fourteenth century through the Mongol-controlled Ilkhanate state that ruled over former Iranian territories (much of which had been ruled by non-Iranian Arab-Muslim empires in one form or another since the seventh century).[15] After the start of the nineteenth century, a number of Irish men and women traveled to Iran; a few among them publishing descriptions of that country. Compared to European and American travelers to some of Iran's neighboring territories during the nineteenth century (i.e., the southern regions of the Russian Empire, the Ottoman Empire, or British India), markedly fewer European/Western travelers visited Iran. There was nonetheless a rapid increase in the number of these travelers by the middle of the century, including visitors from Ireland. Not counting the Irish in the ranks of invading British 'Indian' imperial forces during the 1838 and 1856–57 Anglo-Iranian wars, Irish travelers and residents in Iran included diplomatic staff of the British consular service in Iran, other personnel attached to the consular service, including medical staff such as the Irish-Armenian William Cormick born in Iran (see below), or members of British consular guards, among them Francis Hopkins who in 1835 was briefly attached to the suite of the British representative to Iran, Henry Ellis.[16] There were a number of Irish among the occasional 'British' military advisers engaged by the Iranian state, as well as rare soldiers of fortune serving in the Iranian army, such as Archibald Fitzgerald in the 1820s–30s (see below), or in the ranks of military retinues of British envoys to Iran. For instance, those accompanying the Scottish Sir John Malcolm during his third mission to Iran in 1810 as the representative of the Governor-General of British India included the 17th Dragoons of the English East India Company under Malcolm's command, "who were all (with the exception of one man) from Ireland."[17] Other Irish military personnel of the Indian Army under Malcolm's command included the Anglo-Irish Lieutenant Henry Pottinger of County Down, Ireland, who conducted a military survey of south-western interior of Iran incognito in 1810–11 (along with a British officer Captain Charles Christie).[18] Other Irish travelers to Iran included Christian missionaries (chiefly Anglican), as in the case of Rev. Robert Bruce of the Church Missionary Society and his wife Emily in the 1870s, and individuals with commercial interest in the country or the staff of 'British'-owned commercial enterprises in Iran, as well as the occasional adventurous voyagers and/

or orientalists, journalists, employees of the British-owned Indo-European Telegraph Department later in the century—with the majority of these travelers being men, some accompanied by their wives and/or families—, as well as maids or male attendants employed by the wealthier British and Irish traveling through or residing in Iran. In addition to the few Irish visitors to Iran who published their travel narratives, there were also those, as in the case of William Ouseley, who composed historical, geographical, literary, and other accounts of Iran and/or translated into English 'Iranian' literary and other texts from the original Persian or Arabic. Persian language—by no means limited to the use of Persian in Iran only at the time, since Persian was also used in Afghanistan, Central Asia, India, and parts of the Caucasus, among other locations—was taught at Trinity College (University of Dublin) after the seventeenth century, with Dublin being a leading center in the British Isles of knowledge-production about Iran in the eighteenth and nineteenth centuries. Among other range of 'Iran'-related works, translations into other European languages of historical accounts of Iran, originally written in Persian or Arabic, and of Persian literature and poetry were also available to Irish readers conversant in those other European languages (as noted already in Chapter Three in connection with James Clarence Mangan's reliance on German translations).[19]

Among better known Irish travelers and residents in Iran were the likes of the Anglo-Irish Sir Gore Ouseley (born in Limerick), who served as the first permanent British ambassador to the Qajar court from 1811 to 1814. Setting out for Tehran in 1810 and reaching southern Iran in early spring of 1811, he was accompanied by his brother, the famed orientalist Sir William Ouseley, who served as Sir Gore's secretary, as well as by Sir Gore's wife Harriet Georgina Whitelock and their infant daughter Janie. Lady Ouseley gave birth to another daughter, Eliza Shirin, soon after reaching southern Iran after their long sea voyage, before setting out for Tehran on an arduous overland journey. While Eliza Shirin died a few months later, the Ouseley's also had a son during their stay in Iran (Wellesley Abbas).[20] William Ouseley, born in Wales, was already a renowned orientalist with a particular focus on Persian literature and Iranian history, while Sir Gore was also something of an orientalist himself, if not of the same degree of expertise and stature as his younger brother.[21] Other early nineteenth-century wide-ranging examples of Irish residents in Iran include John Cormick of County Tipperary. An employee of the English East India Company, he arrived in Iran in 1810. He was later appointed special physician to the Iranian crown prince Abbas Mirza and married an Armenian woman, dying in Iran in 1833. His son William (born in Iran), received medical training in England and was attached as a medical officer to the British legation in Tehran and subsequently served as a doctor to the crown prince Nasser al-Din.[22] Between late December 1834 and March 1835, the young George Henry Moore—a future founding member of the Catholic Defence Association (1851) and later also an Independent Irish Party MP, and father of George A. Moore, the prominent late nineteenth- to early twentieth-century Irish Literary Revival playwright and author—traveled to Tabriz and then to Tehran from Russia, and was evidently given an audience by Fath Ali Shah.[23] Reportedly, sometime in the late 1820s or the early 1830s the Irish mercenary adventurer Archibald Fitzgerald briefly joined the Iranian army (although not much is known of Fitzgerald's stay in Iran). Having previously served in the Irish

Brigade of the Spanish Army (Regiment of Hibernia), he was later killed while fighting in the 1841 Santa Fe Expedition aimed at annexing northern parts of Mexico for incorporation into the territory of the Republic of Texas (itself already annexed from Mexico).[24] Arthur MacMurrough Kavanagh, from a recently converted Irish Protestant landowning family in County Carlow and a future Conservative MP, traveled through Iran on his way to British India, where he entered the service of the English East India Company. An inexhaustible traveler, notwithstanding his severe physical disability since birth, he was accompanied on his Iranian journey from late 1849 to late 1850 by his brother Tom, the Rev. David Wood, and a servant (the latter sent back to Ireland mid-journey due to ill health).[25] Kavanagh, amply prone to grandiose hyperbole, was clearly no fan of the celebrated Irish nationalist poet Thomas Moore. Without any allowance for either poetic imagination or the fact that the fictional 'Iranian' settings in Moore's *Lalla Rookh* belonged to almost a millennium earlier, Kavanagh noted in his diary after departing Bushire in southern Iran for Bombay in India on December 26, 1850:

> Passed the island of Ormuz before sunset, about which Moore has written such a false description, as he has of all Persia. The remains of the town and fort were barely visible, and all that could be seen of the island were a series of concave mounds, composed of divers[e] coloured sands and soil, which looked more like the production of some submarine volcanic eruption than the lovely and flourishing island described in *Lalla Rookh*.[26]

Other than the Ouseleys, among the more famous Irish visiting and/or residing in Iran in the nineteenth century were the already-noted Justin Sheil and his wife Mary Leonora Sheil (née Woulfe), both of them from prominent Catholic families in Ireland. Justin Sheil was the British envoy to Iran from 1844 to 1849 and the British minister in that country from 1849 to 1853, having served in different capacities in Iran since 1833—first as an employee of the English East India Company and then in the British diplomatic service. He married Mary Woulfe in Ireland in 1847 while on leave, after which they set out for Iran accompanied by three Irish attendants, two of them maids.[27] Lady Sheil's *Glimpses of Life and Manners in Persia* (1856), which was published the same year the Second Anglo-Iranian War broke out, was the first published book-length account of a residence in Iran written by a woman not only from the United Kingdom but from Europe/the West in general. The first Persian translation of Lady Sheil's book appeared more than a century after the publication of her book, as a condensed serialized 81 part installment by Hussein Aboutorabian in the Tehran newspaper *Ettelā'āt* from December 29, 1980, to May 3, 1981, with some installments of the work by the same translator having appeared earlier in the Tehran periodical *Negin*.[28] As previously mentioned, Justin Sheil was the younger brother of the playwright and prominent O'Connellite nationalist Richard Lalor Sheil, also a co-founder with Daniel O'Connell of the Catholic Association in 1823 and later an Irish nationalist MP, among his other public offices. In the latter decades of the century, Justin and Mary Sheil's son Edward (born in Iran in 1851) joined the Home Rule League and subsequently served as a member of the Home Rule nationalist Irish Parliamentary Party.[29]

Other Irish individuals who played notable commercial, diplomatic, and/or political roles in connection with Iran in the nineteenth century were the Anglican Lynches of County Mayo. Henry Blosse Lynch (d.1873), a naval officer in the service of the English East India Company and subsequently holding diplomatic posts in British India and the Persian Gulf, carried out the negotiations in Paris with the Iranian ambassador that resulted in the March 4, 1857, peace treaty terminating the Anglo-Iranian War of 1856–57. In 1837 Lynch had been conferred the Order of the Lion and the Sun by the Iranian monarch Mohammad Shah (r.1834–48), the highest Iranian order bestowed to non-Iranians for service to the country, in recognition of Lynch's 1836 pioneering of steam navigation from India via the Persian Gulf to the Lower Tigris and Euphrates in the Ottoman Empire. As noted already, in 1861 two of Lynch's brothers, the younger brother Thomas Kerr and the older brother Stephen, co-founded the Euphrates and Tigris Steam Navigation Company serving between the Persian Gulf and British India, with Thomas Kerr appointed the Iranian Consul-General in London in December 1867 and serving also as a member of the Persian Famine Relief Fund committee in London during the Iranian Famine of 1870–72. Thomas Kerr, who was also awarded the Order of the Lion and the Sun, in his case by Nasser al-Din Shah (r.1848–96), was the father of Henry Finnis Blosse Lynch, a partner in Messrs. Lynch Brothers Company. Henry Finnis Blosse Lynch (1862–1913, born in London) expanded the family company far beyond the original steam navigation firm by means of establishing inland commercial enterprises in southern Iran. He secured a concession from the Iranian government in 1890 for the navigation of the Karun River, also in southern Iran, and received a concession from the Bakhtiari chieftains in south-central Iran in 1898 for road construction from the Persian Gulf into Bakhtiari-controlled territories.[30] H. F. B. Lynch later served as a Liberal-Imperialist MP for the constituency of Ripon in Yorkshire, England, and played a central role in the opposition across the United Kingdom to the joint Anglo-Russian intervention in Iranian affairs during the Iranian Constitutional Revolution of 1906–11 (see Chapter Seven).

Ulick Joseph Bourke and the Persistence of the 'Iranian' Theory of Irish Origins in the Second Half of the Nineteenth Century

By the latter decades of the nineteenth century, race and racial categories, specifically with Indo-Europeans/Aryans placed at the apex of the racial hierarchy, had become a key ingredient in Irish and the broader 'Western' scholarly debates on Irish identity, not unlike in debates on English, German, or French identities.[31] These were interlaced cross-territorial dialogical debates, at least in so far as Western Europe (including Ireland) was concerned, without overlooking co-existing constructions, deconstructions, and reconstructions of racial identities by different groups throughout the British Empire and beyond. In the case of Irish constructs of race, as already noted the explicitly Indo-European (or interchangeably "Aryan" or "Caucasian") designations of ancient Irish populations had been in progress as far back as the late eighteenth century, following the rapid dissemination of the racial inflections of so-called Jonesian theory of languages, beginning with Jones himself. This was already evident in some late eighteenth-century Irish antiquarian works, most prominently in Vallancey's writings. By the middle of the nineteenth century, racial designations in Irish historical and literary outputs were occurring in a wide range of contexts, not only in references to Irish or English historical identities, but also in regard to classification of population groups in other parts of the world. A very random example of the extensive absorption of such racial purviews appears in a footnote of Thomas Osborne Davis' celebrated nationalist poem "A Ballad of Freedom," composed in the early 1840s. Relying on the classification of "Caucasian race" by the German Johann Friedrich Blumenbach (d.1840), Davis noted in his condemnation of Russia's annexation of Circassia in the Caucasus that the "Cherkeeses or Abdyes" population of Circassia belonged to the ostensibly superior Caucasian race: "Blumenbach, and other physiologists, assert that the finer European races descend from a Circassian Stock."[32]

Increasingly after the mid-nineteenth century, Irish nationalist commentaries on Ireland's ancient populations operated within the dominant Western European schema of racial hierarchy that placed the Aryans at the top, notwithstanding some continued exceptions to this rule. Whether in the guise of Celticism or other constructs of "Gaelic" origins,[33] racial debates in Ireland most frequently engaged with and incorporated the Aryanist discourse, regarding whether the ancient Gaels and/or other major early population groups of the island had belonged to the so-called Aryan stock. The bottom line here being the often highly racialized modus operandi of commenting on Irish identities and on ancient Ireland in Irish historical and literary works. Included in these debates and commentaries was the topic of the internal gradations of the Aryan racial category itself—ranging from whether some of the earliest Aryan arrivals in European territories from the East had been more advanced civilizationally and, by implication, also racially than other Aryan populations reaching Europe, to whether present-day Western European Aryan groups represented the most historically and civilizationally advanced branch of that racial grouping compared to their kinfolks in the East, or if particular groups of Western European Aryan populations at the time were superior to other Western European Aryan populations, and so on. At the same time, after the second half of the nineteenth century the historical roots of the Aryan race itself, including its original location, came to be ardently contested in Europe, the United States, as well as in Britain's white settlement dominions and in some other parts of the world, including in British India. By the late nineteenth century, these racial theories and debates also resonated in some primarily so-called secular-reformist circles in Iran. This is not to overlook the rejection of Aryanist and/or other hierarchical racial models by various groups around the world.

By the second half of the nineteenth century, the post-Jonesian contestations of the origin of so-called Indo-European/Aryan 'race' had shifted from whether the earliest known Aryans were Indo-Iranian peoples, having originated in the Caucasus or Central Asia, to whether the Aryans had originated in some part of Europe and then spread in different directions, losing their presumable racial purity and/or civilizational aptitude the further east they moved in the direction of what became Indo-Iranian territories. These models alternatively relied on Pre-Darwinian, Darwinian (1859), or post-Darwinian theories of evolution—Darwin's theory gradually gaining wider application in formulations of racial constructs and types by the end of the century, initially in Europe/the West and particularly in the emergent field of anthropology, leaving aside here the Spencerian Social-Darwinist and other such social and political applications of Darwin's theory. The Europe-centered model of Aryan origins, as in the case of the theory of Scandinavian origin of the Aryans, could not be easily reconciled with the biblical Mosaic theory of human origin. Nonetheless, there were adherents of this European theory of Aryan origins who happened to be ordained Christian ministers. For instance, among the most vociferous proponents of the Scandinavian model of Aryan origins in the United Kingdom in the late nineteenth century was the philologist and Anglican canon Isaac Taylor, who maintained the Aryans had originated around Finland and rejected the literariness of the biblical account of post-diluvian population dispersions around the globe, opting instead for evolutionary theory.[34] Meanwhile, the staunchest advocate of the Eastern origin of the Aryans in the United Kingdom in the second half of the century was the German scholar Friedrich Max Müller, professor of comparative philology at Oxford. Müller, whose position was refuted by canon Taylor, claimed a Central Asian origin of the proto Indo-Iranian (Aryan) ancestry. Müller's theory was solidly resounded in many parts of the globe at the time. Similar hypothesis was advanced by the Swiss linguist Adolphe Pictet (d. 1875), and the linguist, archaeologist, and Oxford professor Rev. Archibald Henry Sayce, before he abandoned it in the late 1880s.[35] Ultimately, after the middle of the nineteenth century the dispute over the Asian (whether Caucasian or Central Asian) versus European origin of the Aryans produced new fault lines in debates on the Aryan ancestry of the Gaelic population of Ireland. The contestation over Aryan origins was all the more consequential in light of the mounting emphasis after the middle of the century on the Aryan ancestry of the Gaels in Irish nationalist cultural and/or political circles, which by the end of the century coincided and intersected with the racial "whitening" in the dominant Anglo-centric discourses on race of those Irish who were considered ethnically 'Gaelic' (see below). One of the most resolute Irish proponents of Aryan origins of the Gaels and of the Eastern homeland of the Aryans was canon Ulick Joseph Bourke (1829–87), a Catholic cleric, academic, and a leading authority on Irish language. Despite his eventual break with the stated platform of the nationalist Land League organization during the agrarian agitation in Ireland in 1879 (a.k.a., the "Land War"), Bourke was a well-known moderate political nationalist and a strong advocate of cultural nationalism. He was an instrumental figure in championing the "revival" of Irish language, spearheaded by such organizations as the Society for the Preservation of Irish Language (1876) and the Gaelic Union (1880)—Bourke being a founding member of both organizations—and later in the century by the Gaelic League (1893), founded by Douglas Hyde and Eoin [John] MacNeill.[36]

In his 1875 unambiguously titled *The Aryan Origins of the Gaelic Race and Language*, Bourke claimed philological proof of a direct racial link between the ancient Gaels and the Persians, casting his evidentiary net far and wide. He relied on disputed assertions by the likes of the Swiss linguist Adolphe Pictet, who maintained a linguistic affinity between Gaelic and Sanskrit (i.e., Indo-Iranian languages) as well as the Aryan root of Ireland's name. Bourke also cited recent Sanskrit and Indic studies by Friedrich

Max Müller and his theory of the Aryan race as enumerated, for instance, in Müller's 1861 *Lectures on the Science of Language*. The many other contemporary and past publications on comparative philology enlisted by Bourke in support of his argument included such distinctly contrasting Irish sources as the lectures given by the late Irish philologist and historian Eugene O'Curry (d. 1862) as well as works by Sir William Wilde (d. 1876), and Lady Jane Wilde (discussed below). Pictet, in his 1837 *De l'affinité des langues celtiques avec le sanscrit* (*The Affinity of Celtic Languages with Sanskrit*) and the 1859–63 volumes of *Les origines indo-européennes, ou Les Aryas primitifs: essai de paléontologie linguistique* (*The Origins of Indo-Europeans, or the Primitive Aryans: Essay on Paleontology*), had insisted (erroneously) on the connection between Ireland's name (Éire) and the word "*arya*" (with its various "substantive" meanings avowedly including "'well-born, worthy of respect,' 'lord'") and (wrongly) alleged that Éire, similar to "Irán," was a cognate of *arya*. Pictet also claimed "the Irish [...] were probably the first tribe which detached itself from the ancient Arian [sic] stem to migrate towards the West."[37] Bourke, asserting the purportedly linguistic proof that directly linked ancient Ireland *racially* as well as *culturally* to the East, including ancient 'Iran,' provided a considerable list of those he considered as leading authorities in the field of linguistics in recent decades whose views substantiated his theory. A partial list of these authorities, which was intended to underscore Bourke's adhesion to the latest historical and linguistic methods, in contradistinction with the former antiquarian style of Vallancey, Henry O'Brien, and the like, is worth quoting in some detail:

> The convincing force of what is to be stated is derived from sources of philologic truth not known some fifty years ago. Amongst modern sciences, Comparative Philology has, owing to German scholars, made wonderful strides in the onward march of scientific progress.
>
> Comparative philology, as a science, has not yet seen a complete century roll by. It is only in its infancy, and yet it has effected much. It has shewn, at least, that the early Irish races were of Aryan origin.
>
> The language spoken and written to this day by the Gaels of Ireland, and of the Highlands of Scotland, clearly proves the great fact that the Irish people are from the East. The scholarship of such professors and teachers as Max Müller and Pritchard [sic], in England; Professors Blackie and Geddes, of Scotland; of such German linguists as Zeuss, Bopp, and Ebel; of Swiss savants, like Pictet, Geneva; and Italian litterateurs, like Chevalier Nigra, ambassador at the French Court, and learned antiquarian, make it certain. Our homescholars [sic]—those amongst them who are distinguished for antiquarian research, or for their proficiency in the science of language—admit the same truth. Pre-eminent amongst those are W.K. Sullivan, formerly professor in the Catholic University, and at present Rector of the Queen's College, Cork; Sir William Wilde, Dr. Stokes, the late Dr. O'Donovan, and Mr. O'Curry.
>
> The great objection hitherto against the opinion that the Round Towers are of Pagan origin is, that our Pagan progenitors had not, they say, as far as can be known, knowledge or skill and practical power to erect such superstructures. [...] This objection fades away under the increased knowledge which the light derived from the science of compare[a]tive philology sheds on the early history of the Irish race. The early Irish were Aryan, therefore they were a race possessed of skill and power to erect those Towers.

> [...]
> The language of Ireland, then, has come to the rescue to settle this vexed question of the early origin of the Pillar Towers of Ireland.
> (2) The argument receives additional force from the similarity of style that exists between the architecture of Round Towers and that displayed in the Cyclopian buildings in the East, in Pers[e]polis, Ecbatana, and in Babylon, as far as can be known; in Thebes and in the pyramids along the Nile. ...
> [...] But the Round Towers of Ireland present, in the slanting door-way, in the style of arch, in the material used, in the cement, in the shape and size of stones, and in the manner in which they are laid, architectural features which are nowhere to be found, except in the Cyclopian edifices of the earliest historic period. [...]³⁸

Bourke, repeatedly stressed the "Irish race" had originated in 'Iran' ("Persia"), writing:

> If we admit Mr. Pictet's conclusions all the branches of the Aryan race carried with them, as they migrated from the original home, a knowledge of the arts and sciences and a knowledge of letters. The Romans, Kelts, Greeks, Germans, and [Slavs], all alike, had in early times a knowledge of letters, consequently the early inhabitants of Eire, who were the first colony that had left the cradle of the family in Persia, had, from the start, a knowledge of learning and of letters. [...] No one nation borrowed in the primary al period a knowledge of learning or of rudimentary letters from another. Hence the early Irish did not borrow from the Ph[o]enicians, nor the primeval Greeks from the Phoenicians.³⁹

However, Bourke's attempt to distance himself from the Vallanceyan-style legacy of Irish antiquarianism and his reliance on such philological authorities as Müller, Pictet, or the Scottish linguist and professor of Greek at Aberdeen University, William Duguid Geddes, did not shield Bourke from innuendos "that the Vallancey school is [...] flourishing."⁴⁰

Notwithstanding his references to Eugene O'Curry and John O'Donovan, Bourke countered Petrie's supposition of the relatively recent origin of Ireland's Round Towers (i.e., Christian era), which was shared by O'Curry and O'Donovan. Bourke noted:

> Dr. Petrie has asked—"Does it follow as a logical sequence, because the early Persian race had towers, which, probably were fire temples, that, therefore, towers in Ireland, which are not unlike those in Persia, were fire-temples?["] The only answer to that question is—By no means. No logical sequence can result from a mere accidental resemblance. Mere resemblance does not prove identity of origin, of kind, or sameness of purpose, or of end.
> Dr. Petrie, and those who adopt his views, must, in turn, be asked, does it follow, because the arguments of Dr. O'Conor and of General Vallancey have been refuted, that, therefore, the thesis proposed by them is without convincing proof? The trisection of a given arch is true in fact; in theory, without proof. Again does it follow, logically, that Dr. Petrie is right, if Dr. O'Conor and Vall[ancey] are not? By no means.⁴¹

Incidentally, the first volume of Pictet's *Les origines indo-européennes* had appeared the same year as Charles Darwin's *The Origin of Species*, which substantially impacted the ongoing debates not only on monogenesis versus polygenesis theories in general, but also the studies on so-called racial origins of Ireland's early inhabitants. Bourke, unlike canon Taylor, denounced Darwin's evolutionary theory as "infidel views,"[42] and strictly adhered to the Mosaic theory, noting that all Aryans, including the ancient Gaels as part of the broader Celtic ("Keltic") peoples, belonged to the Japhetic branch of Noah's descendants.[43] Kevin Whelan has mentioned in passing that Bourke belonged to "a generation of Catholic clergy who systematically rewrote Irish history."[44] To this end, Bourke, a fervent enthusiast of Irish language, selectively relied on the latest developments in philology. An overlooked feature of Bourke's assertion of Ireland's civilizational eminence in ancient times, particularly given his standing in the Catholic Church and his staunch defense of the Mosaic account contra evolutionary theories, was his underlying acknowledgment of Ireland's pre-Christian (i.e., 'pagan') cultural splendor. In his 1887 *Pre-Christian Ireland*, Bourke continued to stress Ireland's ancient 'Eastern' ties, most notably the Persian-Aryan connection. By then, he had co-founded the Gaelic Union. In *Pre-Christian Ireland*, as in his earlier book, Bourke recurrently cited Sir William Wilde among the leading scholars of Irish antiquity, and referred to Lady Wilde's works, including her assertion in the 1860s that the 'Keltic' art of illumination and '*ornamentation*' were derived from Eastern traditions, as in the case of '*Hindu Temples*.'[45] In *Pre-Christian Ireland*, Bourke also continued to insist on the inadequacy of the conclusion reached about the Round Towers by Petrie and other proponents of the Christian-era origin of the towers.[46] This was indicative of the still unsettled subject of the towers in Irish historical writing by the end of the century, even if Petrie's position was clearly on the ascendance.

The *Wilde Wilde* Iran: The Ancient Iran of Lady Jane Francesca Agnes Wilde

Indisputably, the most ardent proponent of Ireland's ancient ties to Iran in the latter part of the nineteenth century was the folklorist Lady Jane Francesca Agnes Wilde. Lady Wilde had her fierce critics and vehement supporters. Douglas Hyde, the prominent cultural-nationalist, leading promoter of Irish language at the time, and an eminent and methodical folklorist of Ireland, took serious issue with Lady Wilde's approach and conclusions. Hyde criticized Lady Wilde's lack of familiarity with the Irish language and her failure to disclose the sources and provenance of the tales and legends in her collected volumes. He also noted it was impossible to distinguish in Lady Wilde's publications between the actual lores still circulating in parts of Ireland and her own interpretations and recreations of those lores: "We do not know what is Lady Wilde's and what is not."[47] Of the far-reaching methodological disparity in folklore studies between Lady Wilde and Douglas Hyde, John Wilson Foster has noted that, among other range of differences, Hyde employed both diachronic and synchronic examination "of motifs, tale types, variants, and narrative structures" of folklore. Foster adds that, by following the methodological approach of the prominent English Celticist Alfred Trübner Nutt, "Hyde is among the first of the Irish folklorists to attempt a distinction between originally native and non-native elements in Irish folklore."[48]

On the other hand, another leading cultural-nationalist engaged in Irish folklore and mythology, the poet William Butler Yeats, was among the most enthusiastic admirers of Lady Wilde's studies and her published compilations of Irish folklore. According to Yeats, she possessed a prodigious ability for weaving together national identity, poetic imagination, and the folk culture of ordinary people.[49] The young Yeats in his 1888 edited volume of *Fairy and Folk Tales of the Irish Peasantry* reproduced "The Black Lamb," "The Horned Women," "The Priest's Soul," and "The Demon Cat" from Lady Wilde's 1887 *Ancient Legends, Mystic Charms, and Superstitions of Ireland*, and relied on Wilde's unique elucidations of certain folk traditions, while acclaiming her book "the best" on the subject since publications by Thomas Crofton Croker (d.1854).[50] In his 1892 collection of Irish fairytales, Yeats, who incidentally also attended Lady Wilde's literary salons, included yet another tale that had appeared in Lady Wilde's *Ancient Legends*. Yeats, in acknowledging Lady Wilde and other leading contemporary authorities on Irish folklore from whose works he had reproduced a number of tales in his 1892 collection—the others being Douglas Hyde, Standish O'Grady, and the academic historian Patrick Weston Joyce—noted: "I have to thank Lady Wilde for leave to give 'Seanchan the Bard' from her *Ancient Legends of Ireland* [sic] (Ward and Downey), the most poetical and ample collection of Irish folklore yet published."[51] Yeats had earlier written a sympathetic review of Lady Wilde's 1890 *Ancient Cures, Charms, and Usages of Ireland. Contributions to Irish Lore*, notwithstanding his lament that the material appearing in *Ancient Cures* should have "been better and more scientifically treated." He remarked that "no one," save Douglas Hyde, "may some day [sic] surpass" Lady Wilde's collection of "Irish folk-lore."[52] According to Sinéad Garrigan Mattar, Yeats preferred an "anti-scientific" approach to folklore studies, even though "Yeats could employ scientific methods as a weapon [...] when he wanted to."[53] Conspicuously, in none of his observations on Lady Wilde's two books did Yeats allude to Wilde's theory of Irish origins and her alleged Iranian roots of some of Ireland's oldest folk beliefs and practices. In fact, Yeats rejected the common Irish historical practice of tracing Irish origins back to "the primeval races, Fomorians, Tuatha dé Dannans, Milesians and the rest mentioned in *The Book of Invasions*,"[54] which is not to say he rejected oriental theories of Irish origins (see below).

Lady Wilde (1821(?)–96; née Elgee; a.k.a., "Jane Francesca," "John Fanshawe Ellis," "Speranza"/"Speranza of *The Nation*," and "Ugo Bassi")[55] was of Anglo-Irish descent, even though she also claimed Italian ancestry. Regrettably, best remembered nowadays as the mother of Oscar Wilde than for her own accomplishments, she was a well-known poet, author, feminist, nationalist, antiquarian, and, later in life, a socialite host of celebrated cultural salons. While still surnamed Elgee prior to marriage, she had been a fervent Young Ireland nationalist in the 1840s and a contributor after 1847 to the Young Ireland weekly *The Nation* (Dublin, 1842–48). By her own account, following a conservative Anglo-Irish upbringing, she had embraced the nationalist platform of Young Ireland after reading (evidently the 1843 first edition of) the *Spirit of the Nation*, a collection of Young Ireland poetry by the likes of Thomas Osborne Davis, Richard D'Alton Williams (a.k.a., "Shamrock of *The Nation*"), and others. Starting in 1847, she began submitting poems to *The Nation* under her best known alias 'Speranza,' while signing her letters-to-the-editor "John Fanshawe Ellis."[56] In this respect, she was following in the footsteps of other contemporary Irish nationalist women engaged in political journalism, such as the radical nationalist Ellen Mary Patrick Downing ("Mary of *The Nation*"), who wrote ballads and other works for *The Nation* between 1845 and 1848.[57]

In early July 1848, the editor of *The Nation* Charles Gavan Duffy was arrested as part of an operation by the authorities for rounding up those considered radical republican nationalists ahead of the suspected planned uprising by the militant wing of Young Ireland. Following Duffy's arrest, Jane Elgee (the future Lady Wilde) briefly served as a co-editor of *The Nation* along with Margaret Callan (née Hughes), Duffy's sister-in-law and cousin, before the paper was finally suppressed by the authorities—coincidentally on the very same day as the bungled Young Ireland uprising of July 29 in the midst of the Great Famine. The government's closure of *The Nation* was occasioned by a long unsigned editorial written by Elgee under the caption "Jacta est Alea" in the July 29 issue, calling on "the whole Irish Nation" to take up arms and overthrow English rule. In connection with "Jacta est Alea," it should be mentioned Elgee too deployed the myth of Thermopylae as an analogy for the Irish nationalist struggle, as had Thomas Davis and some other Young Irelanders earlier. This anonymous editorial was used as further evidence by state prosecutors against Duffy, despite public attempts by Elgee to establish her authorship of the piece in Duffy's defense.[58] These developments marked the end of Elgee's overtly political Irish nationalist writing for a few decades. She returned to the subject directly again in connection with her studies of Irish folklore in the 1880s, while having only indirectly alluded to the Irish nationalist struggle in her 1857 narrative poem *Ugo Bassi: A Tale of the Italian Revolution*, published under the pen name Speranza, by which time she was known as Mrs. Wilde following her marriage. The title of the latter work referred to the Italian priest from the Cisalpine Republic and a follower of Giuseppe Garibaldi's Italian unification campaign, who was executed in 1849. As already noted she had earlier adopted 'Ugo Bassi' as one of her many noms de plume. Later in life, Lady Wilde's nationalist writing focused chiefly on cultural commentary, but was not devoid of passing political statements. These scattered forays into nationalist politics also appeared in her two monographs on Irish folk culture, as in the section on "Our Ancient Capital" in the second volume of her 1887 *Ancient Legends* or the sections on "Irish Minstrelsy" and "The American Irish" in the 1890 *Ancient Cures*, among other examples. Later in life she was also active in the political arena of women's rights in the United Kingdom, ranging from her endorsement of women's property rights[59] to the campaign for women's suffrage, in the form of extending the 1884 Household Manhood Suffrage to adult women of property.[60] Incidentally, Lady Wilde also attended at least one meeting of the East India Association in London, during the May 18, 1883, presentation by Henry George Keene on "Liberal Principles in India." The Association was founded by Dadabhai Naoroji in 1866 to promote Indian participation in British administration of India and social reforms.[61] Lady Wilde's earliest publications on folklore were in the form of articles appearing after the late 1870s in periodicals such as the *Dublin University Magazine*.[62] In the interim between her collaboration with *The Nation* in the 1840s and her later studies of folklore, she engaged in translations of various works and published a number of book reviews. Her writings on Irish folklore after the 1870s had an unmistakably cultural-nationalist attribute, largely unacknowledged by her biographers and other commentators.

In 1851, she married the prominent Anglo-Irish ophthalmologist, antiquarian, and folklorist Dr. William Robert Wills Wilde (1815–76) and came to be known as "Lady" Wilde following her husband's knighthood in 1864. William Wilde was the author, among other publications, of the 1852 *Irish Popular Superstitions*, which he dedicated to his wife ("To Speranza").[63] This book, along with William's published 1874 lecture on the subject and his vast collection of unpublished related material, served as Lady Wilde's main sources when composing her own works on Irish folklore following her husband's death. By the early decades of the nineteenth century, among other range of influences (including some earlier antiquarian studies), the Romantic nationalism of the Prussian Johann Gottfried von Herder, with its emphasis on the uniqueness of every nation, was also instrumental in directing Irish nationalist interest to folk traditions and practices—as yet another benchmark of Ireland's distinctive 'national' culture and identity formation. The broader absorption of Herder's views on nation and history were already long evident in Irish nationalist circles, being among the many ideological inspirations for the United Irishmen uprisings of 1798 and 1803 and present in the poetry of Thomas Moore and James Clarence Mangan, among others. In conjunction with this "Herder Effect,"[64] folklore studies itself, having similarly originated during the eighteenth-century European Enlightenment, had become more broadly part and parcel of Irish nationalist discourses by the middle of the nineteenth century. Although the English term 'folklore' was only coined in 1846 by William John Thoms (a.k.a., "Ambrose Merton"),[65] from the 1820s to the 1840s a distinct systematic field of folklore studies took shape in the United Kingdom, beginning with the first English translation from German by Edgar Taylor in 1823 of Jacob and Wilhelm Grimm's fairytales. Early pioneers of concerted compilation and analyses of Ireland's folklore included Thomas Crofton Croker (1798–1854), whose anonymously published *Fairy Legends and Traditions of the South of Ireland* appeared in 1825.[66] This interest in folk culture was reflected, for instance, in some of the undertakings of the Ordnance Survey under George Petrie's supervision between the 1820s and the 1840s, which included the documentation of local lore. The survey's compilers of Irish folklore included the fraternity of George Petrie, John O'Donovan, and Eugene O'Curry, who turned to folk tales, songs, and popular memories and lore in their effort to retrieve original place names of various localities that were being mapped by the survey, along with collecting corollary information on the persistence or decline of cultural beliefs and practices in those localities.[67] Leading pioneers of folklore studies in Ireland in the mid-nineteenth century included Dr. William Robert Wills Wilde, whose acclaimed 1852 monograph on the topic stemmed from a conscious impulse to record as much of Ireland's folktales, or "folks'-lore" as he called them, before they entirely disappeared. His sense of urgency emanated not only from observation of social transformations, but more immediately and precipitously from to the large-scale mortality caused by the Great Famine and the ensuing large-scale Irish emigration, which affected rural regions most direly:

> When now I enquire after the old farmer who conducted me [...] to the ruined Castle or Abbey, and told me the story of its early history and inhabitants, I hear that he died during the famine. On asking for the peasant who used to sit with me in the ancient Rath, and

recite the Fairy legends of the locality, the answer is: "He is gone to America;" and the old woman who took me to the Blessed Well, and gave me an account of its wonderous cures and charms—"where is she?"—"Living in the Workhouse."⁶⁸

For William Wilde, 'folks'-lore,' along with certain ways of life, which were fast vanishing in the post-1845 famine era Ireland, "were after all, *the poetry of the people*, the bond that knit the peasant to the soil." Moreover, as part of a longer process pre-dating the famine, "The old forms and customs, too, are becoming obliterated; the festivals are unobserved, and the rustic festivities neglected or forgotten." Crediting Petrie, O'Donovan, O'Curry, and others involved in the Ordnance Survey for their compilation and documentation of "great amount of traditional, antiquarian, and topographical information," Wilde noted with despondency that much of that mode of information could no longer be amassed in the aftermath of the famine.[69] Even though the preservation of Irish folklore had not constituted the underlying objective of the Ordnance Survey,[70] its mapping, attempted recovery of former names of localities, and, even more significantly, its archiving of interviews with locals, among other range of information, had serendipitously created a repository of knowledge for posterity on the beliefs and practices that were extensively erased from those very localities by the ravages of the famine not long after the Survey's archiving of the data. The implication of William Wilde's reference to the Survey was that Wilde himself was consciously, and in an even more desperate race against time, attempting to compile similar range of information as significant ratio of Ireland's population had already perished in a matter of a few years and many more were joining the ranks of famine-era and post-famine emigrants. Leaving aside here the fluidity and malleability of all so-called traditions, in Wilde's view the latest large-scale additions to the ranks of diasporic Irish populations were stripping away layers of local Irish folk memory and carrying them along to other lands as transplanted and dislocated traditions; but doing so with a burning hatred of England. Wilde pondered: "has future England more to fear from future [Irish-]America in case of national war, than all the rebellions and agitations which puny Ireland could possibly excite, now or hereafter[?]"[71] This view was later echoed by Lady Wilde in her first book on Irish folklore, *Ancient Legends* (1887):

> The new Ireland across the seas, whether in America or in Australia, will still cherish with sacred devotion the beautiful legends, the pathetic songs, the poetry and history and the heroic traditions of the old, well-loved country as eternal verses of the Bible of humanity; all the light and music of the fanciful fairy period, such as I have tried to gather into a focus in these volumes, along with the holy memories of those martyrs of our race whose names are for ever [sic] associated with the words Liberty and Nationhood, but whose tragic fate has illustrated so many mournful pages in the history of the Irish past.[72]

Both Sir William and Lady Wilde regarded the diasporic Irish communities as potentially the main centers of future potent and militant Irish nationalism, given that a large ratio of the newly hyphenated Irish also took along with them a directly experienced collective memory of the famine and its many traumas, which could be channeled into hatred for England and passed on to next generations (assuming next generations of

Irish-Americans and other similarly hyphenated diasporic Irish communities would continue to be interested in the Irish Question). For Sir William, writing not long after the attenuation of the suffering of the Great Famine, and in the aftermath of the abortive Young Ireland rising of 1848, any prospect of speedy attainment of even the moderate nationalist platform of Home Rule in Ireland itself seemed improbable: "Repeal is dead; its ghost was last seen at Ballingarry [i.e., the central location of the dismally abortive 1848 rising], but vanished in smoke and a flash of fire."[73] For her part, Lady Wilde, writing much later in her 1890 *Ancient Cures*, by which time she was also a proponent of "universal suffrage," declared the "fiction" of Home Rule "now almost extinct." Instead, she pinned her hopes of Irish national salvation on "the American Irish, with their bolder views" of a "Republic."[74]

In the two-and-half-decades after the Great Famine, William Wilde alternated between different accounts of Irish origins and cultural traditions. Methodologically, Sir William's interdisciplinary recourse to the latest scientific standards differed vastly from that of most his predecessors who had grappled with the topic. At the same time, there was a notable theoretical and methodological divide between Sir William's and Lady Wilde's later approach to the subject as well. An extract of a long presentation given by Sir William in 1864 at the Young Men's Christian Association in Dublin, titled "Ireland, Past and Present: The Land and the People,"[75] appeared as a supplementary chapter in the second volume of Lady Wilde's 1887 *Ancient Legends, Mystic Charms, and Superstitions of Ireland*. However, Lady Wilde introduced her late husband's 1864 lecture, now titled "On the Ancient Races of Ireland," as the considerably different 1874 lecture by Sir William, given at the anthropological division of the British Association in Belfast. This could not have been an error and was most likely a deliberate attempt by Lady Wilde to present the 1864 presentation as one of her husband's latest and most scientifically formulated works (given also the marked contrast between the 1864 and 1874 venues). Among other things, this allowed Lady Wilde to sidestep Sir William's gravitation away from a firmly monogenesis stance in 1864 to a polygenesis one by 1874; the latter view contrasting with Lady Wilde's own interpretation in *Ancient Legends*. As opposed to his 1864 presentation, in the 1874 British Association lecture William Wilde avoided discussing "the subject of the single or multiple origin of man."[76] Moreover, in his 1864 paper, similar to Lady Wilde in her 1887 book, William Wilde had maintained: "The sacred writings tell us, and the investigations of historians, antiquarians, and philologists confirm the statement, that the cradle of mankind was somewhere between the Caspian Sea and the great River Euphrates. [...] I may state briefly that the human family separated in process of time into three great divisions—the African, the Asiatic, and the Indo-European."[77] In his 1874 British Association paper, however, Sir William was firmly operating within the field of craniological and polygenesis anthropology in the contested shadow of Darwinian evolutionary theory (1859). In 1874 he was not only still a member of the Royal Irish Academy, but was also the director of the Anthropological Department of the Biological section of the Irish chapter of British Association, and was now relying on the latest (pseudo-)scientific trends in the emergent field of physical and psychological anthropology, including the craniological studies of the Swedish anatomist, polygenesist, and craniometrician Andreas Joannes Retzius (d.1821), as well as the works of the Danish Christian Jürgensen Thomsen (who also formulated the Three Age periodization scheme of Stone, Bronze, and Iron, and had also been a corresponding friend of Petrie). In the 1874 presentation, while still tracing the roots of the Celtic population (inclusive of the Gaels) to the area from the Caspian to the Euphrates, that primal region was now designated as the birthplace of a particular human race only: "that great Aryan or Indo-European race which spread from the Euphrates to the Polar regions." He noted that the Aryan population prior to its migration to Europe by different routes, including North Africa, had been initially "creeping round the shores of the Caspian, the Black Sea and the Mediterranean." Although not focusing on folklore in this presentation, in passing William Wilde noted that aspects Celtic folk traditions and beliefs, including those of Ireland, could be traced back to their original racial ancestry and homeland:

> In tracing the footprints of man we have, as I have already stated, to consider the relics he left in the various countries which he trod, the vestiges of his language, and the physical and psychological characteristics still attaching to his modern representatives. In so doing we must consider the dim traditions, genealogies, heroic and bardic tales, rhymes, legends, religions, popular superstitions, folk-lore, romances, and all that description of knowledge which has been handed down from times denominated Prehistoric to the present day.[78]

Within a year after William Wilde's death in 1876, Lady Wilde had taken up her husband's research on Irish origins and folklore, beginning with an 1877 article in the *Dublin University Magazine*,[79] which came to serve as the preliminary outline of her 1887 *Ancient Legends, Mystic Charms, and Superstitions of Ireland*. In that book, Lady Wilde traced both the origins of the early population of Ireland and of the oldest traditions still extant in Irish folklore to the 'Iranian' homeland of the Aryans, in a much more specific manner than her husband had done, with 'Iran' (in its broadest geographic designation here) identified as the birthplace of humanity in general—in a manner that accorded with both the biblical Mosaic model and pre- and post-Darwinian monogenesis evolutionary theories. Interestingly, she made no mention of William Jones' designation in the previous century of 'Iran' as the birthplace of humanity, following the (otherwise mythical) Iranian historical tradition pre-dating the introduction of Islamic conception of human origins.[80] It should be noted that, similar to her late husband in later years, Lady Wilde herself had earlier briefly veered from a monogenesis stance to a polygenesis one, only to re-embrace monogenesis theory. In her 1877 article in the *Dublin University Magazine*, titled "The Fairy Mythology of Ireland," she had been a proponent of monogenesis theory: "there was once a period when the human family was of one creed and one language. [...] From the beautiful Eden-land at the head of the Persian Gulf, where creeds and culture rose to life, the first migrations emanate."[81] It is not known if Lady Wilde had previously shared the polygenesis position of Sir William during his later years. But, in the interval between the appearance of Lady Wilde's "The Fairy Mythology of Ireland" and the publication of *Ancient Legends* in 1887, she deviated to a polygenesis stance. This was the case in her 1884 *Driftwood from Scandinavia*, which even anticipated an impending race war with the expressed victory of Teutonic and Celtic branches of the Aryan race over the so-called

Turanian and other presumably antithetic races.[82] By the time of writing that book, similar to Sir William in his 1874 lecture, she was an adherent of craniological and racial theories of Retzius, Thomsen, and the like, with 'Iran' (in its broadest territorial sense) and northern regions of the Indian subcontinent designated as the fountainhead of what Retzius had classified the Aryan "Dolicephalous [i.e., "dolichocephalic"] or Iranian races."[83] It is unclear when and why Lady Wilde re-embraced the monogenesis theory of human 'races' between 1884 and the appearance of her *Ancient Legends* in 1887.

Further complicating Lady Wilde's designation of Iran as the original location of human race was that—like many of her contemporaries caught between, and seeking to reconcile, biblical faith and particular current trends in anthropological and evolutionary science—she believed in the existence of both "pre-Adamic" (also appearing as "primitive") and "Adamic" humans. The latter was believed to have populated the earth "extending over six thousand years," while the former, which was believed to have existed for millions of years, had eventually died out.[84] Of the various proponents of alternative theories of both pre-Adamites and Adamites, she was at least familiar with the works of the English biologist St. George Jackson Mivart (d. 1900), who also maintained Adam had been born, rather than being created. But, it remains unclear if Lady Wilde shared Mivart's version of Adam.[85] Relying on her husband's extensive research material, among other sources, she formulated her own version of Ireland's Celtic origins and ancient festivals, customs, and folktales, all ultimately traceable back to 'Iran.' She also repudiated Petrie's explanation of the Round Towers. Instead, in the 1887 *Ancient Legends*, she contended "the origin" of the towers "still awaits solution," adding: "One must travel a long way, even to the far East, before finding in the decorations of the ancient Hindoo temples anything approaching to the typical idea that runs through all Irish ornamentation."[86] In this two-volume book, Lady Wilde not only traced the Celts back to the distantly ancient 'Iran,' described as the "source of all life, creed, and culture now on earth,"[87] but, similar to her husband, she emphatically claimed the Milesian ancestry of the Irish had arrived from the East by way of a direct route from the Iberian Peninsula, without any prior contact with mainland Britain. Lady Wilde assigned all human origins to "the eastern cradle of their race," adding that it was from "Persia, Assyria, and Egypt, to Greece and the Isles of the Sea, went forth the wandering tribes." Lapsing into racial craniology, but in the monogenesis form to which her husband had initially subscribed prior to the 1870s, while also rejecting any affinity between Irish and Norse mythology, she designated 'Iran' (in the broadest geographic definition) as the fountainhead of elemental culture, from where peoples, languages, and civilizations spread to other locations such as Greece and Egypt, as well as across Europe, in a not too distant past (i.e., c.3000 years earlier), including to Ireland via different routes. This narrative indirectly avoided the previous disputes between oriental and non-oriental theories of Irish origins (e.g., Persian vs. Phoenician vs. Greek, and so on); since every human population group was now ultimately traced back to an Iranian origin:

> This source of all life, creed, and culture now on earth, there is no reason to doubt, will be found in *Iran*, or Persia as we call it, and in the ancient legends and language of the great

Iranian people, the head and noblest type of the Aryan races. Endowed with splendid physical beauty, noble intellect, and a rich, musical language, the Iranians had also a lofty sense of the relation between man and the spiritual world. They admitted no idols into their temples; their God was the One Supreme Creator and Upholder of all things, whose symbol was the sun and the pure, elemental fire. [...]

[...]

Meanwhile other branches of the primal Iranian stock were spreading over the savage central forests of Europe, where they laid the foundation of the great Teuton and Gothic races [...]

Still the waves of human life kept rolling westward until they surged over all the lands and islands of the Great Sea, and the wandering mariners, seeking new homes, passed through the Pillars of Hercules out into the Western Ocean, and coasting along by the shores of Spain and France, founded nations that still bear the impress of their Eastern origin, and are known in history as the Celtic race; while the customs, usages, and traditions which their forefathers had learnt in Egypt or Greece were carefully preserved by them, and transmitted as heirlooms to the colonies they founded. From Spain the early mariners easily reached the verdant island of the West in which we Irish are more particularly interested. And here in our beautiful Ireland the last wave of the great Iranian migration finally settled. Further progress was impossible—the unknown ocean seemed to them the limits of the world. And thus the wanderers of the primal race, with their fragments of the ancient creed and mythic poet-lore, and their peculiar dialect of the ancient tongue formed, as it were, a sediment here which still retains its peculiar affinity with the parent land—though the changes and chances of three thousand years have swept over the people, the legends, and the language. It is, therefore, in Ireland, above all, that the nature and origin of the primitive races of Europe should be studied. Even the form of the Celtic head shows a decided conformity to that of the Greek races, while it differs essentially from the Saxon and Gothic types. This is one of the many proofs in support of the theory that the Celtic people in their westward course to the Atlantic travelled by the coasts of the Mediterranean, as all along that line the same cranial formation is found. Philologists also affirm that the Irish language is nearer to Sanskrit than any other of the living and spoken languages of Europe; while the legends and myths of Ireland can be readily traced to the far East, but have nothing in common with the fierce and weird superstitions of Northern mythology.[88]

Lady Wilde's underlying objective here was to establish the Milesians as *the last* of the migrating Celtic stock settling in a European territory: "From Spain the early mariners easily reached the verdant island of the West in which we Irish are more particularly interested. And here in our beautiful Ireland the last wave of the great Iranian migration finally settled."[89] This was a significant twist on the former mode of prioritizing Ireland's ancient civilizational grandeur above that of Britain by the likes of Vallancey, L. C. Beaufort, Henry O'Brien, Moore, Betham, John D'Alton, Keane, canon Bourke, and other earlier and contemporary proponents of various oriental origins of the Irish. These other oriental models insisted on Ireland being the location of the earliest arrivals in the entire British Isles of populations from the Orient and, hence, the first great civilizational hub in the British Isles. Lady Wilde, however, was not privileging Ireland as the earliest location of (oriental) civilization in the British Isles. Instead, her account rendered the Milesians as allegedly the last Celtic branch of Iranian peoples to have arrived in the British Isles, presumably also without long periods of prior settlement anywhere along the way, including in the Iberian Peninsula that was their purported final land base before sailing directly to Ireland. Accordingly, the Milesians, as the last Celtic arrival in all of the British Isles and the last oriental wave of Ireland's Gaelic ancestry, were indisputable custodians of the least temporally altered and most historically authentic Iranian traditions to have survived in Western Europe. Whereas time and distance from the original Iranian homeland of prior waves of Iranian arrivals in Europe, who during their prolonged migrations westward and gradual intermixture with other population settlements along the way (all of them eventually traceable to Iranian people in some form), had resulted in the adulteration of the indigenous civilizational attributes of those groups, the Milesian ancestry of the Irish at the time of their arrival in Ireland constituted the most civilizationally sophisticated and uncontaminated Iranian people in all of western Europe, and notably in the British Isles. This was a claim of civilizational authenticity predicated on both the idea of continued purity, if not also continued advancement, of Iranian cultural beliefs and practices in the Iranian homeland itself over time, as well as the lesser susceptibility to change in the Iranian traditions brought over by the Milesians, simply on grounds of their more recent presence in the British Isles:

> And thus the wanderers of the primal race, with their fragments of the ancient creed and mythic poet-lore, and their peculiar dialect of the ancient tongue, formed, as it were, a sediment here which still retains its peculiar affinity with the parent land—though the changes and chances of three thousand years have swept over the people, the legends, and the language. It is, therefore, in Ireland, above all, that the nature and origin of the primitive races of Europe should be studied.[90]

By Lady Wilde's reckoning, following the arrival of Milesians, Ireland had long remained "the most learned and powerful island of the West."[91] She did not, however, elaborate on why and when the Milesians had been divested of that privileged status, nor did she address whether the introduction of Christianity to Ireland in the fifth century had played a part in that alleged civilizational degradation.

Lady Wilde's account of Celtic and post-Celtic migration patterns across Europe, and the various Celtic settlements in Ireland over time, was a mélange of biblical ('Japhetic') as well as particular post-Darwinian evolutionary-biological classification of modern humans (with earlier roots in Carl Linnaeus's writings in the 1750s), along with existing antiquarian varieties of Phoenician, Iranian, Irano-Scythian, Scythian, and other oriental theories of Ireland's ancient populations—albeit, without mentioning the likes of Vallancey or O'Brien. Similar to William Wilde, including in his later 1874 British Association lecture, Lady Wilde had the Celts arriving in Ireland at different stages and by different routes, with the first arrivals vanquishing and eventually annihilating the so-called primitive "pre-Adamic rudimental humanity" already living in the Island. According to Sir William, the early post-'primitive' population settlements in Ireland for whom there was verifiable historical evidence (allegedly the Firbolgs, Tuatha de

Dananns, and Milesians) belonged to "the one Celtic stock" and arrived in Ireland at different periods and through different migratory paths: "Greece," Scandinavia, and "Spain" respectively—with the first two identified paths most certainly requiring these migratory Celts to have passed through other, albeit unnamed, regions of Europe before reaching Ireland. According to this model, each group of these Celtic peoples from the East introduced to Ireland different attributes of civilization (which was ever evolving in their original homeland), ranging from "agriculture" to "the chemistry and mechanics of metal work," and "beauty and governing power." These groups were much later followed by other settlers: "the Danes" (Norse), who brought "commerce and navigation," and the "Anglo-Normans," who introduced "chivalry and organized government," along with other admixture of peoples, such as "French emigrants [who] taught us an improved art of weaving."[92] In contrast to her late husband's account, Lady Wilde's version made room for even earlier post-primitive and non-Iranian settler groups arriving in Ireland from the East, such as "Sidonian fugitives" (i.e., Phoenicians), purportedly led by Partholan.[93] Significantly, Lady Wilde was explicit in her assertion that the ancient Iranian culture transmitted to Ireland continued to shape Irish folk beliefs and customs to the present day: "The present work deals only with the mythology, or the fantastic creed of the Irish respecting the invisible world—strange and mystical superstitions, brought thousands of years ago from their Aryan home, but which still, even in the present time, affect all the modes of thinking and acting in the daily life of the people."[94] She offered examples of such presumably analogous vestigial cultural practices in both contemporary Ireland and Iran (Persia) dating back to a common ancient 'Iranian' origin. For instance, she noted:

> Amongst the earliest religious symbols of the world are the Tree, the Woman, and the Serpent—memories, no doubt, of the legend of Paradise; and the reverence for certain sacred trees has prevailed in Persia from the most ancient times, and become diffused among all the Iranian nations. It was the custom in Iran to hang costly garments on the branches as votive offerings; and it is recorded that Xerxes before going to battle invoked victory by the Sacred Tree, and hung jewels and rich robes on the boughs. And the poet Saadi [i.e., Sa'di] narrates an anecdote concerning trees which has the true Oriental touch of mournful suggestion:—He was once, he says, the guest of a very rich old man who had a son remarkable for his beauty. One night the old man said to him, "During my whole life I never had but this son. Near this place is a Sacred Tree to which men resort to offer up their petitions. Many nights at the foot of this tree I besought God until he bestowed on me this son." Not long after Saadi overheard this young man say in a low voice to his friend, "How happy should I be to know where that Sacred Tree grows, in order that I might implore God for the death of my father."
>
> The poorer class in Persia, not being able to make offerings of costly garments, are in the habit of tying bits of coloured stuffs on the boughs, and these rags are considered to have a special virtue in curing diseases. The trees are often near a well or by a saint's grave, and are then looked upon as peculiarly sacred.
>
> This account might have been written for Ireland, for the belief and the ceremonial are precisely similar, and are still found existing to this day both in *Iran* and in *Erin*. But all trees were not held sacred—only those that bore no eatable fruit that could nourish men; a

lingering memory of the tree of evil fruit may have caused this prejudice, while the Tree of Life was eagerly sought for, with its promised gift of immortality. [...] It is worthy of note, while on the subject of Irish and Iranian affinities, that the old Persian word for tree is *dar*, and the Irish call their sacred tree, the oak, *darragh*.[95]

Lady Wilde's many other examples of corresponding folk beliefs in contemporary Ireland and Iran traceable to presumed ancient 'Iranian' origin, included "*Peris* or *Feroüers* (fairies)" of Iran and the "*Sidhe* or Fairies of Ireland"; the "alder," which "is another of the mystical trees of Ireland, held sacred, as in Persia, on account of its possessing strange mysterious properties and powers to avert evil"; and the ancient celebrations and rituals of Iranian magi and pre-Christian Irish druids, such as the "sacred fire" and the adoration of the sun.[96] More broadly, even leaving aside her theory of Ireland's 'Iranian' racial and civilizational origins, Lady Wilde was overlooking other possible historical scenarios of cross-territorial cultural transmission as well as other probable explanations for perceived similarities between the folk beliefs of peoples in distant lands. She was also neglecting the intervening cultural influences in 'Iran' (in the broad geographic sense) since the time of the supposed migration of Milesians from Iran to Ireland, which may have shaped certain present-day Iranian folk beliefs and practices that now supposedly resembled the Irish folk beliefs and practices. These influences in Iran itself (here in the narrow sense of the country by that name during Lady Wilde's time) ranged from the introduction of Islam to the infusion of Arab, Turkish, and other non-'Persian' legends and cultural practices.

There are some very striking differences between Lady Wilde's and her husband's historical delineation of Irish folk traditions. William Wilde in his 1852 *Irish Popular Superstitions*, by relying in passing on authorities such as John O'Donovan, George Petrie, and Eugene O'Curry, had observed regarding the "Bealtaine" (May Day) celebrations in Ireland that "[m]any of our May Day customs, sports, and games, are of English origin, and were, no doubt, introduced by Anglo-Saxons." He added that in general,

> it is our earnest desire, as far as our knowledge enables us, not to propagate, even in a popular legend, the usual historic fallacies, conjectural etymologies, and far-fetched and often inapplicable and unmeaning analogies to Egyptian, Hindoo, and Persian mythologies—high sounding names often used to cloack the ignorance of writers or to mystify the simplicity or credulity of readers—which obtained credit with Irish readers some years ago; and it is our wish, as far as possible, to correct those opinions which the simplicity or ignorance of our forefathers disseminated.[97]

Lest there be any confusion as to the type of specious theories regarding the roots of Irish traditions and folk practices he had in mind, he cited an example: "Vallancey—whose opinions [...] deserving of little weight, when questions of history or the discussion of theories relative to antiquities and etymologies are concerned."[98] William Wilde rejected such etymological "conjectures" that "the Gaelic appellation *Bealtaine*, the *Beal-fire*" was derived from "Baal" and was, therefore, somehow proof of "the Syrian or Phoenician origin of the Irish."[99] On the other hand, Lady Wilde in her 1887 *Ancient Legends* was categorical in relating the May Day fire festival in Ireland to Iranian roots. However, she was ambiguous as to whether that festival may have been borrowed by ancient Iranians themselves from Phoenicians (who after all in Lady Wilde's model of human origins could also be traced back to the original common Iranian human race), or was possibly borrowed by both groups from some other group (also ultimately traceable back to an original Iranian race), or if Phoenicians had merely continued an earlier Iranian tradition in this case after their branching out of the original Iranian human stock. The possibility of syncretic cross-cultural exchanges between ancient Iranian civilization and other (related) ancient civilizations could have undermined her claim that Milesians had brought to Ireland the purest Iranian civilizational beliefs and practices of the time. According to Lady Wilde, the putatively Iranian May Day tradition in Ireland had undergone certain changes following the introduction of Christianity to the island, being culturally reinterpreted and reconfigured subsequently:

> THERE were four great festivals held in Ireland from the most ancient pagan times, and these four sacred seasons were February, May, Midsummer, and November. May was the most memorable and auspicious of all; then the Druids lit the *Baal-Tinne*, the holy, goodly fire of Baal, the Sun god, and they drove the cattle on a path made between two fires, and singed them with the flame of a lighted torch, and sometimes they cut them to spill blood, and then burnt the blood as a sacred offering to the Sun god.
>
> The great feast of Bel, or the Sun, took place on May Eve; and that of Samhain, or the Moon, on November Eve; when libations were poured out to appease the evil spirits, and also the spirits of the dead, who come out of their graves on that night to visit their ancient homes.
>
> The Phœnicians, it is known, adored the Supreme Being under the name of Bel-Samen, and it is remarkable that the peasants in Ireland, wishing you good luck, say in Irish, "The blessing of Bel, and the blessing of Samhain, be with you," that is, of the sun and of the moon.
>
> These were the great festivals of the Druids, when all domestic fires were extinguished, in order to be re-lit by the sacred fire taken from the temples, for it was deemed sacrilege to have any fires kindled except from the holy altar flame.
>
> St. Patrick, however, determined to break down the power of the Druids; and therefore, in defiance of their laws, he had a great fire lit on May Eve, when he celebrated the paschal mysteries; and henceforth Easter, or the Feast of the Resurrection, took the place of the Baal festival.
>
> The Baal fires were originally used for human sacrifices and burnt-offerings of the first-fruits of the cattle; but after Christianity was established the children and cattle were only passed between two fires for purification from sin, and as a safeguard against the power of the devil.
>
> The Persians also extinguished the domestic fires on the Baal festival, the 21st of April, and were obliged to re-light them from the temple fires, for which the priests were paid a fee in silver money. A fire kindled by rubbing two pieces of wood together was also considered lucky by the Persians; then water was boiled over the flame, and afterwards sprinkled on the people and on the cattle. The ancient Irish ritual resembles the Persian in every particular, and the Druids, no doubt, held the traditional worship exactly as brought from the East, the land of the sun and of tree worship and well worship.

May Day, called in Irish *Là-Beltaine*, the day of the Baal fires, was the festival of greatest rejoicing held in Ireland.[100]

Also commenting on this festival in her next book on Irish folklore, *Ancient Cures, Charms, and Usages of Ireland. Contributions to Irish Lore* (1890), Lady Wilde again provided no sources for her account of the festival.[101] But, there can be no mistake she was working under the lingering influence of older generations of antiquarians committed to varying versions of oriental theories of Irish origins, including Charles Vallancey, Louisa Catherine Beaufort, Henry O'Brien, and Thomas Moore.[102]

Reviews of the 1887 *Ancient Legends* were expectedly mixed. While generally admiring the collection of Irish folktales in the book, a number of reviewers questioned Lady Wilde's comparative methodology and her attribution of Iranian ancestry to the ancient population of Ireland. One of the harshest reviews appeared in the *Academy* (London). The reviewer, Jane Lee, a Dublin-born scholar and student of Sanskrit, and at the time a lecturer and vice-principal of the women's Newnham College at Cambridge, attacked Lady Wilde's Iranian model of cultural diffusion to Ireland in ancient times. Lee relied on a simultaneous, if not necessarily contradictory, appeal to polygenesis theory of human origins, on the one hand, and the universality of basic myths and lore across cultures, on the other hand. She also cited an odd mixture of theories of common as well as distinct origins of languages, and listed such disparate range of authorities as the Grimm brothers, the German August Schleicher, Friedrich Max Müller, the Italian Graziadio Isaia Ascoli, and the German Theodor Benfey (the latter Jane Lee's former Sanskrit professor at the University of Bonn). In keeping with this motley approach to comparative studies of mythology, folklore, and languages, Lee wrote:

> Have not all we students of race and language learned and seen that so far there is no evidence of there ever having been in any part of the world one family, one creed, one language? When was it that Persians, Assyrians, and Egyptians dwelt together in "the beautiful Eden land at head of the Persian Gulf?" Where did those branches of the primal Iranian stock get the ships in which they sailed down Mediterranean Sea, and through the pillars of Hercules to the western shores of Spain, and northward to the island of Erin? Has Wilde been attracted and misled by resemblance of sound between the names Erin and Iran—by the circumstance that first syllable of the words Ir-ish and Ir-anian is the same? Does not all the evidence comparative philology go to prove that *first* people who parted company with ancient Indo-European (not Iranian) stock were the Kelts [i.e., Celts]; that they crossed central and northern Europe until they reached Spain, Gaul, and the British Isles, and were stopped by the waters of the great ocean? Are all Lady Wilde's theories envolved [*sic*] out of her own imagination? Has she never heard or read of Grimm or Ascoli, or Benfey, Schleicher, or Max Müller, not to mention dozen other great names?—and if she has not, why does she write an essay on comparative mythology and comparative philology? *Que diable allait-elle faire dans cette galère*? ["What the devil was she doing in this galley?"][103]

As far as the origin of Indo-European languages was concerned, the one point to which Lee correctly alluded was that in their theories of Indo-European languages the likes of Schleicher, Müller, Benfey, as well as Ascoli in his unique claim of an Indo-Semitic model of languages ("Aryo-Semitic"), had proclaimed a prior original "proto" language from which the later Indo-Iranian languages (Persian and Sanskrit) or the Indo-Semitic languages (in the case of Ascoli's assertion) had evolved. Similarly, the Grimms and Müller in their theories of elementary universal myths (also applicable to fairytales) ascribed a common long-lost primal ancestry to all existing *common* myths. Otherwise, among many of her other claims in this review, Jane Lee's own theory that Celts ("Kelts") were the first of the Indo-Europeans to have left their originary land could not be substantiated.

Another reviewer, this time writing anonymously in the *Saturday Review* (London), also targeted Lady Wilde's identification of a decidedly Iranian extraction of Irish folk tales and of the ancient Irish themselves. Rejecting also Wilde's claim that "Egyptians" too had originated in 'Iran,' the reviewer stated:

> Lady Wilde, if we do not misunderstand her, thinks that the 'Iranian race' (not knowing when they were well off) migrated from Iran to Ireland, taking Egypt by the way, and picking up Egyptian mysteries and beliefs on the road. This is a very natural conclusion, when one is not aware that early ritual is almost as uniformly and widely diffused as early myth, thanks to the similar working of the early human intellect on similar matter.

This anonymous reviewer, instead of directly comparing Lady Wilde's methodology with that of older generation of Irish antiquarians such as Vallancey, likened her work to that of the late eighteenth-century English antiquarian Jacob Bryant, adding: "old antiquarian delusions die hard."[104]

Defying critical reviews of *Ancient Legends*, Lady Wilde in the opening paragraph of her 1890 *Ancient Cures, Charms, and Usages of Ireland. Contributions to Irish Lore* acknowledged certain universal features of ancient beliefs among "All nations," without abandoning the ultimately Iranian origin of all peoples and civilizations, which in her view further sustained the notion of a foundational common origin of certain folk beliefs across the globe. As an example, she listed "the intuitive belief that mystic beings were always around them, influencing, though unseen, every action of life, and all the forces of nature. They felt the presence of a spirit in the winds, and the waves, and the swaying branches of the forest trees, and in the primal elements of all that exists. Fire was to them the sacred symbol of the divine essence, ever striving towards ascension."[105] She defiantly persisted with her particular model of Iran-centered theory of the origin of Ireland's Celtic population, albeit refraining from repeating this assertion as frequently as she had done in her 1887 book. Tracing some of the customs ("usages") of the Irish back to ancient Egypt and pre-Hellenic Aegean region ("Pelasgian"), and in keeping with her theory that all humanity had evolved from the same Iranian stock, she noted, "the Irish, like their Persian ancestors, are fervent tree-worshippers."[106] Some of the folk traditions covered in this book, as in the case of the May Day festival, were mere repetition of what had appeared in her 1887 *Ancient legends*, and the only discernible change in her methodology was the notable avoidance of etymological correspondences between Irish and oriental terms. The chief thematic difference between *Ancient Legends* and *Ancient Cures* was the inclusion in the latter of longer interspersed passages of nationalist commentary, albeit without any elucidation in either work of the precise connection between folklore, on the one hand, and Irish nationalist politics and/or contemporary Irish nationalist literature, on the other hand. However, she clearly believed that, similar to nationalist literature, 'national' folklore too could be utilized for attaining not only the cultural, but also the political objectives of nationalism. With much exaggeration, she noted in the 1890 *Ancient Cures* the manner in which "Moore, in his 'Lalla Rookh,' under the disguise of 'The Fire Worshippers,' incarnated the fierce resolve of Catholic Ireland to break the bondage of the penal yoke."[107] *Ancient Cures* was Lady Wilde's most decidedly political and militant Irish nationalist exhortation since 1848, with an unmistakable advocacy of republicanism, in which the central role in the anticipated armed struggle was assigned to militant Irish nationalists in the United States—who were not subject to the sort of censorship and other restrictions encountered throughout the British Empire. Additionally, gun ownership in the United States was widespread and "[a]rmed clubs are named after the chief leaders of Irish revolt, and solemn processions mark the anniversary of each national tragedy, for there are no triumphs to record in Irish history."[108]

In contrast to her claim of the remote Iranian origin of all peoples, the latter sections of *Ancient Cures* reveal Lady Wilde's lingering vacillation between monogenesis and polygenesis beliefs. The latter sections were replete with craniological racial characterizations of the English and the Irish. The Celts, purportedly similar to "Greeks," represented a higher intelligence and displayed an aptitude for "religion and art," whereas the English were "a people made for commerce and industry." Ignoring here Lady Wilde's a-historical conflation and summation of ancient Hellenic city-states, ranging from Athens and Ithaca to Sparta (with distinct social, cultural, and political structures and dynamics, notwithstanding some common key cultural beliefs), the point she sought to make was that a "war of races" had already been underway in Ireland from the moment of the first Norman incursions in the twelfth century, and intensifying following the complete subjugation of Ireland by the start of the seventeenth century, notably with the establishment of the Plantation of Ulster. This war had reportedly endured to the present time and its final outcome was yet to be decided: "Other nations have had their seven years' war, or thirty years' war, but Ireland has carried on an utterly unavailing war of seven hundred years."[109] This racially divisive analysis of contemporary Ireland was an odd stance for someone of Anglo-Irish ancestry who was advocating cross-ethnic (i.e., cross-"racial") republican Irish nationalism.

A highly critical review of *Ancient Cures*, by the Irish-born Anglican priest and botanist Percy Watkins Fenton Myles, focused primarily on Lady Wilde's Irish nationalist propensity; namely her version of the history of English rule in Ireland, including her particular racial descriptions of the English and the Irish, and her opinion of contemporary Irish nationalist politics since the founding of the Young Ireland movement in 1842. Myles also noted Lady Wilde's methodological weakness in studying folklore, which in Myles' view was also characteristic of most preceding Irish folklorists, including such luminaries as Thomas Crofton Croker and Samuel Lover. Myles pointed out the absence of a hermeneutical approach that would distinguish between folklore rooted in older legends and customs, on the one hand, and more recently formed folk beliefs and practices, on the other hand. In contrast to Lady Wilde's account of the origin and history of Celtic presence in Ireland, Myles recommended the recent book by another Irish scholar, Sophie Bryant (*Celtic Ireland*, 1889), and expressed hope that Douglas Hyde and other Irish folklorists would produce studies of higher quality than Lady Wilde's.[110] It is essential to bear in mind that Lady Wilde's publications on Irish folklore were appearing during the early stages of what came to be known as the Irish Revival.[111] An element of this Revival in connection with Irish identities, which has been largely neglected in prior studies, was the competing Aryanist discourses of Irish origins, with different strands of Aryanism. The feminist, psychologist, mathematician, and historian Sophie Bryant, in contrast to Lady Wilde, belonged to the camp that traced the origin of the Aryans to Scandinavia, whose progenies according to Bryant included the Celtic arrivals in Ireland, from whom the Gaels had descended. Bryant ascribed her own range of racial characteristics to her model of culturally sophisticated Celts. This was part of the broader debate on the origin of Aryan peoples and languages, and their subsequent geographic diffusion. As I discuss later, this Aryanist debate, which became a component of the racial 'whitening' of the Irish in the late nineteenth century, also found notable resonance in the Irish Revival of the turn of the century.

There were also contemporary lesser-known local Irish folklorists who insisted on the Iranian ancestry of some of the earliest population settlements in Ireland. For instance, at the turn of the century an article by the Irish "Miss A.H. Singleton" (the Anglican Annie Elizabeth Harriet Jane Singleton), titled "Customs, Some Old, and Superstitions Yet Surviving in County Meath, Ireland," appeared in the January 1904 issue of *Gentleman's Magazine* (London). This article was subsequently reproduced in some of the provincial Irish press, after it was picked up by the New York periodical *The Gael/An Gaodhal*, with its title now appearing as "Some Old Customs and Superstitions in the County Meath" and without mention of its prior publication in England. Singleton, while following some of Lady Wilde's suppositions about ancient Ireland, nonetheless diverged from Wilde is so far as branding the presumed Iranian settlers in Ireland as the most ancient of the major Celtic population settlements in the island and distinct from the later Celts, albeit with a lasting cultural influence as evident from some contemporary Irish folk beliefs. *The Gael*, published from 1881 to 1904, with an estimated circulation of around 2,000 by the time Singleton's article appeared, was an influential Irish nationalist bi-lingual monthly magazine founded by Mícheál Ó Lócháin (Michael J. Logan) in Brooklyn, New York, and billed itself "a monthly journal devoted to the preservation and cultivation of the Irish language and the autonomy of the Irish nation."[112] Singleton, while citing both Lady Wilde and Bryant among her sources, equated the Irish "Banshees" with "the Peris of Persia," noting: "Many of these old tales have come down to us from very ancient times; for it must be remembered that the Irish is a composite race, beginning with the Iranian, or Persian migration in the most remote period of Irish history, and continuing through an admixture of Basque, Norse and Norman down to the Cromwellian English and Scotch of later times." She added: "Curiously enough the Celtic strain in those tales seems always to have remained the dominant one."[113]

Evident in the conceptual and methodological similarities and disparities on the subjects of Irish origins and folk traditions in works by William Wilde, Lady Jane

Wilde, Sophie Bryant, Singleton, or in the above-mentioned censorious reviews of Lady Wilde's 1887 and 1890 books, or in studies by Douglas Hyde and others for that matter, were various strands of simultaneous discursive transformations as well as continuities in formulations of Irish identity between the late nineteenth and the early nineteenth century. To use Thomas Kuhn's and Michel Foucault's terminologies respectively, the transformations in this setting did not denote a sudden absolute "paradigm shift" or a full-fledged "epistemic rupture" between older and more recent multivocal conceptualizations of Irish identity. There were multiple forces shaping different narratives and methodologies in the quest for Irish origins (including in the Irish diaspora), in addition to growing interest in Irish folklore spurred by as diverse developments as the Great Famine or the persistent plight of the Irish peasantry and the land question. Among the key factors shaping the contours of continued debates on Irish origins at this juncture were the rejection or acceptance of manifold Darwinian and other evolutionary anthropological and ethnographic theories of population groups, as well as the always dynamic formulations of nationhood and nationalism—and their consequent "Irish nationalist" versus "unionist" trajectories—, including the Irish Revival of the latter part of the century, with its own multiple literary and cultural aesthetics and reframing of Irish mythology.

As noted, Lady Wilde's oriental model of Irish origins identified the Gaels as a subgroup of Celtic peoples, with all Celts ultimately traced back to 'Iranian' lands, and Iranians comprising the earliest branch of Aryan peoples, and Milesians (presumably constituting Ireland's main ancestral Gaelic population) as being the last branch of Iranians/Celts to settle in Europe. Her claim that Ireland had attained a more advanced civilizational standing than mainland Britain in ancient times rested on the premise that the Milesians reaching Ireland were the last of the Iranian/Celtic groups settling in Europe, who had departed their original homeland at a time when Iranian civilization was at its pinnacle—with Milesians having bypassed mainland Britain in their relatively rapid migration to their new homeland. This model appeared at a particular juncture in Irish nationalist historiography and was indicative of the influence of distinct, albeit often intersecting, developments in nationalist historiography of Ireland since the mid-nineteenth century, alongside the older lingering antiquarian influences. In effect, Lady Wilde's later writings incorporated some of the old nationalist antiquarian motifs alongside the more recent historiographic departures in Irish nationalist circles (cultural and/or political). Notwithstanding Lady Wilde's abrupt lapse in *Ancient Cures* into a narrative of race hatred between Ireland and England, and completely overlooking here her earlier *Driftwood from Scandinavia* (1884), her works on Irish folklore and history in effect fused the underlying nationalist premises of older and more recent historical depictions of Ireland. While she relegated some of what she considered to be fabulous accounts of ancient Ireland appearing in earlier antiquarian works to the realm of the mythic and lore, she nevertheless shared many of the principal schema of the older historiographic models, ranging from oriental theories of Irish origins to the presumed population groups that had settled in Ireland in ancient times (e.g., Tuatha de Dananns and Milesians), alongside the view that ancient Ireland had been the center of civilization in the British Isles, as well as the assertion of continued contemporary similarities between certain Irish and oriental beliefs and practices. On the other hand, Lady Wilde's account of Ireland since the twelfth century was infused with an unmistakably militant Irish nationalist historical formulation that had emerged in the aftermath of the Great Famine, in works by the likes of John Mitchel, as discussed in the previous chapter.[114] This historical perspective jointly insisted on the irreconcilable civilizational-cultural divide between Ireland and England as well as England's *exclusively* destructive role in Ireland.

Lady Wilde's periodic recourse to a discourse of ongoing race war between the Irish and the English—in spite of the significant non-'Gaelic' ethnic presence in Irish nationalist ranks, including those of English descent such as Lady Wilde herself—needs to be situated in the framework of the historically evolving designations of Gaelic ('mere') Irish and other hyphenated Irish identities in Ireland itself *versus* the 'English.' Irish nationalists belonging to the hyphenated ethnic categories of "Anglo-Irish," "Scots-Irish," and "Welsh-Irish" differentiated between, on the one hand, "England," "Britain," and "English" (denoting an outside colonial power *there*) and, on the other hand, the particular ethnic hyphenations of the 'Irish' (representing segments of Ireland's population and hence being ultimately 'Irish' *here*, regardless of whether or not individuals in question opposed or supported English imperial rule in Ireland). The primary emphasis in this mode of Irish nationalist historical writing was on Ireland's continued and distinctly *non*-'England' cultural-civilizational identity, to borrow Declan Kiberd's terminology of 'not-England' from a different context in Irish nationalist configurations of Ireland.[115] This historical narrative denied any notably positive civilizational impact by England on Ireland. In effect, it consciously or intuitively appropriated and then subverted the assertion made by various English commentators since at least the late sixteenth century that Ireland epitomized all that was *not* England. But, whereas those English commentators had defined not-England as lack of culture, morals, and civility writ large (qualities they associated with England in contrast to Ireland), the Irish nationalist equation of Ireland as not-England turned these English claims of civilizational splendor on their head. It not only denied England any fundamental civilizational leverage in Ireland since the initial Anglo-Norman conquests in the twelfth century, just as some earlier generations of Irish nationalists had done too, but, more significantly, it repudiated England's very claim to any positive civilizational standing since at least the moment of England's colonial encounter with Ireland. This claim went beyond mere accusations of England's culturally destructive role in Ireland (including the erosion of Irish language) or the alleged policy of extermination. The overriding modus operandi of this particular trend in Irish nationalist historical narration was that England, as an imperial power, had forfeited any claim to real civilization in the first place, and that the destructiveness and plunder of English rule in Ireland since the twelfth century was a fundamental and inevitable feature of the specifically 'English' imperial configuration of power (not forgetting many Irish nationalists did not object to all other empires, whether contemporary or in past times). Consequently, this marked an underlying cultural-civilizational disconnect between Ireland and England.

Of essence in this controverting historical narrative, regardless of its characterization of ancient Ireland, was the refutation of any genuine English civilizational advancement since at least the twelfth century. Concentrating on England as an imperial power, and a leading imperialist power around the globe in the nineteenth century (including in the Indian subcontinent, as Irish nationalists frequently reminded their audiences), the objective was to expose England's lack of qualification for the mantle of civilizational grandeur and to rid Ireland of the English cultural, political, and economic parasite. In its sweeping condemnation, this recalibrated Irish nationalist historical ontology targeted English imperialism as the destroyer of existing cultures and civilizations elsewhere under the hypocritical guise of a civilizing mission. Unlike William Wilde's comparatively more measured assessment of England's simultaneous historical contributions to, and devastations in, Ireland, as well as Lady Wilde's own earlier more variegated account of English civilization and empire, even in her *Ancient Legends* (1887), in the 1890 *Ancient Cures* Lady Wilde's verdict was that of England's fundamentally destructive impact in Ireland (as well as in England's other colonial possessions). After describing the alleged official British policy of deliberate neglect during the Great Famine in Ireland—"a country that has been devastated, plundered, and three times confiscated, and reduced by want and famine from eight millions to five millions during the last thirty years"—she observed hyperbolically:

> English statesmen might study with advantage the mode by which the Greeks, the great colonisers of the ancient world, gained the love of all peoples. Like England, the Greeks carried on extensive commerce with many strange nations, but they never sought to exterminate; they humanised. Their trade swept by many shores, but not to destroy, or burn, or ravage. [...] If they wanted land they took it, but civilised the people, and drew them up into their own higher civilization [...].
> [...]
> England never had a divine idea in the treatment of nationalities, least of all in Ireland.
> Nothing grand or noble in policy was ever thought of to lift the people to their true height. Self was the only motive power; greed of land, greed of wealth the only aim; the lust of gold everywhere, the love of God nowhere; spoliation and insult the only policy; the result being that no nation has ever been so unsuccessful in gaining the love of subject states as England.[116]

Moreover, Lady Wilde resorted to the latest, albeit contested, racial and linguistic theories. Leaving aside the recurring contradictions in her account, she adhered to the then-dominant Eastern theory of Aryan origins and claimed at least *some degree* of common Celtic-Aryan (Iranian) ancestry for the majority of Ireland's present population (of varying later ethnic designations: Gaels, English, Welsh, or Scots), even as she maintained that the early Celtic population of England was later significantly altered by the large-scale admixture of "Saxon"/"Teutonic" so-called race; making such racially charged statements as "[t]he round, stolid English head, and pale, cold eyes, denote the nation of practical aims, a people made for commerce and industry; while the small oval head of the Celt, and deep, passionate eyes, denote a people made for religion and art."[117] Given Lady Wilde's tendency to incongruously oscillate between, on the one hand, the rhetoric of racial conflict between the Irish (suddenly designated as the entirely Celtic presumably 'mere Irish') and the English (of ancient Celtic and later primarily Saxon/Teutonic 'racial' admixture), and, on the other hand, the assertion of *some degree of common (Aryan/Iranian) Celtic ancestry among the majority of Irelands population of differing hyphenated ethnic identities*, the political utility of the latter claim for advancing the Irish nationalist project became diluted, if not entirely lost—particularly, since she repeatedly lapsed into statements such as "[i]t would indeed be impossible to find natures more entirely antagonistic than the Saxon and the Celt"[118]—, given that much of the non-Gaelic Celtic population of Ireland had settled in the island after their prior intermixing with Saxons/Teutons. The theory of a predominantly Celtic common ancestry of Britons and the Irish in ancient times, also advocated by William Wilde earlier in the century, had been utilized toward building a cross-ethnic Irish nationalist platform as far back as the 1840s, if not earlier. As already mentioned, the Young Ireland Thomas Osborne Davis, in both his historical writings and poetry, had stressed *some degree* of shared common Celtic ancestry among most contemporary Irish of various British descent (English, Scots, or Welsh) and the Gaelic ('mere') Irish, in an effort to further downplay ethnic divisions among the Irish and bolster cross-ethnic Irish nationalism. There certainly had been much earlier models of a common ancestry of the entire population of the British Isles in ancient times, but these were not formulated as an ideological tool for building cross-ethnic Irish nationalist solidarity.

The chief cultural-political advantage from an Irish nationalist perspective of highlighting a degree of shared ancestry among much of Ireland's population was the blurring, if not complete elision, of inner-Irish ethnic differences.[119] What was lacking from William Wilde's or Thomas Davis' narratives was Lady Wilde's concept of a *naturalized* and *nationalized* race war between the 'Irish' and the 'English.' While there continued to be Irish detractors of varying theories of the common origin of the Gaels and the English, there were also others besides the Irish in the United Kingdom who endorsed the common Aryan origin of the two population groups, among them the famous English poet and highly influential cultural critic Matthew Arnold, who in the second half of the nineteenth century insisted on the common Aryan ancestry of the Celts (including the 'mere Irish'/Gaelic population in this account) and the English (Anglo-)"Saxons." In his 1867 *On the Study of Celtic Literature*, Arnold reminded his readers: "I remember, when I was young, I was taught to think of Celt as separated by an impassable gulf from Teuton [i.e., (Anglo-)Saxons]; my father, in particular, was never weary of contrasting them; he insisted much oftner on the separation between us and them than between us and any other race in the world; in the same way Lord [John Singleton Copley] Lyndhurst, in words long famous, called the Irish, 'aliens in speech, in religion, in blood.'"[120]

By the end of the nineteenth century, there was growing acceptance in Irish nationalist historical writing of the view that the Celts comprised the foremost ancestral common denominator of the populations of both Ireland and Britain, regardless of subsequent heterogenous population arrivals and ethnic blending in the two territories—and, in some versions, with the Saxon ancestral admixture of the English also traced back to the same parent Aryan family as the Celts. Over time, this common Celtic ancestral component effectively enabled Irish nationalist historiography to unburden itself of many (though not all) fabulous accounts of ancient Ireland provided by earlier generations of antiquarians, which were increasingly harder to sustain in keeping with the latest historical and other cross-disciplinary methodological standards. At the turn of the century, a number of leading Irish nationalist and other groups of historians, notably the nationalist Eoin MacNeill, gave the theory of a common ancestry of the earliest populations of the entire British Isles a new and emphatically Europe-centered twist (as opposed to Orient-centered theories of Celtic origins). This was to have significant cultural-political implications (see Chapter Nine). Overall, however, the primary Irish nationalist historical enterprise from the middle of the nineteenth century increasingly focused on confirming Ireland's distinct *cultural* heritage and contemporary cultural beliefs and practices as a bedrock of the not-England 'national' identity of the Irish, rather than fixating on ethnic/'racial' origins. Accordingly, this unique cultural identity by itself warranted Ireland's political autonomy or complete separation from England.

The Persisting Quandary of Irish Origins in the Late Nineteenth and Early Twentieth Century

By the late nineteenth century, Irish mythology was gaining greater prominence in nationalist literary and theatrical productions as part of the wide-ranging "Irish Revival." Existing mytho-histories of Irish origins, even if not treated as authentic history, alongside Ireland's heroic epic cycles and other conventionally recognized legends, offered some in nationalist ranks an imaginative Epimethean bearing in coping with the avowed 'national' tragedy of the present moment and alleviating the trauma of repeatedly failed instances of Irish resistance to English rule since the twelfth century. For the more so-called radical Irish nationalists, these mytho-histories and epic cycles also harbored Promethean inspirational models for the present generation, offering examples of Irish resistance to and/or victory against various enemies. Should the present generation's struggles fail to liberate Ireland, it was hoped their example and the continued utilization of Ireland's heroic legends and mythology would inspire and empower future generations in their pursuit of Ireland's independence, with the failed resistance of the present generation also incorporated into the inspirational legends of future generations. The carefully selected and/or recrafted myths and epics either invoked settings when Ireland was unsullied by English conquests, so as to inspire 'national' pride and foster a desire for national-cultural 'revival,' or, in their rescripted and recontextualized rendering, they evoked heroic episodes of the Irish defending their land and their purported 'national' honor against foreign encroachment[121]—even though in actuality Ireland as a unified territory, let alone as a 'nation,' did not exist in either the original legends or during the historical periods in question. As presumed cultural repositories, mytho-historical and legendary accounts of Ireland, as well as popular lores believed to be rooted in Ireland's pre-Norman past, offered imagined times, places, and traditions that were immune from the *timescape* of Ireland's historical encounters with England. Simply put, England was absent from ancient Irish myths and epic cycles. There was no sign of English military, cultural, or political encroachment and *authority* in those pasts, nor were those pasts *authored* by the English, even if accounts of those pasts recorded by "medieval" Irish scholars and by subsequent antiquarians and littérateurs were on occasion later subjected to the English authorial lens of historical criticism and/or cultural chauvinism and were now largely produced in English language. These legendary pasts were, in effect, Ireland's presumed pre-Norman 'national' halcyon days, regardless of conflicts and battles often taking place between different 'Irish' groups and territories in these same accounts, or between 'Irish' and non-Irish groups, including such tales as the Battle of Clontarf (1014 CE) between the allegedly Irish warriors led by Brian Boru and the foreign Norse (Viking) enemy.

Importantly, in nationalist appeals to both (mytho-)history and readily acknowledged mythology, time became warped and the mythic and ruptured *past* was impregnated in the *present* time with possibilities of a *future* Ireland of *"Irish* making." In all these moments of Ireland's entirely invented and/or re-created pasts, and the instrumentally scripted present and imagined future, Ireland always represented some form of 'not-England,' to again borrow Declan Kiberd's concept from a different context. In their nationalist applications, mytho-history, mythology, folklore, history, and even archaeology became the province of reconstructive projects of a nation-in-the making. Such resuscitative projects of the as of yet inchoate nation-state required particular modes of nationalist poetics. Although ridiculed and reviled by many of his contemporaries and by many scholars of Irish antiquarianism today, Henry O'Brien in the 1830s was possibly the most avant-garde and flamboyant *poetic* mind of all Irish nationalist antiquarians in the nineteenth century, even if he considered his *The Round Towers* (1834) more of a "scientific" than an aesthetic treatise on ancient Ireland. There were also nationalists who extensively reworked existing legends and epics, or who invented entirely new myths without direct recourse to contested Irish antiquarian pasts, as in the case of the 1902 play *Kathleen ni Houlihan* by Lady Isabella Augusta Gregory and W. B. Yeats. Myth-making was (and remains) a creative dimension of all nationalist projects in all ranges of nationalist settings, whether anti-imperialist, imperialist, or otherwise. Even the incrementally more rigorous trend of Irish nationalist historiography by the late nineteenth century (both methodologically and rhetorically), which sought to distance itself from earlier fabulous antiquarian accounts of ancient Ireland, was not immune from myth-making inclinations.

An instance of a direct public appeal for consciously embracing aesthetic styles of "life-affirming"[122] mythic pasts in the service of the Irish nation, as opposed to mere reliance on supposedly conventional history, was the (1863?) poem by Lady Wilde titled "A Remonstrance, addressed to D[enis] Florence M[a]cCarthy." MacCarthy (1817–82) was a renowned nationalist poet, who had belonged to the Young Ireland circle, had utilized the Iran/Erin poetic device following Moore's example, and was now also a member of the Royal Irish Academy. Lady Wilde, herself, it should be recalled, was an erstwhile renowned nationalist poet during her years of collaboration with the Young Ireland mouthpiece *The Nation*, at which time she was better known by her most enduring pseudonym: Speranza. In "A Remonstrance," composed nearly a decade-and-a-half before Lady Wilde largely devoted her attention to investigation of Irish folklore (with her own highly imaginative trademark), MacCarthy was beseeched to concentrate on producing imaginative trans-historical and inspirational nationalist poetry, instead of dabbling in cold historical facts more suitable for "Academies" and "Archivists":

> STAND on the heights O Poet! nor come down
> Amid the wise old serpents, coiled around
> The Tree of Knowledge in Academies.
> The Poet's place is by the Tree of Life,

Whose fruit turns men to Gods, and makes them live,
Not seeking buried treasure in the tombs.
Leave the dim records of a by-gone age
To those great Archivists, who flash the torch
Of Truth along Time's mouldering records,
Illuminating all the fading Past,
Like golden letters on an ancient scroll.
The Poet soars with eagles, breathes pure ether,

Basks in the light that suns the mountain peak,
And sings, from spirit altitudes, such strains,
That all the toilers in life's rugged furrows
Are forced, for once, to lift the bow'd-down head,
And look on Heaven. Flashes from Poet's words
Electric light, strong, swift and sudden, like
The clash of thunder-clouds, by which men read
God's writing legibly on human hearts

O Poet Prophets! God hath sent ye forth
With lips made consecrate by altar fire,
To guide the Future, not to tread the Past;
To chaunt, in glorious music, man's great hymn,
The watchword of humanity—Advance!
Advance in Wisdom, Nobleness, and Truth,
High aims, high purposes, and self-control,
Which is self-reverence, knowing we shall stand
With crownéd angels before God's great throne
The Poet nerves the arm to do great deeds,
Inspires great thoughts, flings o'er the tears of life
The rainbow arch, to save us from despair;
Quickens the stagnant energies to act,
Bears the advancing banner of the age,
Full in the van of all Humanity;
And, with a strength, God-given, rolls the stone,
As angels may, from off the Sepulchre
Where souls lie bound, bidding them rise and live.

O Poet! preach this Gospel once again—
True Life, true Liberty, God's gifts to man;
Freedom from servile aims and selfish ends,
That swathe and bind the kingly spirit down,
Like Egypt's grave-clothes on the royal dead,
Scatter the golden grain of lofty thoughts
From which spring hero-deeds—that so, in truth,
Our Future may be nobler than our Past,
In all that makes a nation's life divine—
This is the Poet's mission, therefore—THINE.[123]

Later in life, Lady Wilde was fully conscious of the 'poetic' dimension of her own collections of Irish folklore and historical commentary. In a characterization of the Irish in her *Ancient Legends*, which in a different setting could be termed self-deprecating, she stated: "Dogmatic religion and science have long since killed the mytho-poetic faculty in cultured Europe. It only exists now, naturally and instinctively, in children, poets, and the child like races, like the Irish—simple, joyous, reverent, and unlettered, and who have remained unchanged for centuries, walled round by their language from the rest of Europe, through which separating veil science, culture, and the cold mockery of the sceptic have never yet penetrated."[124] But, myth-making is always potentially fraught with unsuspected inner tensions and hazards.

In the late nineteenth century, in addition to works on Irish antiquity or folklore by the likes of John O'Hart, canon Ulick Joseph Bourke, Lady Wilde, or Sophie Bryant, there existed other wide-ranging contested accounts of Irish origins imbued with their own distinctive configurations of identity constructs. Among the more imaginative of these accounts, even by the most blasé contemporary criteria, was Standish James O'Grady's *History of Ireland*. By present-day standards this work was chimerical in the manner of former styles of Irish antiquarianism, of which Marcus Keane had once appeared to be one of the last disciples. Only a few years after the publication of Bourke's *The Aryan Origins of the Gaelic Race and Language* in 1875, the cultural-nationalist Standish O'Grady (1846–1928), already a renowned author and literary historian, whose works on Irish mythology were highly influential in the Irish Literary Revival of the late nineteenth century, postulated his mind-twisting theory of Irish origins. In the first volume of his 1878 *History of Ireland (Volume I: The Heroic Period)*, O'Grady, laboring under such a wide range of influences as the eighteenth-century antiquarian Sylvester O'Halloran, on the one extreme, and the pseudo-science of craniology, on the other extreme, and espousing a convoluted geological and paleontological evolutionary scheme of the earth's origin, offered a new theory of the Aryan race and an unprecedented model of Irish origins. Dividing the earth's population into "eight" trans-linguistic categories (although initially listing nine and then even adding other groups along the way), and adopting a polygenesis approach to races, O'Grady came up with uniquely unorthodox racial divisions of humanity and curious geographic distributions of these racial groups contra all contemporary models and standards. His racial categories consisted of "the Australian, the Negrito, the Maorie, the Red Indian, the Eskimo, and the African, the Mongol, the Scythian, and the Turanian." Describing the Turanian race as "well-proportioned, long-headed, brown-skinned, oval-faced, with large dark eyes and soft wavy hair," who supposedly had originated in "Southern Asia," he then had branches of this racial group "spread[ing] eastward till he met the Mongol, and southward till stopped by the Malayan coming up from the isles of the Indian sea; westward along the shores of the Mediterranean, over all Egypt and Barbary, over Phœnecia and Greece and Italy, over Spain, France, Belgium, and the British Isles." He claimed the earliest human settlers in Ireland were in fact descendants of Turanians, rather than descendants of the "tall, fair-haired, blue-eyed, round-headed" Scythians, with the two groups later coming into conflict before eventually bonding to forge the ancestry of present-day Gaelic population of Ireland. Categorizing the Scythians as "Aryans," O'Grady denied that the 'fair-haired, blue-eyed' Aryan population arrivals in Ireland possessed any discernible civilizational aptitude prior to their intermixture with the 'brown-skinned' Turanians—the latter term by that time commonly understood to mean "Turks," but in O'Grady's racial definition representing among others such population groups as the generically titled "Jews," as well as the pre-Hellenic aboriginal peoples of the Aegean region, and also the "Hindoos," Arabs, and Persians! While vitally subverting the predominant European systems of racial categorization and hierarchy and defying the myth of white/Aryan superiority, as well as being inclined toward his own mode of chronological anachronisms, O'Grady summarized his peculiar contrapuntal schema of racial hierarchy as following:

> Glacialis Ierne [i.e., ice-age Ireland] had passed away, and Inis na Veeva [i.e., island of life] appeared upon the liquid surface of the sea, bearing a soil fit for the dent of spade and ploughshare. A new and nobler race of men were now advancing from the south and east. It was not Nemeth and his tribe, or the lady Kasâr, or Partholanus, the ill-starred. Civilization and the means of recording their history they did not bring with them. The annals of the cave do not tally with those of the Four Masters [i.e., the early-seventeenth century *Annals of the Four Masters* covering Irish history since the so-called Middle Ages]. The Book of Invasions [i.e., the eleventh-century *Lebor Gabála Érenn*, a (mythic) history of Ireland] is contradicted by silent witnesses out of the earth. The Lowr Gawla must be re-written, and the time-honoured traditions of the bards interpreted after a new method. It was no branch of Scythic stock, no Aryan-speaking people, who now swarmed over these countries, but a dark small, oval-faced, race between whom and the tall, fierce, blue-eyed Celt there was neither kinship nor resemblance.
>
> [...]
>
> From the Scythian stock shot forth branches—over Europe, the Cymri, the Gael, and the Teuton, the Norseman, and the Sclave, with their many families; and over Asia the terrible name of the Tartar, that ever-impending deluge, banked in by the Caspian, the Balkan, and the Steppes, around the Sea of Aral, but ever and anon bursting its barriers, and under some Timour or Ghengiz Khan, flooding all Southern Asia, and obliterating for a season every vestige of civilization.
>
> From the Turanian stock shot forth branches, not barren. In Asia, the Hindoo, the Arabian, and the Zend [i.e., Persian], the Assyrian, the Phœnician, and the Jew. Further west, the Pelasgian of Greece, the Etruscan of Italy, and in a less pure form the Hellene and the Roman, the Carthaginian, the forgotten Berber, and the Basque.
>
> Of these two mighty divisions of the human race it seems to have been the special task of the latter to found civilizations, and of the former to crush them. They founded the splendid civilizations of Babel, Nineveh, and Babylon, and the Scythians crushed them; of the Pelasgian Greeks and Italians, and the Scythians crushed them. [...]
>
> It is one of the colossal misapprehensions of history, and one which owes its origin to the uncandid egotism of our northern writers, that the exhausted populations of the south were refreshed and invigorated by the young warlike blood of the north. The Cimmerian regions, until they were touched by the quickening contact of the south, bred nought but ignorance, slow melancholy, and war. The peoples whom the father of history beheld upon their knees worshipping the naked sword, seem to have been absolutely incapable of raising themselves without assistance out of the primeval welter. The renaissance and modern civilization made their way through the silt and mire of that northern deluge, in spite of Cimmerian influences, and not through their help. Else how comes it that through the

length and breadth of that vast Aryan land, from the Isles of Britain to the Great Wall of China and the extremities of Kamschatka, we light nowhere upon any trace of the civilization which, upon the theory of chances, their young warlike blood must at least somewhere have succeeded in establishing, somewhere the birth of a noble piety, somewhere the invention of letters, somewhere the existence of beautiful manners and a true theory of life. [...] Whatever may have been the capacities of the northern peoples and their latent aptitudes, it was with the Mediterranean and Semitic peoples that civilizations have had their origin.[125]

O'Grady, himself of dark complexion,[126] then added:

The Irish are a mixed race, the Basque [i.e., "Turanian"] and the Celt [i.e., "Aryan"] went to their formation. The original inhabitants of the country were Basque, but successive Celtic invasions obliterated the ancient Basque language, and altered the physical appearance of the people. In this respect the history of Ireland, and indeed of all North-Western Europe, resembles that of Greece. In the times of which Homer sang, the Greek nobles had yellow hair and blue eyes. At the time when the heroic literature of Ireland was composed, the Irish nobles had yellow hair and blue eyes. Athene seized Achilles by the yellow locks, while she herself was a blue-eyed goddess. Crimthann [a semi-mythic High King of Ireland], who held in check the rebellious sons of Cathair More for Conn of the Hundred Battles, was surnamed Culboy, because the smelted gold was not yellower than his hair; while the locks of Cuculain, the great Ultonian hero, were yellower than the blossom of the sovarchy. On the other hand, the historic Greeks [i.e., Pelasgians] resembled physically the Italians, and were equally with them surprised at the tall stature and fierce blue eyes of the northern warriors, while in Irish bardic literature the lower orders are represented as dark. The history of both countries was the same. The aborigines, a dark Turanian people, were conquered and submerged by successive Celtic invasions, until their language was lost in that of their conquerors. The purest type of Irish beauty has been produced by this blending of races. We often see in Ireland, and not elsewhere, blue eyes fringed with lashes as black as jet, a pure clear skin through which glows the warmth of southern blood.[127]

An anonymous review of *History of Ireland* (*The Heroic Period*) appeared in the *Spectator* (London). The reviewer courteously evaded O'Grady's discussion of the racial origins of Irish people and, instead, focused solely on the content of the book concerning Irish legends:

In speaking of this volume, we do not intend to enter into question of its value from an archaeological point of view; nor does the author's manner of dealing with his subject seem to invite such criticism. The real importance of the book notice lies in this,—that the writer has given to the general reader, in a bold and spirited manner, a succession of wild and poetic stories, each forming a part of that picturesque romance called the heroic period of the history of Ireland.[128]

Given such dismissals of his theory of Irish origins, O'Grady in his 1894 *The Story of Ireland* provided a more concise, unadorned, and conventional account of Irish origins, concentrating primarily on the 'Milesian' ancestry of Gaels.[129] Perhaps, he accordingly should also have swapped the titles of his 1878 and 1894 books. The wrangling over what constituted factual versus fictive accounts of Ireland's past, and the production of discordant accounts of the seemingly inscrutable Irish antiquity, continued into the early years of the twentieth century.

Writing at the end of the century, Douglas Hyde (1860–1949), then the leading revivalist of Irish language and of Irish literature of bygone days, differentiated between mythological and so-called factual 'historical' phases of Ireland's past based on available verifiable documentation. The Anglo-Irish Hyde was a foremost turn-of-the-century cultural nationalist and a co-founder, with Eoin MacNeill, of the Gaelic League in 1893 for promoting the study and use of Irish language, with the objective of popularly 'reviving' that language. Hyde was by then a proponent of Irish Home Rule, having been briefly attracted to militant republicanism earlier. Nonetheless, he publicly refrained from political commentary and endorsement, so as to reach as broad a spectrum of cultural nationalists (including republicans as well as even some unionists) in his quest for broadening the appeal of learning the Irish language. Along with his primary focus on propagation and popularization of Irish language, Hyde was committed to other forms of culturally "de-Anglicizing" Ireland.[130] In his 1899 *A Literary History of Ireland*, in a chapter titled "Confusion between Gods and Men," Hyde sought to assure the "popular estimation" (although he was imprecise as to whether he meant the British, the Irish, both, or an even broader public) that not all accounts of ancient Ireland were to be approached with suspicion on grounds of the existing mythological narratives, and that the continued presence of mythic elements in accounts of ancient Ireland were not some peculiarly Irish oddity and parallels could be found elsewhere around the world. In effect, Hyde was also making the point that the Irish historical imagination, and the Irish mind in general, had been no more susceptible to myth-making than the imaginations of other peoples or 'nations.' Hence, the existence of imaginary histories did not indicate the Irish were trapped in some pre-rational mindset; even if the ostentatious wording of Hyde's "Dedication" in the book cast some doubt on the rational foundations of previous generations of Irish historical scholarship: "To the members of the Gaelic League, the only body in Ireland which appears to realise the fact that Ireland has a past, has a history, has literature, and the only body in Ireland which seeks to render the present a rational continuation of the past." He further noted in the book:

> Of that part of every Irish pedigree which runs back from the first century [CE] to Milesius nothing can be laid down with certainty, nor indeed can there be *any absolute certainty* in affirming that Irish pedigrees from the eleventh to the third century [BCE] are reliable—we have only an amount of cumulative evidence from which we may draw such a deduction with considerable confidence. The mere fact that these pedigrees are traced back a thousand years further through Irish kings and heroes, and end in a son of Milesius, need not in the least affect—as in popular estimation it too often does—the credibility of the last seventeen hundred years, which stands upon its own merits.
>
> On the contrary, such a continuation is just what we should expect. In the Irish genealogies the sons of Milesius occupy the place that in other early genealogies is held by the gods. And the sons of Milesius were possibly the tutelary gods of the Gael. We have seen how one of them was so, at least in folk belief, and was addressed in semi-seriousness as still living and reigning even in the last century.

> All the Germanic races looked upon themselves as descended from gods. The Saxon, Anglian, Danish, Norwegian, and Swedish kings were traced back either to Woden or to some of his companions or sons. It was the same with the Greeks, to whom the Celts bear so close a similitude. [...] It is not in Ireland alone that we see mythology condensing into a dated genealogy. The same thing has happened in Persian history, and the history of Denmark by Saxo Grammaticus affords many such instances.[131]

It should be noted that Hyde was a proponent of Celtic origins of the Gaels, with the Celts in turn ascribed a North European origin. He maintained in his own highly creative narration of ancient history that "the Celtic race and the Celtic language sprang from the heart of what is to-day modern Germany," and that the Celts in ancient times had been allies of the Greek city-states fighting Phoenicians and the Persian Empire, with the Celts also vying with the Carthaginians (Phoenicians), for control of the Iberian Peninsula.[132] In his attempt to circumvent existing legendary narratives of ancient Ireland, Hyde merely provided yet another convoluted model of Irish origins, this time framed within the evolving myth of an exclusively "Western Civilization" somehow traceable in an uninterrupted manner back to ancient 'Greece.' Assertions of oriental origins of the Irish had either explicitly or implicitly countered the prevalent affirmation since the eighteenth-century European Enlightenment of (a homogenized) 'Greece' as the civilizational pinnacle of the ancient world; in essence rejecting the hierarchically framed myth of Western Civilization.

Extensive contestation of the origins of the Gaels and other presumed early major population settlements in Ireland and of the historical roots of Gaelic folk beliefs and practices continued for decades to come, now also within the framework of the Irish Revival of pre-First World War era.[133] In 1906 Stephen Lucius Gwynn's *The Fair Hills of Ireland* was published. Gwynn was a prominent Home Rule nationalist, an Irish Parliamentary Party MP, and a distinguished author and literary critic, with his many publications including the 1905 biography of Thomas Moore. *The Fair Hills of Ireland* coincidentally appeared around the time of the Iranian Constitutional Revolution (1906–11), with Gwynn soon joining the strident multi-party campaign in the United Kingdom waged against the British Liberal foreign secretary Sir Edward Grey's policy of cooperation with Russia in stifling the Iranian constitutionalist-nationalist movement (see the next chapter). In *The Fair Hills of Ireland*, which included an introductory chapter that commenced with poems by Donnchadh Rua Mac Con Mara (1715–1810; a.k.a., Red Donough McNamara) and James Clarence Mangan, Gwynn opted for a vague "Mediterranean"-Scythian origin of Ireland's pre-Milesian population:

> Almost with the first beginnings of Irish legendary history the name of Tara appears. We are told of earlier colonies than the Firbolgs, but no race earlier than they is said to have effected a permanent lodgement in Ireland, and their king Slainge (according to Irish bardic tradition) established at Tara the first monarchy. After the Firbolgs came the Tuatha de Danann, a fair-haired tall people of magical powers, who routed the little dark men, took possession of Tara, and erected there one of their special treasures, the *Lia Fáil*, or Stone of Destiny, on which every High King was inaugurated. Dates are given for these happenings, and the coming of the Tuatha de Danann is confidently put down at the year of the world 3303—that is,

by Irish reckoning, 1896 B.C. Two hundred years later (according to the same tradition) came the last of these pre-historic colonising expeditions—that of the Milesians, who under Eber and Eremon defeated the magic-working de Danann, and got possession of the country.[134]

According to Gwynn, the factual historical precedent for what eventually became the legendary account of the arrival of Tuatha de Dananns in Ireland may have been the escape to safety of Scythians following Persian invasions of Scythia in the late sixth-century BCE and of subsequent Persian invasions of Hellenic territories during the "Persian Wars" (c. 499–449 BCE):

Tradition tells of five invasions or colonisations of Eire, and traces them all back to an origin in the Mediterranean. Parthalon and Nemed, who led the first two colonies, are only shadowy names. Part of the Nemedian colony went back to the Mediterranean and served there as slaves—set to carry earth in wallets from plains to enrich the hill-slopes with vineyards. So, we are told, they got their name of the 'Firbolgs'—men of the leathern sack.

Wearying of their task, the Firbolgs came back to Ireland and they possessed the land: a low statured, dark-skinned, dark-eyed people. Forty years later, according to the annals, came a new body of invaders, the Tuatha de Danann. They also were of Nemedian stock, but had settled in Attica (whereas the Firbolgs went to Thrace), and had learnt magic from the Greeks till they eclipsed their teachers. When Syria [?] overran Greece they fled, and settled in Scandinavia. Here possibly is some track of historic truth, some echo of the Persian wars; and the Tuatha de Danann should be allied to Homer's Danai. But to Ireland they came from the north: a tall, fair, blue-eyed race of magicians, whom the wind wafted over the seas by enchantment, till they settled on the Connaught mountains in the likeness of a blue mist. They demanded from the Firbolgs a share of Ireland, and when it was refused, they fought.[135]

Given the continued appearance of conflicting accounts of Irish origins and Ireland's ancient past by the beginning of the twentieth century, and the irreconcilable chasm between many of the contending versions, some historians of Irish antiquity now simply avoided in-depth commentary on the precise origins of the Irish, and of the Gaels in particular; instead making more general and somewhat oblique references to the distant ancestry of the Gaels. This was the method adopted in the second decade of the twentieth century by the radical nationalist and highly respected historian Alice Stopford Green (d. 1929). Green nonetheless stressed the civilizational sophistication of the pre-Gaelic "Iberian" population of the island, with pre-Gaelic here denoting pre-'Milesian.' She also claimed "Erin" was a pre-Gaelic designation of the island:

We do not know when the Gaels first entered Ireland, coming according to ancient Irish legends across the Gaulish sea. One invasion followed another, and an old Irish tract gives the definite Gaelic monarchy as beginning in the fourth century B.C. They drove the earlier peoples, the Iberians, from the stupendous stone forts and earthen entrenchments that guarded cliffs and mountain passes. The name of Erin recalls the ancient inhabitants, who lived on under the new rulers, more in number than their conquerors. The Gaels gave their language and their organisation to the country, while many customs and traditions of the older race lingered on and penetrated the new people.[136]

Irans of the Irish Revival: Aryanism, Theosophy, Occult, and Magic

The early phase of the Irish Literary Revival, as part of the broader cultural Irish Revival underway by the latter decades of the nineteenth century, also coincided with a renewed surge of interest across the United Kingdom in oriental literatures, particularly the genre of mystical poetry. Edward Fitzgerald's very liberal translation from Persian of *Rubáiyát of Omar Khayyám* was among the more consequential works propelling the renewed and mounting interest in the United Kingdom in Persian literatures in the second half of the nineteenth century. The translation by Fitzgerald (1809–83; born in England to Anglo-Irish parents) was originally published anonymously in 1859 and enjoyed a very limited reception for many years, with subsequent revised editions by him captivating a large readership and profuse praise. Fitzgerald was publicly identified as the translator of the work in the third revised edition in 1872, although those close to him had long known the identity of the translator, who now shot into meteoric fame. Fitzgerald was neither involved in Irish politics nor by any means in the Irish Literary Revival, even if his translation had an impact on some Irish poets engaged in the Revival. Yet, if one of his early biographers is to be trusted, Fitzgerald's initial interest in Persian language was possibly inspired by the presumed Iran-Erin historical connection. Writing in 1887, Michael Kerney (the-then-anonymous American editor of reprint editions of Fitzgerald's collected works), hypothesized on this purported early stimulus for Fitzgerald's learning of Persian:

> EDWARD FITZGERALD [...] was born at Bredfield, in Suffolk, on the 31st March, 1809. He was the third son of John Purcell, of Kilkenny, in Ireland, who, marrying Miss Mary Frances Fitzgerald, daughter of John Fitzgerald, of Williamstown, County Waterford, added that distinguished name to his own patronymic; and the future Omar was thus doubly of Irish extraction. (Both the families of Purcell and Fitzgerald claim descent from Norman warriors of the eleventh century.) This circumstance is thought to have had some influence in attracting him to the study of Persian poetry, Iran and Erin being almost convertible terms in the early days of modern ethnology.
>
> [...]
>
> One of the younger Cambridge men with whom he became intimate during his periodical pilgrimages to the university, was Edward B. Cowell, a man of the highest attainment in Oriental learning [...] From Cowell he could easily learn that the hypothetical affinity between the names of Erin and Iran belonged to an obsolete stage of etymology; but the attraction of a far-fetched theory was replaced by the charm of reading Persian poetry in companionship with his young friend, who was equally competent to enjoy and to analyze the beauties of a literature that formed a portion of his regular studies.[137]

Writing much later, albeit without reference to Irish antiquarianism, Ronald W. Ferrier dismissed suggestions that Fitzgerald was perhaps drawn to the study of Persian language as a result of his early exposure to the oriental-style Romantic poetry in the United Kingdom in the earlier part of the century, with Moore's *Lalla Rookh* among them. Ferrier maintained:

There is no evidence that Fitzgerald was attracted to the Orient like many other contemporary writers and artists. Indeed, when Kinglake's *Eothen* was published, his reaction was distinctly insular. "Have you read," he asked Frederick Tennyson in February 1845, "which all the world talks of? And do you know who it is written by? Why by Devil Kinglake, who was at Cambridge at the same time." As for *The Crescent and the Cross*, which had a great success, "Eliot Warburton has written an Oriental Book! Ye Gods! In Shakespeare's day the nuisance was the Monsieur Travellers who had 'swum in a gundello'; but now the bores are those who have smoked tschibouques with a *Peshaw*! Deuce take it: I say 'tis better to stick to muddy Suffolk.'" It does not appear that Fitzgerald was drawn to the oriental tales of Beckford or others or was impressed by romances such as Moore's *Lalla Rookh* before his acquaintance with Edward Cowell. There is little doubt, however, that the real impetus to his Persian studies was the sorrow of separation which he experienced when "the delightful lady" and "delightful Fellow" left "Bamford all desolate" 'to take up residence in Oxford, leaving himself lonely. He admitted as much to Frederick Tennyson at the end of 1853, "I also amuse myself with poking out some Persian which E. Cowell would inaugurate me with: I go on with it because it is a point in common with him, and enables us to study a little together."[138]

Ferrier's account does not contradict Kerney's theory. Whether or not Kerney, who was writing four years after Fitzgerald's death, was deliberately inventing or deducing with great exaggeration the influence of the lingering Iran/Erin etymological supposition on Fitzgerald's early interest in classical Persian poetry, or conveying information Fitzgerald may actually have shared with friends, or merely repeating some apocryphal account, what is notable is the ongoing familiarity with the theory of Iranian origins of Ireland's ancient civilization in the wider late nineteenth-century literary circles beyond Ireland itself.

Among subsequent English translations of Khayyam's *Rubā'iyāt* was the 1889 partial prose translation (of 466 quatrains) by the author, translator, and Home Rule nationalist (Irish Parliamentary Party MP) Justin Huntly McCarthy (1859–1936; not to be confused with his father Justin McCarthy, also a politician and author). Oscar Wilde was one of the notable literary admirers of both Fitzgerald's and McCarthy's translations of Khayyam's work, among a number of other translations of Persian and "Eastern" poetry.[139] McCarthy, captivated by Fitzgerald's translation of *Rubáiyát*, taught himself some basic Persian by the late 1880s, admitting, "My Persian of to-day is at the best beggarly." With this elementary knowledge of Persian, he began to "translate" Khayyam's poems by working through a number of existing translations and chiefly rendering them into his own preferred prose lyricism. Completing this translation in 1889, the works he consulted were Fitzgerald's work, Edward Henry Whinfield's 1883 English verse translation *The Quatraines of Omar Khayyam*, and the 1867 French prose translation *Les quatrains de Khèyam* by Jean Baptiste Nicolas.[140] In 1893 McCarthy's translation of *Ghazels from the Divan of Hafiz* was published, again rendered in prose form. By then McCarthy was evidently fluent enough in Persian not to have felt the need to mention any existing European translations he had consulted for his own translation of Hafiz's poetry. Meanwhile, in 1892 McCarthy had translated *The Thousand and One Days: Persian Tales* from the exiting French translation of the work by the eighteenth-century François Pétis de La Croix—which in actuality was based on Pétis de La Croix's translation from Persian of what turns out to have been a Persian translation from an earlier Ottoman Turkish version of the text.[141]

By the turn of the century, the increasing recourse to varying formulations of Aryan origins of the Gaels in Irish nationalist accounts of ancient Ireland at times also assumed mystical, occult, magic, and other forms of counter-"rationalist" property, most notably in some works identified with the Irish Revival, as in the case of works by authors embracing theosophy for example. At some level, this was an antithetical stance toward British imperial "modernities." Moreover, for some Irish nationalists, the gravitation toward mystical or non-mystical so-called "Eastern" religions in the parlance of the time, and/or toward occult, to a certain extent stemmed also from a deep disaffection with Ireland's dominant institutional religious traditions (i.e., Catholic and various Protestant institutions). This withdrawal from the main Christian sects in Ireland was at least in part a means of transcending membership in what were still historically and socially rival and exclusionary denominational communities in Ireland, notwithstanding the nonsectarian platforms of most mainstream and 'radical' Irish nationalist organizations at the time—leaving aside here Ireland's smaller non-Christian communities, including the Jewish community. As small-scale as the tendency to abandon parochial Christian allegiances and instead embrace more universalist principles happened to be, ranging from theosophy to deism and atheism, some among these defectors from mainstream Christian denominations were highly influential figures in the intellectual-cultural and political spheres of Irish nationalism at the turn of the century. Among the factors contributing to the willingness of some Irish nationalists to embrace alternative mystical faiths, theosophy in particular, was the increasing exposure by the late nineteenth century to different strands of spiritual belief systems, including cross-colonial cosmopolitan syntheses of different belief systems, most notably drawn from the Indian subcontinent (India also being a major focus of Irish nationalist expressions of cross-territorial anticolonial affinities). In reference to members of Ireland's Protestant community in this regard, Roy Foster has characterized the trend as "a search for psychic control" in response to "the Irish Protestant sense of displacement, their loss of social and psychological integration towards the end of the nineteenth century."[142] John Wilson Foster noted long ago, "It is probable, it seems to me, that occult rites [...] satisfied the cruder need of some Protestants for ritual discipline."[143] Clearly, there can be no singular explanation for the trend, not forgetting also the presence of Catholics among those dissenting from mainstream Christian sects in Ireland.

Some of these individuals entirely broke with their prior Christian affiliation and embraced other faiths, or simply turned deist, agnostic, or atheist, which is not to say all of the latter completely renounced the concept of the sacred. Others simultaneously and heterodoxly embraced different faiths alongside their existing, but now reconstituted, Christian devotion. The various religious realignments did not always necessarily stem from a lingering disaffection with existing Christian denominations, or some politically and/or socially inclined search for a more universalist spiritual affiliation. But, ultimately, these realignments were largely due to increased exposure to other faiths through a wide range of imperial and other globalization processes. There were, in addition, also individuals who had already embraced atheism, after breaking with their denominational upbringing, but later turned to 'Eastern' religions, theosophy, and/or other forms of spirituality associated with the concept of the divine. In the case of the more specifically anti-clerical tendency among those who broke with their former religious traditions, it must be noted this proclivity went far beyond the customary Fenian/Irish Republican Brotherhood (IRB) tradition of politically steering clear of different Christian institutions in Ireland, which in turn happened to publicly denounce republicanism and political militancy—even as most Fenian/IRB members individually retained their personal devotion to their respective Christian denominations (not discounting the existence of some atheists, deists, theosophists, and even possibly adherents of more familiar non-Christian faiths in Fenian/IRB ranks). Despite the divergent contexts, there were some parallels between the dissenting anti-clerical spirit in Irish nationalist circles in the late nineteenth and early twentieth century and a similar tendency on the part of some members of the United Irishmen in the late eighteenth century, who had abandoned conventional Christianity (in the form of atheism, agnosticism, or deism), chiefly under the influence of particular trends in the European Enlightenment.[144] Other earlier examples of Irish nationalist anti-clericalism included, as already discussed, Thomas Moore in the first half of the nineteenth century, who had had a Catholic upbringing.

The orientation toward atheism, deism, or avowedly 'Eastern' spiritual traditions (notwithstanding the fact that the Judeo-Christian traditions had also originated in the so-called East), or the more recent synthetic forms of spirituality, as in the case of theosophy, expectedly placed their adherents in socially marginal positions vis-à-vis the main Christian denominations in Ireland, even if there is no indication of how the majority of the population felt toward such acts of religious dissent. This marginality was, of course, tempered or, alternatively, exacerbated by the individual's social class, gender, other forms of social visibility, and/or social networks, among a range of factors. Representing two divergent poles of these social parameters were the occultist-magician W. B. Yeats from an Anglican background, who no less also briefly flirted with the idea of conversion to Catholicism, and the strictly secular, anti-spiritualist agnostic, socialist, internationalist, pacifist, Irish nationalist Frederick ("Fred") Michael Ryan, from a Catholic background. Yeats and Ryan, as discussed below, variously participated in the Irish Revival at large, both of them also instrumental figures in the founding of the Irish National Theatre Society (1903) and its successor Abbey Theatre (1904). But, they belonged to vastly different, if at times overlapping, social milieus. Outside the immediate circles of the Irish Revival, there were the likes of the Irish-British feminist, radical social reformer, Irish nationalist, outspoken proponents of Indian nationalism and more broadly anti-imperialist, Annie Besant (née Wood; 1847–1933), who started out as an atheist (after having had an Anglican upbringing) and a (Fabian) socialist before embracing co-freemasonry and theosophy and eventually becoming the president of the Theosophical Society in 1907. While not a direct participant in the Irish Revival, Besant influenced the theosophical outlook of some of the key figures in the Revival, among them James and Margaret Cousins. Another prominent Irish-British feminist, socialist, anti-imperialist, and outspoken advocate of Irish and Indian nationalist movements, Charlotte Despard, from a Catholic background, also embraced theosophy.[145] There were, on the other hand, the likes of Hanna and Francis Sheehy Skeffington, close friends of the Cousins and their collaborators in feminist and nationalist movements, who stayed away from theosophy. Also close friends of Fred Ryan, and like him internationalist-leaning socialist pacifists, Sheehy Skeffingtons too were agnostic, if not in fact atheist.[146] Often intersecting with or independently of the disposition to dissent from Ireland's hallowed contemporary religious institutions and traditions, was the tendency among some Irish nationalists to either outright reject normative 'modernities' (e.g., capitalism, bourgeois mores, and so on), or to at least engage with some institutionalized modernities (in the case of imperial modernities, for instance) in a critical and dissonant manner.

The theosophical movement attracted a number of leading figures in the Irish Revival, who either joined the Dublin branch of the Theosophical Society or absorbed its teachings through different channels, without formally joining the organization. The Theosophical Society was founded in New York in 1875 by the "Russian" (Ukrainian) émigré Madame Helena Petrovna Blavatsky and the American Henry Steel Olcott. In its syncretic incorporation of 'Eastern' religious traditions and philosophical systems in the search for occult truth—primarily religious beliefs and practices that had come to be collectively termed in English as "Hinduism" and some variants of Buddhism—theosophy also drew inspiration from some of the teachings and concepts of Zoroastrianism. On the other hand, similar to her views on contemporary Judaism and Christianity, Madame Blavatsky considered Islam and Muslim "dervishes" as lacking access to genuine occult knowledge. She also ahistorically attributed the spread of Islam purely to compulsion by "the sword," notwithstanding her approval of its iconoclastic foundation. Given her statement about dervishes, Blavatsky ironically exempted "sufis" from the charge of occult ignorance and then compounded her fanciful historical characterization of sufism by claiming it was derived from Zoroastrian occult knowledge, itself allegedly in part derived from the ascetic traditions of the Indian subcontinent, among other influences:

> Plato states that the mystic Magian religion, known under the name of *Machagistia*, is the most uncorrupted form of worship in things divine. Later, the Mysteries of the Chaldean sanctuaries were added to it by one of the Zoroasters and Darius Hystaspes. The latter completed and perfected it still more with the help of the knowledge obtained by him from the learned ascetics of India, whose rites were identical with those of the initiated Magi. Ammian [states ...] "he [Darius Hystaspes] transfused them into the creed of the Magi. The latter, coupling these doctrines with their *own peculiar science of foretelling the future*, have handed down the whole through their descendants to succeeding ages." It is from these descendants that the Sufis, chiefly composed of Persians and Syrians, acquired their proficient knowledge in astrology, medicine, and the esoteric doctrine of the ages. "The Sufi doctrine," says C. W. King, "involved the grand idea of one universal creed which could be secretly held under any profession of an outward faith; and, in fact, took virtually the same view of religious systems as that in which the ancient philosophers had regarded such matters."[147]

In Blavatsky's writing Zoroastrianism was also identified with what she classified as magians/magicians, the purported practitioners of venerated occult science in this case. In Blavatsky's and Olcott's view, Judaism and Christianity were debased forms of earlier faiths that had been imbued with the principal doctrines of Zoroastrianism.[148] Henry S. Olcott even claimed, "[t]he scarlet robe of the Roman Catholic cardinal symbolises the heavenly [Zoroastrian] Fire. In an ancient Irish MS. Zarathust [i.e., Zoroaster] is called *Airgiod-Lamh*, or he of the Golden Hand—the hand which received the sacred and scattered celestial Fire [...]. He is also called Mogh Nuadhat, the Magus of the New Ordinance, or dispensation."[149] What Olcott forgot to mention was that his source for this presumed ancient Irish identification of Zoroaster ('*Airgiod-Lamh*') was in fact Charles Vallancey, whose opinion in this regard was later dismissed by as diverse a range of Irish authors as Henry O'Brien and George Petrie.[150] Instead, Olcott disingenuously credited William Ouseley's *Oriental Collections* as his source, which, in this instance, was in fact citing research by Vallancey that the latter had communicated to Ouseley. Blavatsky designated Zoroastrianism as the foundation of central tenets of Judaism (in the latter's post-idol worship reformation, reportedly), as well as of early Christianity (that had been devoid of the later symbolism of the crucifix as well as of the concept of trinity and their associated iconography). She classified contemporary Jews and Christians as "a dissenting sect of the Persians, for they do not even interpret the meaning of all such *Powers* ['*Kabala*'—secret knowledge] as the true kabalists do." Furthermore, according to Blavatsky, Zoroastrian and "Hindu" belief systems had followed divergent paths after the separation of "Iranian" and (a generically categorized) "Indian" peoples, both of which were designated as descendants of the original Aryan stock from Central Asia.[151] In terms of *counter-imperial modernities* in the framework of the Irish Revival, as Catherine Candy has noted, the search for "the essence of [...] a distant precolonial Celtic civilizational past" also "designate[d] 'India' as another archetypal alternative to modernity."[152] This analysis can in fact be extended to the presumed Indo-Iranian "Aryan" traditions in general.

The equation of ancient Persians with occult and magic, also present in some earlier Irish antiquarian writings in connection with Ireland's past druidical tradition, as in the case works by Vallancey or Henry O'Brien, became a commonplace feature of theosophical references to Zoroastrianism and ancient Iran in general. A case in point was the narrator of a short story, "The Story of a Star," by the author and poet George William Russell (later better known as "Æ"), first appearing in the publication of the Theosophical Society of Ireland, the *Irish Theosophist*: "I was, I thought, one of the Magi of old Persia, inheritor of its unforgotten lore, and using some of its powers. I tried to pierce through the great veil of nature, and feel the life that quickened it within. I tried to comprehend the birth and growth of planets, and to do this I rose spiritually, and passed beyond earth's confines into that seeming void which is the matrix where they germinate."[153] Incidentally, Blavatsky embraced Henry O'Brien's view of the importation of Buddhism into ancient Ireland, among other 'oriental' traditions introduced to ancient Ireland according to O'Brien. To this end, she quoted the American Episcopalian Rev. John Patterson Lundy's confused account of O'Brien's theory of the origin of the Round Towers, appearing in

Lundy's 1876 *Monumental Christianity, or the Art and Symbolism of the Primitive Church.*[154] While most Irish nationalists did not directly engage with the theosophical movement—certainly not just because of the condemnation of the movement by Catholic and Protestant institutions—a number of prominent figures in the Irish Revival were enthusiastically drawn to the movement and to 'Eastern' modes of thought in general, as in the case W. B. Yeats. Yeats, who practiced hermetic occult, was attracted to the theosophical movement of Blavatsky and Olcott. Even after later embracing ritual magic, Yeats informally continued his engagement with the spiritual occultism of theosophy. He also maintained a very conflicted and seesawing stance toward "modernity" and literary 'modernism.'[155] The Irish Literary Revival, as part of the broader Irish Revival, in many ways marked a project of literary modernism, despite its pretension of a "renaissance." In 1885, Yeats and a few colleagues formed the occult Dublin Hermetic Society. Other founding members included Yeats' close friend, George William Russell (Æ), and the Indian Mir Aulad Ali, professor of "Hindustani," Persian, Arabic, and Urdu at Trinity College from 1861 to 1898, and a council member of the Society for the Preservation of Irish Language (founded in 1876, with canon Ulick Joseph Bourke among its founders).[156] Mir Aulad Ali was a well-known figure in Dublin, with recurring mention of him over the years in the pages of the *Freeman's Journal* and the *Irish Times*, among other Irish newspapers. Yeats was among those who erroneously presumed Mir Aulad Ali was a "Persian."[157] Yeats served as chairman of the Hermetic Society, which in April 1886 merged into what came to be called the Dublin Theosophical Society. Yeats never formally joined the new organization but worked closely with some members of the theosophical movement and participated in its activities, before eventually joining the Hermetic Order of the Golden Dawn in 1890, so as to be initiated into ritual magic, by which time he was living in London.[158]

The Irish novelist and poet George Augustus Moore noted in what came to be regarded as his scandalous 1911 memoir, *'Hail and Farewell!'*, that there were a number of other leading figures in the Irish Literary Revival of the period, besides Yeats or Russell (Æ), who vigorously participated in theosophy and/or other forms of occult spirituality, 'Eastern' mysticism, or magic. Moore, along with Yeats, Lady Gregory, and Edward Martyn (Moore's cousin), was a founding member of the Irish Literary Theatre in Dublin (1899) and its subsequent reincarnations under different names.[159] Among the major figures of the Literary Revival mentioned by Moore in connection with theosophy and occult was William Kirkpatrick Magee ("John Eglinton"), a prominent literary critic, and journalistic collaborator of Fred Ryan before they went their separate ways a few years after co-founding the short-lived, ground-breaking, modernist Dublin literary journal *Dana: An Irish Magazine of Independent Thought* (1904–05). George A. Moore, who in 1902 converted from Catholicism to Protestantism over a family dispute, wrote mockingly of Magee: "He has certain knowledge of different incarnations. The first was in India, the second in Persia, his third, of which he keeps a distinct memory, happened in Egypt. About Babylon I am not sure."[160] In 1917, Magee himself described his gravitation toward theosophy as a kind of return to authentic pre-Christian druidical tradition of Ireland's ancient bards:

But besides the advantage of [St.] Patrick's personality, Christianity seems to have been able to profit by an imbroglio arising out of the defection from Druidism, about a century and a half previously, of the great king Cormac, who is said finally to have been slain by the Druids for having renounced their teaching. The bards, we may believe, went mostly with their king, and there was a consequent division between bardism and Druidism which proved highly serviceable to Patrick. Even in our own day, when so many of our poets and novelists are agnostics, theosophists, etc., we know that they have done a good deal to undermine established religion, and in the time of Patrick it is clear that with the bards on his side half the battle was gained.[161]

Incidentally, Magee's and Ryan's *Dana* contested the conventional narrow 'national' and religion-induced moralism of many leading figures of the Literary Revival, advocating instead a "Free Thought" and cosmopolitan literary movement in Ireland.[162] This echoed Ryan's joint commitment to political nationalism and internationalism and his opposition to parochialism. Expressing sympathy and solidarity with other colonized and semi-colonized peoples around the world, Ryan famously remarked a few years later:

In the case of Persia, also, we learn the essential unity of the human problem under all its different phases and the futility of the philosophy of Western despots who, anxious to dominate and exploit the East, set up the pleasant doctrine that the peoples of the East love despotism, and thus fundamentally differ from the peoples of the West. The laws of human nature are not suspended east of Suez, and there is not a single political struggle in the East to-day that has not its counterpart either in the recent history or the contemporary convulsions of the West. It is in this realization of human kinship, this shattering of the pride of race and the pride of power and the pride of religion, as well as in the wealth of social experience which now opens before humanity that there lies the greatest hope of moral advance, alike for the Eastern and the Western world.[163]

Magee steered away from nationalist *politics*, merely preferring a continually cosmopolitan Irish nation, much to the chagrin of strait-laced nationalists. Terry Eagleton has noted: "Like [Thomas William Hazen] Rolleston, John Eglinton [i.e., Magee], Frederick Ryan and Stopford Brooke all called for a national art shaped by universal motifs."[164] But, in outlining *Dana*'s literary objective, Magee and Ryan somewhat exaggerated the culturally insular and traditionally moralistic sentiment of the mainstream of Irish Literary Revival. After all, some of the leading figures of the movement were not only atheists, or adherents of theosophy and/or other forms of presumably Eastern spirituality, but also readily turned to 'Eastern' and a wide range of other literatures (including non-English European literary output) as sources of inspiration for their own literary creativity. Hence, cosmopolitanism was not entirely in short supply in the Revival, even if constituting a minority tendency; leaving aside here recurrent Irish nationalist expressions of solidarity and affinity with some other struggles around the world.

What remains generally unacknowledged in discussions of the appeal of theosophy or so-called Eastern religions to Protestant participants in the Irish Revival, ranging from Magee to his staunchly nationalist counterparts such as Yeats and Russell (Æ), is that their turn away from Christianity also allowed these individuals to transcend the Catholic-Protestant divide in Irish culture and politics; even if it alternatively marginalized them in society as non-Christians or as not strictly Christians. As noted already, other better-known Irish nationalist literary figures from Protestant backgrounds drawn to theosophy, and to avowedly 'Indian' thought in particular, included the feminist Margaret Elizabeth Gillespie and her husband, the socialist poet and author James Henry Cousins, whose nationalism was cosmopolitan in a range of manners. They married in 1903 and settled in India in 1915, where they steadfastly campaigned for Indian self-government and women's rights.[165] This is not to deny that there were Irish from other religious backgrounds also drawn to theosophy, other forms of occult spirituality, and/or magic. Nor should we overlook the appeal of these other worldviews to some Irish individuals outside the spheres of literary and cultural Revival and/or of Irish nationalism (cultural or political). Another well-known Irish personality who embraced 'Indian' spirituality and settled in India was the young teacher Margaret Elizabeth Noble (later Sister Nivedita). From a Protestant background and raised in England, she became a follower of the Vedanta teaching of Vivekananda (Narendranath Datta) while the latter was visiting England in 1895–96. She moved to India in 1898, where she later engaged in radical Indian nationalism.[166] On the other hand, the visit to Dublin in 1885 by the Bengali Vedantist and theosophist Mohini Chatterjee, was a notable influence in shaping Yeats' interest in theosophy and Hindu spirituality, which in turn had a marked effect on Yeats' poetry.[167] In the coming decades, in addition to a host of other factors, interest in theosophy and different forms of 'Eastern' spirituality across the United Kingdom was augmented by such visits to England as that of the young Jiddu Krishnamurti in 1911, who was brought over from India along with his younger brother Nityananda by Annie Besant to be educated in Europe; Besant having assumed the presidency of the international network of Theosophical Society in 1907. Krishnamurti was promoted by Besant and her theosophist collaborator Charles W. Leadbeater as the spiritual guide of the Order of the Star in the East, presumably auguring the imminent reincarnation of Lord Maitreya—with Besant having assumed custody of Krishnamurti and his brother against their father's wish.[168] Other range of such visits to the United Kingdom that stimulated greater interest in 'Eastern' spirituality included the 1911 and 1912 tours of England by 'Abdu'l-Bahá, the leader of the Bahái faith, which by then had evolved into a universalist religion, having originated in Iran in the second half of the nineteenth century.[169]

The theosophical promotion of universal "brotherhood," regardless of race, creed, nationality, or *gender*,[170] was certainly no obstacle to simultaneous embrace of anticolonial nationalism as a particularistic mode of self-identification (i.e., the nation). The leading theosophist Annie Besant's own life after she joined the movement is a poignant example. Yet, despite its universalist principles, theosophy operated within the circumscribed parameter of an Aryanist discourse and theosophical writings were permeated with the language of race. While drawing inspiration from a wide range of Eastern belief systems and societies, theosophy clearly privileged what it construed as Aryan civilization, cultures, and presumed intrinsic historical spirituality (the latter in the form of generally cited Hinduism and Buddhism and, to a lesser degree, Zoroastrianism).

Whether in approval or disapproval of certain theories of race, theosophical publications at the time recurrently referred to works on Aryan languages and cultures by Friedrich Max Müller, regarded as the leading authority in the field, alongside older works by Sir William Jones, or works by the likes of the contemporary American Alexander Wilder, and other disparate theoreticians of Aryanism. It is important to stress that—just as in some Irish antiquarian, historical, and folklore studies during the eighteenth and nineteenth centuries, or in the case of the Pan-Aryan Association founded in 1906 in New York by militant pan-Indian and Irish nationalists (see Chapter Seven)—theosophy's formulation of the Aryan race was *not based on skin color*. Nor was theosophy's Aryanist predilection identical to other contemporary Western currents of racial categorization. In the case of theosophy, 'Aryan' primarily denoted peoples with a particular common ancient cultural heritage and a shared contemporary philosophical and spiritual sensibility, albeit as an innate quality. Madame Blavatsky, for example, designated "Eastern Ethiopians" (also appearing as "Eastern Æthiopians"), by which she meant ancient "Egyptians," and which was presumably somehow also inclusive of Phoenicians, as "dark-skinned Caucasians" (i.e., Aryans). Hence, she attributed most of the so-called major civilizations of ancient times, as *then* identified in contemporary Western/European historical writing, to Aryan peoples, including ancient 'Greece.' She also traced the roots of Akkadian, Chaldean, Babylonian, and Assyrian occult knowledge back to what she termed "Hindu" Aryans—leaving aside here her other imaginative association of such otherwise distinct cultural groups as the ancient Hebrews and the later Aztecs, or her view that the original Asian ancestors of many population groups around the globe had at some point imbibed Aryan values to varying degrees and transmitted them to their new locations after leaving their ancestral homelands.[171] Theosophy's 'Aryans' were contrasted with Semitic cultures and thought, the underlying implication being the superiority of Aryan civilization-building and worldviews over Judeo-Christian traditions, with Judaism in its early "reformed" formulation having been influenced by Zoroastrianism, but later deviating from the higher knowledge and doctrines of Zoroastrianism.[172]

At different stages in his life, Yeats's worldview, ranging from occult to magic and spirituality in general, as well as his literary output, were shaped in varying degrees by his engagement with so-called Eastern thoughts, practices, and literatures, as selectively extracted and interpreted by him. These cosmopolitan influences and inspirations included Hinduism, Indian literatures—most famously the Bengali poetry of his contemporary Indian author Rabindranath Tagore, in what became a reciprocal expression of praise by the two poets for their respective literary talent—Buddhism, or Japanese Noh theatre.[173] Among his other Eastern sources of inspiration was the poetry of the fourteenth-century Persian mystic poet (albeit not a sufi) Hafiz (Hafez). Shamsul Islam notes: "In Hafiz, too, Yeats discovered the 'mystical cult of achieving union with the absolute through the senses.'" Islam adds that Yeats "based his poem 'His Bargain' on the one hundred and seventy-third poem of Hafiz's Divan. He quoted Hafiz's poem in a speech in [the play] Diarmuid and Grania, which he and George Moore wrote together in 1902: 'Life of my life, I knew you before I was born, I made a bargain with this brown hair before the beginning of time and it shall not be broken through unending time."'"[174] These lines appear to have been based on the English translation of Hafiz's poetry appearing in the Irish nationalist Justin Huntly McCarthy's 1893 *Ghazels from the Divan of Hafiz*: "From time without beginning, / my heart made covenant with thy tresses to time / without end, my promise shall never be / broken!"[175] While by the late nineteenth century Hafiz (Hafez) was well known in most literary-minded European/Western circles—for instance, Moore, too, had referred to 'Hafez' in his *Lalla Rookh*—an overlooked link in Yeats' interest in Hafiz's poetry is James Clarence Mangan, who had dabbled in a few pseudo-translations of Hafiz's presumed poetry and had hailed Hafiz as an unrivalled oriental poet. For Yeats, the 'East' represented the realm of prized "natural emotions." In what William H. O'Donnell called the "Final" version of Yeats' abandoned novel *The Speckled Bird*, of which Yeats produced at least four versions between 1896 and 1902,[176] the story ends with the protagonist Michael (representing Yeats) "going to the east now, to Arabia and Persia, where he would find among the common people, as soon as he had learned their language, some lost doctrine of reconciliation. [...] surely he would find somewhere in the East a doctrine that would reconcile religion with the natural emotions and at the same time explain these emotions."[177] Yeats' East was an anti-rationalist counterpart to Voltaire's designation of the East in his 1759 *Candide*, in which Voltaire situated the moment of his skeptical protagonist's rational enlightenment in the Ottoman Empire, by way of an encounter between Candide and a sufi, who tells Candide: "we must each cultivate our own garden."[178] Writing in 1924, in the explanatory note for his short play "The Cat and the Moon" (completed in 1917), Yeats stated:

> I have amused myself by imagining incidents and metaphors that are related to certain beliefs of mine as are the patterns upon a Persian carpet to some ancient faith or philosophy. It has pleased me to think that the half of me that feels can sometimes forget all that belongs to the more intellectual half but a few images. The night's dream takes up and plays in the same forgetful fashion with our waking thoughts. Minnaloushe [i.e., the cat in the play] and the Moon were perhaps—it all grows faint to me—an exposition of man's relation to what I have called the Antithetical Tincture, and when the Saint mounts upon the back of the Lame Beggar [in the play,] he personifies a certain great spiritual event which may take place when Primary Tinctures, as I have called it, suspends Antithetical—[...] I have altogether forgotten whether the other parts of the fable have, as is very likely, a precise meaning, and that is natural, for I generally forget in contemplating my copy of an old Persian carpet that is winding and wandering vine had once that philosophical meaning, which has made it very interesting to Josef Strzygowski [the Austrian-Polish art historian and advocate of oriental motifs in European art] and was part of the religion of Zoroaster.[179]

Tracing Ireland's Cuchulain and Conla Legend to an Iranian Epic

A component of the Irish Revival, which also had a particular appeal among republican nationalist camps, was the popularization, reworking, and instrumental reconfiguration of certain episodes from Irish epic cycles, along with the politically calculated creation of *new* "myths." The most famous example of the latter was *Kathleen ni Houlihan* by Yeats and Lady Gregory. The lead character of Yeats' and Gregory's play had also appeared as one of James Clarence Mangan's creative 'translations from Irish.' Stating he had been inspired by James Hardiman's 1831 collection of *Irish Minstrelsy, or Bardic Remains of Ireland*, which in its second volume included a selection of ballads categorized as "Jacobite Relics,"[180] Mangan had anonymously published his highly inventive pseudo-translation (primarily based on existing English translations) in a January 1841 issue of the Dublin paper *Irish Penny Journal* (signed "M.").[181] The poem appeared following an introductory note to the first installment of what was to be a serialized contribution by Mangan to the paper under the heading "The Jacobite Relics of Ireland," which suggested the original ballad in question dated from the mid-eighteenth century. Titled "Kathaleen Ny-Houlahan," Mangan noted that his translation was based on a work that had not been included in Hardiman's collection. In his characteristically contrived provenance for the original ballad, Mangan wrote: "We may observe, that the name of the author of this song, if ever known, is no longer remembered; but there seems to be no doubt that the song itself is of Munster origin." Mangan's poem was in fact a reworking of an English translation of "Caitlin Ni Uallachain" by William Heffernan (Uilliam Dall O'Hearnain/Uilliam Ó hAnnracháin; surnamed "The Blind"). From its opening line, Mangan's 'translation' differed significantly in content and style from Heffernan's.[182] Mangan's version was subsequently included in the 1845 collection of Irish ballads edited by Charles Gavan Duffy, which immediately became a highly popular collection of Irish poetry, particularly in nationalist circles. In the 1866 edition of Duffy's collected volume, Mangan's poem was accompanied by an editorial note: "Kathaleen Ny-Houlahan is one of the names employed by latter bards to signify the country of whose hopes and aim they dare not speak in direct terms."[183] The poem subsequently appeared in a host of other edited volumes of Mangan's works published in the nineteenth century.[184] It was through Mangan's invented translation that Heffernan's ballad was given a new lease of life. Yeats and Gregory further re-invented the legendary Kathleen ni Houlihan as an object of nationalist adoration by transforming her into a contemporary mythologization of Mother Ireland.

An underlying attribute of these reframed or invented epics and legends was their function as literary and theatrical conduits for generating greater interest and pride in a culturally and/or politically charged distinctively Irish 'national' identity, while also inducing a sentiment of pride in a generically defined Irish heritage, if not also ultimately inspiring nationalist heroism and willingness to commit acts of self-sacrifice for the cause of the nation.[185] Or, as Colm Tóibín has reminded us in the case of Lady Gregory's translations of old Irish legends, the literary enterprise of garnering greater interest in Irish epics also aimed "to add dignity to Ireland," by highlighting Ireland's long pre-Norman literary tradition.[186] It was in this context that the stories of Cuchulain (Cú Chulainn) in the Ulster Cycle attracted renewed nationalist literary interest. Cuchulain was now hailed as the preeminent Irish epic hero, transcending all other heroes of the Ulster Cycle and those of the previously better known Fenian Cycle. A generation of Irish nationalist poets, playwrights, and authors at the turn of the century credited Standish O'Grady's literary resuscitation of Cuchulain as the trendsetter in this regard, noting such works as his *History of Ireland. Volume I: The Heroic Period* (1878) and *History of Ireland. Volume II: Cuculain and His Contemporaries* (1880), or *The Coming of Cuculain* (1895). Among those acclaiming O'Grady's works as a major catalyst for their own interest in Irish mythology, and/or their literary or theatrical recreations of Cuchulain stories, were Yeats and Lady Gregory.[187] In turn, Lady Gregory's and Yeats' own rendition of Cuchulain, along with their other theatrical productions, stimulated nationalist fervor and militancy among some of their contemporary audiences, including a number of those who took up arms in Easter week 1916, most notably a leader of the uprising Patrick (Pádraic) Pearse.[188] Lady Gregory, incidentally, in addition to her advocacy of Irish nationalism, had also been one of the earliest champions of "Egypt for Egyptians" in the United Kingdom following the British occupation of Egypt in 1882 (see Chapter Seven).

In 1892, Yeats published a highly influential poem titled "The Death of Cuchulain," urging heroism and nationalist valor (leaving aside here the poem's gendered attributes of nationalist heroism). Even more inspirational in nationalist circles at the turn of the century was Lady Gregory's 1902 *Cuchulain of Muirthemne: The Story of the Men of the Red Branch of Ulster*. This was her own select adaptation and arrangement of the Cuchulain saga in the Ulster Cycle. Lady Gregory's *Cuchulain of Muirthemne* also included the account of the armed encounter between Cuchulain and his son Conla (Conlaoch), an episode occurring in the original Ulster Cycle, but commonly absent from other contemporary nationalist appropriations of the Cuchulain epic. In this story, Conla was born after Cuchulain had left Conla's mother, the warrior Scottish queen Aoife (Aífe), with whom Cuchulain had had a night's affair. Many years later, unbeknownst to both the father and the son, Aoife orchestrated a deadly encounter between the two as her revenge against Cuchulain. Cuchulain and Conla remained unaware of their father-son relationship until shortly before the mortally wounded young hero's death in battle.[189] In his Preface to Lady Gregory's book, Yeats, hailed the work as "the best that has come out of Ireland in my time. Perhaps, I should say that it is the best book that has come out of Ireland; for the stories which it tells are a chief part of Ireland's gift to the imagination of the world—and it tells them perfectly for the first time."[190] Yeats was by then a close collaborator of Lady Gregory at the Irish Literary Theatre (1899), renamed the Irish National Dramatic Society in 1902, the Irish National Theatre Society in 1903, and the Abbey Theatre, 1904–present. In 1903, Yeats wrote a play, *On Baile's Strand*, produced at the Abbey Theatre the following year, which was also based on Cuchulain's and Conla's encounter, and Cuchulain's subsequent grief-maddened death as he fought the waves in the sea until he drowned. This was an adaptation of Lady Gregory's "The Son of Aoife" in *Cuchulain of Muirthemne*. Over the years, Yeats would revisit the overall Cuchulain saga in search of themes and motifs for other poems and plays, as in his 1938 poem "The Statues."[191] In 1939, within weeks after having completed a poem titled "Cuchulain Comforted," he also made the final revisions to a play titled *The Death of Cuchulain*, as Yeats himself now lay in his deathbed.[192]

It should be noted Yeats and Lady Gregory were working within the paradigm of what by then was conventionally accepted as the 'Aryan' roots of Irish mythology, notwithstanding continued disagreements over the cradle of the so-called Aryan race (the East vs. Europe), or Douglas Hyde's distinction between the Aryan carry-over in Irish folklore and mythology and the locally crafted indigenous lore and legends.[193] In addition to Standish O'Grady's publications, Lady Gregory at this stage was also operating under the notable influence of studies by William Larminie (1849–1900), the author of the 1893 *West Irish Folk-Tales and Romances*. Larminie's nebulous Asian theory of Aryan origins and peculiar designation of various racial branches around the world designated the population settlements in northern regions of the Indian subcontinent in ancient times as the earliest known descendants of an Aryan ancestral group, without identifying that group's primal location. Larminie account of the early population of Ireland, evidently a reworking of O'Grady's model appearing in the first volume of the latter's 1878 *History of Ireland*, consisted of an alternative formula of Aryan and non-Aryan population arrivals in Ireland: "Ethnologists know that the so-called Gaelic race is really a compound one, containing in addition to the true Celtic (Aryan) element probably two that are not Aryan—a Mongolian or Finnish element, and an Iberian element."[194] Most notably, Lady Gregory followed Larminie's sequencing of the major epics of Ireland, according to which the main components of the Fenian Cycle (categorized by Larminie as "non-Aryan folk-literature partially subjected to Aryan treatment") were developed by people less civilized than the Aryans and introduced to Ireland by non-Aryan settlers prior to the arrival of Aryans. In this narrative, the Aryan colonists introduced the Cuchulain stories of the Ulster Cycle to Ireland, which in terms of their actual time of creation pre-dated the Fenian sagas of non-Aryan people, even though the Fenian Cycle had reached Ireland first. Larminie wrote:

> Then entered the Aryan Gael, and for him, henceforth, as the ruler of the island, his own gods and heroes were sung by his own bards. His legends became the subject of what I may call the court poetry, the aristocratic literature. [...] Here the heroic cycle has been handed down in remembrance almost solely by the bardic literature. The popular memory retains but few traces of it. Its essentially aristocratic character is shown by the fact that the people have all but forgotten it if they ever knew it. But the Fenian cycle has not been forgotten. Prevailing everywhere, still cherished by the conquered peoples, it held its ground in Scotland and Ireland alike, forcing its way in the latter country even into the written literature, and so securing a twofold lease of existence. That it did not deserve this wider popularity is evident enough. Interesting though it be, it is not equal in interest to the heroic cycle. The tales of the latter, though fewer in number, less bulky in amount, have upon them the impress of the larger constructive sweep of the Aryan imagination. Their characters are nobler; the events are more significant. They form a much more closely compacted epic whole. The Fenian tales, in some respects more picturesque, are less organised. It would be difficult to construct out of them a coherent epic plot; and what is, perhaps, not the least in significance, they have far more numerous, more extended, more intimate connections with the folk-tale.[195]

As a side note here, in the widely known Fenian Cycle story of "Tuatha de Danann and of the Fianna of Ireland," which among other renditions was also translated and edited by Lady Gregory and published in 1905 with a Preface by Yeats, the sons of Tuireann (Brian, Iuchar, and Iucharba) after killing Cian are dispatched by Cian's son, Lugh "of the Long hand," to distant corners of the world. Their mission turns out to be an act of retribution by undergoing ordeals as they fetch items demanded of them by Lugh, who anticipates the brothers will not survive their quest. The three sons of Tuireann fulfill their mission only to die of wounds they have suffered toward the end of their quest.

Lugh instructed Brian and his younger brothers that their mission was to obtain "three apples, and the skin of a pig, and a spear, and two horses, and a chariot, and seven pigs, and a dog's whelp, and a cooking-spit, and three shouts on a hill. That is the fine I am asking." Describing each of these objects in detail to the three brothers, Lugh added:

> "And do you know what is the spear I am asking of you?" he said. "We do not," said they. "It is a very deadly spear belonging to the King of Persia, the Luin it is called, and every choice thing is done by it, and its head is kept steeped in a vessel of water, the way it will not burn down the place where it is, and it will be hard to get it. [...]"[196]

In their odyssey, during which Brian and his brothers variously disguise themselves, after they kill Tuis, the king of Greece, whose magical pig skin they steal, the brothers reach Persia, where they manage to steal the magical spear of the king of Persia named "Pisear," who is killed by being struck on the forehead by a magical apple hurled at him by Brian, which the brothers had taken from the "Garden in the East of the World."[197] Clearly a product of the so-called Middle Ages, than of ancient Ireland as claimed in the myth, the story in effect imputed ancient (i.e., pre-Christian) Irish familiarity with Iran (Persia).

Returning to the story of Cuchulain and Conla in the Ulster Cycle, the fact that Larminie's explanation of the hitherto greater popularity of Fenian Cycle and the near-obscurity of Cuchulain stories resonated with Lady Gregory and Yeats was very likely also due to Larminie's attribution of the Cuchulain saga to the courtly and aristocratic Aryan tradition. Lady Gregory belonged to the landed aristocratic Anglo-Irish Protestant Ascendancy, while Yeats, also from an Anglo-Irish Protestant background and at the time considerably reliant on Lady Gregory's patronage, was well-known for his attraction to values and ambitions of the aristocratic social class, alongside his goal of securing a foremost place among the elite of nationalist literary and cultural "aristocracy" (as presumed shapers of nationalist Ireland's ideals and values).[198] Douglas Hyde, another member of the Anglo-Irish Protestant Ascendancy, shared Larminie's ("My friend Mr. Larminie") model of the Aryan origin of Cuchulain legend and the non-Aryan foundation of Fenian Cycle. In Hyde's view, this theory corresponded in its broader outline to Alfred Nutt's model of two categories of ancient Irish legends: those of Aryan origin sharing common elements with Aryan mythology in other parts of the world, on the one hand, and strictly Irish mythology developed locally. However, Hyde, whose cultural nationalist project and wide-ranging endeavors for popularizing Irish language, as well as his studies on Irish folklore, moved along distinctly different trajectories than the literary and theatrical path taken by Lady Gregory and Yeats, adhered to the theory of the European origin of Aryans, with both ancient Irish and Sanskrit presumably derived from that same origin.[199] This was also the view held by Alfred Nutt, who designated the Baltic region as the original homeland of the Aryans, who had then migrated West and East, including to Iranian lands and the Indian subcontinent.

It was in the setting of a particular segment of the Cuchulain legend that presumed cultural links between Ireland and Iran were again further reinforced at the turn of the twentieth century by a number of leading authorities on Irish mythology. The most debated putative ancient connection between Ireland and Iran in the field of Irish mythology at the turn of the twentieth century centered on the story of the lethal battle between Cuchulain and Conla. For instance, in March 1908 the *Gaelic American*—the New York mouthpiece of Clan na Gael, the main militant Irish nationalist IRB-affiliated organization at the time—published an article titled "Finn and Oisín: An Ossianic Version of the Celebrated Persian Story." This article was based on the work of Kuno Meyer, the renowned German scholar of Celtic studies at the Royal Irish Academy.[200] (Curiously for a militant Irish nationalist periodical, the *Gaelic American*'s choice of the title for this article suggested its editors' continued belief in the authenticity of the Ossianic Cycle of epic poems forged by the eighteenth-century Scottish Protestant poet James Macpherson. As already mentioned, Macpherson's version of the epic cycle, which according to the *Gaelic American* "purported to be translations of the works of a third-century Scottish bard, Ossian," had appeared in the 1760s and immediately generated controversy in Ireland and Scotland over the true Celtic identity of Ossian (i.e., whether he was Irish or Scots), before literary scholars indisputably proved (by the middle of the nineteenth century) that Macpherson's 'translation' was a forgery and the epic was Macpherson's own inventive creation, partly based on a reworking of earlier Celtic sources. In his adaptation of the earlier Celtic epics, Macpherson had blended together episodes from the Fenian Cycle existing in both Scotland and Ireland with episodes from the strictly Irish Ulster Cycle. Although Kuno Meyer's reported study concerned both Fenian and Ulster cycles, Meyer's focus in the above-quoted article was in fact on certain details and motifs of the Ulster Cycle, unrelated to the Fenian epic.)

According to Meyer's study reported in the *Gaelic American*, "That particular version of the story, which in old Irish literature is embodied in the tale of the fight between Chuchulain and his son Conla, is ultimately derived, both in its main features and in all important details, from the Persian story of Rustem and Sohrab."[201] He added: "This occurs as an episode in the Shah Nameh of Firdusi [i.e., *Shāhnāmeh* of Ferdowsi], a poet of the 10th century, who worked by older legends. Long before his time, however, it had passed from Persia Westward. [...] It seems most likely that it was the Anglo-Saxons who handed it on to the Irish sometime during the 7th or 8th century" (i.e., prior to Ferdowsi's compilation and completion of earlier epics by the early eleventh century).[202] Significantly, Meyer was not proposing any ancient racial or other ties between Ireland and the Orient in his model of cultural diffusion. Along with other patrons of the Literary Revival, Yeats was well acquainted with Meyer's studies by the turn of the century, as indicated by Yeats' reference to one of Meyer's works in 1902.[203]

Meyer, frequently cited as a major authority on Irish mythology by the likes of Lady Gregory or Douglas Hyde, had made the imputed connection between the particular episodes in Irish and Iranian epics at least as early as 1906.[204] He was by no means the first commentator to note this similarity, but his verdict on the Iranian origin of the story of Cuchulain and Conla could not be readily overlooked. His renown as a leading contemporary Celtic scholar, and his clout in Irish nationalist circles engaged in promoting different modes of Irish Literary Revival, added greater weight to his analyses. Meyer was also the founder of the School of Irish Learning (Dublin), established in 1903 to promote rigorous scholarship as the bedrock of the Irish Revival and also publishing the journal *Ériu* (1904–), co-edited by Meyer and John Strachan, a professor of Celtic

Studies, Sanskrit, and Greek in Manchester, England. Not only was Meyer a preeminent scholar of Celtic and of Irish mythology, but, as already noted, by the start of the twentieth century the overall epic cycle of Cuchulain had become a ubiquitous motif in the Irish Literary Revival and Cuchulain was reworked by various Irish nationalist purveyors of literary and cultural revival as the prototype of Ireland's 'national' heroism. Michael McAteer writes: "The Theme of the Irish mythical hero Cuchulain, brought into public consciousness through Standish O'Grady, Augusta Gregory and [Thomas William Hazen] Rolleston in their versions of *Táin Bo Cuailnge* [*The Cattle Raid of Cooley*, which featured Cuchulain as a youth], seemed the obvious choice for a national-popular theatre movement in the Ireland of 1900s."[205] Already in 1902, relying on Meyer's earlier translations of the Cuchulain epic in the Ulster Cycle, but before Meyer asserted an Iranian prototype for a segment of that epic, the American Harvard professor Murray Anthony Potter in his *Sohrab and Rustem: the Epic Theme of a Combat Between Father and Son* had drawn attention to similarities between the Iranian legend appearing in Ferdowsi's *Shāhnāmeh* and segments of other epics from around the world, including the mortal battle between Cuchulain and his son Conla. Potter, however, had suggested the universality of the theme of heroic struggle between father and son, rather than proposing a diffusionist template.[206] Even before Potter's study, the correspondence between the Iranian and Irish epics had been noted by numerous scholars dating back to the late eighteenth century, and with many of them maintaining a direct connection between the Irish and Iranian stories. In "The Irish Story of Cucullin and Conloch and the Persian Story of Rustam and Sohrâb" (first presented at a meeting of the Bombay Branch of the Royal Asiatic Society in 1892 and published in 1905), the prominent Indian Parsi dastur (i.e., an authority on Zoroastrianism) and "Shams-ul-Ulama" ("luminary of scholars") Jivanji Jamshedji Modi provided a detailed account of the correspondence between the plots and particulars of the Irish and Iranian epics. Modi noted that the German-French orientalist, and later professor of Persian, Jules (Julius) Mohl "in the preface to his French translation of Shâh-nâmeh, was the first to allude to this resemblance," following Mohl's reading of Charlotte Brooke's English translations from the Irish original in "Conlach, a Poem" and "The lamentation of Cucullin Over the Body of His Son Conlach," which had appeared in Brooke's 1789 *Reliques of Irish Poetry*.[207] Mohl's translation of *Shāhnāmeh* (begun in 1826) appeared in seven volumes after 1838, with the final volume completed and published after his death in 1876 by Charles Barbier de Meynard.[208] This was the first complete European-language translation of the Iranian epic (in the broad sense of Iran). Prior to Modi's 1892 presentation, numerous scholars and other commentators had referred to Mohl's translation of *Shāhnāmeh*, along with references to other partial European translations of the Iranian epic—among them the German-British Helen Zimmern's 1882 translation or Louise Manning Hodgkins's 1890 American edition of the English Matthew Arnold's 1853 poem *Sohrab and Rustum*.[209] There were also various earlier partial translations of *Shāhnāmeh* in European languages that contained the story of the fatal battle between Rustam and Sohrab, such as James Atkinson's *Soohrab; a Poem, Freely Translated from the Original Persian of Firdousee, Being a Portion of the Shahnamu of that Celebrated Poet*, published in India in 1814, which was the first English translation of that particular segment of the Iranian epic.

Modi, in his 1892 "The Irish Story of Cucullin and Conloch," also sought to demonstrate that the resemblance between the Irish and Iranian stories indicated the story was transmitted from Iran to Ireland, rather than the other way around, with the Iranian version being possibly traceable to an even earlier Aryan source. Modi, who as a Parsi traced his ancestral roots to Iran (in its broader historical geographic configuration), was working within the paradigm of a common racial-ethnic ancient connection between Ireland and Iran, which for him explained the occurrence of this purported mythic affinity between the two lands. As already noted in my introductory chapter, Modi stated: "The very name of Ireland suggests that the country was originally inhabited by a tribe of ancient Aryans, the common ancestors of the Irânians of Firdousi and of other adjoining nations. Again, has not the word Erin, used in the above poem of Cucullin as an ancient name of Ireland, a close resemblance with the name of Irân?"[210] Subscribing to the Indo-Iranian Aryanist model, Modi reminded his audience that some German and other European tales and songs also bore close resemblance to the Iranian story. It should be noted Indian Parsi scholars at the turn of the twentieth century also played an instrumental role in the dissemination of Aryanist racial ideology among the Iranian intelligentsia.

Among Irish commentators to have noted the similarity between Rustam and Sohrab, on the one hand, and Cuchulain and Conla, on the other hand, long before Modi's, Potter's, and Meyer's studies, was the antiquarian scholar, member of the Royal Irish Academy, and Catholic priest, James O'Laverty. In his 1859 "Remarkable Correspondence of Irish, Greek, and Oriental Legends" in the *Ulster Journal of Archaeology*, Father O'Laverty noted:

> In examining what little has been published, out of the immense mass of legendary lore yet extant, the reader cannot fail to observe a striking resemblance between the Irish bardic tales and those which have from the most distant antiquity been current in Greece, Persia, and even India. The natural deduction from this is, that at some remote period, a communication existed between those distant countries, by which stories popular in one have been transmitted to others.[211]

Proposing a diffusionist theory of direct ancient transmission of Eastern mythology to Ireland, as opposed to the possibility of gradual diffusion through contact with intermediary territories and cultures, or of universal features of certain myths, O'Laverty wrote under the section on "Rustam and Conloch":

> The beautiful and pathetic story of Rustam, related by the Persian poet Ferdusi in the *Shah Nameh*, is almost identical with the bardic tale of Conlach. The daughter of the King Sitemgum became enamoured of Rustam, when on a visit to her father's court, and she bore him a son, on whom she conferred the name of Sohraub. When he grew up, having learned the story of his birth and his father's fame, he set out in quest of adventures, but in course of time he had the misfortune to encounter his own father. The issue of the combat proved fatal to Sohraub, who, while his life-blood was flowing, related to the victor the history of his birth, and enabled Rustam, when too late, to recognize his own son in the ill-fated youth. The father's grief and the son's affectionate lamentation render the poem of Ferdusi extremely touching.

The Irish tale runs thus. The hero, Cuchullin, when a youth, went to Scotland to study the science of arms, when he became acquainted with Aoife, a lady of that country; she bore him a son, but before his birth the father returned to his own country. He directed the disconsolate Aoife, in case his child should be a son, to call him Conloch, and to have him carefully trained to arms. He gave her a chain of gold to put around his neck [...]
[...]
[...] The result is a combat between the two heroes, in which Cuchullin, when on the point of being worsted, calls for his never-failing dart, which he flings with fatal aim, and transfixes his son. The dying youth declares his name and lineage; and the hoary warrior gives vent to the wild emotions of his grief [...][212]

Even earlier, in 1834, the Anglo-Irish historian and mythologist Thomas Keightley had enumerated the similarities and differences between his selected versions of the two epics.[213] But, unlike O'Laverty, Keightley had outright rejected the likelihood of the Irish myth being a derivative of the Persian original. Noting that his account of the Persian epic was primarily based on other sources than James Atkinson's 1814 translation of *Soohrab* or Atkinson's 1832 abridged translation of *The Shâh Nâmeh of the Persian Poet Firdausí*, Keightley stated:

Mr. Atkinson has translated it into English verse. It will also be found in his epitome of the Shah-Nâmeh. I follow [Johann Joseph von] Görres' epitome of it in his *Heldenbuch von Iran* [1820]. My knowledge of Persian being extremely slight, I always refer in cases of difficulty to my friends MM. [Duncan] Forbes and [Sandford] Arnot, of the London Oriental Institution.

A fine edition of the original poem, edited by Mr. Turner Macan, from a comparison of several of the best MSS., has been printed at Calcutta [in 1829]. It is curious to observe that the reflections with which the following episode opens, are different in it from those in the MS. used by Atkinson, and that Görres' MS. differs from both.[214]

Keightley, based on various footnotes in his book, was familiar with not only works by the likes of the Austrian orientalist Joseph Freiherr von Hammer-Purgstall (e.g., the 1813 *Rosenöl, erstes Fläschchen oder, Sagen und Kunden des Morgenlandes aus arabischen, persischen und türkischen Quellen gesammelt*), but also with a wide range of contemporary English works on Iran, such as John Malcolm's two volume *Sketches of Persia, from the Journals of a Traveller in the East* (1827), Sir William Ouseley's three volume *Travels in Various Countries of the East: More Particularly Persia* (1819–23), and James Morier's satirical *Hajji Baba* fictions. Keightley added:

The tale of Conloch resembles that of Soohrâb in the circumstance of the father in each case having quitted the mother of the unborn babe, and never having returned; and in that of his having left behind him a token of recognition, to be borne by his son (if it should be such) when grown up;—circumstances in which they both agree with the Grecian legend of Theseus. There is a further coincidence in the refusal to tell the name; but in the Persian tale it is the father, in the Irish one the son, who will not reveal himself. [...] and in poetic merit the Irish poem falls immeasurably short of that inspired by the Muse of Irân; yet the coincidence between them is curious, and I think we have here a decided instance of resemblance without imitation.[215]

Keightley, who was at best unsympathetic to Gaelic culture and Catholicism,[216] and who in the above quotation did not miss the opportunity to underrate the Irish poem in comparison with its Iranian counterpart, also went on to accuse Charlotte Brooke and her godfather Sylvester O'Halloran of emblematic "Celtic credulity." This was on grounds that Brooke's Cuchulain, "when bewailing his son, talks of India, Persia, Greece, Spain, and the Picts. Anyone but a Celtic antiquary would, from this, at once infer the late age of the poem. Not so, Mr. O'Halloran, the Celtic Mentor of that accomplished lady. The ancient Irish, according to him, had knowledge far transcending this." Keightley continued:

In a note, Miss Brooke says:

"Our early writers, says Mr. O'Halloran, tell us, and Archbishop Us[s]her affirms the same, that the celebrated champion Conall Cearnach, Master of the Ulster Knights, was actually at Jerusalem at the time of the crucifixion of our Saviour, and related the story to the king of Ulster on his return. He also adds, that one of our great poets in the fifth century traversed the East, and dedicated a book to the Emperor Theodosius. Many similar instances and proofs," continues the fair lady, "could be here subjoined."

It would not, I apprehend, be easy to produce an instance of credulity to exceed or even equal this. I should feel ashamed were I to set seriously about pointing out all the improbabilities which it involves; but I will briefly state my opinion of what the Irish were anterior to the introduction of Christianity in the fifth century. They were then, as far as I can learn, nothing but rude ferocious barbarians (and Christianity does not seem to have made them much better); they were ignorant of arts and letters, utterly unacquainted with any country but their own and the neighbouring Britain, with no vessel beyond the *curragh*, or wicker-boat covered with raw hides.[217]

Brooke, having predicted such line of criticism, had written in her 1789 book *Reliques of Irish Poetry*:

The anti-hibernian critic will here exclaim—"What knowledge could Cucullin possibly be supposed to have had of Greece, or Persia, or of proud India's splendid plain?—Does not the very mention banish every idea of the antiquity of this poem, and mark it out, at once, as a modern production?" It is granted, that this would indeed be the case, had our early ancestors been really such as modern writers represent them:–*Barbarians, descended from barbarians, and ever continuing the same*; but their Phœnician origin of itself sufficiently accounts for their knowledge of the situation, inhabitants, manners, &c. of the various nations of the earth; since the Phœnicians, a maritime and commercial people, traded to every port, and were acquainted with every country.[218]

The Irish cultural-nationalist antiquarian Louisa Catherine Beaufort was among the earliest commentator to have proposed an Iranian archetype for the story of Cuchulain and Conla. In a presentation at the Royal Irish Academy on October 22, 1827, which won the academy's gold prize and relied on the then available partial European translations of *Shāhnāmeh* (although she did not identify her specific translated source), Beaufort noted:

How indeed can the close resemblance between many of the Eastern and Irish legends, that for instance, of the Persian hero Rustam and his son Sohraùb, to the story of the Irish Conloch and his valiant father Cucullin—or the exact similitude which the account Herodotus gives of the Macedonian king Amyntas and Darius the Persian, bears to the Irish history of the destruction of Turgesius the Dane—be accounted for otherwise than by the chronicles and legends of the parent state having been transported to the colony, and there located by the adaptation of names, times, and places.[219]

But, the earliest known assertion of a strong resemblance between these Iranian and Irish epics appears to have been in the essay submitted to the Royal Irish Academy in 1805 by Joseph Cooper Walker, a member of the Academy who had assigned a Phoenician ancestry to Milesians in his earlier works. Walker noted the similarity between the Iranian and Irish stories by way of comparing Sir William Ouseley's account in the 1795 *Persian Miscellanies* of the ill-fated encounter between Rustam and Sohrab in *Shāhnāmeh* and Charlotte Brooke's account of Cuchulain and Conla in her 1789 *Reliques of Irish Poetry*. Walker, too, claimed the Irish tale was based on the Iranian original.[220] The earliest *general* identification of Irish mythology with Iranian mythology had appeared in Vallancey's writings. The publication of Macpherson's Ossianic epics had coincided with the late eighteenth-century surge of Western European interest in Celtic languages and cultures; a development that was more instrumental than is frequently acknowledged in reinforcing contemporary cultural nationalist sentiments in Ireland. The continued interest in Celticism, intersecting with a range of other intellectual, historiographic, and/or political threads over the decades (as already discussed) subsequently impacted the literary, artistic, and cultural Irish Revival of the late nineteenth and early twentieth century in manifold ways. As mentioned before, Vallancey was among leading contributors to the eighteenth-century interest in Celtic studies (more narrowly in the form of Gaelic antiquarianism). In response to Macpherson's claim of the Scottish-Celtic origin of the ascribed Ossianic poems, Vallancey in his 1786 *Vindication of The Ancient History of Ireland* had nebulously insisted not only on the Irish root of both Fenian and Ulster cycles, but also on the ultimately Iranian archetypes of the epic poems in question. To this end, Vallancey had relied on his trademark etymological-linguistic conjuries, while treating the epics as components of his broader overarching theory of Iranian ('Persian') origin of the Gaels. Without ever specifically addressing the lethal encounter between Cuchulain and Conla, Vallancey cited partial summaries of *Shāhnāmeh* he had gleaned from the seventeenth-century French Barthélemy d'Herbelot's *Bibliothèque orientale* and the English John Richardson's 1777 "A Dissertation on the Languages, Literature, and Manners of Eastern Nations."[221]

Walker's, Beaufort's, and O'Laverty's verdicts on the correspondence between specific segments of the Irish and Iranian epics in question had subsequently been highlighted in works by other Irish scholars. For instance, Marcus Keane in his 1867 *The Towers and Temples of Ancient Ireland* relied on O'Laverty's account (with Keane elected a member of the Royal Irish Academy the same year).[222] In effect, long before Modi's 1892 presentation and Meyer's 1906 study, the notion of a remarkably close resemblance between the Iranian and Irish stories, if not also the assertion of an actual Iranian prototype for the episode of the combat between Cuchulain and Conla, was already in circulation in Ireland. This supposition had become so commonplace by the start of the twentieth century that many Irish authors no longer even found it necessary to credit as their precursors the likes of Walker, Beaufort, O'Laverty, or even Mohl, Modi, and Meyer, among other range of such sources—regardless of the occasionally divergent conclusions of these authorities. A case in point was the 1901 *Traces of the Elder Faiths of Ireland* by William Gregory Wood-Martin of the Royal Historical and Archaeological Association of Ireland, who simply stated as a matter of fact and without further elucidation: "There is great similarity between the Persian story of Rustam and the Bardic tale of Conloch."[223]

Nonetheless, the opinion of scholars and literary figures in Ireland, including those engaged in the Irish Revival, concerning the origin of the Cuchulain and Conla segment of the Ulster Cycle remained divided. In his seminal 1899 *A Literary History of Ireland*, Douglas Hyde rejected the view that the story was a derivative of an Iranian version. Relying among other sources on translations and elucidations of Irish epic cycles by Charlotte Brooke and Kuno Meyer—at a time when Meyer had not yet claimed an Iranian prototype for the battle between Cuchulain and Conla—Hyde was of the opinion that the parity between the particular segments of Iranian and Irish epics was due their both having a common origin, as opposed to one being a derivative of the other. Without directly alluding to the Aryan theory in this context, Hyde was in effect suggesting such a connection. Given Hyde's belief in the European origin of Aryans, this would have implied both Irish and Iranian stories were later transmissions of an earlier European-Aryan archetype. He simply wrote that Cuchulain and Conla were "the Irish Sohrab and Rustum, the Celtic Hildebrand and Hadubrand."[224] As noted before, Hyde was writing under the methodological and theoretical influence of Alfred Nutt, the renowned British publisher, Celticist, and folklorist. In 1891 Nutt claimed the "Persian, Teutonic, [and] Celtic" versions of an epic fight between father and son were "variants of a pan-Aryan heroic legend."[225] In subsequent works, Nutt further elaborated on other range of cross-regional Aryan mythological parallels, including in his 1895 "The Happy Otherworld in the Celtic Mythico-Romantic Literature of the Irish," appearing in Kuno Meyer's *The Voyage of Bran*—notably in the section of Nutt's study titled "Scandinavian, Iranian, and Indian Accounts of the Happy Otherworld."[226]

Interestingly, neither Yeats nor Lady Gregory ever publicly commented on the subject of the analogy between the Iranian and Irish epics, despite their extensive use of the Cuchulain legend in general and familiarity with works of leading Celtic scholars such as Hyde, Meyer, and Nutt. Yeats, an adherent of the theory of the Eastern origin of the Aryans, a belief reinforced through his exposure to theosophy, among other range of influences,[227] was also a believer in the more general oriental theory of Irish origins, without being specific about the particular oriental civilizational heritage of ancient Ireland. In fact, he remained a latter-day believer of such theories, as indicated by the date of one of his statement in this regard. In the Preface to his 1924 *The Cat and the Moon and Certain Poems*, which he dedicated to Lady Gregory, Yeats asked: "Why has our school [i.e., literary circle], which has perhaps come to an end, been interested mainly in something in Irish life so old [i.e., the ancient legends] that one can no longer say this is Europe, that is Asia?"[228] The implied connotation being that once upon a time Ireland had been an Asian outpost to the West of Britain, with its myths and sagas reflecting that origin. At least in Yeats' case, a possible explanation for his having steered clear of the debate on the possible Iranian origin of the story of Cuchulain and Conla might be the desire to avoid any suggestion that Ireland's greatest contemporary legendary hero, Cuchulain, whom Yeats and Lady Gregory had done so much to publicize, may in fact be a derivative creation, and hence not an entirely indigenous 'Irish' literary product.

Joseph Jacobs, the Australian-born Jewish English folklorist, Judaica encyclopedist, literary critic, and editor of the 1899 edition of the Anglo-Irish author Louisa Stuart Costello's (d.1870) *The Rose Garden of Persia*—originally published in 1845 and covering a range of (specifically 'Iranian') Persian-language classical poetry after Ferdowsi's time—also referred to the similarity between Iranian and Irish legends of combat between father and son. Jacobs rejected the possibility of the Irish story being based on an Iranian original, or of both stories being derived from some other common source. Instead, similar to Potter's position three years later, Jacobs wrote, while commenting on Ferdowsi's *Shāhnāmeh*, that the close resemblance between the Irish and Iranian stories was a reflection of the universal human condition:

> Curiously enough, the central incident of the whole epic—the single combat of the two heroes, father and son, in which the son falls—is reproduced almost exactly in the early heroic literature of Ireland, and suggestions have been made that there was an original Aryan myth or legend from which both of these Aryan nations took the episode. This is, however, going too far; in a fighting age the natural pathos of such a situation could easily occur independently to two poetic minds.[229]

Jacobs' Introductory essay in Costello's book is worth examining in light of the ongoing Aryanist debates in Irish nationalist circles, even if Ireland did not constitute a particular subject of Jacob's analyses of 'race.' Present in Jacobs's account was a generic counter-Aryanist discourse (without any distinction between the varieties of Aryanism or the imperialist versus anticolonial Aryanist platforms). Jacobs was in fact rejecting the possibility of any direct and continuous Aryan cultural fountainhead. Ironically omitting Ireland from his account of the reception in the United Kingdom of the range of Persian literature covered in Costello's book (by reducing English readership to 'England'), Jacobs equally disallowed any purely Aryan civilizational designation or a thoroughly Aryan foundation of 'European' civilizations and cultures (i.e., inclusive of Ireland). In place of current hierarchical Aryan theories of race and civilization in the West, Jacobs posited a hybridized Aryan-Semitic cultural confluence—with "Semitic" applied in the broad linguistic and trans-Jewish articulation of the category, inclusive of what he termed "Arab" and Christian and Muslim traditions. Jacobs was, in effect, reworking the Italian Graziadio Isaia Ascoli's Indo-Semitic (or Aryo-Semitic) model, while transcending racial categorizations in favor of cultural designations of the same categories. Albeit with some exaggeration, Jacobs criticized the near-exclusive appeal of Persian literature to most contemporary European readers of Eastern literatures, to the extent of almost complete neglect of the literary jewels of South Asia and Arab territories: "Yet nothing is known of Kalidasa [the fourth- to fifth-century Sanskrit poet and author from the Gupta Empire] or Hariri [the eleventh- to twelfth-century

Arab poet from Seljuk-controlled Iraq] by even well-read Englishmen." Through his own peculiar lens of linguistic, literary, (trans-racial) cultural and religious historicizing, Jacobs went on to explain the particular appeal to "English readers" of Ferdowsi's *Shāhnāmeh* and the eleventh- to twelfth-century Persian mathematician, philosopher, astronomer and poet Omar Khayyam's *Rubāiyāt*.[230] While Jacobs was correct in his general observation of the wider availability and appeal of Persian literature (from Iran and beyond) as "household word" in 'England' in comparison with other 'Eastern' literatures, it is still worth noting both his narrow definition of poetry in this context and his somewhat overarching neglect of the growing appeal of Hindu mythology and 'Indian' literatures in the United Kingdom, including in theosophical and other circles frequented by some leading proponents of the Irish Literary Revival. Moreover, by the time Jacobs was writing (1899), besides the much earlier translations into English of various Indian texts, or of translations undertaken more recently by the theosophical movement, there existed 48 volumes of what would become the 50-volume (the last volume comprising the General Index) of *The Sacred Books of the East* translation series (1879–1910), under the general editorship of Friedrich Max Müller (d. 1900). The overwhelming majority of the translations in this series consisted of Sanskrit and other 'Indian' texts.[231]

Jacobs wrote:

> Can we see here some subtle sympathy between the Persian Aryans and their European cousins? Professor Max Müller would probably assent to this explanation, but the high-caste Hindu has also the Aryan cousinship, and yet neither the *Ramayana* or the *Mahabharata* has become a household word in England, and as I have said before, the Kalidasa is equally unknown here. And, even as applied to Persia, the Aryan theory scarcely holds good, for there have been three periods of literary activity in Persia, corresponding to three different forms of the language known to the pundits as Zend, Pahlavi, and Persian. If it were merely a question of racial sympathy, the Zendavesta or the obscure products of the Pahlavi literature should have equal claim to appeal to us as Firdausi or Omar; but it is only when the Pahlavi, or Middle Persian, becomes transformed by its contact with Arabic into Persian properly so called, that poetry written in it seems capable of appealing to the European mind.
>
> Here, then, we seem on the threshold of an explanation of the appeal of Persian poetry to Englishmen. It is when Persia comes into contact with Islam—in other words an Aryan race with a Semitic religion—that we see produced a tone of mind analogous and sympathetic to the European, which may also be described as Aryan tinged with Semitic religion. The analogy may even go further: just as Europe, when it took up the religion of Judæa, gave it a specific form and tone, so the Persians, when they adopted Islam, gave it a special form which constitutes the sole break in the monotony of the Mohammedan religion from Timbuctoo to China. The Shiite heresy is peculiar to Persia, and has given rise (as readers of Matthew Arnold will remember) to a special religious rite represented in a Passion Play, which again has its analogies among the Semitised Aryans of Europe. Altogether, therefore, a good case may be made out for attributing the undoubted sympathy which exists between Persian poetry and the West to the remarkable analogies which exist between their spiritual lives.[232]

Tugged between East and West: Aryanism, the Irish Revival, and Irish Nationalist Historiography

The diverse Irish nationalist articulations of Aryanist theories, just as in Iranian or Indian nationalist circles by the turn of the century, were tied to broader civilizational discourses and frequently served as countervailing matrices of *national self-framing*, if not also premeditated instrumental strategies, apropos of the hierarchical and hegemonic Aryanist currents present in European/Western *imperialist* claims of racial superiority over colonized and semi-colonized population groups. In their manifold formulations over time, some range of anti-imperialist Aryanist configurations spawned cross-territorial pan-Aryan expressions of anti-imperialist nationalist solidarity, as in the case of the 1906 Pan-Aryan Association founded in New York (see Chapter Seven), as well as their own internally and/or externally designated and vilified racial Others—instances of the latter included the targeting of the small Jewish population in Ireland during the 1904 Limerick pogrom, which was justified by some Irish nationalist circles, or the Anti-Arab attribute of certain Perso-centric Iranian nationalist articulations of Aryanism after the late nineteenth century, or the Aryanist strand of Hindu-nationalist civilizational and racial relegation of the (ethnically) Dravidian population in the Indian subcontinent. In a range of these racial articulations of Aryanism, racial pride of the nation was posited as a primary inspiration for securing national independence. An article in *Sinn Féin* in 1910 by Louise Kenny, the Irish nationalist novelist and occasional columnist for that paper, could well have been describing Ireland than Iran from this racial-civilizational perspective, aside from its allusion to the ancient Persian empires and the current Anglo-Russian intervention in Iran:

> Persian historical memories go a deal further back [...] the people never forget that their country was once the seat of one of the four great Empires of the ancient world; moreover, they have the utter pride of being a native white race in the East. So, naturally, they cherish the Nationalist notion that they would like to keep Persia for the Persians. Meanwhile, both the Russian Bear and the British Lion have mouthed down some of the fence rails and slicked inside.[233]

The multiple nationalist (re)arrangements of racial mythologies, including some alternative non-Aryan racial characterizations of the Irish, as well as the overall rejection of racial theories by some nationalists such as Fred Ryan, underscore the always conditional and inherently dissonant and polythetic essence of racial and national constructs. Other than the older patterns of Irish nationalist claims of Ireland's ancient civilizational grandeur—whether in contrast to mainland Britain or framed as a common Celtic heritage of the entire British Isles—at the heart of the counter-hegemonic anti-imperialist Aryanist constructs of the Irish nation was also the topic of Ireland's contemporary status in regard to 'modernity' and notions of national "progress." In this context, nationalists either contested the equation of modernity with empire, by claiming alternative and/or indigenous roots of national modernities, whether alongside, independently of, or contra imperial modernities, or they entirely rejected the notion of national progress being predicated on modernity in any of its manifold definitions.[234]

The particular range of Irish nationalist projects that aimed at preserving and/or recovering (while often in actuality entirely inventing) the putatively authentic national Self by means of returning to certain pre-colonial cultural foundations of the 'nation' as a blueprint for present and future *self*-framing were by definition (albeit not in practice) also projects of resurrecting the pre-modern, For some in the Irish Revival—leaving aside the misleading connotation of the general label 'Revival' that otherwise included different spectrum of revivalist, modernist, and combined purviews—Ireland's presumed historical-cultural links to the Orient served as a means of pursuing a project of specifically "anticolonial" anti-modernities. In this scenario, the insinuated oriental essence of Irish culture represented *the Other of England* and an antidote to imperial modernities, by constituting alternative states of civilizational sophistication and cultural progress in contrast to 'England,' but without necessarily always rendering the "pre-modern" of the pre-colonial condition as an exact *opposite* of 'modernity' in every sense of the term. Yeats and Lady Gregory belonged to this category of Revivalists, even if any notion of cultural *Self*-recovery is as abstruse and absurd as are assertions of modernity unfettered by the past, or somehow not always localized in form and extent, or incomplete and continually deferred projects. Joseph Lennon writes: "Yeats probably did not fully recognize the cultural tradition of a Celtic-Oriental 'something in Irish life,' [but] he nevertheless recognized its subversive, antimodern, and (often) anticolonial resonances and saw how such motifs reverberated within Irish literature and culture. [...] During the Revival [...] cultural nationalists reinvented this pairing ['between the Celt and the Oriental'] by identifying with the Orient as both something new and something traditional."[235] The ancient racial and folk connections between Ireland and the Orient propagated by the likes of Lady Wilde, Standish O'Grady, or Larminie, were imbibed by a host of cultural-stylists of Irish nationalism. Although references to Vallancey and other similar antiquarians of earlier generations had rapidly fallen out of fashion, there was a significant overlap between the new affirmations of Orient-Ireland folk and epic connections and the former antiquarian contentions of Ireland's oriental roots. The main difference, as already noted, lay in methodological and theoretical procedures.

In Irish historiography, however, by the start of the twentieth century the theory of the European origin of the Aryans was rapidly gaining consensus, and hence also the theory of the European origin of the Celts—given the growing identification of Celts as a branch of Aryans in Irish historical narrations since at least the works of Thomas Osborne Davis in the 1840s. This was the model of Irish "Celtic origin" propounded in the late nineteenth century by the likes of Sophie Bryant, or the leading English Celticist Alfred Trübner Nutt, and Douglas Hyde. At the turn of the century, the Irish nationalist Eoin MacNeill, the co-founder with Hyde of the Gaelic League, a leading historian and Celticist, as well as a future professor at the University College Dublin and subsequently also the minister of education in the Irish Free State, became one of the principal shapers of the Europe-centered theory of Ireland's Celtic heritage and the common presence of Celts in ancient times throughout the British Isles. This theory and its cultural and political nationalist implications are examined in Chapter Nine.

Notes

1 "Introduction" in *Handbook for Travellers in Ireland*. London: John Murray, 1864, p.xlvi.
2 Marcus Keane, *The Towers and Temples of Ancient Ireland*, p.42.
3 Jacob Bryant, an English antiquarian, was best known for his 1773 multi-volume *A New System, or, an Analysis of Antient Mythology*, which attempted to provide a comprehensive account of the religious beliefs of ancient pagan peoples in the early period of population dispersions around the globe following the Great Flood, in keeping with the Mosaic theory, particularly the Cuthite (Amonian) descendants of Ham. Bryant's examples included the Phoenicians, Scythians, Chaldeans, Babylonians Egyptians, Persians, Ethiopians, Canaanites, and Dorians.
4 Marcus Keane, *The Towers and Temples of Ancient Ireland*, pp.41–42, 44, 49–50, 97, 170, 172, 231, 233, 235–36 n.*, 242–43, 303, 316–19, 327, 348–49, and passim.
5 Ibid., the misnumbered pages pp.xviii [xxvi]–xix [xxvii], and passim.
6 John O'Hart, *Irish Pedigrees*, vol.II (1892 edition), p.631.
7 "Some Irish War Correspondents" in *United Ireland* (Dublin), January 16, 1892, p.1, cc.f-g. This newspaper, published from 1881 to 1898, was originally owned by Charles Stewart Parnell (d.1891) and edited by William O'Brien from 1881 to 1891. The paper was among the diverse range of Irish nationalist press that routinely condemned British policy in Egypt and the Sudan, attacking the British occupation of Egypt in 1882 and later championing the Mahdi's resistance in the Sudan to British forces in an unmistakably fervent anti-'British' language. On Edmond O'Donovan, see also John Denvir, *The Life Story of an Old Rebel*. Dublin: Sealy, Bryers, & Walker, 1910, pp.90, 160–65; Richard Hayes, "A Famous Irish War Correspondent," *Studies: An Irish Quarterly Review* 36(141), March 1947, pp.40–48; Fitzroy Maclean, *A Person from England*. London: J. Cape, 1958, chapter 3 (passim); Michael Foley, "The Reporting of Edmond O'Donovan: Literary Journalism and the Great Game" in Richard Keeble and John Tulloch, eds., *Global Literary Journalism: Exploring the Journalistic Imagination*. New York: Peter Lang, 2012, chapter 13; Niamh O'Sullivan, *Aloysius O'Kelly: Art, Nation, Empire*. Dublin: Field Day, 2010, pp.112–15; Michael Beard, "European Travelers in the Trans-Caspian Before 1917," *Cahiers du monde russe et soviétique* 13(4), 1973, p.594.
8 Edmond O'Donovan, *The Merv Oasis: Travels and Adventures East of the Caspian During the Years 1879-80-81. Including Five Months Residence among the Tekkés of Merv*. Two volumes. London: Smith, Elder, & Co., 1882.
9 George Nathaniel Curzon, *Persia and the Persian Question*. Volume I. London: Longmans, Green, and Co., 1892, p.23.
10 Edmond O'Donovan, *The Merv Oasis*, vol.I, pp.386–87.
11 Ibid., p.498.
12 Ibid., p.251.
13 Ibid., p.129.
14 Edmond O'Donovan, *The Merv Oasis*, vol.II, p.25.
15 On "Brother James of Ireland," see Alice Stopford Green, *The Making of Ireland and Its Undoing, 1200-1600*. Dublin: Maunsel and company, 1920, p.546; Charles Raymond Beazley, *The Dawn of Modern Geography. Volume III: A History of Exploration and Geographical Science from the Middle if the Thirteenth to the Early Years of the Fifteenth Century (c. A.D. 1260-1420)*. Oxford: Clarendon Press, 1906, p.255. Brother James also visited the Indian subcontinent and Mongol-controlled Tibet and China (ruled by the Mongol Yuan dynasty).
16 David James, "An Irish Visitor to the Court of the Shah of Persia in 1835: Extract from the Unpublished Diary of Sir Francis Hopkins of Athboy," *Studies: An Irish Quarterly Review* 60(238), Summer, 1971, pp.139–54. This article also appears under the same title in Houchang E. Chehabi and Grace Neville, eds., *Erin and Iran*, pp.156–71. On William Cormick and his father, see also Benjamin Schwartz ed., *Letters from Persia*, pp.13, 31, 54, 65, 67, 88–89, 91,112, 117, 123–24, and passim.
17 John Malcolm, *Sketches of Persia, from the Journals of a Traveller in the East*. Volume I. London: John Murray, 1827, pp.23, 98–99.
18 William Broadfoot, "Pottinger, Sir Henry (1789-1856)," *Dictionary of National Biography. Vol. XLVI: Pocock-Puckering*. Sidney Lee editor. London: Smith, Elder, & Co., 1896, pp.224–26.

19 On the teaching of Persian and Iran-related courses (in the very broad historical-territorial sense of Iran) at Trinity College, see also Menahem Mansoor, *The Study of Irish Orientalism*. Dublin: Hodges, Figgis & Co., 1944; Mansour Bonakdarian, "Iranian Studies in 'the United Kingdom' in the 20th Century," *Iranian Studies* 43(2), 2010, pp.280–81 and passim; Vivian Ibrahim, "The Mir of India in Ireland: Nationalism and Identity of an Early 'Muslim' Migrant," *Temenos: Nordic Journal of Comparative Religion* 46(2), 2010, pp.153–74; idem, "Sailors, Merchants, Migrants: From the Sack of Baltimore to World War II" in Oliver Scharbrodt, Tuula Sakaranaho, Adil Hussain Khan, Yafa Shanneik, Vivian Ibrahim, eds., *Muslims in Ireland: Past and Present*. Edinburgh: Edinburgh University press, 2015, pp.5–7; Joseph Lennon, *Irish Orientalism*, p.175.
20 See Denis Wright, "English Memsahibs in Persia," *History Today* 30(9), September 1980, pp.7–9.
21 George Fisher Russell Barker, "Ouseley, Sir Gore (1770-1844), *Dictionary of National Biography. Volume XLII: O'Duinn—Owen*. Sidney Lee, editor. London: Smith, Elder, & Co., 1895, pp.361–62; Stanley Lane-Poole, "Ouseley, Sir William (1767-1842)," ibid., pp.363–64; Peter Avery, "Ouseley, Gore," *Encyclopaedia Iranica* (http://www.iranicaonline.org/articles/ouseley-sir-gore); idem, "Ouseley, William," *Encyclopaedia Iranica* (http://www.iranicaonline.org/articles/ouseley-sir-william).
22 Kamran Ekbal and Lutz Richter-Bernburg, "Cormick, John," *Encyclopaedia Iranica* (http://www.iranica.com/articles/cormick-john); and Moojan Moomen, "Cormick, William" (1993), *Encyclopaedia Iranica* (http://www.iranica.com/articles/cormick-william-b).
23 Maurice George Moore, *An Irish Gentleman: George Henry Moore. His Travels. His Racing. His Politics. With a Preface by George Moore*. London: T. Werner Laurie, n.d., p.32.
24 Frederic von Allendorfer, "Note on An Irish-man (Archibald Fitzgerald) in the Persian Service," *The Irish Sword: The Journal of the Military History Society of Ireland* 7(27), Winter 1965, pp.175–76.
25 On this journey, they also met the Irish Sir Justin Sheil and Lady Mary Leonora Woulfe Sheil at Sultanieh (Iran) in mid-November 1849, as well as the likes of the British Austen Henry Layard and his Ottoman-Iraqi archaeological collaborator Hormuzd Rassam in the outskirts of Mosul near Nineveh (Ottoman-Iraq) in March 1850, after crossing from Iran back into Ottoman territory. Sarah L. Steele, ed., *The Right Honourable Arthur MacMurrough Kavanagh: A Biography*. London: MacMillan and Co., 1891, pp.47, 69–70, and passim.
26 Sarah L. Steele, ed., *The Right Honourable Arthur MacMurrough Kavanagh*, p.101.
27 Lady Mary Leonora Woulfe Sheil, *Glimpses of Life and Manners in Persia*, p.2; Denis Wright, "English Memsahibs in Persia," p.11; idem., "Memsahibs in Persia," *Asian Affairs* 14(1), 1983, p.9.
28 For the first and last installments, see *Ettelā'āt* (Tehran), 8 Dey 1359, p.8; 13 Ordibehesht 1360, p.8. Appearing after the establishment of the Islamic Republic of Iran in 1979, these installments were later published as a book in 1983, titled *Khāterāt-e Lady Sheil* ("The Memoirs of Lady Sheil"). In his introductory commentaries in these different publications, Aboutorabian attributed entirely unfounded conspiratorial and imperialist motives to Lady Sheil.
29 "Sheil, Richard Lalor" in Charles Knight, ed. *Biography, or Third Division of "The English Encyclopedia,"* vol. 5, pp.468–69; "Sheil, Edward. (Meath, South)" in *Dod's Parliamentary Companion. Fifty-Seventh Year*. London: George Bell and Sons, 1889, p.335.
30 Charles Issawi, *The Economic History of Iran 1800-1914*, pp.171–77; Sarah Searight, *The British in the Middle East*. London: Weidenfeld & Nicolson, 1969, pp.123–24; Jon P. Parry, "Steam Power and British Influence in Baghdad, 1820-1860," *Historical Journal* 56(1), March 2013, pp.145–73. On the initial commercial agreement between Messrs. Lynch Brothers' and the Bakhtiaris, see "Inclosure in No.116," in H.M. Durand to Lord Salisbury, received on June 20, 1898, F.O.371/716 (United Kingdom, The National Archive, London).
31 See also Luke Gibbons, "Race Against Time," pp.102–104 and passim.
32 Thomas Osborne Davis, *The Poems of Thomas Davis* (1857 edition), p.18 n.*.
33 See Sinéad Garrigan Mattar, *Primitivism, Science, and the Irish Revival*. Oxford: Oxford University Press, 2004, chapter 1 ("The Rise of Celtology").
34 See, for example, Isaac Taylor, "The Origin and Primitive Seat of the Aryans," *Journal of the Anthropological Institute of Great Britain and Ireland*, vol.17 (1888), pp.238–75; idem, *The Origin*

    of the Aryans: An Account of Prehistoric Ethnology and Civilization of Europe. New York: Humboldt, 1889, pp.5, 10–12, 38, 151, and passim.
35 Max Müller, *Lectures on the Science of Language. Delivered at the Royal Institution of Great Britain in April, May, & June 1861*. London: Longman, Green, Longman, and Roberts, 1861, pp.199–200, 224–27. On Müller, see also various chapters in John R. Davis, and Angus Nicholls, eds., *Friedrich Max Müller and the Role of Philology in Victorian Thought*. New York: Routledge, 2018; Stefan Arvidsson, *Aryan Idols: Indo-European Mythology as Ideology and Science*. Sonia Wickmann translator. Chicago: University of Chicago Press, 2006, pp.66–90. For an interesting early twentieth-century assessment of Max Müller's place in the evolution of comparative philology and mythology, see Salomon Reinach, "The Growth of Mythological Study," *Quarterly Review* 215(429), October 1911, pp.423–41.
36 See Shane Faherty, "'A Few Good Canons?': Canon Ulick Bourke and Clerical Reaction to the Outbreak of the Land War" in Brian Casey, ed., *Defying the Law of the Land: Agrarian Radicals in Irish History*. Foreword by Carla King. Dublin: History Press of Ireland, 2013, chapter 7; Kevin Collins, *Catholic Churchmen and the Celtic Revival in Ireland, 1848-1916*. Dublin: Four Courts Press, 2003, pp.49–50, 125–27.
37 See Adolphe Pictet, "Inquiry into the Origin of the Name of Ireland," *Ulster Journal of Archaeology*, vol.5, 1857, pp.52, 59.
38 Ulick J. Bourke, *The Aryan Origins of the Gaelic Race and Language*. London: Longman's, Green and Co., 1875, pp.380–81, 382. See also the list of names on pp.273–74.
39 Ibid., p.288.
40 See the anonymous joint review of Bourke's 1875 *The Aryan Origins of the Gaelic Race and Language*, titled "The Vallancey School of Philology" in the *Saturday Review of Politics, Literature, Science, and Art* (London), February 12, 1876, pp.214–15.
41 Ulick J. Bourke, *The Aryan Origins of the Gaelic Race*, p.366.
42 Ibid., p.13.
43 Ibid., p.398.
44 Kevin Whelan, "The Revisionist Debate in Ireland," *boundary* 2(31), Spring 2004, p.198 n.49.
45 Ulick Joseph Bourke, *Pre-Christian Ireland*. Dublin: Browne & Nolan, 1887, p.96. See also p.198. The original spelling by Lady Wilde was "Hindoo Temples." See Jane Francesca (Speranza) Wilde, *Ancient Legends, Mystic Charms, and Superstitions of Ireland. With Sketches of the Past. To Which is Appended a Chapter on 'the Ancient Race of Ireland,' by the Late Sir William Wilde*. Volume II. London: Ward and Downey, 1887, p.269.
46 Ulick J. Bourke, *Pre-Christian Ireland*, pp.198–99.
47 Douglas Hyde, ed., *Beside the Fire: A Collection of Irish Gaelic Folk Stories*. Translation and annotations by Douglas Hyde, with additional notes by Alfred Nutt. London: D. Nutt, 1890, pp .xiii–xv.
48 John Wilson Foster, *Fictions of the Irish Literary Revival: A Changing Art*. Syracuse: Syracuse University Press, 1987, pp.221–22.
49 Anne Markey, "The Discovery of Irish Folklore," *New Hibernia Review* 10(4), Winter 2006, pp.36–37; Diarmuid Ó Giolláin, *Locating Irish Folklore: Tradition, Modernity, Identity*. Cork: Cork University Press, 2000, pp.103–108. See also William Butler Yeats, *Writings on Irish Folklore, Legend and Myth*. Edited and with an Introduction by Robert Welch. London: Penguin, 1993, chapter 10; Gregory Castle, *Modernism and the Celtic Revival*. New York: Cambridge University Press, 2001, pp.41, 54.
50 William Butler Yeats, ed., *Fairy and Folk Tales of the Irish Peasantry*. London: Walter Scott, 1888, pp.xv, 47, 128–29, and passim.
51 William Butler Yeats, ed., *Irish Fairy Tales*. London: T. Fisher Unwin, 1892, p.9.
52 William Butler Yeats, "Tales from the Twilight," *The Scots Observer* 3(67), March 1, 1890, pp.408–409, reprinted in William Butler Yeats, *The Collected Works of W.B. Yeats. Volume IX: Uncollected Articles and Reviews Written Between 1886 and 1900*. John P. Frayne and Madeleine Marchaterre editors. New York: Scribner, 2004, pp.113–16. *The Scots Observer*, published in Edinburgh and London, was an avidly conservative Tory, unionist, and imperialist publication. On Yeats' admiration for Lady Wilde's *Ancient Legends*, see also Mary Helen Thuente, *W.B. Yeats and Irish Folklore*, pp.42, 62–63, 89, and passim.
53 Sinéad Garrigan Mattar, *Primitivism, Science, and the Irish Revival*, p.49. See also pp.41–54.

54 Quoted in ibid., p.59 (from Yeats' January 1890 review of Sophie Bryant's 1889 *Celtic Ireland*).
55 Robert Harborough Sherard, *The Life of Oscar Wilde*. Third edition. London: T. Werner Laurie, 1911 [1906], pp.26–73 and passim; Alexander Martin Sullivan, *New Ireland*, vol.I, pp.158–63; Joy Melville, *Mother of Oscar: The Life of Jane Francesca Wilde*. London: John Murray, 1994; Karen Sasha Anthony Tipper, *A Critical Biography of Lady Wilde, 1821?-1896: Irish Revolutionist, Humanist, Scholar and Poet*. New York: Edwin Mellen Press, 2002; "Jane Francesca Elgee (Lady Wilde)" in Angela Bourke, et al., eds., *The Field Day Anthology of Irish Writing. Volume IV: Irish Women's Writing and Traditions*. Cork: Cork University Press, 2002, pp.877–79; "Lady Wilde (Jane Francesca Elgee)" in Angela Bourke, et al., eds., *The Field Day Anthology of Irish Writing. Volume V: Irish Women's Writing and Traditions*. Cork: Cork University Press, 2002, pp.900–902; Terry Eagleton, *Scholars and Rebels*, pp.58–61; Marjorie Howes, "Tears and Blood: Lady Wilde and the Emergence of Irish Cultural Nationalism" in Tadhg Foley and Seán Ryder, eds., *Ideology and Ireland in the Nineteenth Century*, pp.151–72; Marjorie Howes, *Colonial Crossings: Figures in Irish Literary History*. Dublin: Field Day, 2006, pp.5–23.
56 Robert Harborough Sherard, *The Life of Oscar Wilde*, pp.31–32, 41–42, 70; Richard Ellmann, *Oscar Wilde*, pp.5–10 and passim. The pen name "John Fanshawe," spelled "John Fenshaw Ellis" by Sherard, used the first initials of Jane Francesca [Elgee]. At the time, she was also engaged in charitable activities for aiding famine victims in Ireland and Scotland. For instance, she served as one of the many patrons of the "Amateur Dramatic Performance, for the BENEFIT of the DISTRESSED IRISH and SCOTCH" staged at St. James's Theater in London on April 27, 1847 (the play was "The Hunchback"). *The Times* (London), April 13, 1847, p.4. See also Karen Sasha Anthony Tipper, *A Critical Biography of Lady Wilde*, chapters 4, 5, 6 and passim.
57 Alexander Martin Sullivan, *New Ireland*, vol.I, pp.155, 158. Sullivan's account was reproduced under "Political Irish Women" in *Englishwoman's Review of Social and Industrial Questions* (London), March 12, 1878, pp.142–44. See also Robert Harborough Sherard, *The Life of Oscar Wilde*, pp.42–43; Justin McCarthy, "'Eva' of *The Nation*: Biographical Sketch" in Mary Eva Kelly ("Eva of *The Nation*"), *Poems. By 'Eva' of 'The Nation.'* Seumas Mac Manus editor. Dublin: M.H. Gill & Son, 1909, pp.xi–xxi; Rose Novak, "Reviving 'Eva' of *The Nation*?: Eva O'Doherty's Young Ireland Newspaper Poetry," *Victorian Periodicals Review* 45(4), Winter 2012, pp.436–65; Christine Kinealy, *Repeal and Revolution: 1848 in Ireland*. Manchester: Manchester University Press, 2009, pp.65–66; "Ellen Mary Patrick Downing" in Angela Bourke, et al., eds., *The Field Day Anthology of Irish Writing*, vol. V, pp.68, 902–903. In 1848, "Mary of *The Nation*" abandoned the paper in favor of John Mitchel's short-lived breakaway and more militant Young Ireland weekly *The United Irishman*, founded in Dublin in February 1848. See also William Dillon, *Life of John Mitchel*. Vol. I. London: Kegan Paul, Trench, & Co., 1888, pp.176–248. *The United Irishman* was suppressed in May 1848 by the authorities on grounds of sedition, with Mitchel sentenced to 14 years transportation on charge of treason. See also Ann Andrews, *Newspapers and Newsmakers*, pp.121–23.
58 Robert Harborough Sherard, *The Life of Oscar Wilde*, pp.43–55; Alexander Martin Sullivan, *New Ireland*, vol.I, pp.162–63; Christine Kinealy, *Repeal and Revolution*, pp.13, 29, 189; Ann Andrews, *Newspapers and Newsmakers*, p.256; Karen Sasha Anthony Tipper, *A Critical Biography of Lady Wilde*, pp.252–58. Lady Wilde would also allude to Thermopylae in her *Ancient Legends*, vol.II, pp.288–89. The only copy of "The Suppressed Number" of *The Nation* for July 29, 1848, I have been able to access (via the Irish Newspaper Archive website) is missing p.488 on which "Jacta est Alea" had appeared.
59 See Lady Wilde, "A New Era in English and Irish Social Life," *The Irish Law Times and Solicitors' Journal* (Dublin), March 17, 1883, pp.146–47.
60 She was one of the "208 ladies" who in June 1885 signed a petition addressed to the House of Lords in this regard. *The Times* (London), June 5, 1885, p.10.
61 *Journal of the East India Association* (London,) vol.15, 1883, p.94.
62 See, for example, the first instalment of Lady Wilde's "The Fairy Mythology of Ireland," *Dublin University Magazine* 90(535), July 1877, pp.70–83.
63 William Robert Wilde, *Irish Popular Superstitions*. Dublin: James McGlashan, 1852. See also N.a., "Sir William R. Wilde, M.D., M.R.I.A., *Surgeon Oculist to the Queen in Ireland*," *Dublin*

University Magazine 85(509), May 1875, pp.570–89; Colm Tóibín, *Mad, Bad, Dangerous to Know: The Fathers of Wilde, Yeats and Joyce*. London: Viking, 2018, pp.25–76.

64 On the 'Herder Effect,' see Pascale Casanova, *The World Republic of Letters*. M.B. DeBevoise translator. Cambridge, MA: Harvard University press, 2004 (originally published in French in 1999), pp.75–81, 225–26. For Herder's influence on Irish folklore and explorations in mythology, see also Barry Sheils, "'Dark Cognition': W.B. Yeats, J.G. Herder and the Imperfection of Tradition," *Irish Studies Review* 20(3), 2012, pp.299–321; Eva Maria Stöter, "Region vs. Nation: Nineteenth-Century 'Germany' as a Mirror for Irish Regional/National Politics" in Glenn Hooper and Leon Litvack, eds., *Ireland in the Nineteenth Century: Regional Identity*. Dublin: Four Courts Press, 2000, pp.87–94; David Dwan, *The Great Community*, pp.15–16.

65 Anne Markey, "The Discovery of Irish Folklore," p.21; Diarmuid Ó Giolláin, *Locating Irish Folklore*, pp.44–46.

66 Anne Markey, "The Discovery of Irish Folklore," pp.25–27, 29; Diarmuid Ó Giolláin, *Locating Irish Folklore*, pp.100–102 and passim.

67 Stiofán Ó Cadhla, *Civilizing Ireland*, passim; Cóilín Parsons, *The Ordnance Survey*, pp.13–17, 47, 84, and passim.

68 "Preface" in William Robert Wilde, *Irish Popular Superstitions*, pp.v–vi. On William Wilde and folklore studies, see also Anne Markey, "The Discovery of Irish Folklore," pp.30–31; Diarmuid Ó Giolláin, *Locating Irish Folklore*, pp.17, 66, 103, 144.

69 William Robert Wilde, *Irish Popular Superstitions*, pp.9–11, 14, 17.

70 Cóilín Parsons argues "The Ordnance Survey's compulsion […] to make endlessly reproducible images of the landscape in the form of maps, is tinged with the death drive, the compulsion to destroy on the ground what is being preserved on paper. The same holds true for the act of archiving, and preserving for later reproduction, the folklore, history, place names, and archeological remains; in short, the whole preservationist project of the Ordnance Survey." Cóilín Parsons, *The Ordnance Survey*, p.84. On the Survey's preservation of folklore, see also Stiofán Ó Cadhla, *Civilizing Ireland*, chapters 2 and 5 in particular; Alan Gailey, "Folk-life Study and the Ordnance Survey Memoirs" in Alan Gailey and Dáithí Ó hÓgáin, eds., *Gold Under the Furze: Studies in Folk Tradition*. Dublin: Glendale Press, 1982, pp.150–64.

71 William Robert Wilde, *Irish Popular Superstitions*, p.17.

72 Jane Francesca (Speranza) Wilde, *Ancient Legends*, vol.II, pp.337–38.

73 William Robert Wilde, *Irish Popular Superstitions*, p.25.

74 Lady Wilde (Jane Francesca Wilde), *Ancient Cures, Charms, and Usages of Ireland. Contributions to Irish Lore*. London: Ward and Downey, 1890, pp.239–41.

75 William R. Wills Wilde, *Ireland, Past and Present: The Land and the People. A Lecture*. Dublin: McGlashan & Gill, 1864.

76 William R. Wilde, "Address to the Department of Anthropology," *Report of the Forty-Fourth Meeting of the British Association for the Advancement of Science, Held at Balfast in August 1874*. London: John Murray, 1875, p.117 (this pagination is for the "Notices and Abstracts" section of the publication). William Wilde's original paper presented at this 1874 meeting, which was widely reported in the press in the United Kingdom, Canada, and other parts of the British Empire, as well as in the United States, lacked a title. Segments of it were also reproduced in the press under "The Early Races of Mankind in Ireland, their Remains and Present Representatives."

77 Jane Francesca (Speranza) Wilde, *Ancient Legends*, vol.II, p.340.

78 William R. Wilde, "Address to the Department of Anthropology," p.118 (pagination in the "Notices and Abstracts" section pagination of the publication).

79 Lady Wilde, "The Fairy Mythology of Ireland" (part 1), *Dublin University Magazine* 90(535), July 1877, pp.70–83.

80 Jane Francesca (Speranza) Wilde, *Ancient Legends, Mystic Charms, and Superstitions of Ireland. With Sketches of the Past. To Which is Appended a Chapter on 'the Ancient Race of Ireland,' by the Late Sir William Wilde*. Volume I. London: Ward and Downey, 1887, pp.vi, 3, 7.

81 Lady Wilde's "The Fairy Mythology of Ireland" (part 1), *Dublin University Magazine* 90(535), July 1877, pp.70–71.

82 Lady Wilde (Jane Francesca Wilde), *Driftwood from Scandinavia*. London: Richard Bentley & Son, 1884, pp.99–100, 102–11, 135, 166–74, 237, 258–59, 276–77.
83 Ibid., pp.167, 169.
84 Ibid., pp.103, 168; Jane Francesca (Speranza) Wilde, *Ancient Legends*, vol.II, pp.247–49.
85 Jane Francesca (Speranza) Wilde, *Ancient Legends*, vol.II, p.23. On Mivart, see also David N. Livingstone, *Adam's Ancestors: Race, Religion, and the Politics of Human Origins*. Reprint. Baltimore: Johns Hopkins Press, 2011 [2008], pp.138–40.
86 Jane Francesca (Speranza) Wilde, *Ancient Legends*, vol.II, pp.268–69.
87 Ibid., p.3.
88 Jane Francesca (Speranza) Wilde, *Ancient Legends*, vol.I, pp.1–6. As noted before, Sir William Wilde had designated the birth place of the first humans as 'somewhere between the Caspian Sea and the great River Euphrates,' adding: "Without entering too minutely into the subject, I may state briefly that the human family separated in process of time into three great divisions—the African, the Asiatic, and the Indo European." Ibid., p.340.
89 Ibid., vol.II, pp.5–6.
90 Ibid., vol.I, p.6. See also ibid., vol.II, pp.293–97.
91 Ibid., vol.II, p.297. See also pp.250–54.
92 William R. Wilde, "Address to the Department of Anthropology," pp.121–27 (pagination in the "Notices and Abstracts" section of the publication); Jane Francesca (Speranza) Wilde, *Ancient Legends*, vol.II, pp.351–60, 368–69.
93 Jane Francesca (Speranza) Wilde, *Ancient Legends*, vol.II, pp.248–51, 289–97.
94 Ibid., vol.I, Preface, p.vi.
95 Ibid., pp.7–8. On the presumed similarity between the Persian "dar" and the Irish "darragh," she added: "The terms Dryad and Druid may be compared as containing the same root and reference." Ibid., p.8, n1.
96 Ibid., pp.9–10, 194, 242, 236–38, 271–72; ibid., vol.II, pp.162–63.
97 William Wilde, *Irish Popular Superstitions*, p.36. He made a similar observation concerning the theory of the Phoenician origin of the Irish. Ibid., p.41.
98 Ibid., p.39.
99 Ibid., pp.41–47.
100 Jane Francesca (Speranza) Wilde, *Ancient Legends*, vol.I, pp.193–94. See also pp.236–39, passim.
101 Lady Wilde (Jane Francesca Wilde), *Ancient Cures.*, pp.98–105 and passim.
102 See, for example, Charles Vallancey, *A Vindication*, pp.396–97; idem, *An Essay on the Antiquity of the Irish Language*, p.40; Louisa Catherine Beaufort, "An Essay upon the State of Architecture and Antiquities," pp.107–108, 206–208; Henry O'Brien, *The Round Towers* (1834 edition), pp.88–89, 198–201; Thomas Moore, *The History of Ireland*, vol.I, pp.20, 22–23, 24, 25.
103 *Academy* (London), March 14, 1887, pp.338–39. On Jane Lee, see the obituaries in ibid., November 16, 1895, p.410; and *Cambridge Review* 17(417), November 14, 1895, p.74.
104 *Saturday Review of Politics, Literature, Science, and Art* (London) 63(1,629), January 15, 1887, pp.105–106.
105 Lady Wilde (Jane Francesca Wilde), *Ancient Cures*, p.1.
106 Ibid., pp.3–4, 57. See also pp.196–98.
107 Ibid., p.171.
108 Ibid., pp.172–79; 196–211, 238–44, and passim. For the quoted text, see p.200.
109 Ibid., pp.213–36. For the quoted texts, see pp.221, 231.
110 *Academy* (London), September 27, 1890, pp.266–67.
111 On Irish and Gaelic Revivals, see also John Hutchinson, *The Dynamics of Cultural Nationalism: The Gaelic Revival and the Creation of the Irish Nation State*. London: Allen & Unwin, 1987; P. J. Mathews, *Revival: The Abbey Theatre, Sinn Féin, the Gaelic League, and the Co-Operative Movement*. Notre Dame, IN: University of Notre Dame Press, 2004; Timothy G. McMahon, *Grand Opportunity: The Gaelic Revival and Irish Society, 1893-1910*. Syracuse: Syracuse University Press, 2008; and Karen Steele, *Women, Press, and Politics during the Irish Revival*. Syracuse: Syracuse University Press, 2007: Declan Kiberd, *Inventing Ireland*, passim; Declan Kiberd and P. J. Mathews, eds., *Handbook of the Irish Revival: An Anthology of Irish Cultural and Political Writings, 1891–1922*. Reprint. Notre Dame, IN: University of Notre Dame Press, 2016 [2015].

112 Mícheál Ó Lócháin (1836-99) was also the founder of the Brooklyn Philo-Celtic Society (1874). See Gillian Ní Ghabhann, "The Gaelic Revival in the U.S. in the Nineteenth Century," *Chronicon* 2(6), 1998, pp.1–34; Una Ni Bhromeil, "The Gaelic Movement in the United States, 1870-1915," *New Hibernia Review* 5(3), Autumn 2001, pp.88–95. Those conversant in Irish language can also consult Fionnuala Uí Fhlannagáin, *Mícheál Ó Lócháin agus An Gaodhal*. Dublin: An Clóchomhar, 1990.

113 *The Gael/An Gaodhal* (New York), March 1904, pp.90, 92, 93. See also *Gentleman's Magazine* (London), vol.296, January 1904, pp.58–59. In this original publication of the article, the last line in the quoted text read: "Curiously enough, the Celtic strain seems always to have been the dominant one." See also "Some Old Customs and Superstitions in the Co. Meath. By Miss A.H. Singleton in the *New York Gael*," *Meath Chronicle*, April 2, 1904, p.1, cc.e-f; ibid., April 9, 1904, p.6, cc.-a-b. (Similar reproductions of the article appeared in some other provincial Irish press, including the *Dundalk Democrat and People's Journal* on April 30 and May 14, 1904.) Annie Singleton's other reproduced articles on folklore included "Dairy Folklore, and Other Notes from Meath and Tipperary," originally published in *Folklore* (London) 15(4), December 1904, pp.457–62 (the publication of the Folklore Society of the United Kingdom) and "Some Irish Fairies," *National Review* (London) 54(324), February 1910, pp.1008–19. Singleton also wrote short stories.

114 For instance, in his 1861 *The Last Conquest of Ireland (Perhaps)*, reprinted in 1882, John Mitchel stated (p.117): "The very region I have described was once—before British civilization overtook us—the abode of the strongest and the richest clans in Ireland [...] After a struggle of six or seven centuries, after many bloody wars and sweeping confiscations, English 'civilization' prevailed—and had brought the clans to the condition I have related. The ultimate idea of English civilization being that 'the sole *nexus* between man and man is cash payment' [...]" Mitchel added (p.214): "It is absolutely essential to the existence of the British Empire, that the Irish peasant class be kept in a condition which will make them entirely manageable ... Those who are of opinion that British civilization is a blessing and a light to lighten the world, will easily reconcile themselves to the needful condition. Those who deem, it the most base and horrible tyranny that has ever scandalized the earth, will probably wish that its indispensable prop—Ireland—were knocked from under it."

115 Declan Kiberd, *Inventing Ireland*, pp.9–11, 29–31, 279, 289, and passim.

116 Lady Wilde (Jane Francesca Wilde), *Ancient Cures*, pp.232–34.

117 Ibid., p.236.

118 Ibid., p.216.

119 On Celtic theories of Irish origins at the time, see also Richard McMahon, "The Irish Dilemma: Nineteenth-Century Science and Celtic Identity" in Richard McMahon, *The Races of Europe: Construction of National Identities in the Social Sciences, 1839-1939*. London: Palgrave Macmillan, 2016, chapter 5 and passim.

120 Matthew Arnold, *On the Study of Celtic Literature*. London: Smith, Elder, and Co., 1867, pp.17–18. See also idem, *Irish Essays and Others*. London: Smith, Elder, and Co., 1882. Lord Lyndhurst (d.1863) was the American-born, Anglo-Irish British politician and lawyer.

121 On this topic, see also Colm Tóibín, "The Irish Literary Renaissance," lecture presented at Elmhurst College, Illinois, United States, on April 10, 2014 (https://www.youtube.com/watch?v=A7mdEViEU8M).

122 This terminology is borrowed from Friedrich Wilhelm Nietzsche's *On the Advantage and Disadvantage of History for Life*. Peter Preuss translator. Indianapolis: Hackett, 1980 (originally appearing in German as *Vom Nutzen und Nachteil der Historie für das Leben*, 1874).

123 Jane Francesca Wilde, *Poems by Speranza (Lady Wilde)*. Dublin: James Duffy, 1864, pp.73–74.

124 Jane Francesca (Speranza) Wilde, *Ancient Legends*, vol.I, pp.11–12. See also Anne Markey, "The Discovery of Irish Folklore," pp.34–35.

125 Standish James O'Grady, *History of Ireland. Volume I: The Heroic Period*. London: Sampson, Low, Searle, Marston, & Rivington, 1878, pp.10–14. On O'Grady, See also Edward A. Hagan, "The Aryan Myth: A Nineteenth-Century Anglo-Irish Will to Power" in Tadhg Foley and Seán Ryder, eds., *Ideology and Ireland in the Nineteenth Century*, pp.197–204.

126 See Patrick Maume, "Standish James O'Grady," p.16. Maume, correctly noting that O'Grady "asserts that the Irish blend Celtic Aryans and a dark southern race, identified with the Basques," appears however to have misread O'Grady when concluding O'Grady

"firmly repudiates older theories of Phoenician origins for the Irish." Ibid. In fact, O'Grady, as evident from the quotation I have provided, claimed both the Phoenicians and the Basque were of the Turanian racial stock.

127 S. O'Grady, *History of Ireland*, vol.I, pp.15–16. On O'Grady and Irish historiography, see also Marc Cahall, "History and Politics: Interpretations of Early Modern Conquest and Reformation in Victorian Ireland" in Stefan Berger and Chris Lorenz, eds., *Nationalizing the Past: Historians as Nation Builders in Modern Europe*. Houndmills, Basingstoke: Palgrave Macmillan, 2010, pp.149–69.

128 *Spectator*, June 22, 1878, p.799, c.a.

129 Standish James O'Grady, *The Story of Ireland*. London: Methuen & Co., 1894, chapters I and II.

130 See also Seán Ó Lúing, "Douglas Hyde and the Gaelic League," *Studies: An Irish Quarterly Review* 62(246), Summer 1973, pp.123–38; Janet Egleson Dunleavy and Gareth W. Dunleavy, *Douglas Hyde: A Maker of Modern Ireland*. Berkeley: University of California Press, 1991; Declan Kiberd, *Inventing Ireland*, 1995, pp.138–54 and passim; P. J. Mathews, *Revival*, pp.8,14, 19, 41, and passim. On Hyde and Irish folklore, see John Wilson Foster, *Fictions of the Irish Literary Revival*, pp.219–26 and passim.

131 Douglas Hyde, *A Literary History of Ireland: From Earliest Times to the Present Day*. London: Fisher Unwin, 1899, pp.77–78.

132 Ibid., pp.1, 6.

133 See also, for instance, "The Traditional St. Patrick," *The United Irishman* (Dublin), December 2, 1905, p.3.

134 Stephen Gwynn, *The Fair Hills of Ireland*, p.11. Published in 1906 by Maunsel and Co. in Dublin, the book was also published simultaneously by Macmillan & Co. in London and New York.

135 Stephen Gwynn, *The Fair Hills of Ireland*, pp.64–65.

136 Alice Stopford Green, *Irish Nationality*. New York: Henry Holt and Company, 1911, p.8. For a contemporary commentary on this book, see Stephen J. Brown, "The Question of Irish Nationality," *Studies: An Irish Quarterly Review* 1(4), December 1912, pp.653–54. In this article Green is identified as "Mrs. J.R. Green" (i.e., Mrs. John Richard Green, after her husband's name).

137 Edward Fitzgerald, *Rubáiyát of Omar Khayyám in English Verse ... And a Biographical Preface*. New York and Boston: Houghton, Mifflin and Company, 1888, pp.7, 9–10. Kerney's biographical sketch of Fitzgerald had also appeared the previous year, again anonymously, in the American edition of Fitzgerald's collected works (edited by Kerney). Kerney was most certainly also the anonymous author of Fitzgerald's biography appearing in *The Marvellous Year* (with an Introduction by Edwin Markham and drawings by Gertrude Huebsch. New York: B.W. Huebsch, 1909, pp.101–104). In this biographical entry it was stated (p.103): "In the unwise scholarship of his [i.e., Fitzgerald's] university days Persia and Ireland were brought together in a strange family for no better reason than that Erin and Iran suggested each the other. Accepting this opinion without question, for it passed current then in the infancy of ethnology, nothing could come with a warmer appeal to the Irish student than to put into English the poetry of his sister race."

138 R.W. Ferrier, "Edward Fitzgerald, a Reader 'Of Taste', and 'Umar Khayyâm 1809-1883," *Iran*, vol.24, 1986, p.173. Dick Davis too attributes Fitzgerald's interest in Persian solely to his close friendship with Cowell, rather than to any ostensible connection between Iran and Ireland. See Dick Davis, "FITZGERALD, EDWARD" (1999), *Encyclopaedia Iranica* (http://www.iranica.com/articles/fitzgerald-).

139 Thomas Wright, *Built of Books: How Reading Defined the Life of Oscar Wilde*. New York: Henry Holt and Co., 2009, p.128.

140 Omar Khayyam, *Rubaiyat of Omar Khayyam*. Justin Huntly McCarthy translator. London: David Nutt, 1889, pp.vii–xii.

141 On the Turkish original of this work, see Ulrich Marzolph, *Relief After Hardship: The Ottoman Turkish Model for The Thousand and One Days*. Detroit: Wayne State University, 2017.

142 Roy F. Foster, *W.B. Yeats: A Life. Volume 1: The Apprentice Mage, 1865-1914*. Oxford: Oxford University Press, 1998, p.50. See also Roy F. Foster, *Vivid Faces: The Revolutionary Generation in Ireland, 1890-1923*. London: Allen Lane, 2014, pp.99–100 and passim; Terry Eagleton,

Heathcliff and the Great Hunger, pp.286, 290; Gregory Castle, *Modernism and the Celtic Revival*, pp.58–59.
143 John Wilson Foster, *Fictions of the Irish Literary Revival*, p.59.
144 On such anti-clerical tendencies, see Robert E. Burns, "Parsons, Priests, and the People: The Rise of Irish Anti-Clericalism 1785-1789," *Church History* 31(2), June 1962, pp.151–63; Kevin Whelan, "Sectarianism and secularism in nineteenth-century Ireland" in Paul Brennan, ed., *La sécularisation en Irlande*. Caen: Press Universitaires de Caen, 1998, pp.71–90; Douglas Kanter, "Joyce, Irish Paralysis, and Cultural Nationalist Anticlericalism," *James Joyce Quarterly* 41(3), Spring 2004, pp.381–96: Roy F. Foster, *Vivid Faces*, pp.3–4, 56–57, 167–68, and passim.
145 On theosophy and Besant, Cousins, Despard, and others, see also John Wilson Foster, *Fictions of the Irish Literary Revival*, pp.57–59.
146 See also Cliona Murphy, "The Religious Context of the Women's Suffrage Campaign in Ireland," *Women's History Review* 6(4), 1997, pp.552–53.
147 Helena P. Blavatsky, *Isis Unveiled: A Master-Key to the Mysteries of Ancient and Modern Science and Theology*. Volume II. New York: J.W. Bouton; London: Bernard Quaritch, 1877, pp.305–306. See also ibid., p.53; and Helena P. Blavatsky, *Isis Unveiled: A Master-Key to the Mysteries of Ancient and Modern Science and Theology*. Volume I. New York: J.W. Bouton; London: Bernard Quaritch, 1877, pp.xxviii–xxix, 505.
148 Henry S. Olcott, "The Spirit of the Zoroastrian Religion" ("A Lecture delivered at the Town Hall, Bombay, 14th February, 1882") in Henry S. Olcott, *Theosophy: Religion and Occult Science*. London: George Redway, 1885, pp.301–48. On Blavatsky's attack against institutionalized Christianity in general and her references to Zoroastrianism, Persia, and Aryan mythology, see both volumes of her *Isis Unveiled*.
149 Henry S. Olcott, *Theosophy*, p.345.
150 See, for example, Charles Vallancey, *A Vindication*, p.167 and passim. For Henry O'Brien's and George Petrie's dismissive remarks on Vallancey's supposition, see respectively Henry O'Brien, *The Round Towers*, pp.253–54; George Petrie, *The Ecclesiastical Architecture of Ireland*, p.25.
151 Helena P. Blavatsky, *Isis Unveiled*, vol.I, pp. xxxi, xxxiv, xxxvi, 12, 19, 125, 178, 251, 321, 535, 560, and passim; Ibid., vol II, pp.26, 41, 128–29, 140–44, 149, 155, 217–21, 236–37, 306, 361, 409–10, 432–33, 484–86, and passim (the quoted text appears in ibid., pp.205–206).
152 Catherine Candy, "Relating Feminisms, Nationalisms and Imperialisms: Ireland, India and Margaret Cousins's Sexual Politics," *Women's History Review* 3(4), 1994, p.582.
153 *Irish Theosophist* 2(2), August 15, 1894, p.160. On Russell and theosophy, see also Richard M. Kain and James H. O'Brien, *George Russell (A.E.)*. Lewisburg: Bucknell University Press, 1976, chapter 4 ("A.E. as a Theosophist").
154 Helena P. Blavatsky, *Isis Unveiled*, vol.II, pp.290–91 n.* For O'Brien's description, in which the *Budh/Budha* is also identified as *Phallus*, see Henry O'Brien, *The Round Towers* (1834 edition), pp.311–12, 340, 343–45, 353–54, and passim.
155 See also Gregory Castle, *Modernism and the Celtic Revival*, chapter 2.
156 On Mir Aulad Ali, see Vivian Ibrahim, "The Mir of India in Ireland," pp.153–74; Toheed Ahmad, "Nation of Saints and Scholars: A Portrait of Ireland," *Criterion* (Pakistan) 3(3), July-September 2008; Mansour Bonakdarian, "Iranian Studies in 'the United Kingdom'," p.281; *Great Britain Civil Service Commission, Twenty-Seventh Report. Her Majesty's Civil Service Commissioners, Together with Appendices*. London: Eyre and Spottiswoode, 1883, p.493; Oliver Scharbrodt, "'From Hafiz': Irish Orientalism, Persian Poetry, and W.B. Yeats" in Houchang E. Chehabi and Grace Neville, eds., *Erin and Iran*, pp.63–67; Roy F. Foster, *W.B. Yeats: A Life*, vol.1, p.47; Joseph Lennon, *Irish Orientalism*, pp.192, 256.
157 William Butler Yeats, *The Autobiography of William Butler Yeats: Consisting of Reveries Over Childhood and Youth. The Trembling of the Veil, and Dramatis Personae*. New York: Macmillan, 1953, p.56.
158 William Butler Yeats, *The Collected Works of W.B. Yeats*, vol.IV, p.359 n.1. See also the *Irish Theosophist* (Dublin) 1(1), October 1892, which opened with an introductory article by Annie Besant (pp.1–5) that mentioned the activities of Yeats and some of his associates (pp.2, 3); Roy F. Foster, *W.B. Yeats: A Life*, vol.1, pp.45–52, 103–106, and passim; Susan Johnston Graf, *Talking to the Gods: Occultism in the Work of W. B. Yeats, Arthur Machen, Algernon Blackwood,*

and *Dion Fortune*. Albany: State University of New York, 2015, passim; idem, "Heterodox Religions in Ireland: Theosophy, the Hermetic Society, and the Castle of Heroes," *Irish Studies Review*, 11(1), 2003, p.51; Terence Brown, *The Life of W.B. Yeats: A Critical Biography*. Reprint. Oxford: Blackwell Publishers, 2001, pp.69–70; the section on "Magic" in William Butler Yeats, *Essays and Introductions*, pp.28–52; Joy Dixon, *Divine Feminine: Theosophy and Feminism in England*. Baltimore: Johns Hopkins University Press, 2001, pp.57–58.

159 P. J. Mathews, *Revival*, pp.10, 19–23, 61, 79–89 and passim; Declan Kiberd, *Inventing Ireland*, passim; Jerry Nolan, "Edward Martyn's Struggle for an Irish National Theater, 1899-1920," *New Hibernia Review* 7(2), Summer, 2003, pp.88–105.

160 George Moore, '*Hail and Farewell!' Volume II: Salve*. Reprint. London: William Heinemann, 1912 [1911], p.320.

161 John Eglinton, *Anglo-Irish Essays*. Dublin: Talbot Press, 1917, p.15.

162 "Introductory," *Dana: An Irish Magazine of Independent Thought* (Dublin), no.1, May 1904, pp.1–4.

163 Frederick Ryan, "The Persian Struggle," *Irish Review* 1(6), August 1911, p.286.

164 Terry Eagleton, *Heathcliff and the Great Hunger*, p.259.

165 On James Cosuins, see also Gauri Viswanathan, "Ireland, India, and the Poetics of Internationalism," *Journal of World History* 15(1), March 2004, pp.7–30; Joseph Lennon, *Irish Orientalism*, chapter 8. Whereas Viswanathan's provides a Saidian reading of James Cousins, by culturally situating Cousins in 'the West' prior to his arrival in India and, hence, purportedly operating from an 'orientalist' mindset while in India (in the Saidian essentialized definition of Orientalism), Lennon correctly notes that Cousins maintained an underlying cultural affinity between Ireland and India, including an Aryan racial dimension. It should be added, whereas Irish nationalists such as John Dillon regarded Ireland as an indisputably Western European cultural zone, the likes of James Cousins were anchored in the Orient-in-the-West-of-Europe cultural-civilizational grounding of the authentically Irish 'national' existence. On Cousins, Yeats, Lady Gregory, theosophy, and Ireland, see also Mark Williams, *Ireland's Immortals: A History of the Gods of Irish Myth*. Princeton: Princeton University Press, 2016, chapter 10 ("Coherence and Canon: The Fairy Faith and the East").

166 See, for example, Elleke Boehmer, *Empire, the National, and the Postcolonial, 1890-1920: Resistance in Interaction*. Oxford: Oxford University Press, 2002, chapters 2 and 3.

167 Sushil Kumar Jain, "Indian Elements in the Poetry of Yeats: On Chatterji and Tagore," *Comparative Literature Studies* 7(1), March 1970, pp.82–96; Ashim Dutta, "India in Yeats's Early Imagination: Mohini Chatterjee and Kālidāsa," *International Yeats Studies* 2(2), 2018, pp.20–30; Michael Collins, *Empire, Nationalism and the Postcolonial World: Rabindranath Tagore's Writings on History, Politics and Society*. New York: Routledge, 2012, chapter 4.

168 Joy Dixon, *Divine Feminine*, pp.76–80, 94–95, and passim.

169 See also Brendan McNamara, *The Reception of 'Abdu'l-Bahá in Britain*. Leiden: Brill, 2020; Mona Khademi, "Laura Dreyfus-Barney and Abdu'l-Bahá's Visit to the West" in Negar Mottahedeh, ed., *'Abdu'l-Bahá's Journey West: The Course of Human Solidarity*. New York: Palgrave Macmillan, 2013, pp.23–27.

170 See, for example, George W. Russell (Æ), "A Word Upon the Objects of the Theosophical Society," *Irish Theosophist* (Dublin) 1(2), November 15, 1892, p.9.

171 See, for example, Helena P. Blavatsky, *Isis Unveiled*, vol.I, pp.263, 553, 556, 566–67, 570, 576–81, 618–20.

172 Ibid., pp.515–16, 525–26, 566–67; ibid., vol.II, pp.435–37.

173 On Yeats and Noh plays, see Eileen Kato, "W.B. Yeats and the Noh," *Irish Review*, no.42, Summer 2010, pp.104–19. On the Irish Literary Revival and crosscurrents of literary and theatrical influences, see also Roy Foster, "The Irish Literary Revival" in Thomas Bartlett, ed., *The Cambridge History of Ireland. Volume IV: 1880 to the Present*. Cambridge: Cambridge University Press. 2018, pp.168–95.

174 Shamsul Islam, "The Influence of Eastern Philosophy on Yeats's Later Poetry," *Twentieth Century Literature*, 19(4), October 1973, pp.284–85.

175 *Ghazels from the Divan of Hafiz, Done Into English by Justin Huntly McCarthy*. London: David Nutt, 1893, p.77. See also Pamela Bickley, "[Review of] Catherine Cavanaugh, *Love and Forgiveness in Yeats's Poetry*" in Warwick Gould ed., *Yeats Annual, No.7; Including Essays in Memory of Richard Ellmann*. Ronald Schuchard, editor. London: Macmillan, 1990, p.258. On Yeats and Hafiz,

see also Oliver Scharbrodt, "'From Hafiz': Irish Orientalism, Persian Poetry, and W.B. Yeats" in Houchang E. Chehabi and Grace Neville, eds., *Erin and Iran*; pp.57–78; Suheil B. Bushrui, *William Butler Yeats's Search for A Spiritual Philosophy*. London: Temenos Academy, 2013, p.38.

176 See William H. O'Donnell, "Editor's Introduction" in William Butler Yeats, *The Speckled Bird*. William H. O'Donnell editor. Toronto: McClelland and Stewart, 1976, p.xxiii.

177 William Butler Yeats, *The Speckled Bird*, p.106. See also Curtis Bradford, "Yeats and Maud Gonne," *Texas Studies in Literature and Language* 3(4), Winter 1962, p.461.

178 See also Voltaire, *Candide, or Optimism*. John Butt translator. London: Penguin, 1947, pp.142–43. On Yeats' anti-rationalism, among the many other sources on Yeats already cited, see also Lloyd R. Morris, *The Celtic Dawn: A Survey of the Renascence in Ireland, 1889-1916*. New York: Macmillan, 1917, pp.80, 103–104, 129, 211–12, and passim; Mary Helen Thuente, *W.B. Yeats and Irish Folklore*, pp.38, 93, and passim; Frank Kinahan, *Yeats, Folklore and Occultism: Contexts of the Early Work and Thought*. London: Routledge, 1988, pp.12 and passim; Suheil B. Bushrui, *William Butler Yeats's Search for A Spiritual Philosophy*, pp.12–13 and passim.

179 William Butler Yeats, *The Cat and the Moon and Certain Poems*. Dublin: Cuala Press, 1924, pp.35–36.

180 James Hardiman, ed., *Irish Minstrelsy, or Bardic Remains of Ireland*. Volume II. London: Joseph Robins, 1831.

181 *Irish Penny Journal* (Dublin), January 16, 1841, pp.228–29.

182 See also Jacques Chuto, and Rudolf Patrick Holzapfel, Peter MacMahon, and Ellen Shannon-Mangan, eds. *The Collected Works of James Clarence Mangan. Poems: 1838-1844*. Dublin: Irish Academic Press, 1996, pp.239–40, 404. On Heffernan, see "William Dall ua [Ó] h-eifearnáin" in John Daly and Edward Walsh, *Reliques of Irish Jacobite Poetry*. Dublin: John Cumming, 1844, pp.92–120. Mangan later included his own 'translations' of Heffernan's poems in the second instalment of his "Anthologia Hibernica" in the *Dublin University Magazine* 29(173), May 1847, pp.630–34.

183 Charles Gavan Duffy, ed., *The Ballad Poetry of Ireland*. Fortieth edition. Dublin: James Duffy, 1869, pp.79–80.

184 See, for instance, John Mitchel's Introduction in James Clarence Mangan, *Poems by James Clarence Mangan*, pp.22–23, 397–98; David James O'Donoghue, *The Life and Writings of James Clarence Mangan*, p.121.

185 See also John Wilson Foster, *Fictions of the Irish Literary Revival*, pp.9–10, 33, and passim; Martin Williams, "Ancient Mythology and Revolutionary Ideology in Ireland. 1878-1916," *Historical Journal* 26(2), 1983, pp.307–28; Colm Tóibín, "The Irish Literary Renaissance."

186 Colm Tóibín, "The Irish Literary Renaissance."

187 John Wilson Foster, *Fictions of the Irish Literary Revival*, pp.3–14, 32–44 and passim.

188 Reg Skene, *The Cuchulain Plays of W.B. Yeats: A Study*. London: Macmillan, 1974, chapter 2; Colm Tóibín, "Easter 1916," *London Review of Books* lecture. London, British Museum, March 24, 2016 (https://www.lrb.co.uk/2016/03/24/colm-toibin-video-the-story-of-easter-1916); Declan Kiberd, *Inventing Ireland*, pp.196–97 and passim.

189 Isabella Augusta Gregory (Lady Gregory), *Cuchulain of Muirthemne: The Story of the Men of the Red Branch of Ulster*. Arranged and translated from the Irish by Lady Gregory, with a Preface by Yeats. New edition. London: John Murray, 1903 [1902], pp.313–19. Of other aspects of Lady Gregory's reworking of this segment of the Ulster Cyclce, Hazard Adams notes that it "is a syncretic rendering of the tales of the Ulster heroes, taking the life of Cuchulain as the main thread. This device provides and organizational principle, emphasizes the exploits of an incredibly heroic and lone spirit, and yet does not prevent her [Gregory] from offering a few important interludes in which Cuchulain himself does not figure prominently." Hazard Adams, *Lady Gregory*. Lewisburg, PA: Bucknell University Press, 1973, p.49.

190 Isabella Augusta Gregory (Lady Gregory), *Cuchulain of Muirthemne*, p.vii.

191 He wrote in reference to the 1916 Easter Rising: "When Pearse summoned Cuchulain to his side, / What stalked through the Post Office? What intellect / What calculation, number, measurement, replied?" William Butler Yeats, *The Collected Poems of W.B. Yeats*. Richard J. Finneran editor. New York: Macmillan, 1989, pp.336–37.

192 Reg Skene, *The Cuchulain Plays of W.B. Yeats*, p.x. See also Michael McAteer, *Yeats and European Drama*. Cambridge: Cambridge University Press, 2010, p.65.

193 Douglas Hyde, ed., *Beside the Fire*, pp. xix–xx, xxxiv–xlix; John Wilson Foster, *Fictions of the Irish Literary Revival*, pp.221–22. See also Chris Morash, "Celticism: Between Race and Nation" in Tadhg Foley and Seán Ryder, eds., *Ideology and Ireland in the Nineteenth Century*, pp.206–13.
194 William Larminie, *West Irish Folk-Tales and Romances*. London: Elliot Stock, 1893, pp.x, xvi-xx.
195 Ibid., pp.xx–xxiii; Isabella Augusta Gregory (Lady Gregory), ed., *Gods and Fighting Men: The Story of the Tuatha de Danann and of the Fianna of Ireland*. Lady Gregory translator, with a Preface by William Butler Yeats. London: John Murray, 1905, pp.465–68, and pp. xi, xii–xiii, xxii–xxiii in the Preface by Yeats.
196 Isabella Augusta Gregory (Lady Gregory), ed., *Gods and Fighting Men*, pp.32–34.
197 Ibid., pp.40–41.
198 Reg Skene, *The Cuchulain Plays of W.B. Yeats*, pp.224–25.
199 Douglas Hyde, *The Story of Early Gaelic Literature*. London: T. Fisher Unwin, 1895, pp.xvi–xx, 16–17, 68–81, 96–103, and passim. See also John Wilson Foster, *Fictions of the Irish Literary Revival*, pp.203–35. Although Hyde referred to canon Taylor's "The Origin and Primitive Seat of the Aryans," Hyde himself did not specifically pinpoint the European homeland of the Aryans. Douglas Hyde, *A Literary History of Ireland*. pp.11 n.3, 12 n.1, 16 n.1.
200 *Gaelic American*, March 14, 1908, p.3, c.d. On Kuno Meyer, see also Seán Ó Lúing, *Kuno Meyer, 1858-1919: A Biography*. Dublin: Geography Publications, 1991.
201 *Gaelic American*, March 14, 1908, p.3, c.d.
202 Ibid. For other suggested parallels between Irish and 'Iranian' mythologies (in the broadest geographical-cultural definition of Iran), as well as the possibility of the Iranian "medieval" romance *Vis and Ramin* having been resituated in an Irish setting in the European romance *Tristan and Isolde*, see the following chapters in Houchang E. Chehabi and Grace Neville, eds., *Erin and Iran*: Joseph Falaky Nagy, "The 'Conqueror Worm' in Irish and Persian Literature"; John McDonald, "Building Bulls and Crafting Cows: Narratives of Bovine Fabrication from Iran, Ireland, and In-between"; Olga Davidson, "Parallel Heroic Themes in the medieval Irish *Cattle Raid of Cooley* and the Medieval Persian *Book of Kings*"; and Dick Davis, "A Trout in the Milk: *Vis and Ramin* and *Tristan and Isolde*." See also Bruce Lincoln, "The Indo-European Cattle-Raiding Myth," *History of Religions* 16(1), August 1976, pp.42–65.
203 See the Preface by Yeats to Lady Isabella Augusta Gregory, *Cuchulain of Muirthemne*, p.351.
204 See Kuno Meyer "The Quarrel Between Finn and Oisín" in Kuno Meyer, ed., *The Triads of Ireland*. Dublin: Hodges, Figgis, & Co., 1906, p.22; idem, ed., *Fianaigecht: Being a Collection of Hitherto Inedited Irish Poems and Tales Relating to Finn and His Fiana, with an English Translation*. Dublin: Hodges, Figgis, & Co., 1910, p.22. For Meyer's earlier works on the Cuchulain story, without reference to Ferdowsi's epic, see also Kuno Meyer, "The oldest version of Tochmarc Emire" (Kuno Meyer translator), *Revue Celtique*, vol.11 (1890), pp.433–57; and idem, ed., "The death of Connla" (Kuno Meyer translator), *Ériu*, vol.1 (1904), pp.113–21.
205 Michael McAteer, *Yeats and European Drama*, p.65. See also P. Maume, "Standish James O'Grady," p.6. On the Cattle Raid of Cooley, see also Bruce Lincoln, "The Indo-European Cattle-Raiding Myth," pp.42–65.
206 Murray Anthony Potter, *Sohrab and Rustem: The Epic Theme of a Combat Between Father and Son. A Study of its Genesis and Use in Literature and Popular Tradition*. London: David Nutt, 1902, pp.22–27. On the commonality of this theme, see also Ruairi Ó hUiginn, "Cú Chulainn" in John T. Koch, ed., *Celtic Culture: A Historical Encyclopedia*. Vol.II. Santa Barbara: ABC-CLIO, 2006, pp.507–508.
207 Jivanji Jamshedji Modi, *Asiatic Papers*, p.54. See also Charlotte Brooke, *Reliques of Irish Poetry*, pp.15–44.
208 See Frederick Orpen Bower, "Mohl, Julius von," *The Encyclopædia Britannica: A Dictionary of Arts, Sciences, Literature, and General Information. Volume VIII: Medals to Mumps*. Eleventh edition. Hugh Chisholm editor. New York: Encyclopædia Britannica Company, 1911, p.648.
209 Helen Zimmern, "Preface" in Helen Zimmern, *The Epic of Kings: Stories Retold from Firdusi*. London: Fisher Unwin, 1882, p.v; Louise Manning Hodgkins, "Preface" in Louise Manning Hodgkins, ed., *Matthew Arnold's Sohrab and Rustum*. Boston: Leach, Shewell, and Sanborn, 1890. Both Zimmern and Hodgkins also relied on the English James Atkinson's 1814 *Soohrab*;

a Poem, Freely Translated from the Original Persian. It was not until the 1896 American edition of Arnold's *Sohrab and Rustum: An Episode* (Chicago and New York: Werner School Book Company) that the editor of the edition, Merwin Marie Snell, noted, based on the French author Charles Sainte-Beuve's remark, the similarity between the Iranian version of the father and son battle and the battle between Cuchulain and Conla in Macpherson's forged Ossianic saga. See pp.16, 86–87 n.50. But, although Snell did not mention it, Sainte-Beuve's quoted commentary was from his 1850 review of Mohl's translation of the Iranian epic. See also Reza Taher-Kermani, "Persia by Way of Paris: On Arnold's 'Sohrab and Rustum'," *Middle Eastern Literatures* 18(1), 2015, pp.22–40.

210 Jivanji Jamshedji Modi, *Asiatic Papers*, p.65.
211 James O'Laverty, "Remarkable Correspondence of Irish, Greek, and Oriental Legends," *Ulster Journal of Archaeology* (Belfast), vol.7, 1859, p.334.
212 Ibid., pp.335–36.
213 On Keightley, see also Richard M. Dorson, "The First Group of British Folklorists," *Journal of American Folklore* 68(267), January-March 1955, pp.1–8.
214 Thomas Keightley, *Tales and Popular Fictions; Their Resemblance, and Transmission from Country to Country*. London: Whittaker and Co., 1834, p.134 n.1.
215 Ibid., pp.168–69.
216 Keightley maintained, "The lower order of the Irish Catholics are quite proud if they can prove that they have what they call good Protestant blood in their veins. They regard the Protestants as a superior caste." Ibid., p.11 n.2.
217 Ibid., pp.176–78.
218 Charlotte Brooke, *Reliques of Irish Poetry*, p.42.
219 Louisa Catherine Beaufort, "An Essay upon the State of Architecture and Antiquities," p.103.
220 Joseph Cooper Walker, "On the Origin of Romantic Fabling in Ireland," *Transactions of the Royal Irish Academy* (Dublin), vol.10, 1806, pp.7–10 (under the "Antiquities" section (read by William Preston on June 10, 1805)). See also William Ouseley, *Persian Miscellanies: An Essay to Facilitate the Reading of Persian Manuscripts*. London: Richard White, 1795, chapter 5.
221 Charles Vallancey, *A Vindication*, pp.xii–xxii, 217–19, 355–59, 550–51. On the presumed Cuchulain-*Shāhnāmeh* link, see also Clare O'Halloran, *Golden Ages and Barbarous Nations*, 55.
222 Marcus Keane, *The Towers and Temples of Ancient Ireland*, p.39.
223 William Gregory Wood-Martin, *Traces of the Elder Faiths of Ireland. A Folklore Sketch: A Handbook of Irish Pre-Christian Traditions*. Volume I. London: Longmans, Green, and Co., 1901, p.148. On Wood-Martin, see also Aideen M. Ireland, "Colonel William Gregory Wood-Martin Antiquary, 1847-1917," *Journal of Irish Archaeology*, vol.10, 2001, pp.1–11.
224 Douglas Hyde, *A Literary History of Ireland*, p.300.
225 Alfred Nutt, "Bibliographical Notes" in John Gregerson Campbell, *The Fians; or, Stories, Poems, & Traditions of Fionn and His Warrior Band*. London: David Nutt, 1891, p.282. Campbell was a Scottish folklorist and Free Church Minister on the Isle of Tiree, Scotland. On Nutt, see also Juliette Wood, "Folklore Studies at the Celtic Dawn: The Rôle of Alfred Nutt as Publisher and Scholar," *Folklore*, vol.110, 1999, pp.3–12.
226 See Kuno Meyer, *The Voyage of Bran Son of Febal to the Land of the Living ... Edited, wih Translation, Notes, and Glossary, by Kuno Meyer. With an Essay Upon the Irish Vision of the Happy Otherworld and the Celtic Doctrine of Rebirth, by Alfred Nutt. Section I: The Happy Otherworld*. London: David Nutt, 1895, pp.309–16.
227 Reg Skene, *The Cuchulain Plays of W.B. Yeats*, pp.4, 120–21, and passim.
228 William Butler Yeats, *The Cat and the Moon and Certain Poems*, unnumbered second page of the Preface. See also Joseph Lennon, *Irish Orientalism*, p.313.
229 Joseph Jacobs, "Of Persian Poetry" in Louisa Stuart Costello, *The Rose Garden of Persia*. New edition. London: Gibbings and Company, 1899, p.xvii.
230 Ibid., pp.ix–xi.
231 See also Sushil Kumar Jain, "Indian Elements in the Poetry of Yeats," pp.82–96; Ashim Dutta, "India in Yeats's Early Imagination," pp.20–39.
232 Joseph Jacobs, "Of Persian Poetry" in Louisa Stuart Costello, *The Rose Garden of Persia*, pp. xi–xiv.

233 "Persicus Odi," *Sinn Féin*, February 5, 1910, p.2, cc.f–g.
234 On anti-imperialist strands of Irish modernism, see Rónán McDonald, "The Irish Revival and Modernism" in Joe Cleary, ed., *The Cambridge Companion to Irish Modernism*, pp.52–53, 56–57.
235 Joseph Lennon, *Irish Orientalism* pp.249–50.

Chapter Seven

IRISH NATIONALISTS AND THE IRANIAN QUESTION, 1906–21

As noted in previous chapters, on occasion certain Irish nationalist individuals and/or groups voiced opposition to contemporary British policy toward Iran. The most notable example in the nineteenth century was *The Nation*'s coverage of the Anglo-Iranian War of 1856–57 (see Chapter Four). This was an instance of Irish Nationalist expression of cross-territorial anti-imperialist solidarity with Iranians; more specifically with the Iranian state in that setting. Some Irish nationalists also objected to London's handling of Iranian affairs during the 1891–92 Iranian "tobacco protest" movement. However, the most sustained and widespread Irish nationalist condemnation of London's Iranian policy occurred during the Iranian Constitutional Revolution of 1906–11. Irish nationalist critics of London on this occasion ranged from members of various Home Rule parties and organizations to militant republican groups.

The Iranian Tobacco Protest of 1891–92 and London's direct diplomatic intervention in the event elicited parliamentary and extra-parliamentary opposition in the United Kingdom to the Conservative prime minister Lord Salisbury's handling of affairs, with Salisbury also doubling as foreign secretary. This crisis concerned a tobacco concession granted on March 8, 1890, by the Iranian government to a British subject, Major Gerald Francis Talbot (coincidentally also a relative of Lord Salisbury). The comprehensive concession gave Talbot's company a monopoly over the purchase, sale, and export of Iran's entire tobacco output. Talbot then transferred his concession to two consecutive front syndicates (the last being the Imperial Tobacco Corporation of Persia) for grossly inflating the company's share prices and earning Talbot a lucrative profit without the company having undertaken any operations in Iran yet. In Iran itself, the concession sparked off a vehement popular condemnation, before erupting into a nationwide protest movement lasting from January 1891 to early 1892, with protests continuing even after the concession was finally cancelled by Iranian authorities in late December 1891. The Iranian monarch, Nasser al-Din Shah, who had also been on the throne during the Anglo-Iranian War of 1856–57, revoked the concession in light of the fierce domestic opposition that threatened his reign as well as steady diplomatic pressure by Russia, which regarded the concession as a substantial economic reinforcement of Britain's leverage in Iran contra Russia. The annulment of the concession encountered opposition from the British government, and authorities in Tehran were subsequently pressured by London to grant Talbot's Imperial Tobacco Corporation of Persia an exorbitantly inordinate indemnity for the abrogation of the concession. Salisbury was censured by his domestic critics for London's initial diplomatic intercession in preserving a private British commercial undertaking overseas and for later utilizing London's direct diplomatic channels to secure an excessive compensation for the tobacco corporation: a sum of £500,000 awarded by the Iranian government to the corporation in April 1892. This amount was far above both the company's estimated short-term profits and its total expenditures thus far, including bribes paid to Iranian royalty and officials. Moreover, given Tehran's lack of resources for paying the hefty indemnity, the British Foreign Office also pressured Tehran to obtain a loan from the British-owned Imperial Bank of Persia, instead of securing a Russian or some other alternative loan. There had been a precedent for the Iranian Tobacco Protest of 1891–92. This was the mass Iranian opposition to the Reuter concession of 1872 (granted by the shah to the British Baron Julius de Reuter), resulting in the cancellation of that far-reaching concession. In 1872, however, the Liberal British prime minister William Gladstone had refrained from intervening in what the British government rightly considered a private British financial undertaking. From Salisbury's point of view in 1891–92, on the other hand, the cancellation of the tobacco concession without a substantial reimbursement, particularly in light of Russia's opposition to the deal, could undermine Britain's imperial prestige in the region in rivalry with Russia. Moreover, Salisbury regarded private British commercial and financial undertakings in Iran as a legitimate means of solidifying British diplomatic-cum-imperial leverage in that country, by rendering Iran economically more tethered to Britain and the British Empire than to Russia.[1]

British parliamentary critics of Salisbury's handling of the tobacco concession debacle consisted primarily of members of the Radical wing of the opposition Liberal Party,[2] who were joined by the likes of the Socialist MP Robert Bontine Cunninghame-Graham. Also joining them on occasion was the "Home Rule" Irish Parliamentary Party MP for North Longford, Timothy Michael Healy (1855–1931).[3] In addition to Healy, many of Salisbury's critics in the Iranian tobacco dispute were avid supporters of Irish Home Rule, as well as being outspoken critics of British imperial policy in general, notably in regard to India and Egypt.[4] While Healy played a relatively minor role in the parliamentary debates on the Iranian tobacco concession and was the only Irish nationalist MP to take up the Iranian Question at the time, he was nonetheless the first ever distinctly "Irish nationalist" member of the British parliament to condemn London's Iranian policy. The Irish Parliamentary Party (IPP; a.k.a., the Irish Home Rule Party, the Irish Nationalist Party, or the Irish Party) was the only Irish nationalist faction to have parliamentary representation at the time. The IPP had its origins in the (Irish) Home Government Association, formed in 1870 by the Protestant and politically conservative Irish MP Isaac Butt (d.1879). In 1873, the Association was transformed into the

Home Rule League, which following the general election of 1874 constituted the third largest parliamentary party in the United Kingdom, albeit far smaller in its parliamentary representation than the main Conservative and Liberal parties. In 1882 the League was renamed Irish Parliamentary Party under the leadership of the Protestant Anglo-Irish Charles Stewart Parnell. Significantly, Healy's brief parliamentary intervention on the Iranian tobacco concession in 1892 occurred at a time when the IPP was divided and in complete disarray after Parnell's legal entanglement in 1889-90 over his affair with a married woman, Katherine ("Kitty") O'Shea. Parnell was forced out of the party in 1890 in the aftermath of his fierce vilification by both Catholic and Protestant establishments in Ireland and following extensive condemnation within party ranks. Healy, already a critic of Parnell's leadership, emerged as Parnell's most caustic castigator inside the party over the O'Shea affair.[5] It was not until 1899 that the party was reunited under John Redmond's leadership, whom Healy also opposed. In his 1910 *The Persian Revolution of 1905-1909*, the Cambridge orientalist Edward Granville Browne, the most resolute British defender of Iranian sovereignty at the time and a supporter of Irish Home Rule, among his advocacy of other nationalist movements,[6] noted Healy's participation in the debates on the Iranian tobacco concession, but without specifically identifying Healy as an Irish nationalist—although many of Browne's readers in the United Kingdom would have been aware of Healy's political affiliation, given his long parliamentary career.[7] By the time of the publication of Browne's book, Browne had emerged as the leading figure in the extensive campaign across the United Kingdom in opposition to British policy in Iran following the Anglo-Russian Agreement of 1907. This parliamentary and extra-parliamentary campaign included various Irish nationalist individuals and groupings.

The tobacco concession and London's direct diplomatic entanglement in securing an indemnity in return for the cancellation of the concession were also attacked in other venues in the United Kingdom, besides the parliament. Two leading Iranian dissidents in England at the time, Malkum Khan (the former Iranian representative in London) and Sayyid Jamal al-Din Assadabadi (a.k.a., "al-Afghani"; also a well-known pan-Islamic opponent of British occupation of Egypt and a social reformer), attended a number of public gatherings in London in opposition to the concession.[8] Denunciations of Salisbury's Iranian wrangling also appeared in the pages of the "Radical" press across the United Kingdom, most notably in the *Manchester Guardian*, the *Pall Mall Gazette* (London), and *Truth* (London). Little attention was devoted to the Iranian tobacco concession in the pages of the Irish nationalist press. *The Nation* did not lend its voice to Salisbury's critics on this occasion. The generally more moderate nationalist mouthpiece the *Freeman's Journal*, which had earlier carried adverts for the sale of shares in Talbot's Imperial Tobacco Corporation of Persia,[9] was somewhat more responsive to the latest episode in Anglo-Iranian relations. The *Freeman's Journal* also provided passing reports of the activities of Sayyid Jamal al-Din in London in opposition to both the Iranian monarch and the tobacco concession,[10] while occasionally reporting on related British parliamentary criticisms of Salisbury.[11] Moreover, the paper at times reproduced reports from other sources that reflected the popular resentment inside Iran toward the Iranian chief minister ("the Grand Vizier"), who had negotiated the terms of the tobacco concession. One of these reproduced reports also noted the popular disdain in Iran for the official British involvement in the fiasco, including alleged chants by crowds of 'Down with Lord Salisbury.'[12] Some of the provincial Irish nationalist newspapers, such as the Home Rule *Cork Examiner*, also periodically echoed criticisms of Salisbury's handling of the concession. On one instance, noting the large-scale popular opposition to the concession inside Iran and the shah's desperation to stave off "a rebellion," the paper attacked Salisbury for interfering in the matter in order to secure an outrageous compensation for his relative (Talbot), adding:

> No more atrocious piece of jobbery has come to light in modern days. It shows that the Tory Party have not lost the evil character which they bore for corruption in the public departments. We have not heard the last of this scandal. [...] the Shah of Persia should simply refuse, if the money has not been already paid over, to give a single sixpence. Lord Salisbury and his relative dare not go to the country and ask them to coerce the Persian people under circumstances so disgraceful.[13]

The paper also occasionally reported on parliamentary criticisms of Salisbury's handling of the situation.

Overall, however, the coverage of the Iranian tobacco concession in the Irish nationalist press was much more subdued in comparison with *The Nation*'s earlier coverage of the Anglo-Iranian War of 1856–57—not forgetting also the contextual disparity between an armed conflict, with potentially major regional and imperial consequences for London, versus a private economic concession willingly granted by the Iranian government to a British subject, albeit with accompanying ramifications for London's imperial leverage in the region. *The Nation*'s castigation of the British war effort in 1856–57, and the paper's branding of London as an imperialist aggressor, had been the first instance of sustained public expression of contemporary cross-territorial anti-imperialist affinity with Iranians to emanate from a distinctively Irish nationalist platform. At that time, it had been primarily the Iranian state with which *The Nation* had sided, including the paper's rationalization of Iranian military operations in Herat and its environs. The Iranian Tobacco Protest, on the other hand, marked a nationwide Iranian popular movement in opposition to both the Iranian state's continued maladministration of the country and British intervention in Iranian affairs. While the main current of the Iranian Tobacco Protest eventually degenerated into a broadly anti-European xenophobic remonstration before finally petering out, the event marked a major juncture in Iranian popular politics in so far as participation in Iranian anti-government agitations by small groupings of so-called Iranian modernizing "secular"-reformists, alongside the more socially entrenched and powerful (Twelver) Shi'i Muslim clerical camps of varying socio-political proclivities (including some advocates of certain forms of modernization). Both Iranian religious (Shi'i) and secular camps, representing a broad spectrum of political allegiances, later took part in the 1906 Iranian Constitutional Revolution and in the ensuing struggle against domestic tyranny and foreign intervention in Iranian affairs in 1906–11. The Iranian autocracy, too, simultaneously counted on the support of some high-ranking Shi'i clerics and their followers as well as secular-oriented individuals.

Notwithstanding the absence of any resolute Irish nationalist denunciation of London's handling of the Iranian tobacco concession in 1891–92, the concession was nonetheless another indication that Anglo-Iranian relations were now occasionally featuring in Irish nationalist critiques of London's foreign and imperial policies, regardless of whether or not these condemnations were principally self-serving in so far as being ultimately intended to redirect public attention to English domination of Ireland, as had been chiefly the case with *The Nation*'s reporting of the Anglo-Iranian War in 1856–57. At the same time, the relatively insouciant coverage of the Iranian Tobacco Protest by much of the Irish nationalist press, was an indicator of Iran's as of yet marginal position in Irish nationalist expressions of cross-territorial solidarity with other population groups. It was only after 1907 that the topic of Anglo-Iranian relations acquired considerable magnitude in Irish nationalist denunciations of continued British imperial aggression around the world. From 1907 until the founding of the Irish Free State in 1922, British intervention in Iranian affairs constituted one of the leading extra-Irish developments that drew regular commentary from Irish nationalists of differing political platforms, with the fate of the Iranian *nation* now often lumped together in terms of importance with those of Indian and/or Egyptian nations.

Irish Nationalists and the Rights of Other Peoples

Irish nationalists of varying political allegiances had long expressed support for a range of other (anti-imperialist) nationalist as well as certain reformist movements around the world, even if at times in a highly selective manner that disregarded, or even denigrated, the competing rights of other groups. Some Irish nationalist circles and individuals had also long engaged in direct contacts and collaboration with anti-imperialists in other parts of the British Empire, most notably with Indian and Egyptian nationalists by the early years of the twentieth century.[14] These contacts occurred at various locations in the United Kingdom—as in the case of, for example, the 1910 and 1911 Nationalities and Subject Races conferences in London, or at gatherings of the India House in London (founded in 1905), or at the headquarters of Inghinidhe na hÉireann (Daughters of Ireland) in Dublin, or at various private residences, as in the case of Nora Dryhurst's home in London (see below) or the conservative English anti-imperialist Wilfrid Scawen Blunt's country house at Newbuildings Place (Sussex)—, or at different locations in continental Europe, such as during the Egyptian Congress in Brussels in 1910, or in the United States (see below), and in other parts of the world, including in Egypt and India. Some of these locations constituted what I have termed *third contact zones* in reference to places outside the "national" homelands of both Irish nationalists and their counterparts from other colonized and semi-colonized territories—to the exclusion of Great Britain in this setting, given the large presence of Irish communities in Britain, and also excluding locations such as the United States in the case of those participants at such gatherings who were naturalized American citizens of Irish descent, for instance.[15] These direct and indirect political contacts at times also had corollary cultural and other consequences, just as initially cultural contacts could also yield eventual cross-nationalist political collaborations. Wide-ranging examples of such developments include the previously mentioned long residence in India of Margaret and James Cousins after 1915, or the case of Sister Nivedita. In the early twentieth century William Butler Yeats, who also happened to believe in ancient ties between Ireland and the Orient, widely promoted the literary works of his Indian contemporary Rabindranath Tagore (1861–1941) as masterpieces of world literature. Yeats also wrote the Introduction to the English translation of Tagore's 1912 *Gitanjali*, shortly before Tagore was awarded the Nobel Prize in literature.[16] Tagore at the time was still an Indian 'nationalist.' In addition to conventional political and/or cultural cross-territorial nationalist contacts, there were also rare cases of direct Irish republican armed participation in support of other "nationalities," the most famous example being the roughly five hundred Irish and Irish-American volunteers, led by John MacBride, who joined the Boer resistance against British forces in southern Africa during the Boer War of 1899–1902, as already noted. These volunteers were known interchangeably as the Irish Transvaal Brigade, Irish Commandos, or MacBride's Brigade. Of course, largely overlooked by the armed volunteers of the Irish Transvaal Brigade, or for that matter in so-called pro- and anti-Boer platforms in the United Kingdom in general, was the rights of the oppressed "Black" African populations of both Boer- and British-controlled territories in southern Africa.[17] On the other hand, anti-"Black African" and anti-Jewish sentiments were clearly evident among some leading Irish nationalists during the Boer War, such as those resorting to anti-Jewish invectives that blamed all Jews *intrinsically* for what was otherwise the presence of a few Jewish financiers among a much larger gamut of non-Jewish British financiers seeking to gain access to diamond and other mines in the Boer territories.[18] It was the almost unanimous opposition to London's war effort against the Boers by MPs belonging to the splintered post-Parnell Irish Home Rule camps that brought about the reunification of the Irish Parliamentary Party (IPP) under John Redmond's leadership in 1899. Incidentally, whereas Irish members of Britain's imperial armed forces participated in the Boer War, Britain's Indian troops were not deployed in the war on racial grounds (since they would be fighting "white" Boer descendants of earlier Dutch settlers). This again indicates Ireland's different standing in the British Empire.

These modes of cross-territorial Irish nationalist solidarities and cooperation, regardless of whether their ultimate objective was strictly self-regarding or also genuinely other-regarding, were drastically different from some earlier instances of Irish nationalists joining the military forces of Britain's rival powers, as in the case of Theobald Wolfe Tone in the late eighteenth century. Tone, a leader of the United Irishmen, served in the expansionist French revolutionary army in Europe in 1797 that was occupying the territories of other 'nations'[19]—even if it can be claimed that Tone regarded the democratic ideals of the French Revolution and republicanism as universally beneficial to all Europeans, notwithstanding the increasingly authoritarian tendencies of the French state by then. Even in sharper contrast to Irish nationalist armed collaborations with other colonized groups after the late nineteenth century was the military service in *Napoleon's* expansionist imperial army by the celebrated United Irishmen revolutionary Arthur Conner (a.k.a., O'Connor), following the failed United Irishmen uprising of 1798 and the end of the French Revolution the following year.[20] There was also the case of the prominent republican Irish nationalist John Devoy serving in the French Legionnaire force in French-occupied Algeria in 1861, indifferent to the French violation of the territorial sovereignty of "Algerians."[21] Cross-territorial Irish nationalist acts of anti-imperialist solidarity also need to be distinguished from the example of those diasporic Irish living in the United States who joined the Mexican side during the Mexican-American War of 1846–48, as members of San Patricios (Saint Patrick's Battalion).[22] Although this was an anti-imperialist struggle, *many* of the Irish members of the battalion, which largely consisted of non-Irish fighters, happened to be Catholics primarily motivated by their common religious identification with Mexicans and/or aspiring for a better life in Mexico, rather than being inspired by anti-imperialist nationalist sentiments.

Yet, there were also earlier examples of Irish nationalists with extra-Irish commitments concerning the rights of the oppressed that intersected with their broader and more universalist anti-imperialist objectives, most notably the anti-slavery campaign by the likes of Daniel O'Connell and Richard Robert Madden, who in collaboration with the Hibernian Anti-Slavery Society (1837) aimed at the abolition of what was called "African slavery" in the United States and elsewhere, having previously campaigned for the abolition of slavery in the British Empire.[23] Unlike O'Connell and Madden, there were also Irish nationalists who fervently defended the system of enslaving 'Africans,' as in the case of the already-noted John Mitchel's advocacy of slavery in the United States.

The Iranian Constitutional Revolution of 1906, the 1907 Anglo-Russian Agreement, and Irish Nationalist Advocacy of Iran's Sovereignty

After 1907, direct contacts took place between some Irish and Iranian nationalists, with the period from August 1907 to December 1911 marking one of the most extensive and protracted cycles of Irish nationalist expressions of anti-imperialist solidarity with Iranians. This occured following the conclusion of an Agreement between London and St. Petersburg on August 31, 1907, after years of negotiations and nearly a year after the outbreak of the Iranian Constitutional Revolution of 1906. The Agreement delineated the range of the two European powers' respective "interests" and influence in Tibet, Afghanistan, and Iran, with both St. Petersburg and London already having concluded separate formal alliances with France. The 1907 Anglo-Russian Agreement was intended to resolve the regional differences between the two hitherto rival imperial powers and foster cooperation among them for checking Germany's rapid rise as a European military and imperial power—Germany being an ally of the Austro-Hungarian Empire, which more directly concerned Russia. The 1907 Agreement set St. Petersburg and London on a direct collision course with the Iranian constitutionalist-nationalist camps. In Iran, months of mass protests in the capital Tehran and some other cities after December 1905, fueled by economic hardship and government maladministration and autocracy, had eventually culminated in a Constitutional Revolution in the summer of 1906. The revolution was directed at both arbitrary monarchic rule in the country as well as foreign intervention in Iran's domestic affairs, namely by Russia and Britain, the main foreign interlopers in Iranian affairs since the start of the nineteenth century. On August 5, 1906, the ailing Iranian monarch Mozaffar al-Din Shah (r.1896–1906) signed the constitutional proclamation authorizing the formation of a national assembly (majles).

In a world-historical context, the Iranian revolution was one of the many worldwide anti-imperialist, constitutionalist, and/or reformist struggles in the early years of the twentieth century. Some of these struggles variously impacted or even intersected with one another, evoking expressions of cross-territorial solidarity. These struggles ranged from the Russian Revolution of 1905, which had further economic and socio-political bearing on developments in Iran south of the border—with small bands of revolutionaries from Russian territories and beyond later also joining the Iranian constitutionalist-nationalist camp during the Iranian civil war of 1908–09—to Finland's struggle for autonomy from Russia, Norway's secession from Sweden in 1905, the upsurge in Indian nationalist activities following the partition of Bengal in 1905, the intensified Egyptian struggle for independence from Britain following the 1906 "Dinshaway incident," the Young Turk Revolution of 1908, the Mexican Revolution of 1910–11, or the Chinese republican Xinhai Revolution of 1911–12, among other examples. Developments in Iran leading up to the Constitutional Revolution and the subsequent turn of events in that country in the aftermath of the Anglo-Russian Agreement of 1907, also coincided with consequential nationalist political developments in Ireland. In the case of Iran, these developments included the civil war of 1908–09, which pitted the Russian-backed Iranian autocratic monarch Mohammad-Ali Shah (r.1906–09) against constitutionalist-nationalist forces, with the British Liberal foreign secretary Sir Edward Grey publicly justifying Russian aggression in Iran, and the subsequent Anglo-Russian meddling in Iranian affairs after Mohammad-Ali Shah's ouster in the summer of 1909—finally culminating in the termination of the Iranian revolution in late 1911 and the closure of the second Iranian national assembly (i.e., the second majles, 1909-11) under Russian duress with London's backing.

The nationalist political transformations in Ireland in the meantime occurred in tandem with manifold trajectories of the ongoing Irish Revival (ranging from literary output, including plays, to the promotion of Gaelic language, 'Gaelic' sports, and a wide array of other cultural endeavors). During the early twentieth century, the IPP still dominated Ireland's nationalist politics, continuing to do so until the general election of 1918. The IPP was committed to attaining self-government for Ireland within the British Empire through a parliamentary campaign for the creation of a separate Irish parliament in Dublin. The militant Irish Republican Brotherhood (IRB), committed to complete independence from Britain through armed struggle, enjoyed a much smaller support base at the time, albeit attracting steadily larger following in the Irish diaspora, particularly in the United States. In 1905, a new non-violent nationalist organization appeared on the scene, soon establishing branches across Ireland and throughout the Irish diaspora, and emerging as the main rival to the IPP, even if attracting a considerably smaller following than the IPP prior to 1916–18. This party was Sinn Féin ("ourselves"; sometimes also translated as "ourselves alone"). More accurately, prior to the 1918 general election Sinn Féin was more of a "movement" than a party. It was founded in Dublin in November 1905 by the nationalist journalist Arthur Griffith and the playwright, author, and veteran cultural and political nationalist Bulmer Hobson. The playwright Edward Martyn was the organization's first president. The organization came about as a merger of Griffith's Cumann na nGaedheal (the Society *or* League of the Gaels), founded in

1900 to unite all Home Rulers opposed to the IPP, and a number of other smaller groupings. Committed to non-violent attainment of Irish self-government within the British Empire, similar to the chief objective of the IPP, Sinn Féin represented the more radical wing of the Home Rule movement by pursuing an abstentionist platform that opposed Irish nationalist participation in the British parliament, even though it still put up candidates in parliamentary elections as a show of popularity. Sinn Féin's primary political objective had been outlined in Griffith's 1904 book *Resurrection of Hungary*, which called for the establishment of a separate Irish parliament and the transformation of the United Kingdom into a dual kingdom of Great Britain and Ireland on a model similar to the 1867 dual monarchy constitution of the Austro-Hungarian Empire. In 1906, Griffith founded a newspaper as the mouthpiece of this organization, eponymously named *Sinn Féin*, which replaced Griffith's former *The United Irishman* (1899–1906). Moreover, Sinn Féin also promoted Ireland's economic and cultural self-reliance, principally in the form of severing of ties with Britain; a platform analogous to the Indian nationalist swadeshi boycott of British products and institutions following the British partition of Bengal in 1905. This policy of Sinn Féin paralleled the IRB's existing slogan of boycotting British goods, services, and institutions. Within a short time, the IRB set out to infiltrate Sinn Féin, despite the divergent political goals and methods of the two organizations.[24]

There were other smaller Irish nationalist groupings, the activities of some of which overlapped with other nationalist organizations. These included the IPP-affiliated United Irish League, founded in 1898 by William O'Brien to campaign for distribution of land among peasant farmers, and its Young Ireland Branch founded in 1904 by Thomas Michael Kettle. The latter organization, contrary to IPP's platform, shortly also took up the advocacy of women's suffrage and included an amalgam of socialists and/or non-IRB republicans in its ranks.[25] Other nationalist organizations around this time ranged from William O'Brien's All-for-Ireland League (1909), with the *Cork Free Press* (1910–16) as its mouthpiece, to the small labor and/or socialist organizations, such as James Connolly's Socialist Party of Ireland (founded in 1904 as the successor to the 1896 Irish Socialist Republican Party). Besides nationalist political parties, or the officially proscribed IRB (led by Thomas Clarke and Seán MacDermott in the years before the outbreak of the First World War), there were a host of other nationalist organizations, such as the sectarian (Catholic) Ancient Order of Hibernians (AOH), founded in the United States in 1836 and publicly active in Ireland since 1904 (with prior presence in Ireland), and its "Ladies' Auxiliary" formed in 1910. Fiercely loyal to the Catholic establishment, the AOH was a staunch supporter of the otherwise nonsectarian IPP, with its members also engaging in parades, electoral campaigns and demonstrations, as well as disruption of events by rival organizations.[26] Both the IPP and the IRB enjoyed extensive support base in the Irish diaspora, most notably in the United States, which boasted a large population of Irish descent (certainly not all of them Irish nationalists). By the time of the outbreak of the First World War, Sinn Féin too had gained major ground in the diasporic communities, subsequently attaining rapidly mounting popularity after the Easter Rising of 1916, following which Sinn Féin was transformed into a revolutionary republican movement under IRB's leverage. The best organized, and in many ways the most politically and materially consequential, of the American Irish nationalist organizations in these years was the IRB-affiliate Clan na Gael, based in New York and with a vast network of regional branches throughout the United States—although enjoying smaller following than the IPP affiliates in the United States until the events of 1916 in Ireland.

As I have noted in earlier works, "The Iranian Constitutional Revolution was an early example of an *internationalized* revolutionary event in the 'East' par excellence."[27] It attracted expressions of solidarity and varying forms of assistance in different parts of the world, including the participation of hundreds of volunteer and mercenary fighters during the Iranian civil war of 1908-09, mostly from the Russian Empire and with different political agendas (primarily Azeris, Georgians, Armenians, and Russians), as well as a number of Bulgarians and other Europeans, a few Ottomans, and the young American Howard Baskerville, a teacher at the Presbyterian missionary school in Tabriz.[28] In the United Kingdom, before the final signing of the 1907 Anglo-Russian Agreement there was already growing opposition to Sir Edward Grey's handling of Anglo-Iranian affairs, including the rumored ongoing secret talks between London and St. Petersburg. This opposition assumed greater momentum and urgency following the conclusion of the Agreement between London and St. Petersburg on August 31, 1907, signed without any consultation with, or prior notification of, the governments of Iran, Tibet, or Afghanistan. Iran was divided into respective British and Russian spheres of influence (with a putatively neutral, independent zone separating the two spheres). Although negotiations resulting in the Agreement had preceded the outbreak of the Iranian revolution, the Agreement set Russia and Britain on course against Iranian constitutionalist-nationalist camps, with London at first somewhat reluctantly acquiescing to overt Russian acts of aggression against Iranian constitutionalists, before openly joining St. Petersburg in obstructing and intimidating the Iranian majles during its second term (1909–11), following the overthrow of the Russian-backed Iranian autocrat Mohammad-Ali Shah in the summer of 1909 that ended the Iranian civil war. These machinations by the two imperial powers eventually resulted in the termination of the Iranian revolution in December 1911.

Various Irish personalities, both nationalists and unionists, participated in the campaign waged against Sir Edward Grey's Iranian policy in the United Kingdom, with some Irish nationalist outlets in the Irish diaspora also expressing support for the Iranian revolution and defending Iran's territorial sovereignty in the aftermath of the 1907 Agreement. For the small number of Irish unionists MPs who joined this Iranian campaign against Grey—with these unionists belonging to both the ruling Liberal Party and the main opposition Conservative Party (a.k.a., the Unionist Party after 1895)—the question of Iran's sovereignty and the survival of that country's recent constitutional experimentation was chiefly couched in terms of Britain's imperial interests, including the security of British India, and was also reflective of residual sentiments of Russophobia. The (London-born) Irish Henry Finnis Blosse Lynch, Liberal MP for Ripon (Yorkshire), a unionist and self-proclaimed Liberal-Imperialist, was exceptional in unionist ranks for his uncompromising underlying commitment to Iran's independence and its constitutional system. H. F. B. Lynch, also of Messrs. Lynch Brothers Company, which held navigation and other commercial interests in southern Iran, Ottoman Iraq, and the Persian Gulf, became a foremost critic of Grey's handling of Iranian affairs in the United

Kingdom. Lynch, who lost his parliamentary seat in 1910, continued to play a leading role in challenging Grey's Iranian policy, working closely with the Cambridge orientalist Edward Granville Browne, the leading British defender of Iran's independence and, incidentally, a supporter of Irish Home Rule. Lynch was a co-founder and chairman of the Persia Committee, a multi-party parliamentary and extra-parliamentary lobby group founded in London on October 29, 1908, by British critics of Anglo-Russian intervention in Iran. The committee, with Browne as its vice-chairman and the Conservative (Unionist) Lord Lamington (Charles Wallace Alexander Napier Cochrane-Baillie) as its president, inaugurated a more coordinated campaign against Grey's Iranian policy. With over sixty members in its executive committee by 1912, forty-five of them MPs, the committee largely comprised of Radical members of Grey's own party, and smaller number of MPs from Labour and Conservative (Unionist) ranks, along with two IPP members. The committee dogged Grey inside both houses of parliament, in the pages of the press, and at a number of public gatherings, while also maintaining direct contacts with Iranian constitutionalist-nationalists and a number of organizations and individuals in other parts of the world, who were also committed to defending Iran's sovereignty. The committee's activities gradually dwindled after mid-1912—by which time the second Iranian majles had been suppressed—and finally came to a halt on August 4, 1914, after London's entry into what later came to be called the Great War.[29]

For their part, Irish nationalists participating in the campaign against London's Iranian policy, such as the IPP's John Dillon, approached the Iranian Question through the lens of anti-imperialism and the sovereign rights of nations; leaving aside the complexities of 'national' questions in some other parts of the world, where different so-called nations laid claim to the same territories. Moreover, the majority of Grey's critics in the United Kingdom during the protracted Iranian debate, including many unionists, were simultaneously apprehensive of the anti-German contour of improved relations between London and St. Petersburg, which in their view greatly heightened the likelihood of a major war between opposing European imperial powers that had already split into rival alliance systems.[30] Dillon, one of the highest ranking IPP MPs, was the most prominent Irish nationalist politician opposed to London's policy in the Iranian debate from its earliest phase. In addition to Dillon, who worked closely with Browne, another IPP MP, Stephen Lucius Gwynn, also a journalist, poet, and cultural critic, resolutely assisted the Iranian campaign inside and outside the House of Commons, while the IPP leader John Redmond and a number of other IPP MPs, such as Richard Hazleton and John G.S. MacNeill, occasionally joined the debate on the Iranian Question. Dillon and Gwynn formally joined the Persia Committee in 1911, after having all along assisted its campaign since its founding in October 1908, notwithstanding the IPP's proviso that its members refrain from joining extra-Irish political organizations and pressure groups.[31] Another Home Rule Irish nationalist, but not an MP, who participated in the Iranian campaign was the positivist-rationalist Shapland Hugh Swinny, the president of the London Positivist Society and an acquaintance of the likes of Wilfrid Scawen Blunt—the exceptional British conservative anti-imperialist and the leading British champion of Egypt's independence, as well as a proponent of Indian self-government and an outspoken defender of Ottoman and Iranian sovereignty. Swinny joined the

Persia Committee long before Dillon and Gwynn. Blunt also happened to have been the most renowned British campaigner for Irish Home Rule in the late nineteenth century. He became the first Englishman to serve a prison sentence for Ireland's cause (in 1887), following his participation in the Irish National League's Plan of Campaign concerning the agricultural land question in Ireland.[32] In fact, long before Arthur Griffith's 1904 *Resurrection of Hungary*, Blunt had suggested in 1885 that Ireland be granted Home Rule within the empire on similar terms as Hungary under the Austro-Hungarian system of dual monarchy.[33] Swinny encouraged and arranged for the publication of articles by Blunt and many others on topics including the Iranian Question in the *Positivist Review* (London), which Swinny edited and to which he himself contributed occasional notes on Iranian developments, among numerous other subjects. Swinny was a regular participant in such events as the January 1912 conference in London on "Relations between the Mohammedan World and the West," which was also attended by Blunt and the internationalist and socialist Irish nationalist Frederick Michael Ryan (better known as Fred Ryan).[34] At the time Blunt and Ryan were closely collaborating on a host of anti-imperialist causes, including the Iranian Question. Swinny was also the treasurer of the Nationalities and Subject Races Committee, assisting the cause of Iran's territorial and national sovereignty within the scope of that committee's activities too. For instance, he was an organizer, along with Nora ("Nannie") Florence Dryhurst (born Hannah Ann Robinson in Dublin in 1856), of the Nationalities and Subject Races conference held in London in late June 1910.[35]

Dryhurst, an author and a translator, was a suffragist, anti-imperialist, anarchist (also a friend of the Russian anarchist leader Petr Kropotkin), and a staunch champion of Georgian, Indian, Egyptian, and other anti-imperialist nationalist causes. An erstwhile correspondent for the London newspaper *Freedom: A Journal of Anarchist Communism*, she was also a republican Irish nationalist, Sinn Féin activist, and a member of the Gaelic League, as well as being acquainted with some of the leading figures of the Irish Literary Revival, including Yeats. She was also a member of Maud Gonne's pro-Gaelic language women's republican Irish nationalist organization Inghinidhe na hÉireann (Daughters of Ireland, 1900), and a co-founder with Hanna Sheehy Skeffington, Margaret Cousins, and Charlotte Despard (see below) of the Irish Women's Franchise League in 1908.[36] Dryhurst was reportedly also behind the abandoned plan in 1909 to arrange for the prison scape of the militant Indian nationalist student in London Madan Lal Dhingra, who had assassinated Sir Curzon Wyllie, an aide-de-camp to the secretary of state for India and with decades of military and political service in India. Dryhurst was moreover consulted by militant Irish nationalists concerning the ultimately abortive plan in May 1910 to rescue the militant Indian nationalist Vinayak Damodar Savarkar from British police custody.[37] The 1910 gathering in London of the Nationalities and Subject Races conference, organized by Dryhurst and Swinny, included lectures on India, Egypt, Ireland, Georgia, Finland, Iran, Morocco, and Poland. With a few members of the Persia Committee also in attendance, Bernard Temple, a British photojournalist and author who had recently traveled through Iran on his way from India and was assisting the public onslaught against Grey's Iranian policy, spoke on the Iranian Question, while the radical Irish nationalists William Gibson (Lord Ashbourne) and George Gavan

Duffy (later one of the signatories of the 1921 Anglo-Irish Treaty, albeit reluctantly) presented Ireland's case. With participants at the conference coming from different regions of the world, Gibson began his introductory speech in Irish first and then in French, before switching to English ("'the tongue of the stranger' [...] much as I dislike the language").³⁸ The published proceedings of the 1910 Nationalities and Subject Races conference, edited by Dryhurst (*Nationalities and Subject Races*, 1911), included a Preface by Robert Wilson Lynd, a journalist and author, member of the Gaelic League, a socialist-leaning and non-violent republican Irish nationalist, who the previous year had married Dryhurst's daughter Sylvia, and was to later briefly join Sinn Féin. For her part, Dryhurst was personally devoting more attention to Iranian developments by then. Her concern with Anglo-Russian imperial aggression in Iran was in some ways related to her long-standing support for the cause of Georgian nationalism in the Russian Empire. (Incidentally, tens of Georgian nationalists had also joined the Iranian revolutionary camp during the Iranian civil war of 1908–09, directed against the Russian-backed Iranian autocratic monarch Mohammad-Ali Shah.) Dryhurst attempted to recruit the vice-chairman of the Persia Committee, E. G. Browne, as the speaker on the Iranian Question for the next conference of the Nationalities and Subject Races, taking place in London in the summer of 1911. Browne was unable to attend the gathering, but wrote Dryhurst a letter ahead of the conference, in which he outlined his views on European imperialism and the necessity of greater public condemnation of imperialism in the United Kingdom. Dryhurst included segments of Browne's letter in a letter-to-the-editor she submitted to the radical London newspaper the *Nation*.³⁹ Dryhurst's friend, erstwhile lover, and collaborator on many political and social issues, the radical English journalist Henry Woodd Nevinson, worked for the *Nation*. Nevinson, an advocate of Irish Home Rule, happened to be a well-known member of the Persia Committee, among a number of other foreign-policy pressure groups ranging in areas of concern from Russia to the Balkans. Participants at the 1911 conference of the Nationalities and Subject Races included the likes of Wilfrid Scawen Blunt, the British Labour Party leader Keir Hardie (also of the Persia Committee), the Radical British author and critic of imperialism John Atkinson Hobson, the Egyptian nationalist leader Mohamed Farid Bey (president of the Egyptian National Party), and the African American civil rights activist, anti-racism campaigner, and anti-imperialist William Edward Burghardt Du Bois, who was in London ahead of the gathering of the First Universal Races Congress later that month.⁴⁰ Browne was again invited to attend the 1914 conference of the Nationalities and Subject Races as an expert on Iran, but was either unable or unwilling to do so. Instead, S. H. Swinny delivered the presentation on the Iranian Question at that conference on February 16, 1914.⁴¹ Swinny, other than having joined the Persia Committee, periodically reported in the *Positivist Review* on Browne's endeavors on behalf of Iran. Swinny and Browne also took advantage of numerous other venues for championing Iran's independence, as in the case of the 1912 National Peace Congress in London, during which Swinny seconded Browne's motion for a resolution on Iran.⁴²

For her part, the British-Irish Charlotte Despard (née French; 1844–1939), a renowned feminist and suffragist, a resolute socialist, and steadfast anti-imperialist, also occasionally assisted the Iranian campaign. In addition to co-founding the Irish Women's Franchise

League along with Dryhurst and others, Despard was also a co-founder in 1907 of the Women's Freedom League headquartered in London, following her secession from the Women's Social and Political Union. She was an outspoken advocate of Irish Home Rule (later embracing a republican platform) and of Indian self-government, while periodically participating in the Iranian campaign against Grey after the 1907 Anglo-Russian Agreement. She also advocated the struggle for greater rights by Iranian feminists, among her endorsement of feminist endeavors in other parts of the world.[43] It should be noted here that commentaries on the conditions of Iranian and other 'oriental' women by Irish nationalist feminists, including Despard, also frequently replicated some of the negative contemporary European/Western stereotypes of the Orient (even if some of these stereotypes were not necessarily always false in every respect). For instance, Hanna Sheehy Skeffington wrote in a July 1912 article: "An Irishwoman, who has travelled much, told me once that Ireland of all Western countries came nearest to orientalism in its disregard of woman, its exclusion of her in all public occasions, its scarcely veiled contempt of wifehood, while, with regard to motherhood, the Orientals were ahead of us; for in the East the old woman is venerated, while in Ireland the term is synonymous for imbecility."[44]

As I have discussed in great detail in previous publications, John Dillon (at the time the second highest ranking IPP member) was by far the most outspoken Irish nationalist MP defending the Iranian revolution and Iran's sovereignty.[45] A veteran critic of British imperial aggression around the globe,[46] Dillon was also Blunt's long-time collaborator in the ongoing campaign in the United Kingdom in support of Egypt's independence. Being Blunt's closest IPP associate by 1906, their cooperation on Egyptian and other extra-Irish matters dated back to at least 1886, by which time Blunt had already distinguished himself as the leading English advocate of Irish Home Rule. In the aftermath of the 'Dinshaway Incident' in Egypt in 1906, Blunt and Dillon multiplied their efforts for building direct ties between Irish Home Rulers and the National Party in Egypt (al-hizb al-watani), with the IPP MP Thomas Kettle also significantly contributing to these efforts.[47] Blunt was also a friend and erstwhile lover of Lady Gregory, with whom he had jointly campaigned in support of the Egyptian nationalist leader 'Urabi Pasha, who had resisted European intervention in Egyptian affairs during the uprising of 1881–82 and was arrested and exiled following the British occupation of Egypt in 1882.[48] Years later, after much coaxing from Lady Gregory, Blunt accepted to produce a play in three Acts commissioned by the Abbey Theatre in Dublin, titled "Fand of the Fair Cheek" (based on Irish heroic cycles). The play was performed on April 27, 1907. For his part, Dillon was also a fervent critic of imperial inroads by other European/Western powers, as in the case of the French aggression in Morocco. The IPP MPs participating in the British campaign against Grey's Iranian policy, whether only intermittently or resolutely (as did Gwynn and most notably Dillon), undeniably represented only a small fraction of the IPP's parliamentary contingent of roughly 82 seats between the general election of 1906 and the outbreak of the First World War (out of the total 670 parliamentary seats). The same can be said of the overall ratio of members of other political parties who joined the Iranian campaign, or the proportion of MPs from various parties participating in any other foreign-policy or colonial debate. Then again, in each party different members concentrated on particular sets of extra-"domestic" issues, given the time it took to become extensively acquainted with the particulars and broader nuances of each case, not to mention personal preferences. Dillon was among the more exceptional examples in this regard. On top of his IPP duties, and not forgetting his deputy-leadership position in the party, he maintained continued expert engagement in Egyptian, Indian, Iranian, and a host of other imperial and foreign policy debates in the years prior to the outbreak of the First World War. This was, in part, on account of his close association with the likes of Blunt, E. G. Browne,[49] and others who continually apprised him of developments in different regions of the world by means of information they received through their vast networks of contacts in those territories.

As noted earlier, Browne in his 1910 book on the Iranian Constitutional Revolution had mentioned the participation of Timothy Michael Healy in British parliamentary debates surrounding the Iranian tobacco concession in 1891–92. By the time Browne's book was published, Healy, an IPP MP during the time of the Iranian Tobacco Protest, had left the IPP and was returned to parliament in 1910 as a member of the All-For-Ireland League, which he co-founded in 1909 with the veteran journalist and Home Rule politician William O'Brien and a number of other Home Rulers now opposed to the IPP's leadership and tactics and also disinclined to join Sinn Féin. Among their other differences with the IPP, Healy and his associates in the League favored a more gradualist approach to Home Rule and reached out to unionists in the hope of winning them over to their campaign. In regard to the platform of peasant land-ownership, the League adopted a much less confrontational stance toward large landowning interests in Ireland than did the IPP.[50] Healy, who later became the first governor-general of the Irish Free State in 1922, avoided joining the fervent British parliamentary and extra-parliamentary condemnations of London's collusion with St. Petersburg in undermining Iranian sovereignty after 1907. Even more ironically for Browne, on two occasions during the debates in the House of Commons on the Iranian Question in 1911, Healy taunted John Dillon. After returning to parliament as an All-For-Ireland League MP, Healy was no longer interested in espousing causes exterior to the Irish Question. In addition to partisan differences between Healy and Dillon, Healy was now highly critical of what he considered as unwarranted and boundless cosmopolitan anti-imperialism of many Irish nationalists, such as Dillon. Healy was insistent on solely focusing on Irish and Irish-related matters. In the House of Commons on November 14, 1911, in response to Dillon's concern about the possible Russian military occupation of northern Iran, Healy contemptuously asked: "whether Russia has any intention of sending Cossacks to Connemara [in Ireland]?" On December 7, Healy reacted to another parliamentary question by Dillon, this time asking: "Can the Russian Government interfere in Irish questions?"[51] Healy's now insular political disposition was shared by many others in the wide spectrum of Irish nationalist camps both in the United Kingdom and in the Irish diaspora, albeit often expressed in a less categoric manner than by Healy. There were also instances of some Irish nationalists selectively, and often purely rhetorically and in a partisan manner, attacking the internationalist ("cosmopolitan") commitments of other Irish nationalists. A famous case being Arthur Griffith's reproach of Fred Ryan in 1913 (see below).

William Joseph Maloney, Frederick Michael Ryan, and the Iranian Question Before the First World War

A few Irish journalists traveled to Iran to cover the Iranian revolution. These included William Arthur Moore (1880–1962), who served as the special correspondent for the Persia Committee in the city of Tabriz from January to April 1909, during the Iranian civil war, and formally covered the events in Tabriz for a host of British liberal newspapers (*Daily News*, *Manchester Guardian*, and *Daily Chronicle*). Relations between Moore and the Persia Committee soured after Moore took up arms alongside the Tabriz constitutionalist-nationalist combatants fighting the Russian-backed forces of Iranian despot Mohammad-Ali Shah. Moore's action publicly damaged his claim of journalistic objectivity and led to a dispute with the Persia Committee. In his 1914 *The Orient Express*, he publicly reproached both the Persia Committee and the Iranian constitutionalist-nationalist camp, providing his own version of the tangled events.[52] Two other Irish journalists who traveled to Iran together to report on the civil war were Joseph Maunsell Hone (1882–1959), a co-founder in 1905 of the Dublin publishing house Maunsel & Co. ("Maunsell" and "Maunsel" are spelled differently in the two names), and Page Lawrence Dickinson (1881–1958), also a prominent architect. In 1910 Hone and Dickinson published *Persia in Revolution*, in which they were equally disparaging of both the Russian-backed royalist and the constitutionalist-nationalist camps in Iran.[53] Another Irish journalist reporting from Iran on the revolution and on Anglo-Russian meddling in Iranian affairs was the Reuters correspondent William Joseph Maloney (1885–1968),[54] who was stationed in that country from 1909 to 1911.

Unlike the other Irish journalists traveling to Iran to cover the revolution, the Limerick-born Maloney was a well-known Irish nationalist and actively assisted the Iranian resistance to Anglo-Russian machinations.[55] By then, Maloney had already been working closely with Blunt and Frederick Michael Ryan (1873–1913) on the "Egypt for Egyptians" campaign. Both Maloney and Ryan were committed to an expansive internationalist platform of anti-imperialism. Ryan (see also Chapter Six), commonly known as "Fred Ryan," was a positivist-rationalist, socialist, feminist, non-violent republican Irish nationalist, journalist, and cultural critic. From 1908 to 1909 Maloney and Ryan, both friends of Francis Sheehy Skeffington who had first introduced them to one another, served as co-editors of the Cairo nationalist newspaper *The Egyptian Standard*. The paper was founded in 1907 as the English-language edition of *al-Liwa* (*The Standard*) by the Egyptian nationalist leader Mustafa Kamil, with Blunt's encouragement and partial funding—*L'Étendard égyptien* appeared as the French-language edition of the paper.[56] *The Egyptian Standard* had been edited in its first year (1907–08) by the English Charles Rudy It was Blunt who recommended Maloney as the new editor of the paper upon Mustafa Kamil's request. Blunt had first met Maloney in 1906, but it was Thomas Kettle, the IPP MP and a defender of Egypt's independence, who initially recommended Maloney to Blunt for the Cairo post, following Blunt's query to John Dillon about a suitable Irish journalist for the job. Soon after reaching Cairo, Maloney invited his journalist friend Ryan to join him from Dublin. Blunt evidently first met Ryan in person only in April 1909, after Ryan had returned from Egypt.[57] During their editorial tenure at *The Egyptian Standard*, Ryan and Maloney also periodically kept the press in the United Kingdom as well as the diasporic Irish nationalist press abreast of Egyptian developments.[58] Their reporting and other articles in the coming years were also occasionally cited in the pages of the Indian nationalist press.[59]

Ryan's earlier journalistic and literary career in Dublin (where he was born) included active participation in the Irish National Theatre Society (precursor to the Abbey Theatre). He also served as the treasurer of the theatre and composed the theatre's first staged play, "Laying the Foundations" (1902), which dealt with contemporary social issues in Ireland. He opposed the promotion of Irish as the national language of Ireland by organizations such as the Gaelic League and, while of Catholic upbringing, was a vocal secular-rationalist castigator of the Catholic establishment as well as of theosophy, occult, other forms of spiritualism and religions in general, notwithstanding his co-founding and co-editing of the modernist literary journal *Dana* (1904–05) with the theosophist William Kirkpatrick Magee ("John Eglinton"), or his association with Yeats in the Irish National Theatre Society. In 1907 Ryan and Francis Sheehy Skeffington co-founded the short-lived leftist monthly journal *National Democrat* (Dublin), for which Ryan also sporadically wrote articles. Maloney, too, contributed articles to the *National Democrat*. Ryan had previously also written for Arthur Griffith's *The United Irishman* and contributed a number of articles to the *Freeman's Journal* and the *Irish Independent*. Some of his articles appeared under the aliases "Irial" and "Finian," two ancient Gaelic names. Ryan's father, who died when Ryan was in his early teens, had been a Fenian. Fred Ryan, however, opted for non-violent republicanism in combination with socialism, joining James Connolly's Irish Socialist Republican Party (1896–c.1904). Shortly before leaving for Egypt, Ryan served as a founding member and secretary of the Socialist Party of Ireland (1908), with Connolly assuming the party's leadership after his return from the United States in 1910. By then, Ryan had also joined the Young Ireland Branch of the United Irish League.[60]

Years after Ryan's death, he infamously appeared as a character in James Joyce's *Ulysses* (1922), in a scene in which Joyce settled score with Magee and Ryan for *Dana*'s rejection of a submission by Joyce nearly two decades earlier.[61] Incidentally, unlike Joyce and many others, Ryan avoided the subject of Irish origins, focusing instead on contemporary analogies between Ireland and the 'Orient' in the framework of anti-imperialist nationalist struggles; seeking to inspire greater Irish nationalist interest in, and expressed affinities and solidarity with, Egyptian and Iranian nationalist movements (albeit often avoiding the subject of competing nationalist platforms in either of the territories). It was following Ryan's and Maloney's return from Egypt after the closure of *The Egyptian Standard* in 1909, nearly a year after Mustafa Kamil's death in February 1908, that the two Irish journalists devoted their attention to the Iranian Question as a regular international concern. Before long, Maloney was posted as a Reuters journalist in Iran, following a brief stint in Istanbul where he reported for the *Manchester Guardian* on developments in the aftermath of the 1908 Young Turk Revolution. While stationed in Iran, Maloney was in regular communication with Browne and the Persia Committee in London.[62] Ryan resumed his journalistic activities after returning to Ireland, contributing articles on topics ranging from imperialism to nationalism and women's suffrage to periodicals such as the *Irish Review* (Dublin) and the *Positivist Review* (London), the latter edited by Ryan's friend and fellow positivist-rationalist S.H. Swinny.[63] In early 1911 Ryan joined Blunt to work on the monthly newspaper *Egypt* (1911–13), the organ of Blunt's Egyptian Committee, moving between Blunt's house in London and his Sussex country house. The paper was edited by Ryan until his death in 1913 at the age of 40. Maloney, too, contributed a number of articles to *Egypt*, with Blunt and Ryan writing many of the articles themselves, including those on Iranian developments. Ryan also favorably reviewed the American William Morgan Shuster's *The Strangling of Persia* in the September 1912 issue of *Egypt*. Shuster had been Iran's treasurer-general, appointed by that country's constitutional authorities in 1910 and serving in that capacity until the termination of the Iranian revolution under Russian and British coercion in December 1911. Ryan and Maloney championed Iran's political and territorial sovereignty in other fora as well, including Ryan's highly favorable review of E. G. Browne's 1910 *The Persian Revolution*, appearing in the *Irish Review*.[64] On the Iranian Question, Ryan was admittedly influenced by Browne's publications as well as public and private statements. In "Persian Crisis: An Irish Parallel," appearing in the *Irish Independent* (Dublin) in January 1912—only days after the Russian-instigated clampdown on the second Iranian majles, carried out by Iran's Bakhtiari-dominated cabinet, and the ensuing Russian "reign of terror" in northern Iran and Sir Edward Grey's public exculpations of Russian actions—Ryan wrote in the now frequently quoted article:

> Professor Browne of Cambridge, who has done so much to support the Persian cause and to put the case of the Persian nation before English readers, once wrote to me that he always thought there was a considerable likeness between Ireland and Persia, Erin and Iran, both countries having gone through the tragedy of manifold national defeat and invasion, yet both always clinging to an ideal of nationality and striving after that ideal through dark and evil days. One of the myths about the East current in Europe is that the idea of patriotism and national independence is unknown there. It is, of course, a convenient myth enough for those who desire to annex rich slices of Eastern countries, but it sometimes leads to sad accidents, as in the Italian raid on Tripoli. The Oriental people may not have heard of the myth, and may stupidly try to defend their country against the invader.
>
> The Persian movement towards national regeneration is, perhaps, the most striking, with one exception [i.e., Egypt], of these revivals in the East which have been such a feature in the world history of the past two decades. [...][65]

Radical Irish Nationalists and the Iranian Question: *Sinn Féin* (Dublin) and Militant Irish Nationalists in the United States

For the lack of an alternative concise term, here "radicalism" is applied in the general sense of seeking comprehensive transformation of the existing political and/or social order, to jointly describe the abstentionist political platform and self-reliant economic and cultural stance of the 'Home Rule' organization Sinn Féin, founded in 1905, as well as the militant revolutionary republican platform of IRB-affiliated organizations and other similar groups in both Ireland and the Irish diaspora—even though in many ways the label of 'radicalism' properly belongs to Irish nationalists such as Fred Ryan, Hanna and Francis Sheehy Skeffington, and James Connolly, given their more comprehensive and uncompromising progressive commitment to social and political transformation of Ireland and their vision of social justice spanning from workers' rights to feminism and opposition to all forms of religious and racial bigotry. During the time of the Iranian Constitutional Revolution of 1906–11, Arthur Griffith's *Sinn Féin* (Dublin, 1906) and the New York-based IRB-affiliate Clan na Gael mouthpiece the *Gaelic American* (founded in 1903 and edited by John Devoy and George Freeman (a.k.a., "Fitzgerald")) constituted the main radical Irish nationalist papers published in Ireland and in the Irish diaspora respectively. Both papers were slow in taking up the Iranian Question, despite their regularly devoting considerable space to anti-British nationalist developments in different parts of the world. These papers only joined the Iranian debate after the outbreak of the Iranian civil war in the summer of 1908. This delayed reaction appears to have been, at least in part, due to the mistaken diagnosis on the part of the two Irish nationalist outlets that the 1906 Iranian revolution had enjoyed London's backing with the aim of bolstering British leverage in Iran at the expense of St. Petersburg, in keeping with the century-old pattern of Anglo-Russian rivalry in that country. This erroneous view was shared at the time in some other circles around the world, including in Iran itself. Part of the confusion lay in the long history of Anglo-Russian imperial competition in Iran and the fact that the Iranian demand for a constitutional government was first publicly taken up by the large contingent of Iranian anti-government demonstrators who had taken refuge at the British legation in Tehran in the summer of 1906.[66] The more radical Irish nationalists were also approaching Iranian developments in 1906 from the stance of "the enemy of my enemy is my friend." Arthur Griffith had for some time championed Russia's forward imperial policy in Asia in opposition to Britain, not unlike the advocacy of Russian rivalry with Britain by the Dublin nationalist newspaper *The Nation* during the Crimean War or during the Anglo-Iranian War of 1856–57. Following the promulgation of the Iranian constitution on August 5, 1906, it did not take long for St. Petersburg to make known its opposition to the Iranian constitutional movement. With the opening of the first Iranian majles on October 7, 1906, St. Petersburg took steps to frustrate the Iranian constitutional camp, rapidly accelerating its public hostility toward the majles by abetting the obstructionist measures of the new autocratic Iranian monarch Mohammad-Ali Shah, who ascended the throne in January 1907.[67]

The August 1907 Anglo-Russian Agreement, inaugurating formal British and Russian cooperation in Iran among its other clauses, changed the dynamics of Great Power rivalry in that country. Radical Irish nationalists who had previously defended Russia's imperial competition with Britain now jettisoned Tsarist Russia as 'the friend of my enemy.' Nonetheless, these Irish nationalists appear to have also initially accepted at face value, and naively, the stated pledge in the 1907 Agreement by the two powers to safeguard Iran's independence, contrary to mounting evidence of Russian intervention in Iran's domestic affairs in opposition to the majles.[68] Furthermore, many in the more radical Irish nationalist camps were still highly selective in extending their sympathy to the weaker nations struggling for their independence. This proclivity was dissimilar in its overall objective to Timothy Michael Healy's apprehension that what he construed as unfettered cosmopolitan internationalism of the likes of John Dillon supposedly distracted Irish MPs from Irish matters, while also further alienating potential unionist recruits to the nationalist Home Rule platform. Nonetheless, Healy's antagonism toward Irish nationalist involvement in extra-Irish affairs, on the one hand, and the often-skewed selective advocacy of anti-imperialist struggles in other parts of the world by 'radical' Irish nationalists, on the other hand, ultimately emanated from a similar self-regarding premise. To a large degree, both *Sinn Féin* and the *Gaelic American* were at the time preoccupied with the *propaganda dividend for 'Irish nationalism'* of any expressed cross-territorial anti-imperialist solidarity.

This tendency was perhaps most famously exemplified by the Sinn Féin leader Arthur Griffith in his public rebuke of the internationalist commitments of Fred Ryan following Ryan's death in 1913; notwithstanding the regular ample space devoted to anti-British nationalist campaigns in other territories in the pages of *Sinn Féin* itself. In voicing disdain for Ryan's brand of Irish nationalism, Griffith concentrated on what he cast as the blight of internationalist allegiances and active dedication to other *presumably extra-nationalist* concerns, such as women's suffrage and workers' rights. In the case of the latter campaigns, Griffith's disdain was rooted in a number of factors, in addition to personal aversion to such causes at the time. These campaigns were occurring within the broader setting of women's and workers' rights movements throughout the United Kingdom and even internationally, rather than in a strictly Irish context. Ryan's allegedly extra-nationalist commitments to socialism and feminism also ran counter to Griffith's stance of non-cooperation with those who did not specifically and uniformly advocate Irish nationalism—for example, among the British working classes and suffragists, or in Ireland's unionist community. Perhaps more importantly, both Catholic and Protestant establishments in Ireland abhorred laborite, socialist, and feminist platforms, and Griffith hoped to ingratiate himself with the Catholic Church, which backed the rival IPP's Home Rule platform. Griffith characterized Ryan's political and social leanings as detrimental to the nationalist cause in Ireland, by diverting attention to other (allegedly unrelated) highly contentious issues that fueled intra-nationalist divisions. According to Griffith, one could not simultaneously be internationalist and effectively remain a nationalist.[69] Griffith's position was challenged by Ryan's close friend and collaborator Francis Sheehy Skeffington.[70] There was generally also a partisan subtext to Irish nationalist criticisms aimed at purportedly reckless concerns with broader international affairs.[71] In the case of Griffith's rebuke of Ryan's internationalism and cosmopolitanism, there was, moreover, an unstated personal grudge against Ryan. Ryan had contributed articles to Griffith's *Sinn Féin* in its early years, and to its predecessor *The United Irishman*, but had grown increasingly critical of Griffith's nationalist platform as well as Griffith's entrenched anti-Jewish sentiment; a sentiment that incidentally was often expressed in even more rabid form by the *Gaelic American*.[72] Ironically, by the time Griffith attacked Ryan's internationalism, *Sinn Féin* itself had been providing increasingly sympathetic coverage of some of the very same extra-Irish anti-imperialist struggles championed by Ryan, including the Iranian Question.

One major difference between Ryan, on the one hand, and Griffith, John Devoy, and George Freeman, on the other hand, was Ryan's indiscriminate assailing of imperialism, whereas *Sinn Féin* and the *Gaelic American* often refrained from censuring the territorial aggression and colonial policies of Britain's rival imperial powers, if not at times openly endorsing those powers, as in the case of Germany at the time. By the time of the outbreak of the Iranian civil war (June 1908–July 1909), the more 'radical' Irish nationalist outlets, including *Sinn Féin* and the *Gaelic American*, were finally devoting some attention to Iranian developments. This initial interest appears to have been chiefly due to the fact that militant Indian nationalist circles, whose activities enjoyed the support of these Irish news outlets, had been increasingly championing the Iranian constitutionalist-nationalist struggle (see below). But, it was notably following the outbreak of the Iranian civil war (less than a year after the signing of the Anglo-Russian Agreement) that the 'radical' Irish nationalist press finally took up the Iranian Question. The key factor contributing to this transformation was that in the Iranian civil war Russia extensively backed the Iranian autocracy against the constitutionalist-nationalist forces and the British foreign secretary Sir Edward Grey publicly rationalized Russian policy (despite occasional private protests by Grey to St. Petersburg). In light of continued Russian aggression in Iran after the victory of the Iranian constitutionalist-nationalist forces in the civil war in the summer of 1909, and the continued public defense of Russian acts by Grey, reports of Iranian developments in the 'radical' Irish nationalist press multiplied considerably and continued well after of the Russian-instigated clampdown on the second Iranian majles in late 1911 (with London's compliance).[73] Moreover, given the heightened Anglo-German rivalry, which had been a key factor in Grey's conclusion of the 1907 Agreement with Russia, many of the more 'radical' Irish nationalist groupings had now adopted a pro-German stance vis-à-vis Anglo-Russian friendship; hence looking for additional opportunities to denounce the 1907 Agreement, including Anglo-Russian policy in Iran, as indicated in articles appearing in both the *Gaelic American* and *Sinn Féin*.

As noted, both papers were additionally responding to increased advocacy of the Iranian constitutionalist-nationalist platform and Iran's sovereignty by anti-imperialist nationalist organizations and personalities in other regions of the British Empire, most notably in India.[74] Incidentally, while both papers opposed the Muslim-nationalist platform of the All-India Muslim League—founded in 1906 and expressing loyalty to British imperial rule in India until the December 1911 revocation of Bengal's partition—, in November 1910 Griffith, who happened to be in London, attended a gathering of Muslims in support of Iranian sovereignty organized by leading Indian Muslim-nationalists residing in the United Kingdom. In an article in *Sinn Féin* under the heading "The Partition of Persia," Griffith reported:

> On the afternoon of 2nd November I was present at a meeting which was to my mind deeply significant and interesting. The meeting in question was one convened by Mohammedans resident in London as a protest against the recent action of the British Government in landing a naval force in Southern Persian territory, thereby conveying the impression all over the Mussulman world that the partition of Persia was about to be carried out by both England and Russia.[75]

For a complex spectrum of political and other historical factors, Indians of varying outlooks championed the constitutional revolution in neighboring Iran as well as that country's independence. The political affiliations of these Indians ranged from the All-India Muslim League to the moderate mainstream contingent of the Indian National Congress (1885), which at the time was committed to Indian self-government within the British Empire (similar to Irish Home Rule), and militant republican Indian nationalists belonging to different organizations in India and in other parts of the world, mostly advocating nonsectarian pan-Indian nationalism. Pan-Indian nationalists also included members of India's small (Zoroastrian) Parsi community, both in India and in the Indian diaspora, who traced their ancestry to Iran. Some other members of the Parsi community championed the Iranian revolution independently of any Indian political factions (some among them even favoring the existing British administration of India). For these individuals, the Iranian revolution also harbored the potential for social reforms that could improve the conditions of Iran's own remaining small Zoroastrian community.[76] A number of Indian nationalist organizations and individuals were in direct contact with Irish nationalists of differing political orientations in the United Kingdom, India, the United States, France, Switzerland, and elsewhere.

Irish Nationalists, Anti-Imperialist Pan-Aryanism, and Iran

Although the *Gaelic American* had been slow in championing the Iranian revolution, as early as the spring of 1907 the Clan na Gael itself had actually participated in an ultimately unsuccessful scheme, which also involved militant Indian nationalists in the United States, for forging a direct cross-nationalist anti-British united front with Iranian nationalists. This collaboration between militant Indian and Irish nationalists in the United States was launched just a few weeks after the start of the Iranian revolution. This was the Pan-Aryan Association founded in New York, with the United States having a large population of Irish descent as well as a few thousand Indian emigrants and students, many with radical nationalist leanings, who had been arriving in growing numbers after the start of the century. First put into action in the United States through direct collaboration with Indian nationalists, this Irish nationalist Aryanist doctrine of solidarity with other 'Aryan' populations resisting British imperialism drew on nineteenth-century racial theories. This anti-imperialist pan-Aryan formulation, with its own inherent forms of racism, was immediately extended by its planners to the Iranian 'nation' as well. However, Iranians in general, who also happened to have a miniscule presence in the United States at the time, do not appear to have displayed interest in this brand of pan-Aryanism. Instead, those segments of Iranian nationalists who at the time embraced Aryan racial theories preferred to identify as their racial kinsfolk, in addition to such groups as the Parsi population of India, the 'Aryan' populations of Western European territories that happened to be imperial powers, including England.

The Pan-Aryan Association was established in New York City in October 1906. A co-founder and vice-president of the Association was the revolutionary Indian nationalist Mulavi Abdul Hafiz Mohammad Barakatullah, who later joined the militant Indian nationalist Ghadar movement (founded in San Francisco in 1913), serving during the First World War as the prime minister of the German-backed "provisional government of India," based in Afghanistan in 1915. Barakatullah had previously also taught Arabic at Liverpool University, which he subsequently often exaggerated by inferring he actually had a teaching stint at Cambridge University.[77] Another co-founder was the Indian Samuel Lucas Joshi, who served as the Association's corresponding secretary. The Association was launched with the assistance of John Devoy and George Freeman of the Clan na Gael and was presided over by the Irish-American Albert S. Dulin of the Washington, DC, branch of the Vedanta Society. John de Bruyn Kops served as the Associations treasurer and Charlotte Bingham as its secretary.[78] The *Gaelic American* carried reports of the gatherings of the Association—Freeman subsequently also provided journalistic and editorial assistance to the militant *Free Hindustan* (Vancouver, 1907–08; Seattle, 1908–10; New York, 1910) after it began publication in the United States in 1908 under the editorship of Taraknath Das, a militant Indian nationalist student at the University of Washington, with the Free Hindustan Publishing House being based in New York City. Leading members of the Pan-Aryan Association participated at gatherings of Irish-American organizations in New York. In February 1907, for example, Barakatullah gave a presentation at the Brooklyn Gaelic Society, during which he appealed to the common racial identity of Indians and the Irish as grounds for mutual anticolonial solidarity: "Ireland should ally herself with India now. There is a racial question involved. The Irish and the old Aryans of the East are of the same race. Their racial characteristics are the same."[79] The following month, at a gathering of the Pan-Aryan Association, Barakatullah gave a lecture during which he "spoke on the situation in Persia," stating that, "Of all the Oriental lands, India and Persia have always exercised a charm on the American mind. The Pan-Aryan Association has been formed in New York with the object of creating a bond of sympathy and good will between the peoples of those lands and of America."[80] This stated primary focus of the Association on fostering sympathy for Indians and Iranians was yet another nod of approval for the Iranian constitutional movement by Barakatullah and other Indian nationalists and/or reformers in different parts of the world well before the signing of the Anglo-Russian Agreement of 1907. Given Barakatullah's close cooperation with Freeman and other Clan na Gael colleagues in connection with the activities and platform of the Association, it is ironic that it still took nearly another year for the *Gaelic American* to devote serious attention to Iranian developments and to the potential anti-British implications of those developments. Then again, this delay could possibly have been a reaction to the failure of the Association in garnering Iranian expressions of support. In April 1908, the Pan-Aryan Association publicly claimed to be promoting "goodwill and sympathetic cooperation" between Americans, on the one hand, and Indians and Iranians, on the other hand, and with the stated intention of encouraging students from India and Iran to study in the United States, with the Association also pledging to look after the welfare of those students.[81] Seeking to expand its branches to Ithaca (New York), Boston, and Philadelphia, among other US locations, and already boasting a membership of over one hundred by February 1907, the Association's discourse of racial affinity between the Irish, Indians, and Iranians, was in principle intended to unite Irish nationalists with nationalists from these two 'oriental' territories through the twin vectors of purported common ancient racial heritage as well as their common contemporary experience of victimization by British imperialism (at a time when the mainstream of Iranian nationalists had not yet engaged in overt Anti-British posturing); without in any way addressing or denying the

Aryan racial claim of the English. This particular mode of pan-Aryanism selectively identified Ireland with a narrow region of the Orient in a racialized expression of anti-British solidarity, alongside the more sweeping condemnation of British imperialism in general by Irish nationalists, such as in Egypt and the rest of the African continent, as well as in East Asia, and elsewhere. This was a novel form of Irish nationalist recourse to racial identification with the 'Orient'—for instance, in contrast to prior antiquarian and historical accounts of Ireland's oriental Aryan heritage. Notably, this pan-Aryan gesture of common racial front in opposition to British imperialism occurred during a time when the mainstream of Aryanist nationalist discourse in Ireland itself was increasingly claiming Ireland's ancient Celtic 'Aryan' racial affinity with the English. Variants of Aryanist racial identification with the English also existed in India and in Iran, all of them to the exclusion of certain internal population groups who did not qualify as so-called Aryans.

In some ways, and particularly in its implicitly 'anti-British' objective under the guise of cultural activities, the Pan-Aryan Association was modeled after the India House in London, founded by the militant pan-Indian nationalist Shyamji Krishnavarma in 1905, with which Vinayak Damodar Savarkar and, for a time, Madan Lal Dhingra, the assassin of Sir Curzon Wyllie in 1909, were affiliated. Future speakers at gatherings of the Pan-Aryan Association included the likes of the Zoroastrian-Parsi, and Paris-based, militant Indian nationalist and feminist Madame Bhikhaji (also spelled Bhikhaiji) Rustom Cama—the editor of the militant pan-Indian nationalist publication *Bande Mataram* (Geneva)—as well as Sinn Féin's Bulmer Hobson.[82] Bulmer Hobson also spoke at another event at the Grand Central Palace exhibition hall in New York City on February 15, 1907, which was attended by Samuel Joshi, who gave a presentation on the swadeshi movement in India.[83] Within a few months after its founding, the Association reached out to a broader range of foreign students in the United States, regardless of whether these students fit the contemporary 'racial' categorizations of 'Aryans' or even hailed from territories experiencing British imperial domination or aggression. It is unclear whether this was due to the Association's failed attempts to recruit members from among the very small Iranian community in the United States (students and others) and/or was intended to further camouflage its underlying political objectives. Consisting primarily of Indians and their American supporters (notably Irish-Americans), the Association's efforts to now recruit a wider ethnic and geographic pool of foreign students in the United States oddly targeted students from Greece and "Syria" (i.e., the Ottoman province of Greater Syria). Moreover, in addition to lectures, the Association also set out to create "a large collection of Oriental literature and a bureau of general information regarding [its student members'] countries."[84] It is unknown whether the Pan-Aryan Association had any success in its new recruitment drive or if it managed to set up a library and an information bureau. Clearly the organizers of the Association themselves envisioned its long-term institutional development. However, the Association's activities dwindled after Barakatullah moved to Japan in February 1909, to teach Hindi and Urdu at the "newly established department of Indian languages in the Imperial University."[85] His actual mission in Tokyo was to draw Indian students in East Asia into the orbit of militant pan-Indian nationalist activities under the banner of anti-British and Japan-centered "pan-Asianism," notwithstanding the formal alliance at the time between Britain and Japan.⁸⁶ Following Russia's defeat in the Russo-Japanese War of 1904–05, Japan, which after the 1868 Meiji Restoration had adopted a parliamentary system and rapidly industrialized and built a powerful military force, emerged as a beacon of hope and a source of emulation for reformers and anti-imperialists across Asia and beyond, who generally evaded Japan's own imperialist intervention in Chinese Manchuria at the time, soon to be followed by Japan's colonization of Korea. Japanese-sponsored pan-Asianism complicated, if not entirely vitiating, appeals to Aryanism in some Indian and Iranian nationalist circles. In contrast to Indian or Iranian nationalists, many moderate Home Rule and 'radical' Irish nationalists, including Arthur Griffith in the pages of his *The United Irishman* and the Clan na Gael in its *Gaelic American*, had championed the Russian side in the Russo-Japanese War, on grounds of Russian rivalry with Britain at the time and the 1902 Anglo-Japanese Alliance.⁸⁷

The Pan-Aryan Association's emphasis on the common 'racial' origin of Indians, Iranians, and the Irish as grounds for building a joint anti-British platform was a racialized counter-hegemonic political discourse. By then, the dominant English scheme of racial categorization of peoples around the world recognized the 'Aryan' pedigree of many Iranians and Indians, as well as of Ireland's Gaelic population (the latter as belonging to the larger Celtic population group). But, this dominant British racial-civilizational construct placed the English above the 'mere Irish,' Indians, and Iranians in the inner-Aryan hierarchy, with Aryans standing well above all other racial groupings in this model. The term 'pan-Aryan' itself had been in currency for some time, including in reference to the Indo-European 'race,' languages, and mythology. At face value, the presence of Irish-Americans in the Pan-Aryan Association and the publicly stated goal of the Association—to promote 'goodwill and sympathetic cooperation' between Americans, Indians, and Iranians, and to induce more students from India and Iran to study in the United States and to safeguard the interests of students from those territories—could be interpreted as an attempt to overcome the deeply ingrained racism among large segments of the 'white' population of the United States toward peoples from West and South Asia, and as a mode of 'whitening' the South-Asian (Indian) population of the United States, who faced a great degree of racial prejudice and other restrictions even prior to the 1917 US Immigration Act (a.k.a., the Asiatic Barred Zone Act, which included nearly all of the Indian subcontinent, *but did not apply to Iran*). Irish-Americans, particularly the Catholics, had themselves until just a short time earlier been treated as lesser 'whites,' if not as less than white, by the majority of white Americans of purportedly Anglo-Saxon ancestry. For many of the Irish adherents of Aryanism in the United Kingdom, as well as in the United States, regardless of their political orientation, the so-called racial whitening of the Irish through affirming their Aryan origins was first and foremost intended to elevate the Irish (most specifically the 'mere Irish') in the predominant British and American hierarchal matrices of race. Until the latter part of the nineteenth century those of Irish descent in the United States (particularly Catholics) had been branded by Anglo-Saxon Protestants as "white niggers," which produced its own reactionary legacy of racism among many Irish Americans (directed toward African Americans and other non-'Aryan' designated groups, from whom many Irish now sought to distance themselves).⁸⁸

Despite its counter-hegemonic attribute, the Pan-Aryan Association's adoption of an Aryanist racial discourse had its own hegemonic implications in terms of its *internal* applications in the territories it sought to unite in the struggle against British imperialism. It variously conflated and omitted certain population groups within each of the three territories in question. This was an internally exclusionary cross-territorial common racial identification that at closer examination, in accordance with prevailing Aryan-centered models of racial categorization, would have excluded such population groups in Ireland as the small Jewish community, as well as many non-Persian population groups in Iran—such as the sizeable Turkic minorities or the smaller Arab or Assyrian/Chaldean minorities—, and the sizeable Dravidian and some other population groups in India, among other examples. There were different historical and political factors underlying the allure of theories of Aryan racial origin among the Irish, Indians, and Iranians. For instance, Iranians and Indians subscribing to the Aryanist racial myth sought to assert their belonging to the supposed superior race in keeping with the prevalent ('white') Western/European claims of various branches of the Aryan peoples (regardless of the designated location of their original homeland). At the same time, these Indians and Iranians insisted that their own geographic regions constitued some of the earliest homelands of the Aryan race. Such assertions were aimed at racially and civilizationally rendering Iranians and Indians deserving of Western/European admiration and historical and cultural respect. In Iran, the Aryan racial theory resonated at the time within certain predominantly 'secular' circles as a political-historical ingredient of the Iranian nationalist discourse.[89] However, this Iranian strand of Aryanism, in contradistinction to the platform of the Pan-Aryan Association, stressed the racial affinity of Iranians (namely the Persians and related population groups, such as the Kurds) with the populations of Western European *imperialist* countries, the English in particular. Examples of this range from the assertion by the prominent nineteenth-century Iranian secular reformer Mirza Aqa Khan Kermani in his 1895 epic verse composition that "Germans and Anglo-Saxons" were racially descended from 'Aryana' (i.e., ancient 'Iranians')[90] to the statement made by a prominent Iranian constitutionalist-nationalist Yahya Dawlatabadi at the 1911 First Universal Races Congress in London to the same effect.[91] Iranian discourses of Aryanism at this juncture were shaped not only by direct familiarity with post-Jonesian European/Western racial categorizations, but also through the medium of India's Parsi community and some members of Iran's own minority Zoroastrian community—who glorified ancient Iran's so-called Aryan civilization prior to Arab-Muslim domination in the seventh century, with the contemporary Zoroastrian/Parsi narrative itself in part shaped by post-Jonesian Western racial categorizations.

The First World War, the Irish War of Independence, and Irish Nationalist Commentaries on Iranian Sovereignty

By the time of the outbreak of the First World War in the summer of 1914, the Iranian Question had registered in the recent political memory of a broad spectrum of Irish nationalists, with wide-ranging Irish nationalist personalities and organizations having publicly expressed support for the Iranian constitutionalist-nationalist endeavors.

In contrast, Iranian nationalists—who otherwise had extensively expressed solidarity with a host of Egyptian and Indian nationalist platforms and various anticolonial or reform struggles in other parts of the world, including developments in Norway or China—refrained from publicly endorsing any form of Irish nationalist platform until after the Easter Rising of 1916 in Ireland (see Chapter Eight). It was only after the Easter Rising that Irish nationalism, specifically in its militant republican manifestation, first acquired a place among the worldwide anti-imperialist independence movements publicly endorsed by Iranian nationalists.[92] Thereafter an essentialized Irish struggle (subsequently also inclusive of Irish republican aspirations in Northern Ireland after 1921) continued to operate as a prime historical example of worldwide struggles in Iranian condemnations of imperialism (by nationalists, "internationalist" socialists, and other such groups). Notable post-1916 episodes of protracted espousal of the Irish struggle by various Iranian anti-imperialist groups occurred during the Irish War of Independence (1919–21) and, more markedly, during the period known as "The Troubles" in Northern Ireland (1969–98).[93] In the best-selling Iranian novel *Savushun* (1969), written by Simin Daneshvar, the Irish Question featured as the counterpart to the Iranian nationalist struggle against Anglo-Soviet occupation of Iran during the Second World War[94]—in what was either a historically anachronistic framing of the Irish nationalist struggle by Daneshvar, or indicated her receptivity to contemporary Irish nationalist dissatisfaction with Ireland's partition in 1922 and the continued British domination of Northern Ireland; not forgetting that Éire (formerly the Irish Free State, 1922) was still a constituent part of the British Empire during the Second World War. References to the Irish Question (including Northern Ireland) also occurred in different settings and historical framings in Iranian anti-imperialist poetry, primarily by poets also opposed to the authoritarian Pahlavi state in Iran (1925-79).[95]

While Iranians to this day remain unacquainted with miscellaneous appropriations of 'Iran' by Irish nationalists for advancing their own cause against English domination as far back as the late eighteenth century, what is more confounding is that prior to 1916 Iranian nationalists remained *publicly* indifferent to the Irish Question and refrained from reciprocating the broad-based Irish nationalist advocacy of Iranian sovereignty after 1907. At the time, many leading Iranian nationalists were certainly aware of Irish nationalist expressions of solidarity with the Iranian Constitutional Revolution and their endorsement of Iran's independence. Iranian constitutionalist newspapers often reported the presence of the likes of John Dillon in Iranian debates in the United Kingdom in opposition to Grey's policy.[96] A few Iranian nationalists (including political refugees and exiles) even met with the likes of Dillon in London, who were engaged in the Iranian campaign in the United Kingdom both before and after the formation of the Persia Committee. William J. Maloney, who reported from Iran and was in contact with the Persia Committee in London, also got to know some leading Iranian constitutionalist-nationalists. The delayed public espousal of Irish nationalism by various groups of Iranian nationalists appears all the more puzzling given the British parliament's introduction of the (Third) Irish Home Rule Bill on April 11, 1912, and the bill's passage into law on May 25, 1914 (the Irish Home Rule Act)—the implementation of which was postponed due to mounting unionist opposition to Home Rule after 1912 (largely in six counties of the northern province of Ulster that would later comprise Northern Ireland), threatening to plunge Ireland into a civil war. The enforcement of the Home Rule Act was further delayed by the outbreak of the First World War, and the Act was then shelved for the duration of the war, and subsequently abandoned. Surely the better informed Iranian nationalists were aware of the Irish Question following the introduction of the Irish Home Rule Bill of 1912 by the British Liberal government.

With the introduction of the Home Rule Bill, Ireland was beset by unionist v. nationalist disturbances, with rival armed organizations soon engaging in mass recruitment of volunteers: the unionist paramilitary Ulster Volunteers (a.k.a., Ulster Volunteer Force) established in stages after December 1912, and the nationalist Irish Volunteers founded on November 25, 1913. By most accounts, the impending civil war was only averted with the outbreak of what became the First World War—the British Empire joined the war on August 4, 1914. In the absence of military conscription in the United Kingdom at the time, members of Ulster Volunteers, which had earlier smuggled in weapons from Germany, and the main body of the Irish Volunteers (under the designation of National Volunteers and following the IPP's lead), pledged their support for London's war effort. The IPP's decision to formally support the war effort—notwithstanding the party's objections prior to August 4 to London's entanglement in the escalating European conflict—was condemned by militant republican nationalist groupings and also caused dissent in the ranks of the Irish Volunteers, reflecting the existing division between the mainstream of the IPP and the more 'radical' factions. Pacifists of differing nationalist orientations, including Home Rulers, opposed the war itself, while Sinn Féin and a host of republican organizations, including James Connolly's socialist paramilitary Irish Citizen Army (formed during the labor strikes of 1913 and uniquely including women members), also excoriated the war effort on different grounds. Sinn Féin and the IRB even cast Germany as the aggrieved side in the conflict. Many Irish nationalists, as well as some in the ranks of the IPP, such as John Dillon, considered Sr Edward Grey's anti-German posturing prior to the war, including his dalliance with Tsarist Russia after the conclusion of the Anglo-Russian Agreement of 1907, as having significantly contributed to, if not actually triggered, the war. Grey's collusion with Russia in undermining Iran's sovereignty was now cited as a foremost example of London's anti-German policy prior to the war. Meanwhile, Dillon and a few other IPP members continued to publicly voice concern about Iran's independence during the war, while backing London's war effort. In November 1915, Russia and Britain formally occupied Iran, which had declared itself neutral in the armed conflict engulfing the globe.

In contrast to the IPP's official policy of endorsing the British war effort, other range of Home Rule nationalists opposed the war, leaving aside Home Rule pacifists at large. Among Home Rulers objecting to the war was the prominent playwright, author, and Fabian socialist, George Bernard Shaw (1856–1950). Shaw, from a Protestant Irish background and living in London at the time, had been among the earliest critics of Grey's secret negotiations with Tsarist Russia that eventually resulted in the 1907 Agreement between the two powers. Shaw was a signatory of a public letter in June 1907 protesting Grey's policy of improved relations between London and St. Petersburg, particularly in light of Russia's recent dissolution of the second Duma and its general policy of repression at home and pursuit of anti-democratic policies and territorial aggression abroad. The letter, simultaneously casting doubt on Grey's own commitment to liberal principles, appeared in *The Times* of London on June 11, 1907, and in the *Manchester Guardian* the following day, and was later reproduced in other papers.[97] Among the other sixteen signatories of this letter, which included well-known Radicals, socialists, authors, and prominent scholars such as E. G. Browne, was the Irish nationalist historian Alice Stopford Green. As part of his early denunciations of Anglo-Russian talks in 1907, Shaw also participated in a protest rally at Trafalgar Square in London on July 14, 1907, organized by the Society of Friends of Russian Freedom, with Charlotte Despard also speaking at the event.[98] Following the start of the First World War, Shaw became a vocal critic of British Empire's participation in the conflict. In the pamphlet "Common Sense About the War," published in December 1914, he reminded the readers of his early opposition to improved ties between London and St. Petersburg, citing the sacrifice of Iran's sovereignty as an instance of London's capitulation to Russia's expansionist and autocratic policies, which now purportedly had facilitated Russian aggression against Germany with London's blessing, and was bound to result in "sharpening the [Russian] knife for our own […] throat."[99] Overlooked in this style of allegation against London were both the other terms of the 1907 Anglo-Russian Agreement, pertaining to Tibet and Afghanistan, as well as Germany's own intensified imperialist and militarist proceedings prior to the war, which could not be entirely classified as defensive posturing in response British, French, or other rival imperial powers. Denunciations of Anglo-Russian aggression in Iran as part of Sir Edward Grey's pursuit of an anti-German policy, which presumably had instigated the war in 1914, were now frequently echoed by some leading members of the IRB and its US-affiliate Clan na Gael.

As the war dragged on, many armed Irish republican groupings, most notably the IRB (which enjoyed a strong support base in the ranks of the minority faction of Irish Volunteers who refused to join the British war effort), considered London's military preoccupation as an opportunity for staging an uprising against British rule in Ireland. To this end, the IRB and its Clan na Gael affiliate turned to Germany for assistance. These more militant Irish nationalist circles, as well as Sinn Féin, were far more adamant and vitriolic than the likes of Shaw in maintaining Grey's anti-German policy had been the root cause of the global conflict. These ongoing condemnations often alluded to the joint Anglo-Russian suppression of the Iranian constitutional movement. The case of Iran, among other developments, was cited as an indisputable indication of London's callous disregard for the sovereign rights of weaker nations. The official British rationale for entering the war included defending Belgian sovereignty, with Britain having committed itself to preserving Belgium's independence since the 1839 Treaty of London. Radical Irish nationalists argued Iran's fate after 1907, despite the public undertaking by London and St. Petersburg in the 1907 Anglo-Russian Agreement to respect Iranian sovereignty, made a mockery of London's continued efforts to cast itself as the defender of the rights of weaker nations, even if one were to overlook the fact that England as an imperial power had all along violated the sovereign rights of other peoples. The republican Irish nationalist, socialist, and trades-unionist leader James Connolly condemned British policy in Iran as part of London's push to attain Russia's friendship against Germany. Connolly, who became one of the organizers of the Easter Rising (April 24–29, 1916) and was subsequently executed by British authorities, wrote in a September 1914 issue of the *Irish Worker* (Dublin), under the heading "The Friends of Small Nationalities":

> This vicious and rebellious memory of mine will also recur to the recent attempt of Persia to form a constitutional government, and it recalls how, when that ancient nation shook off the fetters of its ancient despotism, and set to work to elaborate the laws and forms in the spirit of a modern civilized representative state, Russia, which in solemn treaty with England had guaranteed its independence, at once invaded it, and slaughtering all [sic] its patriots, pillaging its towns and villages, annexed [sic] part of its territories, and made the rest [sic] a mere Russian dependency. I remember how Sir Edward Grey, who now gushes over the sanctity of treaties [i.e., the British pledge to uphold Belgian sovereignty], when appealed to to stand by and make Russia stand by the treaty guaranteeing the independence of Persia [i.e., the 1907 Anglo-Russian Agreement], coolly refused to interfere.[100]

Analogous statements by Connolly appeared in other publications, as in October 1915 issues of *Workers' Republic* (Dublin).[101] In a November 6, 1915, issue of this newspaper, Connolly reiterated: "Cynical onlookers might say that the rape and betrayal of Persia was regarded as a harmless joke because it was done by England's ally, but the invasion of Belgium was a monstrous crime because it was done by England's enemy."[102]

A similar line of attack on British policy in Iran and on continued Anglo-Russian violations of Iranian sovereignty during the war was taken up by Arthur Griffith in his *Sinn Féin* shortly before the paper was suppressed by British authorities. On November 14, 1914, the paper stated: "Russia saw her opportunity and seized it. Before she came in she exacted a price from England, which England reluctantly paid—the chief part of that price was Persia—a country whom England was bound by her honour to protect. Her honour!"[103] Griffith's subsequent short-lived newspapers *Éire-Ireland* (launched in November 1914) and *Scissors and Paste* (January-March 1915) occasionally carried articles touching on the same subject.[104] Analogous passing statements appeared in the *Gaelic American* (New York) and in other militant Irish nationalist fora. Commentaries on London's violation of Iranian sovereignty appeared in the *Gaelic American* in a range of contexts. On one occasion for instance, in a September 1914 issue, it reproduced the text of a "Manifesto [by Connolly's Irish Citizen Army] Circulated [in Belfast] Urging Irish Workers Not to Fight for Britain," which stated: "Britain guaranteed the independence of Belgium. Yes, as she guaranteed the independence of Egypt, and then swallowed it up and slaughtered and imprisoned its patriot sons and daughters. Britain guaranteed the independence of Belgium. Yes, as she guaranteed the independence of Persia, and then encouraged her Russian ally to invade it and drown its freedom in a sea of blood."[105] Other Clan na Gael channels expressed similar views. For example, in his 1915 *The King, the Kaiser and Irish Freedom*, which was widely advertised in the *Gaelic American*, the Irish-American James Kennedy McGuire, a member of the Clan na Gael executive, and publicly describing himself a *republican* "Sinn Féin" nationalist, reproduced verbatim as his own Arthur Griffith's statement in *Sinn Féin* of November 14, 1914, that the Anglo-Russian Agreement of 1907 and British policy in Iran had allegedly expedited the Great War. McGuire, the former mayor of Syracuse, was canvassing the American public for US support of Germany in the war, or at least continued American neutrality in the armed conflict.[106] In his 1916 *What Could Germany Do for Ireland?*, McGuire echoed Connolly and others on the hypocrisy of London's claim of protecting Belgian independence by entering the war in 1914, while having undermined Iran's independence after 1907. He noted: "Britain is now supposed to be the champion of small peoples [sic], yet we have the example of Persia before our eyes today. Persia, whose independence was guaranteed by Britain and who has been swallowed by Russia."[107] By 1916, the allegation that British policy in Iran after 1907 had all along been designed to expedite St. Petersburg's undermining of Iran's independence as a means of "assuring Russia's aid in the forthcoming war with Germany that was even [t]hen regarded as inevitable," had become a routine assertion in radical Irish nationalist outlets, including in militant nationalist newspapers that could still be published in Ireland, such as *The Hibernian* (Dublin). This paper also noted the formation of organized Iranian armed resistance to English and Russian presence in Iran at the time.[108] Among leading IRB members who lambasted Anglo-Russian policy in Iran as a harbinger of the 1914 Great War was Roger Casement, who wrote: "and to-day we see it [i.e., England] harvesting with hands yet red with the blood of Persian patriots the redder fruit of the seed then sown."[109]

Casement, an IRB representative to Germany during the war, was executed by British authorities on August 3, 1916, in connection with the Easter Rising, although he was not a participant in the uprising and is believed to have arrived in Ireland just ahead of the rising with the objective of halting the planned insurrection due to insufficient German provision of armaments for the rebellion. It was Casement's execution that marked the start of public expressions of solidarity with the Irish struggle in Iranian nationalist circles (see below).[110] Casement served as a representative of IRB/Clan na Gael for the Berlin-based Irish nationalist committee, set up by the IRB under the direction of German authorities after the start of the First World War, with the aim of fomenting anti-British agitation and armed uprising in Ireland. This Irish committee worked alongside other German-backed nationalist committees in Berlin, such as the Egyptian and Indian committees. In 1915, a German-funded and supervised Iranian nationalist committee also began operating in the German capital, primarily composed of Iranian anti-Allied Social Democrats. Despite Tehran's declaration of neutrality in the war, after September 1914 Russian troops already present in northern Iran (since 1911) were drastically reinforced. German spies began operating in different parts of Iran, hoping to incite armed uprising among Iranian nationalists, including some tribes, in opposition to Russia and Britain. Britain expanded its military presence in the Persian Gulf and in southern Iran as a means of averting German advances in the direction of the Gulf, and for curbing the activities of German spies in southern Iran, particularly in the direction of India. Safeguarding the British-owned oil installations in southern Iran (the Anglo-Persian Oil Company), was another leading concern for Britain; petroleum being a vital resource for the British military, especially for the most advanced Dreadnought battleships. Following the Ottoman entry into the war in October 1914, Ottoman forces invaded northwestern Iran in a bid to create another offensive front against Russia. In November 1915 Russia and Britain formally occupied

Iran. Even before the formal Allied occupation of Iran, various Iranian armed groups had clashed with British forces in southern Iran and with Russian forces in the north. In September 1916, Abdul-Hussein Sheybani ("Vahid al-Molk"), the direct representative of the anti-Allied self-proclaimed provisional government of Iran, which was engaged in fighting British occupation forces in southern Iran from 1915 to 1917, arrived in Berlin. The armed units of the provisional government of Iran operated alongside the anti-Allied armed contingents of the Iranian Social Democratic Party, as well as a number of Iranian tribes, German spies and military advisers, Swedish officers who had been serving in the Iranian gendarme force prior to the war, and a small contingent of militant Indian nationalists affiliated with the Indian Independence Committee based in Berlin—while other armed Iranian nationalist groups were independently fighting the Russian occupation force in northern Iran.[111] Iranian nationalists in Berlin were in contact with other Berlin-based anti-British nationalist committees, and members of these different committees attended special events and lectures organized by various committees or by German authorities, including numerous events organized by the Irish committee, under the supervision after 1916 of (the Indian-born) George Chatterton-Hill.[112] Iranian nationalists in Berlin during the war also included Hussein Qoli Khan Navab, a former Iranian foreign minister during the Constitutional Revolution, who was now the official representative of the central Iranian government (which still claimed neutrality in the war, notwithstanding the Allied occupation of the Iranian capital). Navab, who nonchalantly interacted with German-backed Iranian and other anti-Allied nationalists in Berlin, was in Germany with his Irish Catholic wife, Eileen Rainey (married in August 1913).[113]

In effect, during the war Berlin served as what I have previously termed a "third contact zone" for Iranian, Irish, Egyptian, Indian, and other anti-imperialist nationalist groups based there—that is, a location of contacts and/or cooperation between different nationalist groups outside their respective home territories.[114] The renowned German scholar of Celtic languages and Irish mythology, Kuno Meyer, was reportedly present at one of the gatherings in Berlin organized by the Irish committee in celebration of St. Patrick's Day on March 17, 1918, with Iranian nationalists also in attendance.[115] Meyer, who happened to be among scholars convinced of the Iranian origin of the story of Cuchulain and Conla (see Chapter Six), had been assisting the German-backed militant republican Irish nationalist cause during the war. This included his earlier participation at Clan na Gael events in the United States.[116] For its part, the Clan na Gael steadfastly championed the German war effort from the very start of Britain's entry into the war, providing wide range of propaganda assistance to that end, both in the pages of the *Gaelic American* and in other settings. For instance, a member of the Clan na Gael's executive committee, Joseph McGarrity, who was also involved in the war-time Indo-German "conspiracy" in the United States (which included collaboration between the Clan na Gael and militant Indian nationalists), assisted two New York-based pro-German periodicals: *Fatherland* and *World War*, which were edited by the German-American poet George Sylvester Viereck from 1914 to 1917, with funding from the German government.[117] Iranian anti-British campaigns also regularly featured in these weekly periodicals. Casement, for his part, even unsuccessfully attempted to obtain German backing for a plan to dispatch the small number of captured Irish soldiers in German prisoner of war camps who had joined the Irish Brigade (an anti-British republican force organized by Casement) to fight in Ottoman territories against British imperial forces. Casement anticipated this move would impress Indian, Afghan, and Iranian anti-British nationalists on account of the European "racial" identity of the Irish.[118]

The first publicly enunciated Iranian nationalist endorsement of the Irish struggle occurred in the framework of German-sponsored war-time propaganda, following the April 1916 Easter Rising in Ireland. This was in the form of an anonymously authored article (written by Sayyid Mohammad-Ali Jamalzadeh) appearing in the August 15, 1916, issue of German-funded Persian-language Iranian anti-Allied periodical *Kāveh*, published in Berlin and distributed in Iran, the Ottoman Empire, and elsewhere. Titled "The Hanging of Sir Roger Casement," the article excoriated Casement's execution by British authorities on August 3 on charge of treason and hailed the Irish struggle for self-determination.[119]

Irish nationalist advocacy of Iran's independence continued after the end of the First World War in late 1918, as Ireland rapidly plunged into what became the Irish War of Independence (a.k.a., Anglo-Irish War; January 1919 to July 1921), followed by the simultaneous partition of Ireland and creation of the Irish Free State in 1922—with six of the nine northern counties of Ulster remaining within the United Kingdom and the remainder of Ireland administered by the Free State, a self-governing entity within the British Empire and with a governor-general appointed by London until 1936. The Free State's continued membership in the British Empire set in motion the 1922–23 civil war in the Free State between the government forces, backed by Britain, and the separatist republican faction seeking full independence from the British Empire. In turn, since the Easter Rising, differing Iranian anti-imperialist groups had publicly endorsed the Irish republican struggle. They now expressed solidarity with the post-1918 republican campaign in Ireland leading to the formation of the Free State. But, for the most part, Iranian nationalists and other Iranian anti-imperialist circles (including 'internationalist' socialists and communists, or anarchists) refrained from publicly championing either of the rival camps during the Irish Civil War of 1922–23. From 1916 until at least the 1998 Good Friday Agreement, which terminated 'The Troubles' in Northern Ireland (1969–98), the Irish Question periodically featured as a topic of international advocacy by Iranian anti-imperialists.[120] Reportedly, the Iranian Mohammad Mossadeq, a future prime minister whose attempt to nationalize Iran's British-owned oil industry in 1951 led to the joint US- and British-orchestrated coup in 1953, admired "the Irish nationalist Terence MacSwiney, who starved himself to death in October 1920 in protest at his internment by the British" during the Irish War of Independence.[121] Years later, it would be the 1981 paramilitary republican prisoners' hunger strike at the Maze prison in Northern Ireland that drew admiration from a wide range of Iranian political groupings with anti-imperialist aspirations—with the newly created and increasingly authoritarian (post-1979) Islamic Republic of Iran engaging in its own extensive official expression of support for the Irish republican hunger strikers in an unmistakable propaganda utilization of the event.[122] Incidentally, it was during this hunger strike that the semi-official Iranian newspaper *Ettelā'āt* published an article titled "Ireland[:] 2,000 Years of Bloody Struggle for Independence," which dated the history of Ireland's continual colonization to the arrival of the Gaels on the island (c. the first century BCE, according to the article). The Gaels, the article noted, colonized the indigenous Firbolg population of the island and imposed Gaelic language and culture on the Firbolgs after wiping out their native way of life, and with the Gaels in turn colonized by the Norse/Vikings, the Normans, and Scots and English.[123] However, the article did not comment on the disputed origin of the Gaels, nor did the author/s appear to be aware that 'Iran' had once featured in some Irish antiquarian, folklore, and other works as the original homeland of respectively the ancient Gaels or earlier population settlements in Ireland.

As noted before, Irish nationalist expressions of solidarity with Iranian nationalists continued well into the period of the Irish War of Independence (1919–21) and resurfaced intermittently following the establishment of the Irish Free State in 1922. For instance, in 1920—by which time Britain had emerged as the sole imperial power in Iran, following developments in the aftermath of the Russian Revolutions of 1917 and the end of the First World War, including the collapse of the Ottoman Empire—Éamon de Valera, the president of the self-declared Irish Republic, stated during a now much-quoted speech at the gathering of the Friends of Freedom for India in New York: "Our cause is a common cause. We swear friendship tonight; and we send our common greetings and our pledges to our brothers in Egypt and in Persia, and tell them also that their cause is our cause."[124] Among the many other examples of Irish nationalist commentaries on Iran from the period are the passing references in the 1919–21 volumes of the weekly Irish republican *News Letter of the Friends of Irish Freedom National Bureau of Information*, published in Washington, DC. One of these reports in a July 1920 issue, based on news of recent upsurge in anti-British activities by Iranian nationalists, even grandiosely insinuated that awareness of Irish republican agitation against British rule was heartening Iranian nationalists: 'The daily stream of Irish outrages which pours from the telegraph offices and is disseminated through the Teheran press has produced, here as elsewhere, incalculable effect.'[125] The parliament of the self-declared Irish Republic, Dáil Éireann (Irish Assembly), soon after its inauguration in 1919 even sanguinely considered establishing direct contact with Iranian nationalists during the Irish War of Independence (via a representative in Moscow), among proposed contacts with similar anti-imperialist nationalist groups in other territories, as a means of building international "recognition" for the republic.[126] Random examples of intermittent Irish nationalist espousal of Iranian sovereignty after the creation of the Irish Free State in 1922 (renamed Éire in 1937 and, in 1949, the Republic of Ireland), include the November 27, 1952, speech in the Dáil Éireann by John (Jack) McQuillan, an independent leftist member of the Dáil, during the time of the Iranian oil nationalization campaign of 1951–53 directed against British control of Iranian oil industry. McQuillan claimed "the sympathy of the majority of the people in this country" was on the side of the oil nationalization scheme initiated by the Iranian premier Mohammad Mossadeq.[127] Much later, during the Iranian Revolution of 1978–79 that overthrew the Iranian monarchy (Pahlavi dynasty, 1925–79), different Irish nationalist organizations in the Republic of Ireland and in Northern Ireland voiced solidarity with the Iranian masses. These Irish nationalist groups ranged from Sinn

Féin the Workers' Party (1977–82; previously the "Official" Sinn Féin) in the Republic of Ireland to such organizations in Northern Ireland as the Provisional Irish Republican Army, and its political wing the Provisional Sinn Féin (founded in 1969), the Irish National Liberation Army, and its political wing the Irish Republican Socialist Party (founded in 1974), and the republican socialist People's Democracy (founded in 1968).[128]

Notes

1 See my forthcoming "Presenting Dissident Iranian Modernity to British Audiences: Malkum Khan, 'al-Afghani,' and British Debates on the Iranian Tobacco Protest of 1891-1892."
2 The leading Liberal critics included the Radical MPs Henry Labouchere, Arthur Brend Winterbotham, William A. Hunter, Alpheus C. Morton, Sir George Otto Trevelyan, John Seymour Keay, James Allanson Picton, William Pritchard Morgan, along with the Liberal James Bryce (the Belfast-born Scottish politician and later diplomat, and a former under-secretary of state for foreign affairs in 1886).
3 See, for instance, Healy's parliamentary question on the subject on May 23, 1892 in [Great Britain] *Parliamentary Debates* (Commons), 4th Series, 1892, vol.4, c.1523.
4 For example, the Radical John Seymour Keay was a member of the British Committee of the Indian National Congress (1889) and author of *Spoiling the Egyptians: A Tale of Shame Told from the British Blue Books* (1882). On Healy and British imperialism, see also Pauline Collombier-Lakeman, "Ireland and the Empire," pp.64, 69.
5 See also, Frank Callanan, *T.M. Healy: The Rise and Fall of Parnell and the Establishment of the Free State*. Cork: Cork University Press, 1996.
6 Browne, in addition to his general aversion to imperialism (albeit not extended to Japan or the Ottoman Empire) married the Anglo-Irish Alice Caroline Blackburne Daniell in 1906. She was the daughter of the Cambridge (Trinity College) professor of history Francis Henry Blackburne Daniell. Incidentally, Alice Blackburne Daniell's great-grandfather Francis Blackburne, an attorney-general and Lord Chancellor of Ireland, had gained notoriety in Irish nationalist circles for overseeing the government's prosecutions of Daniel O'Connell and William Smith O'Brien in the mid-nineteenth century. See also G. B. Smith, "Blackburne, Francis (1782?-1867)," *Oxford Dictionary of National Biography. Volume 5: Belle—Blackman*. Oxford: Oxford University Press, 2004, pp.934–35.
7 Edward Granville Browne, *The Persian Revolution of 1905-1909*. New edition. Washington, DC: Mage, 1995 [1910], p.58. Incidentally, the Dedication page in this book echoed Thomas Osborne Davis' famous Irish nationalist maxim in his poem "A Nation Once Again." Browne expressed his wish that the "ancient" country of Iran would "rise to life 'a Nation once again.'"
8 On Malkum Khan's and Sayyid Jamal al-Din's participation in the opposition to Salisbury's handling of the tobacco concession, see my forthcoming "Presenting Dissident Iranian Modernity to British Audiences"; Nikki R. Keddie, *Sayyid Jamal ad-Din 'al-Afghani.' A Political Biography*. Berkeley: University of California Press, 1972, pp.357–69, and passim; Hamid Algar, *Mirza Malkum Khan*. Berkeley: University of California Press, 1973, pp.192–93, 210–14.
9 See, for example, *Freeman's Journal*, November 4, 1890, p.8 (under the "Advertisements & Notices" section). In the same issue (p.3), see the report on the corporation appearing under "Commercial Intelligence." See also ibid., December 24, 1891, p.3.
10 Ibid., October 21, 1891, p.5; ibid., December 17, 1891, p.5 (in this report Sayyid Jamal al-Din was misidentified as an "Arab Sheik"). On Iranian protests in opposition to the concession, see also ibid., January 5, 1892, p.5.
11 Ibid., May 24, 1892, p.5; ibid., May 27, 1892, p.6.
12 Ibid., January 20, 1892, p.6.
13 *Cork Examiner*, May 28, 1892, p.5, c.e.
14 For a few examples, see Howard Brasted, "Indian Nationalist Development and the Influence of Irish Home Rule," pp.37–63; Michael Silvestri, *Ireland and India*; idem, "'The Sinn Fein of

India': Irish Nationalism and the Policing of Revolutionary Terrorism in Bengal," *Journal of British Studies* 39(4), October 2000, pp.454–86; Ganesh Devi, "India and Ireland: Literary Relations" in Joseph McMinn, ed., *The Internationalism of Irish Literature and Drama*. Gerrards Cross: Colin Smythe, 1982, pp.294–308; Gauri Viswanathan, "Ireland, India, and the Poetics of Internationalism"; Matthew Erin Plowman, "Irish Republicans and the Indo-German Conspiracy of World War I," *New Hibernia Review* 7(3), Autumn 2003, pp.80–105; Tadhg Foley and Maureen O'Connor, eds., *Ireland and India: Colonies, Culture and Empire*. Dublin: Irish Academic Press, 2007; Barry Crosbie, *Irish Imperial Networks*; Julia M. Wright, *Ireland, India and Nationalism*; Niamh O'Sullivan, *Aloysius O'Kelly*, pp.123–25, and passim.

15 Mansour Bonakdarian, "Iranian Nationalism and Global Solidarity Networks" in Houchang E. Chehabi, et al., eds. *Iran in the Middle East: Transnational Encounters and Social History*. London: I.B. Tauris, 2015, pp.89–91.

16 On Yeats and Tagore, see also Harold M. Hurwitz, "Yeats and Tagore," *Comparative Literature* 16(1), Winter 1964, pp.55–64; Michael Collins, *Empire, Nationalism and the Postcolonial World*, chapter 4.

17 See also Donal P. McCracken, *Forgotten Protest: Ireland and the Anglo-Boer War*. Reprint. Belfast: Ulster Historical Foundation, 2003 [1989], pp. xviii–xix, 93–94, and passim; idem, *MacBride's Brigade: Irish Commandos in the Anglo-Boer War*. Dublin: Four Courts Press, 1999, passim; P.J. Mathews, "Stirring up Disloyalty: The Boer War, the Irish Literary Theatre and the Emergence of a New Separatism," *Irish University Review* 33(1), Spring-Summer 2003, pp.99–116; Pauline Collombier-Lakeman, "Ireland and the Empire," pp.64–68.

18 Donal P. McCracken, *Forgotten Protest*, pp.xviii–xvix.

19 William Theobald Wolfe Tone, ed., *Memoirs of Theobald Wolfe Tone. Written by Himself*. Volime II. London: Henry Colburn, 1827, pp.358–59. See also pp.317–24 and passim.

20 Frank MacDermot, "Arthur O'Connor," *Irish Historical Studies* 15(57), March 1966, pp.48–69.

21 Terry Golway, *Irish Rebel: John Devoy and America's Fight for Ireland's Independence*. New York: St. Martin's, 1998, p.42.

22 Robert Ryal Miller, *Shamrock and Sword: The Saint Patrick's Battalion in the U.S.-Mexican War*. Norman: University of Oklahoma Press, 1989.

23 Nini Rodgers, *Ireland, Slavery and Anti-Slavery: 1612-1865*. Houndmills, Basingstoke: Palgrave, 2007, chapter 11.

24 See also Owen McGee, *Arthur Griffith*. Sallins, Ireland: Irish Academic press, 2015.

25 See also Leah Levenson and Jerry H. Natterstad, *Hanna Sheehy-Skeffington: Irish Feminist*. Syracuse: Syracuse University Press, 1986, pp.25–34; Senia Pašeta, *Irish Nationalist Women, 1900-1918*. Cambridge: Cambridge University Press, 2013, pp.68–80.

26 See also Diarmaid Ferriter, *Transformation of Ireland, 1900-2000*. London: Profile Books, 2005, pp.106–107, 130.

27 Mansour Bonakdarian, *Britain and the Iranian Constitutional Revolution of 1906-1911: Foreign Policy, Imperialism, and Dissent*. Syracuse: Syracuse University Press, 2006, p.123. See also idem, "Iranian Nationalism and Global Solidarity Networks," p.88.

28 See Mansour Bonakdarian, *Britain and the Iranian Constitutional Revolution*; idem, "Iranian Nationalism and Global Solidarity Networks," pp.77–119; idem, "India: IX. Political and Cultural Relations: Qajar Period, Early 20th Century," *Encyclopaedia Iranica*, vol. XIII, fascicle 1, 2004, pp.32–44; Janet Afary, *The Iranian Constitutional Revolution, 1906-1911: Grassroots Democracy, Social Democracy, and the Origins of Feminism*. New York: Columbia, 1996; Houri Berberian, *Armenians and the Iranian Constitutional Revolution of 1905-1911: The Love for Freedom Has No Fatherland*. Boulder: Westview Press, 2001; idem, *Roving Revolutionaries: Armenians and the Connected Revolutions in the Russian, Iranian, and Ottoman Worlds*. Oakland: University of California Press, 2019, passim; Iago Gocheleishvili, "Georgian Connections of the Iranian Constitutional Revolution of 1905-1911," *Central Eurasian Studies Review* 5(1), 2006, pp.10–14; Fariba Zarinebaf, "From Istanbul to Tabriz: Modernity and Constitutionalism in the Ottoman Empire and Iran," *Comparative Studies of South Asia, Africa, and the Middle East* 28(1), 2008, pp.154–69; Nader Sohrabi, *Revolution and Constitutionalism in the Ottoman Empire and Iran*. New York: Cambridge University Press, 2011; essays by Charles Kurzman, Yidan Wang, Kamran Rastegar, Touraj Atabaki, Farzin Vejdani, and Mansour Bonakdarian in H. E. Chehabi and Vanessa Martin, eds., *Iran's Constitutional Revolution: Politics, Cultural*

Transformations and Transnational Connections. London: I.B. Tauris, 2010; Touraj Atabaki, "Constitutionalism in Iran and its Asian Interdependencies," *Comparative Studies of South Asia, Africa and the Middle East* 28(1), 2008, pp.142–53.
29 See Mansour Bonakdarian, *Britain and the Iranian Constitutional Revolution*, passim.
30 Ibid., passim.
31 See also Dillon's letter-to-the-editor in the *Manchester Guardian*, January 22, 1909, p.7, c.c; as well as the explanation offered in this regard by the vice-chairman of the Persia Committee, E.G. Browne, in *The Times* (London), September 20, 1909, p.4, c.b; Mansour Bonakdarian, "Erin and Iran Resurgent: Ireland and the Iranian Constitutional Revolution of 1906-1911" in Houchang Chehabi and Vanessa Martin, eds., *Iran's Constitutional Revolution*, pp.291–318.
32 See *United Ireland* (Dublin), October 29, 1887, p.2; *Statement of Facts Relating to Mr. Wilfrid Blunt's Arrest at Woodford, October 23, 1887. Together with the Joint Opinion of Sir Charles Russell [...] R.T. Reid [...] H.H. Asquith [...] and W.S. Robson*. London: Home Rule Union, 1887; *Journal of the Home Rule Union* (London) 1(1), March 1888, pp.9–11, 14–15; ibid., no.2, April 1888, pp.19, 28–29; ibid., no.3, May 1888, pp.39, 45, 46; ibid., no.6, August 1888, pp.81–83, 95; ibid., no.7, September 1888, p.107; ibid., no.8, October 1888, p.127; ibid., no.11, January 1889, p.176; ibid., no.14, April 1889, p.224; ibid., no.19, September 1889, p.307; ibid., no.20, October 1889, p.315; *Freeman's Journal* (Dublin), October 24, 1887, p.5; ibid., October 26, 1887, p.6; ibid., October 28, 1887, p.5; ibid., January 17, 1888, p.5; ibid., January 28, 1888, pp.5–6; ibid., February 13, 1888, pp.5–6; ibid., March 7, 1888, p.5; "The Deptford Irish National League," *The Tablet* (London), March 17, 1888, p.443; "Mr. Wilfrid Scawen Blunt," *Illustrated London News*, March 3, 1888, p.224; Wilfrid Scawen Blunt, *My Diaries: Being a Personal Narrative of Events 1888-1914. Part One [1888-1900]*. Reprint, with a Foreword by Lady Gregory. New York: Alfred Knopf, 1921, pp.1–2; James Mitchell, "The Imprisonment of Wilfrid Scawen Blunt in Galway: Cause and Consequences," *Journal of the Galway Archaeological and Historical Society* 46, 1994, pp.65–110; Anna Pilz, "'All Possessors of Property Tremble': Constructions of Landlord-Tennant Relations in Lady Gregory's Writings" in Heidi Hansson and James H. Murphy, eds., *Fictions of the Irish Land War*. Bern: Peter Lang, 2014, pp.144–47.
33 Wilfrid Scawen Blunt, *Gordon at Khartoum: Being a Personal Narrative of Events in Continuation of "A Secret History of the English Occupation of Egypt."* London: Stephen Swift and Co., 1911, pp. 392, 610–11.
34 See *Positivist Review* (London) 20(231), March 1, 1912, p.71.
35 Nora F. Dryhurst, ed., *Nationalities and Subject Races. Report of Conference Held in Caxton Hall, Westminster June 28-30, 1910*. With a Preface by Robert Lynd. London: P.S. King & Son, 1911. See also *Manchester Guardian*, July 2, 1910, p.8, c.e.
36 See Dryhurst's obituaries in *Freedom: A Journal of Libertarian Thought, Work and Literature* (London), January 1931, p.2, and in *The Times* (London), November 1, 1930, p.17, c.d. See also Angela V. John, *War, Journalism and the Shaping of the Twentieth Century: The Life and Times of Henry W. Nevinson*. New York: I.B. Tauris, 2006, pp.85–92 and passim; Ronald Schuchard, "'An Attendant Lord': H.W. Nevinson's Friendship with W.B. Yeats" in Warwick Gould ed., *Yeats Annual, No.7*, pp.95, 97, 101 (in which Dryhurst's first name erroneously appears as "Norah"). See also Dana Hearne, "The Irish Citizen 1914-1916: Nationalism, Feminism, and Militarism," *Canadian Journal of Irish Studies* 18(1), July 1992, pp.1–14.
37 Helen Smith, *An Uncommon Reader: A Life of Edward Garnett, Mentor and Editor of Literary Genius*. New York: Farrar, Strauss and Giroux, 2017, pp.191–92; Conor Mulvagh, *Irish Days, Indian Memories: V.V. Giri and Indian Law Students at University College Dublin, 1913-1916*. Sallins, Ireland: Irish Academic Press, 2016, pp.23–24. Mulvagh quotes the Irish republican Patrick Sarsfield O'Hegarty, who erroneously assumed this rescue attempt took place sometime in 1908, although adding: "I do not recollect the year."
38 Nora F. Dryhurst, ed., *Nationalities and Subject Races*, p.87. On the 1910 conference, an article in *Sinn Féin*, signed "G.D." (most certainly George Gavan Duffy, who had participated at the conference and at times signed his name G.D.), welcomed the gathering, but noted many more such events needed to take place before British public opinion could turn against imperialism. The article went on to criticize the choice of some of the participants at the conference, based on their imputed lack of familiarity with their subject matter, as well as the fact that "the Congress was not as thoroughly international as it might be." It added: "Most of the promoters are Englishmen who have courted national unpopularity in the past

through daring to 'decry their own country' and it is a thousand pities that the international work which they have initiated and carried on in the face of considerable difficulties should be comparatively fruitless." *Sinn Féin*, July 16, 1910, p.3, c.c. See also ibid., July 9, 1910, p.1, c.g; August 6, 1910, p.3, cc.f-g. The latter coverage of the conference was also signed "G.D." An anonymous hostile review of the published report of the 1910 Conference (edited by Dryhurst) appeared under the heading "A Conference of Cranks" in the London literary journal *Academy* (July 29, 1911, p.142). The review focused chiefly on Gibson's speech. On the other hand, the Syrian L.B. Joureidini who attended the 1910 conference, considered some of the speeches "seditious," pondering: "What impression these speeches left on the minds of the Egyptian young men present—and they were not few—and what their echo in Egypt will be." *Spectator* (London), July 30, 1910, pp.163–65.

39 *Nation* (London), July 29, 1911, pp.642–43.
40 See also *Manchester Guardian*, July 19, 1911, p.6, c.f; ibid., June 29, 1910, p.8, c.b.
41 Shapland Hugh Swinny, "Nationalities and Subject Races Conference," *Positivist Review* (London) 22(255), March 1, 1914, pp.66–68.
42 *Positivist Review* (London) 20(234), June 1, 1912, p.143. See also Swinny's highly favorable review of Browne's 1910 *The Persian Revolution of 1905-1909* in *Positivist Review* 19(218), February 1, 1911, pp.42–45.
43 Mansour Bonakdarian, "British suffragists and Iranian women, 1906-1911" in Ian Christopher Fletcher, Laura E. Nym Mayhall, and Philippa Levine, eds., *Women's Suffrage in the British Empire: Citizenship, Nation, and Race*. London: Routledge, 2000, pp.164–67.
44 Hanna Sheehy Skeffington, "The Women's Movement—Ireland," *Irish Review* 2(17), July 1912, p.226.
45 Mansour Bonakdarian, *Britain and the Iranian Constitutional Revolution*, passim; idem, "Erin and Iran Resurgent" in Houchang Chehabi and Vanessa Martin, eds., *Iran's Constitutional Revolution*, pp.291–318.
46 For example, on Dillon's support of the Zulu resistance to British aggression in southern Africa during the war of 1879, see Paul A. Townend, *The Road to Home Rule*, pp.78–79; idem, "Between Two Worlds," p.160.
47 See, for instance, Wilfrid Scawen Blunt, *My Diaries: Being a Personal Narrative of Events 1888-1914. Part Two [1900-1914]*. Reprint, with a Foreword by Lady Gregory. New York: Alfred a. Knopf, 1922 [1921], pp.271, 317–19, 323, 412, and passim; "Letter to Egyptian Nationalist Congress at Brussels," *The Times*, September 23, 1910, p.3. Dillon had visited Egypt in 1903.
48 Among numerous sources, see Sinéad Garrigan Mattar, "'Wage for Each People Her Hand Has Destroyed': Lady Gregory's Colonial Nationalism," *Irish University Review* 34(1), Spring-Summer, 2004, pp.49–66; Lucy McDiarmid, "Lady Gregory, Wilfrid Blunt, and London Table Talk," ibid, pp.67–80; William T. Going, "A Peacock Dinner: The Homage of Pound and Yeats to Wilfrid Scawen Blunt," *Journal of Modern Literature* 1(3), March 1971, p.303; Andrea Bobotis, "From Egypt to Ireland: Lady Augusta Gregory and Cross-Cultural Nationalisms in Victorian Ireland," *Romanticism and Victorianism on the Net* 48, November 2007 (http://www.erudit.org/revue/ravon/2007/v/n48/017439ar.html).
49 See also Dillon's statement following a 1912 lecture by E.G. Browne on Iranian literature at a gathering of the Persia Society in London, in Edward Granville Browne, *The Literature of Persia*. London: Persia Society, 1912 (published by John Hogg), pp.38–41. In his speech, while expressing solidarity with the Iranian nation and crediting Browne for illuminating Iran's ancient civilization and major contributions to history, Dillon also noted:

> [...] I confess that my sympathies go out to all these races. My sympathies go out to Morocco and to Egypt, and to all these races [...] who have a historic past, a national self-consciousness, which in my opinion is the necessary seed-bed of great achievement; and though it may appear somewhat of a paradox, I say that my sympathy goes out especially to those countries which still have succeeded in resisting the introduction of railways. [...] I venture to offer my advice [...] if you allow railways to be laid down without paying for them yourselves, your country will pass into the hands of others.

The Persia Society was founded in London in March 1911 by Lord Lamington, the president of the Persia Committee, and Mirza Mahdi Khan ("Moshir al-Molk"), the Iranian minister in London (1907–20). The objective of the society was to promote Iranian culture and literature in the United Kingdom and greater cultural understanding and appreciation between the two countries. Many of the original members of the society belonged to the Persia Committee.

50 Joseph V. O'Brien, *William O'Brien and the Course of Irish Politics, 1881-1918*. Berkeley: University of California Press, 1976, chapter 8 ("The All-For-Ireland League").

51 [Great Britain] *Parliamentary Debates* (House of Commons), 4th series, 1911, vol.31, c.177; ibid., vol.32, c.1559.

52 Mansour Bonakdarian, *Britain and the Iranian Constitutional Revolution*, pp.187–88, 190, and passim. See also *Habl al-Matin* (Calcutta), vol.16, no.41, Monday, 19 Rabi' al-Thāni 1327 (May 10, 1909), p.19.

53 Joseph Maunsell Hone and Page L. Dickinson, *Persia in Revolution. With Notes of Travel in the Caucasus.* London: T. Fisher Unwin, 1910.

54 On Maloney, see also Myles Dillon, *The Correspondence of Myles Dillon, 1922-1925: Irish-German Relations and Celtic Studies.* Joachim Fischer and John Dillon editors. Dublin: Four Courts Press, 1999, pp.36–37, 44, 46, and passim; Lesa Ní Mhunghaile, "Moloney, William J. (1885-1968)" in James McGuire and James Quinn, eds., *Dictionary of Irish Biography from the Earliest Times to the Year 2002. Volume 6: McGuire-Nutt.* Cambridge: Cambridge University Press, 2009, p.560. Maloney, not to be confused with the American William Joseph Marie Alois Maloney, who was involved in militant Irish republican activities in the United States during the First World War, was also known to his friends such as Francis and Hanna Sheehy Skeffington as "Willie Moloney" and later in life formally spelled his surname "Moloney."

55 Mansour Bonakdarian, "Erin and Iran Resurgent" in Houchang Chehabi and Vanessa Martin, eds., *Iran's Constitutional Revolution*, pp.309–10.

56 Wilfrid Scawen Blunt, *My Diaries*, Part Two, pp.217, 228, 242, 243, 368, 405, 407, 410–11; Fred Ryan, "Egypt Through English Eyes," *Egypt* (London), vol.II, no.5, July 1912, pp.56–57; Frederick Ryan, *Sinn Féin and Reaction*. With an Introduction by Manus O'Riordan. Dublin: Labour History Workshop, 1984; Francis Sheehy Skeffington, "Frederick Ryan," *Irish Review*, May 1913, p.118.

57 Wilfrid Scawen Blunt, *My Diaries*, Part Two, pp.154, 243, 368; Francis Sheehy Skeffington, "The Irish National Theatre," *T.P.'s Weekly* (Dublin), 2 May, 1913, p.566.

58 See for example, *Gaelic American* (New York), May 4, 1907, p.8; ibid., July 6, 1907, p.7; ibid., August 3, 1907, p.4; ibid., August 10, 1907, p.7; ibid., September 7, 1907, p.3; ibid., October 12, 1907, pp.2, 4; ibid., June 27, 1908, p.2; ibid., January 1, 1909, p.4; ibid., August 3, 1912, p.4; ibid., September 14, 1912, p.5.

59 See, for example, the coverage of an article by Ryan, under the heading "A Vindication of the Turk," *Modern Review* (Calcutta) 13(3), March 1913, pp.354–55.

60 Shapland Hugh Swinny, "In Memoriam: Frederick Ryan," *Positivist Review* (London) 21(246), June 1, 1913, pp.138–39; Francis Sheehy Skeffington, "Frederick Ryan," *Irish Review*, May 1913, pp.113–19; Francis Sheehy Skeffington, "The Irish National Theatre," *T.P.'s Weekly* (London), May 2, 1913, p.566; Frederick Ryan, *Sinn Féin and Reaction*; Manus O'Riordan, "The Second Greatest Event Of 1916?," *Irish Political Review and Northern Star* (Belfast) 26(2), February 2011, pp.20–21; Seamus Deane, "Frederick Ryan (1874-1913)" in Seamus Deane, ed., *The Field Day Anthology of Irish Writing: Volume III: From James Joyce (1882-1941) through contemporary Irish poetry (-1900)*. Reprint. Derry: Field Day Publications, 1992 [1991], pp.703–707; John Kelly, "Ryan, Frederick Michael (1873–1913)," *Oxford Dictionary of National Biography. Volume 48: Rowell—Sarsfield.* Oxford: Oxford University Press, 2004, pp.434–35; David Pierce, *Irish Writing in the Twentieth Century: A Reader.* Cork: Cork University Press, 2000, pp.74–77; Nicholas Allen, "Ryan, Frederick Michael (1873-1913)" in James McGuire and James Quinn, eds., *Dictionary of Irish Biography from the Earliest Times to the Year 2002. Volume 8: Patterson-Stagg.* Cambridge: Cambridge University Press, 2009, pp.690–91; William O'Brien, *Forth the Banners Go.* Dublin: Three Candles Limited, 1969, pp.14–19; Terry Eagleton, *Crazy John and the Bishop*, pp.249–72; Leah Levenson, *With Wooden Sword: A Portrait of Francis Sheehy-Skeffington, Militant Pacifist.* Boston: Northeastern University Press,

1983, pp.54, 64, 65, 66, 67, 73, 75, 89–90, 93, 95–96, 99, 105, 126, 139, 148–49; Patrick Maume, *The Long Gestation: Irish Nationalist Life, 1891-1918*. New York: St. Martin's Press, 1999, pp.25, 55, 57–58, 83, 85–88, 98, 243–44; Joseph Lennon, *Irish Orientalism*, pp.234–39; Elizabeth Longford, *A Pilgrimage of Passion: The Life of Wilfrid Scawen Blunt*. London: Wedenfeld and Nicolson, 1979, pp.360, 373, 384. On Francis Sheehy Skeffington and Fred Ryan, see also Robert Lynd, *If the Germans Conquered England*, pp.141–46; Mansour Bonakdarian, "Erin and Iran Resurgent" in Houchang Chehabi and Vanessa Martin, eds., *Iran's Constitutional Revolution*, pp.309–11; idem, *Britain and the Iranian Constitutional Revolution*, pp.156, 264; idem, "The Easter Rising," pp.57–58.

61 See Terry Eagleton, *Crazy John and the Bishop*, p.253.
62 For example, see the account of the private meeting between Maloney and Blunt in the entry for October 23, 1911, in *Wilfrid Scawen Blunt Papers. General Memoirs, 1910-12, Ms.11-1975*, pp.299–301 (Fitzwilliam Museum, Cambridge); Wilfrid Scawen Blunt, *My Diaries*, Part Two, pp. 217, 228, 242, 368, 542, 631; Maloney to Browne, March 3, 1912, *Correspondence of E.G. Browne: 1. Letters to Browne from Persia 1910-11*. Add. Mss.7604, ff.20-21 (Cambridge University Library); E.G. Browne, *The Persian Revolution*, pp.275, 300, 303; William Morgan Shuster, *The Strangling of Persia*. Reprint, Washington, DC: Mage, 1987 [1912], p.124. Browne wrongly assumed Maloney was reporting for the *Manchester Guardian* and other British papers from Iran. Blunt and Shuster respectively spelled Maloney's name as "Malony" and "Moloney." Later in life, Maloney also spelled his own name "Moloney."
63 See, for example, Frederick Ryan, "The Suffrage Tangle," *Irish Review* (Dublin) 2(19), September 1912, pp.346–51; Frederick Ryan, "An Open Letter to the Young Turks," *Positivist Review* 17(193), January 1, 1909, pp.13–16; Shapland Hugh Swinny, "Some Minor Currents in Irish Life" [which included a review of Frederick Ryan's 1906 *Criticism and Courage and Other Essays*], *Positivist Review* 15(171), March 1, 1907, pp.56–62; Shapland Hugh Swinny, "[Review of Frederick Ryan's English translation of] *Egyptian-French Letters, Addressed by Kamel Pasha to Madame Juliette Adam, 1895-1908*," *Positivist Review* 17(194), July 1, 1909, pp.164–65. See also Shapland Hugh Swinny, "In Memoriam: Frederick Ryan," *Positivist Review* (London) 21(246), June 1, 1913, pp.138–39.
64 "The Persian Struggle," *Irish Review* (Dublin) 1(6), August 1911, pp.281–86.
65 *Irish Independent*, December 29, 1911, p.4, c.e. This article was partially reproduced in *Egypt* (London), no.11, January 1912, p.122. See also Frederick Ryan, "The Persian Struggle," *Irish Review* 1(6), August 1911, p.286.
66 On this subject, see Mansour Bonakdarian, *Britain and the Iranian Constitutional Revolution*, pp.53–56.
67 Ibid., pp.59–67.
68 See, for instance, *Gaelic American*, September 22, 1906, p.4, c.a.
69 *Sinn Féin*, April 12, 1913, p.5. See also April 26, 1912, p.5.
70 Francis Sheehy Skeffington, "Frederick Ryan," *Irish Review* 2(27), May 1913, pp.113–19. In reaction to Sheehy Skeffington's rebuttal to Griffith's characterization of Ryan, Griffith's stance was defended by Tomas MacSeamus in a future issue of the same periodical, appearing under "Correspondence," *Irish Review*, June 1913, p.216.
71 See, for example, the *Gaelic American*'s attack on the 'Home Rule' IPP MP, William Redmond on June 2, 1906 (p.4, c.f), on grounds of Redmond's concern with the rumored Anglo-Russian talks (which later resulted in the 1907 Anglo-Russian Agreement).
72 See Frederick Ryan, *Sinn Féin and Reaction*, p.13. Both the *Gaelic American* and *Sinn Féin* were unmistakably anti-Jewish. In 1904, then as the editor of *The United Irishman*, Griffith had publicly rationalized the Limerick pogrom, even though in 1912 he anachronistically praised the Zionist project in Palestine at the time as a laudable 'nationalist' movement: "Israel represents the triumph of Sinn Féin." *Sinn Féin*, March 16, 1912, p.2, cc.a-b. On the Jewish community and anti-Jewish sentiments in Ireland at the time, see Frederick Ryan, *Criticism and Courage and Other Essays*. Dublin: Maunsel & Co., 1906, pp.30–31; Cormac Ó Gráda, *Jewish Ireland in the Age of Joyce*; Neil R. Davison, *James Joyce, Ulysses, and the Construction of Jewish Identity: Culture, Biography, and 'The Jew' in Modernist Europe*. Cambridge: Cambridge University Press, 1996.
73 See, for instance, the report of the Persia Committee's allegations against Grey in *Gaelic American*, July 17, 1909, p.4, c.f; or the confused report of Iranian developments

appearing under "Persia and China," ibid., January 6, 1912, p.4, c.d. The latter report was also once again indicative of the paper's anti-Jewish propensity. See also the reproduced report in the *Gaelic American* of September 14, 1912 (p.4, cc.e-f), of Browne's letter in condemnation of Russian atrocities in Iran after the closure of the second majles, originally appearing in W.S. Blunt's paper *Egypt*, which was edited by Fred Ryan. This particular article in the *Gaelic American* was most likely forwarded to the paper by Ryan himself. As already noted, from 1908 to 1909 Ryan and William J. Maloney, while still based in Cairo, had periodically sent articles and reports on Egyptian developments to the *Gaelic American* and *Sinn Féin*, despite Ryan's and Maloney's opposition to the political agendas of both of these Irish nationalist papers.

74 For some early examples of this, see the reference to Iranian developments in Vinayak Damodar Savarkar's appeal to Indian Muslims under the heading "Wake Up, Sons of Islam," reproduced in the *Gaelic American*, December 8, 1906, p.2, cc.c-d; "Persians' Eyes Open," based on a report from the Lahore *Panjabee* in the *Gaelic American*, December 22, 1906, p.6, cc.c-d; the reference to Iranian developments in an article reproduced from the Lahore *Panjabee* in *Sinn Féin*, March 23, 1907, p.3, c.a; or the article on the "general political awakening of Asia" reproduced from the Pune *Mahratta* in *Sinn Féin*, October 10, 1908, p.3, c.a.

75 November 26, 1910, p.3, cc.g-h. On the November 1910 meeting, see Mansour Bonakdarian, *Britain and the Iranian Constitutional Revolution*, pp.229–31.

76 On Indian groupings and the Iranian Constitutional Revolution and subsequent cooperation between Iranian and Indian nationalists, see Mansour Bonakdarian, *Britain and the Iranian Constitutional Revolution*, passim; idem, "India: IX. Political and Cultural Relations: Qajar Period, Early 20th Century," pp.32–44; idem, "Iranian Nationalism and Global Solidarity Networks," pp.80–81, 84–85, 92–95.

77 On Barakatullah's actual and reported teaching experience, see "Enterprising Orientals," *Evening Post* (New York), February 16, 1907, p.10; Maia Ramnath, *Haj to Utopia: How the Ghadar Movement Charted Global Radicalism and Attempted to Overthrow the British Empire*. Berkeley: University of California Press, 2011, p.223.

78 *Gaelic American* (New York), February 2, 1907, p.5, c.d; ibid., March 2, 1907, p.5, c.b; *New York Tribune*, June 9, 1907, p.6, c.f; *The Sun* (New York), October 20, 1907, p.4, c.a; *New York Times*, January 15, 1908, p.16; "Enterprising Orientals," *Evening Post* (New York), February 16, 1907, p.10; "India and Pan-Aryanism," *Review of Reviews* (US edition; New York) 35(4), April 1907, p.409; "The Bonds of Brotherhood," *Century Path: A Magazine Devoted to the Brotherhood of Humanity and Promulgation of Theosophy* ... (Point Loma, California) 10(23), April 14, 1907, p.17; *Marion Daily Mirror* (Marion, Ohio), March 2, 1907, p.9, c.d; *Hindusthanee Student: Official Bulletin of the Hindustan Association of America* (Urbana, Illinois, US), second series, 3(1–2), 1927, p.11; Tilak Raj Sareen, *Indian Revolutionary Movement Abroad (1905-1921)*. New Delhi: Sterling. 1979, pp.51–55; Aravind Ganachari, *Nationalism and Social Reform in Colonial Situation*. Delhi: Kalpaz Publications, 2005, pp.137–40, 152–53; Maia Ramnath, *Haj to Utopia*, pp.104, 222–23; Joan M. Jensen, *Passage from India: Asian Indian Immigrants in North America*. New Haven: Yale University Press, 1988, pp.19, 168. See also Harald Fischer-Tiné, "Indian Nationalism and the 'world forces': transnational and diasporic dimensions of the Indian freedom movement on the eve of the First World War," *Journal of Global History* 2(3), November 2007, pp.325–44; M. Bonakdarian, 'Erin and Iran Resurgent' in H. Chehabi and V. Martin, eds., *Iran's Constitutional Revolution*, pp.306–307.

79 *Gaelic American*, February 2, 1907, p.5, c.d.

80 Ibid., March 2, 1907, p.5, c.b.

81 Some sources took the stated formal objective of the Association at face value. See the report on Joshi's work with the Association appearing in the *Times of India* (Bombay), April 13, 1908, p.8, c.e.

82 *The Sun* (New York), October 20, 1907, p.4, c.a; Bhikhaiji Rustom Cama, "India as Seen by a Parsee Lady," *Independent* (New York) 63(3080), December 12, 1907, p.1430; Tilak Raj Sareen, *Indian Revolutionary Movement Abroad*, pp,56–57; Maia Ramnath, *Haj to Utopia*, p.104.

83 *Gaelic American*, February 23, 1907, pp.1–5. See also the interview with the Paris-based militant pan-Indian nationalist Madame Bhikhaji Rustom Cama during her stay in New York in *The Sun* (New York), October 20, 1907, p.4, c.a.

84 *New York Tribune*, June 9, 1907, p.6, c.f.

85 *The Sun* (New York), February 6, 1909, p.3, c.c.
86 In Tokyo, Barakatullah also took over the editorship of the Ottoman-funded pan-Islamic monthly publication *Islamic Fraternity*, after the departure from Japan in 1910 of the periodical's existing editor, the Egyptian Fadli Bey. "An Anti-British Periodical in Japan," *Manchester Guardian*, September 4, 1912, c.f; "Seditious Magazine Suppressed," *Times of India* (Bombay), November 6, 1912, p.11, c.d; Tilak Raj Sareen, *Indian Revolutionary Movement Abroad*, p 159 n.64; Aravind Ganachari, *Nationalism and Social Reform in Colonial Situation*, p.144; Maia Ramnath, *Haj to Utopia*, p.223. For an example of reports on the *Islamic Fraternity* in the Iranian constitutionalist-nationalist press, see *Irān-e Nou* (Tehran), 18 Shawal 1328 (October 23, 1910), p.4, cc.d-e. The *Islamic Fraternity* was a component of the Young Turks' international efforts (already initiated prior to the 1908 Young Turk Revolution) to build a pro-Young Turk pan-Islamic reformist and anti-"European imperialist" front, with earlier examples including La Fraternité Musulmane founded in Paris in 1907, which was in contact with Muslims from different territories, including Indians (both pan-Indian nationalists and Muslim-nationalists, among other groups), as well as with Iranian nationalists and reformers. Subsequent offshoots of this organization would include the London-based Society of Islamic Fraternity founded in March 1910 (a.k.a., the Muslim Brotherhood of Progress, among its other names) and led by prominent Indian Muslims residing in the United Kingdom, who were in contact with Iranian revolutionaries. See, for example, "Russia and Persia," *Manchester Guardian*, March 24, 1910, p.7, c.e. See also *Irān-e Nou* (Tehran), 17 Rabi' al-Awal 1328 (April 28, 1910), p.2, c.b.
87 See also Susan A. Rosenkranz, "'To Hold the World in Contempt': The British Empire, War, and the Irish and Indian Nationalist Press, 1899-1914." PhD dissertation, Florida International University, 2013, pp.214–32.
88 Michael de Nie, *The Eternal Paddy*; Robert J.C. Young, *Colonial Desire*, pp.68–89; Catherine Hall, "The Nation Within and Without" in Catherine Hall, Keith McClelland, and Jane Rendall, eds., *Defining the Victorian Nation*, pp.204–20; Amy E. Martin, "'Becoming a Race Apart'" in Terrence McDonough, ed., *Was Ireland a Colony?*, pp.186–211; Noel Ignatiev, *How the Irish Became White*; David R. Roediger, *The Wages of Whiteness*.
89 For a random example, see Ali-Akbar Dehkhoda's article on Russian aggression in Iran, appearing in *Soroush* (Istanbul), 19 Jamādi al-Thāni 1327 (July 8, 1909), reproduced in Ali-Akbar Dehkhoda, *Maqālāt-e Dehkhodā*. Volume 2. Mohammad Dabir-Siyaqi editor. Tehran: Tirazheh, 1362 (1983), pp.222–30.
90 This epic poem was subsequently amended and published by Ahmad ibn Mula Hafez in 1898. See Ahmad ibn Mula Hafez, ed., *Sālārnāmeh*. Volume I. Shiraz: Matba'eh-ye Mohammadi, 1316 A.H. (1898), p.12.
91 Hadji Mirza Yahya, "Persia" in Gustav Spiller, ed., *Papers on Inter-Racial Problems. Communicated to the First Universal Races Congress Held at the University of London July 26-29, 1911*. London: P.S. King & Son, 1911, p.145; Mansour Bonakdarian, "Negotiating Universal Values and Cultural and National Parameters," pp.120–21; Mansour Bonakdarian, "Iran at the Universal Races Congress: Yahya Dawlatabadi, Global Networks, International Platform, and National Allegiance" (forthcoming).
92 Mansour Bonakdarian, "The Easter Rising." On the global cosmopolitan-nationalist reverberations of the Easter Rising elsewhere around the world, see also Declan Kiberd, *Inventing Ireland*, pp.197, 203; Luke Gibbons, "Recasting the Rising: 1916 on the World Stage." Lecture presented at "The Theatre of War Symposium," Abbey Theatre (Dublin), January 22, 2015 (https://www.youtube.com/watch?v=Xv10_s3X4FA).
93 Mansour Bonakdarian, "Iranian Consecration of Irish Nationalist 'Martyrs'"; idem, "Iranian coverage of the 1981 paramilitary republican prisoners' hunger strike in Northern Ireland," *Social History* Blog Post, May 2018 (http://socialhistoryblog.com/iranian-coverage-of-the-1981-paramilitary-republican-prisoners-hunger-strike-in-northern-ireland-by-mansour-bonakdarian/).
94 Simin Daneshvar, *Savushun: A Novel about Modern Iran*. Mohammad R. Ghanoonparvar translator. Washington, DC: Mage, 1990. See also Mohammad R. Ghanoonparvar "Sharing Poetic Sensitivity and Misery: Encounters of Iranians with the Irish in Travel Writings and Fiction," in H. E. Chehabi and Grace Neville, eds., *Erin and Iran*, pp,119–26.
95 Mansour Bonakdarian, "The Easter Rising," p.72.

96 Mansour Bonakdarian, "Erin and Iran Resurgent" in Houchang Chehabi and Vanessa Martin, eds., *Iran's Constitutional Revolution*, passim; idem, *Britain and the Iranian Constitutional Revolution*, passim.
97 See for instance the Fabian socialist *New Age* (London), June 20, 1907, p.115.
98 *The Times* (London), July 15, 1907, p.12 c.c; *New Age* (London), July 18, p.184; *Justice* (London), July 20, p.6 cc.c-b.
99 George Bernard Shaw, "Common Sense About the War," *The New York Times* Current History of the European War series. Volume 1, no.1 ("What Men of Letters Say"). New York: New York Times, December 1914, pp.43–46. See also George Bernard Shaw, *Collected Letters. Volume III: 1911-1925*. Dan H. Laurence editor. New York: Viking, 1985, pp.71–72.
100 *Irish Worker*, September 12, 1914, p.2. On Connolly, see also Joseph Lennon, *Irish Orientalism*, pp.239–41.
101 See October 9 and October 30, 1915, issues of *Workers' Republic* in James Connolly, *Labour and Easter Week*, pp.84, 89. The articles are respectively titled in this book "In Praise of the Empire" and "A War for Civilisation."
102 Ibid., p.95 (titled "Diplomacy").
103 "The Mission of King Edward VII," *Sinn Féin* (Dublin), November 14, 1914, p.2.
104 See, for example, the report of the radical English journalist and war correspondent, and a former member of the Persia Committee, Henry Noel Brailsford under "Persia: 'The Small Nationalities'," *Éire-Ireland* (Dublin), November 24, 1914, p.1; "England and Neutral States" and "Persia and England" and "Germany's Friends" in *Scissors and Paste* (Dublin), January 27, 1915, p.2.
105 *Gaelic American*, September 12, 1914, p.7, c.b.
106 James K. McGuire, *The King, The Kaiser and Irish Freedom*. New York: Devin-Adair Company, 1915, p.291. See also p.283. On McGuire, see Charles Johnston, "Sinn Fein Record as to Germany," *New York Times*, May 26, 1918, p.XI (Arts and Leisure section); David Fitzpatrick, *Harry Boland's Irish Revolution, 1877-1922*. Cork: Cork University Press, 2003, passim; and Joachim Fischer, "A Future Ireland under German Rule: Dystopia as Propaganda During World War I," *Utopian Studies* 18(3), 2007, pp.348–49.
107 James K. McGuire, *What Could Germany Do for Ireland?* With an Introduction by Thomas Addis Emmet. New York: Wolfe Tone Company, 1916, p.103.
108 *The Hibernian* (Dublin), February 19, 1916, p.6.
109 Roger Casement, *The Crime Against Europe: A Possible Outcome of the War of 1914*. Berlin: The Continental Times, 1915, p.7.
110 Mansour Bonakdarian, "The Easter Rising," pp.58–61, 64–66.
111 See Mansour Bonakdarian, "Iranian Nationalism and Global Solidarity Networks," pp.91–95.
112 On the presence of Sheybani and other Iranians (including Sayyid Hassan Taqizadeh, the leader of the German-backed Iranian nationalist committee) at Irish nationalist gatherings in Berlin, as well as a few references by Sheybani in his memoirs to the Irish Question, see Abdul-Hussein Sheybani, *Khāterāt-e Mohājerat: az Dowlat-e Movaqat-e Kermānshāh tā Komiteh-ye Melliyun-e Berlin*. Iraj Afshar and Kaveh Bayat editors. Tehran: Shirazeh, 1378 (1999), pp.238, 313, 416, 463, 500. On July 1, 1917, while attending the International Socialist Peace Conference in Stockholm, Sheybani and Chatterton-Hill got together with the Berlin-based militant Indian nationalist Virendranath Chattopadhyaya (Chatto), whom they both knew from prior contacts. Ibid., p.317. On October 1, 1917, Sheybani and Chatterton-Hill had a long conversation at the latter's residence in Berlin, during which Chatterton-Hill expressed frustration with Germany's lack of a coherent war policy. Ibid., p.416. Among other examples, Iranian nationalists also attended a gathering of the German-Irish Society in Berlin on December 2, 1917, as well as the celebration of St. Patrick's Day organized by the same society on March 17, 1918. At the latter gathering, attended also by Indians, Egyptians, and other groups, Chatterton-Hill "thanked in particular friends from India, Egypt, and Iran." *Irische blätter* (Berlin) 2(3), April 1918, pp.174, 176, 178; *Documents Relative to the Sinn Fein Movement*. London: H.M. Stationary Office, 1921, p.44. See also "Vigilant," "Sinn Fein and Germany," *Quarterly Review* (London) 230(456), July 1918, pp.232–33; Richard Dawson, *Red Terror and Green: The Sinn Fein-Bolshevist Movement*. New York: E.P. Dutton, 1920, pp.203–205. On the gathering at the German-Irish Society in Berlin on December 2, 1917, see also

Irische blätter 1(8), December 1917, p.583. Chatterton-Hill and Iranians were also present at the Ottoman Club in Berlin on September 14, 1917. *Irische blätter* 1(6), October 1917, p.469. Besides Iranians and Germans attending a reception hosted by the Iranian nationalist committee in Berlin on January 9, 1918, other guests included Ottoman, Egyptian, Syrian, Algerian, Tunisian, Indian, and Irish nationalists in the city, notably Chatterton-Hill. See *Die Islamische Welt: Illustrierte Monatsschrift für Politik, Wirtschaft und Kultur* (Berlin) 2(1), January 1918, p.37.

113 For Rainey's and Navab's marriage notices, see *Cork Examiner*, August 20, 1913, p.1; "Co. Cork Lady Weds and Indian," *Freeman's Journal*, August 21, 1913, p.10.

114 Mansour Bonakdarian, "Iranian Nationalism and Global Solidarity Networks," pp.89–91.

115 *Documents Relative to the Sinn Fein Movement*, pp.42–44.

116 See, for example, *Gaelic American*, December 12, 1914, pp.1, 8; August 14, 1915, p.8. Among his other war-related activities, Meyer also translated into English from German Theodor Schiemann's 1915 "Russia on the Road to Revolution," which was published in the *Gaelic American*, among other militant Irish nationalist papers in the United States. See *Gaelic American*, September 11, 1915, p.8; September 18, 1915, p.3. For a study refuting Meyer's involvement in German-Irish war-time activities, see Seán Ó Lúing, *Kuno Meyer*.

117 See Roger Casement to Joseph McGarrity, November 11, 1914 (from Berlin) in "Papers of William J. Maloney relating to Sir Roger Casement," *Maloney Collection of Irish Historical Papers, 1857-1965* (New York Public Library), Box 1, folder "Joseph McGarrity, 1914 Nov.-Dec."; Kuno Meyer to John Devoy, September 2, 1915 (from Berlin) in William O'Brien and Desmond Ryan, eds. *Devoy's Post Bag, 1871-1928. Volume II: 1880-1928*. With an Introduction by Patrick Sarsfield O'Hegarty. Dublin: C.J. Fallon, 1953, pp.475–76; "Vigilant," "Sinn Fein and Germany," *Quarterly Review* (London) 230(456), July 1918, pp.214–35.

118 Reinhard R. Doerries, *Prelude to the Easter Rising: Sir Roger Casement in Imperial Germany*. London: Frank Cass, 2000, pp.172–73.

119 *Kāveh* (Berlin) 1(11), 4 Ordibehesht 1286 Yazdgerdi (August 15, 1916), pp.7–8. See also Mansour Bonakdarian, "The Easter Rising," pp.64–65.

120 Mansour Bonakdarian, "The Easter Rising," pp.72–73; idem, "Iranian Consecration of Irish Nationalist 'Martyrs'," pp.295–302.

121 Christopher de Bellaigue, *Patriot of Persia: Muhammad Mossadegh and a Tragic Anglo-American Coup*. New York: Harper Collins, 2012, p.61. The practice of political hunger-striking in Ireland dated back to 1912, when suffragettes jailed in the summer of that year resorted to the tactic. The following summer it was the socialist Irish nationalist James Connolly who went on hunger strike while in prison for his part in organizing (along with Jim Larkin) the labor dispute in Dublin that turned violent as employers and the authorities resorted to armed force against strikers (the Lockout of 1913).

122 Mansour Bonakdarian, "Iranian Consecration of Irish Nationalist 'Martyrs'"; idem, "Iranian coverage of the 1981 paramilitary republican prisoners' hunger strike in Northern Ireland."

123 *Ettelā'āt* (Tehran) 17 Ordibehesht 1360 (May 7, 1981), p.5.

124 Éamon de Valera, *India and Ireland*. New York: Friends of Freedom for India, 1920 (speech delivered on February 28, 1920, at the Central Opera House, New York City), p.24.

125 *News Letter of the Friends of Irish Freedom National Bureau of Information* 2(4), July 24, 1920, p.7.

126 Gerard Keown, *First of the Small Nations: The Beginnings of Irish Foreign Policy in the Interwar Years, 1919-1932*. Oxford: Oxford University Press, 2016, p.36.

127 *Dáil Debates*, vol.135, no.2, 1952, c.255. Incidentally, at that time Ireland was not a major importer of Iranian petroleum. Prior to 1921, Ireland's oil imports were primarily supplied by the Anglo-American Oil Company, founded in 1905 as a subsidiary of Standard Oil. Following the establishment of the Free State in 1922, the Irish-American Oil Company was formed as an independent branch of the parent company. *The Economist* (London), April 28, 1923, p.908. British control of Iran's oil industry originated with a bilateral concession in 1901 between the Iranian state and a private British entrepreneur, William Knox D'Arcy. The concession, in violation of its terms, was gradually taken over by the British government through the purchase of shares in the oil company, initially in the form of the British Admiralty's purchase of majority shares (51%) in July 1914. The attempt by Reza Shah to

renegotiate the concession and at least secure more favorable terms for Iran, while failing to fully terminate the concession, had mixed results due to British diplomatic and economic pressure on Iran. A new concession in 1933 granted Iran a modicum of greater supervision and increased financial leverage, but also substantially extended the duration of the concession.

128 See Bonakdarian, "Iranian coverage of the 1981 paramilitary republican prisoners' hunger strike in Northern Ireland"; and Sinn Féin the Workers' Party's *United Irishman* (Dublin), September 1979, p.4.

Chapter Eight

PERSPECTIVAL DETOUR: IRANIAN FAMILIARITY WITH IRELAND AND THE IRISH QUESTION PRIOR TO THE EASTER RISING

As noted in previous chapters—in addition to the general lack of awareness among Iranians (to this day) of the place of 'Iran' in certain corpus of Irish-nationalist antiquarian and other range of historical, folklore, literary, and/or more narrowly political writing during the time period covered in this book—, in the early twentieth century Iranian nationalists continued to to be apathetic toward Irish nationalist politics (until the Easter Rising of 1916), notwithstanding fervent Irish nationalist expressions of solidarity with the Iranian constitutionalist-nationalist struggle of 1906–11 and subsequently. By the turn of the twentieth century, at least educated Iranians following world events were not entirely ignorant of Irish political developments in general. Since the latter decades of the nineteenth century, summary coverage of Irish nationalist activities had appeared in a spectrum of Iranian publications. The topics covered in these reports ranged from Home Rule campaigns to agitation for land reform or armed republican activities. The delayed Iranian nationalist expressions of support for their Irish counterparts appears all the more confounding given the rapidly multiplying Iranian condemnations after 1907 of British imperial domination of India and Egypt. As discussed below, the Iranian neglect of the Irish Question prior to 1916 appears to have been considerably due to Ireland's somewhat ambiguous position as an English colonial entity. Notably, other than being England's oldest substantial colonial territory outside mainland Britain, as well as being a European colony, Ireland had its own separate parliament from 1264 to 1800 and was later incorporated into the new territorial-administrative amalgam of the United Kingdom in 1801. It was around this time that the British Empire emerged as a major outside player in Iranian affairs and attracted increasing Iranian diplomatic, military, commercial, historical, and cultural attention, with also a small (albeit gradually increasing) number of Iranian travelers visiting England during the nineteenth century, but rarely venturing into Ireland. Yet, some Iranians in the nineteenth century directly encountered the Irish not only in England, India, Egypt, the Ottoman Empire, and other locations outside Ireland, but also in the form of a small number of Irish residing in, or passing through, Iran itself—as in the case members of the British diplomatic service, or those serving as agents of commercial firms or as Christian missionaries, along with the occasional Irish traveler (including journalists), among others—without my implying that all such direct contacts necessarily generated familiarity with Irish politics. Furthermore, throughout the nineteenth century, educated Iranians interested in world affairs and in the British Empire incrementally acquired greater knowledge of Ireland's geographic location and social, economic, and political status within the British Isles, while also having greater opportunity to learn about certain major episodes in Irish history (generally only after the Norman conquests in the island beginning in the twelfth century).

Yet, the Iranian lack of familiarity at the time with Iran-centered Irish antiquarianism, or with other modes of Irish nationalist referentialities to 'Iran' in a wide array of historical, folklore, mythological, and allegoric framings (ultimately as a means of commenting on Ireland's own history), was itself symptomatic of the relatively limited Iranian knowledge of Ireland in general. Certainly, by the late nineteenth century, some among the more educated Iranians were aware of Ireland's geographic location in the British Isles, its administration as a constituent part the English realm, and had some vague inkling of the communal, religious, and/or political divisions in the island. The overall limited Iranian familiarity with Ireland was not entirely due to Ireland's presumably marginal position in Europe as an English colony. Distance and extremely scarce direct Iranian contacts with the island were also major factors. After all, educated Iranians were highly informed of developments in nearby British-controlled territories, notably the Indian subcontinent (gradually occupied by Britain after 1757, initially under the auspices of the English East India Company) and Egypt (occupied in 1882), given that Iran had had a long history of reciprocal contacts and exchanges with these territories—not forgetting also varying degrees of linguistic familiarity (primarily Persian or Arabic), or the shared frontier between British India and Iran after the 1870s and the long presence of émigré communities from Iran and the Indian subcontinent in the respective territories, as well as of Iranian émigré communities in Egypt, among the many other factors. In addition to this contrast between direct Iranian historical encounters with the Indian subcontinent or Egypt, on the one hand, and the extreme rarity of direct contacts with Ireland during the period, on the other hand, there was also the significant factor of the range of sources available to Iranians in their knowledge formation about Ireland. Information available to Iranians about Ireland was primarily acquired from translations of standard British histories of Ireland and from the mainstream, and often conservative, British newspapers, such as *The Times* of London—including translations of these English-language sources into Persian in the Indian subcontinent or into Arabic in Egypt, or into Turkish in the Ottoman Empire, for instance—, as well as from translations of conventional material about Ireland originally appearing in French-language (primarily published in France, Belgium, or Switzerland), given the predominance of French as the European lingua franca among the highly educated Iranians at the time (who were a very small fraction of the population to begin with), among other potential European language sources accessible to some Iranians. Furthermore, that Iranians should have been in any way interested in Ireland in the first place during the nineteenth century was also largely a by-product of Iranian interest in England and in the British Empire, given the expanded of British diplomatic, economic, and other range of interactions with Iran after the start of the nineteenth century—Britain being one of the two leading European imperial powers in Iran, alongside Russia—, and the proximity to Iran of Britain's expanding Indian territories or of British military engagements in Afghan territories during the century, two Anglo-Iranian wars, as well as the expanded British hegemony in the Persian Gulf (including the Arab littoral). In other words, Ireland was primarily approached through a British (more appropriately an "English") lens. Understandably, educated Iranians residing in British India during the nineteenth century would, in general, have had greater familiarity with information related to Ireland. In Iran itself, however, well up to the 1916 Easter Rising in Ireland, Iranians primarily approached Ireland through the medium of Iran's engagement with England and the British Empire, in a manner that in Iranian perspective "provincialized" Ireland as a fringe realm of the English monarchy within the British Isles, similar to Scotland or Wales, which also attracted little direct attention in Iran compared to England.

In the framework of Iranian geographical and historical familiarity with Ireland at the time, it is necessary to bear in mind that by the nineteenth century Ireland had long been provincialized in standard *British* accounts and maps of the British Isles. By the time the earliest notable direct contacts between Iran and the British Isles took place, beginning in the sixteenth century, Ireland was already under English rule, with Iranian knowledge of contemporary and historical Ireland largely filtered through either the conventional English lens, or through other European sources accessible to Iranians, which also treated Ireland as an English dominion, even if some of the European powers at the time, namely France and Spain, periodically backed Catholic uprisings against English rule in Ireland. The first direct diplomatic contact between England and a territorially independent and unified Iranian state occurred in 1562. There had been at least two prior diplomatic exchanges in the thirteenth century between the English crown and 'Iranian' territories in their varying politically administered configurations.[1] In 1562, Anthony Jenkinson, an agent of the private English chartered Muscovy Company (1555), arrived at the court of the Iranian Safavid ruler Shah Tahmasp I. Jenkinson, who was later reviled in James Clarence Mangan's 1846 "To the Ingleezee Khafir," carried a royal authorization from Queen Elizabeth I for negotiating English trading rights in Iran. This mission and subsequent attempts by the Muscovy Company (a.k.a., the Russia Company) to secure special trading privileges in Iran proved futile, as in the case of the delegations to the Afsharid court in Iran in the eighteenth century, led by the Englishmen John Elton and Jonas Hanway. In 1615, however, another private English chartered joint-stock company, the English East India Company (EIC, 1600), succeeded in acquiring trading privileges in southern Iran (Persian Gulf) from the Safavid ruler Shah Abbas I (r.1587–1629). This was accomplished through the intercession of the English brothers Robert and Anthony Sherley, who along with a number of other English adventurers had joined the military and diplomatic service of the Safavid court. In return for expanded operations in southern Iran and securing a special leverage in the Persian Gulf, in 1622 the EIC provided naval military assistance to the Safavid state for ending the Portuguese occupation of the island of Hormuz in the

Persian Gulf. Incidentally, the older brother of the two Sherleys who were then residing in Iran, Thomas Sherley, an MP and a military adventurer himself, had been knighted in 1589 by the Lord Deputy of Ireland William FitzWilliam for his service in Ireland.[2] The Safavid court dispatched its first diplomatic missions to England in the seventeenth century. In 1611, during the reign of the English Stuart monarch James I (James VI of Scotland), Robert Sherley arrived in England in pursuit of what proved to be an abortive attempt to secure English military assistance to Iran against the Ottomans. In 1625, during the reign of the English king Charles I, another Iranian diplomatic mission led by Naqd-Ali Beg arrived in England to again obtain English assistance against the Ottomans, and to arrange for overall Anglo-Iranian diplomatic and commercial cooperation. Naqd-Ali Beg was one of a number of Iranians to reach England in the seventeenth century, not counting other members of his delegation. After arriving in England, he famously engaged in a dispute with Robert Sherley, who happened to be in England again. Naqd-Ali Beg refuted Sherley's claim of once again serving as the Iranian ambassador to the English court. Ultimately, Naqd-Ali Beg's mission too failed to yield a desired outcome. However, Charles I dispatched Sir Dodmore Cotton as ambassador to Iran in 1626 in the joint company of Sherley and the ill-fated Naqd-Ali Beg. Cotton died of illness soon after arriving in Iran in 1628.[3] These early Anglo-Iranian contacts, no doubt provided at least Iranian courtiers and some other officials, if not also other Iranians dealing with the EIC and/or with the Sherleys, a modicum of general knowledge of Ireland (biased or otherwise).

With the violent collapse of the Safavid dynasty in 1722, following the Gilzai Afghan conquest of Safavid capital Isfahan, Iran was beset by regional power struggles and short-lived dynasties until the founding of the Qajar dynasty (1796–1925). It was at this juncture at the turn of the nineteenth century that Iran first featured as a major regional factor in the European balance of power. This occurred toward the end of the French Revolutionary Wars (1792–99) and the start of Napoleonic Wars (1799–1815), including Anglo-Russian rivalry in the region and British concern with the security of Britain's expanding Indian territories, as well as with British trade in the Indian Ocean and the Persian Gulf. Coinciding with these developments, Iran and Russia clashed militarily over Georgian territories from 1804 to 1813, with Russia annexing Georgia and then substantial Iranian territory in the Caucasus. As Iran rapidly gained prominence in the regional calculations of British India and London, the first British diplomatic mission to the Qajar court was dispatched (1799–1801), led by John Malcolm as the representative of the Governor-General of British India, Marquess Wellesley. Thereafter, Britain and Russia emerged as foremost European imperial players in Iranian affairs.

The Earliest First-Hand Persian-Language Accounts of Ireland

Based on the available information (memoirs, newspaper reports, published letters, census records, and so on), evidently only a handful of Iranians visited Ireland in the nineteenth century; none of them taking up long-term residence there. From the middle of the nineteenth century, modestly increasing number of Iranians traveled to England, compared to the earlier part of the century when such visits were uncommon and largely restricted to diplomatic missions and a small group of students dispatched by

Iranian government to study in England. With rare exceptions, throughout the nineteenth century these travelers did not venture into Ireland. As a result, well into the early twentieth century very few first-hand accounts of Ireland by Iranians were available to Iranian readers (with this readership itself representing a very small fraction of Iran's population, who were overwhelmingly illiterate). Of course, some Iranians acquainted with other languages could have had access to first-hand travel accounts of Ireland by authors from other territories.

The first published Persian-language personal account of travel through Ireland appeared outside Iran. This was the travelogue of Mirza Abu Taleb Khan Tabrizi-Isfahani (d.1805). A Muslim from Lucknow in British India of Iranian descent on his father's side, and an erstwhile employee of various Indian regional governments, Abu Taleb Khan visited Ireland at the turn of the nineteenth century on his way to mainland Britain. The manuscript of his travelogue, written in Persian (Persian being the dominant literary language in much of the Indian subcontinent at the time, as well as the language of official transactions in British India prior to the 1830s), first appeared in print in English translation in 1810, published in London in two volumes, long after Abu Taleb Khan had returned to India. Titled *The Travels of Mirza Abu Taleb Khan, in Asia, Africa and Europe, during the Years 1799, 1800, 1801, 1802, and 1803*, this translation was by Charles Stewart, an Irish-born employee of the East India Company, and an orientalist instructor at the company's college at Haileybury, Hertfordshire (England). The Persian edition of Abu Taleb Khan's book was published in India posthumously two years later as *Massir-e Tālebi* (a.k.a., *Massir-i Tālibi fi Bilād-i Afranji*).[4] This book is also noted for providing one the first Persian language descriptions of contemporary European theaters, including two Dublin "play-houses" visited by Abu Taleb Khan: the Crow Street Theatre (a.k.a., Theatre Royal) and Astley's Amphitheater.[5]

Abu Taleb Khan, who during his travels was designated in the European press as "the Persian traveller," arrived in Cork on December 6, 1799, and spent 40 days in Ireland before crossing over to Britain on January 16, 1800. In Ireland, he settled in Dublin, where the famed Indian Deen Mahomet happened to be living at the time, although they appear to have kept their distance from each other.[6] Abu Taleb Khan, whose Irish contacts consisted of the wealthier classes in Dublin, and chiefly members of the Anglican Ascendancy, described his stay in Ireland as most delightful: "In the course of my whole life, never spent my time so agreeably." Evidently prior to his arrival in Ireland he had acquired prejudicial views of the Irish from his British acquaintances in the Indian subcontinent, and/or on board the ship during his voyage to Ireland as he claimed—his closest British friend was the Scottish captain David Richardson of the English East India Company, whom Abu Taleb Khan had accompanied on this journey. In his travelogue, Abu Taleb Khan characterized the Irish people as affable and kind, noting, "It affords me much satisfaction, thus to record the amiable qualities of the Irish; as previous to my landing I had conceived strong prejudices against them, in consequence of the misrepresentation of some of the passengers on board our ship, who had described them as rude, irascible, and savage." He nevertheless regarded Irish men as prone to excessive drinking. Abu Taleb Khan also remarked that the majority Catholic population of Ireland "are not so intolerant as the English, neither have they the austerity and bigotry of the Scotch" in religious principles.⁷ He noted the wretched conditions of the Irish peasantry ("the peasants of India are rich when compared to them"), pointing out also the heavy reliance of peasants on the potato crop for subsistence, despite the land being "well cultivated, and very fertile." He wrote that Ireland produced "great quantities of wheat, barley, peas, turnips, and, above all, potatoes," while "Rice, both of Bengal and America, is procurable every where [sic], though at a high price."⁸ Interestingly, the *Dublin Penny Journal* in its first year of publication in 1832 would rely almost entirely on Abu Taleb Khan's account in an entry under the "The Irish." The entry read: "Abu Taleb, the Persian traveller, whose remarks on national characteristics are generally distinguished by no small degree of discrimination, is of opinion that in 'bravery and determination, hospitality and prodigality, freedom of speech, and open heartedness, the Irish surpass the English and Scotch, but are deficient in prudence and sound judgment, though nevertheless witty and quick of comprehension.' Their great national defect, he allows, 'is excess in drinking.'"⁹ The *Dublin Penny Journal* was a self-avowedly nonsectarian and non-partisan weekly periodical with close ties to the Royal Irish Academy. On another occasion, also in 1832, the *Dublin Penny Journal* cited Abu Taleb Khan's travel narrative as an objective testament of Kilkenny's idyllic scenery: "The situation of Kilkenny is so beautiful, the views from the bridges so picturesque, and the air so clear and wholesome, that Mirza Abu [sic], the Persian [sic] nobleman, compared it to a paradise."¹⁰

In the first volume of Abu Taleb Khan's travelogue, there were only vague allusions to general political developments in Ireland, which could be of little value, if any, to readers unacquainted with Irish history, notably in the case of contemporary and later generations of Iranian readers who had access to the travelogue—although, Iranians residing in, or traveling to, India, where news of Irish developments circulated more widely in some venues, may have grasped some of the historical connotations of Abu Taleb Khan's statements. Abu Taleb Khan arrived in the British Isles during the ongoing French Revolutionary and Napoleonic wars, with Britain and France at war since 1793 (to which he alluded in passing). Significantly, he reached Ireland just over a year after the failed United Irishmen uprising with French assistance (May to September 1798). The 1801 Act of Union (creation of the United Kingdom) had not yet gone into effect, and by the time Abu Taleb Khan reached Dublin the Irish parliament (a.k.a., "Grattan's Parliament") was still in existence (until January 1800).¹¹ His references to Ireland's violent events of the previous year were extremely succinct, possibly a conscious decision so as not to cause offense to British authorities (in Britain and the Indian subcontinent) or to the Anglo-Irish Ascendancy who had hosted him during his stay in Ireland. The first of his references to the large-scale uprising of 1798 was in the context of his expressed eagerness to see Lord Cornwallis: "During my visit to Cork, I learned that Lord Cornwallis (late Governor of India), who was the representative of the King in this island, having quelled the rebellion which had disturbed this country for several years [sic], was settled in Dublin."¹² Charles Cornwallis had assumed the office of the Lord Lieutenant of Ireland in June 1798 in the midst of the uprising and just ahead of the Battle of Vinegar Hill and the gruesome atrocities committed by both revolutionary and government forces. Abu Taleb Khan's next mention of the uprising, which practically reduced the event to a personal insurrection by a member of the nobility aided by people beholden to him, occurred during his description of the titles of the nobility in the British Isles and the system of primogeniture:

> The title next in rank to Prince is Duke. Several of these Dukes are the King's sons [...]. Their property, contrary to the general custom of England, is not divided among the children, but goes to the eldest son. By this means, the wealth and influence of the family remain stationary; and, as they are always generous and liberal to their tenants, they acquire such a host of dependants [sic], that the Government has had frequent occasions to be jealous or distrustful of them. Thus, some years ago, a brother of the Duke of L-----r rebelled in Ireland against the King, and, having been joined by a great number of the Irish, very nearly effected a revolution in that kingdom. At length, however, by the great wisdom and military abilities of Lord C-----s, the rebels were vanquished, and Lord F-----d was taken prisoner.
> I had the honour of being acquainted with several of these Dukes.[13]

The above redacted names were respectively the Duke of Leinster (William Robert FitzGerald), whose younger brother "Lord F-----d" (Lord Edward FitzGerald) was a radical leader of the United Irishmen and was apprehended by the authorities during the uprising, dying in prison of a bullet wound and other injuries he had sustained during his capture. "Lord C-----s" was Lord Cornwallis. Not surprisingly, during his stay in Dublin Abu Taleb Khan met Charles Vallancey, who was present at a dinner reception hosted by the Duke of Leinster in Abu Taleb Khan's honor. Curiously, the passage refereeing to this meeting was excised in the original 1810 published English translation of Abu Taleb Khan's travelogue by Charles Stewart, but was included in the 1814 second edition of the same translation by Stewart and printed by the same publisher, which now appeared in three volumes in contrast to the original two volumes.[14] Abu Taleb Khan remarked: "I here had the pleasure of forming an acquaintance with General Vallanc[e]y, an officer of artillery, who, although of a remarkable short stature, had a most expanded heart[;] he was a great adept in acquiring languages, and was much delighted with the Hebrew, Arabic, and Persian dialects[;] he informed me, that there was a considerable analogy between the Hindoostany and Irish languages."[15] Unfortunately, it cannot be ascertained from this statement whether Vallancey had in fact acquired some command of Persian and Arabic languages by the time, or if he even exchanged a few words in either language with Abu Taleb Khan, who was conversant in both of those languages. Of course, to anyone unacquainted with Vallancey's broader theory of oriental origins of ancient Irish civilization, the above remark would not have inferred anything more than an implied linguistic affinity between the Irish language and Sanskrit or Persian, rather than conveying Vallancey's general theory at the time of the Iranian origin of Ireland's Gaelic population. Incidentally, at the Trinity College library Abu Taleb Khan "was much pleased to find [...] several Persian books; among which were two very elegant manuscript copies of the *Shahnameh* and the Five Poems of Nizamy."[16] *Shāhnāmeh* was one of the key sources cited in Irish antiquarian claims of Ireland's ancient ties to Iran, beginning with Vallancey's works.

In the second volume of the original 1810 English edition of Abu Taleb Khan's travelogue there was a more explicit reference to events of 1798 in Ireland, while underestimating London's grave concern over the crisis. However, there was a major conscious editorial modification of Abu Taleb Khan's wording in the English translation of the travelogue regarding the cause of that insurrection, which was now bizarrely characterized as having been motivated by purely religious factors. He commented on the French Revolutionary Wars and French attempts to draw Britain's attention away from the continental war, as in the case of the 1798 occupation of Egypt led by Napoleon (then still only a French General) and the alleged continued French threats posed to India—which also had served as a British pretext for waging war against Tipu Sultan of Mysore in 1790–92, before Britain formally went to war against revolutionary France. Abu Taleb Khan then stated that France had also sent forces to Ireland to abet an uprising against the English monarchy. Whereas in the Persian original, Abu Taleb Khan, albeit acknowledging the legitimacy of British rule in Ireland, remarked the rebellion in Ireland had been occasioned "not by a sympathy with France, but by a local dispute [with England dating back a] few hundred years,"[17] Stewart's English translation altered this to "on account of some religious differences":

> Although the French found themselves masters of the Continent, they durst not send an army to invade England, because of the superiority of the British navy: they therefore resolved, as they could not approach the stem or root of the tree, that they would endeavour to lop off the branches. They, in consequence, sent an army to take possession of and plunder Hanover. They also sent an army to assist the disaffected party in Ireland, who, on account of some religious differences, and the intrigues of the French, have frequently rebelled against their legitimate Sovereign.
>
> [...]
>
> These schemes were quickly discovered by English, who, trusting to the superiority their navy, were not at all alarmed by these undertakings of the enemy. They, in the first place, easily defeated the army sent to Ireland; and, having subdued the rebellion in that country, they despatched [sic] a fleet in pursuit of Bonaparte.[18]

In effect, readers of the published original Persian travelogue should have gotten at least a vague hint of an enduring discord between England and some of Ireland's population.

The first recorded traveler from Iran itself to reach Ireland was Mirza Abul Hassan Khan Shirazi in 1819, during his second mission as the special Iranian representative to England. Thomas Moore's 1817 *Lalla Rookh* was published between Mirza Abul Hassan Khan's two journeys to England in 1809–10 and 1819–20, respectively during the reigns of George III and George IV. These visits by Abul Hassan Khan, better known as "Ilchi" (the Envoy), helped pique public curiosity about Iran in the United Kingdom.[19] As already noted (see Chapter Two), Abul Hassan Khan, whose visits generated much public and press fascination—also on account of his female companion during his stay in England on the second trip, who was dubbed by the British press as the legendary "Fair Circassian"—became the subject of some contemporary European and American satirists. The most famous example was that of the British diplomat and author James Justinian Morier's lampooning of Iranians and Iranian cultural mores in his highly popular works of fiction:

The Adventures of Hajji Baba of Ispahan (1824) and its somewhat lesser acclaimed sequel *The Adventures of Hajji Baba, of Ispahan, in England* (1828). Greater space was devoted to Abul Hassan Khan in the latter work in the form of the absurdities of "Mirza Firouz."[20] Morier, who had served as the secretary to the British representative in Iran from 1808 to 1810, Sir Harford Jones (later Jones Brydges), personally knew Abul Hassan Khan and had accompanied him from Iran during the latter's first visit to England. Other examples of Abul Hassan Khan's literary incarnations in the United Kingdom included a biographical account of him, accompanied with a portrait, and followed by a spoof "Genuine Letter" allegedly written by Abul Hassan Khan in broken English, appearing in the June 1810 issue of *The European Magazine and London Review* and reproduced in other publications in the same year, including in the United States, as in the case of the Philadelphia *Select Reviews, and Spirit of the Foreign Magazines*.[21] This was most likely authored by Morier, portending the fabricated, but avowedly authentic, letter attributed to Abul Hassan Khan in Morier's *The Adventures of Hajji Baba, of Ispahan, in England*, which was written in a comical language akin to Rudyard Kipling's future ascription of derisory pidgin English to his Indian characters. Similar jocular representations of Abul Hassan Khan appeared during his second visit to the United Kingdom in 1819–20.[22]

Surprisingly ignored by historians and other commentators today, during his second mission to England Abul Hassan Khan also sojourned in Ireland, following a tour of Scotland.[23] Abul Hassan Khan's visit to Ireland stimulated a great deal of public interest, with some long-lasting personal impressions. Thomas Moore, who had been living in England for many years by the time of Abul Hassan Khan's second visit to the United Kingdom, was at the time residing in France and traveling through continental Europe. Unfortunately, we also do not know what the 16-year-old James Clarence Mangan made of the Iranian who visited his hometown of Dublin. But, according to various early sources, which may merely have been repeating an apocryphal story, Abul Hassan Khan during his visit to Dublin in November 1819 received a letter composed in Persian by the polyglot teenager William Rowan Hamilton, the future famed Irish mathematician and scientist, as well as a president of the Royal Irish Academy. Reportedly, in the letter the young Hamilton unsuccessfully requested an audience with the Iranian ambassador.[24] Among the many entertainments and receptions in Dublin, on November 19 Abul Hassan Khan attended a specially scheduled concert of songs at the Rotunda, performed by Clarinda Mary Byrne and other vocalists and composed by Charles Frederick Horn. The concert, evidently arranged following a special request by Abul Hassan Khan, also consisted of both Irish and "Persian" airs, including "The National Persian air, with appropriate words" by the renowned Anglo-Irish songwriter Samuel Lover, and "arranged for this occasion by Horn." The concert concluded with the finale chorus of "God Save the King."[25] In the public announcement for this concert, Abul Hassan Khan was inaccurately elevated to the status of a "prince," although it is unclear whether he was personally responsible for this appellation: "His Highness, Prince Mirza Abul Hassan Khan, the Persian Ambassador."[26] Abul Hassan Khan's attendance at the Crow Street Theatre in Dublin on November 20 for the performance of the play "The Gamester," by the early eighteenth-century English playwright Edward Moore (again reportedly staged at the special request of Abul Hassan Khan[27]), is said to have resulted in the second "largest sum ever received there for one stock performance," with Abul Hassan Khan himself, "in all his oriental magnificence,"[28] presumably the central attraction and main spectacle of the event. During the Crow Street play, there was also a musical performance of a "Grand March and Waltz" composed specifically for this event by the noted Irish composer William Michael Rooke (originally O'Rourke), called "Prince Mirza Abul Hassan Khan's March." The march was performed again at the Crow Street Theatre on the evening of November 23 in honor of the Iranian visitor, who was not in attendance on that later date.[29]

As a side note, in 1845 Abul Hassan Khan's made a fleeting appearance in the form of a recollection in *The Falcon Family; or, Young Ireland* by the Irish satirist and journalist Marmion Wilme ("Wilard") Savage. Appearing just as the Great Famine was casting its shadow over Ireland, this book was equally critical of what Savage regarded as extremist nationalist politics of the recently formed Young Ireland movement as well as the conceited callous range of English attitudes toward Ireland and the (Gaelic) Irish. The plot line displayed a degree of sympathy with O'Connell's early Catholic Relief campaign for the removal of remaining restrictions on Catholics in the United Kingdom, but not with O'Connell's Repeal movement for Ireland's self-government through the reinstitution of a separate Irish parliament (with equal political rights for Protestants and Catholics). Abul Hassan Khan appeared in a reminiscence of earlier times in the Falcon family's life and as having been smitten by the young English Miss Emily Falcon, now aged and with diminished charms. The Iranian Envoy had presented Miss Falcon a ring following her performance at a garden party of "a popular Italian air in a style which" Abul Hassan Khan reportedly "had not heard equaled in the gardens of Gul or the meadows of Cashmere."[30] This insipid reference to Abul Hassan Khan, indicative of the enduring public impression he had made during his stay in Ireland a quarter of a century earlier, was not the first fictional casting of the Iranian Envoy in quirky British or Irish romantic settings. Among other earlier works was the first volume of the jocular 1820 *The Orientalist, or Electioneering in Ireland; a Tale, by Myself* (appearing under the pseudonym "Myself" and vaguely attributed later to a "Mrs. Purcell"), which was published prior to the appearance of Morier's famous Hajji Baba sequels.[31] The plot of this book revolves around the India-born Stuart Jesswunt, of a Sikh mother and English father (the latter an officer in British India), "as he strives to win both the hand of Lady Eleanor, daughter of Irish absentee landlord Lord Clanroy, and the parliamentary seat incorporating the Clanroy's Irish estate at Glenarm Castle, North Antrim."[32] As also noted by Joseph Lennon, during Abul Hassan Khan's second journey to the United Kingdom there also appeared the "Dublin pamphlet, *The History of Mirza Abul Hassan Khan ... with Some Account of the Fair Circassian* (1819)." Lennon recounts that this pamphlet, written by an anonymous "Irish officer," "depicts the Persian ambassador to England on a visit to Ireland—which he admires and compares to Persia."[33] Lennon, who assumes Abul Hassan Khan did not visit Ireland, comments on this pamphlet by making an important observation central to the present study: "The link between the Irish and the Persian echoes the centuries-old Irish link to the Orient. Significantly, it is not a mere projection of Irish desires onto the Orient; it is reported as a mutually imagined link, similar to later cross-colony identifications between Irish and Asian writers and nationalists."[34] Yet, as suggested by the 'Fair Circassian' in the title of this pamphlet in reference to Abul Hassan Khan's female companion during his second visit to England, who generated much press chatter (there are no contemporary reports of her accompanying Abul Hassan Khan to Ireland), or by the particular casting of Abul Hassan Khan in the fictional works of the Irish novelists 'Mrs. Purcell' and Marmion Wilme Savage, it is evident the Iranian envoy was also saddled with a not too obscure idiom of cross-cultural (if not also cross-ethnic/racial) sexual desire and fantasy, often typical of the exoticizing trend in Western imaginations of the Orient.[35]

Abul Hassan Khan kept a diary of his first journey to England in 1809–10, at which time he did not visit Ireland. It is not known if he also kept a diary of his second journey to the United Kingdom, which included a tour of Ireland. As of yet, no such diary has surfaced; meaning that no Persian-language account of his stay in Ireland would have been available to Iranians. However, in the diary for his first trip to England in 1809–10, Abul Hassan Khan made some remarks about Ireland. He referred to Ireland as a constituent territory of "Great Britain" (i.e., here used as a shorthand for the United Kingdom). In an entry in the diary for March 11, 1810, he provided a brief account of England, Scotland, and Ireland (Wales was not mentioned), reportedly based on information gleaned from an encyclopedia or an almanac he evidently was given by the Anglo-Irish orientalist Sir Gore Ouseley (later the British representative to Iran), who was then living with Abul Hassan Khan and serving as his guide, while improving his own knowledge of conversational Persian and of Iran. The source of the information about Ireland consulted by Abul Hassan Khan was possibly the 1810 or another recent edition of the *Encyclopaedia Britannica*, notwithstanding the factual errors and the discrepancies appearing in his description of Ireland, Irish history, and the Irish population.[36] With his scant knowledge of English, Abul Hassan Khan would have relied on Ouseley's assistance for translating the text he was consulting for this entry in his diary, with Ouseley even possibly supplementing the textual information with his own descriptions of Ireland. In either case, there was clearly some miscommunication in translation and/or in Abul Hassan Khan's recording of the information, given some of his descriptions of Ireland and the Irish:

> The distance by sea of the isle of Ireland from England [i.e., Britain] is estimated at two hundred miles [sic]. [...] Its largest city, which is considered its capital, is "Dublin" [...] its population are martial ["*jangi*"] and brave, and three hundred years ago its king was defeated by the king of England [sic], and that island too came under English control[.] Nonetheless[,] as of ten years ago[,] Ireland had a parliament similar to that in London and its representatives attended the parliament, conducting the affairs of that island without following [sic] the legislation of the English [government]. Presently the parliament in Ireland is suspended and the representatives of the Irish people come to London at the start of the [parliamentary session] and consult with the authorities[,] barring those who object to this condition. The people of that land are tenacious and brave with no middle ground[;] they are either absolutely virtuous or absolutely dissolute. ... The people of Ireland have pleasing features [...][37]

In light of the frequent and continued denigration of the predominantly-Catholic population of Ireland in many late eighteenth and nineteenth-century British and Anglo-Irish

Protestant sources, it is noteworthy that Mirza Abul Hassan Khan did not differentiate among the Irish population based on religion or ethnicity, regardless of whether he cast them in a positive or a negative light. He also notably alluded to 'those who object to' the dissolution of the Irish parliament, even as he regarded Ireland as a land captured by England long ago and comprising part of England's provinces in the British Isles.

Another Iranian who left behind a record of his visit to Ireland was the famed late nineteenth/early twentieth-century Iranian traveler Mirza Mohammad Ali Mahallati (later "Haj Sayyah"—that is, *Hāji* the traveler, signifying his pilgrimage to Mecca and extensive travels to different lands). He visited Dublin, Cork, and Belfast sometime around late 1866 or in early 1867. Similar to Mirza Abu Taleb Khan, Sayyah too considered the Irish as "more lively and much kinder than the English," but he did not comment on Irish history or politics; only mentioning that Catholics formed the majority of the island's population and noting their alleged partiality toward French-speaking foreigners, while remarking on the general layout of the cities he visited, their primary production and occupations, as well as libraries and Trinity College (Dublin), among other places he toured during his short sojourn.[38] In Spring of 1893, another Iranian who recorded a travelogue, Hajji Mirza Mohammad-Ali "Mo'in al-Saltaneh", traveled to Ireland after visiting Britain and then proceeding to Ireland from Liverpool en route to the United States to attend the 1893 World's Columbian Exposition in Chicago. His published travelogue, however, is devoid of any description of his short stay in Ireland.[39] In the nineteenth century, with rare exceptions, Iranian travelers to European (not counting the Russian Caucasus or European provinces of the Ottoman Empire) or to other destinations besides the predominantly Muslim territories or the Indian subcontinent were men; the majority of rare exceptions to this rule being members of Iran's non-Muslim religious minority communities. The first Iranian thus far known to have married an Irish individual was Hussein Qoli Khan Navab, who in August 1913 married the Irish-Catholic Eileen Rainey in Aghada, County Cork (see Chapter Seven). Navab, a secular reformer and Social Democrat at the time, of a Shi'i Muslim background, had served as the Iranian foreign minister during the latter part of the Constitutional Revolution, with prior diplomatic service, including as an interpreter at the Iranian legation in London.[40]

Although the rare nineteenth century first-hand Iranian commentaries on Ireland and on the Irish entailed degrees of sympathy toward the Irish in general, and even occasional remarks on contemporary cultural resemblances, Ireland largely remained an obscure geographic and political zone for Iranians (of the educated classes) until the twentieth century.

Provincializing of Ireland in Iranian Historical Imaginations Prior to 1916

In the context of Irish history, the phrase "provincializing Ireland," with multiple connotations, long pre-dated the (re)inception of the concept following the emergence of colonial/postcolonial studies in the latter decades of the twentieth century. For example, the prominent Irish author John Banim in his anonymously published 1828 nationalist novel, *The Anglo-Irish of the Nineteenth Century*, inserted the following passage into a conversation concerning the "Anglo-Irish":

> Descendants of colonists, English and Scotch, whom to this day, in addresses presented to the throne, call themselves colonists, and decline the name of Irishmen—these, in the first instance; next descendants of colonists, who openly advocate or encourage anti-Irish measures of any kind.
>
> 'Your English-Irish, in fact,' commented Gerald.
>
> Even so, if you like the phrase; for I certainly do mean all persons who would strive to make Ireland English; and lastly, I mean all pretended English-Irish friends of the people, who, to carry a county, or a town, or, perhaps, with a commendable foresight towards cherishing their Irish estates, (though I pronounce them in no danger,) give a vote, now and then, upon the great wrangling question, (as you would throw a piece of bread to a hungry mastiff, or to a critic, merely to pass him by,) and afterwards zealously, though perhaps covertly, engage in one or all of the absurd schemes for *provincializing Ireland*: such as converting, transporting, or unhousing a million at a time of her population. Long ago, Sir, such half measures, and such half Irishmen, might have succeeded in recommending themselves to our generous credulity; but even the burnt child now teaches us a lesson.[41] (Emphasis added.)

Even more directly germane to the particular application of 'provincializing Ireland' as I intend the concept here was the use of the term by Young Ireland's Thomas Osborne Davis in his poem "A Nation Once Again," composed sometime in the early 1840s, as already noted: "And Ireland long a province be / A nation once again." Similarly, the Irish nationalist John Cornelius O'Callaghan in his 1845 *The Green Book* made use of the phrase under the Index heading for "Volunteers, Irish," and in reference to the 1801 Act of Union, which he condemned: "Ingratitude of England, in provincializing Ireland by the Union, notwithstanding the preservation of the connection between the two islands by the Volunteers, illustrated by an anecdote from Inglis's tour in the Tyrol." In O'Callaghan's estimation, the Act of Union had reduced Ireland to the status of a "Mameluke medium of a numerically-insignificant, contemptibly-bigoted, shamelessly-antinational, individually-rapacious and collectively-odious aristocracy," which "can not [*sic*], and, what is more, ought not, to last."[42] He was using the Arabic term 'Mameluke' (*mamluk*/enslaved) that referred to territories governed originally by enslaved military and administrative personnel of Muslim sultans, with these enslaved groups or their descendants at times establishing their own dynastic rule. In an alternative simile of "slavery," Daniel O'Connell had earlier likened Ireland's status under the Act of Union to that of a slave of the English slave master. O'Connell incidentally preferred to describe Ireland's status as that of a British 'province,' rather than a 'colony.'[43] Among many other examples, the Irish Parliamentary Party leader Charles Stewart Parnell during an 1875 speech in the House of Commons similarly condemned the treatment of Ireland as "a geographical fragment of England."[44] In his 1904 *Ireland: The People's History of Ireland*, John Frederick Finerty, the Irish-American Irish nationalist and president of the "Parnellite" United Irish League of America, dated the 'provincializing' of Ireland to the reign of Queen Elizabeth I and the reappointment in 1588 of

Sir William FitzWilliam as the Lord Deputy of Ireland. Blaming the queen's policy and FitzWilliam's appointment for developments leading to the outbreak of the "Nine Years' War" of 1594–1603 (also known as the failed "Tyrone's Rebellion") and the subsequent "Flight of the Earls" in 1607, Finerty wrote: "In a word, the recall of Lord Fitzwilliam was the first step in the direction of provincializing Ireland."[45]

There were, of course, major differences among Irish nationalists on whether their particular brand of nationalism should *deprovincialize* Ireland through the creation of a separate nation-state or by means of re-establishing a self-governing territory within the British Empire under the ultimate jurisdiction of London. At the heart of these disputes among Irish nationalists was the acceptance or rejection of Ireland's continued existence as a constituent part of the British Empire. Writing from self-imposed exile in New York in 1894, Patrick Tynan, a member of the militant republican Irish National Invincibles (an extremist group that had split from the Irish Republican Brotherhood), alleged the Home Rulers were mere "Provincialists" in the Irish struggle. He characterized Daniel O'Connell (d.1847) as the architect of Home Rule provincialism. Ironically, in light of O'Connell's own earlier analogy of slavery in describing London's direct rule over Ireland and O'Connell's renown as an opponent of the system of 'African slavery,' Tynan stated:

> After the death of Emmet, there came upon the scene a great Irishman, a giant in intellect and physique, and one of the most brilliant and gifted orators the Irish nation has produced. [...] He could master and control the Irish heart, as the great master Mozart inspired the organ. [...]
>
> And yet this man, with almost godlike genius and gifts, inherited to the full, the slavish curse of generations. His soul was steeped in slavery. Slavery circulated in his veins. Slavery haunted his noblest aspirations. He not only bowed down before the British Gessler's cap; he abased himself before that foreign symbol. He ate dirt, and beslavered [*sic*] himself with ashes, in the presence of the invader's insignia. His most exalted ambition for his nation, was that she should be enslaved with chains of gold; or, as he termed it, be fastened to the robber's rule by "the golden link of the Crown." The flag of Britain, which in Ireland is a pirate's banner, he recognised as his country's standard. The illegal measures passed by an alien assembly, he recognised as law; and told his unhappy enslaved countrymen that he could, at his pleasure drive a coach and six through any Act of the British Parliament. [...]
>
> [...] He was the father of the modern school of political thought in Ireland; the creator of that abnormal movement in the history of nations which Nationalists [i.e., republicans] call Provincialism, and Provincialists, "constitutional agitation."[46]

Whether Ireland was considered a colony, a country, or a territory, what was undeniable from the perspective all Irish nationalist platforms was the *double* provincialization of Ireland following the 1801 Act of Union, inaugurating direct "English" ascendancy over Ireland through the formal abrogation of a separate Irish parliament, which assigned Ireland an even lesser subordinate and peripheral status in what became the United Kingdom and, by implication, also in the British Empire—even if others could counter this view by claiming that Ireland's direct representation in the Westminster parliament in London in fact in some ways privileged Ireland as an English territorial possession. The Act of Union stripped Ireland of its former status under the designation of "The Kingdom of Great Britain and the Kingdom of Ireland." The latter Kingdom was ruled indirectly from London between 1542 and 1800—not forgetting, of course, that Ireland had not constituted a single unified territory prior to the gradual Anglo-Norman domination after the twelfth century, and that it was English rule over the island that subsequently created a unified ('national'-) territorial entity called Ireland, similar to English domination of the Indian subcontinent. In 1801 England, which already held the center of executive power in Ireland, deprived Ireland of its own separate legislative parliament that had existed in different forms since 1264, leaving aside here the various ethnically and/or religiously exclusionary policies of the Irish parliaments prior to 1800. The English double provincialization of Ireland in 1801, initially in the form of occupying/colonizing of Ireland after the twelfth century and now by means of annulling Ireland's internal administrative institution in Dublin, deprived Ireland of its special standing as an English-ruled territory in the British Isles. After 1801 Ireland was directly represented at the parliament in London, just as Wales and Scotland had been since much earlier times. It now enjoyed far less autonomy than before, not the least in comparison with the much smaller Crown Dependencies of the Isle of Man or the Channel Islands. Viewed from outside the United Kingdom, too, the Act of Union by implication further marginalized both Ireland's political standing in the British Isles and many other things 'Irish.' This was true also of the status of Dublin as the capital of the island.

Ireland's post-1801 'provincialized' status vis-à-vis England in the United Kingdom and in the British Empire was an indisputable factor shaping the collective Iranian perspective of Ireland (among better informed Iranians) from the start of the nineteenth century to 1916; not forgetting that any, at best negligible, prior Iranian familiarity with Ireland would already have contemplated the territory as a province of the English crown, whether regarded as colony or as some sort of a self-administering province. By the time Iranians first came into direct contact with England as a major European power during the reign of the English monarch Elizabeth I—in the form of Anthony Jenkinson's failed 1562–63 commercial and diplomatic mission to Safavid Iran and the later commercial, diplomatic, and military contacts between Iran and the English East India Company—Ireland was already accessed and processed in the Iranian imagination through the medium of England in some form. This was in marked contrast to Iranian interactions with, and imaginations of, territories in the Indian subcontinent before and after 1757 or of Egypt before and after 1882. Moreover, at least since the publication of the English antiquarian William Camden's *Britannia* in 1586 and John Speed's 1612 map, called the "Theatre of the Empire of Great Britaine," Ireland in its entirety was situated in standard English historical, geographical, and cartographic productions within the domain of 'English' territories in the British Isles; even if in actuality it took a few more decades after Camden's book for all of Ireland to be brought under England's firm control[47]—notwithstanding the fact that Camden, along with Edmund Spenser and many other English contemporaries who followed suit, drew a clear line of ethnic, cultural, religious, and inner-geographic demarcation between so-called indigenous 'wild Irish' and the 'English-Irish.' In 1833 Sir Harford Jones Brydges' *The Dynasty of the Kajars* was published, being a translation from Persian of the earlier and longer manuscript draft (1811) of Abdul-Razzaq Beg Donboli's *Ma'āsser-e Sultāniyeh* (*Royal Memorials*, published in 1826), which had been presented to Jones Brydges by the Iranian government shortly prior to his departure from Iran as the British representative to that country (1808–11). Jones Brydges quoted the following statement from his Iranian source: "At the present date, the provinces belonging to the English in Hindustan [i.e., India] are more numerous and extensive than the countries they possess in Aroopa (*i.e.* Europe), and the island of Irlandah (Ireland), which was under their sway before these events: therefore we may truly say they have added kingdoms to their kingdom." In a footnote referring to Ireland in this quoted text, Jones Brydges crudely remarked: "I am afraid I must admit the Persians to be not far advanced in geographical knowledge." Presumably he misunderstood the Iranian source as implying that Ireland was not situated in Europe.[48] The point, however, is that the Iranian source considered Ireland as part of the English domain (a single "kingdom"), similar to Wales and Scotland.

This is not to suggest that Iranians who followed news of developments around the world during the period under examination were entirely ignorant of all internal developments in Ireland as well as of the uprisings in Ireland against English rule and of the existence of Irish nationalism. As discussed below, by the latter decades of the nineteenth century some literate Iranians would be able to read about such subjects in Persian-language sources available inside Iran. Yet, the available evidence indicates that until the 1916 Easter Rising—by which time some Iranian nationalist groups were fighting British forces with German (and/or Ottoman) backing—Iranian observers generally considered Irish political matters as *internal* provincial affairs of an English-ruled realm in the British Isles, similar to developments in Scotland and Wales at the time, as opposed to challenges posed to English hegemony in the Indian subcontinent or in other parts of the British Empire during the same time period. Among many other factors (not the least being the geographic proximity of Ireland to Britain), Ireland's incorporation into the United Kingdom in 1801 and its parliamentary representation in London after that date (with propertied adult male Irish Catholics, along with other propertied adult male Catholics in the United Kingdom, also allowed to hold seats in the Westminster parliament after 1829), as well as the subsequent presence of Repeal (Home Rule) Irish MPs in the British parliament, also set Ireland apart from England's other colonies in Iranian perspective. From this vantage point, the very notion of demanding self-government as a semi-autonomous domain of England's territorial possessions in the British Isles, through the mechanism of "British" electoral process no less, further fortified Ireland's provincial, as opposed to colonial, status in Iranian estimation. The view of Ireland as an English-controlled province (similar to Scotland and Wales) and with a territorial standing distinct from England's other colonies is further corroborated from the absence of any distinction made in contemporary Iranian sources between Irish and other British imperial military personnel. Examples include general Iranian references to British consular guards stationed in Iran or to soldiers participating in British armed operations in southern Iran on a few occasions after 1838. In these cases, no distinction was made between Irish and other 'British' forces, who were uniformly designated 'British,' in contradistinction to Indian sepoys and sowars serving in the same British armed forces, who were regularly identified in the same Iranian sources as "Indians." This is not to deny that on occasion Iranian sources mentioning certain individual British officials or military and other personnel, such as John Malcolm or Marquess Wellesley (Richard Colley Wellesley), did not allude to these individuals being natives of Scotland or Ireland. For instance, in his 1826 *Ma'āsser-e Sultāniyeh* (*Royal Memorials*), the Iranian historian Abdul-Razzaq Beg Donboli described Wellesley as "the former governor-general of India [...] who has attained ministerial position" (i.e., Lord Lieutenant of Ireland, 1821–28), adding: "Marquess Lord Wellesley is from the domain of Ireland and of the nobility of that land[,] and [of] old and prominent lineage[,] and was among members of the English parliament" (i.e., a member of the House of Commons from 1784 to 1797).[49]

Iranian Geographical Knowledge of Ireland Prior to 1916

Ireland's first recorded appearance on surviving so-called medieval world maps produced in Muslim-controlled territories dated back to the twelfth century, by which time 'Iran' (in its broad territorial definition) had been absorbed into Muslim-dominated lands (after the seventh century). The Irish-American militant nationalist James Kennedy McGuire, for example, noted in his 1916 *What Could Germany Do for Ireland?* that long ago "in far-away Arabia, too, our country was known as 'Irandah-al-Kaberah' (Ireland the Great)."[50] What McGuire was clumsily referring to was the geographic identification of *"irlandah al-kabirah"* on the twelfth-century map produced by the renowned Moroccan geographer Abu Abdullah Muhammad al-Idrisi. The first drafting of this map, which had long been well-known in European cartographic circles, dated to 1154 CE, prior to the earliest Norman conquests in Ireland in 1171.[51] Given al-Idrissi's imprecise positioning of 'Ireland the Great,' some sources since the nineteenth century have fabulously postulated the improbable idea that he was in fact referring to the American continents, with which the Norse had made contact by that time.[52] It should not be forgotten that geographers in "medieval" Muslim-controlled territories had access to ancient Hellenic and Roman sources (including Ptolemaic sources from Roman-controlled Egypt), a few of which contained minimal and confused references to Ireland. Moreover, there were substantial cartographic exchanges within the Muslim-ruled territories and between these territories and Christian Europe from the 'Middle Ages' on, including the mutual flow of information between the predominantly Muslim lands to the East and in North Africa and the Muslim-controlled lands in the Iberian Peninsula from 711 to 1492, as well as between Muslim-ruled Iberian territories and the rest of Europe, which also expedited Europe's Scholasticism and "Renaissance."[53] Similarly, by the twelfth century there were contacts between the Norse and Muslim-controlled territories, with the Norse having ample knowledge of at least the Eastern shores of Ireland.[54] Ireland again appeared on another widely reproduced 'medieval' map in the thirteenth century by the Persian geographer Zakaria ibn Mohammad Qazvini in the Ilkhanid Mongol-controlled former Abbasid territories (the latter itself including former Iranian lands).[55] Among other cursory medieval references to Ireland with which a fraction of the educated population of 'Iranian' territories would have been familiar, was the early fourteenth-century mention of Ireland in the multi-volume world history *Jāmi' al-Tawārikh* (*Compendium of Histories*, 1306–11) by the Persian historian Rashid al-Din of Hamedan, working under Ilkhanid Mongol patronage, considered to be the first significant Persian-language attempt at writing the history of the known world. Obviously indirectly drawing on older Latin sources (most likely pre-twelfth century CE), according to Rashid al-Din, whose description of other lands was of the fabulous quality of the Age (including in Europe and elsewhere), in the vicinity of Portugal and Spain (i.e., to the north) were situated two islands, (the smaller) one named Hibernia and the other England. Reportedly, a property of Hibernia's soil was that venomous creatures could not survive and mice could not be born there. People there lived long lives, had rosy features, strong upper bodies, and were of heroic built. Moreover, in Hibernia there existed a spring into which if a piece of wood was placed the wood would turn to stone within a week.[56]

Even though by the nineteenth century Iran lagged behind the West/Europe in cartographic techniques, with the trend continuing well into the twentieth century, Iranian geographers in the nineteenth century relied on a wide spectrum of contemporary cartographic knowledge and descriptive geographies of the world, ranging from European works to Indian, Ottoman, or Egyptian sources, with the latter sources themselves heavily reliant on European world mapping and geographic accounts.[57] Hence, as the nineteenth century progressed greater cartographic and historical knowledge of Ireland become available inside Iran, and literate Iranians interested in world events had increasing access to a broad range of geographical and historical descriptions of Ireland. Informed Iranians' knowledge of world geography and history in the nineteenth century underwent a drastic refinement. Among the many contributing factors during the century were Iran's entanglement in European imperial rivalries in the region, the expanded Western/European diplomatic and commercial presence in Iran and Iran's correspondingly expanded diplomatic presence in Western/European countries among some other parts of the world, as well as the gradually growing number of European and American travelers to Iran during the century, including Christian missionaries, who also founded schools with curricula that on occasion included basic information about the West/Europe alongside other regions of the globe. There was also increased Iranian travel to the West/Europe, particularly after the middle of the century, which also resulted in the occasional publication of travelogues. These Iranian travelers included a small number (but gradually increasing) of Iranians studying in Western/European countries, notably after the latter decades of the century. By the latter part of the century, there were also multiplying Persian translations of wide-ranging body of texts originally published in European languages, including works of history, biographies of "great men," and works of fiction. The founding of Iran's first modern institution of higher learning in 1851, and such other diverse range of developments as the rapidly expanding world trade and other globalization processes, including scientific, literary, and other forms of knowledge exchange, also led to greater Iranian familiarity with the West/Europe and with some other regions of the world.[58]

So far as the dissemination of textual knowledge about Ireland is concerned, the development of the printing press in Iran was a delayed phenomenon (without my wishing to suggest any requisite timeline by which certain technologies should be adopted in different societies). The introduction of the printing press in Iran largely dated to the nineteenth century and, even then, it was a piecemeal process. There had been much earlier fleeting experimentations with the printing press in Iran during the seventeenth century, in both Persian and Armenian languages.[59] The first Persian-language newspaper published inside Iran was the monthly state-owned *Kāqaz-e Akhbār* (literally *News Paper*;

Tehran, 1837–40?), even though earlier Persian language newspapers had appeared in the Indian subcontinent, primarily aimed at Indian readership, given that Persian at the time was a common medium of education and until the mid-1830s also the language of official correspondence in many parts of the Indian subcontinent. The next Persian-language newspaper published inside Iran, the state-owned *Rouznāmeh-ye Vaqāye'-e Ettefāqiyeh* (*Current Events Newsletter*) did not appear until 1851. Certainly, more limited and dated textual information about world events had appeared in Iran in copied hand-written manuscript form long before the introduction of the printing press and newspapers. But, it was with the publication of *Rouznāmeh-ye Vaqāye'-e Ettefāqiyeh* that occasional news of *contemporary* developments in Ireland became more widely available inside Iran. *Rouznāmeh-ye Vaqāye'-e Ettefāqiyeh*, published until 1860, carried regular reports of major international political and commercial events as well as sensational trivia, and included periodic synopses of main items of discussion in the British parliament. In the latter decades of the century, occasional reports of Irish developments appeared in the small number of Iranian newspapers, whether state-owned or privately-owned (both types subject to state censorship regulations). The number of Iranian newspapers and periodicals rapidly multiplied following the outbreak of the Constitutional Revolution in 1906.[60]

After the first decades of the nineteenth century, there were also Persian-language newspapers and books published by Indians and Iranians in the Indian subcontinent or by Iranians residing in the Ottoman Empire or in Egypt. These too often included periodic coverage of events related to Ireland. Most of these printed sources, just as those published inside Iran, acquired their information about contemporary Irish developments from reports originally appearing in European newspapers and periodicals, barring rare eyewitness accounts by travelers to or from Ireland or by means of diplomatic channels, and so on. In addition, information about Ireland and the Irish diaspora also occasionally appeared in books published in Iran, as well as in books printed outside Iran, whether in Persian language or in other languages that were accessible to those Iranians conversant in any of those languages, most notably Arabic, Turkish, and increasingly also French, and to a much lesser degree at the time English, German, or Russian. Most educated Iranians (whether receiving so-called traditional or modern education) had degrees of fluency in Arabic, while for the much smaller number of Iranian speakers of European languages, primarily after the second half of the nineteenth century, French constituted the preferred European literary and diplomatic medium; French also being the diplomatic European/Western lingua franca of the period. By the late nineteenth century, with the emergence of the Azeri-Turkish press in the Russian Caucasus following the publication in 1875 of the short-lived *Akinchi*, that incorporated information gleaned from Russian and other sources, yet another avenue of printed information became available for some Iranian readers. Turkish sources in Azeri, as well as in Ottoman Turkish, were accessible to literate Iranians of Turkic ethnicities, with different dialects of that language spoken by a substantial portion of Iran's populations. There were also members of other Iranian ethnic groups who for various reasons, including commerce, had acquired knowledge of at least spoken Turkish language (with both Azeri and Ottoman Turkish then appearing in print in the familiar Arabic script, similar to Persian). As in other parts of the world, books and newspapers often switched hands in Iran, particularly those that were rare and or expensive to purchase. And, lastly, it is important not to forget the role of oral transmission of knowledge, including information in newspapers and books (printed or otherwise) that were read to those who lacked literacy or simply lacked reading proficiency in the language in which the written information appeared.

The most salient developments in the Iranian genre of world geography, as well as in cartographic expertise and reproduction technology, occurred in the second half of the nineteenth century. This also included the availability of the most accurate latest mapping and topographical descriptions of Ireland in Iranian world maps by the late nineteenth century; not forgetting the prior and contemporary availability of maps (re-)produced outside Iran that were also available to an even more limited circle of educated Iranians inside and outside Iran (the latter including Iranian travelers, diplomatic staff, and members of émigré communities). Geography also emerged as one of the *main* subjects taught at Iran's first (state-founded) modern institutions of higher learning staffed by both Iranian and international instructors: Dar al-Fonun (1851) and the School of Political Science (1899).[61] The Qajar monarch Nasser al-Din Shah, a number of princes, and various government officials in different parts of the country, were among patrons of expanded Iranian geographic knowledge of the world. By the end of the nineteenth century, many privately founded schools with modern curricula, primarily for boys, whether run by Iranians of various ethnoreligious backgrounds or by Western Christian missionaries, also promoted greater geographical knowledge of the world.[62] The earliest of Iranian cartographic representations and descriptive geographic accounts of the world in keeping with the latest contemporary standards in the West appeared around the middle of the nineteenth century. These works, at first mostly translations of European publications infused with additional details about Iran by their compilers, included the 1847 *"World Geography"* (Persian title unknown) by the English Edward Burgess, a long-time resident in Iran serving as a royal translator and, later, the first editor of the official newspaper *Rouznāmeh-ye Vaqāye'-e Ettefāqiyeh* (founded in 1851) and, hence, effectively also the state press censor. Burgess' *World Geography*, compiled in Tabriz at the request of the Iranian prince Bahram Mirza, was based on a "Turkish work [...] written above a hundred years ago, but [...] a good work, and [corrected] with the most modern Gazetteers I can find."[63] Another such world geography compendium was the 1851 *Jahān-namā* (*Display of the World*) by a Mr. "Raphael" ("Fologun Refayel"), who described himself as an "English national" or "English subject" residing in Tabriz and employed by the provincial authorities in Azerbaijan; Tabriz serving as the seat of Qajar crown princes.[64] These and subsequent geographical works and world maps, which adhered to the latest standards of the time, firmly located Ireland as one of the main constituent territories of the English realm, distinct from the many other English-controlled islands or English colonies and later protectorates around the world. While the 1922 edition of *A Catalogue of the Persian Printed Books in the British Museum* identifies Raphael's *Jahān-namā* as "A geography, compiled from English works at the request of the Shah," according to Raphael himself the Persian translation was based on (an unidentified) original French source.[65] The French work must have been published at least after 1835. Its brief description of Ireland included the existence of railroads across the island.⁶⁶ The first passenger railroad in Ireland was the Dublin line that began operation in December 1834.

The most detailed *historical*-geographical account of Ireland in a nineteenth-century Iranian publication appeared as two chapter entries in the 1856 Persian translation of a work by the English William Pinnock (d.1843). This translation, by the Qajar prince Farhad Mirza ("Nayeb al-Eyaleh"; later "Mo'tamed al-Dowleh") was in fact a revised and updated translation of the original English text by way of consulting more contemporary sources, among them European newspapers, and included the translator's own (clearly identified) amended notes throughout.⁶⁷ In this amended translation, titled *Jām-e Jam* ("World-Revealing Chalice"; referring to the mythological ancient Iranian cup of divination possessed by the Pishdādiān ruler Jamshid), Farhad Mirza identified his original source as Pinnock's *Modern Geography and History*.⁶⁸ This was Pinnock's *A Comprehensive Grammar of Modern Geography and History; for the Use of Schools and for Private Tuition*, first published in 1830 (London: Poole and Edwards). It was the 1834, second and vastly expanded, edition of Pinnock's book (London: Holdsworth & Ball) that Farhad Mirza translated, which, similar to the first edition, included maps and illustrations, only one of which was reproduced in Farhad Mirza's *Jām-e Jam* along with a few simple illustrations added by Farhad Mirza himself.⁶⁹ Farhad Mirza also added his own tables of information throughout. Primarily targeting a younger student readership, *A Comprehensive Grammar of Modern Geography and History* was also comprehensive in its survey of the disciplines of geography (including historical and political geography), cartography, climatology, and so on, as well as the topic of the evolution of the science of geography since ancient times. It was also relatively detailed in its coverage of many regions of the world. Missing from *Jām-e Jam* were the original "Questions for Examination" at the end of each chapter in Pinnock's book. Pinnock was a former schoolmaster-turned-publisher and compiler of highly popular and frequently reprinted school texts on a wide range of historical, geographical, religious, scientific, and other educational subjects in the form of "catechisms," including incidentally an 1825 school text on the history of Ireland (*A Catechism of the History of Ireland*). In *A Comprehensive Grammar of Modern Geography and History*, the two short chapters on Ireland ("Ireland" and "Historical Memoranda of Ireland"), followed chapter entries on England, Wales, and Scotland. Whereas these entries on Ireland in Pinnock's book constituted chapters 82 and 83, they appeared in Farhad Mirza's translation as chapters 83 and 84. This discrepancy was due to the fact that, while in Pinnock's book only two chapters were devoted to Russia, Farhad Mirza's amended translation included an extra entry on Russia (given the importance of Russia as Iran's northern neighbor and their commercial ties, the vast annexation of Iranian territory by Russia in two wars between 1804 and 1828, as well as Russia's continued imperial intervention in Iranian affairs, along with Britain). The first entry on Ireland commenced with a general geographical description of Ireland and its major cities and their population, with Farhad Mirza updating some of the information intermittently. For instance, in Pinnock's book (1834) Dublin's population was listed as "about 200,000," but Farhad Mirza noted: "According to the translator[,] the population of Dublin is now above two hundred and ten thousand" (in actuality it would have been closer to 250,000). It should be remembered Farhad Mirza was providing the population of the city following the Great Famine of 1845–1851, which, despite the ravages of the famine and large-scale emigration from Ireland, had nonetheless increased due to internal population migrations from rural areas to towns and cities during the famine and subsequently, not counting new births in the city since the famine and other factors. Farhad Mirza also repeated the original statement by Pinnock that Dublin as a city "ranks the second in the British dominions" (i.e., after London).[70] The entry also described Ireland's climate. It listed a few renowned natives of Dublin and Galway, including Sir Philip Francis (born in Dublin in 1740 and believed to be the author of *Junius*, among other works) and Richard Brinsley Sheridan (born in Dublin in 1751 and best known for his *School for Scandal*), with Farhad Mirza ('According to the translator') briefly elaborating on the plotline of these books, among his other elucidations throughout this entry and in the remainder of the book.[71] (Incidentally, Pinnock's contemporary Irish poet Thomas Moore was missing from this slender shortlist of famous Dubliners.)

There are occasional omissions in Farhad Mirza's amended translation. Although it is unclear whether the missing information simply skipped his attention or was considered repetitious or trivial. For example, the following remark by Pinnock is missing from *Jām-e Jam*: "The *laws* of Ireland differ but little from those of England." At the same time, on one occasion Farhad Mirza toned down Pinnock's bigoted statement about Irish Catholics. On this occasion, Farhad Mirza both misunderstood part of the following passage appearing in Pinnock's book and excluded Pinnock's condescending comment about Catholics: "The established religion of Ireland is the same as that of England, but the Roman Catholic [faith] is almost universally professed by the middling and lower orders, and, from their deplorable ignorance, the clergy possess almost an absolute power over them."[72] Farhad Mirza translated this passage as following: "The common [sic] religion of Ireland is the same as that of the population of England[,] and there are also Roman Catholics[,] and the majority of middling and lower [class] people are followers of Roman Catholicism."[73] Similarly, Farhad Mirza deleted Pinnock's further prejudicial statements about the Irish, after having described their hospitality and kindness. While Farhad Mirza repeated the original statement that "[t]he lower [class] Irish are warm in their attachments, courteous to strangers, and patient of hardship," Farhad Mirza excluded the remainder of this paragraph (instead only noting "they are generally cantankerous"). Pinnock had contended: "but from intemperance, riot, and rebellion, their manner of life is but little removed from that of a savage, and their ignorance is extreme." Both Pinnock's text and Farhad Mirza's translation also asserted that "[t]he higher orders are noted for their bravery, and generous hospitality" (with this statement appearing in a different order in this paragraph in Farhad Mirza's translation).[74] After a general commentary on Irish manufactures, this chapter proceeded with Ireland's overall population. While Pinnock's *A Comprehensive Grammar of Modern Geography and History* maintained that at the time (i.e., 1834) the population numbered at "6,800,000," in *Jām-e Jam* Farhad Mirza added: "According to the translator[,] in the Christian year eighteen-hundred-and-forty-one [...] eight million and one hundred and seventy-five thousand one hundred and twenty-four [people] were counted [in Ireland]." Farhad Mirza then briefly mentioned episodes of famine in Ireland; inexplicably not only failing to mention the Great Famine of 1845–1851 (which had occurred after the publication of Pinnock's book), but also getting the 1851 population of Ireland drastically wrong as well ("above eight million and five hundred thousand"). Whereas he had the 1841 data correct, the 1851 census counted only around six-and-a-half-million people in Ireland (a sharp reduction of well over two million). Farhad Mirza, nevertheless, noted (with some exaggeration) that of his stated 1851 population, six million subsisted primarily on the potato crop and butter, and added that periodic potato blight resulted in repeated famines and sizeable annual emigration to the United States.[75] The entry then proceeded with brief commentaries on Irish language (identified as Celtic and similar to the languages of Scottish Highlanders and Welsh), Irish literature (with Farhad Mirza's appended information, and Thomas Moore again missing from the shortlist), and the repetition in *Jām-e Jam* of Pinnock remark that Ireland had only one university (in Dublin), "founded by Queen Elizabeth in the year 1591." Pinnock also mentioned, "The old natives of this land [...] dispute the honour of the *Poems of Ossian* with the Scotch *Highlanders*, insisting that he was a native of Ireland." Farhad Mirza identified the Dublin university in question as "Trinity College," while entirely skipping the section on Ossianic poems, which must have been an entirely baffling piece of information for him.[76] Pinnock had left out the Maynooth seminary college in Ireland (1795), and by the time *Jām-e Jam* was composed there was also Queen's University (Belfast, 1845); neither of which are mentioned in Farhad Mirza's addenda.

In effect, the range of information Farhad Mirza appended to his translation of Pinnock's book demonstrates the increased availability of information about Ireland by the mid-nineteenth century for those literate Iranians interested in pursuing that information (albeit evidently not inclusive of Irish antiquarian theories of Iranian or other 'oriental' origins), while at the same time indicating the difficulty encountered by these Iranians in decoding some of that information (e.g. the so-called Ossianic Cycle). Also of relevance in regard to Iranian familiarity with Ireland at the time is the representation of Ireland as an old realm of the English crown, similar to Wales and Scotland (see also below), and distinct from British "colonies" in other parts of the world. The sequence of entries in Pinnock's book, reproduced by Farhad Mirza, is itself illustrative of Ireland's special standing as a territory ruled by England; conveying the impression to the average Iranian reader of *Jām-e Jam* that Ireland was an integral part of English dominions, apart from English colonies. In so far as British territories were concerned, Pinnock's book began with a general chapter entry on "The British Empire." Missing from *Jām-e Jam* in this section was only Pinnock's preambular patriotic poem glorifying England. This entry stated, "The British Empire is the most powerful on the earth. Its dominions in Europe consist of the two large islands of *Great Britain* and *Ireland*, and others of inferior note." It added: "Great Britain has colonial possessions in every quarter of the Globe. In Asia [...] In Austral-Asia [...] In Africa [...] In North-America [...] On the continent of South-America [...]" Pinnock next stated, and Farhad Mirza followed suit, that "Great Britain comprehends [sic] the kingdoms of *England*, and *Scotland*, and the Principality of *Wales*."[77] In this formulation, there was clearly a hint of Ireland's somewhat ambivalent status. While Ireland was not considered a colony of England, it was unclear from this description whether Ireland was considered a kingdom (as in the separate "Kingdom of Ireland" ruled by English monarchs prior to the 1801 Act of

Union, or "The United Kingdom of Great Britain and Ireland" after 1801), or as another 'principality' of England, similar to Wales—although, in the final entry on Ireland (see below) Pinnock referred to Ireland as a "kingdom" under English rule (meaning 'The United Kingdom of Great Britain and Ireland'). Regardless, it was unmistakable in this account that Ireland constituted a province of English territorial possessions in the British Isles. The remainder of this general introductory chapter on "The British Empire" made no more mention of Ireland. The next set of chapter entries progressed from England to Wales, Scotland, and then Ireland, *before* proceeding with Britain's specifically designated "Colonial Possessions" (respectively in "America," "West Indies," "Africa," "East Indies," and "Australasia" [spelled differently here]).

Curiously, in the first chapter entry on Ireland appearing in *Jām-e Jam*, following the reference to Ireland's "only" university and prior to the listing of a few literary luminaries of Ireland, there appeared information missing from Pinnock's *A Comprehensive Grammar of Modern Geography and History*, but without Farhad Mirza's usual 'According to the translator' that marked his appended descriptions. The following out-of-place detail was inserted by Farhad Mirza: "Ireland is represented in the imperial parliament ['*perlement-e shāhanshāi*'] by twenty-eight members in the House of Lords and one hundred and fifty members in the House of Commons."78 This again denoted Ireland's special standing as an English territorial possession. This introductory entry on Ireland was followed by another chapter on Ireland, titled "Historical Memoranda of Ireland" (appearing in Persian as "a brief account of Irish history"). In Pinnock's *A Comprehensive Grammar of Modern Geography and History*, this entry began by dismissing as "fable and obscurity" the so-called medieval accounts of ancient Ireland by "Irish monks," without providing any detail of those accounts. The entry then proceeded with the introduction of Christianity to the island, "The invasion of the DANES and NORWEGIANS," the Norman raids from the East, the gradual Anglo-Norman conquests of Irish territories ruled by various local kings (beginning in the twelfth century, during the reign of the English monarch Henry II), the establishment of English rule over Ireland, and the subsequent absolute English consolidation of power over the island during the reign of Queen Elizabeth I (r.1558–1603), who "reduc[ed] *Ireland* into a state of greater order and submission."79 Pinnock's historical account of Ireland then came to an abrupt halt, with no mention of continued uprisings against Protestant/English rule since the sixteenth century. He simply averred the presumably civilizing influence of English rule in Ireland, albeit adding enigmatically: "Although Ireland is in a very unsettled state, as regards to the QUESTION of CATHOLIC EMANCIPATION [i.e., the Catholic Emancipation Act of 1829], she is [*sic*] now become a very respectable kingdom."80 Farhad Mirza's *Jām-e Jam* truncated the latter part of Pinnock's narrative, by omitting the specific reference to Queen Elizabeth for some unknown reason.81 Importantly, however, both Pinnock's and Farhad Mirza's texts clearly stated that the coverage of Britain's "colonial possessions" would appear in subsequent chapter entries; again denoting that Ireland did not belong to that latter category of England's territorial possessions.82

Another example of a translated descriptive world geography from roughly around the time of Raphael's and Farhad Mirza's translations was the undated *Jahān-namā -ye Jadid* ("*The New Display of the World*"), by the Iranian-Armenian Jean David ("Jān Dāvud").83

Jean David was also commissioned to translate another French text of a descriptive world geography into Turkish, which was then translated into Persian by Mohammad Hussein Farahani, with the translation evidently completed in 1848 and finally printed in hand script under the popular Persian title of *Jahān-namā* (*Display of the World*) in 1861(1277 A.H). In this publication, too, like other such Persian-language accounts of world geography produced in Iran during the century, Ireland was again unambiguously defined as an integral constituent territory of the English realm in the British Isles, similar to Scotland, and distinct from British colonies, dependencies, or later protectorates around the globe.[84] Similar classification of Ireland was replicated in other range of sources, as in the case of a geographic account of the British Isles appearing in *Rouznāmeh-ye Elmi* ("*Scientific Gazette*") of April 16, 1877, published in Tehran.[85] By the latter part of the nineteenth century, translations of works in the genre of descriptive world geography, along with re-productions of the then most accurate and detailed world maps, as well as continental and regional cartographies, inclusive of the British Isles, were more widely available inside Iran.[86] By then, cartographic expertise in Iran itself was vastly improving as well; Iran being a member of international geographical organizations such as the Lisbon Geographical Society (founded in 1875) and participating in international geographical congresses, such as the May 1889 congress held in Paris.

Iranian Historical Familiarity with Ireland and the Irish Question in the Nineteenth Century

Other than a small circle of educated Iranians proficient enough in European languages, and who had access through various channels to books on European history published in European languages or could glean historical information appearing in European newspapers and periodicals available to them, the majority of literate Iranians relied on translations of such material in the more familiar local and regional languages, ranging from Persian and Arabic to Ottoman Turkish. For much of the nineteenth century, the Indian subcontinent served as the main conduit for translations of English-language texts into Persian that were also accessible to some Iranians in the Indian subcontinent, inside Iran, and at various locations of Iranian émigré communities throughout the region. Based on the available information I have thus far managed to process, there were no Persian translations of texts available in the nineteenth century to Iranian readers in any of the familiar regional languages that dealt exclusively with Irish history. The available Persian translations of texts dealing with English or British history during the century at best contain only a smattering of references to Irish history. Many of these translations, or those dealing with general European or world history, were based on texts in European languages that frequently happened to have been intended for classroom usage in their original country of publication. The extremely limited coverage of Irish history in these translated texts is occasionally due to selective omissions by the translators, who frequently condensed the already summary original content of the books. For example, an undated Persian translation by Shaykh Reza of a text appearing as *Tārikh-e Ingiliss* (*History of England*) covered the period from Roman times until the end of the Napoleonic Wars in 1815, with only minor passing coverage of Ireland in connection with Anglo-Irish relations. Since the translation was dedicated to Nasser al-Din Shah, it would have been completed sometime between 1848 and 1896. This appears to have been a summary translation of the 1823 abridged and updated edition by Robert Simpson of the multi-volume *The History of England* composed by the Anglo-Irish Dr. Oliver Goldsmith and intended for school children, with the student exercises omitted in the Persian translation.[87] The paltry references to Anglo-Irish developments in Shaykh Reza's translation included the creation of the United Kingdom (1801) through the incorporation of Great Britain and Ireland.[88] An alternative example of such histories is a late nineteenth century Persian translation from the English original of a history of England that included far more references to Ireland in comparison with Shaykh Reza's translation. This was *Tārikh-e Engelesstān* (*History of England*) by Esmail Sahaf-bashi, a former graduate of Dar al-Fonun. This translation, based on Leonhard (Leonard) Schmitz's 1873 *A History of England for Junior Classes*, covered the twelfth-century Norman conquests in Ireland, England's break with the Catholic Church during the reign of Henry VIII in the sixteenth century and the subsequent religious divide between England and Ireland, the Protestant Plantations ("Colony") in Ireland during the reign of James I (1603–25) by English and Scottish settlers (in "Ulster, Munster, Londonderry, and elsewhere"), Oliver Cromwell's military campaigns in Ireland in the mid-seventeenth century for subduing Catholic rebel forces (i.e., during the Confederate War), James II's conversion to Catholicism and his ouster by the English Parliament in the "Glorious Revolution" of 1688 and James' subsequent rallying of Catholic forces in Ireland with French backing until his final defeat by the Protestant forces of King William III (of Orange) during the wars of 1690–91, the 1798 (United Irishmen) uprising in Ireland, the 1801 Act of Union, and Daniel O'Connell's campaign for Catholic Emancipation and the subsequent admission of Catholics as members of British parliament after 1829. The work also included a very brief allusion to the Great Famine of 1845–51 in Ireland.[89] But, even in this book, Ireland was, in effect, presented as an English domain (at least since the sixteenth century), albeit convulsed by periodic religious and/or political turmoil that were eventually curtailed by the authorities in London. Other range of works on English or British history available to Iranian readers during the century included Persian translations of European originals carried out in British India. One of these translations published in stone lithograph print in 1888/1889 (1306 A.H.) was based on a work attributed to the famed English orientalist Jonathan Scott (1754–1829), who worked in India in the service of the English East India Company: *Tārikh-e Engelesstān* (*History of England*) translated by the Iranian Mirza Mohammad Shirazi ("Malek al-Kotab") and printed in Bombay. However, there is no extant copy of such a history composed by Scott, nor is there any mention of it in Scott's biographical accounts. It is possible this was either an unfinished and unpublished work by Scott, or Mirza Mohammad Shirazi was confusing Scott with another author.

In addition to passing references to Ireland in translated books on the history or descriptive geographies of the British Isles, the most regular, and often more detailed, source of information about Ireland available to Iranians inside Iran from the middle of the nineteenth century were newspapers (and, later on, periodicals as well). Following a slow start, Iranian newspapers rapidly multiplied by the latter decades of the century, including newspapers published by members of Iranian émigré communities in India, the Ottoman Empire, the Russian Caucasus, Egypt, end even briefly in England. There was further rapid proliferation of newspapers after the Iranian Constitutional Revolution of 1906. *Rouznāmeh-ye Vaqāye'-e Ettefāqiyeh* (1851–60), the state-controlled gazette published in Tehran, is the earliest Persian-language newspaper published inside Iran in the nineteenth century of which most copies are thus far known to have survived. This was the same newspaper from which the Irish nationalist Dublin newspaper *The Nation* periodically quoted during the Anglo-Iranian War of 1856–57 (referred to as the "*Teheran Gazette*"). The occasional Ireland-related news items in this paper ranged from marginal to detailed. Random examples during the first year of the paper's publication include the report of a plan to reduce trans-Atlantic steamship navigation time between England and the United States, by having passengers travel from Liverpool to the eastern shore of Ireland and then transported by rail to the western shore of Ireland, in order to board ships en route to the United States (presumably New York). Another news item dealt with the 1851 census in the United Kingdom, mentioning emigration from the United Kingdom to other parts of the British Empire and to the United States, and noting the significant recent emigration to the United States from Ireland.[90] This particular report did not specify that the surge in Irish emigration was occurring in the midst of the Great Famine in Ireland. The Irish famine was briefly mentioned in a separate 1851 report in *Rouznāmeh-ye Vaqāye'-e Ettefāqiyeh* that dealt with the extensive emigration of Irish peasantry to the United States: "a few years ago the potato crop, which is the dietary staple of the majority of that land's inhabitants, was devastated by a blight, resulting in famine and countless deaths." The article added that following the famine and mass emigration, the remaining population of Ireland were expected to enjoy higher living standards, since it was said pre-famine Ireland was overpopulated.[91] Reports of large-scale Irish emigration to the United States during the remainder of the famine years, particularly that of the Irish peasantry, appeared in other issues of the paper.[92] Ireland's depopulation and extensive Irish emigration to the United States, as well as to Australia and Canada among other locations in the British Empire, became the prevalent theme in the paper's occasional reports in connection with Ireland in the coming years.[93]

It should be noted that in these news reports, just as in Persian translations of historical and geographical texts at the time, Ireland was generally designated as a "country" (*mamlekat*), similar to Scotland and Wales (on the rare occasions that Wales was even mentioned). But, this did not connote that Ireland was treated as a territorial entity independent of English rule. Nineteenth-century Iranian sources considered Ireland as an integral component of English domain in the British Isles, with 'English' or 'England' in this setting frequently referring to both Britain and the United Kingdom interchangeably, with either *velāyat-e ingiliss* ("territory of England") or *mamlekat-e ingiliss* ("country of England") used as a shorthand for the United Kingdom. For instance, a member of the Iranian delegation to London following the First Anglo-Iranian War of 1838 over Herat, Mirza Abdul-Fattah Khan Garmroudi, noted the "State [i.e., administrative realm] of England" ("*dowlat-e ingiriz*"), "with the exception of Indian and other territories that lie in other quarters," was comprised of "triple islands [*sic*] of England,

Ireland, and Scotland" (with Wales again left unmentioned and frequently overlooked as part of Britain in Iranian sources at the time).[94]

Reports of European events in *Rouznāmeh-ye Vaqāye'-e Ettefāqiyeh* were primarily taken from European newspapers (frequently those in French language) as well as from newspapers published in India and elsewhere. On occasion, errors in the original sources were duplicated in the paper, while on other occasions details of original reports got confused, as in the case of a brief report of the British Whig prime minister Lord John Russell's "surprise" visit to Dublin in September 1851 during the famine, which in actuality had taken place in 1848.[95] In this report, Dublin was described as the capital of "the country of Ireland" situated "in the English Isles" (i.e., the British Isles). Other periodic Irish-related reports in *Rouznāmeh-ye Vaqāye'-e Ettefāqiyeh* included Queen Victoria's (second) visit to Ireland in the summer of 1853 during the Great Industrial Exhibition in Dublin, also known as the Irish Industrial Exhibition, or, as the paper too called it, the Dublin "Crystal Palace" exhibit.[96] Another random example of reports in this paper related to Ireland was that of troops being transported to Cape Colony in southern Africa from Ireland (during the 1850–53 British war against the indigenous Xhosa population).[97] An 1856 report covered the suicide of John Sadleir, following revelations of his banking and financial misappropriations and misuse of political power.[98] The report did not specify that Sadleir was a former prominent Irish MP and a member of George Henry Moore's "Irish Brigade" in the House of Commons, as well as a co-founder of the Catholic Defence Association. But this report again unambiguously designated Ireland an English province or district (a territory within *'velāyat-e ingiliss'*/country or territory of England). Following the cessation of *Rouznāmeh-ye Vaqāye'-e Ettefāqiyeh*'s publication in 1860, subsequent Iranian newspapers continued to periodically report Ireland-related events. Samples of these news items include a report in 1866 on the population of the "domain of England" (i.e., the United Kingdom), appearing in the official Iranian newspaper *Rouznāmeh-ye Dowlat-e Āliyeh-ye Irān* ("*Newsletter of the Majestic State of Iran*," published in Tehran). This report defined the 'domain of England' (*'mamlekat-e ingiliss'*) as consisting of England, Scotland, and Ireland (with Wales again getting short shrift).[99] After 1868, with the extension of the Indo-European Telegraph lines to Iran, news of some developments in other parts of the world reached Iran in a considerably more rapid manner than before, with some of the telegraphed information appearing in the Iranian press.

The above random examples should not imply an absolute absence of reports on ongoing socio-political conflicts in Ireland and of Irish nationalist platforms in Iranian newspapers throughout the nineteenth century. Yet, these latter types of reports were overwhelmingly, if not entirely, treated as *domestic matters* within English-administered territories in the British Isles. For instance, an 1898 article under the heading "Monsieur Gladstone" in the Tehran newspaper *Sherāfat* ("*Honor*") on the occasion of Gladstone's recent death, provided an account of the British Liberal prime minister William Ewart Gladstone's disestablishment of the Church of Ireland (1871) and agrarian reforms in Ireland (i.e., Irish Land Acts of 1870 and 1881), which the paper maintained had significantly removed "danger" to "British government." The article, however, added that Gladstone had ultimately failed to introduce self-government in Ireland (i.e., the Irish Home Rule Bills of 1886 and 1893).[100] While it should be kept in mind that Home Rule nationalists did not seek Ireland's full independence from the British Empire, which further buttressed the general Iranian impression that Home Rule campaigns were an *internal* provincial political matter within the United Kingdom, it is simultaneously germane to note that militant republican Irish nationalist activities were generally reported in Iranian newspapers in the same manner as other professedly *illegitimate* acts of violence and disorder around the world. This was in part symptomatic of the Iranian state's censorship of the press; in this case intended to vilify rebellion and other armed activities against the state as illicit acts, not forgetting the failed Babi religious-political assassination attempt on Nasser al-Din Shah's life in 1852—the shah was later assassinated by a follower of a different socio-political cause in 1896. This style of reporting was indicative of the general fear on the part of authorities of armed disorder in Iranian society. In the Iranian political parlance of the late nineteenth century, acts of political violence and terror, other than those carried out by the state and its various regional agents, were frequently designated as "anarchy." Regardless, it is safe to assume that literate Iranians interested in world affairs, and some other Iranians who acquired their knowledge of world events solely through oral communication, had acquired some general familiarity with at least the broader political contours of contemporary Ireland by the late nineteenth century. This was all the more so the case for regular readers of newspapers, considering Iranian newspapers well into the early twentieth century consisted of no more than four pages in large script print, which meant various news items were not entirely buried in the multitude of reportage, not to mention that most individuals would have read the entire paper given the relatively high price of newspapers and the fact that most newspapers were published as weeklies.

The most extensive, albeit still summary, coverage of contemporary Irish developments and recent history in a single Iranian source in the nineteenth century appeared in the form of two overlapping, and on occasion identical, multi-volume compendia of domestic, regional, and world events. These were, in effect, almanacs of annual records of major political and social occurrences around the globe, compiled in the latter part of the nineteenth century by Mohammad Hassan Khan ("E'temad al-Saltaneh"). E'temad al-Saltaneh held various government posts, including his tenure as the minister of publications and his supervision of the official newspaper *Rouznāmeh-ye Dowlat-e Āliyeh-ye Irān*. He was also Nasser al-Din Shah's regular personal translator of newspapers and other publications in French language. The first of E'temad al-Saltaneh's collections was *Mer'āt al-Boldān-e Nāsseri* ("*Mirror of the Lands During the Reign of Nasser al-Din Shah*"; or roughly translating as *"World Occurrences in Nasser al-Din Shah's Era"*), published between 1877 and 1880 in four volumes and chronicling major events during the reign of Nasser al-Din Shah (r.1848–96). The other collection, which was far more detailed in its coverage of Irish-related events, was *Tārikh-e Montazem-e Nāsseri* (roughly translating as "*Methodical History of Nasser al-Din Shah's Era*"), published in three volumes from 1881 to 1883. Ireland-related events appeared in the third volume of this collection, beginning around the time of the United Irishmen Uprising of 1798. This final volume concluded with entries on domestic and global developments between March 1882 and March 21, 1883 (with the Iranian New Year beginning on 20–21 March). Considering E'temad al-Saltaneh's status, these two collections of world events would have been highly sought after by readers interested in domestic and foreign developments. The European sources consulted for these two compendia, with the exception of previously translated foreign news items culled from existing Iranian sources (ranging from newspapers to books), were most certainly translations from publications in French language, given E'temad al-Saltaneh's fluency in French and his use of Persian transliterations of French terms and his substitution of French terms, idioms, and names in place of English equivalents, such as "Comte" instead of Lords or Earls when referring to British and Irish personalities, or the French name "Guillaume" instead William, as well as rendering of John as "Jean," or the Persian transcription of "Nouvelle-Zélande" in place of New Zealand. Moreover, the reports of political developments in Ireland in these collected volumes occasionally exhibit an underlying tone of sympathy toward Irish nationalists as well as Catholics, while critical of English policymakers, particularly regarding anti-Catholic policies. This further suggests E'temad al-Saltaneh's reliance on French sources. On the other hand, E'temad al-Saltaneh added his own analytical touch to some of the entries, such as equating militant Irish republican groups like the Fenians/Irish Republican Brotherhood (IRB) with members of the Babi faith that was officially proscribed and persecuted by the Iranian state and by the Shi'i religious establishment as an expression of apostasy with socially and politically destructive objectives.

Both of the above collections by E'temad al-Saltaneh treated Ireland and the Irish under the heading of "England," in contradistinction to "occupied" ("*motessarefi*") English territories in other parts of the world. The annual entries of events listed under "England," in the section on major European developments, would have been of particular interest to the average Iranian reader, given the Anglo-Russian rivalry and competing range of influences in Iran at the time. From the entries under 'England,' the reader could gain basic familiarity with the contours of Irish campaigns for Home Rule as well as about Irish republican activities. Given the book format of these compendia, the readers' absorption and retention of information about major contemporary Ireland-related events would have been more thorough, instantaneous, and lasting than sporadic information about Ireland acquired from regular reading of newspapers over many years or from amassing fragmentary information appearing in general surveys of English and/or European history. A brief outline of Ireland-related entries in *Mer'āt al-Boldān-e Nāsseri* ranges from events such as Daniel O'Connell's death in 1847 to the Young Ireland uprising of 1848, the sizeable emigration from Ireland to North America (of "65,000 households") in 1851 (i.e., toward the end of the Great Famine), "the renowned Irish poet" Thomas Moore's death in 1852 (by then Moore's *Lalla Rookh* was known in some Iranian circles, even though the Iran/Erin interchange in the poem eluded them), the Great Industrial Exhibition in Dublin in 1853, violent protests in 1861 against landowners by peasants ("*ro'ayā*"; i.e., tenant farmers),[101] the revelation and suppression of a planned Fenian/IRB uprising in Ireland in 1865 and the ensuing violence in England (which was recorded in more detail than usual), the failed 1867 "Fenian Rising" in Ireland (there is no mention of the Fenian raids into Canada from the United States in the same year under the entries for either "England" or "the US"), or the high rate of continued Irish emigration to the United States.[102] Significantly, in an entry for 1865 in the third volume of *Mer'āt al-Boldān-e Nāsseri* (erroneously appearing under 1864, with some of the entries in this volume being off by a year due to a calendar conversion error), the Fenian "sect" ("*tāyefeh*") was equated with communists and Babis,[103] both of which were widely reviled in both Iranian state and Shi'i religious circles. In the standard Iranian political idiom of the late nineteenth century, communists and Babis were in the same category as the undifferentiated "anarchists" and "nihilists," even as some among the slowly-expanding small group of 'secular'-oriented Iranian intellectuals and reformers were privately opposed to the ongoing persecution of Babis and/or were receptive to communism or anarcho-populism.

The third volume of E'temad al-Saltaneh's *Tārikh-e Montazem-e Nāsseri* (1883)[104] carried a much more extensive range of Ireland- and Irish-related entries, duplicating many of the entries in the earlier *Mer'āt al-Boldān-e Nāsseri*, but providing more detail in some cases and covering additional events, including those since the publication of *Mer'āt al-Boldān-e Nāsseri*. The entries for developments in Ireland in *Tārikh-e Montazem-e Nāsseri* again appeared under the main heading of "England," as a sub-category of developments in "Europe," and repeated some of the calendar conversion errors in calculating the years for the annual entries. However, in this publication Canada and British-controlled territories in India were also occasionally described as "provinces of England," similar to Ireland or Scotland, and developments in those territories too were frequently listed under major events in England. Below is the full range of information about Ireland and the Irish which the reader of the third volume of *Tārikh-e Montazem-e Nāsseri* could have gleaned:

- Under the entry for major events in *Europe* in 1796 and alluding to the formation of the Society of United Irishmen in 1791: "Ireland which has witnessed the developments in France and approves of them and wishes to secede from England and become a republic similar to France" (p.64).
- Under the entry for major events in England in 1798: "Uprising in Ireland and the declaration of a republic"—i.e., the United Irishmen uprising of 1798 with French backing (p.71).
- Under the entry for major events in England in 1800: "Ireland no longer has a separate parliament and will be sending its deputies to the parliament in London"—i.e., the 1801 Act of Union (p.75).
- Under the entry for major events in England in 1801: "[William] Pitt [the Younger], the prime minister [...] pledges [Catholic] relief to the people of Ireland[.] But, given that the population of Ireland are Catholic and the [English] king is Protestant and is extremely fanatical in this regard, [the king] refrains from granting relief to the Irish[.] Pitt, after seventeen years as [prime] minister, resigns from his post and a person named [Henry] Addington becomes prime minister"—this was in reference to Pitt's resignation on avowed grounds of having failed to carry out his promised Catholic Emancipation Act (p.76).
- Under the entry for major events in England in 1803: "Insurrection in Ireland"—this cursory entry was an allusion to the failed republican uprising in Ireland led by Robert Emmet and fellow former members of the Society of United Irishmen (p.80).

- Under the entry for major events in England in 1821: "In this year the population of England [i.e., Britain], with the exception of Ireland, numbered fourteen million and four hundred thousand persons and the population of Ireland numbered six and a half million and thirteen thousand persons" (p.124).
- Under the entry for major events in England in 1822: "The inhabitants of Ireland riot in reaction to the outbreak of famine and government interference in religious affairs"—i.e., disturbances resulting from the potato crop failure due to excessive rain that affected Western parts of Ireland in particular, and the pervasive refusal by the poorer Catholics to the pay compulsory tithes to the [Anglican] Church of Ireland, as well as the spread of Ribbonism and attacks against landed interests, leading to the passage of the Insurrection Act in that year and the formation of the Royal Irish Constabulary (p.127).
- Under the entry for major events in England in 1828: "[Daniel] O'Connell, an inhabitant of Ireland, incites the population of this *province* ['*eyālat*'] against the English government" (p.146)—emphasis added.
- Under the entry for major events in England in 1829: "The Irish O'Connell demands a [separate] parliament for Ireland, but this is rejected"—this was a reference to the campaign for the Repeal of the Union and promulgation of Home Rule in Ireland led by Daniel O'Connell and the Catholic Association (p.148). The entry did not mention the success of O'Connell's campaign for Catholic Emancipation in that year, allowing Catholics in the United Kingdom to stand in general elections and take up seats in the parliament at Westminster.
- Under the entry for major events in England in 1833: "O'Connell incites Ireland against England"—this was a reference to the intensified Tithe War in Ireland (p.157).

*** There were no entries for either domestic or foreign events for the year 1840, while there were two entries for the year 1844, indicating E'temad al-Saltaneh erroneously marked 1840 as 1841, 1841 as 1842, 1843 as 1844, and then had yet another (correct) general entry for the year 1844.***

- Under the entry for major events in England in 1846: "Unrest in Ireland"—this cursory entry was evidently a reference to the disorders in Ireland during the first year of what subsequently came to be called the Great Famine of 1845-51, even though there is no mention of the Irish famine in any of the entries for those years; whereas ironically the much milder famine of 1822 had been mentioned earlier, as already noted (p.193).
- Under the entry for major events in England in 1847: "O'Connell, who was one of Ireland's luminaries ['*ma'āref*'], passed away" (pp.198–99).
- Under the very brief entry for major events in England in 1848: a passing mention of "insurrection in some of Ireland's cities"—i.e., the failed Young Ireland uprising, the main scene of which was in fact a very minor rural affair (p.202).
- Under the entry for major events in England in 1851: a brief mention of large-scale emigration from Ireland to North America ("65,000 households")—again without any reference to the Great Famine (p.222). The entry also noted the death of the "renowned Irish poet [...] Thomas Moore" (p.227).

- Under the entry for major events in England in 1853: a passing mention of the opening of the [Great Industrial] Exhibition in Dublin (p.234).
- Under the entry for major events in England in 1864: mention of "Minor disturbances in Ireland" and the "appearance of the Fenian sect ['*tāyifeh*'] in Ireland, which is akin to communists and the Babis[, and] the capture of many of them and killing of some"—these events actually occurred in October–November of 1865, with British authorities uncovering a plot for a Fenians/IRB rising in that year and suppressing the weekly IRB mouthpiece *Irish People* (Dublin), edited by James Stephens, as well as carrying out mass arrests of Fenian/IRB members throughout the United Kingdom (p.291).
- Under the entry for major events in England in 1865: "The Fenian sect's unrest and insurrection ['*shuresh va enqelāb*'] in Ireland" and "unrest and insurrection in the city of London and numerous [other] locations[, and] the capture of one hundred and fifty thousand counts of Snider[-Enfield] breech-loading rifles ['*tofang-e tah-por*']," as well as the "insurrection of Fenian members in Ireland resulting in the incarceration of a few thousand people"—these events actually occurred in 1866, during which John O'Reilly and John Devoy were also detained (pp.295–96).
- Under the entry for major events in England in 1867: a brief mention of "Fierce unrest and insurrection in Ireland"—in reference to the Fenian uprising in 1867, with no mention of Fenian raids into Canada from the United States in the same year (p.307).
- Under the entry for major events in England in 1872, there were tallies of the number of emigrants to the United States departing from English and Irish ports (not forgetting that emigrants from England—meaning "Britain"—would also have included some of the Irish residing in Britain): "In the span of thirteen years, nine hundred and ten thousand and four hundred and twenty five inhabitants of Germany, half a million and sixty thousand and eight hundred and thirty inhabitants of Ireland, and seven hundred and fifty one thousand and seven hundred and sixty nine people [from] England have emigrated to the United States' soil" (p.327). Interestingly, a separate account in the same entry of a pistol being pointed at Queen Victoria's carriage (p.326) did not mention that the apprehended individual who had pointed the pistol at a very close range was a young Irish nationalist (Arthur O'Connor). Moreover, this event had actually occurred in 1871.
- Under the entry for major events in England in 1880: mention of public assemblies calling for reforms in Ireland and of [agrarian] unrest—this was a highly unusual entry for Irish events, in so far as this report significantly appeared alongside reports of Afghan resistance to British military incursion (during the second Anglo-Afghan War, 1878–80), signs of planned agitation among Indian Muslims against the British Raj, an uprising against British rule in Basutoland in southern Africa, and the Boer resistance to British territorial aggression in southern Africa (during the First Boer War of 1880–81), followed by yet another mention of intensified disturbances in Ireland "day-by-day" (p.365). This was the first occasion that reports of disturbances in Ireland in this book were classed together with resistance to British imperial aggression in other parts of the world. This arrangement was repeated in an entry the following year (see below).

- Under the entry for major events in England in 1881: "the expulsion of Irish MPs from parliament"—there was no mention of the arrests in October 1881 (under that year's Coercion Act) of Charles Stewart Parnell and a number of other leading "Home Rule" Irish Parliamentary Party (IPP) MPs, including John Dillon and William Redmond, on grounds of their Land League agitation in Ireland, as well as the detention of Michael Davitt, the architect of the Land League and a former IRB activist, and of the Irish nationalist journalist William O'Brien. The entry also noted the dispatch of 30,000 additional British forces to Ireland for pacifying the disturbances, with yet another mention of "fierce unrest and insurrection in Ireland" appearing later in the same account alongside reports of the British defeat in the war against the Boer republics, and British withdrawal from Kandahar in Afghanistan (p.373).
- Under the entry for major events in England in the year 1882 and up to March 21, 1883: mention of severe unrest in Ireland, while also adding that "the rebellion in Ireland against the government is intensifying, with a few homicides ["*ghatl-e nafss*"] occurring every day," and the appointment of Lord [John] Spencer as Lord Lieutenant of Ireland, and the murder of the [newly appointed] chief secretary for Ireland Lord [Frederick Charles] Cavendish along with his under-secretary [Thomas Henry] Burke in Dublin by rebels ["*yāghiān*"]—i.e., the Phoenix Park murders on 6 May 1882, carried out by the Irish National Invincibles, a breakaway faction from the IRB. This was followed by yet another mention of "continued Irish […] insurgency" and ongoing "insurrection of the masses against the aristocracy and landowners," while noting that actions taken by "the police force responsible for safeguarding people and apprehending the offenders, was further emboldening the masses to commit murder" (p.384).

Parenthetically, E'temad al-Saltaneh also recorded some information related to Ireland in his diaries (published posthumously), which, despite some degree of confusion on his part, underscore his, and evidently Nasser al-Din Shah's, perception of Ireland as an integral territorial unit of the English realm in the British Isles, as opposed to a colony. This was apparently reflective of a more general Iranian perspective at the time (that is, among Iranians who knew about Ireland in the first place). A diary entry for April 13, 1886 (Tuesday, 8 Rajab 1303 A.H.) noted: "The English government has inexorably given Ireland, which is part of English soil, actual autonomy, granting it a parliament."[105] In reality, the Home Rule Bill introduced by the Liberal government of William Gladstone in 1886, with the IPP backing, was defeated in parliament. (The introduction of the Bill split the Liberal Party, leading to Liberal-Unionist defections from the party and the collapse of the Liberal administration.) On November 27, 1886 (Saturday, 1 Rajab 1304 A.H.), E'temad al-Saltaneh correctly, albeit generically, recorded in his diary the disturbances in Ireland in the aftermath of the abortive Home Rule Bill of that year. The events to which he was vaguely alluding had ranged from sectarian-communitarian clashes over the summer (following the annual July 12 Protestant Orange marches) to evictions of tenant-farmers by landowners in the midst of the "Great Depression" of 1873–96, and the consequent nationalist revival of the Land War campaign. In this entry, E'temad al-Saltaneh added that the Iranian monarch "had dreamt [last night] the situation in England was very dire. This morning, when the telegraph of the disorders in Ireland arrived, he considered [the news as] his divination. Since the shah has pretentions of sainthood ['*emāmat*'] and prophecy ['*nobo'vat*'], [it is only fitting that] he should also have performed [such] a miracle!"[106] E'temad al-Saltaneh kept his diaries a secret, given his often unflattering portrayal of the shah.[107]

As indicated by the above examples from Iranian newspapers, or of Persian translations of European surveys of "English" history, or translations of descriptive world geographies that also covered Ireland, as well as E'temad al-Saltaneh's *Mer'āt al-Boldān-e Nāsseri* and *Tārikh-e Montazem-e Nāsseri*, among numerous other range of possible sources, by the end of the nineteenth century the informed politically-minded Iranians interested in world events would have been sufficiently familiar with the general tenor of Irish agitation for attaining different modes of sovereignty from London. Nevertheless, by the early years of the twentieth-century violent republican Irish nationalist aspirations were commonly condemned in Iranian publications, if not often entirely ignored, while Irish nationalism in its parliamentary Home Rule configuration was consigned to the realm of domestic provincial quarrels in the United Kingdom over regional administration and autonomy. Prior to the 1916 Easter Rising in Ireland, this pattern of assessing Irish nationalist politics appears to have been widely shared in Iranian nationalist circles as well, including among the more radical groups, even as many leading Iranian nationalists after the outbreak of the Iranian Constitutional Revolution in 1906 were aware of the public advocacy of the Iranian constitutionalist-nationalist struggle by at least a few prominent Irish Home Rule nationalists, if not by other nationalists as well. Some Iranian nationalists traveling to England even met the likes of John Dillon. In effect, the multivalent Irish nationalism failed to elicit the same kind of publicly expressed solidarity on the part of Iranian nationalists at the start of the twentieth century as did campaigns for the territorial autonomy of Finland from Russia or of Norway from Sweden, let alone of the sort of expansive solidarity expressed by Iranian nationalists with Indian or Egyptian nationalists in the British Empire, or with such events as the Young Turk Revolution of 1908 and the Chinese Xinhai Revolution of 1911-12. The Iranian constitutionalist-nationalist press during these years frequently approved of campaigns against British imperial rule in other parts of the British Empire, including the activities of the Indian National Congress (1885), which at the time, similar to the IPP platform in Ireland, pursued a policy of self-government within the confines of the British Empire. Moreover, Iranian revolutionaries periodically drew analogies between the Iranian resistance to European imperialism, on the one hand, and Egyptian and Indian nationalist opposition to British rule, on the other hand, among other range of such analogies. The Irish Question, however, remained absent from the Iranian list of worldwide examples. Furthermore, to reiterate, despite their growing familiarity with Ireland and Irish affairs after the late nineteenth century, Iranians remained unaware of the contested Irish theories of Iranian origins and the various appropriations of Iranian history and mythology in the service of Irish nationalism.

Iranian Familiarity with the Irish Question after the Iranian Constitutional Revolution of 1906–11

The Iranian Constitutional Revolution of 1906–11 inaugurated a new phase in Iranian awareness of Irish politics. As already noted, following the 1907 Anglo-Russian Agreement, a broad spectrum of Irish nationalists (in Ireland and in the Irish diaspora) joined the opposition to British policy of cooperation with Russia in undermining the Iranian constitutional struggle and Iran's overall sovereignty. This opposition extended from the United Kingdom itself to other parts of the world (including different regions of the British Empire). This time around, unlike *The Nation's* advocacy of Iranian sovereignty during the Anglo-Iranian War of 1856–57, some Iranians, notably in the ranks of Iranian nationalists, were fully cognizant of at least some range of Irish nationalist advocacy of the Iranian revolutionary camp (leaving aside here the inner factional politics of the latter). A few Iranian nationalists traveling to England during this period crossed paths with a few prominent Irish Parliamentary Party members who had joined the mounting parliamentary and extra-parliamentary campaigns in the United Kingdom against Sir Edward Grey's Iranian policy after 1907. These endeavors, most notably by John Dillon, were reported in the Iranian press. For his part, William J. Maloney, stationed in Iran as a Reuters correspondent after 1909, was in direct contact with Iranian revolutionaries and the Persia Committee in London, which coordinated the organized multi-party campaign against Grey's Iranian policy in the United Kingdom after late 1908. Moreover, by then there was much greater flow of information available through different channels about world affairs to Iranians interested in such matters. Increasing number of Iranians were also traveling to more distant regions of the world, than had been the case in the nineteenth century; albeit, Iranian travelers to England still rarely ever ventured as far west in the British Isles as Ireland. Iranian nationalists were also aware of the advocacy of varying Irish nationalist platforms by groups of Indian, Egyptian, and other nationalists with whom Iranians were in contact and with whose struggles Iranian nationalists publicly sympathized.

Yet, Iranian nationalists in general appear to have continued with their assessment of Ireland as a long-standing constituent territory under English jurisdiction in the British Isles and with segments of Ireland's population having primarily "domestic" or "inner" political squabbles with London over matters of regional (provincial) governance, occasionally with some religious and/or ethnic overtones. To give an example illustrative of this Iranian trend, during the Iranian civil war of 1908–09 the prominent Iranian constitutionalist-nationalist Yahya Dawlatabadi—who would shortly also travel to England and meet with John Dillon among other critics of Grey's Iranian policy—wrote in his posthumously-published memoirs: "the [segment of the] English nation [i.e., the population of the United Kingdom] that can be characterized as opposed to the [Iranian policy of its] government, consists of English [i.e.'British'] Radical-Liberals and Irish critics of the English government[. These critics] do not desist from loathing Russian actions [in Iran], [the latter acting] with England's compliance[,] even though [these critics' campaigns] cannot have a significant effect."[108] Essentially, similar to those Radicals in Grey's own Liberal Party who opposed London's cooperation with Russia in the Iranian arena, Dawlatabadi characterized the Irish critics of Grey's Iranian policy too (i.e., members of the IPP in this case) as a domestic political opposition force in the United Kingdom (i.e., opposed to the policy of their *own* government), rather than regarding them as opponents of British "imperial" rule in Ireland—which in the case of the IPP's Home Rule platform was not entirely off the mark. As apparent from the tone of Dawlatabadi's remark, as well as from some reports appearing in Iranian nationalist newspapers at the time, a key factor in Ireland's distinct place as a constituent part of England's combined territorial domain in the British Isles was Ireland's direct parliamentary representation in London, including the sizeable IPP Irish nationalist bloc. This was in contrast to British colonies around the world, including self-governing so-called "white-settlement" dominions in the British Empire, such as Canada (1867) or the Union of South Africa (1910). It should be kept in mind that by the time of the Iranian revolution there were also Scottish and Welsh Home Rule campaigns underway in the United Kingdom, with no less a figure than the leading Liberal politician David Lloyd George (chancellor of the exchequer after 1908) being a staunch champion of Welsh self-government.[109] Otherwise, periodic Iranian news reports of Irish political affairs were certainly not lacking during the time of the Iranian revolution.

The Iranian revolution coincided with intensified Irish campaigns for Home Rule, whether in the form of the IPP's parliamentary action, or the newly founded Sinn Féin (1905) with its 'abstentionist' approach to participation in the British parliament, or by some smaller political groups. In the United Kingdom's general election of 1906, the IPP secured 83 parliamentary seats (later gaining an additional seat in 1910), with the governing Liberal Party after the two general elections of 1910 depending on IPP's backing (along with the support of the much smaller number of Labour Party MPs) for maintaining its parliamentary majority.[110] Ireland-related political news available to Iranian readership during the Constitutional Revolution ranged from indirect coverage of Irish affairs to more specifically Ireland-focused political developments. Some of these reports clearly underscored the protracted background of campaigns for parliamentary Home Rule in Ireland. For instance, a May 1907 article in the Tehran constitutionalist paper *Habl al-Matin* ("*The Firm Cord*") concerning the willingness of the "British" Liberal Party to consider domestic devolution of power in the British Isles (Irish Home Rule in this case) and to curb England's imperial expansion around the globe (which was a clear exaggeration by the paper), contrasted this Liberal platform with the "British" Conservative Party's (a.k.a., Unionists) opposition to decentralization of power in the British Isles and that party's pursuit of aggressive imperialism abroad. *Habl al-Matin* commented on this political and ideological disparity between the two main parties in the United Kingdom by way of an oversimplified characterization of the stance of the two parties on the Irish Question. Alluding to the defeated 1886 and 1893 Irish Home Rule Bills in the British parliament, the paper noted that whereas the Conservative Party was committed to British imperial expansion, the Liberals conversely were "as far as possible desirous of self-determination of peoples ['*tavāyef*'; literally 'clans']—for this reason during the premiership of Mr. Gladstone, who was the leader of the Liberal faction ['*tāyefeh*'/'clan'], [even] the question of self-rule for the island of Ireland was taken up, but [this Bill] was defeated due to the overwhelming opposition of Conservatives."[111] The paper forgot to mention Gladstone's occupation of Egypt in 1882, among other examples of Liberal perpetuation of British imperialism. Other occasional Ireland-related reports in the Iranian press during this time period again generally treated the Irish Question as an internal, rather than an imperial, concern of the authorities in London. For instance, in August 1907 *Habl al-Matin* of Tehran reported (albeit without historical contextualization) the clashes that had taken place earlier in the month between security forces and some crowds in Belfast and the resulting injuries and deaths.[112] This was, in fact, a cryptic coverage of the August 11, 1907, rioting in the predominantly Catholic (and largely nationalist) Falls Road district of Belfast, where the residents supported the recent dockers' strike in the city. The Royal Irish Constabulary had responded to stone-throwing crowds by bayoneting and shooting them, with the violence continuing over the next few days.[113] Other scope of reports on Irish political developments periodically appeared in major Iranian constitutionalist-nationalist papers, including in the radical social-democratic *Irān-e Nou* ("*New Iran*"), published in Tehran following the Iranian civil war of 1908–09. These ranged from John Redmond's re-election as the IPP leader in early 1910 to a very brief report of the planned protests against local authorities in Belfast in late 1910.[114] In December 1910, *Irān-e Nou* provided one of the extremely rare Iranian press commentaries during these years on Ireland as a British *imperial* territory; that of British misrule in Ireland in the form of the paper's critique of capitalist-imperialism.[115] Yet, the paper did not comment on Irish nationalist platforms; nor did it endorse any form of Irish nationalism.

Once again, it should be remembered that reports of Irish developments available to Iranian readers also consisted of material in other languages published outside Iran and accessible to some educated Iranians, whether in the pages of the European press, including the Russian press (either in Russian language or in other local languages in the Russian Empire), or in Ottoman, Indian (the latter also inclusive of English language newspapers), Egyptian, or other press that reached small numbers of readers inside Iran. Some of these sources clearly covered the Irish Question as an imperial/colonial topic. There were also instances of contemporary Iranian press reports in which references by non-Iranian commentators to the Irish Question appeared in the unmistakable framework of British imperial rule, with similar reports also appearing in Persian language newspapers published outside Iran and accessible to Iranian readers. A random example is the 1908 translation of a speech by Marquess Okuma Shigenobu on British rule in India. Appearing in a foremost Tehran constitutionalist-nationalist paper *Majles* ("*National Assembly*"). In his discussion of Britain's "divide and rule" imperial politics, Marquess Okuma Shigenobu (the former Japanese foreign minister and a founder of the Constitutional Progressive Party of Japan) alluded to London's policy in Ireland.[116] Similar range of reporting occurred in the Iranian émigré press that reached Iran. Among these, the highly-renowned and influential weekly Calcutta Persian-language newspaper *Habl al-Matin* ("*The Firm Cord*") alluded to the Irish Question in various settings and with much greater frequency and detail than papers published inside Iran. Founded in December 1893, with Indian, Iranian, and Central Asian readership (among other locations), since its inception this paper was distributed inside Iran through subscription and served as a major source of information about international events for Iranian readers, particularly of news related to the United Kingdom and the British Empire (not surprisingly, given its place of publication). The paper was owned by

Sayyid Jalal al-Din Kashani (a.k.a., "Mo'ayed al-Eslam"), whose brother later launched the Tehran *Habl al-Matin*. Having long resided in British-India and well-versed in the history of British imperial rule and domestic politics, including parliamentary debates at Westminster, Kashani was a leading proponent of various reform platforms in Iran. By the time of the Iranian revolution, his paper also simultaneously, and paradoxically, espoused pan-Indian nationalist campaigns for self-government, waged by the Indian National Congress, alongside the paper's advocacy of the Muslim-nationalist platform of the All-India Muslim League (1906), which opposed Indian self-government prior to the 1911 British revocation of Bengal's 1905 partition into predominantly Muslim and Hindu parts. The content of Ireland-related reports appearing in the Calcutta *Habl al-Matin* before and after the Iranian revolution were highly varied and indicate a more layered familiarity with Irish affairs than most papers published inside Iran. For instance, in two separate reports on July 28, 1902, the paper covered British parliamentary exchanges between John Redmond, the IPP leader, and George Wyndham, chief secretary for Ireland. The topics of discussion were the latest government statistics on "the number of persons prosecuted in Ireland" that year (i.e., under the Criminal Law and Procedure Act) as well as the land agitation in Ireland and the Land Purchase Act (of 1887).[117] Most likely the complexities of these exchanges would not have been readily comprehensible to the average reader of the paper inside Iran. Another random example of the paper's coverage of Ireland-related news from these earlier years was a brief report in November 1903 on the refusal of US authorities to extradite to the United Kingdom a fugitive "resident of Ireland" now living in the American state of Indiana, on grounds that the United States considered the said individual's offense political and not criminal.[118] (While the article implied that Irish "political" activists fleeing British prosecution took refuge in the United States, the paper's readers would not have known that this time around it was the highly controversial case of an Irish Catholic named James Lynchehaun. He had made it to the United States after escaping from prison in Ireland in 1902, where he had been serving a life sentence for an extremely sadistic assault in 1894 on his former Protestant landowning employer following his dismissal as the "rent collector" on her property on Achill Island, County Mayo.[119]) The same expansive range of Irish reports continued in the Calcutta *Habl al-Matin* after the outbreak of the Iranian revolution in 1906. Some reports also contained Kashani's own editorial addenda. For instance, on December 30, 1907, under the heading "Iran and its Trinary Neighbors" (i.e., British India, Russia, and the Ottoman Empire), the paper commented on continued tensions between London and Berlin and, based on a report from an unnamed German source, noted that Germany's "political options" in the event of war with Britain included the Irish struggle for independence from Britain, which could be utilized "as a major instrument of a German military advance."[120]

Among other passing reports in the Calcutta *Habl al-Matin* on Irish developments in the coming years was a vaguely worded and inadequately concise mention of the opposition in the British House of Commons to proposed amendments by the House of Lords to the 1909 Irish Land Purchase Bill (introduced by Augustine Birrell, chief secretary for Ireland).[121] Another insufficiently detailed report from the point of view of average readers inside Iran was that of William O'Brien's speech in Cork following the January 1910 general election in the United Kingdom in which the Liberal government managed to narrowly maintain its hold on power. O'Brien echoed Irish nationalist objections to certain additional taxes in the Liberal government's proposed budget of 1909. This account of O'Brien's speech was followed by the ambiguously-worded report of the Liberal chancellor of the exchequer's (David Lloyd George) rejection of O'Brien's recommended tax exemptions in Ireland.[122] (It should again be reminded that the narrow Liberal electoral victory in 1910 had rendered the government dependent on the IPP's backing for a parliamentary majority. The taxes in question, including on liquor, were contained in the government's "People's Budget" that was eventually passed on April 29, 1910.) The actual contour of such reports could only be grasped by readers already well-versed in both Irish developments and key political debates in the United Kingdom. Whereas this degree of familiarity may have existed among some of the paper's readers in India (including members of the Iranian émigré community), the average reader in Iran would have failed to draw relevant connections. However, the next issue of the paper carried a clearer account of the recent general election in the United Kingdom and the parliamentary crisis generated by the opposition in the House of Lords to the Liberal government's proposed budget. This report, by the "London correspondent" (most likely in actuality taken from an English-language paper which had a correspondent in London), commented on the significantly diminished electoral majority of the Liberal Party after 1910 and the party's ability to remain in office only with the support of the Irish (i.e., the IPP) and Labour ("*amaleh*"). The report added that some commentators caustically remarked the current government was in actuality an Irish-coalition administration and that the real prime minister was the leader of the "Irish bloc," John Redmond. The report continued that it was expected the current parliament would be dissolved shortly over (1) the obstruction of the budget, (2) the proposed reform of the House of Lords by the Liberal government, and (3) Irish self-government ("*esteqlāl*"; i.e., Home Rule), which the current Liberal administration had to promise in return for the Irish parliamentary support.[123] In the case of the Calcutta *Habl al-Matin*'s coverage of Irish affairs too, which at times were framed in reference to the British Empire at large, what stood out was Ireland's special political and administrative status in the British Empire, distinct from territories such as India or Egypt. In effect, Ireland was not represented as a colony. This distinction was most evident in a 1909 report in the paper that treated the Irish Question separately from Britain's colonial concerns. Appearing not long after the end of the Iranian civil war, under the caption of "What do Russia and England Want from Iran[?]," the paper stated: "do not believe that the English [i.e., the British state] are altruistic, freedom-nurturers, and enthusiasts of Iran's sovereignty. [...] If this were the case[,] the extensive unrest and universal uproar in India and Egypt would not have broken out, and the disputes with the population of Ireland would have been resolved."[124] Other range of Ireland-related news in the paper during the time of the Iranian revolution included such mundane matters as the September 19, 1910, report from the Dublin *Daily Express* (very likely obtained indirectly from another publication in India) of the pending vacation trip to Ireland by the new British monarch George V and his wife Mary, following the king's forthcoming coronation.[125]

Although the Calcutta *Habl al-Matin* devoted greater attention to Irish affairs than newspapers published inside Iran, this coverage during the Iranian revolution was much less frequent in comparison with the paper's reporting of colonial developments and/or reform movements in other parts of the world (not counting the paper's regular coverage of Indian and Iranian affairs for obvious reasons). The frequency of Ireland-related reports did not even remotely approach the regularity with which the paper covered Japanese-occupied Korea or the Belgian Congo during the same time frame. Whereas the lesser coverage of Irish news in comparison with some other world events during certain periods is understandable, the overall scarcity of the Calcutta *Habl al-Matin*'s reportage on Irish developments is ultimately indicative of the minor place of the Irish Question on the Iranian nationalist horizon of world events at the time—no less by a newspaper published in British India and with a substantial target readership there. For instance, the frequent reports by the paper of the Boer War during 1899–1902, compared to its meager coverage of Ireland during the same period, can readily be accounted for by the fact that the Boer War was a major armed conflict that also concerned Britain's imperial position in southern Africa, as well as generating extensive condemnation of London's unwarranted aggression by other European powers. But the volume of Irish news in the paper remained scarce overall and paled in comparison with many other developments around the world (ranging from Korea and the Belgian Congo to Finland, China, and Egypt), including during the time of the Iranian revolution of 1906–11. Regardless, even the paper's rare imperial framing of Ireland failed to evoke Iranian nationalist expressions of support for any Irish nationalist platforms at the time, and Iranian revolutionaries did not reciprocate any of the Irish nationalist gestures of solidarity until after 1916.

In fact, the avoidance of public cross-identification with Irish nationalists by Iranian nationalists during the Iranian revolution provoked commentary from two Irish journalists covering the Iranian civil war of 1908–09: Joseph Maunsell Hone and Page L. Dickinson. Whether or not Hone and Dickinson were deliberately embellishing their account, they pointed out the irony of the disinclination on the part of Iranian nationalists to be in any way identified with Irish nationalists at a time when a leading representative of the latter, John Dillon, was busy defending the Iranian revolution. On this occasion, Dillon was objecting to the decision by *The Times* of London to recall from Iran its reporter known for "objective" coverage of the Iranian civil war. Commenting on the purported aversion of some Iranian revolutionaries to being branded "Nationalist," Hone and Dickinson wrote:

> Several Nationalists were at pains to point out that the term was an unfortunate one. Being in bad odour owing to "those Irish," it would not attract the sympathy of English people. The point was brought before us by the [Persian] correspondent of the *Times* among others. Curiously enough at this very moment an Irish M.P., under misapprehension that the *Times* had dismissed this gentleman from its service, asked a question on his behalf in the English House of Commons. This gentleman's use of the phrase "those Irish" and his anxiety lest a parallel should be drawn between the Irish and Persian Nationalists were, in the circumstances, unkind. The ingratitude was of course unconscious; the English newspapers containing the Irish M.P.'s question and the *Times*' explanation of the facts had not yet arrived in Teheran.[126]

For many years after "the English newspapers containing the Irish M.P.'s question and the *Times*' explanation of the facts" finally reached Tehran, Iranian nationalists continued their public silence on the Irish Question, even if Hone and Dickinson may have been consciously exaggerating their case, given their overall lack of sympathy with any of the camps involved in the Iranian civil war.

Following the termination of the Iranian revolution in late 1911, the Iranian press continued reporting on political developments in Ireland. General Iranian press reports of Irish affairs modestly increased in frequency in the immediate aftermath of the passage of the Irish Home Rule Bill by the British parliament in April 1912 and the eruption of disturbances in Ireland between unionist and nationalist factions over the Bill in the period leading up to the outbreak of the First World War in 1914. An exceptionally lengthy Iranian coverage of organized unionist opposition to Irish Home Rule that culminated in the signing of the unionist Ulster Covenant on September 28, 1912, appeared in the Tehran newspaper *Āftāb* in late October of that year.[127] But this heightened Iranian interest in the Irish Question did not assume any tenor of cross-nationalist solidarity and/or publicly expressed sympathy with any Irish nationalist platform. Then again, a Scottish Home Rule Bill also passed into law by the Westminster parliament in 1914, as did the Irish Home Rule Act in that year, and Scottish Home Rule too failed to elicit public advocacy from Iranian nationalists, whom, it should be noted, did not consider Scotland an English colony either. Incidentally, both Home Rule Acts were suspended during the First World War and abandoned by London after the war.

As mentioned in the previous chapter, it was only following the outbreak of the Easter Rising in Ireland from April 24 to 29, 1916, that Iranian nationalists (and later also other Iranian anti-imperialist groups) began to publicly voice solidarity with the Irish struggle (in its radical republican manifestation).[128] More precisely, this Iranian cross-identification with Irish nationalists occurred after the execution of Roger Casement by British authorities on August 3, 1916, in alleged connection with the rising. This transformation in Iranian nationalist appraisal of the Irish struggle took place in the broader framework of the First World War and German war-time propaganda and backing for militant Iranian, Irish, Indian, and other anti-Allied nationalist groupings. Following the Easter Rising, Ireland (and Northern Ireland after 1922) in various settings and configurations continued to resurface periodically in wide-ranging Iranian anti-imperialist expressions of cross-territorial solidarity. Yet, it needs to be stressed that the growing Iranian interest in Ireland was not restricted to political matters alone. For instance, for an increasing number of literate Iranians (certainly after the 1930s, if not earlier) Ireland in general (i.e., the Irish Free State/Éire/Republic of Ireland as well as Northern Ireland) was also of interest because of works fiction, theatrical plays, and poetry produced by Irish authors. This is yet another indication of the mounting international stature and appeal of Irish authors in the arena of world literature, ranging from Oscar Wilde to George Bernard Shaw, William Butler Yeats, James Joyce, and Samuel Beckett, among others, and with growing recognition in more recent years of works by some women luminaries of Irish literature as well, such as Elizabeth Bowen (d.1973). Thomas Moore's 1817 *Lalla Rookh* had been the first work of literature by an Irish author to attract some attention among Iranians, but as of yet Moore's narrative poem has not been translated into Persian. Of course, nowadays many Iranians are conversant enough in English to read the work in its original language, as is the case with other works of Irish literature composed in English language as well. Works of numerous Irish authors and playwrights have been translated and published in Persian inside and outside Iran. Bram Stoker's *Dracula* and works by Samuel Beckett rank among the best known of these translations. Beckett's *Waiting for Godot* (1953) is the most frequently adapted theatrical work by an Irish playwright staged in Iran. In addition to Beckett, Iranian translations of plays and/or theatrical productions by Irish authors include works by Flann O'Brien, John Banville, William Trevor, or Marian Keyes, either in their entirety or in partial adaptations, to offer just a random incomplete listing. James Joyce (d. 1941) remains the most widely *recognized* example of an Irish author influencing a highly-celebrated Iranian author. As already noted in my Introduction, Joyce's works had a major impact on the modernist style of Sadeq Hedayat (d.1951). Today, of course, Ireland and Northern Ireland also serve as locations of Iranian diaspora, travel abroad, as well as of international study, among other range of Irish attractions for Iranians, such as music, cinema, and the arts. The greater appeal of Joyce, or Beckett for that matter, than Yeats—as difficult as it has been to translate the works of Beckett into Persian and practically impossible to translate even very brief portions of Joyce's *later* works—is doubtless largely a symptom of particular modes of *worlding the human experience* by Joyce and Beckett, in contrast to most of Yeats' writings. Perhaps because of their authors' exilic identities, works by Joyce and Beckett ultimately address universal human conditions (even in the case of Joyce's Ireland-centered *Ulysses* and *Finnegans Wake*). As Terry Eagleton put it, "for Yeats, at least in one of his incarnations, the race in question is Irish, whereas for Joyce it is human; so that the cosmopolitan vision of the literal exile outflanks the totalizing standpoint of the metaphorical one."[129]

Notes

1 In 1238, the Isma'ili leader of Alamut, northern Iran, dispatched an abortive mission to the court of the English monarch Henry III, seeking a military alliance against the invading Mongol forces. The earliest English diplomatic mission to an 'Iranian' territory took place in the last decade of the thirteenth century. The mission was led by Geoffrey de Langley, the representative of King Edward I, and was an official English deputation to the Mongol Ilkhanid state that controlled 'Iranian' and other territories. This failed mission, occurring in what became the last years of the Crusades, was intended to forge a Christian-Mongol alliance against Muslim forces resisting the Crusaders. See Percy Sykes, *A History of Persia*, vol.II, pp.172, 185–86, 191. On the 1562 English embassy of Anthony Jenkinson (of the Muscovy Company) to the Safavid court, see ibid., pp.249–53.
2 John Malcolm, *The History of Persia*, vol.I (1815 edition), pp.531–37, 544–52, 559; Percy Sykes, *A History of Persia*, vol.II, pp.259–62, 273–83, 363–67; John Piggot, *Persia*, pp. 205–207; William Noel Sainsbury, ed., *Calendar of State Papers. Colonial Series*, vol.6, passim. On the Sherley brothers, see Evelyn Philip Shirley, *The Sherley Brothers: An Historical Memoir of the Lives of Sir Thomas Sherley, Sir Anthony Sherley, and Sir Robert Sherley, Knights*. Chiswick: Charles Wittingham, 1848; Edward Denison Ross, ed. *Sir Anthony Sherley and His Persian Adventure: Including Some Contemporary Narratives Relating Thereto*. Abingdon, Oxford: Routledge Curzon, 2005 [1933], passim; Jane Grogan, *The Persian Empire in English Renaissance Writing, 1549-1622*. Basingstoke: Palgrave Macmillan, 2013, chapter 4.

3 John Malcolm, *The History of Persia*, vol.I (1815 edition), pp.531–37, 544–52, 559; Percy Sykes, *A History of Persia*, vol.II, pp.259–62, 273–83, 363–67; John Piggot, *Persia*, pp. 205–207. See also, for example, John Bruce, ed., *Calendar of State Papers. Domestic Series: of the Reign of Charles I. 1625, 1626*. London: Longman, Brown, Green, Longmans, & Roberts, 1858, pp.315, 345; William Noel Sainsbury, ed., *Calendar of State Papers. Colonial Series*, vol.6, passim. On contacts between Safavid Iran and Europe and Europeans, see also Rudi Matthee, "The Safavids Under Western Eyes: Seventeenth-Century European Travelers to Iran," *Journal of Early Modern History* 13(2–3), 2009, pp.137–71. Another 'Iranian' traveler to seventeenth-century England was Teresia Sampsonia, the Christian Circassian-Iranian wife of Robert Sherley. See Jonathan Burton, "The Shah's Two Ambassadors: *The Travels of the Three English Brothers* and the Global early Modern" in Brinda Charry and Gitanjali Shahani, eds., *Emissaries in Early Modern Literature and Culture: Mediation, Transmission, Traffic, 1550-1700*. Farnham, Surrey: Ashgate, 2009, pp.23–40; Manoutchehr Eskandari-Qajar, "Persian Ambassadors, their Circassians, and the Politics of Elizabethan and Regency England," *Iranian Studies* 44(2), March 2011, pp.251–71. An Iranian, possibly originally a Christian or a convert to Christianity, or having later merely adopted a Christian/English first name, called "Nicholas Argoro" (?), is mentioned as living in London c.1614-15, and on July 27, 1630 an Iranian resident in London, Yosuf Ali (listed as "Joseph Alley"), was buried at the parish of St. Botolph's Church in Aldgate, London. See "St Michael Cornhill, Churchwardens: Accounts 1614-1615: Given Nicholas Argoro a Persian that boughte letters from the Lords of the Council but the like is not to be allowed hereafter" (Ms 4071/2 f. 26, top of page); and "St Botolph Aldgate: July 27, 1630, burial of Joseph Alley, a Persian borne" (GL Ms 9222/2 p.87), Guildhall Library Manuscripts Section (http://www.history.ac.uk/gh/baentries.htm).

4 Abu Taleb Khan, *Massir-e Tālebi* [mash'ar bar hālāt-e landan va keyfiāt-e jami'-e jazireh-ye england va [...].]. [Horace Hayman?] Wilson, Hassan Ali ibn Abu Taleb ibn Mohammad Esfahani, and Mir Qodrat-Ali editors. Calcutta: Hindustani Press, 1812. Other editions of the work appeared throughout the nineteenth century, including an abridged Persian edition edited by David MacFarlane. See, for instance, Abu Taleb Khan, *The Travels of Mirza Aboo Talib Khan, in the Persian Language (Masir-e talebi)*. Abridged by David MacFarlane. Second edition. Calcutta: Baptist Mission Press, 1836. See also Daniel O'Quinn, "Introduction" and "Mirza Abu Talib and Charles Stewart: A Brief Chronology" in Abu Taleb, *The Travels of Mirza Abu Taleb Khan, in Asia, Africa and Europe, during the Years 1799, 1800, 1801, 1802, and 1803*. Translated by Charles Stewart and edited by Daniel O'Quinn. Peterborough, Canada: Broadview, 2009, pp.9–52; Houchang Chehabi, "An Indo-Persian in Ireland, anno 1799: Mirzā Abu Tāleb Khān" in Houchang E. Chehabi and Grace Neville, eds., *Erin and Iran*, pp.129–55; Juan R.I. Cole, "Invisible Occidentalism: Eighteenth-Century Indo-Persian Constructions of the West," *Iranian Studies* 25(3–4), 1992, pp.3–16; Denis Wright, *The Persians Amongst the English*, pp.44–46; Mohammad R. Ghanoonparvar, *In a Persian Mirror: Images of the West and Westerners in Iranian Fiction*. Austin: University of Texas Press, 1993, pp.13–18.

5 Abu Taleb Khan, *The Travels of Mirza Abu Taleb Khan, in Asia, Africa and Europe, during the Years 1799, 1800, 1801, 1802, and 1803*. Volume I. Charles Stewart translator. London: Longman, Hurst, Rees, and Orme, 1810, pp.131–34. See also, Jamshid Malekpour, *Adabiyāt-e Namāyeshi dar Irān: Nokhostin Koushesh-hā tā Doureh-ye Qājār*. Volume I. Reprint. Tehran: Touss, 1385 (2006), pp.57–58.

6 Mirza Abu Taleb Khan, *The Travels of Mirza Abu Taleb Khan*, vol.I (1810 edition), chapters 6, 7, and 8. On Deen Mahomet, see Michael H. Fisher's "Introduction" and biographical essay in Sake Deen Mahomet, *The Travels of Dean Mahomet: An Eighteenth Century Journey through India*. Edited by Michael H. Fisher. Berkeley: University of California Press, 1997.

7 Abu Taleb Khan, *The Travels of Mirza Abu Taleb Khan*, vol.I (1810 edition), pp.135–36.

8 Ibid., pp.106–107.

9 *Dublin Penny Journal* 1(4), July 21, 1832, p.3, c.a.

10 Ibid. 1(12), September 15, 1832, p.93, c.a.

11 Abu Taleb Khan, *The Travels of Mirza Abu Taleb Khan*, vol.I (1810 edition), pp.127–28.

12 Ibid., p.99.

13 Ibid., pp.296–97.

14 Compare the original edition (Abu Taleb Khan, *The Travels of Mirza Abu Taleb Khan*, vol.I (1810 edition), p.150) with Abu Taleb Khan, *The Travels of Mirza Abu Taleb Khan, in Asia, Africa and Europe, during the Years 1799, 1800, 1801, 1802, and 1803*. Volume I. Charles Stewart translator. Second edition. London: Longman, Hurst, Rees, Orme, and Brown, 1814, pp.180–81.
15 Abu Taleb Khan, *The Travels of Mirza Abu Taleb Khan*, vol.I (1814 edition), pp.180–81; Abu Taleb Khan, *Massir-e Tālebi*, 184.
16 Abu Taleb Khan, *The Travels of Mirza Abu Taleb Khan*, vol.I (1810 edition), p.126.
17 It read "*da'āvi-e nafssānieh-ye khod*" (i.e., "their own worldly disputes"). See Abu Taleb Khan, *Massir-e Tālebi*, p.518.
18 Abu Taleb Khan, *The Travels of Mirza Abu Taleb Khan, in Asia, Africa and Europe, during the Years 1799, 1800, 1801, 1802, and 1803*. Volume II. Charles Stewart translator. London: Longman, Hurst, Rees, and Orme, 1810, pp.79–82.
19 On Abul Hassan Khan's travels to the United Kingdom, see Abul Hassan Khan Shirazi, *Hayratnāmeh: Safarnāmeh-ye Mirzā Abulhassan Khān Ilchi beh Landan*. Hassan Morselvand editor. Tehran: Farhang-e Rassa, 1364 (1985); and Margaret Morris Cloake, ed., *A Persian at the Court of King George, 1809-10: The Journal of Mirza Abul Hassan Khan*. London: Barrie & Jenkins, 1988. Both publications cover Abul Hassan Khan's first visit to the United Kingdom. See also Harford Jones Brydges, *The Dynasty of the Kajars*, pp.370, 444–45; *London Gazette*, May 22, 1819, p.881; ibid., June 5, 1819, p.976. Abul Hassan was granted the honorific title "Khan" following his return to Iran in 1811 from his first ambassadorial appointment to England.
20 On Abul Hassan Khan and James Morier, among numerous sources, see also Henry B. McKenzie Johnston, "Hajji Baba and Mirza Abul Hasan Khan: A Conundrum," *Iran*, vol.33 (1995), pp.93–96; James Watt, "James Morier and the Oriental Picaresque" in Graeme Harper, ed., *Comedy, Fantasy, Colonialism*. London: Continuum, 2002, pp.58–72; Naghmeh Sohrabi, "Looking behind *Hajji Baba of Ispahan*: The case of Mirza Abul Hassan Khan Ilchi Shirazi" in Amy Singer, Christoph K. Neumann, Selçuk Akşin Somel, eds., *Untold Histories of the Middle East: Recovering Voices from the 19th and 20th Centuries*. New York: Routledge, 2011, pp.159–75; Daniel O'Quinn, "Tears in Tehran / Laughter in London: James Morier, Mirza Abul Hassan Khan, and the Geopolitics of Emotion," *Eighteenth-Century Fiction* 25(1), Fall 2012, pp.85–114; Abbas Amanat, "Hajji Baba of Ispahan" (2003), *Encyclopaedia Iranica* (http://www.iranica.com/articles/hajji-baba-of-ispahan); Mohamad Tavakoli-Targhi, *Refashioning Iran*, pp.41–43; Amir Ahmadi Arian, "The Unstable People of a Tumultuous Land: Persia Through the Eyes and Feet of Hajji Baba of Isfahan," *Iranian Studies* 49(1), 2016, pp.57–75; Manoutchehr Eskandari-Qajar, "Persian Ambassadors," pp.251–71.
21 *European Magazine and London Review*, vol. 57, June 1810, pp.403, 456–57; *Select Reviews, and Spirit of the Foreign Magazines* (Philadelphia) 4(23), November 1810, pp.334–36.
22 See, for example, "Manners of the Persian Ambassador, Drawn in England," *Asiatic Journal and Monthly Register for British India and Its Dependencies* (London), vol.9, March 1820, pp.246–49.
23 See also ibid., vol.8, December 1819, p.621; *Edinburgh Magazine* 84(2), November 1819, p.469.
24 See Robert Perceval Graves, *Life of Sir William Rowan Hamilton*. Vol. I. Dublin: Hodges, Figgis, & Co., 1882, pp.71–74; Bertram C.A. Windle, "Irish Men of Science" in Joseph Dunn and Patrick Joseph Lennox, eds., *The Glories of Ireland*, p.46.
25 John C. Greene, *Theatre in Dublin, 1745-1820: A Calendar of Performances*. Volume 6. Lanham, MD: Rowman & Littlefield, 2011, pp.4425–26. Regarding the performance of 'The National Persian air' at the concert, it should be noted the very first Iranian national anthem was only composed in 1873 during the reign of Nasser al-Din Shah by the French Alfred Jean-Baptiste Lemaire, a music instructor at the Dar al-Fonun, Iran's first modern institution of higher learning founded in 1851.
26 Ibid., pp.4425–26.
27 Ibid., p.4426; John Thomas Gilbert, *History of the City of Dublin*. Volume II. Dublin: McGlashan and Gill, 1859, p.247.
28 John Thomas Gilbert, *History of the City of Dublin*, vol.II, p.247.
29 John C. Greene, *Theatre in Dublin*, Vol.6, p.4426. On O'Rourke, see also ibid., p.4190.

30 Marmion Wilard Savage, *The Falcon Family; or, Young Ireland*. London: Chapman and Hall, 1845, pp.52–53. Incidentally, a review of this book appeared in the same issue of the *Dublin University Magazine* as the sixth installment of James Clarence Mangan's "Literæ Orientales," which immediately preceded the review. *Dublin University Magazine* 27(157), January 1846, pp.58–67. "Gul" and "Cashmere" had both appeared in Moore's *Lalla Rookh*.

31 Myself [Mrs. Purcell], *The Orientalist, or Electioneering in Ireland; a Tale, by Myself*. Volume I. London: Baldwin, Cradock, and Joy, 1820, pp.13–15, 25–31. In this work Abul Hasan Khan appeared in Ballinaglera (County Leitrim). For an announcement of this book's publication, see also *Freeman's Journal* (Dublin), April 26, 1820, p.2.

32 See Sonja Lawrenson, "'The country chosen of my heart': the comic cosmopolitanism of *The Orientalist, or Electioneering in Ireland; a Tale, by Myself*" in Simon Davis, Daniel Sanjiv Roberts, and Gabriel Sánchez Espinosa, eds., *India and Europe in the Global Eighteenth Century*. Oxford: Voltaire Foundation, 2014, pp.101–22. Lawernson's nuanced essay, even though it does not mention Abul Hasan Khan, is the only study of *The Orientalist, or Electioneering in Ireland* that I have come across.

33 Joseph Lennon, *Irish Orientalism*, p.130.

34 Ibid.

35 See also Myself [Mrs. Purcell], *The Orientalist*, vol.I, pp.13–15, 25–31.

36 See, for example, "Ireland" in *Encyclopaedia Britannica; or A Dictionary of Arts, Sciences, and Miscellaneous Literature; Enlarged and Improved*. Volume 11. Fourth edition. Edinburgh: Archibald Constable and Company, 1810, pp.320–56. Notwithstanding the disparities between Abul Hasan Khan's entry and the information in the *Encyclopaedia Britannica*, the latter comes closest in tone and content to Abul Hassan Khan's entry in comparison with other possible range of contemporary textual sources that may have been available to him, such as the section on "Ireland" in *A System of Geography; or, A Descriptive, Historical, and Philosophical View of the Several Quarters of the World* …. Volume 4. Glasgow: W. and D. Brownlie, 1807, pp.314–64. On Sir Gore Ouseley and his brother the orientalist William Ouseley and Abul Hassan Khan, see also Stanley Lane-Poole, "Ouseley, Sir William (1767-1842)," p.363; Peter Avery, "Ouseley, Gore"; idem, "Ouseley, William"; Hasan Javadi, "Abu'l-Ḥasan Khan Īlčī," *Encyclopaedia Iranica* (http://www.iranicaonline.org/articles/abul-hasan-khan-ilci-mirza-persian-diplomat-b).

37 Abul Abul Hassan Khan Shirazi, *Hayratnāmeh*, pp.232–33. This entry, for Sunday, March 11, 1810, does not appear in M. Cloake, ed., *A Persian at the Court of King George*.

38 Mohammad Ali Sayyah, *Safarnāmeh-ye Hāj Sayyāh beh Farang*. Ali Dehbashi editor. Tehran: Nasher, 1363 (1984) p.510. See also Mohammad Ali Sayyah, *An Iranian in Nineteenth Century Europe: The Travel Diaries of Hâj Sayyâh, 1859-1877*. Translation and an Introduction by Mehrbanoo Nasser Deyhim, and with a Foreword by Peter Avery. Bethesda: Ibex, 1999, pp.362–67. On Hajj Sayyah, see also Ali Ferdowsi, "Ḥājj Sayyāḥ," *Encyclopaedia Iranica* (http://www.iranicaonline.org/articles/hajj-sayyah).

39 Hajji Mirza Mohammad-Ali Mo'in al-Saltaneh, *Safarnāmeh-ye Shikago: Khāterāt-e Hāji Mirzā Mohammad-Ali Mo'in al-Saltaneh beh Orupā va Amrikā, 1310 Hejri-e Qamari*. Homayoun Shahidi editor. Tehran: Elmi, 1363 (1984), pp.280–81.

40 See also Abbas Zaryab and Iraj Afshar, eds., *Nāmeh-hā-ye Edvārd Brāvn beh Sayyid Hassan Taqizādeh*. Tehran: Jibi, 1356 (1975), p.99; Iraj Afshar, ed., *Zendegi-e Tufāni*: Khāterāt-e *Sayyid Hassan Taqizādeh*. Tehran: Elmi, 1368 (1989). p.355.

41 John Banim, *The Anglo-Irish of the Nineteenth Century. A Novel*. Volume III. London: Henry Colburn, 1828, pp.124–25.

42 John Cornelius O'Callaghan, *The Green Book, or Gleanings from the Writing-desk of a Literary Agitator*. Dublin: James Duffy, 1845, pp.60, 348–49.

43 Sean Ryder, "Defining Colony and Empire in Early Nineteenth-Century Nationalism" in Terrence McDonough, ed., *Was Ireland a Colony?*, pp.178–80; Pauline Collombier-Lakeman, "Ireland and the Empire," p.60.

44 Francis S. L. Lyons, *Charles Stewart Parnell*. London: Collins, 1977, p.51.

45 John Frederick Finerty, *Ireland: The People's History of Ireland*. Volume II. New York: Co-operative Publication Society, 1904, p.528.

46 Patrick J.P. Tynan, *The Irish National Invincibles*, pp.5–6. See also pp.6–13, and passim.

47 On English cartography of Ireland's *interior* in the sixteenth and seventeenth centuries, see John Harwood Andrews, *The Queen's Last Map-Maker; Richard Bartlett in Ireland, 1600-3*. Dublin: Geography Publications, 2008; idem, "Colonial Cartography in a European Setting: The Case of Tudor Ireland" in David Woodward, ed., *The History of Cartography. Volume 3: Cartography in the European Renaissance*. Chicago: University of Chicago Press, 2007, pp.1670–83.
48 Sir Harford Jones Brydges, *The Dynasty of the Kajars*, pp.110–11.
49 Abdul-Razzaq Beg Donboli, *Ma'āsser-e Sultāniyeh*. Tehran: Mirza Zayn al-Abedin Tabrizi printers, 1241 A.H. (1826), no pagination (p.63).
50 James K. McGuire, *What Could Germany Do for Ireland?*, p.221.
51 Ignaty Yulianovich Krachkovsky, *Tārikh-e Neveshteh-hā-ye joqrāfiāyi dar Jahān-e Eslāmi*. Persian translation by Abolqassem Payandeh from the Arabic translation of the Russian original *Istoriia arabskoi geograficheskoi literatury* / History of Geographical Works in the Arab World. Second edition. Tehram: Entesharat-e Elmi va Farhangi, 1384 [1379] (2005), pp.153–57.
52 For refutations of the supposition that al-Idrissi was alluding to the Americas, see for example William Laird Clowes, *The Royal Navy: A History from the Earliest Times to the Present*. Volume I. London: Sampson Low, Marston and Company, 1897, pp.65–66; Geoffrey Ashe, *The Quest for America*; New York: Praeger, 1971, p.48. Ashe, on the other hand, maintains that by 'Ireland the Great' al-Idrissi most likely intended Greenland.
53 The British Sir Percy Sykes noted in 1915 that so-called medieval "Moslem Exploration and Geography" were among the "departments of intellectual activity [in which] the East was incomparably superior to the then benighted West, and this continued through during a period of some five hundred years; for not until the twelfth century did Christendom cease to depend on the East for its light. *Ex Oriente Lux*: no aphorism ever crystallized a profounder truth." Percy Sykes, *A History of Persia*, vol.II, pp.75–77. Leaving aside Sykes' neglect of continued forms of 'Western' dependence on exchanges with the 'East' after the twelfth century, he nevertheless underscored the advanced interest in learning about, and charting, the geography of the known world by 'medieval' Arab, Turkish, Persian and other scholars and scientists, including non-Muslims, living in Muslim-controlled territories.
54 See also Ignaty Yulianovich Krachkovsky, *Tārikh-e Neveshteh-hā-ye joqrāfiāyi*, pp.78–79, 108–109, 148, 149, 160.
55 Edward Granville Browne, *A Literary History of Persia. Volume II: From Firdawsi to Sa'di*. London: T. Fisher Unwin, 1906, pp.482–83; Ignaty Yulianovich Krachkovsky, *Tārikh-e Neveshteh-hā-ye joqrāfiāyi*, pp.192–95.
56 Rashid al-Din Fazlullah Hamedani, *Jāmi' al-Tawārikh: Tārikh-e Afranj, Pāpān, va Qiyāssiri*. Mohammad Roushan editor. Tehran: Mirass-e Maktoub, 1384 (2005), p.47. For a summarized version of Rashid al-Din's descriptions of Ireland, England, and Scotland ("the Scotch paid tribute to the English and that there were no snakes in Ireland"), see Edward Granville Browne, *A Literary History of Persia. Volume III: Under the Tartar Dominion (A.D. 1265-1502)*. Cambridge: Cambridge University Press, 1920, pp.43–44. See also ibid., pp.101–102.
57 On the development of cartographic expertise in Iran in the second half of the nineteenth century, see also Ignaty Yulianovich Krachkovsky, *Tārikh-e Neveshteh-hā-ye joqrāfiāyi*, pp.287–88, 289–94.
58 See also Fereydoun Adamiyat (Thomas M. Ricks translator), "Problems in Iranian Historiography," *Iranian Studies* 4(4), Autumn 1971, pp.136–38.
59 Willem M. Floor, "The First Printing-Press in Iran," *Zeitschrift der Deutschen Morgenländischen Gesellschaft* 130(2), 1980, pp.369–71.
60 See also Edward Granville Browne, *The Press and Poetry of Modern Persia*, pp.7–19, 27–153.
61 Mohammad Hassan Ganji, *Joqrāfiyā dar Irān: az Dār al-Funun tā Enqelāb*. Mashhad: Astan-e Qods-e Razavi, 1367 (1988), pp.23–31, 144–64, 436–40, and passim. For a partial listing of some of the publications and translations by the instructors at Dar al-Fonun, the School of Political Science, and by others see Edward Granville Browne, *The Press and Poetry of Modern Persia*, pp.157–67.
62 See also Javad Safi-Nejad, "Mo'arefi-e Kotob-e Chā'pi-e Joqrāfiyāi-e Dourān-e Qājār," *Roshd-e Āmouzesh-e Joqrāfiyā* (Tehran) 1(2), Summer 1364 (1985), pp.28–36; Abbas Amanat, *Pivot of the Universe: Nasir al-Din Shah Qajar and the Iranian Monarchy, 1831-1896*. Berkeley:

University of California Press, 1997, pp.73–78; Firoozeh Kashani-Sabet, *Frontier Fictions*, pp.15, 57, 62–74; Monica Ringer, *Education, Religion, and the Discourse of Cultural Reform in Qajar Iran*. Costa Mesa, CA: Mazda, 2001, passim; Maryam Ekhtiar, *Modern Science, Education and Reform in Qajar Iran: The Dar al-Fonun*. Richmond, UK: Curzon, 2008, passim; Afshin Marashi, *Nationalizing Iran*, pp.57–59.

63 Benjamin Schwartz ed., *Letters from Persia*, pp.93, 95, 96- 97, 110–11, 113, 115, 116–17. See also Denis Wright, *The English Amongst the Persians*, pp.96–98; Abbas Amanat, *Pivot of the Universe*, p.74.

64 Fologun Refayel, *Jahān-namā*. Tabriz: Molla Saleh Tabrizi, 1267 A.H. (1851), pp.128–37. The actual identity of this author remains unknown. Phonetically spelling his name in Persian as 'Fologun Refayel,' it is possible he was a naturalized British subject of other prior nationality. Given his own account in the Introduction to the book, he had travelled to Iran and learned Persian in that country. He identified himself in the two different existing Persian long-hand and script-printed versions of the manuscript available at the National Library of Iran (Tehran) as variously "English subject" and "English national." He was also fluent in the French language, given that he translated the book from a French source. He is listed as "P. Raphael" in the March 31, 1871, issue of the London journal *Trübner's American and Oriental Literary Record* (p.139) and in *A Catalogue of the Persian Printed Books in the British Museum*. Compiled by Edward Edwards. London: William Clowes and Sons, 1922, p.625. These sources corroborate that Raphael was indeed his surname. (Incidentally, *Trübner's* erroneously rendered the title of Raphael's book as *Tārikh-e Jahān-namā* (*The History of the Display of the World*). I have been unable to find anything resembling the name of this author in the available United Kingdom naturalization records or in published historical and travel narratives of Tabriz from the period in different languages. Over time, other sources have provided very different renderings of the author's name. Edward Granville Browne referred to him as "Mirzá Rafá'il," using the standard Persian term "mirza, denoting a learned person or a scribe in this context. See Browne, *The Press and Poetry of Modern Persia*, pp.9, 160. For another example of other possible renderings of Raphael's name, see Abbas Amanat, *Pivot of the Universe*, p.463 n.47. The publication of Raphael's *Jahān-namā* and its distribution for sale in Tehran was announced in the official Iranian newspaper *Rouznāmeh-ye Vaqāye'-e Ettefāqiyeh* (Tehran), year 1, no. 68, 30 Rajab 1368 A.H. (May 20, 1852), p.8. A more detailed description of the book appeared in a sale advert in the following weekly issue of the same paper. Ibid., year 1, no.69, on 7 Sha'bān 1368 A.H. (May 27, 1852), p.8. The author's name in these announcements was given as only "Refayeli." On Raphael's *Jahān-namā*, see also Mohammad Hassan Ganji, *Joqrāfiyā dar Irān*, pp.145–51; Javad Safi-Nejad, "Mo'arefi-e Kotob-e Chā'pi-e Joqrāfiyāi-e Dourān-e Qājār," pp.28–29.

65 See respectively *A Catalogue of the Persian Printed Books in the British Museum*, p.625; and Fologun Refayel, *Jahān-namā*, p.286.

66 Fologun Refayel, *Jahān-namā*, p.136.

67 Farhad Mirza Qajar, *Jām-e Jam*. Tehran: n.p., 1273 A.H. (1856), p.629.

68 Ibid., p.625. This acknowledgment was written in English.

69 This was the illustration of "Armillary Sphere." See William Pinnock, *A Comprehensive Grammar of Modern Geography and History; for the Use of Schools and for Private Tuition*. London: Holdsworth & Ball, 1834, unnumbered page between pp.32 and 33; Farhad Mirza Qajar, *Jām-e Jam*, p.57.

70 William Pinnock, *A Comprehensive Grammar of Modern Geography and History*, p.285; Farhad Mirza Qajar, *Jām-e Jam*, p.365.

71 Farhad Mirza Qajar, *Jām-e Jam*, pp.364–65; William Pinnock, *A Comprehensive Grammar of Modern Geography and History*, pp.284–85.

72 William Pinnock, *A Comprehensive Grammar of Modern Geography and History*, p.285.

73 Farhad Mirza Qajar, *Jām-e Jam*, p.365.

74 William Pinnock, *A Comprehensive Grammar of Modern Geography and History*, pp.285–86; Farhad Mirza Qajar, *Jām-e Jam*, pp.365–66.

75 Farhad Mirza Qajar, *Jām-e Jam*, p.366.

76 William Pinnock, *A Comprehensive Grammar of Modern Geography and History*, p.286; Farhad Mirza Qajar, *Jām-e Jam*, p.366.

77 William Pinnock, *A Comprehensive Grammar of Modern Geography and History*, p.241; Farhad Mirza Qajar, *Jām-e Jam*, p.328.
78 Farhad Mirza Qajar, *Jām-e Jam*, p.366.
79 William Pinnock, *A Comprehensive Grammar of Modern Geography and History*, pp.286-90.
80 Ibid., p.290.
81 Farhad Mirza Qajar, *Jām-e Jam*, pp.367-69.
82 William Pinnock, *A Comprehensive Grammar of Modern Geography and History*, p.290; Farhad Mirza Qajar, *Jām-e Jam*, pp.369.
83 Andranik Hovian, "Jahān-namā-ye Jadid[:] Nokhostin assar-e Farssi-zaban-e Joqrāfiyā-ye Jahān," Payām-e Bahārestān (Tehran), second series 2(6), Winter 1388 (2010), pp.593-94.
84 Jān Dāvud (Jean David) and Mohammad Hussein Farahani, *Jahān-namā*. Tehran: Reza-Qoli Sarabi, 1277 A.H. (1861), pp.134-161, and passim.
85 *Rouznāmeh-ye Elmi* (Tehran), 2 Rabi' al-Thāni 1294 (April 16, 1877), p.4.
86 For examples of such maps, see Abdul-Qaffar Najm al-Dowleh, *Atlass-e Tāzeh-ye Joqrāfi-e Ahd-e Jadid*. Tehran: Dar al-Funun, 1302 (1884), maps 27 and 28. See also Mohammad Hassan Ganji, *Joqrāfiyā dar Irān*, pp.144-62; Javad Safi-Nejad, "Mo'arefi-e Kotob-e Chā'pi-e Joqrāfiyāi-e Dourān-e Qājār," p.33.
87 *Dr. Goldsmith's Abridgment of the History of England, Brought Down to the General Peace of Europe, Concluded at Paris, in 1815. With Exercises on Each Chapter, for the Use of Schools*. Abridged and updated by Robert Simpson. Sixth edition. Edinburgh: Oliver and Boyd, 1823. The Persian translation does not appear to have been based on other works covering the same time period, such as Mrs. Markham's [Elizabeth Cartwright Penrose] *A History of England from the First Invasion by the Romans to the End of the Reign of George III* (1823), or John Bigland's 1815 two volume *The History of England, from the Earliest Period to ... 1814*, or John Lingard's multi-volume 1840 *A History of England, from the First Invasion by the Romans*, or Charles Dickens' 1851-1853 *A Child's History of England*.
88 Shaykh Reza ("akhavi-e Hajji Mohsen Khan"), *Tārikh-e Ingiliss*. Tehran: n.p., n.d, p.177.
89 Esmail Sahaf-bashi, *Tārikh-e Engelesstān*. Tehran: [Dar al-Funun?], [no later than 1880s], pp.74-75, 79, 205, 218-20, 248-52, 284-85, 295-97, 308.
90 *Rouznāmeh-ye Vaqāye'-e Ettefāqiyeh*, no.6, Friday, 10 Jamādi al-Awal 1267 (March 4, 1851), pp.2 and 3.
91 Ibid., no.47, Thursday, 2 Rabi' al-Awal 1268 (December 25, 1851), p.5.
92 In one of these reports, the paper referred to Ireland in the plural as the "islands of Ireland." Ibid., no.64, Thursday, 2 Rajab 1268 (April 22, 1852), p.5.
93 See, for example, ibid., no.161, Thursday, 2 Jamādi al-Thāni 1270 (March 2, 1854), p.5; no.180, Thursday, 17 Shawal 1270 (July 13, 1854), p.8.
94 Mirza Abdul-Fattah Khan Garmroudi, *Safarnāmeh-ye Mirzā Fattāh Khān Garmroudi beh Orupā dar Zamān-e Mohammad Shāh Qājār*. Fath al-Din Fattahi editor. Tehran: Bank-e Bazargani, 1347 (1969), pp.823-24.
95 *Rouznāmeh-ye Vaqāye'-e Ettefāqiyeh*, no.40, Thursday, 11 Muharram 1268 A.H. (November 6, 1851), p.4.
96 Ibid., no.141, Thursday, 9 Muharram 1270 A.H. (October 13, 1853), p.4. (Queen Victoria was accompanied on this official royal visit by Prince Albert, as had been the case on her first visit to Ireland in 1849 during the Great Famine.)
97 Ibid., no.42, Thursday, 26 Muharram 1268 A.H. (November 20, 1851), p.5.
98 Ibid., no.277, Thursday, 17 Ramadān 1272 A.H. (May 22, 1856), p.7.
99 Rouznāmeh-ye Dowlat-e Āliyeh-ye Irān (Tehran), Thursday, 23 Muharram 1283 (June 7, 1866), p.7.
100 *Sherāfat*, no.23, Dhu'l-Hijja 1315 A.H. (April/May 1898), pp.153-54.
101 Mohammad Hassan Khan E'temad al-Saltaneh, *Mer'āt al-Boldān-e Nāsseri*. Volume 2. Tehran, n.p., 1294 A.H. (1878), pp.14, 26, 118, 136, 151, 295.
102 Mohammad Hassan Khan E'temad al-Saltaneh, *Mer'āt al-Boldān-e Nāsseri*. Volume 3. Tehran, n.p., 1296 A.H. (1879), pp.50, 94, 96, 168.
103 Ibid., p.39.
104 Mohammad Hassan Khan E'temad al-Saltaneh, *Tārikh-e Montazem-e Nāsseri*. Volume 3. Tehran: n.p., 1300 A.H. (1883). The first volume of *Tārikh-e Montazem-e Nāsseri* (1298 A.H. (1881)) covers events from the year 622 (i.e., the founding of the Muslim *umma* (community)

in Medina) to the collapse of the Abbasid dynasty in 1258, following the Mongol capture of Baghdad. The second volume (1299 A.H. (1882)) covers domestic and regional developments during the period from 1259 to 1778, also including an appended summary of domestic and world events for the years 1882 to 1883 (i.e., the time of the publication of the third volume).

105 Mohammad Hassan Khan E'temad al-Saltaneh, *Rouznāmeh-ye Khāterāt-ei E'temād al-Saltaneh*. Iraj Afshar editor. Fourth edition. Tehran: Amir Kabir, 1377 (1999), p.427.
106 Ibid., p.465.
107 See also Ali Gheissari, "Authorial Voices and the Sense of an Ending in Persian Diaries: Notes on E'temād al-Saltaneh and 'Alam," *Iranian Studies* 49(4), 2016, pp.693–723.
108 Yahya Dawlatabadi, *Hayāt-e Yahyā*. Volume II. Reprint. Tehran: Attar, 1362 (1983), p.361.
109 Of Welsh descent, Lloyd George served as the Liberal president of the Board of Trade (1905-08), chancellor of the exchequer (1908–15), munitions minister (1915, during the First World War), secretary of state for war (1916), and prime minister of war-time and post-war coalition government (1916–22).
110 David Butler and Gareth Butler, *British Political Facts 1900-1985*. New York: St. Martin's, 1986, p.224; Trevor O. Lloyd, *Empire to Welfare State: English History 1906-1985*. Third edition. New York: Oxford University Press, 1991, p.22.
111 *Habl al-Matin* (Tehran), 12 Rabi al-Thāni 1325 (May 25, 1907), p.2.
112 Ibid., 14 Rajab 1325 (August 24, 1907), p.4.
113 On these clashes, see also John McHugh, "The Belfast Labour Dispute and Riots of 1907," *International Review of Social History* 22(1), 1977, pp.1–20.
114 *Irān-e Nou*, 6 Safar 1328 A.H. (February 17, 1910), p.4, c.a; 18 Dhu'l-Hijja 1328 A.H. (December 21, 1910), p.3, cc.c-d.
115 Ibid., 22 Dhu'l-Hijja 1328 A.H. (December 25, 1910), p.4, c.d.
116 *Majles*, no.73, 12 Safar 1326 (March 15, 1908), p.4. Marquess Okuma Shigenobu was an advocate of Japan-led Pan-Asian platform against Western/European imperial inroads into Asia, notwithstanding Japan's own imperialism or the Anglo-Japanese Alliance of 1902 (in regard to his direct condemnation of British imperialism).
117 See under "Telegraphs" section in *Habl al-Matin* (Calcutta), vol.9, no.38, Monday, 22 Rabi' al-Thāni 1320 A.H. (July 28, 1902), pp.2b–3a, 3a–3b. On these parliamentary exchanges on July 23, 1902, see [Great Britain] *Parliamentary Debates* (Commons), 4th series, vol.111 (1902), cc.1010–11; ibid., 1088–91.
118 *Habl al-Matin* (Calcutta), vol.11, no.11, Monday, 25 Sha'bān 1321 A.H. (November 16, 1903), p.5, c.a.
119 Lynchehaun, who had also set fire to his employer's sheds, stable, and house, had brutally assaulted the landowner: "her nose was bitten off, her right eye crushed to a pulp, her stomach stomped, and spines of whin bush (gorse) kicked deep into her vagina." Faced with extradition in the United States, Lynchehaun claimed, and his claim was upheld by American authorities, "that he had attacked the woman not out of spite, but as part of a movement of oppressed tenants belonging to the Irish Republican Brotherhood, who sought to drive her out of Ireland and regain her lands for Irish people," adding also: "that the bulk of her injuries were inflicted by members of the crowd that pretended to help fight the fires." Christopher H. Pyle, *Extradition, Politics, and Human Rights*. Philadelphia: Temple University Press, 2001, pp.115–16.
120 *Habl al-Matin* (Calcutta), vol.15, no.23, 24 Zul'qada 1325 A.H. (December 30, 1907), p.2, cc.a-b.
121 Ibid., vol.17, no.23, Monday, 29 Ziqa'da 1327 A.H. (December 13, 1909), p.14, c.a.
122 Ibid., vol.17, no.38, Monday, 8 Rabi' al-Thāni 1328 A.H. (April 18, 1910), p.24.
123 Ibid., vol.17, no.39, Monday, 15 Rabi' al-Thāni 1328 A.H. (April 25, 1910), p. 4.
124 Ibid., vol.17, no.12, Monday, 11 Ramadān 1327 A.H. (September 27, 1909), p.8.
125 Ibid., vol.18, no.13, Monday, 14 Ramadān 1328 A.H. (September 19, 1910), p.24.
126 Joseph Maunsell Hone and Page L. Dickinson, *Persia in Revolution*, pp.90–91; Mansour Bonakdarian, "The Easter Rising," pp.56–58.
127 *Āftāb*, 11 Zul'qada 1330 A.H. (October 23, 1912), p.2, cc.a–c.
128 See also Mansour Bonakdarian, "The Easter Rising," pp.60–73.
129 Terry Eagleton, *Heathcliff and the Great Hunger*, pp.257–58. On the inherent tension between the universalism and particularism of "nationalism as an international phenomenon," see ibid., pp.259–60. See also Mansour Bonakdarian, "Iranian Nationalism and Global Solidarity Networks."

Chapter Nine

NATION, HISTORY, AND MEMORY: THE IRISH FREE STATE, EUROPE-CENTERED WORLDING OF IRELAND, AND JAMES JOYCE'S *FINNEGANS WAKE* (1939)

Irish nationalist antiquarian and (mytho-)historical, literary, political, folklore, racial, and other range of commentaries about Ireland through the medium of "Iranian" referentialities (past and present) were among the many divergent instances of locating Ireland in a world historical setting. Both full-fledged and residual traces of theories of "oriental" origins of the Irish reappeared well into the early twentieth century, but with rapidly diminished frequency and declining power of persuasion, at least in Irish historical circles. Such works were still being produced during the Irish War of Independence (1919–21) and even after the creation of the Irish Free State in 1922. A case in point is the references to Scythians, Egyptians, and Phoenicians, in Seumas MacManus' 1921 *The Story of the Irish Race*.[1] This was despite the fact that such theories were compellingly cast aside as legendary and mythological in the new historiographic models that emerged in Ireland after the latter decades of the nineteenth century and were further reinforced by the likes of Patrick Weston Joyce, Eoin MacNeill, Mary Teresa Hayden and George Aloysius Moonan, or Alice Stopford Green in the early twentieth century.[2] In her 1925 *History of the Irish State to 1014*, Alice Stopford Green noted the past appeal of legendary accounts of ancient Ireland by casting her glance over a much broader time frame than just the period since the eighteenth century:

> Irish tradition told of a series of invasions, wars, and successive colonies ending in pestilence and death. All distinct knowledge of the past, however, has been obscured by the learned fictions of the annalists and genealogy makers of Christian times. Overawed by the authority of classic authors, and the pride of empire which Rome had bequeathed to the world, they set themselves to shape Irish history after the fashionable manner of Latin models. In the interests of symmetry, and to give Ireland a good place in the orthodox framework of world history,

patriot scholars devised a fantastic scheme of genealogies and chronologies by which the invasions of the island should be forced into line with the Empires known to classic fame. The learned men's terror of provincialism, and of a merely national history, ended in double disaster—the complete discrediting down to our own day of all early Irish history; and the confusion or destruction of a mass of genuine tradition of great importance for the study of European civilization. Four great legendary invasions of Ireland were reported or invented in the old Irish schools:—the coming of Parthalon, of Nemed, of the Fir Bolg, and of the Gaedhil.[3]

Accordingly, in defending contemporary Ireland's historical *inheritance*, "patriot scholars" in the so-called Middle Ages, overcome by the "terror of provincialism," sought to situate Ireland in a world historical configuration that privileged the island's ancient past by appending that past to accounts of other known so-called high civilizations of ancient times (even if, as Green later noted (see below), these scholars ultimately considered the pre-Christian heritage of the island as being inferior to its later Christian "civilization"). This interpretation in principle (minus the ultimate exaltation of Christianity over the so-called pagan past by these 'medieval' scholars) is also applicable to the (mythic) narratives of oriental origins of the Irish and/or of Ireland's civilizational Golden Age by Irish nationalist antiquarians after the eighteenth century. The main difference was that by the late eighteenth century a "national" attribute was grafted onto this schema of *deprovincializing* Ireland (both politically and civilizationally), notwithstanding the admittedly diverse ethnic backgrounds of the 'Irish' population at the time, including the nationalist antiquarians themselves. Many in the ranks of these nationalist antiquarians and later generations of historians were of Anglo-Irish, Scots-Irish, Welsh-Irish and other ancestry, as in the case of Vallancey, an Englishman of French parentage who resided in Ireland. As Green noted in her Preface, she was writing under the acknowledged influence of Eoin MacNeill's more rigorous historiographic methodology, which placed no historical premium in the old pseudo-historical and mythic traditions—even though MacNeill's and Green's own approaches were undeniably also tendentious in their nationalist underpinnings.

In Green's view, the *world-historical* mythologization of Ireland's past had been a remedial antidote to the historical provincialization of Ireland as a European outpost (and later also a European outpost of the English Empire specifically), although it is unclear whether she meant this was an entirely conscious or unconscious reaction on the part of 'medieval' and later Irish scholars—and not forgetting that so-called medieval "Ireland" was actually a leading center of monastic intellectual vitality and literacy in western Europe. Leaving aside also Green's anachronistic application of a territorially unified entity called 'Ireland' in the Middle Ages and her elastic extension of the category of 'nation' to as early a period as the sixth century CE, she noted additional methods by which medieval Irish writers had incorporated ancient Ireland into world history with the aim of privileging Ireland's past.[4] One of these was the cross-referencing of dates for major events in the island's history with (near-)contemporary events that had unfolded in a select range of professedly major civilizations of ancient times known to these Irish scholars. This periodization schema for narrating Ireland's past, through selective rummaging of world history in search of extra-'Irish' events that were considered worthy of cross-referencing, inexorably relied on miscellaneous assortment of sources and documentation styles produced by others outside the island over an extended period:

The writing down of Irish legend and history probably began in the sixth and seventh centuries [...]. *Filid* [poets] and monks alike, the "synthetic historians" as they have been called, proposed to construct the story of the Irish people, duly harmonized and fitted with dates—a traditional record from Adam down to S. Patrick, after which historians could rely on their own knowledge. Accounts of ancient Irish peoples, their descent and migrations, show how closely Virgil was read. From Orosius scholars took the description of the world in which the legendary "Scotti" roamed before they reached Ireland. The Scythian origin of the Gaels, the geographical details of their wanderings, the tower of Bregon, the landing at an unknown Inber Scéne—such were the inventions suggested to the Irish by the continental scholars and writers of the time [...]. The chronicle of Eusebius [...], in its Latin translation by S. Jerome and its continuation to 445 by Prosper of Aquitaine, became the model and framework of their Irish history—a form of world-history in parallel columns, with the reigns and chief events ranged in due order under the four accepted epochs established by Latin writers, the Assyrian Empire, the Median Empire, the usurpation of the Magi in Persia, Alexander's Empire. To give Ireland its due place in the record, biblical and classical, a skeleton of Irish history was added in these columns. The early chroniclers faithfully copied the Latin columns of empires and kings, the scanty lists of events, and added their dry and formal notes, according to the limited end they had in view. Tradition and history however were not delegated to the Latinists alone. Many of the early synthetists were lay poets. The *filid* took their share in gathering fragments of tradition to form the groundwork; old sagas and stories were woven together, and blanks boldly filled up. Calendars kept in the churches for the regulation of festivals were used for entering brief notices of interesting events, such as the one at Iona in the seventh century which was drawn upon by Irish historians: all these alike perished in the Norse invasions. As ancient traditions found their way into the monastic schools[,] national influence became paramount. Christian monks who had lost none of their affection for the old lore of their country collected all that they could find regarding Ireland and its pagan records; even if at the end of their manuscript they felt bound to add a prayer or a profession of Christian faith repudiating devil-worship.[5]

Green, was not the first commentator to underscore the attempt by 'medieval' Irish annalists to situate ancient Ireland in world history through various means of cross-referentiality to so-called great civilizations of ancient times (as these were defined and known to Europeans at the time). Among others, writing in 1923 and mentioning Green's earlier studies as among the finest historical accounts of Ireland, Stephen Lucius Gwynn noted that the book of *Synchronisms* by "Flann, professor in the monastery at Monasterboice, near Drogheda," which dated to the year 1056, "set out in parallel columns the story of Assyrian, Median, Persian, Greek, and Roman history alongside of the history of Irish kings—a text-book of world history as he understood it."[6] Gwynn's particular account of the *Synchronisms* of Flann was based on a 1903 study by Patrick Weston Joyce (discussed below). As John Carey has put it more recently:

> The various settlements which successively occupied Ireland were placed more or less in parallel with the sequence of 'world kingships' which had been developed by Eusebius; and the spatial setting for the whole extended story was supplied by the ancient geographers, as mediated by the Christian historian Orosius. This schema, the main outlines of which had been thought out by the end of the eighth century at the latest, had burgeoned into an enormously complex body of doctrines by the eleventh, when it was recorded in the treatise called *Lebor Gabála* or 'The Book of Taking'.[7]

There were parallels in other parts of the world to these attempts at locating one's own ancient history (always imagined to a substantial degree) in the broader world-historical framework (also similarly imagined to some extent). For example, as Séamus Mac Mathúna has noted of the Armenian Movsēs Khorenatsi's *The History of Armenia*, which covered Armenian history from the time of Noah to 440 CE, "Khorenatsi's purpose is more or less the same as that of the compilers of the Irish *Lebor Gabála* and of Geoffrey Keating who wrote a renowned and influential history of Ireland in the seventeenth century [...] It was to reconstruct as fully as possible the earlier histories, including invasions and colonisations, of the countries concerned and [...] to locate these histories in the scheme of biblical and world history."[8] There were also similar genres of Iranian history, as in the case of, for instance, Mirkhond's fifteenth-century *Universal History* that relied on a fusion of Qur'anic as well as Iranian pre-Islamic (mytho-)historical sources for reconstructing the ancient history of the Persian peoples (in the broad sense of the term), while also remarking on the inconsistencies between Qur'anic and pre-Islamic sources. However, there was a key difference in the case of Iranian histories such as Mirkhond's and the medieval and later antiquarian Irish world-historical accounts of ancient Ireland. In Mirkhond's history, the Iranian Keyoumars (whether identified as Adam, a descendant of Adam, or a descendant of Noah in various post-Islamic accounts that incorporated pre-Islamic sources) was the very first law-giver and sovereign on the planet.[9] Accordingly, the origin of humanity itself was, in effect, Iran-centered, in a manner that universalized world history by tracing it back to Iranian lands (not unlike what William Jones, Vallancey, Henry O'Brien, or Lady Wilde would do much later). In other words, unlike the different Irish narratives, the post-Islamic Iranian (Persian in this case) stories of their ethnic-"national" inception privileged their earliest ancestors as the direct and immediate descendants of the first generation of human beings, whether in the form of Adamite-style creation or Noah-like regeneration of humanity, rather than being descendants of population arrivals from other lands, as was the case in accounts of early population settlements in Ireland to whom the Gaelic Irish traced their ancestry. Hence, whereas the earliest privileged ancestry of the Irish were transplants and colonizers, the earliest proclaimed ancestry of the Persians in Iranian (mytho-)history of pre-Islamic Iran, as well as in sources that combined Islamic and pre-Islamic accounts, comprised the very first aboriginal peoples on the planet.

The works of Irish nationalist antiquarians after the late eighteenth century and of subsequent generations of Irish nationalist historians writing on ancient Ireland in the nineteenth century exhibit a similar pattern of situating ancient Ireland in a world-historical schema as that found in 'medieval' Irish sources, even if to a different end. By the time Geoffrey Keating in the seventeenth century engaged in his project of constructing Ireland's glorious pre-Christian ancient past, Ireland was much more firmly and indisputably an English imperial province. A key difference between the accounts of ancient Ireland produced by Irish nationalist antiquarian and historians after the late eighteenth century and the accounts written by 'medieval' Irish scholars, or by Keating for that matter, was the always dynamic historiographic suppositions and evidential parameters of *worlding* ancient Ireland. These included, for instance, the influence of such developments as the circulation of Indo-European theories of languages after the late eighteenth century, which impacted the debates on ancient Ireland by those prescribing to varying theories of oriental or non-oriental origins of the Irish. Among a host of other related factors and developments was the increasingly more extensive availability (and in much greater detail) of historical information about other regions of the world, whether largely accurate or not, including greater awareness of, and familiarity with, other literatures and mythologies. By the late eighteenth century, the geographic range of extra-'Irish' evidential sources consulted by antiquarians seeking to (re-)affirm the oriental roots of Ireland's ancient past had vastly expanded, embracing now also texts in oriental languages (besides the primarily scriptural Hebrew and other biblical sources previously available)—even if these oriental texts were almost uniformly consulted by Irish antiquarians in the form of available translations in European languages, as in the case of Vallancey, L. C. Beaufort, or Henry O'Brien. The more expansive integration into historical reconstructions of ancient Ireland of knowledge production concerning the Orient was itself a sign of increased *worlding* of Irish historiographic methodologies and documentary scope. These ranged from information generated in the Orient itself—including through collaborative efforts between Europeans and natives in the Indian subcontinent and elsewhere, as in the case of research conducted by the Asiatic Society of Bengal for instance—to works by scholars in mainland Britain and in other parts of Europe. This gravitation away from mere reliance on biblical and Greco-Roman and other presumably 'Western' sources of knowledge about the world also entailed a process of legitimizing knowledge produced by orientals (i.e., outside the narrow range of more traditional sources consulted, in writing Western 'national' histories).

Iran and New Modes of Irish Nationalist *Worlding* of Ireland

By 1925, when Green's *History of the Irish State to 1014* was published, Irish historians of ancient Ireland, as mainstream historians elsewhere in the British Isles, had increasingly turned to incrementally more scrupulous, and analytically more self-reflexive, so-called scientific methodologies, including more rigorous standards of historical verification *from our standpoint*, in comparison with the frequently speculative and largely deductive antiquarian criteria of previous centuries.[10] By then, with extremely rare exceptions, they also had abandoned sifting through non-European/non-Western sources for reconstructing Ireland's ancient past (except biblical sources in some cases). The continuous and heterogeneous development of new historical methods, albeit still strongly tinged with Romantic suppositions and particular extrapolations in the case of nationalist historiographies, among other historiographic trends, can be traced to the self-avowedly "scientific" historical methods developed in the nineteenth century. Unfortunately, detailed work on the evolution of Irish historiography during the period under examination in this book is lacking. Since at least George Petrie's publications on the Round Towers after the 1830s, the notion of inductive historical method, with empirically skeptical and comparatively verifiable evidentiary basis, gradually gained grounds in Irish historical studies, marking the transition from former styles of antiquarianism to so-called modern historical writing in Ireland. It is unclear to what extent, if at all, Petrie was influenced in the 1830s by the emerging continental trends in historiography. In many ways, Petrie's approach corresponded to the methodological groundwork already undertaken by the Prussian historian Leopold von Ranke (1795–1886)—commonly considered as the progenitor of what came to be known as 'scientific' historiographic methods (inaccurately also generally designated as being "objective"), which to some extent had been in gestation since the latter part of the eighteenth century.[11] By the latter part of the nineteenth century, so-called scientific history rapidly assumed different, competing, and continually evolving trajectories, mainly in the form of historicism versus the teleological variations of positivism developed by the French Auguste Comte (d.1857) and drawing on distinct and even earlier pre-Rankean jointly 'scientific' and teleological traditions of Georg Wilhelm Friedrich Hegel, Immanuel Kant, and earlier and subsequent trends in "secular" teleological conceptions of the world since the 'European' Enlightenment, including works by Karl Marx and Friedrich Engels in the mid-nineteenth century.

Without here delving into the foundational myth of scientific 'objectivity' in general, let alone its wide-ranging spurious applications in historical undertakings, by the early twentieth century there was an overwhelming consensus in Irish historiography (nationalist or otherwise) on the Celtic origins of the earliest verifiably documented population settlements across the British Isles, including Ireland. This conclusion was corroborated by contemporary related disciplines of archaeology, art history, linguistics, and ethnography and anthropology, which were also continually developing their own more rigorous standards—even as flawed as these disciplines at the time may appear from our present-day perspectives. In these accounts, the Celts were also almost unanimously acknowledged as a branch of the Aryan peoples. Regardless of continued debates on the origin of the Celts, their migratory routes and prior settlements across Europe, and of the primal homeland of their Aryan ancestry for that matter, the various Celtic models of ancient Ireland acknowledged the very gradual and long-duration process of Celtic expansions across Western Europe. These new models constituted *Europe-centered* accounts of ancient Ireland. In regard to oriental theories of Irish origins, the current Celtic models at the very least debunked the fiction of population arrivals in ancient Ireland from the Orient (as well as from other locations) through very rapid migratory processes (whether or not independently of prior settlements in mainland 'Britain'). Nonetheless, varying formulations of oriental origins of the Irish persisted, albeit with a rapidly shrinking number of professional enthusiasts.[12] The latter-day promoters of these theories often selectively incorporated into their accounts some of the most recent historiographical methods and the new range of evidence supplied by related disciplines for sustaining their own claims.

The Europe-centered theory of a common distant Celtic ancestry of most Britons and the Gaelic Irish, irrespective of later ethnic ('racial') admixtures among the different population groups, had a substantial political capital for those Irish nationalists committed to cross-ethnic 'Irish' nationalism—whether the Celts were explicitly defined as Aryans, as in Hayden's and Moonan's 1922 study, for instance, or otherwise. Without my wishing to imply a politically premeditated *fabrication* of this model of a distant common Celtic ancestry of the overwhelming population of the British Isles, Thomas Osborne Davis had already in the 1840s recognized a key political advantage of such a theory: the blurring of ethnic differences among early population settlements in the two neighboring islands of Britain and Ireland and, hence, between the ancestry of the Gaelic Irish and the early ancestry of subsequent Welsh, Scots, and even English arrivals in Ireland after the twelfth century, who now jointly comprised the Irish 'nation.' The notion of some degree of common Celtic origin among most Britons and the Gaelic Irish, irrespective of later ethnic fusions, whether Norse, Saxon, or Norman (among other groups), inferred a primordial hereditary ethnic link among the majority of Ireland's population—not forgetting, of course, that in its nationalist applications this could be turned into a *majoritarian* and exclusionary praxis that marginalized and ultimately denied other smaller population groups of Ireland, who were not traceable to some degree of Celtic ancestry, an equal claim of genuinely belonging to the Irish nation. The Gaels were almost unanimously identified by Irish historians at the time as a Celtic sub-branch of the Aryan family and designated as belonging to the same family of Celtic migrations that had previously reached mainland Britain from originally either central or northern Europe. At the heart of this narrative of ancient Ireland in Irish nationalist historiography was ultimately a fixation with *contemporary* Ireland, even as many unionist and other Irish historians also shared the pan-Celtic model of ancient Ireland.[13] By the turn of the twentieth century, the new pan-Celtic nationalist paradigm had rapidly overtaken former contentious antiquarian accounts of Ireland's distinct ancient peopling—even in the case of older nationalist brands of the Celtic theory that claimed a distinct Celtic ancestry for the Gaels compared to the Celtic settlements in mainland Britain and, hence, of Ireland's ancient civilizational uniqueness.[14] The newly dominant historiographic standard emphasized a shared ancient ethnic and civilizational identity across the British Isles prior to subsequent historical separations that produced a strongly Gaelic cultural identity. This was a belated historiographic-cum-political gesture with the potential for ethnically unifying the (majority of the) Irish 'nation' contra London's control over Ireland, by means of eclipsing, if not entirely eradicating, ethnic divisions in the tortuous history of the formation of contemporary Irish 'nation.'

Comparable in its objective to the aim of the Society of United Irishmen (1791) and the Young Ireland circle of the 1840s, which had attempted to bring together Ireland's multi-ethnic and multi-religious, as well as secular, communities for forging an independent nation, the new nationalist historiography consciously or unconsciously expunged as much as possible the emphasis on ethnic distinctions between the major hyphenated Irish identities (Gaelic-Irish, Anglo-Irish, Welsh-Irish, and Scots-Irish). Instead, this historiography attributed the inter-communal tensions between the Irish of Gaelic lineage and the other primary hyphenated Irish groups not to some deep historically rooted ethnic disparity among them, but to the political-cultural sphere of English rule in Ireland since the earliest Anglo-Norman conquests, with added Christian denominational divisions having surfaced after the sixteenth century—which is not to deny initial differences in service and ritual between the native Christian tradition of Ireland and the Christian practices of the Anglo-Normans. (Needless to say, this pan-Celtic historiographic model later circumvented other forms of hyphenated Irish identities, notably the small Jewish community by the early twentieth century, whose members had settled in Ireland from other parts of Europe, or those of presumably "full" African or South Asian ancestry; leaving aside here the broader question of racism.) From the standpoint of nationalists, the hyphenated Irish identities were politically and culturally manipulated for maintaining England's domination of Ireland, but could be readily transcended, if not entirely dissolved, through the alternative political-cultural embrace of an independent, or at least autonomous, Irish nation. The '-Irish' modifier in these hyphenated designations had originated in consequence of population arrivals in the island from mainland Britain. Overtime, the descendants of those arriving from mainland Britain, in their own estimation and from the point of view of the descendants of existing Gaelic population of the island, had come to be regarded as both *part* of the population of the land and yet *apart* from the descendants of indigenous Gaelic population based on rights and privileges accorded to them by London. Further complicating these divisions was the inter-denominational split following the English and Scottish Reformations, which happened to precede the largest phase of population settlements in Ireland from mainland Britain after the mid-sixteenth century—establishing a minority Protestant hierarchy over the existing predominantly Catholic population of the island (Gaelic and non-Gaelic), with Anglicans at the very top in terms of religious and political privilege; not forgetting also class and gender determinants.

Since the emergence of cross-ethnic and cross-denominational Irish nationalism in the late eighteenth century, these nationalists had reductively attributed the persistence of accompanying religious, social, and political distinctions among separate hyphenated Irish groups to continued English administration of the island. The pan-Celtic narrative that gained ascendance in Irish nationalist historiography at the turn of the twentieth century, in effect, differentiated between, on the one hand, the English (i.e., 'Anglo') component of Anglo-Irish ethnic identity (as a secondary ethnic factor within the primary national marker of Irish identity) and, on the other hand, England's hegemony over Ireland (i.e., 'English' rule)—glossing over other possible contributing factors to the earlier divisions and tensions between the Gaelic Irish and other groups settling in the island, such as language, clan affiliations, and so on. Although unstated, this demarcation of two separate connotations of 'English' implied that the presence of both Scots-Irish and Welsh-Irish was an ancillary historical appendage of England's presence in Ireland, tacitly also allocating the Stuart policy of establishing plantations in Ireland to the English realm of the Stuart monarchs, who jointly ruled Scotland and England (as well as Wales) from 1603 to 1649 and 1660 to 1688, with London as their imperial capital but hailing from a Scottish dynasty. The one divisive communal element in Ireland that continually threatened to destabilize the nationalist project of pan-Celticism or other modes of cross-ethnic unification in opposition to London's rule was Christian denominational differences. While denominational politics was largely checked, or held at bay, in most nationalist platforms after the late eighteenth century, in ways unparalleled in the otherwise predominantly *Protestant* unionist platforms—with the (exclusively Catholic) Ancient Order of Hibernians being the most notable exception among nationalist groupings in this regard—the specter of denominational divisions later came to haunt the new Irish nation-state (Irish Free State) following the Irish Civil War of 1922–23, with the rising supremacy of the Catholic Church and the obeisance of many leading politicians to the church establishment for personal and/or political and social reasons.

By the start of the twentieth century, popular historical surveys of Ireland, as well as publications more specifically focusing on ancient Irish history that subscribed to the pan-Celtic model, which was now garnering increased consensus in the Irish historical profession, were being promoted through different nationalist channels in Ireland and in the Irish diaspora. These included works by the likes of the cultural-nationalist Patrick Weston Joyce (1827–1914), a historian, member of the Royal Irish Academy, and a commissioner of the Education Department in Ireland. Among P. W. Joyce's many publications on a wide range of Irish historical subjects were the two-volume 1903 *A Social History of Ancient Ireland* (with an abridged edition in 1908 and subsequent editions), along with revised editions of his *A Concise History of Ireland*—which had first appeared in 1897 under the title *A Child's History of Ireland*, before the title change in 1903, and was primarily aimed at a younger readership. In the first volume of *A Social History of Ancient Ireland*, Joyce underlined his primary objective (besides instructing the Irish in their own history) as that of situating ancient Ireland within the broader world-historical frame of great "nations" of ancient times and, thereby, reclaiming Ireland's deserved status among 'nations' that had accomplished major achievements and made substantial contributions to world history:

> The social condition of most of those ancient nations that have made any figure in the world has been investigated and set forth in books; and perhaps it will be acknowledged that Ireland deserves to be similarly commemorated. For, besides the general importance of all such studies in elucidating the history of the human race, the ancient Irish were a highly intellectual and interesting people; and the world owes them something, as I hope to be able to show.[15]

This project of 'national' recovery and resuscitation of the memory of Ireland's professed distinguished place in the ancient world was an unambiguous commemoration of ancient Ireland directed at not only domestic and diasporic Irish audiences in pursuit of national pride, but also at a broader world audience unaware of Ireland's avowed rightful place in ancient history. Ancient Ireland, in other words, belonged in the pantheon of so-called great civilizations of ancient times and had contributed to the development of world civilizations. This perspective, however, no longer required the claim of unique Irish origins in the British Isles, as had been the case in the works of nationalist antiquarians of previous centuries. P. W. Joyce stated at the outset that his 'words of truth and soberness' were bound to meet with disapproval from both camps of "those English and Anglo-Irish people [...] who think, merely from ignorance, that Ireland was a barbarous and half-savage country before the English came among the people and civilised them; and, on the other hand, [...] those of my countrymen who have an exaggerated idea of the greatness and splendour of the ancient Irish nation." Joyce belonged to what was by then the mainstream of professional Irish historians who traced the earliest documentable populations of the island to the wider (Europe-centered) Celtic sub-branch of the Aryan race. In addition to the latest archaeological theories, Joyce relied on the available research concerning glossaries of earliest surviving Irish texts dating as far back as the seventh century CE, carried out by the likes of the renowned nineteenth-century Bavarian Celtic linguist Johann Kaspar Zeuss, who had demonstrated the affinity between Celtic and other "Aryan or Indo-European languages" such as Sanskrit.[16] Working under the influence of the Aryan theory of Ireland's ancient Gaelic population, with the Aryans in this case having originated in the East but with a prolonged presence in Europe before reaching the British Isles, Joyce noted in his Preface: "I have taken occasion all along to compare Irish Social Life with that of other ancient nations, especially pointing out correspondences that are the natural consequence of common Aryan origin," with ancient Persia ('Iran') constituting one of these passing comparisons.[17] For Joyce, the Irish Celts belonged to the larger Celtic family that had also settled in mainland Britain prior to arriving in Ireland on their westward migration, even if some of their practices diverged over time due to distance and limited interactions: "It is pretty certain, indeed, that the druidic system of Gaul, Britain, and Ireland were originally one and the same. But, the Gaels of Ireland and Scotland were separated and isolated for many centuries from the Celtic races of Gaul; and thus, their religious system, like their language, naturally diverged, so that the druidism of Ireland, as pictured forth in the native records, differed in many respects from that of Gaul."[18]

P. W. Joyce's works were not only referenced as authoritative sources in historical accounts of Ireland produced by other leading Irish authors, as in the case of the Home Rule Irish nationalist Stephen Gwynn as previously noted, but were also recommended by the Irish nationalist press as standard texts to be adopted in teaching Irish history, including in the diasporic communities. For instance, in January 1903 the bi-lingual Irish nationalist monthly magazine *The Gael/An Gaodhal* (New York) recommended the adoption of Joyce's *A Concise History of Ireland*, also published in New York in 1903, as well as other works by him, as required texts in those American parochial schools that were introducing Irish history as part of their curriculum.[19] In *A Concise History of Ireland*, Joyce consigned Parthalon, Nemedians, Fomorians, Firbolgs, Tuatha de Dananns, and Milesians to the realm of legend, noting: "We have no means of finding out for a certainty how Ireland was first peopled. It is highly probable that part at least of its earliest colonists came across the narrow sea from Great Britain, which had been itself colonised by some of the Celtic tribes that in those days occupied a large part of the west of Europe."[20] While in many ways written in the generally sober style of such studies as Sophie Bryant's 1889 *Celtic Ireland* or her 1913 *The Genius of the Gael: A Study in Celtic Psychology and its Manifestations*, P. W. Joyce was working within the tradition of the ultimately Eastern origins of the Aryan 'race,' whereas Bryant had claimed a European ancestry for the Aryans. Moreover, remarkably, in Joyce's attempt to underscore familiarity in other parts of the ancient world with Ireland's civilizational grandeur, he was not entirely dismissive of Ireland's direct or indirect contacts with Phoenicians or other 'eastern' population groups mentioned in the old antiquarian legends:

> In those days of imperfect navigation, Ireland was so remote that foreign writers knew very little about it; but the few notices of it they have left us are very important. It was known to the Phœnicians, who probably visited it[,] and Greek writers mention it under the names of

Iernis and *Ierne* [I-er-nè], and as the "Sacred Island" thickly inhabited by the *Hiberni*. The Greek geographer Ptolemy, writing in the second century, who drew his information from Phœnician authorities, has given us a description of Ireland much more accurate than the account he has left us of Great Britain. And that the people of Ireland carried on a considerable trade with foreign countries in those early ages we know from the statement of the Roman historian Tacitus, that in his time—the end of the first century—the harbours of Ireland were better known to trading nations than those of Britain. People that carry on commerce cannot be altogether barbarous[,]: and these few notices show that the country had some settled institutions and a certain degree of civilisation as early at least as the beginning of the Christian era. So that the native writers, with all their legends and overdrawn pictures of ancient Ireland, have some truth on their side.[21]

Such historiographic endeavors were still intended to counter continued claims by English and other die-hard castigators of ancient Ireland's civilizational standing (with varying degrees of success). For example, Goldwin Smith, the English historian and professor at Cornell University in the United States (previously a professor at Oxford) wrote in 1905 that not only were the ancient Celts "kinsmen of the primitive races of Gaul and Britain," but that they were also of an impure "Aryan stock" compared to Teutons, whom Smith valorized as the primary ancestors of English people, with their allegedly intrinsic racial characteristics observable to the present day, including in their religious orientation, poetry, art, warfare, and so forth.[22] Ironically, Smith insouciantly cited as one of his main sources P. W. Joyce's 1903 *A Social History of Ancient Ireland*.

The growing subtextual appeal of *intra-Irish* pan-Celticism after the latter decades of the nineteenth century in Irish nationalist narrations of ancient Ireland, whether articulated in implicit or pronounced manner, had an additional component beyond serving as a signifier of a shared ethnic ingredient of contemporary Irishness. This was what Terry Eagleton and Declan Kiberd have identified in different settings as the Irish nationalist impulse of "Europeanizing" Ireland (see below). By all Celticist accounts, the Celts had evolved as a distinct ethnic group in central or northern Europe, even if the remote 'racial' origin of the Celts (whether or not defined as a sub-branch of Aryans) could ultimately be traced back to the Orient. Eoin MacNeill, the most celebrated Irish nationalist historian in the period from the end of the nineteenth century to the first decade after the creation of the Irish Free State in 1922, and also the first education minister of the Free State, was more definitive than P. W. Joyce in Europeanizing the Celts and promoting a pan-Celtic Irish national identity. In 1909 MacNeill became a professor of early and 'medieval' Irish history at the University College Dublin. In addition to his academic career, MacNeill was a co-founder of the Gaelic League (1893) and served as the chief of staff in the paramilitary Irish Volunteers force from 1913 to 1916, famously countermanding the plan to stage the Easter Rising in 1916, but nonetheless imprisoned following the event. In his 1919 *Phases of Irish History*, partly based on much earlier articles and lectures dating to before the First World War, MacNeill outright dismissed simplistic notions of clear-cut racial differences between various European population groups designated as Latin, Teutonic, Anglo-Saxon, and Celtic. Maintaining these groups were all admixtures of various races in different degrees, he claimed, "There must have been a time when the Celts of Ireland, Britain and Gaul were fully aware that they were nearer akin to each other than to the Germans and Italians, but this knowledge perished altogether from the popular memory and the popular consciousness." He credited the sixteenth-century Scottish George Buchanan as the earliest authority on the common genealogy of initial large-scale Celtic population settlements in the British Isles, following prior smaller-scale settlements in Ireland by groups known as Picts and, before them, the Iverni, from whom, according to MacNeill, Ireland's ancient indigenous designation "Erin" was derived (i.e., Éire, and its genitive and dative cases of Éireann and Éirinn). MacNeill dated the continued arrivals of Celtic peoples in Ireland through Britain (as part of the westward migration of the Celts from central European territories) to the period after the Bronze Age in Ireland, meaning roughly after the fourth century BCE.[23] Accordingly, regardless of subsequent arrivals of other ethnic groups in England, Wales, Scotland, and Ireland—whether the Romans or others in England and Wales, or the Norse and Normans in Ireland—the contemporary Irish and Britons shared a common Celtic ethnic admixture and cultural heritage. Moreover, without specifically using either of the terms 'Aryan' or 'Indo-European' in this work, MacNeill was rather vague on the original location of the parent population stock from whom the Celts had descended (meaning 'Aryans'), seemingly preferring the theory of their European origin:

> It need hardly be re-stated here that the Celts are a linguistic offshoot of a prehistoric people whose descendants—also in the line of language—comprise many ancient and modern populations in Europe and Asia. It would be out of place now to discuss the central location from which the various branches of this prehistoric people spread themselves over so wide an area. Indeed, it is a facile and fanciful assumption to suppose that the spreading took place from one central habitat. It is enough to say that, whereas the earlier philologists took for granted that the original population, before its division into various linguistic groups, was located in Western Asia, the later philologists are strongly inclined to place its home in Europe, in the region south-east of the Baltic Sea.[24]

In his notes on Celtic populations, which MacNeill later shared with Alice Stopford Green and were reproduced in Green's 1925 *History of the Irish State to 1014*, he was cautiously more explicit about the European origin of the Aryans: "A region [...] stretches from the marshes of East Prussia and the slopes of the Carpathian mountains eastward to the mountain ranges of India. In this region and at first probably in the western part of it was the home of an ancient people," adding that "the farthest eastern group [of this branch of people] is called Indo-Iranian."[25] Leaving aside the general fiction of separate continents of 'Asia' and 'Europe' in the first place (which are otherwise coterminous lands stretching over a wide region of the world and encompassing a wide array of ethno-linguistic and cultural groups since ancient times), MacNeill's statements were exemplary of a growing Irish historiographic trend for more firmly grounding the Celts, and hence the ancient Irish, within the *European sphere* of identities.[26] In this model, not only did the earliest major population settlements throughout the British Isles share a common ethnic identity, but the Gaelic Irish, similar to their kin in mainland Britain, were ultimately of European descent. In present-day commentaries on MacNeill's style of (Irish nationalist) historiographic methodology—which stressed the European essence of Ireland's ancient Gaelic (Celtic) identity—what is generally neglected is the fact that his historical narrative accommodated the idea of *a* common ancient ancestral pedigree of the Gaelic Irish and much of the subsequent English, Welsh, and Scottish settlers in Ireland, regardless of other prior or subsequent ancestral admixtures in this model. This insinuated, and historically elastic, shared ethnic essence of the majority of Ireland's population at the time was at the heart of MacNeill's nationalist historical project. On the other hand, and noteworthy for a nationalist account of ancient Ireland (in contrast to much earlier antiquarian nationalist models), MacNeill's version also dispensed with the premise of ancient Ireland's civilizational alterity from, and/or superiority over, mainland Britain (England, more specifically). Without in any way disregarding its *comparative* methodological rigor vis-à-vis earlier antiquarian accounts, the general political appeal of MacNeill's model of ancient Ireland in Irish nationalist circles was inevitable. This was a historiographic initiative that conveniently dovetailed the politically unifying impulse of mainstream Irish nationalism (of both parliamentary and militant inclinations), traceable back to the cross-ethnic project of the United Irishmen in the late eighteenth century and Young Ireland's vision of Irish national identity in the 1840s. Whereas Young Ireland had called for transcending ethnic differences, MacNeill's *European* Celtic model of ancient Ireland ethnically harmonized and assimilated the overwhelming majority of the Irish. However, in contrast to Young Ireland's joint objective of also transcending religious sectarianism, there was a latent disruptive religious dimension to MacNeill's historicization of Irish 'national' identity. He interjected into his model of Irish authenticity a generic form Christianity, which according to him marked the primary cultural attribute of Ireland's Europe-centered Celtic population after the fifth century, and which initially had also been independent of Rome and, hence, unique to Ireland. By overemphasizing the Christian component, MacNeill's historicization of Irishness left room for the potentially disunifying force of Christian sectarianism as a defining constituent of Irishness. In fact, this potential propensity for a sectarian formulation of genuine or *purer* Irish identity surfaced in the Irish Free State. At issue was the contestation of Irishness based solely on ethnicity (itself to some extent an already exclusionary construct of national identity) versus the even more constricted exclusionary formulation of Irishness based jointly on ethnic (Celtic) and denominational (primarily Catholic) identity. Notwithstanding this potentially destabilizing dynamic, MacNeill's model of Irish identity was yet another form of deprovincializing Ireland—by means of purging (the internally contested) 'oriental' models of Irish heritage and, hence, culturally divesting Ireland of its former status as an aberrant *orientalized* land in the West of Europe, and now firmly affixing Irish identity and civilization to Europe and its dominant Christian traditions.

MacNeill's version of ancient Ireland rapidly assumed a normative status, being reproduced by other Irish historians, including the likes of Alice Stopford Green as well as by influential amateur historians such as Stephen Lucius Gwynn. The latter, in the Preface to his 1923 *The History of Ireland*, while listing publications by P. W. Joyce and Green among the main sources he had consulted, noted: "Finally, without the books of Professor MacNeill, his *Phases of Irish History* and his *Celtic Ireland*[,] I should never have attempted even in this rudimentary fashion to trace the history as a whole. Out of the chaotic mass which is in the *Annals* he has produced an intelligible fabric." Writing after the creation of the Irish Free State in 1922, Gwynn was by then a former leading 'Home Rule' Irish Parliamentary Party (IPP) MP and a co-founder of the short-lived (Home Rule) Irish Centre Party (1919). In the opening chapter of *The History of Ireland*, Gwynn immediately and emphatically proceeded to underscore Ireland's European civilizational identity and the racial affinity of the Irish with the (specifically "white") Aryan branch of world's populations: "History is concerned with the development of civilisation, and the civilisation to which Ireland belongs is that of Europe, not of the British Isles. Ireland should always be viewed as a part of Europe; and to-day as part of that greater Europe which includes the continent of America, as well as Australia, New Zealand, and South Africa." In effect also deprovincializing Ireland by expanding its geo-cultural location beyond the frontiers of the British Isles, Gwynn added: "Ireland came late into European history."[27] This was a major modification of Gwynn's already quoted view in his 1905 *The Fair Hills of Ireland*, which had echoed some of the older antiquarian suppositions, such as in Gwynn's view at the time of a highly probable Scythian origin of Tuatha de Danann arrivals in ancient Ireland. The 'Europeanizing' of Ireland's oldest documentable large-scale population settlements was a key facet of the newly dominant Celtic theory of ancient Irish origins advocated by MacNeill, Gwynn, Green, and others.

In short, the predominant Europe-centered Celticist orientation of Irish nationalist historiography after the turn of the twentieth century—also generally distinguishing itself from former styles of Irish historical inquiry by its claim of bona fide scientific methodology—overwhelmingly categorized the Celts as an unequivocally European branch of the wider Aryan populations (regardless of where the Aryans may have originated according to these accounts). Furthermore, this model identified the earliest Celtic settlers in Ireland as part of the *longue durée* westward migration of Celts to the British Isles. This historiographic trend coincided with other increasingly Europe-centered nationalist imaginings of Ireland, which in turn coincided with the process of racially 'whitening' the Irish. In this regard, the Pan-Aryan Association in the United States in the early years of the twentieth century was an anomaly, given its articulation of an Aryan 'race' not based on skin color; even if individual Irish participants at the gatherings of the Association may personally have subscribed to a 'white' Europe-centered definition of the Aryan race. The causal interconnection between the burgeoning Europe-centered historiographic trend in reconstructing ancient Ireland and other contemporary Europe-centered Irish configurations of 'national' identity during this period requires further and more focused analyses—including the intersection of these developments with other potential range of crisscrossing developments, among them the political discourses of certain Home Rule or republican movements in both Ireland and the Irish diaspora. Regardless, what is undeniable is the general ascendant pattern of Irish nationalist *Europeanizing* of Ireland and of the Irish by the early twentieth century.

In some of its variations, as in the case of Eoin MacNeill's writing on ancient Ireland, this Europeanizing pattern also marked the sharpest hitherto break with claims of oriental origins of the Irish, as well with many other prior accounts of the arrival of early large-scale waves of settlers in the island by routes bypassing mainland Britain or at least without extensive period of prior residence on mainland Britain. The historiographic shift in what became the mainstream of Europe-centered Irish nationalist renditions of Ireland's ancient past also pushed forward in time the starting date for Ireland's earliest substantiated population settlements that could be categorically identified and documented in ethno-cultural terms (i.e., the Celts). This date was now moved to as late as the fourth century BCE. Moreover, in MacNeill's template, and accepted by many other leading Irish nationalist historians of his generation, what could be construed as accurate chronology of authentically 'Irish' history began only in the fifth century CE, following the introduction of Christianity to the island, which marked the island's true civilizational flourishing.[28] For MacNeill the twin cardinal defining historical qualities of Irishness all the way up to the present time were a common European-Celtic ethnic essence along with the Christian heritage of the land. Due to combined forces of exposure to this rapidly ascendant historiographic framing of Ireland after the start of the twentieth century and to other alternative modes of firmly situating Ireland and Irishness within a European framework (including the Europe-centered Aryanist discourses in general and the 'whitening' of the Irish in the late nineteenth century), the *Europeanization* of Ireland fast assumed a normative status in the sphere of Irish nationalist political discourse. The politically oriented Europeanizing of Ireland appeared in heterogeneous forms. For instance, John Dillon, a prominent IPP MP and a leading critic of the British foreign secretary Sir Edward Grey's handling of the Iranian Question, stated in 1912:

> My interest in that country [i.e., Iran] was aroused some years ago by the writings and the speeches of Professor Browne, and my interest to it was attracted because I have all my life thought that one of the greatest outrages against humanity that can be perpetrated is to kill the soul or the civilisation of any nation. [...] I am afraid that in these modern days the vast majority, at all events in Western Europe, have set up a false standard for the guidance of their own judgment as to what is really valuable in the civilization of to-day. We in Western Europe are so handed over to materialism that we seem to think the amount of manufactures produced and the wealth realised is really the only standard by which you can judge a people, or that a nation like Persia [/Iran], or many other nations who are no longer [...] able to defend themselves very well, do not matter; and that it is no loss to mankind if they are wiped out of existence and forgotten. ...
>
> [...]
>
> Another thing is perfectly plain: that we in the West have inflicted great injustice and injury on many of the Eastern races.[29]

Present in Dillon's statement, in which "we" and "the West" were conflated and the 'we' was consequently also assigned some of the onus of "inflict[ing] great injustice and injury on many of the Eastern races," was a particular geo-political grounding of Ireland in Europe, which contrasted with the earlier nineteenth-century Irish nationalist imaginations and representations of Ireland as both simultaneously *belonging to* and *situated between* the West and the East,[30] in so far as its meta-geographic national, cultural, and later on also political designation were concerned.[31] In regard to its political designation, the West had formerly been evocative of empire/colonizer and the East of the colonized and semi-colonized. Dillon's specific mode of worlding Ireland was at the same time at odds with some other Irish nationalist gestures of Europeanizing Ireland, which disingenuously absolved the Irish 'nation' of all responsibility for the 'injustice and injury' wreaked 'on many of the Eastern races.' Regardless, Dillon's and other alternative Irish nationalist modes of Europe-centered configurations of Ireland left no room for any consideration of former antiquarian theories of oriental origins. As evident from Dillon's statement, it is nonetheless imperative to emphasize that these distinct Europeanizing formulations of the Irish nation did not by themselves impede Irish nationalist expressions of sympathy with the suffering of colonized and semi-colonized "Eastern races," at least prior to the formation of the Irish Free State. Articulations of cross-territorial and cross-nationalist solidarity between Ireland and 'oriental' colonized and semi-colonized territories and peoples continued, and assumed even greater tenor in some Irish nationalist circles following the outbreak of the First World War and well up to the creation of the Irish Free State—only to substantially wane in the aftermath of the outbreak of the Irish Civil War of 1922–23, which inaugurated a more insular climate of Irish nationalist politics apropos of non-European "international" developments for at least nearly two decades, with India being among the most notable exceptions to this pattern.

In the early twentieth century, political identification of contemporary Ireland with Europe by Irish nationalists assumed many other forms than in Dillon's statement. These included Arthur Griffith's particular *Central* European template for Ireland's future political administration. Griffith's pre-1914 espousal of the Austro-Hungarian model of dual monarchy as Ireland's future system of government was yet another mode of worlding the Irish nation as a political entity. Notwithstanding the incompatibility of Griffith's pairing of Austria and England as imperial powers in this model, his recommended institutional-administrative status for a future Ireland resembling the singularly European imperial administrative status of Hungary, approached Ireland as a distinctly unique *European* imperial territory within the broader imperial dominions of England. Griffith was not absent-mindedly overlooking other Austro-Hungarian subject territories in Europe, ruled by the system of dual monarchy that Griffith advocated as the prototype for his proposed simultaneous Anglo-Irish administrative separation (i.e., the break-up of the United Kingdom with separate British and Irish parliaments), on the one hand, and the union of Britain and Ireland as an imperial entity under a new arrangement, on the other hand. What his model of future Anglo-Irish political realignment called for was both self-government for Ireland as well as a shared administrative status for Ireland as a steering cog in the re-christened imperial machine of Great Britain and Ireland, in contradistinction to other regions of England's current imperial dominions, even if at the same time espousing self-government for territories such as India within the British Empire. Even more so than the IPP's platform of Home Rule, and despite Griffith's advocacy of self-government in some other parts of the British Empire, the proposed system of dual monarchy anticipated a privileged imperial standing for the future Ireland, even compared to Scotland and Wales, and of Ireland's formal participation as a European partner with England in the governance of the remodeled Empire—in the form of a partnership that no future self-governing India within the British Empire, for example, could hope to attain without first dismantling the system of dual monarchy of Great Britain and Ireland. In contrast, republican Irish nationalists sought to sever ties with not only England, but with England's imperial enterprise as well.

Regardless of Griffith's vision of the future Ireland *at this stage*, or Dillon's premise for equating Ireland with the West—leaving aside here economic, political, and other disparities between Ireland and the dominant Western powers at the time—the incremental Irish embrace of the theory of Europe-centered Celtic origin of the Irish further facilitated the broader Europeanizing of nationalist self-imaginations of Ireland. Declan Kiberd, in a different setting, traces the process of 'Europeanizing' of Ireland to the establishment of the Irish Free State in 1922. Remarking on the more politically insular orientation of both Pro-Treaty and Anti-Treaty factions following the creation of the Free State (more appropriately after the outbreak of the Irish Civil War). Kiberd has perceptively noted: "many Irish leaders and artists, having glimpsed the potentials of a global alliance with other emerging peoples [*sic*], could so easily forget them in the drive to Europeanize the emerging Irish state."[32] Terry Eagleton has more accurately observed even earlier signs of this Europeanizing tendency, even if Eagleton's assertion in *Heathcliff and the Great Hunger* (in his discussion of "divided sensibility of modernism" in Ireland) that the "union of Celt and Gael" in the Irish Literary Revival can be singled out as a project of specifically Anglo-Irish Ascendancy committed to cultural nationalism is highly debatable. By the time the Irish Free State was founded, the theory of common Celtic origins of the earliest large-scale settlements throughout the British Isles, with those in Ireland arriving by different routes over an extended period, including via mainland Britain, was the accepted conventional account of ancient Ireland in most Irish academic and non-academic scholarly circles. Although, Eagleton is correct in noting that cultural nationalists of the Revival "could also draw on an antiquarian tradition stretching back to the eighteenth century."[33] In the arena of Irish historiography, this Celtic union was *also* the enterprise of Catholic 'mere Irish' cultural nationalists, whether committed to sectarian or ecumenical nationalism, even if the roots of this mode of historiography can be traced back to the likes of Anglo-Irish Protestant historians such as Walter Harris in the mid-eighteenth century. Harris had undertaken to exalt ancient Ireland against charges of savagery by claiming a glorious past for the island and upholding that past as part of the cultural heritage of all of Ireland's (European) population, regardless of their (European) ethnic ancestry, (Christian) denominational affiliation, or the time frame of their ancestral arrival in the island.[34] In fact, earlier in *Heathcliff and the Great Hunger*, Eagleton admits as much, noting: "the notion of some pure Gaelic race was lambasted by nationalist thinkers from George Sigerson and Eoin MacNeill to Aodh de Blacam and Thomas MacDonagh."[35]

That the manifold Europeanizing trends in Irish nationalist historiography in general prior to 1922 should have coincided with both intensified Irish nationalist expressions of cross-territorial solidarity and cross-identification with colonized and semi-colonized peoples in different parts of the world, as well as with the rising appeal among some Irish Revivalists before the First World War of Eastern literatures and/or religions (notably as reconstituted components of theosophy), poses no contradiction. Even many Irish theosophists and the like, who were committed to so-called political as well as more narrowly defined 'cultural' nationalism, and who overwhelmingly believed in Eastern origins of the Irish, conceived of contemporary Ireland and of the Irish as solidly European in their current geo-political and cultural grounding. The same was true of many of the staunchest 'internationalist' Irish nationalists committed to erasing all delusion of the West's privileged standing above the rest of humanity, as in the case of Fred Ryan. Yeats, who personally abhorred literary modernism, notwithstanding his own unmistakable modernist interventions in Irish literature, along with a number of his cultural and/or political Irish nationalist associates (whether avowedly modernist or anti-modernist), ranging from Lady Gregory and Edward Martyn to Maude Gonne, and briefly including Fred Ryan (a purveyor of literary as well as socio-political modernism), were variously obsessed with situating Ireland (Dublin to be more precise) in the hub of European cultural-spatial prominence. The literary-cultural deprovincializing of Dublin as a European capital, and deprovincializing of Ireland by implication, whether through expressed recuperation or re-inscription and (re-)invention of Irish mythology and folklore, or through the medium of other new literary genres, had been a key factor in founding the Irish Literary Theatre in 1899, later known as the Irish National Dramatic Society (1902), the Irish National Theatre Society (1903), and finally the Abbey Theatre (1904–present). It should be added, however, that the political and/or cultural Europeanizing trends in Irish nationalism were in their own ways indicative of the advent of new modes of cosmopolitanism, rather than a complete negation of cosmopolitanism, with most practices of cosmopolitanism ultimately having their own limited scope, insularities, and centers and margins. Irish nationalist Europeanizing gestures, too, were in their own ways alternative means of worlding Ireland of both past and present times. It should also be kept in mind that any discussion of Europeanizing or other historiographic, cultural, literary, and political trends, only pertain to segments of Irish nationalists who have been given historical prominence in this study solely on account of the available recorded articulations of their views (textual or otherwise). It is, therefore, not suggested here that the average nationalist public overwhelmingly shared these trends prior to the formation of the Free State. Following the creation of the Free State, *however*, the Europeanizing of Ireland assumed official status and was propagated through the educational system of the country (see below).

There were, of course, the occasional lingering practitioners of older antiquarian (legendary) models of distinct Irish origins and of the arrival of the Gaels in Ireland independently of Britain, evidently with their own intractable audiences. This was the case with the unambiguously titled 1921 *Ireland: Elements of Her Early Story from the Coming of Ceasair to the Anglo-Norman Invasion* by John Joseph O'Kelly (Seán Ua Ceallaigh)— Ceasair being presumably Noah's granddaughter and believed to have arrived in Ireland with her companions on board a separate ark during the Great Flood and prior to the arrival of Partholan and his followers. A firebrand Catholic, O'Kelly was an early member of Sinn Féin at its founding in 1905 and subsequently a prominent republican nationalist, and the editor of *Catholic Bulletin and Book Review* from 1916 to 1922. He was also the president of the Gaelic League from 1919 to 1923, and, more relevantly here, the minister of education in the Second Dáil Éireann (Irish Assembly or Parliament, 1921 to 1922) under the self-proclaimed government of the Irish Republic prior to Ireland's division and the founding of the Free State in 1922. In effect, O'Kelly was a successor to Eoin MacNeill as president of the Gaelic League and, in a less formal manner, MacNeill's predecessor as education minister, with the two men also incidentally supporting opposite nationalist factions following the establishment of the Free State; MacNeill siding with the Pro-Treaty camp and O'Kelly with the republican opposition during the Irish Civil War of 1922–23. O'Kelley's book commenced with the mythical accounts of Ireland's early population arrivals in a chapter titled "The Traditional Background," which comprised his entire chronological history of the land prior to the arrival of Christianity in Ireland in the fifth century. This was more than just an ambiguous rejection of the Europe-centered Celtic account of ancient Ireland, even as O'Kelley relied on P. W. Joyce's *A Social History of Ancient Ireland* among his sources (but only for the post-legendary period covered in O'Kelley's book).

Notably, there was no mention of the likes of the now démodé antiquarian Charles Vallancey in O'Kelly's book. Instead, he relied on what for him constituted the earliest surviving authoritative Irish sources on Ireland's ancient past, such as Geoffrey Keating's 1634 *The History of Ireland (Foras Feasa ar Éirinn)* and the eleventh-century *Lebor Gabála Érenn (The Book of Invasions)*. In the "Introduction," O'Kelly quickly dispelled Eoin MacNeill's account of the origin of the Celts, tracing instead the early population arrivals in Ireland to the East (as a branch of the Aryan Celts). O'Kelly's historiographic rationality was no less outlandish than the likes of Vallancey. O'Kelly traced the origin of the post-diluvian Aryan peoples to Armenia by way of blending the biblical Mosaic narrative with the hypothesis of the lost land of Atlantis based on the 1882 *Atlantis: The Antediluvian World* by the American Ignatius Donnelly. It this rendering of ancient Ireland that may have met with some degree of approval from the likes of Vallancey and Henry O'Brien, it was from Armenia that the Aryan colonists, who were originally from Atlantis, had spread West and East, including to Ireland and Iran.[36] By 1922, however, the O'Kellys of Irish historiographic enterprise were a fast diminishing vestigial breed of nationalist historians. There were also those who preferred a combined Eastern and European ancestry for the ancient Irish, as a means of both claiming at least somewhat distinct population settlement in Ireland than in Britain in ancient times as well as according ancient Ireland the blessing of multiple early civilizations.

These rapidly waning obdurate historiographic trends were also present in the Irish diaspora. For instance, in his 1916 war-time propaganda tract, *What Could Germany Do for Ireland?*, the Irish-American republican Irish nationalist James Kennedy McGuire resorted to (mythic) racial accounts of Ireland's earliest population settlements, harkening back to the eighteenth- and nineteenth-century debates on the origins of the Gaels. In a tangled manner, and carelessly claiming reliance on the authority of prominent nineteenth-century Royal Irish Academy historian Sir John Thomas Gilbert (1829–98), McGuire maintained a joint Greco-Tyrian (i.e., Hellenic-Phoenician) 'racial' origin for the Gaels as well as subsequent hodgepodge 'oriental' cultural influences in Ireland prior to the Norse invasions in the 'Middle Ages':

> [...] it is desirable and necessary briefly to state the true historic facts of the Irish situation for the enlightenment of democracies the world over. Sir J.T. Gilbert, Ireland's foremost archivist and archaeologist, tells us that the earliest tribes to reach Ireland, back in the twilight of history, long ere England was even known to exist, were

> familiar with all science necessary to preserve existence and organize a new country into human habitation. They cleared the forests, worked the mines, built chambers for their dead after the manner of their kindred left in Tyre and Greece, wrought arms, defensive and offensive, such as the heroes of Marathon used against the long-haired Persian; they raised altar and pillar stones, still standing amongst us, mysterious and eternal symbols of a simple, primitive creed; they had bards, priests, and law-givers, the old tongue of Shinar, the dress of Nineveh, and the ancient faith whose ritual was prayer and sacrifice.

Of the second people who found their way to Ireland the same authority tells us that they

> brought with them the Syrian arts and civilization, such as dyeing and weaving, working in gold, silver and brass, besides the written characters, the same as Cadmus afterward gave to Greece, and which remained in use amongst the Irish for above a thousand years, until modified by St. Patrick into their present form to assimilate them to the Latin.

Continuing, this same writer, from his researches, ascertained that

> continued intercourse with their Tyrian kindred soon filled Ireland with the refinements of a luxurious civilization. From various sources we learn that in those ancient times the native dress was costly and picturesque, and the habits and modes of living of the chiefs splendid and Oriental. [...] The ladies wore the silken robes and flowing veils of Persia, or the rolls of linen wound round the head like the Egyptian Isis [...]

This half-Tyrian, half-Greek race occupied Ireland for centuries and traded with Tyre, and subsequently with Carthage.[37]

Whether or not McGuire, who throughout his book displayed a distinctive plagiaristic proclivity, had on this occasion directly taken the text attributed to Gilbert from one of Gilbert's own publications, the quoted passage had also appeared earlier in an article by "Sean-Ghall" (Henry Egan Kenny) in the 1908 *Irish Year Book/Leabar na hÉireann* (published in Dublin)[38] and previously had also appeared in Lady Wilde's 1887 *Ancient Legends, Mystic Charms, and Superstitions of Ireland*, where in the section on "Our Ancient Capital" in the second volume of her book she cited Gilbert's three volume *A History of the City of Dublin* (1854–59).[39] The quoted text had, in fact, appeared in Gilbert's 1853 article "History of the City of Dublin."[40]

The old antiquarian mytho-histories of ancient Ireland (in their oriental or other manifestations), while fast falling out of favor in historical circles by the time of the creation of the Irish Free State, continued to be produced with varying degrees of former antiquarian resonances for some years to come, including works that otherwise utilized avowedly new 'scientific' methodologies. Most notable in this category was the 1931 *And So Began the Irish Nation* by Seamus MacCall, who also, incidentally, wrote biographies of Thomas Moore and John Mitchel, among his other publications. MacCall set out to reconcile a particular oriental narrative of Ireland's distant ancient past with contemporary archaeological and anthropological claims of insufficient evidence for definitively establishing Irish origins prior to the Celtic migrations to Ireland by different routes. In MacCall's account, the ancient Celtic Ireland could still be directly traced back to a broad-based 'Iranian' culture centered around the Caspian Sea and embracing Scythians, Persians, and Ossetians.[41]

Worlding Practices of Irish Nationalism, from the Late Eighteenth Century to 1921

The inception of cross-denominational and cross-ethnic Irish nationalism in the late eighteenth century—both politically and culturally in the form of the Society of United Irishmen (1791), as well on a more narrowly defined 'cultural' spectrum in some antiquarian works prior to the society's formation—was among the earliest examples of distinctly 'nationalist' anticolonial struggles. While the American War of Independence (1776–83) had further inspired and galvanized Protestant "Patriots" in Ireland, culminating in the 1782 "Grattan's Parliament," the United Irishmen identified much more with the democratic ideals of the post-1792 republican revolutionary France than with the precedent of Britain's former American colonies.[42] This was also reflected in the extent and mode of references to the two events in the 1795, 1796, 1798, and 1803 editions of the United Irishmen publication of patriotic songs titled *Paddy's Resource*;[43] without overlooking, of course, that the formation of the United Irishmen and its 1798 uprising coincided with the evolving French Revolution that was continually convulsing Europe, and with France threatening to militarily invade the British Isles itself. Even though the American War of Independence undeniably featured in the propaganda of the United Irishmen, and both American and French models shared a tolerant view of religion and irreligion (the latter more applicable to the French Revolution), the features of the nationalist struggle in Ireland, and the Irish situation in general, were drastically different from that of the thirteen former North-American colonies of Britain, as were their nebulous ideals of a future society. Unlike the American colonies, the nation envisaged by the United Irishmen was inclusive of both so-called settler and *native* populations of Ireland, with the latter comprising a majority, and 'African slavery' was loathed in the propaganda of the United Irishmen, which is not to say some Irish nationalists may not have economically benefited from the system of slavery overseas, directly or indirectly.[44] Ideologically influenced much more extensively by events in Europe than in North America, the United Irishmen followed the more democratic (albeit still exclusionary) example of the French Republic, which in theory embraced universal manhood suffrage—not extended to French colonies until 1793 during the Reign of Terror, notably in the aftermath of the 1791 uprising in the French colony of Saint-Domingue by the enslaved and freed former enslaved population, backed by some of the French residents in the colony. For instance, many of the poems in different editions of the revolutionary-republican *Paddy's Resource*, unequivocally castigated the plight of enslaved people of African descent in the newly independent United States, even if some of the poems in passing alluded to the "Freedom" of American colonies from Britain. In fact, laudatory cross-identification with the American War of Independence in Irish nationalist circles appears to have multiplied only in the aftermath of the failed United Irishmen uprisings of 1798 and 1803.

It was not merely developments in theoretical formulations and conceptualizations of nation and nationalism in other territories that resonated with different Irish nationalist platforms after 1791 (whether of the Enlightenment, Romantic, or the late nineteenth-century positivist ideological molds and/or of other variations and combinations).

Without overlooking numerous examples of blinkered Irish nationalist individuals who in the period between 1791 and 1922 justified and/or sponsored various forms of bigotry, or rationalized the imperialist expansion of Britain's rival powers as an anti-British gesture, it is undeniable that Irish nationalism since its inception in the late eighteenth century was *trans-territorial* and *trans-temporal* (past and present) in its historical self-grounding and frames of analyses, as well as in its expressions of solidarity with other peoples. As increasingly insular and religiously parochial as the "independent" Irish nation-state became in at least the first decades following the 1922 establishment of the Free State in partitioned Ireland—without here addressing the worsening communal relations in Northern Ireland after 1922 as well—Irish nationalist historiography up to that point had been marked by various practices of *worlding* Ireland. Even Arthur Griffith, the anti-Jewish and self-avowedly (albeit unconvincingly) anti-internationalist co-founder of Sinn Féin (1905), had turned to world-historical examples in framing his brand of Irish nationalism and anti-imperialism, such as the Boer struggle against the British Empire from 1899 to 1902, various Indian nationalist platforms, the Austro-Hungarian imperial system of dual monarchy as a model for Irish Home Rule within the British Empire, or (somewhat paradoxically) even in his approbation of the Zionist quest for a Jewish homeland (see below). Moreover, and possibly more so than any other anti-imperialist nationalist settings around the globe during the period covered in this book, Irish nationalist historiography in general cast its dialectical and dialogic gaze far and wide, well beyond Anglo-Irish relations and Ireland's internal socio-political configurations, even if these were its principal underlying modus operandi. Hence, Irish nationalists at large not only observed, drew lessons from, and expressed parity and varying degrees of sympathy with what they characterized as anti-imperialist resistance in other parts of the world throughout history, but they also frequently engaged in dialogic interconnections with those other histories (imagined or real).

As already noted, expressions of solidarity with other anti-imperialist struggles could often be highly selective, as in the case of Theobald Wolfe Tone or John Mitchel, who also in distinct ways promoted the subjugation of other population groups. For his part, Ireland's pre-eminent nineteenth-century nationalist balladeer Thomas Moore had earlier in life pursued imperial careers. He briefly served as the registrar for the Admiralty in Bermuda from February to May 1804 through the intercession of his Anglo-Irish friend Lord Moira (Marquess Hastings), before turning over his duties to an intermediary agent as his deputy and returning to England (with the agent absconding in late 1817 and saddling Moore with a huge debt). In 1812, Moore unsuccessfully entertained the prospect of an administrative post in British India through the office of Lord Moira, recently appointed governor-general of British India. In 1841, Moore procured an officer's rank in the British imperial army in India for his oldest son Tom and, the following year, facilitated his son's transfer from that appointment to a new post in the French Foreign Legion stationed in Algeria, a territory colonized by France in 1830.[45] Yet, there were also the likes of Daniel O'Connell, John Dillon, Hugh Shapland Swinny, Charlotte Despard, Nora Dryhurst, Fred Ryan, and many more, who, despite their own respective sets of ideological limitations, were as expansive in their support for struggles against imperialism and racism as one could hope for in any corner of the world at the time. Irish nationalists were attentive to what they termed 'nationalist' struggles not only in other parts of Europe, including Poland, or the Italian territories in the nineteenth century for instance, but also in the rest of the world, such as in Afghan territories, British India, Iran, Egypt, or the Sudan (the latter example being more complicated given the joint Anglo-Egyptian military expeditions in the Sudan after the 1880s, with Egypt both occupied by Britain in 1882 and maintaining an imperial territorial claim over the Sudan at the same time).[46]

Heterogeneous styles of worlding Ireland in nationalist accounts of ancient Ireland both pre-dated and persisted after the emergence of the United Irishmen (regardless of whether these accounts espoused oriental or non-oriental theories of Irish origins and/or relied on biblical or other narratives). There were, in addition, works of Irish nationalist literature that situated Ireland's experience of colonization and resistance in broader comparative and/or allegoric world-historical contexts, as in the case of the songs appearing in *Paddy's Resource* or the poetry of Thomas Moore, Thomas Osborne Davis, James Clarence Mangan, Denis Florence MacCarthy, or Jane Francesca Agnes Wilde, among numerous other such examples already mentioned. Thomas Moore, during his prolific literary and antiquarian career in the early nineteenth century, combined the literary and antiquarian worlding of Ireland. Celebrating Ireland's ancient grandeur through Phoenician and Iranian civilizational ties, among other global connections (appearing in the first volume of his *The History of Ireland*, 1835), he alternatively *worlded* more recent episodes in Irish history, such as the seventeenth-century Catholic uprising in Ireland and the more contemporary nonsectarian United Irishmen uprisings in allegoric forms in *Lalla Rookh* (1817), alongside other examples of such historical parallels in his other poems and ballads. The many currents of extra-Irish referentialities as components of Irish nationalist self-identification and/or self-historicization served as modes of worlding the Irish experiences of colonization, resistance, and struggle for self-government, whether through purely conceptual techniques of affiliation or also through direct exchanges and cooperation—with these referentialities including mythologized account of ancient Spartan resistance to Persian imperial aggression and equally mythologized accounts of Iranian (Persian) resistance to Arab-Muslim imperial conquest of the seventh century. As with worlding practices of nationalist movements elsewhere (anti-imperialist or other forms of nationalisms in general), these cross-referentialities required conscious narrative alterations and elisions in particular details of certain episodes of Ireland's past and present configurations, as well as in representations of peoples and/or territories that were the subject of comparative and/or affiliative analyses.

Incorporated into some of these worlding practices were also different strategies of de-provincializing Ireland. The likes of the Young Ireland leader Thomas Osborne Davis sought to transform Ireland from a 'province' to 'A nation once again,' leaving aside here that 'Ireland' had had no prior existence as a 'nation.' Davis' style of nationalism turned its back on the standard Irish antiquarian fixation with establishing Ireland's ancient indigenous identity. For Davis, the Irish nation came into being with the emergence of nonsectarian and multi-ethnic Irish nationalism—with nationalism, in effect, begetting the nation—and that nation required the re-invention of its past in order to successfully propel itself into an independent future. At the same time, Davis' poetry worlded Irish nationalism by way of not only alluding to the myth of Thermopylae, but also through condemnation of recent English acts of imperial aggression in the Indian subcontinent and in Afghan territories, the extensive violence committed against the indigenous populations of the United States ("Red Indians"), or French colonization of Algeria, alongside imperialist aggression by Russia in Circassia and Poland, or by Austria in Hungary, Serbia, or the Italian territories.[47] Meanwhile, James Clarence Mangan's inimitable genre of nationalist poetry operated on another level of worlding Ireland. Turning also to oriental and other non-Irish settings for his anti-England themed poems, including the Iranian historical setting of "To the Ingleezee Khafir" (1846), Mangan claimed his 'oriental' poems were translations from original poems in oriental languages. Whereas the antiquarians Charles Vallancey, Henry O'Brien, and the like, had turned to oriental sources for authenticating their versions of Ireland's ancient history, Mangan claimed to be presenting to his readers oriental sources that were otherwise entirely or substantially his own creations. This was an act of holding up world history to the Irish, with the intent of not only inspiring the Irish to engage in nationalist resistance of their own, but to also draw some vicarious gratification from England's imperial humiliation by others, in times past in this case. Through his self-plagiarizing format, Mangan's 'translations' in effect produced a genre of cosmopolitan poetry that was ultimately in its entirety, or in part, the product of an Irish poet (hence 'Irish'). By assigning a number of his invented poems to actual historical poets from the 'Orient,' whose works were hailed by leading orientalist authorities in Europe since the eighteenth century as specimens of great poetry, Mangan facetiously claimed to be translating original works of renowned poets, while crediting himself with fluency in a wide range of languages, including those of the Orient. By claiming to be translating oriental and other poems and peppering his poems and works of prose with real or invented oriental lexicon, Mangan was, in his own unique way, contributing to the already extensive worlding of Irish literary sensibilities (including nationalist sensibilities), while for the most part actually offering his Irish readers nothing more than the works of an ingenious Irish author; long foreshadowing James Joyce's polyglot and cosmopolitan texts in the twentieth century (see below). At the same time, as noted before, Mangan refrained from submitting his works for publication in British periodicals. This posture, along with Mangan's purported original sources of 'translated' poems (including some 'translations' from Irish) was itself a negation of Ireland's provincial literary status and its reliance on Britain (specifically England) as the arbiter of literary standards and tastes in the British Isles—not forgetting Mangan's reliance on English as his primary medium communication, and hence his ultimately contributing to 'English' literature.

The Irish Literary Revival that got underway in the late nineteenth century engendered its own modes of worlding and deprovincializing Ireland, by both further exposing Ireland to the world and further exposing other parts of the world to Ireland. Even as many participants in the Literary Revival turned to Irish legends and folklore for their subject matter, they nevertheless experimented with styles of playwriting, poetry, and fiction developed in other parts of the world, ranging from the Norwegian Henrik Ibsen's plays to the Noh theatre of Japan. There were also more personal trajectories in this deprovincializing of Ireland. Yeats' friendship and dialogue with the Indian Rabindranath Tagore is a case in point. The 1912 English translation of Tagore's Bengali poems titled *Gitanjali* included an Introduction by Yeats. The award of the Nobel Prize in Literature to Tagore in 1913, further propelled Yeats' already meteoric fame in different parts of the world as a world-class poet and playwright from Ireland, who had also recognized and endorsed the quality of Tagore's poetry in general.[48] Malcolm Sen has incisively directed attention to the function of "cultural memory" in these diverse worlding techniques spanning the interconnected realms of Irish antiquarianism, on the one hand, and the Literary and broader Irish Revival after the late nineteenth century, on the other hand:

> The antiquarian and orientalist projects were ideologically attempting the restoration of ancient cultural memory at a time of intensive national and political self-definition. [...]
> Although the tradition of antiquarian discourse waned during the Celtic Revival, the internationalist and universalist aims of many antiquarians may be said to be have been amalgamated into a religious dialect of supernatural interconnections. For example, the most important pseudoreligious organization of the nineteenth century, the Theosophical Society, had among its three tenets one that necessitated the study and understanding of Eastern literature. By a curious transformation of methodologies, the focus on the global reach of Irish history that antiquarians had earlier supplied finds expression in such pseudoscientific and spiritualist organizations that often built their visionary vocabulary on an ideology of remembering.[49]

Sporadic Irish nationalist and other modes of Irish historicization and contemporary representations of 'Iran' (in its manifold historical, geographic, and cultural sense) are examples of extra-Iranian imaginings of Iran (sympathetic, neutral, and denigrating) that in some ways overlapped with, but did not entirely correspond to, manifold Iranian self-imaginings (contemporary and historical). In this regard, the specific narrations of Iran that situated Iran in the sympathetic framework of Irish nationalist historical *and* political affinities are an unprecedented instance of non-Iranian utilization of Iranian history, as a component of world history, for countering imperialism in such an extensive array of formats and self-referentialities during the period covered in this book.

A Shrinking World of Possibilities: History, Memory, Anti-Imperialist Affinities, and the Post-1921 Worlding of Irish National Identity

The increasingly dominant Europe-centered Celticist historical paradigm of ancient Ireland engendered its own modes of worlding Ireland, while initiating a gradual process of *cultural forgetting* of the former antiquarian and other theories of Ireland's oriental origins. The transition from earlier antiquarian variations of Irish origins to the new Europe-centered Celtic narrative had itself been a gradual, and initially overlapping, paradigm shift, rather than a sudden epistemic rupture, which *re-located* ancient Ireland on the spatial-temporal horizon of world history as seen through the Irish lens—with Irish fragments of that world history now re-written. This now-dominant narrative, notwithstanding its much sounder historiographic grounding, was nevertheless a much narrower geo-cultural framing of Ireland's historical place in the world. In this new historiography, the overwhelming majority of the Irish 'nation' could claim some degree of common historical Celtic ancestry, regardless of whether their ancestry had settled in Ireland much earlier than the ancestors of other groups (who could claim the same common Celtic ingredient in their ancestral makeup, among any other possible range of so-called ethnic traces). According to this historical model, regardless of the time frame of their ancestral arrivals in the island the present Irish nation also shared a *contemporary cultural identity*, beyond the defining Christian identity of Ireland since the fifth century, that was distinct from the cultures of mainland Britain. This vaguely defined cultural identity of Ireland (whether presented as something uniquely 'not-England' or as former English, Scots, and Welsh cultural beliefs and practices now imbued with varying degrees of the core Gaelic traditions of the land) was seen as yet another justification for an Irish nation-state (whether within the British Empire or as a completely separate entity). With the exception of a few fringe organizations after the late eighteenth century, it was the claim of Irish *cultural* distinctiveness (rather than ethnic or 'racial' uniqueness), as well as the quest for *political* self-governance, that were pitched as the primary rationale for a separate Irish state. The centrality of Irish language as a marker of the national culture remained a contested subject. One major selling point of the new Celticist nationalist historiography by the start of the twentieth century—leaving aside whether it was more 'scientific' and accurate than former antiquarian accounts—was its ultimate *expunging* of the Gael versus the Celt and other such ethnic/racial wranglings.

Moreover, notwithstanding the emphasis on a common national culture (as a universalizing force) and the frequently avowed nonsectarian approach of the new historiography, similar to the platforms of most nationalist organizations (even if some of the latter often sought to ingratiate themselves with the Catholic Church), the majority of Ireland's population and the competing church establishments in Ireland were clearly *unwilling* to leave denominational religion out of their own particularistic formulations of culture and identity. This resistance to extracting religion from the 'national' was later manifested in the rapid merger of religion (Catholicism) with the state-sponsored concept of the Irish nation after the founding of the Free State in 1922. In the process, the Catholic Church also assumed 'cultural' control over the state-funded primary educational system of the new Irish state, including the teaching of the compulsory school subject of "history." The teaching of the new Europe-centered Celticist history of ancient Ireland, which became the primary means by which younger generations of the Irish were initiated into this historical paradigm, also stressed the Christian component of Irish identity since ostensibly the proselytization efforts of St. Patrick in the fifth century—in keeping with Eoin MacNeill's own version of history, and with MacNeill also serving as the Free State's minister of education from 1922 to 1925.[50] Perhaps it should not be surprising that under the growing influence of the Catholic Church, and the political pandering to that church by some leading Pro-Treaty nationalist politicians in the years immediately after the founding of the Free State, that the already exclusionary parameters of the cultural realm of the Irish nation began to contract even further after 1922—to the point of incrementally marginalizing the minority Protestant communities in the Free State. The much smaller number of non-Christians residing in the Free State had already been largely situated in the margins of the Irish nation prior to 1922, if not entirely excluded from or stigmatized in *mainstream* nationalist discourses—as a small number of nationalists, such as the likes of Fred Ryan, had vehemently protested before 1922 in connection with the discriminatory treatment of the Jewish community, for instance. The marginalization of the Free State's already small Protestant community (with most Protestants having lived in the six northern counties within Ulster prior to 1921 and, hence, living in Northern Ireland after 1922) occurred despite the presence on public stage of 'nationally' well-established Protestants, ranging from Douglas Hyde, the first president of Éire (1938–1945), to Yeats (d.1939), the celebrated national poet who won the Nobel Prize in literature in 1923.

By the start of the twentieth century, in the sphere of nationalist historiography, as well as in nationalist solidarity networks, Irish national identity had been mapped in multiple heterogeneous Europe/non-Europe configurations in world-historical and world-political framings. This extended from the residual oriental theories of Irish origins (among other theories) to the Eastern model of the Aryan ancestry of the Celts or the Europe-centered Celticist model of ancient Ireland, along with cross-identification of the Irish struggle with Egyptian, Indian, Polish, Iranian, and other anti-imperialist nationalist struggles. However, not long after the turn of the century, with the growing dominance in historical circles of the emergent Europe-centered Irish historiography, the overall nationalist horizon of worlding the Irish nation was now incrementally circumscribed, even as the political horizon of Irish nationalist expressions of cross-territorial solidarity continued to encompass Europe as well as the rest of the world for sometime to come. This is not to suggest the practitioners and adherents of the new historiographic model of ancient Ireland themselves somehow necessarily ceased to express support for anti-imperialist struggles outside Europe/the West. Nor had Irish historiography previously served as the determining factor in expressions of support for anti-imperialist struggles in other parts of the world. In fact, the two decades prior to the founding of the Irish Free State marked a high point of expressed Irish nationalist solidarity with other struggles, most of them outside Europe/the West. However, following the founding of the Irish Free State, the political horizon of Irish nationalist endorsement of other anti-imperialist struggles also rapidly contracted, coming to focus more and more on European developments due to Ireland's new status and the political-ideological realignments in the European balance of power following the First World War, among other factors. Particularly after the Irish Civil War of 1922–23, the state, its political institutions, the foundations of its educational system, the outlines of its economy and "modernization" schemes, and Ireland's mainstream 'modernist' literary and cultural practices, among other forces, increasingly situated the Free State firmly within a 'European' geo-political, historical, ethnic, and cultural orbit.

During at least the first decade-and-a-half after the creation of the Free State, the focus on building and solidifying the new state, navigating the deep intra-national chasm exposed by the civil war, commemorating the founding of the state and the struggles of the past, debating the future of the state (including its constitution and ties to London), deliberating the future status of Northern Ireland, building a viable independent economy, pondering the proximity of the Catholic Church and the state—with the Church closely scrutinizing an array of social issues from education to women's rights, marriage and family, legislation of alcohol consumption, "morality" in general, and other such domestic issues—became the overarching preoccupations of veteran and younger generations of Irish nationalists in the Free State. The same can be said of most nationalists in the Irish diaspora. In this setting, there was a corresponding diminished interest in anti-imperialist struggles elsewhere around the world; India being the most notable exception.

Irish nationalist expressions of solidarity with other struggling nations facing imperial domination had multiplied in the period leading up to the creation of the Free State, exponentially peaking after the end of the First World War, with Ireland itself gripped in the tumult of the Irish War of Independence (a.k.a., Anglo-Irish War, 1919–21), before these cross-territorial expressions plummeted following the creation of the Free State. That broadening horizon of nationalist solidarities and affinities prior to 1922 was also reflective of the proliferation of anticolonial and other anti-imperialist struggles around the world in reaction to intensified European, American, and Japanese imperialisms. The First World War merely fueled anticolonial/anti-imperialist aspirations, even if creating new fissures within and between some of the anti-imperialist nationalist constituencies, as in Ireland itself. Ireland entered the war with prior anticipation of self-government secured by Home Rule nationalists and corresponding apprehension and defiance by unionists, along with continued disaffection with both the status quo and the promised Home Rule on the part of republican nationalists. Following the outbreak of the war, the mainstream Home Rule nationalists for the most part—similar to unionists, who had shortly before threatened London with an armed mutiny in opposition to the Home Rule Bill of 1912—offered their support for London's war effort, even if some among them objected to London's handling of affairs leading up to the war. Opponents of the war effort consisted of Irish pacifists and conscientious objectors in general, militant republican nationalists, and the more radical Sinn Féiners. During the war, Irish republicans associated with the Irish Republican Brotherhood (IRB) continued their anti-British activities with German sponsorship in both Ireland and in the Irish diaspora. (Germany, incidentally, had supplied weapons to the unionist Irish paramilitary group the Ulster Volunteers prior to the war, with the latter preparing to circumvent the introduction of Home Rule through armed resistance.) The militant republican nationalists forged closer ties with the more militant nationalist organizations in some other parts of the world that also enjoyed German sponsorship, including Indian, Iranian, and Egyptian nationalist groupings headquartered in Berlin, alongside German-backed Indo-Irish covert operations in the United States, among other examples.[51] In the midst of the raging bloodbath of the First World War, 1916 witnessed a failed republican uprising in Dublin (the Easter Rising). As noted already, it was this failed uprising (largely limited to the center of Dublin) that resulted in the first instance of a public espoual of the Irish Question by Iranian nationalist factions. This occurred at a time when the more militant Iranian nationalists were engaged in armed operations against British and Russian occupation forces in Iran, with Germany and/or the Ottoman Empire backing different Iranian factions in these armed conflicts. German war-time propaganda was a key factor in the public endorsement of the Irish nationalist struggle by Iranian nationalists.

The Irish Question was avoided in president Woodrow Wilson's Fourteen Points (January 8, 1918), which on paper bombastically pledged the United States to the principle of national self-determination after the end of the war, while in intent this promise of self-determination was to only encompass the *European* imperial possessions of the Central Powers (with their non-European colonies later swallowed up by the Allied Powers). Nor was Ireland (similar to Iran) allowed a nationalist deputation at the Paris/Versailles peace talks after the war, with Britain as one of the Big Four powers dominating the talks. The Irish Home Rule Act of 1914 was now also a distant memory and Irish nationalism rapidly veered in the direction of militant republicanism in response to developments following the Easter Rising of 1916 and the abandonment of the 1914 Home Rule Act by London. In 1919 widespread nationalist armed struggle against English rule erupted in Ireland. The IRB republican camp had by now absorbed Sinn Féin and many other militant groups and was gaining rapid popularity in nationalist communities across Ireland, proclaiming itself in 1919 the government of the Irish Republic, with the Irish Republican Army as its paramilitary force. In the meantime, the IPP, which had enjoyed the support of the overwhelming majority of Irish nationalist constituency prior to at least the Easter Rising, if not even up to the end of the First World War, experienced a rapid decline in popular support. Yet, in the midst of these major post-war disturbances and changed fortunes of nationalist camps, both republican and Home Rule factions (in Ireland and in the Irish diaspora) continued their advocacy of anti-imperialist struggles in other parts of world—with the IPP members having earlier largely suspended their condemnations of British imperialism during the war. These extra-Irish causes included the ongoing Iranian struggle for national sovereignty, with Britain now the sole imperial power in Iranian affairs following the collapse of Tsarist Russia in 1917 (the March Revolution) and the Ottoman defeat in the First World War and the partition of former Ottoman territories, excluding Anatolia, by Britain and France. To the existing list of Iranian nationalist grievances against London was added the abortive Anglo-Iranian Agreement of 1919, with the potential of extending full British suzerainty over Iran. In the immediate years following the end of the First World War there was a surge in anti-imperialist nationalist campaigns around the world, along with an escalation in the activities of their distinctive or overlapping global networks, including a range of activities centered in so-called imperial metropoles.

Following the founding of the Free State and the Irish Civil War of 1922–23, new fault lines emerged in the now reconfigured, re-aligned, and competing Irish nationalist camps vying for control of the new state.[52] Although there were continued periodic expressions of solidarity with other anti-imperialist struggles, notably in India, the general trend in Irish nationalism after 1923 was one of overwhelmingly insular and/or chiefly Europe-centered outlooks. After 1922, as with mainstream Irish historiography (albeit without any implied direct connection), the 'internationalist' and 'transnational' political horizon of Irish nationalism too shrank rapidly, becoming predominantly Europe-centered.[53] The now-republican Sinn Féin party that dominated Irish nationalist politics after the United Kingdom general election of 1918—with the party declaring the establishment of the Irish Republic and the creation of a Provisional Irish government in 1919, during the Irish War of Independence, and later negotiating the terms of the Anglo-Irish Treaty of December 6, 1921, leading to the creation of the Free State—immediately splintered following the conclusion of the Treaty. One faction of Sinn Féin (Pro-Treaty) assumed the government of the new Free State in 1922, while the other faction (Anti-Treaty) waged war against the new government under the banner of the Irish Republican Army, inaugurating the Irish Civil War of 1922-23. The Pro-Treaty faction briefly reclaimed the party after 1923, with the defeat of the Anti-Treaty faction in the armed conflict. Many of the latter subsequently joined Fianna Fáil, founded in 1926 under Éamon de Valera's leadership after his release from prison in 1924. Meanwhile, the Pro-Treaty ruling faction reconstituted itself as a new political party, supplanting the Pro-Treaty Sinn Féin faction. This was Cumann na nGaedheal (founded in 1923, led by William Thomas Cosgrave, and named after an earlier organization founded in 1900 that was the precursor to the original Sinn Féin). This new party lasted until 1932, and was in turn superseded by Fine Gael in 1933, following Cumann na nGaedheal's 1932 and 1933 electoral defeats by Fianna Fáil. From 1923 to Fianna Fáil's electoral victory in 1932, it was the (Pro-Treaty) Labour Party that constituted the main Opposition party in the Free State.[54] Fianna Fáil, despite its acceptance of the oath of allegiance to the British crown after 1927, in order to hold seats in the Dáil Éireann, pursued an underlying republican goal of incrementally severing all ties with the British Empire in the foreseeable future.

During these years, Cumann na nGaedheal, the Labour Party, and Fianna Fáil focused increasingly on internal Irish politics (including the future status of Northern Ireland) and on gaining or retaining control of the state, as well as a host of pressing domestic issue such as the economy, with correspondingly diminished active attention to anti-imperialist struggles elsewhere. These domestic concerns also included Cumann na nGaedheal's partisan ingratiating of the Catholic establishment in Ireland for bolstering its electoral support base; further underscoring the Catholic essence of the young Irish state's vision of national identity. The rapidly dwindling tenor of cross-territorial anti-imperialist solidarities in the Free State, at least up to 1935, was by no means absolute. Leaving aside the very small-scale anarchist and communist groupings—the latter comprising such organizations in the 1920s as the Communist Party of Ireland (1921-24) and James Larkin's Irish Worker League (1923-28), both affiliates of the Comintern, which at least gave lip service to anticolonial struggles[55]—the Labour Party and, to a lesser extent, Fianna Fáil, were the two main nationalist political factions during this period that occasionally voiced support for anti-imperialist nationalist campaigns in other parts of the world, most specifically within the British Empire, and by far in regard to India. The Labour Party, and to a lesser degree also Fianna Fáil, continued to exhibit some interest in anticolonial developments elsewhere, in sharp contrast to the ruling Cumann na nGaedheal. Other than their latent ideological commitment to anticolonial solidarities, the fact that the staunchly Anti-Treaty elements of the nationalist constituency—defeated in the civil war of 1922-23, during which the Pro-Treaty government of the Free State relied on British military backing—should have been more vociferous in their advocacy of anticolonial movements in other parts of the British Empire, namely in India, is no surprise. Whether these Anti-Treaty groups ended up supporting Fianna Fáil, continued their allegiance to the outlawed Irish Republican Army, or joined other groups ultimately opposed to the Free State's current standing as an imperial dominion, they harbored a bitter resentment of Ireland's existing ties to the British Empire (with Northern Ireland still under direct British rule no less).

The overarching focus on India in Irish nationalist endorsement of other anti-imperialist struggles during the period was also evident among the small-scale Irish Left-wing organizations represented in the Comintern, whose members interacted with Left-leaning Indian nationalists through the Comintern-affiliated League Against Imperialism (1927–37).[56] The Indian nationalist movements had assumed mass popular following in the aftermath of the massacre of civilians by the British Indian army in Amritsar in April 1919, in addition to the unpopularity of various post-war repressive measures introduced by British authorities in the subcontinent, such as the Rowlatt Acts in February 1919, and the dashed hope of many moderate Indian nationalists that India might at least attain some degree of self-government following the end of the First World War in return for the sacrifices made by Indians in defense of the British Empire during the war. The League Against Imperialism had a broader socio-economic global approach to anti-imperialism. For example, the first issue of the Dublin *Anti-Imperialist* in 1926, billed as the "Official Organ of the Anti-Imperialist Vigilance Association," which was an extension of the League, stated its opposition to the Irish Free State's continued membership in the British Empire in the following terms: "We are to share the spoils of a 'commonwealth' wrung from the widow and the orphan, to fill our own coffers by seizing the riches of the Indian, the Egyptian, and the Chinese. [...] Irishman! Do you want to share in the co-equality of oppression, of child labour in China, of force and fraud in every foreign land where, as partners of England, you will do her dirty work while she pockets the gains?"[57] The banned Irish Republican Army's mouthpiece during these years, *An Phoblacht (The Republic)*, edited by the socialist republican Peadar O'Donnell from 1926 to 1929, was also a venue for expressions of anticolonial solidarity, again with a special concentration on India.[58] Later, O'Donnell, along with Maud Gonne MacBride, Charlotte Despard, Frank Ryan, and the Indian Vithalbhai Jhaverbhai Patel organized the Indian–Irish Independence League (1932), 'with a view to work by every possible means to secure the complete independence of India and Ireland, and to achieve the closest solidarity between the Irish and the Indian masses in their common struggle against British imperialism.'[59] Not only was India the largest and most populous British colony, but there was a long precedence to Indo-Irish nationalist expressions of solidarity and cross-territorial cooperation. Indian nationalists, too, devoted particular attention to developments in the Irish Free State during these years, with majority of Indian nationalists after 1919 desiring full independence from Britain (swaraj), albeit through non-violent means, and wishing to avoid a fate similar to that of Ireland's partitioning and the Free State's limited autonomy within the empire. Meanwhile, collaborations between diasporic militant Irish and Indian nationalists in the United States also continued after the creation of the Free State, as in the case of the Ghadar monthly publication *The United States of India*, published in San Francisco from 1923 to 1926.[60]

At any rate, at the official level in the Free State, Patrick Sarsfield O'Hegarty's 1922 desire to align the Free State with other "Small Nations" as well as with the imperial dominions of Britain that enjoyed representation in the League of Nations for building an anti-imperialist front was far too optimistic and anachronistic in the current climate of Irish politics. O'Hegarty, a long-time militant Irish nationalist and now a Pro-Treaty nationalist and the secretary of the Department of Posts and Telegraphs of the Free State, wrote in a letter dated September 15, 1922, to James Joseph Walsh, the Postmaster-General of the Free State:

> Ireland's position is unique. By virtue of our special history, our special position, we can not only lead the British Dominions in an anti-Imperial policy against the British Empire, but we can, through the League, organise the small Nations in a Small Nations League against the Empires. We can make of the League a reality by going into it and supplying honesty and passion and decency in its Councils. We can become a pivot for Europe and for America as well.
>
> It is Utopian, but it is possible, and we ought to neglect nothing in which there is any promise.[61]

Had there even been a realistic possibility of such an anti-imperialist front led by the Irish Free State, that state's dependence on British military support during the Irish Civil War that was still raging as O'Hegarty composed his letter, certainly quashed that possibility. The overall foreign affairs orientation of principal nationalist platforms in the Free State, until at least 1935, was one of increasingly Europe-centered, if not predominantly insular, outlook. This was further impacted by European ramifications of new state ideologies of, on the one hand, the post-1917 Bolshevism (later Soviet communism), and, on the other hand, the post-1922 fascism, and the intense mutual antagonism between these ideologies.

The dwindling internationalist horizon of the post-"independence" Irish nation-state was certainly not a uniquely Irish phenomenon. More importantly, world events doubtless played a part in the post-1922 diminished extra-European gaze of Irish nationalism in general. To avoid an overarching account of the overall Irish nationalist insularity during the initial decade-and-a-half after the formation of the Free State in 1922, it is essential to take into consideration also developments outside Ireland itself. Some territories that had previously elicited Irish nationalist expressions of solidarity were no longer in their former circumstances. In the case of Iran, conditions in that country and wider international developments were also contributing factors. Although the same mode of explanation does not apply to all other colonized and semi-colonized territories, in the case of Iran prior to at least John (Jack) McQuillan's already noted 1952 speech in the Dáil in support of the Iranian opposition to Britain's control of Iran's oil industry, the rapid decline in Irish nationalist expressions of solidarity with the Iranian 'nation' in the first three decades after the creation of the Free State cannot be solely characterized as a symptom of Irish nationalist preoccupation with developments inside the Free State itself—particularly following the violent rupture in nationalist ranks with the outbreak of the Irish Civil War. Nor was the diminished interest in the Iranian Question during this time largely a reflection of the urgent foreign policy priorities of the Free State. After the establishment of the Pahlavi dynasty in Iran in 1925, the founder of that dynasty Reza Shah (r.1925–41) pursued a policy of authoritarian modernization of the country, while engaging in a largely successful nationalist policy of diplomatically curtailing much of Britain's imperial leverage in Iran (the main exception being the Anglo-Iranian Oil Company). These measures included the withdrawal of British forces stationed in the country since 1915 (during the First World War). For its part, Egypt, which along with India had routinely featured in Irish nationalist declarations of anti-imperialist solidarity before 1922, secured its conditional independence in February 1922 (following the Egyptian Revolution of 1919). Among other random examples, in 1919 Afghans successfully rebuffed the British attempt to establish a protectorate over their territory. With the collapse of the Austro-Hungarian, German, and Russian empires in the First World War, Hungary and Poland gained their independence, along with the newly created Czechoslovakia and Yugoslavia. But, as in the case of India, imperialism was by no means dead and buried. Furthermore, former German imperial territories outside Europe were divided among the Allied victors, including Japan. The Allied powers continued their possession of former African colonies. The Ottoman Empire, except Anatolia, was carved out by England and France. In effect, the British Empire actually expanded its geographic reach following the end of the First World War, notwithstanding the (partitioned) Irish Free State's and Egypt's circumscribed independence. Hence, the post-1922 brisk dwindling of Irish nationalist advocacy of liberation movements elsewhere was clearly not due to the shrinking of the British Empire or the waning of imperialism in general.

It is undeniable that after the creation of the Irish Free State Irish nationalism for the most part turned its gaze inward, until at least the Abyssinian Crisis of 1935,[62] and much more notably following the outbreak of the Spanish Civil War of 1936-39—not forgetting that both events were simultaneously national, regional, European, and more broadly international events with far-reaching global consequences, ranging from ideological-political and militarist polarization of the major powers to the credibility of the League of Nations, as well as "rules" of warfare. The Abyssinian (Ethiopian) and Spanish crises not only animated the foreign affairs stance of the governing Fianna Fáil party in the Free State, but also reinforced the internationalist activism of Irish communists, socialists, anarchists and other anti-fascist groups, while also boosting the extra-Irish profile of Eoin O'Duffy's fascist Blueshirts, founded in 1932. The overwhelming religiously-conservative sector of trade unionists, with the encouragement of the Catholic Church, favored the fascists against the republican government of Spain during the Spanish Civil War and chiefly either ignored or defended the Italian aggression in Abyssinia. Some supporters of these disparate Irish political groupings joined the opposing sides in the Spanish Civil War as legions of international volunteers flocking to Spain, with public opinion in Ireland concerning that conflict believed to have been chiefly pro-fascist, in part due to the urging of the Catholic establishment. De Valera's governing Fianna Fáil also found its rank and file split over the contending camps in Spain.[63] It should be added, however, that both the Spanish Civil War and the Italian invasion of Abyssinia were still approached in most of the statements made by Irish nationalists of different ideological leanings through a primarily 'European' lens, rather than through a more global lens, in so far as their potential implications for unleashing a major European conflict that could also embroil Ireland.

As on certain occasions in the past, the latest expressions of concern with the rights of so-called weaker nations, such as Abyssinia, were at times diluted by overtly self-centric Irish apprehensions. A case in point is that of the frequently mentioned, yet inadequately analyzed, statement by the Irish Taoiseach (de Valera) before the League of Nations in Geneva on July 2, 1936. De Valera's commentary on the Italian invasion of Abyssinia, in which he expressed grave alarm at the blatant violation of the right of an independent territory, and a member of the League of Nations no less, is uniformly cited by historians of Ireland as an instance of the Free State's formal endorsement of the rights of weaker nations. Entirely lost in this verdict, is the additional self-centric subtext of de Valera's statement, which ultimately called on the League to do nothing beyond verbal condemnations and diplomatic negotiations among the major European powers, while Italy slaughtered Abyssinians and gruesomely conquered their country. This seemingly paradoxical statement on the one hand expressed sympathy with Abyssinia, as the League of Nations stood by and did nothings, while simultaneously (and realistically) recognizing any armed conflict between the major European powers would potentially turn into another devastating global conflict much worse than the First World War. But, there was another underlying and overlooked dimension to de Valera's concern for avoiding an armed conflict between the major European powers. Implicit in his speech before the League was his anxiety that a European war over the Abyssinian crisis would oblige the Irish Free State to militarily contribute to any large-scale British war effort, given the Free State's continued membership in the British Empire. His statement deserves to be quoted in some detail here:

> Perhaps as the representative of a small nation that has itself experience of aggression and dismemberment, the members of the Irish Delegation may be more sensitive than others to the plight of Ethiopia. But is there any small nation represented here which does not feel the truth of the warning that what is Ethiopia's fate today may well be its own fate tomorrow, should the greed or the ambition of some powerful neighbour prompt its destruction.
> [...] Unless the League can inspire confidence it clearly cannot stand. Subscribing to what has been proved to be a delusion is not the way to secure confidence. [...] Let us face the fact that economic and financial sanctions can be made effective only if we are prepared to back them up by military measures. Let us face the fact that every nation may when the test comes have many good reasons for shirking the terrible responsibility of entering upon a war. Let us face the fact that not one of the fifty nations represented here is prepared to face war to preserve the principles of the League in the present dispute. For the sake of a nation in Africa, apparently no one is ready to risk now a war that would be transferred to Europe.
> [...]
> Europe is obviously the danger point. If we want to be realists we will concentrate upon Europe without delay [...] let us, if we are thinking only of the future, set about the urgent task of preserving peace in Europe and leave aside for the moment such questions as how the Covenant should be altered to make it as a world organisation effective and universal.
> The peace of Europe depends, as everybody knows, on the will of the great Powers. If the great Powers of Europe would only meet now in that Peace conference which will have to be held after Europe has once more been drenched in blood; if they would be prepared to make now in advance only a tithe of the sacrifice each of them will have to make should the war be begun, the terrible menace which threatens us all today could be warded off.
> The problems that distract Europe should not be left to the soldiers to decide. They should be tackled now by the statesmen. If these problems cannot be settled by conciliation, let them be submitted to arbitration. I will be told that there are difficulties. Of course there are difficulties. [...]
> [...]

Despite our judicial equality here, *in matters such as European peace, the small States are powerless.* As I have already said, peace is dependent upon the will of the great States. *All the small States can do, if the statesmen of the greater States fail in their duty, is resolutely to determine that they will not become the tools of any great Power and that they will resist with whatever strength they may possess every attempt to force them into a war against their will.*[64] (Emphasis added.)

It was only after the 1937 amendment of the constitution of the Irish Free State, under de Valera's supervision (which also officially changed the name of the Free State to Éire), that the Irish parliament (Dáil Éireann) assumed complete control over the country's foreign relations and declaration of war, while still remaining in the British Empire—a constitutional adjustment that later enabled the Irish state to declare neutrality in what became the Second World War.

Concomitant with these and other political transformations in Irish nationalist outlooks after 1922, the narrowly defined and strictly *European* ethnic identity of the overwhelming majority of the Irish population, and its accompanying assertion of Ireland's common historical rootedness in a 'European' Celtic civilizational heritage, was also being firmly consolidated. This occurred in the form of the official historiographic standard in the Free State (in conjunction with a fervently Catholic undergirding of national identity in contrast to Northern Ireland). This dominant construct of Irishness was robustly disseminated through the state-operated educational system, among other venues, and was now conferred an unprecedented official and hegemonic status. No previous account of ancient Ireland had received an official seal of state and church approval and active endorsement, even after acquiring consensus in the ranks of the Royal Irish Academy. Regardless of the comparative methodological reliability and verifiability of the Europe-centered Celticist historical narrative, contra the preceding diverse antiquarian accounts of Ireland's oriental or other origins, the point here is that this historiographic model also proved a better ideological fit for the emergent Irish state after 1922. This is not to suggest a conscious strategic convergence between this official nationalist historiography and the incremental tendency of the Free State authorities (notwithstanding intra-nationalist divisions) to position the Free State principally in the arena of European politics. These were separate modes of 'Europeanizing' the Irish identity, ethno-historically and politically, that merely *happened* to coalesce after 1922, following the proliferation of the European-Celtic paradigm for a few decades prior to the formation of the Free State. Moreover, in the diplomatic arena from 1922 to 1932 there was an attempt to align the Free State (inside and outside the League of Nations) with existing British dominions comprised of 'white'/'European'-settler territories: Canada, Newfoundland, Australia, New Zealand, and South Africa.[65]

While the European-Celtic model of ancient Ireland assumed official endorsement through the educational system in the Free State, it already long before had attained normative historiographic status among leading Irish historians, operating as the dominant narrative in Northern Ireland as well. After 1922, this historiographic model in the Free State operated in a new environment of nationalist-controlled Irish politics, which turned out to be highly receptive to this model. As part of the state's nation-building efforts at institutional levels, this model also enjoyed the backing of the Catholic Church, given that the particular version of Irish historical identity propagated by the likes of Eoin MacNeill grounded the roots of Irishness in both Europe and Christianity—in this case, a Christianity long preceding the Protestant Reformation. This convergence process resulted in a contextually symbiotic configuration, and the historiographic model was disseminated through official state and church sponsorship as part of the curriculum in the new state's system of compulsory primary education. But, there is another dimension of nationalist historiography that needs to be addressed. This is the relatively recent formation of the particular European-Celtic narrative of ancient Ireland, now functioning as the dominant historiographic paradigm in which so-called postcolonial citizens of the Free State were inculcated (the Free State more accurately being in a liminal stage between colonial and postcolonial). Oona Frawley makes an important general observation concerning "idealization" of the pre-colonial past in nationalist historiography. However, her application of this template to Ireland (similar to many other 'national' contexts) requires certain adjustments. She notes:

> if a colonized society moving toward postcoloniality recovers or attempts to recover its cultural memory, there is usually a sense that the recovered memory (a) belongs to a pre-colonial period and is not marked by the trauma usually associated with colonization and is seen as somehow pretraumatic; and (b) is somehow to be seen as "positive" as a result. This conscientious, literal remembering and hearkening back to a precolonial period often result in the fetishization of that period as idyllic and utterly removed from the vagaries of the times to come—and, indeed, utterly removed from the actual historical record. In an Irish context, this idealization can be clearly seen, as has been endlessly noted, in the work of early Revivalists in the mid–nineteenth century. Such an idealization can mark a stage in the process that moves a nation toward postcoloniality; the recovered cultural memory tends to swerve toward a more historically based and so "accurate" construction of the past as the culture begins to critique its own nostalgia and moves into a postcolonial time/space. The nostalgic impulse can, and often does, persist, however, not only in abstract projections of the nation's idealized future, as Malcolm Sen points out (2005), but also, practically, in the teaching of history within a newly postcolonial space, and in any burgeoning tourist / heritage industries (Thompson 2000).[66]

Yet, the version of ancient Ireland taught in the Free State would have been inconceivable to many "early Revivalists in the mid-nineteenth Century."[67] Leaving aside that by 1922 the specifically 'oriental' theories of ancient Ireland, including Iranian theories, were largely a flickering shadow of bygone historical mentalities and methodologies, there was another element of disconnect between more recent and former nationalist accounts of the Irish past. This was the different pre-colonial timescapes subject to nationalist historical 'idealization.' The European-Celtic model dismissed as legends all accounts of Irish origins and civilization prior to roughly the fourth century BCE, whereas prior antiquarian accounts had sought to trace Irish origins and civilizations to a much more archaic temporal frame.

Without here delving into present-day, and still unsettled, genetic re-mappings of Irish identities, the last notable attempt at reconciling the model of European-Celtic identity of the Irish with the purportedly much earlier presence of the Celts in Ireland, as well as ultimately tracing the Celts back to an ancestral home in the Orient, occurred just prior to the formation of the Free State. This was Seumas MacManus' previously mentioned 1921 *The Story of the Irish Race*, which relied on an ample dose of antiquarian beliefs, albeit avoiding any reference to more controversial antiquarians such as Vallancey or Henry O'Brien. MacManus commenced the first chapter of his book in the following vein:

> THE Irish Race of to-day is popularly known as the Milesian Race, because the genuine Irish (Celtic) people were supposed to be descended from Milesius of Spain, whose sons, say the legendary accounts, invaded and possessed themselves of Ireland a thousand years before Christ.
>
> But it is nearly as inaccurate to style the Irish people pure Milesian because the land was conquered and settled by the Milesians, as it would be to call them Anglo-Norman because it was conquered and settled by the twelfth century English.
>
> The Races that occupied the land when the so-called Milesians came, chiefly the Firbolg and the Tuatha De Danann, were certainly not exterminated by the conquering Milesians. Those two peoples formed the basis of the future population, which was dominated and guided, and had its characteristics moulded, by the far less numerous but more powerful Milesian aristocracy and soldiery.
>
> All three of these races, however, were different tribes of the great Celtic family, who, long ages before, had separated from the main stem, and in course of later centuries blended again into one tribe of Gaels — three derivatives of one stream, which, after winding their several ways across Europe from the East, in Ireland turbulently met, and after eddying, and surging tumultuously, finally blended in amity, and flowed onward in one great Gaelic stream.

Significantly, in the very first footnotes of this first page of his opening chapter, MacManus stated: "Many scientific historians deny [...] in toto" that Milesians "invaded [...] Ireland a thousand years before Christ." He added defiantly:

> [Marie Henri d'Arbois de] Jubainville denies a De Danann race to Ireland. He asserts they were mythological. [Eoin] MacNeill agrees with him. But many students of the question disagree with both of these able men. The fact that myths grow around great people must not lead us to conclude that the people were mythical. Fortunately[,] Fionn and his Fian fell within historical time when actual facts, countering the myths that have gathered around them, were set down; otherwise, by the same process of reasoning, they might have been classed with the De Danann as an entirely imaginary people.[68]

MacManus, originally from Donegal and an Irish nationalist, was by then living in the United States, where he also periodically lectured at the University of Notre Dame in Indiana. *The Story of the Irish Race* was published in the United States and immediately gained popularity in Irish circles, including in Ireland itself, judging by its numerous reprint editions.[69] MacManus' book was among what, with hindsight, can be regarded as anachronistic last gasps of old-style antiquarian convictions of Irish origins. Significantly, from the early twentieth century onward, with rare exceptions, it was only *contemporary Iran* that featured in Irish nationalist imaginations in the form of cross-territorial expressions of solidarity until the creation of the Free State and then again much later on. Previously, for over a century, 'Iran' had also functioned as a civilizational prism through which some Irish nationalists (as well as other Irish commentators) regarded Ireland's own ancient past and/or its contemporary folk beliefs and legends, as well as serving as an Irish nationalist allegoric device for representing Ireland's history of resistance to English domination.

Nevertheless, the lingering traces of oriental models of Irish origins persisted well into the 1930s and beyond, the most ambitious in its methodological scope being the 1931 *And So Began the Irish Nation* by the nationalist (former 'Anti-Treaty') amateur historian Seamus MacCall. Published in Dublin, London, and New York, this was a revisionist take on the dominant contemporary European-Celtic grounding of ancient Ireland. Utilizing new interdisciplinary historiographic trends, MacCall engaged with the latest geological, archaeological, and anthropological theories to construct what he regarded as "a coherent and comprehensive story of the origin and evolution of the Irish nation."[70] He sought to demonstrate that human arrivals in Ireland in the Mesolithic and Neolithic periods would most likely have come by way of the Iberian Peninsula via the Bay of Biscay, and dated the first-known modern human inhabitants of Ireland to the end of the Paleolithic Age, based on the excavated skeleton of the "Kilgreany Man" that was discovered in 1928 (which subsequently proved to belong to a much later period). MacCall rejected as mythic the antiquarian and 'medieval' accounts of Ireland's early inhabitants.[71] Providing a much more complex and protracted diffusionist model of ancient migrations to Ireland than anything found in Irish historical writing thus far, including in works by MacNeill and his cohorts, MacCall instead asserted an identifiable 'Early Celtic' culture in Ireland, traceable back to "the Danubian valley" in eastern Europe and, from there, further east to Iranian (Persian) people and Iranian culture around the Caspian. This Iranian nexus was inclusive of Scythians, "Ossethians," and Persians. He differentiated the ancient Celtic settlers in Ireland from those in Britain in terms of their degree of preservation and observance of ancestral 'Iranian' customs, with the Irish having retained many of those customs well into the time of their settlement in Ireland. As proof of similarities between the ancient Irish Celts and ancient Persians, MacCall offered such examples as the common style of ornamentation and dress, including the braiding of (male) rulers' beards. He broadly defined the ancient Iranian culture surrounding the Caspian as "the proto-Celtic culture," classifying the Celtic language as a sub-branch of the Aryan language that had already reached Ireland "during the second millennium B.C.," even before the initiation of "Celtic civilisation" on the island. MacCall was claiming an Iranian-Aryan 'racial' ancestry for the Celts, while maintaining the Aryan racial-civilizational grandeur of ancient Ireland well before the arrival of later Celtic migrations into mainland Britain; the latter occurring following a much longer Celtic stopover in continental Europe, which had diluted and stripped away their original civilizational characteristics.

As with other range of self-aggrandizing and commemorative historiographies (from religious to ethnic/'racial'), it is now commonly acknowledged that all national histories ultimately entail varieties of founding myths and the pretense of historically stable *core* identity constructs. This was also the case in all accounts of ancient Ireland from

Vallancey's different versions of oriental origins to Eoin MacNeill's European-Celtic and Christian essence of Irish identity, with some of these models being more (although not entirely) inclusive of Ireland's current population groups. Whether or not at some level the likes of Vallancey, Henry O'Brien, and other antiquarians, or latter-day proponents of oriental roots of ancient Ireland, such as Seumas MacManus and MacCall, were conscious of the mythic propensities of their historical accounts, mythology has been a key component of all nationalist historiographies. Prior to the 1916 Easter Rising, William Butler Yeats had been a strong proponent of blatant nationalist mythology. The younger Yeats, himself a propagator of nationalist legends in various settings, readily and unapologetically acknowledged his preference for nationally empowering myths over prosaic history (not unlike Lady Wilde's previously quoted poem in this regard). For Yeats, these myths were an essential source of nationalist inspiration. As noted earlier, sometime around 1887 he had written in the weekly Dublin paper *The Gael*:

> Under all the old legends there is, without doubt, much fact, though, I confess, I care but little whether there be or not. A nation's history is not in what it does, this invader or that other; the elements or destiny decides all that; but what a nation imagines that is its history, there is its heart; than its legends, a nation owns nothing more precious. Without her possible mythical siege of Troy, perhaps, Greece would never have had her real Thermopylae. Learn those of your own country, let the young love them.[72]

Following the 1916 Easter rising, Yeats credited his own theatrical creations and renditions of Irish mythology as a major force in compelling the 1916 rebels to commit the ultimate nationalist act of self-sacrifice; which he then went on to lament publicly and with typical conceit. In a poem titled "Easter 1916," he now in turn mythologized the Easter Rising itself as the selfless heroic transcendence of otherwise seemingly ordinary people one daily encountered in Dublin. With the chilling refrain of "A terrible beauty is born," the poem lionized the leaders of the insurgency, while simultaneously bemoaning the sanctity of nationalist violence. (The poem was also yet another opportunity for Yeats to further elevate himself as a key nationalist figure by underscoring his acquaintance with many of the executed and sentenced leaders of the rising, including his despised nemesis in romance, John MacBride.[73])

Again, it is crucial to keep in mind that the present book is an interrogation of Irish nationalism only at the level of available written sources, which happen to primarily reflect the more textually articulate, albeit not necessarily always elite, segments of the nationalist community, as well as those other members of the nationalist community whose views were indirectly represented in some of the available sources (assuming these views were accurately reproduced). Moreover, within this small cross-section of Irish nationalist community over a period of roughly a century-and-a-half, this book has only covered a select range of Irish nationalist self-imaginings and representations of Ireland through the narrow lens of Irish nationalist commentaries on, imaginative engagements with, and allegoric deployments of, 'Iran.' Given the available sources, it is impossible to gauge how the Irish 'nation' as a whole came to terms with contending versions of ancient Ireland and the major historiographic 'paradigm shift' resulting from the proliferation, and subsequent institutionalization, of the European-Celtic model of ancient Ireland, let alone to prognosticate on such topics as *collective* "forgetting" of antiquarian accounts of ancient Ireland and any potentially consequent collective "trauma" that the transition between the acceptance of former and the embrace of new accounts of the past may have entailed. It is one thing to note the occurrence of a historical paradigm shift among historians and/or literary or political figures, whether gradual or rapid, and quite another matter to determine the precise patterns of its reception and absorption by the society at large. This quandary is related to the indeterminate intersection of *history* (in the sense of so-called reconstructing and "knowing" the past) and what can be termed *'collective memory.'* Historians never stand entirely outside the broader cultural collective, even when working against the cultural grain, and new accounts of the 'national' past are always processed, filtered through, and situated within the existing parameters of cultural coordinates and collective memory. But, in the absence of any available general survey during the period covered in this study of contemporary Irish adherence to various theories of Irish origins and the reactions of *the population at large* to the changing consensus over time among antiquarians and later historians—besides the information I have gleaned from newspapers and periodicals, including letters-to-the-editor—renders imprecise the manner in which history and collective memories intersected in this case. Yet, *it is possible to speak of some general patterns*. It is much less complicated to presuppose a post-1922 generational exposure to, and overall embrace, of the European-Celtic model of Irish origins among school children, given the state-sponsored history curriculum at primary schools, notwithstanding alternative views of the past to which some students may have been exposed at home or in other venues, or other range of what Roy Foster has called "simplified notions [of the past . . .] buried deep in the core of popular consciousness," or 'myth.'[74] The increasingly normative Europeanizing historiographic model incontrovertibly assumed a collective quality following the standardization of Irish history curricula in the primary schools of the Free State. The institutionalization of this particular version of ancient Ireland, despite ongoing methodological and narrative debates within this normative historiographic paradigm, was the paramount source of the vanishing generational recollection of alternative models of ancient Ireland in the new nation-state during subsequent decades. The extent and generational pace of the absorption of European-Celtic model of ancient Ireland outside the Free State, namely in the Irish diaspora and in Northern Ireland after 1922, are not as easy to discern.[75] Incidentally, it was also in 1922 that *A Short History of the Irish People from the Earliest Times to 1920* by Mary Hayden and George Aloysius Moonan was published. In short, that year marked a decisive juncture in the 'national' dissemination of the already ascendant Europe-centered historiographic model of ancient Ireland. As John O'Callaghan has noted, not only was Ireland-centered history made a compulsory school subject, but for decades after the founding of the Free State "many teachers had no historical knowledge beyond what they found in elementary textbooks." Moreover, "The textbooks of Alice Stopford Green (1847-1929) and P.W. Joyce (1827-1914) were widely used in schools."[76] Even though Joyce had suggested a distant Eastern Aryan ancestry for the Celts, he too had situated the gestation of the specifically 'Celtic' cultural identity squarely within Europe and maintained a pan-Celtic identity of all notable population settlements throughout the British Isles.

Ultimately, the different Europeanizing initiatives of Irish nationalists were at various levels marked by contemporary grounding of the Irish nation in the '*modern*' world of the West, even as an extant colonized territory from the republican standpoint in the case of the Free State. Terry Eagleton, evidently using a much later definition of "historicism" than what was current in the late nineteenth and early twentieth century, makes an observation in another setting that is equally applicable to the Europeanizing currents of Irish nationalism discussed here (including the historicist alignments of ancient Ireland with Europe): "Anti-historicist consciousness blends the archaic with the absolutely contemporary, squeezing out the dreary continuum between them; and this, as we shall see, is as true of Ireland's modernism as it is of its nationalism. It is a time-warping."[77] The gradually evolving Europeanizing historiographic paradigm of Irish nationalism required continuous readjustments and reorientations in the dominant 'collective' or 'cultural' historical memory of those Irish who were familiar with alternative models of Ireland's ancient history (to borrow the categories of memory coined by Maurice Halbwachs and Jan Assmann respectively), or, of the more loosely termed "social memory" of the Irish (to borrow a term coined by James Fentress and Chris Wickham)[78]—so far as one can speak of collective, cultural, or social memory of the *Irish nation-in-the-making*, at least as indicated by the range of publications on ancient Irish history in the couple of decades leading up to the creation of the Irish Free State and subsequently.[79] However, it must be observed the categories of collective, cultural, or social memory, in so far as shared views of the past are concerned, range from mutual or overlapping memories among segments of the population regarding particular sets of events personally experienced—even if these memories are subsequently molded by other sources of information and opinions and are never entirely identical, exact, and "accurate"—all the way to collective knowledge of events (contemporary or past) that are acquired through various channels without direct personal experience or observation of those events. These categories of *knowledge-memory* continually intersect and influence one another at both individual and collective levels, with a whole array of other personal or inner-group intersectional, polythetic, and other factors also determining the contours and applications of the always fluid memories—including current motives and/or interface with other internal or external matrices of knowledge, and so on.

The point here is not that of the actual accuracy of memory, since all memories, particularly with the passage of time and the circumstances of their transmission, acquisition, preservation, retrieval, and application are tinged with layers of forgetting, changing perspectives, conscious reinterpretation or re-framing, and so on; without overlooking prior personal or collective predispositions that can cloud initial personal and collective experiences and observations and that also impact the direct and indirect reception of information about events in the first place. Historical knowledge of the distant past, transcending the realm of direct observations, can be variously conceptualized as personal or collective/cultural/social modes of *transmitted* and *acquired* information (in effect, the act of remembering as members of particular "mnemonic communities," to borrow Eviatar Zerubavel's terminology), that are constructed and circulated through different channels. These modes of knowledge, too, are influenced by multiple personal or collective factors and cross-influences. Yet, whereas nowadays in the social sciences and the humanities there is routine acknowledgment of both the attribute of "false memory" in the act of remembering (with the concept here borrowed from the field of neuroscience)[80] and of the underlying "subjectivity" and imaginative component of historical knowledge and narration (particularly following the publication of Hayden White's 1973 *Metahistory: The Historical Imagination in Nineteenth-century Europe*), it is important to note not all memories are false in the sense of being somehow entirely inaccurate, nor can the entirety of all historical knowledge be reduced to fiction in the narrowest (and generally misconstrued) sense of their being totally imaginary. It would be more accurate in this case to describe memories as "imprecise," or as partially "faulty" and subjective modes of recollections, since without some element of, and criteria for, their "truth" value, and correspondence to "reality," there would be no validation for presupposing their "falsity." The challenge is to sort out and untangle the plausibly "true" and the "false" in what is recalled, which is a complex but not entirely impossible task in all circumstances. The same proposition applies to historical narrations. Without engaging in a detailed thematic diversion here, it is important to also distinguish between false memory and outright lies. Similarly, we need to differentiate between the enterprise of historical research and narration in keeping with conventional scholarly parameters (albeit subject to change and always susceptible to interpretive and methodological disputes), on the one hand, and deliberate fabrications of the past, on the other hand—not counting situations where historical standards themselves are predetermined by other institutionally enforced criteria with a prescribed desired effect (propaganda or otherwise), as in the case of accounts of the past mandated by a state, religious establishment, cult, political party, and so forth.

However, more germane to my discussion of the normative Irish nationalist historiography by 1922 is the recognition of the diminishing, but nonetheless persistent, dissenting imaginations of ancient Ireland among the Irish, regardless of their truth or falsity—at least briefly militating against what Robert Proctor and Iain Boal have termed cultural "agnotology" (in this setting as culturally generated modes devaluing and erasing particular forms of knowledge). In this respect, to borrow Michel Foucault's concepts (but without entirely embracing his problematic approach to history), one can speak of lingering and/or resurgent historical beliefs constituting "counter-history" and "counter-memory" of Ireland's ancient past vis-à-vis the post-1922 official historical canon geared toward forging a collective acquired memory of the very remote past of the 'nation.' Some of these counter-canonical historical models, as in the case of competing theories of Eastern origins of the Irish, had once enjoyed degrees of historiographic consensus in Irish nationalist circles, in so far as one can gauge from surviving written sources. In addition to enduring memories of earlier accounts of ancient Ireland among some groups in the population of the Free State after 1922, such alternative versions of ancient Ireland were also accessible to some among the younger generations in the Free State, either orally transmitted by the older generations or in the form of the availability of former antiquarian texts (whether as reprints at bookstores, second-hand books, or in family, municipal, and institutional libraries, for instance), as well as by way of quotations from those texts appearing in contemporary publications, even if intended to demolish the credibility of those accounts. There were also the rare new publications, as already mentioned, that either reproduced in toto former antiquarian visions of ancient Ireland, including various oriental theories of Irish origins, or echoed the former antiquarian accounts by way of new methodological, documentary, and descriptive formulations. In other words, not all Irish individuals (in the Free State, Northern Ireland, and the Irish diaspora) restricted their acquisition of historical knowledge throughout their lives to school textbooks and examinations only. To what degree some among the younger generations imbibed the older versions of ancient Ireland is impossible to conjecture. There is at least textual evidence that some among the older generations in Ireland and in the Irish diaspora, just before 1922 and after the formation of the Free State, rejected the European-Celtic model of ancient Ireland, adhering instead to varying models of oriental origins of the Irish. These sources ranged from articles in various publications to the already mentioned 1921 *The Story of the Irish Race* by Seumas MacManus or James Joyce's fictional take on Irish history in *Finnegans Wake* (1939), with earlier hints of the oriental origins of the Irish appearing also in Joyce's *Ulysses* (1922). These texts represent some of the disparate assortment and modes of recalcitrant resistance to the newly normative historiography of ancient Ireland. By subscribing to diverse range of alternative views of the distant Irish past, these works also belatedly defied the homogenization of that past.

Evident in these alternative representations of the Irish past is the overlooked quality of their distinctively broader cosmopolitan imaginations of Ireland in comparison with the European-Celtic model, in so far as simultaneously locating Ireland *in* and *between* alternative modalities of the East and the West (as these presumed cultural-geographical categories were articulated at the time) and, in essence, also in a broader world-historical scheme of ancient civilizations. The contrasting cosmopolitan historical proclivities, no matter how constricted or expansive, were even present to a lesser degree in the more narrowly defined Celtic-Catholic Europeanizing articulation of Irish identity prior to and after 1922—not taking into account here the varying degrees of cosmopolitan visions present in manifold Irish nationalist expressions of political solidarity with anti-imperialist and other range of struggles elsewhere in the world. There were also cosmopolitan imaginations of contemporary Irish identity that were not necessarily anchored in any historically grounded formulations of Irishness. For instance, before the First World War Fred Ryan had assailed xenophobic and exclusionary constructs of Irish national identity, as in the case of widespread discrimination against the Jewish population of Ireland. This critique was based on ethical humanist principles and the necessity of 'national' inclusivity alongside a more expansive vision of humanity in general, without recourse to historical and/or ethnic/'racial' foundational theories of Irish identity. On the other hand, James Joyce, who later in life also condemned anti-Jewish sentiments in Ireland, believed in Ireland's own ancient "Semitic" roots in the form of Phoenician colonization (and of Phoenician and Iranian civilizational presence in ancient Ireland).[81] Ryan's vision of Irishness entirely transcended the East-West civilizational configurations of Irish identity, whereas Joyce's approach to Irish identities was grounded in both presumed Irish history as well as philosophical and ethical humanism. On the other hand, Ryan's political cosmopolitanism and expressed solidarity with Egyptian, Iranian, or Indian anti-imperialists operated at both levels of contemporary ethical humanist considerations and historical *experiential* affinities. In Ryan's already quoted 1912 reference to 'Erin and Iran' in the *Irish Independent* (Dublin), the 'likeness between Ireland and Persia, Erin and Iran,' was one of historical proximity in the experience of both territories that had been constantly overrun by foreign occupiers, 'yet [...] always clinging to an ideal of nationality and striving after that ideal.' As Romantic and ahistorical as Ryan's comparative synopsis of Irish and Iranian histories happened to be, it was nonetheless Ireland's and Iran's *present* resistance to imperialism that correlated the two territories and their people's. Ryan's Iran/Erin analogy, rather than being grounded in antiquarian theories of Irish origins, consciously hearkened back to Thomas Moore's allegoric literary deployment of Iran/Erin, leaving aside here Moore's own simultaneous antiquarian belief in ancient contacts between Iran and Ireland. For Ryan the principal worlding context for Ireland was that of positioning contemporary Ireland in the global orbit of colonized and semi-colonized territories struggling for national sovereignty, along with the additional trajectories of worldwide struggles for workers' and women's rights and for human rights in general. Joyce, on the other hand, for the most part remained publicly aloof from 'political' worlding of Ireland, even as he too was concerned with Ireland's place in the contemporary world and was troubled by the general pattern of escalating Irish nationalist suspicion of cosmopolitanism—notwithstanding the extensive cosmopolitan foundations of different strands of Irish nationalism.[82]

Similar to Ryan, Joyce was alarmed by the festering 'national' prejudices of most Irish, including the prevalent anti-Jewish sentiments directed at both Irish Jews and Judaism in general, at times with an approving nod from higher ranks of the Catholic establishment. In fact, what has not been addressed previously is whether Joyce's highlighting of the Jewish Question in Ireland in his *Ulysses* was at some deeper level also an act of personal atonement related to Joyce's erstwhile admiration for Arthur Griffith's Sinn Féin, at a time when Griffith was a public apologist for anti-Jewish sentiments in Ireland. Before the First World War, Joyce was attracted to Griffith's non-violent Sinn Féin campaign for Irish self-reliance, without publicly commenting on Griffith's legitimization of the Limerick pogrom of 1904. But, by the time Joyce began work on *Ulysses*, he had grown to abhor the broader implications of the concept and practice of Sinn Féin ("ourselves") as a kind of exclusionary nationalist filter through which some groups could not pass. While there is a circuitous discussion of Griffith's narrow horizon of Irishness in *Ulysses*,[83] it was in *Finnegans Wake* that Joyce parodied various exclusionary renditions of 'ourselves' (Sinn Féin; also often erroneously translated as "ourselves alone" or "we alone"). For example, "the pancosmic urge the allimmanence of the which Itself is Itself Alone (hear, O hear, Caller Errin!) exteriorises on this ourherenow plane in disunited solod [...]."[84] As Joyce put it in another section of *Finnegans Wake* (with a clear slur at xenophobic nationalism as well as the form of Catholic chauvinism evocative of the Limerick pogrom instigated by a priest, even though the Catholic hierarchy later condemned the event): "The racist to the racy, rosy. The soil is for the self alone. Be ownkind, be kithkinish, be bloodysibby. Be irish. Be inish. Be offalia. Be hamlet. Be the property plot. [...] Be cool. Be mackinamucks of yourselves. Be finnish. No martyr where the preature is there's no plagues like rome. [...]"[85] In connection with the diverse ethnic makeup of Irish identities, Joyce, unlike Ryan, was also deeply preoccupied with Ireland's history stretching back to ancient times. *Ulysses*, among its other distillations of Irish society and history, condensed manifold contrasting imaginings of Ireland and of the Irish nation into the events of a single day in Dublin (June 16, 1904), with the lives of the Jewish Leopold Bloom and Joyce's alter ego Stephen Dedalus intersecting. Most notable among the range of other characters outside Bloom's and Dedalus' immediate circles in the story is "the citizen," the embodiment of the average (male) Irish Catholic radical nationalist, who taunts Bloom at Barney Kiernan's pub as to whether a Jew can belong to the Irish 'nation.' This exchange occurs in an episode of the book vividly titled "Cyclops." As Declan Kiberd has noted, "The men in the pub in 'Cyclops' [...] are not anti-foreign, evincing a real sympathy for people of colour living under the lash in other corners of the empire. [...] their range of reference is not Eurocentric." Nonetheless, Kiberd adds:

> The patriotic Citizen [...] possesses a one-track mind, which leaves him intolerant of all foreigners [i.e., in the midst of the Irish,] among whom, of course, he includes the Jews. Bloom, as an internationalist, profoundly tests the Citizen's tolerance, enabling Joyce to do two things [...] to distinguish Bloom's liberationism from the Citizen's nationalism, and show how closely the latter's ideas were based on English models which he claimed to contest. Against that backdrop, Bloom emerges as much 'more Irish' than the Citizen.[86]

The citizen's selectively insular and bifurcating nationalist gaze was exemplary of Arthur Griffith's anti-Jewish proclivity, but so was the citizen's politically instrumentalist extra-Irish cosmopolitan gaze. For instance, in 1912 the same anti-Jewish Griffith could praise the Zionist endeavor to establish a Jewish homeland, which in Griffith's view was indicative of advanced 'nationalism' and "the triumph of Sinn Fein" among the Jews.[87] Just like the citizen, Griffith, who by the way did not regard the Anglo-Irish or Scots-Irish or Welsh-Irish as foreign elements in Ireland, deemed Irish Jews as "foreigners," and yet had no problem defending the rights 'foreigners' in other lands (even if not necessarily *their own land*). Doubtless, citizen would also have had no 'sympathy for people of colour living' among the Irish.

Joyce in his works of fiction, particularly in *Ulysses* and *Finnegans Wake*, accentuated the polymorphous construct of Irish identities and disputed any historically stable and fundamentally European and Christian formation of Irishness across time.[88] Although *Ulysses* and, far more so, *Finnegans Wake* were greatly circumscribed in their popular reach by their arduous Joycean language—and without my wishing to reduce these works solely to their exploration of Irishness—they nonetheless constituted as of yet unprecedented literary foregrounding of the historically cosmopolitan underpinnings of Irish identities past and present (as highly imaginative as such a foregrounding was). *Finnegans Wake* is of particular relevance here also in connection with its Iranian motifs. While it was published a decade-and-a-half after the founding of the Irish Free State, and hence after the cut-off date for my main project, its coverage spanned the known record of Irish historiography apropos of the formation of Irish identities and of alternative accounts of ancient Ireland produced from the so-called Middle Ages to the 1920s. *Finnegans Wake* offers a grand tour of the perceived historical heterogeneity of Irish identities at different stages prior to the ascendance of the Europe-centered historical model (the latter itself also being receptive to various range of heterogeneities) and of the continual *worlding* of Ireland throughout its history (ethnically, culturally, linguistically, religiously, and so on). Moreover, *Finnegans Wake*, which is written as interconnected sequences of dreams, contemplated Ireland's historically shifting placement in distinct *geographic* orbits of cultures and people's originally hailing from other parts of the world, extending from Phoenicians (as a Semitic people related to Jews and Arabs, and primarily based in Carthage in this case—i.e., Carthaginians) to influences of ancient 'Iranian' and other non-Phoenician cultures (as well as contemporary Iranian and other 'oriental' consumer goods and motifs), to Norse, Anglo-Norman, and other cultural influences and ethnic intermixtures, among a much wider assortment of such synchronic and diachronic cosmopolitan effects. Foregrounded against a whirling historical backdrop of disparate population arrivals and cultural transmission and fusion since ancient times, Joyce's Ireland had been an evolving cross-ethnic, cross-cultural, and and cross-*geographic* arena that now, in so far as the majority of the Irish were concerned, stubbornly refused to see itself as a *substantially worlded* place and peoples. This latter insular impulse, and ultimately also self-provincializing proclivity, was seen as having been reinforced under the tutelage of the dominant Europeanizing Celtic-Catholic nationalist delineations of Irish authenticity in the Free State (Éire after 1937). In *Finnegans Wake*, the consciously repressed traces of alternative Irish pasts and presents are reanimated and rendered accessible to the Irish subconscious in dream-time and through the polyglot babel of dream-speak—historically re-connecting Ireland with other parts of the world, including Iran, and of Irish language with Persian, among tens of other languages. The *conscious* history of the nation engages in self-parochializing, while its *subconscious* history reveals the extent of its cosmopolitan formation and current character. The story occurs in the realm of dreams in which the characters mutate and fragment into other characters and are transported back and forth between cycles of the past, the present, and the imagined future, with desires and anxieties emanating from the deep recesses of imagination and memory.[89]

Without my intending to in any way validate the entire range of Joyce's interpretation of the Irish past, most notably his oriental construct of ancient Ireland, it should be observed there was another relevant element to his cosmopolitan rendering of Ireland and Irishness. Joyce also turned to Irish antiquarianism, and more particularly the tradition of antiquarianism that connected ancient Ireland to the Orient, as a means of refuting Ireland's provincialism in a different sense; underscoring Ireland's always, and continually incremental, cosmopolitan identity, even if the average contemporary Irish may have grown to complacently regard Ireland as the boondocks of Europe. In *Finnegans Wake*, Joyce made it abundantly clear that the writing of Irish history since the so-called Middle Ages had always continually cross-referenced Irish history with developments in other parts of the world as a comparative and temporal framework, situating Ireland in the *world*. Moreover, as *Finnegans Wake*, *Ulysses*, and *Dubliners* jointly denoted, Ireland prior to the Anglo-Norman conquests and subsequently had been and remained a site of continuous migrations and emigrations, substantiating the always elastic and heterogeneous matrices of identity formations in Ireland. This was Joyce's template for the subtext of the-world-in-Ireland in *Finnegans Wake*. In effect, the source of Joyce's disaffection with Ireland's stultifying cultural milieu that drove him to what he regarded as the more cosmopolitan continental Europe, was not Ireland and the Irish per se, but what he considered as the provincialist and conservative mindset of Ireland's self-proclaimed cultural custodians, who among other things had also shunned Joyce's early writings.

Joyce's writing intrepidly and recalcitrantly crashed against Europeanizing and other insular currents of Irish nationalism. This inclination was present in some of Joyce's short stories in *Dubliners*, published before the First World War, and appeared much more extensively in *Ulysses* and *Finnegans Wake*, both published after the war. Joyce wished to shake Dublin out of what he perceived of as its overwhelmingly provincial state of mind, despite its actual cosmopolitan formation and continued existence. But, unlike Yeats and his associates in the Abbey Theatre, Joyce's goal was not to merely claim Dublin's prominent standing on the map of European capital cities, but rather on the map of the entire world, while also reminding Dubliners that they themselves for the most part were denying their own city's cosmopolitan identity. After all, Joyce was fixated with Dublin. *Dubliners* and his other works were all situated in Dublin, even as his major works *Ulysses* and *Finnegans Wake* were composed while living as a self-exile away from Dublin. Richard Ellmann noted long ago with great exaggeration that Joyce swapped being "an Irishman" for being "A European."[90] Joyce, having earlier in his writing and translation career unsuccessfully nurtured the ambition of participating in the program of the Irish Literary Theatre (later Abbey Theatre) and failing to publish his short stories in journals such as *Dana*, edited by William Kirkpatrick Magee ("John Eglinton") and Fred Ryan, eventually opted to live and write outside Ireland (in continental Europe) for the remainder of his life.[91] Joyce gradually developed a new literary style that far outstripped the existing parameters of literary modernism, including Dada and Surrealist poetry and prose, which may in fact have influenced Joyce's style in *Finnegans Wake*, but were structurally dissimilar in their linguistic, cultural, and historical evocations than what appeared in Joyce's later work. Joyce also avoided the rampant contemporary anxiety and insecurity about Irish literary-culture, and ultimately about Irishness, which otherwise permeated the prevailing Irish modernist horizons of Ireland←→Europe (even in the case of Yeats' poetry that drew on both non-European as well as European traditions). Joyce, an author fixated with Dublin—the city serving as the setting for all his works of fiction—wrote of Dublin and its people, and by implication of Ireland and the Irish, without joining the drive to attain recognition for Dublin *only in the literary-cultural pantheon of the West*. The diasporic Joyce simultaneously gave Ireland and the world in general (i.e., far beyond the West's/Europe's literary frontiers) a new portal into literature and literary imagination, with its own neoteric literary ethos.

By the time he wrote *Finnegans Wake*, Joyce had invented an entirely new style and literary format, also incorporating some of the polyglot and multivocal literary techniques of his nineteenth-century predecessor, the poet James Clarence Mangan (whose works had not reached a broad extra-Irish audience), as well as utilizing Mangan's temporal and spatial literary interface between here/there and now/then, and the collaging of 'oriental' and other literatures and histories, among some other similarities between their works. Joyce's literary interest in Mangan dated back to Joyce's student days at the University College Dublin, where in 1902 he presented a paper on Mangan at the Literary and Historical Society. He later revised the paper for a 1907 lecture while living in Trieste, Italy (the planned lecture did not materialize).[92] It needs to be pointed out, however, that while *Ulysses* and, even more so, *Finnegans Wake* were written in a polyglot style, *English* still functioned as the primary medium of this Joycean language.

James Joyce, Ireland, the World, and "persianly literatured" Irish History[93]

In *Ulysses*, among other subjects Joyce reflected on the increasingly contracting Irish nationalist configurations of the Irish nation.[94] Joyce had left Ireland in late 1904 for continental Europe as his adopted homeland. His last visit to Ireland was in 1912. As is well known now, *Ulysses* is set in Dublin in a single day (June 16, 1904), the day on which Joyce went on his first date with Nora Barnacle, who became Joyce's life-long partner. By the time Joyce began working on *Ulysses* in 1914, based on his earlier thoughts for a novel, he had grown to abhor the increasingly exclusionary mainstream nationalist mood in Ireland, albeit never abandoning the principle of nonviolent and inclusive Irish nationalism.[95] *Ulysses* was published in February 1922, less than a month before the passage of the Irish Free State Act. By then, Joyce would also have amply taken stock of alternative expressions of rabidly exclusionary nationalism and xenophobia in the otherwise more outwardly 'cosmopolitan' societies of continental Europe, given the bloodbath of the First World War. As in Ireland itself, different modes of cosmopolitanism and chauvinism existed side by side in continental Europe as well, not necessarily always in a dialectical manner. Of course, the same can be said of most forms of anti-imperialist nationalisms too. Nor did the bigoted Irish nationalist characters in *Ulysses*, who badgered Leopold Bloom to confess his national otherness, live in some sort of an Irish bubble, cut off from the rest of the world. These nationalists happened to be well-informed about world events, be it a report appearing in Arthur Griffith's *United Irishman* of the visit of the Zulu chief to England, or of Sir Roger Casement's exposé of the atrocities committed against the indigenous populations in the Congo Free State of King Leopold of Belgium.[96] The speeches of Dubliners in general in *Ulysses* are filled with references to such things as the Russo-Japanese War, Christian missionary endeavors in China, or the "Shah of Persia," and Dubliners are surrounded by products from various corners of the world mentioned throughout the book. At the same time, it would be a mistake to consider Bloom as representing a *broadly* European and cosmopolitan character (on account of his Hungarian-Jewish father) in contrast to a narrowly and inwardly exclusionary Irish identity. Bloom is both Irish and Jewish, and cosmopolitan in his cultural taste while adamant about his Irishness and living in the same Dublin where most Irish nationalists in Joyce's view were growing increasingly suspicious of cosmopolitanism and intolerant of inner-Irish heterogeneities. As Joyce later remarked on the structure of the book, "It is the epic of two races (Israel-Ireland) and at the same time the cycle of the human body as well as a little story of a day (life)."[97] Key here is the use of the phrase 'Israel-Ireland' instead of "Israel and Ireland." The story is not about Israel, on the one hand, and Ireland, on the other hand, but rather about the existence of 'Israel' *in* Ireland. More precisely, it is about the Orient in Ireland, including the 'Semitic' Phoenicians in ancient times.[98] Similarly, Joyce's 'cycle of the human body' when applied anthropomorphically to the Irish nation (in the form of body-politic) is applicable to Bloom's generic definition of a 'nation,' when he is quizzed by the 'citizen' and the latter's Sinn Féin mates in the pub. Bloom's definition of a nation is "the same people living in the same place." He later clarifies that *his* nation is "Ireland [...]. I was born here, Ireland," subsequently adding: "And, I belong to a race too, [...] that is hated and persecuted. Also now. This very moment. This very instant."[99] Leaving aside what Bloom's political and social commitments may have been, regardless of his Jewish father Bloom is secular in his cosmopolitanism and tastes, not all that unlike Joyce, Fred Ryan, William Kirkpatrick Magee, or James Connolly. On the other hand, in terms of his mixed ancestry (Irish-Catholic and Hungarian-Jewish), Bloom represents the historicity of Irishness, which from Joyce's point of view in some ways had always been *of both* and *in between* the East and the West, with all the oscillating inner tensions of that variegated liminal identity. It is important here to recognize that it was not merely Bloom's father who represented the East in Ireland as a relatively recent 'Eastern' arrival (in this case in so far as Jews in the West/Europe were still regarded as 'oriental,' as well as being from Eastern Europe). Bloom's mother, too, in Joyce's schema of Irish history, may have had some degree of distant oriental ancestry, Phoenician most likely (hence also possibly partly 'Semitic' in terms of her ancestral makeup), just as some of Bloom's nationalist tormentors in the pub (the citizen and his mates) could also have had very distant purportedly Eastern ancestry. In fact, Bloom only travels to the Orient in his imagination, never having left Ireland. The Orient, in its manifold representations, fantasies, and materialities repeatedly pervades the narrative of *Ulysses*.[100] Joyce was reacting to both the increasingly European-Celtic as well as Christian (here specifically Catholic) delineations of Irish national identity.

Today hailed as a seminal figure in the development of literary modernism,[101] Joyce was a contemporary of Yeats. Similar to Yeats and many other Irish nationalist authors, poets, and playwrights at the time, Joyce developed his own particular cosmopolitan literary style while fixated on Ireland as his subject matter (more specifically Dublin in Joyce's case). However, Joyce's approach in this regard transcended the mere incorporation of literary motifs, narrative styles, literary or historical references, or specific belief systems and other forms of knowledge production derived from other parts of the world. Joyce, the foremost paragon of Irish cosmopolitan literature since James Clarence Mangan in the 1830s–40s, followed Mangan's example of producing his own uniquely polyglot and multi-culturally referenced Ireland-centered literature (particularly in *Ulysses* and most extensively in *Finnegans Wake*). These techniques also included compound words with parts made up from different languages. This additional cosmopolitan fabric of Joyce's writing, while a reminder of languages in general—which always consist of loan words and other borrowed linguistic effects—more specifically resembled the pidgin or patois melded languages of colonizers and the colonized, as well as of other dislocated peoples besides colonizers, ranging from many people of enslaved ancestry across the world to many so-called migrant communities, among other examples. Certain parallels can be found in the Jamaican Claude McKay's 1929 *Banjo: A Story Without a Plot*. Only, Joyce took this hybrid style of language to a new consciously vertiginous level. In Joyce's works, this linguistic effect echoed the idea of the-world-in-Ireland and of Ireland-in-the-world. At the same time, it was a reminder that English language, and more specifically Irish-English, had historically incorporated vocabulary from numerous other languages—in the case of Irish-English from Joyce's point of view, this also included Irish-Gaelic itself, which he regarded as a language originally derived from the Orient. In this Joycean (and Manganesque) style, the worlded literary product of an Irish author acquired a unique place in world literature (as opposed to Mangan's works that were hardly known to the average Irish, let alone to a global readership; not that Joyce's later works readily appeal to the average reader around the world). Similar to Mangan, Joyce also embraced oriental theories of Irish origins, albeit in an age when oriental models of ancient Ireland were considered a highly eccentric anomaly in historical circles than had been the case in Mangan's time. Joyce indisputably subscribed to a model of Phoenician origins of ancient Ireland, as also evident from the text of one of his Trieste lectures in 1907, based on his critical engagement with Charles Vallancey's *earliest* writings.[102] There are traces of this oriental theory of Irish origins in Joyce's *Ulysses*.[103] *Finnegans Wake*, as I note below, was saturated with such references. Although it has generally been suggested that allusions to the Phoenician theory in Joyce's later works were it the mode of the mythic and parodic, this was far from the case. Joyce did in fact consider certain range of older Irish antiquarian works, such as Vallancey's, as quite absurd in much of their underlining analytical methodology, but not in their overall suppositions. In this setting, Joyce engaged with Vallancey's earlier Phoenician theory, rather than with Vallancey's later Iranian theory of Irish origins. By the time Joyce was working on *Finnegans Wake*, he not only still held on to the Phoenician theory of Irish origins, but had concurrently embraced Vallancey's later Iranian (Persian) theory of Irish origins as well (while again dissenting from Vallancey's overall methodology). There is even a direct allusion in *Finnegans Wake* to *Collectanea de Rebus Hibernicis* (appearing as "Rebus de Hibernicis" in Joyce's work), which was the publication of the Hibernian Antiquarian Society, edited in six volumes by Vallancey from 1770 to 1804.[104] Joyce now shared a vision of ancient Ireland not dissimilar to Thomas Moore's Iranianized-Phoenician model.

It was in the 1939 *Finnegans Wake* that Joyce, with a good dose of humor, specifically tackled the question of Irish identities since ancient times in the framework of his rejection of the dominant European-Celtic (and Catholic) paradigm in Irish historiography that delineated Irish authenticity at the time. For Joyce, Vallanceyan-style methodology had been farcical. However, in the case of the circumscribed constructs of Irishness by MacNeill, and even by Patrick Weston Joyce, it was their conclusions that were illogical; eliding the significant mixed ancestry of many of the Irish, who in Joyce's view were an amalgam of historically more varied ethnic backgrounds than primarily Celts, Norse, Anglo-Normans and other 'Europeans.' Joyce sarcastically maligned what to him was the parochial Europeanizing myth of Ireland's past and present, which in his view further culturally provincialized the post-'independence' Irish Free State/Éire as a European hinterland, as opposed to its previous status as an English-controlled hinterland in the British Isles. Unquestionably, *Finnegans Wake* is textually cumbersome, eclectically polyglot, and to this day attempts at decoding and interpreting different sections of the text remain highly contentious, let alone deciphering the full meaning of the work. Regardless, at one level it unequivocally serves as a literary counter-narrative to the dominant contemporary Irish historiographic paradigms that stripped ancient Ireland, and hence also Joyce's contemporary Ireland, of its purported oriental heritage. Thomas C. Hofheinz has provided the most comprehensive treatment to date of *Finnegans Wake* in light of the modes of Irish historiography Joyce was contesting,[105] while also providing a detailed discussion of Joyce's fascination with the general theory of history as outlined by the Neapolitan philosopher and historian Giambattista Vico (1668–1744).[106] Hofheinz also deftly notes, albeit without further elucidation, "MacNeill's sort of confidence in the 'secure foundation' of scientific Irish history and [Standish James] O'Grady's sort of mystical belief in the heroic age each receive rough handling in *Finnegans Wake*, where the former's positivism collapses along with the latter's sentimentalism. Joyce explicates the motives and procedures of historical writing by transposing it upon seemingly unrelated material, disclosing as he does so the dissonance, anxiety, and primitive motives inherent in reflexive historical thought."[107] Although Hofheinz addresses Joyce's interest in mythology (see below), he appears to have overlooked Joyce's partiality for Ireland's (otherwise *mythic*) ancient history of Eastern origins, as opposed to both alternatively heroic-mystical renditions as well as the more-recent 'scientific' modes of recreating that past. There are clear hints in *Finnegans Wake* that Joyce had not abandoned his earlier belief in the veracity of Irish antiquarian theories of Eastern origins of the Irish, among the many subsequent ethnic ingredients in the historical formation of Irish identity and culture. In *Finnegans Wake*, the main difference regarding Joyce's vision of oriental civilizational traces in ancient Ireland in contrast to his earlier writing was that, instead of the earlier solidly Phoenician theory, in *Finnegans Wake* he adopted a more general, diffuse theory of oriental presence and influences in ancient Ireland, stretching from Phoenicians to Iranians, Indo-Iranians, Hebrews, Egyptians, and so on. This was a medley of 'oriental' civilizations of the Near East and North Africa that ostensibly had been transmitted to Ireland, and was much later supplemented by Celts, the Norse, Anglo-Normans, and other population groups and cultures all the way to the present.

In short, for Joyce the historical formation of the present Irish 'nation' had been a cosmopolitan mélange from the very start, with that history and the remaining collective memory of that past being swiftly undermined through the rapid elevation of the European-Celtic model—just as Ireland's literary *imagination* had been richly cosmopolitan prior to the onslaught of the cultural-nationalist Irish Revival after the late nineteenth century, even in the case of works by the likes of Yeats. Hofheinz notes: "In *Finnegans Wake* [...] the 'broken lights of Irish myth' shine persistently through the murk, with Joyce's treatments of Irish mythical figures such as the Tuatha Dé Danaan and legendary figures such as Finn MacCool [a.k.a., Fionn mac Cumhaill] beckoning and mocking readers at the same time like chimeras of an irrecoverable past."[108] As a matter of fact, it is the term 'irrecoverable' in Hofheinz's statement that correctly point out Joyce's take on the inevitable loss of Ireland's ancient past in light of the new dominant historiography that had gained ground under the guise of scientific inquiry. Otherwise, Joyce was far from 'mocking' the readers by inserting references to Tuatha de Danann, whom Joyce certainly did not regard as entirely mythic—in this setting, Finn MacCool belongs to a very different category of 'myth' and was universally acknowledged as a legendary figure (as opposed to Milesians, Tuatha de Dananns, or Firbolgs). Missing from Hofheinz's listing of Irish antiquarian and historical sources familiar to Joyce are the works of Vallancey or Thomas Moore's *The History of Ireland*—, even though Hofheinz notes Joyce's references to Moore's literary oeuvre in the case of *Irish Melodies*, but not Moore's *Lalla Rookh*. There are, in fact, a few references to *Lalla Rookh* in *Finnegans Wake*.

One is "plane of Khorason," a clear allusion to Thomas Moore's poem "The Veiled Prophet of Khorassan."[109] Another is "Hill of Hafid," an allusion to the death in battle of Hafed, the Iranian hero of Thomas Moore's "The Fire-Worshippers." Moore had written, "This rock, his monument aloft, / shall speak the tale to many an age."[110] Even one of Joyce's references to Moore's *Irish Melodies* ("*Inglo–Andeen Medoleys from Tommany Moohr*"), played on Mangan's already-mentioned pun regarding Moore's *Lalla Rookh*, in which Mangan orientalized Moore's last name as 'Moorish,' identifying him as 'Tom Moorish.'[111] Moreover, Joyce's theory of a broadly oriental "Phoenician" culture transplanted to ancient Ireland, including Iranianized influences, parallels Moore's model of ancient Ireland in the first volume of *The History of Ireland*. Far more influential than Moore's history in this regard, was the Iranianized-Phoenician account of ancient Ireland advocated by the antiquarian John D'Alton (see below). Hofheinz notes Joyce's familiarity with the *Annals of the Four Masters*, compiled in the seventeenth-century, as well as works by the likes of the eighteenth-century antiquarian Charles O'Conor.[112] But, there is no specific mention by Hofheinz of Eastern theories of Irish origins in these antiquarian sources, which were of paramount importance to Joyce.

To put it superficially, *Finnegans Wake* comprises an interweaving sequence of dreams within dreams in a single night, and of interconnecting histories of Ireland (of Dublin more specifically) set in the broader contexts of world history, with Ireland's present and past variously entangled in that world history—even though Dublin in actuality did not exist before the Norse arrivals. It is the publican Mr. Porter, who initiates, or more aptly is initiated into, the opening and continuing cycles of dreams within dreams plot of the book. Of Scandinavian (Norse) ancestry,[113] Porter's dreams—in which he is transformed, among other characters, into "Harold or Humphrey Chimpden [Earwicker]" ("H.C.E."), as well as "Persse O'Reilly"—also consist of his family, each of whose own dreams interlink with Porter's changing dream sequences and who are also transformed into different characters themselves. These are his wife, better known as "Anna Livia Plurabelle" (ALP), their twin sons, generally appearing as "Shem" and "Shaun," and their daughter Isobel, who frequently appears and is alluded to as two individuals, with her dualism also marking her simultaneous existence as Porter's daughter as well as his secret object of sexual desire. In *Finnegans Wake*, there are myriad episodes of back-and-forth lexical slippage from *English as spoken by the Irish* in various dialects to so-called patois English spoken by natives of India (including an admixture of Persian and other Urdu words) to Arabic, Hebrew, and Persian, among a wide range of world languages, inclusive also of other 'European' languages in addition to Irish and English. There are also recurring historical and literary references to the 'Orient,' often (but most certainly not always) by means of incorporating characters and/or scenes and terminology from *One Thousand and One Nights* (a.k.a., *Arabian Nights*). The cycle of dreams traverses the history of present-day Dublin against a patchwork backdrop of the entire human history, including British imperial history, and underscores Joyce's view of Ireland as having always been interconnected with other parts of the world since the first human arrivals in the island. In this worlded vision of Ireland since ancient times in the dream cycles, Joyce drew on stories of creation and/or human regeneration appearing in different traditions, ranging from the biblical story of the Flood to stories of life-sustaining rivers and seas in other accounts. These stories occur in connection with the

River Liffey that runs through Dublin and where the book begins in mid-cycle and ends in mid-cycle of a continual history and interlocking dream cycles. There are also allusions to the Tower of Babel (itself a metaphor for the languages appearing in Joyce's book), the various waves of new population arrivals in Ireland and so on, all the way to politics, society, religion, and literature in contemporary Ireland in the broader context of various developments around the world. Continually toying with the slippery threshold between the mythical, historical, and literary representations, inventions, and interpretations of the past, Joyce alluded to such Irish historical sources as the *Annals of the Four Masters*, with the Four Masters appearing in different forms throughout the book, including as "Mat and Mar and Lu and Jo" or collectively alluded to as "mamalujo," and as various combinations of "four." Some examples of Irish antiquarian texts appearing in Joyce's novel are works by Keating, Vallancey, John D'Alton, and Thomas Moore—with all of these sources in turn drawing on a vast range of sources and traditions from other parts of the world. There are also allusions to works by a host of historians from other regions of the world, past and present. In addition, there are references to authors, poets, and playwrights from Ireland and other parts of the world, ranging from Homer to Sappho, Dante ("Daunty"), Mangan ("Mengarments"—derived from Mangan + Mangan's alias "The Man in the Cloak"), Lady Jane Francesca Agnes Wilde ("Doña Speranza of the Nacion"), and a range of Joyce's contemporaries from Ibsen to Yeats. One of the references to Yeats is a jocular gibe at Yeats' famous rendition of a line from the fourteenth-century Persian poet Hafiz (Hafez), here appearing as "I have met with you, bird, too late, or if not, too worm and early."[114] In essence, Joyce was underscoring the always already cosmopolitan undergirding of Irish history, literature, and culture. In its world-historical, polyglot, and dizzying narration of Irish history, *Finnegans Wake* unmistakably straddled the antiquarian style of the likes of Charles Vallancey and Henry O'Brien as well as Mangan's unique literary style.

Throughout *Finnegans Wake*, there are numerous references to 'Iran' of differing historical settings (in its broadest and narrowest historical, geographic, and cultural configurations), as well as references to certain Iranian myths, along with sporadic use of Persian words. Some of these also occur in the form of Joyce's engagement with works of other authors, such as Mangan's poetry. Without my wishing to in any way imply these references constitute a central motif of the book, or my privileging 'Iran' as the key extra-Irish cultural and territorial trope in *Finnegans Wake*, these references and my highly selective sampling of passages from Joyce's book nevertheless provide valuable clues to Joyce's particular perspective on ancient Ireland in contrast to the mainstream contemporary current of European-Celtic model. Early on in *Finnegans Wake*, Joyce introduces some of the many disparate ethnic infusions into Ireland in times past. Moving from biblical mythology to (mythic) accounts of ancient Ireland, he also transitions from the Hebrew Book of Ecclesiastes—"all that farfatch'd and peragrine or dingnant or clere lift we our ears, eyes of the darkness, from the tome of *Liber Lividus*"[115]—to the account of "[…] the Formoreans [i.e., Fomorians] have brittled the tooath of the Danes [meaning the Tuatha de Danann here, rather than the Danes/Norse] and the Oxman has been pestered by the Firebugs [i.e., Firbolgs] […]"[116] This passage concerning Ireland's (otherwise mythic) ancient past then segues to the early (historical) Saxon raids into Ireland in the seventh century CE, during a scene in the book in which two contemporary characters, the unambiguously named "Jute" (in allusion to those of Anglo-Saxon descent) and "Mutt" (in reference to the Gaels), first meet in a pub after figuring out in which of the many languages historically introduced to Ireland they can converse together:

> In the name of Anem this carl on the kopje in pelted thongs a parth a lone [i.e., Partholan] who the joebiggar be he? Forshapen his pigmaid hoagshead, shroonk his plodsfoot. He hath locktoes, this short-shins, and, Obeold that's pectoral, his mammamuscles most mousterious. It is slaking nuncheon out of some thing's brain pan. Me seemeth a dragon man. He is almonthst on the kiep fief by here, is Comestipple Sacksoun [i.e., Saxon], be it junipery [i.e., January] or febrew-ery [i.e., February], marracks [i.e., March] or alebrill [i.e., April] or the ramping riots of pouriose and froriose. What a quhare soort of a mahan [i.e., What a queer sort of months?—Joyce uses the Persian plural for "months' here: "*māhān*"]. [...] Scuse us, chorley guy! You toller-day donsk [Do you speak Danish?]? N. You tolkatiff scowegian? [i.e., Do you speak Scandinavian-Norwegian?—in other words, the Dano-Norwegian dialect, which Joyce had learned in order to read Henrik Ibsen's works in the original.[117]] Nn. You spigotty anglease? [i.e., Do you speak English?] Nnn. You phonio saxo? [i.e., Do you speak Saxon German?] Nnnn. Clear all so! 'Tis a Jute. Let us swop hats and excheck a few strong verbs weak oach ea-ther yapyazzard abast the blooty creeks.[118]

Realizing they are of distinct Irish ethnic backgrounds (at least in part), Mutt tells Jute: "Let eerhim ruhmuhrmuhr. Mermerge two races, swete and brack" (Let Ireland remember. We unite two races, sweet and briny; i.e., light and dark/oriental).[119] But the two men eventually establish that Jute is a descendant of (in actuality the now-extinct) early Stone Age hominids, with the Irish consisting of "Miscegenations on miscegenations":

> Mutt.— Ore you astoneaged [i.e., Stone Aged], jute you?
>
> Jute.— Oye am thonthorstrok, thing mud.
>
> (Stoop) if you are abcedminded, to this claybook, what curios of signs (please stoop), in this allaphbed! Can you rede (since We and Thou had it out already) its world? It is the same told of all. Many. Miscegenations on miscegenations. Tieckle. They lived und laughed ant loved end left. Forsin. Thy thingdome is given to the Meades and Porsons [i.e., Medes and Persians]. The meandertale [i.e., Neanderthal], aloss and again, of our old Heidenburgh [i.e., Heidelberg man] in the days when Head-in-Clouds walked the earth. [...] A hatch, a celt, an earshare [Irisher] [...] Face at the eased [i.e., Face to the East]! O I fay! Face at the waist [Face to the West]! [...] mace to mace! [...] Right rank ragnar rocks and with these rox orangotangos rangled rough and rightgorong. [...] Our durlbin [i.e., Dublin] is sworming in sneaks. They came to our island from triangular Toucheaterre [i.e., Britain] beyond the wet prairie rared up in the midst of the cargon of prohibitive pomefructs but along landed Paddy Wippingham [i.e., St. Patrick] and the his garbagecans cotched the creeps of them [...]. Racketeers and bottloggers.[120]

This first section of *Finnegans Wake*, with a somewhat anachronic historical arrangement progresses to the arrival of the Norse in Ireland,[121] before proceeding to the Anglo-Norman conquests. Significant in this segment of the narrative is Joyce's references to the indigenous Irish as "Foenix" (Phoenician), "Eirenesians" (Irish-Asian).[122] These references to the Phoenician, and more broadly 'oriental', origins of Ireland's earlier population settlements, in a manner similar to John D'Alton's and Thomas Moore's Iranianized-Phoenician account of ancient Ireland, persist throughout the book. Among the many examples is the account of the initial Norman conquests in Ireland at the invitation of the ousted king of Leinster, Dermot MacMurrough (Diarmaid [or Diarmait] Mac Murchadha), who, as a reward for Norman assistance against MacMurrough's regional rivals, offered his daughter Aoife in marriage to the Norman warlord Richard de Clare (Strongbow) in 1170 in the town of Waterford. In this passage Joyce also alludes to Mangan's 1846 poem "To the Ingleezee Khafir," in which Mangan's Iranian (Shi'i Muslim) Qizilbash cursed the English Anthony Jenkinson as "Thou dog," which Mangan then in a footnote to the poem deliberately mistranslated as the English equivalent of the Persian "Ei Gaour!" (in actuality meaning "infidel" from the Muslim point of view)—so that the presumed Persian original of the word would sound like a cognate of the Irish word for a hunting dog ("*A Gadar*"), in order to establish the proximity between Persian and Irish and, hence, between Iran and Erin in their defiance of English imperialism. Joyce rendered this as "dog of a dgiaour, ye! Angealousmei!" ('Angealousmei' implying "you, my jealous English"—a contraction of Angeal+gealous+mei = English+jealous+my). Another factor to note in this passage is Joyce's reference to Ireland as "Phenicia or Little Asia," with the acronym for this designation (PLA) mirroring of the ethnicity of a leading character in *Finnegan's Wake*, Mr. Porter's wife Anna Livia Plurabelle (ALP):

> Houri [i.e., the Persianized Arabic term for heavenly nymphs, also appearing in poems by Moore and Mangan, among other examples] of the coast of emerald [i.e., Ireland], arrah of the lacessive poghue, Aslim-all-Muslim [i.e., "peace upon all Muslims" in Arabic], the resigned to her surrender, did not she, come leinster's even, true dotter of a dearmud, (her pitch was Forty Steps and his perch old Cromwell's Quarters) with so valkirry a licence as sent many a poor pucker packing to perdition, again and again, ay, and again sfidare him, tease fido, eh tease fido, eh eh tease fido, toos top-ples topple, stop, dug of a dog of a dgiaour, ye! Angealousmei! And did not he, like Arcoforty, farfar off Bissavolo, missbrand her behaveyous with iridescent huecry of down right mean false sop lap sick dope? Tawfulsdreck! A reine of the shee, a shebeen quean [the queen of Sheba, also appearing in the poetry of Hafiz (Hafez) and referenced by Mangan], a queen of pranks. ... Nor needs none shaft ne stele from Phenicia or Little Asia to obelise on the spout, neither pobalclock neither folksstone, nor sunkenness in Tomar's Wood to bewray how erpressgangs score off the rued.[123]

Among other random examples of allusions to the oriental ethnic ingredient of the Irish in this book are: "But to return to the atlantic and Phenitia Proper" (Ireland); "in the shape of betterwomen with bowstrung hair of Carrothagenuine [i.e., genuine Carthaginian] ruddiness"; "Asia in Ireland"; "Europasianised" (Europe Asianized); "the week of wakes is out and over; as a wick weak woking from ennemberable [i.e., innumerable] Ashias [i.e., Asias] unto fierce force fuming, temtem tamtam, the Phoenican wakes."[124] In addition, there are numerous references to the Carthaginian arrivals in Ireland by way of Spain in the form of the supposed Milesian settlements, such as "Celtiberian"; "But is was all so long ago. Hispano-Cathayan-Euxine, Castillian-Emeratic-Hebridian, Espanol- Cymric-Helleniky?"; or "Hiberio-Miletians."[125]

As already stated, Joyce's acceptance of the oriental roots of ancient Ireland was not tantamount to his acceptance of Vallanceyan-style antiquarian methodologies. Parodying Vallancey's abstruse mode of verification, Joyce wrote: "[...] (A most cursery reading into the Persic–Uraliens hostery shows us how Fonnumagula picked up that propper numen out of a colluction of prifixes though to the permienting cannasure the Coucousien oafsprung of this sun of a kuk is [...])"—i.e., a most cursory reading of the Persian-Uralian history shows how Finn McCool picked up that proper name out of a collection of prefixes [...] the Caucasian offspring of this son of a dick is [...].[126] Malcolm Sen has correctly noted in general that "James Joyce may have parodied such antiquarianism [...], but he returns positively to philological debates elsewhere as if to show that although mistaken on a few counts, the antiquarian discourse was nonetheless useful and pervasive."[127] Joyce, applying the cyclical Viconian model of history to national memory and Irish historiography (hence also the dreams within dreams cycles in the book), surmised that the European-Celtic construct of ancient Ireland, which denied Ireland's oriental heritage, would ultimately fail to fully repress the memories and historical records of that oriental past, which like the subconscious world of dreams in *Finnegans Wake*, and "highly charged with electrons," defied permanent historical amnesia:

> Begin to forget it. It will remember itself from every sides, with all gestures, in each our word. Today's truth, tomorrow's trend.
> Forget, remember!
> Have we cherished expectations? Are we for liberty of perusiveness? Whyafter what forewhere? A plainplanned liffeyism assemblements Eblania's conglomerate horde. By dim delty Deva.
> Forget!
> Our wholemole millwheeling vicociclometer, a tetradomational gazebocroticon (the "Mamma Lujah" known to every schoolboy scandaller, be he Matty, Marky, Lukey or John-a-Donk [i.e., the compilers of the *Annals of the Four Masters*]), autokinatonetically preprovided with a clappercoupling smeltingworks exprogressive process, [...] receives through a portal vein the dialytically separated elements of precedent decomposition for the verypetpurpose of subsequent recombination so that the heroticisms, catastrophes and eccentricities transmitted by the ancient legacy of the past; type by tope, letter from litter, word at ward, with sendence of sundance, since the days of Plooney [i.e., Pliny the Elder, who had characterized Ireland's population as savages] and Columcellas [most likely meaning Pliny's first-century CE contemporary Lucius Junius Moderatus Columella, who wrote about agricultural topics, and not the Irish Christian monk Columba (a.k.a., Colmcille, 521–97 CE)] when Giacinta, Pervenche and Margaret [names of flowers] swayed over the all-too-ghoulish and illyrical and innumantic in our mutter nation, all, anastomosically assimilated and preteridentified paraidiotically, in fact, the sameold gamebold adomic structure of our Finnius the old One [i.e., Fénius Farsaid], as highly charged with electrons as hophazards can effective it, may be there for you, Cockalooralooraloo—menos, when cup, platter and pot come piping hot, as sure as herself pits hen to paper and there's scribings scrawled on eggs.
> Of cause, so! And in effect, as?[128]

Similar to Vico's model of historical repetition, in different dream sequences of *Finnegans Wake*, the history of Ireland is retold, with different temporal emphasis and spatial world-configurations, again and again, inevitably returning once again to first principles. As Joyce put it, "The Vico road goes round and round to meet where terms begin."[129] Joyce mentioned some of the antiquarian authors with whose works he was familiar and who had claimed various Eastern ancestry for the ancient populations of Ireland.[130] These included Sir James Ware, the editor among other works of *The Historie of Ireland* (1633), who believed the early population arrivals in the island included Scythians; John D'Alton's *The History of Ireland* (1845), which propounded a model of the Phoenician populating of Ireland and their introduction of ancient Iranian cultural practices to the island; Sir John Thomas Gilbert (d.1898), author of the three volume *A History of the City of Dublin* (1854–59); Luke Wadding (d.1657) the Franciscan friar and scholar noted for initiating the celebration of "St. Patrick's Day"; as well as most likely the antiquarian Charles Haliday (d.1866)—rather than his brother William Haliday, the author of *Uraicecht na Gaedhilge: A Grammar of the Gaelic Language* (1808, published under the pseudonym "E.O.C."/ "Edmond O'Connell"), which highly endorsed Vallancey's commentaries on the oriental origins of Irish language and drew a number of grammatical and literary parallels between Irish and Persian. Charles Haliday had published pamphlets on the history of Dublin, and his unfinished manuscript on *The Scandinavian Kingdom of Dublin* was posthumously edited and published by John P. Prendergast in 1881.[131] Then again, it is possible Joyce had in mind both Haliday brothers.

Thanks to previous generations of scholars, it is already commonplace today to acknowledge that in writing *Ulysses* Joyce relied on Victor Bérard's theory in *Les Phéniciens et l'Odyssée* (1902–03), which maintained Homer's *The Odyssey* was fundamentally based on Phoenician archetypes and that Homer's hero Ulysses was unmistakably a Phoenician.[132] Bérard's theory suggested to Joyce that *The Odyssey*, and the account of Ulysses in particular, in effect belonged to ancient Ireland's own Phoenician epic heritage, since Ireland in Joyce's view had been a Phoenician satellite. This connection appealed to Joyce, who both believed in Ireland's oriental past and was creating a modern Irish version of *Ulysses*. But, there had been precedents for Bérard's interpretation in the much older corpus of Irish antiquarianism itself, although it is not known if Joyce was either previously familiar with these works or possibly came across them after reading *Les Phéniciens et l'Odyssée*. These Irish sources include works by John D'Alton (1792–1867), who postulated a Phoenician prototype for much of the territorial descriptions appearing in Homer's *The Odyssey*, including what D'Alton claimed to be unmistakable Irish settings in the Homeric references to Phoenician/Carthaginian locales. Even though Joyce mentions D'Alton in *Finnegans Wake*, it is not known whether Joyce had actually read the particular works by D'Alton in which this idea was expressed.[133] However, it is clear that by the time Joyce wrote *Finnegans Wake*, if not sooner, he had moved on to a more diffused theory of Ireland's oriental roots in contrast to his earlier belief in a strictly Phoenician model of ancient Ireland, which he had derived from Vallancey's early writings as indicated in Joyce's 1907 Trieste lecture on "Ireland: Island of Saints and Sages."[134] With some hints of this more heterogeneous oriental vision of ancient Ireland in Joyce's *Ulysses*, by the time he composed *Finnegans Wake* he had embraced a far more eclectic theory of Eastern origins of the Irish, supplementing Iranian and other oriental ingredients (populations and/or cultures) to the Phoenician model. This was a fusion of Vallancey's earlier Phoenician and later Iranian theories of Irish origins, and not unlike the Phoenician theories of the likes of D'Alton and Thomas Moore that cast the Phoenician arrivals in Ireland as already culturally, and even in part ethnically, Iranianized, among a host of other similar models that had been proposed by Irish antiquarians. Joyce's Phoenicians/Carthaginians were an amalgam of Phoenicians and other 'Semitic' groups (e.g., "Arabs," Chaldeans, "Jews"), as well as non-Semitic ancient South-Asians, Iranians, Armenians, and Egyptians. (I am using the term 'Semitic' here in reference to linguistic and *presumably* cultural and, hence, at most 'ethnic' sense, and not in the garbled 'racial' sense commonly used in Joyce's time and even today.) Accordingly, for Joyce the very earliest oriental ancestry of the Irish was already cosmopolitan in its ethnic, historical, and cultural characteristics at the very moment of its arrival in Ireland—to which in later centuries were added other population groups and cultures, notably the Norse and Anglo-Normans. This is indeed what Joyce had meant when responding to the question of what his next book after the completion of *Ulysses* would be: "I think I will write the history of the world."[135] More specifically, it was to be a history of the *world* in Ireland and of *Ireland* in the world. In its splintering and reconnecting temporal and spatial narrative structure, *Finnegans Wake* also interchangeably replicates the structural pattern of various creation stories, as already mentioned, as well as the temporal elasticity and overlapping narrative ambiguities evocative of Irish antiquarian and earlier 'medieval' accounts of Ireland's ancient past, including their chronicling of developments in Irish history via referencing major contemporaneous events in other parts of the world—in the style of the eleventh-century *The Book of Invasions* (*Lebor Gabála Érenn*) or Geoffrey Keating's and later histories.[136] Significantly, moreover, for Joyce this historical admixture of ethnicities in Ireland also collapsed any contemporary easy distinction between Semitic and Indo-European constructs of race in the case of most Irish—note also his constant switching between varying names and pronunciations of Ireland and Phoenicia and "Aryan"/"Aryania," etc.[137]

The heteroglossic and polyglot text of *Finnegans Wake*, described by Emer Nolan as "a post-colonial novel,"[138] was not merely Joyce's tribute to his imagined Ireland's prior cosmopolitan historical and literary sensibilities. The book reveals Joyce's belief in the continued lexical equivalence between Irish language and the languages currently spoken in places or among peoples from where or whom the mixed ancestry of the Irish had derived, albeit in a very unorthodox approach to linguistics, and ironically not entirely unlike the philological acrobatics of Vallancey and other similar Irish antiquarians. For Joyce, these lexical correspondences also included Persian and Irish cognates. Furthermore, he incorporated various existing Irish literary patterns of utilizing the Iran/Erin interchange, ranging from works by Thomas Moore to Mangan, but evidently not Denis Florence MacCarthy, who is mentioned in the book in a different setting. The perplexing language of *Finnegans Wake* is simultaneously English, Irish-English, and significantly not English in any shape or form (even if it also often happens not to be remotely close to Irish).[139] Whereas Oscar Wilde's riposte to English mockery of the Irish had been to master the English language better than the best of the English—not unlike Shakespeare's Caliban in *The Tempest*—, Joyce mastered the English language and then rendered his text doubly illegible for the English reader (whether these readers were ethnically English, Irish, or other), both by introducing Irish (Dubliner) pronunciations of English terms into his text, as well as Irish terminology and a multitude of words and phrases from many other languages.[140] This was akin to English as spoken by the Irish, also known as "Hiberno-English." While Joyce had used Hiberno-English extensively in *Ulysses* and, to a lesser degree, in earlier works as well, in *Finnegans Wake* he further complicated the Irish component of that speech, which throughout Ireland was already suffused with local dialects and accents. In *Finnegans Wake,* Joyce went a step further and additionally obfuscated the text with both Ireland's (real and presumed) past legacy, as well as with the continued legacy of the British Empire and world history in general. It was specifically the Irish component of Hiberno-English language that Joyce in *Finnegens Wake* rendered additionally polyglossic by means of incorporating into it languages spoken by different presumed ancestries of the Irish, including recent immigrants—even though most of the terminology in these other languages used by Joyce were taken from the contemporary forms of those languages, which happened to be significantly different from their 'ancient' or 'medieval' forms. This Irish-English was rendered in Joyce's own inventive composite lexical effects, with creative and constantly changing spellings, and with the text also drawing on literatures, histories, myths, and cosmogonies of those *other-yet-not-altogether-other* cultures. The multitude of passages in which Persian words appear (either in the form of the language spoken in contemporary Persian-speaking territories, or as part of the vocabulary present in Urdu and Hindi in the Indian subcontinent), suggest either Joyce had some very basic (and as of yet undocumented) familiarity with Persian or, most likely, had painstakingly perused through a descriptive Persian dictionary or phrasebook, given the complex ways in which the lexicon in question is used and arranged in the text. Joyce was exceptionally multi-lingual, but is not known to have formally studied any so-called oriental languages. It is also not known if Joyce's friend and volunteer literary assistant in Paris while Joyce was working on *Finnegans Wake*, the Jewish-Russian émigré Paul Léon, who is reputed to have spoken many more languages than Joyce himself, had any knowledge of Persian. The following passage from *Finnegans Wake* is one of the many examples where Persian terms appear in highly complex arrangements of clauses and meaning that would have required more than just glossary familiarity with Persian words from a dictionary. This passage is a description of Mr. Porter, who has initiated the intersecting dream cycles in the book. He is now secretly leafing through an illustrated "(suppressed) book" of sexual content while hiding in the toilet at home. In this scene, Porter fantasizes about anal sex, something Joyce himself famously enjoyed with his wife Nora:

> [...] the wordcraft of this early woodcutter, a master of vignettiennes and our findest grobsmid among all dieir orefices, (and, shukar in chowdar, so splunderdly English!) Mr Aubeyron Birdslay. Chubgoodchob, arsoncheep and wellwillworth a triat! Bismillafoulties. But the hasard you asks is justly ever behind his meddle throw! Those sad pour sad forengistanters, dastychappy dustyrust! Chaichairs. It is that something, awe, aurorbean in that fellow, hamid and damid, (did he have but Hugh de Brassey's beardslie his wear mine of ancient guised) which comequeers this anyway perssian which we, owe, realisinus with purups a dard of pene. There is among others pleasons whom I love and which are favourests to mind, one which I have pushed my finker in for the movement and, but for my

sealring is none to hand I swear, she is highly catatheristic and there is another which I have fombly fongered freequuntly and, when my signet is on sign again I swear, she is deeply sangnificant. *Culpo de Dido*! Ars we say in the classics. *Kunstful* we others said. What ravening shadow! What dovely line! Not the king of this age could richlier eyefeast in oreillental longuardness with alternate night joys of a thousand kinds but one kind. A shahrryar cobbler on me when I am lying![141]

Keeping in mind Joyce's disjointed phrases and sentences, indicating the dream-state stream of consciousness, as well as the choppy dream sequences and his invention of composite words and word compounds, sometimes in different languages, and often with playful combinations of meanings, the above passage can be rendered as following, with the translated Persian words and English-Persian compound phrases marked here in bold font:

> [...] the word-craft of this early woodcutter, a master of vignettes and our finest Grub-smith [i.e., a reference to the infamous eighteenth-to-early-nineteenth century Grub Street in London] among all their offices [with "offices" also evocative of orifices] (and, **sugar in a veil**, so splendidly English!) Mr. Aubrey Beardsley [the famed late nineteenth century English illustrator, who also illustrated Oscar Wilde's *Salome* and whose later works were considered obscene by the mainstream public, with a number of his illustrations depicting veiled or unveiling figures]. **Wood** good **wood** [i.e., a reference to woodblock printing, even though Beardsley's works were actually line block prints], arson [a possible joint allusion to ejaculation and arse?] cheap and well, well worth a trial! In the name of god of all faults [appearing in the transliteration of the Arabic "bismillah"+faults] transgressive. But the risk you are thinking of is just ever behind his middle throw! Those sad, poor, sad **foreigners** [appearing as a Joycean transliteration of the Persian term *farangesstan*, meaning European/Western lands]. **Left hand, right hand**! [i.e., an allusion to masturbation] Tea Chair [also a wordplay on "teacher"?]. There is something, ah, Arabian in that fellow, [akin to] Hamid [the name *possibly* taken from *One Thousand and One Nights*, to whom is attributed a bawdy song in the original story, and with many of Beardsley's erotic illustrations portraying men in drag] and **damid** [the past-tense of the Persian word for "to blow," and rhyming with the Arabic name Hamid meaning "praiseworthy," the latter also a name that is still current among Iranians and some other non-Arab population groups], (if he had Hugh de Bras' beard [a reference to the title character of Samuel Butler's 1663-78 serialized anti-puritanical satirical poem titled *Hudibras*, which also included woodblock illustrations[142]—evidently also drawing a contrast here with the men in drag lacking facial hair appearing in Beardsley's illustrations] his wear mine of ancient guise) which anyhow is odd that the person whom we, all, realize in us with perhaps a **discomfort** of the penis. There is among other turn-ons in which I delight, and which is a prime longing, the body part in which I have pushed in my finger for probing that, but for my seal ring, I swear is unmatched [in the pleasure it gives me], she is highly cathartic [?] and there is another one whom I have awkwardly fingered frequently and, when my signet is on sign again I swear, she is deeply significant [here playing on multiple meanings of the letters "sign"]. *Blame it on Dido* [a reference to the legendary Carthaginian queen in Virgil's *The Aeneid*]! Ars [craft] we say in the classics. *Kunstful* we others said [given the content of the passage and the references to Beardsley's illustrations of risqué nudity, it is very possible Joyce also intended "arse" by using the Latin Ars, which otherwise means "craft," as well as by the German English compound "Kunstful,"

technically implying highly artistic, but with "**kun**," ("kuns" in the plural), also meaning arse in Persian; hence "arse-full"]. What ravening shadow! What beautiful line! The king of this age could not better feast the eyes with oriental languidness of alternative wet dreams of a thousand kinds but one kind [again a reference to *One Thousand and One Nights*, scenes from which Beardsley also illustrated]. May the cobbler of a **king's** [the Persian word "shahryār" here also taken from *One Thousand and One Nights*] punish me if I am lying!

After further references to anal sex,[143] Porter concludes his description of masturbating to Beardsley's illustrations of nudes, and then another dream sequence gets underway, in which Joyce utilizes the Iran/Erin interchange, which is also intended to establish a linguistic and ethnic affinity between the Irish and Iranians (in the broadest sense of 'Iran'): "the harpermaster told all the living conservancy, know Meschiameschianah, how that win a gain was in again. Flying the Perseoroyal. Withal aboarder, padar and madar, hal and sal, the sens of Ere with the duchtars of Iran. Amick amack amock in a mucktub."[144] In this section 'Meschiameschianah' is a reference to the ancient Iranian mythical male-female twins, Mashya and Mashyana, born from the semen of the first being, the androgynous founder of the legendary Pīshdādīān dynasty, named Keyoumars (Gayōmard), according to the Zoroastrian texts *Avesta*, *Zend* [*Avesta*], and *Bundahishn*. Born of the rhubarb plant, fertilized by Keyoumars' sperm, Mashya and Mashyana procreated the first of the world's human-born population, having seven sets of twins, the first of which they devoured.[145] Despite being male and female, Mashya and Mashyana in *Finnegans Wake* are indirect allusions to Mr. Porter's twin sons, Kevin and Jerry (a.k.a., Shem and Shaun), as well as Isobel's splitting persona. In the next sentence of the above-quoted section of the book, Joyce playfully blended Iran and Ireland, using Persian words and utilizing the Iran/Erin interchange. With the Persian terms rendered into English (here appearing in bold font again), the sentence would read: "Withal on board the fantasy are **father** and **mother**, hal and sal, the sons of Ireland with the **daughters** of Iran," keeping in mind here again Isobel's splitting persona in the text. In the following sentence, the two 'loulous' (the singular Persian term 'lulu' meaning a bogey) juxtaposed with griffins (which has distinct symbolism in Iranian and Irish mythology), refers to Mr. Porter's twins. Meanwhile Joyce conflated one of Mr. Porter's many monikers in Porter's dream sequences, that of Persse O'Reilly (also appearing as "Persic–Uralien"—meaning Persian-Uralian [i.e., Ural Mountains, which were once part of the Scythian Empire]), with the term also connoting Persian+royal (hence 'Perseoroyal' that also occurs in the book). 'Perseoroyal' in this scene appears to denote a flying vessel, in other words the lofty and highfalutin fantasy that will convey Mr. Porter and his family to another dream cycle, with their separate, but intersecting, dreams evocative of the narrative structure and fantasy quality of *One Thousand and One Nights*, which is recurrently alluded to in *Finnegans Wake*.

As previously noted, various creation myths occur throughout *Finnegans Wake*. Earlier in the book, there appears yet another ancient Iranian myth of creation—in this case, of much more central relevance to Dublin's identity and to the opening sentence of *Finnegans Wake* that invokes the River Liffey and the recurring Joycean-Viconian cyclical flow of Ireland's worlded history, paralleling the flowing cycles of dreamscapes in the book (i.e., "riverrun, past Eve and Adam's,[146] from swerve of shore to bend of bay, brings us by a commodius vicus of recirculation back to Howth Castle[147] and Environs"). The Iranian myth in this case was that of "Arvanda" (Aredvi), the original source of all rivers, which appears in *Finnegans Wake* alongside references to Dublin's Grand and Royal canals, in obvious reference to the Liffey. This is tellingly followed by the designation of Mr. Porter (who has Scandinavian ancestry) as a "fellow of Iro-European ascendances."[148] The hyphenated Irish-European designation insinuates a distinction and simultaneous connection between 'Irish' and 'European,' evocative of and paralleling the related Indo-(/Iranian-)European population groups in both the Orient and in Europe—in this case with Ireland itself designated as the Orient in Europe, given the hyphenation. Just as Arvanda was the primal river, and River Liffey was the life-source of Dublin (the modern city having been founded by the Norse), the Orient was the primal source of Ireland's ancient civilization, onto which had been forged other civilizations and cultures along the way. Ultimately, Joyce's vision of ancient Ireland was a direct negation of the contemporary, and fast-ascendant, stance of Eoin MacNeill and other leading Irish historians, who, in MacNeill's words, maintained: "The fact is that the whole story of the origin of the Gaels in Scythia or in Armenia, their wanderings by land and sea, their settlement in Spain, and their landing in Ireland, is an artificial product of the schools, and does not represent a primitive tradition. It must have displaced the popular tradition."[149] For Joyce, it was the oriental roots of ancient Ireland that constituted the now rapidly vanishing *popular tradition*, nestled in the deepest recesses of Irish collective memory—currently occluded by the dominant Irish historiographic paradigm, and yet impossible to entirely erase from the subconscious of the nation. Without my assigning any "Truth" value to Joyce's version of history, Ellen Carol Jones' incisive reading of Joyce's *Ulysses* (in light of Walter Benjamin's "the now of recognizability") is even more applicable to *Finnegans Wake*. Jones writes:

> To attend the catastrophe of memory is to experience the present as an awakening in which the dream we call the past is brought into relation to truth [vid. Walter Benjamin's *Arcades Project*]. To awaken is to seize the past in what Benjamin terms the 'now of recognizability': that epiphanic moment when a "historical constellation of past and present, formed as in a dream, becomes legible and demands interpretation" [...] This awakening is a [...] process of recollection that gives access to a different kind of knowledge of the past, to a 'not yet conscious knowledge of what has been', or to the "dream form of the past which has left its traces in the present".[150]

To put it differently, for Joyce Ireland's latent national memory of its ancient past and Ireland's currently dominant national historiographic paradigm would face off again in the future, with memory retrieval certain to prevail over the present epistemic pretensions. Even though MacNeill's strictly European-Celtic construct of Irish national identity did not survive unscathed into the twenty-first century—leaving aside the ongoing debates as to which population groups in ancient Europe can even be categorized as Celts—, Joyce's anticipated collective self-recovery of national memory, which would trigger the recuperation of suppressed history of ancient Ireland, as Joyce regarded it, proved abortive for obvious reasons already discussed in connection with the mythic dimensions of various oriental theories of ancient Ireland. This is not to deny that recent studies point to the arrival in Ireland in ancient times of population groups that had originated in the so-called Near East, but these were population migrations in a far more distant past and across a very long gradual time span than suggested by the oriental theories of Irish origins propounded by the likes of Vallancey, Beaufort, Moore, D'Alton, Lady Wilde, or Joyce. The problem with collective memory, the future resuscitation of which Joyce had anticipated, is that memory (here in the form of acquired knowledge of the past not directly experienced, whether in personal or collective forms) is a constantly changing and imperfect recollection of the past that also relies on other form of knowledge and information for sustainment—in this case also historical knowledge. More importantly, the remembrance of alternative histories of ancient Ireland that Joyce personally valued now lacked any significantly meaningful value and political cachet in the post-'independence' Irish Free State/Éire. In fact, those alternative histories had been incrementally stripped of their political relevance and value since the mid-nineteenth century, even overlooking their fundamental methodological and evidentiary weaknesses as seen through the lens of more recent historical practices. In effect, Joyce was invoking the re-orientation of a memory that had already been deprived of its power of "affirmative historiography" (to borrow Allan Megill's concept[151]). This is not to say the European-Celtic and Christian attributes in the dominant historiographic model of the core ancient Irish identity at the time was the singular correct interpretation of ancient Ireland. Regardless of its historicity, the latter historiographic model, which enjoyed official state and church backing through the educational system of the Free State, was stacked with political and religious affirmation. This was, at the time, a simultaneously "affirmative" and "didactic" historiography.[152] Moreover, through the educational system, this historiography was afforded a repetitive commemorative status as well, enhancing its recollective value and potency.

Notes

1 Seumas MacManus, *The Story of the Irish Race: A Popular History of Ireland*. Revised edition. New York: Devin-Adair, 1977 [1921], pp.8–9, 21, 91, 315. On the Round Towers, the book followed George Petrie's dating of the towers to the Christian era. See ibid., pp.302–303. According to MacManus's "Foreword," there was to be "an article on The Ancient Language, History and Literature of Ireland, which Dr. Douglas Hyde kindly contributed for this volume—but which was unfortunately received too late for inclusion."

2 Patrick Weston Joyce, *A Social History of Ancient Ireland* (1903); Eoin MacNeill, *Phases of Irish History* (1920); Mary Hayden and George Aloysius Moonan, *A Short History of the Irish People from the Earliest Times to 1920*. London: Longman, Green, and Co., 1922, pp.1–10; Alice Stopford Green, *History of the Irish State to 1014* (1925). See also Thomas C. Hofheinz, *Joyce and the Inventions of Irish History: Finnegans Wake in Context*. Cambridge: Cambridge University Press, 1995, pp.116–20.

3 Alice Stopford Green, *History of the Irish State to 1014*. London: Macmillan and Co., 1925, pp.11–12. See also pp.12–16, 20, 177, and passim. Anna Davin has noted, "As Alice Stopford Green pointed out in 1917, consciousness of Ireland as an entity developed very early, even though political power was not centralized.' From the eighth century Ireland had a strong cultural identity[...]" Anna Davin, "Introduction," p.95.

4 On 'medieval' biblical as well "pagan" accounts of Irish origins, see Donnchadh Ó Corráin, "Creating the Past: The Early Irish Genealogical Tradition," *Peritia* 12 (1998), pp.201–208.

5 Alice Stopford Green, *History of the Irish State to 1014*, pp.176–77. See also pp.13, 178. Writing of the Irish John Lynch's Latin translation of Keating's *The History of Ireland* (*Foras Feasa ar Éirinn*) in the 1650s, Bernadette Cunningham notes: "In an attempt to focus attention on Ireland's rightful place in world culture[,] Lynch made special mention of the synchronisms attached to *Foras Feasa*[,] which fitted Irish kings into the wider chronology of Persian and Greek kings and Roman emperors." Bernadette Cunningham, *The World of Geoffrey Keating*, pp.187, 189.
6 Stephen Gwynn, *The History of Ireland*. London: MacMillan & Co., 1923, pp.v, 72; Patrick Weston Joyce, *A Social History of Ancient Ireland*. Volume I. London: Longmans, Green, and Co., 1903, p.521.
7 John Carey, "Lore of Origins in Medieval Ireland" in Séamus Mac Mathúna, Maxim Fomin, and Alvard Jivanyan, eds. *Journal of Indo-European Studies*, p.140.
8 Séamus Mac Mathúna, "Creative Witness in Ireland and Armenia: Parallels in Historiography, the Eremetical Tradition, Myth and Legend" in ibid., pp.5,7. See also Maxim Fomin, "Armenia in Ireland: Indo-European Cognates, Medieval Legends and Pseudo-Historical Accounts" in ibid., pp.103–104.
9 David Shea, *History of the Early Kings of Persia*, pp.47–51.
10 On the methodological *transformation*, rather than a complete rupture, between older antiquarian and newer "historical" research and writing, see also the interview by Guy Beiner with Joep Leerssen, "Why Irish History Starved," pp.71–72.
11 On von Ranke, see also Andreas Dieter Boldt, *The Role of Ireland in the Life of Leopold Von Ranke (1795-1886): The Historian and Historical Truth*. Lewiston, New York: Edwin Mellen, 2007.
12 On this theme, see also Malcolm Sen, "Memory, Modernity, and the Sacred" in Oona Frawley, ed., *Memory Ireland*, vol.1, pp.106–10; Guy Beiner interview with Joep Leerssen, "Why Irish History Starved," p.77.
13 See also Eoin MacNeill, *Phases of Irish History*, pp.3–4.
14 See, for example, Sophie Bryant, *Celtic Ireland*. London: Kegan Paul, Trench & Co., 1889, pp.26–29.
15 Patrick Weston Joyce, *A Social History of Ancient Ireland*, vol.I, Preface, p.vii.
16 Ibid., pp.474–75.
17 Ibid., pp.xi, 149, 169, 366–67.
18 Ibid., p.221. See also pp.95, 267–68, 277–78, 471–72, 558.
19 "Irish History in American Schools," *The Gael/An Gaodhal* (New York), new series, 22(1), January 1903, pp.11–12.
20 Patrick Weston Joyce, *A Concise History of Ireland*. New York: Longmans, Green, and Co., 1903, Chapter 7.
21 Ibid., p.65.
22 Goldwin Smith, *Irish History and the Irish Question*. New York: McClure, Phillips, and Co., 1905, pp.v, 3–4.
23 Eoin MacNeill, *Phases of Irish History*, chapters 1–3.
24 Ibid., p.10.
25 Alice Stopford Green, *History of the Irish State to 1014*, p.20.
26 On MacNeill's historical legacy in general, see also Francis John Byrne, "Ireland before the Norman invasion" in Theodore William Moody, *Irish Historiography, 1936-70*. Dublin: Irish Committee of Historical Sciences, 1971, pp.1–15.
27 Stephen Gwynn, *The History of Ireland*, pp.v–vi, 1, 4, 31.
28 See, for example, Eoin MacNeill, *Phases of Irish History*, pp.48–52, 248, and passim; Alice Stopford Green, *History of the Irish State to 1014*, pp.25–26 and passim. See also Thomas C. Hofheinz, *Joyce and the Inventions of Irish History*, pp.116–20.
29 In Edward Granville Browne, *The Literature of Persia*, pp.38–41.
30 In reference to antiquarian theories of Eastern origins of the Gaelic Irish, Joep Leerssen concludes that "By projecting a tacitly implied idea of contemporary identity into a historical Otherness, it accommodated the alienness of the far past into a recognizable proto-present, a proto-European rather than a non-European tradition." Joseph Theodoor Leerssen, "On the Edge of Europe," p.109.
31 On the conceptual application of "meta-geography" in reference to particular political and other hegemonic mappings of the world, see also Martin W. Lewis and Kären E. Wigen, *The Myth of Continents A Critique of Metageography*. Berkeley: University of Clifornia Press, 1997.

32 Declan Kiberd, *Inventing Ireland*, p.259.
33 Terry Eagleton, *Heathcliff and the Great Hunger*, pp.300–303.
34 John Patrick Delury, "Ex Conflictu Et Collisione," pp.12–13.
35 Terry Eagleton, *Heathcliff and the Great Hunger*, p.259.
36 John Joseph O'Kelly (Seán Ua Ceallaigh), *Ireland: Elements of Her Early Story from the Coming of Ceasair to the Anglo-Norman Invasion*. Dublin: M.H. Gill & Son, 1921, pp.xxi–xxiii. Gill & Son also published the monthly magazine *Catholic Bulletin and Book Review*, edited by O'Kelly at the time.
37 James K. McGuire, *What Could Germany Do for Ireland?*, pp.218–20.
38 Sean-Ghall, "Early Irish Trade and Commerce," *Irish Year Book/Leabar na hÉireann, 1908*. Dublin: James Duffy & Co., 1908, p.124. As additional sources for the last sentence of the quoted text, Sean-Ghall referred to the Swiss archaeologist Ferdinand Keller and Madeline Anne Wallace-Dunlop's 1882 *Glass in the Old World*.
39 Jane Francesca (Speranza) Wilde, *Ancient Legends*, vol.II, pp.288–91.
40 John Thomas Gilbert, "History of the City of Dublin," *Dublin University Magazine* 47(279), March 1856, pp.320–42 (for the quoted text, see pp.323–24).
41 On 'Persia' and 'Persians,' see Seamus MacCall, *And So Began the Irish Nation*. Dublin: Talbot Press, 1931, pp.9–22 (under "Author's Note"), and pp.290–96, and passim
42 See also Ian McBride, *Eighteenth-Century Ireland*, chapter 10. As of yet, there are no studies, and hence no indication, of any potential interest in, and/or influence of, other late eighteenth-century democratic revolutions in connection with the ideological formation of the United Irishmen, such as the revolutions in South America (i.e., Túpac Amaru or Comunero uprisings) or in Saint-Domingue (later Haiti)
43 On *Paddy's Resource* in general, see Mary Helen Thuente, *The Harp Re-Strung*, pp.103–104, 130–69, and passim; Jacques Chuto, "Militant Nationalist Verse," pp.239–69; Ian McBride, *Eighteenth-Century Ireland*, pp.369–70, 384, 388–89.
44 See also Nini Rodgers, "Ireland and the Black Atlantic in the Eighteenth Century," *Irish Historical Studies* 32(126), November 2000, pp.174–92.
45 See, for example, Thomas Moore, *Memoirs, Journal, and Correspondence of Thomas Moore*, vol.1, pp.128–33, 138, 140–44, 148, 150, 154–58, 184, 245, 280, 317, 319–23, 326–28, 333, 338, 369; idem, *Memoirs, Journal, and Correspondence of Thomas Moore*, vol.2, pp.140, 187, 339–41, 343–44; idem, *Memoirs, Journal, and Correspondence of Thomas Moore*, vol.7, pp.289, 294–95, 307–308, 324–29, 332–33, 340, 342–43.
46 On Irish nationalists and the Sudan, where the journalist and militant Irish republican activist Edmond O'Donavan was killed while covering the "Mahdist" uprising against Anglo-Egyptian forces, and where O'Donovan's Irish nationalist associates (and former IRB members), the journalist and artist brothers James and Aloysius O'Kelly also covered the conflict, see Niamh O'Sullivan, *Aloysius O'Kelly*, chapters 5 and 6; Michael de Nie, "'Speed the Mahdi!' The Irish Press and Empire during the Sudan Conflict of 1883–1885," *Journal of British Studies* 51(4), October 2012, pp.883–909. On James O'Kelly (a Parnellite Home Rule member of the British Parliament at the time) see also the diary entries for April 29 and July 22, 1884. and April 27, 1885 in Wilfrid Scawen Blunt, *Gordon at Khartoum*, pp.231, 272, 422.
47 On this topic, see also Terry Eagleton, *Heathcliff and the Great Hunger*, pp.91, 152/
48 For the languages and dates of some of the earliest translations of Yeats' works, not forgetting the accessibility of his works in the original English in many parts of the world, see Colin P. Smythe, "Yeats in Translation" (https://www.dublincity.ie/story/yeats-translation).
49 Malcolm Sen, "Memory, Modernity, and the Sacred" in Oona Frawley, ed., *Memory Ireland*, vol.1, pp.108–109. See also p.110.
50 On the earlier roots of the affinity between MacNeill and the Catholic Church, see Kevin Collins, *Catholic Churchmen and the Celtic Revival*, pp.77–79, 161–62.
51 On German-backed Indo-Irish activities in the United States, see also French Strother, *Fighting Germany's Spies*. Garden City, New York: Doubleday, 1919, pp.234–36; Matthew Erin Plowman, 'Irish Republicans and the Indo-German Conspiracy,' pp.80–105.
52 Among many other works on Irish political developments during the period, see Diarmaid Ferriter, "The Historical Climate of James Joyce's *Finnegans Wake*, 1922-39." Lecture presented at the 23rd International James Joyce Symposium. University College Dublin, June 14, 2012 (https://www.youtube.com/watch?v=3UUtsYMZf7k); idem, *A Nation and*

Not a Rabble: The Irish Revolution 1913-1923. New York: Overlook Press, 2015 (particularly chapters 17 to 24); idem, *Transformation of Ireland*, chapter 3; Bill Kissane, *The Politics of the Irish Civil War*. Oxford: Oxford University Press, 2005, John Dorney, *'Peace After the Final Battle': The Story of the Irish Revolution, 1912-1924*. Dublin: New Island Books, 2014.

53 For a slightly different take on this development, see Bruce Nelson, *Irish Nationalists and the Making of the Irish Race*. Princeton: Princeton University Press, 2012, chapters 6,7, 8 and Epilogue.

54 Among numerous other works, see also Joseph J. Lee, *Ireland, 1912-1985: Politics and Society*. Cambridge: Cambridge University Press, 1989, chapter 2; Diarmaid Ferriter, *Transformation of Ireland*, chapter 4; Terence Brown, *Ireland: A Social and Cultural History, 1922-2002*. Revised edition. London: Harper Perennial, 2004, chapters 1–4; Enda McKay, "Changing with the Tide: The Irish Labour Party, 1927-1933," *Saothar* 11, 1986, pp.27–38.

55 Matt Treacy, *The Communist Party of Ireland, 1921–2011. Volume 1: 1921–1969*. Dublin: Brocaire Books, 2012, chapter 1.

56 Kate O'Malley, "Indo-Irish radical connections in the interwar period," *Saothar* 29, 2004, pp.45–55.

57 "Imperial Piracy," *Anti-Imperialist* (Dublin), no.1, Samhain 1926, p.1. See also "Fascism in Ireland" and the reproduction of the nineteenth century English socialist Henry Labouchere's "Where is the Flag of England?" in ibid., p.2.

58 Kate O'Malley, *Ireland, India and Empire: Indo-Irish Radical Connections, 1919-64*. Manchester: Manchester University Press, 2008, chapter 2. See also Joseph Lennon, *Irish Orientalism*, p.219; Richard English, "Peadar O'Donnell: Socialism and the Republic, 1925-37," *Saothar* 14, 1989, pp.47–58.

59 Kate O'Malley, *Ireland, India and Empire*, chapter 2 (see p.77 for the quoted text).

60 See also Michael Silvestri, *Ireland and India*, pp.43–45.

61 "Memorandum on Irish membership of the League of Nations by Patrick Sarsfield O'Hegarty with covering note by J.J. Walsh, Dublin, 15 September 1922" (document no.320 NAI DT S3332) in Ronan Fanning, Michael Kennedy, Dermot Keogh, and Eunan O'Halpin, eds., *Documents on Irish Foreign Policy. Volume I: 1919-1922*. Dublin: Royal Irish Academy, 1998 (https://www.difp.ie/docs/Volume1/1922/320.htm). See also Michael Kennedy, *Ireland and the League of Nations, 1919-1946: International Relations, Diplomacy and Politics*. Dublin: Irish Academic Press, 1996; Dermot Keogh, *Ireland and Europe, 1919-48*. Dublin: Gill and Macmillan, 1988.

62 Cian McMahon, "Irish Free State newspapers and the Abyssinian crisis, 1935-6," *Irish Historical Studies* 36(143), May 2009, pp.368–88; Martha Kavanagh, "The Irish Free State and Collective Security, 1930-6," *Irish Studies in International Affairs* 15, 2004, pp.103–22.

63 J. Bowyer Bell, "Ireland and the Spanish Civil War, 1936-1939," *Studia Hibernica*, no.9, 1969, pp.137–63; Fearghal McGarry, *Irish Politics and the Spanish Civil War*. Cork; Cork University Press, 1999; Robert Stradling, *The Irish and the Spanish Civil War 1936-1939*. Manchester: Mandolin, 1999. Brian Hanley, *The IRA, 1926-1936*. Dublin: Four Courts Press, 2002.

64 "Speech by Eamon de Valera at the League of Nations Assembly, Geneva, 2 July 1936" (document no.347 NAI DFA 26/94) in Catriona Crowe, Ronan Fanning, Michael Kennedy, Dermot Keogh, and Eunan O'Halpin, eds., *Documents on Irish Foreign Policy. Volume IV: 1932–1936*. Dublin: Royal Irish Academy, 2004 (https://www.difp.ie/docs/Volume4/1936/1716.htm). For an alternative interpretation of this speech, see Michael Kennedy, *Ireland and the League of Nations*, pp.13, 205–22.

65 On the Free State and Britain's imperial "white-settlement" dominions, see David W. Harkness, *The Restless Dominion: The Irish Free State and the British Commonwealth of Nations 1921-31*. London: Macmillan, 1969; Michael Kennedy, *Ireland and the League of Nations*, Chapter 5; Donal Lowry, "The captive dominion: imperial realities behind Irish diplomacy, 1922-49," *Irish Historical Studies* 36(142), November 2008, pp.202–26; Francis M. Carroll, "Ireland Among the Nations of the Earth: Ireland's Foreign Relations from 1923 to 1949," *Études irlandaises* 41(1), 2016, pp.35–52.

66 Onna Frawley, "Toward a Theory of Cultural Memory in an Irish Postcolonial Context" in Oona Frawley, ed., *Memory Ireland*, vol.1, p.32.

67 For a brief summary of manifold disparate versions of the Irish past "in the two centuries previous to" the establishment of the Free State, see also Malcolm Sen, "Memory,

Modernity, and the Sacred" in Oona Frawley, ed., *Memory Ireland*, vol.1, pp.106–10; as well as Joep Leerssen, "Setting the Scene for National History" in Stefan Berger and Chris Lorenz, eds., *Nationalizing the Past*, pp.79–80.
68 Seumas MacManus, *The Story of the Irish Race*, p.1. See also pp.8–20.
69 On the popularity of the book, see also Bruce Nelson, *Irish Nationalists and the Making of the Irish Race* (pp.242–43), which does not delve into MacManus' theory of oriental origins of ancient Ireland.
70 Seamus MacCall, *And So Began the Irish Nation*, p.vii.
71 Ibid., pp.9–21, 26–32.
72 William Butler Yeats, *The Collected Works of W.B. Yeats. Vol. XII*, pp.xi–xii. John O'Leary, Yeats's friend and at the time a leader of the IRB, soon to assume the presidency of the organization, was the literary editor of *The Gael*, which was published by the Gaelic Athletic Association.
73 For alternative modes of contextualizing Yeats' 1916 poem, see also Colm Tóibín, "Easter 1916"; Roy F Foster, *The Irish Story: Telling Tales and Making It Up in Ireland*. London: Allen Lane, 2001, pp.62–66; Declan Kiberd, *Inventing Ireland*, pp.213–17.
74 Roy F. Foster, "History and the Irish Question," *Transactions of the Royal Historical Society* 33(1983), pp.191–92.
75 Diarmaid Ferriter, *A Nation and Not a Rabble*, chapters 5 and 6; Sean Farren, *The Politics of Irish Education, 1920-65*. Belfast: Queen's University of Belfast Institute of Irish Studies, 1995, pp.52–58, 104, 106–108, and passim; Philip O'Leary, *Gaelic Prose in the Irish Free State, 1922-1939*. University Park, PA: Pennsylvania State University Press, 2004 (see especially pp.252–54, 274–75); Colm Mac Gearailt, "Writing the Irish Past: An Investigation into Post-Primary Irish History Textbook Emphases and Historiography, 1921-69," *History Education Research Journal* 15(2), October 2018, pp.235–37, 240–41; Gabriel Doherty, "National Identity and the Study of Irish History," *English Historical Review* 111(441), April 1996, pp.324–49; Thomas Walsh, "100 years of primary curriculum development and implementation in Ireland: a tale of a swinging pendulum," *Irish Educational Studies* 35(1), 2016, pp.5–6; Roy F. Foster, "History and the Irish Question," pp.187–88; Alan McCully and Fionnuala Waldron, "'A Question of Identity' Purpose, Policy and Practice in the Teaching of History in Northern Ireland and the Republic of Ireland" in Hilary Cooper and John Nichol, eds., *Identity, Trauma, Sensitive and Controversial Issues in the Teaching of History*. Newcastle upon Tyne: Cambridge Scholars, 2015, pp.3–4, 10–11; Tony Gallagher, "Addressing Conflict and Tolerance Through the Curriculum" in Michelle J. Bellino and James H. Williams, eds. *(Re)Constructing Memory: Education, Identity, and Conflict*. Boston: Sense Publishers, 2017, pp.194–95.
76 John O'Callaghan, "Politics, Policy and History: History Teaching in Irish Secondary Schools 1922-1970," *Études irlandaises* 36(1), 2011, pp.25–41.
77 Terry Eagleton, *Heathcliff and the Great Hunger*, p.279.
78 For a broad overview of these concepts in the framework of Irish history, see Ian McBride, "Introduction: memory and national identity in modern Ireland" in Ian McBride, ed., *History and Memory in Modern Ireland*, pp.5–13 in particular; Barbara A. Misztal, "Memory and History" in Oona Frawley, ed., *Memory Ireland*, vol.1, pp.3–17; Onna Frawley, "Toward a Theory of Cultural Memory in an Irish Postcolonial Context" in ibid., pp.18–34; and Malcolm Sen, "Memory, Modernity, and the Sacred" in ibid., pp.101–14; Guy Beiner, "A Short History of Irish Memory in the Long Twentieth Century" in Thomas Bartlett, ed., *The Cambridge History of Ireland*, vol.IV, pp.708–25. On "History as Social Memory" in general, see also Peter Burke, *Varieties of Cultural History*. Ithaca: Cornell University Press, 1997, pp.43–59. On applications and limitations of these concepts, see Astrid Erll and Ansgar Nünning, eds., *Cultural Memory Studies: An International and Interdisciplinary Handbook*. New York: de Gruyter, 2008; Allan Megill, *Historical Knowledge, Historical Error*, chapters 1 and 2.
79 On national memory and history, see also Stefan Berger and Bill Niven, "Introduction" and "Writing the history of national memory" in Stefan Berger and Bill Niven, eds., *Writing the History of Memory*. London: Bloomsbury, 2014.
80 Among other sources, see Marcia K. Johnson, Carol L. Raye, Karen J. Mitchell, and Elizabeth Ankudowich, "The Cognitive Neuroscience of True and False Memories" in Robert F. Belli, ed., *True and False Recovered Memories: Toward a Reconciliation of the Debate*. New York: Springer, 2012, pp.15 52.

81 On this topic, see also Maria Tymoczko, *The Irish Ulysses*. Berkeley: University of California Press, 1997, pp.37–43, 319–23.
82 On Joyce's alleged repudiation of Irish nationalism, see "Joyce and Nationalism" in Seamus Deane, *Celtic Revivals: Essays in Modern Irish Literature, 1880-1980*. London: Faber and Faber, 1985, pp.92–107.
83 See the reference to Griffith and his pseudonyms "Shanganah" and "P." (under which Griffith had published some of his own opinions in his *United Irishmen*) in James Joyce, *Ulysses*. London: Egoist Press (published by John Rodker in Paris), 1922, p.320. On this topic, see also Gerald Y. Goldberg, "'Ireland Is the Only Country [...]': Joyce and the Jewish Dimension," *The Crane Bag* 6(1), 1982, p.7. On the Jewish background of Joyce's fictional character Bloom in *Ulysses* and Arthur Griffith's anti-Jewish proclivity, see also Abby Bender, *Israelites in Erin: Exodus, Revolution, & the Irish Revival*. Syracuse: Syracuse University Press, 2015, pp.131–33.
84 James Joyce, *Finnegans Wake*, p.394. See, for example, also "Ourselves, oursouls alone" in ibid., p.623.
85 Ibid., p.465.
86 Declan Kiberd, *Inventing Ireland*, pp.344–45., 350–51.
87 See "Israel represents the triumph of Sinn Fein," *Sinn Féin*, March 16, 1912, p.2, cc.a–b.
88 On Joyce and "the doctrine of cultural diversity," see Terry Eagleton, *Heathcliff and the Great Hunger*, pp.270, 316.
89 On Joyce's choice of the dreamscape in this regard, see also Richard Ellmann, *James Joyce*. Revised edition. Oxford: Oxford University Press, 1982 [1959], pp.703, 716–17.
90 Ibid., p.75.
91 See also ibid., pp.88, 144–47.
92 Ibid., pp.94–96, 259; Kevin Barry, ed. *James Joyce*, pp. pp.53–60, 127–36.
93 For the phrase "persianly literatured" see James Joyce, *Finnegans Wake*, p.183.
94 Among many other sources, see also Emer Nolan, *James Joyce and Nationalism*. Second edition. New York: Routledge, 2002 [1995], pp.50–52 and passim; "Introduction: Democratic and Cosmopolitan Joyce" in Margot Norris, *The Value of James Joyce*. Cambridge: Cambridge University Press, 2016, pp.1–7 (and passim); Rebecca L. Walkowitz, *Cosmopolitan Style: Modernism Beyond the Nation*. New York: Columbia University Press, 2006, pp.73–77 and passim; Jason King, "'Memory of These Migrations': Joyce, Interculturalism, and the Reception of *Ulysses* in the Irish Immigration Debate" in R. Brandon Kershner and Tekla Mecsnóber, eds., *Joycean Unions: Post-Millennial Essays from East to West*. Amsterdam: Rodopi, 2013, pp.95–108; Thomas F. Halloran, "Joyce and postcolonial literature: creating an inclusive Irish identity" in Ruth Connolly and Ann Coughlan, eds., *New Voices in Irish Criticism 5*, pp.187–97.
95 On the complexities of Joyce's attitude toward nationalism, see also Marjorie Howes, "Joyce, colonialism, and nationalism" in Derek Attridge, ed., *The Cambridge Companion to James Joyce*. 2nd edition. Cambridge: Cambridge University Press, 2004 [1990], pp.254-71.
96 James Joyce, *Ulysses*, pp.319–20.
97 Quoted in Richard Ellmann, *James Joyce*, p.521 n.†.
98 See also Maria Tymoczko, *The Irish Ulysses*, pp.285–89; Norman Vance, *Irish Literature*, p.194.
99 James Joyce, *Ulysses*, pp.317–18.
100 On oriental crossings and theories of Irish origins in Joyce's *Ulysses* see also Ian Almond, "Tales of Buddha, Dreams of Arabia"; Joseph Lennon, *Irish Orientalism*, pp.213–14; Carol Loeb Shloss, "Joyce in the Context of Irish Orientalism," *James Joyce Quarterly* 35(2 & 3), Winter-Spring, 1998, pp.266–70; R. Brandon Kershner, "'Ulysses' and the Orient," ibid., pp.273, 277, 281–84, 291–93 See also the articles on Joyce and the Orient in the same issue of *James Joyce Quarterly* (devoted to "ReOrienting Joyce") by Zack Bowen, Heyward Ehrlich, Mary C. King, Susan Cannon Harris, Aida Yared, and again Carol Loeb Shloss.
101 For a detailed treatment of Joyce and Modernism, see Emer Nolan, *James Joyce and Nationalism*. See also idem, "James Joyce and the Mutations of the Modernist Novel" in Joe Cleary, ed., *The Cambridge Companion to Irish Modernism*, chapter 6.
102 See James Joyce, "Ireland: Island of Saints and Sages" in Kevin Barry, ed. *James Joyce*, p.110.

103 On the allusion to the theory of Phoenician (i.e., Semitic) origins of Ireland in *Ulysses* and Joyce's familiarity with Vallancey's works, see James Joyce, *Ulysses*, p.641; Maria Tymoczko, *The Irish Ulysses*, pp.285 and passim. See also R. Brandon Kershner, "'Ulysses' and the Orient"; Carol Loeb Shloss, "Joyce in the Context of Irish Orientalism."
104 James Joyce, *Finnegans Wake*, p.104.
105 See also Thomas C. Hofheinz, *Joyce and the Inventions of Irish History*, chapter 2 ("Conditions for historical study of *Finnegans Wake*").
106 On Joyce and Vico, see also Scott Samuelson, "Joyce's *Finnegans Wake* and Vico's Mental Dictionary," *New Vico Studies* 17, 1999, pp.53–66. For some of Joyce's references to Vico, see James Joyce, *Finnegans Wake*, pp.246, 260, 452, 497, 614.
107 Thomas C. Hofheinz, *Joyce and the Inventions of Irish History*, p.120.
108 Ibid., p.49. See also James Joyce, *Finnegans Wake*, pp.139, 381. On the latter page, Joyce mentioned "the unimportant Parthalonians with the mouldy Firbolgs and the Tuatha de Danaan googs."
109 James Joyce, *Finnegans Wake*, p.347. There are references to Moore in *Ulysses* as well.
110 Ibid., p.595.
111 Ibid., p.106. On Mangan's joke, see also Heyward Ehrlich, "'Araby' in Context," p.325; Melissa Fegan, "'Every Irishman is an Arab'," p.200. See also Emer Nolan, "'The Tommy Moore Touch'," pp.64–77; Lynne A. Bongiovanni, "'Turbaned faces going by': James Joyce and Irish Orientalism," pp.25–49.
112 Thomas C. Hofheinz, *Joyce and the Inventions of Irish History*, pp.69–81.
113 See "The Ballad of Persse O'Reilly" in James Joyce, *Finnegans Wake*, pp.44–47.
114 Ibid., p.37. The actual line, to which I have already alluded in Chapter Six, appeared in the 1902 play "Diarmuid and Grania" by Yeats and George Moore: "Life of my life, I knew you before I was born, I made a bargain with this brown hair before the beginning of time and it shall not be broken through unending time.'
115 Ibid., p.14. Joyce had earlier referred to this as "the bluest book in baile's annals," establishing its connection with the Jewish tradition through the use of Hebrew names of months in the Jewish calendar. Ibid., p.13. Among other subsequent references to Ecclesiastes in *Finnegans Wake* is "usylessly unreadable Blue Book of Eccles, *édition de ténèbres*." Ibid., p.179.
116 Ibid., p.15. See also pp.13–14, 381.
117 On Joyce learning the Dano-Norwegian dialect, see Richard Ellmann, *James Joyce*, p.76.
118 James Joyce, *Finnegans Wake*, pp.15–16.
119 Ibid., p.17. Emer Nolan correctly interprets this as "the eventual merging of Viking and Irish," albeit without clarifying Joyce's intended ancestries of the indigenous Irish prior to the arrival of the Norse. Emer Nolan, *James Joyce and Nationalism*, p.152.
120 James Joyce, *Finnegans Wake*, pp.18–19.
121 Ibid., pp.21–30, and passim.
122 Ibid., pp.23, 25.
123 Ibid., p.68. It is unclear whether Joyce's reference to Queen of Sheba in this passage was a random reference or based on Mangan's already discussed purported translation of a poem he attributed to Hafiz (in which Mangan alludes to "Solomon and Sheba," with 'Sheba' appearing recurrently in Hafiz's *Rubā'iyāt*). The term "giaours" appears again in Joyce's book. Ibid., p.107. For a different interpretation of 'Phenicia or Little Asia,' see Donald A. Lashomb, "Working Through Tradition Alone — Joyce's Mythic Return," PhD dissertation, New York University, 2008, pp.117–18. Lashomb, however, correctly recognizes that by the time Joyce was working on *Finnegans Wake*, Joyce had developed a more heterogeneous theory of Ireland's ancient oriental roots than just the Phoenician connection.
124 James Joyce, *Finnegans Wake*, pp.85, 87, 182, 191, 608.
125 Ibid., pp.78, 263, 309.
126 Ibid., p.162.
127 Malcolm Sen, "Memory, Modernity, and the Sacred" in Oona Frawley, ed., *Memory Ireland*, vol.1, p.108.
128 James Joyce, *Finnegans Wake*, pp.614–15. Richard Ellmann notes that a section of this quoted passage was taken from the work of the French historian Edgar Quinet, echoing Vico's theory of history, but "without Vico's apparatus." Richard Ellmann, *James Joyce*, p.664.

129 James Joyce, *Finnegans Wake*, p.452. On Joyce and Vico, see Thomas C. Hofheinz, *Joyce and the Inventions of Irish History*, chapter 5; Richard Ellmann, *James Joyce*, p.554 and passim; Emer Nolan, *James Joyce and Nationalism*, pp.152–55. On history, memory, and repetition, see also Harry D. Harootunian, "The Benjamin Effect," pp.62–87.
130 James Joyce, *Finnegans Wake*, pp.572–73.
131 John V. Kelleher, "Identifying the Irish Printed Sources for *Finnegans Wake*" in John V. Kelleher, *Selected Writings of John V. Kelleher on Ireland and Irish America*. Charles Fanning editor. Carbondale: Southern Illinois University Press, 2002, pp.57–72 (this essay was originally published in 1971). See also Thomas C. Hofheinz, *Joyce and the Inventions of Irish History*, p.69; Maria Tymoczko, *The Irish Ulysses*, pp.283–85, 289, 292, 299–301.
132 On Joyce and Bérard's *Les Phéniciens et l'Odyssée* see, for example, Richard Ellmann, *James Joyce*, pp.408, 550; Michael Seidel, *Epic Geography: James Joyce's Ulysses*. Princeton: Princeton University Press, 1976, pp.3–5, 19, and passim; Maria Tymoczko, *The Irish Ulysses*, pp.20, 37–43, 285. On other influences shaping Joyce's Phoenician hypothesis of ancient Ireland, see also Salvatore Pappalardo, "Waking Europa: Joyce, Ferrero and the Metamorphosis of Irish History," *Journal of Modern Literature* 34(2), Winter 2011, pp. 154–77.
133 See, for instance, John D'Alton, "Essay on the Ancient History, Religion, Learning, Arts, and Government of Ireland," pp.26–37 (under the "Antiquities" section); idem, *The History of Drogheda, with Its Environs*. Volume II. Dublin: privately published, 1844, pp.7–8.
134 See the text of the lecture in Kevin Barry, ed. *James Joyce*, p.110.
135 Although this interpretation is mine, Joyce's own statement is reproduced in Richard Ellmann, *James Joyce*, pp.536–37.
136 Among many other variations of this, see the listing of historical names appearing in the margin of following pages in James Joyce, *Finnegans Wake*, pp.306–308.
137 Ibid., pp.68, 85, 129, 197, 567, 608, and passim.
138 Emer Nolan, *James Joyce and Nationalism*, chapter 5.
139 On this topic, see also Norman Vance, *Irish Literature*, pp.192, 195.
140 See also Emer Nolan, *James Joyce and Nationalism*, pp.50–52 and passim.
141 James Joyce, *Finnegans Wake*, pp.356–57.
142 See Edmund L. Epstein, "James Joyce and the Way of All Flesh," *James Joyce Quarterly* 7(1), Fall 1969, pp.22–29.
143 "[I]f you wil excuse for me this informal leading down of inexpressibles, enlivened toward the Author of Nature by the natural sins liggen gobelimned theirs before me, (how differended with the manmade Eonochs Cunstuntonopolies!), weathered they be of a general golf stature, assasserted, or blossomly emblushing thems elves underneed of some howthern folleys, am entrenched jipxontemplating of myself, wiz my naked I, for relieving purposes in our trurally virvir vergitabale (garden). [...]" James Joyce, *Finnegans Wake*, pp.357–58.
144 Ibid., p.358. The term 'mucktub' in this section may be a play on the Arabic term for traditional elementary schools (*maktab*), including in Iran. For alternative and extremely facile, Persian- and Iran-focused readings of select passages in *Finnegans Wake*, disconnected from Irish literary and historical framings, see the essays by Leila Barandan Jamili and Bahman Zarrinjooee, who attempt to decode certain passages in *Finnegans Wake* through Persian lexical elucidation or references to Iran independently of the remainder of the text, with Jamili's over-eagerness to establish as many Persian and/or Iran connections in the text, resulting in such erroneous associations of certain terms and names, as in the case of the English name "Inglis" (meaning "English"/"Angles" in the Anglo-Saxon Old English), which she confuses with the Persian designation for England ("Ingiliss"), or of "Arras" (a region in France) being misidentified as the Arras River in Iran, or the Irish expression "Arrah" being misconstrued as the Persian word for "Yes." Bahman Zarrinjooee, "Joyce's Finnegans Wake: A Universal Culture," *Hypermedia Joyce Studies* 11, 2010-2011 (http://hjs.ff.cuni.cz/main/essays.php?essay=zarrinjooee); Leila Barandan Jamili, "On the Footsteps of Shahrzad in James Joyce's *Finnegans Wake*: The Rustle of Persian Language," ibid. (http://hjs.ff.cuni.cz/archives/vl1_1/main/essays.php?essay=jamili); Leila Barandan Jamili, "'The Chaosmos of Alle': Chaos, the Persian Culture, and James Joyce's *Finnegans Wake*" (http://lbjamili.8m.com/);; Leila Baradaran Jamili and Bahman Zarrinjooee, "An Artistic Metempsychosis: James Joyce and Sadeq Hedayat's Nonlinear and Chaotic Imagination" in Martha C. Carpentier, ed., *Joycean Legacies*. New York: Plagrave Macmillan, 2015, pp.230–57.

145 See also endnote 155 in Chapter One of the present book.
146 Meaning the Church of the Immaculate Conception in Dublin, known as "Adam and Eve's."
147 The oldest surviving medieval castle in Dublin and a reminder of the Norman conquests of Ireland in the twelfth century.
148 James Joyce, *Finnegans Wake*, p.37. There are other, more cursory, allusions to ancient Iranian mythical-religious belief systems in *Finnegans Wake*, as in the case of the cosmic force of evil, "ahriman." Ibid., p.426.
149 Eoin MacNeill, *Phases of Irish History*, p.95
150 Ellen Carol Jones, "Memorial Dublin" in Maurizia Boscagli and Enda Duffy, eds., *Joyce, Benjamin and Magical Urbanism*. (European Joyce Studies 21.) Amsterdam: Rodopi, 2011, pp.113–14. See also Luke Gibbons, "Race Against Time," pp.109–12.
151 On Memory and affirmative historiography, see Allan Megill, *Historical Knowledge, Historical Error*, pp.22–36.
152 Ibid., p.27. Even though here Megill only discusses these categories as two different modes of historiography, he later addresses the possibility of their overlap. See ibid., pp.37–38.

CONCLUSION: HISTORICAL APOPHENIA, AFFINITIES, DEPARTURES, AND NESCIENCE

Rather than merely focusing on the stated platforms, activities, and appeal of different Irish nationalist organizations or individuals from the late eighteenth century to 1921, this study has probed particular contours of Irish nationalism during that time frame through the perspectival lens of multivocal and multivalent Irish nationalist imaginations and *self-representations* by way of references to a distant land ('Iran' in this case, in its broadest historical, geographic, and cultural configurations). This approach has underscored the always *worlded* dimension of nativist and/or nationalist Irish self-imaginings (in the case of nationalism, particularly after the emergence of the multiethnic and cross-communal Society of United Irishmen). This method has relied on an array of new analytical trajectories for interrogating particular trends in the history of Irish nationalism, yielding both information that is at times familiar and an extensive range of material and interpretations that are entirely new and otherwise inaccessible through other existing modes of engaging with the history of Irish nationalism. It is also imperative to emphasize once again that the focus of this study has been the exploration of particular strands of thought in the multifaceted sphere of Irish nationalism over a broad time span through the heuristic lens of 'Iran,' and not the study of Irish–Iranian relations during the period covered in this book or of solely *political* (in its narrowest definition) dimensions of Irish nationalist engagement with contemporary Iran.

The Iranian frame of reference in this book is only one of many potential modes of investigating the evolution and diversity of Irish nationalism in a comparative world-historical setting—keeping in mind also that this study has only probed particular trends in Irish nationalist historical, literary, cultural, and political expressions, and that in doing so, like other studies of Irish nationalism dealing with the period under investigation, this study too has relied throughout on the available *recorded* Irish and other sources and, hence, makes no pretence of either reflecting the entire range of continuities and transformations in Irish nationalist articulations and "mentalities" (to borrow from the Annales School), or shedding light on the otherwise undocumented attitudes of ordinary Irish people during the period who gravitated to different strands of nationalism. Such a world-historical approach can be carried out at micro or macro levels, both synchronically and diachronically, each with its own advantages and limitations. In contrast to Poland, Scythia, Phoenicia, or Armenia, the choice of Iran as the extra-Irish historical medium for ultimately framing and probing particular articulations of the always manifold Irish nationalist self-referentialities during the time period has had a particular temporal-spatial advantage, leaving aside my own greater familiarity with Iranian history. The Iranian lens has made it possible to interrogate certain trends (by no means exhaustive) in Irish nationalist narrations of Irish history since ancient times—not forgetting Iran's own continually changing territorial, cultural, political, and other contours over time—as well as contemporary political expressions of cross-territorial affinities and solidarity.

The present study has opted for the micro approach, through a narrow diachronic (albeit historically fluid) Iran-centered (mytho-)historical, cultural, geographic, literary, and political portal into the evolution of particular strands of cross-communal Irish nationalism during the century-and-a-half leading up to the creation of the Irish Free State; even while repeatedly drawing comparisons with some other regions of the world that also appeared in Irish nationalist imaginations and commentaries. This broad temporal frame of examining Irish nationalist self-imaginings and their modes of charting Irish history and the Irish Question has made it possible to investigate a wide array of Irish nationalist expressions after the late eighteenth century, besides just the narrowly defined 'political' articulations, as in the case of antiquarian debates or nationalist poetry. In both narrowly and broadly defined nationalist political and cultural spheres, Iran was one of many territories—alongside such locations as Egypt, Afghan territories, India, Poland, Algeria, Morocco, or even ancient Sparta, to give just a few examples—that cropped up in instrumentalized forms in Irish nationalist narrations of the Irish struggle against English domination. With somewhat different historical contours and nuances, a similar micro approach of spatially narrow, but temporally broad, *worlding* survey of Irish nationalism, by utilizing an identical range of topics as in the present study (extending from antiquarian search for Irish origins to expressions of contemporary anti-imperialist affinities), can well be conducted by focusing on the Indian subcontinent or 'Egypt,' instead of 'Iran.' Only these other territorial constructs can function (in different degrees and combinations) as candidates for a study of this kind, which examines Irish nationalist imaginations apropos of another spatial setting in such panoramic temporal and thematic sweep, extending from theories of Irish origins to allegoric literary utilizations, Irish folklore, mythology, 'racial' delineations of contemporary Irish people, and Irish nationalist expressions of cross-territorial solidarities. In contrast, a joint synchronic world-historical comparative analyses of simultaneous Irish nationalist expressions of solidarity with Iranian and Polish and/or Indian and Egyptian nationalist struggles in the early years of the twentieth century, for instance, might well shed light on other aspects of various Irish nationalist platforms and modus operandi at that particular historical juncture.

Most other territories variously referenced by Irish nationalists in connection with ancient Ireland, or serving as allegoric literary devices for commenting on the ongoing

Irish struggle, or appearing in Irish nationalist expressions of cross-territorial solidarity, lack the same temporal and thematic world-historical fit as Iran. Poland, for instance, while allegorically appearing in Irish nationalist literature (particularly poetry) as well as eliciting contemporary Irish nationalist expressions of solidarity at particular junctures after the eighteenth century, was not identified as the original home of the ancient populations or civilizations of Ireland or as sharing a common foundational folk tradition with contemporary Ireland, among other key topics covered in this book. Scythia and Phoenicia, for their part, had ceased to exist as specifically designated territorial entities after ancient times. So, naturally, there could be no expressions of solidarity with contemporary anti-imperialist struggles in those territories, among other factors. Armenia, which was identified in some antiquarian accounts as the original homeland of of some of the earliest population settlements in Ireland, did not feature as an allegoric nationalist motif in Irish literature and was not a focus of cross-territorial expressions of anti-imperialist solidarity in the same manner as contemporary Iran, India, Afghanistan, Poland, or Egypt—which is not to deny instances of expressed Irish sympathy for the plight of Armenian victims of massacres committed against them in the Ottoman Empire after the late nineteenth century and, especially, during the Armenian Genocide of the First World War. Where and when possible, the present study has engaged in a more panoramic world-historical comparative coverage of Irish nationalism by juxtaposing Irish nationalist commentaries on Iran with commentaries on other territories and peoples in similar settings. Just as varying articulations of the 'national' Self are contingent on co-existing constructs of Others (without restricting Self/Other here to reductionist and always oppositional binary conceptualization of alterity), so too nationalist self-projections and historiographies operate within various matrices of Self/Other grounded in the broader world history. Irish nationalists did not solely define the 'Irish nation' in contradistinction to 'England.' In defining Ireland and Irishness, whether in opposition to England or imperialism more broadly, or in other configurations, Irish nationalists also resorted to various modes of cross-identification with, and distancing from, particular groups elsewhere around the world, past and present. In effect, the envisioned Irish national Self transcended the narrow confines of Anglo-Irish history, even if that history was its primary focus and *political* raison d'être. Nationalist constructs of the Irish Self were also articulated and narrated by means of utilizing the broader world for historically and politically contextualizing, representing, and refashioning Ireland, Irishness, and the Irish struggle (as well as for particular corresponding representations of England). Such techniques of grounding the Irish Self in the broader world predated the emergence of nationalism, or even the earlier attempts at defending and acclaiming the presumably indigenous Irish culture in the always dynamic conflictual settings of post-Norman invasions. 'Medieval' Irish celebrations of Ireland's specifically "Christian" cultural heritage by means of references to world history preceded the earliest examples of Anglo-Norman derision of Ireland's cultural standing and of all things Irish. These medieval sources, whether or not they also provided blanket condemnations of Ireland's pre-Christian 'pagan' past, sought to variously locate contemporary Ireland as a center of culture in the known Christian world. Many of these sources traced Ireland's pre-Christian ancient past to non-European lands mentioned in the Bible and/or in Greco-Roman texts, even if those sources had cast that presumed ancestry as uncivilized or lesser-civilized, as in the case of descriptions of Scythians appearing in Greco-Roman accounts. This impulse to *world* Ireland was not unlike the earliest cartographic depictions of the known world (terra cognito) produced in different parts of the globe, as cultural and/or political expressions of locating the Self in the world. What changed over time was the particular connections drawn by Irish commentators with other regions of the world—including the choice of locations, time frames, as well as sympathetic, antithetical, or other configurations of those referentialities, at times with overlapping or even competing trends. In the case of Irish nationalists specifically (after the late eighteenth century), references to other regions of the world also assumed particular politically and/or culturally charged modes of expressed affinities or dissimilitude.

In the context of selective Irish nationalist articulations of solidarity with anti-imperialist struggles elsewhere in the world, Irish nationalists resorted to distinctly different and at times conflicting ideological arsenals in evoking historical parallels and/or affinities with other so-called nations resisting imperialism. In this regard, it should be noted that Róisin Healy in her important study, *Poland in the Irish Nationalist Imagination, 1772–1922*, has overstated the underlying "anti-Islamic" dimension in Irish nationalist articulations of solidarity with the Polish struggle in the years immediately before and, particularly, during the First World War, when remarking: "Poland served as a proxy for anti-Islamic feeling."[1] Such a sentiment of Irish nationalism during the time period in question was most certainly absent from Irish declarations of solidarity with Egyptians, Afghans, Moroccans, Algerians, or Iranians; not to mention some of the *much earlier* Irish nationalist political and fictional recourse to Iranian, Afghan, Moroccan, Algerian, or Egyptian history, and/or contemporary struggles. It also should not be forgotten that the German-backed militant Irish nationalists during the First World War, certainly did not openly revile Germany's Ottoman ally, which was conducting anti-Russian and anti-British campaigns under joint stated platforms of pan-Islam and pan-Turkism. Moreover, members of the Irish nationalist committee in Berlin during the war worked in tandem with members of Egyptian, Iranian, Moroccan, Algerian, and other such committees based in the German capital. Even though there had been an antipathetic component in regard to Islam in Thomas Moore's 1817 *Lalla Rookh*—in the setting of Zoroastrian Persian resistance to the Arab-Muslim invasion of Iran—this was cast in an imperial-political rather than fundamentally religious configuration. Moreover, in Moore's work the poet Feramorz (Aliris), who regaled Lalla Rookh, and with whom Moore seemingly identified as both a poet and as a religiously tolerant character, also happened to be a Muslim. The main subtext of Moore's narrative poem was not so much the choice of one's religion, but the condemnation of religious intolerance, manipulation of religion for political ends, and/or the cultural devastation unleashed by colonialism, as also evident again in *Lalla Rookh* in the form of Moore's depiction of the love affair between the Zoroastrian Hafed and the Muslim Hinda, or in Azim's enmity toward Mokanna, or Moore's characterization of the fanatical Fadladeen in prose sections of the text, or in Moore's portrayal of the eleventh-century invasion of predominantly Hindu territories in the Indian subcontinent by Muslim forces of Mahmud of Ghazni in the second section of *Lalla Rookh* ("Paradise and the Peri"). Similarly, in Moore's earlier 1813 *Intercepted Letters* ("Letter VI"), it was the prejudicial treatment of contemporary Iran's minority Sunni Muslim population by the majority Shi'i Muslim population of the country that was Moore's target, as an allegoric condemnation of Protestant mistreatment of Catholics in the United Kingdom. Any fundamentally 'anti-Islamic' underpinning of Irish nationalism in the earlier period was certainly also missing from Mangan's "To the Ingleezee Khafir," or from Thomas Osborne Davis' simultaneous advocacy of the Polish struggle against Russia and the Algerian resistance to French occupation, as well as from his celebration of the Afghan routing of invading British imperial forces.

Moore, who conveniently overlooked the fact that Iran itself had constituted an imperial power prior to the Arab-Muslim conquest in the seventh century, introduced the Iran/Erin allegoric parity that continued to resonate as an Irish nationalist literary device for decades to come. Mangan, on the other hand, in his 1846 poem "To the Ingleezee Khafir," turned to (Shi'i Muslim) Safavid Iran—ironically, yet another imperial state, and a religiously intolerant one no less—as an allegoric site of resistance to an imputed episode of English imperial aggression. Prior to 1856, disparate modes of Irish nationalist representations of 'Iran' *in connection with Ireland* extended from antiquarian/historical to the realm of literature (namely allegoric poetry), each with multiple ranges of motifs—inclusive also of contemporary Iran appearing in Thomas Moore's 1813 *Intercepted Letters*. However, in connection with Irish condemnations of contemporary British imperial aggression in other parts of the world, Iran first entered the lexicon of Irish nationalism during the Anglo-Iranian War of 1856–57. After 1907—with a more vociferous and sustained advocacy of Iranian sovereignty by a much larger and diverse spectrum of Irish nationalist groupings than in 1856–57—the rights of the Iranian 'nation' and the constitutionalist and reformist platforms in that country also featured as attributes of Irish nationalist espousal of Iranian resistance to British imperial aggression (as well as now also of Iranian resistance to Russian imperialism, at least in many Irish nationalist circles, if not all). In this transformed setting, the question of Iranian sovereignty was no longer merely a component of Irish nationalist formulations of 'the enemy of my enemy is my friend,' as had been the case in 1856–57.

There are clear indications that at least some Irish nationalists participating in the post-1907 Iranian Question were increasingly operating from a more comprehensive premise of the *rights* of nations or peoples—even if some of these individuals still variously fell short of defending the rights of all groups or nations resisting imperialism around the world, or failed to advocate the rights of all inner members of a given 'nation,' as in the case of women's suffrage and/or workers' rights in Ireland itself. To some extent, this development was also indicative of manifold ongoing globalization processes that influenced the ideological contours of competing Irish nationalist platforms as well as the flow of information about, and contacts with, anti-imperialist agendas and activists in other parts of the world (also applicable to the Irish diaspora). Among the constellation of globalization processes (including imperialism) that shaped Irish nationalist discursive deployments of 'Iran' after the late eighteenth century (historical, political, cultural, and literary) were such factors as the emergence of Indo-European theory of languages and the subsequent evolution of Aryan 'racial' theories. In so far as related global modes, circulation, and circuits of transmission of knowledge are concerned, one can point to increased availability of information about and familiarity with Iranian history and wider access to Iranian and other Iran-related textual sources, including works produced in the Indian subcontinent, such as *Dabestān-e Mazāheb* and *Dasātir* that were first brought to the attention of other 'Europeans' by 'British' (including Irish) members of the Asiatic Society of Bengal, among them the Irish orientalist David Shea (notwithstanding the later revelation that the historical claims made in these two particular texts were entirely concocted). Greater familiarity with other range of Iranian sources (in the broader sense of Iran) and the wider availability of European translations of Persian-language texts, including the *Shāhnāmeh*, or of Iran-related sources in Arabic or other 'oriental' languages, were also instrumental in this regard, alongside works produced in other parts of Europe (such as Thomas Moore's reliance on Iran-related entries in the French Barthélemy d'Herbelot's 1697 *Bibliothèque orientale*, or Mangan's reliance on translations of Turkish, Arabic, and Persian poetry by the Austrian Joseph Freiherr von Hammer-Purgstall). Other relevant global developments consisted of advances in modes of communication in general. For instance, during the Anglo-Iranian War of 1856–57, Irish press coverage of the faraway conflict often directly or indirectly reproduced reports from French or Belgian newspapers, as well as from such sources as the *Bombay Times* and even indirectly from the official Tehran newspaper *Rouznāmeh-ye Vaqāye'-e Ettefāqiyeh*, among other range of available accounts of the conflict. Other technological and communication advances ranged from modes of travel to the spread of telegraph lines in the latter part of the nineteenth century. These developments not only expedited faster and more frequent Irish coverage (in both Ireland and the Irish diaspora) of developments during the Iranian revolution of 1906–11, and subsequently, but also facilitated direct encounters between John Dillon and some Iranian constitutionalist-nationalists traveling to London during the Iranian revolution, or William J. Maloney's reporting on the Iranian struggle as a Reuters correspondent based in Iran.

This monograph has also, at least tangentially, outlined the ways in which representations of Iran by varying Irish nationalists before and during the time of the Iranian Constitutional Revolution paralleled or diverged from some of the contemporary Iranian 'modernist'-nationalist self-imaginings and self-representations. An example is the reliance on *Dabestān-e Mazāheb* by some Iranian nationalists in late nineteenth century for reconstructing and/or reaffirming and glorifying particular narratives of Iran's ancient past, similar to attempts by some Irish nationalists many decades earlier to reconstruct Ireland's ancient past by means of consulting the same source. Conversely, the dominant strand of Iranian discourses of Aryanism in the early twentieth century diverged from the anticolonial Aryanist discourse of the Pan-Aryan Association in New York. Iranian adherents of the Aryan theory preferred to 'racially' identify with the populations of Western European imperial powers—even if these Iranians also considered some of the population of the Indian subcontinent, in addition to the Parsi community there, as belonging to the Aryan family, and not forgetting, of course, the complete avoidance of racial theories by many Irish and Iranian nationalists. These analogous, as well as dissimilar, Irish and Iranian national self-imaginings were indicative of both the confluences and incongruencies of different anti-imperialist nationalist worlding projects and tactics of self-grounding, which were in turn shaped by and contributed to distinct, albeit intersecting, globalization processes, including various anti-imperialist global solidarity networks.

To recap, the previous chapters have interrogated certain trends in the evolution of multivalent Irish nationalism from the late eighteenth century to the founding of the Irish Free State in 1922 through the narrow lens of Irish nationalist imaginations, appropriations, and representations of Iran. The many renderings of Iran across time in Irish nationalist commentaries (fictional, mytho-historical, historical, and contemporary) have served as means of exploring an amalgam of Irish constructs of the Irish 'nation' itself, and of heterogeneous formulations of the Irish struggle for autonomy or full independence from England. On the other hand, the particular instance of *The Nation*'s disregard of Iran during the Iranian famine of 1870–72 was illustrative of conscious and politically calculated apathy on the part of the more 'radical' Irish nationalist groupings at the time, as a means of denying England a humanitarian mantle, given the involvement of British diplomatic channels in relief efforts for Iranian famine victims. By investigating Irish nationalism through the narrow lens of Irish nationalist imaginations of 'Iran' across time and geographic space—antiquarian, folklore, archaeological, philological, literary, and/or more narrowly 'political,' among other spectrums—this book has maintained above all that Irish nationalism from the time of its inception in the eighteenth century until the formation of the Irish Free State in 1922 was always in different ways and degrees cosmopolitan in its multiple self-imaginings of Ireland and of the Irish 'nation.' This persistently dynamic process continued after 1922, albeit in forms that precluded some of the earlier cosmopolitan ambits. During at least the first decade-and-a-half after the creation of the Free State (later Éire and the Republic of Ireland), the Irish nationalist gaze grew more insular in general, but without ever entirely losing all traces of its diversely worlded quality. In this context, the worlding practices of most Irish nationalist groupings became *primarily* Europe-centered/Westcentric, with the continued focus on India being a notable exception in this regard. For a wide array of reasons, a rapid reversal of this trend occurred after the 1950s. Most notable among later examples of more broadly worlded imaginations of Irish nationalism beyond European/Western horizons was the platform of the post-1957 revived Sinn Féin, particularly following its gradual embrace of Marxist internationalism by the 1960s, with the organization later known as the Official Sinn Féin and then Sinn Féin the Workers' Party, headquartered in the Republic of Ireland. Another similar example was the breakaway Sinn Féin organization in Northern Ireland following the outbreak in 1969 of what came to be known as "The Troubles," this time in the form of the Provisional Sinn Féin and its military wing, the Provisional Irish Republican Army. During this period, a similar trend was evident among such other organizations in Northern Ireland as the Irish Republican Socialist Party (1974), with its own paramilitary wing, the Irish National Liberation Army, and a host of other violent and nonviolent nationalist organizations during 'The Troubles' that embraced various forms of internationalism (if not also always adopting varying degrees of anticolonial analyses resembling Third Worldist platforms). Other examples include People's Democracy (also spelled "Peoples' Democracy"; 1968) or the parliamentary Social Democratic and Labour Party (1970), which at the time was by far the most popular Irish nationalist and republican organization in Northern Ireland. Iran, too, periodically featured in these later modes of worlding the Irish struggle, but now only in the confines of narrowly defined political expressions of cross-territorial solidarity with segments of the Iranian opposition to the autocratic reign of Mohammad Reza Shah Pahlavi (r.1941–79).[2]

Knowledge Production, Recollection, and Forgetting

Among other topics, the previous chapters have addressed instances of imagined, or apophenic, historical connections between ancient Ireland and 'Iran.' These Iran-centered Irish nationalist accounts of Irish origins (whether of the Irish people and/or of Ireland's alleged glorious ancient civilization) also claimed fundamental errors and gaps in alternative non-Iranian as well as in competing Iranian models of ancient Ireland. These other accounts were professedly marked by historical inaccuracies, nescience, and/or outright fabrications. Beginning with Vallancey's pioneering Iranian model, Iran-centered antiquarian reconstructions of ancient Ireland variously addressed and probed the silence in alternative prior as well as contemporary historical narrations of ancient Ireland that either entirely failed to recognize or did not correctly grasp the presumed Iranian connection. The earlier alleged persistence of nescience was attributed to the loss of some key evidentiary documentation—presumably rectified by the recent availability of works such as *Dabestān*—along with enduring joint processes of forgetting and distorted interpretations of surviving evidence, as in the case of supposedly the origin of the Round Towers after at least the introduction of Christianity to Ireland in the fifth century CE, if not much earlier (according to Henry O'Brien, for instance). Expectedly, there were rival claims of historical nescience, amnesia, and rediscovery in other competing oriental or non-oriental accounts of Irish origins. In Iranian models of Ireland's ancient past, Irish history extended back to ancient Iranian history, not only up to the moment that Ireland's Iranian ancestors departed from their original homeland—or, in the case of Moore's and D'Alton's Iranianized-Phoenician model, back to the time when those indirect conveyors of Iranian civilization left their original homeland—but up to the actual transplantation of those ancestors in Ireland itself. It was only after the process of transplantation in Ireland that a specifically 'Ireland'-*accented* form of Iranian identity and/or culture began to gradually take shape, whatever historical characteristics that Iranian prototype purportedly possessed at the moment of arrival (e.g., Mahābādiān, Pishdādiān, Scytho-Iranian, Mede, Persian, Parthian, and so on). The particular components of this (imagined) 'Irish' chapter of Iranian history in ancient times were a combined by-product of existing beliefs and practices brought to the new land, adaptation to new surroundings, incrementally diminished or complete loss of contact between the ancestral land and the Irish colony, conflicts and/or syncretic intermingling with prior and subsequent population arrivals in the island (including, in some accounts, other Iranian arrivals with historically transformed cultural values and practices), among the many other scenarios.

In effect, in these Iranian models of Irish origins, a distinctly Irish history of transplanted Iranians (or of Iranianized-Phoenicians and other such groups) developed beyond the knowledge range of 'Iranians' who did not emigrate to Ireland. This allegedly accounted for the absence of references to the Irish branch of Iranians in surviving Iranian historical sources available in the ancestral Iranian lands, including in contemporary Iran. In this formulation, ancient Irish history, as a history of an Iranian colony and/or of Iranian civilization established in Ireland, began beyond the spatial, temporal, and cognitive threshold of *mainstream* Iranian history. There were also Irish antiquarian accounts that claimed initial continued contacts between Ireland and the ancestral Iranian lands of the Irish for a few generations before these contacts ceased. In these accounts, whereas ancient Iranians in the ancestral land of the Irish knew about their migrating kinsfolk and the new homeland of these Iranian transplants in Ireland, that particular chapter of the Iranian colony in Ireland had simply been lost or erased and forgotten in surviving historical narratives and, hence, in present-day memory of Iranians. Yet, interestingly, no attempt was made by any Irish antiquarian embracing an Iranian model to also amend contemporary Iranian historiography by introducing current "discoveries" of Ireland's ancient ties to Iran to contemporary Iranians. In other words, while claiming to resuscitate the world-historical narrative of Iranian presence in ancient Ireland, these antiquarians were perpetuating the presumed continued deficiency and nescience in contemporary Iranian world-historical awareness of Iran's past connections to Ireland and their once shared heritage. Iranians remained completely unaware of various contemporary claims of Ireland's shared heritage with Iran and of Ireland's alleged place in the "Persianate" world, including such information as Lady Wilde's assertion of continued correspondence between certain folk beliefs and practices in both territories; notwithstanding even the occasional acknowledgment, and further elaboration of, such claims in a range of works by some non-Iranian 'oriental' scholars who were known in Iranian circles on other grounds (e.g., works on Iranian and Irish legends by the Indian Parsi scholar Jivanji Jamshedji Modi).

The recuperative projects of "national memory" undertaken by Irish nationalist antiquarians and later historians were undergirded by particular, albeit fluid, modes of epistemological grounding and nationalist positionality. In their overlapping, as well as at times divergent, efforts to "restore" Irish historical familiarity with Ireland's purported ancient Iranian heritage, some Irish nationalist antiquarians from the late eighteenth to the early nineteenth century, and a host of subsequent Irish nationalist historians, archaeologists, linguists, folklorists, and scholars of mythology, drew attention to what they considered as substantial surviving evidential traces of that past. The range of proof cited also included many instances of presumed present-day affinities between Ireland and Iran. These extant comparative correspondences between Ireland and Iran consisted of (otherwise entirely apophenic) presumed similarities between Ireland's Round Towers and Zoroastrian edifices, a range of other seeming archaeological resemblances, the supposed proximity between ancient Irish and Iranian scripts (Ogham and Old Persian cuneiform), and certain sets of alleged linguistic, folklore, and/or mythological correspondences. The models of Ireland's ancient Iranian past, as internally contentious as these were in their historical and epistemological claims, had to contend with competing models of Ireland's alternative oriental and non-oriental pasts. By the early twentieth century, however, all Orient-centered models of Ireland's ancient past were vigorously swept aside by an incrementally ascendant Europe-centric Celticist model, marking what proved to be an irreversible historiographic departure from oriental theories, notwithstanding the occasional flare-up of resurgent oriental models, including in fictional form in Joyce's *Finnegans Wake*. Within a few generations thereafter a new form of historical nescience had occurred in Ireland: that of general unfamiliarity with the once-dominant Orient-centered historiography of ancient

Ireland. As the Orient-centered antiquarian theories had once been, this particular Europe-centered historiographic departure (in contrast to much older Europe-centered models, such as the Scandian theory) and the eventual generational amnesia about former oriental models of Ireland's ancient heritage were *also* products of nationalist historiography. The original underlying aim of the new dominant historiography was to erase any assertion of absolute ethnic distinctions between the majority of Ireland's current population, whether of Gaelic, English, Scots, or Welsh ancestry. At first, this Europe-centric model retained many of the (otherwise mythic) prior structural elements of ancient Ireland, as in the case of allusions to such groups as the Fomorians or the Tuatha de Danann. Gradually, those elements too were debunked as untenable aberrations and utter fables, if not entirely expunged from narratives.

Ultimately, at the heart of all these distinct nationalist projects of historical recovery and recollection was the same anxiety about ancient Ireland being relinquished to the realm of the unknown or misconception, of non-knowledge or erroneous knowledge. The recovery of ancient Ireland in these diverse nationalist epistemological endeavors rested on the belief in knowledge as power (to use the Baconian-cum-Foucauldian formulation of that concept), in this case that of enabling and empowering the 'nation.' This included countering former modes of domestic ignorance of early Ireland (in the form of loss of knowledge, by at least the so-called Middle Ages), as well as of even earlier misinformed or consciously falsified Hellenic and Roman depictions of the presumed ancestors of the Irish. More immediately and much more urgently, however, these claims of corrective nationalist historiography were aimed at resisting and countering the alleged distortions (in the form of instrumentally manufactured false knowledge) about Ireland's past that had been perpetuated by defenders of English imperial domination of Ireland. In effect, all of the competing self-avowedly corrective Irish nationalist historiographic trends aimed at demolishing what they considered to be falsified narratives of ancient Ireland in the service of *imperial* power/knowledge production as well as other modes of distorted historical accounts of that past, and with an underlying objective of historically redeeming the 'Irish nation' (more specifically the 'mere Irish' element of that nation)—without my personally subscribing to any notion of an absolute split between colonial and counter-colonial knowledge and power formations. As Thomas G. Kirsch and Roy Dilley note in *Regimes of Ignorance*:

> ignorance and knowledge are mutually constitutive, and [...] ignorance is not simply the absence of, or a gap in, knowledge. Ignorance is a social fact. [...] the positivity of ignorance [...] has generative social effects, [...] it is produced in specific socio-cultural contexts and [...] there are political consequences that flow from its production and reproduction. [...] Rather than knowledge and ignorance ["not-knowing"] being seen as the negation of each other, they are instead constructed as intimately related, each one deriving its character and meaning from a mutual interaction. As Giorgio Agamben states: "The ways in which we do not know things are just as important (and perhaps even more important) as the ways in which we know them" [...] and he points out that "the articulation of a zone of non-knowledge is the condition [...] of all our knowledge." [...] as Andrew Mathews [...] has [...] pointed out, Michel Foucault's analyses of the reorganization of knowledge in its interconnectedness with the emergence of new forms of power neglects that idea that these

processes are not just about 'knowledge' but also about 'non-knowledge.' In other words, there needs to be an acknowledgment of the fact that the emergence of new forms of power is linked to the momentous transformation of one field of non-knowledge into another field of non-knowledge. Following from the above, we argue that every "regime of knowledge" simultaneously is a "regime of ignorance": by determining legitimate types, modes and objects of knowing [...] The Foucauldian conceptual pair power/knowledge must consequently be broadened to include those aspects of power relations that are associated with people's unknowing, non-knowledge, nescience and ignorance.[3]

The historiographic dominance of the Europe-centric model of ancient Ireland coincided with another form of departure and its accompanying sets of imagined constructs of affinities. This departure followed the partition of Ireland, the establishment of the Irish Free State, and the subsequent civil war in the Free State from 1922 to 1923. It so happened that as the political guardians of the Free State stressed the country's standing as a Western European nation-state (notwithstanding its limited independence and continued subordination to the English crown in certain matters), the educational system of the new state inculcated a template of Irish historical identity as comprised of both Christian (more specifically Catholic) and European-Celtic foundations. There was no underlying premeditated interconnecting logic to these joint developments—which now accorded the Europe-centered model an unequivocally official and hegemonic historiographic status in the Free State—other than the broader nationalist anxiety of Ireland's perceived lack of, or lagging behind, 'modernity' seen through the lens of other "Western" observers (including in the United Kingdom).

The World, History, and Techniques of Worlding Ireland

Through the thematic portal of 'Iran,' this book has interrogated certain applications of, and appeals to, *world history* in a wide range of Irish nationalist framings of the Irish 'nation' and/or the Irish Question. In doing so, it has traced various historical and contemporary Irish nationalist referentialities to Iran, itself a historically changing territorial, political, social, and cultural entity with manifold instrumentalized Irish nationalist interpretive functions. This has served as a means of commenting on different episodes and particular features of heterogeneous and multivalent Irish nationalist imaginations in the context of the broader world from the late eighteenth century up to 1921. Joyce's 1939 *Finnegans Wake*, because of its relevance to this *worlded* perspectives of Irish history and Irishness, has been the only major post-1921 exception to the time frame covered in the book. Ultimately, this study has investigated the ways in which another location in the world (territorial, historical, cultural, and political) served as one of many components of envisioning and forging the Irish national Self, and/or commenting on different modes of Irish struggle against English domination since the early Norman conquests. Needless to say, by no means does the present book pretend to provide a comprehensive account of the range of subjects examined; neither have my selected thematic approach and range of examples covered all aspects of the always evolving and multivocal Irish nationalist expressions of the 'Irish nation' (whether in-the-making or in the presumed past) or of characterizations of the Irish struggle for autonomy or for complete independence.

As in any other work of history, my selective assemblage and arrangement of material for interrogating the past expectedly lack the full range of social, political, religious (or secular) attributes, historical knowledge formations, and/or other forms of individual and collective experiences, aspirations, anxieties, and accumulated memories of those Irish nationalists discussed in this study. We also need to take into account such other factors as the available sources (that may not necessarily encompass the full range of what particular individuals or organizations expressed or envisioned in other settings). Similarly, our modes of interpreting the past also hinge upon the types of questions we pose apropos of the particular past under investigation—with that "past" itself also ultimately circumscribed by our particular mode and focus of inquiry. Moreover, it is important to bear in mind that the particular arrangement of the chapters and topical sequences appearing in this book, as chronological and thematically interconnected as they happen to be, is nonetheless a historiographic organizational choice and a selective form of conceptual and narrative engagement with the history of Irish nationalism during the period under study.

It is imperative to emphasize once again that there was no "natural" or logical underlying interconnection between, or contextual continuum to, all of the frequently distinct patterns of 'Iranian' referentiality in Irish nationalist imaginations. To put it differently, it does not follow that Irish nationalists who championed Iran during the Anglo-Iranian War of 1856–57 also necessarily believed in antiquarian theories of Iranian origins of Ireland's Golden Age and were somehow motivated by such beliefs in condemning the British war effort against Iran. Nor does it follow that those individuals were somehow familiar with the Iran/Erin literary allegories, or that they later embraced Aryanist theories of racial affinity between the ancient Gaels and Iranians due to their advocacy of the Iranian state at the time of the Anglo-Iranian War. We also need to consider the historian's vantage point when looking back in time and determining continuities and discontinuities that could not have been perceived by individuals and organizations who are the subjects of this study. For instance, whereas Vallancey would have known about prior Scythian and Phoenician theories of Irish origins, he would have had no knowledge of Henry O'Brien's subsequent version of the Iranian theory of Irish origins or of Lady Wilde's much later studies of Irish folklore, or of even William Betham's 1842 variant of the Phoenician theory of Irish origins, which also credited the Phoenicians as founders of the Etruscan civilization. Nor did folklore studies in general at the time when Lady Wilde was writing on the subject incorporate the full plethora of cultural and literary theories available today in the field of comparative folklore studies. Similarly, Lady Wilde did not know the theory of Aryan (Iranian) origins of the Irish that she and others had been promoting in the nineteenth century would assume a politically instrumentalist nationalist application in the form of the Pan-Aryan Association (1906), which aimed to unite nationalists from India, Ireland, and Iran. Hence, the chronological and thematic progression of the present book from Vallancey to Lady Wilde and then to the Pan-Aryan Association, and so on, should not be misconstrued as suggesting an interdependent and unified and logical chronological progression between different Aryanist trends in Irish nationalism.

What cannot be disputed is the extent to which Irish nationalist imaginations over such a vast temporal plane were always *worlded*, whether it was in references to Iran, India, Poland, Afghanistan, the Boers in southern Africa, Algerians resisting French imperialism after the 1830s, enslaved peoples of African descent in the United States (in this case, without overlooking the likes of John Mitchel who later defended the system of 'African slavery' in the United States), British occupation of Egypt, and so on. This is not to say the underlying cosmopolitan framing of Irish nationalist platforms and purviews always resulted in universal validation of the struggles of every other group of people against imperialist aggression and/or other forms of repression. Rather, it merely underscores the fact that Irish nationalists overwhelmingly framed their struggle in some form of a world-historical context. While this may be stating the obvious, nationalist *cosmopolitan imaginations* remain a greatly neglected dimension of not only studies of Irish nationalism but of nationalisms in general, notwithstanding the increasing number of studies over the past decades of intersecting nationalist struggles (anti-imperialist or otherwise), such as those in India and Ireland. Even in the case of prior studies that have focused on Irish nationalist advocacy of anti-imperialist struggles in other parts of the world, the theoretical significance of these modes of situating Ireland in various currents of world history (including contrived settings) has generally escaped systematic attention. Within the broader Irish nationalist practices of worlding the Irish experience of colonization and resistance, contemporary Iran after 1907 also featured in Irish nationalist expressions of solidarity with other anti-imperialist struggles—with a more limited and ambivalent precedent for this during the 1856–57 Anglo-Iranian War when only the more 'radical' Irish nationalist factions endorsed the Iranian war effort against the British Empire, and not forgetting that Iran itself in that setting was also a territorial aggressor (in Herat), or that it was the Iranian monarch Nasser al-Din Shah and Iran as a territorial entity that were the object of radical Irish nationalist endorsement at that time, as opposed to the Iranian 'nation' and territorial sovereignty after 1907. During the Anglo-Iranian War, as well as after 1907 (during the Iranian Constitutional Revolution), the Iran/Erin analogy, as in the case of statements made by Frederick Ryan and others, assumed a contemporary political quality in contrast to Thomas Moore's, Denis Florence MacCarthy's, or James Clarence Mangan's distinct literary pairings of Irans of past historical settings with various moments in Irish history, or Lady Wilde's Iran/Erin cultural parity (in terms of alleged present-day folk beliefs dating back to ancient connections between the two lands and peoples), among other such examples.

Different configurations of Irish nationalism, even during the same time frames, had their own temporally, spatially, and politically malleable instrumentalist modes of self-imagining and self-grounding in world-historical settings. After 1922, some of the prior formulations of the Irish Self no longer served the objectives of leading ideologues of the 'nation' in the Free State, and/or were simply no longer applicable under changed domestic, regional, and transregional circumstances, or acceptable in keeping with conventional standards. Nations and nationalist struggles over time contrive for themselves new (and at times simultaneously competing sets of) 'national' genealogies as well as professed future trajectories based on continually dynamic situations, even if retaining key elements of former genealogical and future-oriented templates. With some notable exceptions, as in the case of the likes of Frederick Ryan, Nora Florence Dryhurst, or John Dillon for instance, Irish nationalist world-historical framings of Ireland were generally Ireland-centered in the final analysis and primarily *Self*-regarding. The same can be said of most 'nationalisms' in general. This is not to deny that even the most universalist humanist expressions ultimately proceed from some sense of the Self. Rather, it underscores the fact that expressions of cross-territorial anti-imperialist solidarity with other nations were not *necessarily* predicated on some requisite broader ethical expression of fellow feeling with the population of the particular nation in question as circumstances changed. Whereas during the Anglo-Iranian War of 1856–57 *The Nation* (Dublin) selectively portrayed the Iranian war effort against the invading British forces as bearing some resemblance to the ongoing plight of the Irish and mirroring the Irish struggle against English domination, the same paper refrained from expressing sympathy with the victims of the large-scale Iranian famine of 1870–72, instead of choosing to compare that calamity with Ireland's Great Famine of 1845–51. On the other hand, the competing Irish nationalist mouthpiece *Freeman's Journal* (Dublin), which had supported the British war effort against Iran in 1856–57, was far more responsive to the suffering of Iranian famine victims later on.

Furthermore, in regard to nationalist historiographies, the example of Ireland prior to the formation of the Irish Free State (with Ireland situated in the west of Europe, no less) contradicts across the board statements by the likes of Vinay Lal that "Europe [has functioned] as the Loadstar" of "History," adding that "This is the condition of colonized people everywhere,"[4] or Dipesh Chakrabarty's already quoted verdict that "Europe works as a silent referent in historical knowledge. [...] Third-World historians feel the need to refer to works in European history; historians of Europe do not feel the need to reciprocate." Without even taking into account the long existence in the West of "world history" and, much more recently, also of "global history," such extravagant ahistorical statements more than merely disregard numerous examples of 'European' historical interest in other parts of the world (at the very least since the eighteenth century, even if overlooking the many earlier examples)—and not solely on account of European/Western imperial expansion and/or commercial and military competition around the world. Many 'European' Enlightenment, Romantic, theosophist, and other thinkers, for instance, eagerly and admittedly rummaged through other histories in search of philosophical, scientific, literary, and socio-ethical knowledge. One can certainly make the case that there was a gradual and notable shift in many parts of the world toward adopting methodological approaches first developed in certain regions of the West after the eighteenth century (albeit to different degrees and in different configurations based on localized circumstances)—without disregarding the fact that some of these historiographic methods were themselves products of a long intellectual interaction between the so-called West and other parts of the world, dating back to well before the "European" Renaissance, which itself was heavily indebted to the flow of knowledge from other regions of the world, even if these interconnections frequently remained unacknowledged in later Western historical narratives. Leaving aside that historiographic transformations cannot be entirely reduced to formulaic colonizer-colonized arrangement, and while it is undeniable that in many (but certainly not all) colonized and semi-colonized regions the nationalist elite turned to the West as models of technological progress and/or parliamentary systems (and in some cases also turning to Japan as such a model after the late nineteenth century), it would be a gross oversimplification to suggest "their intellectual outlook appears to have been shorn of any reference to [… their own respective] civilizational pasts"—be it in the case of the Bengali nationalist elite whom Lal writes about, or pan-Africanists in different parts of the world, or many other nationalist elites elsewhere, including in Ireland and Iran.[5] A feature of most anti-imperialist nationalist and/or nativist resistance to imperialism has been the glorification of their own pasts (in the form of a Golden Age), certainly in some dialogical, if not always dialectical, manner. Furthermore, what is entirely overlooked by Lal, Chakrabarty, and others sharing such essentializing historical verdicts is the emergence and rapid expansion of cross-territorial anti-imperialist solidarity networks among the colonized and semi-colonized populations (particularly after the late nineteenth century), with a corresponding expanded interest among nationalist and/or nativist elites (including in post-independence eras) of learning about the histories of other colonized/semi-colonized regions, including historical periods prior to the advent of 'Western' imperial contacts with those regions.

In other words, imperialism, albeit inadvertently, fostered greater interest in *world history*, as evident also in the Irish context—not counting here the history curricula of colonial administrators in many colonies that, while privileging the history of so-called imperial metropoles, also covered different reaches of the empire, albeit in an imperially self-aggrandizing manner. Moreover, leaving aside obvious reasons why many nationalists in colonized and semi-colonized regions of the world would have been more focused on histories of imperial powers, as opposed to other regions of the world, as well as having greater interest after gaining their independence in studying the militarily, economically, industrially and/or scientifically more powerful states, overarching verdicts by the likes of Lal and Chakrabarty suffer from numerous other flawed analytical underpinnings. These include the presumption that interest and referentialities to other regions of the world are solely predicated on *writing* of histories, rather than also of *reading* available histories (including translations in the more familiar languages) about other regions of the world. The average Irish nationalist would have learned about India, Egypt, or Iran not by reading Sanskrit, Hindi, Persian, Arabic, or other such sources, but by perusing available works in more familiar range of languages, including translations of local histories available in English, French, or German, for instance. Similarly, Iranians interested in Chinese history read Persian translations of China's history originally compiled in more familiar European languages, or of works initially translated from Chinese to those European languages, before being translated into Persian. In effect, this was also a question of where, and by whom, such available range of works had been initially produced and access to such works. Iranian nationalists, for example, were certainly interested in India's history, particularly that of the gradual British colonization and subsequent administration of the subcontinent, as well as various forms of nationalist resistance to British rule and India's subsequent partition and Independence (leaving aside the extensive commercial, literary, and other cultural exchanges between the two lands). The overarching verdicts additionally overlook literary and journalistic coverage of non-'Western' regions of the world in colonized, semi-colonized, and postcolonial settings (not to mention in other non-print media by the middle of the twentieth century), among other modes of exposure to those histories and societies—and not even considering here both non-European, as well as European, historical references to pre- and post-1949 China, or the Algerian, Palestinian, Vietnamese, and numerous other liberation movements in different parts of the world. It was often not some ostensible universal lack of interest in 'non-Western' regions of the globe or a presumably "colonized mind" (to borrow from Ngũgĩ wa Thiong'o's concept "decolonizing the mind") that plagued nationalist attitudes to world history in colonized, semi-colonized, and postcolonial societies, but also an array of pragmatic priorities and considerations (whether or not we agree with those choices from our present-day standpoint), as well as practical limitations (communication, print and/or other technology, language, and so on).

The world-historical outlooks coexisting alongside a historical interest in the West, rather than some presumed absolute fixation with Europe as 'the Loadstar' of history, were in part also corollaries of the condition of colonization/semi-colonization, among a wide spectrum of other determining factors, ranging from cross-territorial religious, linguistic, ethnic, and other co-identifications to long-distance commerce, literary exchanges, and numerous other such examples, including the embrace of racial theories. It was at the confluence of the late eighteenth-century so-called European Enlightenment movement and British imperialism that the earliest Iranian theories of ancient Ireland were formulated. British imperial expansion also further *contributed* to the search for, and transmission of, new information and sources that were then selectively utilized by Irish nationalist antiquarians to various ends. It was also imperialism in general that engendered Irish nationalist expressions of solidarity and/or affinity with other contemporary colonized and semi-colonized groups around the world. Imperialism also further necessitated, and in varying degrees facilitated, Irish nationalist familiarity with, and analyses of, British imperial policies, administration, expansion, weaknesses, compromises, and so on in other parts of the world—which is not to imply 'nationalists' were solely concerned with imperial affairs and not with other range of world events and developments (ideological, literary, scientific, artistic, etc.). The overarching notion of a *singular* Europe-oriented gawking historical gaze of the colonized and semi-colonized nationalist elite before and/or after independence is a fiction generated by some self-proclaimed "postcolonial" scholars in search of "grand narratives" (to borrow Jean-François Lyotard's term), in their attempts to essentialize imperial encounters and, inevitably, also (the otherwise manifold) anti-imperialist nationalist imaginations. Otherwise, such totalizing narratives do not reflect the documented multifaceted and multivocal historical experience of actual imperial and counter-imperial encounters (including cross-territorial anti-imperialist solidarities by those residing in so-called imperial metropoles). Nationalist and/or nativist imaginations of the Self under particular conditions of colonization and semi-colonization, as well as following independence, may at times have prioritized certain range of histories, but those imaginations were ultimately world-historical in their conceptualizations of the Self, particularly in regard to other colonized and semi-colonized regions. Ireland was certainly not an exception in this regard. One can easily cite parallels in the case of Egypt, Iran, India, China, the Philippines, Cuba, and numerous other regions. The world-historical Irish nationalist imaginations cross-referenced Ireland (historically and politically) beyond the mere confines of the West/Europe (and certainly well beyond the British Isles). Without overlooking the earlier biblical Mosaic models of population dispersions, or 'medieval' Irish methods of chronicling Ireland's past through cross-referencing actual or fictional contemporaneous major events in other parts of the known world, after the late eighteenth century Irish nationalists continually *worlded* Ireland by means of referring to both Western/European and non-Western/non-European regions of the world. At the same time, these worlding strategies and practices, whether in antiquarian, literary, cultural, and/or political settings, were always carefully crafted and relied on *truncated* histories of elsewhere, taking select slices from histories of Others to interweave or juxtapose with histories of the Self. 'Iran' was one of these (both real and imagined) referential zones appearing in antiquarian, literary, folklore, political, and other settings.

Notes

1. Róisin Healy, *Poland in the Irish Nationalist Imagination*, p.224.
2. See Mansour Bonakdarian, "Iranian coverage of the 1981 paramilitary republican prisoners' hunger strike in Northern Ireland"; idem, "Iranian Consecration of Irish Nationalist 'Martyrs'."
3. Thomas G. Kirsch and Roy Dilley, "An Introduction" in Roy Dilley and Thomas G. Kirsch, eds., *Regimes of Ignorance: Anthropological Perspectives on the Production and Reproduction of Non-Knowledge*. Reprint. New York: Berghahn, 2017 [2015], pp.15, 20, 22–23.
4. Vinay Lal, "Provincializing the West: World History from the Perspective of Indian History" in Benedikt Stuchtey and Eckhardt Fuchs, eds., *Writing World History*, p.278.
5. Ibid., p.283. In this case I am also ignoring Lal's presupposition that the likes of Rammahon Roy, who was far from being a Bengali "nationalist," should somehow have thought of themselves as historically "Indian," rather than Bengalis living in Britain's *Indian* Empire.

BIBLIOGRAPHY OF WORKS CITED

Government Documents

Republic of Ireland

Dáil Debates, vol.135, no.2, 1952.

United Kingdom

[Great Britain] *Correspondence Respecting Relations with Persia*. London: Harrison and Sons, 1857.
[Great Britain] Foreign Office Correspondence. F.O.371 (The National Archives of the United Kingdom, London).
[Great Britain] Foreign Office Correspondence. F.O.539 (The National Archives of the United Kingdom, London).
[Great Britain.] *Parliamentary Debates* (Commons), 3rd series.
[Great Britain] *Parliamentary Debates* (Commons), 4th series.
[Great Britain] *Parliamentary Debates* (Commons), 5th series.

Private Correspondence

Wilfrid Scawen Blunt Papers. General Memoirs, 1910–12. Ms.11-1975 (Fitzwilliam Museum, Cambridge).
Correspondence of E.G. Browne: 1. Letters to Browne from Persia 1910-11. Add. Mss.7604 (Cambridge University Library).
"Papers of William J. Maloney relating to Sir Roger Casement," *Maloney Collection of Irish Historical Papers, 1857-1965* (New York Public Library).

Maps

Arrowsmith, John, "Central Asia; comprising Bokhara, Cabool, Persia, The River Indus, & Countries Eastward of it … By his obliged Servant, J. Arrowsmith. June 1834. (Map) 29. London, Pubd. 15 Feby. 1842, by J. Arrowsmith, 10 Soho Square." Digital Public Library America map collection: (https://dp.la/search?q=john+arrowsmith+persia).

George, Philip and Son, 1852 map of Persia and Kabul (http://www.cais-soas.com/CAIS/Images2/persian_gulf/British_map_of_Persia__Kabul_by_Philip_George_and_Son_1852WM.png).
Johnston, Alexander Keith, 1843 map of Persia (http://www.cais-soas.com/CAIS/Images2/persian_gulf/Persia_A_K_Johnston_National_Atlas_1843WM.png).
Speed, John, "The theatre of the empire of Great Britaine: presenting an exact geography of the kingdomes of England, Scotland, Ireland, . . .," 1612 (https://cudl.lib.cam.ac.uk/view/PR-ATLAS-00002-00061-00001/1).

Periodicals and Encyclopedias

Academy (London)
Āftāb (Tehran)
Anti-Imperialist (Dublin)
The Argus (Melbourne)
Asiatic Journal and Monthly Register for British India and Its Dependencies (London)
Assr-e Jadid (Tehran)
Blackwood's Edinburgh Magazine
Belfast News-Letter
British Critic (London)
British Review and London Critical Journal
Cambridge Review
Catholic Progress (London & Dublin)
Century Path: A Magazine Devoted to the Brotherhood of Humanity and Promulgation of Theosophy ... (Point Loma, California)
Chambers's Encyclopædia: A Dictionary of Universal Knowledge for the People (Edinburgh)
Church Missionary Gleaner (London)
Church Missionary Intelligencer: A Monthly Journal of Missionary Information (London)
Church Missionary Intelligencer and Record (London)
The Citizen (New York)
The Economist (London)
Cork Examiner
Critical Review (London)
Daily News (London)
Dana: An Irish Magazine of Independent Thought (Dublin)
Democratic Review of British and Foreign Politics, History, & Literature (London)
Diplomatic Review (London)
Dublin Evening Post
Dublin Monthly Magazine
Dublin Penny Journal
Dublin University Magazine
Eclectic Review (London)
Edinburgh Monthly Magazine
Edinburgh Magazine
Edinburgh Review
Egypt (London)
Éire-Ireland (Dublin)
Encyclopaedia Britannica; or A Dictionary of Arts, Sciences, and Miscellaneous Literature; Enlarged and Improved (Edinburgh; London)
Englishwoman's Review of Social and Industrial Questions (London)
Ettelā'āt (Tehran)
European Magazine and London Review

Evening Post (New York)
Folklore (London)
Fraser's Magazine (London)
Freedom: A Journal of Libertarian Thought, Work and Literature (London)
Freeman's Journal (Dublin)
The Gael/An Gaodhal (New York)
Gaelic American (New York)
Gentleman's Magazine (London)
Habl al-Matin (Calcutta)
Habl al-Matin (Tehran)
The Hibernian (Dublin)
Hindusthanee Student: Official Bulletin of the Hindustan Association of America (Urbana, Illinois, US), Second Series
Illustrated London News
The Independent (New York)
Irān-e Nou (Tehran)
Irische blätter (Berlin)
The Irish-American (New York)
Irish Independent (Dublin)
The Irish Law Times and Solicitors' Journal (Dublin)
Irish Literary Gazette (Dublin, Cork, Belfast and Galway)
Irish News (New York)
Irish Penny Journal (Dublin)
Irish Review (Dublin)
The Irish Shield and Monthly Milesian (New York)
Irish Theosophist: A Monthly Magazine Devoted to Universal Brotherhood, The Study of Eastern Literature and Occult Science (Dublin)
Irish Times (Dublin)
Irish Worker (Dublin)
Die Islamische Welt: Illustrierte Monatsschrift für Politik, Wirtschaft und Kultur (Berlin)
Journal of the East India Association (London)
Journal of the Home Rule Union (London)
Journal of the Ivernian Society (Cork)
Justice (London)
Kāveh (Berlin)
Literary Gazette (London)
London Gazette
Literature (New York)
Majles (Tehran)
Manchester Guardian
Marion Daily Mirror (Marion, Ohio)
Meath Chronicle
The Meddler (Dublin)
Modern Review (Calcutta)
Morning Post (London)
The Nation (Dublin)
Nation (London)
National Review (London)
New Age (London)
New York Times
New York Tribune
New Zealand Herald (Auckland)
News Letter of the Friends of Irish Freedom National Bureau of Information (Washington, D.C.)

Northern Star (Belfast)
Old Jonathan: The District and Parish Helper (London)
Pall Mall Gazette (London)
Parry's Literary Journal (Salt Lake City, US)
Penny Cyclopædia of the Society for the Diffusion of Useful Knowledge (London)
The Penny Illustrated Paper and Illustrated Times (London)
Positivist Review (London)
Proceedings of the Royal Irish Academy (Dublin)
Quarterly Review (London)
Review of Reviews (US edition, New York)
Rouznāmeh-ye Dowlat-e Āliyeh-ye Irān (Tehran)
Rouznāmeh-ye Elmi (Tehran)
Rouznāmeh-ye Vaqāye'-e Ettefāqiyeh (Tehran)
Saturday Review of Politics, Literature, Science, and Art (London)
Scissors and Paste (Dublin)
Scots Observer (Edinburgh; London)
Select Reviews, and Spirit of the Foreign Magazines (Philadelphia)
Sentimental and Masonic Magazine (Dublin)
Sherāfat (Tehran)
Sinn Féin (Dublin)
Spectator (London)
The Standard (London)
Straits Times (Singapore)
The Sun (New York)
The Sun and Central Press (London)
The Tablet (London)
The Times (London)
Times of India (Bombay)
T.P.'s Weekly (London)
Trübner's American and Oriental Literary Record (London)
United Ireland (Dublin)
The United Irishman (Dublin, 1848)
The United Irishman (Dublin, 1899–1906)
Ulster Journal of Archaeology (Belfast)
Workers' Republic (Dublin)

Journal Articles, Book Chapters, Encyclopedia Entries, Presentations, Data Bases

Abu el-Haj, Nadia, "Reflections on Archaeology and Israeli Settler-Nationhood," *Radical History Review* 86, Spring 2003, pp.149–63.

Adamiyat, Fereydoun (Thomas, M. Ricks Translator), "Problems in Iranian Historiography," *Iranian Studies* 4(4), Autumn 1971, pp.132–56.

Ahmad, Toheed, "Nation of Saints and Scholars: A Portrait of Ireland," *Criterion* (Pakistan) 3(3), July–September 2008.

Ahmadi Arian, Amir, "The Unstable People of a Tumultuous Land: Persia Through the Eyes and Feet of Hajji Baba of Isfahan," *Iranian Studies* 49(1), 2016, pp.57–75.

Allen, Nicholas, "Ryan, Frederick Michael (1873–1913)" in James McGuire and James Quinn, eds., *Dictionary of Irish Biography from the Earliest Times to the Year 2002. Volume 8: Patterson-Stagg.* Cambridge: Cambridge University Press, 2009, pp.690–91.

Almond, Ian, "Tales of Buddha, Dreams of Arabia: Joyce and Images of the East," *Orbis. Littererum* 57, 2002, pp.18–30.

Al-Qattan, Najwa, "When Mothers Ate Their Children: Wartime Memory and the Language of Food in Syria and Lebanon," *International Journal of Middle East Studies* 46(4), November 2014, pp.719–36.

Amanat, Abbas, "Hajji Baba of Ispahan" (2003), *Encyclopaedia Iranica* (http://www.iranica.com/articles/hajji-baba-of-ispahan).

Amanat, Abbas, "Herat vi. The Herat Question" (2003, 2012), *Encyclopaedia Iranica* (http://www.iranicaonline.org/articles/herat-vi).

Amanat, Abbas, "Historiography viii. Qajar Period," *Encyclopaedia Iranica* (http://www.iranicaonline.org/articles/historiography-viii).

Amanat, Abbas, "The Kayanid Crown and Qajar Reclaiming of Royal Authority," *Iranian Studies* 34(1–4), 2001, pp.17–30.

Amanat, Abbas, "Pur-e ḵāqān wa andiša-ye bāzyābi-e tāriḵ-e melli-e Irān," *Iran Nameh* 17, Winter 1999, pp.5–54.

Amanat, Abbas and Farzin Vejdani, "Jalāl-al-Din Mirzā," *Encyclopaedia Iranica* (iranicaonline.org/articles/Jalal-al-Din Mirza).

Andrews, John Harwood, "Charles Vallancey and the Map of Ireland," *Geographical Journal* 132(1), March 1966, pp.48–61.

Andrews, John Harwood, "Colonial Cartography in a European Setting: The Case of Tudor Ireland" in David Woodward, ed., The History of Cartography. Volume 3: Cartography in the European Renaissance. Chicago: University of Chicago Press, 2007, pp.1670–83.

Assmann, Aleida, "How History Takes Place" in Indra Sengupta, ed., *Memory, History, and Colonialism: Engaging With Pierre Nora in Colonial and Postcolonial Contexts*. London: German Historical Institute, 2009, pp.151–65.

Atabaki, Touraj, "Constitutionalism in Iran and Its Asian Interdependencies," *Comparative Studies of South Asia, Africa and the Middle East* 28(1), 2008, pp.142–53.

Avery, Peter, "Ouseley, Gore," *Encyclopaedia Iranica* (http://www.iranicaonline.org/articles/ouseley-sir-gore).

Avery, Peter, "Ouseley, William," *Encyclopaedia Iranica* (http://www.iranicaonline.org/articles/ouseley-sir-william).

Barker, George Fisher Russell, "Ouseley, Sir Gore (1770–1844)" in Sidney Lee, ed., Dictionary of National Biography. *Volume XLII: O'Duinn—Owen*. London: Smith, Elder, & Co., 1895, pp.361–62.

Bartlett, Robert, "Ancient Iran in the Imagination of Medieval West" in Ali Ansari, ed., *Perceptions of Iran: History, Myths and Nationalism From Medieval Persia to the Islamic Republic*. London: I.B, Tauris, 2014, pp.37–46.

Beard, Michael, "European Travelers in the Trans-Caspian Before 1917," *Cahiers du monde russe et soviétique* 13(4), 1973, pp.590–96.

Beaufort, Louisa Catherine, "An Essay Upon the State of Architecture and Antiquities, Previous to the Landing of the Anglo-Normans in Ireland," *Transactions of the Royal Irish Academy* (Dublin) 15, 1828, pp.101–241.

Beiner, Guy and Joep Leerssen, "Why Irish History Starved: A Virtual Historiography," *Field Day Review* 3, 2007, pp.67–81.

Bell, J. Bowyer, "Ireland and the Spanish Civil War, 1936–1939," *Studia Hibernica* 9, 1969, pp.137–63.

Bender, Jill, "The Imperial Politics of Famine: The 1873–74 Bengal Famine and Irish Parliamentary Nationalism," *Éire-Ireland* 42(1&2), Spring/Summer 2007, pp.132–56.

Benstock, Bernard, "Persian in *Finnegans Wake*," *Philological Quarterly* 44(1), January 1965, pp.100–109.

Bobotis, Andrea, "From Egypt to Ireland: Lady Augusta Gregory and Cross-Cultural Nationalisms in Victorian Ireland," *Romanticism and Victorianism on the Net* 48, November 2007 (http://www.erudit.org/revue/ravon/2007/v/n48/017439ar.html).

Bonakdarian, Mansour, "India: IX. Political and Cultural Relations: Qajar Period, Early 20th Century," *Encyclopaedia Iranica*, Vol. XIII, Fascicle 1. New York: Encyclopaedia Iranica Foundation, 2004, pp.32–44.

Bonakdarian, Mansour, "Iranian Consecration of Irish Nationalist 'Martyrs': The Islamic Republic of Iran and the 1981 Republican Prisoners' Hunger Strike in Northern Ireland," *Social History* 43(3), August 2018, pp.293–331.

Bonakdarian, Mansour, "The Easter Rising as a Milestone in Iranian Nationalist Appraisals of the Irish Question," *American Journal of Irish Studies* 14, 2017, pp.51–81.

Bonakdarian, Mansour, "Iranian Coverage of the 1981 Paramilitary Republican Prisoners' Hunger Strike in Northern Ireland," *Social History* Blog Post, May 2018 (http://socialhistoryblog.com/iranian-coverage-of-the-1981-paramilitary-republican-prisoners-hunger-strike-in-northern-ireland-by-mansour-bonakdarian/).

Bonakdarian, Mansour, "Iranian Nationalism and Global Solidarity Networks" in Houchang E. Chehabi, ed., *Iran in the Middle East: Transnational Encounters and Social History*. London: I.B. Tauris, 2015, pp.77–119.

Bonakdarian, Mansour, "Iranian Studies in 'the United Kingdom' in the 20th Century," *Iranian Studies* 43(2), 2010, pp.265–93.

Bonakdarian, Mansour, "Locating Ireland in Iran of Thomas Moore's 'The Veiled Prophet': Allegory, History, and Unsettled Interpretive Trajectories," *European Romantic Review* 30(5–6), November 2019, pp.519–40.

Bonakdarian, Mansour, "Negotiating Universal Values and Cultural and National Parameters: Iran and Turkey at the First Universal Races Congress (London, 1911)," *Radical History Review* 92, Spring 2005, pp.118–32.

Bonakdarian, Mansour and Manoutchehr Eskandari-Qajar, "Malcolm, Major-General Sir John (1769–1833)," *Encyclopaedia Iranica Online*, October 2021 (https://referenceworks.brillonline.com/entries/encyclopaedia-iranica-online/malcolm-sir-john-COM_362631).

Bongiovanni, Lynne A., "'Turbaned Faces Going By': James Joyce and Irish Orientalism," *Ariel: A Review of International English Literature* 38(4), October 2007, pp.25–49.

Bos, Jacques, "Nineteenth-Century Historicism and Its Predecessors: Historical Experience, Historical Ontology and Historical Method" in Rens Bod, Rapp Maat, and Thijs Weststeijn, eds., *The Making of the Humanities. Volume II: From Early Modern to Modern Disciplines*. Amsterdam: Amsterdam University Press, 2012, pp.131–47.

Boyne, Patricia and John O'Donovan, "Letters From the County Down: John O'Donovan's First Field Work for the Ordnance Survey," *Studies: An Irish Quarterly Review* 73(290), Summer 1984, pp.106–16.

Bradford, Curtis, "Yeats and Maud Gonne," *Texas Studies in Literature and Language* 3(4), Winter 1962, pp.452–74.

Brasted, Howard, "Indian Nationalist Development and the Influence of Irish Home Rule, 1870–1886," *Modern Asian Studies* 14(1), 1980, pp.37–63.

"Brief Notices of Persian, and of the Language called Zend. By John Homer, Esq., M.R.A.S., Formerly President of the Society. Communicated by the Rev. Dr. Wilson, Honorary President" (Presented on January 20, 1853), *Journal of the Bombay Branch of the Royal Asiatic Society* 5(18), July 1853, pp.95–108.

Brown, Michael Philip and Lesa Ní Mhunghaile, "Futures Past: Enlightenment and Antiquarianism in the Eighteenth Century" in Thomas Bartlett and James Kelly, eds., *The Cambridge History of Ireland: Volume III: 1730–1880*. Cambridge: Cambridge University Press. 2018, pp.380–405.

Brown, Stephen J., "The Question of Irish Nationality," *Studies: An Irish Quarterly Review* 1(4), December 1912, pp.634–54.

Brown, Wallace Cable, "Thomas Moore and English Interest in the East," *Studies in Philology* 34(4), October 1937, pp.576–88.
Buckley, Mary, "John Mitchel, Ulster and Irish Nationality (1842–1848)," *Studies: An Irish Quarterly Review* 65(257), Spring 1976, pp.30–44.
Bulliet, Richard W., "Naw Bahār and the Survival of Iranian Buddhism," *Iran* 14, 1976, pp.140–45.
Burns, Robert E., "Parsons, Priests, and the People: The Rise of Irish Anti-Clericalism 1785–1789," *Church History* 31(2), June 1962, pp.151–63.
Burton, Antoinette, "On the First Anglo-Afghan War, 1839–42: Spectacle of Disaster" (http://www.branchcollective.org/?ps_articles=antoinette-burton-on-the-first-anglo-afghan-war-1839-42-spectacle-of-disaster).
Burton, Jonathan, "The Shah's Two Ambassadors: *The Travels of the Three English Brothers* and the Global early Modern" in Brinda Charry and Gitanjali Shahani, eds., *Emissaries in Early Modern Literature and Culture: Mediation, Transmission, Traffic, 1550–1700.* Farnham, Surrey: Ashgate, 2009.
Butler, Marilyn, "Orientalism" in David B. Pirie, ed., *The Penguin History of Literature. Volume 5: The Romantic Period.* London: Penguin, 1994, pp.395–447.
Byrne, Francis John, "Ireland Before the Norman Invasion" in Theodore William Moody, ed., *Irish Historiography, 1936–70.* Dublin: Irish Committee of Historical Sciences, 1971, pp.1–15.
Calmard, Jean, "Anglo-Persian War (1856–57)" (1985, 2011), *Encyclopaedia Iranica* (http://www.iranicaonline.org/articles/anglo-persian-war-1856-57).
Campbell, Lyle, "Why Sir William Jones Got it All Wrong, or Jones' Role in How to Establish Language Families," *Anuario del Seminario de Filologia Vasca Julio de Urquijo/International Journal of Basque Linguistics and Philology* 40, 2006, pp.245–64.
Campbell, Matthew, "Lyrical Unions: Mangan, O'Hussey and Ferguson," *Irish Studies Review* 8(3), December 2000, pp.325–38.
Candy, Catherine, "Relating Feminisms, Nationalisms and Imperialisms: Ireland, India and Margaret Cousins's Sexual Politics," *Women's History Review* 3(4), 1994, pp.581–94.
Cannon, Garland Hampton, "Sir William Jones's Persian Linguistics," *Journal of the American Oriental Society* 78(4), October–December 1958, pp.262–73.
Canny, Nicholas, "The Formation of the Irish Mind: Religion, Politics and Gaelic Irish Literature 1580–1750," *Past & Present* 95(1), May 1982, pp.91–116.
Carey, John, "The Ancestry of Fénius Farsaid," *Celtica* 21(1990), pp.104–12.
Carroll, Francis M., "Ireland Among the Nations of the Earth: Ireland's Foreign Relations from 1923 to 1949," *Études irlandaises* 41(1), 2016, pp.35–52.
Chuto, Jacques, "James Clarence Mangan: In Exile at Home," *Études irlandaises* 1(1), 1976, pp.35–50.
Chuto, Jacques, "Militant Nationalist Verse From 1798 to 1848," *Études irlandaises* 4(1), 1979, pp.239–69.
Cole, Juan R. I., "Invisible Occidentalism: Eighteenth-Century Indo-Persian Constructions of the West," *Iranian Studies* 25(3–4), 1992, pp.3–16.
Collombier-Lakeman, Pauline, "Ireland and the Empire: The Ambivalence of Irish Constitutional Nationalism," *Radical History Review* 104, 2009, pp.57–76.
Conacher, James Blennerhasset, "British Policy in the Anglo-American Enlistment Crisis of 1855–1856," *Proceedings of the American Philosophical Society* 136(4), December 1992, pp.533–76.
Conrad, Sebastian, "Enlightenment in Global History: A Historiographical Critique," *American Historical Review* 117(4), October 2012, pp.999–1027.
Corbin, Henry, "Āẕar Kayvān," *Encyclopaedia Iranica* (http://www.iranicaonline.org/articles/azar-kayvan-priest).
Coughlan, Patricia, "'Fold over Fold, Inveterately Convolv'd': Some Aspects of Mangan's Intertextuality" in Birgit Bamsbäck and Martin Croghan, eds., *Anglo-Irish and Irish Literature: Aspects of Language and Culture Volume 2.* Uppsala: S. Academiae Ubsaliensis, 1988, pp.191–200.

Cunningham, Bernadette, "'Foras Feasa ar Éirinn' and the Historical Origins of Irish Catholic Identity," *New Hibernia Review* 5(4), Winter 2001, pp.144–47.

Crone, Patricia, "MOQANNA'" (2011, 2012) *Encyclopaedia Iranica* (https://iranicaonline.org/articles/moqanna).

D'Alton, John, "Essay on the Ancient History, Religion, Learning, Arts, and Government of Ireland" ("Introduction" and "Period First From the Birth of Christ to the Arrival of St. Patrick, A.D. 431"), *Transactions of the Royal Irish Academy (Dublin)* 16(II), 1831, pp.3–170 Under the "Antiquities" Section.

Davin, Anna, "Introduction" (Irish History Feature), *History Workshop* 31, Spring 1991, pp.95–104.

Davis, Dick, "FITZGERALD, EDWARD" (1999), *Encyclopaedia Iranica* (http://www.iranica.com/articles/fitzgerald-).

De Bruijn, J. T. P., "Hammer-Purgstall, Joseph Freiherr von," *Encyclopaedia Iranica* (http://www.iranicaonline.org/articles/hammer-purgstall).

De Nie, Michael, "'Speed the Mahdi!' The Irish Press and Empire During the Sudan Conflict of 1883–1885," *Journal of British Studies* 51(4), October 2012, pp.883–909.

Delury, John Patrick, "Ex Conflictu Et Collisione: The Failure of Irish Historiography, 1745 to 1790," *Eighteenth-Century Ireland/Iris an dá chultúr* 15, 2000, pp.9–37.

Dickson, David, "No Scythians Here: Women and Marriage in Seventeenth Century Ireland" in Margaret MacCurtain and Mary O'Dowd, eds., *Women in Early Modern Ireland*. Edinburgh: Edinburgh University Press, 1991, pp.223–35.

Dillon, Myles, "Lebor Gabála Érenn," *Journal of the Royal Society of Antiquaries of Ireland* 86(1), 1956, pp.62–72.

Doherty, Gabriel, "National Identity and the Study of Irish History," *English Historical Review* 111(441), April 1996, pp.324–49.

Dorson, Richard M., "The First Group of British Folklorists," *Journal of American Folklore* 68(267), January–March 1955, pp.1–8.

Dunne, Fergus, "The Politics of Translation in Francis Sylvester Mahony's 'The Rogueries of Thomas Moore,'" *European Romantic Review* 23(4), August 2012, pp.453–74.

Dutta, Ashim, "India in Yeats's Early Imagination: Mohini Chatterjee and Kālidāsa," *International Yeats Studies* 2(2), 2018, pp.20–39.

Dwan, David, "Romantic Nationalism: History and Illusion in Ireland," *Modern Intellectual History* 14(3), 2017, pp.717–45.

Ehrlich, Heyward, "'Araby' in Context: The 'Splendid Bazaar,' Irish Orientalism and James Clarence Mangan," *James Joyce Quarterly* 35, 1998, pp.309–31.

Ekbal, Kamran and Lutz Richter-Bernburg, "Cormick, John," *Encyclopaedia Iranica* (http://www.iranica.com/articles/cormick-john).

English, Richard, "Peadar O'Donnell: Socialism and the Republic, 1925–37," *Saothar* 14, 1989, pp.47–58.

Epstein, Edmund L., "James Joyce and the Way of All Flesh," *James Joyce Quarterly* 7(1), Fall 1969, pp.22–29.

Ernst, Carl W., "The *Dabistan* and Orientalist Views of Sufism" in Jamal Malik and Saeed Zarrabi-Zadeh, eds., *Sufism East and West: Mystical Islam and Cross-Cultural Exchange in the Modern World*. Leiden: Brill, 2019, pp.33–52.

Erskine, William, "Account of the Cave-Temple of Elephanta" (read on November 2, 1813) in *Transactions of the Literary Society of Bombay (Volume I)*. London: Longman, Hurst, Rees, Orme, and Brown; and John Murray, 1819, pp.198–250.

Erskine, William, "Observations on Two Sepulchural Urns Found at Bushire, in Persia" (read on July 6, 1813) in *Transactions of the Literary Society of Bombay (Volume I)*. London: Longman, Hurst, Rees, Orme, and Brown; and John Murray, 1819, pp.191–97.

Erskine, William, "On the Authenticity of the Desatir, With Remarks on the Account of the Mahabadi Religion Contained in the Dabistan" (Read on May 25, 1819) in *Transactions of the*

Literary Society of Bombay. Volume II. London: Longman, Hurst, Rees, Orme, and Brown; and John Murray, 1820, pp.342–76.

Erskine, William, "On the Sacred Books and Religion of the Parsis" (Read on April 27, 1819) in *Transactions of the Literary Society of Bombay. Volume II.* London: Longman, Hurst, Rees, Orme, and Brown; and John Murray, 1820, pp.295–341.

Eskandari-Qajar, Manoutchehr, "Persian Ambassadors, their Circassians, and the Politics of Elizabethan and Regency England," *Iranian Studies* 44(2), March 2011, pp.251–71.

Faherty, Shane, "'A Few Good Canons?': Canon Ulick Bourke and Clerical Reaction to the Outbreak of the Land War" in Brian Casey, ed., *Defying the Law of the Land: Agrarian Radicals in Irish History.* Foreword by Carla King. Dublin: History Press of Ireland, 2013, Chapter 7.

Fegan, Melissa, "'Every Irishman is an Arab': James Clarence Mangan's Eastern "Translations"," *Translation and Literature* 22, 2013, pp.195–214.

Fenton, Laurence, "Charles Rowcroft, Irish-Americans, and the 'Recruitment Affair', 1855–1856," *Historical Journal* 53(4), December 2010, pp.963–82.

Ferdowsi, Ali, "Ḥājj Sayyāḥ," *Encyclopaedia Iranica* (http://www.iranicaonline.org/articles/hajj-sayyah).

Ferrier, R. W., "Edward Fitzgerald, a Reader 'Of Taste', and 'Umar Khayyâm 1809–1883," *Iran* 24, 1986, pp.161–87.

Ferriter, Diarmaid, "The Historical Climate of James Joyce's *Finnegans Wake,* 1922–39." Lecture Presented at the 23rd International James Joyce Symposium. University College Dublin, June 14, 2012 (https://www.youtube.com/watch?v=3UUtsYMZf7k).

Fischer, Joachim, "A Future Ireland under German Rule: Dystopia as Propaganda During World War I," *Utopian Studies* 18(3), 2007, pp.345–63.

Fischer-Tiné, Harald, "Indian Nationalism and the 'World Forces': Transnational and Diasporic Dimensions of the Indian Freedom Movement on the Eve of the First World War," *Journal of Global History* 2(3), November 2007, pp.325–44.

Fisher, Michael H., "Persian Professor in Britain: Mirza Muhammad Ibrahim at the East India Company's College, 1826–44," *Comparative Studies of South Asia, Africa and the Middle East* 21(1&2), 2001, pp.24–32.

Floor, Willem M., "The First Printing-Press in Iran," *Zeitschrift der Deutschen Morgenländischen Gesellschaft* 130(2), 1980, pp.369–71.

Foley, Michael, "Colonialism and Journalism in Ireland," *Journalism Studies* 5(3), 2004, pp.373–85.

Foley, Michael, "The Reporting of Edmond O'Donovan: Literary Journalism and the Great Game" in Richard Keeble and John Tulloch, eds., *Global Literary Journalism: Exploring the Journalistic Imagination.* New York: Peter Lang, 2012, Chapter 13.

Foster, Roy F., "History and the Irish Question," *Transactions of the Royal Historical Society* 33, 1983, pp.169–92.

Foucault, Michel, "Of Other Spaces: Utopias and Heterotopias" in Neil Leach, ed., *Rethinking Architecture: A Reader in Cultural Theory.* New York: Routledge, 1997, pp.330–36.

Fozdar, Vahid, "'That Grand Primeval and Fundamental Religion': The Transformation of Freemasonry into a British Imperial Cult," *Journal of World History* 22(3), 2011, pp.493–525.

Gailey, Alan, "Folk-Life Study and the Ordnance Survey Memoirs" in Alan Gailey and Dáithí Ó hÓgáin, eds., *Gold Under the Furze: Studies in Folk Tradition.* Dublin: Glendale Press, 1982, pp.150–64.

Gallagher, Tony, "Addressing Conflict and Tolerance Through the Curriculum" in Michelle J. Bellino and James H. Williams, eds., *(Re)Constructing Memory: Education, Identity, and Conflict.* Boston: Sense Publishers, 2017, pp.191–208.

Garrigan Mattar, Sinéad, "'Wage for Each People Her Hand Has Destroyed': Lady Gregory's Colonial Nationalism," *Irish University Review* 34(1), Spring–Summer, 2004, pp.49–66.

Gheissari, Ali, "Authorial Voices and the Sense of an Ending in Persian Diaries: Notes on E'temād al-Saltaneh and Alam," *Iranian Studies* 49(4), 2016, pp.693–723.

Gibbons, Luke, "Race Against Time: Racial Discourse and Irish History," *Oxford Literary Review* 13(1–2), 1991, pp.95–117.

Gibbons, Luke, "Recasting the Rising: 1916 on the World Stage." Lecture Presented at "The Theatre of War Symposium," Abbey Theatre (Dublin), January 22, 2015 (https://www.youtube.com/watch?v=Xv10_s3X4FA).

Gibbons, Luke, "Romantic Ireland: 1750–1845" in James Chandler, ed., *The Cambridge History of English Romantic Literature*. Cambridge: Cambridge University Press, 2009, pp.182–203.

Gocheleishvili, Iago, "Georgian Connections of the Iranian Constitutional Revolution of 1905–1911," *Central Eurasian Studies Review* 5(1), 2006, pp.10–14.

Going, William T., "A Peacock Dinner: The Homage of Pound and Yeats to Wilfrid Scawen Blunt," *Journal of Modern Literature* 1(3), March 1971, pp.303–10.

Goldberg, Gerald Y., "'Ireland Is the Only Country...': Joyce and the Jewish Dimension," *The Crane Bag* 6(1), 1982, pp.5–12.

Goldsmid, Frederic, "Notes on Recent Persian Travel," *Journal of the Royal Geographical Society (London)* 44, 1874, pp.183–203.

Good, Peter, "The East India Company's *Farmān*, 1622–1747," *Iranian Studies* 52(1–2), 2019, pp.181–97.

Gray, Peter, "Famine and Land in Ireland and India, 1845–1880: James Caird and the Political Economy of Hunger," *Historical Journal* 49(1), 2006, pp.193–215.

Green, Abigail, "Sir Moses Montefiore and the Making of the 'Jewish International'," *Journal of Modern Jewish Studies* 7(3), November 2008, pp.287–307.

Gregory, Allan, "Thomas Moore's Orientalism" in Peter Cochran, ed., *Byron and Orientalism*. Newcastle: Cambridge Scholar's Press, 2006, pp.173–82.

Grey, Louis Herbert, "The Kings of Early Irān According to the Sidrā Rabbā," *Zeitschrift für Assyriologie und verwandte Gebiete* 19, 1905–1906, pp.272–87.

Grogan, Jane. *The Persian Empire in English Renaissance Writing, 1549–1622*. Basingstoke: Palgrave Macmillan.2013.

Halloran, Clare, "Harping on the Past: Translating Antiquarian Learning into Popular Culture in Early Nineteenth-Century Ireland" in Melissa Calaresu, Filippo de Vivo and Joan-Pau Rubies, eds., *Exploring Cultural History: Essays in Honour of Peter Burke*. Farnham, England: Ashgate, 2010, pp.327–43.

Harootunian, Harry D., "The Benjamin Effect: Modernism, Repetition, and the Path to Different Cultural Imaginaries" in Michael P. Steinberg, ed., *Walter Benjamin and the Demands of History*. Ithaca: Cornell University Press, 1996, pp.62–87.

Haslam, Richard, "'Broad Farce and Thrilling Tragedy': Mangan's Fiction and Irish Gothic," *Éire-Ireland* 41(3&4), Fall/Winter 2006, pp.215–44.

Hayes, Richard, "A Famous Irish War Correspondent," *Studies: An Irish Quarterly Review* 36(141), March 1947, pp.40–48.

Heaney, Seamus, "Singing High: James Clarence Mangan," *Poetry Ireland Review* 77, 2003, pp.10–17.

Hearne, Dana, "The Irish Citizen 1914–1916: Nationalism, Feminism, and Militarism," *Canadian Journal of Irish Studies* 18(1), July 1992, pp.1–14.

Heine, Heinrich. *Tragödien, nebst einem lyrischen Intermezzo*. Berlin: Ferdinand Dümmler, 1823.

Hill, Roland, "Lord Acton and the Catholic Reviews," *Blackfriars* 36(429), December 1955, pp.469–82.

Hogan, Ciara, "'Lost Hero of the Past': Ruin, Wound, and the Failure of Idealism in the Poetry of James Clarence Mangan," *Études irlandaises* 35(1), 2010, pp.131–46.

Holzapfel, Rudolf Patrick, "Mangan's Poetry in the 'Dublin University Magazine': A Bibliography," *Hermathena* 105 (Autumn 1967), pp.40–54.

Hovian, Andranik, "Jahān-namā-ye Jadid[:] Nokhostin assar-e Farssi-zaban-e Joqrāfiyā -ye Jahān," *Payām-e Bahārestān* (Tehran), second series 2(6), Winter 1388 (2010), pp.593–94.

Howes, Marjorie, "Joyce, colonialism, and nationalism" in Derek Attridge, ed., *The Cambridge Companion to James Joyce*. 2nd edition. Cambridge: Cambridge University Press, 2004 [1990], pp.254–271.
Hurwitz, Harold M., "Yeats and Tagore," *Comparative Literature* 16(1), Winter 1964, pp.55–64.
Ibrahim, Vivian, "Sailors, Merchants, Migrants: From the Sack of Baltimore to World War II" in Oliver Scharbrodt,Tuula Sakaranaho,Adil Hussain Khan,Yafa Shanneik, and Vivian Ibrahim, eds.,*Muslims in Ireland: Past and Present*. Edinburgh: Edinburgh University Press, 2015, pp.27–48.
Ibrahim, Vivian, "The Mir of India in Ireland: Nationalism and Identity of an Early 'Muslim' Migrant," *Temenos: Nordic Journal of Comparative Religion* 46(2), 2010, pp.153–74.
Ingersoll, Earl G., "The Psychic Geography of Joyce's 'Dubliners'," *New Hibernia Review* 6(4), Winter 2002, pp.98–107.
Ireland, Aideen M., "Colonel William Gregory Wood-Martin Antiquary, 1847–1917," *Journal of Irish Archaeology* 10, 2001, pp.1–11.
Irslinger, Brita, "Geographies of Identity: Celtic Philology and the Search for Origins in Ireland and Germany" in Joachim Grage and Thomas Mohnike, eds., *Geographies of Knowledge and Imagination in 19th Century Philological Research on Northern Europe*. Newcastle upon Tyne: Cambridge Scholars, 2017, pp. 174–218.
Islam, Shamsul, "The Influence of Eastern Philosophy on Yeats's Later Poetry," *Twentieth Century Literature* 19(4), October 1973, pp.283–90.
Jacobs, Joseph, "Anglo-Israelism" in Isidore Singer, ed., *The Jewish Encyclopedia. Volume I*. New York: Funk and Wagnalls Company, 1901, pp.600–601.
Jain, Sushil Kumar, "Indian Elements in the Poetry of Yeats: On Chatterji and Tagore," *Comparative Literature Studies* 7(1), March 1970, pp.82–96.
James, David, "An Irish Visitor to the Court of the Shah of Persia in 1835: Extract From the Unpublished Diary of Sir Francis Hopkins of Athboy," *Studies: An Irish Quarterly Review* 60(238), Summer, 1971, pp.139–54.
Javadi, Hasan, "'Abul'l-Ḥasan Khan Īlčī," *Encyclopaedia Iranica* (http://www.iranicaonline.org/articles/abul-hasan-khan-ilci-mirza-persian-diplomat-b).
Johnson, Marcia K., Carol L. Raye, Karen J. Mitchell and Elizabeth Ankudowich, "The Cognitive Neuroscience of True and False Memories" in Robert F. Belli, ed., *True and False Recovered Memories: Toward a Reconciliation of the Debate*. New York: Springer, 2012, pp.15–52.
Johnston Graf, Susan, "Heterodox Religions in Ireland: Theosophy, the Hermetic Society, and the Castle of Heroes," *Irish Studies Review* 11(1), 2003, pp.51–59.
Jones, Ellen Carol, "Memorial Dublin" in Maurizia Boscagli and Enda Duffy, eds., *Joyce, Benjamin and Magical Urbanism* (European Joyce Studies 21). Amsterdam: Rodopi, 2011, pp.59–121.
Joyce, James, "Anna Livia Plurabelle" (Samuel Beckett, Alfred Perron, et al., translators), *Nouvelle revue française* 19(212), May 1, 1931, pp.637–46.
Kanter, Douglas, "Joyce, Irish Paralysis, and Cultural Nationalist Anticlericalism," *James Joyce Quarterly* 41(3), Spring 2004, pp.381–96.
Kato, Eileen, "W.B. Yeats and the Noh," *Irish Review* 42, Summer 2010, pp.104–19.
Kavanagh, Martha, "The Irish Free State and Collective Security, 1930–6," *Irish Studies in International Affairs* 15, 2004, pp.103–22.
Keach, William. "'Trade and Poesy' in Moore's Lalla Rookh: An Oriental Romance," *La Questione Romantica* 18–19, Autumn 2005, pp.91–98.
Kelly, John, "Ryan, Frederick Michael (1873–1913)" in *Oxford Dictionary of National Biography. Volume 48: Rowell-Sarsfield*. Oxford: Oxford University Press, 2004, pp.434–35.
Kelly, James, "The Last Will and Testament of Henry Flood: Context and Text," *Studia Hibernica* 31, 2000/2001, pp.37–52.
Kelly, Matthew, "Irish Nationalist Opinion and the British Empire in the 1850s and 1860s," *Past and Present* 204(1), 2009, pp.127–54.

Kelly, Ronan, "Another Side of Thomas Moore," *History of Ireland* 11(3), Autumn 2003, pp.39–43.

Kelly, Ronan, "Thomas Moore and Irish Historiography" in Karen Vandevelde, ed., *New Voices in Irish Criticism 3*. Dublin: Four Courts Press, 2002, pp.70–75.

Kennedy, Máire, "Reading the Enlightenment in Eighteenth-Century Ireland," *Eighteenth-Century Studies* 45(3), Spring 2012, pp.355–78.

Kershner, R. Brandon, "'Ulysses' and the Orient," *James Joyce Quarterly* 35(2&3), Winter–Spring, 1998, pp.273–96.

Kidd, Colin, "Gaelic Antiquity and National Identity in Enlightenment Ireland and Scotland," *English Historical Review* 109(434), November 1994, pp.1197–1214.

Killeen, J. F., "Ireland in the Greek and Roman Writers," *Proceedings of the Royal Irish Academy. Section C: Archaeology, Celtic Studies, History, Linguistics, Literature* 76, 1976, pp.207–15.

King, Jason, "'Memory of These Migrations': Joyce, Interculturalism, and the Reception of *Ulysses* in the Irish Immigration Debate" in R. Brandon Kershner and Tekla Mecsnóber, eds., *Joycean Unions: Post-Millennial Essays From East to West*. Amesterdam: Rodopi, 2013, pp.95–108.

Kotwal, Firoze M., Jamsheed K. Choksy, Christopher J. Brunner and Mahnaz Moazami, "Hataria, Manekji Limji," *Encyclopaedia Iranica* (iranicaonline.org/articles/hataria-manekji-limji).

Kra, Pauline, "Montesquieu's Lettres persanes and George Lyttelton's Letters From a Persian in England," *Studies on Voltaire and the Eighteenth Century* 304, 1992, pp.871–74.

Krappe, Alexander, "The Sovereignty of Erin," *American Journal of Philology* 63(4), 1942, pp.444–54.

Kurzman, Charles, "Weaving Iran into the Tree of Nations," *International Journal of Middle East Studies* 37(2), May 2005, pp.137–66.

Lal, Vinay, "Provincializing the West: World History From the Perspective of Indian History" in Benedikt Stuchtey and Eckhardt Fuchs, eds., *Writing World History, 1800–2000*. Oxford: Oxford University Press, 2003, pp.271–89.

Lane-Poole, Stanley, "Ouseley, Sir William (1767–1842)," *Dictionary of national Biography. Volume XLII: O'Duinn—Owen*. Sidney Lee Editor. London: Smith, Elder, & Co., 1895, pp.363–64.

Law, Vivien, Language and Its Students: The History of Linguistics" in Neville Edgar Collinge, ed., *Encyclopedia of Language*. London: Routledge, 1990, pp.426–55.

Lawrenson, Sonja, "'The Country Chosen of My Heart': The Comic Cosmopolitanism of *The Orientalist, or Electioneering in Ireland; a Tale, by Myself*" in Simon Davis, Daniel Sanjiv Roberts and Gabriel Sánchez Espinosa, eds., *India and Europe in the Global Eighteenth Century*. Oxford: Voltaire Foundation, 2014, pp.101–22.

Leerssen, Joep, "Celticism" in Terence Brown, ed., *Celticism*. Amsterdam: Editions Rodopi B.V., 1996, pp.1–20.

Leerssen, Joep, "Setting the Scene for National History" in Stefan Berger and Chris Lorenz, eds., *Nationalizing the Past: Historians as Nation Builders in Modern Europe*. Houndmills, Basingstoke: Palgrave Macmillan, 2010.

Leerssen, [Joep] Joseph Theodoor, "On the Edge of Europe: Ireland in Search of Oriental Roots, 1650–1850," *Comparative Criticism* 8, 1986, pp.91–112.

Lennon, Joseph, "Antiquarianism and Abduction: Charles Vallancey as Harbinger of Indo-European Linguistics," *European Legacy* 10(1), February 2005, pp.5–20.

Lincoln, Bruce, "The Indo-European Cattle-Raiding Myth," *History of Religions* 16(1), August 1976, pp.42–65.

Lloyd, David, "Great Gaps in Irish Song: James Clarence Mangan and the Ideology of the Nationalist Ballad," *Irish University Review* 14(2), Autumn 1984, pp.179–90.

Lloyd, David, "James Clarence Mangan's Oriental Translations and the Question of Origins," *Comparative Literature* 38(1), Winter 1986, pp.20–35.

Lloyd, David, "Translator as Refractor: Towards a Re-Reading of James Clarence Mangan as Translator," *Dispositio* 7(19–21), 1982, pp.141–62.

Loeffler, Toby H., "'Erin go Bragh': 'Banal Nationalism' and the Joycean Performance of Irish Nationhood," *Journal of Narrative Theory* 39(1), Winter 2009, pp.29–56.

Love, Walter D., "Edmund Burke and an Irish Historiographical Controversy," *History and Theory* 2(2), 1962, pp.180–98.

Love, Walter D., "The Hibernian Antiquarian Society: A Forgotten Predecessor to the Royal Irish Academy," *Studies: An Irish Quarterly Review* 51(203), Autumn 1962, pp.419–31.

Lowry, Donal, "The Captive Dominion: Imperial Realities Behind Irish Diplomacy, 1922–49," *Irish Historical Studies* 36(142), November 2008, pp.202–26.

Lynch, Niamh, "Defining Irish Nationalist Anti-Imperialism: Thomas Davis and John Mitchel," *Éire-Ireland* 42(1&2), Spring/Summer 2007, pp.82–107.

MacDermot, Frank, "Arthur O'Connor," *Irish Historical Studies* 15(57), March 1966, pp.48–69.

Mac Gearailt, Colm, "Writing the Irish Past: An Investigation into Post-Primary Irish History Textbook Emphases and Historiography, 1921–69," *History Education Research Journal* 15(2), October 2018, pp.233–47.

Markey, Anne, "The Discovery of Irish Folklore," *New Hibernia Review* 10(4), Winter 2006, pp.21–43.

Martin, Andrew, "The Mask of the Prophet: Napoleon, Borges, Verne," *Comparative Literature* 40(4), Autumn 1988, pp.318–34.

Martin, Vanessa, "Social Networks and Border Conflicts: The First Herat War 1839–1841" in Roxane Famanfarmaian, ed., *War and Peace in Qajar Persia: Implications Past and Present*. New York: Routledge, 2008, pp.110–21.

Mathews, P. J., "Stirring up Disloyalty: The Boer War, the Irish Literary Theatre and the Emergence of a New Separatism," *Irish University Review* 33(1), Spring–Summer 2003, pp.99–116.

Matthee, Rudi, "The Safavids Under Western Eyes: Seventeenth-Century European Travelers to Iran," *Journal of Early Modern History* 13(2–3), 2009, pp.137–71.

Maume, Patrick, "Standish James O'Grady: Between Imperial Romance and Irish Revival," *Éire-Ireland* 39(1&2), Spring/Summer 2004, pp.11–35.

Maume, Patrick, "Unionists and Patriots: James Whiteside, the Irish Bar and the Dilemmas of the Protestant Nation in Victorian Ireland" in Allan Blackstock and Frank O'Gorman, eds., *Loyalism and the Formation of the British World, 1775–1914*. Woodbridge, England: Boydell Press, 2014, pp.145–61.

McBride, Ian, "The Edge of Enlightenment: Ireland and Scotland in the Eighteenth Century," *Modern Intellectual History* 10(1), April 2013, pp.135–51.

McCarthy, Michael, "The Franco-Irish Ambulance Brigade 1870–71," *Old Limerick Journal (Limerick)* 25, Summer 1989, pp.132–38.

McDiarmid, Lucy, "Lady Gregory, Wilfrid Blunt, and London Table Talk," *Irish University Review* 34(1), Spring–Summer 2004, pp.67–80.

McHugh, John, "The Belfast Labour Dispute and Riots of 1907," *International Review of Social History* 22(1), 1977, pp.1–20.

McKay, Enda, "Changing With the Tide: The Irish Labour Party, 1927–1933," *Saothar* 11, 1986, pp.27–38.

McKenzie, Johnston and B. Henry, "Hajji Baba and Mirza Abul Hasan Khan: A Conundrum," *Iran* 33, 1995, pp.93–96.

McMahon, Cian, "Irish Free State Newspapers and the Abyssinian Crisis, 1935–6," *Irish Historical Studies* 36(143), May 2009, pp.368–88.

Meagher, Shelley, "Politics and Persian Mythology in Irish Poetry," *La Trobe Journal (Melbourne)* 91, June 2013, pp.76–85.

Melville, Charles P., "The Persian Famine of 1870–1872: Prices and Politics," *Disasters* 12(4), 1988, pp.309–25.

Menon, Dilip, "Writing History in Colonial Times: The Space and Time of Religious Polemic in Late 19th and Early 20th Century Southern India." Presented at the Center for South Asian Studies, University of Michigan, November 16, 2015 (https://www.youtube.com/watch?v=vMzMoG96YlQ).

Meyer, Kuno, "The Death of Connla" (Kuno Meyer Editor and Translator), *Ériu* 1, 1904, pp.113–21.

Meyer, Kuno, "The Oldest Version of Tochmarc Emire" (Kuno Meyer Editor and Translator), *Revue Celtique* 11, 1890, pp.433–57.

Mitchell, Colin Paul, "Shāh 'Abbās, the English East India Company and the Cannoneers of Fārs," *Itinerario* 24(2), 2000, pp.104–25.

Mitchell, James, "The Imprisonment of Wilfrid Scawen Blunt in Galway: Cause and Consequences," *Journal of the Galway Archaeological and Historical Society* 46, 1994, pp.65–110.

Modi, Jivanji Jamshedji, "A Glimpse into the Work of the Bombay Branch, 'Royal Asiatic Society, During the Last 100 Years (November 1804 to 1904) From a Parsee Point of View," *Journal of the Asiatic Society of Bombay* 21(59), 1905, pp.163–334.

Modi, Jivanji Jamshedji, "The Dantes of Iran and Erin," *The Indian Review (Madras)* 23(7), July 1922, pp.451–56.

Mojtaba'i, Fath-Allah, "Dabestān-e maḏāheb," *Encyclopaedia Iranica* (http://www.iranicaonline.org/articles/dabestan-e-madaheb).

Mojtaba'i, Fath-Allah, "Dasātīr," *Encyclopaedia Iranica* (http://www.iranicaonline.org/articles/dasatir).

Moojan, Moomen, "Cormick, William" (1993), *Encyclopaedia Iranica* (http://www.iranica.com/articles/cormick-william-b).

Moore, Jane, "Nineteenth-Century Irish Anacreontics: The Literary Relationship of James Clarence Mangan and Thomas Moore," *Irish Studies Review* 21(4), 2013, pp.387–405.

[Moore, Thomas], "[Review of Henry O'Brien's] The Round Towers of Ireland; or the Mysteries of Freemasonry, of Sabaism, and of Budhism, for the First Time Unveiled," *Edinburgh Review* 59(119), April 1834, pp.143–54.

Murphy, Cliona, "The Religious Context of the Women's Suffrage Campaign in Ireland," *Women's History Review* 6(4), 1997, pp.549–65.

Murphy, Seán, "Irish Jacobitism and Freemasonry," *Eighteenth-Century Ireland/Iris an dá chultúr* 9, 1994, pp.75–82.

Ni Bhromeil, Una, "The Gaelic Movement in the United States, 1870–1915," *New Hibernia Review* 5(3), Autumn 2001, pp.87–100.

Ní Ghabhann, Gillian, "The Gaelic Revival in the U.S. in the Nineteenth Century," *Chronicon* 2, 1998, pp.1–34.

Ní Mhunghaile, Lesa, "Anglo-Irish Antiquarianism and the Transformation of Irish Identity, 1750–1800" in David A. Valone and Jill Marie Bradbury, eds., *Anglo-Irish Identities, 1571–1845*. Lewisburg: Bucknell University Press, 2008, pp.181–98.

Ní Mhunghaile, Lesa, "Moloney, William J. (1885–1968)" in James McGuire and James Quinn, eds., *Dictionary of Irish Biography From the Earliest Times to the Year 2002. Volume 6: McGuire-Nutt*. Cambridge: Cambridge University Press, 2009, p.560.

Nolan, Emer, "'The Tommy Moore Touch': Ireland and Modernity in Joyce and Moore," *Dublin James Joyce Journal* 2, 2009, pp.64–77.

Nolan, Jerry, "Edward Martyn's Struggle for an Irish National Theater, 1899–1920," *New Hibernia Review* 7(2), Summer 2003, pp. 88–105.

Nolan, Jerry C. M., "In Search of an Ireland in the Orient: Tom Moore's *Lalla Rookh*." *New Hibernia Review* 12(3), Autumn 2008, pp.63–80.

Nolan, Jerry C. M., "Standish James O'Grady's Cultural Nationalism," *Irish Studies Review* 7(3), 1999, pp.347–57.

Norris, James Alfred, "Anglo-Afghan Wars ii. Second Anglo-Afghan War (1878–80)," *Encyclopaedia Iranica* (http://www.iranicaonline.org/articles/anglo-afghan-wars#pt2).

Novak, Rose, "Reviving 'Eva' of *The Nation*?: Eva O'Doherty's Young Ireland Newspaper Poetry," *Victorian Periodicals Review* 45(4), Winter 2012, pp.436–65.

O'Brien, Eugene, "The Epistemology of Nationalism," *Irish Studies Review* 5(17), Winter 1996/1997, pp.15–20.

O'Callaghan, John, "Politics, Policy and History: History Teaching in Irish Secondary Schools 1922–1970," *Études irlandaises* 36(1), 2011, pp.25–41.

Ó Ciosáin, Niall, "Review: Round Towers and Square Holes: Exoticism in Irish Culture," *Irish Historical Studies* 31(122), November 1998, pp.259–73.

Ó Corráin, Donnchadh, "Creating the Past: The Early Irish Genealogical Tradition," *Peritia* 12, 1998, pp.177–208.

O'Halloran, Clare, "Irish Re-Creations of the Gaelic Past: The Challenge of Macpherson's Ossian," *Past and Present* 124, August 1989, pp.69–95.

Ohlmeyer, Jane, "Ireland, India and the British Empire," *Studies in People's History* 2(2), 2015, pp.169–88.

Okazaki, Shoko. "The Great Persian Famine of 1870–71," *Bulletin of the School of Oriental and African Studies, University of London* 49(1), 1986, pp.183–92.

O'Laverty, James, "Remarkable Correspondence of Irish, Greek, and Oriental Legends," *Ulster Journal of Archaeology (Belfast)* 7, 1859, pp.334–346.

Ó Lúing, Seán, "Douglas Hyde and the Gaelic League," *Studies: An Irish Quarterly Review* 62(246), Summer 1973, pp.123–38.

O'Malley, Kate, "Indo-Irish Radical Connections in the Interwar Period," *Saothar* 29, 2004, pp.45–55.

O'Neill, William, "Joyce's Esthetic and Some Earlier Irish Writers," *Études irlandaises* 21(1), 1996, pp.33–41.

O'Quinn, Daniel, "/Laughter in London: James Morier, Mirza Abul Hassan Khan, and the Geopolitics of Emotion," *Eighteenth-Century Fiction* 25(1), Fall 2012, pp.85–114.

O'Reilly, Seán, "Birth of a Nation's Symbol: The Revival of Ireland's Round Towers," *Irish Arts Review Yearbook* 15, 1999, pp.27–33.

O'Reilly, William, "Orientalist Reflections: Asia and the Pacific in the Making of Late Eighteenth-Century Ireland," *New Zealand Journal of Asian Studies* 6(2), December 2004, pp.127–47.

O'Riordan, Manus, "The Second Greatest Event of 1916?" *Irish Political Review and Northern Star (Belfast)* 26(2), February 2011, pp.20–23.

Pappa, Eleftheria, "Tropicalismo in Classics. Contemporary Brazilian Approaches to the Value of Classical Antiquity in Higher Education: Between Colonial Legacy and Post-Colonial Thinking," *Journal for Critical Education Policy Studies* 18(2), 2020, pp.358–408.

Pappalardo, Salvatore, "Waking Europa: Joyce, Ferrero and the Metamorphosis of Irish History," *Journal of Modern Literature* 34(2), Winter 2011, pp. 154–77.

Parry, Jon P. "Steam Power and British Influence in Baghdad, 1820–1860," *Historical Journal* 56(1), March 2013, pp.145–73.

Pazargad, Bahauddin, "Āyā irlandihā hameh irāni-al-asl hasstand?," *Irān va Āmrikā* (Tehran) 26(24), Dey 1326 (December 1947), pp.11–13.

Penet, Jean-Christophe, "Thomas Davis, 'The Nation' and the Irish Language," *Studies: An Irish Quarterly Review* 96(384), Winter 2007, pp.433–43.

Pictet, Adolphe, "Inquiry into the Origin of the Name of Ireland," *Ulster Journal of Archaeology* 5, 1857, pp.52–60.

Plowman, Matthew Erin, "Irish Republicans and the Indo-German Conspiracy of World War I," *New Hibernia Review* 7(3), Autumn 2003, pp.80–105.

Pordzik, Ralph, "A Postcolonial View of Ireland and the Irish Conflict in Anglo-Irish Utopian Literature Since the Nineteenth Century," *Irish Studies Review* 9(3), 2001, pp.331–46.

Quiggin, Edmund Crosby, "Ireland: Early History," *The Encyclopædia Britannica*, 11th Edition, 1910, vol.14 (Hugh Chisholm editor). New York: The Encyclopædia Britannica Company, pp.756–70.

Rangarajan, Padma, "Lalla Rookh and the Afterlife of Allegory," *English Language Notes* 54(1), Spring/Summer 2016, pp.77–92.

Regan, Jennifer M., "'We Could Be of Service to Other Suffering People': Representations of India in the Irish Nationalist Press, c. 1857–1887," *Victorian Periodicals Review* 41(1), Spring 2006, pp.61–77.

Rodgers, Nini, "Ireland and the Black Atlantic in the Eighteenth Century," *Irish Historical Studies* 32(126), November 2000, pp.174–92.

Roling, Bernd, "Phoenician Ireland: Charles Vallancey (1725–1812) and the Oriental Roots of Celtic Culture" in Karl A. E. Enenkel and Konrad Adriaan Ottenheym, eds., *The Quest for an Appropriate Past in Literature, Art and Architecture*. Leiden: Brill, 2018, pp.750–70.

Rolston, Bill, "Bringing It All Back Home: Irish Emigration and Racism," *Race & Class* 45(2), 2003, pp.39–53.

Rudd, Andrew, "'Oriental' and 'Orientalist' Poetry: The Debate in Literary Criticism in the Romantic Period," *Romanticism* 13(1), 2007, pp.53–62.

Ryder, Sean, "Male Autobiography and Irish Cultural Nationalism: John Mitchel and James Clarence Mangan," *Irish Review* 13, Winter 1992/1993, pp.70–77.

Safi-Nejad, Javad, "Mo'arefi-e Kotob-e Chā'pi-e Joqrāfiyāi-e Dourān-e Qājār," *Roshd-e Āmouzesh-e Joqrāfiyā (Tehran)* 1(2), Summer 1364 (1985), pp.28–36.

Salter-Townshend, Charlotte, "Round Towers and the Birth of Irish Archaeology: George Petrie and Changing Perceptions of Irish Archaeology in the 19th Century," *Archaeology Online*, September 2013.

Samuelson, Scott, "Joyce's *Finnegans Wake* and Vico's Mental Dictionary," *New Vico Studies* 17, 1999, pp.53–66.

Sean-Ghall (Henry Egan Kenny), "Early Irish Trade and Commerce," *Irish Year Book/Leabar na hÉireann, 1908*. Dublin: James Duffy & Co., 1908, pp.123–45.

Sharma, Sunil, "Woven Worlds and Painted Pictures: The Persian Book in India." Lecture Presented at the Library of Congress, June 11, 2014 (https://www.loc.gov/today/cyberlc/feature_wdesc.php?rec=6468).

Shaw, George Bernard, "Common Sense About the War," The New York Times *Current History of the European War Series* 1(1) ("What Men of Letters Say"). New York: New York Times, December 1914, pp.11–60.

Shedd, John Haskell, "Communications From the Missions. Famine in Persia," *The Foreign Missionary* (New York) 30(3), August 1871, pp.72–76.

Sheils, Barry, "'Dark Cognition': W.B. Yeats, J.G. Herder and the Imperfection of Tradition," *Irish Studies Review* 20(3), 2012, pp.299–321.

Shloss, Carol Loeb, "Joyce in the Context of Irish Orientalism," *James Joyce Quarterly* 35(2&3), Winter–Spring, 1998, pp.264–71.

Silvestri, Michael, "'The Sinn Fein of India': Irish Nationalism and the Policing of Revolutionary Terrorism in Bengal," *Journal of British Studies* 39(4), October 2000, pp.454–86.

Smith, G. B., "Blackburne, Francis (1782?–1867)" in *Oxford Dictionary of National Biography. Volume 5: Belle—Blackman*. Oxford: Oxford University Press, 2004, pp.934–35.

Smythe, Colin P., "Yeats in Translation" (https://www.dublincity.ie/story/yeats-translation).

Snyder, Edward D., "The Wild Irish: A Study of Some English Satires Against the Irish, Scots, and Welsh," *Modern Philology* 17(12), April 1920, pp.687–725.

Sohrabi, Naghmeh, "Looking Behind *Hajji Baba of Ispahan*: The Case of Mirza Abul Hassan Khan Ilchi Shirazi" in Amy Singer, Christoph K. Neumann and Selçuk Akşin Somel, eds., *Untold Histories of the Middle East: Recovering Voices From the 19th and 20th Centuries*. New York: Routledge, 2011, pp.159–75.

"St Botolph Aldgate: 27 July 1630, Burial of Joseph Alley, a Persian Borne" (GL Ms 9222/2 p.87), Guildhall Library Manuscripts Section (http://www.history.ac.uk/gh/baentries.htm).

"St Michael Cornhill, Churchwardens: Accounts 1614–1615: Given Nicholas Argoro a Persian That Boughte Letters From the Lords of the Council But the Like is Not to be Allowed Hereafter" (Ms 4071/2 f. 26, top of page), Guildhall Library Manuscripts Section (http://www.history.ac.uk/gh/baentries.htm).

Sturgeon, Sinéad, "'False, Fleeting, Perjured Clarence': Pseudonymity and Criminality in the Writings of James Clarence Mangan," *Canadian Journal of Irish Studies* 36(2), Fall 2010, pp.76–99.

Taher-Kermani, Reza, "Persia by Way of Paris: On Arnold's 'Sohrab and Rustum'," *Middle Eastern Literatures* 18(1), 2015, pp.22–40.

Tavakoli-Targhi, Mohamad, "Contested Memories: Narrative Structures and Allegorical Meanings of Iran's Pre-Islamic History," *Iranian Studies* 29(1&2), Spring 1996, pp.149–75.

Taylor, Isaac, "The Origin and Primitive Seat of the Aryans," *Journal of the Anthropological Institute of Great Britain and Ireland* 17, 1888, pp.238–75.

The Irish Famine Project (https://www.irishfamineproject.com/data.html).

Tóibín, Colm "Easter 1916," London Review of Books lecture. London, British Museum, March 24, 2016 (https://www.lrb.co.uk/2016/03/24/colm-toibin/video-the-story-of-easter-1916).

Tóibín, Colm, "The Irish Literary Renaissance," Lecture Presented at Elmhurst College, Illinois, US, on 10 April 2014 (https://www.youtube.com/watch?v=A7mdEViEU8M).

Townend, Paul, "Between Two Worlds: Irish Nationalists and Imperial Crisis, 1878–1880," *Past and Present* 194(1), February 2007, pp.139–74.

Trigger, Bruce G., "Alternative Archaeologies: Nationalist, Colonialist, Imperialist," *Man, New Series* 19(3), September 1984, pp.355–70.

Twomey, Christina and Andrew J. May, "Australian Responses to the Indian Famine, 1876–78: Sympathy, Photography and the British Empire," *Australian Historical Studies* 43(2), 2012, pp.233–52.

Vail, Jeffrey W., "'The Standard of Revolt': Revolution and National Independence in Moore's Lalla Rookh," *Romanticism on the Net* 40, November 2005, no pagination.

Vail, Jeffrey, "Thomas Moore in Ireland and America: The Growth of a Poet's Mind," *Romanticism* 10(1), 2004, pp.41–62.

Viswanathan, Gauri, "Ireland, India, and the Poetics of Internationalism," *Journal of World History* 15(1), March 2004, pp.7–30.

Von Allendorfer, Frederic, "Note on an Irish-Man (Archibald Fitzgerald) in the Persian Service," *The Irish Sword: The Journal of the Military History Society of Ireland* 7(27), Winter 1965, pp.175–76.

Walker, Joseph Cooper, "On the Origin of Romantic Fabling in Ireland," *Transactions of the Royal Irish Academy (Dublin)* 10, 1806, pp.3–21 (under the "Antiquities" section (read by William Preston on June 10, 1805)).

Walsh, Paul, "George Petrie: His Life and Work" in Próinséas Ní Chatháin, Siobhán Fitzpatrick and Howard Clarke, eds., *Pathfinders to the Past: The Antiquarian Road to Irish Historical Writing, 1640–1960*. Dublin: Four Courts Press, 2012, pp.44–71.

Walsh, Thomas, "100 Years of Primary Curriculum Development and Implementation in Ireland: A Tale of a Swinging Pendulum," *Irish Educational Studies* 35(1), 2016, pp.1–16.

Watt, James, "James Morier and the Oriental Picaresque" in Graeme Harper, ed., *Comedy, Fantasy, Colonialism*. London: Continuum, 2002, pp.58–72.

Weston, John C. Jr., "Edmund Burke's Irish History: A Hypothesis," *PMLA* 77(4), September 1962, pp.397–403.

Whelan, Kevin, "The Revisionist Debate in Ireland," *Boundary* 2(31), Spring 2004, pp.179–205.

Whelan, Kevin, "Sectarianism and Secularism in Nineteenth-Century Ireland" in Paul Brennan, ed., *La sécularisation en Irlande*. Caen: Press Universitaires de Caen, 1998, pp.71–90.

White, Alan, "An Appalling or Banal Reality," *Variaciones Borges* 15, 2003, pp.47–91.

Wickens, George M., "*Lalla Rookh* and the Romantic Tradition of Islamic Literature in English," *Yearbook of Comparative and General Literature* 20, 1971, pp.61–66.

Wilde, William R. "Address to the Department of Anthropology," *Report of the Forty-Fourth Meeting of the British Association for the Advancement of Science, Held at Balfast in August 1874*. London: John Murray, 1875, pp.116–28 (pagination in the "Notices and Abstracts" section of the publication).

Wilford, Francis, "On Egypt and Other Countries Adjacent to the Ca'li' River, or Nile of Ethiopia, From the Ancient Books of the Hindus" (including a commentary by William Jones, the president of the Asiatic Society of Bengal) in *Asiatic Researches; or Transactions of the Society Instituted in Bengal*. Volume 3. London: J. Sewell and Co., 1799, pp.295–468.

Williams, Martin, "Ancient Mythology and Revolutionary Ideology in Ireland. 1878–1916," *Historical Journal* 26(2), 1983, pp.307–28.

Wood, Juliette, "Folklore Studies at the Celtic Dawn: The Rôle of Alfred Nutt as Publisher and Scholar," *Folklore* 110, 1999, pp.3–12.

Wright, Denis, "English Memsahibs in Persia," *History Today* 30(9), September 1980, pp.7–13.

Wright, Denis, "Fraser, James Baillie," *Encyclopaedia Iranica* (iranicaonline.org/articles/fraser-).

Wright, Denis, "Memsahibs in Persia," *Asian Affairs* 14(1), 1983, pp.5–14.

Wright, Jonathan Jeffrey and Diarmid A. Finnegan, "Rocks, Skulls and Materialism: Geology and Phrenology in Late-Georgian Belfast," *Notes and Records: The Royal Society Journal of the History of Science* 72(1), 2017, pp.25–55.

Wright, Nadia, "The Armenians of Singapore: An Historical Perspective," *Armenian Weekly* (https://armenianweekly.com/2015/01/06/armenians-of-simgapore).

Yarshater, Ehsan, "Iran III. Traditional History," *Encyclopaedia Iranica* (http://www.iranicaonline.org/articles/iran-iii-traditional-history).

Yohannan, John D., "The Persian Poetry Fad in England, 1770–1825," *Comparative Literature* 4(2), Spring 1952, pp.137–60.

Zarinebaf, Fariba, "From Istanbul to Tabriz: Modernity and Constitutionalism in the Ottoman Empire and Iran," *Comparative Studies of South Asia, Africa, and the Middle East* 28(1), 2008, pp.154–69.

Books, Pamphlets, Unpublished Dissertations, and other Monographs

A Catalogue of the Persian Printed Books in the British Museum. Compiled by Edward Edwards. London: William Clowes and Sons, 1922.

A System of Geography; or, A Descriptive, Historical, and Philosophical View of the Several Quarters of the World .... Volume 4. Glasgow: W. and D. Brownlie, 1807.

Abu Taleb Khan, *The Travels of Mirza Aboo Talib Khan, in the Persian Language (Masir-e talebi)*. Abridged by David MacFarlane. Second Edition. Calcutta: Baptist Mission Press, 1836.

Abu Taleb Khan, *The Travels of Mirza Abu Taleb Khan, in Asia, Africa and Europe, During the Years 1799, 1800, 1801, 1802, and 1803*. Two Volumes. Charles Stewart Translator. London: Longman, Hurst, Rees, and Orme, 1810.

Abu Taleb Khan Massir-e Tālebi [mash'ar bar hālāt-e landan va keyfiāt-e jami'-e jazireh-ye england va ....]. [Horace Hayman?] Wilson, Hassan Ali ibn Abu Taleb ibn Mohammad Esfahani, and Mir Qodrat-Ali Editors. Calcutta: Hindustani Press, 1812.

Abu Talib [Khan], *The Travels of Mirza Abu Taleb Khan, in Asia, Africa and Europe, During the Years 1799, 1800, 1801, 1802, and 1803*. Translated by Charles Stewart and edited by Daniel O'Quinn. Peterborough, Canada: Broadview, 2009.

Adams, Hazard, *Lady Gregory*. Lewisburg, Pennsylvania: Bucknell University Press, 1973.

Afary, Janet, *The Iranian Constitutional Revolution, 1906–1911: Grassroots Democracy, Social Democracy, and the Origins of Feminism*. New York: Columbia, 1996.

Afshar, Iraj, ed., *Zendegi-e Tufāni: Khāterāt-e Sayyid Hassan Taqizādeh*. Tehran: Elmi, 1368 (1989).

Ahmad ibn Mula Hafez, ed., *Sālārnāmeh*. Volume I. Shiraz: Matba'eh-ye Mohammadi, 1316 A.H. (1898).

Algar, Hamid, *Mirza Malkum Khan*. Berkeley: University of California Press, 1973.
Amanat, Abbas, *Pivot of the Universe: Nasir al-Din Shah Qajar and the Iranian Monarchy, 1831–1896*. Berkeley: University of California Press, 1997.
Anderson, Benedict, *Imagined Communities: Reflections on the Origin and Spread of Nationalism*. London: Verso, 1983.
Anderson, Kevin B., *Marx at the Margins: On Nationalism, Ethnicity, and Non-Western Societies*. Chicago: University of Chicago Press, 2010.
Anderson, Olive, *A Liberal State at War: English Politics and Economics During the Crimean War*. New York: St. Martin's Press, 1967.
Andrews, Ann, *Newspapers and Newsmakers: The Dublin Nationalist Press in the Mid-Nineteenth Century*. Liverpool: Liverpool University Press, 2014.
Andrews, John Harwood, *The Queen's Last Map-Maker; Richard Bartlett in Ireland, 1600–3*. Dublin: Geography Publications, 2008.
Ansari, Ali M., *The Politics of Nationalism in Modern Iran*. Cambridge: Cambridge University Press, 2012.
Appadurai, Arjun, *Modernity at Large: Cultural Dimensions of Globalization*. Minneapolis: University of Minnesota Press, 1996.
Arnold, Matthew, *Irish Essays and Others*. London: Smith, Elder, and Co., 1882.
Arnold, Matthew, *On the Study of Celtic Literature*. London: Smith, Elder, and Co., 1867.
Arnold, Matthew, *Sohrab and Rustum: An Episode*. Reprint. Merwin Marie Snell Editor. Chicago and New York: Werner School Book Company, 1896.
Aronoff, Mark and Janie Rees-Miller, eds., *The Handbook of Linguistics*. Second Edition. Wiley Blackwell, 2007.
Arvidsson, Stefan, *Aryan Idols: Indo-European Mythology as Ideology and Science*. Sonia Wickmann Translator. Chicago: University of Chicago Press, 2006.
Ashe, Geoffrey, *The Quest for America*; New York: Praeger, 1971.
Asimov, Muhammad S. and Clifford E. Bosworth, eds., *History of Civilizations of Central Asia. Volume IV. The Age of Achievement: A.D. 750 to the End of the Fifteenth Century. Part One: The Historical, Social and Economic Setting*. Paris: UNESCO Publishing, 1998.
Avery, Peter, Gavin Hambly and Charles Melville, eds., *The Cambridge History of Iran. Volume 7: From Nadir Shah to the Islamic Republic*. Cambridge: Cambridge University Press, 1991.
Bakhtin, Mikhael M., *The Dialogic Imagination: Four Essays by M.M. Bakhtin*. Michael Holquist Editor, and Caryl Emerson and Michael Holquist Translators. Austin: University of Texas Press, 1981.
Ballantyne, Tony, *Orientalism and Race: Aryanism in the British Empire*. Houndmills, Basingstoke: Palgrave, 2002.
Banim, John, *The Anglo-Irish of the Nineteenth Century. A Novel*. Three Volumes. London: Henry Colburn, 1828.
Barfoot, C. C. and Theo D'haen, eds., *Oriental Prospects: Western Literature and the Lure of the East*. Amsterdam: Rodopi, 1998.
Barry, Kevin, ed., *James Joyce: Occasional, Critical, and Political Writing*. With and Introduction by K. Barry, and Translations from Italian by . Oxford: Oxford University Press, 2000.
Barry, Michael Joseph, ed., *The Songs of Ireland*. Second Edition. Dublin: James Duffy & Sons, 1846.
Bartlett, Thomas, ed., *The Cambridge History of Ireland. Volume IV: 1880 to the Present*. Cambridge: Cambridge University Press. 2018.
Bashiri, Iraj, *The Fiction of Sadeq Hedayat*. Lexington, Kentucky: Mazda Publishers, 1984.
Beard, Michael, *Hedayat's "Blind Owl" as a Western Novel*. Princeton: Princeton University Press, 1999.
Beazley, Charles Raymond, *The Dawn of Modern Geography. Volume III: A History of Exploration and Geographical Science From the Middle if the Thirteenth to the Early Years of the Fifteenth Century (c. A.D. 1260–1420)*. Oxford: Clarendon Press, 1906.

Bell, Herbert C. F., *Lord Palmerston*. Volume II. Reprint. Hamden, Connecticut: Archon, 1966 [1936].

Bender, Abby, *Israelites in Erin: Exodus, Revolution, & the Irish Revival*. Syracuse: Syracuse University Press, 2015.

Benjamin, Walter, *Selected Writings. Volume 4: 1938–1940*. Howard Eiland and Michael W. Jennings Editors, and Edmund Jephcott, et al., Translators. Cambridge, MA: Harvard University Press, 2003.

Berberian, Houri, *Roving Revolutionaries: Armenians and the Connected Revolutions in the Russian, Iranian, and Ottoman Worlds*. Oakland: University of California Press, 2019.

Berberian, Houri, *The Love for Freedom Has No Fatherland: Armenians and the Iranian Constitutional Revolution of 1905–1911*. Boulder, CO: Westview, 2001.

Berger, Stefan and Bill Niven, eds., *Writing the History of Memory*. London: Bloomsbury, 2014.

Berger, Stefan and Chris Lorenz, eds., *Nationalizing the Past: Historians as Nation Builders in Modern Europe*. Houndmills, Basingstoke: Palgrave Macmillan, 2010.

Berger, Stefan and Christoph Conrad, *Past as History: National Identity and Historical Consciousness in Modern Europe*. Houndmills, Basingstoke: Palgrave, 2015.

Betham, William, *Etruria-Celtica: Etruscan Literature and Antiquities Investigated*. Two Volumes. Dublin: Philip Dixon Hardy and Sons, 1842.

Betham, William, *The Gael and Cymbri: An Inquiry into the Origin and History of the Irish Scoti, Britons, and Gauls, and of the Caledonians, Picts, Welsh, Cornish and Bretons*. Dublin: William Curry, Jun, and Co., 1834.

Blavatsky, Helena Petrovna, *Isis Unveiled: A Master-Key to the Mysteries of Ancient and Modern Science and Theology*. Two Volumes. New York: J.W. Bouton; London: Bernard Quaritch, 1877.

Blunt, Wilfrid Scawen, *Gordon at Khartoum: Being a Personal Narrative of Events in Continuation of "A Secret History of the English Occupation of Egypt."* London: Stephen Swift and Co., 1911.

Blunt, Wilfrid Scawen, *My Diaries: Being a Personal Narrative of Events 1888–1914. Part One [1888–1900]*. Reprint, With a Foreword by Lady Gregory. New York: Alfred Knopf, 1921.

Blunt, Wilfrid Scawen, *My Diaries: Being a Personal Narrative of Events 1888–1914. Part Two [1900–1914]*. Reprint, With a Foreword by Lady Gregory. New York: Alfred a. Knopf, 1922 [1921].

Boehmer, Elleke, *Empire, the National, and the Postcolonial, 1890–1920: Resistance in Interaction*. Oxford: Oxford University Press, 2002.

Boldt, Andreas Dieter, *The Role of Ireland in the Life of Leopold Von Ranke (1795–1886): The Historian and Historical Truth*. Lewiston, New York: Edwin Mellen, 2007.

Bonakdarian, Mansour, *Britain and the Iranian Constitutional Revolution of 1906–1911: Foreign Policy, Imperialism, and Dissent*. Syracuse: Syracuse University Press, 2006.

Bourke, Angela, Siobhán Kilfeather, Maria Luddy, Margaret Mac Curtain, Gerardine Meaney, Máirín Ní Dhonnchadha, Mary O'Dowd and Clair Wills, eds., *The Field Day Anthology of Irish Writing. Volume IV: Irish Women's Writing and Traditions*. Cork: Cork University Press, 2002a.

Bourke, Angela, Siobhán Kilfeather, Maria Luddy, Margaret Mac Curtain, Gerardine Meaney, Máirín Ní Dhonnchadha, Mary O'Dowd and Clair Wills, eds., *The Field Day Anthology of Irish Writing. Volume V: Irish Women's Writing and Traditions*. Cork: Cork University Press, 2002b.

Bourke, Ulick Joseph, *Pre-Christian Ireland*. Dublin: Browne & Nolan, 1887.

Bourke, Ulick Joseph, *The Aryan Origins of the Gaelic Race and Language*. London: Longman's, Green and Co., 1875.

Bradshaw, Brendan, Andrew Hadfield and Willy Male, eds., *Representing Ireland: Literature and the Origins of Conflict 1534–1660*. Cambridge: Cambridge University Press, 1993.

Brady, Ciaran, ed., *Interpreting Irish History: The Debate on Historical Revisionism, 1938–1994*. Blackrock, Ireland: Irish Academic Press, 1994.

Brake, Laurel and Marysa Demoor, general eds., *Dictionary of Nineteenth-Century Journalism in Great Britain and Ireland*. Ghent: Academia Press, 2009.

Breed, Brennan W., *Nomadic Text: A Theory of Biblical Reception History*. Bloomington: Indiana University Press, 2014.

Brittlebank, William, *Persia During the Famine: A Narrative of a Tour in the East and of the Journey Out and Home*. London: Basil, Montagu, Pickering, 1873.
Broadfoot, William, "Pottinger, Sir Henry (1789–1856)" in *Dictionary of National Biography. Vol. XLVI: Pocock-Puckering*. Sidney Lee Editor. London: Smith, Elder, & Co., 1896, pp.224–26.
Brooke, Charlotte, *Reliques of Irish Poetry: Consisting of Heroic Poems, Odes, Elegies, and Songs, Translated into English Verse; with Notes Explanatory and Historical, and the Originals in Irish Character, to which is Subjoined an Irish Tale*. Reprint, with "A Memoir of Her Life and Writings" by Aaron Crossly Seymour. Dublin: J. Christie, 1816 [1789].
Brown, Ken S., Alison L. Joseph and Brennan Breed, eds., *Reading Other Peoples' Texts Social Identity and the Reception of Authoritative Traditions*. London: t&tclark (Bloomsbury), 2020.
Brown, Terence, *Ireland: A Social and Cultural History, 1922–2002*. Revised Edition. London: Harper Perennial, 2004.
Brown, Terence, *The Life of W.B. Yeats: A Critical Biography*. Reprint. Oxford: Blackwell Publishers, 2001.
Browne, Edward Granville, *A Literary History of Persia. Volume I: From the Earliest Times Until Firdawsi*. Reprint. London: T. Fisher Unwin, 1908 [1902].
Browne, Edward Granville, *A Literary History of Persia. Volume II: From Firdawsi to Sa'di*. London: T. Fisher Unwin, 1906.
Browne, Edward Granville, *A Literary History of Persia. Volume III: Under the Tartar Dominion (A.D. 1265–1502)*. Cambridge: Cambridge University Press, 1920.
Browne, Edward Granville, *The Literature of Persia*. London: Persia Society (Published by John Hogg), 1912.
Browne, Edward Granville, *The Persian Revolution of 1905–1909*. New Edition. Washington, DC: Mage, 1995 [1910].
Browne, Edward Granville, *The Press and Poetry of Modern Persia. Partly Based on the Manuscript Work of Mirzâ Muhammad Ali Khân "Tarbiyat" of Tabriz*. Cambridge: University Press, 1914.
Bruce, John, ed., *Calendar of State Papers. Domestic Series: Of the Reign of Charles I. 1625, 1626*. London: Longman, Brown, Green, Longmans, & Roberts, 1858.
Bryant, Jacob, *A New System, or, an Analysis of Antient Mythology*. Volume I. London: P. Elmsly, 1773.
Bryant, Sophie, *Celtic Ireland*. London: Kegan Paul, Trench & Co., 1889.
Burke, Peter, *Varieties of Cultural History*. Ithaca: Cornell University Press, 1997.
Bushrui, Suheil B., *William Butler Yeats's Search for a Spiritual Philosophy*. London: Temenos Academy, 2013.
Butler, David and Gareth Butler, *British Political Facts 1900–1985*. New York: St. Martin's, 1986.
Byron, George Gordon, *Don Juan*. New Edition. Boston: Phillips, Sampson, and Co., 1858.
Byron, George Gordon, *The Complete Works of Lord Byron*. Volume III. J.W. Lake Editor. Paris: Baudry, 1825.
Byron, George Gordon, *The Corsair, a Tale*. Reprint. Boston: West & Blake, 1814.
Callanan, Frank, *T.M. Healy: The Rise and Fall of Parnell and the Establishment of the Free State*. Cork: Cork University Press, 1996.
Camden, William, *Britannia: Or a Chorographical Description of Great Britain and Ireland, Together With the Adjacent Islands*. Volume II. Second Edition. Edmund Gibson Editor. London: Awnsham Churchill, 1722 [1586].
Campbell, John Gregerson, *The Fians; or, Stories, Poems, & Traditions of Fionn and His Warrior Band*. London: David Nutt, 1891.
Campbell, Lyle and William J. Poser, *Language Classification: History and Method*. Cambridge: Cambridge University Press, 2008.
Campbell, Matthew, *Irish Poetry Under the Union, 1801–1924*. New York: Cambridge University Press, 2014.
Carroll, Clare and Patricia King, eds., *Ireland and Postcolonial Theory*: With an Afterword by Edward Said. Notre Dame, Indiana: University of Notre Dame Press, 2003.

Casanova, Pascale. *The World Republic of Letters*. M.B. DeBevoise Translator. Cambridge, MA: Harvard University Press, 2004 (Originally Published in French in 1999).

Casement, Roger, *The Crime Against Europe: A Possible Outcome of the War of 1914*. Berlin: The Continental Times, 1915.

Castle, Gregory, *Modernism and the Celtic Revival*. New York: Cambridge University Press, 2001.

Chakrabarty, Dipesh, *Provincialising Europe: Postcolonial Thought and Historical Difference*. Princeton: Princeton University Press, 2000.

Chatterjee, Partha, *The Nation and Its Fragments: Colonial and Postcolonial Histories*. Princeton: Princeton University Press, 1993.

Chehabi, Houchang E. and Grace Neville, eds., *Erin and Iran: Cultural Encounters Between the Irish and the Iranians*. Boston: Ilex, 2015.

Chehabi, Houchang E. and Vanessa Martin, eds., *Iran's Constitutional Revolution: Popular Politics, Cultural Transformations and Transnational Connections*. London: I.B. Tauris, 2010.

Chuto, Jacques, Peter Van de Kamp, Augustine Martin and Ellen Shannon-Mangan, eds., *The Collected Works of James Clarence Mangan. Prose: 1840–1882*. Dublin: Irish Academic Press, 2002.

Chuto, Jacques, Rudolf Patrick Holzapfel and Ellen Shannon-Mangan, eds., *The Collected Works of James Clarence Mangan. Poems: 1845–1847*. Dublin: Irish Academic Press, 1997.

Chuto, Jacques, Rudolf Patrick Holzapfel, Peter MacMahon and Ellen Shannon-Mangan, eds., *The Collected Works of James Clarence Mangan. Poems: 1838–1844*. Dublin: Irish Academic Press, 1996.

Clancy, James Joseph, *The Land League Manual: With Portraits and Sketches of Parnell and Davitt*. New York: Thomas Kelly, 1881.

Cleary, Joe, ed., *The Cambridge Companion to Irish Modernism*. Cambridge: Cambridge University Press, 2014.

Cloake, Margaret Morris, ed., *A Persian at the Court of King George, 1809–10: The Journal of Mirza Abul Hassan Khan*. London: Barrie & Jenkins, 1988.

Clowes, William Laird, *The Royal Navy: A History From the Earliest Times to the Present*. Volume I. London: Sampson Low, Marston and Company, 1897.

Codfelter, Micheal, *Warfare and Armed Conflicts: A Statistical Encyclopedia of Casualty and Other Figures, 1492–2015*. Jefferson, North Carolina: McFarland, 2017.

Cohn, Norman, *Noah's Flood: The Genesis Story in Western Thought*. Reprint. New Haven: Yale University Press, 1999 [1996].

Collini, Stefan, Richard Whatmore and Brian Young, eds., *History, Religion, and Culture: British Intellectual History 1750–1950*. Cambridge: Cambridge University Press, 2000.

Collins, Kevin, *Catholic Churchmen and the Celtic Revival in Ireland, 1848–1916*. Dublin: Four Courts Press, 2003.

Collins, Michael, *Empire, Nationalism and the Postcolonial World: Rabindranath Tagore's Writings on History, Politics and Society*. New York: Routledge, 2012.

Connolly, James, *Labour and Easter Week: A Selection From the Writings of James Connolly*. Desmond Ryan Editor, with an Introduction by William O'Brien. Dublin: Sign of the Three Candles, 1949.

Connolly, Ruth and Ann Coughlan, eds., *New Voices in Irish Criticism 5*. Dublin: Four Courts Press, 2005.

Connolly, Sean J., *Divided Kingdom: Ireland 1630–1800*. Oxford: Oxford University Press, 2008.

Cook, Scott B., *Imperial Affinities: Nineteenth Century Analogies and Exchanges Between India and Ireland*. New Delhi: Sage, 1993.

Coquelin, Olivier, Patrick Galliou and Thierry Robin, eds., *Political Ideology in Ireland: From the Enlightenment to the Present*. Newcastle: Cambridge Scholars Press, 2009.

Costello, Louisa Stuart, *The Rose Garden of Persia*. Joseph Jacobs Editor. New Edition. London: Gibbings and Company, 1899 [1845].

Craik, George Lillie and Charles MacFarlane, *The Pictorial History of England: Being a History of the People, as Well as a History of the Kingdom*. Volume I. London: Charles Knight and Co., 1837.

Crawley, John, William J. Smyth and Mike Murphy, eds., *The Atlas of the Great Irish Famine*. Cork: Cork University Press, 2012.
Crosbie, Barry, *Irish Imperial Networks: Migration, Social Communication and Exchange in Nineteenth-Century India*. Cambridge: Cambridge University Press, 2012.
Crowe, Catriona, Ronan Fanning, Michael Kennedy, Dermot Keogh and Eunan O'Halpin, eds., *Documents on Irish Foreign Policy. Volume IV: 1932–1936*. Dublin: Royal Irish Academy, 2004.
Cunningham, Bernadette, *The Annals of the Four Masters: Irish History, Kingship and Society in the Early Seventeenth Century*. Dublin: Four Courts Press, 2009.
Cunningham, Bernadette, *The World of Geoffrey Keating: History, Myth and Religion in Seventeenth-Century Ireland*. Dublin: Four Courts Press, 2000.
Curran, Stuart, *Poetic Form and British Romanticism*. New York: Oxford University Press, 1986.
Curzon, George Nathaniel, *Persia and the Persian Question*. Volume I. London: Longmans, Green, and Co., 1892.
Cusack, Margaret Anna, *An Illustrated History of Ireland: From the Earliest Period*. London: Longmans. Green, and Co., 1868.
Cusack, Margaret Anna, *The Student's Manual of Irish History*. London: Longmans. Green, and Co., 1870.
Dalberg-Acton, John Emerich Edward, *The History of Freedom, and Other Essays*. John Neville Figgis and Reginald Vere Laurence Editors. London: MacMillan and Co., 1907.
D'Alton, John, *The History of Drogheda, With Its Environs*. Volume II. Dublin:Privately Published, 1844.
D'Alton, John, *The History of Ireland: From the Earliest Period to the Year 1245*. Volume II. Dublin:Privately Published, 1845.
Daly, John and Edward Walsh, *Reliques of Irish Jacobite Poetry*. Dublin: John Cumming, 1844.
Daneshvar, Simin, *Savushun: A Novel About Modern Iran*. Mohammad R. Ghanoonparvar Translator. Washington, DC: Mage, 1990.
Daniel, Elton, *The Political and Social History of Khurasan Under Abbasid Rule, 747–820*. Minneapolis: Bibliotheca Islamica, 1979.
Darcy, Eamon, *The Irish Rebellion of 1641 and the Wars of the Three Kingdoms*. Woodbridge: Royal Historical Society, 2013.
Davidson, Neil, *Origins of Scottish Nationhood*. London: Pluto Press, 2000.
Davis, John R. and Angus Nicholls, eds., *Friedrich Max Müller and the Role of Philology in Victorian Thought*. New York: Routledge, 2018.
Davis, Thomas Osborne, *Literary and Historical Essays*. Edited by Charles Gavan Duffy. Dublin: James Duffy, 1846.
Davis, Thomas Osborne, *Prose Writings of Thomas Davis*. Edited and With an Introduction by Thomas William Rolleston. London: Walter Scott, 1889.
Davis, Thomas Osborne, *The Poems of Thomas Davis*. Edited With an Introduction by John Mitchel. New York: D. & J. Sadlier & Co., 1866.
Davis, Thomas Osborne, *The Poems of Thomas Davis*. Thomas Wallis Editor. Dublin: James Duffy, 1857.
Davison, Neil R., *James Joyce, Ulysses, and the Construction of Jewish Identity: Culture, Biography, and 'The Jew' in Modernist Europe*. Cambridge: Cambridge University Press, 1996.
Dāvud, Jān (Jean David) and Mohammad Hussein Farahani, *Jahān-namā*. Tehran: Reza-Qoli Sarabi, 1277 A.H. (1861).
Dawlatabadi, Yahya, *Hayāt-e Yahyā*. Volume II. Reprint. Tehran: Attar, 1362 (1983).
Dawson, Richard, *Red Terror and Green: The Sinn Fein-Bolshevist Movement*. New York: E.P. Dutton, 1920.
de Bellaigue, Christopher, *Patriot of Persia: Muhammad Mossadegh and a Tragic Anglo-American Coup*. New York: Harper Collins, 2012.

De Nie, Michael, *The Eternal Paddy: Irish Identity and the British Press, 1798–1882.* Madison: University of Wisconsin Press, 2004.

De Valera, Eamon, *India and Ireland.* New York: Friends of Freedom for India, 1920.

Deane, Seamus, *Celtic Revivals: Essays in Modern Irish Literature, 1880–1980.* London: Faber and Faber, 1985.

Deane, Seamus, *Strange Country: Modernity and Nationhood in Irish Writing Since 1790.* Oxford: Clarendon Press, 1997.

Deane, Seamus, ed., *The Field Day Anthology of Irish Writing: Volume III: From James Joyce (1882–1941) Through Contemporary Irish Poetry (–1900).* Reprint. Derry: Field Day Publications, 1992 [1991].

Dehkhoda, Ali-Akbar, *Maqālāt-e Dehkhodā.* Volume 2. Mohammad Dabir-Siyaqi Editor. Tehran:Tirazheh, 1362 [1983].

Denvir, John, *The Life Story of an Old Rebel.* Dublin: Sealy, Bryers, & Walker, 1910.

Desai, Palanji Barjorji, "The Ostracism of the Achæmenids From the Pahlavi Works and the Shâh Nameh" in Jivanji Jamshedji Modi, ed., *The K. R. Cama Memorial Volume: Essays on Iranian Subjects Written by Various Scholars in Honour of Mr. Kharshedji Rustamji Cama on the Occasion of His Seventieth Birthday.* Bombay: Fort Printing Press, 1900, pp.29–39.

Dew, Nicholas, *Orientalism in Louis XIV's France.* Oxford: Oxford University Press, 2009.

Dickson, David, Dáire Keogh and Kevin Whelan, *The United Irishmen: Republicanism, Radicalism, and Rebellion.* Dublin: Lilliput Press, 1993.

Digby, William, *Famine Campaign in Southern India (Madras and Bombay Presidencies and Province of Mysore), 1876–1878.* Volume II. London: Longmans, Green, and Co., 1878.

Dilley, Roy and Thomas G. Kirsch, eds., *Regimes of Ignorance: Anthropological Perspectives on the Production and Reproduction of Non-Knowledge.* Reprint. New York: Berghahn, 2017 [2015].

Dillon, William, *Life of John Mitchel.* Two Volumes. London: Kegan Paul, Trench, & Co., 1888.

Dillon, Myles, *The Correspondence of Myles Dillon, 1922–1925: Irish-German Relations and Celtic Studies.* Joachim Fischer and John Dillon Editors. Dublin: Four Courts Press, 1999.

Dixon, Joy, *Divine Feminine: Theosophy and Feminism in England.* Baltimore: Johns Hopkins University Press, 2001.

Documents Relative to the Sinn Fein Movement. London: H. M. Stationary Office, 1921.

Dod's Parliamentary Companion, Fifty-Seventh Year. London: George Bell and Sons, 1889.

Doerries, Reinhard R., *Prelude to the Easter Rising: Sir Roger Casement in Imperial Germany.* London: Frank Cass, 2000.

Donboli, Abdul-Razzaq Beg, *Ma'āsser-e Sultāniyeh.* Tehran:Mirza Zayn al-Abedin Tabrizi Printers, 1241 A.H. (1826).

Dorney, John, *'Peace After the Final Battle': The Story of the Irish Revolution, 1912–1924.* Dublin: New Island Books, 2014.

Dowden, Wilfred S., ed., *The Journal of Thomas Moore. Volume 5: 1836–1842.* Newark: University of Delaware Press, 1988.

Downham, Clare, *Medieval Ireland.* Cambridge: Cambridge University Press, 2018.

Drummond, William Hamilton, *Ancient Irish Minstrelsy.* Dublin:Hodges and Smith, 1852.

Dryhurst, Nora F., ed., *Nationalities and Subject Races. Report of Conference Held in Caxton Hall, Westminster June 28–30, 1910.* With a Preface by Robert Lynd. London: P.S. King & Son, 1911.

Duffy, Charles Gavan, ed., *The Ballad Poetry of Ireland.* Fortieth Edition. Dublin: James Duffy, 1869.

Duffy, Charles Gavan, *Thomas Davis: The Memoirs of an Irish Patriot, 1840–1846.* London: Kegan Paul, Trench, Trubner, & Co., 1890.

Dunn, Joseph and Patrick Joseph Lennox, eds., *The Glories of Ireland.* Washington, DC: Phoenix, 1914.

Dwan, David, *The Great Community: Culture and Nationalism in Ireland.* Dublin: Field Day, 2008.

Eagleton, Terry, *Crazy John and the Bishop and Other Essays on Irish Culture.* Cork: Cork University Press, 1998.

Eagleton, Terry, *Heathcliff and the Great Hunger: Studies in Irish Culture.* London: Verso, 1995.

Eagleton, Terry, *Scholars and Rebels in Nineteenth-Century Ireland*. Oxford: Blackwell Publishers, 1999.
Egleson Dunleavy, Janet and Gareth W. Dunleavy, *Douglas Hyde: A Maker of Modern Ireland*. Berkeley: University of California Press, 1991.
Eglinton, John, *Anglo-Irish Essays*. Dublin: Talbot Press, 1917.
Ekhtiar, Maryam, *Modern Science, Education and Reform in Qajar Iran: The Dar al-Fonun*. Richmond, England: Curzon, 2008.
Ellmann, Richard, *James Joyce*. Revised Edition. Oxford: Oxford University Press, 1982 [1959].
Ellmann, Richard, *Oscar Wilde*. New York: Alfred A. Knopf, 1988.
The Encyclopædia Britannica: A Dictionary of Arts, Sciences, Literature, and General Information. Eleventh Edition. Hugh Chisholm editor. New York: Encyclopædia Britannica Company, 1911.
English, Barbara, *John Company's Last War*. London: Collins, 1971.
Erll, Astrid and Ansgar Nünning, eds., *Cultural Memory Studies: An International and Interdisciplinary Handbook*. New York: de Gruyter, 2008.
E'temad al-Saltaneh, Mohammad Hassan Khan, *Mer'āt al-Boldān-e Nāsseri*. Volume 2. Tehran: n.p., 1294 A.H. (1878).
E'temad al-Saltaneh, Mohammad Hassan Khan, *Mer'āt al-Boldān-e Nāsseri*. Volume 3. Tehran: n.p., 1296 A.H. (1879).
E'temad al-Saltaneh, Mohammad Hassan Khan, *Rouznāmeh-ye Khāterāt-ei E'temād al-Saltaneha*. Iraj Afshar Editor. Fourth Edition. Tehran: Amir Kabir, 1377 [1999].
E'temad al-Saltaneh, Mohammad Hassan Khan, *Tārikh-e Montazem-e Nāsseri*. Volume 3. Tehran: n.p., 1300 A.H. (1883).
Eze, Emmanuel Chukwudi, *Race and the Enlightenment: A Reader*. Cambridge, Massachusetts: Blackwell, 1997.
Faber, George Stanley, *The Origin of Pagan Idolatry Ascertained From Historical Testimony and Circumstantial Evidence*. Three Volumes. London: F.C. and J. Rivington, 1816.
Fanning, Ronan and Michael Kennedy, Dermot Keogh and Eunan O'Halpin, eds., *Documents on Irish Foreign Policy. Volume I: 1919–1922*. Dublin: Royal Irish Academy, 1998.
Farren, Sean, *The Politics of Irish Education, 1920–65*. Belfast: Queen's University of Belfast Institute of Irish Studies, 1995.
Farzaneh, Masoud F., *Āshenā-yi bā Sādeq-e Hedāyat. Part I: ĀnchehSādeq-e Hedāyat beh man goft*. Paris: Self-Published, 1988.
Farzaneh, Masoud F., *Āshenā-yi bā Sādeq-e Hedāyat. Part II: Sādeq-e Hedāyat cheh migoft?* Paris: Self-Published, 1988.
Fegan, Melissa, *Literature and the Irish Famine, 1845–1919*. New York: Oxford University Press, 2002.
Ferrier, Joseph Pierre, *Caravan Journeys and Wanderings in Persia, Afghanistan, Turkistan, and Beloochistan; With Historical Notices of the Countries Lying Between Russia and India*. William Jesse Translator and Henry Danby Seymour Editor. London: John Murray, 1856.
Ferriter, Diarmaid, *A Nation and Not a Rabble: The Irish Revolution 1913–1923*. New York: Overlook Press, 2015.
Ferriter, Diarmaid, *Transformation of Ireland, 1900–2000*. London: Profile Books, 2005.
Findlater, Alex, *Findlaters: The Story of a Dublin Merchant Family, 1774–2001*. Dublin: A. & A. Farmer, 2001.
Finerty, John Frederick, *Ireland: The People's History of Ireland*. Volume II. New York:Co-Operative Publication Society, 1904.
Fisher, Michael H., *Counterflows to Colonialism: Indian Travellers and Settlers in Britain 1600–1857*. New Delhi: Permanent Black, 2004.
Fitzgerald, Edward, *Rubáiyát of Omar Khayyám in English Verse … And a Biographical Preface*. Edited by Michael Kerney. New York and Boston: Houghton, Mifflin and Company, 1888.
Fitzpatrick, David, *Harry Boland's Irish Revolution, 1877–1922*. Cork: Cork University Press, 2003.

Flannery, Eoin, *Versions of Ireland: Empire, Modernity and Resistance in Irish Culture*. Cambridge: Scholars Press, 2006.

Fletcher, Ian Christopher, Laura E. Nym Mayhall and Philippa Levine, eds., *Women's Suffrage in the British Empire: Citizenship, Nation, and Race*. London: Routledge, 2000.

Foley, Tadhg and Maureen O'Connor, eds., *Ireland and India: Colonies, Culture and Empire*. Dublin: Irish Academic Press, 2007.

Foley, Tadhg and Seán Ryder, eds., *Ideology and Ireland in the Nineteenth Century*. Dublin: Four Courts Press, 1998.

Foroughi, Mohammad Hussein Khan (Zoka' al-Molk), *Doureh-ye Ebtedā'i az Tārikh-e Ālam. Volume I: Tārikh-e Irān*. 1318 A.H. (1901).

Foster, John Wilson, *Fictions of the Irish Literary Revival: A Changing Art*. Syracuse: Syracuse University Press, 1987.

Foster, John Wilson, ed., *Nature in Ireland: A Scientific and Cultural History*. Montreal: McGill-Queen's University Press, 1997.

Foster, Roy F., *The Irish Story: Telling Tales and Making It Up in Ireland*. London: Allen Lane, 2001.

Foster, Roy F., *Vivid Faces: The Revolutionary Generation in Ireland, 1890–1923*. London: Allen Lane, 2014.

Foster, Roy F. W. B., *Yeats: A Life. Volume 1: The Apprentice Mage, 1865–1914*. Oxford: Oxford University Press, 1998.

Franklin, Michael J., *'Orientalist Jones': Sir William Jones, Poet, Lawyer, and Linguist, 1746–1794*. Oxford: Oxford University Press, 2011.

Fraser, James Baillie, *An Historical and Descriptive Account of Persia: From the Earliest Ages to the Present Time. With a Detailed View of its Resources, Government, Population, Natural History, and Character of Its Inhabitants, Particularly of Its Wandering Tribes; Including a Description of Afghanistan and Beloochistan*. Edinburgh: Oliver and Boyd, 1834.

Fraser, James Baillie, *The Kuzzilbash: A Tale of Khorasan*. Three Volumes. London: Henry Colburn, 1828.

Fraser, James Baillie, *Travels and Adventures in Persian Provinces on the Southern Banks of the Caspian Sea*. London: Longman, Rees, Orme, Brown, and Green, 1826.

Frawley, Oona, ed., *Memory Ireland. Volume 1: History and Modernity*. Syracuse: Syracuse University Press, 2011.

Gadamer, Hans-Georg, *Truth and Method*. Joel Weinsheimer and Donald G. Mar Translators. Second Revised Edition. London: Continuum, 2004.

Gamble, Eliza Burt, *The God-Idea of the Ancients or Sex in Religion*. New York and London: G.P. Putnam's Sons, 1897.

Ganachari, Aravind, *Nationalism and Social Reform in Colonial Situation*. Delhi: Kalpaz Publications, 2005.

Ganji, Mohammad Hassan, *Joqrāfiyā dar Irān: az Dār al-Funun tā Enqelāb*. Mashhad: Astan-e Qods-e Razavi, 1367 [1988].

Garmroudi, Mirza Abdul-Fattah Khan, *Safarnāmeh-ye Mirzā Fattāh Khān Garmroudi beh Orupā dar Zamān-e Mohammad Shāh Qājār*. Fath al-Din Fattahi Editor. Tehran: Bank-e Bazargani, 1347 [1969].

Garrigan Mattar, Sinéad, *Primitivism, Science, and the Irish Revival*. Oxford: Oxford University Press, 2004.

Gaskill, Howard, ed., *The Reception of Ossian in Europe*. London: Thoemmes Continuum, 2004.

Geary, Laurence M., ed., *Rebellion and Remembrance in Modern Ireland*. Dublin: Four Courts Press, 2001.

Ghanoonparvar, Mohammad R., *In a Persian Mirror: Images of the West and Westerners in Iranian Fiction*. Austin: University of Texas Press, 1993.

Gharavi, Mahmoud, *Majerā-ye Dowlat-e Ingilis va Mirzā Hāshem Khān*. Tehran: Nashr-e Tarikh-e Iran, 1363 [1984].

Ghazels From the Divan of Hafiz, Done Into English by Justin Huntly McCarthy. London: David Nutt, 1893.
Gibbons, Luke, *Limits of the Visible: Representing the Great Hunger*. Cork: Cork University Press, 2015.
Gibbons, Luke and Kieran O'Conor, eds., *Charles O'Conor of Ballinagare*. Dublin: Four Courts Press, 2012.
Gilbert, John Thomas, *History of the City of Dublin*. Volume II. Dublin: McGlashan and Gill, 1859.
Giles, John Allen, ed., *The British History of Geoffrey of Monmouth*. Translated from the Latin by Aaron Thompson. London: James Bohn, 1842.
Gladstone, William Ewart, *The Gladstone Diaries. Volume V: 1855–1860*. Henry Colin Gray Matthew Editor. Oxford: Clarendon Press, 1978.
Godwin, Joscelyn, *The Theosophical Enlightenment*. Albany: State University of New York Press, 1994.
Golway, Terry, *Irish Rebel: John Devoy and America's Fight for Ireland's Independence*. New York: St. Martin's Press, 1998.
Gott, Richard, *Britain's Empire: Resistance, Repression and Revolt*. London: Verso, 2011.
Gould, Warwick, ed., *Yeats Annual, No.7; Including Essays in Memory of Richard Ellmann*. Ronald Schuchard editor. London: Macmillan, 1990.
Graves, Robert Perceval, *Life of Sir William Rowan Hamilton*. Volume I. Dublin: Hodges, Figgis, & Co., 1882.
Graves-Brown, Paul, Siän Jones and Clive Gamble, eds., *Cultural Identity and Archaeology: The Construction of European Communities*. New York: Routledge, 1996.
Great Britain Civil Service Commission, Twenty-Seventh Report. *Her Majesty's Civil Service Commissioners, Together with Appendices*. London: Eyre and Spottiswoode, 1883.
Green, Alice Stopford, *History of the Irish State to 1014*. London: Macmillan and Co., 1925.
Green, Alice Stopford, *Irish Nationality*. New York: Henry Holt and Company, 1911.
Green, Alice Stopford, *The Making of Ireland and Its Undoing, 1200–1600*. Dublin: Maunsel and Company, 1920.
Greene, John C., *Theatre in Dublin, 1745–1820: A Calendar of Performances*. Volume 6. Lanham, MD: Rowman & Littlefield, 2011.
Green, Nile, *The Love of Strangers: What Six Muslim Students Learned in Jane Austen's London*. Princeton: Princeton University Press, 2016.
Gregory, Lady Isabella Augusta, *Cuchulain of Muirthemne: The Story of the Men of the Red Branch of Ulster*. Arranged and Translated From the Irish by Lady Gregory, With a Preface by Yeats. New Edition. London: John Murray, 1903 [1902].
Gregory, Lady Isabella Augusta, ed., *Gods and Fighting Men: The Story of the Tuatha de Danann and of the Fianna of Ireland*. Lady Gregory Translator, With a Preface by William Butler Yeats. London: John Murray, 1905.
Grover, Henry Montague, "The Identity of Cyrus and the Times of Daniel," *Journal of Sacred Literature*, New Series 7(14), January 1855, pp.364–81.
Guiney, Louise Imogen, *James Clarence Mangan: His Selected Poems, With a Study*. With a Dedication to Sir Charles Gavan Duffy. Norwood, MA: Norwood Press, 1897.
Gurney, John and Mansour Sefat-gol, *Qom dar Qahti-e Bozorg-e 1288 Qamari*. Qom:Ketabkhaneh-ye Bozorg-e Hazrat-e Ayatollah-e Ozma Mar'ashi-Najafi, 2008.
Gwynn, Stephen Lucius, *The Fair Hills of Ireland*. Dublin: Maunsel and Co., 1906.
Gwynn, Stephen Lucius, *The History of Ireland*. London: MacMillan & Co., 1923.
Gwynn, Stephen Lucius, *Thomas Moore*. London: MacMillan and Co., 1905.
Hachey, Thomas E. and Lawrence J. McCaffrey, eds., *Perspectives on Irish Nationalism*. Lexington: University Press of Kentucky, 1989.
Hales, William, *A New Analysis of Chronology and Geography, History and Prophecy: In Which Their Elements Are Attempted to be Explained, Harmonized, and Vindicated, Upon Scriptural and Scientific Principles; Tending to Remove the Imperfection and Discordance of Preceding Systems, and to Obviate the*

Cavils of Sceptics, Jews, and Infidels. Volume IV: Profane Chronology. Second Edition. London: G.J.G. and F. Rivington, 1830.

Hall, Catherine, Keith McClelland and Jane Rendall, eds., *Defining the Victorian Nation: Class, Race, Gender and the Reform Act of 1867.* Cambridge: Cambridge University Press, 2000.

Hall, Samuel Carter and Anna Maria Hall, *Ireland: Its Scenery, Character, &c.* Volume III. London: Jeremiah How, 1843.

Hall, Stuart and Bram Gieben, eds., *Formations of Modernity.* Cambridge: Open University, 1992.

Halpin, William G. and Other Defendants, *In the District Court of the United States for the Southern District of Ohio. United States vs. W. G. Halpin, David Reidy, Edward Kenifeck, Samuel Lumsden, et al. Charged With Conspiracy, for Exciting Insurrection in Ireland, and Aiding It by an Armed Force From the United States. Preliminary Examination Before the Hon. H. H. Leavitt, Sitting as Commissioner.* Cincinnati: Moore, Wilstach, Keys & Overend, 1856.

Hamedani, Rashid al-Din Fazlullah, *Jāmi ' al-Tawārikh': Tārikh-e Afranj, Pāpān, va Qiyāssiri.* Mohammad Roushan Editor. Tehran: Mirass-e Maktoub, 1384 [2005].

Handbook for Travellers in Ireland. London: John Murray, 1864.

Hanley, Brian, *The IRA, 1926–1936.* Dublin: Four Courts Press, 2002.

Hansson, Heidi and James H. Murphy, eds., *Fictions of the Irish Land War.* Bern: Peter Lang, 2014.

Hardiman, James, ed., *Irish Minstrelsy: Or Bardic Remains of Ireland.* Volume II. London: Joseph Robins, 1831.

Harkness, David W., *The Restless Dominion: The Irish Free State and the British Commonwealth of Nations 1921–31.* London: Macmillan, 1969.

Hart, Kevin, *Samuel Johnson and the Culture of Property.* Reprint. Cambridge: Cambridge University Press, 2004 [1999].

Hayden, Mary and George Aloysius Moonan, *A Short History of the Irish People From the Earliest Times to 1920.* London: Longman, Green, and Co., 1922.

Hayrat-Irani, Ismail, *Ketāb-e Tārikh-e Navāb-e Mostetāb Ser Jān Malkom Sāheb Bahādor.* Volume I. Bombay: n.p., 1876.

Healy, John, *Irish Essays: Literary and Historical.* Dublin: Catholic Truth Society of Ireland, 1908.

Healy, Róisín, *Poland in the Irish Nationalist Imagination, 1772–1922: Anti-Colonialism Within Europe.* New York: Palgrave Macmillan, 2017.

Hedayat, Rezaqoli Khan, *Ajmal al-Tawārikh.* Tabriz: Aqa Reza and Karbala'i Mohammad Hussein Publishers, 1283 A.H. (1866).

Hedayat, Sadeq, *Toup-e Morvari.* Tehran: n.p., 1358 (1979).

Herbelot de Molainville, Barthélemy, *La Bibliothèque orientale, ou Dictionnaire universel contenant generalement tout ce qui regarde la connossance des peuples de l'Orient.* Paris: Compagnie des Libraires, 1697.

Herder, John Godfrey (Johann Gottfried von Herder), *Outlines of a Philosophy of the History of Man.* Volume I. Second Edition. T. Churchill Translator. London: J. Johnson, 1803 [First Edition, 1800].

Higgins, Padhraig, *A Nation of Politicians: Gender, Patriotism, and Political Culture in Late Eighteenth-Century Ireland.* Madison: University of Wisconsin Press, 2010.

Hobsbawm, Eric J. and Terence O. Ranger, eds., *The Invention of Tradition.* Cambridge: Cambridge University Press, 1983.

Hobson, John Atkinson, *Richard Cobden: The International Man.* New York: Henry Holt and Company, 1911.

Hodgkins, Louise Manning, ed., *Matthew Arnold's Sohrab and Rustum.* Boston: Leach, Shewell, and Sanborn, 1890.

Hofheinz, Thomas C., *Joyce and the Inventions of Irish History: Finnegans Wake in Context.* Cambridge: Cambridge University Press, 1995.

Hone, Joseph Maunsell and Page L. Dickinson, *Persia in Revolution: With Notes of Travel in the Caucasus.* London: T. Fisher Unwin, 1910.

Hooper, Glenn and Leon Litvack, eds., *Ireland in the Nineteenth Century: Regional Identity*. Dublin: Four Courts Press, 2000.
Howes, Marjorie, *Colonial Crossings: Figures in Irish Literary History*. Dublin: Field Day, 2006.
Huddie, Paul, *The Crimean War and Irish Society*. Liverpool: Liverpool University Press, 2015.
Humbachm, Helmut and Klaus Faiss, *Herodotus's Scythians and Ptolemy's Central Asia: Semasiological and Onomasiological Studies*. Weisbaden: Ludwig Reihert, 2012.
Hunter, Douglas, *The Place of Stone: Dighton Rock and the Erasure of America's Indigenous Past*. Chapel Hill: University of North Carolina Press, 2017.
Hutchinson, John, *The Dynamics of Cultural Nationalism: The Gaelic Revival and the Creation of the Irish Nation State*. London: Allen & Unwin, 1987.
Hyde, Douglas, *A Literary History of Ireland: From Earliest Times to the Present Day*. London: Fisher Unwin, 1899.
Hyde, Douglas, ed., *Beside the Fire: A Collection of Irish Gaelic Folk Stories*. Translation and Annotations by Douglas Hyde, With Additional Notes by Alfred Nutt. London: D. Nutt, 1890.
Hyde, Douglas, *The Story of Early Gaelic Literature*. London: T. Fisher Unwin, 1895.
Ignatiev, Noel, *How the Irish Became White*. New York: Routledge, 1995.
Ingram, Edward, *In Defence of British India: Great Britain in the Middle East, 1775–1842*. London: Cass, 1984.
Ingram, John Kells, *Sonnets and Other Poems*. London: Adam and Charles Black, 1900.
Issawi, Charles, *The Economic History of Iran 1800–1914*. Chicago: University of Chicago Press, 1971.
Jackson, Peter and Laurence Lockhart, eds., *The Cambridge History of Iran. Volume 6: The Timurid and Safavid Periods*. Reprint. Cambridge: Cambridge University Press, 2006 [1986].
Javadi, Hasan, *Persian Literary Influence on English Literature*. New Edition. Costa Mesa, CA: Mazda, 2005.
Jenkins, Brian, *Fenians and Anglo-American Relations During Reconstruction*. Ithaca, NY: Cornell University Press, 1969.
Jenkins, Kirk C., *The Battle Rages Higher: The Union's Fifteenth Kentucky Infantry*. Lexington: University of Kentucky Press, 2003.
Jenkinson, Anthony and Other Englishmen, *Early Voyages and Travels to Russia and Persia*. Two Volumes. E. Delmar Morgan and C. H. Coote Editors. London: Hakluyt Society, 1886.
Jennings, Hargrave, *Phallic Objects, Monuments and Remains: Illustrations of the Rise and Development of the Phallic Idea (Sex Worship) and Its Embodiment in the Works of Nature and Art*. Anonymously and Privately Published, 1889.
Jensen, Joan M., *Passage From India: Asian Indian Immigrants in North America*. New Haven: Yale University Press, 1988.
John, Angela V., *War, Journalism and the Shaping of the Twentieth Century: The Life and Times of Henry W. Nevinson*. New York: I.B. Tauris, 2006.
Johnston Graf, Susan, *Talking to the Gods: Occultism in the Work of W. B. Yeats, Arthur Machen, Algernon Blackwood, and Dion Fortune*. Albany: State University of New York, 2015.
Jones, Howard Mumford, *The Harp That Once: A Chronicle of the Life of Thomas Moore*. New York: Henry Holt and Company, 1937.
Jones, Rowland, *The Origin of Language and Nations, Hieroglyfically, Etymologically, and Topografically Defined and Fixed, After the Method of an English, Celtic, Greek and Latin English Lexicon*. London: J. Hughs, 1764.
Jones, William, *The Works of Sir William Jones. Volume I*. Anna Maria Jones Editor. London: G.G. and J. Robinson, Pater-Noster-Row, and R.H. Evans, 1799.
Jones Brydges, Harford, *An Account of the Transactions of His Majesty's Mission to the Court of Persia in the Years 1807–11, to Which is Appended, a Brief History of the Wahauby*. Volume I. London: James Bohn, 1834.

Jones Brydges, Harford, *The Dynasty of the Kajars. Translated From the Original Persian Manuscript Presented by His Majesty Faty Aly Shah* ... (Based on the Translation of *Abdul-Razzaq Beg Donboli's Ma'āser-e Sultānīyeh, 1811*). London: John Bohn, 1833.

Joyce, James, *Dubliners*. With an Introduction by Laurence Davies. Ware, Hertfordshire: Wordsworth, 2001.

Joyce, James, *Finnegans Wake*. Reprint. New York: Viking Press, 1966 [1939].

Joyce, James, *Ulysses*. London: Egoist Press (Published by John Rodker in Paris), 1922.

Joyce, Patrick Weston, *A Concise History of Ireland*. New York: Longmans, Green, and Co., 1903.

Joyce, Patrick Weston, *A Social History of Ancient Ireland*. Volume I. London: Longmans, Green, and Co., 1903.

Kain Richard M. and James H. O'Brien, *George Russell (A.E.)*. Lewisburg: Bucknell University Press, 1976.

Kashani-Sabet, Firoozeh, *Frontier Fictions: Shaping the Iranian Nation, 1804–1946*. Princeton: Princeton University Press, 1999.

Keane, Marcus, *The Towers and Temples of Ancient Ireland; Their Origin and History Discussed From a New Point of View*. Dublin: Hodges, Smith and Co., 1867.

Keating, Geoffrey, *The History of Ireland*. Two Volumes. David Comyn Translator and Editor. London: Irish Texts Society, 1902.

Keating, Geoffrey, *The History of Ireland, From the Earliest Period to the English Invasion*. John O'Mahony Translator. New York: P.M. Haverty, 1857.

Keddie, Nikki R., *Sayyid Jamal ad-Din 'al-Afghani.' A Political Biography*. Berkeley: University of California Press, 1972.

Keightley, Thomas, *Tales and Popular Fictions; Their Resemblance, and Transmission From Country to Country*. London: Whittaker and Co., 1834.

Kelleher, John V., *Selected Writings of John V. Kelleher on Ireland and Irish America*. Charles Fanning Editor. Carbondale: Southern Illinois University Press, 2002.

Kelly, James and Susan Hegarty, eds., *Schools and Schooling, 1650–2000: New Perspectives on the History of Education*. Dublin: Four Courts Press, 2017.

Kelly, Laurence, *Diplomacy and Murder in Tehran: Alexander Griboyedov and Imperial Russia's Mission to the Shah of Persia*. Reprint. London: I.B. Tauris, 2006 [2002].

Kelly, Mary Eva ("Eva of *The Nation*"), *Poems. By 'Eva' of 'The Nation.'* Seumas Mac Manus Editor. Dublin: M.H. Gill & Son, 1909.

Kelly, Ronan, *Bard of Erin: The Life of Thomas Moore*. Dublin: Penguin, 2008.

Kennedy, Michael, *Ireland and the League of Nations, 1919–1946: International Relations, Diplomacy and Politics*. Dublin: Irish Academic Press. 1996.

Keogh, Dermot, *Ireland and Europe, 1919–48*. Dublin: Gill and Macmillan, 1988.

Keown, Gerard, *First of the Small Nations: The Beginnings of Irish Foreign Policy in the Interwar Years, 1919–1932*. Oxford: Oxford University Press, 2016.

Khayyam, Omar, *Rubaiyat of Omar Khayyam*. Justin Huntly McCarthy Translator. London: David Nutt, 1889.

Kiberd, Declan, *Inventing Ireland: The Literature of the Modern Nation*. Cambridge, MA: Harvard University Press, 1995.

Kiberd, Declan and P. J. Mathews, eds., *Handbook of the Irish Revival: An Anthology of Irish Cultural and Political Writings, 1891–1922*. Reprint. Notre Dame, IN: University of Notre Dame Press, 2016 [2015].

Kidd, Colin, *British Identities Before Nationalism: Ethnicity and Nationhood in the Atlantic World, 1600–1800*. Reprint. Cambridge: Cambridge University Press, 2004 [1999].

Kilroy, James, *James Clarence Mangan*. Cranbury, NJ: Associated University Press, 1970.

Kilroy, James, ed., *The Autobiography of James Clarence Mangan*. Dublin: Dolmen, 1969.

Kinahan, Frank, *Yeats, Folklore and Occultism: Contexts of the Early Work and Thought*. London: Routledge, 1988.

Kinealy, Christine, *Charity and the Great Hunger in Ireland: The Kindness of Strangers*. London: Bloomsbury, 2013.
Kinealy, Christine, *Repeal and Revolution: 1848 in Ireland*. Manchester: Manchester University Press, 2009.
Kinealy, Christine, *The Great Irish Famine: Impact, Ideology and Rebellion*. Houndmills, Basingstoke: Palgrave, 2001.
Kirwan, Richard, *Geological Essays*. London: D. Bremner, 1799.
Kissane, Bill, *The Politics of the Irish Civil War*. Oxford: Oxford University Press, 2005.
Knight, Charles, ed., *Biography, or Third Division of "The English Encyclopedia."* Volume 5. London: Bradbury, Evans, & Co., 1867.
Koch, John T., ed., *Celtic Culture: A Historical Encyclopedia*. Five Volumes. Santa Barbara: ABC-CLIO, 2006.
Kopf, David, *British Orientalism and the Bengal Renaissance*. Berkeley: University of California Press, 1969.
Krachkovsky, Ignaty Yulianovich, *Tārikh-e Neveshteh-hā-ye joqrāfiāyi dar Jahān-e Eslāmi*. Persian translation by Abolqassem Payandeh from the Arabic translation of the Russian original *Istoriia arabskoi geograficheskoi literatury/History of Geographical Works in the Arab World*. Second Edition. Tehram: Entesharat-e Elmi va Farhangi, 1384 [1379] (2005).
Krappe, Alexander Haggerty, *Mythologie universelle*. Paris: Payot, 1930.
Kristeva, Julia, *The Kristeva Reader*. Toril Moi Editor. New York: Columbia University Press, 1986.
Lake, Edward John, *The Church Missionary Society Atlas*. Sixth Edition. London: Church Missionary House, 1879.
Larminie, William, *West Irish Folk-Tales and Romances*. London: Elliot Stock, 1893.
Lashomb, Donald A., "Working Through Tradition Alone – Joyce's Mythic Return," PhD Dissertation, New York University, 2008.
Ledwich, Edward, *The Antiquities of Ireland*. Second Edition. Dublin: John Jones, 1804 [1790].
Lee, Joseph J., *Ireland, 1912–1985: Politics and Society*. Cambridge: Cambridge University Press, 1989.
Leerssen, Joep (Joseph Theodoor), A. H. van der Weel and Bart Westerweel, eds., *Forging in the Smithy: National Identity and Representation in Anglo-Irish Literary History*. Amsterdam:Editions Rodopi B.V., 1995.
Leerssen, Joep (Joseph Theodoor), *Remembrance and Imagination: Patterns in the Historical and Literary Representation of Ireland in the Nineteenth Century*. Cork: Cork University Press, 1996.
Leerssen, Joseph Theodoor (Joep), *Mere Irish & Fíor-ghael: Studies in the Idea of Irish Nationality, Its Literary Expression and Development*. Amsterdam: John Benjamins, 1986.
Legg, Marie-Louise, *Newspapers and Nationalism: The Irish Provincial Press, 1850–1892*. Dublin: Four Courts Press, 1999.
Lenihan, Pádraig, *Confederate Catholics at War, 1641–1649*. Cork: Cork University Press, 2000.
Lennon, Joseph, *Irish Orientalism: A Literary and Intellectual History*. Syracuse: Syracuse University Press, 2004.
Levenson, Leah and Jerry H. Natterstad, *Hanna Sheehy-Skeffington: Irish Feminist*. Syracuse: Syracuse University Press, 1986.
Levenson, Leah and Wooden Sword, *A Portrait of Francis Sheehy-Skeffington, Militant Pacifist*. Boston: Northeastern University Press, 1983.
Levine, Philippa, *The Amateur and the Professional: Antiquarians, Historians and Archaeologists in Victorian England, 1838–1886*. Cambridge: Cambridge University Press, 1986.
Lewis, Arthur, *George Maxwell Gordon, M.A., F.R.G.S.: The Pilgrim Missionary of the Punjab. A History of His Life and Work, 1839–1880*. Second Edition. London: Seeley & Co., 1889.
Lewis, Martin W. and Kären E. Wigen, *The Myth of Continents a Critique of Metageography*. Berkeley: University of California Press, 1997.

Livingstone, David N., *Adam's Ancestors: Race, Religion, and the Politics of Human Origins*. Reprint. Baltimore: Johns Hopkins Press, 2011 [2008].

Lloyd, David, *Counterpoetics of Modernity: On Irish Poetry and Modernism*. Edinburgh: Edinburgh University Press, 2022.

Lloyd, David, *Nationalism and Minor Literature: James Clarence Mangan and the Emergence of Irish Cultural Nationalism*. Berkeley: University of California Press, 1987.

Lloyd, Trevor O., *Empire to Welfare State: English History 1906–1985*. Third Edition. New York: Oxford University Press, 1991.

Lock, Frederick Peter, *Edmund Burke, Volume II: 1784–1797*. Oxford: Clarendon Press, 2006.

Loewe, Louis, ed., *Diaries of Sir Moses and Lady Montefiore: Comprising Their Life and Work as Recorded in Their Diaries From 1812 to 1883*. Two Volumes. Chicago: Belford-Clarke Co., 1890.

Longford, Elizabeth, *A Pilgrimage of Passion: The Life of Wilfrid Scawen Blunt*. London: Wedenfeld and Nicolson, 1979.

Lynd, Robert, *If the Germans Conquered England, and Other Essays*. Dublin: Maunsel and Company, 1917.

Lyons, Claire, "Sylvester O'Halloran's General History: Irish Historiography and the Late Eighteenth-Century British Empire." PhD Dissertation, National University of Ireland, Galway, 2011.

Lyons, Francis S. L., *Charles Stewart Parnell*. London: Collins, 1977.

MacCall, Seamus, *And So Began the Irish Nation*. Dublin: Talbot Press, 1931.

MacCarthy, Anne, *James Clarence Mangan, Edward Walsh and Nineteenth-Century Irish Literature in English*. New York: Edwin Mellen, 2000.

MacCarthy, Denis Florence, *Ballads, Poems, Lyrics, Original and Translated*. Dublin: James McGlashan, 1850.

Maclean, Fitzroy, *A Person From England*. London; J. Cape, 1958.

MacManus, Seumas, *The Story of the Irish Race: A Popular History of Ireland*. Revised Edition. New York: Devin-Adair, 1977 [1921].

MacMathúna, Séamus, Maxim Fomin and Alvard Jivanyan, eds., *Journal of Indo-European Studies, Monograph 61: "Ireland and Armenia: Studies in Language, History and Narrative."* Washington, DC, 2013.

MacNeill, Eoin, *Phases of Irish History*. Dublin: M.H. Gill & Son, 1920.

MacSweeney, Patrick, *A Group of Nation Builders: O'Donovan-O'Curry-Petrie*. Dublin: Catholic Truth Society of Ireland, 1913.

Mahomet, Sake Deen, *The Travels of Dean Mahomet: An Eighteenth Century Journey Through India*. Edited With and Introduction and Biographical Essay by Michael H. Fisher. Berkeley: University of California Press, 1997.

Majeed, Javed, *Ungoverned Imaginings: James Mill's the History of British India and Orientalism*. Oxford: Clarendon Press, 1992.

Malcolm, John, *Sketches of Persia, From the Journals of a Traveller in the East*. Two Volumes. London: John Murray, 1827.

Malcolm, John, *The History of Persia From the Most Early Period to the Present Time: Containing an Account of the Religion, Government, Usages, and Character of the Inhabitants of that Kingdom*. Volume I. London: John Murray, 1815.

Malcolm, John, *The History of Persia From the Most Early Period to the Present Time: Containing an Account of the Religion, Government, Usages, and Character of the Inhabitants of that Kingdom*. Volume I. Second Revised Edition. London: John Murray, 1829.

Malekpour, Jamshid, *Adabiyāt-e Namāyeshi dar Irān: Nokhostin Koushesh-hā tā Doureh-ye Qājār*. Volume I. Reprint. Tehran: Touss, 1385 [2006].

Mangan, James Clarence, *Anthologia Germanica. German Anthology: A Series of Translations from the Most Popular of the German Poets*. Volume II. Dublin: William Curry, Jun. and Company, 1845.

Mangan, James Clarence, *Poems*. David Wheatley Editor. Oldcastle, Ireland: Gallery Press, 2003.

Mangan, James Clarence, *Poems by James Clarence Mangan*. With Biographical Introduction by John Mitchel. New York: P.M. Harvey, 1859.
Mansoor, Menahem, *The Study of Irish Orientalism*. Dublin: Hodges, Figgis & Co., 1944.
Marashi, Afshin, *Nationalizing Iran: Culture, Power, & the State, 1870–1940*. Seattle: University of Washington Press, 2008.
Markham, Clements Robert, *A General Sketch of the History of Persia*. London: Longmans, Green, and Co., 1874.
Marquardt, Janet T. and Alyce A. Jordan, eds., *Medieval Art and Architecture After the Middle Ages*. Newcastle upon Tyne: Cambridge Scholars, 2009.
The Marvellous Year, With an Introduction by Edwin Markham and Drawings by Gertrude Huebsch. New York: B.W. Huebsch, 1909.
Marzolph, Ulrich, *Relief After Hardship: The Ottoman Turkish Model for the Thousand and One Days*. Detroit: Wayne State University, 2017.
Mathews, P.J., *Revival: The Abbey Theatre, Sinn Féin, the Gaelic League, and the Co-Operative Movement*. Notre Dame, IN: University of Notre Dame Press, 2004.
Matthew, Henry Colin Gray, *Gladstone 1809–1874*. Oxford: Clarendon Press, 1986.
Maume, Patrick, *The Long Gestation: Irish Nationalist Life, 1891–1918*. New York: St. Martin's Press, 1999.
McAteer, Michael, *Yeats and European Drama*. Cambridge: Cambridge University Press, 2010.
McBride, Ian, *Eighteenth-Century Ireland: The Isle of Slaves*. Dublin: Gill & Macmillan, 2007.
McBride, Ian, ed., *History and Memory in Modern Ireland*. Cambridge: Cambridge University Press, 2001.
McCarthy, Justin, Charles Welsh, Maurice Francis Egan, Douglas Hyde, Lady Gregory and James Jeffrey Roche, eds., *Irish Literature*. Volume 9. Philadelphia: J.D. Morris & Company, 1904.
McCracken, Donal P., *Forgotten Protest: Ireland and the Anglo-Boer War*. Reprint. Belfast: Ulster Historical Foundation, 2003 [1989].
McCracken, Donal P., *MacBride's Brigade: Irish Commandos in the Anglo-Boer War*. Dublin: Four Courts Press, 1999.
McCully, Alan and Fionnuala Waldron, "A Question of Identity" Purpose, Policy and Practice in the Teaching of History in Northern Ireland and the Republic of Ireland" in Hilary Cooper and John Nichol, eds., *Identity, Trauma, Sensitive and Controversial Issues in the Teaching of History*. Newcastle upon Tyne: Cambridge Scholars, 2015, pp.2–24.
McDonough, Terrence, ed., *Was Ireland a Colony? Economics, Politics and Culture in Nineteenth-Century Ireland*. Dublin: Irish Academic Press, 2005.
McGarry, Fearghal, *Irish Politics and the Spanish Civil War*. Cork: Cork University Press, 1999.
McGee, Owen, *Arthur Griffith*. Sallins, Ireland: Irish Academic Press, 2015.
McGee, Thomas D'Arcy, *A History of the Irish Settlers in North America: From the Earliest Period to the Census of 1850*. Boston: American Celt, 1851.
McGovern, Bryan P., *John Mitchel: Irish Nationalist, Southern Secessionist*. Knoxville: University of Tennessee Press, 2009.
McGuire, James K., *The King, the Kaiser and Irish Freedom*. New York: Devin-Adair Company, 1915.
McGuire, James K., *What Could Germany Do for Ireland?* With an Introduction by Thomas Addis Emmet. New York: Wolfe Tone Company, 1916.
McLean, Stuart, *The Event and Its Terrors: Ireland, Famine, Modernity*. Stanford: Stanford University Press, 2004.
McMahon, Richard, *The Races of Europe: Construction of National Identities in the Social Sciences, 1839–1939*. London: Palgrave Macmillan, 2016.
McMahon, Timothy G., *Grand Opportunity: The Gaelic Revival and Irish Society, 1893–1910*. Syracuse: Syracuse University Press, 2008.

McMinn, Joseph, ed., *The Internationalism of Irish Literature and Drama*. Gerrards Cross: Colin Smythe, 1982.

McNamara, Brendan, *The Reception of 'Abdu'l-Bahá in Britain*. Leiden: Brill, 2020.

Meehan, Charles Patrick, ed., *Essays in Prose and Verse by James Clarence Mangan*. Dublin: James Duffy & Sons, 1884.

Megill, Allan, *Historical Knowledge, Historical Error: A Contemporary Guide to Practice*. With Contributions by Steven Shepard and Phillip Honenberger. Chicago: University of Chicago Press, 2007.

Melville, Joy, *Mother of Oscar: The Life of Jane Francesca Wilde*. London: John Murray, 1994.

Meyer, Kuno, ed., *Fianaigecht: Being a Collection of Hitherto Inedited Irish Poems and Tales Relating to Finn and His Fiana, With an English Translation*. Dublin: Hodges, Figgis, & Co., 1910.

Meyer, Kuno, ed., *The Triads of Ireland*. Dublin: Hodges, Figgis, & Co., 1906.

Meyer, Kuno, *The Voyage of Bran Son of Febal to the Land of the Living ... Edited, With Translation, Notes, and Glossary, by Kuno Meyer. With an Essay Upon the Irish Vision of the Happy Otherworld and the Celtic Doctrine of Rebirth, by Alfred Nutt. Section I: The Happy Otherworld*. London: David Nutt, 1895.

Mill, James, *The History of British India*. Volume I. London: Baldwin, Cradock, and Joy, 1817.

Miller, Robert Ryal, *Shamrock and Sword: The Saint Patrick's Battalion in the U.S.-Mexican War*. Norman: University of Oklahoma Press, 1989.

Mink, Louis O., *A Finnegans Wake Gazetteer*. Bloomington: Indiana University Press, 1978.

Mitchel, John, *The Last Conquest of Ireland (Perhaps)*. Author's Edition. Glasgow: R. & T. Washbourne, 1882 [1861].

Modi, Jivanji Jamshedji, *Asiatic Papers: Papers Read Before the Bombay Branch of the Royal Asiatic Society*. Part I. Bombay: Bombay Education Society, 1905.

Mo'in al-Saltaneh, Hajji Mirza Mohammad-Ali, *Safarnāmeh-ye Shikāgo: Khāterāt-e Hāji Mirzā Mohammad-Ali Mo'in al-Saltaneh beh Orupā va Amrikā, 1310 Hejri-e Qamari*. Homayoun Shahidi Editor. Tehran: Elmi, 1363 [1984].

Montaño, John Patrick, *The Roots of English Colonialism in Ireland*. Cambridge: Cambridge University Press, 2011.

Moore, George, *'Hail and Farewell!' Volume II: Salve*. Reprint. London: William Heinemann, 1912 [1911].

Moore, Maurice George, *An Irish Gentleman: George Henry Moore. His Travels. His Racing. His Politics*. With a Preface by George Moore. London: T. Werner Laurie, n.d.

Moore, Thomas, *Corruption and Intolerance: Two Poems. With Notes. Addressed to an Englishman by an Irishman*. London: J. Carpenter, 1808.

Moore, Thomas, *Irish Melodies*. London: Longman, Brown, Green, and Longmans, 1852.

Moore, Thomas, *Lalla Rookh: An Oriental Romance*. New Edition With a New Preface. New York: C.S. Francis & Co., 1849 [1817].

Moore, Thomas, ed., *Letters and Journals of Lord Byron: With Notices of His Life*. Volume II. Reprint. New York: Harper, 1831 [1830].

Moore, Thomas, *Memoirs, Journal, and Correspondence of Thomas Moore*. 8 Volumes. Edited by Lord John Russell. London: Longman, Brown, Green, and Longmans, 1853–1856.

Moore, Thomas, *Memoirs of Captain Rock, the Celebrated Irish Chieftain, With Some Account of His Ancestors. Written by Himself*. Edited and With an Introduction by Emer Nolan, and With Annotations by Seamus Deane. Dublin: Field Day, 2008.

Moore, Thomas, *The History of Ireland*. Volume I. London: Longman, Rees, Orme, Brown, Green, & Longman, 1835.

Moore, Thomas, *The History of Ireland*. Volume II. London: Longman, Rees, Orme, Brown, Green, & Longman, 1837.

Moore, Thomas, *The History of Ireland*. Volume IV. London: Longman, Rees, Orme, Brown, Green, & Longman, 1846.

Moore, Thomas, *The Poetical Works of Thomas Moore, Collected by Himself*. Volume VI. London: Longman, Orme, Brown, Green, & Longmans, 1841.

Moore, Thomas, *The Poetical Works of Thomas Moore: As Corrected by Himself in 1848*. Volume I. New York: Robert Martin, 1851.
Moore, Thomas, *Travels of an Irish Gentleman in Search of Religion: With Notes and Illustrations, by the Editor of "Captain Rock's Memoirs." In Two Volumes*. London: Longman, Rees, Orme, Brown, Green, & Longman, 1833.
Moore, Thomas and Thomas Brown, *Intercepted Letters; or, the Twopenny Post-Bag. To Which Are Added, Trifles Reprinted*. Third Edition. London: J. Carr, 1813.
Morris, Lloyd R., *The Celtic Dawn: A Survey of the Renascence in Ireland, 1889–1916*. New York: Macmillan, 1917.
Mostufi Qazvini, Hamdollah, *Tarikh-e Gozideh*. Abdul-Hussein Nava'i Editor. Tehran: Amir Kabir, 1339 (1960–1961) [Composed in 1330 CE].
Mottahedeh, Negar, ed., *'Abdu'l-Bahá's Journey West: The Course of Human Solidarity*. New York: Palgrave Macmillan, 2013.
[Mrs. Purcell], *The Orientalist, or Electioneering in Ireland; a Tale, by Myself*. Volume I. London: Baldwin, Cradock, and Joy, 1820.
Müller, Max, *Lectures on the Science of Language. Delivered at the Royal Institution of Great Britain in April, May, & June 1861*. London: Longman, Green, Longman, and Roberts, 1861.
Mulvagh, Conor, *Irish Days, Indian Memories: V.V. Giri and Indian Law Students at University College Dublin, 1913–1916*. Sallins, Ireland: Irish Academic Press, 2016.
Mulvey, Helen, *Thomas Davis and Ireland: A Biographical Study*. Washington, DC: Catholic University of America, 2003.
Murphy, David, *Ireland and the Crimean War*. Dublin: Four Courts Press, 2002.
Murphy, James H., ed., *The Oxford History of the Irish Book. Volume IV: The Irish Book in English, 1800–1891*. Oxford: Oxford University Press, 2011.
Muthu, Sankar, *Enlightenment Against Empire*. Princeton: Princeton University Press, 2003.
Najm al-Dowleh, Abdul-Qaffar, *Atlass-e Tāzeh-ye Joqrā fi-e Ahd-e Jadid*. Tehran: Dar al-Funun, 1302 [1884].
Nelson, Bruce, *Irish Nationalists and the Making of the Irish Race*. Princeton: Princeton University Press, 2012.
Nietzsche, Friedrich Wilhelm, *On the Advantage and Disadvantage of History for Life*. Peter Preuss Translator. Indianapolis: Hackett, 1980 (Originally Appearing in German as *Vom Nutzen und Nachteil der Historie für das Leben*, 1874).
Noack, Christian, Lindsay Janssen and Vincent Comerford, eds., *Holodomor and Gorta Mór: Histories, Memories and Representations of Famine in Ukraine and Ireland*. Reprint. London: Anthem Press, 2014 [2012].
Nolan, Emer, *Catholic Emancipations: Irish Fiction From the Thomas Moore to James Joyce*. Syracuse: Syracuse University Press, 2007.
Nolan, Emer, *James Joyce and Nationalism*. Second Edition. New York: Routledge, 2002 [1995].
Nora, Pierre, ed., *Realms of Memory: Rethinking the French Past. Volume I: Conflicts and Divisions*. New York: Columbia University Press, 1996 (Originally Published in French in 1984).
Norris, Margot, *The Value of James Joyce*. Cambridge: Cambridge University Press, 2016.
O'Brennan, Martin A., *A School History of Ireland, From the Day of Partholan to the Present Time*. Volume II. Dublin: n.p., 1858.
O'Brennan, Martin A., *O'Brennan's Antiquities*. Volume I. Second Edition. Dublin: n.p., 1858.
O'Brien, Henry, *The Round Towers of Ireland, or the History of Tuath-de-Dananas. Reprint of O'Brien's 1834 The Round Towers of Ireland, or the Mysteries of Freemasonry .... With an "Introduction" by W.H.C*. Calcutta: Thacker, Spink, and Co., 1898.
O'Brien, Henry, *The Round Towers of Ireland, or the Mysteries of Freemasonry, of Sabaism, and of Budhism, for the First Time Unveiled*. London: Whittaker and Co., 1834.
O'Brien, Joseph V., *William O'Brien and the Course of Irish Politics, 1881–1918*. Berkeley: University of California Press, 1976.

O'Brien, William, *Forth the Banners Go*. Dublin: Three Candles Limited, 1969.

O'Brien, William and Desmond Ryan, eds., *Devoy's Post Bag, 1871–1928. Volume II: 1880–1928*. With and Introduction by P.S. O'Hegarty. Dublin: C.J. Fallon, 1953.

ÓCadhla, Stiofán, *Civilizing Ireland: Ordnance Survey 1824–1842, Ethnography, Cartography, Translation*. Dublin: Irish Academic Press, 2007.

O'Callaghan, John Cornelius, *The Green Book, or Gleanings From the Writing-Desk of a Literary Agitator*. Dublin: James Duffy, 1845.

O'Connor, Thomas Power, ed., *The Cabinet of Irish Literature: Selections From the Works of the Chief Poets, Orators, and Prose Writers of Ireland*. Volume IV. London: Blackie and Son, 1880.

O'Conor, Charles, *Dissertations on the Ancient History of Ireland*. New Edition. Dublin: G. Faulkner, 1756 [1753].

O'Curry, Eugene, *On the Manners and Customs of the Ancient Irish: A Series of Lectures*. Three Volumes. Edited With an Introduction by William Kirby Sullivan. Dublin: W.B. Kelly, 1873.

O'Donoghue, David James, *The Life and Writings of James Clarence Mangan*. Edinburgh: Patrick Geddes and Colleagues, 1897.

O'Donoghue, David James, *The Poets of Ireland: A Biographical and Bibliographical Dictionary of Irish Writers of English Verse*. Dublin: Hodges Figgis, & Co., 1912.

O'Donoghue, David James, ed., *The Prose Writings of James Clarence Mangan*. Dublin: O'Donoghue & Co., 1904.

O'Donovan, Edmond, *The Merv Oasis: Travels and Adventures East of the Caspian During the Years 1879–80-81. Including Five Months Residence Among the Tekkés of Merv*. Two Volumes. London: Smith, Elder, & Co., 1882.

O'Donovan, John, *Annals of the Kingdom of Ireland by the Four Masters, From the Earliest Period to the Year 1616*. Volume I. Dublin:Hodges and Smith, 1848.

Official Guide: Dublin. Dublin: Bord Fáilte Éireann, 1950.

O'Flaherty, Roderic, *Ogygia, or a Chronological Account of Irish Events*. Two Volumes. James Hely Translator and Editor. Dublin:W. McKenzie, 1793.

O'Flaherty, Roderic, *The Ogygia Vindicated, Against the Objections of Sir George MacKenzie*. With "A Dissertation on the Origin and Antiquities of the Ancient Scots, and Notes, critical and explanatory, on Mr. O'Flaherty Text" by Charles O'Conor, Translator and Editor. Dublin: G. Faulkner, 1775.

Ó Giolláin, Diarmuid, *Locating Irish Folklore: Tradition, Modernity, Identity*. Cork: Cork University Press, 2000.

Ó Gráda, Cormac, *Black '47 and Beyond: The Great Irish Famine in History, Economy, and Memory*. Princeton: Princeton University Press, 2000.

Ó Gráda, Cormac, *Eating People is Wrong, and Other Essays on Famine, Its Past, and Its Future*. Princeton: Princeton University Press, 2015.

Ó Gráda, Cormac, *Jewish Ireland in the Age of Joyce: A Socioeconomic History*. Princeton: Princeton University, 2006.

O'Grady, Standish James, *History of Ireland. Volume I: The Heroic Period*. London: Sampson, Low, Searle, Marston, & Rivington, 1878.

O'Grady, Standish James, *Selected Essays and Passages*. With an Introduction by Ernest A. Boyd. Dublin: Talbot Press, 1918.

O'Grady, Standish James, *The Story of Ireland*. London: Methuen & Co., 1894.

O'Halloran, Clare, *Golden Ages and Barbarous Nations: Antiquarian Debate and Cultural Politics in Ireland, c.1750–1800*. Cork: Cork University Press, 2004.

O'Halloran, Sylvester, *A General History of Ireland, From the Earliest Accounts to the Close of the Twelfth Century* …. Volume I. London: A. Hamilton, 1778.

O'Hart, John, *Irish Pedigrees; or, the Origin and Stem of the Irish Nation*. Two Volumes. Fifth Edition. Dublin: James Duffy and Co., 1892 [1876].

O'Kelly, John Joseph (Seán Ua Ceallaigh), *Ireland: Elements of Her Early Story From the Coming of Ceasair to the Anglo-Norman Invasion*. Dublin: M.H. Gill & Son, 1921.

Olcott, Henry S., *Theosophy: Religion and Occult Science*. London: George Redway, 1885.
O'Leary, John, *Recollections of Fenians and Fenianism*. Two Volumes. London: Downey & Co., 1896.
O'Leary, Philip, *Gaelic Prose in the Irish Free State, 1922–1939*. University Park, Pennsylvania: Pennsylvania State University Press, 2004.
Ó Lúing, Seán, *Kuno Meyer, 1858–1919: A Biography*. Dublin: Geography Publications, 1991.
O'Malley, Kate, *Ireland, India and Empire: Indo-Irish Radical Connections, 1919–64*. Manchester: Manchester University Press, 2008.
O'Reilly, John Boyle, ed., *Poetry and Song of Ireland*. New York: Gay Brothers & Co., 1887.
Ó Siochrú, Micheál. *Confederate Ireland, 1642–1649: A Constitutional and Political Analysis*. Dublin: Four Courts Press, 1999.
O'Sullivan, Niamh, *Aloysius O'Kelly: Art, Nation, Empire*. Dublin: Field Day, 2010.
Ouseley, William, *Epitome of the Ancient History of Persia. Extracted and Translated From the Jehan Ara, a Persian Manuscript*. London: Cadell and Davis, 1799.
Ouseley, William, *Persian Miscellanies: An Essay to Facilitate the Reading of Persian Manuscripts*. London: Richard White, 1795.
Ouseley, William, *Travels in Various Countries of the East; More Particularly Persia*. Volume I. London: Rodwell and Martin, 1819.
Paddy's Resource: Being a Select Collection of Original and Modern Patriotic Songs, Toasts and Sentiments, Compiled for the Use of the People of Ireland. N.p., 1795.
Pakdaman, Nasser, ed., *Sādeq Hedāyat: Hāshtād-o do nāmeh beh Hassan Chahid Nourāi*. With a Preface by Behzad Noël Chahid. Second Edition. Paris: Cheshmandaz, 2001.
Parsons, Cóilín, *The Ordnance Survey and Modern Irish Literature*. Oxford: Oxford University Press, 2016.
Pašeta, Senia, *Irish Nationalist Women, 1900–1918*. Cambridge: Cambridge University Press, 2013.
Petrie, George, *The Ecclesiastical Architecture of Ireland, Anterior to the Anglo-Norman Invasion: Comprising and Essay on the Origin and Uses of the Round Towers of Ireland*. Second Edition. Dublin: Hodges & Smith, 1845.
Petrie, George, *The Petrie Collection of the Ancient Music of Ireland: Arranged for the Piano-Forte*. Volume I. Dublin: M.H. Gill, 1855,
Pezron, Paul, *Celtic Linguistics, 1700–1850. Volume I: The Antiquities of Nations*. Edited With a New Introduction by Daniel R. Davis. London: Routledge, 2000.
Pierce, David, *Irish Writing in the Twentieth Century: A Reader*. Cork: Cork University Press, 2000.
Piggot, John, *Persia: Ancient and Modern*. London:Henry S. King & Co., 1874.
Pinkerton, John, *A Dissertation on the Origin and Progress of the Scythians or Goths*. London: John Nichols, 1787.
Pinnock, William, *A Comprehensive Grammar of Modern Geography and History; for the Use of Schools and for Private Tuition*. London: Holdsworth & Ball.
Pollock, Sheldon, ed., *Forms of Knowledge in Early Modern Asia: Explorations in the Intellectual History of India and Tibet, 1500–1800*. Durham: Duke University Press, 2011.
Porter, Robert Ker, *Travels in Georgia, Persia, Armenia, Ancient Babylonia, etc., During the Years 1817, 1818, 1819, and 1820*. Volume I. London: Longman, Hurst, Rees, Orme, and Brown, 1821.
Potter, Murray Anthony, *Sohrab and Rustem: The Epic Theme of a Combat Between Father and Son. A Study of Its Genesis and Use in Literature and Popular Tradition*. London: David Nutt, 1902.
Prichard, James Cowles. *The Eastern Origin of the Celtic Nations Proved by a Comparison of Their Dialects with the Sanskrit, Greek, Latin, and Teutonic Languages*. London: Sherwood, Gilbert, and Piper, 1831.
Prichard, James Cowles, *Researches into the Physical History of Man*. London: John and Arthur Arch, 1813.
Pyle, Christopher H., *Extradition, Politics, and Human Rights*. Philadelphia: Temple University Press, 2001.
Qajar, Farhad Mirza, *Jām-e Jam*. Tehran: n.p., 1273 A.H. [1856].

Qajar, Jalal Pour-Fath-Ali Shah (Jalal al-Din Mirza), *Nāmeh-ye Khosrovān: Dāstan-e Pādeshāhān-e Pārs beh Zabān-e Pārsi keh Soudmand-e Mardān, beh-vizheh Koodakān asst: Az Āqāz-e Ābādiān tā Anjām-e Sāssāniān*. Volume I. Tehran: Mohammad-Taqi Publisher, 1285 A.H./1868.

Radford, Mark, *The Policing of Belfast, 1870–1914*. London: Bloomsbury, 2015.

Ramaswamy, Sumathi, *The Lost Land of Lemuria: Fabulous Geographies, Catastrophic Histories*. Berkeley: University of California Press, 2004.

Ramnath, Maia, *Haj to Utopia: How the Ghadar Movement Charted Global Radicalism and Attempted to Overthrow the British Empire*. Berkeley: University of California Press, 2011.

Refayel, Fologun, *Jahān-namā*. Tabriz: Molla Saleh Tabrizi, 1267 A.H. (1851).

Renan, Ernest, *What is a Nation? And Other Political Writings*. M.F.N. Giglioli Translator. New York: Columbia University Press, 2018.

Richardson, John, *A Dictionary: Persian, Arabic*. Oxford: Clarendon Press, 1777.

Ricoeur, Paul, *Memory, History, Forgetting*. Kathleen Blamey and David Pellauer Translators. Second Edition. Chicago: University of Chicago Press, 2006 [2004] (Originally Published in French as La mémoire, l'histoire, l'oubli in 2000).

Ricoeur, Paul, *Time and Narrative*. Volume 2. Kathleen McLaughlin and David Pellauer Translators. Chicago: University of Chicago Press, 1985 (Originally Published in French in 1984).

Ridley, Jasper, *Lord Palmerston*. New York: E.P. Dutton, 1970.

Ringer, Monica, *Education, Religion, and the Discourse of Cultural Reform in Qajar Iran*. Costa Mesa, CA: Mazda, 2001.

Rodgers, Nini, *Ireland, Slavery and Anti-Slavery: 1612–1865*. Houndmills, Basingstoke: Palgrave, 2007.

Roediger, David R., *The Wages of Whiteness: Race and the Making of the American Working Class*. New York: Verso, 1999.

Rosenkranz, Susan A., "'To Hold the World in Contempt': The British Empire, War, and the Irish and Indian Nationalist Press, 1899–1914." PhD Dissertation, Florida International University, 2013.

Ross, Edward Denison, ed., *Sir Anthony Sherley and His Persian Adventure: Including Some Contemporary Narratives Relating Thereto*. Abingdon, Oxford: Routledge Curzon, 2005 [1933].

Ryan, Desmond, *The Fenian Chief: A Biography of James Stephens*. Dublin: Gill and Son, 1967.

Ryan, Frederick, *Criticism and Courage and Other Essays*. Dublin: Maunsel & Co., 1906.

Ryan, Frederick, *Sinn Féin and Reaction*. With an Introduction by Manus O'Riordan. Dublin: Labour History Workshop, 1984.

Ryder, Sean, ed., *James Clarence Mangan: Selected Writings*. Dublin: University College Dublin Press, 2004.

Sahaf-bashi, Esmail, *Tārikh-e Engelesstān*. Tehran: [Dar al-Fonun?], [No Later Than 1880s].

Said, Edward W., *Orientalism*. New York: Vintage, 1979 [1978].

Said, Edward W., *The World, the Text, and the Critic*. Cambridge, MA: Harvard University Press, 1983, pp.226–47.

Sainsbury, William Noel, ed., *Calendar of State Papers. Colonial Series. Volume 6: East Indies, China and Persia, 1625–1629*. London: Her Majesty's Stationary Office, 1884.

Sandner, David, *Critical Discourses of the Fantastic, 1712–1831*. Farnham, Surrey: Ashgate, 2011.

Sareen, Tilak Raj, *Indian Revolutionary Movement Abroad (1905–1921)*. New Delhi: Sterling, 1979.

Savage, Marmion Wilard, *The Falcon Family; or, Young Ireland*. London: Chapman and Hall, 1845.

Sayyah, Mohammad Ali, *An Iranian in Nineteenth Century Europe: The Travel Diaries of Hâj Sayyâh, 1859–1877*. Translation and an Introduction by Mehrbanoo Nasser Deyhim, and with a Foreword by Peter Avery. Bethesda: Ibex, 1999.

Sayyah, Mohammad Ali, *Safarnāmeh-ye Hāj Sayyāh beh Farang*. Ali Dehbashi Editor. Tehran: Nasher, 1363 [1984].

Schwab, Raymond, *The Oriental Renaissance: Europe's Rediscovery of India and the East, 1680–1880* (Translation of Schwab's 1950 *La Renaissance Orientale* by Gene Patterson-Black and Victor Reinking). New York: Columbia University Press, 1984.

Schwartz, Benjamin, ed., *Letters From Persia: Written by Charles Burgess and Edward Burgess, 1828–1855*. New York: New York Public Library, 1942.

Searight, Sarah, *The British in the Middle East*. London: Weidenfeld & Nicolson, 1969.

Seidel, Michael, *Epic Geography: James Joyce's Ulysses*. Princeton: Princeton University Press, 1976.

Sergeev, Evgeny, *The Great Game, 1856–1907: Russo-British Relations in Central and East Asia*. Baltimore: Johns Hopkins University Press, 2013.

Shannon-Mangan, Ellen, *James Clarence Mangan: A Biography*. Dublin: Irish Academic Press, 1996.

Sharma, Sunil, *Mughal Arcadia: Persian Literature in an Indian Court*. Cambridge, MA: Harvard University Press, 2017.

Shaw, George Bernard, *Collected Letters. Volume III: 1911–1925*. Dan H. Laurence Editor. New York: Viking, 1985.

Shaykh Reza ("akhavi-e Hajji Mohsen Khan"). *Tārikh-e Ingiliss*. Tehran: n.p., n.d. (Second Half of the Nineteenth Century).

Shea, David, *History of the Early Kings of Persia, From Kaiomars, the First of the Peshdadian Dynasty, to the Conquest of Iran by Alexander the Great*. London: Oriental Translation Fund of Great Britain & Ireland, 1832 (English translation from the Arabic original of the section on rulers of ancient Iran appearing in *Rowzat al-Safā' fi Sirat al-Anbiyā' wa al-Moluk wa al-Kholafā*, also known as *Universal History*, by Muhammad ibn Khāvandshāh Mirkhvānd, 1433–98).

Shea, David and Anthony Troyer, eds. and trans., *Dabistan, or the School f Manners*. Three Volumes. Paris: Oriental Translation Fund of Great Britain and Ireland, 1843.

Sheil, Lady Mary Leonora Woulfe, *Glimpses of Life and Manners in Persia*. London: John Murray, 1856.

Sherard, Robert Harborough, *The Life of Oscar Wilde*. Third Edition. London: T. Werner Laurie, 1911 [1906].

Shirley, Evelyn Philip, *The Sherley Brothers: An Historical Memoir of the Lives of Sir Thomas Sherley, Sir Anthony Sherley, and Sir Robert Sherley, Knights*. Chiswick: Charles Wittingham, 1848.

Sheybani, Abdul-Hussein, *Khāterāt-e Mohājerat: Az Dowlat-e Movaqat-e Kermānshāh tā Komiteh-ye Melliyun-e Berlin*. Iraj Afshar and Kaveh Bayat Editors. Shirazeh, 1378 [1999].

Shirazi, Abul Hassan Khan, *Hayratnāmeh: Safarnāmeh-ye Mirzā Abulhassan Khān Ilchi beh Landan*. Hassan Morselvand Editor. Tehran: Farhang-e Rassa, 1364 [1985].

Shuster, William Morgan, *The Strangling of Persia*. Reprint. Washington, DC: Mage, 1987 [1912].

Silvestri, Michael, *Ireland and India: Nationalism, Empire and Memory*. Houndmills, Basingstoke: Palgrave Macmillan, 2009.

Simon, John Y., ed., *The Papers of Ulysses S. Grant. Volume 20: November 1, 1869–October 31, 1870*. Carbondale, IL: Southern Illinois University Press, 1967.

Skene, Reg, *The Cuchulain Plays of W.B. Yeats: A Study*. London: Macmillan, 1974.

Smith, Anthony D., *National Identity*. Reno: University of Nevada Press, 1991.

Smith, Goldwin, *Irish History and the Irish Question*. New York: McClure, Phillips, and Co., 1905.

Smith, Helen, *An Uncommon Reader: A Life of Edward Garnett, Mentor and Editor of Literary Genius*. New York: Farrar, Strauss and Giroux, 2017.

Sohrabi, Nader, *Revolution and Constitutionalism in the Ottoman Empire and Iran*. New York: Cambridge University Press, 2011.

Soupault, Philippe, *Souvenirs de James Joyce*. Parsi:Alger E. Charlot, 1943.

Spenser, Edmund, *A View of the State of Ireland as It Was in the Reign of Queen Elizabeth*. Reprint. Dublin: L. Flin and Ann Watts, 1763.

Spiller, Gustav, ed., *Papers on Inter-Racial Problems: Communicated to the First Universal Races Congress Held at the University of London July 26–29, 1911*. London: P.S. King & Son, 1911.

Stanford, Charles Villiers, *Pages From an Unwritten Diary*. London: Edward Arnold, 1914.

Stanley, Henry Morton, *My Early Travels and Adventures in America and Asia*. Volume 2. Second Edition. London: Sampson Low, Marston and Company, 1895.

Statement of Facts Relating to Mr. Wilfrid Blunt's Arrest at Woodford, October 23, 1887. Together with the Joint Opinion of Sir Charles Russell … R.T. Reid … H.H. Asquith … and W.S. Robson. London: Home Rule Union, 1887.

Steele, Karen, *Women, Press, and Politics During the Irish Revival*. Syracuse: Syracuse University Press, 2007.

Steele, Sarah L., ed., *The Right Honourable Arthur MacMurrough Kavanagh: A Biography*. London: MacMillan and Co., 1891.

Stevens, John, *The History of Persia: Containing, the Lives and Memorable Action of Its Kings From the First Erecting of That Monarchy to This Time; an Exact Description of All Its Dominions … Written in Arabick, by Mirkond, a Famous Eastern Author; That of Ormuz, by Torunxa, King of That Island, Both of Them Tr. Into Spanish, by Antony Teixeira …*. London: Jonas Brown, 1715.

Stokes, William, *The Life and Labours in Art and Archæology, of George Petrie, LL.D., M.R.I.A*. London: Longmans, Green, & Co., 1868.

Stradling, Robert, *The Irish and the Spanish Civil War 1936–1939*. Manchester: Mandolin, 1999.

Strother, French, *Fighting Germany's Spies*. Garden City, New York: Doubleday, 1919.

Sturgeon, Sinéad, ed., *Essays on James Clarence Mangan: The Man in the Cloak*. Houndmills, Basingstoke: Palgrave, 2014.

Sullivan, Alexander Martin, *New Ireland: Political Sketches and Personal Reminiscences*. Volume I. Fifth Edition. London: Sampson Law, Marston, Searle, & Rivington, 1878.

Sullivan, Alexander Martin, *Speeches and Addresses in Parliament, on the Platform, and at the Bar, 1859 to 1881*. Second Edition. Dublin: T.D. Sullivan, 1882.

Sullivan, Alexander Martin, *The Story of Ireland: A Narrative of Irish History from the Earliest Ages to the Insurrection of 1867 … Continued to the Present Time by James Luby, of New York*. New Edition. New York: Patrick Joseph Kennedy, 1898 (This Was a Posthumous American Edition of A.M. Sullivan's 1885 Publication).

Sullivan, Timothy Daniel, *Penny Reading for the Irish People*. Volume I. Dublin: T.D. Sullivan, 1879.

Sullivan, Timothy Daniel, *Recollections of Troubled Times in Irish Politics*. Dublin: Sealy, Bryers & Walker, 1905.

Sullivan, Timothy Daniel, Alexander Martin Sullivan and Denis Baylor Sullivan, eds., *Speeches From the Dock; or, Protests of Irish Patriotism*. New York: Patrick Joseph Kennedy, Excelsior Catholic Publishing House, 1904.

Sweet, Rosemary, *Antiquaries: The Discovery of the Past in Eighteenth-Century Britain*. London: Hambledon and London, 2004.

Sykes, Percy Molesworth, *A History of Persia*. Volume II. London: MacMillan and Co., 1915.

Tavakoli-Targhi, Mohamad, *Refashioning Iran: Orientalism, Occidentalism, and Historiography*. Houndmills, Basingstoke: Palgrave, 2001.

Taylor, Isaac, *The Origin of the Aryans: An Account of Prehistoric Ethnology and Civilization of Europe*. New York: Humboldt, 1889.

Thuente, Mary Helen, *The Harp Re-Strung: The United Irishmen and the Rise of Irish Literary Nationalism*. Syracuse: Syracuse University Press, 1994.

Thuente, Mary Helen, *W.B. Yeats and Irish Folklore*. Dublin: Gill and Macmillan, 1980.

Tipper, Karen Sasha Anthony, *A Critical Biography of Lady Wilde, 1821?–1896: Irish Revolutionist, Humanist, Scholar and Poet*. New York: Edwin Mellen Press, 2002.

Tóibín, Colm, *Mad, Bad, Dangerous to Know: The Fathers of Wilde, Yeats and Joyce*. London: Viking, 2018.

Tone, William Theobald Wolfe, ed., *Memoirs of Theobald Wolfe Tone. Written by Himself*. Volume II. London: Henry Colburn, 1827.

Townend, Paul A., *The Road to Home Rule: Anti-Imperialism and the Irish National Movement*. Madison: University of Wisconsin Press, 2016.

Trautmann, Thomas R., *Aryans and British India*. Berkeley: University of California Press, 1997.
Treacy, Matt, *The Communist Party of Ireland, 1921–2011. Volume 1: 1921–1969*. Dublin: Brocaire Books, 2012.
Tsadik, Daniel, *Between Foreigners and Shi'is: Nineteenth-Century Iran and Its Jewish Minority*. Stanford: Stanford University Press, 2007.
Turner, Sharon, *History of the Anglo-Saxons: Comprising the History of England From the Earliest Period to the Norman Conquest*. Volume 1. London, Longman, Hurst, Rees, Orme, and Brown, 1820.
Tymoczko, Maria, *The Irish Ulysses*. Berkeley: University of California Press, 1997.
Tynan, Patrick J. P., *The Irish National Invincibles and Their Times*. London: Chatham and Co., 1894.
Vallancey, Charles, *A Grammar of the Iberno-Celtic, or Irish Language*. Dublin: G. Faulkner, T. Ewing, and R. Moncrieffe, 1773.
Vallancey, Charles, *A Vindication of the Ancient History of Ireland*. Dublin: Luke White, 1786.
Vallancey, Charles, *An Essay on the Antiquity of the Irish Language. Being a Collation of the Irish With the Punic language. With a Preface Proving Ireland to be the Thule of the Ancients. Addressed to the Literati of Europe*. Dublin: S. Powell, 1772.
Vallancey, Charles, *An Essay on the Primitive Inhabitants of Great Britain and Ireland. Proving From History, Languages, and Mythology, That They Were Persians or Indo.Scythæ, Composed of Scythians, Chaldæans, and Indians*. Dublin: Graisberry and Campbell, 1807.
Vallancey, Charles, *Collectanea de Rebus Hibernicis*. Volume 6, Part I. Dublin: Graisberry and Campbell, 1804.
Vallancey, Charles, *Prospectus of a Dictionary of the Language of the Aire Coti, or Ancient Irish, Compared With the Language of the Cuti, or Ancient Persians, With the Hindoostanee, the Arabic, and Chaldean Languages*. Dublin: Graisberry and Campbell, 1802.
Vance, Norman, *Irish Literature: A Social History: Tradition, Identity, and Difference*. Oxford: Blackwell, 1990.
Vejdani, Farzin, *Making History in Iran: Education, Nationalism, and Print Culture*. Stanford: Stanford University Press, 2015.
Venables Vernon-Harcourt, Leveson, *The Doctrine of the Deluge, Vindicating the Scriptural Account From the Doubts Which Have Recently Been Cast Upon It by Geological Speculations*. Volume II. London: Longman, Orme, Brown, Green, and Longmans, 1838.
Villanueva, Joachimo Laurentio (Joaquín Lorenzo Villanueva), *Phœnecian Ireland*. Henry O'Brien Translator and Editor. London: Longman & Co., 1833.
Voltaire, *Candide, or Optimism*. John Butt Translator. London: Penguin, 1947.
Voltaire, *The Philosophy of History*. Reprint. No Translator. Glasgow: Robert Urie, 1766 [1765].
Von Hammer-Purgstall, Joseph [Freiherr], *Der Diwan von Mohammed Schemsed-din Hafis*. Volume I. Stuttgart: J.G. Gottaschen, 1812.
Von Hammer-Purgstall, Joseph [Freiherr], *Geschichte der Osmanischen Dichtkunst bis auf unsere Zeit*. Volume 1. Pesth: Conrad Adolph Hartleben, 1836.
Von Hammer-Purgstall, Joseph [Freiherr], *Rosenöl, erstes Fläschchen oder, Sagen und Kunden des Morgenlandes aus arabischen, persischen und türkischen Quellen gesammelt*. Volume I. Stuttgart: J.G. Gottaschen, 1813.
Walcher, Heidi A., *In the Shadow of the King: Ẓill al-Sulṭān and Isfahān Under the Qājārs*. London: I.B. Tauris, 2008.
Walker, Joseph Cooper, *Historical Memoirs of the Irish Bards*. Volume I. Second Edition. Dublin: J. Christie, 1818.
Walkowitz, Rebecca L., *Cosmopolitan Style: Modernism Beyond the Nation*. New York: Columbia University Press, 2006.
Waterfield, Robin E., *Christians in Persia: Assyrians, Armenians, Roman Catholics and Protestants*. Reprint. New York: Routledge, 2011 [1973].

Watson, Robert Grant, *A History of Persia From the Beginning of the Nineteenth Century to the Year 1858*. London: Smith, Elder and Co., 1866.
Weber, Max, *From Max Weber: Essays in Sociology*. Hans H. Gerth and C. Wright Mills, eds. and trans. With a New Preface by Bryan S, Turner. New London: Routledge, 2009.
Wilde, Jane Francesca (Lady Wilde), *Ancient Cures, Charms, and Usages of Ireland. Contributions to Irish Lore*. London: Ward and Downey, 1890.
Wilde, Jane Francesca (Speranza), *Ancient Legends, Mystic Charms, and Superstitions of Ireland. With Sketches of the Past. To Which is Appended a Chapter on 'the Ancient Race of Ireland,' by the Late Sir William Wilde*. Two Volumes. London: Ward and Downey, 1887.
Wilde, Jane Francesca (Lady Wilde), *Driftwood From Scandinavia*. London: Richard Bentley & Son, 1884.
Wilde, Jane Francesca (Lady Wilde), *Notes on Men, Women, and Books*. London: Ward and Dawney, 1891.
Wilde, Jane Francesca, *Poems by Speranza (Lady Wilde)*. Dublin: James Duffy, 1864.
Wilde, Jane Francesca, *Social Studies*. London: Ward & Downey, 1893.
Wilde, William R. Wills, *Ireland, Past and Present: The Land and the People. A Lecture*. Dublin: McGlashan & Gill, 1864.
Wilde, William Robert [Wills], *Irish Popular Superstitions*. Dublin: James McGlashan, 1852.
Williams, Mark, *Ireland's Immortals: A History of the Gods of Irish Myth*. Princeton: Princeton University Press, 2016.
Wills, Charles James, *In the Land of the Lion and Sun or Modern Persia*. London: William Clowes and Sons, 1883.
Winter, Jay, *Sites of Memory, Sites of Mourning: The Great War in European Cultural History*. Cambridge: Cambridge University Press, 1995.
Wolf, Nicholas, *An Irish-Speaking Island: State, Religion, Community, and the Linguistic Landscape in Ireland, 1770–1870*. Madison: University of Wisconsin, 2014.
Wood-Martin, William Gregory, *Traces of the Elder Faiths of Ireland. A Folklore Sketch: A Handbook of Irish Pre-Christian Traditions*. Volume I. London: Longmans, Green, and Co., 1901.
Woodman, Peter, *Ireland's First Settlers: Time and the Mesolithic*. Oxford: Oxbow, 2015.
Wright, Denis, *The English Amongst the Persians: Imperial Lives in Nineteenth-Century Iran*. London: I.B. Tauris, 1977.
Wright, Denis, *The Persians Amongst the English*. London: I.B. Tauris, 1986.
Wright, Julia M., *Ireland, India and Nationalism in Nineteenth-Century Literature*. Cambridge: Cambridge University Press, 2007.
Wright, Thomas, *Built of Books: How Reading Defined the Life of Oscar Wilde*. New York: Henry Holt and Co., 2009.
Wylie, Paul R., *The Irish General: Thomas Francis Meagher*. Norman: University of Oklahoma Press, 2007.
Yapp, Malcolm E., *Strategies of British India: Britain, Iran and Afghanistan 1789–1850*. Oxford: Clarendon Press, 1980.
Yarshater, Ehsan, ed., *The Cambridge History of Iran. Volume 3(1): The Seleucid, Parthian and Sasanian Periods*. Reprint. Cambridge: Cambridge University Press, 2003 [1983].
Yeats, William Butler, ed., *A Book of Irish Verse: Selected From Modern Writers*. Revised Edition. London: Methuen and Co., 1900 [1895].
Yeats, William Butler, *Essays and Introductions*. Reprint. New York: Collier Books, 1986 [1968].
Yeats, William Butler, ed., *Fairy and Folk Tales of the Irish Peasantry*. London: Walter Scott, 1888.
Yeats, William Butler, ed., *Irish Fairy Tales*. London: T. Fisher Unwin, 1892.
Yeats, William Butler, *The Autobiography of William Butler Yeats: Consisting of Reveries Over Childhood and Youth. The Trembling of the Veil, and Dramatis Personae*. New York: Macmillan, 1953.
Yeats, William Butler, *The Cat and the Moon and Certain Poems*. Dublin: Cuala Press, 1924.

Yeats, William Butler, *The Collected Poems of W.B. Yeats*. Richard J. Finneran Editor. New York: Macmillan, 1989.
Yeats, William Butler, *The Collected Works of W.B. Yeats. Volume IV: Early Essays*. Richard J. Finneran and George Bornstein, eds. New York: Scribner, 2007.
Yeats, William Butler, *The Collected Works of W.B. Yeats. Volume IX: Uncollected Articles and Reviews Written Between 1886 and 1900*. John P. Frayne and Madeleine Marchaterre Editors. New York: Scribner, 2004.
Yeats, William Butler, *The Collected Works of W.B. Yeats. Volume XII: John Sherman and Dhoya*. Richard J. Finneran Editor. New York: Macmillan, 1991.
Yeats, William Butler, *The Collected Works of William Butler Yeats*. Volume 8. Stratford-on-Avon: Shakespeare Head Press, 1908.
Yeats, William Butler, *The Speckled Bird*. William H. O'Donnell Editor. Toronto: McClelland and Stewart, 1976.
Yeats, William Butler, *Writings on Irish Folklore, Legend and Myth*. Edited and With an Introduction by Robert Welch. London: Penguin, 1993.
Yerosushalmi, David, *The Jews of Iran in the Nineteenth Century: Aspects of History, Community, and Culture*. Leiden: Brill, 2009.
Yohannan, John D., *Persian Poetry in England and America*. Delmar, New York: Caravan Books, 1977.
Young, Robert J. C., *Colonial Desire: Hybridity in Theory, Culture and Race*. New York: Routledge, 1995.
Zaryab, Abbas and Iraj Afshar, eds., *Nāmeh-hā-ye Edvārd Brāvn beh Sayyid Hassan Taqizādeh*. Tehran: Jibi, 1356 [1975].
Zerubavel, Yael, *Recovered Roots: Collective Memory and the Making of Israeli National Tradition*. Chicago: University of Chicago Press, 1995.
Zimmern, Helen, *The Epic of Kings: Stories Retold From Firdusi*. London: Fisher Unwin, 1882.

INDEX

Abbas I, Shah 273, 515; *see also* English East India Company; Safavid dynasty (Iran, 1501–1722/36)

Abbas Mirza (Qajar crown prince) 186, 187, 389; *see also* Iranian students in England (early 19th century); Qajar dynasty (Iran, 1796–1925)

Abbasid caliphate 175, 239, 241, 261, 529, 562n104; *see also* Baghdad; *Lalla Rookh. An Oriental Romance* (by Thomas Moore, 1817); "al-Muqanna" (Hashim ibn Hakim)

Abbey Theatre 429, 438, 480, 483, 580, 609; *see also* Blunt, Wilfrid Scawen; Gregory, Isabella Augusta (née Persse); Irish Literary Theatre; Irish National Dramatic Society; Irish National Theatre Society; Yeats, William Butler

Abdallah: *see Intercepted Letters; or, The Twopenny Post-bag* (by Thomas Moore, 1813)

'Abdu'l-Bahá 434; *see also* Baha'i faith

Abdülbāki, Mahmud (a.k.a., Baki) 251, 259

Aberdeen, Lord (George Hamilton-Gordon) 335, 354n14; *see also* Conservative Party (UK; a.k.a., Unionist Party after 1895); Crimean War (1854–56)

Abu Taleb Khan (Mirza Abu Taleb Khan Tabrizi-Isfahani) 517–20, 524; *Massir-e Tālebi* [a.k.a., *Massir-i Tālibi fi Bilād-i Afranji* …] (by Abu Taleb Khan (Mirza Abu Taleb Khan Tabrizi-Isfahani), 1812) 517; *see also* Astley's Amphitheater (Dublin); Crow Street Theatre (a.k.a., Theatre Royal, Dublin); Richardson, David; *The Travels of Mirza Abu Taleb Khan, in Asia, Africa and Europe, during the Years 1799, 1800, 1801, 1802, and 1803* (trans. By Charles Stewart, 1810)

Abyssinian Crisis 595–97; *see also* de Valera, Éamon; Ethiopia; Italy (and Italian)

Academy (London) 409

Achaemenid dynasty (Persian Empire, c.550–330 BCE) 52, 64, 130, 133, 136, 172, 219, 221, 223–24, 228, 293n33; *see also* Alexander the Great; Cyrus (Achaemenid emperor); Darius I (Achaemenid emperor); Marathon, Battle of (490 BCE); Persians; Thermopylae, Battle of (480 BCE); Xerxes I (Achaemenid emperor)

Acker, Kathy 294n55

Act of Union (of the United Kingdom of Great Britain and Ireland, 1801) 9, 34, 50, 90, 99, 167, 168, 237, 284, 349, 351, 513, 518, 525–28, 535–36, 538, 543, 202n1; termination of "The Kingdom of Great Britain and the Kingdom of Ireland" 349, 526–27, 535; *see also* Irish Home Rule; Repeal movement; United Irishmen uprising (1798); United Kingdom

Acton, Lord: *see* Dalberg-Acton, John Emerich Edward

Adam 50, 95, 106, 112, 118, 403, 565–66, 623; Adamic/Adamite 61, 403, 566; *see also* The Bible; Cain; Eve; Garden of Eden; The Hebrew Bible ("Old Testament"); pre-Adamic/pre-Adamite

Adam and Eve's Church (Church of the Immaculate Conception, Dublin) 623

Addington, Henry 543

"Æ": *see* Russell, George William ("Æ")

Aegean 96, 118, 410, 421

"al-Afghani": *see* Assadabadi, Sayyid Jamal al-Din (a.k.a., "al-Afghani")

Afghanistan 5, 10, 33, 36, 74, 87, 105, 147, 239, 244, 261, 304, 305, 308, 317, 319–20, 322–26, 329–30, 332, 334, 336, 339, 341–42, 345, 347, 389, 473, 476, 488, 495, 515, 516, 545, 546, 585, 586, 595, 636–39, 647; *see also* Anglo-Afghan War (1839–42); Anglo-Afghan War (1878–80); Anglo-Iranian War (1856–57); Anglo-Russian Agreement (1907); Dost Mohammad Khan; Herat; Kabul; Kandahar (/Qandahar); Peshawar Valley

Afghans 147, 225, 261, 267, 310, 319, 349, 499, 638; *see also* Pashtun (Pathan) Barakzai tribe; Pashtun (Pathan) Durrani/Abdāli clan; Pashtun (Pathan) Gilzai confederacy; Pashtun (Pathan) Sadozai tribe

Afrasiab 83, 84, 119; *see also* mythology (Iranian mythology); *Shāhnāmeh*; Vallancey, Charles

Africa 11, 12, 73, 77, 190, 315, 357n71, 490, 517, 535, 536, 595, 596; East Africa 139; North Africa 3, 17, 54, 72, 81, 241, 254, 402, 529, 613; northeast Africa 12; southern Africa 234, 312, 313, 351, 472, 540, 545, 553, 647; *see also* Fomorians; South Africa

African-American 479, 491

"African slavery": *see* slavery

Africans 30, 49, 352, 373, 401, 420, 472, 473, 504n46, 569, 583, 647

Afro-Asian 129

Afsharid dynasty (Iran, 1736–51/96) 267, 515; *see also* Elton, John; Fraser, James Baillie (*The Kuzzilbash: A Tale of Khorasan* (by James Baillie Fraser, 1828)); Hanway, Jonas; Nader Shah

Āftāb (Tehran) 554

"after-life" of a work of art: *see* Benjamin, Walter

Aga Khan I (Hassan Ali Shah) 377n15; *see also* Iranian famine (1870–72)

Agamben, Giorgio 644

Agnosticism 428–30, 433

agnotology 604; *see also* Boal, Iain; Proctor, Robert

Ahvaz 342; *see also* Anglo-Iranian War (1856–57)

Ajmal al-Tawārikh (by Rezaqoli Khan Hedayat, 1866): *see* Hedayat, Rezaqoli Khan

Akinchi (Baku) 431

Akkadian 435

Albania 261

Albion 376; *see also* England; Great Britain

Alexander the Great 52, 115, 132–33, 326, 565; *see also* Achaemenid dynasty (Iran, c.550–330 BCE); Macedonia; Seleucid Empire

Algeria 472, 584, 586, 636, 650; Algerians 225, 472, 510n112, 638, 639, 647; *see also* Devoy, John; French Legionnaires (i.e., Foreign Legion force)

Alighieri, Dante 615

Alison, Charles 366, 370; *see also* Iranian famine (1870–72)

All-for-Ireland League 475, 481; *see also Cork Free Press*; Healy, Timothy Michael; Irish Home Rule; O'Brien, William

All-India Muslim League 487, 488, 551; "Muslim-nationalist" 487, 508n86, 551; *see also* Bengal (partition of (1905–11))

Althusser, Louis 134; *see also* "interpellation"

"ambivalence" 126–27, 143, 231, 251, 265, 267, 270, 280, 282; *see also* Kristeva, Julia

America: *see* United States

American Civil War 355n35; antebellum United States 217; Union Army 355n35; *see also* Halpin, William George

American colonies 30, 320, 352, 583; *see also* American War of Independence ("American Revolution"); United States

American War of Independence ("American Revolution") 30, 352, 473, 583; *see also Paddy's Resource* (1795–1803); United States; Washington, George

Americas 108, 261, 360n127, 382, 559n52; American continents 108, 529

Amonian 452n3; *see also* Cuthite, Hamitic

Amritsar massacre (1919) 593; *see also* India

Anarchism 478, 541; anarchists 478, 499, 543, 592, 595; anarcho-populism 543; *see also* Dryhurst, Nora ("Nannie") Florence; *Freedom: A Journal of Anarchist Communism* (London); Kropotkin, Petr; workers' rights

Anatolia 72, 239, 244, 296n92, 387, 591, 595

Ancient Cures, Charms, and Usages of Ireland. Contributions to Irish Lore (by Jane Francesca Agnes Wilde, 1890) 397–98, 401, 409–11, 413, 415; *see also* Wilde, Jane Francesca Agnes (née Elgee)

Ancient Legends, Mystic Charms, and Superstitions of Ireland (by Jane Francesca Agnes Wilde, 1887) 397–98, 400–403, 407, 409, 410, 415, 420, 447, 582; *see also* Wilde, Jane Francesca Agnes (née Elgee)

Ancient Order of Hibernians 366, 475, 570; Ladies' Auxiliary 475; *see also* Catholics; Irish nationalism

Anderson, Benedict 139, 217; *see also* "imagined communities"

Angles 632n144; Anglian 424; *see also* Anglo-Normans; Anglo-Saxons

Anglican Ascendancy (in Ireland) 30, 170, 181, 440, 517, 518, 579; *see also* Anglo-Protestants (in Ireland)

Anglican Church 5, 18, 88, 170, 171, 195, 366, 544; Anglican missions in Iran 366, 367, 370, 388; Anglicans 18, 68, 89, 108, 117, 119, 120, 146, 168, 170, 171, 180–82, 194, 223, 265, 270, 365–67, 388, 391, 393, 411, 412, 429, 570; Oath of Supremacy 171; *see also* Anglican Ascendancy (in Ireland); Anglo-Protestants (in Ireland); Bruce, Robert (Rev.); Catholic Emancipation; Church of Ireland; English Reformation; Ireland (English and Protestant penal laws)

Anglican Church (in Ireland): *see* Church of Ireland

Anglo-Afghan War (1839–42) 261, 304, 325, 329, 347; *see also* Dost Mohammad Khan; Keane, John; Login, John Spencer; Sale,

INDEX 699

Florentia (née Wynch); Sale, Robert; sepoys; sowars
Anglo-Afghan War (1878–80) 545; Gandamak Treaty (1879) 345
Anglo-Catholics 24; *see also* Catholic Church (in Ireland)
Anglo-Chinese War (1839–42) 319
Anglo-Chinese War (1856–60) 306, 307, 309, 310, 312, 316–18, 322, 324, 332, 333, 343, 345, 346
Anglo-German rivalry 36, 473, 477, 487, 494–97, 551, 590
Anglo-Iranian Agreement (1919) 591
Anglo-Iranian Oil Company: *see* Anglo-Persian Oil Company
Anglo-Iranian treaties (1801) 33, 34; *see also* Malcolm, John
Anglo-Iranian Treaty (1814) 330; *see also* Herat
Anglo-Iranian Treaty (1853) 309, 330, 334, 338; *see also* Herat
Anglo-Iranian War (1838) 303, 388, 515, 539; "most-favored nation" status granted to Britain in trade with Iran (1841) 329; peace treaty (1841) 303, 304, 329, 330; *see also* Herat
Anglo-Iranian War (1856–57) 1, 8, 22, 36, 37, 149, 199, 231, 303–53, 354n19, 367–71, 388, 390, 391, 467, 468, 470, 471, 485, 515, 539, 548, 639, 640, 646–48; Treaty of Paris (March 4, 1857) 305, 342, 343, 345, 391; *see also* Ahvaz; Ayrton, Acton Smee; Bushire; Canning, Charles John; Canning, Stratford (Viscount Stratford de Redcliffe); Cobden, Richard; *Cork Examiner*; Cowley, Lord (Henry Wellesley); Dost Mohammad Khan; Dunkellin, Lord (Ulick de Burgh); Engels, Friedrich; Farrokh Khan ("Amin al-Molk"); France; *Freeman's Journal* (Dublin); Gladstone, William Ewart; Havelock, Henry; Jones, Felix; Kharg Island; Khushab; Layard, Austen Henry; Lynch, Henry Blosse; Marx, Karl; Mohammad Yusuf; Mohammareh (Khorramshahr); Nasser al-Din Shah; *The Nation* (Dublin); Outram, James; Palmerston, Lord (Henry John Temple); Pashtun (Pathan) Durrani/Abdāli clan; Pashtun (Pathan) Gilzai confederacy; Roebuck, John Arthur; Russia; sepoys; Seymour, Henry Danby; Stalker, Foster; Utterson, Mathews Corsellis; Warren, William Blackburn
Anglo-Irish Treaty (December 6, 1921) 479, 591; *see also* Anti-Treaty (Irish nationalists); Irish Civil War (1922–23); Irish Free State; Irish War of Independence; Pro-Treaty (Irish nationalists)
Anglo-Irish War: *see* Irish War of Independence
Anglo-Japanese Alliance (1902) 491, 562n116
Anglo-Norman conquests in Ireland (12th century CE) 5, 11, 24, 31, 35, 47, 54, 63, 65, 88, 93, 100, 102, 123, 143, 182, 183, 195, 215, 216, 225–27, 406, 414, 527, 536, 569, 599, 608, 616, 637; *see also* Henry II, King
Anglo-Normans 5, 11, 24, 29, 31, 35, 47–49, 54, 63, 65, 68, 69, 77, 88, 93, 101, 102, 123, 127, 138, 141–44, 182, 183, 191, 195, 201, 215–18, 225–28, 257, 271, 287, 383, 406, 411, 412, 414, 417, 426, 437, 500, 514, 527, 529, 536, 538, 569, 574, 580, 599, 608, 612, 613, 616, 617, 620, 637, 645; *see also* Angles; "Old English"
Anglo-Persian Oil Company 497, 499, 500, 510–11n127, 594; *see also* Iranian oil nationalization (1951); Mossadeq, Mohammad; petroleum
Anglo-Protestants (in Ireland) 5, 11, 24, 29, 50, 51, 63, 66, 68, 69, 77, 88, 137, 168, 170, 174, 180, 182, 212, 237, 267, 268, 270, 279, 303, 308, 323, 336, 344, 352, 366, 367, 428, 432, 434, 440, 469, 486, 523–24, 538, 546, 570, 579, 583; *see also* Anglican Ascendancy (in Ireland)
Anglo-Russian Agreement (1907) 8, 36, 37, 145, 347, 391, 424, 450, 469, 473, 474, 476, 477, 479, 480, 482, 484, 485, 487, 489, 494–97, 506n71, 506–7n73, 548, 552, 590; *see also* Afghanistan; Browne, Edward Granville; Despard, Charlotte; Dillon, John; Germany; Green, Alice Stopford; Grey, Edward; Gwynn, Stephen Lucius; Iranian Constitutional Revolution (1906–11); Iranian Question; Lamington, Lord (Charles Wallace Alexander Napier Cochrane-Baillie); Lynch, Henry Finnis Blosse; MacNeill, John G. S.; Persia Committee (London); Shaw, George Bernard; Society of Friends of Russian Freedom (London); Tibet
Anglo-Russian rivalry (general) 1, 6, 33, 36, 138, 273, 274, 303, 304, 306–11, 313, 314, 317, 318, 320, 322, 324–30, 332–33, 335–37, 341–43, 346–48, 354n8, 357n61, 370, 375, 468, 473, 491, 515, 516, 533, 542
Anglo-Saxons 290, 407, 416, 441, 491, 492, 573, 616, 632n144; *see also* Angles; Saxon
Anglo-Soviet occupation of Iran 493; *see also* Second World War
Anklesaria, Bahramgor Tahmuras 41; *see also* Hedayat, Sadeq

Anklesaria, Tehmuras Dinshaw (Dinshah/ Dinshaji) 41; *see also* Modi, Jivanji Jamshedji
"Anna Livia Plurabelle": *see Finnegans Wake* (by James Joyce, 1939)
Annales School 636; *see also* "mentalities"
Annals of the Four Masters (17th century) 147, 200, 421, 614, 615, 618; *see also* "Four Masters"
Annals of the Kingdom of Ireland by the Four Masters (English translation by John O'Donovan, 1848–51): *see* O'Donovan, John
Annual Register (London) 235; *see also* Burke, Edmund
Anquetil-Duperron, Abraham Hyacinthe 57, 62, 81, 116; *Zend Avesta* (French translation by Abraham Hyacinthe Anquetil-Duperron, 1771) 62, 116; *see also* Indo-European language; *Zend Avesta*; Zoroastrianism
Anster, John 251
Anthropology 24, 118, 149, 296n79, 381, 393, 401, 403, 413, 568, 582, 600; *see also* Prichard, James Cowles
anti-clericalism 429
anticolonial 26, 320, 346, 434, 448, 451, 489, 493, 583, 590, 592, 593, 640, 641; anticolonial "modernities" 141, 428, 430, 431, 450, 451; *see also* anti-imperialism; colonialism (colonization); imperialism; "modernity"/"modernities"
anti-imperialism 1, 4, 6, 8, 9, 11, 31, 36–38, 129, 139, 145, 222, 224, 303, 318, 320, 346, 348–53, 418, 429, 430, 450, 467, 470–74, 477–79, 481–83, 486–88, 491, 493, 498–500, 554, 584, 585, 589–95, 605, 610, 636–40, 647–50; *see also* anticolonial; colonialism (colonization); imperialism
Anti-Imperialist (Dublin) 593; *see also* Anti-Imperialist Vigilance Association; League Against Imperialism (1927–37)
Anti-Imperialist Vigilance Association 593; *see also Anti-Imperialist* (Dublin); League Against Imperialism (1927–37)
anti-Jewish 472, 486, 506n72, 507n73, 584, 605–7; *see also* Jewish people; Limerick pogrom (Ireland, 1904); racial theories; "Semitic" (racial designation)
Anti-Treaty (Irish nationalists) 348, 579, 592, 600; *see also* Anglo-Irish Treaty (December 6, 1921); Irish Civil War (1922–23); Irish Free State; Irish Republican Army (1922); Pro-Treaty (Irish nationalists)
The Antiquities of Ireland (by Edward Ledwich, 1790): *see* Ledwich, Edward

Antrim 51, 522
"anxiety of influence" 128; *see also* Bloom, Harold
Aoife (Aífe) 438, 444, 617; *see also* Conla (Conlaoch); Cuchulain (Cú Chulainn); Ulster Cycle
Apollo (Hellenic deity) 94, 96
Arab 74, 83, 86, 239, 241–43, 421, 622
Arab-Muslim invasion of Iran (7th century CE) 4, 5, 25, 41, 112, 119, 131–33, 137, 172–75, 179–82, 184, 194, 205n46, 237, 239, 241, 261, 269, 272–75, 318, 348, 388, 492, 585, 638, 639; *see also Lalla Rookh. An Oriental Romance* (by Thomas Moore, 1817); MacCarthy, Denis Florence ("The Clan of Mac Caura")
Arabia 75, 133, 246, 270, 436, 529
Arabian Nights: *see One Thousand and One Nights* (a.k.a., *Arabian Nights*)
Arabian Sea 10
Arabic language 7, 14, 17, 22, 40, 67, 74, 79, 81–83, 115, 124, 130–33, 138, 174, 178, 186, 205n46, 233, 237, 239, 241–43, 246, 249, 250, 254, 259, 262, 264, 268, 273, 278, 387, 389, 432, 449, 488, 514, 519, 525, 531, 537, 614, 617, 622, 632n144, 640, 649; *see also* Semitic languages
Arabs 12, 138, 147, 162n235, 178, 238, 239, 252, 264, 421, 608, 620; *see also* "Semitic" (racial designation)
Aran Islands 25, 44n38
Ararat, Mount 126
Araxes: *see* Arras River
archaeology 13, 24, 56, 64, 85, 88, 91, 98–100, 109, 110, 123, 124, 131, 149, 197–200, 257, 276, 296n79, 381, 385, 386, 393, 418, 422, 447, 453n25, 568, 571, 581, 582, 600, 641, 643
architecture 13, 23, 24, 56, 64, 88, 100–102, 104, 121, 123–25, 190, 195, 196, 226, 339, 382, 383, 386, 387, 395
Ardestani, Mir Zulfaqar 85; *see also Dabestān-e Mazāheb*; Keyvan, Azar; "neo-Zoroastrianism"
aristocracy 440, 525, 546, 599; aristocratic 439, 440
Armagh 18
Armenia 2, 4, 52, 56, 63, 71, 72, 84, 186, 193, 581, 624, 636, 637
Armenian 19, 77, 81, 84, 226, 272, 328, 365, 377n17, 377n18, 476, 530, 536, 566, 620; Irish-Armenian 388, 389; *see also* Christians in Iran; Cormick, William; Iranian famine of (1870–72); Moses (Movsessian), Catchick; Singapore; *The Strait Times* (Singapore)
Armenian Genocide (Ottoman Empire) 637

INDEX 701

"Armenian" theories of Irish origins 2, 4, 19, 52, 56, 72, 77, 84, 226, 581, 624, 636, 637; *see also* theories of Irish origins
"Armenian-Scythians" 77; *see also* Vallancey, Charles
Arnold, Matthew 416, 442, 449; *On the Study of Celtic Literature* (by Matthew Arnold, 1867) 416; *Sohrab and Rustum* (by Matthew Arnold, 1853) 442
Arnot, Sandford 444
Arras River 78, 632n144
Arrowsmith, Aaron 329
Arrowsmith, John 329, 330
Artapanus (of Alexandria) 108
"Arvanda" (River Aredvi) 624
Aryan (languages) 8, 14, 15, 35, 42, 44n38, 57–59, 61–63, 67, 394, 435, 600, 639; *see also* Indo-European languages; Indo-Europeans; Jones, William; "Jonesian" theory of Indo-European languages; Persian language; philology; Sanskrit
The Aryan Origins of the Gaelic Race and Language (by Ulick Joseph Bourke, 1875) 277, 393, 420; *see also* Bourke, Ulick Joseph
"Aryan" theories of Irish origins 8, 44n38, 58–61, 79, 145–48, 200, 201, 277, 382, 391–96, 402–6, 412, 413, 415, 416, 420–22, 428, 431, 435, 438–40, 443, 447–51, 461n165, 488–92, 568, 569, 571–74, 576, 577, 581, 589, 600, 602, 620, 639, 640, 646; *see also* Bourke, Ulick Joseph; "Europe-centered" theories of Irish origins; Green, Alice Stopford; Hayden, Mary; "Indo-European" theories of Irish origins; "Iranian" theories of Irish origins; Joyce, Patrick Weston; MacNeill, Eoin (John); Moonan, George Aloysius; "Scandinavian" (Scandian) theories of Irish origins; Taylor, Isaac; theories of Irish origins; Vallancey, Charles; Wilde, Jane Francesca Agnes (née Elgee)
Aryana 492; *see also* Aryanism (racial theories); Kermani, Mirza Aqa Khan
Aryanism (racial theories) 8, 9, 35, 58, 59, 137, 139, 145–46, 148, 353, 392, 412, 434, 435, 443, 448, 450, 488, 490–92, 577, 620, 640, 646; Asian origins of Aryans 58, 61, 74, 146, 147, 200, 391–93, 435, 439, 443, 447, 449, 489, 572, 573, 576, 581, 620; Nordic (Scandinavian) origins of Aryans 58, 59, 393, 412, 424, 440, 447, 451, 571–74, 576, 577, 581; *see also* Aryana; Caucasians; "Europe-centered" theories of Irish origins; "Indo-European" theories of Irish origins; "Indo-Iranian" theories of Irish origins; "Iranian" theories of Irish origins; Pan-Aryan Association;

racial theories; "whitening" of the "mere Irish"
Aryans 42, 57–60, 146, 201, 382, 391–94, 396, 402, 412, 420, 435, 439, 440, 443, 447, 449, 451, 489–91, 568, 572–74, 576; *see also* Indo-Europeans; Indo-Iranians; Indo-Scythians; Irano-Scythians; Scythians
Aryo-Semitic (Aryan-Semitic; Indo-Semitic) 410, 448; *see also* Ascoli, Graziadio Isaia; Jacobs, Joseph
Ascoli, Graziadio Isaia 409–10, 448; *see also* Aryo-Semitic (Aryan-Semitic; Indo-Semitic)
"Asfendyar": *see* Esfandiyar
Asia (and Asians) 58–61, 73–75, 106, 108, 118, 128, 129, 186, 195, 196, 214, 215, 311, 325, 401, 421, 435, 439, 442, 485, 491, 522, 535, 536, 574, 616, 617; Central Asia 3, 12, 17, 58, 72, 74, 87, 88, 174, 183, 320, 324, 329, 349, 385, 389, 392, 393, 431, 550; East Asia 12, 143, 490; South Asia 3, 17, 31, 58, 72, 94, 146, 147, 244, 420, 421, 448, 491, 570, 620; West Asia 3, 17, 53, 58, 72, 77, 111, 126, 190, 193, 324, 382, 491, 574
Asiatic Researches 116, 117; *see also* Asiatic Society of Bengal
Asiatic Society of Bengal 57, 73, 75, 76, 81–86, 91, 105, 111, 115–17, 132, 567, 640; *see also Asiatic Researches*; "Bengal Renaissance"; *Dabestān-e Mazāheb*; *Dasātir*; Gladwin, Francis; Jones, William; "Oriental Renaissance"; Shea, David; Troyer, Anthony
Assadabadi, Sayyid Jamal al-Din (a.k.a., "al-Afghani") 469, 501n8, 501n10; *see also* "Egypt for Egyptians"; pan-Islam; tobacco concession (Iran, 1890)
Assmann, Aleida 275; *see also* memory
Assmann, Jan 603; *see also* memory ("cultural" memory)
Assyria (and Assyrians) 12, 21, 146, 147, 403, 409, 421, 435, 565; theories of Irish origins 21, 146, 147, 403, 409; *see also* "Semitic" (racial designation)
Astley's Amphitheater (Dublin) 517
astronomy 63, 95, 277, 382, 449; *see also* O'Brien, Henry; Round Towers (Ireland)
atheism 180, 428–30, 433
Athens 220, 221, 224, 225, 411; *see also* Greece; Marathon, Battle of (490 BCE); Thermopylae, Battle of (480 BCE)
Atkinson, James 184, 185, 242, 442, 444, 463n209; *Lailā and Majnūn: A Poem* (translated by James Atkinson, 1836) 243; *The Shâh Nâmeh of the Persian Poet Firdausí* (by James Atkinson, 1832) 184, 185, 242, 444; *Soohrab; a Poem, Freely Translated*

from the Original Persian ... (translated by James Atkinson, 1814) 184, 242, 442, 444, 463n209; *see also* English East India Company; *Shāhnāmeh*; Sohrab; Ulster Cycle

Atlantis 139, 142, 581; *see also* Donnelly, Ignatius; O'Kelly, John Joseph (Seán Ua Ceallaigh)

Aurangzeb (Mughal emperor) 174, 204n20; *see also* Mughal dynasty

Australasia 536; "Austral-Asia" 535

Australia 11, 139, 147, 234, 312, 313, 364, 377n17, 400, 420, 448, 539, 576, 597; *see also* St. Kilda (Australia)

Austria (and Austrian) 36, 225, 240, 242, 308, 436, 444, 578, 586, 640; Austro-Hungarian Empire 473, 475, 478, 578, 584, 595; "dual monarchy" 475, 478, 578, 584; *see also* Blunt, Wilfrid Scawen; First World War; Griffith, Arthur

Avestan language and script (Old Iranian) 83, 449

Ayrton, Acton Smee 354n18; *see also* Anglo-Iranian War (1856–57); Whig Party (Radical wing)

Azerbaijan (Iranian province) 532; *see also* Tabriz

Azerbaijan, Republic of 244

Azeris (Iran) 531

Azeris (from Russian controlled Caucasus) 476, 531

Aztec 435

Baal 407–9; *see also* Bealtaine (May Day festival)

Baath (/Baoth) 47, 61; *see also* Fénius Farsaid (Fenius Farsa); Magog

Babi faith 542; Babis 543, 545

Babur (Mughal emperor) 326; *see also* Mughal dynasty

Babylon: *see* Babylonia

Babylonia 64, 75, 108, 395, 421, 432; Neo-Babylonian/Chaldean 75

Babylonians 12, 147, 383, 435, 452n3; theories of Irish origins 108, 147, 383, 395, 432; *see also* Cuthite; Nebuchadnezzar II; "Semitic" (racial designation)

Bacon, Francis 644; knowledge/power 644

Bactria 74

Baghdad 175, 268, 342, 562n104; *see also* Iraq

Baha'i faith 434; *see also* 'Abdu'l-Bahá

Bahram Mirza 532; *see also* Burgess, Edward ("*World Geography*" (Persian title unknown, 1847)); Qajar dynasty (Iran, 1796–1925)

Bailly, Jean-Sylvain 71

Bakhtiari 391, 484; *see also* Lynch, Henry Finnis Blosse

Bakhtin, Mikhail 126, 286; *see also* "dialogic imagination"; heteroglossia

Bakki: *see* Abdülbāki, Mahmud (a.k.a., Baki)

Balaklava 335; Congress of Paris 329; *see also* Crimean War (1854–56)

Balkan 421, 479

Balkh 239, 244; *see also* Afghanistan

Baltic 214, 336, 440; Baltic Sea 574

Balzac, Honoré de 279; *Melmoth Réconcilié* (by Honoré de Balzac, 1835) 279; *see also* Maturin, Charles Robert

Bandar Abbas 378n23

Banim, John 524; *The Anglo-Irish of the Nineteenth Century* (by John Banim, 1828) 525; *see also* "provincializing Ireland"

Banville, John 555

Barakatullah, Abdul Hafiz Mohammad 488–90, 508n86; *see also* Ghadar; Japan (Imperial University (Tokyo)); Pan-Aryan Association; pan-Asianism

Barberino, Raphael 267; *see also* Jenkinson, Anthony; Muscovy Company; Urban VIII, Pope (Maffeo Barbarini)

Barbier de Meynard, Charles Adrien Casimir 442; *see also* Mohl, Jules (Julius)

Barckly, John 49

Barmakids 239, 265, 267; *see also* Hammer-Purgstall, Joseph Freiherr von; Heman, Felicia; Mangan, James Clarence; *One Thousand and One Nights* (a.k.a., *Arabian Nights*)

Barnacle, Nora 610; *see also* Joyce, James

Barry, Michael Joseph 167; *see also* Moore, Thomas; Young Ireland

Barthes, Roland 247; "the Death of the Author" 247

Baskerville, Howard 476; *see also* I Iranian Constitutional Revolution (1906–11)

Basque 412, 421, 422, 458n126

Basra 332; *see also* Iraq; Pyrault, Claude

Bassi, Ugo (Italian revolutionary priest) 398; Cisalpine Republic 398; *see also* Wilde, Jane Francesca Agnes (née Elgee)

Basutoland 545; *see also* southern Africa

Bataille, Georges 141; *see also* "labors of loss"

Bateman-Champain, John Underwood 377n22; *see also* Iranian famine (1870–72)

Bealtaine (May Day festival) 407, 409; *see also* Baal

Beardsley, Aubrey 622, 623

Beauford ("Beaufort"), William 85, 93, 124, 196, 208n81; *see also* Irish antiquarianism; "Scandinavian" (Scandian) theories of Irish origins

Beaufort, Louisa Catherine 17, 79, 120, 123–27, 129, 135, 142, 143, 185, 189, 206n63, 207n81, 211, 280, 382, 384, 404,

409, 445–47, 567, 625; "An Essay upon the State of Architecture and Antiquities ..." (1827) 123, 208n81; gold prize of the Royal Irish Academy 445; *see also* Conla (Conlaoch); Cuchulain (Cú Chulainn); Ferdowsi, Abul-Qassem; "fire worship"; historiography and history; Iran/Erin; "Iranian" theories of Irish origins; Irish antiquarianism; Jones, William; Round Towers (Ireland); Royal Irish Academy; Rustam; *Shāhnāmeh*; Sohrab; *Transactions of Royal Irish Academy*; Ulster Cycle; Vallancey, Charles; Zoroastrian

Becanus, Jan Goropius (Jan van Gorp van der Beke) 57; *see also* Indo-European languages

Beckett, Samuel 554, 555; *Waiting for Godot* (by Samuel Beckett, 1953) 555

Belfast 26, 106, 109, 121, 198, 308, 366, 367, 371–73, 401, 496, 524, 535, 550; Falls Road district 550

Belfast News-Letter 308, 367, 371–73; *see also* unionists (Ireland)

Belgium 39, 350, 420, 496, 514, 610; Belgian 208n87, 640; sovereignty guaranteed by Britain (1839) 495–97; *see also* Congo (Belgian Congo); First World War; Leopold II, King

Belize 314

Beltaine: *see* Bealtaine (May Day festival)

Benfey, Theodor 409

Bengal 57, 73, 75, 76, 81, 82, 84–86, 91, 105, 111, 115–17, 132, 434, 435, 474, 518, 567, 586, 640, 649, 651n5; partition of (1905–11) 474, 475, 487, 551; *see also* All-India Muslim League; Asiatic Society of Bengal; "Bengal Renaissance"; swadeshi

"Bengal Renaissance" 81; *see also* Asiatic Society of Bengal; "Oriental Renaissance"

Benjamin, Walter 116, 135, 136, 226, 248, 280, 624; "after-life" of a work of art 116, 135; "messianic time" 136, 226; "the now of recognizability" 624; "now-time" (Jetztzeit) 135, 136, 226, 227; "reception" of a work of art 116, 135

Bérard, Victor 619; *Les Phéniciens et l'Odyssée* (by Victor Bérard, 1902–03) 619

Berger, Stefan 61

Berlin 497–99, 509n112, 551, 590, 638; *see also* Germany

Bermuda 584

Besant, Annie (née Wood) 429, 434; *see also* Fabian socialism; freemasonry (co-freemasonry); Indian nationalism; Irish nationalism; Theosophical Society; theosophy; women's rights

Betham, William 93, 94, 99, 100, 105, 106, 121, 122, 126, 141, 142, 154n78, 157n161, 190, 196, 198, 199, 211, 278, 283, 404, 646; *Etruria-Celtica: Etruscan Literature and Antiquities Investigated* (by William Betham, 1842) 121; *The Gael and Cymbri: An Inquiry into the Origin and History of the Irish Scoti, Britons, and Gauls ...,* (by William Betham, 1834) 121; Phoenician theory of Irish origins 99, 105, 106, 121, 122, 154n78, 190, 646; presumed sepulchral function of the Round Towers 105, 196; *see also* Irish antiquarianism; O'Brien, Henry; Petrie, George; "Phoenician" theories of Irish origins; Round Towers (Ireland); Royal Irish Academy; theories of Irish origins; Vallancey, Charles

The Bible 17, 64, 95, 107, 116, 400, 637; *see also* Adam; Cain; Eve; Garden of Eden; Japheth; Magog; Mosaic theory; Nephilim; Noah

biblical sources 13, 15–19, 22, 30, 57, 60, 61, 64, 69, 73–76, 79, 80, 82, 92, 95, 106–9, 112, 115, 117, 124, 131, 135, 146, 393, 402, 403, 405, 565–67, 581, 585, 614, 615, 651; Judeo-Christian sources 16, 49, 79, 429

Bibliothèque orientale (by Barthélemy d'Herbelot, 1697) 75, 81, 83, 84, 115, 175, 184, 205n46, 446, 640; *see also* Herbelot [de Molainville], Barthélemy d'; *Kashf al-ẓunūn 'an asāmī al-kutub wa-al-funūn* (by Mustafa bin Abdullah (a.k.a., Hadji Khalfa "Katip Çelebi"), 17th century); Mangan, James Clarence; Moore, Thomas; Vallancey, Charles

Bin Kaus, Firuz (Mulla) 111; *see also Dasātir*

Bingham, Charlotte 489; *see also* Pan-Aryan Association

Birmingham 310

Birrell, Augustine 551; *see also* Land Purchase Bills (Ireland)

Black Sea 73, 74, 193, 303, 402

Blackburne, Francis 335, 501n6; Lord Chancellor of Ireland 501n6; *see also* Blackburne Daniell, Alice Caroline; O'Brien, William Smith; O'Connell, Daniel

Blackburne Daniell, Alice Caroline 501n6; *see also* Blackburne, Francis; Browne, Edward Granville

Blackie, John Stuart 394

Blackwood's Edinburgh Magazine 235, 353n8

Blavatsky, Helena Petrovna 139, 430–32, 435, 460n148; *see also* Theosophical Society; theosophy

"The Blind," William Heffernan (Uilliam Dall O'Hearnain/Uilliam ÓhAnnracháin)

437; "Caitlin Ni Uallachain" 437; *see also* Mangan, James Clarence ("Kathaleen Ny-Houlahan" (1841))
Bloom, Harold 128; *see also* "anxiety of influence"
Bloom, Leopold 606, 607, 610, 611; Israel-Ireland 610; *see also Ulysses* (by James Joyce, 1922)
Blumenbach, Johann Friedrich 392
Blunt, Wilfrid Scawen 471, 477–82, 484, 506n62, 507n73; "Fand of the Fair Cheek" (play, performed in 1907) 480; *see also* Abbey Theatre; Austria (Austro-Hungarian Empire); *Egypt* (London); "Egypt for Egyptians"; Egyptian Committee (UK); Iranian Constitutional Revolution (1906–11); Irish Home Rule; Nationalities and Subject Races conferences (London, 1910, 1911, 1914)
Boal, Iain 604; *see also* agnotology
Bochart, Samuel 71, 384; *see also* O'Hart; Vallancey, Charles
Boer War (1880–81) 545; *see also* southern Africa
Boer War (1899–1902) 351, 472, 553; *see also* Irish Parliamentary Party; Irish Transvaal Brigade (a.k.a., Irish Commandos/MacBride's Brigade); southern Africa
Bolshevism 594
Bombay (Mumbai) 111, 113, 131, 309, 327, 335, 369, 377n15, 390, 442, 538, 640; *see also* India; Literary Society of Bombay
Bombay Times 327, 335, 640
Bonaparte, Charles-Louis Napoleon (Napoleon III) 311, 325, 364; *see also* Crimean War (1854–56); Franco-Prussian War (1870–71)
Bonaparte, Napoleon 6, 33, 170, 171, 173, 204n26, 206n56, 288, 337, 472, 516, 518, 520, 537; *see also* Egypt (French invasion (1798)); Napoleonic Wars
Bongiovanni, Lynne A. 302n208
Bopp, Franz 57, 394; *see also* Indo-European languages
Borneo 331; *see also* Brooke, James (Rajah Brooke)
Bornstein, George 228
Bosphorus (Bosporus) 74
Boston 368, 489
Bourke, Ulick Joseph 277, 382, 383, 391, 393–96, 404, 420, 432; ancient Gaels and Persians 393–96, 404; *Pre-Christian Ireland* (by Ulick Joseph Bourke, 1887) 189, 396; *see also The Aryan Origins of the Gaelic Race and Language* (by Ulick Joseph Bourke, 1875); "Aryan" theories of Irish origins; Gaelic League; Gaelic Union; "Iranian" theories of Irish origins; Land League; "Land War"; pillar towers; Round Towers (Ireland); Royal Irish Academy; Society for the Preservation of Irish Language; theories of Irish origins

Bowen, Elizabeth 554
Boxhorn, Marcus Zuerius van 57; *see also* Indo-European languages
Brahminical 82, 85
"Brahminical" language and script: *see* Sanskrit
Brahmins 89
Brazil 159n191
Breed, Brennan 134; "other peoples' texts" 134; *see also* "interpellation"
Brian Boru 219, 283, 418; *see also* Clontarf, Battle of; Norse ("Vikings")
Brigger, Francis Joseph 201; *see also The Glories of Ireland* (Joseph Dunn and Patrick Joseph Lennox, eds., 1914); Petrie, George; Round Towers (Ireland); Royal Irish Academy
Britain: *see* Great Britain; United Kingdom
Britannia: Or a Chorographical Description of Great Britain and Ireland, Together with the Adjacent Islands (by William Camden, 1586): *see* Camden, William
Britannic Isles: *see* British Isles
British Association 401, 405; Anthropological Department of the Biological section of the Irish chapter of the British Association 401
British Committee of the Indian National Congress (1889) 501n4; *see also* Keay, John Seymour
British Empire 1, 8–11, 26, 33, 38, 115, 140, 149, 168, 183, 212, 223, 284, 303, 313, 317, 320, 321, 329, 330, 335, 337, 348, 351, 352, 362, 364, 365, 369–71, 391, 411, 456n76, 458n114, 468, 471–75, 487, 488, 493–95, 499, 513–15, 526–28, 535, 536, 539, 541, 547–50, 552, 578, 584, 588, 592–97, 621, 647; *see also* Celtic Sea; Egypt; English Channel; Great Britain; Great Britain (imperial leverage in Iran); India; Irish Sea; Mediterranean Sea; North Sea; Palestine
British Isles 16, 18, 21, 23, 25, 30, 51, 53, 55, 59, 60, 65–67, 79, 80, 138, 149, 190, 191, 214–16, 272, 283, 387, 389, 404, 405, 409, 413, 416, 417, 420, 450, 451, 514, 515, 518, 519, 524, 527, 528, 536–40, 546, 548, 549, 567–69, 571, 572, 574, 576, 579, 583, 586, 602, 612, 651; *see also* England; Great Britain; Ireland; Scotland; Wales; United Kingdom
British legation (Tehran) 305, 338, 389, 485; *see also* Murray, Charles; Thomson, William Taylour

British parliament 9, 34, 140, 165n301, 168, 171, 202n8, 284, 305–7, 309–12, 321, 323, 324, 329, 339, 349, 351, 354n14, 354n18, 467–70, 474, 475, 477, 480, 481, 493, 522, 523, 526–29, 531, 536, 538, 543, 544, 546, 548, 549, 551, 552, 554, 578; "Home Rule" Irish nationalist representation 9, 36, 145, 302n214, 309, 312, 314, 317, 355n28, 358n98, 368, 390, 424, 427, 468, 472, 475, 480, 481, 486, 494, 528, 540–41, 546, 547, 549, 552, 576, 584, 590, 591, 627n46; House of Commons 9, 145, 307, 312, 354n14, 354n15, 477, 481, 525, 529, 536, 541, 551, 553; House of Lords 536, 551, 552; *see also* Anglo-Iranian War (1856–57); Iranian Constitutional Revolution (1906–11); Tobacco Protest (Iran, 1891–92)

"Briton" 12, 20, 25, 66, 68, 70, 74, 170, 185, 283, 319, 335, 343, 416, 568, 569, 574

Brittlebank, William 378n23; *see also* Iranian famine (1870-72)

Brooke, Charlotte 42, 46n48, 53, 68, 69, 185, 442, 445–47; *Reliques of Irish Poetry* (by Charlotte Brooke, 1789) 42, 69, 185, 442, 445, 446; Royal Irish Academy 69; *see also* Conla (Conlaoch); Cuchulain (Cú Chulainn); O'Conor, Charles; O'Halloran, Sylvester (Silvester); Ulster Cycle; Vallancey, Charles

Brooke, James (Rajah Brooke) 331; *see also* Borneo

Brooke, Stopford Augustus 433

Brooklyn (New York) 412, 458n112, 489; *see also* New York

Brooklyn Gaelic Society 489

"Brother James of Ireland" 388, 452n15; *see also* Odoric of Venetia (a.k.a., Odoric of Pordenone)

Brown, Ken S. 134; "other peoples' texts" 134; *see also* "interpellation"

Browne, Edward Granville 118, 137, 138, 469, 477, 479, 481, 483, 484, 495, 501n6, 504n49, 506n62, 507n73, 560n64, 577; *The Persian Revolution of 1905–1909* (by Edward Granville Browne, 1910) 469; *The Press and Poetry of Modern Persia* (by Edward Granville Browne, 1914) 138; *see also* Anglo-Russian Agreement (1907); Blackburne Daniell, Alice Caroline; Iranian Constitutional Revolution (1906–11); National Peace Congress (London, 1912); orientalism; Persia Committee (London)

Bruce, Emily 366, 388; *see also* Anglican Church; Bruce, Robert (Rev.); Church Missionary Society; Iranian famine (1870–72)

Bruce, Robert (Rev.) 366, 367, 370, 377n17, 377n23, 388; *see also* Anglican Church; Bruce, Emily; *Church Missionary Intelligencer*; Church Missionary Society; Iranian famine (1870–72)

Brutus 20; *see also* Troy

Bryant, Jacob 382, 410, 452n3; *A New System, or, an Analysis of Antient Mythology* (by Jacob Bryant, 1777) 452n3

Bryant, Sophie 412, 413, 420, 451, 572; *Celtic Ireland* (by Sophie Bryant, 1889) 412, 572; *The Genius of the Gael: A Study in Celtic Psychology and its Manifestations* (by Sophie Bryant, 1913) 572; *see also* "Aryan" theories of Irish origins

Bryce, James 501n2; *see also* tobacco concession (Iran, 1890)

Buchanan, George 191, 574

Buchanan, James (US president) 315, 356n37; *see also* Democratic Party (US); slavery

Büchner, Karl Georg 254

Buddha 117–18; Buddhism 96, 106, 239, 382, 430, 431, 434, 435; *see also* Round Towers (Ireland)

Buffon, Comte de 18, 61; *see also* Neptunism (geology)

Bukhara 174, 175, 241, 320; *see also* Conolly, Arthur; *Lalla Rookh. An Oriental Romance* (by Thomas Moore, 1817); Transoxania; Uzbekistan

Bulgarians 476

Bundahishn 95, 623; *see also* Keyoumars; Zoroastrianism

Bunting, Edward 214

Burgess, Edward 358n98, 532; "World Geography" (Persian title unknown, 1847); *see also* Bahram Mirza; *Rouznāmeh-ye Vaqāye'-e Ettefāqiyeh* (Tehran; a.k.a., "*Teheran Gazette*")

Burke, Edmund 156n124, 235

Burke, Thomas Henry 546; under-secretary for Ireland 546; *see also* Phoenix Park murders (Dublin, 1882)

Bushire 305, 309, 311, 323, 335, 336, 341, 343, 367, 378n23, 390; British Residency in the Persian Gulf 336; *see also* Anglo-Iranian War (1856–57)

Butler, Samuel 622; *Hudibras* (by Samuel Butler, 1663–78) 622

Butt, Isaac 468; *see also* Home Government Association; Home Rule League

Byrne, Clarinda Mary 521

Byron, Lord (George Gordon Byron) 173, 175, 188, 203n17, 207n74, 221, 228, 229, 236, 247; *The Corsair* (by Lord Byron, 1814) 188; *Don Juan* (by Lord Byron, 1818–24) 207n74, 221, 228; *see also* Greek War of

Independence (1821–29); Hellenophilia; Marathon, Battle of (490 BCE); Moore, Thomas; "oriental-style" literature; Romanticism
Byzantine Empire 175, 176, 204n29; Empress Irene 175; *see also Lalla Rookh. An Oriental Romance* (by Thomas Moore, 1817)

Cain 110, 285; *see also* Adam; The Bible; Eve; The Hebrew Bible ("Old Testament")
Calcutta (Kolkata) 57, 73, 75, 85, 86, 91, 132, 184, 305, 309, 320, 337, 444, 550–53; *see also* India
Caliban 233, 284, 620; *see also* Shakespeare, William (*The Tempest*)
Callan, Margaret (née Hughes) 398; *see also The Nation* (Dublin)
Callanan, Jeremiah John 241
Cama [Rustom Cama], Bhikhaji (also spelled Bhikhaiji) 490, 507n83; *Bande Mataram* (Geneva) 490; *see also* Pan-Aryan Association
Cambrensis, Giraldus 49
Camden, William 21, 23, 43n15, 48, 49, 78, 384, 527; *Britannia: Or a Chorographical Description of Great Britain and Ireland, Together with the Adjacent Islands* (by William Camden, 1586) 21, 48, 527; Celto-Scytæ 21; English-Irish 21, 527; "wild Irish" 21, 48, 78, 527
Campbell, Thomas 93; *see also* Irish antiquarianism; "Scandinavian" (Scandian) theories of Irish origins
Campion, Edmund 49, 83
Canaanites 75, 383, 452n3; *see also* Cuthite
Canada 11, 159n191, 313, 363, 366, 456n76, 539, 542, 543, 545, 549, 597; *see also* Fenian raids into Canada (1870 and 1871); Irish diaspora (in Canada)
Candia: *see* Crete
Candy, Catherine 431
cannibalism: *see* Great Famine (Ireland, 1845–51) (reported incidences of anthropophagy); India (famines) (reported incidences of anthropophagy); Iranian famine (1870–72) (reported incidences of anthropophagy)
Canning, Charles John 305, 342, 370; governor-general of British India 304, 342; Viceroy of India 370; *see also* Anglo-Iranian War (1856–57); Indian uprising (1857–58)
Canning, Stratford (Viscount Stratford de Redcliffe) 207n67, 342; *see also* Anglo-Iranian War (1856–57); Moore, Thomas; Ottoman Empire
Cape Colony 540; *see also* southern Africa
Carey, John 565

Carlow (County) 143, 390; *see also* Kavanagh, Arthur MacMurrough
Carpathian Mountains 574
Carthage: *see* Phoenicia
Carthaginian: *see* Phoenicians
cartography 20, 142, 253, 255, 329, 330, 527, 529, 530, 532, 533, 537, 559n47, 559n57, 638, *passim*; *see also* geography; Lisbon Geographical Society
Casanova, Pascale 456n64; *see also* Herder, Johann Gottfried von
Casement, Roger 201, 209n115, 497–99, 610; execution (1916) 497, 499, 554 "The Romance of Irish History" (1914) 20; *see also* Easter Rising (Ireland, 1916); *The Glories of Ireland* (Joseph Dunn and Patrick Joseph Lennox, eds., 1914); Irish Brigade (Irish nationalist volunteers recruited from the ranks of Irish prisoners of war in Germany during the First World War); Irish Nationalist Committee (Berlin; a.k.a., German-Irish Society); Irish Republican Brotherhood; *Kāveh* (Berlin)
Caspian Sea 70, 71, 74, 77, 191, 194, 333, 343, 378n23, 401, 402, 421, 582, 600
A Catalogue of the Persian Printed Books in the British Museum (1922) 532
Catherine "the Great" (Empress of Russia) 151n20
Catholic Association (1823) 171, 339, 390, 544; *see also* Catholic Emancipation; Catholic Relief Act (1829); O'Connell, Daniel; Sheil, Richard Lalor
Catholic Association (a.k.a., Catholic Committee, 1756) 70; *see also* Curry, John; O'Conor, Charles
Catholic Bulletin and Book Review (Dublin) 580; *see also* O'Kelly, John Joseph (Seán Ua Ceallaigh)
Catholic Church (in Britain) 538
Catholic Church (in Ireland) 24, 171, 195, 212, 268, 309, 313, 316, 396, 475, 483, 486, 570, 588, 589, 592, 595, 597, 606; *see also* Anglo-Catholics; Catholics; Irish Free State
Catholic Church (in Rome) 20, 177, 195, 262, 263, 265–69, 273, 363, 575, 606
Catholic Counter-Reformation 48, 316; *see also* Keating, Geoffrey
Catholic Defence Association (1851) 389, 540; *see also* Moore, George Henry; Sadleir, John
Catholic Emancipation 90, 168, 171, 293n33, 339, 349, 536, 538, 543, 544; *see also* Anglican Church (Oath of Supremacy); Catholic Association (1823); Catholic Relief Act (1829); Church of Ireland

(tithes); Moore, Thomas; O'Connell, Daniel; Pitt, William ("the Younger"); Woulfe, Stephen
Catholic Progress (London and Dublin) 196; Young Men's Catholic Association 196; *see also* D'Alton (Dalton), John; Lanigan, John; Round Towers (Ireland); Vallancey, Charles
Catholic Relief Act (1778) 50, 170; *see also* Hely, James; Trinity College (University of Dublin)
Catholic Relief Act (1829) 171; *see also* Catholic Association (1823); Catholic Emancipation; O'Connell, Daniel
Catholic University of America 201; *see also* Dunn, Joseph; Lennox, Patrick Joseph
Catholic University of Ireland (Dublin) 199, 394; *see also* O'Curry, Eugene
Catholics 5, 7, 34, 50, 51, 68, 101, 144, 145, 168–71, 178, 223, 231, 136, 250, 252, 268–71, 301n199, 308, 313, 316, 349, 351, 352, 362, 365, 367, 428, 464n216, 473, 491, 522, 524, 528, 534, 538, 542, 544, 639, *passim*; "papists" 171, 178, 301n199; "Popish" 195; "Romish" 195; *see also* Ancient Order of Hibernians; Catholic Association (a.k.a., Catholic Committee, 1756); Catholic Association (1823); Catholic Church; Catholic Counter-Reformation; Catholic Emancipation; Catholic Relief Act (1778); Catholic Relief Act (1829); John XXII, Pope; papacy; Ribbonism (Ireland)
Caucasians 146, 147, 328, 391–93, 435, 618; *see also* Aryanism (racial theories); Indo-Europeans; racial theories
Caucasus 3, 12, 58, 71, 72, 74, 126, 208n81, 272, 389, 392, 516, 524, 531, 539
Cavendish, Frederick Charles 546; chief secretary for Ireland 546; *see also* Phoenix Park murders (Dublin, 1882)
Ceanchora 89; *see also* O'Brien, Henry; O'Brien, James McEdward
ceann 278, 279; *see also* khan
Ceasair 580; *see also* "Great Flood"; Noah
"celestial" alphabet 82; "celestial" ("heavenly") language 106, 112, 118
Celtic 16, 23, 25, 26, 41, 50, 53, 56, 57, 60, 61, 63, 65–67, 70, 71, 78, 79, 106, 119, 121–22, 143, 146–47, 149, 190–93, 200, 215, 216, 279, 383, 387, 394, 396, 402–6, 410, 412, 413, 415–17, 422, 424, 431, 439, 441, 442, 445–47, 450, 451, 458n113, 458n126, 490, 491, 498, 535, 568–77, 579, 581, 582, 587, 588, 597–602, 605, 608, 611–13, 615, 618, 624, 625, 645; *see also* Celts
The Celtic Druids; or, An Attempt to Shew, That the Druids Were the Priests of Oriental Colonies who Emigrated from India... (by Godfrey Higgins, 1827): *see* Higgins, Godfrey
Celtic languages 57, 63, 65, 70, 121, 383, 394, 424, 446, 498, 600
Celtic Sea 9, 54
Celticism 25, 55, 64, 70, 392, 446, 570, 573; *see also* Aryanism (racial theories); Celts; civilization; *Fragments of Ancient Poetry, Collected in the Highlands of Scotland* (by James Macpherson, 1760); Green, Alice Stopford; Hayden, Mary; Jones, Rowland; Joyce, Patrick Weston; MacNeill, Eoin (John); Macpherson, James; Moonan, George Aloysius; mythology (Irish heroic cycles); O'Brien, Henry; O'Conor, Charles; O'Halloran, Sylvester (Silvester); Ossian; pan-Celticism; theories of Irish origins; Vallancey, Charles
Celto-Scyths: *see* Camden, William; Jones, Rowland
Celts 16, 23, 25, 66, 67, 74, 78, 89, 106, 119, 121, 122, 144–47, 191–93, 215–17, 219, 226, 383, 387, 395, 403, 405, 406, 409–13, 416, 424, 451, 568, 572–74, 576, 577, 581, 589, 599, 600, 602, 612, 613, 624; *see also* Celtic; Celtic languages; Celticism; "Europe-centered" theories of Irish origins; "Iranian" theories of Irish origins; James II, King; Jones, Rowland; Lhuyd, Edward; O'Conor, Charles; O'Halloran, Sylvester (Silvester); "oriental" theories of Irish origins; Pezron, Paul; theories of Irish origins; Vallancey, Charles
Central America 306, 331; *see also* Costa Rica; Latin America; Mosquito Coast (Nicaragua and Honduras); Washington (diplomatic row with London (1854–56))
Ceylon (/Sri Lanka) 331
Chakrabarty, Dipesh 17, 26, 127–29, 648, 649; "provincialising Europe" 127, 128
Chaldea 85, 108, 197, 277, 430, 435; Neo-Babylonian/Chaldean 75; *see also* Nebuchadnezzar II
Chaldeans 2, 72, 75, 365, 452n3, 492, 620; Chaldean alphabet and language 82, 84; theories of Chaldean origins of the Irish 72, 75, 277; *see also* Round Towers (Ireland); theories of Irish origins
Chambers's Encyclopædia (Edinburgh) 197
Champion, Joseph 184; *The Poems of Ferdosi* (by Joseph Champion, 1785) 184; *see also* Ferdowsi, Abul-Qassem
Charles I, King 516; *see also* Cotton, Dodmore; Naqd-Ali Beg; Safavid dynasty (Iran, 1501–1722/36); Sherley (Shirley), Robert; Stuart dynasty (1603–49, 1660–1714)

Chartism 265; *see also* Harney, George Julian
Chatterjee, Mohini 434; *see also* theosophy; Vedanta
Chatterjee, Partha 144
Chatterton-Hill, George 498, 509n112; *see also* Irish Nationalist Committee (Berlin; a.k.a., German-Irish Society)
Chattopadhyaya, Virendranath ("Chatto") 509n112
Chicago 524; the Great Chicago Fire (1871) 371–73; *see also* Heron, Denis Caulfield; Mansion House (Dublin)
China 105, 246, 363, 422, 449, 452n15, 493, 553, 593, 610, 649, 650; Manchuria 491; *see also* Anglo-Chinese War (1839–42); Anglo-Chinese War (1856–60); Japan; Peking (Beijing); Xinhai Revolution (1911–12); Yuan dynasty
Chinese (language) 233
Chinese (people) 12, 67, 143, 144, 162n235
Chinese Famine (1876–79) 369, 378n38
Chippewa (Ojibwe) 246
Christianity (general) 101, 131, 183, 429, 430, 431, 432, 434, 460n148, 556n3, 564, 575, 598, *passim*; *see also* Catholics; Protestants (general)
Christianity (introduction to Ireland) 15, 24, 48, 54, 65, 68, 70, 85, 93, 100, 142, 190, 195, 201, 386, 405, 408, 433, 445, 536, 577, 581, 588, 642; "Asiatic" Christian proselytizers in Ireland 195; "Greek and Asiatic missionaries" in Ireland 195; *see also* Ledwich, Edward; Moore, Thomas
Christians in Iran 272, 328, 365, 431; Armenian 365, 377n18, 389, 536; Assyrian 365; Catholic Armenian Rite church 365; Chaldean 365; Nestorian Assyrian 365; *see also* Iranian famine (1870–72)
Christie, Charles 388; *see also* Malcolm, John; Pottinger, Henry
The Chronology of Ancient Kingdoms Amended (by Isaac Newton, 1728): *see* Newton, Isaac
Church Missionary Intelligencer 366; *see also* Anglican Church; Bruce, Robert (Rev.); Church Missionary Society; Iranian famine (1870–72)
Church Missionary Society 366, 388; *see also* Anglican Church; Bruce, Emily; Bruce, Robert (Rev.); *Church Missionary Intelligencer*; Iranian famine (1870–72)
Church of England: *see* Anglican Church
Church of Ireland 88, 170, 171, 540; disestablishment (1871) 540; tithes 171, 544; *see also* Gladstone, William Ewart; Tithe War
Chuto, Jacques 257, 284; *see also* "there and then"

Cincinnati (Ohio, US) 314
Circassia 186, 225, 326, 392, 520, 522, 523, 556n3, 586; *see also* Sampsonia, Teresia; Shirazi, Mirza Abul Hassan Khan ("Ilchi") ("Fair Circassian")
The Citizen (New York) 318, 323, 343; *see also* McClenahan, John; Mitchel, John
civilization 2, 7, 10–15, 17, 19, 21–25, 27–31, 35, 38, 48, 50, 51, 53–60, 63–67, 69, 72, 77–80, 87, 88, 90–95, 97–99, 102–4, 106, 109–11, 116–18, 121–23, 127–30, 132, 133, 136, 138, 141–45, 148, 157n155, 160n207, 172, 174, 185, 188–92, 204n29, 208n87, 216, 218–21, 225, 226, 230, 255, 277, 278, 280, 290, 321, 331, 334, 336, 341, 383, 392, 396, 403–8, 410, 413–15, 421, 422, 424, 425, 427, 431, 434, 435, 447, 448, 450, 451, 458n114, 461n165, 491, 492, 504n49, 519, 564, 565, 569, 571, 572, 573, 575, 576, 577, 581, 582, 585, 597, 598, 600, 605, 613, 624, 637, 642, 646, 649; Gaelic civilization 23, 600, *passim*; "Golden Age" 11, 30, 35, 48, 54, 58–60, 92, 102, 121, 131, 132, 137, 139, 141, 142, 276, 278, 331, 564, 646, 649; "Western Civilization" 23, 28, 30, 31, 58, 220, 424; *see also* Aryanism (racial theories); Celticism; the Enlightenment; Moore, Thomas; O'Brien, Henry; Vallancey, Charles; "wild Irish" (civilizational accusation)
Clan na Gael (United States) 2209n115, 229, 441, 476, 485, 488, 489, 491, 495–98; *see also* Devoy, John; Freeman, George ("Fitzgerald"); *Gaelic American* (New York); Irish Republican Brotherhood; McGarrity, Joseph; Pan-Aryan Association
Clancy, James Joseph 79, 227–28; *see also* Irish-American; Irish diaspora (United States); Irish Home Rule; Irish nationalism; Land League; Parnellite; United States
Clarke, Thomas James 475; *see also* Irish Republican Brotherhood
Claudius (Roman emperor) 191
Cloncurry, Lord (Valentine Brown Lawless, 2nd Baron Cloncurry) 93; *see also* Royal Irish Academy's 1833 prize essay
Clontarf 89, 212, 418; *see also* O'Brien, James McEdward; O'Connell, Daniel; Repeal Association (1840)
Clontarf, Battle of 89, 418; *see also* Brian Boru; Norse ("Vikings")
Clüver, Philipp 193
Cobden, Richard 354n19; *see also* Anglo-Iranian War (1856–57); Whig Party (Radical wing)
Coercion Acts (Ireland) 376, 546

Collectanea de Rebus Hibernicis (Volume 6, Part I; by Charles Vallancey, 1804): *see* Vallancey Charles
colonial/postcolonial studies: *see* "postcolonial"
colonialism (/colonization) 2, 5, 9, 11, 17, 19, 20, 23, 26, 31, 32, 36, 44n38, 66, 69, 82, 84, 89, 97, 122, 125, 127, 129, 138–42, 146, 174, 190–92, 196, 197, 225–27, 231, 243, 259, 260, 265, 274, 275, 284, 286–88, 319, 320, 322, 347–49, 351, 362, 363, 414, 415, 425, 433, 439, 450, 471, 472, 480, 486, 491, 500, 525, 527, 566, 572, 577–79, 581, 584–86, 594, 598, 605, 606, 611, 638, 644, 647–50; colony 9, 23, 30, 51, 53, 64, 78, 79, 91, 94, 100, 106, 121, 122, 128, 147, 148, 190–92, 194, 208n87, 249, 255, 258, 262, 284, 308, 310, 314, 320, 345, 349, 352, 363, 369, 373, 382, 384, 395, 404, 415, 424, 425, 428, 446, 513, 514, 522, 525–28, 532, 535–38, 540, 546, 549, 550, 552–54, 563, 583, 591, 593, 595, 603, 642, 643, 649; semi-colonized 19, 20, 36, 44n38, 129, 139, 223, 226, 433, 450, 471, 577–79, 594, 606, 648–50; *see also* anticolonial; anti-imperialism; imperialism
Colum, Padraic 40; "Anna Livia Plurabelle," 40; *see also Finnegans Wake* (by James Joyce, 1939)
Comerford, Vincent 368
The Comet (Dublin) 254
Comintern (Third / Communist International) 592, 593; *see also* Communist Party of Ireland (1921–24); Irish Worker League (1923–28); Larkin, James; League Against Imperialism (1927–37)
communism 364, 478, 499, 543, 545, 592, 594, 595
Communist Party of Ireland (1921–24) 592; *see also* Comintern (Third / Communist International)
Confederate War (Ireland, 1642–52) 177, 207n78, 267, 269, 538; *see also* English Civil War (1642–49); *The History of Ireland*, vol.IV (by Thomas Moore, 1846); O'Neill, Owen Roe; O'Neill, Phelim; Urban VIII, Pope (Maffeo Barbarini)
Congo (Belgian Congo) 553; Congo Free State 610; *see also* Belgium; Leopold II, King
Conla (Conlaoch) 41, 42, 143, 185, 436, 438, 440–43, 445–48, 464n209, 498; *see also* Aoife (Aífe); Brooke, Charlotte; Cuchulain (Cú Chulainn); epics; Meyer, Kuno; Modi, Jivanji Jamshedji; Mohl, Jules (Julius); mythology (Irish heroic cycles); Sohrab; Ulster Cycle

Conlaoch: *see* Conla (Conlaoch)
Connaught (Connacht) 147, 148, 278, 288, 320, 425; *see also* Cahal (Cáhal Mór; Cathal) of the Red Hand; Mangan, James Clarence
Connaught Rangers Mutiny (Punjab, 1920) 320; *see also* Irish War of Independence
Connemara 481
Conner (a.k.a., O'Connor), Arthur 472; *see also* Society of United Irishmen; United Irishmen (1798 uprising)
Connolly, James 350, 475, 483, 485, 494–97, 510n121, 611; *see also* Easter Rising (Ireland, 1916); Irish Citizen Army; Irish Socialist Republican Party; *The Irish Worker* (Dublin); Socialist Party of Ireland; *Workers' Republic* (Dublin)
Conolly, Arthur 320; *see also* Bukhara; English East India Company
Conservative Party (UK; a.k.a., Unionist Party after 1895) 145, 306, 307, 311, 323, 324, 354n18, 385, 390, 467–69, 476, 477, 549; *see also* Aberdeen, Lord (George Hamilton-Gordon); Curzon, George Nathaniel; Kavanagh, Arthur MacMurrough; Salisbury, Lord (Robert Arthur Talbot Gascoyne-Cecil); Sykes, Mark; Whiteside, James
Constitutional Society of India 312; *see also* British parliament; Sullivan, Alexander Martin
"contrapuntal" 127, 128, 256, 421; counterpoint 127; *see also* Said, Edward W.
Corcoran, Michael 314; *see also* Emmet Monument Association (New York); Fenian Brotherhood
Cork (County) 524; Aghada 524; Cork 157n161, 198, 308, 371, 394, 517, 518, 524, 551
Cork Constitution 367; *see also* unionists (Ireland)
Cork Examiner 52, 202n1, 212, 291n2, 316, 323, 367, 470; *see also* Anglo-Iranian War (1856–57); O'Connellite; Repeal movement; tobacco concession (Iran, 1890)
Cork Free Press 475; *see also* All-for-Ireland League
Cormick, John 389; *see also* Cormick, William
Cormick, William 388; *see also* Armenian (Irish-Armenian); Cormick, John
Cornwallis, Charles 518, 519; governor-general of India 518; Lord Lieutenant of Ireland 518
Cosgrave, William Thomas 592; *see also* Cumann na nGaedheal (1923); Fine Gael; Irish Free State
cosmopolitan 3, 7, 82, 128, 149, 219, 227, 259, 284, 347, 433, 435, 555, 580, 605, 608–11,

613, 615, 620; Irish polyglot cosmopolitan texts 7, 39, 82, 206n53, 232, 586, 611; nationalist cosmopolitanism 229, 293n34, 347, 351, 428, 433, 434, 481, 485, 486, 508n92, 605–8, 610, 613, 641, 647; *see also* Irish antiquarianism; Joyce, James; Mangan, James Clarence; Vallancey, Charles

Costa Rica 316; *see also* Central America; Latin America; Walker, William

Costello, Louisa Stuart 448; *The Rose Garden of Persia* (by Louisa Stuart Costello, 1845) 448; *see also* Jacobs, Joseph

"Coti" (ancient population of Ireland) 82, 83, 86; *see also* Vallancey, Charles

Cotton, Dodmore 516; *see also* Charles I, King; Naqd-Ali Beg; Safavid dynasty (Iran, 1501–1722/36); Sherley (Shirley), Robert

Coughlan, Patricia 300n177

Cousins, James 429–30, 434, 461n165, 471; *see also* Indian nationalism; internationalism; Irish nationalism; pacifism; socialism; women's rights

Cousins, Margaret Elizabeth (née Gillespie) 429–30, 434, 471, 478; *see also* Indian nationalism; internationalism; Irish nationalism; Irish Women's Franchise League; pacifism; socialism; women's rights

Cowell, Edward B. 426–27, 459n138; *see also* Fitzgerald, Edward (poet)

Cowley, Lord (Henry Wellesley) 342; *see also* Anglo-Iranian War (1856–57)

Craik, George Lillie 121–22; *see also The Pictorial History of England: Being a History of the People, as Well as a History of the Kingdom*, vol.I (by George Lillie Craik and Charles Macfarlane, 1838)

craniology 215, 401, 403, 411, 420

creation stories and beliefs 15, 17, 18, 20, 51, 69, 92, 106, 113, 135, 566, 614, 620, 623; Judeo-Christian-Islamic concept of "Special Creation" 60, 106; *see also* The Bible; The Hebrew Bible ("Old Testament"); mythology; The Qur'an

Crete 384; Cretans 12, 222

Crimean War (1854–56) 303, 306, 310, 312, 314, 317, 318, 322, 324–26, 329, 331–33, 335, 346, 347, 354n14, 357n61, 485; Congress of Paris 329; *see also* Aberdeen, Lord (George Hamilton-Gordon); Balaklava; Bonaparte, Charles-Louis Napoleon (Napoleon III); France; Great Britain; Kars; Ottoman Empire; Palmerston, Lord (Henry John Temple);

Russell, William Howard; Russia; Sevastopol; Stopford, James

Criminal Law and Procedure Act (Ireland) 551; *see also* Wyndham, George

Croker, Thomas Crofton 397, 399, 411; *Fairy Legends and Traditions of the South of Ireland* (by Thomas Crofton Croker, 1825) 399

Crom-Cruach (Crom Crúaich; pre-Christian Irish deity) 193–94; golden stone of Clogher 194; *see also The History of Ireland*, vol.I (by Thomas Moore, 1835); Kerman

Cromwell, Oliver 50, 412, 538, 617

Cromwellian Commonwealth Republic 50, 272

Cromwellian Puritan Republic: *see* Cromwellian Commonwealth Republic

Crow Street Theatre (a.k.a., Theatre Royal, Dublin) 517, 521–22; *see also* Moore, Edward ("The Gamester" (1753))

Crown Dependencies 527; Channel Islands 527; Isle of Man 527

Crusades 555n1; *see also* Edward I, King; Ilkhanid Empire; Langley, Geoffrey de

Ctesias 193

Cú Chulainn: *see* Cuchulain (Cú Chulainn)

Cuba 650

Cuchulain (Cú Chulainn) 41, 42, 143, 185, 436–48, 462n189, 463n204, 464n209, 498; *see also* Aoife (Aífe); Brooke, Charlotte; Conla (Conlaoch); epics; Larminie, William; Meyer, Kuno; Modi, Jivanji Jamshedji; Mohl, Jules (Julius); mythology (Irish heroic cycles); O'Grady, Standish James; Rustam; *Táin Bo Cuailnge* (*The Cattle Raid of Cooley*); Ulster Cycle

Cuculain: *see* Cuchulain (Cú Chulainn)

culture-making 142

Cumann na nGaedhael (Society/League of the Gaels 1900–05) 474; *see also* Griffith, Arthur; Sinn Féin

Cumann na nGaedheal (1923) 592; *see also* Cosgrave, William Thomas

Cunninghame-Graham, Robert Bontine 468; *see also* tobacco concession (Iran, 1890)

Curran, Sarah 181; *see also* Emmet, Robert; *Lalla Rookh. An Oriental Romance* (by Thomas Moore, 1817)

Curry, John 69, 70; *see also* Catholic Association (a.k.a., Catholic Committee, 1756); O'Conor, Charles

Curzon, George Nathaniel 385; *Persia and the Persian Question* (by George Nathaniel, 1892) 385; Viceroy of India 385; *see also* Conservative Party; O'Donovan, Edmond

Cusack, Margaret Anna 146; *An Illustrated History of Ireland* (by Margaret Anna Cusack, 1868) 146

INDEX 711

Cuthite 118, 382, 383, 452n3; *see also* Amonian; Babylonians; Canaanites; Cuthite-Iranians; Ham; Keane, Marcus; Sanskrit; Scythians

Cuthite-Iranians 382, 383; *see also* Cuthite; Keane, Marcus

Cuvier, Georges 95; *see also* extinctionism; O'Brien, Henry

Cyrus (Achaemenid emperor) 45n42, 64, 120, 221; *see also* Achaemenid dynasty (Persian Empire, c.550–330 BCE)

Czechoslovakia 595

Dabestān-e Mazāheb 13, 85, 86, 90–92, 94, 95, 108–20, 130, 132–36, 160n204, 640, 642; *see also* Ardestani, Mir Zulfaqar; *Dabistan, or the School of Manners* (by David Shea and Anthony Troyer, 1843); *Dasātir*; Fani, Mohsen; "Iranian" theories of Irish origins; Jalal al-Din Mirza (Jalal Pour-Fath-Ali Shah); Keyvan, Azar; Mahābādiān; Malcolm, John; "neo-Zoroastrianism"; O'Brien, Henry; Pishdādiān; Vallancey, Charles

Dabistan: see *Dabestān-e Mazāheb*

Dabistan, or the School of Manners (by David Shea and Anthony Troyer, 1843) 86, 111, 113; *see also Dabestān-e Mazāheb*; Mahābādiān; Shea, David; Troyer, Anthony

Dáil Éireann (Irish Assembly) 500, 580, 592, 597; *see also* Irish Free State; Irish parliament; "Irish Republic" (1919–21); taoiseach

Daily Chronicle (London) 482; *see also* Moore, William Arthur

Daily Express (Dublin) 552

Daily News (London) 384, 482; *see also* Moore, William Arthur; O'Donovan, Edmond

Dalberg-Acton, John Emerich Edward 143; *The Rambler* 143–45

D'Alton (Dalton), John 54, 103, 104, 106, 124, 158n177, 158n178, 196, 199, 211, 404, 614, 615, 617, 619, 620, 625, 642; *The History of Ireland* (by John D'Alton, 1845) 104, 619; Phoenician-Iranian theories of ancient Ireland's "Golden Age" 54, 103, 104, 158n178, 614, 617, 619, 620, 642; *see also* "fire worship"; Moore, Thomas; Round Towers (Ireland); Royal Irish Academy; Zoroastrianism

Damghan 385

Dana: An Irish Magazine of Independent Thought (Dublin) 432, 433, 483, 609; *see also* Magee, William Kirkpatrick ("John Eglinton"); Ryan, Frederick Michael (Fred)

Daneshvar, Simin 493; *see also Savushun*

Danish 124, 381, 402, 424, 616; Danes 200, 201, 215, 217–19, 225, 283, 406, 446, 536, 615; *see also* Denmark; Norse; Round Towers (Ireland)

Dar al-Fonun 532, 538, 557n25, 559n61; *see also* geography; Sahaf-bashi, Esmail

Darius I (Achaemenid emperor) 45n42, 50, 51, 222, 224, 225, 293n33, 430, 446; *see also* Achaemenid dynasty (Persian Empire, c.550–330 BCE); Persians; Scythia; Zorababel

"Darius Hystaspis": *see* Darius I (Achaemenid emperor)

Darwin, Charles 18, 24, 60, 107, 120, 392–93, 395–96, 401, 402, 405, 413; Darwinian evolutionary theory 24, 392, 401, 402, 405, 413; *On the Origin of Species* (by Charles Darwin, 1859) 18, 107, 395; *see also* evolutionary theories; Social-Darwinism

Das, Taraknath 489; *see also* Free Hindustan

Dasātir 92, 94, 95, 110–19, 130, 132–36, 640; *see also* Bin Kaus, Firuz (Mulla); Browne, Edward Granville; *Dabestān-e Mazāheb*; Gladwin, Francis; Jalal al-Din Mirza (Jalal Pour-Fath-Ali Shah); Jones, William; Mahābādiān; Malcolm, John; Mir Muhammed Husain (Isfahani); "neo-Zoroastrianism"; O'Brien, Henry

Dasātir-e Āsemāni: see *Dasātir*

Datta, Narendranath: see Vivekananda (Narendranath Datta)

David, Jean ("Jān Dāvud") 536–37; *Jahān-namā-ye Jadid* (by Jean David, n.d.) 536

Davies, John 49, 150n10

Davin, Anna 48, 68, 624n3; "Catholic antiquarianism" 68

Davis, Thomas Osborne 7, 22, 24, 165n300, 167, 172, 212–22, 224–25, 227, 232, 256, 258, 261, 277, 284, 312, 317–19, 324–26, 344, 347–49, 392, 397, 398, 416, 451, 525, 568, 585, 639; "A Ballad of Freedom" 225, 261, 319, 325, 347, 392; "Celts and Saxons" 217, 219; "Ethnology of the Irish Race" 215; Irish republic and virtue 216, 344–45; "A Nation Once Again" 22, 172, 220, 344, 348, 349, 525, 585; "Oh! For a Steed" 219, 225; "The Sack of Baltimore" 225; "A Second Plea for the Bog-Trotters" 224; *see also* "deprovincializing" Ireland; Dost Mohammad Khan; Ireland as a "province"; Irish antiquarianism; Irish nationalism; Moore, Thomas; *The Nation* (Dublin); "oriental" theories of Irish origins; *The Spirit of the Nation* (by Thomas Osborne Davis, et al., 1843); Sublicius Bridge; Thermopylae, Battle of (480 BCE); Young Ireland

Davitt, Michael 546; *see also* Land League
Dawes, Edwyn Sandys 366, 377n22; British India Steam Navigation Company 377n22; *see also* Iranian famine (1870–72)
Dawlatabadi, Yahya 492, 548–49; *see also* First Universal Races Congress (London, 1911)
"de-Anglicizing" Ireland 138, 423; *see also* Hyde, Douglas
de Blácam, Aodh Sandrach (Harold Saunders Blackham) 579
de Bruyn Kops, John 489; *see also* Pan-Aryan Association
de Clare, Richard (Strongbow) 617; *see also* MacMurrough, Aoife
de Man, Paul 234
de Valera, Éamon 500, 592, 595–97 amendment of the Irish Free State constitution 597; *see also* Abyssinian Crisis; Éire; Fianna Fáil; Friends of Freedom for India (New York); "Irish Republic" (1919–21); taoiseach
Declaration of Arbroath (1320) 20; *see also* John XXII, Pope
Dedalus, Stephen 606, 607; *see also Ulysses* (by James Joyce, 1922)
deism 168, 180, 428, 429
Delhi 174, 240, 326, 327; *see also* India; *Lalla Rookh. An Oriental Romance* (by Thomas Moore, 1817)
Delhi Gazette 327
"Deluge": *see* "Great Flood"
Delury, John Patrick 69
Democratic Party (US) 315; *see also* Buchanan, James (US president)
Democratic Review (London) 265; *see also* Harney, George Julian; Mangan, James Clarence
Denmark 424; *see also* Danish
"deprovincializing" Ireland 8, 318, 349, 526, 564, 575, 576, 580, 586; *see also* Davis, Thomas Osborne; Ireland as a "province"; Joyce, James; "provincializing Ireland"
Derrida, Jacques 248, 258; "trace" or "residue" 248, 257
Derry 538
Desātir: *see* Dasātir
Desmond Rebellions in Ireland 268; *see also* Elizabeth I, Queen; Munster; Plantation of Munster
Despard, Charlotte 430, 478–80, 495, 584, 593; *see also* Anglo-Russian Agreement (1907); Indian-Irish Independence League (1932); Indian nationalism; Iranian Constitutional Revolution(1906–11); Irish nationalism; Irish Women's Franchise League; socialism; suffragist; theosophy; Women's Freedom League; women's rights; Women's Social and Political Union
Devanagari 82
Devoy, John 472, 485, 486, 489, 545; *see also* Algeria; Clan na Gael (United States); French Legionnaires (i.e., Foreign Legion force); *Gaelic American* (New York); Pan-Aryan Association
Dhingra, Madan Lal 478, 490; *see also* Dryhurst, Nora ("Nannie") Florence; Wyllie, Curzon
dialogic (/dialogical) 29, 126–28, 286, 391, 584, 649; *see also* Bakhtin, Mikhail
"dialogic imagination" 126; *see also* Bakhtin, Mikhail
Dickens, Charles 294n55
Dickinson, Page Lawrence 482, 553–54; *see also Persia in Revolution* (by Joseph Maunsell Hone and Page Lawrence Dickinson, 1910)
Dighton Rock (Massachusetts) 108; *see also* Stiles, Ezra
Dilley, Roy 644; *Regimes of Ignorance* ... (by Roy Dilley and Thomas G. Kirsch, 2015) 644
Dillon, John 145, 165n300, 165n301, 302n214, 324, 351, 461n165, 477, 478, 480–82, 485, 493, 494, 503n31, 504n46, 504n47, 504n49, 546–48, 553, 577–79, 584, 640, 648; *see also* Anglo-Russian Agreement (1907); "Egypt for Egyptians"; Iranian Constitutional Revolution(1906–11); Irish Parliamentary Party; Land League; Persia Committee (London)
Dillon, John Blake 165n300, 212, 314; *see also The Nation* (Dublin); Young Ireland
Dillon, Myles 165n300
"Dinshaway incident" (1906): *see* Egypt
"disenchantment" (*Entzauberung*) 140, 141, 268; *see also* Weber, Max
Dissertation on the Origin and Progress of the Scythians or Goths, A: *see* Pinkerton, John
Dissertations on the Ancient History of Ireland (by Charles O'Conor, 1753): *see* O'Conor, Charles
The Doctrine of the Deluge, Vindicating the Scriptural Account from the Doubts which Have Recently Been Cast Upon it by Geological Speculations (by Leveson Venables Vernon-Harcourt, 1838): *see* Venables Vernon-Harcourt, Leveson (Rev.)
Dodona (oracle) 98
Doheny, Michael 314; *see also* Emmet Monument Association (New York); Fenian Brotherhood
Don River 74

INDEX 713

Donboli, Abdul-Razzaq Beg 527, 529;
  Ma'āsser-e Sultāniyeh (by Abdul-Razzaq Beg
  Donboli, 1811/1826) 527, 529; *see also* Jones
  Brydges, Harford (*The Dynasty of the Kajars.
  Translated from the Original Persian Manuscript
  Presented by His Majesty Faty Aly Shah* ... (by
  Harford Jones Brydges, 1833))
Donegal 148, 203n16, 599
Donnelly, Ignatius 581; *Atlantis: The
  Antediluvian World* (by Ignatius Donnelly,
  1882) 581; *see also* Atlantis
Dorian 452n3; *see also* Hellenic
Dost Mohammad Khan 304, 305, 318, 325,
  326, 329, 330, 332–34, 336, 337, 342, 345,
  347, 348; *see also* Afghanistan; Anglo-
  Afghan War (1839–42); Anglo-Iranian
  War (1856–57); Davis, Thomas Osborne;
  Herat; Issa Khan; Kabul; Kandahar (/
  Qandahar); Pashtun (Pathan) Barakzai
  tribe; Peshawar Treaty (1857)
Down (County) 388; *see also* Pottinger, Henry
Downing, Ellen Mary Patrick 398; a.k.a.,
  "Mary of *The Nation*" 398; *see also The
  Nation* (Dublin)
Dravidian 450, 492; *see also* Aryanism (racial
  theories); Indian subcontinent
Droitwich (England) 310; *see also* Pakington,
  John
druids 13, 106, 192, 199, 219, 407, 408, 433,
  572; druidic 56, 62, 106, 122, 199, 382,
  431, 432, 572; *see also* "fire worship"
Drummond, William Hamilton 86; *see also*
  Royal Irish Academy
Dryhurst, Nora ("Nannie") Florence
  [born Hannah Ann Robinson] 471,
  478–90, 503n36, 503n38, 584, 648; *see
  also* anarchism; Anglo-Russian Agreement
  (1907); Dhingra, Madan Lal; "Egypt for
  Egyptians"; *Freedom: A Journal of Anarchist
  Communism* (London); Gaelic League;
  Georgia (Georgian nationalism); Indian
  nationalism; Inghinidhe na hÉireann
  (Daughters of Ireland); Iranian Question;
  Irish nationalism; Irish Women's Franchise
  League; *Nationalities and Subject Races* (ed.
  by Dryhurst, Nora ("Nannie") Florence,
  1911); Nationalities and Subject Races
  conferences (London, 1910, 1911, 1914);
  Nevinson, Henry Woodd; Savarkar,
  Vinayak Damodar; Sinn Féin; suffragist
Dryhurst, Sylvia 479; *see also* Lynd, Robert
  Wilson
Du Bois, William Edward Burghardt 479;
  see also First Universal Races Congress
  (London, 1911); Nationalities and Subject
  Races conferences (London, 1910, 1911,
  1914)

Dublin 8, 22, 26, 34, 37, 39, 50, 52, 67, 70, 82,
  88–91, 93, 97, 102, 104, 105, 108, 115, 149,
  167–69, 185, 187, 189, 194–96, 198, 199,
  212, 229, 230, 233, 235–37, 239–41, 244,
  247, 251, 254–56, 260, 265, 278, 280, 282,
  283, 285, 288, 290, 291, 301n195, 308–10,
  315, 316, 349, 353, 364, 367, 368, 371, 372,
  389, 397, 398, 401, 402, 409, 430, 432,
  434, 437, 441, 471, 474, 478, 480, 482–85,
  496, 497, 510n121, 517–19, 521–24, 527,
  533–35, 539, 540, 542, 545, 546, 552, 573,
  580, 582, 590, 593, 600, 601, 605, 606,
  608–11, 614–16, 619, 621, 623, 624, 648
Dublin Evening Mail 367; *see also* unionists
  (Ireland)
Dublin Penny Journal 93, 104, 105, 235–36, 437,
  518; *see also* Folds, John S.; Hardy, Philip
  Dixon; Otway, Caesar; Petrie, George;
  Royal Irish Academy
Dublin Society: *see* Royal Dublin Society
Dublin University Magazine 88, 97, 102, 194,
  195, 235, 237, 239–41, 245, 256, 278, 280,
  282, 308, 389, 402, 558n30; *see also The
  History of Ireland*, vol.I (by Thomas Moore,
  1835); McGlashan, James; O'Brien, Henry;
  Petrie, George; Tory
Dubliners (by James Joyce, 1914) 39, 45n40,
  298n123, 608, 609; "The Sisters" 39,
  45n40; *see also* Joyce, James
Duffy Charles Gavan 165n300, 212, 254,
  312, 314, 319, 398, 437; *see also The Nation*
  (Dublin); Young Ireland
Duffy, George Gavan 478–79, 503n38; *see
  also* Anglo-Irish Treaty (December 6,
  1921); Nationalities and Subject Races
  conferences (London, 1910, 1911, 1914)
Dulin, Albert S. 489; *see also* Pan-Aryan
  Association; Vedanta (Vedanta Society)
Dunkellin, Lord (Ulick de Burgh) 323; *see also*
  Anglo-Iranian War (1856–57)
Dunn, Joseph 201; *see also The Glories of Ireland*
  (Joseph Dunn and Patrick Joseph Lennox,
  eds., 1914)
Dunne, Fergus 234
Dutch East India Company 273, 332
Dwan, David 216, 317, 345
Dyke, Elizabeth ("Bessy") 168; *see also* Moore,
  Thomas
*The Dynasty of the Kajars. Translated from the
  Original Persian Manuscript Presented by His
  Majesty Faty Aly Shah* ... (by Harford Jones
  Brydges, 1833): *see* Jones Brydges, Harford

Eagleton, Terry 288, 433, 555, 573, 579,
  603; *Heathcliff and the Great Hunger* (by
  Terry Eagleton, 1995) 579; *see also*
  "Europeanizing" Ireland

East India Association (London) 398; *see also* Naoroji, Dadabhai

Easter Rising (Ireland, 1916) 9, 38, 350, 352, 475, 493, 496, 497, 499, 513, 515, 528, 547, 554, 573, 590, 591, 601; *see also* Casement, Roger; Connolly, James; First World War; Iranian nationalism (and the Easter Rising (Ireland, 1916)); Irish Citizen Army; Irish nationalism; MacNeill, Eoin (John)

The Eastern Origin of the Celtic Nations Proved by a Comparison of Their Dialects with the Sanskrit, Greek, Latin, and Teutonic Languages (by James Cowles Prichard 1831): *see* Prichard, James Cowles

Eastern origins of the Irish: *see* "oriental" theories of Irish origins

Ebel, Hermann Wilhelm 394

Ecbatana 395

The Ecclesiastical Architecture of Ireland, Anterior to the Anglo-Norman Invasion (by George Petrie, 1845) 100, 121, 124, 195, 211, 277; *see also* Petrie, George

Eco, Umberto 94; *see also* "the limits of interpretation"

Edgeworth, Maria 123, 254; *see also* Royal Irish Academy

Edinburgh Cabinet Library 236

Edinburgh Review 102, 235

Edward I, King 555n1; *see also*; Crusades; Ilkhanid Empire; Langley, Geoffrey de

Eglinton, John: *see* Magee, William Kirkpatrick ("John Eglinton")

Egypt 2, 4, 6, 9, 11, 12, 19–21, 49, 52, 53, 56, 67, 72, 79, 94, 106, 116, 131, 145, 195, 199, 218, 227, 363, 384, 403, 404, 407, 409, 410, 419, 420, 422, 435, 452n3, 504n38, 504n47, 514, 529–31, 539, 563, 582, 585, 613, 620, 636, 649, 650; British occupation of (1882) 6, 9, 10, 20, 36, 145, 165n301, 313, 350–52, 384, 438, 452n7, 468, 469, 471, 474, 477–84, 490, 493, 496–98, 500, 504n49, 507n73, 508n86, 509n112, 513, 514, 520, 527, 547–50, 552, 553, 585, 589, 590, 593–95, 605, 627n46, 636–38, 647; "Dinshaway incident" (1906) 474, 480; French invasion (1798) 31; *see also* Bonaparte, Napoleon; British Empire; "Egypt for Egyptians"; Egyptian nationalists; Suez

Egypt (London) 484, 507n73; *see also* Blunt, Wilfrid Scawen; Egyptian Committee (UK); Ryan, Frederick Michael (Fred)

"Egypt for Egyptians" 438, 482; *see also* Assadabadi, Sayyid Jamal al-Din (a.k.a., "al-Afghani"); Blunt, Wilfrid Scawen; Dillon, John; Egyptian Congress (Brussels, 1910); Egyptian nationalists; *The Egyptian Standard* (Cairo); Farid Bey, Mohamed; Gregory, Isabella Augusta (née Persse); Kamil, Mustafa; Kettle, Thomas Michael; Maloney, William Joseph; Ryan, Frederick Michael (Fred); 'Urabi Pasha

Egyptian Committee (UK) 484; *see also* Blunt, Wilfrid Scawen; *Egypt* (London)

Egyptian Congress (Brussels, 1910) 471; *see also* "Egypt for Egyptians"; Egyptian nationalists

Egyptian National Committee (Berlin) 497, 498; *see also* Egyptian nationalists; First World War

Egyptian nationalists 352, 471, 479, 480, 482, 547, 590, 636; *see also* "Egypt for Egyptians"; Egyptian Congress (Brussels, 1910); Egyptian National Committee (Berlin); Farid Bey, Mohamed; Kamil, Mustafa; National Party (Egypt; *al-hizb al-watani*); 'Urabi Pasha

Egyptian Revolution (1919) 595; Egypt's "independence" (1922) 595

The Egyptian Standard (Cairo) 482, 483; *al-Liwa* (*The Standard*) 482; *see also* "Egypt for Egyptians"; Kamil, Mustafa; Maloney, William Joseph; Rudy, Charles; Ryan, Frederick Michael (Fred)

"Egyptian" theories of Irish origins 20, 52, 56, 227, 613, 620, 636; *see also* Fénius Farsaid (Fenius Farsa); Nectanebo II, Pharaoh; "Oriental Renaissance"; Scota; theories of Irish origins

"*Ei Gaour!*" 264, 266, 617; *see also Finnegans Wake* (by James Joyce, 1939); Mangan, James Clarence ("To the Ingleezee Khafir, Calling Himself Djuan Bool Djenkinzun")

Éire 1, 5, 26, 38, 42n1, 44–45n38, 148, 384, 394, 395, 425, 493, 496, 500, 554, 574, 589, 597, 608, 612, 625, 641; *see also* de Valera, Éamon; Éireann; Éirinn; Erin; Hedayat, Sadeq; Ireland; Irish Free State; Republic of Ireland

Éire-Ireland (Dublin) 496; *see also* Griffith, Arthur

Éireann 42n1, 44n38, 574; *see also* Éire; Éirinn; Erin; Ireland

Eirin: *see* Erin

Éirinn 1, 42n1, 574; *see also* Éire; Éireann; Erin; Ireland

Elamites 12, 56, 63, 130; theories of Irish origins 56, 63

Elizabeth I, Queen 33, 266, 268, 272, 299n158, 515, 525, 527, 535, 536; *see also* Desmond Rebellions in Ireland; Jenkinson, Anthony; Mangan, James Clarence ("To the Ingleezee Khafir, Calling Himself Djuan Bool Djenkinzun"); Nine Years'

War (/Tyrone's Rebellion, Ireland); Protestant plantations in Ireland; Safavid dynasty (Iran, 1501–1722/36); Tahmasp I, Shah; Tudor dynasty (1485–1603)
Ellis, Henry 388
Ellmann, Richard 609, 631n128
Elton, John 515; *see also* Afsharid dynasty (Iran, 1736–51/96)
Emmet, Robert 168, 180–81, 222, 526, 543; *see also* Curran, Sarah; *Lalla Rookh. An Oriental Romance* (by Thomas Moore, 1817); Moore, Thomas; United Irishmen; United Irishmen uprising (1803)
Emmet Monument Association (New York) 314, 355n34; *see also* Corcoran, Michael; Doheny, Michael; Fenian Brotherhood; O'Mahony, John
Encyclopædia Britannica 149, 523, 558n36
Engels, Friedrich 346–47, 568; on the Anglo-Iranian War (1856–57) 347
England *passim;* Roman invasion (43 CE) 80; *see also* Great Britain; United Kingdom
English Channel 9
English Civil War (1642–49) 177; *see also* Confederate War (Ireland, 1642–52)
English East India Company 10, 31, 91, 112, 114, 174, 184, 273, 309, 310, 320, 322, 351, 388–91, 514–17, 527, 538; *see also* Abbas I, Shah; Atkinson, James; Conolly, Arthur; Haileybury College (Hertfordshire, England); India; Lynch, Henry Blosse; Macnaghten, William Hay; Mohammad Ebrahim (Mirza); Mughal dynasty; Richardson, David; Safavid dynasty (Iran, 1501–1722/36); Stewart, Charles
English language 13, 32–34, 40, 42n1, 69, 82, 83, 110, 112, 113, 131, 168, 170, 184, 187, 203n19, 205n46, 221, 232–35, 239, 240, 242, 249, 250, 253, 256, 257, 258, 266, 267, 283, 284, 287, 327, 417, 482, 514, 517, 521, 537, 550, 552, 555, 611, 620, 621, 649
"English Letters" genre (Iran) 169; *see also Irān-e Nou* (Tehran); *Lettres persanes* (by Montesquieu, Baron de, 1721)
English Reformation 1, 5, 26, 50, 68, 90, 101, 162n243, 272, 570; *see also* Anglican Church; Protestant Reformation
the Enlightenment (general) 27–28, 436; "European" Enlightenment 22, 27, 28, 30–32, 42n5, 51, 61, 140, 152n36, 169, 216, 220, 301n195, 315, 352, 399, 424, 429, 436, 568, 583, 648, 650; *see also* civilization ("Western Civilization"); "Oriental Renaissance"; rationalism; Voltaire (François-Marie Arouet)
Enniskillen 323

"Entruria": *see* Betham, William; Etruria (Italian territory)
Enzeli 378n23
epics 41–42, 46n48, 65, 66, 69, 74, 75, 83, 105, 112, 114, 124, 133, 137, 138, 143, 184–85, 187, 206n63, 417, 418, 436–39, 441–42, 444, 446–48, 451, 463n204, 464n209, 492, 508n90, 610, 619; *see also* mythology
epistemology 13, 60, 79, 80, 106, 124, 135, 224, 250, 257, 643, 644; epistemic 14, 22, 31, 81, 413, 587, 624; *see also* Foucault, Michel
Erin 4, 5, 7, 8, 13, 35–42, 42n1, 44n38, 52, 76, 84, 120, 122, 123, 125, 127, 142, 148, 174, 178, 180–82, 187, 189, 199, 227, 236, 237, 241, 252, 259–62, 264, 273, 280, 282, 283, 331, 383, 384, 406, 409, 418, 425–27, 443, 459n137, 484, 542, 574, 605, 606, 617, 620, 623, 639, 646, 647; *see also* Éire; Iran-Erin; Iran/Erin (Irish nationalist allegory); Ireland
Ériu (Dublin) 441; *see also* Meyer, Kuno; School of Irish Learning (Dublin); Strachan, John
Erskine, William 113, 115, 160n207; *see also Dabestān-e Mazāheb*; *Dasātir*; Jones, William; Literary Society of Bombay; *Transactions of the Literary Society of Bombay*
Erzurum ("Erzeroum") 311; *see also* Ottoman Empire
Esfandiyar 83, 84, 185; *see also* mac Cumhaill, Fionn (a.k.a., Finn MacCool); mythology (Iranian mythology); Rustam; *Shāhnāmeh*; Vallancey, Charles
An Essay on the Antiquity of the Irish Language. Being a Collation of the Irish with the Punic language (by Charles Vallancey, 1772): *see* Vallancey, Charles
An Essay on the Primitive Inhabitants of Great Britain and Ireland. Proving from History, Languages, and Mythology, that They were Persians or Indo.Scythæ, Composed of Scythians, Chaldæans, and Indians (by Charles Vallancey, 1807) 64, 73, 82–84, 86, 91, 115; categorical assertion of Iranian (Persian) theory of Irish origins 72–73; *see also* "Iranian" theories of Irish origins; Vallancey, Charles
Estonia 254
"E'temad al-Saltaneh" (Mohammad Hassan Khan) 541–44, 546–47, 581; *Mer'āt al-Boldān-e Nāsseri* (by "E'temad al-Saltaneh," 1877–80) 541–43, 547; *Tārikh-e Montazem-e Nāsseri* (by "E'temad al-Saltaneh," 1881–83) 541, 543, 547; *see also Rouznāmeh-ye Dowlat-e Āliyeh-ye Irān* (Tehran)

Ethiopia 596; Ethiopians 67, 435, 452n3, 595; see also Abyssinian Crisis
ethnicity 3–5, 15, 16, 24, 71, 84, 90, 126, 134, 143, 146, 180, 214, 216, 227, 239, 262, 266, 271, 272, 287, 317, 363, 393, 450, 524, 527, 531, 532, 569, 575, 607, 617, 620; ethnic 11, 14, 16, 24–27, 29–31, 34, 48, 65, 68, 72, 81, 92, 94, 107, 113–16, 128, 133, 137, 139, 151n20, 174, 178, 180, 183, 191, 201, 212, 215, 216, 218, 219, 225, 235, 239, 251, 252, 264, 266, 287, 316, 317, 331, 346, 352, 361, 411, 414–17, 443, 490, 423, 527, 531, 548, 564, 568–70, 573–75, 577, 579, 583, 585, 588, 589, 597, 600, 605, 606, 608, 612, 613, 615–17, 620, 623, 635, 644, 650; ethno-nationalism 416, 566, 597, 606
ethnography 197, 215, 381, 383, 413, 568; see also craniology; Wilde, William Robert Wills
ethnology 215, 254, 298n123, 426, 439, 459n137
Etruria (Italian territory) 53, 121
Etruria-Celtica: Etruscan Literature and Antiquities Investigated (by William Betham, 1842): see Betham, William
Etruscan 105–6, 121, 220, 421, 646; see also Rome; Sublicius Bridge
Ettelā 'āt (Tehran) 390, 453n28, 499
etymology 13, 21, 38, 39, 52, 67, 71, 73, 77, 81–83, 85, 86, 94, 97–99, 102, 104, 110, 117, 123, 125, 146, 147, 150n3, 162n237, 174, 185, 189, 193, 197, 199, 206n53, 264, 278, 283, 383, 407, 410, 426, 427, 446; see also lexicon; linguistics; philology
Euphrates and Tigris Steam Navigation Company 342, 391; see also Lynch, Stephen; Lynch, Thomas Kerr
Euphrates River 342, 391, 401, 402, 457n88
Europe (general) 3, 6, 7, 9, 10, 12–20, *passim*; eastern Europe 12, 25, 66, 297n95, 316, 600, 611; northern Europe 409, 569, 573; southern Europe 12; western Europe 15–18, 22, 23, 27, 31, 57, 58, 67, 80, 98, 99, 111, 113, 117, 121, 122, 130, 138, 145, 159n199, 235, 343, 387, 391, 392, 405, 422, 435, 446, 461n165, 488, 492, 530, 562n116, 564, 568, 577, 640, 645, 651
"Europe-centered" theories of Irish origins 10, 16, 25, 26, 226, 393, 417, 451, 568, 571, 575–79, 581, 587–89, 591, 594, 597, 602, 607, 641, 644, 645; see also Celticism; "Europeanizing" Ireland; Green, Alice Stopford; Hayden, Mary; Joyce, Patrick Weston; MacNeill, Eoin (John); Moonan, George Aloysius; theories of Irish origins
European-Celtic origin of the Gaels: see "Europe-centered" theories of Irish origins

The European Magazine and London Review 521
"Europeanizing" Ireland 10, 16, 573, 576–80, 597, 602, 603, 605, 608, 609, 612; Europe-centered "Celtic-Catholic" conception of Ireland 10, 16, 23, 25, 26, 149, 417, 451, 568, 571, 575–79, 581, 587–89, 591, 594, 597, 598, 600–602, 605, 607, 608, 611–13, 615, 618, 624, 625, 643–45; *Ireland* ← → *Europe* 609; see also Eagleton, Terry; "Europe-centered" theories of Irish origins; Kiberd, Declan
Euxine: see Black Sea
Eve 95, 106; see also Adam; The Bible; Cain; Garden of Eden; The Hebrew Bible ("Old Testament")
evolutionary theories 18, 61, 95, 118, 120, 392–93, 396, 401–3, 405, 413, 420; see also Darwin, Charles; Lyell, Charles; Prichard, James Cowles
extinctionism 95; see also Cuvier, Georges

Faber, George Stanley 117, 118, 120, 382; *The Origin of Pagan Idolatry Ascertained from Historical Testimony and Circumstantial Evidence* (by George Stanley Faber, 1816) 117; see also Buddha; *Dasātir*; Indo-Scythians; Jones, William; Mahābādiān; Mosaic theory; "oriental" theories of Irish origins; phallic worship; Pishdādiān; Vallancey, Charles; *Zend Avesta*; Zoroaster
Fabian socialism 429, 494, 509n97; see also Besant, Annie (née Wood); Shaw, George Bernard; socialism
Faizi, Abul-Fayz ibn Mubarak 244; see also Mangan, James Clarence
Fani, Mohsen 85, 111; see also *Dabestān-e Mazāheb*
Farah province 345; see also Afghanistan
Farahani, Mohammad Hussein 537; *Jahān-namā* (trans. by Mohammad Hussein Farahani, 1848; pub. 1861) 537
Farhad Mirza ("Nayeb al-Eyaleh"; later "Mo'tamed al-Dowleh") 533–36; *Jām-e Jam* (by Farhad Mirza, 1856) 533–36; see also Pinnock, William; Qajar dynasty (Iran, 1796–1925)
Farid Bey, Mohamed 479; see also Egyptian nationalists; National Party (Egypt; *al-hizb al-watani*); Nationalities and Subject Races conferences (London, 1910, 1911, 1914)
farman (royal decree) 273, 359n117; "firman" 271, 343–44
Farrokh Khan ("Amin al-Molk") 311, 333, 337, 342; see also Anglo-Iranian War (1856–57)
Fars Province (Iran) 72, 84, 147, 188
Farsi: see Persian language

Farzaneh, Mostafa F. 41; *see also* Hedayat, Sadeq
fascism 594, 595; *see also* O'Duffy, Eoin
Fath Ali Shah 389; *see also* Qajar dynasty (Iran, 1796–1925)
"Father Prout": *see* Mahony, Francis Sylvester (alias "Father Prout")
Fatherland (New York) 498; *see also* Viereck, George Sylvester
feminism: *see* women's rights
Fenian Brotherhood 314; Fenians 223, 229, 230, 281, 285, 289, 290, 314, 355n35, 363, 366, 379n63, 429, 483, 542–43, 545; *see also* Corcoran, Michael; Doheny, Michael; Emmet Monument Association; Halpin, William George; Irish Republican Brotherhood; O'Mahony, John; O'Reilly, John Boyle; Young Ireland uprising (1848)
Fenian Cycle 65, 69, 83, 137, 143, 185, 437, 439–41, 446; the brothers Brian, Iuchar, and Iucharba 439–40; Cian 439; Lugh "of the Long hand" 439–40; "Pisear," king of Persia 440; "Tuatha de Danann and of the Fianna of Ireland" 439; Tuireann 439; *see also* Celticism; epics; *Fragments of Ancient Poetry, Collected in the Highlands of Scotland* (by James Macpherson, 1760); Larminie, William; Macpherson, James; mythology (Irish heroic cycles); Ossian
Fenian raid into Canada (1866) 363, 542
Fenian raids into Canada (1870 and 1871) 366, 542
Fenian Rising (1867): *see* Irish Republican Brotherhood uprising (a.k.a., "Fenian Rising," 1867)
Fenius Farsa: *see* Fénius Farsaid
Fénius Farsaid (Fenius Farsa) 47–49, 61, 72, 79, 147, 618; *see also* Baath (/Baoth); Egypt; Gaels; Iberian Peninsula; Japheth; *Lebor Gabála Érenn (The Book of the Taking of Ireland / The Book of Invasions*, 11th century); Magog; Milesians; Milesius (Miledh/Míl Espáine); Niul; Noah; Scythia; Spain
Fentress, James 603; *see also* memory ("social" memory)
Ferdowsi, Abul-Qassem 41, 75, 83, 95, 108, 114, 119, 130, 136, 184, 243, 261, 441, 442, 448, 449; *see also Bibliothèque orientale* (by Barthélemy d'Herbelot, 1697); Champion, Joseph; epics; Herbelot [de Molainville], Barthélemy d'; Modi, Jivanji Jamshedji; mythology; O'Brien, Henry; *Shāhnāmeh*; Vallancey, Charles
Ferrier, Joseph Pierre 339, 341; *Caravan Journeys and Wanderings in Persia, Afghanistan, Turkistan, and Beloochistan* (by Joseph Pierre Ferrier; English translation from the French by William Jesse, edited by Henry Danby Seymour, 1856) 339, 341; *see also* Jesse, William; Seymour, Henry Danby
Ferrier, Ronald W. 426–27
Fianna Fáil 592, 595; *see also* de Valera, Éamon
filí (a class of poet scholar "seers" in Old Gaelic; pl. filíd/filídh) 47, 565
Findlater, Alexander 364; *see also* Iranian famine (1870–72)
Fine Gael 592; *see also* Cosgrave, William Thomas
Finerty, John Frederick 525–26; *Ireland: The People's History of Ireland* (by John Frederick Finerty, 1904) 525; *see also* Nine Years' War (/Tyrone's Rebellion, Ireland); "provincializing Ireland"; United Irish League of America
Finland 350, 393, 474, 478, 547, 553; *see also* Finnish
Finnegans Wake (by James Joyce, 1939) 3, 7, 10, 39–41, 45n42, 45n43, 46n45, 54, 82, 182, 206n53, 240, 302n208, 555, 605–9, 611–21, 623–24, 631n115, 631n123, 632n143, 632n144, 643, 645; "Anna Livia Plurabelle" 40, 46n45, 614, 617; reference to William Butler Yeats 615; *see also* Colum, Padraic; Hedayat, Sadeq; Joyce, James; Lavergne, Philippe; *One Thousand and One Nights* (a.k.a., *Arabian Nights*); references to Charles Vallancey 206n53, 612, 613, 615, 618; references to Iran and incorporation of Persian terms 39, 40, 45n42, 608, 612–15, 617, 620–24; references to James Clarence Mangan 206n53, 609, 614, 615, 617, 620; references to Thomas Moore 206n53, 613–15, 617, 620
Finneran, Richard J. 228
Finnish 79, 439; *see also* theories of Irish origins; Scythians
Firbolgs 49, 72, 107, 147, 197, 200, 218, 226, 405, 424, 425, 500, 572, 599, 613, 615, 631n108; *see also* Irish antiquarianism; Keating, Geoffrey; Nemed; Scythia
"fire worship" 5, 13, 25, 72, 75, 88, 95, 97, 98, 101, 102, 104, 110, 123, 124, 163n250, 180, 182, 189, 192–94, 196, 199, 207–8n81, 211, 213, 215, 237, 270, 277, 382, 395; *see also* D'Alton (Dalton), John; druids; *The History of Ireland*, vol.I (by Thomas Moore, 1835); *Lalla Rookh. An Oriental Romance* (by Thomas Moore, 1817); magi; Moore, Thomas; O'Brien, Henry; Round Towers (Ireland); Vallancey, Charles; Zoroastrianism
"The Fire-Worshippers": *see Lalla Rookh. An Oriental Romance* (by Thomas Moore, 1817)

"firman": *see farman* (royal decree)
"First Anglo-Persian War": *see* Anglo-Iranian War (1838)
"First Opium War": *see* Anglo-Chinese War (1839–42)
First Universal Races Congress (London, 1911) 479, 492; *see also* Dawlatabadi, Yahya; Du Bois, William Edward Burghardt
First World War 9, 10, 45n42, 148, 165n301, 209n155, 350, 424, 475, 480, 481, 488, 492–500, 505n54, 507n78, 554, 562n109, 573, 578, 579, 589–91, 593–97, 605, 606, 609, 610, 637, 638; Allied Powers 497–99, 554, 591, 595; Anglo-Russian occupation of Iran (1915) 498; Central Powers 591; Paris/Versailles peace talks 591; *see also* Belgium; Germany; Great Britain; Russia; Egyptian National Committee (Berlin); Indian Independence Committee (Berlin); Iranian Nationalist Committee (Berlin); Irish Nationalist Committee (Berlin; a.k.a., German-Irish Society)
Fitzgerald, Archibald 388–90; in Iranian army 388, 389; *see also* Irish Brigade of the Spanish Army (Regiment of Hibernia); Santa Fe Expedition
Fitzgerald, Edward (poet) 426–27, 459n137, 459n138; *Rubáiyát of Omar Khayyám* (by Edward FitzGerald, 1859 and subsequent editions) 426, 459n137; *see also* Cowell, Edward B.; Fitzgerald, Mary Frances; Kerney, Michael; poetry; Khayyam, Omar; Purcell, John
FitzGerald, Edward (United Irishmen) 181, 139, 519; *see also Lalla Rookh. An Oriental Romance* (by Thomas Moore, 1817); United Irishmen uprising (1798)
Fitzgerald, Mary Frances 426; *see also* Fitzgerald, Edward (poet)
Fitzgerald, Thomas (10th Earl of Kildare) 349; uprising (1534–35) 349
FitzGerald, William Robert (Duke of Leinster) 519
FitzWilliam, William (Lord Deputy of Ireland) 516, 526; *see also* Elizabeth I, Queen
Flann (Mainistrech) 565; *Synchronisms* (by Flann, n.d.) 565
Flood, Henry 77
"Fluellen, Captain" 86; *see also* Drummond, William Hamilton; Vallancey, Charles
Folds, John S. 93; *see also Dublin Penny Journal*
folklore 4, 6, 8, 148, 381, 396–400, 402, 409, 411–13, 418, 420, 435, 438, 440, 456n64, 456n70, 458n113, 500, 513, 514, 563, 580, 586, 636, 641, 643, 646, 651; presumed Iranian roots of Irish folk beliefs and practices 6, 8, 148, 396, 402, 409, 412, 513, 514, 563, 641, 643, 646, 651; *see also* Hyde, Douglas; Thoms, William John; Wilde, Jane Francesca Agnes (née Elgee); Wilde, William Robert Wills
Fomorians 49, 226, 382, 397, 572, 615, 644; *see also* Africa; Irish antiquarianism; Keating, Geoffrey
Forbes, Duncan 444
Foreign Office (UK) 307, 366, 369, 468; *see also* Grey, Edward; Iranian famine (1870–72); Salisbury, Lord (Robert Arthur Talbot Gascoyne-Cecil)
forgetting (/amnesia) 5, 129, 142, 227, 231, 258, 274, 275, 320, 325, 349, 351, 587, 602, 603, 618, 642, 644; "collective" forgetting 602; cultural forgetting 587; forgetting and nationalism 227, 231, 258, 274, 275, 351; *see also* memory (counter-memory); nescience
Foroughi, Mohammad Hussein Khan ("Zoka' al-Molk") 136
Foster, John Wilson 396, 428
Foster, Roy 428, 602
Foucault, Michel 126, 140, 413, 604, 644; "epistemic rupture" 413, 587; 'insurrection of subjugated knowledges' 140; power/knowledge 334, 644, 645; *see also* epistemology; "heterotopia"; history ("counter-history"); memory ("counter-memory")
"Four Masters" 61, 147, 200, 421, 614, 615, 618; Conary O'Clery 200; Cucogry [or *Peregrine*] O'Clery 200; Ferfeasa O'Mulconry 200; Michael O'Clery 200; *see also Annals of the Four Masters* (17th century); *Annals of the Kingdom of Ireland by the Four Masters* (English translation by John O'Donovan, 1848–51)
Fozdar, Vahid 117
Fragments of Ancient Poetry, Collected in the Highlands of Scotland (by James Macpherson, 1760) 65; and the Fenian Cycle 65; Ossian 65, 66, 69, 83, 143, 441, 446, 464n209, 535; and the Ulster Cycle 65; *see also* Macpherson, James; Ossian
France 6, 33, 36, 39, 40, 165n301, 170, 188, 197, 206n56, 207n70, 217, 281, 303, 310, 311, 325, 332–33, 335, 337, 342–43, 366, 372, 404, 420, 473, 488, 514, 515, 518, 520, 521, 543, 583, 584, 591, 595, 632n144; invasion of Ottoman Egypt (1798) 520; *see also* Anglo-Chinese War (1856–60); Anglo-Iranian War (1856–57); Bonaparte, Charles-Louis Napoleon (Napoleon III); Bonaparte, Napoleon; Crimean War (1854–56); Franco-Prussian War (1870–71); French Revolution (1789–99); French

Revolutionary Wars; Hedayat, Sadeq; Kharg Island; Louis XIV (French king); Napoleonic Wars; "Oriental Renaissance"
Francis, Philip 534
Franco-Prussian War (1870–71) 364, 372, 376n9; Battle of Sedan 364; German unification 364; Paris Commune 364, 376n9; Third French Republic 364; *see also* Bonaparte, Charles-Louis Napoleon (Napoleon III)
Franks 268; "farangi" 268; "Ferindjee" 263, 268, 273, 345; *see also* Mangan, James Clarence ("To the Ingleezee Khafir, Calling Himself Djuan Bool Djenkinzun")
Fraser, James Baillie 187, 267–68; *The Kuzzilbash: A Tale of Khorasan* (by James Baillie Fraser, 1828) 267; "Mohammad Reza Mirza" 187; *see also Lalla Rookh. An Oriental Romance* (by Thomas Moore, 1817); Nader Shah; Qizilbash
Fraser's Magazine (London) 104, 120
Frawley, Oona 598; "idealization" of the pre-colonial past 598
Free Hindustan 489; *see also* Das, Taraknath; Free Hindustan Publishing House (New York)
Free Hindustan Publishing House (New York) 489; *see also Free Hindustan*
Freedom: A Journal of Anarchist Communism (London) 478; *see also* anarchism; Dryhurst, Nora ("Nannie") Florence
Freeman, George ("Fitzgerald") 485, 486, 489; *see also* Clan na Gael (United States); *Gaelic American* (New York); Pan-Aryan Association
Freeman's Journal (Dublin) 8, 212, 235, 309–13, 316, 323, 356n51, 363–65, 367, 369–71, 373, 432, 469, 483, 648; *see also* Anglo-Iranian War (1856–57); Iranian famine (1870–72); Irish Home Rule; Irish nationalism; O'Connellite; Repeal movement; tobacco concession (Iran, 1890)
freemasonry 88, 91, 92, 105, 116, 117, 229, 293n41, 364, 383; co-freemasonry 429; *see also* Besant, Annie (née Wood); O'Brien, Henry
French Legionnaires (i.e., Foreign Legion force) 472, 584; *see also* Algeria; Devoy, John
French Revolution (1789–99) 28, 30, 135, 352, 472, 583; *see also* Jacobins; *Paddy's Resource* (1795–1803); United Irishmen uprising (1798)
French Revolution (1848) 313
French Revolutionary Wars 33, 516, 518, 520
Friends of Freedom for India (New York) 500; *see also* de Valera, Éamon

"Fudge Family" epistolary poems (1818, 1823): *see* Moore, Thomas
futurity 216, 280; future-oriented 138, 218, 248–49, 260, 261, 647

Gadamer, Hans-Georg 134–35; *see also* hermeneutics
Gaedhil 564
The Gael (Dublin) 601
The Gael and Cymbri: An Inquiry into the Origin and History of the Irish Scoti, Britons, and Gauls ... (by William Betham, 1834): *see* Betham, William
The Gael/An Gaodhal (New York) 412, 572; *see also* Ó Lócháin, Mícheál (Michael J. Logan)
Gaelic 6, 14, 16, 21, 23, 25, 27, 31, *passim*; *see also* Gaels; Irish language
Gaelic American (New York) 441, 485–89, 491, 496, 498, 506n71, 506n72, 506–7n73, 507n74, 510n116; "Finn and Oisín: An Ossianic Version of the Celebrated Persian Story" (1908) 441; *see also* Clan na Gael (United States); Devoy, John; Freeman, George ("Fitzgerald")
Gaelic Athletic Association 387; *see also* hurling (sport)
Gaelic League 393, 423, 451, 478, 479, 483, 573, 580; *see also* Bourke, Ulick Joseph; Dryhurst, Nora ("Nannie") Florence; Hyde, Douglas; Lynd, Robert Wilson; MacNeill, Eoin (John); O'Kelly, John Joseph (Seán Ua Ceallaigh)
Gaelic Union 393, 396; *see also* Bourke, Ulick Joseph
"Gaelicized" 48, 68, 140, 145
Gaels 15, 20, 21, 24, 25, 47–56, 59, *passim*; *see also* civilization (Gaelic civilization); Fénius Farsaid (Fenius Farsa); Gaodhal; "Iranian" theories of Irish origins; Irish antiquarianism; "Irishness"; Mahābādiān; "mere Irish"; Milesians; O'Brien, Henry; Pishdādiān; theories of Irish origins; Vallancey, Charles; "wild Irish" (civilizational accusation)
Galland, Antoine 235, 244; *see also One Thousand and One Nights* (a.k.a., *Arabian Nights*)
Galway 198, 534
Gamble, Eliza Burt 120; *The God-Idea of the Ancients or Sex in Religion* (by Eliza Burt Gamble, 1897) 120–21; *see also* Lingam; Mahābādiān; O'Brien, Henry; Pishdādiān; Round Towers (Ireland); Tuatha de Dananns; Yoni
Gancher, David 45n38; *see also* Iran/Erin; Pazargad, Bahauddin

Gaodhal 61, 412, 572; *see also* Gaels
"Gaodhil": *see* Gaodhal
Garden of Eden 106; *see also* Adam; The Bible; Eve; The Hebrew Bible ("Old Testament")
Garibaldi, Giuseppe 398
Garmroudi, Mirza Abdul-Fattah Khan 539
Gaul 70, 74, 122, 144, 147, 190, 191, 197, 199, 409425, 572, 573; Gallic 122, 191, 197
Gayōmard: *see* Keyoumars
Geddes, William Duguid 394, 395
Geertz, Clifford James 269, 272; "thick description" 257, 269, 272
Genealogy 142, 424, 563, 574; *see also* O'Hart, John
A General History of Ireland (by Sylvester (Silvester) O'Halloran, 1778): *see* O'Halloran, Sylvester (Silvester)
Geneva 394, 490, 595
Genii (Genie) 286
Gentleman's Magazine (London) 412
Geoffrey of Monmouth 20; *Historia Regum Britanniae* (*The History of the Kings of Britannia*; by Geoffrey of Monmouth, 1136) 20
Geography 108, 125, 131, 139, 257, 275, 329, 336, 530, 532–34, 536–38, 547, 559n53, 565, 573, 626n31; geographical 9, 23, 41, 65, 76, 77, 81, 116, 124–26, 128, 130, 139, 183, 240, 250, 254, 255, 265, 279, 284, 313, 350, 351, 361, 389, 402, 403, 407, 412, 420, 443, 463n202, 490, 492, 514, 515, 524, 525, 527–30, 532, 533, 537, 539, 565, 567, 577, 587, 595, 605, 607, 608, 615, 635, 636, 641; *see also* cartography; Dar al-Fonun; Lisbon Geographical Society; School of Political Science (Tehran)
George III, King 72, 293n33, 520; *see also* Hanover (royal House of Hanover); *A Vindication of the Ancient History of Ireland* (by Charles Vallancey, 1786)
George IV, King 170, 520; Prince Regent 170, 186; *see also Intercepted Letters; or The Twopenny Post-bag* (by Thomas Moore, 1813)
George V, King 552; and Queen Mary 552
Georgia 33, 272, 328, 341, 350, 476, 516; Georgian nationalism 476, 478, 479; *see also* Dryhurst, Nora ("Nannie") Florence
Geraldine Rebellion: *see* Desmond Rebellions in Ireland
German (language) 233, 240, 242, 243, 245–47, 253, 259, 264, 270, 279, 286, 288, 301n199, 389, 399, 531, 616, 622, 661; *see also* Germans; Germany
German-Irish Society (Berlin): *see* Irish Nationalist Committee (Berlin; a.k.a., German-Irish Society)

Germans 36, 41, 57, 121, 144, 150n3, 228, 234, 254, 391–95, 409, 441–43, 492, 574; Germanic 78, 197, 424
Germany 9, 32, 36, 41, 208n87, 209n115, 214, 288, 333, 350, 364, 365, 424, 473, 477, 487, 488, 494–99, 509n112, 510n116, 528, 529, 545, 551, 554, 581, 590, 595, 627n51, 638; *see also* Anglo-Russian Agreement (1907); Berlin; First World War; Egyptian National Committee (Berlin); Franco-Prussian War (1870–71); Indian Independence Committee (Berlin); Iranian Nationalist Committee (Berlin); Irish Nationalist Committee (Berlin; a.k.a., German-Irish Society); Irish nationalism; unionists (Ireland)
Ghadar 488, 593; *see also* Barakatullah, Abdul Hafiz Mohammad; *The United States of India* (San Francisco)
Ghaznavid dynasty 326, 386; Mahmud of Ghazni (Ghaznavid ruler) 326, 638; *see also* Indian subcontinent
Ghazni 261, 638; *see also* Afghanistan; Ghaznavid dynasty; MacCarthy, Denis Florence
"Gheber": *see* Zoroastrian
Gibbons, John 364; *see also* Iranian famine (1870–72)
Gibson, William (Lord Ashbourne) 478–79, 504n38; *see also* Nationalities and Subject Races conferences (London, 1910, 1911, 1914)
Gilbert, John Thomas 581–82, 619; *A History of the City of Dublin* (by John Thomas Gilbert, 1854–59) 582; "History of the City of Dublin" (1853) 582; *see also* Royal Irish Academy
Gilzai: *see* Pashtun (Pathan) Gilzai confederacy
Ginza Rabbā (*Sidrā Rabbā*) 119; *see also* Mandean
Gladstone, William Ewart 306, 307, 323, 339, 354n14, 367, 468, 540, 546, 549; *see also* Anglo-Iranian War (1856–57); Church of Ireland (disestablishment (1871)); Irish Land Acts (1870, 1881); Liberal Party (UK); Peelite; Reuter concession (Iran, 1872); Whig Party
Gladwin, Francis 111; *see also* Asiatic Society of Bengal; *Dasātir*; Jones, William
global history 3, 648; *see also* world history
globalization processes 429, 530, 639, 640
The Glories of Ireland (Joseph Dunn and Patrick Joseph Lennox, eds., 1914) 201; *see also* Brigger, Francis Joseph; Casement, Roger; Dunn, Joseph; Lennox, Patrick Joseph; Milligan, Alice

INDEX

"Glorious Revolution" (1688) 538; *see also* William III, King (William of Orange); James II, King
"Golden Age": *see* civilization
Goldsmith, Oliver 538; *The History of England* (by Oliver Goldsmith; abridged and updated by Robert Simpson, 1823) 538; *see also* Shaykh Reza (?) (*Tārikh-e Ingiliss* (by Shaykh Reza, n.d.)); Simpson, Robert
Gomer 70, 74; *see also* Japheth; Mosaic theory
Gonne, Maud (Maud Gonne MacBride) 478, 580, 593; *see also* Indian-Irish Independence League (1932); Inghinidhe na hÉireann (Daughters of Ireland); MacBride, John
Görres, Johann Joseph von 444
"an Gorta Mór" (the Great Hunger): *see* Great Famine (Ireland, 1845–51)
Goths 20, 67, 78, 200, 404; Gothic languages 78, 111, 200
Gowharshad mosque 386; *see also* Imam Reza shrine (Mashhad)
"Grattan's Parliament" 29, 352, 518, 583; *see also* Irish Constitution (1782)
Great Britain 9, 21, 34, 48, 50, 51, *passim*; imperial leverage in Iran 1, 36, 37, 273, 306, 324, 325, 342, 346, 368, 473, 485, 511n127, 594, *passim*; *see also* Anglo-Iranian War (1838); Anglo-Iranian War (1856–57); Anglo-Japanese Alliance (1902); Anglo-Russian Agreement (1907); Anglo-Soviet occupation of Iran; British Empire; British parliament; Crimean War (1854–56); Egypt (British occupation of (1882)); England; First World War (Anglo-Russian occupation of Iran (1915)); Foreign Office (UK); India (British colonization); Iran (Anglo-Iranian relations (general)); Scotland; United Kingdom; Wales; Washington (diplomatic row with London (1854–56))
Great Depression (1873–96) 546; *see also* "Land War" (Ireland)
Great Famine (Ireland, 1740–41) 233, 331, 367; "Year of Slaughter" 331, 367
Great Famine (Ireland, 1845–51) 6, 8, 25, 32, 36, 145, 182, 230, 244, 246, 259, 260, 281, 284, 289, 331, 332, 361–63, 367–69, 373, 374, 381, 398, 399, 401, 413–15, 522, 534, 538, 539, 542, 544, 561n96, 648; famine relief aid from Indian rajahs 363; famine relief aid from the Chinese Emperor (Daoguang) 363; famine relief aid from the Egyptian Pasha (Ibrahim) 363; famine relief aid from the Iranian Shah (Nasser al-Din) 363; famine relief aid from the Ottoman Sultan (Abdulmejid I) 363; famine relief aid from the Pope (Pius IX) 363; famine relief aid from the Tsar (Nicholas I) 363; impact on Irish-speaking population 284, 362, 376n3; in Irish nationalist memory 6, 25, 145, 331, 361, 362, 367, 400; reported incidences of anthropophagy 373–74; *see also* India (famines); Iranian famine (1870–72); Irish diaspora; Mangan, James Clarence; McGee, Thomas D'Arcy; Mitchel, John; *Old Jonathan: The District and Parish Helper* (London); O'Rourke, John; Society of Friends (Quaker); Sullivan, Alexander Martin; Victoria, Queen; Young Ireland uprising (1848)
"Great Flood" 15, 17–19, 30, 50, 60, 61, 64, 72, 76, 115, 118, 126, 393, 452n3, 580, 581; *see also* Ceasair; Mosaic theory; Noah; Ussher, James
Great Industrial Exhibition (Dublin, 1853; a.k.a., Irish Industrial Exhibition) 540, 542, 545; *see also* Victoria, Queen
Greco-Roman sources 17, 22, 28, 23, 30, 31, 48, 63, 80, 567, 637–38, *passim*; accounts of ancient Persians 22, 63, 80, *passim*; *see also* Hellenic (Hellenic sources); Roman
"Greco-Tyrian" 581, 582; *see also* Hellenic; Phoenicia
Greece 53, 72, 74, 100, 147, 175, 176, 220–23, 230, 384, 403, 404, 406, 420–22, 424, 425, 435, 440, 443, 445, 490, 582, 601, *passim*; *see also* Athens; Greek language; Greeks; Hellenic; Marathon, Battle of (490 BCE); "Migdonia"; Thermopylae, Battle of (480 BCE)
Greek language 53, 67, 81, 82, 119, 221, 395, 442
Greek sources: *see* Greco-Roman sources; Hellenic (Hellenic sources)
"Greek" theories of Irish origins 19, 20, 49, 200; *see also* theories of Irish origins
Greek War of Independence (1821–29) 221; *see also* Byron, Lord; Ottoman Empire
Greeks: *see* Greece; Greek language; Greco-Roman sources; Hellenic; Marathon, Battle of (490 BCE); "Migdonia"; Thermopylae, Battle of (480 BCE)
Green, Alice Stopford 26, 425, 495, 563–65, 567, 574–76, 602, 635n3; *History of the Irish State to 1014* (by Alice Stopford Green, 1925) 563, 567, 574; *see also* Anglo-Russian Agreement (1907); Celticism; "Europe-centered" theories of Irish origins; historiography and history
Gregory, Isabella Augusta (née Persse) 138, 432, 436–41, 447, 448, 451, 461n165, 462n189, 480, 580; *Cuchulain of Muirthemne*:

The Story of the Men of the Red Branch of Ulster (by Isabella Augusta Gregory, 1902) 438; *see also* Abbey Theatre; "Egypt for Egyptians"; Irish Literary Theatre; Irish National Dramatic Society; Irish National Theatre Society; *Kathleen ni Houlihan* (by Isabella Augusta Gregory and William Butler Yeats, 1902)

Grey, Edward 307, 404, 424, 474, 476–78, 480, 484, 487, 493–96, 506n73, 548, 549, 577; *see also* Anglo-Russian Agreement (1907); Foreign Office (UK); Iranian Constitutional Revolution (1906–11); Liberal Party (UK)

Griboyedov, Alexander Sergeyevich 328, 341, 357n71; *see also* Russo-Iranian War (1826–28)

Griffith, Arthur 474, 475, 478, 481, 483, 485–87, 491, 496, 506n70, 506n72, 578–79, 584, 606–7, 610, 630n83; *Resurrection of Hungary* (by Arthur Griffith, 1904) 475, 478; *see also* Austria (Austro-Hungarian Empire); Boer War (1899–1902); Cumann na nGaedhael (Society/League of the Gaels); *Éire-Ireland* (Dublin); Limerick pogrom (Ireland, 1904); *Scissors and Paste* (Dublin); Sinn Féin; *Sinn Féin* (Dublin); *The United Irishman* (Dublin, 1899–1906); Zionism

Grimm brothers (Jacob and Wilhelm) 399, 409, 410

Grover, Henry Montague (Rev.) 120

Gudarz 75; *see also* Nebuchadnezzar II; Vallancey, Charles

"Guebre": *see* Zoroastrian

Guiney, Louise Imogen 247, 290, 295n67; *James Clarence Mangan: His Selected Poems, with a Study* (edited by Louise Imogen Guiney, 1897) 290–91; *see also* Mangan, James Clarence

Gupta Empire 448; *see also* Indian subcontinent; Kalidasa (poet)

Gurkhas (Nepalese) 321; *see also* Indian uprising (1857–58)

Gwynn, Stephen Lucius 291, 302n214, 424, 425, 477, 478, 480, 565, 572, 575–76; *The Fair Hills of Ireland* (by Stephen Lucius Gwynn, 1906) 291, 424, 576; *The History of Ireland* (by Stephen Lucius Gwynn, 1923) 575, 576; *see also* Anglo-Russian Agreement (1907); Iranian Constitutional Revolution (1906–11); Irish Parliamentary Party; Mangan, James Clarence; Moore, Thomas; Persia Committee (London)

Habl al-Matin (Calcutta) 165n301, 550–53; *see also* Kashani, Sayyid Jalal al-Din ("Mo'ayed al-Eslam")

Habl al-Matin (Tehran) 549–51

Hafez, Shams al-Din Mohammad 205n46, 243, 244, 246–48, 251, 261, 279, 427, 435–36, 615, 617, 631n123; possible source of the name Hafed in Thomas Moore's 1817 *Lalla Rookh. An Oriental Romance* 205n46; *Rubā 'iyāt* 247, 631n123; "Solomon and Sheba" 631n123; *see also* Malcolm, John; Mangan, James Clarence; McCarthy, Justin Huntly; Moore, Thomas; Yeats, William Butler

Hafiz: *see* Hafez (Khajeh Shams al-Din Mohammad)

Haileybury College (Hertfordshire, England) 131, 517; *see also* English East India Company; Mohammad Ebrahim (Mirza); Stewart, Charles

Haiti 360n127, 627n42; Saint-Domingue 360n127, 627n42

Hakluyt, Richard 266; Hakluyt Society 299n158; *The Principal Navigations, Voyages, Traffiques, and Discoveries of the English Nation* (published by Richard Hakluyt, 1598–1600) 266; *see also* Jenkinson, Anthony

Halbwachs, Maurice 603; *see also* memory ("collective" memory)

Hales, William (Rev.) 108, 109; *New Analysis of Chronology and Geography, History and Prophecy, A*, vol.IV (by William Hales, 1830) 108; *see also Dabestān-e Mazāheb*; Jones, William; Mahābādiān; Pishdādiān; *Shāhnāmeh*; Trinity College (University of Dublin); *Universal History* of Mirkhond (15th century)

Haliday, Charles 619; *The Scandinavian Kingdom of Dublin* (by Charles Haliday; ed. by John P. Prendergast, 1881) 619

Haliday, William ("Edmond O'Connell") 619; *Uraicecht na Gaedhilge: A Grammar of the Gaelic Language* (by William Haliday, 1808) 619

Hall, Anna Maria (née Fielding): *see Ireland: Its Scenery, Character, &c.*, vol.III (by Anna Maria Hall and Samuel Carter Hall, 1843)

Hall, Samuel Carter: *see Ireland: Its Scenery, Character, &c.*, vol.III (by Anna Maria Hall and Samuel Carter Hall, 1843)

Halpin, William George 314, 355n35; *see also* American Civil War; Fenian Brotherhood; Fenian (Irish Republican Brotherhood) uprising (Ireland, 1867)

Ham 61, 73, 162n235, 383, 452n3; *see also* Amonian; Cuthite; Noah

Hamburgische Börsenhalle 333

Hamedani, Rashid al-Din 529–30; *Jāmi' al-Tawārikh* (by Rashid al-Din of Hamedan, 1306–11) 529

INDEX 723

Hamilton, William Rowan 106, 521; *see also* Royal Irish Academy; Shirazi, Mirza Abul Hassan Khan ("Ilchi")
Hamitic: *see* Ham
Hammer-Purgstall, Joseph Freiherr von 240, 242, 243, 245, 246, 296n93, 444, 640; *Der Diwan von Mohammed Schemsed-din Hafis* (translated by Joseph Freiherr von Hammer-Purgstall, 1812) 246; *Rosenöl, erstes Fläschchen oder, Sagen und Kunden des Morgenlandes aus arabischen, persischen und türkischen Quellen gesammelt* (by Joseph Freiherr von Hammer-Purgstall, 1813) 240, 444; *see also* Mangan, James Clarence; *One Thousand and One Nights* (a.k.a., *Arabian Nights*)
Handbook for Travellers in Ireland (John Murray publisher, 1864) 381
Hanmer, Meredith 49
Hanover 520; Prince Ernest Augustus 293n33; royal House of Hanover 224; *see also* George III, King
Hanway, Jonas 208n81, 515; *see also* Afsharid dynasty (Iran, 1736–51/96)
Hardie, (James) Keir 479; *see also* Labour Party (UK); Nationalities and Subject Races conferences (London, 1910, 1911, 1914); Persia Committee (London)
Hardiman, James 437; *Irish Minstrelsy, or Bardic Remains of Ireland* (by James Hardiman, 1831) 437
Hardy, Philip Dixon 105; *see also Dublin Penny Journal*; Royal Irish Academy
harem (/haram) 173, 175, 176, 235, 271, 308, 328, 340, 341, 359n107
Hariri (poet) 448; *see also* Iraq; Seljuks
Harney, George Julian 265; *see also* Chartism; *Democratic Review* (London); Mangan, James Clarence
Harootunian Harry 248
Harris, Walter 69, 579
Hashem Khan (Mirza) 305, 327, 328, 340, 353n3, 358n97; *see also* "Hashem Khan," Mrs. Murray, Charles
"Hashem Khan," Mrs. 305, 306, 327, 328, 340, 341, 353n3, 358n97; *see also* Hashem Khan (Mirza); Murray, Charles
Haslam, Richard 279
Hastings, Marquess of: *see* Moira, Lord (Francis Rawdon-Hastings; Marquess of Hastings)
Hataria, Manekji Limji 132; *see also* Jalal al-Din Mirza (Jalal Pour-Fath-Ali Shah); Parsi; Society for the Amelioration of the Condition of Zoroastrians in Persia; Zoroastrian

Havelock, Henry 342, 345; *see also* Anglo-Iranian War (1856–57)
Hayden, Mary Teresa 26, 563, 568, 602, 604; *A Short History of the Irish People from the Earliest Times to 1920* (by Mary Hayden and George Aloysius Moonan, 1922) 602; *see also* "Aryan" theories of Irish origins; Celticism; "Europe-centered" theories of Irish origins; historiography and history; Moonan, George Aloysius
Hayrat-Irani, Ismail 131; *see also* Malcolm, John (*The History of Persia from the Most Early Period to the Present Time* ... (1815))
Hazleton, Richard 477; *see also* Anglo-Russian Agreement (1907); Irish Parliamentary Party
Healy, Róisín 203n18, 299n139, 638; *Poland in the Irish Nationalist Imagination, 1772–1922* (by Róisín Healy, 2017) 638
Healy, Timothy Michael 468–69, 481, 485–86; first governor-general of the Irish Free State (1922) 481; *see also* All-For-Ireland League; Irish Parliamentary Party; tobacco concession (Iran, 1890)
Heaney, Seamus 232, 294n51; *see also* Mangan, James Clarence
Heber 79, 201, 269; *see also* Milesians; Milesius (Miledh/Míl Espáine)
Hebrew (language and script) 40, 67, 74, 81, 82, 283, 519, 614, 631n115; *see also* Semitic languages
The Hebrew Bible ("Old Testament") 17, 75, 115, 116, 567; "Book of Ecclesiastes" 615; *see also* Adam; Cain; Eve; Garden of Eden; Japheth; Magog; Mosaic theory; Nephilim; Noah
Hebrews (people) 12, 435, 613; Hebraic 52, 56; *see also* Jewish People; theories of Irish origins
Hedayat, Rezaqoli Khan 133; *Ajmal al-Tawārikh* (by Rezaqoli Khan Hedayat, 1866) 133; *see also Dabestān-e Mazāheb*; *Dasātir*; Keyvan, Azar; Kiāniān; Mahābādiān; Pishdādiān
Hedayat, Sadeq 38–41, 44n38, 46n47, 555; Alexander Haggerty Krappe's *Mythologie universelle* (1930) 41, 46n47; and "Anna Livia Plurabelle" 40; "Aran" 38, 44n38; and Bahramgor Tahmuras Anklesaria 41; in Belgium 39; "Éire" 38, 44n38; and *Finnegans Wake* (by James Joyce, 1939) 39–41, 44n38, 45n43; folklore 38; in France 39; in India 39, 41; Iran/Erin analogy 38, 39, 44n38; James Joyce 38–41; and Jules (Julius) Mohl 41; magian 38; *Toup-e Morvari* (*The Pearl Cannon*, 1947) 38, 41; *Ulysses* (by

James Joyce, 1922) 39; *see also* Farzaneh, Mostafa F.; Joyce, James
Hegel, Georg Wilhelm Friedrich 568; Hegelian 208n87
Heidegger, Martin 276
Heine, Heinrich 270; *see also* Mangan, James Clarence
Hellenic 4, 7, 20–22, 52, 63, 94, 96, 116, 176, 191, 223, 225, 235, 410, 411, 421, 425, 581; accounts of ancient Persians 22, 63–64, 80, 130, 131, 138, 228, 229; Hellenic sources 13, 22, 50, 51, 63, 64, 79, 80, 130, 131, 138, 190, 228, 529, 644; *see also* Apollo (Hellenic deity); civilization; Dorian; Greco-Roman sources; "Greco-Tyrian"; Greek language; Greeks; Hellenophilia
Hellenophilia 176, 221; *see also* Byron, Lord (George Gordon Byron); Moore, Thomas; Romanticism
Hely, James (Rev.) 50, 77, 78; Catholic Relief Act (1778) 50; *Ogygia, or a Chronological Account of Irish Events* (1793 translation of Roderic O'Flaherty's 1685 *Ogygia: seu Rerum Hibernicarum Chronologia*) 50, 77, 78; Trinity College (University of Dublin) 50, 77; *see also* Vallancey, Charles
Heman, Felicia 239
Henry II, King 93, 178, 536; *see also* Anglo-Norman conquests in Ireland (12th century CE)
Henry III, King 555n1; *see also* Isma'ili Shi'i Muslims
Henry VIII, King 272, 349, 538; *see also* Tudor dynasty (1485–1603)
Herat 291n2, 304–6, 308–9, 317–18, 321–22, 325–27, 329–34, 336–39, 342, 344–47, 353n8, 358n97, 470, 539, 647; mass starvation of the population during the Iranian siege (1856) 331, 332, 336, 371; *see also* Afghanistan; Anglo-Iranian Treaty (1814); Anglo-Iranian Treaty (1853); Anglo-Iranian War (1838); Anglo-Iranian War (1856–57); Dost Mohammad Khan; Issa Khan; Kamran Shah Durrani; Mohammad Khan (Sayyid Mohammad Khan); Mohammad Yusuf; Nasser al-Din Shah; Pashtun (Pathan) Barakzai tribe; Pashtun (Pathan) Durrani/Abdāli clan; Pashtun (Pathan) Gilzai confederacy; Peshawar Treaty (1857); Yar Mohammed Khan
Herbelot [de Molainville], Barthélemy d' 75, 81, 83, 84, 115, 175, 184, 204n26, 205n46, 237, 446, 640; *see also Bibliothèque orientale* (by Barthélemy d'Herbelot, 1697); Moore, Thomas; *Shāhnāmeh*; *Universal History of Mirkhond* (15th century); Vallancey,

Charles; *Zardoshtnāmeh* ("The Book of Zoroaster")
Herbert, Algernon 103, 104; *Nimrod: A Discourse on Certain Passages of History and Fable* (by Algernon Herbert, 1828–29) 103, 104; *see also* Nimrod
Herder, Johann Gottfried von 28, 243, 297n95, 399; "Herder Effect" (coined by Pascale Casanova) 399, 456n64; *Ideen zur Philosophie der Geschichte der Menschheit* (1784, 1791) 28; *see also* historiography and history; Romanticism
Heremon (Érimón) 79; *see also* Milesians; Milesius (Miledh/Míl Espáine)
hermeneutics 7, 12–14, 98, 117, 135, 411; *see also* historiography and history
Hermetic Order of the Golden Dawn 432; *see also* Yeats, William Butler
Hermetic Society (Dublin) 432, 461n158; *see also* Mir Aulad Ali; Russell, George William ("Æ"); Yeats, William Butler
Herodotus 131, 147, 228, 229, 446; *The Histories* 131, 228; *see also* Greco-Roman sources; Hellenic (Hellenic sources; Mohammad Ebrahim (Mirza))
Heron, Denis Caulfield 371; *see also* Chicago (the Great Chicago Fire (1871))
Herwegh, Georg 264; *see also* Mangan, James Clarence
heteroglossia 24, 126, 286, 620; *see also* Bakhtin, Mikhail; polyphony
"heterotopia" 39, 126, 127; *see also* Foucault, Michel
Hibernia 67, 94, 96, 109, 185, 197, 366, 390, 445, 530; Hiberni 50, 77, 82, 185, 282, 573; *see also* O'Brien, Henry; Vallancey, Charles
The Hibernian (Dublin) 497
Hibernian Antiquarian Society 67, 185, 612; *see also* Irish antiquarianism; Vallancey Charles
Hibernian Anti-Slavery Society 473; *see also* Madden, Richard Robert; O'Connell, Daniel
Hiberno-English 82, 256, 621
Hiempsal I (2nd century BCE Numidian king) 77
Hiemsal: *see* Hiempsal I (2nd century BCE Numidian king)
Higgins, Godfrey 106; *The Celtic Druids; or, An Attempt to Shew, That the Druids Were the Priests of Oriental Colonies who Emigrated from India...* (by Godfrey Higgins, 1827) 106; *see also* Royal Asiatic Society (London)
Hildebrand and Hadubrand 447
Hill of Tara 270
Hincks, Thomas (Rev.) 106; *see also* Jamshid; Pishdādiān

INDEX 725

Hindi 40, 490, 621, 649; "Hindoostany" 519; "Hindostanee" 82, 233
"Hindoo": *see* Hindu
"Hindoostany": *see* Hindi; Sanskrit
Hindostan: *see* Indian subcontinent
"Hindostanee": *see* Hindi; Sanskrit
"Hindostanic": *see* Hindi; Sanskrit
Hindu 67, 86, 96, 113, 116, 119, 160n207, 173, 204n20, 269, 345, 396, 430–32, 434, 435, 449, 450, 551, 638; "Hindoo" 118, 143, 144, 147, 280, 403, 407, 421
Hindustan: *see* Indian subcontinent
Historia Regum Britanniae (*The History of the Kings of Britannia*): *see* Geoffrey of Monmouth
Historia religionis veterum Persarum eorumque magorum (by Thomas Hyde, 1700): *see* Hyde, Thomas
"historical arrival" of texts 134; *see also* Benjamin, Walter ("after-life" of a work of art)
Historical Memoirs of the Irish Bards (by Joseph Cooper Walker, 1818): *see* Walker, Joseph Cooper
historicism 23, 24, 43n21, 136, 568, 603; *see also* historiography and history
historicity 12, 115, 201, 208n87, 218, 267, 287, 611, 625; historicizing 55, 132, 133, 138, 226, 231, 449, 575, 585, 587
historiography and history 8, 10, 11, 14–18, 20, 22–26, 60, 69, 73, 75, 79, 80, 82, 93, 107, 111, 117, 118, 120, 122–24, 126, 129, 133, 136, 138, 159n199, 164n267, 201, 275, 383, 413, 446, 451, 563, 566–70, 573, 576, 577, 579–81, 587–89, 591, 597, 598, 600–605, 607, 612, 613, 618, 624, 625, 637, 643–48; "counter-history" 604; "didactic" historiography 625; "empirical" and "scientific" methods 24, 117, 118, 122, 123, 381, 413, 563, 564, 567–69, 574, 600, 613, 648; fragmented histories 248–49, 256, 274, 276, 347, 587; historical knowledge 19, 26, 48, 115, 117, 200, 530, 602–5, 625, 646, 648; history as a separate branch of knowledge from theology (in Europe) 61; history-making 139; homogenization of the past 605; "nationalist" historiography 3, 6, 11, 17, 22, 25, 69, 82, 129, 138, 139, 141, 142, 208n87, 225, 413, 416, 418, 567, 569, 570, 574–77, 579, 580, 584, 587–89, 597, 598, 601, 603, 604, 624, 637, 644, 648; truncated histories 258, 268, 274, 651; *see also* Berger, Stefan; Foucault, Michel; Green, Alice Stopford; Hayden, Mary; Herder, Johann Gottfried von; hermeneutics; historicism; Irish antiquarianism; Irish nationalism; Joyce, Patrick Weston; MacNeill, Eoin (John); Mangan, James Clarence; Megill, Allan; Moonan, George Aloysius; Moore, Thomas; O'Brien, Henry; Petrie, George; teleology; Vallancey, Charles; Vico, Giambattista
The History of Ireland (*Foras Feasa ar Éirinn*) (by Geoffrey Keating, 1634) 15, 21, 35, 48, 55, 73, 139, 146, 201, 316, 581, 626n5; *see also* Keating, Geoffrey; O'Connor, Dermod; O'Mahony, John
The History of Ireland, vol.I (by Thomas Moore, 1835) 35, 89, 102, 104, 167, 172, 180, 189, 190, 193–95, 197, 199, 585, 613, 614; *see also* Celts; *Dublin University Magazine*; "fire worship"; Longman, Rees, Orme, Brown, and Green; magi; Moore, Thomas; Persianate heritage; Phoenician-Iranian theories of ancient Ireland's "Golden Age"; Round Towers (Ireland); Vallancey, Charles; Zoroastrianism
The History of Ireland, vol.II (by Thomas Moore, 1837) 195; *see also* Moore, Thomas; Round Towers (Ireland)
The History of Ireland, vol.IV (by Thomas Moore, 1846) 103, 178, 195; *see also* Confederate War (Ireland, 1642–52); *History of Ireland from the Invasion of Henry II* (by Thomas Leland, 1773); *An History of the Life of James Duke of Ormonde, from His Birth in 1610, to His Death in 1688* (by Thomas Carte, 1736); *The Irish Rebellion; Or, An History of the Irish Papists to Extirpate the Protestants in the Kingdom of Ireland* (by John Temple, 1646); Moore, Thomas; O'Neill, Phelim
History of Ireland from the Invasion of Henry II (by Thomas Leland, 1773) 178; *see also The History of Ireland*, vol.IV (by Thomas Moore, 1846); O'Neill, Phelim
The History of Mirza Abul Hassan Khan ... with Some Account of the Fair Circassian (by anon., 1819) 522; *see also* Shirazi, Mirza Abul Hassan Khan ("Ilchi")
History of the Early Kings of Persia, from Kaiomars the First of the Peshdadian Dynasty, to the Conquest of Iran by Alexander the Great (by David Shea, 1832): *see* Shea, David
An History of the Life of James Duke of Ormonde, from His Birth in 1610, to His Death in 1688 (by Thomas Carte, 1736) 178; *see also The History of Ireland*, vol.IV (by Thomas Moore, 1846); O'Neill, Phelim
Hobsbawm, Eric 35; *see also* "invention of tradition"
Hobson, (John) Bulmer 474, 490; *see also* Pan-Aryan Association; Sinn Féin

Hobson, John Atkinson 479; *see also* Nationalities and Subject Races conferences (London, 1910, 1911, 1914)
Hodgkins, Louise Manning 442, 463n209
Hoey, John Cashel 312; *see also The Nation* (Dublin)
Hofheinz, Thomas C. 612–14
Hogan, Ciara 261
Holkar, Maharaja (Tukoji Rao II) 377n15; *see also* Iranian famine (1870–72)
Holzapfel, Rudolf Patrick 245
Home Government Association 468; *see also* Butt, Isaac; Home Rule League; Irish Parliamentary Party
Home Rule: *see* Irish Home Rule; Scotland (Scottish Home Rule); Wales (Welsh Home Rule)
Home Rule League 390, 469; *see also* Butt, Isaac; Home Government Association; Irish Parliamentary Party; Parnell, Charles Stewart; Sheil Edward
Homer 83, 422, 425, 615, 619; *The Odyssey* (by Homer, c.8th century BCE) 619; Ulysses 619
Honduras 314; *see also* Central America; Latin America; Mosquito Coast (Nicaragua and Honduras); Walker, William
Hone, Joseph Maunsell 482, 553–54; Maunsel & Co. (Dublin) 482; *see also Persia in Revolution* (by Joseph Maunsell Hone and Page Lawrence Dickinson, 1910)
Hopkins, Francis 388
Hormuz Island 273, 515
Horn, Charles Frederick 521
Hungary 12, 475, 478, 578, 586, 595; Hungarian 610, 611; *see also* Austria (Austro-Hungarian Empire); Bloom, Leopold; Irano-Alan people; Jász people
hunger strike (Irish republican prisoners) 38, 499, 510n121; Maze prison (Northern Ireland, 1981) 499; *see also* Connolly, James; MacSwiney, Terence
Hunter, William A. 501n2; *see also* tobacco concession (Iran, 1890)
hurling (sport) 387; *see also* Gaelic Athletic Association
Hutton, James 18; *see also* Plutonism (geology); uniformitarian theory (geology)
Hyde, Douglas 393, 396, 397, 412, 413, 423, 424, 438, 440, 441, 447, 451, 463n199, 589, 625n1; *A Literary History of Ireland* (by Douglas Hyde, 1899) 423; *see also* Aryans; Conla (Conlaoch); Cuchulain (Cú Chulainn); "de-Anglicize"; Fenian Cycle; folklore; Gaelic League; Rustam; Sohrab; Ulster Cycle
Hyde, Thomas 62, 85, 116, 158n178; *Historia religionis veterum Persarum eorumque magorum* (by Thomas Hyde, 1700) 62, 85, 158n178; *Veterum Persarum et Parthorum et Medorum religionis historia*, also known as *De vetere religione Persarum* (by Thomas Hyde, 1760) 62; *see also* Zoroastrianism

Iberian Peninsula 19, 21, 47, 49, 54, 65, 81, 102, 190, 191, 362, 403, 405, 424, 425, 439, 529, 600, 617; *see also* Milesians; Scytho-Iberiaus; Spain
Ibernia Phoenicea (by Joaquín Lorenzo Villanueva 1831; translated as *Phoenecian Ireland* by Henry O'Brien, 1833) 89; *see also Phoenecian Ireland* (1833 translation by Henry O'Brien of Joaquín Lorenzo Villanueva's 1831 *Ibernia Phoenicea*); Villanueva, Joaquín Lorenzo
Ibn Khalakan (Ibn Khallikan, Abul-Abbas Ahmad) 285
Ibn Khaldun, Abd al-Rahman ibn Muhammad 241
Ibsen, Henrik 586, 615, 616
Ideen zur Philosophie der Geschichte der Menschheit (1784, 1791): *see* Herder, Johann Gottfried von
Identity 1, 23, 25, 29, 32, 33, 39, 42n4, 55, 56, 66–69, 93, 129, 134, 137, 139, 149, 180, 216, 219, 222, 225, 227, 231, 233, 239, 245, 258, 260, 272, 273, 275, 283, 284, 287, 322, 361, 387, 391, 397, 399, 413, 414, 417, 420, 437, 489, 499, 569, 570, 573–76, 585, 588, 589, 592, 597–602, 605, 608, 610, 611, 613, 624, 625, 626n30, 642, 645, *passim*; the fiction of identity 349–50; intersectionality 29, 603; polythetic identities 29, 348, 450, 603
al-Idrisi, Abu Abdullah Muhammad 529, 559n52; "irlandah al-kabirah" ("Ireland the Great") 529; *see also* McGuire, James Kennedy ("Irandah-al-Kaberah" ("Ireland the Great"))
Ilkhanid Empire 244, 286, 388, 529, 555n1; *see also* Crusades; Edward I, King; Langley, Geoffrey de; Mongol
"imagined communities" 139, 217; *see also* Anderson, Benedict
Imam Reza shrine (Mashhad) 386; *see also* Gowharshad mosque; *Merv Oasis: Travels and Adventures East of the Caspian During the Years 1879–80–81 ..., The* (by Edmond O'Donovan, 1882)
Imperial Bank of Persia 568; *see also* tobacco concession (Iran, 1890)
imperialism (general) 3–5, 19, 20, 22, 23, 31, 36, 38, 44n38, 124, 129, 137, 172, 204n20, 219, 222, 224–26, 231, 237, 260–62, 265, 269–72, 274, 283, 284, 286, 303, 304, 309,

311, 315–22, 324–26, 334, 344, 346–53, 370, 374, 385, 391, 415, 418, 448, 450, 470, 476, 479, 483, 486, 488–93, 495, 501n6, 503n38, 508n86, 547, 549, 550, 562n116, 584, 586, 587, 591–95, 606, 617, 637–40, 647, 649, 650, *passim*; *see also* anticolonial; anti-imperialism; British Empire; China; colonialism (/colonization); Egypt; France; India; Iran; Ireland; Japan; Ottoman Empire; Russia

Inca 382; *see also* Peru

L'Indépendance Belge (Brussels) 327

Independent Irish Party 389; *see also* Moore, George Henry

India 4, 6, 9–13, 18, 20, 34, 37, 39, 41, 55, 58, 62, 67, 72, 73, 74, 80, 82, 85, 87, 88, 91, 94, 95, 105, 108, 111, 113, 114, 116–18, 124, 128–34, 139, 149, 173, 174, 183, 184, 185, 187, *passim*; British colonization of 20, 31, 33, 112, 114, 174, *passim*; British imperial administration of (British Raj) 6, 9–11, 20, 26, 33, 34, 36, 73, 114, 148, 168, 183, 184, *passim*; partition an independence from Britain (1947) 11, 337, 649; *see also* All-India Muslim League; Amritsar massacre (1919); Anglo-Iranian War (1838); Anglo-Iranian War (1856–57); British Empire; Bombay (Mumbai); Calcutta (Kolkata); Delhi; English East India Company; Hedayat, Sadeq; Hindi; India (famines); Indian subcontinent; Indian uprising (1857–58); Mughal dynasty; Peshawar Treaty (1857); Peshawar Valley; Rowlatt Acts (India, 1919); Sanskrit; Santal ("Santhal") uprising; sepoys; sowars

India (famines) 363, 369, 370, 374; famine in northwestern provinces (1861) 369; famine relief finds (UK) 365, 370; Great Indian Famine (1876–78) 363, 369; Orissa Famine (1865–67) 363, 365, 368, 369, 373, 374; reported incidences of anthropophagy 374; *see also* Great Famine (Ireland, 1845–51); Iranian famine (1870–72); *The Nation* (Dublin)

India House (London) 471, 490; *see also* Krishnavarma, Shyamji

Indian Independence Committee (Berlin) 498, 509n112; *see also* First World War

Indian-Irish Independence League (1932) 593; *see also* Despard, Charlotte; Gonne, Maud (Maud Gonne MacBride); O'Donnell, Peadar; Patel, Vithalbhai Jhaverbhai; Ryan, Frank

Indian National Congress 488, 501n4, 547, 551; *see also* Indian nationalism; Indian nationalists

Indian nationalism 9, 11, 149, 363, 429, 430, 434, 450, 474, 475, 478, 483, 487–90, 493, 498, 508n86, 509n112, 547, 551, 584, 593, *passim*; pan-Indian nationalists 435, 488, 490, 507n83, 508n86, 551; *see also* Amritsar massacre (1919); Indian National Congress; Indian nationalists; Pan-Aryan Association; swadeshi; swaraj

Indian Ocean 516

Indian subcontinent 6, 10, 12, 13, 18, 20, 33, 34, 37, 55, 58, 62, 67, 73, 74, 80, 82, 85, 87, 88, 91, 95, 111, 113, 116, 117, 124, 129, 132, 134, 139, 174, 183, 185, 193, 196, 204n20, 241, 269, 272, 320, 331, 351, 382, 403, 415, 428, 430, 439, 440, 450, 452n15, 491, 514, 517, 518, 524, 527, 528, 531, 537, 567, 586, 621, 636, 638–40; Hindostan 53, 147, 200, 326; Hindustan 489, 528; lascars and ayahs 185; *see also* Dravidian; English East India Company; Ghaznavid dynasty; Gupta Empire; Hindu; India; Mughal dynasty

Indian uprising (1857–58) 307, 312, 318, 345, 346; *see also* Canning, Charles John; Gurkhas (Nepalese); sepoys, sowars;

Indic studies 393; *see also* Sanskrit

Indo-European languages 14, 15, 17, 34, 35, 52, 56–59, 61–64, 67, 70, 72–74, 78–79, 91, 113, 387, 401, 566, 572, 639; *see also* Anquetil-Duperron, Abraham Hyacinthe; Aryan (languages); Becanus, Jan Goropius (Jan van Gorp van der Beke); Bopp, Franz; Boxhorn, Marcus Zuerius van; Jäger, Andreas; Jones, William; "Jonesian" theory of Indo-European languages; Lhuyd, Edward; linguistics; Müller, Friedrich Max; philology; Pictet, Adolphe; Sanskrit; Saumaise, Claude (Claudius Salmasius); Schleicher, August; Young, Thomas; Zeuss, Johann Kaspar

Indo-European Telegraph Department 366, 367, 379n55, 389, 540; *see also* Iranian famine (1870–72); telegraph; Wills, Charles James

"Indo-European" theories of Irish origins 58, 61, 72, 78, 79, 197, 200, 391, 401, 402, 409, 410, 491, 474, 620, *passim*; *see also* "Aryan" theories of Irish origins; Aryanism (racial theories); "Europe-centered" theories of Irish origins; "Iranian" theories of Irish origins; racial theories; theories of Irish origins; Vallancey, Charles

Indo-Europeans 179, 197, 200, 391, 392, 394, 402, 409, 410, 491, 574, 620; *see also* Aryans; Caucasians; "Indo-European" theories of Irish origins

"Indo-Iranian" theories of Irish origins; *see also* "Indo-European" theories of Irish

origins; Indo-Iranians; theories of Irish origins
Indo-Iranians 17, 19, 21, 57, 72, 102, 113, 188, 214, 393, 394, 410, 431, 443, 574, 613, 624; *see also* Aryans; Indo-Europeans; "Indo-Iranian" theories of Irish origins; Indo-Scythians; Irano-Scythians
Indo-Scythians 52, 57, 59, 64, 66, 71, 75, 82, 118, 121, 122, 151n31, 214, 215, 219, 382; "Sanscritic" 214; *see also* Aryans; Davis, Thomas Osborne; Indo-Iranians; Irano-Scythians
Indo-Semitic: *see* Aryo-Semitic (Aryan-Semitic; Indo-Semitic); Ascoli, Graziadio Isaia
Inghinidhe na hÉireann (Daughters of Ireland) 471, 478; *see also* Dryhurst, Nora ("Nannie") Florence; Gonne, Maud (Maud Gonne MacBride)
Ingram, John Kells 212; "The Memory of the Dead" 212–13; *see also The Nation* (Dublin)
Innes, Thomas 191
Intercepted Letters; or, The Twopenny Post-bag (by Thomas Moore, 1813) 5, 35, 169, 170, 172, 173, 178, 186, 231, 143, 269, 303, 348, 638, 639; "Letter VI": From Abdallah, in London, to Mohassan, in Ispahan 169, 170, 186, 203n16, 143, 269, 638; *see also* Catholic Emancipation; George IV, King (Prince Regent); Leckie, Gould Francis; Moore, Thomas; "Persian Letters" genre
International Socialist Peace Conference (a.k.a., Third Zimmerwald Conference; Stockholm, 1917) 509n112
Internationalism 293n34, 351, 429, 430, 433, 478, 481, 482, 485, 486, 493, 499, 580, 584, 587, 591, 594, 595, 607, 641; *see also* cosmopolitan (nationalist cosmopolitanism); "third contact zones"
"interpellation" 42n4, 134; *see also* Althusser, Louis
"Intertextuality" 7, 126–27; *see also* Kristeva, Julia
"invention of tradition" 35, 139; *see also* Hobsbawm, Eric; "modernity"/"modernities"; mythology (myth-making); Ranger, Terence; "tradition"
Iran (general) *passim;* Anglo-Iranian relations (general) 1, 9, 33, 34, 36, 271, 308, 370, 469–71, *passim*; and English East India Company 114, 273, 310, 332, 388–91, 515, 527; Gilzai Pashtun invasion (1722) 5, 516; Irish travelers to 185, 384–91, 482, 483, 493, 541, 553–54, 548, 640; *see also* Achaemenid dynasty (Iran, c.550–330 BCE); Alexander the Great; Anglo-Iranian War (1838); Anglo-Iranian War (1856–57); Anglo-Russian Agreement (1907); Anglo-Soviet occupation of Iran; Arab-Muslim invasion of Iran (7th century CE); First World War (Anglo-Russian occupation of Iran (1915)); folklore; Great Britain (imperial leverage in Iran); Iranian famine (1870–72); Pahlavi dynasty (Iran, 1925–79); Parthians; Persianate heritage; Persians; Qajar dynasty (Iran, 1796–1925); Russia (imperial leverage in Iran); Russo-Iranian War (1804–13); Russo-Iranian War (1826–28); Safavid dynasty (Iran, 1501–1722/36); Sassanian dynasty (Iran, 224–650 CE); Seleucid Empire; Zand dynasty (Iran, 1751–94)
Iran/Erin 38–41, 189, 260, 264, 280, 282, 404, 426, 605, 606, 620, 623, 647; Iran-Erin connections 8, 13, 38–40, 76, 120, 142, 282, 426; Iran-Ireland connections 34, 44n38, 92, 102, 110, 123, 125; Irish nationalist allegory 5, 7, 35–37, 127, 174, 178, 180–82, 187, 236, 237, 241, 252, 259–62, 264, 273, 280, 282, 331, 418, 542, 606, 617, 620, 639, 646; presumed common linguistic origin of "Erin" and "Iran" 13, 21, 38–41, 52, 62, 84, 125, 174, 383–84, 409, 426, 427, 459n137, 623, *passim*; *see also* Beaufort, Louisa Catherine; Gancher, David; Hedayat, Sadeq; Joyce, James; Keane, Marcus; MacCarthy, Denis Florence; Mangan, James Clarence; Moore, Thomas; O'Brennan, Martin A.; O'Brien, Henry; O'Hart, John; Pazargad, Bahauddin; Vallancey, Charles; Wilde, Jane Francesca Agnes (née Elgee)
Irān-e Nou (Tehran) 170, 550; *see also* "English Letters" genre (Iran)
Iranian Constitutional Revolution (1906–11) 1, 8, 36, 37, 137, 145, 165n301, 302n214, 322, 324, 346, 374, 391, 424, 467, 470, 473, 474, 476, 477, 479–85, 487–89, 492, 493, 495, 500, 508n86, 513, 539, 547–54, 640, 647; Iranian civil war (1908–09) 474, 476, 479, 482, 485, 487, 548, 550, 552–54; *see also* Anglo-Russian Agreement (1907); Baskerville, Howard; Browne, Edward Granville; Dillon, John; Grey, Edward; Gwynn, Stephen Lucius; Iranian nationalism; Iranian Question; Lynch, Henry Finnis Blosse; majles (Iranian national assembly); Mohammad-Ali Shah; Mozaffar al-Din Shah; Persia Committee (London); Shuster, William Morgan
Iranian famine (1870–72) 6, 8, 37, 346, 363–75, 379n55, 391, 641, 648; the City of London Mansion House "Persian Famine

Relief Fund" 364–67, 369–70, 372, 373; famine relief finds (UK) 364, 366, 370, 373, 391; funds raised at a football match between Lloyd's and the Stock Exchange 364; funds raised by Fishmongers' Company (City of London) 364; funds raised by the Order of Freemasons (the United Grand Lodge of England) 364; funds received from Australia 364; funds received from India 364, 377n15; funds received from New Zealand 364; funds received from the German Emperor (Wilhelm I) 365; reported incidences of anthropophagy 373–74, 379n55; *see also* Aga Khan I (Hassan Ali Shah); Alison, Charles; Bateman-Champain, John Underwood; Brittlebank, William; Bruce, Robert (Rev.); Christians in Iran; Dawes, Edwyn Sandys; Findlater, Alexander; *Freeman's Journal* (Dublin); Gibbons, John; Great Famine (Ireland, 1845–51); Holkar, Maharaja (Tukoji Rao II); India (famines); Lynch, Thomas Kerr; Mansion House (Dublin); Mansion House (the City of London); Mehrban brothers of Bombay; Messrs. Rothschild & Sons; Mohsen Khan ("Mo'in al-Molk", later "Amin al-Molk"); Montefiore, Moses Haim; *The Nation* (Dublin); *Old Jonathan: The District and Parish Helper* (London); Ongley, Henry Hardy; Pelly, Lewis; Rao of Kutch (Pragmalji II); Rawlinson, Henry Creswicke; Sassoon, Albert Abdullah David; Waterlow, Sydney Hedley; Wills, Charles James

Iranian nationalism 9, 36, 38, 76, 132–34, 136–39, 145, 149, 275, 324, 350, 352, 424, 450, 473, 474, 476, 482, 483, 487, 488, 489, 491, 492, 493, 494, 513, 528, 547–50, 553, 554, 591, 640, 649, *passim*; Iranian nationalists and Irish nationalists 476–82, 483–88, 493, 494–500, 509n112, 547, 548, 549, 553, 554, 590, *passim*; Iranian nationalists and the Easter Rising (Ireland, 1916) 493, 497, 528, 547, 590, *passim*; *see also* historiography and history; Iranian Constitutional Revolution; Iranian Question; Jalal al-Din Mirza (Jalal Pour-Fath-Ali Shah)

Iranian Nationalist Committee (Berlin) 497, 509–10n112; *see also* First World War; Jamalzadeh, Mohammad-Ali; *Kāveh* (Berlin); Social Democratic Party (Iran); Taqizadeh, Hassan

Iranian oil nationalization (1951) 500; *see also* Anglo-Persian Oil Company; McQuillan, John (Jack); Mossadeq, Mohammad; petroleum

Iranian Question 6, 337, 339, 468, 477–79, 481, 483–87, 492, 577594, 639; *see also* Anglo-Russian Agreement (1907); Iranian Constitutional Revolution; Iranian nationalism

Iranian students in England (early 19th century) 186, 187; Mirza Jafar 186; Mohammad Reza Mirza 187; *see also* Abbas Mirza (Qajar crown prince); *Lalla Rookh. An Oriental Romance* (by Thomas Moore, 1817); Moore, Thomas

"Iranian" theories of Irish origins 2, 4, 10, 13, 14, 17–19, 22, 27, 33–35, 37–39, 45n38, 52–56, 62, 63, 64, 67, 70, 73, 77, 79, 81, 86, 87, 89, 90, 91, 99, 100, 102, 111, 114, 117, 121, 130, 133, 139, 143, 172, 174, 185, 189, 190, 238, 254, 277, 278, 321, 348, 382, 384, 391, 403, 406, 407, 409, 410, 427, 446, 514, 519, 547, 598, 612, 620, 642, 643, 646, 650, *passim*; diffusionist model of Irish Golden Age 12, 14, 25, 104, 117, 142, 409, *passim*; *see also* Aryan; Aryanism; Beaufort, Louisa Catherine; Bourke, Ulick Joseph; *Dabestān-e Mazāheb*; "fire worship"; Gaels; Jones, Rowland; Keane, Marcus; Mahābādiān; Mangan, James Clarence; Medes; Milesians; Moore, Thomas; O'Brien, Henry; Persians; Phoenician-Iranian theories of ancient Ireland's "Golden Age"; Pishdādiān; Round Towers (Ireland); theories of Irish origins; Vallancey, Charles; Wilde, Jane Francesca Agnes (née Elgee)

Iranian travelers to Ireland 10, 169, 187, 514, 520–24, 548

"Iranianized (/Persianized) Phoenician civilization" in ancient Ireland: *see* Phoenician-Iranian theories of ancient Ireland's "Golden Age"

Iranians 4, 5, 8–10, 12, 13, 18, 36–38, 42, 52, 54, 56, 57, 63, 64, 70, 72, 74, 77, 84, 87, 91, 94, 96, 104, 114, 118, 121, 130–33, 142, 148, 175, 177, 178, 180, 184–89, 191, 192, 220, 223, 229, 233, 238, 261, 270, 272, 293n37, 311, 343, 344, 353, 359n117, 383, 391, 392, 404, 405, 408, 413, 443, 467, 470, 473, 488, 489, 491–93, 509n112, 513–18, 520, 523, 524, 527, 528, 530–32, 535, 537, 538, 541, 546–48, 550, 554, 555, 613, 620, 622, 623, 638, 640, 642, 643, 646, 649; *see also* Aryanism (racial theories); Aryans; Cuthite; Indo-Europeans; Indo-Iranians; Indo-Scythians; Irano-Alan people; Irano-Sarmatians;

Irano-Scythians; Medes; Parthians; Persianate heritage; Persians; Scythians
Irano-Alan people 12; *see also* Jász people (Hungary); Persianate heritage
Irano-Sarmatians 12; *see also* Persianate heritage; Polish Sarmatianism
Irano-Scythians 12, 17, 19, 21, 52, 53, 57, 59, 64, 69, 71, 75, 84, 92, 121, 146, 405, 642; *see also* Aryanism (racial theories); Aryans; Indo-Europeans; Indo-Iranians; Indo-Scythians; Irano-"Scythian" theories of Irish origins; Vallancey, Charles
Iraq 449; Ottoman Iraq 332, 453n25, 476; *see also* Baghdad; Mosul
Ireland (general) *passim*; *see also* Anglican Church; Catholic Church; Coercion Acts (Ireland); Confederate War (Ireland, 1642–52); Easter Rising (Ireland, 1916), Éire; Éireann; Éirinn; English and Protestant penal laws; Erin; "Europeanizing" Ireland; folklore; Gaels; Great Famine (Ireland, 1845–51); Irish Civil War (1922–23); Irish Free State; Irish Land Acts (1870, 1881); Irish War of Independence; "Irishness"; Kingdom of Ireland (under English rule); "Land War" (Ireland); Northern Ireland; Protestant plantations in Ireland; Repeal of the Party Processions Act (Ireland, 1871); Republic of Ireland; Scotia; Ulster; United Kingdom; theories of Irish origins
Ireland: Its Scenery, Character, &c., vol.III (by Anna Maria Hall and Samuel Carter Hall, 1843) 196; *see also* "fire worship"; Moore, Thomas; Round Towers (Ireland); "sun worship"; Vallancey, Charles
Ireland as a "province" 138, 220, 227, 349, 525, 527, 528, 536, 540, 543, 544, 566, 585; *see also* Davis, Thomas Osborne; "deprovincializing" Ireland; "provincializing" Ireland
Ireland's "Golden Age": *see* civilization; Phoenician-Iranian theories of ancient Ireland's "Golden Age"
Irish-American 79, 148, 227, 253, 314, 316, 361, 372, 401, 472, 489–91, 496, 525, 529, 581; *see also* Irish diaspora (United States); Irish nationalism
The Irish-American (New York) 315, 343
Irish antiquarianism 2–4, 6–8, 11–27, 29–31, 34–39, 42, 47–72, 76–82, 84–89, 93, 94, 97–107, 109, 110, 115–21, 123–30, 132–36, 138–43, 146–47, 153n59, 156n124, 172–74, 180, 185, 188–90, 193–94, 196–99, 201, 208n87, 212–15, 219, 226–27, 235–36, 253, 276–78, 282, 296n79, 303, 321, 331, 346, 348, 353, 382–84, 392, 394–95, 397, 399–401, 405, 409–10, 413–18, 420, 426, 431, 435, 443, 445, 446, 451, 490, 500, 513, 514, 519, 527, 535, 563–64, 566–57, 569, 571–72, 575–78, 580–83, 585–88, 597–602, 604, 605, 608, 612–15, 618–20, 626n10, 626n30, 636–37, 639, 641–44, 646, 650–51; *see also* Beaufort, Louisa Catherine; Betham, William; cosmopolitan (Irish polyglot cosmopolitan texts); historiography and history; Irish nationalism; Keane, Marcus; Keating, Geoffrey; Milesians; Moore, Thomas; O'Brien, Henry; O'Conor, Charles; O'Flaherty, Roderic; Persianate heritage; Round Towers (Ireland); Royal Irish Academy; theories of Irish origins; Vallancey, Charles
"Irish Brigade" (in the British House of Commons) 549; *see also* Moore, George Henry; Sadleir, John
Irish Brigade (Irish nationalist volunteers recruited from the ranks of Irish prisoners of war in Germany during the First World War) 499; *see also* Casement, Roger
Irish Brigade of the Spanish Army (Regiment of Hibernia) 398–99; *see also* Fitzgerald, Archibald
Irish Citizen Army 494, 496; *see also* Connolly, James; Easter Rising (Ireland, 1916); Larkin, James
Irish Civil War (1922–23) 10, 348, 494, 499, 570, 578, 579, 581, 589, 591, 592, 594, 645; *see also* Anglo-Irish Treaty (December 6, 1921); Anti-Treaty (Irish nationalists); Irish Free State; Irish Republican Army (1922); Pro-Treaty (Irish nationalists)
Irish Constitution (1782) 28; *see also* "Grattan's Parliament"
Irish diaspora (general) 9, 11, 20, 29, 30, 36, 38, 86, 142, 303, 313–15, 343, 361–63, 368–69, 387, 400–401, 413, 473–76, 481, 483–85, 531, 548, 571–72, 576, 581, 590, 591, 602, 605, 609, 639, 640, *passim*; in Australia 11, 313; in Britain 11, 313; in Canada 11, 313; in India 11; in Latin America 11; in southern Africa 11, 313; *see also* Irish diaspora (United States); Irish-American
Irish diaspora (United States) 9, 11, 209n115, 303, 313–15, 323–24, 343, 361, 473–75, 572, 581, 593, *passim*
Irish Free State 2, 3, 7, 10, 16, 26, 44n38, 348, 451, 471, 481, 493, 499, 500, 510n127, 554, 563, 570, 573, 575, 576, 578–82, 584, 588–600, 602–5, 607, 608, 610, 612, 625, 637, 641, 645, 647, 648; and the Catholic Church 570, 575, 588–89, 592, 595, 597, 598; Ireland's partition) 10, 11, 38, 348,

493, 499, 584, 593, 595, 645; *see also* Anglo-Irish Treaty (December 6, 1921); Anti-Treaty (Irish nationalists); Communist Party of Ireland (1921–24); Cosgrave, William Thomas; Fianna Fáil; Fine Gael; Irish Civil War (1922–23); Irish War of Independence; Irish Worker League (1923–28); Labour Party (Irish Free State); Pro-Treaty (Irish nationalists)

Irish heroic cycles: *see* epics; Fenian Cycle; mythology; Ulster Cycle

Irish Home Rule 165n301, 168, 183, 212, 307–10, 312, 314, 322–24, 346, 348, 364, 367, 368, 401, 423, 468–70, 475, 477–80, 491, 494, 513, 526, 541, 542, 544, 546, 547, 549, 552, 554, 576, 578, 584, 590; Irish Home Rule Act (1914) 493, 494, 554, 591; Irish Home Rule Bill (1886) 540, 546, 549; Irish Home Rule Bill (1893) 540, 549; Irish Home Rule Bill (1912) 9, 493, 494, 554, 590; Irish Home Rule nationalists 9, 24, 36, 145, 227, 302n214, 309, 312, 317, 348, 355n28, 358n98, 364, 366–68, 390, 424, 427, 467, 468, 472, 475, 477, 480, 481, 484, 486, 488, 491, 494, 526, 528, 540–41, 547, 549, 572, 590, 591, 627n46; *see also* All-for-Ireland League; British parliament ("Home Rule" Irish nationalist representation); Irish Parliamentary Party; Irish Volunteers; O'Connell, Daniel; O'Connellite; Repeal Association (1840); Repeal movement; Sinn Féin; Ulster Covenant; Ulster Volunteers (a.k.a., Ulster Volunteer Force); unionists (Ireland)

The Irish Independent (Dublin) 483, 484, 605

Irish Industrial Exhibition: *see* Great Industrial Exhibition (Dublin; a.k.a., Irish Industrial Exhibition) 540, 542, 545

Irish Land Acts (1870, 1881) 367, 540; *see also* Gladstone, William Ewart; peasantry (Ireland); Ribbonism (Ireland)

Irish language 32, 42n1, 45n38, 56–57, 63–65, 67, 70, 73, 76, 78, 79, 82–84, 86, 87, 98, 121, 122, 126, 138, 144, 146–48, 168, 196, 197, 200, 201, 214, 219, 222, 234, 240, 245, 246, 250, 253, 256–58, 277, 278, 280, 284, 286–87, 302n208, 317, 383, 384, 393–96, 402, 404, 405, 412, 414, 420, 422–25, 432, 440, 446, 474, 478, 479, 483, 498, 500, 519, 535, 570, 572, 574, 588, 600, 608, 611, 614, 616, 619–21; *see also* Gaelic

Irish Literary Gazette (Dublin, Cork, Belfast and Galway) 198; "Half Hours with Irish History" 198; *see also* "fire worship"; Moore, Thomas

Irish Literary Revival 8, 148, 238, 389, 420, 426, 432, 433, 441, 442, 449, 478, 579, 586; *see also* Irish Revival

Irish Literary Theatre 432, 438, 580, 609; *see also* Abbey Theatre; Gregory, Isabella Augusta (née Persse); Irish National Dramatic Society; Irish National Theatre Society; Martyn, Edward; Moore, George Augustus; Yeats, William Butler

Irish Melodies (by Thomas Moore): *see* Moore, Thomas (*Irish Melodies*)

Irish National Dramatic Society 438, 580; *see also* Abbey Theatre; Gregory, Isabella Augusta (née Persse); Irish Literary Theatre; Irish National Theatre Society; Yeats, William Butler

Irish National Invincibles 221, 526, 546; *see also* Phoenix Park murders (Dublin, 1882); Tynan, Patrick

Irish National Liberation Army 501, 641; *see also* Irish Republican Socialist Party; *The Starry Plough* (Belfast); "The Troubles" (Northern Ireland, 1969–98)

Irish National Theatre Society 429, 438, 483, 580; *see also* Abbey Theatre; Gregory, Isabella Augusta (née Persse); Irish Literary Theatre; Irish National Dramatic Society; Yeats, William Butler

Irish nationalism *passim*; *see also* Ancient Order of Hibernians; Easter Rising (Ireland, 1916); historiography and history ("nationalist" historiography); Irish antiquarianism; Irish diaspora (general); Irish diaspora (United States); Irish Home Rule; Irish National Invincibles; Irish National Liberation Army; Irish Parliamentary Party; Irish Question; Irish Republican Socialist Party; "Land War" (Ireland); Official Sinn Féin; Pan-Aryan Association; People's Democracy; Provisional Irish Republican Army; Provisional Sinn Féin; Sinn Féin; Sinn Féin the Workers' Party; Society of United Irishmen; United Irishmen; Young Ireland

Irish Nationalist Committee (Berlin; a.k.a., German-Irish Society) 497–98, 509n112; *see also* Casement, Roger; Chatterton-Hill, George; First World War

The Irish News (New York) 315; *see also* Meagher, Thomas Francis

Irish parliament 34, 90, 168, 349, 474, 475, 518, 522, 524, 526, 527, 578, 597; *see also* Dáil Éireann (Irish Assembly)

Irish Parliamentary Party 145, 165n300, 302n214, 390, 424, 427, 468, 469, 472, 525, 546, 548, 576; a.k.a., Irish Home Rule Party 468; a.k.a., Irish Nationalist

Party 468; a.k.a., Irish Party 468; *see also* Boer War (1899–1902), British parliament ("Home Rule" Irish nationalist representation); Dillon, John; Gwynn, Stephen Lucius; Hazleton, Richard; Healy, Timothy Michael; Home Government Association; Home Rule League; Irish Home Rule; MacNeill, John G. S.; McCarthy, Justin; McCarthy, Justin Huntly; National Volunteers; Parnell, Charles Stewart; Parnellite; Redmond, John; Redmond, William; Sheil, Edward

Irish Pedigrees; or, the Origin and Stem of the Irish Nation (by John O'Hart, 1876 and later editions) 61, 146, 148, 384, 423

Irish Penny Journal (Dublin) 437

Irish People (Dublin) 229, 545; *see also* Irish Republican Brotherhood; O'Leary, John; Stephens, James

Irish Question 9, 10, 303, 309, 311, 318, 324, 345, 346, 401, 481, 493, 494, 499, 509n112, 513, 537, 547–54, 590, 591, 636, 645; *see also* Irish Home Rule; Irish nationalism

The Irish Rebellion; Or, An History of the Irish Papists to Extirpate the Protestants in the Kingdom of Ireland (by John Temple, 1646) 178; *see also The History of Ireland*, vol.IV (by Thomas Moore, 1846); O'Neill, Phelim

"Irish Republic" (1919–21) 500, 580, 591; *see also* Dáil Éireann (Irish Assembly); de Valera, Éamon; *News Letter of the Friends of Irish Freedom National Bureau of Information* (Washington, DC)

Irish Republican Army (1919–22) 591; *see also* Irish War of Independence

Irish Republican Army (1922) 592, 593; *see also* Anti-Treaty (Irish nationalists); Irish Civil War (1922–23); *An Phoblacht* (Dublin)

Irish Republican Brotherhood 209n115, 221, 228, 314, 355n35, 363, 386, 379n63384, 429, 474, 526, 542, 562n119, 590; *see also* Casement, Roger; Clan na Gael (United States); Clarke, Thomas James; Fenian Brotherhood; *Irish People* (Dublin); Irish Volunteers; MacDermott (Mac Diarmada), Seán; O'Donovan, Edmond; O'Leary, John; Reddin, Daniel; Stephens, James;

Irish Republican Brotherhood uprising (a.k.a., "Fenian Rising," 1867) 355n35, 363, 366, 379n63, 542, 545; *see also* Halpin, William George

Irish Republican Socialist Party 501, 641; *see also* Irish National Liberation Army; *The Starry Plough* (Belfast); "The Troubles" (Northern Ireland, 1969–98)

Irish Review (Dublin) 484

Irish Revival 25, 136, 138, 393, 412, 413, 417, 423, 424, 426, 428–34, 436, 441, 442, 446, 447, 451, 474, 579, 587, 598, 613; *see also* Irish Literary Revival (Ireland)

Irish Sea 9, 143

The Irish Shield and Monthly Milesian (New York) 86

Irish Socialist Republican Party 475, 483; *see also* Connolly, James; Socialist Party of Ireland

Irish Theosophist (Dublin) 431; *see also* Theosophical Society

The Irish Times (Dublin) 308, 367, 432; *see also* unionists (Ireland)

Irish Transvaal Brigade (a.k.a., Irish Commandos/MacBride's Brigade) 351, 472; *see also* Boer War (1899–1902); MacBride, John

The Irish Tribune (Dublin) 368

Irish Volunteers 494, 495, 573; *see also* Irish Home Rule (Irish Home Rule Bill (1912)); Irish Republican Brotherhood; MacNeill, Eoin (John); National Volunteers

Irish War of Independence 320, 493, 499, 500, 563, 590, 591; provisional government of the Irish Republic (1919–22) 591; *see also* Anglo-Irish Treaty (December 6, 1921); Connaught Rangers Mutiny (Punjab, 1920); Irish Free State; Irish Republican Army (1919–22)

Irish Women's Franchise League 478; *see also* Cousins, Margaret Elizabeth (née Gillespie); Despard, Charlotte; Dryhurst, Nora ("Nannie") Florence; Sheehy Skeffington, Hanna

The Irish Worker (Dublin) 496; *see also* Connolly, James

Irish Worker League (1923–28) 592; *see also* Comintern (Third / Communist International); Larkin, James

Irish Year Book/Leabar na hÉireann (Dublin) 582

The Irishman (Dublin) 261, 265, 285

"Irishness" 25, 33, 253, 283, 284, 573, 575, 577, 597, 598, 605–12, 637, 645; *see also* Gaels; Mangan, James Clarence; "mere Irish"

Isfahan 169–71, 186, 358n106, 376, 377n17, 377n22, 377–78n23, 516, 521

Isfahani, Abdul-Motaleb 133; *see also* Jalal al-Din Mirza (Jalal Pour-Fath-Ali Shah) (*Nāmeh-ye Khosrovān: Dāstān-e Pādeshāhān-e Pārs beh Zabān-e Pārsi* ... (by Jalal al-Din Mirza (Jalal Pour-Fath-Ali Shah), 1868))

Isfahani, Mir Muhammad Hussein 111

Ishrāqiyyun 112; *see also Dabestān-e Mazāheb; Dasātir;* Keyvan, Azar; "neo-Zoroastrianism"

Islam 17, 114, 131, 172, 173, 175, 194, 205n46, 237, 239, 246, 262, 268, 269, 272, 306, 322, 326, 329, 344, 359n117, 371, 385, 386, 402, 407, 430, 449, 566, 638–39; Muslims 4, 5, 20, 25, 35, 41, 45n42, 61, 62, 81, 108, 112, 114, 119, 131–33, 137, 169, 170, 172–75, 178–82, 184, 194, 204n20, 204n29, 205n46, 225, 237, 241, 252, 261, 262, 264, 266, 269, 270, 272–75, 318, 328, 340, 343–45, 348, 365, 371, 373, 385, 386, 388, 430, 448, 470, 487, 488, 492, 507n74, 508n86, 517, 524, 525, 529, 545, 551, 555n1, 559n53, 561n104, 585, 617, 638, 639; pre-Islamic Iran 17, 76, 85, 112, 114, 131–33, 138, 172, 174, 242, 386, 566; Shi'i Islam 35, 170–72, 178, 203n15, 237, 262, 269–73, 308, 311, 322, 328, 340, 343, 345, 348, 365, 385, 386, 470, 524, 542, 543, 617, 638, 639; Sunni Islam 35, 170–72, 175, 178, 262, 269–72, 308638; *see also* Isma'ili Shi'i Muslims; MacCarthy, Denis Florence; Mangan, James Clarence; Moore, Thomas; Muhammad (prophet); pan-Islam; The Qur'an

Islam, Shamsul 435

Isma'ili Shi'i Muslims 555n1; Alamut 555n1; *see also* Henry III, King; Islam

Ispahan: *see* Isfahan

Issa Khan 332, 334; *see also* Dost Mohammad Khan; Herat

Istanbul 341, 483; 1870 fire 373; Constantinople 186, 354n12; *see also* Ottoman Empire

Italy (and Italian) 74, 121, 171, 220, 246, 350, 394, 398, 409, 420–22, 448, 484, 522, 574, 585, 586, 595, 596, 609; *see also* Abyssinian Crisis; Libya

Ithaca 411

Ithaca (New York) 489

ithna' ashari (Twelver) Shi'i Islam: *see* Islam (Shi'i Islam)

Iverni 574

Jacobins 265; Jacobite 245, 437; *see also* French Revolution (1789–99); *Paddy's Resource* (1795–1803)

Jacobs, Joseph 448–49; *see also* Aryanism (racial theories); Aryo-Semitic (Aryan-Semitic; Indo-Semitic); Conla (Conlaoch); Costello, Louisa Stuart; Cuchulain (Cú Chulainn); Ferdowsi, Abul-Qassem; folklore; Khayyam, Omar; Rustam; *Shāhnāmeh*; Sohrab; Ulster Cycle

Jäger, Andreas 57; *see also* Indo-European languages

Jalal al-Din Mirza (Jalal Pour-Fath-Ali Shah) 132–34, 136; *Nāmeh-ye Khosrovān*: *Dāstan-e Pādeshāhān-e Pārs beh Zabān-e Pārsi* … (by Jalal al-Din Mirza (Jalal Pour-Fath-Ali Shah), 1868) 132, 133; *see also Dabestān-e Mazāheb*; *Dasātir*; Hataria, Manekji Limji; Iranian nationalism; Isfahani, Abdul-Motaleb; Kiānīān; Mahābādiān; Pishdādiān; Qajar dynasty (Iran, 1796–1925)

Jamalzadeh, Mohammad-Ali 499; *see also* Casement, Roger; Iranian Nationalist Committee (Berlin); *Kāveh* (Berlin)

James I of England (James VI of Scotland) 51, 516, 538; *see also* Plantation of Ulster; Safavid dynasty (Iran, 1501–1722/36); Sherley (Shirley), Robert; Stuart dynasty (1603–49, 1660–1714)

James II, King 50, 352, 538; *see also* "Glorious Revolution" (1688); O'Flaherty, Roderic; Scotland; Stuart dynasty (1603–49, 1660–1714); Stuart Restoration (1660)

Jami, Nur al-Din Abd al-Rahman 244; *see also* Mangan, James Clarence

Jamshid (Jam) 106, 264, 286, 533; *see also* Hincks, Thomas (Rev.); Mangan, James Clarence ("To the Ingleezee Khafir, Calling Himself Djuan Bool Djenkinzun"); Pishdādiān

Japan 67, 490–91, 501n6, 508n86, 550, 553, 562n116, 586, 590, 595, 610, 649; Imperial University (Tokyo) 490; Japanese 63; *see also* Anglo-Japanese Alliance (1902); China (Manchuria); Korea; Meiji Restoration; Noh theatre; Okuma, Shigenobu; pan-Asianism; Russo-Japanese War (1904–05)

Japheth 47, 61, 73, 74, 79, 162n235; "Japhetic ("Ya'fet")" branch of languages 57, 61, 73, 74, 147, 396, 405; *see also* The Bible; Fénius Farsaid (Fenius Farsa); Gomer; The Hebrew Bible ("Old Testament"); Jones, William; "Jonesian" theory of Indo-European languages; Madai; Magog; Mosaic theory; Noah

Jász people (Hungary) 12; *see also* Persianate heritage

Jenkinson, Anthony 33, 262, 265–68, 273, 322, 515, 527, 617; *see also* Elizabeth I, Queen; Hakluyt, Richard (*The Principal Navigations, Voyages, Traffiques, and Discoveries of the English Nation* (published by Richard Hakluyt, 1598–1600)); Malcolm, John (*The History of Persia from the Most Early Period to the Present Time* … (1815)); Mangan, James Clarence ("To the Ingleezee Khafir, Calling Himself Djuan Bool Djenkinzun"); Muscovy Company; Safavid dynasty (Iran, 1501–1722/36); Tahmasp I, Shah

Jennings, Hargrave 383; *Phallic Objects, Monuments and Remains: Illustrations of the Rise and Development of the Phallic Idea* (*Sex Worship*) *and Its Embodiment in the Works of Nature and Art* (by Hargrave Jennings, 1889) 383; *see also* O'Brien, Henry (Round Towers and phallic worship); phallic worship; Round Towers (Ireland)

Jesse, William 339; *see also* Ferrier, Joseph Pierre (*Caravan Journeys and Wanderings in Persia, Afghanistan, Turkistan, and Beloochistan* (by Joseph Pierre Ferrier; English translation from the French by William Jesse, edited by Henry Danby Seymour, 1856)); Seymour, Henry Danby

Jewish people 21, 25, 51, 52, 64, 74, 82, 108, 147, 162n235, 272, 364, 365, 376–77n11, 377n17, 421, 431, 448, 472, 486, 506n72, 507n73, 584, 608, 610, 620, 621, 631n115; Eastern European Jews 25, 316, 610, 611; Ireland's Jewish communities 25, 316, 428, 450, 486, 492, 506n72, 507n73, 569, 584, 589, 605–7, 610, 611; Judaism 17, 61, 131, 430, 431, 435, 606, 631n115; *see also* anti-Jewish; The Hebrew Bible ("Old Testament"); Hebrews (people); Limerick pogrom (Ireland, 1904); "Semitic" (racial designation); Shem; theories of Irish origins

jihād (denoting Muslim "holy war" in this case) 342, 343

"John Bull" 259, 262, 265–66, 322; *see also* Mangan, James Clarence ("To the Ingleezee Khafir, Calling Himself Djuan Bool Djenkinzun")

"John Bull Company": *see* English East India Company

John XXII, Pope 20; *see also Declaration of Arbroath* (1320); Catholics; papacy

Jones, Ellen Carol 624

Jones, Felix 335; *see also* Anglo-Iranian War (1856–57)

Jones, John 229; *see also Sentimental and Masonic Magazine* (Dublin)

Jones, Rowland 73–74; Celto-Scyths 74; on Welsh language 74; *see also* Celticism; Celts; "Iranian" theories of Irish origins; Wales

Jones, William 15, 57, 59, 60, 63, 67, 70, 72, 76, 80, 84–86, 91, 92, 94, 96, 105, 108, 111–13, 115–18, 123, 125, 126, 132, 134, 146, 160n207, 161n222, 174, 193, 237, 391, 392, 402, 435, 492, 566; February 1786 lecture (at the Asiatic Society of Bengal) 57, 67; "On the Origin and Families of Nations" 92, 112; *see also* Aryan (languages); Asiatic Society of Bengal; Browne, Edward Granville; *Dabestān-e Mazāheb*;

Dasātir; Erskine, William; Faber, George Stanley; Gladwin, Francis; Indo-European languages; Indo-Europeans; Japheth ("Japhetic ("Ya'fet")" branch of languages); "Jonesian" theory of Indo-European languages; Mahābādiān; Mir Muhammed Husain (Isfahani); O'Brien, Henry; Ogham; Persian language; Persian script; philology; Sanskrit; Vallancey, Charles

Jones Brydges, Harford 18, 34, 115, 161n217, 521, 527–28; British representative to the Qajar court (1808–11) 34, 521, 528; *The Dynasty of the Kajars. Translated from the Original Persian Manuscript Presented by His Majesty Faty Aly Shah ...* (by Harford Jones Brydges, 1833) 115, 527; *see also Dabestān-e Mazāheb*; Donboli, Abdul-Razzaq Beg; Jones, William; Mahābādiān; orientalism; Pishdādiān

"Jonesian" theory of Indo-European languages 57, 59, 60, 63, 70, 76, 80, 146, 391, 392, 492; *see also* Indo-European languages; Japheth ("Japhetic ("Ya'fet")" branch of languages); Jones, William

Josephus, Flavius 74

Joshi, Samuel Lucas 489, 490; *see also* Pan-Aryan Association

Journal de St. Petersburg 327

Journal of Sacred Literature 120; *see also* Grover, Henry Montague (Rev.)

Joyce, James 3, 7, 10, 39–41, 44n38, 46n45, 54, 82, 149, 182, 232, 236, 240, 258, 265, 285, 289–91, 298n123, 302n208, 483, 554, 555, 586, 605–25, 643, 645; "Ireland: Island of Saints and Sages" (1907) 619; Joycean 39, 40, 607, 609, 611, 622, 623; Phoenician-Iranian theories of ancient Ireland's "Golden Age" 289, 302n208, 605, 608, 611–14, 616–20, 624, 625, 643; *see also* Barnacle, Nora; cosmopolitan (Irish polyglot cosmopolitan texts); "deprovincializing" Ireland; *Dubliners* (by James Joyce, 1914); *Finnegans Wake* (by James Joyce, 1939); Hedayat, Sadeq; Léon, Paul; *Ulysses* (by James Joyce, 1922); Vico, Giambattista

Joyce, Patrick Weston 26, 397, 563, 565, 571–73, 575, 581, 602, 612; *A Concise History of Ireland* (by Patrick Weston Joyce), 1903; previously appearing as *A Child's History of Ireland* (1897) 571, 572; *A Social History of Ancient Ireland* (by Patrick Weston Joyce, 1903) 571, 573, 581; *see also* "Aryan" theories of Irish origins; Celticism; "Europe-centered" theories of Irish origins; historiography and history; Royal Irish Academy

INDEX 735

Jubainville, Marie Henri d'Arbois de 599

Ka'ba 119, 270; *see also* Arabia; Islam; Mecca
Kabul 304, 310, 319, 320, 326, 329, 330, 333, 347; *see also* Afghanistan; Dost Mohammad Khan; Macnaghten, William Hay
"Kaimours": *see* Keyoumars
kalandars (/qalandars) 239; *see also* Mangan, James Clarence; *One Thousand and One Nights* (a.k.a., *Arabian Nights*)
Kalidasa (poet) 448, 449; *see also* Gupta Empire
Kamil, Mustafa 482, 483; *see also* "Egypt for Egyptians"; *The Egyptian Standard* (Cairo)
Kamran Shah Durrani 338; *see also* Herat
Kandahar (/Qandahar) 304, 326, 330, 334, 337, 546; *see also* Afghanistan; Dost Mohammad Khan
Kant, Immanuel 568
Kāqaz-e Akhbār (Tehran) 530
Karaman (Anatolia) 239–41, 265; Karamanid dynasty 239; *see also* Mangan, James Clarence
Karim Khan (Zand ruler) 332; *see also* Kharg Island; Zand dynasty (Iran, 1751–94)
Kars 325, 336; *see also* Crimean War (1854–56); Ottoman Empire
Karun River 391; *see also* Lynch, Henry Finnis Blosse
Kashani, Sayyid Jalal al-Din ("Mo'ayed al-Eslam") 551; *see also* Habl al-Matin (Calcutta)
Kashf al-ẓunūn 'an asāmī al-kutub wa-al-funūn (by Mustafa bin Abdullah (a.k.a., Hadji Khalfa "Katip Çelebi"), 17th century) 81
Kashmir 85, 111, 174; *see also* *Lalla Rookh. An Oriental Romance* (by Thomas Moore, 1817)
Kathleen ni Houlihan (by Isabella Augusta Gregory and William Butler Yeats, 1902) 137, 138, 418, 436, 437; *see also* Gregory, Isabella Augusta (née Persse); Mangan, James Clarence ("Kathaleen Ny-Houlahan" (1841)); Yeats, William Butler
Kavanagh, Arthur MacMurrough 390; *see also* Kavanagh, Thomas; Moore, Thomas; Wood, David
Kavanagh, Thomas 390; *see also* Kavanagh, Arthur MacMurrough; Wood, David
Kāveh (Berlin) 499; *see also* Casement, Roger; Jamalzadeh, Mohammad-Ali
Keane, John 319, 356n51; *see also* Anglo-Afghan War (1839–42)
Keane, Marcus 18, 120, 382–84, 404, 420, 446; *The Towers and Temples of Ancient Ireland; Their Origin and History Discussed from a New Point of View* (by Marcus Keane, 1867) 120,
382, 446; *see also* Cuthite; Cuthite-Iranians; Iran/Erin; "Iranian" theories of Irish origins; Irish antiquarianism; Mahābādiān; phallic worship; Pishdādiān; Round Towers (Ireland); Royal Irish Academy
Keating, Geoffrey (Céitinn, Seathrún) 15, 19, 21–23, 31, 35, 48–50, 52, 53, 55, 60, 64, 68, 72, 73, 80, 128, 139, 146, 198, 201, 316, 384, 566, 581, 615, 620; *see also* Anglo-Normans; Catholic Counter-Reformation; *The History of Ireland (Foras Feasa ar Éirinn)* (by Geoffrey Keating, 1634); Irish antiquarianism; O'Mahony, John; "Scythian" theories of Irish origins; "wild Irish" (civilizational accusation)
Keay, John Seymour 501n2, 501n4; *Spoiling the Egyptians: A Tale of Shame Told from the British Blue Books* (by John Seymour Keay, 1882) 501n4; *see also* British Committee of the Indian National Congress (1889); tobacco concession (Iran, 1890)
Keene, Henry George 398
Keightley, Thomas 444–45, 464n216; "Grecian legend of Theseus" 444; *see also* Conla (Conlaoch); Cuchulain (Cú Chulainn); Ferdowsi, Abul-Qassem; Rustam; *Shāhnāmeh*; Sohrab; Ulster Cycle
Kelly, Matthew 357n61
Keltic: *see* Celtic
Kelts: *see* Celts
Kennedy, Máire 301n195
Kenny, Henry Egan ("Sean-Ghall") 582, 627n38
Kenny, Louise 450; *see also* Anglo-Russian Agreement (1907); Aryanism; *Sinn Féin* (Dublin)
Kerman 194; *see also* Crom-Cruach (Crom Crúaich; pre-Christian Irish deity); *The History of Ireland*, vol.I (by Thomas Moore, 1835); *Lalla Rookh. An Oriental Romance* (by Thomas Moore, 1817); Zoroastrianism
Kerman Kelstach ("Cermand Cestach"): *see* Crom-Cruach (Crom Crúaich; pre-Christian Irish deity)
Kermani, Mirza Aqa Khan 137, 492; *Sālārnāmeh* (by Mirza Aqa Khan Kermani, 1895) 137; *see also* Aryana; Aryanism (racial theories)
Kerney, Michael 426, 427, 459n137; *see also* Fitzgerald, Edward (poet)
Kettle, Thomas Michael 475, 480, 482; *see also* "Egypt for Egyptians"; Irish nationalism; United Irish League; Young Ireland Branch of the United Irish League
Keyes, Marian 555
Keyoumars 95, 110, 157n115, 566, 623; *see also Bundahishn*; Mashya and Mashyana;

Noah; O'Brien, Henry; *Universal History of Mirkhond* (15th century); *Zend Avesta*; Zoroastrianism
Keysler, Johann Georg 193
Keyvan: *see* Saturn
Keyvan, Azar 85, 112, 133; *see also* Ardestani, Mir Zulfaqar; *Dabestān-e Mazāheb*; *Dasātir*; ishrāqiyyun; "neo-Zoroastrianism"
khan 45n42, 278–79, 289, 295n69; *see also* ceann
Kharg Island 305, 308, 332, 334, 336, 337, 343; *see also* Anglo-Iranian War (1856–57); France; Karim Khan (Zand ruler); Louis XIV (French king); Pyrault, Claude
Khayyam, Omar 239, 247, 426, 427, 429; *see also* Fitzgerald, Edward (poet); McCarthy, Justin Huntly; Nicolas, Jean Baptiste; Whinfield, Edward Henry
"Khizzilbash": *see* Qizilbash
Khorasan: *see* Khorassan
Khorassan 172–75, 182204n28, 241, 267, 614; *see also Lalla Rookh. An Oriental Romance* (by Thomas Moore, 1817)
Khujandi, Kamal al-Din 244; *see also* Mangan, James Clarence
Khushab 342; *see also* Anglo-Iranian War (1856–57)
Kiāniān dynasty 83, 119, 130, 131, 133, 136; *see also* mythology (Iranian mythology); *Shāhnāmeh*
Kiberd, Declan 414, 418, 573, 579, 607; *see also* "Europeanizing" Ireland; "not-England"
Kidd, Colin 2
Kildare 349, 386; *see also* Fitzgerald, Thomas (10th Earl of Kildare); *Merv Oasis: Travels and Adventures East of the Caspian During the Years 1879–80–81 ..., The* (by Edmond O'Donovan, 1882); Round Towers (Ireland)
"Kilgreany Man" 600
Kilkenny 245, 426, 518
Killeshandra rectory 108; *see also* Hales, William (Rev.)
Kilroy, James 291; *The Autobiography of James Clarence Mangan* (edited by James Kilroy, 1969) 291; *see also* Mangan, James Clarence
Kingdom of Ireland (under English rule) 178, 200, 349, 527, 535
Kinglake, Alexander William 427; *Eothen, Or, Traces of Travel Brought Home from the East* (by Alexander William Kinglake, 1844) 427
Kinsley, Charles 228
Kipling, Rudyard 521
Kirsch, Thomas G. 644; *Regimes of Ignorance ...* (by Roy Dilley and Thomas G. Kirsch, 2015) 644

Kirwan, Richard 60; *see also* Neptunism (geology)
"Kizzilbash": *see* Qizilbash
knowledge 3–4, 7, 13, 15–19, 22, 26, 27, 34, 37, 48–50, 62, 69, 71, 78, 80, 81, 115–17, 130, 131, 134, 140, 141, 149, 198, 200, 201, 214, 227, 257, 271, 278, 334, 394, 395, 400, 402, 407, 418, 430, 431, 435, 445, 514–16, 523, 529, 530, 532, 541, 565, 567, 602–5, 624, 625, 639, 648; circulation 3–4, 7, 13, 86, 134, 187, 190, 212, 532, 639, 642, 644–46, 648; production 18, 22, 26, 30, 33, 34, 36, 39, 56, 62, 80, 91, 130, 389, 611; reception 13, 26, 116, 135, 286, 602, 603
Korea 491, 553; *see also* Japan
Koselleck, Reinhart 276
Krappe, Alexander Haggerty 41; *Mythologie universelle* (1930) 41; *see also* Hedayat, Sadeq; Mohl, Jules (Julius)
Krishnamurti, Jiddu 434; "Order of the Star in the East" 434; *see also* Besant, Annie (née Wood); Maitreya, Lord; theosophy
Krishnavarma, Shyamji 490; *see also* India House (London)
Kristeva, Julia 126; *see also* "ambivalence"; "Intertextuality"
Kropotkin, Petr 478; *see also* anarchism
Kuhn, Thomas 413; *see also* "paradigm shift"
Kumarināṭu 12; Kumarikkaṇṭam 139; *see also* Lemuria; Pillai, Kandiah; Ramaswamy, Sumathi; Tamil people
Kurds 147, 387, 492; Kurdistan 147
"Kûzel-bash": *see* Qizilbash
"Kuzzil-bâsh": *see* Qizilbash
"Kuzzilbash": *see* Qizilbash

"labors of loss" 140–42; *see also* Bataille, Georges
Labouchere, Henry 501n2, 628n57; *see also* tobacco concession (Iran, 1890)
Labour Party (Irish Free State) 592
Labour Party (UK) 479, 549; *see also* Hardie, (James) Keir
Laing, Samuel 214, 215; *Journal of a Residence in Norway* (by Samuel Laing, 1836) 214
Lal, Vinay 128, 648
Lalla Rookh. An Oriental Romance (by Thomas Moore, 1817) 5, 25, 31, 32, 37, 39, 53, 84, 109–10, 167, 168, 171–89, 193, 194, 205n46, 206n64, 231, 235–37, 241, 261, 269, 270, 272, 275, 295n71, 295n75, 299n152, 322, 344, 348, 390, 411, 426, 427, 436, 520, 542, 554, 585, 613, 614, 638; Allah ("Alla") 178; Azim 172, 175–79, 183, 204n209, 205n46, 638; "Bendemeer's Stream" song 188; Fadladeen 174, 178, 187, 269, 638; Feramorz/Aliris 172, 174,

178, 204n20, 241, 269, 638; "The Fire-Worshippers" 5, 25, 168, 172–74, 179–83, 188, 189, 237, 270, 275, 295n71, 322, 344, 411, 614; Hafed 5, 180, 181, 205n46, 275, 295n71, 344, 614, 638; Al Hassan 180, 205n46; Hinda 172, 180, 181, 205n46, 295n71, 638; "The Light of the Haram" 173, 235; Mahadi 175; Mokanna 175–79, 204n28, 204n29, 207n74, 241, 295n75, 638; "Paradise and the Peri" 109, 173, 204n20, 295n75, 638; "The Veiled Prophet of Khorassan" 172–83, 188, 204n25, 204n28, 205n46, 241, 270, 614; Zelica 175–79, 183; *see also* Arab-Muslim invasion of Iran (7th century CE); Aurangzeb (Mughal emperor); Curran, Sarah; Emmet, Robert; fire worship"; FitzGerald, Edward (United Irishmen); Fraser, James Baillie; Iran/Erin (Irish nationalist allegory); Iranian students in England (early 19th century); Longman, Rees, Orme, Brown, and Green; Malcolm, John; Mangan, James Clarence ("Al Makeenah"); Moore, Thomas; Mughal dynasty; "al-Muqanna" (Hashim ibn Hakim); O'Neill, Owen Roe; O'Neill, Phelim; Ouseley, William; *The Poetical Works of Thomas Moore*, vol. VI (by Thomas Moore, 1841); Round Towers (Ireland); Sassanian dynasty (Iran, 224–650 CE); Zoroastrian, Zoroastrianism

Lamii Çelebi 259; *see also* Mangan, James Clarence

Lamington, Lord (Charles Wallace Alexander Napier Cochrane-Baillie) 477, 505n49; *see also* Anglo-Russian Agreement (1907); Persia Committee (London)

Land League 227, 393, 546; *see also* Bourke, Ulick Joseph; Davitt, Michael; Dillon, John; "Land War" (Ireland); O'Brien, William; peasantry (Ireland); Parnell, Charles Stewart; Redmond, William

Land Purchase Bills (Ireland) 551; *see also* Birrell, Augustine; "Land War" (Ireland)

"Land War" (Ireland) 313, 393, 546; *see also* Bourke, Ulick Joseph; Great Depression (1873–96); Land League; Land Purchase Bills (Ireland); peasantry (Ireland)

Langley, Geoffrey de 555n1; *see also* Crusades; Edward I, King; Ilkhanid Empire

language: *see* philology; linguistics

Lanigan, John 124, 196, 211, 277, 382; *see also* Round Towers (Ireland)

Lapps (i.e., Sámi people) 147

Larkin, James 510n121, 592; *see also* Comintern (Third / Communist International); Irish Citizen Army; Irish Worker League (1923–28)

Larminie, William 439, 440, 451; *West Irish Folk-Tales and Romances* (by William Larminie, 1893) 439; *see also* "Aryan" theories of Irish origins; Cuchulain (Cú Chulainn); Fenian Cycle; folklore; Ulster Cycle

Latin America 11, 315, 317; *see also* Central America

Lavergne, Philippe 40; *see also Finnegans Wake* (by James Joyce, 1939)

Lawrence, John Laird Mair 370; Viceroy of India 370

Layard, Austen Henry 306, 307, 339–41, 354n12, 453n25; *see also* Anglo-Iranian War (1856–57); Liberal Party (UK)

Leadbeater, Charles Webster 434; *see also* Theosophical Society; theosophy

League Against Imperialism (1927–37) 593; *see also Anti-Imperialist* (Dublin); Anti-Imperialist Vigilance Association; Comintern (Third / Communist International)

League of Nations 593, 595–97

Lebor Gabála Érenn (*The Book of the Taking of Ireland* / *The Book of Invasions*, 11th century) 47, 55, 201, 421, 565, 566581, 620; *see also* Fénius Farsaid (Fenius Farsa)

Leckie, Gould Francis 170; *see also Intercepted Letters; or, The Twopenny Post-bag* (by Thomas Moore, 1813)

Leclerc, Georges-Louis: *see* Buffon, Comte de

Ledwich, Edward 66, 77, 85, 88, 93, 94, 195; *The Antiquities of Ireland* (by Edward Ledwich, 1790) 66; "Asiatic" Christian proselytizers in Ireland 195; *see also* "Scandinavian" (Scandian) theories of Irish origins; "wild Irish" (civilizational accusation)

Lee, Jane 409–10; Newnham College, Cambridge 409

Leeds Mercury 305

Leerssen, Joep (Joseph Theodoor) 2, 23, 79, 105, 126, 159n186, 194, 208n87, 317, 626n30

legends: *see* mythology

Leinster 519, 617; *see also* FitzGerald, William Robert; MacMurrough, Aoife; MacMurrough, Dermot (Diarmaid [Diarmait] Mac Murchadha)

Lemuria 12, 139–42; *see also* Kumarinātu; Pillai, Kandiah; Ramaswamy, Sumathi; Tamil people

Lennon, Joseph 2, 18, 35, 44n36, 55, 153n55, 189, 243, 280, 451, 461n165, 522; *see also* orientalism

Lennox, Patrick Joseph 201; *see also The Glories of Ireland* (Joseph Dunn and Patrick Joseph Lennox, eds., 1914)

Léon, Paul 621; *see also* Joyce, James
Leopold II, King 610; *see also* Belgium; Congo (Belgian Congo)
Lettres persanes (by Montesquieu, Baron de, 1721) 169; *see also* "English Letters" genre (Iran); *Intercepted Letters; or, The Twopenny Post-bag* (by Thomas Moore, 1813); Lyttelton, George (*Letters from a Persian in England to His Friend at Ispahan* (by George Lyttelton, 1735)); *The Meddler* ("A Letter from a *Persian* in *Ireland* to His Friend in *Sheraz*"); Ozell, John (*The Persian Letters* (English translation of *Lettres persanes* by John Ozell, 1722)); "Persian Letters" genre; *Remarks of a Persian Traveller on the Principal Courts of Europe with a Dissertation upon that of England, the Nation in General, and the Prime Minister...* (anon., 1736)
Levant 53; *see also* Middle East; Near East; Orient
lexicon 7, 81, 82, 264, 586, 621, 639, *passim*; lexicography 82; *see also* etymology; linguistics; philology
Lhuyd, Edward 57, 65, 191; *see also* Celticism; Celts; Indo-European languages
Liberal Party (UK) 306, 468, 476, 546, 548, 549, 552; *see also* Gladstone, William Ewart; Grey, Edward; Layard, Austen Henry; Lloyd George, David; Lynch, Henry Finnis Blosse; Palmerston, Lord (Henry John Temple); Roebuck, John Arthur; Whig Party
Libya 254; Italian invasion (1911) 484; Tripoli 484
Liffey (river) 615, 618, 623, 624; *see also* Dublin
"The Light of the Haram": *see Lalla Rookh. An Oriental Romance* (by Thomas Moore, 1817)
Limerick 389, 450, 482, 506n72, 606
Limerick pogrom (Ireland, 1904) 450, 506n72, 606; *see also* anti-Jewish; Griffith, Arthur; Jewish people (Ireland's Jewish communities); Ryan, Frederick Michael (Fred)
"the limits of interpretation" 71, 94; *see also* Eco, Umberto
Lingam 95, 121; *see also* Mahābādiān; O'Brien, Henry; phallic worship; Tuatha de Dananns
Lingham: *see* Lingam
linguistics 2, 8, 13, 14, 39, 40, 52, 57, 58, 65, 68, 72, 73, 76, 81, 84, 86, 116, 119, 121, 125, 135, 146, 147, 196, 197, 235, 246, 251, 283, 284, 286, 289, 383, 393–95, 415, 420, 446, 448, 449, 514, 519, 568, 572, 574, 607, 609, 611, 620, 623, 643, 650; *see also* etymology; lexicon; philology
Linnaeus, Carl 405

Lisbon Geographical Society 537; *see also* cartography; geography
literary "modernism" 432, 580, 609, 611, *passim*; *see also* Joyce, James; Mangan, James Clarence; "modernity"/"modernities"; Yeats, William Butler
Literary Society of Bombay 113; *see also* Erskine, William; *Transactions of the Literary Society of Bombay*
Liverpool 189, 329, 524, 539
Liverpool University 488
Livy (Titus Livius) 83
Lloyd, David 231, 237–38, 255, 257, 277, 282; "irony," "parody," and "refraction" in the poetry of James Clarence Mangan 238, 255, 278; *see also* Mangan, James Clarence
Lloyd George, David 549, 552, 562n109; *see also* Liberal Party (UK); Wales (Welsh Home Rule)
Login, John Spencer 341; *see also* Anglo-Afghan War (1839–42)
London *passim*
Londonderry: *see* Derry
Longman, Rees, Orme, Brown, and Green 194; "Cabinet Cyclopaedia" series 194; Messrs. Longman 173, 203n18; Thomas Longman 180; *see also The History of Ireland*, vol.I (by Thomas Moore, 1835); *The History of Ireland*, vol.II (by Thomas Moore, 1837); *The History of Ireland*, vol.IV (by Thomas Moore, 1846); *Lalla Rookh. An Oriental Romance* (by Thomas Moore, 1817)
lore: *see* folklore
Louis XIV (French king) 337; *see also* France; Kharg Island
Lover, Samuel 411, 521
Lucknow 517
Lundy, John Patterson 431–32; *Monumental Christianity, or the Art and Symbolism of the Primitive Church* (by John Patterson Lundy, 1876) 432
Luristan 147
Lyell, Charles 18; *Principles of Geology* (1830) 18; *see also* Plutonism (geology); uniformitarian theory (geology);
Lynch, Henry Blosse 342, 391; Order of the Lion and the Sun 391; *see also* Anglo-Iranian War (1856–57); English East India Company
Lynch, Henry Finnis Blosse 391, 476–77; *see also* Anglo-Russian Agreement (1907); Bakhtiari; Iranian Constitutional Revolution (1906–11); Karun River; Liberal Party (UK); Lynch, Thomas Kerr; Messrs. Lynch Brothers Company; Persia Committee (London); Yorkshire (Ripon)

INDEX 739

Lynch, Stephen 391; *see also* Euphrates and Tigris Steam Navigation Company
Lynch, Thomas Kerr 342, 366, 391; Iranian Consul-General in London 342, 366, 391; Order of the Lion and the Sun 391; *see also* Euphrates and Tigris Steam Navigation Company; Iranian famine (1870–72); Lynch, Henry Finnis Blosse; Messrs. Lynch Brothers Company
Lynchehaun, James 551, 562n119
Lynd, Robert Wilson 350, 479; *If the Germans Conquered England, and Other Essays* (by Robert Wilson Lynd, 1917) 350; *see also* Dryhurst, Sylvia; Gaelic League; *Nationalities and Subject Races* (ed. by Dryhurst, Nora ("Nannie") Florence, 1911); Nationalities and Subject Races conferences (London, 1910, 1911, 1914); Sinn Féin
Lyndhurst, Lord (John Singleton Copley) 416, 458n120
Lyotard, Jean-François 650; "grand narrative" ("metanarrative") 650
Lyttelton, George 169, 202n7; *Letters from a Persian in England to His Friend at Ispahan* (by George Lyttelton, 1735) 169; *see also Lettres persanes* (by Montesquieu, Baron de, 1721)
Lytton, Lord (Robert Bulwer-Lytton) 370; Viceroy of India 370

Mac Con Mara, Donnchadh Rua (Red Donough McNamara) 291, 424
mac Cumhaill, Fionn (a.k.a., Finn MacCool) 83, 185, 613; *see also* Esfandiyar; Fenian Cycle; mythology (Irish heroic cycles); Vallancey, Charles
Macan, Turner 444
MacBride, John 351, 472, 601; *see also* Gonne, Maud (Maud Gonne MacBride); Irish Transvaal Brigade (a.k.a., Irish Commandos/MacBride's Brigade)
MacCall, Seamus 582, 600, 601; *And So Began the Irish Nation* (by Seamus MacCall, 1931) 582, 600
MacCarthy, Denis Florence 5, 24, 172, 182, 261, 269–72, 274, 299n152, 418, 585, 620, 647; "The Clan of Mac Caura" 182, 269, 270, 299n152; *see also* Arab-Muslim invasion of Iran (7th century CE); Iran/Erin (Irish nationalist allegory); Islam; Royal Irish Academy; Young Ireland; Zoroastrianism
MacDermott (Mac Diarmada), Seán 475; *see also* Irish Republican Brotherhood
MacDonagh, Thomas Stanislaus 579
Macedonia 4, 49, 52, 446; *see also* Alexander the Great; "Migdonia"; Seleucid Empire

Macfarlane, Charles 121–22; *see also The Pictorial History of England: Being a History of the People, as Well as a History of the Kingdom*, vol.I (by George Lillie Craik and Charles Macfarlane, 1838)
Mackenzie, George 70; *see also* O'Flaherty, Roderic
Mackintosh, James 194; *The History of England* (by James Mackintosh, 1830–40) 194; *see also* Longman, Rees, Orme, Brown, and Green
MacManus, Seumas 16, 563, 599, 601, 605, 625n1; *The Story of the Irish Race* (by Seumas MacManus, 1921) 16, 563, 599, 605
Mac Mathúna, Séamus 566
MacMurrough, Aoife 617; *see also* de Clare, Richard (Strongbow); Leinster
MacMurrough, Dermot (Diarmaid [Diarmait] Mac Murchadha) 617; *see also* Leinster
Macnaghten, William Hay 320; *see also* English East India Company; Kabul
MacNeill, Eoin (John) 26, 149, 222, 393, 417, 423, 451, 563, 564, 573–77, 579–81, 588, 598–601, 612, 613, 624; chief of staff of the Irish Volunteers 573; minister for education of the Irish Free State 451, 573, 580, 588; *Phases of Irish History* (by Eoin MacNeill, 1919) 573, 575; *see also* "Aryan" theories of Irish origins; Celticism; Easter Rising; "Europe-centered" theories of Irish origins; Gaelic League; historiography and history
MacNeill, John G. S. 477; *see also* Anglo-Russian Agreement (1907); Irish Parliamentary Party
MacNeill, Laoghaire (Lóegaire mac Néill) 197
Macpherson, James 65–66, 69, 83, 143, 441, 446, 464n209; *see also* Celticism; Fenian Cycle; *Fragments of Ancient Poetry, Collected in the Highlands of Scotland* (by James Macpherson, 1760); Ossian
MacSweeny, Connor 104; *see also* Moore, Thomas; O'Brien, Henry
MacSweeney, Patrick 197–99; *A Group of Nation Builders: O'Donovan-O'Curry-Petrie* (by Patrick MacSweeney, 1913) 199; *see also* O'Curry, Eugene; O'Donovan, John; Petrie, George; "Petrie & Co."
MacSwiney, Terence 499; *see also* hunger strike (Irish republican prisoners)
Madai 73; *see also* Japheth; Mosaic theory
Madden, Richard Robert 473; *see also* Hibernian Anti-Slavery Society
Magee, William Kirkpatrick ("John Eglinton") 432–33, 483, 609, 611; *see*

also Dana: *An Irish Magazine of Independent Thought* (Dublin); theosophy
magh: *see* magi
magi 13, 72, 96, 110–11, 191–93, 199, 219, 407, 424–25, 430, 431, 435, 565; magian 38, 219, 430; *see also* "fire worship"; Hedayat, Sadeq; Zoroastrianism
magic 96, 140, 226, 424–25, 428, 429, 431, 432, 434, 435, 440; *see also* Yeats, William Butler
Magog 49, 61, 69, 72, 74; *see also* The Bible; Fénius Farsaid (Fenius Farsa); The Hebrew Bible ("Old Testament"); Japheth; Mosaic theory
Mahābād: *see* Mahābādiān
Mahābādiān 14, 19, 86, 92, 94–96, 108–10, 112, 114–20, 132, 133, 159n199, 382, 642; *see also* Dabestān-e Mazāheb; *Dabistan, or the School of Manners* (by David Shea and Anthony Troyer, 1843); Dasātir; "Iranian" theories of Irish origins; Jones, William; Malcolm, John; mythology (Iranian mythology); O'Brien, Henry; Pishdādiān; Tuatha de Dananns
Mahabharata 449
Mahadeva 120
Mahallati, Mirza Mohammad Ali (later known as "Haj Sayyah") 524
Mahdi: *see* "Mahdist" uprising
Mahdi Khan ("Moshir al-Molk") 505n49
"Mahdist" uprising 384, 452n7, 627n46; *see also* O'Donovan, Edmond; Sudan
Mahomet, Deen ("Dean") 517
"Mahommedan": *see* Islam
Mahony, Francis Sylvester (alias "Father Prout") 104; *see also* Moore, Thomas; O'Brien, Henry
Mainz-Kastel 288; Hesse-Darmstadt 288; *see also* Mangan, James Clarence; Napoleonic Wars
Maitreya, Lord 434; *see also* Krishnamurti, Jiddu
majles (Iranian national assembly) 473, 474, 476, 477, 484, 485, 487, 507n73; *see also* Iranian Constitutional Revolution (1906–11)
Majles (Tehran) 550
Malcolm, John 16–19, 33, 34, 110, 111, 113–15, 122, 124, 130, 131, 159n199, 160n207, 183–84, 206n56, 243, 266, 267, 293n37, 329, 388, 444, 516, 528; Anglo-Iranian treaties (1801) 33; envoy of British India to Iran (1799–1801, 1808, 1810) 33, 34, 114; *The History of Persia from the Most Early Period to the Present Time ...* (by John Malcolm, 1815) 16, 19, 110, 113–15, 124, 131, 183, 184, 266, 267, 293n37, 329; mostly-Irish 17th Dragoons of the English East India Company 388; *Sketches of Persia* (by John Malcolm, 1827) 243, 444; *see also* Christie, Charles; Dabestān-e Mazāheb; Dasātir; English East India Company; Hayrat-Irani, Ismail; Kiāniān; *Lalla Rookh. An Oriental Romance* (by Thomas Moore, 1817); Mahābādiān; orientalism; Pishdādiān; *The Poetical Works of Thomas Moore*, vol. VI (by Thomas Moore, 1841); Pottinger, Henry; Wellesley, Richard Colley (Lord Mornington; Marquess Wellesley)
Malkum Khan 469; *see also* tobacco concession (Iran, 1890)
Maloney, William Joseph ["Moloney" later in life] 482–84, 493, 505n54, 506n62, 507n73, 548, 640; *see also* Anglo-Russian Agreement (1907); "Egypt for Egyptians"; *The Egyptian Standard* (Cairo); internationalism; Iranian Constitutional Revolution (1906–11); Irish nationalism; Reuters; Young Turk Revolution (1908)
Manchester 379n63, 442
Manchester Guardian 469, 482, 483, 495, 506n62; *see also* Moore, William Arthur
Mandean 119; *see also* Ginza Rabbā (*Sidrā Rabbā*)
Mangan, James Clarence 1, 5, 7, 10, 24, 32, 33, 39, 81, 127, 172, 175, 182, 202n6, 204n28, 206n53, 219, 231–62, 264–74, 276–91, 296n89, 296n93, 297n100, 301n192, 301n195, 301n199, 318, 322, 331, 345, 347, 348, 362, 389, 399, 424, 436–37, 462n182, 515, 521, 558n30, 585, 586, 609, 611–12, 614, 615, 617, 621, 631n123, 639, 640, 647; "Anthologia Germanica" 279, 297n95; "Anthologia Hibernica" 282, 301n195, 462n182; anti-England poems 32, 586, *passim*; "the antithesis of plagiarism" 233; "authenticity" 24, 231, 234, 237–38, 242, 245, 247–50, 253, 256–58, 265, 267, 274, 284; "An Extraordinary Adventure in the Shades" 254, 255, 288; "Herr Hoppandgoön Von Baugtrauter" 240, 241, 253; "Herr Poppandgoöff Von Tutschemupp" 240, 241, 296n93; "Iranian" theories of Irish origins 231, 238, 254, 276–85, *passim*; irrecoverability of the past 248–49, *passim*; "Irish National Hymn" 232, 252, 260–61, 278, 280–82, 289; "Kathaleen Ny-Houlahan" (1841) 437; "Literæ Orientales" series 237, 239, 241–46, 249, 250, 252, 254, 256, 259, 260, 278, 279, 285, 558n30; "Al Makeenah" 175, 204n28, 241; "oriental" poems (pseudo-translations) 32, 231, 234, 238, 248, 254, 262, 233, 235, 236, 237, 242,

250, 254, 255, 262, 267, 270, 287, 436, *passim*; poetry of "hate" 263–65, 274; "A Polyglott Anthology" 240, 241, 253, 260, 279, 288; refractive history (*see also*, Lloyd, David) 255–56; "Siberia" 259–61, 264, 288, 299n154, 362; "Sketches of Modern Irish Writers" 277, 279, 285; "To the Ingleezee Khafir, Calling Himself Djuan Bool Djenkinzun" 5, 33, 236, 237, 241, 260–65, 267, 268, 270, 271, 273, 276, 278, 280, 282, 286, 299n154, 318, 322, 345, 515, 586, 617, 639; "A Vision of Connaught in the Thirteenth Century" 278, 288; *see also* Balzac, Honoré de; *Bibliothèque orientale* (by Barthélemy d'Herbelot, 1697); cosmopolitan (Irish polyglot cosmopolitan texts); *Dublin University Magazine*; the Enlightenment ("European" Enlightenment); *Finnegans Wake* (by James Joyce, 1939); Great Famine (Ireland, 1845–51); Hafez, Shams al-Din Mohammad; Hammer-Purgstall, Joseph Freiherr von; Heine, Heinrich; history (truncated); Iran/Erin (Irish nationalist allegory); Irish nationalism; "Irishness"; Islam; Jenkinson, Anthony; Jones, William; *Lalla Rookh. An Oriental Romance* (by Thomas Moore, 1817); "Manganesque"; Maturin, Charles Robert; "modernity"/"modernities"; Moore, Thomas; *The Nation* (Dublin); O'Donovan, John; *One Thousand and One Nights* (a.k.a., *Arabian Nights*); Ordnance Survey of Ireland; orientalism; Ouseley, William; Petrie, George; Romanticism; Sa'di; Safavid dynasty (Iran, 1501–1722/36); self-plagiarism; *The United Irishman* (Dublin, 1848); Vallancey, Charles; Wilde, Jane Francesca Agnes (née Elgee); Young Ireland

"Manganesque" 262, 264, 295n67, 611; *see also* Guiney, Louise Imogen; O'Donoghue, David James; Mangan, James Clarence

Mansion House (the City of London) 364–67, 369, 370, 372; *see also* Iranian famine (1870–72)

Mansion House (Dublin) 371, 372; *see also* Chicago (the Great Chicago Fire (1871)); Iranian famine (1870–72)

Mansoor, Menahem 2; *see also* orientalism

map; mapping: *see* cartography

Marathon, Battle of (490 BCE) 221–22, 225, 228, 582; *see also* Achaemenid dynasty (Persian Empire, c.550–330 BCE); Athens; Byron, Lord (George Gordon Byron); Greece; Sparta

Mariti, Giovanni 171; *see also Intercepted Letters; or, The Twopenny Post-bag* (by Thomas Moore, 1813); *Lalla Rookh. An Oriental Romance* (by Thomas Moore, 1817)

Martyn, Edward 432, 474, 580; *see also* Irish Literary Theatre; Sinn Féin

Marx, Karl 346, 568, 641; on the Anglo-Iranian War (1856–57) 346

Mashhad 386; *see also* Gowharshad mosque; Imam Reza shrine (Mashhad)

Mashya and Mashyana 157n155, 623; *see also* Joyce, James; Keyoumars

Masjed-e Shah (mosque; Tehran) 343

Mathews, Andrew 644

Mattar, Sinéad Garrigan 397

Maturin, Charles Robert 279, 285; *Melmoth the Wanderer* (by Charles Robert Maturin, 1820) 279; *see also* Balzac, Honoré de

Maynooth 198, 535

Mayo (County) 391, 551; *see also* Lynch, Henry Finnis Blosse

Mazandaran Province (Iran) 191, 207–8n81; *see also* pillar towers; Round Towers (Ireland)

Mazzini, Giuseppe 350

McAteer, Michael 442

McCarthy, Justin 427

McCarthy, Justin Huntly 427, 436; *Ghazels from the Divan of Hafiz* (by Justin Huntly McCarthy, 1893) 427, 436; *The Thousand and One Days: Persian Tales* (by Justin Huntly McCarthy, 1892) 427; *see also* Hafez, Shams al-Din Mohammad; Irish Parliamentary Party; Khayyam, Omar; Pétis de La Croix, François

McClenahan, John 318; *see also The Citizen* (New York)

McDonnell, Randal 51; *see also* O'Flaherty, Roderic

McGarrity, Joseph 498; *see also* Clan na Gael (United States)

McGee, Thomas D'Arcy 363, 368; *A History of the Irish Settlers in North America* (by Thomas D'Arcy McGee, 1851) 368; *New Era* (Montreal) 363; *see also* Great Famine (Ireland, 1845–51); O'Connellite; Young Ireland

McGlashan, James 280; *see also Dublin University Magazine*; Mangan, James Clarence

McGuire, James Kennedy 496–97, 529, 581, 582; "Irandah-al-Kaberah" ("Ireland the Great") 529; *The King, the Kaiser and Irish Freedom* (by James Kennedy McGuire, 1915) 496; *What Could Germany Do for Ireland?* (by James Kennedy McGuire, 1916) 497, 529, 581; *see also* al-Idrisi, Abu Abdullah Muhammad ("irlandah al-kabirah" ("Ireland the Great"))

McKay, Claude 611; *Banjo: A Story Without a Plot* (by Claude McKay, 1929) 611
McQuillan, John (Jack) 500, 594; *see also* Iranian oil nationalization (1951)
Meagher, Thomas Francis 281, 315; *see also The Irish News* (New York); Nicaragua; Young Ireland; Young Ireland uprising (1848)
Meath 147, 245, 412
Mecca 119, 270, 524; *see also* Arabia; Islam; Ka'ba
The Meddler 169; "A Letter from a *Persian* in *Ireland* to His Friend in *Sheraz*" 169; *see also Lettres persanes* (by Montesquieu, Baron de, 1721); Wilson, Peter
Medes 57, 69, 72, 74, 78, 119, 147, 616; Media 73, 74, 277; Median 125, 565
medieval: *see* "Middle Ages"
Mediterranean Sea 9, 12, 54, 69, 72, 77, 122, 402, 404, 409, 420, 422, 424, 425
"Meer Djafrit": *see* Mangan, James Clarence ("To the Ingleezee Khafir, Calling Himself Djuan Bool Djenkinzun")
Megill, Allan 625, 633n152; "affirmative historiography" 625; *see also* historiography and history
Mehrban brothers of Bombay 377n15; *see also* Iranian famine (1870–72); Parsi
Meiji Restoration 491; *see also* Japan
Mela (Pomponius Mela) 80
Memoirs of Captain Rock, The Celebrated Irish Chieftain ... (by Thomas Moore, 1824) 173, 177; *see also* Moore, Thomas; O'Neill, Phelim
memory 6, 8, 10, 25, 33, 87, 100, 128–29, 142, 145, 179, 181, 212–13, 219, 267, 273–75, 287, 290, 291, 300n176, 321, 322, 328, 361, 362, 367, 400, 407, 432, 439, 492, 496, 571, 574, 587, 591, 598, 602–4, 608, 613, 618, 624, 625, 643; "acquired" memory 219, 603, 604, 625; "collective" memory 6, 361, 362, 400, 587, 602, 613, 624, 625; "counter-memory" 604; "cultural" memory 8, 25, 598, 602, 603; "false" memory 604; "folk" memory 100, 400; "historical" memory 213, 219, 274, 287, 321, 361, 603; "knowledge-memory" 603; "labor" of memory 275; "literary" memory 290, 291; "melancholy memory of suffering and death" 361; "national memory" 33, 142, 213, 274, 275, 300n176, 321, 367, 591, 618, 624, 643; "political" memory 6, 213, 275, 492, *passim*; recollection, recovery, resuscitation, and retrieval 362, 571, 598, 624; "remembering" 189, 289, 369, 587, 598, 603–4, 616, 618; "re-orientation" of memory 625; "repressed" memory 8, 608; "social" memory 275, 367, 603; "trauma" and memory 258, 274, 284, 367, 374, 417, 598, 602; *see also* Assmann, Aleida; Assmann, Jan; Fentress, James; forgetting (/amnesia); Foucault, Michel; Halbwachs, Maurice; "mnemonic communities"; Nora, Pierre ("Tyranny of Memory"); Ricoeur, Paul; "sites of memory"; Wickham, Chris
Menon, Dilip 141; "abbreviated time" 141
"mentalities" 598, 636; *see also* Annales School
Menu Satyavrata: *see* Satyavrata (Vaivasvata Manu)
Menu-Swayambhuva: *see* Svayambhuva Manu
Mer'āt al-Boldān-e Nāsseri (by "E'temad al-Saltaneh," 1877–80): *see* "E'temad al-Saltaneh" (Mohammad Hassan Khan)
"mere Irish" 24, 25, 68, 90, 137, 148, 180, 182, 215, 224, 230, 240, 250, 253, 254, 264, 287, 317, 414, 415, 416, 491, 579, 644, *passim*; *see also* Gaels; "Irishness"; "wild Irish" (civilizational accusation)
Merv Oasis: Travels and Adventures East of the Caspian During the Years 1879–80–81 ..., The (by Edmond O'Donovan, 1882) 385, 386; *see also* Gowharshad mosque; Imam Reza shrine (Mashhad); Kildare; "Nadir Tepé" (Nader tapeh); O'Donovan, Edmond; Round Towers (Ireland); Turkmen
Mesolithic period 600
"messianic time": *see* Benjamin, Walter
Messrs. Lynch Brothers Company 391, 476; *see also* Lynch, Henry Finnis Blosse; Lynch, Thomas Kerr
Messrs. Rothschild & Sons 376n11; *see also* Iranian famine (1870–72)
Methodists 365
Mexican-American War (1846–48) 473; *see also* San Patricios (Saint Patrick's Battalion)
Mexican Revolution (1910–11) 474
Mexico 390, 473, 474; *see also* Santa Fe Expedition; Republic of Texas
Meyer, Kuno 150n3, 441–43, 446, 447, 463n204, 498, 510n116; *The Voyage of Bran Son of Febal to the Land of the Living ...* (ed. by Kuno Meyer, 1895) 447; *see also* Conla (Conlaoch); Cuchulain (Cú Chulainn); *Ériu* (Dublin); Ferdowsi, Abul-Qassem; Rustam; School of Irish Learning (Dublin); *Shāhnāmeh*; Sohrab; Ulster Cycle
"Middle Ages" 12, 14, 15, 19, 20, 35, 42n5, 47, 48, 53, 59, 60, 65, 77, 79, 82, 100, 125, 126, 131, 151n22, 198–201, 215, 226, 417, 421, 440, 529, 536, 559n53, 564–66, 573, 581, 600, 607, 608, 620, 621, 637, 644, 651; Irish monks and monastic scholars 15, 46,

60, 193, 195, 200, 276, 277, 341, 388, 536, 564, 565, 618
Middle East 3, 12, 129; *see also* Levant; Near East; Orient
"Migdonia" 49, 72; *see also* Greece; Macedonia; Partholan (Partholón)
Míl Espáine: *see* Milesius (Miledh/Míl Espáine)
Miledh: *see* Milesius (Miledh/Míl Espáine)
Milesians 14, 21, 47–49, 51, 53, 56, 64, 69, 71, 72, 75, 79, 85–87, 89, 91, 92, 94–97, 100, 102, 107, 141, 147, 190, 191, 195, 197, 199, 201, 208n87, 214, 215, 218, 226–28, 277, 283, 312, 383, 397, 403–8, 413, 422, 424, 425, 446, 572, 599, 613, 617; *see also* Fénius Farsaid (Fenius Farsa); Gaels; Iberian Peninsula; "Iranian" theories of Irish origins; Irish antiquarianism; Milesius (Miledh/Míl Espáine); O'Brien, Henry; "oriental" theories of Irish origins; Pishdādiān; Scytho-Iberiaus; Spain; Vallancey, Charles
Milesius (Miledh/Míl Espáine) 48, 49, 72, 79, 226, 269, 423, 599; *see also* Fénius Farsaid (Fenius Farsa); Heber; Heremon (Érimón); Iberian Peninsula; Irish antiquarianism; Milesians; Spain
Mill, James 160n207, 183; *The History of British India* (by James Mill, 1817–26) 183
Milligan, Alice 138, 201; *Hero Lays* 138; *see also The Glories of Ireland* (Joseph Dunn and Patrick Joseph Lennox, eds., 1914)
Mir Aulad Ali 432; *see also* Hermetic Society (Dublin); Society for the Preservation of Irish Language
Mir Muhammed Husain (Isfahani) 111; *see also Dasātir*; Jones, William
Mirkhond (a.k.a. "Mirkhound"; Muḥammad ibn Khāvandshāh Mīr Khvānd) 62, 74, 81, 108, 113, 115, 118, 119, 130, 132–34, 566; *see also Universal History* of Mirkhond (15th century)
Mitchel, John 212, 217, 247, 254, 260, 262, 280, 281, 286, 301n192, 301n199, 315, 318, 368, 373, 414, 455n57, 458n114, 473, 582, 584, 647; *The Last Conquest of Ireland (Perhaps)* (by John Mitchel, 1861) 368, 458n114; *Poems by James Clarence Mangan* (ed. by John Mitchel, 1859) 290, 297n102, 301n192; *see also The Citizen* (New York); Fenian Brotherhood; Great Famine (Ireland, 1845–51); Mangan, James Clarence; *The Nation* (Dublin); slavery; *Southern Citizen* (Knoxville, Tennessee); *The United Irishman* (Dublin, 1848); Young Ireland; Young Ireland uprising (1848)

Mivart, St. George Jackson 403
"mnemonic communities" 603; *see also* memory; Zerubavel, Eviatar
"modernity"/"modernities" 35, 39, 127, 132, 140, 141, 232, 254, 256, 257, 428, 430–32, 450–51, 470, 483, 555, 579, 580, 589, 594, 603, 609, 611, 640, 645; anticolonial "modernities" 141, 431, 450–51; counter-discourses of modernity 127, 431, 450–51, 580; imperial "modernities" 140–41, 428, 430, 451; *see also* "invention of tradition"; literary "modernism"; nationalism; "tradition"
Modi, Jivanji Jamshedji 41–42, 46n48, 442–43, 446, 447, 643; "The Irish Story of Cucullin and Conloch and the Persian Story of Rustam and Sohrâb" (by Jivanji Jamshedji Modi, 1892; 1905) 41–42, 442, 443; *see also* "Aryan" theories of Irish origins; Brooke, Charlotte; Conla (Conlaoch); Cuchulain (Cú Chulainn); Ferdowsi, Abul-Qassem; Iran-Erin; Mohl, Jules (Julius); Rustam; *Shāhnāmeh*; Sohrab; Ulster Cycle
Mohammad-Ali ("Mo'in al-Saltaneh") 524
Mohammad-Ali Shah 474, 476, 479, 482, 485; *see also* Iranian Constitutional Revolution (1906–11); Qajar dynasty (Iran, 1796–1925)
Mohammad Ebrahim (Mirza) 131; *see also* Haileybury College (Hertfordshire, England); Herodotus (*The Histories*); English East India Company
Mohammad Khan (Sayyid Mohammad Khan) 304, 330, 338; *see also* Anglo-Iranian War (1856–57); Herat
Mohammad Shah 338, 391; *see also* Qajar dynasty (Iran, 1796–1925)
Mohammad Reza Shah 641; *see also* Pahlavi dynasty (Iran, 1925–79)
Mohammad Yusuf 304, 331–32; *see also* Anglo-Iranian War (1856–57); Herat; Pashtun (Pathan) Sadozai tribe
Mohammareh (Khorramshahr) 342; *see also* Anglo-Iranian War (1856–57)
Mohassan: *see Intercepted Letters; or, The Twopenny Post-bag* (by Thomas Moore, 1813)
Mohl, Jules (Julius) 41, 42, 442, 447; *see also* Barbier de Meynard, Charles Adrien Casimir; Brooke, Charlotte; Conla (Conlaoch); Cuchulain (Cú Chulainn); Ferdowsi, Abul-Qassem; Modi, Jivanji Jamshedji, Rustam; *Shāhnāmeh*; Sohrab; Ulster Cycle
Mohsen Khan ("Mo'in al-Molk", later "Amin al-Molk") 365, 377n20; *see also* Iranian famine (1870–72)

"Mo'in al-Saltaneh": *see* Mohammad-Ali ("Mo'in al-Saltaneh")
Moira, Lord (Francis Rawdon-Hastings; Marquess of Hastings) 168, 584; *see also* Moore, Thomas
Molesworth, William 354n13
Mongol 4, 131, 132, 138, 162n235, 244, 272, 279, 296n92, 388, 420, 439, 452n15, 529, 555n1, 562n104; *see also* Ilkhanid Empire; Yuan dynasty
monogenesis 61, 146, 395, 401–3, 411
Montefiore, Moses Haim 364; *see also* Iranian famine (1870–72)
Montesquieu, Baron de (Charles Louis de Secondat): *see Lettres persanes* (by Montesquieu, Baron de, 1721)
Moonan, George Aloysius 26, 563, 568, 602; *A Short History of the Irish People from the Earliest Times to 1920* (by Mary Hayden and George Aloysius Moonan, 1922) 602; *see also* "Aryan" theories of Irish origins; Celticism; "Europe-centered" theories of Irish origins; Hayden, Mary Teresa; historiography and history
Moore, Edward 521; "The Gamester"(1753) 521; *see also* Crow Street Theatre (a.k.a., Theatre Royal, Dublin)
Moore, George Augustus 389, 432, 435, 631n114; "Diarmuid and Grania" (by William Butler Yeats and George Augustus Moore, 1901) 435, 631n114; *'Hail and Farewell!'* (by George Augustus Moore, 1911) 432; *see also* Irish Literary Revival; Irish Literary Theatre; Moore, George Henry
Moore, George Henry 389, 540; *see also* Catholic Defence Association (1851); Independent Irish Party; "Irish Brigade" (in the British House of Commons); Moore, George Augustus
Moore, Thomas 1, 5, 7, 25, 31, 32, 35, 37, 39, 53, 54, 81, 84, 89, 90, 102–4, 107, 109, 124, 126, 127, 141, 142, 167–75, 177–99, 201, 202n1, 203n18, 203n19, 204n20, 204n29, 205n46, 206n53, 206n56, 206n67, 207n74, 207n81, 208n87, 211, 214, 231–38, 241, 243, 259–61, 264, 265, 269–72, 274, 275, 277, 280, 291, 295n69, 295n71, 299n152, 303, 318, 322, 331, 344, 347, 348, 390, 399, 404, 409, 411, 418, 424, 426, 427, 429, 436, 520, 521, 534, 535, 542, 544, 554–55, 558n30, 582, 584, 585, 606, 612–15, 617, 620, 625, 638–40, 642, 647; Catholic rights 5, 7, 35, 167, 169, 172, 178, 182, 231, 236, 269, 270, *passim*; "Fudge Family" 173; Iran/Erin (Irish nationalist allegory) 5, 7, 35, 37, 127, 174, 180–82, 187, 236, 237, 241, 259, 261, 264, 280, 331, 418, 542, 606, 620, 639; *Irish Melodies* 168, 180, 189, 206n51, 295n71, 613, 614; "Let Erin Remember the Days of Old" (1808) 189; Phoenician-Iranian theories of ancient Ireland's "Golden Age" 39, 54, 142, 174, 189, 192, 612, 614, 617, 620, 642, *passim*; *see also* Barry, Michael Joseph; *Bibliothèque orientale* (by Barthélemy d'Herbelot, 1697)); Byron, Lord (George Gordon Byron); Canning, Stratford (Viscount Stratford de Redcliffe); Catholic Emancipation; D'Alton (Dalton), John; Davis, Thomas Osborne; Dyke, Elizabeth ("Bessy"); *The Ecclesiastical Architecture of Ireland, Anterior to the Anglo-Norman Invasion* (by George Petrie, 1845); Emmet, Robert; the Enlightenment ("European" Enlightenment rationalism); *Finnegans Wake* (by James Joyce, 1939); "fire worship"; Hellenophilia; Herbelot [de Molainville], Barthélemy d'; *The History of Ireland*, vol.I (by Thomas Moore, 1835); *The History of Ireland*, vol.IV (by Thomas Moore, 1846); *Intercepted Letters; or, The Twopenny Post-bag* (by Thomas Moore, 1813); Iranian students in England (early 19th century); "Iranian" theories of Irish origins; Islam; Kavanagh, Arthur MacMurrough; *Lalla Rookh. An Oriental Romance* (by Thomas Moore, 1817); MacSweeny, Connor; Mahony, Francis Sylvester (alias "Father Prout"); *Memoirs of Captain Rock, The Celebrated Irish Chieftain …* (by Thomas Moore, 1824); Moira, Lord; Moors ("Moorish"); Morier, James Justinian; O'Brien, Henry; O'Neill, Phelim; "Oriental Renaissance"; "oriental" theories of Irish origins; "oriental-style" literature; orientalism; "Phoenician" theories of Irish origins; *The Poetical Works of Thomas Moore*, vol. VI (by Thomas Moore, 1841); Repeal movement; Romanticism; Round Towers (Ireland); Royal Irish Academy; Russell, John; United Irishmen; United Irishmen uprising (1798); United Irishmen uprising (1803); Wellesley, Richard Colley (Lord Mornington; Marquess Wellesley); Zoroastrianism
Moore, William Arthur 482; *The Orient Express* (by William Arthur Moore, 1914) 482; *see also Daily Chronicle* (London); *Daily News* (London); Iranian Constitutional Revolution (1906–11); *Manchester Guardian*; Persia Committee (London)
Moors 147, 286; "Moorish" 236, 614; *see also* Moore, Thomas

Morgan, William Pritchard 501n2; *see also* tobacco concession (Iran, 1890)
Morganwg, Iolo (Edward Williams) 65
Morier, James Justinian 186, 206n67, 444, 520–22, 557n20; *The Adventures of Hajji Baba of Ispahan* (by James Justinian Morier, 1824) 186, 444, 521, 522; *The Adventures of Hajji Baba, of Ispahan, in England* (by James Justinian Morier, 1828) 186, 444, 521, 522; *A Journey Through Persia, Armenia, and Asia Minor, to Constantinople, in the Years 1808 and 1809* (by James Justinian Morier, 1812) 186; *see also* Moore, Thomas; "Persian Letters" genre; Shirazi, Mirza Abul Hassan Khan ("Ilchi")
The *Morning Post* (London) 364; *see also* Iranian famine (1870–72)
Mornington, Lord: *see* Wellesley, Richard Colley (Lord Mornington; Marquess Wellesley)
Morocco 478, 480, 504n49, 529, 636, 638
Morton, Alpheus C. 501n2; *see also* tobacco concession (Iran, 1890)
Moryson, Fynes 49
Mosaic theory 15–18, 21, 49–51, 57, 60, 61, 64, 73, 76, 79, 88, 95, 107, 116–18, 126, 135, 146, 393, 396, 402, 452n3, 581, 651; *see also* The Bible; "Great Flood"; Ham; The Hebrew Bible ("Old Testament"); Japheth; Madai; Magog; Moses; Noah; O'Brien, Henry; Shem; theories of Irish origins; Vallancey, Charles
Moscovy Company: *see* Jenkinson, Anthony
Moscow 500
Moses 19, 21; *see also* The Bible; "Great Flood"; The Hebrew Bible ("Old Testament"); Mosaic theory; Noah
Moses (Movsessian), Catchick 377n18; *see also* Armenian; Singapore; *The Strait Times* (Singapore)
Moses of Chorene (Movsēs Khorenatsi) 77, 566; *The History of Armenia* (by Moses of Chorene, n.d.) 566
"Moses Choronesis": *see* Moses of Chorene
Mosquito Coast (Nicaragua and Honduras) 314, 315, 317, 324; *see also* Central America; Latin America; Walker, William
Mossadeq, Mohammad 499, 500; *see also* Anglo-Persian Oil Company; Iranian oil nationalization (1951); MacSwiney, Terence
Mosul 453n25; *see also* Iraq
Mozaffar al-Din Shah 346, 473; *see also* Iranian Constitutional Revolution (1906–11); Qajar dynasty (Iran, 1796–1925)
Mughal dynasty 112, 134, 174, 204n20, 244, 326; *see also* Aurangzeb (Mughal emperor); Babur (Mughal emperor); English East India Company; Indian subcontinent; *Lalla Rookh. An Oriental Romance* (by Thomas Moore, 1817)
Muhammad (prophet) 133, 270; *see also* Islam; The Qur'an
Müller, Friedrich Max 146, 229, 383, 393–95, 409–10, 435, 449, 454n35; *Lectures on the Science of Language* (by Friedrich Max Müller, 1861) 394; *The Sacred Books of the East* [translation series] (gen. ed., Friedrich Max Müller, 1879–1910) 449; *see also* Aryans; Indo-European languages; *Zend Avesta*
Müller, Günther 161n224; "time of narrating" 161n224
Munster 268, 269, 437, 538; *see also* Desmond Rebellions in Ireland; Oilioll Olum (Oloill Olum), King of Munster; Plantation of Munster
"al-Muqanna" (Hashim ibn Hakim) 175, 178, 204n26, 204n29, 241, 270; *see also Lalla Rookh. An Oriental Romance* (by Thomas Moore, 1817 (Mokanna)); Transoxania
Murray, Charles 305, 306, 308, 327–29, 337, 338, 340–42, 354n12; *see also* British legation (Tehran); Hashem Khan (Mirza); "Hashem Khan," Mrs.
Muscovy Company 266, 515; *see also* Barberino, Raphael; Jenkinson, Anthony; Mangan, James Clarence ("To the Ingleezee Khafir, Calling Himself Djuan Bool Djenkinzun"); Russia; Safavid dynasty (Iran, 1501–1722/36); Tahmasp I, Shah
Myles, Percy Watkins Fenton 411–12
mysticism 244, 249, 250, 406, 407, 410, 426, 428, 430, 432, 435, 613; *see also* poetry ("mystical" poetry)
Mythologie universelle (1930): *see* Krappe, Alexander Haggerty; *see also* Hedayat, Sadeq
mythology 2, 6, 7, 11–13, 16, 18, 22, 35, 41, 56, 58, 64, 65, 75, 76, 83, 84, 92, 94, 95, 106, 107, 112, 113, 125, 127, 129–33, 136, 137, 139, 140, 142, 143, 184, 185, 190, 200, 201, 208n87, 219–23, 226, 228, 230, 254, 264, 280, 321, 347, 381, 382, 396, 398, 402–7, 409, 410, 413, 417, 418, 420, 421, 423, 424, 436–38, 440–44, 446–50, 463n202, 484, 491, 492, 498, 514, 533, 547, 563, 564, 566, 567, 580–82, 585, 599, 601, 613, 615, 623, 624, 636, 641, 643, 644; Celtic mythology 41, 447, 498, *passim*; Iranian mythology 11, 12, 18, 41, 65, 75, 76, 81, 83, 84, 92, 94, 95, 112, 113, 130, 131, 132, 133, 136, 137, 143, 184, 185,

264, 280, 402, 407, 446, 533, 566, 585, 615, 623, 624, 636, 641, *passim*; Irish heroic cycles 6, 13, 41, 46n48, 65, 66, 69, 83, 137, 143, 185, 321, 417, 436, 439, 442, 480, *passim*; "life-affirming" mythology 418; myth-making 35, 418, 420, 423; mytho-history 19, 41, 64, 65, 75, 81, 83, 84, 92, 94, 95, 112, 113, 127, 130–33, 184, 219, 226, 264, 280, 321, 347, 402, 417, 418, 421, 436, 563, 566, 582, 636, 641; "mytho-poetic" 405, 420; nationalist mythology 6, 137, 347, 417, 418, 436, 437, 547, 601, 641, *passim*; *see also* creation stories and beliefs; epics; Fenian Cycle; *Shāhnāmeh*; Ulster Cycle

Nader Shah 267, 308, 326; *see also* Afsharid dynasty (Iran, 1736–51/96); Fraser, James Baillie (*The Kuzzilbash: A Tale of Khorasan* (by James Baillie Fraser, 1828))
Nadir Shah: *see* Nader Shah
"Nadir Tepé" (Nader tapeh) 387; *see also Merv Oasis: Travels and Adventures East of the Caspian During the Years 1879–80–81 …, The* (by Edmond O'Donovan, 1882)
Nāmeh-ye Khosrovān: Dāstan-e Pādeshāhān-e Pārs beh Zabān-e Pārsi … (by Jalal al-Din Mirza (Jalal Pour-Fath-Ali Shah), 1868): *see* Jalal al-Din Mirza (Jalal Pour-Fath-Ali Shah)
Naoroji, Dadabhai 398; *see also* East India Association (London)
Napoleonic Wars 6, 33, 170, 171, 173, 288, 337, 516, 518, 537; Peace of Amiens (1802–03) 170; *see also* Bonaparte, Napoleon; Mainz-Kastel
Naqd-Ali Beg 516; *see also* Charles I, King; Cotton, Dodmore; Safavid dynasty (Iran, 1501–1722/36); Sherley (Shirley), Robert
Nasser al-Din Shah 230, 304, 343, 346, 375, 389, 391, 467, 532, 538, 541, 546, 557n25, 647; assassination of 230, 541; Bracey Vane's "Have You Seen the Shah?" 230; Francis Cawley Burnand's "Kissi-Kissi, or the Pa, the Ma, and the Padishah" 230; *see also* Anglo-Iranian War (1856–57); Herat; Qajar dynasty (Iran, 1796–1925); Reuter concession (Iran, 1872); tobacco concession (Iran, 1890); Tobacco Protest (Iran, 1891–92)
The Nation (Dublin) 8, 22, 37, 149, 165n300, 167, 169, 182, 189, 211–13, 215–19, 222, 231, 233, 237, 238, 260–62, 278, 309–38, 342–53, 357n61, 363, 364, 367–75, 397, 398, 418, 467, 469–71, 485, 539, 548, 641, 648; "THE BULLY ENGLAND" 331, 334; *see also* Anglo-Iranian War (1856–57); Callan, Margaret (née Hughes); Davis, Thomas Osborne; Dillon, John Blake; Downing, Ellen Mary Patrick; Duffy Charles Gavan; Great Famine (Ireland, 1845–51); Hoey, John Cashel; India (famines); Ingram, John Kells; Iranian famine (1870–72); Irish nationalism; Mangan, James Clarence; Mitchel, John; O'Brien, William Smith; Repeal movement; Sullivan, Alexander Martin; Wilde, Jane Francesca Agnes (née Elgee); Williams, Richard D'Alton; Young Ireland
The Nation (London) 479
National Democrat (Dublin) 483; *see also* Sheehy Skeffington, Francis; Ryan, Frederick Michael (Fred)
National Party (Egypt; *al-hizb al-watani*) 479, 480; *see also* Egyptian nationalists
National Peace Congress (London, 1912) 479; *see also* Browne, Edward Granville; Swinny, Shapland Hugh
National Volunteers 494; *see also* Irish Parliamentary Party; Irish Volunteers
nationalism *passim*; *see also* cosmopolitan (nationalist cosmopolitanism); Iranian nationalism; Irish nationalism; "invention of tradition"; "modernity"/"modernities"; "third contact zones"; "tradition"
Nationalities and Subject Races (ed. by Dryhurst, Nora ("Nannie") Florence, 1911) 479
Nationalities and Subject Races conferences (London, 1910, 1911, 1914) 471, 478, 479; *see also* Blunt, Wilfrid Scawen; Dryhurst, Nora ("Nannie") Florence; Du Bois, William Edward Burghardt; Duffy, George Gavan; Farid Bey, Mohamed; Gibson, William (Lord Ashbourne); Hardie, (James) Keir; Hobson, John Atkinson; Lynd, Robert Wilson; Swinny, Shapland Hugh; Temple, Bernard
"nationalizing" 136, 282
nativism 35, 129, 172, 175, 225, 282, 348, 635, 649, 650
natural theology 60
Navab, Hussein Qoli Khan 498, 524; *see also* Rainey, Eileen
Near East 15, 57, 81, 183, 254, 288, 613, 625; *see also* Levant; Middle East; Orient
Nebuchadnezzar II 75; *see also* Babylonia (Neo-Babylonian/Chaldean); Chaldea (Neo-Babylonian/Chaldean); Gudarz; Vallancey, Charles
Nectanebo II, Pharaoh 49; *see also* Egypt; Fénius Farsaid (Fenius Farsa); Scota
Negin (Tehran) 390
Nemed 49, 72, 382, 421, 425, 564; Nemedians 49, 72, 199, 226, 382, 383, 425, 572; *see also*

Firbolgs; Irish antiquarianism; Keating, Geoffrey; Scythia
Nemeth: *see* Nemed
Neolithic period 600
"neo-Zoroastrianism" 85, 112, 133; neo-Platonic influence 112; *see also* Ardestani, Mir Zulfaqar; *Dabestān-e Mazāheb*; *Dasātir*; ishrāqiyyun; Keyvan, Azar; Zoroastrianism
Nephilim 106; *see also* The Bible; The Hebrew Bible ("Old Testament")
Neptunism (geology) 18, 60; *see also* Buffon, Georges de; Kirwan, Richard
nescience 642, 643, 645; *see also* forgetting (/amnesia)
Nevinson, Henry Woodd 479; *see also* Anglo-Russian Agreement (1907); Dryhurst, Nora ("Nannie") Florence; Irish Home Rule; Persia Committee (London)
New Analysis of Chronology and Geography, History and Prophecy, A, vol.IV (by William Hales, 1830): *see* Hales, William (Rev.)
New Ireland Review (Dublin) 149
New York 10, 36, 45n38, 86, 221, 290, 314–16, 318, 323, 343, 346, 367, 412, 430, 435, 441, 450, 476, 485, 488–90, 496, 498, 500, 526, 539, 572, 600, 640; *see also* Pan-Aryan Association
New York Tribune 346
New Zealand 234, 331, 364, 542, 576, 597
News Letter of the Friends of Irish Freedom National Bureau of Information (Washington, DC) 500; *see also* "Irish Republic" (1919–21)
Newton, Isaac 85; *The Chronology of Ancient Kingdoms Amended* (by Isaac Newton, 1728) 85
Nezami-Ganjavi 243, 244, 519; *see also* Atkinson, James; Malcolm, John; Mangan, James Clarence
Nicaragua 314–17; *see also* Central America; Latin America; Mosquito Coast (Nicaragua and Honduras); Walker, William
Nicolas, Jean Baptiste 427; *Les quatrains de Khèyam* (by Jean Baptiste Nicolas, 1867) 427; *see also* Khayyam, Omar
Nietzsche, Friedrich 39, 219, 229; "life-affirming" history 219, 418; *On the Use and Abuse of History for Life* 219; *Thus Spoke Zarathustra* 229
Nigra, Costantino 394
"nihilism" 543
Nile River 116, 218, 395
Nimrod 103, 104, 108, 118, 190; *see also* Herbert, Algernon (*Nimrod: A Discourse on Certain Passages of History and Fable* (by Algernon Herbert, 1828–29))

Nine Years' War (/Tyrone's Rebellion, Ireland) 268, 526; "Flight of the Earls" 526; *see also* Elizabeth I, Queen; O'Neill, Hugh
Nineveh 255, 421, 453n25, 582
Nityananda, Jiddu 434; *see also* Besant, Annie (née Wood); theosophy
Niul 79; *see also* Fénius Farsaid (Fenius Farsa); Japheth; Scota
Nizamy: *see* Nezami-Ganjavi
Noah 15, 17, 18, 47, 50, 51, 60, 61, 73, 95, 106, 115, 117, 118, 126, 162n235, 396, 566, 580; *see also* The Bible; Ceasair; Fénius Farsaid (Fenius Farsa); "Great Flood"; Ham; The Hebrew Bible ("Old Testament"); Japheth; Keyoumars; Mosaic theory; O'Brien, Henry; Shem; Vallancey, Charles
Noble, Margaret Elizabeth ("Sister Nivedita") 434, 471; *see also* Indian nationalism; Vedanta; Vivekananda (Narendranath Datta); women's rights
Noh theatre 435, 586; *see also* Japan; Yeats, William Butler
Nolan, Emer 620
non-knowledge: *see* forgetting (/amnesia); nescience
Nora, Pierre 142, 274, 275; "Tyranny of Memory" 274; *see also* memory; "sites of memory" (lieux de mémoire)
Le Nord (Brussels) 328–29
Normans: *see* Anglo-Normans
Norse ("Vikings") 65, 101, 141, 167, 214–16, 219, 225–28, 287, 403, 406, 412, 418, 421, 500, 529, 565, 569, 574, 581, 608, 612–16, 620, 624; Northmen 200; *see also* Brian Boru; Clontarf, Battle of; Danish; Norway; Odin
North Sea 9
Northern Ireland 10, 26, 38, 51, 493, 494, 499–501, 554, 555, 584, 589, 592, 597, 602, 605, 641; *see also* Ireland; "The Troubles" (Northern Ireland, 1969–98); Ulster
Norway 214, 474, 493, 547; Norwegian 424, 536, 586, 616; *see also* Norse ("Vikings")
"not-England" (/non-'England'/not England) 414, 417, 418, 588, 620; *the Other of England* 32, 451; *see also* Kiberd, Declan
"not knowing": *see* forgetting (/amnesia); nescience
"now-time" (Jetztzeit): *see* Benjamin, Walter
Nutt, Alfred Trübner 396, 440, 447, 451; "The Happy Otherworld in the Celtic Mythico-Romantic Literature of the Irish" (1895) 447; *see also* Aryans; Conla (Conlaoch); Cuchulain (Cú Chulainn); Rustam; Sohrab; Ulster Cycle

O Suilleabhain, Eoghan Rua (Owen Roe O'Sullivan) 245; *see also* Mangan, James Clarence

O'Brennan, Martin A. 52–53; 1858 lecture at the Mechanics' Institute (Dublin) 52; *A School History of Ireland, from the Day of Partholan to the Present Time* (by Martin A. O'Brennan, 1858) 52; *see also* Iran/Erin

O'Brien, Eugene 224; "aetiology of nationalism" 224

O'Brien, Flann 555

O'Brien, Henry 17, 79, 87–127, 129, 133, 135, 142, 148, 159n186, 163n250, 167, 189, 193, 194, 196, 198, 199, 207n81, 211, 254, 277, 278, 280, 382–84, 394, 404, 405, 409, 418, 431, 566, 567, 581, 586, 599, 601, 615, 642, 646; 1833 prize essay of the Royal Irish Academy 89, 90, 92, 93, 97, 100, 104, 106, 107, 123; Mahābādiān ancestry of the Irish ("Tuatha de Dananns") 92, 94–96, 108–10, 112, 114–16, 117, 118, 120, 133, *passim*; Pishdādiān ancestry of the Irish ("Milesians") 92, 94–96, 108, 110, 114, 115, 117, 120, *passim*; Round Towers and phallic worship 89, 93, 94, 95, 97, 102, 109, 111, 120, 163n250, 189, 278, 383, *passim*; *see also* Betham, William; Celticism; civilization; Cuvier, Georges; *Dabestān-e Mazāheb*; *Dasātir*; *Dublin University Magazine*; Faber, George Stanley; freemasonry; Gaels; Hibernians; "Iranian" theories of Irish origins; Irish antiquarianism; Jones, William; Keyoumars; Lingam; MacSweeny, Connor; Mahābādiān; Mahony, Francis Sylvester (alias "Father Prout"); Milesians; Moore, Thomas; Mosaic theory; Noah; Petrie, George; *Phoenecian Ireland* (1833 translation by Henry O'Brien of Joaquín Lorenzo Villanueva's 1831 *Ibernia Phoenicea*); Pishdādiān; Puranas; Round Towers (Ireland); *The Round Towers of Ireland, or the Mysteries of Freemasonry, of Sabaism, and of Budhism, for the First Time Unveiled* (by Henry O'Brien, 1834); Royal Irish Academy's 1833 prize essay; *Shāhnāmeh*; theories of Irish origins; Tuatha de Dananns; Vallancey, Charles; *Zend Avesta*; Zoroastrianism; Yoni

O'Brien, James McEdward 89; *see also* Ceanchora; Clontarf; *Phoenecian Ireland* (1833 translation by Henry O'Brien of Joaquín Lorenzo Villanueva's 1831 *Ibernia Phoenicea*); Thomond, Marquess of

O'Brien, John 146, 147; *Dictionary* (1768) 146, 147

O'Brien, William 452n7, 475, 481, 546, 551; *see also* All-for-Ireland League; Land League; United Irish League

O'Brien, William Smith 212, 281, 283, 323, 501n6; *see also* Blackburne, Francis; *The Nation* (Dublin); Whiteside, James; Young Ireland; Young Ireland uprising (1848)

The Observer (London) 356n56

O'Callaghan, John 602

O'Callaghan, John Cornelius 525; *The Green Book* (by John Cornelius O'Callaghan, 1845) 525; Ireland as a "Mameluke" (*mamluk*/enslaved) province 525; *see also* "provincializing Ireland"

occult 383, 428–32, 434, 435, 483; *see also* Yeats, William Butler

O'Connell, Daniel 90, 171, 202n1, 212, 221, 224, 276, 308, 312, 315, 323, 324, 339, 390, 473, 501n6, 522, 525, 526, 538, 542, 544, 584; *see also* Blackburne, Francis; Catholic Association (1823); Catholic Church; Catholic Emancipation; Catholic Relief Act (1829); Clontarf; Hibernian Anti-Slavery Society; Irish Home Rule; Irish nationalism; O'Connellite; "provincializing Ireland"; Repeal Association (1840); Repeal movement; Whiteside, James

O'Connellite 24, 202n1, 212, 308, 312, 355n31, 356n51, 363, 390; *see also* Cork Examiner; O'Connell, Daniel; Irish Home Rule; Irish nationalism

O'Connor, Arthur 545; *see also* Victoria, Queen

O'Connor, Arthur (United Irishmen): *see* Conner (a.k.a., O'Connor), Arthur

O'Connor, Dermod 316; *General History of Ireland … The* (*Foras Feasa ar Éirinn*) (by Geoffrey Keating, 1634; English translation by Dermod O'Connor, 1723) 316

O'Conor, Cahal (Cáhal Mór; Cathal) of the Red Hand 288, 289; *see also* Connaught (Connacht); Mangan, James Clarence

O'Conor, Charles 51, 63, 68–70, 85, 88, 124, 196, 277, 384, 395, 614; connection between Persians and Scythians 70 *passim*; "A Dissertation on the Origin and Antiquities of the antient Scots …," 70; *Dissertations on the Ancient History of Ireland* (by Charles O'Conor, 1753) 69, 70; English translation of Roderic O'Flaherty's *The Ogygia Vindicated* 70, 85; presumed connection between Celtic and Persian languages 63; *see also* Catholic Association (a.k.a., Catholic Committee, 1756); Celticism; Celts; Curry, John; Gomer;

Irish antiquarianism; O'Flaherty, Roderic; "Phoenician" theories of Irish origins; Royal Irish Academy; Vallancey, Charles

O'Curry, Eugene 110, 149, 197–99, 211, 255, 394, 395, 399, 400, 407; magi and druids 199; "Scythian" theory of Irish origins 199; Zoroaster 199; *see also* Catholic University of Ireland (Dublin); O'Donovan, John; Ordnance Survey of Ireland; Petrie, George; "Petrie & Co."

Odin 193; *see also* Norse ("Vikings")

O'Donnell, Peadar 593; *see also* Indian-Irish Independence League (1932); *An Phoblacht* (Dublin)

O'Donnell, William H. 436

O'Donoghue, David James 239, 290, 295n67; *The Life and Writings of James Clarence Mangan* (by David James O'Donoghue, 1897) 290; *The Prose Writings of James Clarence Mangan* (by David James O'Donoghue, 1904) 290; *see also* Mangan, James Clarence

O'Donovan, Edmond 382, 384–88, 627n46; *see also* Curzon, George Nathaniel; Irish Republican Brotherhood; "Mahdist" uprising; *Merv Oasis: Travels and Adventures East of the Caspian During the Years 1879–80–81 ..., The* (by Edmond O'Donovan, 1882); O'Donovan, John; Round Towers (Ireland); Turkmen; Sudan

O'Donovan, John 79, 99, 101, 110, 122, 127, 149, 197, 198, 200, 211, 256, 257, 276–78, 384, 394, 399, 400, 407; *Annals of the Kingdom of Ireland by the Four Masters* (English translation by John O'Donovan, 1848–51) 200; *see also Annals of the Four Masters* (17th century); "Four Masters"; Mangan, James Clarence; O'Curry, Eugene; O'Donovan, Edmond; Ordnance Survey of Ireland; Petrie, George; "Petrie & Co."

Odoric of Venetia (a.k.a., Odoric of Pordenone) 388; *see also* "Brother James of Ireland"

O'Duffy, Eoin 595; Blueshirts 595; *see also* fascism

Official Guide: Dublin (Tourist Board of the Republic of Ireland, 1950) 291; *see also* Mangan, James Clarence

Official Sinn Féin 501, 641; *see also* Sinn Féin the Workers' Party; *The United Irishman* (Dublin; post-1948 publication)

O'Flaherty, Roderic 50, 51, 70, 77–78, 85, 139, 140, 142, 149, 198, 384; English translation of Roderic O'Flaherty's *The Ogygia Vindicated*, (by Charles O'Conor, 1775) 51, 70, 85; *Ogygia: seu Rerum Hibernicarum Chronologia* (1685) 50, 51, 77–78, 139, 142; *Ogygia Vindiciae* 70, 149;

Scythian origins of the Irish 51, 70; *see also* Irish antiquarianism; Hely, James; James II, King; Mackenzie, George; McDonnell, Randal; O'Conor, Charles

O'Gallagher, Felix 253; *see also* Mangan, James Clarence

O'Gara, Fergal (Ferall) 201; "toisach" (taoiseach; chieftain) 201; *see also Annals of the Four Masters* (17th century); "Four Masters"

Ogham 48, 84, 123, 643; presumed similarity with ancient Persian script 123, 643; *see also* Jones, William; Vallancey, Charles

O'Grady, Standish James 223–24, 227, 397, 420–22, 437–39, 442, 451, 458n126, 613; *The Coming of Cuculain* (by Standish James O'Grady, 1895) 437; *History of Ireland. Volume I: The Heroic Period* (by Standish James O'Grady, 1878) 420, 422, 437; *History of Ireland. Volume II: Cuculain and His Contemporaries* (by Standish James O'Grady, 1880) 437; *Story of Ireland* (by Standish James O'Grady, 1894) 422; *see also* Cuchulain (Cú Chulainn); Thermopylae, Battle of (480 BCE); Ulster Cycle

Ogygia, or a Chronological Account of Irish Events (1793 translation of Roderic O'Flaherty's 1685 *Ogygia: seu Rerum Hibernicarum Chronologia*): *see* Hely, James

Ogygia: seu Rerum Hibernicarum Chronologia (Roderic O'Flaherty, 1685): *see* O'Flaherty, Roderic

Ogygia Vindicated, (English translation of Roderic O'Flaherty's book by Charles O'Conor 1775): *see* O'Conor, Charles; O'Flaherty, Roderic

O'Halloran, Clare 2

O'Halloran, Sylvester (Silvester) 53–55, 61, 63, 68–70, 211, 214, 420, 445; *A General History of Ireland* (by Sylvester (Silvester) O'Halloran, 1778) 53; "Phoenician" theories of Irish origins 53–55, 61, 69; "Scytho-Phoenician" theory of Irish origins 53–55, 61, 69; *see also* Brooke, Charlotte; Celticism; Celts; Royal Irish Academy

O'Hart, John 61, 146–48, 384, 420; *see also* Aryans; Baath (/Baoth); Celtic; Fénius Farsaid (Fenius Farsa); "Four Masters"; Gaels; Gaodhal; genealogy; Iran/Erin; *Irish Pedigrees; or, the Origin and Stem of the Irish Nation* (by John O'Hart, 1876 and later editions); Japheth; Phoenicians; Scythians

O'Hegarty, Patrick Sarsfield 503n37, 593–94

Oilioll Olium (Olioll Olum), King of Munster 269

O'Kelly, John Joseph (Seán Ua Ceallaigh) 580–81; *Ireland: Elements of Her Early Story from the Coming of Ceasair to the Anglo-Norman Invasion* (by John Joseph O'Kelly, 1921) 580; minister of education in the Second Dáil Éireann (1921–22) 580; *see also* Atlantis; *Catholic Bulletin and Book Review* (Dublin); Gaelic League; Sinn Féin

Okuma, Shigenobu 550, 562n116; Constitutional Progressive Party (Japan) 550; *see also* Japan; pan-Asianism

O'Laverty, James 443, 444, 446, 447; "Remarkable Correspondence of Irish, Greek, and Oriental Legends" (1859) 443; *see also* Conla (Conlaoch); Cuchulain (Cú Chulainn); Ferdowsi, Abul-Qassem; Royal Irish Academy; Rustam; *Shāhnāmeh*; Sohrab; Ulster Cycle

Olcott, Henry Steel 430–32; *see also* Theosophical Society; theosophy

"Old English" 48, 68, 180, 182; *see also* Anglo-Normans

"Old Irish": *see* "mere Irish"; Gaels

Old Jonathan: The District and Parish Helper (London) 374; *see also* Great Famine (Ireland, 1845–51); Iranian famine (1870–72)

Old Persian (language and script) 83, 155n105, 643; *see also* Rawlinson, Henry Creswicke

O'Leary, John 228–30; *see also Irish People* (Dublin); Irish Republican Brotherhood

Ó Lócháin, Mícheál (Michael J. Logan) 412, 458n112; *see also The Gael/An Gaodhal* (New York)

O'Mahony, John 49, 229, 314, 316–17; English translation by John O'Mahony, 1857 49, 316; on Geoffrey Keating 49, 316; *The History of Ireland (Foras Feasa ar Éirinn)* (by Geoffrey Keating, 1634); *see also* Emmet Monument Association (New York); Fenian Brotherhood; Young Ireland

On the Origin of Species (by Charles Darwin, 1859): *see* Darwin, Charles

One Thousand and One Nights (a.k.a., *Arabian Nights*) 40, 45n42, 235, 239, 240, 244, 614, 622, 623; *see also Finnegans Wake* (by James Joyce, 1939); Galland, Antoine; Hammer-Purgstall, Joseph Freiherr von; Joyce, James; Mangan, James Clarence

O'Neill, Hugh 268; "Red Hand" 268; *see also* Nine Years' War (/Tyrone's Rebellion, Ireland)

O'Neill, Owen Roe 177, 207n78; *see also* Confederate War (Ireland, 1642–52); *Lalla Rookh. An Oriental Romance* (by Thomas Moore, 1817); O'Neill, Phelim

O'Neill, Phelim 177, 178; *see also* Confederate War (Ireland, 1642–52); *The History of Ireland*, vol.IV (by Thomas Moore, 1846); *History of Ireland from the Invasion of Henry II* (by Thomas Leland, 1773); *An History of the Life of James Duke of Ormonde, from His Birth in 1610, to His Death in 1688* (by Thomas Carte, 1736); *The Irish Rebellion; Or, An History of the Irish Papists to Extirpate the Protestants in the Kingdom of Ireland* (by John Temple, 1646); *Lalla Rookh. An Oriental Romance* (by Thomas Moore, 1817); *Memoirs of Captain Rock, The Celebrated Irish Chieftain …* (by Thomas Moore, 1824); O'Neill, Owen Roe

Ongley, Henry Hardy 366; *see also* Iranian famine (1870–72)

ontology 13, 218, 225, 249, 250, 415; ontic mapping 142

Orange Order: *see* Orange organizations

Orange organizations 366–67, 546; clashes between the Irish-American Orange Order and Catholics in New York (1870–71) 366–67; Orange marches 366, 546; *see also* unionists (Ireland)

Ó Rathaille, Aogán 247

Ordnance Survey of Ireland 88, 122, 127, 211, 255–57, 276–78, 284, 399, 400, 456n70; Ordnance Department 255–58, 274, 276; *see also* Mangan, James Clarence; O'Curry, Eugene; O'Donovan; John; Petrie, George

O'Reilly, John Boyle 223, 290, 545; *Poetry and Song of Ireland* (edited by John Boyle O'Reilly, 1887) 290; *see also* Fenian Brotherhood; Irish Republican Brotherhood; Mangan, James Clarence

Orient *passim*; oriental *passim*; *see also* Levant; Middle East; Near East; "Oriental" theories of Irish origins

"Oriental Renaissance" 31, 62, 81; *see also* "Bengal Renaissance"; the Enlightenment ("European" Enlightenment); "oriental-style" literature; orientalism; Romanticism; Schwab, Raymond

"oriental-style" literature 31, 173, 175, 184, 233, 236, 279, 426, *passim*; *see also* Byron, Lord (George Gordon Byron); Moore, Thomas; Romanticism; Yahannan, John D.

"oriental" theories of Irish origins 3, 6, 7, 14, 17, 19, 23, 39, 47, 51, 55, 56, 59, 62, 65, 67, 69, 102, 123, 142, 143, 146, 188–91, 195, 199, 208n87, 214, 227, 248, 254, 278, 289, 381, 383, 384, 404, 424, 519, 535, 563, 564, 567, 568, 576, 578, 587, 601, 605, 617, 619, 629n69, *passim*; *see also* Celts; Faber,

George Stanley; "Iranian" theories of Irish origins; theories of Irish origins;
orientalism 2, 18, 32, 35, 36, 41, 44n36, 55, 57, 62, 74, 80, 81, 111–13, 116, 118, 124, 137, 184, 189, 242, 243, 252, 286, 352, 370, 389, 442, 444, 461n165, 467, 477, 480, 517, 522, 523, 538, 558n36, 586, 587, 640; "Irish nationalist" orientalism 18; orientalizing 102, 144, 575, 614; "self-orientalizing gestures" 35–36, 55, 143, 352; *see also* Browne, Edward Granville; Leerssen, Joep (Joseph Theodoor); Lennon, Joseph; Mangan, James Clarence; Mansoor, Menahem; Moore, Thomas; "Oriental Renaissance"; "oriental-style" literature; Said, Edward W.; Schwab, Raymond; theories of Irish origins ("Iranian" theories of Irish origins); theories of Irish origins ("oriental" theories of Irish origins)
The Origin of Pagan Idolatry Ascertained from Historical Testimony and Circumstantial Evidence (by George Stanley Faber, 1816): *see* Faber, George Stanley
Ormuz: *see* Hormuz Island
O'Rourke, John 368, 522; *The History of the Great Irish Famine of 1847* (by John O'Rourke, 1875) 368; *see also* Great Famine (Ireland, 1845–51)
O'Shea, Katherine ("Kitty") 469; *see also* Parnell, Charles Stewart
Ossetians ("Ossethians") 583, 600
Ossian 65, 66, 69, 83, 143, 441, 446, 464n209, 535; *see also* Fenian Cycle; *Fragments of Ancient Poetry, Collected in the Highlands of Scotland* (by James Macpherson, 1760); Macpherson, James; Ulster Cycle
Ost Deutsche Post (Vienna) 327
Ottoman Empire 4, 31, 33, 45n42, 131, 162n238, 165n301, 185, 187, 188, 233, 237–39, 242, 243, 246, 250, 262, 268, 270, 297n95, 303, 325, 329, 332, 335, 342, 345, 346, 366, 385, 388, 391, 428, 436, 453n25, 476, 477, 490, 497, 499, 500, 501n6, 508n86, 510n112, 514, 516, 524, 528, 530, 531, 537, 539, 550, 551, 590, 591, 595, 637, 638; Ottomans 81, 239, 244, 251, 259, 268, 453n25, 476, 510n112; *see also* Armenian genocide (Ottoman Empire); Crimean War (1854–56); Erzurum ("Erzeroum"); First World War; Greek War of Independence (1821–29); Istanbul; Kars; Russo-Ottoman War (1877–78); Turkey; Turkish (languages); Turks; Young Turk Revolution (1908)
Otway, Caesar 93; *see also Dublin Penny Journal*; Royal Irish Academy

Ouseley, Eliza Shirin 389; *see also* Ouseley, Gore; Whitelock, Harriet Georgina
Ouseley, Gore 34, 389, 390, 523; *see also* Ouseley, Eliza Shirin; Ouseley, Janie; Ouseley, Wellesley Abbas; Shirazi, Mirza Abul Hassan Khan ("Ilchi"); Whitelock, Harriet Georgina
Ouseley, Janie 389; *see also* Ouseley, Gore; Whitelock, Harriet Georgina
Ouseley, Wellesley Abbas 389; *see also* Ouseley, Gore; Whitelock, Harriet Georgina
Ouseley, William 34, 83, 112, 160n204, 184, 185, 193, 237, 296n76, 389, 390, 431, 444, 446; *Oriental Collections* (by William Ouseley, 1797–1800) 184, 431; *Persian Miscellanies* (by William Ouseley, 1795) 184, 185, 446; *Travels in Various Countries of the East: More Particularly Persia* (by William Ouseley, 1819–23) 444; *see also Lalla Rookh. An Oriental Romance* (by Thomas Moore, 1817)
Outram, James 332, 342, 345; *see also* Anglo-Iranian War (1856–57)
Owenson, Sydney (Lady Morgan) 53; *The Wild Irish Girl* (by Sydney Owenson (Lady Morgan), 1806) 53
Oxus River (Amu Darya) 84
Ozell, John 169; *The Persian Letters* (English translation of *Lettres persanes* by John Ozell, 1722) 169; *see also Lettres persanes* (by Montesquieu, Baron de, 1721); "Persian Letters" genre

pacifism 429, 430, 494, 590; conscientious objector 590
Paddy's Resource (1795–1803) 265, 583, 585; *see also* American War of Independence; French Revolution (1789–99); Jacobins; Society of United Irishmen; United Irishmen
Pahlavi dynasty (Iran, 1925–79) 493, 500, 594, 641; *see also* Mohammad Reza Shah; Reza Shah
Pahlavi language (ancient "Middle Persian") 41, 45n38, 78, 79, 83, 84, 113, 122, 382, 449
Pahlavi script (ancient "Middle Persian") 41, 45n38; *see also* de Sacy, Silvester
Pakington, John 310; *see also* Tory
Pakistan 334
Paleolithic period 600
Palestine 11, 118, 506n72, 650; *see also* Zionism
Pall Mall Gazette (London) 469
Palmerston, Lord (Henry John Temple) 305–11, 321–23, 328, 338–41, 353n8, 354n11,

354n18, 354n19; *see also* Anglo-Iranian War (1856–57); Crimean War (1854–56); Liberal Party (UK); Washington (diplomatic row with London (1854–56)); Whig Party

Palmyra 255

"Palus Meotis": *see* Don River

pan-African 649

Pan-Aryan Association 9, 10, 36, 435, 450, 488–92, 576, 640, 646; *see also* Barakatullah, Abdul Hafiz Mohammad; Bingham, Charlotte; Cama [Rustom Cama], Bhikhaji (also spelled Bhikhaiji); Clan na Gael (United States); de Bruyn Kops, John; Devoy, John; Dulin, Albert S.; Freeman, George ("Fitzgerald"); Hobson, (John) Bulmer; Joshi, Samuel Lucas; pan-Aryanism

pan-Aryanism 148, 149, 353, 447, 488, 490, 491

pan-Asianism 490, 491, 562n116; *see also* Okuma, Shigenobu

pan-Celticism 569–71, 573, 602; *see also* Celticism

pan-Islam 469, 508n86, 638; *see also* Assadabadi, Sayyid Jamal al-Din (a.k.a., "al-Afghani")

pan-Turkism 638

papacy 20, 177, 195, 240, 262, 263, 265–69, 273, 363; *see also* Catholics; John XXII, Pope; Urban VIII, Pope (Maffeo Barbarini)

"papists": *see* Catholics

"paradigm shift" 118, 122, 212, 413, 587, 601–2; *see also* Kuhn, Thomas

"Paradise and the Peri": *see* Lalla Rookh. An Oriental Romance (by Thomas Moore, 1817)

Paris 230, 305, 329, 337, 342, 343, 345, 364, 376n9, 391, 490, 507n83, 508n86, 537, 621

Parnell, Charles Stewart 452n7, 469, 472, 525, 546; *see also* Home Rule League; Irish Home Rule; Irish Parliamentary Party; Land League; O'Shea, Katherine ("Kitty"); Parnellite; "provincializing Ireland"

Parnellite 227, 355n28, 525, 627n46; *see also* Parnell, Charles Stewart; United Irish League of America

Parsee: *see* Parsi

Parsi dastur: *see* Modi, Jivanji Jamshedji

Parsis 37, 41, 113, 132, 133, 196, 309, 377n15, 442, 443, 488, 490, 492, 640, 643; *see also* Hataria, Manekji Limj; Society for the Amelioration of the Condition of Zoroastrians in Persia; Zoroastrian

Parsons, Cóilín 127, 247, 255–58, 456n70; *see also* Ordnance Survey of Ireland

Parthians 50, 52, 57, 63, 69, 72, 78, 81, 146, 147, 151n22, 642; *see also* Aryanism (racial theories); Aryans; Indo-Europeans; Indo-Iranians

Partholan (Partholón) 49, 52, 62, 72, 146, 226, 406, 421, 580, 616; *see also* Irish antiquarianism; "Migdonia"

Pashtun (Pathan) Barakzai tribe 304; *see also* Afghans; Anglo-Iranian War (1856–57); Dost Mohammad Khan; Herat

Pashtun (Pathan) Durrani/Abdāli clan 304, 338; *see also* Afghans; Anglo-Iranian War (1856–57); Herat; Pashtun (Pathan) Gilzai confederacy

Pashtun (Pathan) Gilzai confederacy 5, 516; *see also* Afghans; Anglo-Iranian War (1856–57); Herat; Pashtun (Pathan) Durrani/Abdāli clan; Safavid dynasty (Iran, 1501–1722/36)

Pashtun (Pathan) Sadozai tribe 304; *see also* Afghans; Anglo-Iranian War (1856–57); Herat; Mohammad Yusuf

Patel, Vithalbhai Jhaverbhai 593; *see also* Indian-Irish Independence League (1932); Indian nationalism; swaraj

Pazargad, Bahauddin 45n38; *see also* Gancher, David; Iran/Erin

The Pearl Cannon: *see* Hedayat, Sadeq (*Toup-e Morvari* (*The Pearl Cannon*, 1947))

Pearse, Patrick (Pádraic) 438

peasantry (Ireland) 25, 397, 399, 400, 408, 413, 458n114, 475, 481, 518, 539, 542; *see also* Irish Land Acts (1870, 1881); Land League; "Land War" (Ireland); Ribbonism (Ireland)

Peelite 306, 339, 354n13, 354n18; Liberal Conservatives 354n18; *see also* Gladstone, William Ewart

"Pehlavi": *see* Pahlavi language; Pahlavi script

"Pehlvi": *see* Pahlavi language; Pahlavi script

Peking (Beijing) 333; *see also* China

Pelasgi (Pelasgian) 96, 118, 410, 421, 422

Pelloutier, Simon 121–22, 162n243, 193

Pelly, Lewis 367; *see also* Iranian famine (1870–72)

penal laws: *see* Ireland (English and Protestant penal laws)

Penny Cyclopædia of the Society for the Diffusion of Useful Knowledge (London) 197

"People's Budget" (United Kingdom, 1910) 552

People's Democracy 501, 641; *see also* Socialist Republic (Belfast); "The Troubles" (Northern Ireland, 1969–98)

periodization schemes 12, 18, 20, 42n5, 60, 107, 402, 564

Persepolis 84, 123, 255

INDEX 753

Persia: *see* Iran
Persia Committee (London) 477–79, 482, 483, 493, 503n31, 504n49, 506n73, 509n104, 548; *see also* Anglo-Russian Agreement (1907); Browne, Edward Granville; Dillon, John; Gwynn, Stephen Lucius; Hardie, (James) Keir; Iranian Constitutional Revolution (1906–11); Lamington, Lord (Charles Wallace Alexander Napier Cochrane-Baillie); Lynch, Henry Finnis Blosse; Moore, William Arthur; Nevinson, Henry Woodd; Swinny, Shapland Hugh
Persia in Revolution (by Joseph Maunsell Hone and Page Lawrence Dickinson, 1910) 482
Persia Society (London) 504n49
Persian Gulf 10, 31, 33, 66, 72, 273, 305, 308, 310, 321, 327, 332, 333, 336, 338, 342, 345, 358n93, 367, 377n22, 391, 402, 409, 476, 497, 515, 516
Persian language 18, 38, 45n38, 75, 83, 90, 111, 133, 148, 169, 273, 280, 32, 7, 328, 384, 389, 426, 448, 499, 517, 523, 528–31, 537, 539, 550, 640, *passim*; Dari dialect 112; Farsi 78
"Persian Letters" genre 169, 186, 243, 244, 303; *see also Intercepted Letters; or, The Twopenny Post-bag* (by Thomas Moore, 1813); *Lettres persanes* (by Montesquieu, Baron de, 1721); Ozell, John
Persian script 7, 41, 67, 71, 81, 82, 123, 155n105, 273, 531, 560n64, 643; *see also* Pahlavi script (ancient "Middle Persian")
"Persian" theories of Irish origins: *see* "Iranian" theories of Irish origins
Persianate heritage 12–13, 41, 235, 643; Ireland's presumed Persianate heritage 12–13, 643; *see also* Irano-Alan people; Irano-Sarmatians; Jász people (Hungary); Polish Sarmatianism; "Shirazis" of Zanzibar; Swahili coast
Persians 2, 14, 15, 20, 22, 40, 45n42, 50, 52, 56, 57, 63–67, 69–75, 77, 78, 84, 89, 91, 92, 94, 96, 102, 108, 112–14, 116, 118, 119, 121, 122, 130, 131, 137, 144, 147, 161n217, 162n235, 190, 192–93, 196, 220–23, 228, 229, 234, 238, 239, 252, 277, 310, 335, 341, 354n11, 365, 375, 393, 408, 409, 421, 430, 431, 449, 450, 452n3, 470, 492, 528, 566, 582, 600, 616; *see also* Aryanism (racial theories); Aryans; Greco-Roman sources (accounts of ancient Persians); Hellenic (accounts of ancient Persians); Indo-Europeans; Indo-Iranians; Iranians
Perso-centric 64, 76, 133, 450
Perso-Scythian: *see* Irano-Scythians
Peru 382; Peruvians 67; *see also* Inca

Peshawar Treaty (1857) 336; *see also* Dost Mohammad Khan; Herat; India
Peshawar Valley 334, 336; *see also* Afghanistan; India; Pakistan
Pétis de La Croix, François 428; *see also* McCarthy, Justin Huntly
Petrie, George 23, 24, 88–90, 93, 97–102, 104–10, 120–24, 127, 142, 146, 157n145, 163n250, 167, 195–201, 211, 213, 215, 237, 255, 256, 276–78, 283, 288, 381–83, 385–86, 395, 396, 399, 400, 402, 403, 407, 431, 567, 568; 1833 prize essay of the Royal Irish Academy 90, 93, 101, 104, 106, 107, 124, 157n145, 195; archaeology 88, 98, 100, 198, 200; architectural history 23, 100, 110; Christian origin of the Round Towers 24, 93, 97, 99–101, 104, 107, 109, 142, 195, 196, 201, 277, 381, 385, 386, 395, 396; musicology 88, 200; "The Origins and Uses of the Round Towers of Ireland" (1833) 90, 100; Round Towers as belfries 100, 101, 196, 382; Royal Irish Academy 90, 93, 99, 104, 121, 200; *see also* Beaufort, Louisa Catherine; Betham, William; *Dublin Penny Journal; Dublin University Magazine; The Ecclesiastical Architecture of Ireland, Anterior to the Anglo-Norman Invasion* (by George Petrie, 1845); historiography and history; Mangan, James Clarence; O'Brien, Henry; O'Curry, Eugene; O'Donovan, John; Ordnance Survey of Ireland; "Petrie & Co."; Round Towers (Ireland); Royal Irish Academy's 1833 prize essay; Society for the Preservation and Publication of the Melodies of Ireland; Stokes, William; Windele, John
"Petrie & Co." 99, 107, 122, 197, 198, 278; *see also* O'Curry, Eugene; O'Donovan, John; Petrie, George
petroleum 497, 510n127; *see also* Anglo-Persian Oil Company; Iranian oil nationalization (1951)
Pezron, Paul 65; *see also* Celticism; Celts
phallic worship 89, 93–95, 97, 102, 109, 111, 116, 117, 120, 157n161, 163n250, 189, 278, 382, 383, 460n154; priapic 109; *see also* Faber, George Stanley; Keane, Marcus; Mahābādiān; O'Brien, Henry (Round Towers and phallic worship); Lingam; Jennings, Hargrave; Round Towers (Ireland); Tuatha de Dananns; Wilford, Francis
Philadelphia 489, 521
Philippines 650
philology 14, 31, 52, 56, 57, 64, 65, 67, 74, 76, 86, 97, 110, 115, 116, 125, 146, 149, 151n31, 174, 193, 237, 278, 381, 387, 393–96,

401, 404, 409, 574, 618, 620, 641; *see also* Aryan (languages); etymology; Indo-European languages; Indo-Europeans; Jones, William; lexicon; linguistics; Persian language; Sanskrit; Vallancey, Charles

An Phoblacht (Belfast) 26; *see also* Provisional Irish Republican Army; Provisional Sinn Féin; "The Troubles" (Northern Ireland, 1969–98)

An Phoblacht (Dublin) 593; *see also* Irish Republican Army (1922); O'Donnell, Peadar

Phoenicia 2, 4, 7, 11, 12, 14, 15, 19–21, 25, 27, 39, 42, 47, 52, 53, 55, 56, 59, 61, 63, 64, 66, 67, 69–73, 85, 89, 90, 99, 102, 104–6, 108, 121, 122, 130, 142, 146, 153n55, 154n78, 156n124, 159n191, 174, 189–93, 197, 199, 215, 216, 218, 222, 226, 227, 253, 289, 302n208, 382, 395, 403–8, 421, 424, 435, 445, 446, 452n3, 457n97, 459n126, 563, 572, 573, 581, 585, 605, 608, 610–14, 616, 617, 619–20, 631n103, 631n123, 632n132, 636, 637, 642, 646; Carthage 2, 53, 54, 56, 70, 71, 190, 191, 421, 424, 582, 608, 617, 619, 620, 622; Sidon 190, 406; Tyre 190, 582; Tyrian 21, 581, 582; *see also* "Greco-Tyrian"; "Phoenician" theories of Irish origins

Phoenician/Carthaginian language (Punic) 70, 77, 79, 102, 283

Phoenecian Ireland (1833 translation by Henry O'Brien of Joaquín Lorenzo Villanueva's 1831 *Ibernia Phoenicea*) 89, 90, 114, 207n81; James McEdward O'Brien 89; Tuatha de Dananns as *"true, Iranian, Milesian,* Irish" 89; *see also Ibernia Phoenicea* (by Joaquín Lorenzo Villanueva, 1831; translated as *Phoenecian Ireland* by Henry O'Brien, 1833)

"Phoenician" theories of Irish origins 15, 27, 39, 69, 61, 64, 106, 190, 253, 407, 445, 446, 612, *passim*; *see also* Betham, William; "Phoenician-Iranian" theories of ancient Ireland's "Golden Age"; "Scytho-Phoenician" theory of Irish origins; theories of Irish origins; Vallancey, Charles

"Phoenician-Iranian" theories of ancient Ireland's "Golden Age" 54, 85, 189, 192, 612, 614, 617, 620, 642, *passim*; origins of "historical documentation" in Ireland 192; *see also* civilization; D'Alton (Dalton), John; Joyce, James; Moore, Thomas

Phoenician-Scythian theories of ancient Ireland's "Golden Age": *see* "Scytho-Phoenician" theory of Irish origins

Phoenicians 2, 7, 12, 20, 53, 54, 59, 61, 63, 66, 67, 69, 91, 89, 90, 102, 104, 106, 108, 121, 122, 142, 189–92, 199, 215, 222, 395, 406, 408, 424, 435, 445, 452n3, 459n126, 563, 572, 608, 610, 613, 620, 642, 646; *see also* "Semitic" (racial designation)

Phoeniusa Farsaidh: *see* Fénius Farsaid (Fenius Farsa)

Phoenix Park murders (Dublin, 1882) 221, 292n27, 546; *see also* Burke, Thomas Henry; Cavendish, Frederick Charles; Irish National Invincibles; Tynan, Patrick

Pictet, Adolphe 393–95; *De l'affinité des langues celtiques avec le sanscrit* (by Adolphe Pictet, 1837) 394; *Les origines indo-européennes, ou Les Aryas primitifs: essai de paléontologie linguistique* (by Adolphe Pictet, 1859–63) 394, 395; supposition of "Éire" and "Iran" as cognates 394; *see also* Aryans; Indo-European languages

Picton, James Allanson 501n2; *see also* tobacco concession (Iran, 1890)

The Pictorial History of England: Being a History of the People, as Well as a History of the Kingdom, vol.I (by George Lillie Craik and Charles Macfarlane, 1838) 121–22, 162n243; on presumed common linguistic origin of "Erin" and "Iran" 122; *see also* Betham, William; "Iranian" theories of Irish origins; Malcolm, John; O'Brien, Henry; Pelloutier, Simon; Vallancey, Charles

Pillai, Kandiah 12; *see also* Kumarināṭu; Lemuria; Ramaswamy, Sumathi; Tamil people

pillar temples: *see* pillar towers

pillar towers 191, 193, 194, 207n81, 277, 395, 404, 409, 582; *see also* Bourke, Ulick Joseph; Mazandaran; Round Towers (Ireland)

Pinkerton, John 20, 78; *A Dissertation on the Origin and Progress of the Scythians or Goths* (1787) 20, 78

Pinnock, William 533–36; *A Catechism of the History of Ireland* (by William Pinnock, 1825) 533; *A Comprehensive Grammar of Modern Geography and History; for the Use of Schools and for Private Tuition* (by William Pinnock, 1830, 1834) 533, 534, 536; *see also* Farhad Mirza

Pishdād: *see* Pishdādiān

Pishdādiān 14, 19, 64, 65, 72, 76, 81, 83, 84, 86, 92, 94–96, 106, 108, 110, 112–20, 130–33, 136, 159n199, 160n204, 280, 382, 533, 623, 642; *see also Dabestān-e Mazāheb*; Hincks, Thomas (Rev.); "Iranian" theories of Irish origins; Jamshid; Mahābādiān; Malcolm, John; Milesians; mythology (Iranian mythology); O'Brien, Henry; *Shāhnāmeh*; *Universal History* of Mirkhond (15th century); Vallancey, Charles; Yoni

Pitt, William ("the Younger") 543; *see also* Catholic Emancipation
"place-making" 56, 140, 142; *see also* Ramaswamy, Sumathi
plagiarism 98, 104, 109, 233, 242, 243, 274, 279, 294n55; *see also* self-plagiarism
Plantation of Munster 268, 538; *see also* Desmond Rebellions in Ireland; Elizabeth I, Queen; Munster; Protestant plantations in Ireland
Plantation of Ulster 411, 538; *see also* James I of England (James VI of Scotland); Protestant plantations in Ireland; Ulster
Plutarch 191
Plutonism (geology) 18, 60, 61; *see also* Hutton, James; Lyell, Charles; uniformitarian theory (geology)
Plymouth 329
The Poetical Works of Thomas Moore, vol. VI (by Thomas Moore, 1841) 182, 184; *see also Lalla Rookh. An Oriental Romance* (by Thomas Moore, 1817); Malcolm, John; Moore, Thomas
Poetry 1, 5, 7, 24, 25, 29, 30, 32, 33, 39, 42, 42n1, 53, 68, 69, 81, 109, 131, 138, 144, 149, 167, 168, 182, 183, 185, 188, 214, 216, 231–33, 235, 236, 238, 241–44, 246, 247, 249–55, 257, 258, 262, 263, 274, 278, 280, 288, 289, 296n93, 397, 399, 400, 416, 418, 426, 427, 434, 435, 437, 439, 449, 459n137, *passim*; "classical" Persian poetry 18, 64, 183, 232, 233, 235, 237, 240–44, 246, 249, 253, 273, 296n93, 389, 426, 427, 436, 448, 449, *passim*; "mystical" poetry 244, 249, 250, 297n100, 426, 435; *see also* Davis, Thomas Osborne; Fitzgerald, Edward (poet); Irish nationalism; MacCarthy, Denis Florence; Mangan, James Clarence; Moore, Thomas; Wilde, Jane Francesca Agnes (née Elgee)
Poland 4, 325, 326, 350, 351, 478, 585, 595, 636–38, 647; Poles 225, 326, 436; Polish nationalism 4, 299n138, 589, 636, 638, 639
Polish Sarmatianism 1; *see also* Irano-Sarmatians; Persianate heritage
polygenesis 107, 395, 401, 402, 409, 411, 420
polyphony 127; *see also* heteroglossia
Pope, Alexander 240
popes: *see* papacy
Porter, Robert Ker 112
Portugal 147, 530; Portuguese 273, 515
positivism 198, 258, 477–79, 482, 484, 568, 583, 613; *see also* Comte, Auguste
Positivist Review (London) 478, 479, 484; *see also* Positivist Society (London); Swinny, Shapland Hugh

Positivist Society (London) 477; *see also Positivist Review* (London); Swinny, Shapland Hugh
"postcolonial" 17, 26, 27, 42, 128, 257, 275, 524, 598, 649, 650; colonial/postcolonial studies 524
potato blight (Ireland, 1871) 366, 535, 539, 544; *see also* Iranian famine (1870–72)
Potter, Murray Anthony 442, 443, 448; *Sohrab and Rustem: the Epic Theme of a Combat Between Father and Son* (by Murray Anthony Potter, 1902) 442; *see also* Conla (Conlaoch); Cuchulain (Cú Chulainn); Ferdowsi, Abul-Qassem; Meyer, Kuno; Rustam; *Shāhnāmeh*; Sohrab; Ulster Cycle
Pottinger, Henry 388; *see also* Christie, Charles; Down (County); Malcolm, John
pre-Adamic/pre-Adamite 403, 405; *see also* Adam
Presbyterians 68, 180, 212, 364, 365, 378n23, 476; *see also* Scots-Protestants
La Presse (Paris) 332
Prichard, James Cowles 118, 119; *The Eastern Origin of the Celtic Nations Proved by a Comparison of Their Dialects with the Sanskrit, Greek, Latin, and Teutonic Languages* (by James Cowles Prichard 1831) 119; *see also* anthropology; evolutionary theories; Mahābādiān; Pishdādiān
printing press 82, 132, 580, 581; technological innovations 81
Proctor, Robert 604; *see also* agnotology
Prospectus of a Dictionary of the Language of the Aire Coti, or Ancient Irish, Compared with the Language of the Cuti, or Ancient Persians, with the Hindoostanee, the Arabic, and Chaldean Languages (by Charles Vallancey, 1802): *see* Vallancey, Charles
Protestant plantations in Ireland 268, 336, 411, 538, 570; *see also* Elizabeth I, Queen; James I of England (James VI of Scotland); Plantation of Munster; Plantation of Ulster
Protestant Reformation 1, 5, 26, 48, 50, 68, 90, 101, 162n243, 272, 316, 570, 598; *see also* Anglican Church; Church of England; English Reformation
Protestants (general) 11, 50, 51, 68, 69, 88, 168, 177, 178, 212, 252, 262, 270, 303, 428, 464n216, 491, 522, 589
Pro-Treaty (Irish nationalists) 348, 579, 581, 588, 592, 593; *see also* Anglo-Irish Treaty (December 6, 1921); Anti-Treaty (Irish nationalists); Irish Civil War (1922–23); Irish Free State
"provincializing" England 127
"provincializing Ireland" 8, 138, 220, 227, 318, 349, 515, 524–28, 536, 540, 541,

547, 548, 564, 566, 575, 585, 608, 613, *passim*; provincialists 526, 564, 608; self-provincializing of Ireland 608; *see also* Banim, John; Davis, Thomas Osborne; "deprovincializing" Ireland; Finerty, John Frederick; Ireland as a "province"; O'Callaghan, John Cornelius; O'Connell, Daniel; Parnell, Charles Stewart

Provisional Irish Republican Army 501, 591, 641; *see also An Phoblacht* (Belfast); Provisional Sinn Féin; "The Troubles" (Northern Ireland, 1969–98)

Provisional Sinn Féin 501, 641; *see also An Phoblacht* (Belfast); Provisional Irish Republican Army; "The Troubles" (Northern Ireland, 1969–98)

Prussia 28, 240, 245, 254, 364, 365, 372, 376n9, 399, 568, 574; *see also* Franco-Prussian War (1870–71)

Ptolemy 573; Ptolemaic 529

Punch (London) 266

Punic: *see* Phoenician/Carthaginian language (Punic)

Puranas 95, 117; *see also* O'Brien, Henry

Purcell, John 426; *see also* Fitzgerald, Edward (poet)

[Purcell, Mrs.] 522, 523; *The Orientalist, or Electioneering in Ireland; a Tale, by Myself* (by [Mrs. Purcell], 1820) 522; *see also* Shirazi, Mirza Abul Hassan Khan ("Ilchi")

Pyrault, Claude 332; *see also* Basra; France; Kharg Island

Qajar dynasty (Iran, 1796–1925) 33, 115, 132, 187, 304, 348, 389, 516, 532, 533; *see also* Abbas Mirza (Qajar crown prince); Bahram Mirza; Farhad Mirza; Fath Ali Shah; Jalal al-Din Mirza (Jalal Pour-Fath-Ali Shah); Mohammad Shah; Mohammad-Ali Shah; Mozaffar al-Din Shah; Nasser al-Din Shah

Qazvini, Hamdollah Mostufi 162n235

Qazvini, Zakaria ibn Mohammad 529

Qizilbash 259, 262–74, 276, 345, 617; *see also* Fraser, James Baillie; Mangan, James Clarence ("To the Ingleezee Khafir, Calling Himself Djuan Bool Djenkinzun"); Nader Shah

Quarterly Review (London) 339

Queen's College (Belfast) 121, 209n105

Queen's College (Cork) 394

Quiggin, Edmund Crosby 149

Qunavi, Sadr al-Din 244; *see also* Mangan, James Clarence

The Qur'an 133, 205n46, 270, 566; *see also* Islam; Muhammad (prophet)

"race": *see* racial theories

racial theories 8, 16, 28, 30, 31, 35, 36, 52, 57–59, 86, 92, 100, 107, 108, 113, 121, 134, 137–39, 143–49, 181, 191, 197, 200, 201, 214, 215, 217, 233, 260, 262–64, 277, 278, 280, 282, 291, 316, 341, 346, 353, 371, 387, 391–97, 400–405, 407–22, 424–25, 433–35, 438–39, 441, 443, 448–51, 458n126, 459n137, 461n165, 471, 472, 478–79, 485, 488–92, 499, 504n49, 523, 563, 568, 570–73, 576–79, 581, 582, 584, 588, 599, 600, 605, 606, 610–11, 616, 620, 636, 639, 640, 646, 650; *see also* Aryanism (racial theories); "whitening" of the "mere Irish"

Rainey, Eileen 498, 524; *see also* Navab, Hussein Qoli Khan

rajah 89, 331, 363, 377n15, 546

"rajas": *see* rajah

Ramaswamy, Sumathi 12, 56, 139–41; *The Lost Land of Lemuria: Fabulous Geographies, Catastrophic Histories* (by Sumathi Ramaswamy, 2004) 139; *see also* Kumarināṭu; Lemuria; "place-making"; Tamil people

Ramayana 449

The Rambler: *see* Dalberg-Acton, John Emerich Edward

Ranger, Terence 35; *see also* "invention of tradition"

Ranke, Leopold von 568

Rao of Kutch (Pragmalji II) 377n15; *see also* Iranian famine (1870–72)

Rashid al-Din of Hamedan: *see* Hamedani, Rashid al-Din

Rasht 187, 378n23

Rassam, Hormuzd 453n25

rationalism 27, 28, 30–32, 428, 436, 462, 477, 482–84; counter- "rationalism" 428; *see also* the Enlightenment ("European" Enlightenment rationalism)

Rawlinson, Henry Creswicke 370, 373; *see also* Iranian famine (1870–72); Old Persian (language and script)

"reception" of a work of art: *see* Benjamin, Walter

Reddin, Daniel 375, 379n63; *see also* Coercion Acts (Ireland); Irish Republican Brotherhood

Redmond, John 165n300, 469, 472, 477, 550–52; *see also* Irish Parliamentary Party

Redmond, William 506n71, 546; *see also* Irish Parliamentary Party; Land League

"Refayel, Fologun" 532, 560n64; *Jahān-namā* (by "Fologun Refayel," 1851)

Reliques of Irish Poetry (by Charlotte Brooke, 1789): *see* Brooke, Charlotte

Remarks of a Persian Traveller on the Principal Courts of Europe with a Dissertation upon that of England, the Nation in General, and the Prime Minister... (anon., 1736) 169; *see also Lettres persanes* (by Montesquieu, Baron de, 1721)
"Renaissance" ("European") 421, 529, 648
Renan, Ernest 216; "What is a Nation?" 216
Repeal Association (1840) 212; *see also* Clontarf; Irish Home Rule; O'Connell, Daniel; O'Connellite; Repeal Movement
Repeal movement 90, 99, 168, 202n1, 212, 236, 522, 544, *passim*; *see also* Act of Union (of the United Kingdom of Great Britain and Ireland, 1801); *Cork Examiner*; *Freeman's Journal* (Dublin); Irish Home Rule; Irish Parliamentary Party; *The Nation* (Dublin); O'Connell, Daniel; O'Connellite; Repeal Association (1840); Sinn Féin
Repeal of the Party Processions Act (Ireland, 1871) 366
Republic of Ireland 26, 45n38, 291, 500, 501, 554, 641; *see also* Éire; Erin; Ireland; Irish Free State
Republic of Texas 390; *see also* Mexico; Santa Fe Expedition
republicanism: *see* Fenian Brotherhood; Irish National Liberation Army; Irish Republican Socialist Party; Official Sinn Féin; People's Democracy; Provisional Irish Republican Army; Provisional Sinn Féin; Sinn Féin; Sinn Féin the Workers' Party; Society of United Irishmen; United Irishmen; Young Ireland
Retzius, Andreas Joannes 401–3; *see also* craniology; Wilde, Jane Francesca Agnes (née Elgee)
Reuter concession (Iran, 1872) 346, 375, 468; *see also* Gladstone, William Ewart; Nasser al-Din Shah; Reuter, Julius de
Reuter, Julius de 375, 468; *see also* Reuter concession (Iran, 1872)
Reuters 482, 483, 548, 640
Reza Shah 511n127, 594, 641; *see also* Pahlavi dynasty (Iran, 1925–79)
Rhys, John 149
Ribbon Society: *see* Ribbonism
Ribbonism (Ireland) 367, 544; *see also* Catholics; Irish Land Acts (1870, 1881); peasantry (Ireland)
Richardson, David 517; *see also* Abu Taleb Khan (Mirza Abu Taleb Khan Tabrizi-Isfahani); English East India Company
Richardson, John 22, 251, 446; *A Dictionary: Persian, Arabic* (by John Richardson, 1777) 22; "A Dissertation on the Languages, Literature, and Manners of Eastern Nations" (1777) 446

Ricoeur, Paul 161n224, 273–76, 280, 300n176; "debt" 256, 275–76, 280, 281; "heritage" 275, 280; "narrated time" 161n224; "obligation" to the past 274, 276, 280, 281; "traces" of the past 274–76, 280; "work of memory, work of mourning" 274; *see also* memory
Robespierre, Maximilien 135
Roebuck, John Arthur 307, 354n13, 354n14, 354n18; *see also* Anglo-Iranian War (1856–57); Liberal Party (UK); Whig Party (Radical wing)
Roling, Bernd 71
Rolleston, Thomas William Hazen 433, 442
Roman 47, 48, 50, 54, 63, 64, 74, 79, 80, 89, 96, 115, 116, 124, 130, 131, 136, 138, 144, 150n3, 183, 190, 195, 197, 220, 290, 384, 395, 421, 529, 534, 537, 565, 573, 574, 626n5, 644; *see also* Greco-Roman sources; Rome
Romanticism 28, 32, 236; Romantic 25, 27, 28, 30–32, 89, 167, 173, 175, 176, 184, 188, 203n19, 212, 232, 235, 236, 270, 279, 289, 399, 426, 447, 522, 567, 583, 640; *see also* Byron, Lord (George Gordon Byron); Hellenophilia; Herder, Johann Gottfried von; Irish nationalism; Moore, Thomas; "oriental-style" literature
Rome 135, 195, 217, 220, 563, 575, 606; *see also* Sublicius Bridge
Rooke, William Michael (originally O'Rourke) 522
Rotunda concert hall (Dublin) 521
Round Towers (Ireland) 7, 13, 14, 24, 53, 56, 63, 66, 72, 75, 79, 85–95, 97–107, 109–15, 117, 120–25, 133, 142, 147, 148, 167, 180, 189–93, 195, 196, 198, 199, 201, 207n81, 211–13, 215, 227, 261, 269, 277, 278, 381–86, 394–96, 403, 418, 431, 567, 625n1, 642, 643; *see also* archaeology; architecture; astronomy; Beaufort, Louisa Catherine; Betham, William; Bourke, Ulick Joseph; Chaldeans; D'Alton (Dalton), John; "fire worship"; "Iranian" theories of Irish origins; Irish antiquarianism; Keane, Marcus; Kildare; Lanigan, John; Moore, Thomas; O'Brien, Henry; O'Donovan, Edmond; Petrie, George; phallic worship; "sun worship"; Vallancey, Charles; Wilde, Jane Francesca Agnes (née Elgee); Windele, John
The Round Towers of Ireland, or the Mysteries of Freemasonry, of Sabaism, and of Budhism, for the First Time Unveiled (by Henry O'Brien, 1834) 87, 88, 90–92, 97, 99, 100, 104, 106, 111–15, 117, 120–23, 133, 167, 208n81, 277, 278, 418; *see also Dabestān-e Mazāheb*;

Dasātir; Erskine, William; "Iranian" theories of Irish origins; Jones, William; Mahābādiān; Milesians; O'Brien, Henry; Petrie, George; Pishdādiān; Round Towers (Ireland); Tuatha de Dananns; Vallancey, Charles

Rouznāmeh-ye Dowlat-e Āliyeh-ye Irān (Tehran) 540, 541; *see also* "E'temad al-Saltaneh" (Mohammad Hassan Khan)

Rouznāmeh-ye Elmi (Tehran) 537

Rouznāmeh-ye Vaqāye'-e Ettefāqiyeh (Tehran; a.k.a., "*Teheran Gazette*") 327, 333, 337, 343, 531, 532, 539, 540, 560n64, 640; *see also* Burgess, Edward

Rowlatt Acts (India, 1919) 593

Rowzat al-Safā' fi Sirat al-Anbiyā' wa al-Moluk wa al-Kholafā : *see Universal History* of Mirkhond (15th century)

Roy, Rammahon 651n5

Royal Asiatic Society (London) 91, 106; Bombay branch of the Society 442; *see also* Higgins, Godfrey; Modi, Jivanji Jamshedji

Royal Dublin Society 67, 70; *see also* Irish antiquarianism; Vallancey, Charles

Royal Historical and Archaeological Association of Ireland 447; *see also* Wood-Martin, William Gregory

Royal Irish Academy 7, 24, 60, 61, 63, 67, 69, 77, 86, 89–93, 97, 99, 104–7, 120, 121, 123, 140, 185, 195, 198, 200, 201, 206n63, 209n105, 211, 382, 401, 418, 441, 443, 445, 446, 518, 521, 571, 581, 597; *see also* Beaufort, Louisa Catherine; Betham, William; Bourke, Ulick Joseph; Brigger, Francis Joseph; D'Alton (Dalton), John; Drummond, William Hamilton; *Dublin Penny Journal*; Edgeworth, Maria; Gilbert, John Thomas; Hamilton, William R.; Hardy, Philip Dixon; Irish antiquarianism; Joyce, Patrick Weston; Keane, Marcus; MacCarthy, Denis Florence; Moore, Thomas; O'Brien, Henry; O'Conor, Charles; O'Halloran, Sylvester (Silvester); O'Laverty, James; Otway, Caesar; Petrie, George; *Transactions of the Royal Irish Academy*; Vallancey, Charles; Walker, Joseph Cooper; Wilde, William Robert Wills

Royal Irish Academy's 1833 prize essay 89, 90, 92, 93, 97, 104, 106, 123, 157n145, 195; *see also* Cloncurry, Lord (Valentine Brown Lawless, 2nd Baron Cloncurry); D'Alton (Dalton), John; O'Brien, Henry (1833 prize essay of the Royal Irish Academy); Petrie, George (1833 prize essay of the Royal Irish Academy)

Royal Irish Constabulary 544, 550

Rudy, Charles 482; *see also The Egyptian Standard* (Cairo)

Rumi, Moulana Jalal al-Din Mohammad 243, 244, 297n100; *see also* Malcolm, John; Mangan, James Clarence

Russell, George William ("Æ") 431–33; "The Story of a Star" (1894) 431; *see also* Hermetic Society (Dublin); Irish Literary Revival; theosophy

Russell, John 168, 195, 540; *see also* Moore, Thomas

Russell, William Howard 335; *see also* Crimean War (1854–56); *The Times* (London)

Russia 4, 33, 36, 131, 138, 151n20, 185, 207n81, 225, 260, 266, 267, 273, 303, 304, 307–11, 313, 314, 317, 318, 320, 322, 324–30, 332–33, 335–37, 341–43, 346, 347, 353n8, 354n12, 355n34, 357n61, 362, 364, 366, 370, 375, 378n23, 385, 388, 389, 392, 430, 468, 473, 474, 478, 479, 481, 491, 494–98, 500, 510n116, 515, 516, 524, 531, 533, 539, 547, 550, 551, 586, 591, 595, 621, 638, 639; imperial leverage in Iran 1, 6, 8, 33, 36, 37, 138, 145, 273, 274, 304, 306, 307, 324, 328, 333, 347, 348, 354n12, 370, 375, 391, 424, 450, 468, 469, 473, 474, 476, 477, 479–82, 484, 485, 487, 489, 493–98, 506n71, 506n73, 508n88, 515, 516, 533, 542, 548, 551, 552, 590, 639; Soviet Union 493, 594; *see also* Anglo-Iranian War (1856–57); Anglo-Russian Agreement (1907); Anglo-Soviet occupation of Iran; Bolshevism; Catherine "the Great" (Empress of Russia); Comintern (Third / Communist International); Crimean War (1854–56); First World War (Anglo-Russian occupation of Iran (1915)); Moscow; Muscovy Company; Russo-Iranian War (1804–13); Russo-Iranian War (1826–28); Russo-Japanese War (1904–05); Russo-Ottoman War (1877–78); St. Petersburg; Tsar (Czar)

Russian Revolution (1905) 474

Russian Revolutions (1917) 500

Russo-Iranian War (1804–13) 33, 206n56, 273, 516, 533

Russo-Iranian War (1826–28) 328, 330, 533; "most-favored nation" status granted to Russia in trade with Iran 329–30; *see also* Griboyedov, Alexander Sergeyevich

Russo-Japanese War (1904–05) 491, 610

Russo-Ottoman War (1877–78) 345

Rustam 41, 42, 83, 184, 185, 442, 443, 446, 447; *see also* Cuchulain (Cú Chulainn); epics; Esfandiyar; Meyer, Kuno; Modi, Jivanji Jamshedji; Mohl, Jules (Julius);

INDEX 759

mythology (Iranian mythology);
  Shāhnāmeh; Sohrab; Ulster Cycle
Ryan, Frank 593; *see also* Indian-Irish
  Independence League (1932)
Ryan, Frederick Michael (Fred) 324, 351,
  429, 430, 432, 433, 450, 478, 481–84,
  486, 507n73, 580, 584, 589, 605, 609,
  611; "Finian" 483; "Irial" 483; "Laying
  the Foundations" (a play by Fred Ryan,
  performed in 1902) 483; *see also* Anglo-
  Russian Agreement (1907); *Dana: An Irish
  Magazine of Independent Thought* (Dublin);
  Egypt (London); "Egypt for Egyptians"; *The
  Egyptian Standard* (Cairo); internationalism;
  Iranian Constitutional Revolution (1906–
  11); Irish National Theatre Society; Irish
  nationalism; Limerick pogrom (Ireland,
  1904); *National Democrat* (Dublin); pacifism;
  positivism; socialism; women's rights

Sabian 96, 112, 277; Sabean-Mandaean 112;
  Sabians of Harran 112;*see also* O'Brien,
  Henry; Vallancey, Charles
de Sacy, Silvester 155n105; *see also* Pahlavi
  script (ancient "Middle Persian")
Sa'di 240, 243, 244, 279, 406; *see also*
  Malcolm, John; Mangan, James Clarence
Sadleir, John 540; *see also* Catholic Defence
  Association; "Irish Brigade" (in the British
  House of Commons)
Safavid dynasty (Iran, 1501–1722/36) 4, 5,
  33, 134, 172, 262, 265–74, 348, 515, 516,
  527, 639; *see also* Abbas I, Shah; Charles
  I, King; Cotton, Dodmore; Elizabeth I,
  Queen; English East India Company;
  James I of England (James VI of Scotland);
  Jenkinson, Anthony; Mangan, James
  Clarence ("To the Ingleezee Khafir,
  Calling Himself Djuan Bool Djenkinzun");
  Muscovy Company; Naqd-Ali Beg;
  Pashtun (Pathan) Gilzai confederacy; Safi,
  Shah; Sherley (Shirley), Anthony; Sherley
  (Shirley), Robert; Tahmasp I, Shah
Safi, Shah 268; *see also* Safavid dynasty (Iran,
  1501–1722/36)
Sahaf-bashi, Esmail 538; *Tārikh-e Engelesstān*
  (by Esmail Sahaf-bashi, n.d.) 538; *see
  also* Dar al-Fonun; Schmitz, Leonhard
  (Leonard) (*A History of England for Junior
  Classes* (by Leonhard (Leonard) Schmitz,
  1873))
"Sahib Company": *see* English East India
  Company
Said, Edward W. 127, 134; Saidian 36,
  44n36, 129, 153n59, 461n165; *see also*
  "contrapuntal"; orientalism; "Traveling
  Texts"

Sainte-Beuve, Charles Augustin 463n209
Salārnāmeh (by Mirza Aqa Khan Kermani,
  1895): *see* Kermani, Mirza Aqa Khan
Sale, Florentia (née Wynch) 319; *A Journal
  of the Disasters in Affghanistan, 1841–2* (by
  Florentia Sale, 1843) 319; *see also* Anglo-
  Afghan War (1839–42); Sale, Robert
Sale, Robert 319; *see also* Anglo-Afghan War
  (1839–42); Sale, Florentia (née Wynch)
Salisbury, Lord (Robert Arthur Talbot
  Gascoyne-Cecil) 467–70, 501n8; *see also*
  Conservative Party (UK; a.k.a., Unionist
  Party after 1895); Foreign Office (UK);
  tobacco concession (Iran, 1890); Tobacco
  Protest (Iran, 1891–92)
Sallust (Gaius Sallustius Crispus) 77
Sampsonia, Teresia 556n3; *see also* Circassia;
  Sherley (Shirley), Anthony
San Patricios (Saint Patrick's Battalion) 473;
  see also Mexican-American War (1846–48)
Sanscrit: *see* Sanskrit
Sanskrit 17, 57, 79, 81, 83, 84, 95, 119, 125,
  147, 214, 383, 393, 394, 404, 409, 410,
  440, 442, 448, 449, 519, 572, 649; *see also*
  Cuthite; Indic studies; Indo-European
  languages; Jones, William
Santa Fe Expedition 390; *see also* Fitzgerald,
  Archibald; Mexico; Republic of Texas
Santal ("Santhal") uprising 325, 327; *see also*
  India
Sappho 615
Sarmatians 12, 78, 119; *see also* Irano-
  Sarmatians; Polish Sarmatianism
Sarmatic: *see* Sarmatians
Sassanian dynasty (Iran, 224–650 CE)
  155n105, 182; *see also Lalla Rookh. An
  Oriental Romance* (by Thomas Moore, 1817)
Sassoon, Albert Abdullah David 376n11; *see
  also* Iranian famine (1870–72)
*Saturday Review of Politics, Literature, Science, and
  Art* (London) 410
Saturn 119–20
Satyavrata (Vaivasvata Manu) 117, 118;
  see also Faber, George Stanley; Wilford,
  Francis
Saumaise, Claude (Claudius Salmasius) 57,
  151n31; *see also* Indo-European languages
Savage, Marmion Wilme ["Wilard"] 522–23;
  The Falcon Family; or, Young Ireland (by
  Marmion Wilme Savage, 1845) 522; *see
  also* Shirazi, Mirza Abul Hassan Khan
  ("Ilchi")
Savarkar, Vinayak Damodar 478, 490,
  507n74; *see also* Dryhurst, Nora ("Nannie")
  Florence
Savushun 493; *see also* Daneshvar, Simin
Saxo Grammaticus 424

Saxon 20, 43n13, 71, 193, 217–19, 228, 283, 404, 407, 415, 416, 424, 569, 615, 616; *see also* Anglo-Saxons

Sayce, Archibald Henry 393; *see also* Aryans

"Scandian" theories of Irish origins: *see* "Scandinavian" (Scandian) theories of Irish origins

Scandinavia 56, 58, 77, 119, 124, 193, 200, 216, 317, 393, 402, 412, 425; Scandinavian 198, 215, 447, 614, 616, 619, 624; *see also* Norse ("Vikings")

"Scandinavian" (Scandian) theories of Irish origins 16, 19, 25, 56, 66, 77, 85, 88, 93, 124, 199, 215, 216, 317, 406, 644; *see also* Aryanism (racial theories Nordic (Scandinavian) origins); Beauford ("Beaufort"), William; Campbell, Thomas; Ledwich, Edward; theories of Irish origins

Schiller, Friedrich 247, 248, 259, 288; *see also* Mangan, James Clarence

Schleicher, August 409

Schmitz, Leonhard (Leonard) 538; *A History of England for Junior Classes* (by Leonhard (Leonard) Schmitz, 1873) 538; *see also* Sahaf-bashi, Esmail (*Tārikh-e Engelesstān* (by Esmail Sahaf-bashi, n.d.))

Scholasticism 529

School of Irish Learning (Dublin) 441; *see also* *Ériu* (Dublin); Meyer, Kuno

School of Political Science (Tehran) 136, 532, 559n61; *see also* geography

Schwab, Raymond 151n31; *The Oriental Renaissance: Europe's Rediscovery of India and the East, 1680–1880* (*La Renaissance Orientale*, by Raymond Schwab, 1950) 151n31; *see also* "Oriental Renaissance"; orientalism

Scissors and Paste (Dublin) 496; *see also* Griffith, Arthur

Scota 49, 79; *see also* Egypt; Fénius Farsaid (Fenius Farsa); Ireland; Nectanebo II; Niul; Pharaoh; Scotia; Scotland

Scotia 96, 150n3, 197, 214; Scoti 96, 147, 150n3, 197, 214; "Scotia Major"(Ireland) 214; "Scotica" 91; Scotti 150n3, 565; *see also* Ireland; Scota; Scotland; Scythia

Scotland 20, 21, 50, 51, 65, 66, 68, 70, 78, 96, 190, 194, 197, 202n2, 283, 368, 387, 394, 439, 441, 444, 455n56, 464n225, 515, 516, 521, 523, 527, 528, 533, 535–37, 539, 540, 543, 554, 559n56, 570, 572, 574, 578; Caledonia 197; Scottish Home Rule 549, 554; Scottish people (also "Scotch" and "Scots") 20, 43n15, 50, 51, 65, 69, 70, 78, 83, 112, 113, 121, 143, 187, 206n56, 214, 267, 293n37, 357n74, 357n75, 388, 395, 438, 441, 446, 464n225, 501n2, 517, 535, 538, 570, 574, 575; Scottish Reformation 570; theories of Scottish origins 20, 51, *passim*; *see also* James I of England (James VI of Scotland); James II, King; Scota; Scotia; Stuart dynasty (1603–49, 1660–1714)

Scots-Protestants 24; *see also* Presbyterians

Scott, Jonathan 538; *see also* Shirazi, Mirza Mohammad ("Malek al-Kotab")

Scott, Walter 194; *The History of Scotland* (by Walter Scott, 1830) 194; *see also* Longman, Rees, Orme, Brown, and Green

"Scuitte": *see* Scotia

Scythia 2, 4, 12, 15, 20, 21, 47, 49, 50, 52, 53, 61, 63, 72, 74, 96, 150n3, 151n20, 277, 425, 623, 636, 637; *see also* Darius I (Achaemenid emperor); Scotia

"Scythian" theories of Irish origins 2, 4, 14, 15, 17, 19–21, 27, 47–56, 59, 61, 63, 64, 66, 69–75, 77–79, 82, 84, 85, 89, 91, 92, 94–96, 102, 104, 121, 122, 144, 146, 147, 150n3, 199, 214–16, 219, 226, 227, 277, 312, 382, 383, 405, 420–21, 424, 563, 565, 576, 582, 619, 624, 636, 637, 642, 646; *see also* Keating, Geoffrey; O'Curry, Eugene; "Scytho-Phoenician" theory of Irish origins; theories of Irish origins

Scythian-Phoenician: *see* "Scytho-Phoenician" theory of Irish origins

Scythians 2, 4, 12, 15, 19–22, 47–55, 57, 62–64, 66, 67, 69–75, 77–81, 91, 94–96, 104, 108, 116, 118, 119, 144, 146, 147, 151n22, 151n32, 214, 215, 420–21, 425, 452n3, 563, 600, 638; *see also* Aryanism (racial theories); Aryans; "Coti"; Cuthite; Fénius Farsaid (Fenius Farsa); Finnish; Firbolgs; Indo-Europeans; Indo-Iranians; Indo-Scythians; Irano-Scythians; Nemed; Nemedians; Tuatha de Dananns; Voltaire (François-Marie Arouet)

Scytho-Iberiaus 102; *see also* Iberian Peninsula; Milesians; Spain

Scytho-Iranians: *see* Irano-Scythians

Scytho-Persians: *see* Irano-Scythians

"Scytho-Phoenician" theory of Irish origins 55, 64, 71, 72; *see also* O'Halloran, Sylvester (Silvester); Vallancey, Charles

seanchaí (traditional Gaelic chroniclers and storytellers) 397; "seanachie" 193; "Seanchan the Bard" 397

Seattle 489

"Second Anglo-Persian War": *see* Anglo-Iranian War (1856–57)

"Second Opium War": *see* Anglo-Chinese War (1856–60)

Second World War 493, 597; *see also* Anglo-Soviet occupation of Iran

INDEX 761

Select Reviews, and Spirit of the Foreign Magazines (Philadelphia) 521
Seleucid Empire 52; *see also* Alexander the Great; Macedonia
self-plagiarism 232–33, 238, 242, 243, 253, 274, 279, 586; *see also* plagiarism; Mangan, James Clarence
Seljuks 296n92, 386, 449
"Semitic" (racial designation) 20, 59, 73, 422, 435, 448, 449, 605, 608, 610, 611, 620, 631n103; *see also* anti-Jewish; Arabs; Assyria (and Assyrians); Babylonians; Chaldeans; Jewish people; Phoenicians; Shem
Semitic languages 387, 409–10, 448, 620; *see also* Arabic; Hebrew; Phoenician/Carthaginian language (Punic)
Semnani, Ala al-Dawla 244; *see also* Mangan, James Clarence
Sen, Malcolm 587, 598, 618
Sentimental and Masonic Magazine (Dublin) 229; *see also* freemasonry; Jones, John
"Sepoy Mutiny": *see* Indian uprising (1857–58)
sepoys 303, 307, 320, 327, 345, 528; *see also* Anglo-Afghan War (1839–42); Anglo-Iranian War (1856–57); Indian uprising (1857–58); sowars
Sevastopol 335; Battle of the Great Redan Fort 335–36; *see also* Crimean War (1854–56)
Seymour, Henry Danby 339, 358n99; *see also* Anglo-Iranian War (1856–57); Ferrier, Joseph Pierre (*Caravan Journeys and Wanderings in Persia, Afghanistan, Turkistan, and Beloochistan* (by Joseph Pierre Ferrier; English translation from the French by William Jesse, edited by Henry Danby Seymour, 1856)); Jesse, William
Shâh-Nâma: *see* Shāhnāmeh
Shāhnāmeh 41, 42, 74, 95, 108, 112, 114, 119, 130, 132–34, 136–37, 157n155, 184–85, 441, 442, 445, 446, 448, 449, 519, 640; *see also* Atkinson, James; *Bibliothèque orientale* (by Barthélemy d'Herbelot, 1697); epics; Ferdowsi, Abul-Qassem; Herbelot [de Molainville], Barthélemy d'; Kiāniān dynasty; Meyer, Kuno; Modi, Jivanji Jamshedji; Mohl, Jules (Julius); mythology (Iranian mythology); O'Brien, Henry; Pishdādiān; Rustam; Sohrab; Ulster Cycle; Vallancey, Charles
Al-Shahrastani (Muhammad) 119
"Al Shahrastani": *see* Al-Shahrastani (Muhammad)
Shakespeare, William 86, 98, 233, 284, 427, 620; *The Tempest* 284, 620; *see also* Caliban

"Shams-ul-Ulama": *see* Modi, Jivanji Jamshedji
Shannon-Mangan, Ellen 247, 264, 278, 281
Sharma, Sunil 134
Shaw, George Bernard 494–95, 554; "Common Sense About the War" (1914) 495; *see also* Anglo-Russian Agreement (1907); Fabian socialism; Irish Home Rule
Shaykh Reza (?) 537–38; *Tārīkh-e Ingilīss* (by Shaykh Reza, n.d.) 537; *see also* Goldsmith, Oliver (*The History of England* (by Oliver Goldsmith; abridged and updated by Robert Simpson, 1823))
Shea, David 86, 111, 113, 115, 640; *History of the Early Kings of Persia, from Kaiomars, the First of the Peshdadian Dynasty, to the Conquest of Iran by Alexander the Great* (by David Shea, 1832) 115; *see also* Asiatic Society of Bengal; *Dabestān-e Mazāheb*; *Dabistan, or the School of Manners* (by David Shea and Anthony Troyer, 1843); Troyer, Anthony; *Universal History of Mirkhond* (15th century)
Sheehy Skeffington, Francis 430, 482, 483, 485, 486, 505n54, 506n70; *see also* internationalism; Irish nationalism; *National Democrat* (Dublin); pacifism; socialism; women's rights
Sheehy Skeffington, Hanna 430, 478, 480, 484, 505n54; *see also* internationalism; Irish nationalism; Irish Women's Franchise League; pacifism; socialism; women's rights
Sheil Edward 358n98; *see also* Home Rule League; Irish Parliamentary Party; Sheil, Justin; Sheil, Lady (Mary Leonora Woulfe Sheil)
Sheil, Justin 330, 337–40, 358n97, 358n98, 390, 453n25; Molla Akram 338; Sultan Khan 338; *see also* Anglo-Iranian Treaty (1853); Sheil, Edward; Sheil, Lady (Mary Leonora Woulfe Sheil)
Sheil, Lady (Mary Leonora Woulfe Sheil) 339–41, 358n98, 358n105, 358n106, 359n107, 390, 453n25; *Glimpses of Life and Manners in Persia* (by Lady Sheil, 1856) 339, 390; *see also* Sheil, Edward; Sheil, Justin; Woulfe, Stephen
Sheil, Richard Lalor 339, 358n98, 390; *see also* Catholic Association (1823)
Shelley, Percy Bysshe 247
Shem 61, 73, 162n235; *see also* Noah
Shemitic: *see* "Semitic" (racial designation); Semitic languages; Shem
Sherāfat (Tehran) 540
Sheridan, Richard Brinsley 534
Sherley (Shirley), Anthony 273, 515, 516; *see also* Safavid dynasty (Iran, 1501–1722/36)

Sherley (Shirley), Robert 273, 515, 516, 556n3; *see also* Charles I, King; Cotton, Dodmore; James I of England (James VI of Scotland); Naqd-Ali Beg; Safavid dynasty (Iran, 1501–1722/36); Sampsonia, Teresia

Sherley (Shirley), Thomas 516

Sheybani, Abdul-Hussein ("Vahid al-Molk") 498, 509n112

Shiraz 279, 305, 328, 358n106, 377n22, 378n23; British mission 305, 328; *see also* Hashem Khan (Mirza)

Shirazi, Mirza Abul Hassan Khan ("Ilchi") 186, 187, 520–24, 558n36; "Fair Circassian" 186, 520, 522, 523; *see also* Hamilton, William Rowan; *The History of Mirza Abul Hassan Khan ... with Some Account of the Fair Circassian* (by anon., 1819); Morier, James Justinian; Ouseley, Gore [Purcell, Mrs.] (*The Orientalist, or Electioneering in Ireland; a Tale, by Myself* (by [Mrs. Purcell], 1820)); Savage, Marmion Wilme ["Wilard"] (*The Falcon Family; or, Young Ireland* (by Marmion Wilme Savage, 1845))

Shirazi, Mirza Mohammad ("Malek al-Kotab") 538; *Tārikh-e Engelesstān* (by Mirza Mohammad Shirazi, 1888/1889) 538; *see also* Scott, Jonathan

"Shirazis" of Zanzibar 12; *see also* Persianate heritage; Swahili coast

Shuster, William Morgan 484, 506n62; *The Strangling of Persia* (by William Morgan Shuster, 1912) 484; *see also* Anglo-Russian Agreement (1907); Iranian Constitutional Revolution (1906–11)

Siberia 259–61, 264, 288, 299n139, 299n154, 362; *see also* Mangan, James Clarence

Sigerson, George 579

Sikh 345, 522

Simpson, Robert 538; *see also* Goldsmith, Oliver (*The History of England* (by Oliver Goldsmith; abridged and updated by Robert Simpson, 1823))

Singapore 365, 377n18; Rev. Petros of the Armenian Church 377n18; *see also* Armenian; Iranian famine (1870–72); Moses (Movsessian), Catchick; *The Strait Times* (Singapore)

Singleton, Annie Elizabeth Harriet Jane 412, 413, 458n113; "Customs, Some Old, and Superstitions Yet Surviving in County Meath, Ireland" (1904) 412; *see also* "Iranian" theories of Irish origins

Sinn Féin 474–75, 478, 479, 481, 484, 486, 490, 494–96, 549, 580, 584, 590–92, 606, 607, 610; *see also* Cumann na nGaedheal (Society/League of the Gaels); Dryhurst, Nora ("Nannie") Florence; Griffith, Arthur; Hobson, (John) Bulmer; Irish Home Rule; Irish nationalism; Lynd, Robert Wilson; Martyn, Edward; O'Kelly, John Joseph (Seán Ua Ceallaigh); *Sinn Féin* (Dublin)

Sinn Féin (Dublin) 450, 475, 485–87, 496; *see also* Griffith, Arthur; Sinn Féin

Sinn Féin the Workers' Party 501, 641; *see also* Official Sinn Féin; *The United Irishman* (Dublin; post-1948 publication)

Sister Nivedita: *see* Noble, Margaret Elizabeth ("Sister Nivedita")

"sites of memory" (lieux de mémoire) 142, 275; *see also* Nora, Pierre

"sites of mourning": *see* Winter, Jay

Slavery 30, 175, 213, 217, 221, 224, 225, 228, 314–15, 352, 359n107, 360n128, 425, 473, 525, 526, 583, 647; enslavement 49, 214, 315, 352, 373, 385, 525, 526, 583, 611, 647; *see also* Hibernian Anti-Slavery Society; Mitchel, John

Slavs 395

Smith, Goldwin 144, 573

Snell, Merwin Marie 463n209

Social-Darwinism 393; *see also* Spencer, Herbert

Social Democratic and Labour Party (Northern Ireland) 641; *see also* "The Troubles" (Northern Ireland, 1969–98)

Social Democratic Party (Iran) 170, 497, 498, 524, 550; *see also* First World War; Iranian Nationalist Committee (Berlin); Taqizadeh, Hassan

socialism 265, 350, 429, 430, 434, 468, 475, 478, 479, 482, 483, 486, 493–95, 499, 501, 509n112, 510n121, 593, 595, 628n58; *see also* Fabian socialism; Irish Republican Socialist Party; Irish Socialist Republican Party; People's Democracy; Socialist Party of Ireland; worker's rights

Socialist Party of Ireland 475, 483; *see also* Connolly, James; Irish Socialist Republican Party

Socialist Republic (Belfast) 26; *see also* People's Democracy; "The Troubles" (Northern Ireland, 1969–98)

Society for the Amelioration of the Condition of Zoroastrians in Persia 132; *see also* Hataria, Manekji Limji; Parsi; Zoroastrian

Society for the Diffusion of Useful Knowledge 91, 197

Society for the Preservation and Publication of the Melodies of Ireland 200; *see also* Petrie, George

Society for the Preservation of Irish Language 393, 432; *see also* Bourke, Ulick Joseph; Mir Aulad Ali

INDEX 763

Society for the Suppression of Vice 170
Society of Friends (Quaker) 368; *see also* Great Famine (Ireland, 1845–51)
Society of Friends of Russian Freedom (London) 495; *see also* Anglo-Russian Agreement (1907)
Society of United Irishmen 2, 27, 29, 345, 352, 543, 569, 583, 635; *see also* Emmet, Robert; *Paddy's Resource* (1795–1803); Tone, Theobald Wolfe; United Irishmen; United Irishmen uprising (1798); United Irishmen uprising (1803)
Society of Useful Knowledge: *see* Society for the Diffusion of Useful Knowledge
Sogdians 72
Sohrab 41, 42, 185, 441–43, 446, 447; *see also* Atkinson, James; Conla (Conlaoch); epics; Meyer, Kuno; Modi, Jivanji Jamshedji; Mohl, Jules (Julius); mythology (Iranian mythology); Rustam; *Shāhnāmeh*; Ulster Cycle
South Africa 576, 597; Union of South Africa 549; *see also* Africa (southern Africa); Basutoland; Boer War (1880–81); Boer War (1899–1902); Cape Colony; Xhosa
Southern Citizen (Knoxville, Tennessee) 368; *see also* Mitchel, John
sowars 320, 327, 345, 528; *see also* Anglo-Afghan War (1839–42); Anglo-Iranian War (1856–57); Indian uprising (1857–58); sepoys
Spain 47, 49, 53, 63, 66, 71, 72, 75, 77, 125, 156n124, 190–92, 197, 269, 387, 390, 404, 406, 409, 420, 445, 515, 530, 595, 599, 617, 624; Spaniard 286; Spanish 21, 77, 89, 190, 191, 262, 286; Spanish Americas 360n127; *see also* Iberian Peninsula; Milesians; Scytho-Iberiaus
Spanish Civil War 595
Sparta 5, 22, 220, 222, 223, 225, 411, 585, 636; *see also* Greece; Marathon, Battle of (490 BCE); Thermopylae, Battle of (480 BCE)
"Speaking Truth to Power" 51, 228
Spectator (London) 422
Speed, John 527; "The theatre of the empire of Great Britaine: presenting an exact geography of the kingdomes of England, Scotland, Ireland, ..." (map, 1612) 527
Spencer, Herbert 393; *see also* Social-Darwinism
Spencer, John 546; Lord Lieutenant of Ireland 546
Spenser, Edmund 21, 23, 48, 49, 71, 78, 93, 527; *A View of the Present State of Ireland* (by Edmund Spenser, completed in 1596 and published in 1633) 48; *see also* "wild Irish" (civilizational accusation)

"Speranza": *see* Wilde, Jane Francesca Agnes (née Elgee)
The Spirit of the Nation (by Thomas Osborne Davis, et al., 1843) 397; *see also* Davis, Thomas Osborne; Williams, Richard D'Alton
spiritualism 429, 483, 587
St. Kilda (Australia) 377n17; *see also* Iranian famine (1870–72); Jewish people
St. Patrick 283, 387, 408, 498, 616; St. Patrick's Day 509n112, 582, 588, 619
St. Patrick's College (Maynooth) 198
St. Petersburg 36, 145, 302n214, 303, 333, 345, 473, 476, 477, 481, 485, 487, 494, 495, 497; *see also* Russia
Stalker, Foster 332; *see also* Anglo-Iranian War (1856–57)
Stanford, Charles Villiers 223
Stanihurst, Richard 49, 150n10
Stanley, Edward (Earl of Derby) 324; *see also* Anglo-Chinese War (1856–60)
Stanley, Henry Morton 357n71
The Starry Plough (Belfast) 26; *see also* Irish National Liberation Army; Irish Republican Socialist Party
Stephens, James 229, 545; *see also Irish People* (Dublin); Irish Republican Brotherhood; Young Ireland; Young Ireland uprising (1848)
Stevens, John 16, 64, 115; *The History of Persia. Containing, the Lives and Memorable Action of its Kings from the First Erecting of that Monarchy to this Time* (by John Stevens, 1715) 16, 64, 115; *see also Universal History* of Mirkhond (15th century)
Stewart, Charles 452n7, 469, 517, 519, 520, 525, 546; *see also* Abu Taleb Khan (Mirza Abu Taleb Khan Tabrizi-Isfahani); English East India Company; Haileybury College (Hertfordshire, England); *The Travels of Mirza Abu Taleb Khan, in Asia, Africa and Europe, during the Years 1799, 1800, 1801, 1802, and 1803* (trans. By Charles Stewart, 1810)
Stiles, Ezra 108; *see also* Dighton Rock (Massachusetts)
Stoker, Bram 555; *Dracula* (by Bram Stoker, 1897) 555
Stokes, William 101, 199–200, 394; *see also* Petrie, George
Stoler, Ann Laura 257
Stopford, James 335; *see also* Crimean War (1854–56)
The Story of the Irish Race (1921): *see* MacManus, Seumas
Strabo 48, 80
Strachan, John 441; *see also Ériu* (Dublin)

The Strait Times (Singapore) 377n18; *see also* Armenian; Moses (Movsessian), Catchick; Singapore

Strzygowski, Josef Rudolph Thomas 436

Stuart dynasty (1603–49, 1660–1714) 50, 352, 516, 570; *see also* Charles I, King; James I of England (James VI of Scotland); James II, King

Stuart Restoration (1660) 50; *see also* James II, King

Sturgeon, Sinéad 223

Sublicius Bridge 220; *see also* Davis, Thomas Osborne; Etruscan; Rome

Sudan 384, 452n7, 585, 627n46; *see also* O'Donovan, Edmond; "Mahdist" uprising

Suez 433

suffragist 120, 401, 478, 479, 486, 510n121; suffragette 398; *see also* women's rights

sufism 244, 430, 435, 436

Sullivan, Alexander Martin 189, 312, 324–26, 331, 339, 347, 353, 355n31, 368; *New Ireland* (by Alexander Martin Sullivan, 1877) 368; *see also* Constitutional Society of India; Great Famine (Ireland, 1845–51); *Lalla Rookh. An Oriental Romance* (by Thomas Moore, 1817); Moore, Thomas; *The Nation* (Dublin); "oriental" theories of Irish origins; Round Towers (Ireland); Zulus

Sullivan, Timothy Daniel 254, 324; *Penny Readings for the Irish People* (edited by Timothy Daniel Sullivan, 1879) 254

Sullivan, William Kirby 394

Sultanieh 453n25

Sumerians 12

"sun worship" 62, 85, 196, 386; *see also* Round Towers (Ireland)

Svayambhuva Manu 118

swadeshi 475, 490; *see also* Bengal (partition of (1905–11)); Indian nationalism

Swahili coast 12

swaraj 593; *see also* Indian nationalism

Sweden 214, 424, 474, 547; Swedish 57, 401; Swedish officers in the Iranian gendarme force 498

Swinny, Shapland Hugh 477–79, 484, 504n42, 584; *see also* Anglo-Russian Agreement (1907); Iranian Constitutional Revolution (1906–11); Irish Home Rule; National Peace Congress (London, 1912); Nationalities and Subject Races conferences (London, 1910, 1911, 1914); Persia Committee (London); *Positivist Review* (London); Positivist Society (London)

Switzerland 488, 514; Swiss 310, 393, 394, 627n38

Sykes, Mark 145, 165n301; *see also* Conservative Party (UK; a.k.a., Unionist Party after 1895); Sykes-Picot Agreement

Sykes, Percy 559n53

Sykes-Picot Agreement 165n301; *see also* Sykes, Mark

Syracuse (New York) 497

Syria 21, 53, 147, 407, 425, 430, 490, 503n38, 509n112, 582; *see also* Assyria

Tabari, Abu Jafar Mohammad 83

Tabreez: *see* Tabriz

Tabriz 120, 162n237, 389, 476, 482, 517, 532, 560n64; *see also* Azerbaijan (Iranian province)

Tacitus 573

Tagore, Rabindranath 435, 586–87; English translation of *Gitanjali* (by Rabindranath Tagore, 1912) 472, 587; Nobel Prize in literature (1913) 472, 587; *see also* Yeats, William Butler

Tahmasp I, Shah 266, 299n158, 515; *see also* Elizabeth I, Queen; Jenkinson, Anthony; Mangan, James Clarence ("To the Ingleezee Khafir, Calling Himself Djuan Bool Djenkinzun"); Muscovy Company; Safavid dynasty (Iran, 1501–1722/36)

Táin Bo Cuailnge (The Cattle Raid of Cooley) 442; *see also* Cuchulain (Cú Chulainn)

Talbot, Gerald Francis 467–70; *see also* tobacco concession (Iran, 1890); Tobacco Protest (Iran, 1891–92)

Tamerlane 326; *see also* Timurid dynasty

Tamil people 12, 139, 140; *see also* Kumarināṭu; Lemuria; Ramaswamy, Sumathi

taoiseach 595; *see also* Dáil Éireann (Irish Assembly); de Valera, Éamon

Taqizadeh, Hassan 509n112; *see also* Iranian Nationalist Committee (Berlin); Social Democratic Party (Iran)

Tara: *see* Hill of Tara

Tārikh-e Montazem-e Nāsseri (by "E'temad al-Saltaneh," 1881–83): *see* "E'temad al-Saltaneh" (Mohammad Hassan Khan)

"Tartar": *see* Tatar

Tatar 84, 86, 246, 279, 421

Tauris: *see* Tabriz

Taylor, Edgar 399

Taylor, Isaac 393, 396; *see also* Aryans

taziyeh (Shi'i Muslim passion plays) 385; *see also* Islam (Shi'i Islam); O'Donovan, Edmond

Teheran: *see* Tehran

Tehran 33, 34, 136, 170, 187, 304–6, 308–11, 318, 321, 322, 327–31, 333, 334, 336–39, 341, 343, 345, 354n12, 358n106, 366, 369, 378n23, 385, 389, 390, 468, 473, 485, 497, 500, 531, 537, 539, 540, 549–51, 553, 554, 560n64, 640; *see also* British legation (Tehran); Masjed-e Shah (mosque; Tehran)

INDEX 765

telegraph 305, 341, 342, 366, 367, 375, 379n55, 389, 500, 540, 547, 593, 640; *see also* Indo-European Telegraph Department; Iranian famine (1870–72); Wills, Charles James

teleology 107, 568; *see also* historiography and history

Temple, Bernard 478; *see also* Anglo-Russian Agreement (1907); Nationalities and Subject Races conferences (London, 1910, 1911, 1914)

Tennessee 318, 368

Tennyson, Alfred 251

Tennyson, Frederick 427

Teuton 70, 119, 144, 193, 200, 288, 289, 402, 404, 415, 416, 421, 447, 573

Thailand (/Siam) 365, 377n18; King Chulalongkorn 377n18; *see also* Armenian; Iranian famine (1870–72)

theories of Irish origins 2, 7, 8, 10, 11, 14–27, 33, 34, 36, 42, 48, 52, 53, 55–57, 62–64, 67, 68, 71–74, 79, 80, 86, 88, 93, 98–100, 102, 103, 105, 108, 121, 123, 126, 127, 130, 134, 135, 140–43, 145, 146, 148, 149, 153n55, 167, 188, 190, 191, 197, 199, 201, 212, 214–16, 226, 228, 231, 238, 276–79, 282, 284, 385, 388, 397, 401–3, 409, 412, 413, 417, 420, 422, 424, 425, 447, 458n119, 483, 568, 571, 576, 580, 582, 585, 587, 589, 598–600, 602, 604, 606, 612, 614, 620, 625, 636, 642, 646; *see also* "Armenian" theories of Irish origins; "Aryan" theories of Irish origins; Assyria (and Assyrians); Babylonians; Beaufort, Louisa Catherine; Bourke, Ulick Joseph; Celticism; Celts; Chaldeans; "Egyptian" theories of Irish origins; Elamites; "Europe-centered" theories of Irish origins; folklore (presumed Iranian roots of Irish folk beliefs and practices); "Greek" theories of Irish origins; Hebrews (people); "Indo-European" theories of Irish origins; "Indo-Iranian" theories of Irish origins; "Iranian" theories of Irish origins; "Irano-Scythian" theories of Irish origins; Irish antiquarianism; Keane, Marcus; Milesians; Moore, Thomas; O'Brien, Henry; "oriental" theories of Irish origins; Persianate heritage (Ireland's presumed Persianate heritage); "Phoenician" theories of Irish origins; Phoenician-Iranian theories of ancient Ireland's "Golden Age": "Scandinavian" (Scandian) theories of Irish origins; "Scythian" theories of Irish origins; "Scytho-Phoenician" theory of Irish origins; Vallancey, Charles

Theosophical Society 139, 429–32, 434, 587; *see also* Besant, Annie (née Wood); Blavatsky, Helena Petrovna; *Irish Theosophist* (Dublin); Leadbeater, Charles Webster; Olcott, Henry Steel

theosophy 116, 121, 139, 148, 428–35, 447, 449, 483, 579, 587, 648; *see also* Besant, Annie (née Wood); Blavatsky, Helena Petrovna; Chatterjee, Mohini; Cousins, James; Cousins, Margaret Elizabeth (née Gillespie); Despard, Charlotte; Leadbeater, Charles Webster; Magee, William Kirkpatrick ("John Eglinton"); Olcott, Henry Steel; rationalism (counter-"rationalism"); Russell, George William ("Æ"); Theosophical Society; Yeats, William Butler

"there and then" 257, 276, 284, 288, 289, 347, 609; *see also* Chuto, Jacques

Thermopylae, Battle of (480 BCE) 5, 7, 22, 220–24, 228, 348, 398, 455n58, 585, 601; *see also* Achaemenid dynasty (Persian Empire, c.550–330 BCE); Athens; civilization ("Western Civilization"); Davis, Thomas Osborne; Greece; O'Grady, Standish James; Sparta; Xerxes I (Achaemenid emperor)

Thiong'O, Ngugi Wa 650; "decolonizing the mind" 650

"third contact zones" 471, 498; *see also* cosmopolitan (nationalist cosmopolitanism); internationalism; nationalism

"Third World" 17, 26, 648; "Third-Worldist" 26, 641

"Thomas Brown, the younger" (pseud.): *see* Moore, Thomas

Thomond, Marquess of 89; *see also* O'Brien, James McEdward

Thoms, William John 399; a.k.a., "Ambrose Merton" 399; coined the English term "folklore" 399

Thomsen, Christian Jürgensen 198, 402, 403; *see also* craniology

Thomson, William Taylour 305, 306, 337, 338; *see also* British legation (Tehran); "Hashem Khan," Mrs.

Thonus Concolerus 118

Thracian Bosphorus: *see* Bosphorus (Bosporus)

Tibet 36, 452n15, 473, 476, 495; *see also* Anglo-Russian Agreement (1907)

"time in the text" 117

"time of the text" 117

The Times (London) 102, 165n301, 235, 305, 307, 308, 310, 311, 327, 335, 353n8, 377n20, 495, 514, 553, 554; Russell, William Howard 335

The Times of India (Bombay) 369, 373
timescape 417, 598
Timurid dynasty 386; *see also* Tamerlane
Tipperary (County) 371, 389, 458n113; *see also* Heron, Denis Caulfield; Cormick, John
Tipu Sultan of Mysore 520
Tithe War (Ireland, 1831–36) 544; *see also* Church of Ireland (tithes)
tobacco concession (Iran, 1890) 346, 375, 467–70, 481; cancellation 468; Imperial Tobacco Corporation of Persia 4467, 68, 469; indemnity 468, 469; *see also* Assadabadi, Sayyid Jamal al-Din (a.k.a., "al-Afghani"); Bryce, James; Cunninghame-Graham, Robert Bontine; Foreign Office (UK); Healy, Timothy Michael; Hunter, William A.; Imperial Bank of Persia; Keay, John Seymour; Labouchere, Henry; Malkum Khan; Morgan, William Pritchard; Morton, Alpheus C.; Nasser al-Din Shah; Picton, James Allanson; Salisbury, Lord (Robert Arthur Talbot Gascoyne-Cecil); Talbot, Gerald Francis; Tobacco Protest (Iran, 1891–92); Trevelyan, George Otto; Winterbotham, Arthur Brend
Tobacco Protest (Iran, 1891–92) 374, 467, 468, 470, 471, 481; *see also* Nasser al-Din Shah; Salisbury, Lord (Robert Arthur Talbot Gascoyne-Cecil); Talbot, Gerald Francis; tobacco concession (Iran, 1890)
Tóibín, Colm 437
Tone, Theobald Wolfe 222, 315, 472, 584; *see also* Society of United Irishmen; United Irishmen (1798 uprising)
topography 255–57, 385, 400, 532
Tory 88, 170, 310, 353n8, 354n13, 454n52, 470; *see also Dublin University Magazine*; Pakington, John
Toup-e Morvari (*The Pearl Cannon*, 1947): *see* Hedayat, Sadeq
Touran: *see* Turan
Towers and Temples of Ancient Ireland; Their Origin and History Discussed from a New Point of View, The (by Marcus Keane, 1867): *see* Keane, Marcu
"tradition" 8, 14, 17, 28, 30, 35, 49, 54, 59–62, 65–66, 68–70, 72, 78, 80, 82, 84, 92, 106–7, 109, 128, 130–31, 134, 136–37, 139–40, 143, 148, 152n36, 157n155, 179, 191, 193, 196–97, 208n87, 214, 220–21, 232–35, 249, 256, 290, 317, 326, 345, 381, 387, 396–97, 399–402, 404–5, 407–8, 410, 412, 417, 421, 424–25, 428–33, 435, 437, 440, 448, 451, 531, 563–65, 567–69, 572, 575, 579, 581, 587–88, 608–9, 614–15, 624, 626n30, 631n115,

637; *see also* "invention of tradition"; "modernity"/"modernities"
Transactions of the Literary Society of Bombay 113; *see also* Erskine, William; Literary Society of Bombay
Transactions of the Royal Irish Academy 92, 104; *see also* Beaufort, Louisa Catherine; Royal Irish Academy
Transoxania 119, 175, 241; *see also* Bukhara; "al-Muqanna" (Hashim ibn Hakim); Uzbekistan
"Traveling Texts" 134; *see also* Said, Edward W.
The Travels of Mirza Abu Taleb Khan, in Asia, Africa and Europe, during the Years 1799, 1800, 1801, 1802, and 1803 (trans. By Charles Stewart, 1810) 517, 557n14; *see also* Abu Taleb Khan (Mirza Abu Taleb Khan Tabrizi-Isfahani); Stewart, Charles
Trevelyan, George Otto 501n2; *see also* tobacco concession (Iran, 1890)
Trevor, William 555
Trieste 609, 612, 619; *see also* Italy (and Italian)
Trinity College (University of Dublin) 50, 77, 108, 168, 280, 389, 432, 453n19, 519, 524, 535; *see also* Catholic Relief Act (1778); Emmet, Robert; Flood, Henry; Hales, William (Rev.); Hely, James; Mir Aulad Ali; Moore, Thomas
"The Troubles" (Northern Ireland, 1969–98) 26, 493, 499, 641; Iranian expressions of solidarity with paramilitary Irish nationalist prisoners' hunger strike (1981) 493; *see also* Irish National Liberation Army; Irish Republican Socialist Party; Northern Ireland; People's Democracy; Provisional Irish Republican Army; Provisional Sinn Féin; Ulster
Troy 601; Trojans 20, 28, 193; *see also* Brutus
Troyer, Anthony 86, 111, 113, 115; *see also* Asiatic Society of Bengal; *Dabestān-e Mazāheb*; *Dabistan, or the School of Manners* (by David Shea and Anthony Troyer, 1843); Shea, David
Truth (London) 469
Tsar (Czar) 261, 326, 362, 363, 485, 494, 591; *see also* Russia
Tuatha de Dananns 14, 49, 64, 72, 89–92, 94–96, 100, 107, 111, 112, 121, 141, 147–48, 200, 201, 208n87, 226, 227, 277, 382, 383, 397, 405–6, 413, 424–25, 439, 572, 576, 599, 613, 615, 631n108, 644; *see also* Firbolgs; "Iranian" theories of Irish origins; Irish antiquarianism; Keating, Geoffrey; Mahābādiān; Nemedians; O'Brien, Henry; *Phoenecian Ireland* (1833

translation by Henry O'Brien of Joaquín Lorenzo Villanueva's 1831 *Ibernia Phoenicea*); Scythia; Vallancey, Charles
Tudor dynasty (1485–1603) 349; *see also* Elizabeth I, Queen; Henry VIII, King
Tunisia 241, 509n112
Turan 66, 72, 81, 83, 84, 119, 403, 420–22, 458n126
Turkey 3, 308, 311; *see also* Ottoman Empire
Turkish (languages) 40, 233, 237, 240–46, 249, 250, 259, 264, 266, 278, 279, 295n69, 387, 407, 428, 444, 514, 531, 532, 537, 640
Turks 4, 50, 84, 132, 133, 137, 147, 162n235, 239, 262, 264, 266, 271, 272, 296n92, 421, 492, 559n53; Turkmen 339, 385, 387; Yomut tribe 387; *see also Merv Oasis: Travels and Adventures East of the Caspian During the Years 1879–80–81 ..., The* (by Edmond O'Donovan, 1882); pan-Turkism; Tatar
Tynan, Patrick 221, 292n27, 526; *see also* Irish National Invincibles; Phoenix Park murders (Dublin, 1882)
Tyrone (County) 245, 268; *see also* Nine Years' War (/Tyrone's Rebellion, Ireland); O'Neill, Hugh; Ulster
Tyrone's Rebellion: *see* Nine Years' War (/Tyrone's Rebellion, Ireland)

Ulster 109, 194, 245, 411, 443, 445, 462n189, 494, 499, 538, 554, 589, 590; Anagh 245; Ultonian 194, 422; *see also* Northern Ireland; Plantation of Ulster; Tyrone (County); Ulster Cycle
Ulster Covenant 554; *see also* Irish Home Rule; unionists (Ireland)
Ulster Cycle 41, 65, 66, 137, 143, 185, 437–42, 446, 447; *see also* Aoife (Aífe); Beaufort, Louisa Catherine; Brooke, Charlotte; Celticism; Conla (Conlaoch); Cuchulain (Cú Chulainn); epics; *Fragments of Ancient Poetry, Collected in the Highlands of Scotland* (by James Macpherson, 1760); Larminie, William; Meyer, Kuno; Modi, Jivanji Jamshedji; Mohl, Jules (Julius); mythology (Irish heroic cycles); Ossian; Rustam; *Shāhnāmeh*; Sohrab; Vallancey, Charles; Walker, Joseph Cooper
Ulster Journal of Archaeology (Belfast) 109, 443
Ulster Volunteers (a.k.a., Ulster Volunteer Force) 494, 590; *see also* Irish Home Rule (Irish Home Rule Bill (1912)); unionists (Ireland)
Ulysses (by James Joyce, 1922) 39, 483, 555, 605–12, 619–21, 624; *see also* Bloom, Leopold; Dedalus, Stephen; Hedayat, Sadeq; Joyce, James
Umayyad caliphate 204n29, 261

uniformitarian theory (geology) 18; *see also* Hutton, James; Lyell, Charles; Plutonism (geology)
unionists (Ireland) 18, 25, 145, 165n301, 223, 237, 308, 317, 323, 344, 348, 349, 362, 366, 367, 371, 413, 423, 454n52, 476, 477, 481, 486, 493, 494, 546, 549, 554, 569, 570, 590; *see also* Orange organizations; Ulster Covenant; Ulster Volunteers (a.k.a., Ulster Volunteer Force)
Unitarian 86, 262
United Irish League 475, 483; *see also* Kettle, Thomas Michael; O'Brien, William; Young Ireland Branch of the United Irish League
United Irish League of America 525; *see also* Parnellite
The United Irishman (Dublin, 1848) 260, 280, 281, 368, 455n57; *see also* Great Famine (Ireland, 1845–51); Mangan, James Clarence; Mitchel, John; Young Ireland uprising (1848)
The United Irishman (Dublin, 1899–1906) 475, 483, 486, 491, 506n72, 610, 630n83; *see also* Griffith, Arthur
The United Irishman (Dublin; post-1948 publication of the Official Sinn Féin and, subsequently, Sinn Féin the Workers' Party) 26, 511n128; *see also* Official Sinn Féin; Sinn Féin the Workers' Party
United Irishmen 5, 11, 24, 25, 29, 30, 34, 37, 68, 69, 138, 168, 174, 180, 181, 216, 219, 265, 274, 315, 348, 352, 429, 472, 519, 575, 583, 585, 627n42; *see also* Emmet, Robert; Moore; Thomas; *Paddy's Resource*(1795–1803); Society of United Irishmen; Tone, Theobald Wolfe; United Irishmen uprising (1798); United Irishmen uprising (1803)
United Irishmen uprising (1798) 68, 168, 174, 180, 181, 183, 213, 315, 399, 472, 518, 519, 538, 541, 543, 583, 585; *see also* Act of Union (of the United Kingdom of Great Britain and Ireland, 1801); FitzGerald, Edward (United Irishmen); Moore, Thomas; Society of United Irishmen; Tone, Theobald Wolfe; United Irishmen; Vinegar Hill, Battle of (Ireland)
United Irishmen uprising (1803) 181, 183, 399, 583, 585; *see also* Emmet, Robert; Moore, Thomas; Society of United Irishmen; United Irishmen
United Kingdom 1, 5, 7–10, 33, 34, 40, 50, 60, 82, 90, 107, 113, 116, 119, 121, 145, 159n199, 167–72, 175, 176, 180–86, 194, 197, 221, 223, 227, 231, 234, 236, 242, 246, 269–71, 283, 284, 293n37, 308, 312, 318,

319, 321, 331, 337, 339, 340, 342, 345, 349, 351, 363–67, 369–73, 377n20, 381, 385, 390, 391, 393, 398, 399, 416, 424, 426, 434, 438, 448, 449, 456n76, 467, 469, 471, 472, 475–77, 479–81, 483, 486–88, 491, 493, 494, 499, 504n49, 508n86, 513, 518, 520–23, 526–28, 536, 538–41, 544, 545, 547–52, 560n64, 578, 591, 639, 645; 1918 general election 474, 591; *see also* Act of Union (of the United Kingdom of Great Britain and Ireland, 1801); England; Great Britain; Ireland; Scotland; Wales

United States 9, 11, 30, 108, 148, 149, 173, 186, 209n115, 217, 225, 229, 290, 292n27, 303, 306, 313–18, 324, 327, 346, 352, 354n14, 360n128, 363, 366, 368, 371, 372, 392, 411, 456n76, 471, 473–76, 483, 488–91, 498, 505n54, 521, 524, 535, 539, 542, 545, 551, 562n119, 573, 576, 583, 586, 590, 591, 593, 599, 627; *see also* African-American; American Civil War; American War of Independence; Dighton Rock (Massachusetts); Irish-American; Irish diaspora (United States); Mexican-American War (1846–48); slavery; Washington; Wilson, Woodrow (US president)

United States 1917 Immigration Act (a.k.a., "Asiatic Barred Zone Act") 491

The United States of India (San Francisco) 593; *see also* Ghadar

Universal History of Mirkhond (15th century) 62, 74, 108, 113, 115, 119, 130, 132–34, 566; *see also Bibliothèque orientale* (by Barthélemy d'Herbelot, 1697); Herbelot [de Molainville], Barthélemy d'; Keyoumars; Mirkhond (a.k.a. "Mirkhound"; Muḥammad ibn Khāvandshāh Mīr Khvānd); Pishdādiān

universalism *vs.* particularism 27, 28, 30, 117, 315, 352, 428, 434, 473, 587, 588, 648

University College Dublin 451, 573, 609

University of Cambridge 137, 149, 171, 409, 426, 427, 469, 477, 484, 489, 501n6

University of Dublin 389; *see also* Trinity College (University of Dublin)

University of Oxford 62, 146, 171, 186, 393, 427, 573

University of Washington 489

'Urabi Pasha 480; *see also* Egypt (British occupation of (1882)); "Egypt for Egyptians"; Egyptian nationalists

Ural Mountains 623; Uralian 618, 623

Urban VIII, Pope (Maffeo Barbarini) 262, 265–69, 273; "Maphaeus Barberino" 267; *see also* Barberino, Raphael; Confederate War (Ireland, 1642–52); Mangan, James Clarence ("To the Ingleezee Khafir, Calling Himself Djuan Bool Djenkinzun")

Urdu 432, 490, 614, 621

Ussher, James 18; dating of the "Great Flood" 18–19

Utterson, Mathews Corsellis 335; *see also* Anglo-Iranian War (1856–57)

Uzbekistan 74, 175; *see also* Bukhara; Transoxania

Vallancey, Charles 8, 17, 18, 22, 29, 30, 34, 35, 39, 40, 54, 55, 63–88, 90–92, 94–97, 100–103, 105, 107–12, 115, 116, 118–27, 129, 131, 133, 135, 142, 143, 146, 148, 153n55, 153n59, 155n88, 156n124, 174, 185, 189–91, 193, 196–99, 206n53, 207–208n81, 211, 213–15, 236, 238, 252–55, 260, 264, 276–80, 282, 289, 296n79, 382–85, 387, 392, 394, 395, 404, 405, 407, 409, 410, 431, 446, 451, 519, 564, 566, 567, 581, 586, 599, 601, 612, 613, 615, 618–20, 625, 642, 646; *Collectanea de Rebus Hibernicis* (Volume 6, Part I; by Charles Vallancey, 1804) 82, 185, 612; *An Essay on the Antiquity of the Irish Language. Being a Collation of the Irish with the Punic language* (by Charles Vallancey, 1772) 79; *A Grammar of the Iberno-Celtic* (by Charles Vallancey, 1773) 71; "Irish History *corresponding with the preceding* Persian History" 75–76; *Prospectus of a Dictionary of the Language of the Aire Coti, or Ancient Irish, Compared with the Language of the Cuti, or Ancient Persians, with the Hindoostanee, the Arabic, and Chaldean Languages* (by Charles Vallancey, 1802) 82, 86; Tuatha de Dananns as Pishdādiān 64, 65, 72, 76, 92, *passim*; *see also* "Armenian-Scythians"; Aryans; Betham, William; *Bibliothèque orientale* (by Barthélemy d'Herbelot, 1697); Celticism; Celts; cosmopolitan (Irish polyglot cosmopolitan texts); "Coti" (ancient population of Ireland); *Dabestān-e Mazāheb*; *An Essay on the Primitive Inhabitants of Great Britain and Ireland. Proving from History, Languages, and Mythology, that They were Persians or Indo.Scythæ, Composed of Scythians, Chaldæans, and Indians* (by Charles Vallancey, 1807); Fenian Cycle; *Finnegans Wake* (by James Joyce, 1939); "fire worship"; Flood, Henry; Gudarz; Hely, James; Herbelot [de Molainville], Barthélemy d'; Hibernian Antiquarian Society; Indo-European languages; "Iranian" theories of Irish origins; Irano-Scythians; Irish antiquarianism; Jones, William; Milesians; Mosaic theory; O'Brien, Henry;

O'Conor, Charles; "oriental" theories of Irish origins; "Phoenician" theories of Irish origins; Pishdādiān; Round Towers (Ireland); Royal Dublin Society; Royal Irish Academy; "Scytho-Phoenician" theory of Irish origins; *Shāhnāmeh*; Trinity College (University of Dublin); Tuatha de Dananns; Ulster Cycle; United Irishmen uprising (1798); *Universal History* of Mirkhond (15th century); Vallanceyan; *A Vindication of the Ancient History of Ireland* (by Charles Vallancey, 1786); *Zardoshtnāmeh* ("The Book of Zoroaster"); Zoroastrianism

Vallanceyan 67, 86, 108, 123, 146, 213, 254, 264, 278, 289, 296n79, 387, 395, 612, 618; *see also* Vallancey, Charles

Van Diemen's Land (Tasmania) 315

Vancouver 489

Vedanta 434; Vedanta Society 489; *see also* Chatterjee, Mohini; Dulin, Albert S.; Vivekananda (Narendranath Datta)

"The Veiled Prophet of Khorassan": *see Lalla Rookh. An Oriental Romance* (by Thomas Moore, 1817)

Venables Vernon-Harcourt, Leveson (Rev.) 119; *The Doctrine of the Deluge, Vindicating the Scriptural Account from the Doubts which Have Recently Been Cast Upon it by Geological Speculations* (by Leveson Venables Vernon-Harcourt, 1838) 119–20; *see also* Beaufort, Louisa Catherine; *Dabestān-e Mazāheb*; Petrie, George; Round Towers (Ireland); Tabriz

Veterum Persarum et Parthorum et Medorum religionis historia, also known as *De vetere religione Persarum* (by Thomas Hyde, 1760): *see* Hyde, Thomas

Vico, Giambattista 613, 618–19, 623, 631n128; *see also* historiography and history; Joyce, James

Victoria, Queen 230, 363, 540, 545; *see also* Great Famine (Ireland, 1845–51); Great Industrial Exhibition (Dublin, 1853; a.k.a., Irish Industrial Exhibition); O'Connor, Arthur

"Victorian" values 109, 340

Viereck, George Sylvester 498; *see also Fatherland* (New York); *World War* (New York)

Vietnam 650

A View of the Present State of Ireland (by Edmund Spenser, completed in 1596 and published in 1633): *see* Spenser, Edmund

Vikings: *see* Norse ("Vikings")

Villanueva, Joaquín Lorenzo 89–90, 114, 207n81, 384; *see also Ibernia Phoenicea* (by Joaquín Lorenzo Villanueva, 1831;

translated as *Phoenecian Ireland* by Henry O'Brien, 1833); O'Brien, Henry; *Phoenecian Ireland* (1833 translation by Henry O'Brien of Joaquín Lorenzo Villanueva's 1831 *Ibernia Phoenicea*)

A Vindication of the Ancient History of Ireland (by Charles Vallancey, 1786) 34, 63–64, 71–72, 75–78, 82, 84–85, 185, 238, 277; *see also* Vallancey, Charles

Vinegar Hill, Battle of (Ireland) 518; *see also* United Irishmen uprising (1798)

Virgil 565, 622; *Aeneid* (by Virgil, 19 BCE) 622

Vivekananda (Narendranath Datta) 434; *see also* Vedanta

Voltaire (François-Marie Arouet) 51, 151n20, 436; *Candide* (by Voltaire, 1759) 436; *The Philosophy of History* (by Voltaire, 1765) 51; on Scythians 51, 151n20; *see also* Enlightenment ("European" Enlightenment)

Vulcanism (geology) 60–61

Wadding, Luke 619

Wales 20, 51, 66, 78, 144, 170, 283, 389, 515, 523, 527, 528, 533, 535, 536, 539, 540, 570, 574, 578; theories of Welsh origins 74, 216, 416; Welsh Home Rule 549; Welsh language 74, 535; Welsh people 11, 16, 24, 50, 57, 65, 73, 74, 133, 180, 191, 215, 216, 225–27, 285, 287, 317, 321, 414, 416, 562n109, 564, 569, 570, 575, 588, 607, 644; *see also* Jones, Rowland; Lloyd George, David

Walker, Joseph Cooper 185, 214, 446, 447; *Historical Memoirs of the Irish Bards* (by Joseph Cooper Walker, 1818) 185; *see also* Brooke, Charlotte; Conla (Conlaoch); Cuchulain (Cú Chulainn); Ferdowsi, Abul-Qassem; mythology; Ouseley, William; Royal Irish Academy; Rustam; *Shāhnāmeh*; Sohrab; Ulster Cycle

Walker, William 314–18, 324; *see also* Costa Rica; Honduras; Mosquito Coast (Nicaragua and Honduras); Nicaragua; slavery

Walpole, Spencer Horatio 354n18

Walsh, Edward 221, 292n26

Walsh, James Joseph 594

Warburton, Eliot 427; *The Crescent and the Cross; or Romance and Realities of Eastern Travel* (by Eliot Warburton, 1852) 427

Ware, James 619; *The Historie of Ireland* (ed. by James Ware, 1633) 619

Warren, William Blackburn 335; *see also* Anglo-Iranian War (1856–57)

Washington 306, 312, 314, 316, 317, 489, 500; diplomatic row with London (1854–56)

306, 314; *see also* Palmerston, Lord (Henry John Temple); United States
Washington, George 320; *see also* American colonies; American War of Independence ("American Revolution"); United States
Waterford 426, 617
Waterlow, Sydney Hedley 364; *see also* Iranian famine (1870–72)
Webb, William 196
Weber, Max 141; *see also* "disenchantment" (*Entzauberung*)
Weld, Isaac 196
Wellesley, Richard Colley (Lord Mornington; Marquess Wellesley) 33, 516, 528–29; *see also* Malcolm, John; Moore, Thomas
West Indies 371–73, 536; 1871 hurricane 371–73
"Western Civilization": *see* civilization
Westminster: *see* British parliament
Wheatley, David 253–54, 298n123, 302n204
Whelan, Kevin 396
Whig Party 168, 169, 235, 305, 306, 309, 339, 540; Radical wing 306, 307, 321, 323, 354n13, 354n18; *see also* Gladstone, William Ewart; Liberal Party (UK); Palmerston, Lord (Henry John Temple)
Whinfield, Edward Henry 427; *The Quatraines of Omar Khayyam* (by Edward Henry Whinfield, 1883) 427; *see also* Khayyam, Omar
White, Hayden 604; *Metahistory: The Historical Imagination in Nineteenth-century Europe* (by Hayden White, 1973) 604
Whitelock, Harriet Georgina 389; *see also* Ouseley, Eliza Shirin; Ouseley, Gore; Ouseley, Janie; Ouseley, Wellesley Abbas
"whitening" of the "mere Irish" 144, 148, 393, 412, 491, 576, 577; *see also* Aryanism (racial theories); racial theories
Whiteside, James 323; *see also* Anglo-Iranian War (1856–57); Conservative Party (UK; a.k.a., Unionist Party after 1895); O'Brien, William Smith; O'Connell, Daniel
Whitty, Michael James 207n81
Wickham, Chris 603; *see also* memory ("social" memory)
"wild Irish" (civilizational accusation) 21, 48, 67, 71, 78, 144, 150n8, 527; *see also* Camden, William; Keating, Geoffrey; Ledwich, Edward; "mere Irish"; Spenser, Edmund
The Wild Irish Girl (by Sydney Owenson (Lady Morgan), 1806): *see* Owenson, Sydney (Lady Morgan)
Wilde, Jane Francesca Agnes (née Elgee) 8, 35, 148, 181, 238, 245, 291, 382–84, 394, 396–416, 418, 420, 451, 455n58, 566, 582, 585, 601, 615, 625, 643, 646, 647; "Dolicephalous" (i.e., "dolichocephalic" Aryan race, coined by Andreas Joannes Retzius) 403; *Driftwood from Scandinavia* (by Jane Francesca Agnes Wilde, 1884) 402, 413; "The Fairy Mythology of Ireland" (1877) 402; "in *Iran* and in *Erin*" 406; "Jacta est Alea" (1848) 398; a.k.a., "John Fanshawe Ellis" 397, 455n56; presumed Iranian roots of Irish folk beliefs and practices 8, 35, 148, 382–84, 396, 397, 401–10, 412, 413, 625, 643, 646, 647; "A Remonstrance, addressed to D[enis] Florence M[a]cCarthy" (1863?) 418–19; a.k.a., "Speranza"/"Speranza of *The Nation*" 181, 397–99, 418, 615; a.k.a., "Ugo Bassi" 397, 398; *Ugo Bassi: A Tale of the Italian Revolution* (by Jane Francesca Agnes Wilde, 1857) 398; "war of races"/race war between the Irish and the English 402, 411, 414, 416; *see also Ancient Cures, Charms, and Usages of Ireland. Contributions to Irish Lore* (by Jane Francesca Agnes Wilde, 1890); *Ancient Legends, Mystic Charms, and Superstitions of Ireland* (by Jane Francesca Agnes Wilde, 1887); Aryan theories; Bassi, Ugo (Italian revolutionary priest); craniology; folklore; "Iranian" theories of Irish origins; Irish nationalism; *The Nation* (Dublin); Round Towers (Ireland); women's rights
Wilde, Oscar 232, 233, 397, 427, 554, 620, 622
Wilde, William Robert Wills 215, 394, 396, 398–402, 405, 407, 412, 415, 416, 456n76; "folks' lore" 399, 400; "Ireland, Past and Present: The Land and the People" (1864) 401; *Irish Popular Superstitions* (by William Robert Wills Wilde, 1852) 399, 407; "On the Ancient Races of Ireland" (1874) 401; *see also* British Association; craniology; ethnography; folklore; Royal Irish Academy
Wilder, Alexander 435
Wilford, Francis 116–17; *see also Asiatic Researches*; phallic worship
William III, King (William of Orange) 538; *see also* "Glorious Revolution" (1688)
Williams, Richard D'Alton 397; a.k.a., "Shamrock of *The Nation*" 397; *see also The Nation* (Dublin); *The Spirit of the Nation* (by Thomas Osborne Davis, et al., 1843); Young Ireland; Young Ireland uprising (1848)
Wills, Charles James 379n55; *see also* Iranian famine (1870–72); telegraph (Indo-European Telegraph Department)
Wilson, Peter 169; *see also The Meddler*

Wilson, Woodrow (US president) 591; "Fourteen Points" 591
Windele, John 101, 124, 163n250, 198, 211, 382; *see also* Petrie, George; Round Towers (Ireland)
Winter, Jay 142; "sites of mourning" 142
Winterbotham, Arthur Brend 501n2; *see also* tobacco concession (Iran, 1890)
Women's Freedom League 480; *see also* Despard, Charlotte
women's rights 398, 434, 475, 478–80, 483, 486, 590, 606, 639; feminism 294n55, 351, 397, 412, 429, 430, 434, 479, 480, 482, 485, 486, 490; *see also* suffragist
Women's Social and Political Union 480; *see also* Despard, Charlotte
Wood, David 390; *see also* Kavanagh, Arthur MacMurrough; Kavanagh, Thomas
Wood-Martin, William Gregory 447; *Traces of the Elder Faiths of Ireland* (by William Gregory Wood-Martin, 1901) 447; *see also* Conla (Conlaoch); Royal Historical and Archaeological Association of Ireland; Rustam; *Shāhnāmeh*; Ulster Cycle
Workers' Republic (Dublin) 496; *see also* Connolly, James
workers' rights 485, 486, 606, 639; *see also* anarchism; socialism
world history 3, 17, 21, 23, 31, 35, 41, 60, 77, 116, 126–29, 142, 276, 346, 484, 529, 537, 563–66, 571, 586, 587, 614, 621, 637, 645, 647–50; "Iran"-centered world history 566; world-historical 4, 6, 11, 20, 27, 40, 41, 45n42, 64, 76, 87, 116, 126, 135, 219, 322, 346–48, 351, 352, 474, 563, 564, 566, 571, 584, 585, 589, 605, 615, 635–37, 643, 647, 648, 650; *see also* global history
World War (New York) 498; *see also* Viereck, George Sylvester
"worlding" 3, 5, 8, 10, 11, 36, 129, 318, 319, 331, 346, 347, 349, 351, 352, 555, 566–67, 577, 578, 580, 584–87, 589, 606, 607, 636, 640, 641, 647, 651; Ireland-in-the-world 611; the-world-in-Ireland 608, 611; "worlded" 6, 82, 352, 585, 608, 611, 614, 623, 635, 641, 645, 647, 651; worlding of Ireland 3, 10, 36, 585, 606, 607; worlding the nation 347, 351
World's Columbian Exposition (Chicago, 1893) 524
Worsaae, Jens Jacob Asmussen 198
Woulfe, Stephen 339; *see also* Catholic Emancipation
Wyllie, Curzon 478, 490; *see also* Dhingra, Madan Lal
Wyndham, George 551; *see also* Criminal Law and Procedure Act (Ireland)

Xenophon 228
Xerxes I (Achaemenid emperor) 222, 223, 406; *see also* Thermopylae, Battle of (480 BCE)
Xhosa 540; *see also* southern Africa
Xinhai Revolution (1911–12) 474, 547; *see also* China

Yar Mohammed Khan 338; *see also* Herat
Yazd 194; *see also* Iranian famine (1870–72); *Lalla Rookh. An Oriental Romance* (by Thomas Moore, 1817); Zoroastrianism
Yeats, William Butler 136–38, 211, 228, 232, 279, 291, 396–97, 418, 429, 432–41, 447, 448, 451, 460n158, 461n175, 472, 478, 483, 554, 580, 586–87, 589, 601, 609, 611, 613, 615, 627n48; "The Cat and the Moon" (1917) 436; *The Cat and the Moon and Certain Poems* (by William Butler Yeats, 1924) 447; "Cuchulain Comforted" (1939) 438; "The Death of Cuchulain" (1892) 438; *The Death of Cuchulain* (by William Butler Yeats, 1939) 438; "Diarmuid and Grania" (by William Butler Yeats and George Augustus Moore, 1901) 435; "Easter 1916" (1916) 601; *Fairy and Folk Tales of the Irish Peasantry* (by William Butler Yeats, 1888–1902) 397; *On Baile's Strand* (by William Butler Yeats, 1903) 438; *The Speckled Bird* (by William Butler Yeats, 1896) 436; "The Statues" (1938) 438; *see also* Abbey Theatre; Aryans; *Finnegans Wake* (by James Joyce, 1939); Hafez, Shams al-Din Mohammad; Hermetic Order of the Golden Dawn; Hermetic Society (Dublin); Irish Literary Theatre; Irish National Dramatic Society; Irish National Theatre Society; *Kathleen ni Houlihan* (by Isabella Augusta Gregory and William Butler Yeats, 1902); magic; Noh theatre; occult; "oriental" theories of Irish origins; Tagore, Rabindranath; theosophy
Yezd: *see* Yazd
Yima: *see* Jamshid
Yohannan, John D. 188; "pseudo-Oriental" poetry" 188, 241; *see also* "oriental-style" literature
Yoni 95, 121; *see also* O'Brien, Henry; Pishdādiān
Yorkshire 391, 476; Ripon 391, 476; *see also* Lynch, Henry Finnis Blosse
Young, Thomas 57; *see also* Indo-European languages
Young Ireland 7, 8, 24, 25, 35, 37, 138, 143, 161, 165n300, 167, 172, 181, 182, 212, 213, 215–19, 223, 227–34, 236–38, 247, 254, 260–62, 269, 281–84, 289, 290, 311–19,

323–25, 344–45, 347, 355n31, 362, 363, 397, 398, 401, 411, 416, 418, 455n57, 475, 483, 522, 525, 542, 544, 569, 575, 585; *see also* Barry, Michael Joseph; Davis, Thomas Osborne; Dillon, John Blake; Duffy Charles Gavan; MacCarthy, Denis Florence; Mangan, James Clarence; Meagher, Thomas Francis; Mitchel, John; *The Nation* (Dublin); O'Brien, William Smith; O'Mahony, John; Stephens, James; Williams, Richard D'Alton; Young Ireland uprising (1848)

Young Ireland Branch of the United Irish League 475, 483; *see also* Kettle, Thomas Michael; United Irish League

Young Ireland uprising (1848) 182, 217, 223, 228–30, 269, 290, 363, 398, 542, 544; *see also* Great Famine (Ireland, 1845–51); Mangan, James Clarence; Meagher, Thomas Francis; Mitchel, John; O'Brien, William Smith; *The United Irishman* (Dublin, 1848); Williams, Richard D'Alton; Young Ireland

Young Men's Catholic Association 196

Young Men's Christian Association (Dublin) 401

Young Turk Revolution (1908) 474, 483, 547; *see also* Maloney, William Joseph; Ottoman Empire

Yuan dynasty 452n15; *see also* China; Mongol

Yugoslavia 595

Zand dynasty (Iran, 1751–94) 332; *see also* Karim Khan (Zand ruler); Kharg Island

Zardoshtnāmeh ("The Book of Zoroaster") 75; *see also Bibliothèque orientale* (by Barthélemy d'Herbelot, 1697); Herbelot [de Molainville], Barthélemy d'; Vallancey, Charles; Zoroastrianism

"Zend": *see* Avestan language and script (Old Iranian)

Zend Avesta 62, 116, 117, 229; *see also* Anquetil-Duperron, Abraham Hyacinthe; Keyoumars; Müller, Friedrich Max; Zoroastrianism

Zend Avesta (French translation by Abraham Hyacinthe Anquetil-Duperron, 1771): *see* Anquetil-Duperron, Abraham Hyacinthe

Zerubavel, Eviatar 603; *see also* "mnemonic communities"

Zeuss, Johann Kaspar 394, 572; *see also* Indo-European languages

Zimmern, Helen 442, 463n209

Zionism 506n72, 584, 607; *see also* Griffith, Arthur; Palestine

Zohal: *see* Saturn

Zorababel 51; *see also* Darius I (Achaemenid emperor)

Zoroaster 39, 63, 75, 112, 117, 121, 191, 311, 430, 431, 436; in *Ulysses* (by James Joyce, 1922) 39; *see also* Vallancey, Charles; *A Vindication of the Ancient History of Ireland* (by Charles Vallancey, 1786)

Zoroastrian 5, 7, 25, 41, 53, 56, 62, 63, 72, 85, 88, 95, 97, 101–4, 112, 113, 116, 120, 124, 132, 133, 158n178, 172, 178–80, 182, 184, 189, 192–94, 213, 215, 219, 237, 261, 269–72, 309, 344, 365, 377n15, 386, 430, 431, 488, 490, 492, 623, 638, 643; "Guebre" 182, 194, 196, 215, 269, 299n152, 386; *see also* Hataria, Manekji Limj; Parsi; Society for the Amelioration of the Condition of Zoroastrians in Persia; Zoroastrianism

Zoroastrianism 62, 85, 86, 95, 113, 132, 158n178, 264, 269, 430, 431, 434, 435, 442, 460n148; *see also* Bundahishn; D'Alton (Dalton), John; *The History of Ireland*, vol.I (by Thomas Moore, 1835); Hyde, Thomas (*Historia religionis veterum Persarum eorumque magorum* (by Thomas Hyde, 1700); Hyde, Thomas (*Veterum Persarum et Parthorum et Medorum religionis historia*, also known as *De vetere religione Persarum* (by Thomas Hyde, 1760)); Keyoumars; *Lalla Rookh. An Oriental Romance* (by Thomas Moore, 1817); "neo-Zoroastrianism"; Parsi; Round Towers (Ireland); Vallancey, Charles; *Zardoshtnāmeh* ("The Book of Zoroaster"); *Zend Avesta*; Zoroastrian

Zulus 312, 504n46, 610

www.ingramcontent.com/pod-product-compliance
Lightning Source LLC
Chambersburg PA
CBHW021128230426
43667CB00005B/63